QUEST FOR GOLD

QUEST FOR GOLD

THE ENCYCLOPEDIA OF AMERICAN OLYMPIANS

BY BILL MALLON & IAN BUCHANAN   WITH JEFFREY TISHMAN

LEISURE PRESS

NEW YORK

A publication of
Leisure Press.
597 Fifth Avenue; New York, N.Y. 10017

Book & cover design: Brian Groppe
Front cover illustration: Halsted Craig Hannah
Production: Kate Back

Library of Congress Cataloging in Publication Data

Mallon, Bill
  Quest for gold.

  1. Athletes—United States—Biography.   2. Olympic
games.   I. Buchanan, Ian.   II. Tishman, Jeffrey.
III. Title.
GV697.A1M275 1984   796.4'8'0922 [B]   84-966
ISBN 0-88011-217-4

To the 1980 United States Olympic Team.

TABLE OF CONTENTS

PREFACE

It was a throaty, emotional cheer, one that was even deeper than that—it came from near all of our hearts. The cheer was "U-S-A" and it was for the 1980 United States' Olympic ice hockey team—the team that beat the Soviet Union.

The cheer did not stop with that victory. In fact, it has grown and is now heard whenever the U.S. athletes compete internationally. It is a cheer in honor of the athletes who represent us in international competition. And this, then, is a book about that cheer.

Specifically our book deals with those athletes who've heard that cheer at the highest echelon of international sport—the Olympic Games. Within these pages can be found the most comprehensive history ever done of the United States' Olympic athletes.

Many European countries have published similar books on their own Olympic athletes. But no country even remotely approaches the overall success enjoyed by the United States' Olympians. Our country has produced the most Olympic athletes, the most Olympic gold medalists, and the most Olympic medalists—by far. It seems to us that a book of this sort is long overdue—a book in honor of our Olympic athletes and their quest for gold.

Bill Mallon
Ian Buchanan
Jeffrey Tishman

ACKNOWLEDGMENTS

This book would not have been possible without the assistance of many, many people. However a small group of sport historians has been especially helpful, so we extend our special thanks to : Hal Bateman (Colorado Springs), Peter Diamond (New York), Erich Kamper (Graz, Austria), John and Evelyn Mallon (Boston), Don Sayenga (Bethlehem, PA), Ture Widlund (Stockholm). And we especially tip our hat to Gary Webb, former curatorial assistant at the Harvard Archives who first advised the authors that we were both, independently, researching the same subject.

We would also like to give our thanks to the following: Max Ammann (Geneva, Switzerland), June Becht (St. Louis), Andy Buckley (Boston), the Duke University Library Reference Staff (especially Ken Berger, Bessie Carrington, Ilene Nelson and Jane Vogel), David Ellison (Durham, NC), Pim Huurman (Laren, Holland), Steve Ivy (Palo Alto, CA), Alice Landon and all the chapter presidents of the U.S. Olympian Society, Michael Raab (Hong Kong), Fran Perkins, Gloria Reid and Tony Seaber (Durham, NC), Bob Rhode (Tucson), Jack Shea (Lake Placid, NY), David Wallechinsky (Los Angeles), and Paula Welch (Gainesville, FL).

Many colleges and universities sent us a great deal of material on their athletes. We would especially like to thank the alumni and sports information departments of the schools who had many Olympians and went out of their way to offer help: Cornell, Dartmouth, Harvard, Michigan, Penn, Princeton, Southern Cal, Stanford, UCLA, U.S. Military Academy, U.S. Naval Academy, and Yale.

Of course, many U.S. Olympians and their families have responded to our many questions graciously, and we offer here a collective thank you.

Finally, Bill and Ian would like to thank our wives, Karen and Jeanne, for graciously putting up with the many hours the project demanded.

INTRODUCTION

The bulk of this book is made up of biographies of every American who has ever won a medal in the Olympic Games. The biographies are grouped by sports, and include the athlete's full name, date and place of birth, date and place of death (if applicable), a list of the medals won, and a short synopsis of that person's life—both athletic and, if significant, nonathletic. If vital information is missing, it is only because it could not be found.

The research for this book has taken us down fascinating and often sportingly obscure avenues and the space devoted to a biography should not be taken as the authors' assessment of the relative merit of any particular performance. We have, in fact, often taken the opposite view and devoted more space to some of the lesser known medalists, rather than restate, at length, the well-documented careers of the more famous champions.

Each section also includes a short history of our overall record in the sport, as well as specific U.S. Olympic records pertaining to that sport—most medals, oldest gold medalist, oldest medalist, etc. Please note that we do not include an age record for oldest or youngest medalist if it is held by an already listed gold medalist. In a few sports we have omitted this section because information on the ages of the medalists was scarce, mainly for the many medalists from 1904.

The United States has not won Olympic medals in a few sports. These sports, along with demonstration sports, and sports soon to appear on the Olympic program, are included in the chapter entitled "Other Sports."

Periodically throughout the book, we have also inserted interesting little asides about our Olympic athletes—biggest, tallest, special honors won, short bios about nonmedalists who acheived some unique honor, pro athletes, and many others. In addition we have tried to include a cross-section of photographs from many of the sports.

Finally at the end of the book we have included overall U.S. Olympic records, tables of participation, an honor roll of the most successful competitors, and an index which includes every United States athlete who has ever competed in the Olympics.

Whenever we use the term "U.S. Olympian," or "U.S. Olympic athlete," we mean a person who actually competed in the Games, and all records and lists deal exclusively with those athletes. Also, to avoid repetition, when we have written that the "U.S. has never failed to be represented" in a particular sport at the Summer Olympics, this must be taken in the light of the boycott of the 1980 Olympic Games, at which, obviously, no Americans competed.

We have tried to make all records and lists as complete as possible but it is likely that omissions and errors do exist. We would appreciate being informed of any error or omission, however small, or any information about the athletes, biographical or otherwise, which we may have missed. You can reach us at:

Quest for Gold
510 Island View Road
Rock Falls, IL 61071

ABBREVIATIONS

Organizations

AA   Athletic Association
AC   Athletic Club
AAU   Amateur Athletic Union
AAA   Amateur Athletic Association
ABA   Amateur Boxing Association or American Basketball Association
AFLA   American Fencer's League of America AIAW Association for Intercollegiate Athletics for Women
BC   Boat Club
CC   Country Club
ECAC   Eastern Collegiate Athletic Conference
FIS   Federation Internationale de Ski
FISA   Federation Internationale des Societes d'Aviron
FITA   Federation Internationale de Tir a l'Arc
GA   Golf Association
GC   Golf Club
HC   Hockey Club
IAAF   International Amateur Athletic Federation
IC4A   Intercollegiate Amateur Athletic Association of America
IFA   Intercollegiate Fencing Association
IHL   International Hockey League
IOC   International Olympic Committee
IRA   Intercollegiate Rowing Association
NBA   National Basketball Association
NCAA   National Collegiate Athletic Association
NFL   National Football League
NHL   National Hockey League
RC   Rowing Club SC Swim Club
TC   Track Club
USOC   United States Olympic Committee
WBA   World Boxing Association
WBC   World Boxing Council
WHA   World Hockey Association
YC   Yacht Club

Sports

Many times, when discussing an athlete, we try to help the reader by telling in what sport he may have competed. For space considerations, we use a three-letter abbreviation for all the sports.

ARC   Archery
ASK   Alpine Skiing
BAS   Basketball
BIA   Biathlon
BOB   Bobsledding
BOX   Boxing
CAN   Canoe & Kayaking
CYC   Cycling
DIV   Diving
EQU   Equestrian Events
FEN   Fencing
FIH   Field Hockey
FSK   Figure Skating
GOL   Golf
GYM   Gymnastics
HAN   Handball
ICH   Ice Hockey
JDP   Jeu de Paume
JUD   Judo
LAX   Lacrosse
LUG   Luge
MOP   Modern Pentathlon
NSK   Nordic Skiing
POL   Polo
ROQ   Roque
ROW   Rowing
RUG   Rubgy Football
SHO   Shooting
SOC   Soccer
SSK   Speed Skating
SWI   Swimming
TAF   Track & Field
TEN   Tennis
VOL   Volleyball
WAP   Water Polo
WLT   Weightlifting
WRE   Wrestling
YAC   Yachting

(Continued on next page)

State and Country Abbreviations

State abbreviations, where used, are the standard two-letter U.S. Postal Service abbreviation. To save space where necessary, we occasionally use the International Olympic Committee's three-letter abbreviations, or a variant, for certain countries. The ones used are as follows:

AUT   Austria
CZE   Czechoslovakia
DAN   Denmark
FIN   Finland
FRA   France
FRG   West Germany
GBR   Great Britain
GER   Germany (pre-World War II)
HUN   Hungary
ITA   Italy
NOR   Norway
PUR   Puerto Rico
ROM   Romania
SAF   South Africa
SUI   Switzerland
SWE   Sweden
URS   Soviet Union

Special Abbreviations

y   —yards (e.g., 100y = 100 yards)
m   —meters (e.g., 100m = 100 meters)
Ddi —*decessit, dies incognatum* (died, date unknown)
nka —now known as

ALPINE SKIING

MEN

The United States has had limited success in men's alpine skiing. Though competing every year the sport has been held, they have won only three medals—two silver and one bronze. However, in recent years, the success of Phil Mahre and his brother, Steve, augurs well for the future of the U.S. Olympic ski team.

HEUGA, James Frederic.

B. 22 SEP 1943 San Francisco, CA. Bronze: 1964 Slalom. Jimmy Heuga first became nationally known in 1960 when he won the U.S. Junior and U.S. Senior Slalom titles. He continued to win alpine races through 1963 and then in 1964 acheived two of his biggest wins with a first in the Harriman Cup downhill and a victory in the famed Arlberg Kandahar Combined Race. A few weeks later he followed Billy Kidd to become the second American man to win a medal in Olympic alpine skiing. Heuga continued to compete and do well, mainly in the technical events of slalom and giant slalom, through the 1968 Olympics.

However, Jimmy Heuga was not totally well at the 1968 Olympics. In the past year he had begun to have problems which were eventually diagnosed as multiple sclerosis. The disease hastened his retirement a short time after the 1968 Olympics. Heuga has since gone on to a successful business career as a consultant and spokesman for various firms in the ski industry. He has also coached and helped raise funds for the U.S. ski team. In the late 70's, with his disease in remission thanks in part to his own intensive therapy of diet and exercise, he began to ski again recreationally.

KIDD, William Winston.

B. 13 APR 1943 Burlington, VT. Silver: 1964 Slalom. Billy Kidd first gained world-wide attention when he finished eighth in slalom and 12th in giant slalom at the 1962 FIS World Championship's. Although he had to sit out much of the 1963 season with a sprained ankle, he came back in 1964 to win the first U.S. medal ever in alpine skiing, when he finished second in the slalom at Innsbruck. In the next few years, Kidd laid claim to the title of America's greatest ski racer. In 1965 he won eight consecutive races in the United States and in 1966 he won several European races, dueling head-to-head with the great Jean Claude Killy.
However a broken leg in 1967, and sprained ankles prior to the 1968 Olympics, hampered his chances at

Grenoble. After the Olympics, Kidd competed as an amateur for two more years, during which time, in 1970, he won the first U.S. gold medal at the FIS World's Championships. Kidd then turned pro and won the 1970 World Professional Championships in giant slalom and combined.

Billy Kidd has gone on to a very successful career in the ski industry. He has been ski director at Steamboat Springs, Colorado, for many years, represented various ski industry manufacturers as a spokesman, been a ski commentator for television, written columns for ski magazines, and written two books on skiing. He also has served on the President's Council for Physical Fitness and Sports and been a part-time coach to the U.S. ski team.

MAHRE, Phil.

B. 10 MAY 1957 Yakima, WA. Silver: 1980 Slalom. Phil Mahre is the most successful ski racer the United States has ever produced. Mahre first made the U.S. team in 1974, just after graduating from high school. He went on to compete in the 1976 Olympics, finishing fifth in the giant slalom, the best performance that year by a U.S. alpine ski racer. In the next two years, Phil and his twin brother, Steve, had very successful seasons, but Phil had by far the better of it. He won several World Cup races and was a challenger to Ingemar Stenmark for world domination of the technical races. But at the pre-Olympic races at Lake Placid in 1979, Phil Mahre fell, so severely fracturing his ankle that he required surgery and seven pins and a metal plate to hold the bones together. His Olympic chances looked slim with the Games less than a year away.

But Mahre made an amazing recovery. Understandably, he had a so-so early season in 1979-80 but recovered to win a silver medal, behind Stenmark, in the slalom at Lake Placid. Since then, Phil Mahre has become the best alpine skiier in the world. He has won the men's all-round World Cup title three years in succession, 1981-1983, something done before only by Stenmark and Gustavo Thoeni.

WOMEN

Beginning with the successes of Gretchen Fraser and Andy Mead Lawrence, the United States has always done well in women's alpine skiing. Though we have never been the top nation in a sport usually dominated by the Austrians, Swiss and French, we have always been near the top. Overall, eight U.S. women have accounted for twelve medals—four gold, five silver and three bronze.

OUTSTANDING PERFORMANCES

Most Gold Medals
  2 Andrea Mead Lawrence
Most Medals
  2 Andrea Mead Lawrence, Gretchen Fraser, Penny Pitou, Jean Saubert
Oldest Gold Medalist
  28y359d Gretchen Fraser
Youngest Gold Medalist
  19y301d Andrea Mead Lawrence

COCHRAN, Barbara Ann.

B. 04 JAN 1951 Claremont, NH. Gold: 1972 Slalom. Barbara Cochran is the best known of the skiing Cochran family, which has contributed three women and one man to the U.S. Olympic ski team. Taught by her father, Mickey, who later became U.S. alpine coach, she started skiing at age four and won her first big title at the 1966 Junior Nationals when she took the giant slalom. At the 1970 FIS World Championships, Cochran finished second in the slalom and repeated that finish in the 1970 World Cup. She also placed third in the giant slalom in the 1970 World Cup. She continued to rank among the top three technical skiiers during the 1971 season which led to her 1972 gold medal at Sapporo, a medal which was achieved by the margin of only .02 second over Danielle Debarnard of France.

Since retiring from skiing, Barbara Cochran has graduated from college (Vermont), married (now Mrs. Williams), written a book (*Skiing for Women*), and is now a writer for *The Washington Post*.

CORROCK, Susan.

B. 30 NOV 1951 Seattle, WA. Bronze: 1972 Downhill. Although Susan Corrock was rated the best downhiller among the U.S. women in 1972, she had actually had more success in the technical races in the years lead-ing up to the Olympics. In 1970, she won the U.S. Junior Nationals at slalom and giant slalom, also winning the Senior title in the giant slalom. Her first international experience came in 1971 and she had a good season, but gave no hint that she could win a medal at the 1972 Olympics. However she had the best run of her ski career in the Sapporo downhill, a run about which she said, "I didn't make any mistakes." Corrock left the U.S. ski team in 1973, skiing that year in the United States and then turned professional. She retired after 1975 and has since married.

FRASER, Gretchen Kunigk.

B. 11 FEB 1919 Vancouver, WA. Gold: 1948 Slalom = Silver: 1948 Alpine Combined. Gretchen Fraser first became known as a top skier years before the 1948 Olympics. She won the first revival of the Silver Belt trophy in 1940, won the 1941 National Alpine Combined, and the 1942 National Slalom titles. At St. Moritz in 1948, Fraser took another slalom title and her proficiency in the technical event helped her to an overall second place in the now defunct alpine combined (downhill and slalom). For her performance she was awarded the National Ski Association's Beck International Trophy. After retiring from competition, Gretchen Fraser became an officer of the National Ski Association and active in ski development in the Pacific Northwest.

LAWRENCE, Andrea B. Mead.

B. 19 APR 1932 Rutland, VT. Gold(2): 1952 Slalom, 1952 Giant Slalom. Andy Mead started skiing at the age of three and began entering races before she was ten. Her first big international moment came in 1948 when she placed third in the Arlberg Kandahar race. She also competed in the Olympics that year. Between 1948 and 1952 she won virtually every women's race available to her. She also married—to men's ski team member, David Lawrence. In 1952, as Andrea Mead Lawrence, she continued her domination of women's skiing by winning the two technical events at the Olympics. She continued her winning ways in 1953 with victories in the North American Downhill and Slalom championships, the U.S. National Giant Slalom, and won the Harriman Cup that year. In 1954 and 1955 she tailed off a little but still won several races. She competed at the 1956

Olympics, finishing fourth in the giant slalom, and then retired.

In the 60's Andrea Mead Lawrence was visible as an expert ski commentator on television. She and David Lawrence have since been divorced.

MEAD, Andrea

B. (see Andrea Mead Lawrence)

NELSON, Cynthia.

B. 19 AUG 1955 Duluth, MN. Bronze: 1976 Downhill. Cindy Nelson is probably the greatest downhill racer the U.S. has ever produced male or female. In addition, for most of the late 70's, she was the top U.S. woman at all the alpine events. Her career is remarkable not only for her success in the downhill but for its longevity. She first made the U.S. ski team in 1971 and is still competing through 1983.

Nelson was forced to miss the 1972 Olympics with a dislocated hip, but before the 1976 Olympics, she won two World Cup downhills, a World Cup giant slalom, and was ranked in the top ten in the World overall. After her bronze medal in 1976 she continued to race, winning another World Cup downhill in 1979, and ranking fourth overall in that year. A medal hopeful at Lake Placid in 1980, she was unable to come through. However in three years on the World Cup circuit since, she has continued to be a force in the downhill races.

PITOU, Penelope Theresa.

B. 08 OCT 1938 Bayside, NY. Silver(2): 1960 Downhill, 1960 Giant Slalom. After several successful seasons with the U.S. ski team, Penny Pitou competed at the 1956 Winter Olympics, but with little success. She continued to ski the European circuit, however, and by 1958 had gained a reputation as one of the world's top skiiers. Her European experience also included becoming fluent in several languages and climbing the Matterhorn—without a guide.

In 1959 Penny Pitou began to win downhills and giant slaloms with frequency and was a gold medal favorite at Squaw Valley in 1960. She just missed the gold in two races at Squaw Valley but her name made the headlines there in another way. She was linked romantically with Austrian star, Egon Zimmerman, a gold medalist in 1964, and they would later marry and then divorce. After retiring from competition, Penny

Pitou began to run ski schools in New England. She also has served as a fashion consultant to the ski industry, and a participant in ski shows and ski promotions.

SAUBERT, Jean Marlene.

B. 01 MAY 1942 Roseberg, OR. Silver: 1964 Giant Slalom (tied); Bronze: 1964 Slalom. A winner of national titles in the late 50's, Jean Saubert failed to be named to the 1960 Olympic team but continued to improve. At the 1962 FIS World Championships she placed in the top ten in all four events (three races and alpine combined). In 1963 and 1964 she was dominating United States' skiing and beginning to win races on the European circuit. She was one of the favorites at the 1964 Olympics and did not disappoint, although she was unable to beat France's Goitschel sisters, who nipped her in the two technical races. Saubert's silver medal was actually shared with Christine Goitschel, with whom she tied in the giant slalom. After the Olympics, Jean Saubert continued to race successfully through 1966 when she retired just after the FIS summer championships.

Saubert graduated from Oregon State and did graduate work at Brigham Young. Since retiring she has had a career as a teacher and a ski coach.

SNITE, Betsy

B. 20 DEC 1938 Grand Rapids, MI. Silver: 1960 Slalom. After high school in Hanover, New Hampshire, Betsy Snite joined the U.S. ski team and competed mostly in Europe in the late 50's. She was a rare skiier in that she seemed equally adept at all three disciplines. Her finest moment prior to the Olympics came in Grindelwald, Switzerland, where she finished second in the downhill, and won the giant slalom and combined titles. She retired shortly after her Olympic silver medal and has since become Mrs. Bill Reilly.

JESSE AND LUZ

At the 1936 Olympics in Berlin, Jesse Owens fouled on his first two long jumps in the qualifying round. In the 1960's he was the best man at a wedding in Germany. Not related? Hardly.

After fouling those first two jumps in 1936, Owens felt a tap on his shoulder. It was his strongest competitor, Luz Long of Germany. There, in the Olympic stadium, in front of 100,000 Germans and Adolf Hitler, Luz Long befriended the black American, Jesse Owens. He told Owens he should move his mark back one foot, not even try to hit the take-off board. Long told him that with his skill, he would still qualify easily. Owens listened and did just that. He did qualify easily and the next day won the gold medal. The silver medalist was Luz Long.

Long and Owens became fast friends during the Berlin Olympics, they spent many hours together talking of their lives. But their friendship extended way beyond that. Owens would never forget the blonde Aryan who had befriended him in front of Hitler and after the Olympics were over, they wrote each other frequently.

War broke out and Long was called to fight for Germany, but the letters between the two athletes did not stop. One letter from Luz to Jesse, written from the North African desert, spoke of Long's infant son, whom he barely knew. It read:

> My heart tells me, if I be honest with you, that this is the last letter I shall ever write. If it is so, I ask you something. It is you go to Germany when this war is done, someday find my son Karl, and tell him about his father. Tell him, Jesse, what times were like when we were not separated by war. I am saying—tell him how things can be between men on this earth. (*Jesse* by Jesse Owens with Paul Neimark. Plainfield: Logos, 1978.)

Owens promised he would someday visit Karl Long, but fervently wished he could also see Luz again. It was not to be. Luz Long was killed shortly after he wrote that letter, but the promise would not be forgotten by the man that was Jesse Owens.

In the 1960's, Owens went to Germany and met Karl Long. He told him of his father and the courage he had displayed that August day in Berlin. He told him of the love that had developed between them. A few years later, Karl Long was to be married, and although he would have liked a brother, or his father, to be his best man, there was none that could be. But he knew there could be only one choice and that is how Jesse Owens, the son of a black Alabama sharecropper, came to stand by Karl Long, the son of a blonde, Aryan hero, on the most important day of Long's life.

Not the boycotts, not the protests or the rules hassles, not the massacre in Munich, or the political mechanizations—that is what the Olympic Games were meant to be.

ARCHERY

MEN

Archery appeared on the Olympic program in 1900, 1904, 1908 and 1920, but then was not again an Olympic sport until 1972. The United States did not participate in 1900 or 1920, had only one archer present at London in 1908, and has entered full teams in 1972 in 1976. In 1972 and 1976 United States' archers won both gold medals. In 1904 the Olympic archery events doubled as the United States' championships and there were no foreign competitors. Many people do not consider these truly to be Olympic events, but they were on the program and although no foreigners competed, there were foreign entrants, causing us to include the 1904 archers.

OUTSTANDING PERFORMANCES

Most Gold Medals
2 G. Phillip Bryant
Most Medals
3 G. Phillip Bryant, Robert Williams,
William Thompson
Oldest Medalist
68y194d Samuel Duvall
Youngest Medalist
15y125d Henry Richardson

BRYANT, George Phillip.
B. 22 FEB 1878 Melrose, MA. D. 18 APR 1938 Marshfield, MA.
Gold(2): 1904 Double York Round, 1904 Double American Round, Bronze: 1904 Team Round. The 1904 Olympic archery events were the first big wins for Phil Bryant. But he later went on to win the United States title in 1905, 1909, 1911 and 1912.

Bryant graduated from Harvard and Harvard Law School. He practiced law in Boston for 18 years before taking an executive's position with the Brant Rock Water Company in his hometown of Marshfield. He also served on the Marshfield Board of Selectman.

BRYANT, Wallace.
B. 19 DEC 1863 Melrose, MA. D. 02 MAY 1953 Gloucester, MA. Bronze: 1904 Team Round. Wallace Bryant shot for the Boston Archery Club in 1904. He was probably their best known archer, as he had been national champion in 1903, although his younger brother, Phil, eventually surpassed him. Wallace Bryant later became a very famous portrait artist.

CLARK, William A.
D. 20 OCT 1913. Silver: 1904 Team Round. William Clark represented the Cincinnati Archers in 1904 and helped them win the silver medal, as well as finishing sixth in the Double American Round individual event. Clark was U.S. champion in 1886, 1887 and 1897 and also won the Ohio State Championship at the Double York Round in 1900, 1903-04 and 1908.

DALLIN, Cyrus Edwin.
B. 22 NOV 1861 Springfield, UT. D. 14 NOV 1944 Arlington Heights, MA. Bronze: 1904 Team Round. Cyrus Dallin shot for the Boston Archery Club in 1904 but, individually, was not one of the top archers in the country. His primary fame came as an outstanding sculptor.

Dallin came to Boston in 1880 from Salt Lake City and studied art at night with the well-known Truman Bartlett. He later studied in Paris under Henri Chapu and Jean Dampt.

In 1884 the city of Boston commissioned a statue to be built of Paul Revere and Dallin later won two open competitions to be named the sculptor. He did the statue and considered it his best work but had to fight for over 50 years to have it erected by the city. In 1940 the statue was dedicated on the Paul Revere Mall behind the Old North Church.

DUVALL, Samuel Harding.
B. 11 MAR 1836. D. 26 SEP 1908 Liberty, IN. Silver: 1904 Team Round. Samuel Duvall, from Liberty, Indiana, was a member of the Cincinnati Archers in 1904. By shooting on the winning team at the 1904 Olympics he set a still-standing record as the oldest American to ever participate, or win a medal, in the Olympic Games. Duvall never won a national championship but was Ohio champion in 1889 (Double York Round) and 1890 (Double American Round). He made his living as a farmer and livestock buyer.

HUBBARD, Charles R.
Silver: 1904 Team Round. Charles Hubbard shot for the Cincinnati Archers in 1904. In addition to competing in the Olympic team round, he finished 11th in the Double American Round at the 1904 Olympics.

MAXSON, Lewis W.

B. c1850. D. 20 JUL 1918 Washington, DC. Gold: 1904 Team Round. Lewis Maxson was one of the best known archers at the turn of the century. He had been United States champion from 1889 until 1894 and again in 1898 and he also served many years as secretary of the National Archery Association. Maxson shot for the Potomac Archers, the top team in the country from 1901 until 1904. In addition to the team event at the Olympics, he also competed in both individual events—but with little success. Maxson was a patent attorney.

PACE, Darrell Owen.

B. 23 OCT 1956 Cincinnati, OH. Gold: 1976 Double FITA Round. Darrell Pace was probably the world's top archer in the 1970's. He was United States Champion from 1973-76 and first competed internationally in 1973, finishing 23rd at the World Championships. But his next three appearances would be a bit more successful as he won the World title in 1975 and 1979, becoming the first person in the "modern" era of archery to win the title twice.

In addition to his Olympic gold, Pace also won a silver medal at the 1979 Pan-American Games and was a member of the 1980 Olympic team. He has set several world records and his FITA Round of 1,341 shot in 1979 has lasted through 1982. Though official world records are not kept for Double FITA Rounds, the two highest scores on record are the 2,571 which Pace shot to win the Olympic gold and the 2,570 which he shot at the 1976 U.S Olympic Trials.

RICHARDSON, Henry Barber.

B. 19 MAY 1889 Boston, MA. D. 19 NOV 1963 New York, NY. Bronze(2): 1904 Team Round, 1908 York Round. Aged only 15 in 1904, Henry Richardson is one of the youngest medalists ever among United States men. Though his 1904 medal came as a member of the Boston Archery Club he won an individual medal at the London Olympics of 1908. In addition to his Olympic successes, Richardson won the U.S. title at the Double York Round in 1906-07 and 1910, and at the Double American Round in 1906 and 1910.

Richardson graduated in 1910 from Harvard, in 1914 from Harvard Medical School and then began a career in internal medicine on the staff of the Cornell University Medical School. But in 1945, at the age of 56, he returned to school as a student at Columbia to study psychiatry. He went on to become a practicing psychiatrist serving on the staffs of both the Columbia and New York University Medical Colleges.

SPENCER, Galen Carter.

B. 19 SEP 1840 New York, NY. D. 19 OCT 1904 Greenwich, CT. Gold: 1904 Team Round. At the 1904 Olympics, "G. C." Spencer competed in the Double American Round on September 19—his 64th birthday. He finished 13th in that event but two days later helped his Potomac Archers team win the gold medal, thereby becoming the oldest American to ever win a gold medal. At the time of the 1904 Olympics, Spencer was from Greenwich, Connecticut where he was a retired minister.

THOMPSON, William Henry.

B. 10 MAR 1848 Calhoun, GA. D. 1918 Seattle, WA. Gold: 1904 Team Round; Bronze(2): 1904 Double York Round, 1904 Double American Round. In 1879 Will Thompson became the first American to be crowned our national archery champion. He repeated that victory four times, the last of which was in 1908, almost 30 years after the first. He continued to compete in the National Championships until 1913, when he was 65 years old, still placing ninth.

Thompson was from Seattle, Washington in 1904 but he had grown up in the hills of Georgia. He and his brother, Maurice, grew up hunting in those hills with bow and arrow and Maurice later wrote of these tales in his book, *Witchery of Archery*. Will Thompson also did some writing about the sport of archery but his primary occupation was as an attorney.

WILLIAMS, John Chester.

B. 12 SEP 1953 Erie, PA. Gold: 1972 Double FITA Round. John Williams finished second at the 1969 World Championships but for the next several years he was never beaten. He won the World title in 1971 and 1972 as well as winning the World Field Championships in 1972. At the 1972 Olympics his score of 2,528 was a world's best for the Double FITA Round.

Williams attended Texas A & M briefly but eventually graduated from Cal State (San Bernadino) with a degree in business and management. He has put the degree to good use as the product manager for Yamaha International's archery division.

WILLIAMS, Robert W., Jr.

B. 24 JAN 1841 Franklin County, PA. D. 10 DEC 1914 Washington, DC. Gold: 1904 Team Round; Silver(2): 1904 Double York Round, 1904 Double American Round. In 1883, 1885 and 1902, Robert Williams won the National Championship by winning the Double York Round. He also won the Double American Round six times at the American championships.

Williams can probably claim to be the only American Olympian to have fought in the Civil War. He entered the Union Army in 1861 as a private, was afterwards elected captain of Company B of the 54th Ohio Volunteers and later was promoted to colonel of the regiment. He participated in the battles of Shiloh, Vicksburg, Chickasaw and Bayou.

In 1899 Williams was appointed the first deputy commissioner of the Internal Revenue Service, a post he held until his death. Death came as the result of pneumonia, which had bothered Williams constantly after suffering several bad war wounds.

WOODRUFF, C. S.

Silver: 1904 Team Round. Besides competing in the Olympic team competition, C. S. Woodruff competed in both individual events at the 1904 Olympics—finishing eighth in the Double York Round and fourth in the Double American Round. Woodruff's only national championship came in the Double American Round in 1901, an event he also won at the Ohio State Championships in 1904 and 1906. Woodruff's wife, Laura, was also a fine archer who finished fourth in both the women's individual events in the 1904 Olympics.

WOMEN

Women competed in archery at the 1904 Olympics but not again until 1972, when it became part of the regular Olympic program. In both 1972 and 1976, United States' archers won the women's championship at the Olympics. The 1904 Olympic contests, like the men's events of the same year, are of disputed Olympic caliber.

COOKE, Emma C.

Silver(2): 1904 Double Columbia Round, 1904 Double National Round. Emma Cooke of the Potomac Archers finished second to Lida Howell in both Olympic events in 1904. It was a common occurence for Miss Cooke as the only national titles she won in target shooting came in 1906 when Mrs. Howell did not compete. Emma Cooke also won the flight shooting national championship in 1902 with a distance of 190 yards.

HOWELL, Lida Scott.

B. 28 AUG 1859. D. 20 DEC 1939. Gold(2): 1904 Double Columbia Round, 1904 Double National Round. Lida Scott became interested in archery in the 1870's and won her first titles, the Ohio State Championship, in 1881 and 1882. In the spring of 1883 she married Millard C. Howell and also won her first national championship.

Lida Scott Howell won 17 national championships of the 20 she contested between 1883 and 1907—surely one of the most amazing records in any sport. Her scores in the 1895 championship set records which were not broken until 1931—35 years later. As an archer, she was clearly a woman ahead of her time.

POLLACK, Jessie.

Bronze(2): 1904 Double Columbia Round, 1904 Double National Round. Mrs. H. W. "Jessie" Pollack made a career of finishing second to Lida Scott Howell. They competed for the same club, the Cincinnati Archers, and virtually in all the same tournaments. As a result, Jessie Pollack can claim no national titles and only one Ohio State championship—that being the 1887 Double National Round. Mrs. Pollack's husband was also an accomplished archer.

Courtesy Des Moines Register

The 1972 women's archery gold medalist, Doreen Wilber.

RYON, Luann.

B. 13 JAN 1953 Long Beach, CA. Gold: 1976 Double FITA Round. Luann Ryon took up the sport of archery rather late, beginning only in 1971. By the time of the 1976 Olympics, she had competed in only one U.S. Championship, finishing 11th in 1975, and had never competed internationally. She had won the 1976 Olympic trials with the best score of her life, 2,457, but she bettered that with 2,499 at Montreal to take the gold medal.

After the 1976 Olympics, Luann Ryon proved her victory was no fluke. She won the U.S. title in 1976 and in 1977, won the World Championships as an individual, and led the U.S. to a team title as well. Her score at the 1977 Worlds—2,515—was a world's best for a woman in the Double FITA Round.

WILBER, Doreen Viola Hansen.

B. 08 JAN 1930 Rutland, IA. Gold: 1972 Double FITA Round. Between 1965 and 1975, Doreen Wilber was undoubtedly the top woman archer in the United States. Participating in eight National Championships in that decade, she won four (1969, 1971, 1973-74), was second twice, and third once. Although she was primarily a target shooter, Mrs. Wilber also entered the 1967 National Field Archery Championship—and won it in her only attempt.

Internationally, Doreen Wilber also distinguished herself. She competed in two World Championships, finishing second in both 1969 and 1971. She also shot several times in international invitationals, and these, combined with her Olympic gold, gave her an international record of four wins and three seconds in eight appearances. At the 1972 Olympics, her gold medal was earned by scoring 2,424—at the time a world's best for women.

BASKETBALL

MEN

The United States domination of basketball is unparalleled in Olympic annals. Since the first official Olympic tournament, in 1936, the United States has won every Olympic basketball championship, save 1972 (and 1980 when they did not compete). Amazingly, the only game the United States has ever lost was the 1972 final. Two moments stand out.

Probably the most memorable U.S. Olympic basketball team was the 1960 team. Certainly the greatest Olympic team ever, it was also the greatest amateur basketball team ever assembled. In fact, a starting line-up of Oscar Robertson and Jerry West at guards, Jerry Lucas and Terry Dischinger at forwards, and Walt Bellamy at center, would match up well head-to-head against even the greatest of pro teams. From 1961 to 1964 the NBA Rookie of the Year came from the above group—all save Lucas, who went on to earn a spot in the Basketball Hall of Fame, as did West and Robertson. The 1960 team was never pressed enroute to the gold and its like will probably not be seen again.

Munich—1972, are words that always bring consternation to U.S. basketball fans. It was there that the U.S. lost its only basketball game in the Olympics—or did it? It was a close final against the Soviet Union, but the Soviets led most of the way. However the U.S. fought back and was behind only 49-48 with a few seconds to play—but Russia controlled the ball. Then Doug Collins stole a pass and broke downcourt for a sure lay-up, only to be fouled on a smart play by a Russian defender. With the pressure of 36 years of tradition weighing upon him, Collins sunk both free throws. U.S. 50, USSR 49. Three seconds on the clock. The USSR tried to inbound the ball but failed and there was jubilation on our side. But in a series of unbelievable rulings the Soviets were given two more chances, and finally they scored—on the third try—to win 51—50. A series of appeals to everyone from the IOC on down was rejected. In dismay, the United States' team, feeling it had been wronged, declined to accept the silver medals.

OUTSTANDING PERFORMANCES

Most Gold Medals
 2 Bob Kurland, Bill Hougland,
  Burdette Haldorson
Youngest Gold Medalist
 19y186d Spencer Haywood
Oldest Gold Medalist
 30y319d Jesse Renick

ARMSTRONG, Michael Taylor.
B. 05 OCT 1955 Houston, TX. Gold: 1976. "Tate" Armstrong attended Duke University and was the star of that team for four years in the mid-70's, graduating in 1977. The 6'-3" guard was known for his shooting touch and defensive skills. After earning his gold medal and graduating from Duke he played briefly in the NBA for two years with the Chicago Bulls, although without distinction. After his retirement from basketball he worked briefly as a stock broker but is now enrolled in business school.

ARNETTE, Jay Hoyland.
B. 19 DEC 1938. Gold: 1960. Jay Arnette was a 6'-2" guard from the University of Texas who graduated in 1963. He took his gold medal to the NBA where he played for two full seasons, and three games of a third, with the Cincinnati Royals. Between seasons of professional basketball Arnette attended dental school at his alma mater. He eventually became licensed in both dentistry and as a pharmacist but is today a successful orthodontist.

BALTER, Samuel J., Jr.
B. 15 OCT 1909 Detroit, MI. Gold: 1936. Signed by the Chicago White Sox out of high school, Sam Balter instead attended UCLA in the late 20's where he was a star of the basketball team and its captain in 1929. As pro basketball was virtually nonexistent in the depression days, he continued playing as an amateur with a team sponsored by Universal Pictures. When basketball made its first Olympic appearance in 1936 he helped the United States win its first gold medal in this sport and retains the dubious distinction of being our shortest (5'-9¾") basketball Olympian ever.

Balter later went on to a short career as a teacher and basketball coach. However he became quite famous as a sportscaster and radio announcer in the southern California area, so much so that in 1945 *Variety* voted him the top news commentator of the U.S. He was the first person to do coast-to-coast radio sports commentary and also the first person to cover a college football game for television. In 1970 he was voted into the Helms Basketball Hall of Fame.

BANTOM, Michael Allen.
B. 03 DEC 1951 Philadelphia, PA. Silver: 1972. A 6′-9″ forward, Mike Bantom played for St. Joseph's University in his hometown of Philadelphia before joining the ill-fated 1972 U.S. Olympic basketball team. He was drafted in the first round by the Phoenix Suns in 1973 the eighth pick overall in that year's NBA draft—and established himself immediately by making the NBA All-Rookie team and averaging 10.1 points a game that year. He has continued to play in the NBA as a solid but not spectacular performer and since 1977 has been a member of the Indiana Pacers.

BARKER, Clifford Eugene.
B. 15 JAN 1921. Gold: 1948. Cliff Barker starred with the great Kentucky teams of the late 40's. The 1948 gold medal winning basketball team was largely composed of Kentucky players, as five of them were on the team. In 1949 the NBA was formed from a merger of the National Basketball League and the Basketball Association of America. Though most of the teams in the new league were already established, a new team was formed called the Indianapolis Olympians, composed of (and partly owned by) the five Kentucky Olympians—including Cliff Barker, who served a dual role as player-coach. That first year, 1949-50, Barker helped the Indianapolis team to a division championship though they did not win the league title. Barker played for two more years, and coached for one more, before retiring.

BARKSDALE, Donald Argee.
B. 31 MAR 1923. Gold: 1948. Don Barksdale was the first black to play on the U.S. Olympic basketball team. Unfortunately he could not then join the pro ranks—they did not allow blacks at that time. The 6′-6″ UCLA product then played four years of AAU ball with the Oakland Bittners before the ban on blacks in the NBA was lifted. In the NBA he played for two years with the original Baltimore Bullets and was the top player on that team—averaging 12.6 and 13.8 points per game in the

days of much lower scores. In 1953 Barksdale was traded to the Boston Celtics where he played only two more years, but he was elected to play in the NBA All-Star Game in 1953.

Barksdale was also an outstanding track star, having won the 1944 AAU triple jump championship. Since retirement from pro basketball, he has worked as a real estate investor and nightclub and radio station owner.

BARNES, James.
B. 13 APR 1941 Tuckerman, AK. Gold: 1964. At 6′-8″ and a muscular 240 lbs., "Bad News" Barnes played mostly center in his college days at Texas Western (now Texas at El Paso). He also played center for the 1964 Olympic team alternating with Mel Counts at that position. He was the first round choice of the New York Knicks in 1964 and played well for two years with them, averaging in double figures. In 1966 they traded Barnes, a forward in the NBA, to the Baltimore Bullets (now of Washington). Barnes never again approached his first two years, finishing up his career as a journeyman with four more teams before his retirement in 1971.

BARRETT, Michael.
B. 05 SEP 1943 Montgomery, WV. Gold: 1968. Mike Barrett went to college at West Virginia Tech but later played AAU ball while he was in the navy. It was then that he played for the U.S. in the 1967 World's Championship and won a gold medal as a member of the 1968 Olympic team. Barrett then played three years in the now-defunct ABA. A 6′-2″ guard, he was perfectly suited to that league as his long suit was the ability to burn it up from outside. In 1969-70, with Washington, he had his best year in pro basketball as he averaged 15 points per game, which was aided by his 62 3-point goals.

BEARD, Ralph Milton, Jr.
B. 02 DEC 1927 Louisville, KY. Gold: 1948. Ralph Beard was a member of the Kentucky basketball team which sent five members to the London Olympics. He then joined his teammates on the Indianapolis Olympians and played for only two seasons in the nascent NBA. Beard's two years were very successful, however. He was a playmaking guard who was among the assists leaders in both years and was voted first-team all-NBA

Seven members of our first Olympic basketball team, all from the Universal Pictures AAU squad. Kneeling (L-R) — manager Lloyd Goldstein, Duane Swanson, Don Piper, Sam Balter. Standing (L-R) — Carl Shy, Art Mollner, Carl Knowles, Frank Lubin.

Courtesy Frank Lubin

Courtesy Indiana University

Walt Bellamy, the center from the "greatest amateur basketball team of all time," the 1960 U.S. Olympic team.

in 1951 after having made the second team as a rookie. Beard later went into the wholesale drug business.

BECK, Louis W., Jr.
B. 19 APR 1922. D. 25 APR 1970. Gold: 1948. Lou Beck never played college basketball but was an AAU star in the 40's with the great Phillips '66 teams. He also never played professional basketball, instead accepting a position with the Phillips company.

BELLAMY, Walter Jones, Jr.
B. 24 JUL 1939 New Bern, NC. Gold: 1960. Walt Bellamy was the starting center on the 1960 Olympic gold medalists. He played for Indiana University and made most all-America teams in 1960 and 1961 before being drafted in 1961 by the Chicago Packers. Bellamy starred in the NBA from the start—he was Rookie of the Year in 1962, leading the league in field-goal percentage (with a new record of .519) and averaging 31.6 points and 19 rebounds a game. During a 14-year career which saw him play for five teams, he was one of the top centers in the league and ended up with career averages of over 20 points and 14 rebounds. Bellamy's 14th year was a short one as he played just one game with the New Orleans Jazz but this made him the last of the 1960 Olympians to be playing pro basketball.

Bellamy had an active business career while he played pro basketball. Investing wisely in real estate and office buildings his career since leaving basketball has been managing his investments and doing public relations for several Southern firms.

BISHOP, Ralph English.
B. 01 JAN 1915. D. c1978. Gold: 1936. Ralph Bishop was a center at the University of Washington. In 1936 their team finished third in the Olympic Trials and was therefore allowed to select one player to join the 14-man Olympic basketball roster. Bishop did not play a lot at the Games but he had great success on the trip to Berlin. He won the U.S. Olympic team's ping-pong tournament by defeating fellow hoopster Sam Balter in the finals. After the Olympics Bishop played AAU basketball for several years.

BONTEMPS, Ronald Yngve.
B. 11 AUG 1926 Taylorville, IL. Gold: 1952. After playing for tiny Beloit College and graduating from there in

1951, Ron Bontemps qualified for the 1952 Olympic team as a member of the Peoria Caterpillars AAU basketball team. Bontemps never played pro basketball, but instead opted for the AAU leagues where he starred for three years with the Caterpillars. It also worked out to be a fine career move as he took a job with the Caterpillar Tractor Co. in 1951 and has worked for them ever since.

BOOZER, Robert Lewis.

B. 26 APR 1937. Gold: 1960. Bullet Bob Boozer was an all-American forward at Kansas State who graduated in 1959. A sure bet to play pro basketball, he had a dream of playing in the Olympics, so although he was drafted by Cincinnati in 1959, he made them wait a year while he played AAU basketball with the Peoria Cats—and won a gold medal.

Boozer was worth the wait. He only played four years with Cincinnati but he had an 11-year NBA career during which he averaged 15 points per game and played in one NBA All-Star Game—in 1968. During his last season, he helped the Milwaukee Bucks win the 1971 championship.

Boozer returned to his hometown of Omaha after leaving pro basketball. He has worked for Northwestern Bell Telephone as well as owning several radio stations in partnership with baseball great Bob Gibson. Boozer has also done some sportscasting on local college basketball games.

BORYLA, Vincent Joseph.

B. 11 MAR 1921 East Chicago, IN. Gold: 1948. Vince Boryla took 10 years to get out of college—World War II interrupted his studies. Beginning at Notre Dame he also spent a semester at the U.S. Naval Academy, but eventually graduated from the University of Denver in 1949. He was one of the oldest collegiate all-Americans ever at 28 years old. He played in 1947-48 with the Denver Nuggets in AAU leagues and also made AAU all-America. He played in the NBA for five years with the New York Knicks. In 1954 he retired as a player but coached the Knicks until 1958.

BOUSHKA, Richard James.

B. 29 JUL 1934 St. Louis, MO. Gold: 1956. Dick Boushka played for St. Louis University and graduated in 1955, twice having received all-America mention. He

NBA MVP'S AND ROOKIE STARS

With so many Olympic basketball players going on to the NBA, did you ever wonder how many of them became big, big stars in that league? Well, there are several criteria by which to measure that.

Only two American Olympians have been named the NBA MVP. Oscar Robertson won that award in 1964, but Bill Russell was named the league MVP five times, in 1958, 1960, 1961, 1962, 1963, and 1965.

Seven times the NBA Rookie of the Year has come from the ranks of the U.S. Olympic basketball team. It has occurred in two streaks of four and three consecutive years. The first streak came right after the 1960 team graduated to the pros and the winners were Oscar Robertson (1961), Walt Bellamy (1962), Terry Dischinger (1963), and Jerry Lucas (1964). The second streak came from the 1976 team and included Adrian Dantley (1977), Walter Davis (1978), and Phil Ford (1979).

Now our last criterion is making the official NBA All-Star teams. The league announces a first and second team and twelve U.S. Olympians have been selected. Jerry West leads here with ten selections to the first team and two to the second, which is a record matched only by non-Olympian, Bob Cousy. Oscar Robertson is next with nine first team selections and two second team. The others were Bill Russell (3-8), Jerry Lucas (3-2), Spencer Haywood (2-2), Alex Groza (2-0), Ralph Beard (1-1), Walter Davis (0-2), Jo Jo White (0-2), Adrian Dantley (0-1), Phil Ford (0-1), and Clyde Lovelette (0-1).

played several seasons of AAU ball but never played in the NBA. He played most of his AAU career with the Wichita Vickers and had a career high game of 54 points.

The Wichita Vickers were sponsored by Vickers Petroleum for whom Boushka also worked. Boushka gradually rose up the company ladder until he was president of the firm. In 1980 Vickers was sold and Boushka left the company to start several of his own ventures, which have been very successful. Dick Boushka's sons have carried on the family's athletic fame—two of them have started for the Notre Dame football team, one played football and track at Kansas, and another, a heavily recruited high school quarterback, is now going to Stanford. The family basketball games are fierce affairs but the sons report that the 6'-5" Boushka can still hit from outside.

BRADLEY, William Warren.
B. 28 JUL 1943 St. Louis, MO. Gold: 1964. A renaissance man if ever there was one, Bill Bradley was the greatest college basketball player of the mid-60's. Eschewing the normal route of immediate pro stardom, he instead accepted a Rhodes Scholarship to study at Oxford. While at Oxford he played occasional basketball in European leagues and found that he missed the competition of top-flight basketball.

Bradley joined the New York Knicks in the middle of the 1968 amidst much media hoopla. He was basically a disappointment that first season and it was attributed to the fact that, at 6'-5" and of only average speed, he fit in at neither guard nor forward. Eventually Bradley became a star in the NBA but not of the individual variety. Never an all-star or an outstanding one-on-one player, he became the consummate team player and helped the New York Knicks to win two NBA championships. After an 11-year pro career, all with the Knicks, he retired in 1977.

Bradley's accomplishments did not end with professional sports. Today he serves the state of New Jersey as one of their United States Senators.

BREWER, James Turner.
B. 03 DEC 1951 Maywood, IL. Silver: 1972. A 6'-9" power forward, Jim Turner played for the University of Minnesota before taking his talents to the Olympics and the NBA. Never a great scorer he still made several all-America teams while in college because of his defensive skills. In 1973 he was the second pick of the NBA draft as the Cleveland Cavaliers hoped he would be the one to lead their young team out of the league basement. Brewer played six years at Cleveland before being traded to several other teams. His pro career was similar to his college days, as he has been a defensive star, twice being named to the NBA All-Defensive Second Team.

BROWN, Lawrence Harvey.
B. 14 SEP 1940 Brooklyn, NY. Gold: 1964. At a shade under 5'-10", Larry Brown shares with Sam Balter the distinction of being the shortest U.S. Olympic basketball players. Brown played his college ball at North Carolina and then played two years of AAU hoop with the Akron Goodyears. At his height, and with his deadly outside shot, he was far better suited for the ABA with its 3-point goals, and from 1967-1972 he played in that league as a steady performer. In 1969 he played with the champion Oakland Oaks and led the league in assists that year.

Since retiring as a player, Larry Brown has been one of the game's best, and most peripatetic, coaches. He started with the Carolina Cougars of the ABA and moved in 1974 to the Denver Nuggets. He stayed with the Nuggets when they joined the NBA in 1976 but in 1979 left to take over the UCLA college coaching job. He left there after two seasons to return to the NBA, but again lasted only two seasons before accepting the head coaching job at the University of Kansas.

BUCKNER, William Quinn.
B. 20 AUG 1954 Phoenix, IL. Gold: 1976. While at Indiana University, Quinn Buckner had a difficult decision to make. He was a college star on both the football and basketball teams, and if he had wanted to, could probably have played defensive back in the NFL. Instead he elected to play pro basketball, first with the Milwaukee Bucks and of late with the Boston Celtics. A 6'-3" guard, Buckner is known primarily as a defensive specialist and has four times been made a member of the NBA All-Defensive Team. Buckner was a member of both an NCAA and an Olympic champion in 1976—one of the few players to pull off this double.

BURLESON, Tommy Loren.

B. 24 FEB 1952 Crossnore, NC. Silver: 1972. One of the most ironic sights to American Olympic fans must be the memory of 7'-4" Tommy Burleson exulting at Munich in 1972, as twice it appeared the U.S. had beaten the Russians in the final game. But it was not to be.

Burleson was used to success. In 1974 he led his NC State team to the NCAA championship after defeating UCLA in the semi-finals to end their string of eight straight championships. The very tall, yet very thin, Burleson has gone on to be a good center in the NBA, but he has probably lacked the muscle and athletic skills to be a dominant force. Burleson remains the tallest United States Olympian ever.

CAIN, Carl Cecil.

B. 02 AUG 1934 Freeport, IL. Gold: 1956. Carl Cain attended the University of Iowa, graduating from there in 1956. He was the star at Iowa when they twice won the Big Ten Championship and went to the finals of the NCAA tournament before losing. Cain never played pro basketball but went on to a career as a bookkeeper. For a time he was the brother-in-law of 1956 Olympic teammate, K.C. Jones.

CALDWELL, Joe Louis.

B. 01 NOV 1941 Texas City, TX. Gold: 1964. Jumping Joe Caldwell, the human pogo stick, played for Arizona State in the early 60's. He went on to play for 11 years in the NBA and the ABA, always as a top performer. Caldwell was only 6'-5" tall, short for a forward, but he played that position well thanks to his prodigious leaping ability.

In 1970 Caldwell jumped leagues, going from Atlanta of the NBA to Carolina of the ABA. He later became enmeshed in a bitter contract dispute as a result of his changing leagues and some later developments.

CARPENTER, Gordon.

B. 24 SEP 1919 Saddle, AK. Gold: 1948. "Shorty" Carpenter never played either college or pro basketball. He was an AAU legend, however, in the 1940's. From 1943 thru 1948, Carpenter was a member of the AAU champion Phillips Oilers. He was a six-time AAU all-America, five with Phillips and one with the Denver Chevrolets.

Carpenter later became a basketball coach with the Denver Chevrolets and was their coach when they represented the United States at the 1950 World's Championship.

CARR, Kenneth Alan.

B. 15 AUG 1955 Washington, DC. Gold: 1976. DeMatha High School in Hyattsville, Maryland is one of the greatest high school basketball powers in the country—year-in and year-out. It was there that Kenny Carr got his basketball roots and they eventually led him to be an ACC star at North Carolina State, an Olympic star as a forward in 1976, and a good professional player, first with Los Angeles and later with Cleveland.

CLAWSON, John Richard.

B. 15 MAY 1944 Duluth, MN. Gold: 1968. John Clawson attended the University of Michigan from where he graduated in 1966. At 6'-4" he was a good solid swingman, but never was a great collegiate player. Although he played on three Big Ten championship teams, the likes of Cazzie Russell and Bill Buntin made it difficult for Clawson to get much playing time. After graduation he joined the Army and played for several seasons on their teams, being a member of three AAU championship teams and also representing the United States in 1967 at the World's Championship. After the Olympics, Clawson played one year of pro basketball with the Oakland Oaks of the ABA. He played in almost all the team's games, primarily as a playmaking guard. After his year in the pros he returned to law school and now makes his living as an attorney.

COLLINS, Paul Douglas.

B. 28 JUL 1951 Christopher, IL. Silver: 1972. In the final game in 1972, Doug Collins stole the ball from a Russian and broke downcourt for the lay-up that would have given the U.S. a one-point victory. He was intentionally fouled to prevent this and missed the lay-up, but in one of the Olympics' great clutch performances he calmly sank both free throws to seemingly give the U.S. another Olympic gold. Several minutes later, however, the joy turned to sorrow as the officials and Alexandr Belov combined to give the Soviet Union a one-point victory.

Collins returned for his senior year at Illinois State where he made many all-America teams. He was the first-pick in the 1973 NBA draft—by the Philadelphia 76ers—and a great NBA career was predicted for him. Collins played for nine years in the NBA and undoubtedly had a good career. But the greatness predicted for him never emerged, held back by a never-ending string of injuries. At his best he was one of the top guards in the NBA.

Doug Collins is now an assistant coach at Arizona State and occasionally does basketball commentary for television.

COUNTS, Mel Grant.
B. 16 OCT 1941 Coos Bay, OR. Gold: 1964. Before Tommy Burleson came along in 1972, Mel Counts was the tallest U.S. Olympian ever. The 7'-0", 230 lb. hoopster from Oregon State played center for the 1964 U.S. Olympic team and helped lead the team to victory. Counts then began a 12-year professional career, starting out as a back-up center to Bill Russell of the Boston Celtics. Counts played little in those years, as Russell was the dominant force in the league, but his association with the Celtics provided him with the rare double of an Olympic gold medal and an NBA championship. Counts later played for the Los Angeles Lakers (backing up Wilt Chamberlain), the Phoenix Suns, and the New Orleans Jazz. He was never a great center, and, in fact, rarely started, but his height and size made him a player to be reckoned with.

DANTLEY, Adrian Delano.
B. 28 FEB 1955 Washington, DC. Gold: 1976. Adrian Dantley came from basketball powerhouse DeMatha High School in suburban Washington and then attended Notre Dame. As a sophomore and junior he was a first-team all-America in college. After playing on the 1976 gold medal winning team, he claimed hardship and declared himself eligible for the NBA draft. Dantley started out his NBA career with Buffalo, but has since played for Indiana, Los Angeles, and Utah. He has been one of the stars of the league, making the all-rookie team in 1977 as well as being named Rookie of the Year. His best year to date has been 1981 when he was an NBA All-Star Second Team selection as well as leading the league in scoring.

DARLING, Charles Frick.
B. 20 MAR 1930 Denison, IA. Gold: 1956. Chuck Darling was a star at every level of basketball he played, although he never attempted a career in the NBA. In high school he was all-state in both Montana and Colorado before moving on to the University of Iowa. At Iowa he made all-Big Ten in 1951 and 1952, and was voted the league's most valuable player, and an all-American, in 1952—all this while making Phi Beta Kappa academically. Although Darling was drafted first by the Rochester Royals, he spurned their offers and instead played AAU ball with the Phillips '66 Oilers. This put to good use his geology background as he also become an executive of the corporation.

DAVIES, Richard Allen.
B. 21 JAN 1936 Harrisburg, PA. Gold: 1964. Dick Davies was a 6'-1" guard out of Louisiana State who was passed over by the NBA draft. As a result he joined up with the Goodyear Wingfoots AAU team and also got an excellent job as a management trainee with the Goodyear Company. While playing with the Wingfoots he was selected for the U.S. team in 1964 and won a gold medal as a result.

DAVIS, Kenneth Bryan.
B. 12 SEP 1948 Slat, KY. Silver: 1972. Ken Davis went to the small school of Georgetown College in Kentucky. He became their greatest player, scoring 3,003 points in four years there and making NAIA all-America three straight years. After graduation in 1971, Davis continued to play, mainly with the Marathon Oil AAU team. However he also won a gold medal in the 1971 Pan-American Games as a U.S. team member.

DAVIS, Walter Paul.
B. 09 SEP 1954 Pineville, NC. Gold: 1976. Walter Davis played high school basketball in South Mecklenburg, NC, so the choice of the University of North Carolina was a natural one for him. While at UNC, Davis starred all four years, never averaging less than 14 points in any season, despite Dean Smith's team approach to basketball. Davis also played for Smith on the 1976 Olympic team and was one of the primary reasons the U.S. regained the Olympic basketball gold medal.

In 1977 Walter Davis was drafted first by the Phoenix Suns and easily made the transition into the

NBA. He was voted Rookie of the Year in 1978 and named to the all-rookie team. With 24 points, six rebounds, and four assists per game, he was also voted second-team all-NBA, a feat he repeated in 1979.

DEE, Donald F.

B. 09 AUG 1943 Booneville, MO. Gold: 1968. Don Dee first attended St. Louis University but did not like it and transferred to little St. Mary of the Plains in Kansas— nearer his home of Dodge City. While at St. Mary, Dee set all sorts of school records for scoring and rebounding and made NAIA all-America. He went on to play AAU ball briefly after his graduation in 1968, but joined the U.S. Olympic team and went to Mexico City to pick up a gold medal. Upon his return he played one year of pro basketball with the Indiana Pacers of the ABA.

DISCHINGER, Terry Gilbert.

B. 21 NOV 1940. Gold: 1960. Terry Dischinger was one of the stars of the great 1960 U.S. Olympic gold medalists. He joined the team after his sophomore year at Purdue where it was obvious he was going to be a great player. In both his junior and senior years, the 6'-7" Dischinger made all-America and then was drafted in the second round by the Chicago Zephyrs. He immediately produced, averaging 25.5 points and becoming the third of four consecutive NBA rookies of the year to come from the 1960 Olympic team. Dischinger had two more excellent years, averaging 21 and 18 points, but then had to join the army for two years. He was never the same player again although he remained in the NBA for six more years, averaging about 10 points per game.

In his last few years, Dischinger attended dental school in the off season, and even did a two-game stint as player-coach of the Pistons in 1971. He ended his career with the Portland Trail Blazers and now is a dentist in Oregon.

EVANS, William Best.

B. 13 SEP 1932 Berea, KY. Gold: 1956. Bill Evans was a 6'-1" guard for the University of Kentucky in the early 50's. For him it was choice of whether to play tennis or basketball. In high school he was twice Kentucky state tennis champion and he eventually played three years of varsity tennis at Kentucky as well as basketball. After graduation in 1954 he remained at Kentucky for an-

other year to earn a master's degree. He then joined the service and was chosen for the 1956 Olympic team while playing for the Air Force All-Stars.

FORBES, James.

B. 18 JUL 1952. Silver: 1972. Jim Forbes was not originally selected to be a member of the 1972 Olympic team but was added to the squad after John Brown came down with an injury. Forbes was a 6'-8" forward.

FORD, Gilbert.

B. 14 SEP 1931 Tulia, TX. Gold: 1956. Gib Ford played for the University of Texas, graduating in 1954. While there he led the team to three Southwest Conference titles and co-captained the team in his senior year. He later played for the Phillips '66 Oilers before joining the air force. It was while playing for the air force team that he was selected to play in the 1956 Olympics.

FORD, Phil Jackson, Jr.

B. 09 FEB 1956 Rocky Mount, NC. Gold: 1976. Phil Ford attended the University of North Carolina and in the 1976 Olympics played for his college coach, Dean Smith, also of UNC. Ford was a college superstar, making various all-America teams in each of his last seasons. At 6'-2" he was small for an NBA guard but he was also one of the quickest players to ever step on a basketball court, and although a good scorer, he made his mark as a playmaker. He proved his size no handicap when, playing for the Kansas City Kings, he was named NBA Rookie of the Year in 1979, as well as making the NBA All-Rookie Team and being selected a second team NBA All-Star.

FORTENBERRY, Joseph Cephis.

B. 01 APR 1911 Slidell, TX. Gold: 1936. Joe Fortenberry was 6'-8" tall and many people think he was the first person to dunk a basketball in an organized game. Fortenberry was three-times named all-Conference center while he played at West Texas State and later played AAU ball with the Ogden Boosters, the McPherson Globe Refiners, and the Phillips '66 powerhouses. It was while he was playing with the Globe Refiners that he played for the 1936 Olympic team. Fortenberry is now a member of the Amateur Basketball Hall of Fame.

FOWLER, Calvin.
B. 11 FEB 1940 Pittsburgh, PA. Gold: 1968. Calvin Fowler attended tiny St. Francis College in Pennsylvania. He received almost no national acclaim as a collegian but after graduation joined up with the Goodyear Wingfoots and became an AAU star. In 1967 he led the Wingfoots to the AAU championship and made AAU all-America that year and the next. He played for the U.S. at the 1967 World's Championship as well as winning a gold medal at the 1967 Pan-American Games. In 1968 Fowler, a 6'-0" guard, was the sparkplug of the Olympic team which won the gold medal in Mexico City. After the Olympics he returned to AAU ball and had one year in the ABA, playing with the Carolina Cougars in 1969-70.

FRIEBERGER, Marcus Ross.
B. 27 NOV 1928 Amarillo, TX. Gold: 1952. At 6'-10", Marc Frieberger was the tallest of four brothers, all of whom were at least 6'-8" tall. Backed by those genes, he had a distinguished career as a center at the University of Oklahoma, graduating in 1951. After graduation he joined the Peoria Caterpillars of the AAU leagues and played with them for two years, during which time he qualified for the 1952 Olympics. He left Peoria in 1953 to play with the Ada Oil Company team in 1954-55 before retiring from competitive basketball. Frieberger started his business career in Peoria but later left that company to become a manufacturer's rep for machinery sales.

GIBBONS, John Haskell.
B. 07 OCT 1907 Elk City, OK. Gold: 1936. In the early 30's, John Gibbons played his basketball at Southwestern College of Winfield, Kansas, but after graduation, like many of the stars of his day, he joined the AAU leagues. He played for several AAU teams but it was as a member of the McPherson Oilers that he qualified for the 1936 Olympic team. He later joined the employ of Phillips Oil and spent his entire business career in the oil business.

GLASGOW, Victor Wayne.
B. 17 JAN 1926 Dacoma, OK. Gold: 1952. Wayne Glasgow played both baseball and basketball at the University of Oklahoma in the late 40's, graduating in 1950, but his main sport was basketball. He went on to play with the Phillips 66ers from 1950 until 1954, during

which time he was named to the Olympic team. He also accepted a position with the oil company, and 30 years later, is still working for them.

GROZA, Alexander John.
B. 07 OCT 1926. Gold: 1948. Alex Groza was the biggest star of the Kentucky teams of the late 40's. The 6'-7" forward certainly came from an athletic family as his older brother, Lou, became quite well known as a place-kicker for the Cleveland Browns. After college Groza played for two seasons in the NBA with the Indianapolis Olympians, of which he was part-owner. He was an excellent player, making first-team all-league both years, and was twice runner-up for the scoring title to big George Mikan. He was also one of the league's top rebounders.

Groza later returned to his home state of Kentucky. When the ABA was formed in the late 60's, Groza was instrumental in bringing a team to play in his home state, the Kentucky Colonels. In 1970, as general manager, Alex Groza also took over the reins as an interim coach for two games and left undefeated—2-0. In 1974 the call of coaching lured him back and he coached one-half of a season, with little success, for the San Diego Conquistadors of the ABA, succeeding Wilt Chamberlain.

GRUNFELD, Ernest.
B. 24 APR 1955 Satu-Mare, Romania. Gold: 1976. Ernie Grunfeld's family emigrated from Romania when he was nine years old, although he did not become a naturalized U.S. citizen until 1975. Living near New York city, he quickly became a basketball star and accepted a scholarship to the University of Tennessee. Grunfeld was one of the Volunteer's greatest players ever, and with teammate Bernard King, led Tennessee to some of its best years. Grunfeld won a gold medal in 1975 in the Pan-American Games before he added his Olympic gold in 1976. After graduation in 1977 Grunfeld was drafted in the first round by the Milwaukee Bucks. After two fair seasons with the Bucks he was traded to the Kansas City Kings.

After graduation from college Ernie Grunfeld felt it necessary to repay the school that had helped him so much. A true measure of the man is that he immediately donated a portion of his first-year NBA salary to start a scholarship fund at the University of Tennessee.

While many professional athletes have formed such funds, school officials said they knew of no one who had ever done this in his first year in pro sports.

HALDORSON, Burdette Eliele.

B. 12 JAN 1934 Austin, MN. Gold(2): 1956, 1960. Burdette Haldorson is one of only three people to have won two Olympic gold medals in basketball. Haldorson attended the University of Colorado, making all-conference twice, and being named all-American in his senior year in his last year. He also led the Big Eight in scoring in his last two years. Besides his Olympic successes Haldorson also won a gold medal in 1959 with the Pan-American team. Haldorson never played pro basketball but instead joined up with the Phillips teams and played AAU ball. He was four times AAU all-American and after retirement settled into an executive's position with Phillips for 15 years. After leaving Phillips he set up his own business as a franchise holder in a Dallas based oil company.

HAYWOOD, Spencer.

B. 22 APR 1949 Silver City, MS. Gold: 1968. The 1968 Olympic basketball team was not expected to be one of the greatest teams we have ever sent to the Olympics and many people thought the 1968 team might be the first ever to lose the gold medal. But the experts had not heard of Spencer Haywood, who was then an unknown freshman at the University of Detroit. Haywood was a 6'-8" player who could play either center or forward. In the Olympics he completely dominated the big men from other countries to lead the U.S. to another gold medal.

After the Olympics, Haywood returned to school for only one year. He joined the Denver Rockets of the ABA in 1969 and began an outstanding professional career. In his first year he was the Rookie of the Year, the Most Valuable Player and made first-team all-ABA. He then jumped leagues to join the NBA's Seattle Supersonics and took up where he left off by becoming one of the great forwards in the NBA. He made first-team all-NBA three straight years, and then was named to the second-team for the two years after that. In 1975 he was traded to the New York Knicks, where he played for four seasons before finishing up his career with the Los Angeles Lakers in 1980.

Mahdi Abdul-Rahman, during his NBA days with the Seattle Super Sonics. As Walt Hazzard, Abdul-Rahman won a gold medal in the 1964 Olympics.

Courtesy Seattle Super Sonics

HAZZARD, Walter Raphael.

B. 15 APR 1942 Wilmington, DE. Gold: 1964. Walt Hazzard played collegiate basketball at UCLA, but when he started there it was not the legendary basketball power it would later become. He had a big hand in that reputation getting its start, as he was the star of the team when they won their first NCAA title in 1964. For his efforts he was named all-American that year.

After the 1964 Olympics, Hazzard joined the Los Angeles Lakers and played with them for three seasons. In 1967 he was traded to the Seattle Super Sonics where he had his best year, averaging 23.9 points per game, and playing in the NBA All-Star Game that year. Hazzard played in the NBA through the 1974 season,

A Triple Crown Of Basketball Titles

Unlike baseball dozens of United States' Olympians have gone on to play pro basketball. But only four of these Olympians have been able to play on an Olympic gold medal winner, an NBA champion, and an NCAA basketball champion. Got any ideas who these were??? This is a toughy.

The four US Olympians to wear a triple crown of basketball titles were Bill Russell (1956 Olympics, 1955–56 NCAA with University of San Francisco, and multiple NBA titles with the Boston Celtics), K. C. Jones (a teammate of Russell's for all the above titles), Jerry Lucas (1960 Olympics, 1960 NCAA title with Ohio State, and the 1973 NBA championship with the New York Knicks), and, the real toughy, Clyde Lovelette (1952 Olympics, 1952 NCAA title with Kansas, and two NBA titles with the Boston Celtics — 1963–1964).

ending up in Seattle after several seasons with Atlanta, Buffalo and Golden State. During his career, he embraced the Muslim faith and played his last seasons under the name, Mahdi Abdul-Rahman.

HENDERSON, Thomas Edward.

B. 26 JAN 1952 Newberry, SC. Silver: 1972. Tom Henderson learned his basketball in the Bronx and played for high school power DeWitt Clinton. He initially attended San Jacinto Junior College, where he averaged almost 30 points per game, but later transferred to the University of Hawaii. While at Hawaii he made first-team all-America in 1974. The 6'-3" guard was drafted in the first round of the NBA draft by the Atlanta Hawks in 1974. He has since played for the Washington Bullets and the Houston Rockets and in 1978 he helped the Bullets to win the NBA championship. He has been a steady NBA performer without ever really developing into a great star.

HOAG, Charles Monroe.

B. 19 JUL 1931 Tulsa, OK. Gold: 1952. Hoag was a member of the Kansas team which won the NCAA championship in 1952 and was one of the five Kansas team members who played for the 1952 Olympic champions. However, Hoag was primarily thought of as a football player. He was the starting halfback for Kansas in his junior year, and was named all-Big Eight halfback that year. After the Olympics he returned to Kansas for another football season but injured his knee very badly, and never played either football or basketball again. Since college he has made his living as an insurance broker.

HOSKETT, Wilmer Frederick.

B. 20 DEC 1946 Dayton, OH. Gold: 1968. Bill Hoskett followed Gary Bradds and fellow Olympian Jerry Lucas as star forwards for the Ohio State Buckeyes. He was a 6'-8", 225 lb. bruiser who three times was Ohio State basketball MVP, twice was named all-Big Ten, and in 1968 was NCAA District IV Player of the Year. In addition he was an honor student who won an NCAA fellowship for graduate study. The fellowship did not prevent Hoskett from playing in the NBA however. He was drafted by the New York Knicks as their first choice and he played two years for them and finished up his NBA career by playing two more years for the Buffalo Braves. Hosket did not have a great professional career but part of the problem was he had chronically injured knees which prevented him from ever playing a full season.

HOUGLAND, William Marion.

B. 20 JUN 1930 Caldwell, KS. Gold(2): 1952, 1956. Bill Hougland played for Kansas University, graduating in 1952, and helping them win the NCAA championship in that year. He was not drafted by the NBA and so went on to play two years of service ball with the air force. After leaving the service, he played AAU ball with the Phillips teams until 1958 and became a salesman for the Phillips Petroleum Co. He left the Phillips company in 1961 to join up with Koch Industries.

HUBBARD, Phillip Gregory.

B. 13 DEC 1956 Canton, OH. Gold: 1976. Phil Hubbard was only a freshman at Michigan when he made the 1976 Olympic basketball team as its youngest member.

At 6'-8" he had played center for the Wolverines that year, although as a natural forward, he was out of position. On the Olympic team he contributed as a forward and played that position later in college and the NBA. He missed one year of college basketball due to a knee injury and left school after his junior year. He joined the NBA's Detroit Pistons and has played forward for them, averaging 10-15 point per game.

IMHOFF, Darrell T.

B. 11 OCT 1938. Gold: 1960. Darrell Imhoff attended Cal/Berkeley and in 1959, playing against West Virginia, his tip-in with 17 seconds remaining gave Cal the NCAA championship. At 6'-10" he played center exclusively, but was only a back-up center on the 1960 Olympic team, behind Lucas and Bellamy. He went on to have a solid 12-year NBA career, starting out with the New York Knicks, and eventually playing for Detroit, Los Angeles, Philadelphia, Cincinnati, and Portland. He liked the Portland area so much that he settled there and became a part-time radio commentator for the Trail Blazers' games. In addition he has worked as a representative for a Seattle sporting goods firm.

JACKSON, Lucius Brown.

B. 31 OCT 1941 San Marcos, TX. Gold: 1964. At 6'-9" and 240 lbs., Luke Jackson was one of the strongest forwards to ever play basketball. He played collegiate basketball at little known Pan American University and from there was the first round draft pick of the Philadelphia 76ers in 1964. Jackson had an eight-year career in the NBA, all with Philadelphia. In his first year in the league he made the NBA All-Rookie team and later played in two NBA All-Star games. Jackson was never mentioned as the greatest forward in the league, but he had a job to do and did it to perfection. He was an outstanding defensive player and strong rebounder who was never asked to score a lot of points. The culmination of his role as a team player came in 1966-67 when the Philadelphia team on which he played won 68 games and lost only 13. Jackson was an indispensable cog in this machine which some people think is the greatest NBA team ever.

JEANGERARD, Robert Eugene.

B. 20 JUN 1933 Evanston, IL. Gold: 1956. Bob Jeangerard attended the University of Colorado in the

---

THE BUFFALO GERMANS

There was a basketball tournament at the 1904 Olympics but it was really just the U.S. National Championship. But the winners were easily of Olympic quality—the team from the Buffalo German YMCA in New York.

The Buffalo Germans are one of only four teams to have been inducted into the Basketball Hall of Fame as a group. They were formed in 1895 and went on to have a career record of 792–86, winning 111 games in a row at one point. Led by captain Alfred Heerdt, they won games at the 1904 Olympics by scores of 77–6, 36–28, 105–50, 39–28, and 97–8. Other team members included Albert Manweiler, Ed Miller, William Rhode, George Redlein, and Charles Monahan.

---

early 50's, winning all-Big Eight honors in both his junior and senior years. He also was chosen as MVP of the NCAA western regionals in his senior year—1955. Jeangerard went on to play AAU ball, winning AAU all-America honors and leading his team to the 1955 AAU National Championship.

JOHNSON, Francis Lee.

B. 05 AUG 1910 Hartford, KS. Gold: 1936. At Wichita University in the early 30's, Frank Johnson played football, basketball, and pole vaulted and ran hurdles for the track team. He earned three letters all three years of varsity competition. After his 1934 graduation, he played AAU basketball with the Globe Refiners for two years, winning a national championship and making the Olympic team while with them in 1936. He then played three more years of AAU ball, winning another national title in 1938 with the Healey Motors team. Johnson worked most of his life with the John Deere Company and also became a noted rancher, raising Apaloosa horses. His ranch eventually produced 15 national or world champions.

Courtesy Boston Celtics

The new head of the Boston Celtics, K. C. Jones — a 1956 Olympic gold medalist.

JONES, Dwight Elmo.

B. 27 FEB 1952 Houston, TX. Silver: 1972. Dwight Jones attended the University of Houston where, at 6'-10", he usually played center. He won a gold medal playing for the 1971 Pan-American team and then, after playing for the 1972 Olympic team, he played one more season of collegiate before declaring himself eligible for the NBA hardship draft. In the 1973 NBA draft, Jones was selected first by the Atlanta Hawks, and was the ninth pick overall. As a professional, Dwight Jones has played either power forward or back-up center. Since leaving Atlanta in 1976 he has played for the Houston Rockets, the Chicago Bulls, and the Los Angeles Lakers.

JONES, K. C.

B. 25 MAY 1932 Taylor, TX. Gold: 1956. K. C. Jones is one of four men to have played on an Olympic champion, an NCAA champion, and an NBA champion and is one of the most titled men in basketball history. Jones' college career was at the University of San Francisco which won NCAA titles in 1955 and 1956 (although Jones missed the 1956 NCAA tourney due to an eligibilty technicality). After college he played for nine years in the NBA, the first eight of which saw his Boston Celtics win the NBA championship. He played his entire collegiate and professional career in the company of Bill Russell, and although Russell was usually given as the reason for all the championships, K. C. Jones was the exact same type of player. He was a defensive stalwart who always guarded the opposition's leading guard and he was the ultimate team player.

After he retired as a player, K. C. Jones began a career as a professional coach, first as an assistant on the Celtics. His first head coaching job came for the San Diego Conquistadors in 1972, although his most successful head coaching experience came in a three-year stint in the mid 70's with the Washington Bullets. Jones went back to the Celtics as an assistant coach and, in 1983, was named their head coach.

JONES, Robert Clyde.

B. 18 DEC 1951 Charlotte, NC. Silver: 1972. Bobby Jones played his high school ball in Charlotte and attended his home state school, the University of North Carolina. He had an illustrious basketball career in college, and also high jumped for the track team, before being drafted in the first round in 1973 by the ABA and again in the first round in 1974 by the NBA. He opted for the ABA and through a complicated series of trades became the property of the Denver Nuggets after his senior year in college. Jones stayed with Denver when they joined the NBA but was traded to Philadelphia in 1978. Throughout his pro career he has been known as one of the top defensive forwards in the game, being named to either the NBA or ABA All-Defensive team for seven straight years.

In the late 70's Bobby Jones was found to have a mild form of epilepsy. He has continued to play while on medication for the disease and has been a spokesman for epilepsy research groups as well as an inspiration to many epileptics.

JONES, Wallace Clayton.
B. 14 JUL 1926. Gold: 1948. Wally "Wah-Wah" Jones set a national high school record by scoring 2,398 points before playing on the great Kentucky teams that won two NCAA championships in the late 40's. But basketball was not the only sport this 6'-4" forward could play. While in college he also lettered in football and baseball, although basketball was his best sport. As a hoopster he was named all-America in 1947, 1948 and 1949, as well as all-Southeastern Conference four straight years—1946-1949. In football he was also named all-Conference in 1946 and 1947, and received occasional all-America mention in 1947. After graduation in 1949, Jones played three years of NBA ball with the Indianapolis Olympians—the 'Kentucky' team. He ended his NBA career in 1952 with a 10 points per game scoring average.

JOYCE, Kevin Francis.
B. 27 JUN 1951 Bayside, NY. Silver: 1972. Kevin Joyce came out of New York to attend the University of South Carolina where he briefly played alongside another great guard, John Roche. After Roche graduated, Joyce was the star of the South Carolina team and played for the Olympic team in 1972 after his junior year. He went on to have a short career (three years) in the ABA, first with Indiana, and then with San Diego and Kentucky in his last year.

KELLER, John Frederick.
B. 10 NOV 1928 Page City, KS. Gold: 1952. John Keller played for the University of Kansas team which won the NCAA championship in 1952. He graduated that year and after playing on the 1952 Olympic team, never again played competitive basketball. He instead went into teaching and coaching.

KELLEY, Earl Allen.
B. 24 DEC 1932. Gold: 1960. Al Kelley was a 6'-0" guard at the University of Kansas, graduating in 1954. After graduation he was drafted in the seventh round by the Milwaukee Hawks but spurned their offers. Instead he played AAU ball until 1960 for the Peoria Caterpillars, the powerhouse in AAU basketball at that time, and helped them win several national championships. Kelley has been a long-time employee of the Caterpillar Tractor firm which sponsored those great teams.

KELLEY, Melvin Dean.
B. 23 SEP 1931 McCune, KS. Gold: 1952. A 1953 graduate of the University of Kansas, Dean Kelley went on to play for four years with the Peoria Cats. He also began working with the Caterpillar Tractor Co. which sponsored that team and has remained with them since that time.

KENNEY, Robert Earl.
B. 23 JUN 1931 Arkansas City, KS. Gold: 1952. Bob Kenney was another member of the Kansas Jayhawk 1952 NCAA championship team. After his graduation in the same year he joined the Air Force, and played on the service team. He also later played for the Wichita Vickers in AAU basketball. He put his engineering degree to use for five years, then moved up to engineering sales, and now makes his living as a real estate broker.

KING, James.
B. 09 FEB 1943 Gold: 1968. Jim King was a 6'-7" forward at Oklahoma State who was named all-Big Eight conference in 1966. He never played in the NBA but played several years of AAU ball with the Goodyear Wingfoots, and then played for several seasons in some European professional leagues.

KNOWLES, Carl Stanley.
B. 24 FEB 1910. D. 04 SEP 1981 Los Angeles, CA. Gold: 1936. Carl Knowles played for UCLA in the late 20's and early 30's, captaining the team in his senior year. He then played for the Universal Studios team which won the final Olympic trials in 1936 and contributed seven members of the 1936 Olympic team. He was several times named as AAU all-America and all-Pacific Coast in the late 30's. After his basketball days ended he worked for Universal Studios, mostly as a grip on movie sets. In his later years he was in ill health much of the time before passing away in 1981.

KUPCHAK, Mitchell.
B. 24 MAY 1954 Hicksville, NY. Gold: 1976. Mitch Kupchak played for the University of North Carolina and also for its coach, Dean Smith, in the 1976 Olympic Games. He was drafted in the first round of the 1976 NBA draft by the Washington Bullets and was shortly thereafter named to the NBA's all-rookie team.

Kupchak has been described as a 6'-10" banger who didn't start but led the league in floor burns and contributed significantly to every team he has played on. After five excellent years in Washington, including an NBA championship in 1978, Kupchak signed a multi-million dollar contract with the Los Angeles Lakers. But injuries have hindered what could have been a great career. In college, and again after the 1979 NBA season, he has had to undergo back surgery, but in December 1981 he suffered the worst blow. On that night he crashed to the floor in a game against San Diego, suffering ligament, cartilage and bone damage to his left knee which has required two operations, but has not been totally successful in allowing him to play again.

KURLAND, Robert Albert.
B. 23 DEC 1924 St. Louis, MO. Gold(2): 1948, 1952. Bob "Foothills" Kurland was the first dominating seven-footer to play college basketball; so dominant, in fact, that he caused the rulesmakers to outlaw goal-tending, because he could block almost every shot from going into the basket. In 1945 and 1946 he led his Oklahoma A&M team to the NCAA championship and then went on to play for six years with the Phillips 66ers, being named AAU all-America every year he played. While playing with Phillips, Kurland became the first man to play on two Olympic championship teams. He recalls his greatest athletic thrill as being selected to carry the United States' flag at the closing ceremonies of the 1952 Games, a thrill which he says still brings tears to his eyes.

After the 1952 Olympics Kurland joined Phillips Petroleum's marketing division. He has moved up in the company to division manager of several offices, as well as having been sales manager of the Atlanta and Denver office.

LaGARDE, Thomas Joseph.
B. 10 FEB 1955 Detroit, MI. Gold: 1976. From the University of North Carolina, Tom LaGarde went on to play for his college coach, Dean Smith, at the Montreal Olympics. He then returned to Chapel Hill for one more season of college ball, during which he earned second-team all-America honors, before joining the NBA as a first round draft pick of the Denver Nuggets. After one season with Denver, LaGarde was traded to the Seattle Supersonics, which worked out well as he helped them

win an NBA championship in that first year with them. After one more year with Seattle, LaGarde was drafted by the Dallas Mavericks in the expansion draft of 1980.

LANE, Lester E.
B. 06 MAR 1932 Purcell, OK. D. 06 SEP 1973 Norman, OK. Gold: 1960. At 5'-10" tall, Les Lane is one of our shortest Olympic basketball players ever, but also one of the best allround athletes to ever grace the squad. At the University of Oklahoma in the early 50's, Lane played basketball, football, and pole vaulted for the track team. He was a starting defensive back on Bud Wilkinson's powerhouse squads, and on the hardcourt scored 1,180 points, a Sooner record which would not be broken for 11 years.

After his college days, Lane played AAU ball, mostly with the Wichita Vickers, whom he helped win a national championship in 1959. After the Olympics in 1960, Les Lane coached on the AAU level for several years, but then was hired by both Mexico and Spain to coach their national teams. Under Lane's guidance, the Mexican team finished fifth at the 1968 Olympics. In the spring of 1973 he was named head basketball coach at his alma mater, but never held a practice—he succumbed to a heart attack during a pick-up game later that year.

LIENHARD, William Barner.
B. 14 JAN 1930 Slaton, TX. Gold: 1952. Bill Lienhard played on the great Kansas team which won the 1952 NCAA championship, but really played very little basketball after college. He played in Helsinki on the 1952 gold medalists, but after returning from Europe joined up with the air force and played two years of service basketball. He retired from competitive basketball after that, spurning a chance to play AAU ball. Since leaving the air force he has become a very successful banker in Kansas.

LOVELETTE, Clyde Edward.
B. 07 SEP 1929 Terre Haute, IN. Gold: 1952. Clyde Lovelette has won championship basketball titles at every major level of competition NCAA, Olympic and NBA. The 6'-9" center was a two-time all-American at the University of Kansas and, in 1952, led them to the NCAA title. That year he also led the nation's colleges in scoring with 28.4 points per game. After his Olympic

success, Lovelette was drafted by the Minneapolis Lakers in 1953 and he had four good years for them. He subsequently played for both Cincinnati and St. Louis, playing in three NBA All-Star games and making second team all-NBA one year. Lovelette finished out his career with the Boston Celtics, as a back-up center to Bill Russell, and it was with them, in 1963 and 1964, that he played on NBA championship teams.

Lovelette was a burly fellow on the court and was known as a bit of an enforcer. He apparently took the reputation with him after his playing days—he served several years as sheriff of his hometown.

LUBIN, Frank John.
B. 07 JAN 1910 Los Angeles, CA. Gold: 1936. Frank Lubin was one of the greatest basketball players this country produced in the days before professional basketball. He started his big-time career with UCLA, graduating in 1931, and then went on to star in AAU competition for over 30 years, until he was 54 years old. He was on the Universal Studios team which contributed seven players to the 1936 Olympic team, and also played with the 20th Century Fox team at various times, including 1941 when they won the national championship. He was 10 times named AAU all-America. He also coached the Lithuanian national team to the 1939 European championship, before he was forced to flee the country at the outbreak of war. Many honors have come his way, including Helms Basketball Hall of Fame, and being selected as one of the top 200 local athletes at the 1981 Los Angeles Bi-Centennial.

Lubin worked most of his life in movies and television, mainly as a grip. His nickname was Frankenstein, given him by the make-up man for the Frankenstein series at Universal Studios. Contrary to reports, however, he never actually played the part of Frankenstein, but was only a stand-in and stunt-man for the role.

LUCAS, Jerry Ray.
B. 30 MAR 1940 Middletown, OH. Gold: 1960. Ejrry Aclsu (see below) was one of the greatest forwards to ever play basketball. In 1960, besides playing on the Olympic team, he led his Ohio State team to the NCAA championship as a sophomore center. He played mostly center in college and made all-America in 1960, 1961, and 1962 as well as twice being named College Player of the Year. He also led the nation in rebounding in his junior and senior years, and in field goal percentage all three of his varsity years, setting a collegiate career mark in that category. He was drafted by Cincinnati of the NBA in 1962 but instead signed with the Cleveland Pipers of the soon-to-be-defunct American Basketball League. Cleveland folded before playing a game and Lucas sat out a season before beginning his NBA career.

Lucas had an excellent 11-year pro career, starting out with a Rookie of the Year award in 1964. He three times was named to the NBA first-team All-Stars, and three times was named second-team. In 1965 he was the MVP of the NBA All-Star game and he finished his career with the New York Knicks by helping them win an NBA title in 1973.

Since his basketball career ended, Lucas has been involved in several entrepreneurial pursuits, the most well known of which are his books and schools of memory training. Lucas' own memory is phenomenal and he and partner, Harry Lorayne, have devised a system of memory which they have marketed into a big business. Lucas also has the unusual distinction of being able to instantly "alphabetize" words—pronounce the words with all the letters spelled in alphabetical order. Hence his name becomes Ejrry Aclsu!

LUMPP, Raymond G.
B. 11 JUL 1923 Brooklyn, NY. Gold: 1948. Ray Lumpp was a star at New York University in the late 40's. He went from there to play pro basketball, mainly with the New York Knicks, but also briefly with the Indianapolis Olympians and the Baltimore Bullets. Lumpp was a 6'-1" guard whose main forte was playmaking. Since his basketball days have ended he has been director of the New York Athletic Club and active on the board of the U.S. Olympians club. He has also served as an official at track meets and has been meet director of the U.S. Olympic Invitational Track Meet.

MAY, Scott Glenn.
B. 19 MAR 1954 Sandusky, OH. Gold: 1976. At the University of Indiana, Scott May played on two of the greatest collegiate teams ever in 1975 and 1976, although only the 1976 team succeeded in winning the NCAA championship. May was acknowledged to be the leader of that team, and later in 1976, he was the

Scott May, a 1976 Olympian, shoots over Paul Westphal while playing for the Chicago Bulls in the NBA.

backbone of the U.S. Olympic team, as well. A great pro career was expected of the 6'-7" forward, but it was not to be. May never became the dominant force he was in college, although he played for parts of seven seasons, mostly with Chicago. In the middle of the 1982-83 season, May was released by the Detroit Pistons, and he retired to devote full time to a real estate business he had established for himself.

McCABE, Frank Reilly.
B. 30 JUN 1927 Grand Rapids, MN. Gold: 1952. A 6'-8" center for Marquette University, Frank McCabe graduated in 1950 after four good, but not spectacular, years at the Catholic school. He was their top player only in his senior year when he led the team in scoring with 13 points per game. McCabe really came into his own after his college days as he joined the Peoria Caterpillars AAU team and helped them to win three straight national titles in 1952, 1953 and 1954. Frank McCabe was named AAU all-America from 1951 thru 1954 consecutively. Since joining the Caterpillar Tractor company in 1951 he has remained with the firm to this day.

McCAFFREY, John Paul.
B. 24 DEC 1938 Tucson, AZ. Gold: 1964. The 6'-6" forward, "Pete" McCaffrey, played for St. Louis University in the late 50's but really blossomed as a player after college. He played AAU basketball for several years, mainly with the Goodyear Wingfoots, and it was while he was playing with them that he was named to the 1964 Olympic team.

McMILLEN, Charles Thomas.
B. 26 MAY 1952 Mansfield, PA. Silver: 1972. When Tom McMillen was in high school, he was one of the nation's most coveted basketball recruits—he even graced the cover of Sports Illustrated while a high school senior. The University of Maryland won the recruiting war and McMillen had an excellent college career, though it was perhaps a bit less than expected of him. While at Maryland, McMillen earned Phi Beta Kappa honors and was his class's graduation speaker. He then followed 1964 Olympian, Bill Bradley, to Oxford, England, as the recipient of a Rhodes Scholarship. While at Oxford, McMillen studied politics, philosophy, and economics and played basketball with the Virtus Sinudyne team in an Italian league.

In 1975 Tom McMillen returned to play in the NBA, finishing up his Rhodes work during summers. He at first played with the Buffalo Braves, but of late has been with the Atlanta Hawks. His pro career has not been spectacular but he has taken some limited natural ability and made the best of it, improving his strength and defense to where he is known as a "tough player."

Off the court, Tom McMillen is also highly successful. He has been the youngest member of the President's Council on Physical Fitness and Sports, a member of a U.S. Senate advisory committee on national sports development, and been active in politics. The question about Tom McMillen's future after basketball is not if he will run for public office, but which one and when.

MOLLNER, Arthur Owen.
B. 20 DEC 1912 Saranac Lake, NY. Gold: 1936. After briefly attending a junior college in Los Angeles, Art Mollner joined the Los Angeles police force. He also took his talent to playing basketball to the local AAU teams and became a regular with the Universal Studios team which sent seven players to Berlin in 1936. After playing for several years in the AAU leagues, Mollner coached the Fibber McGee and Molly team until 1952. He also continued his career with the LAPD until he retired as a sergeant.

MULLINS, Jeffry Vincent.
B. 19 MAR 1942 Astoria, NY. Gold: 1964. In the early 60's Jeff Mullins started the Duke Blue Devils on the road to being one of the collegiate basketball powers of the decade. After graduation from Duke, Mullins went on to a fine career in the NBA, playing 12 years. He started out with St. Louis, but after two years moved to the San Francisco (later Golden State) Warriors, where he stayed for the rest of his career. Mullins was a 6'-4" guard who had his best years from 1967 through 1974 when he consistently averaged over 20 points per game and played in three NBA All-Star games.

After leaving the NBA, Mullins took up a post as assistant athletic director at his alma mater, but left that to devote fulltime to an automobile dealership.

PIPER, Donald Arthur.
B. 05 MAR 1911 Peoria, IL. D. 25 MAR 1963 Temple City, CA. Gold: 1936. Don Piper was a UCLA grad who

Jeff Mullins, a 1964 Olympic basketball gold medalist.

played for the Universal Studios team and the U.S. Olympic team in 1936. Piper had an illustrious career in college and was probably the greatest collegiate player of the 1936 team, but he did not play as much afterwards.

Piper's business career began with a credit investigation firm but he later worked for a television distributor, eventually rising to general manager of that company. He died rather young and the eulogy at his funeral was given by fellow Olympian, Sam Balter.

PIPPIN, Daniel Luther.
B. 20 OCT 1926. D. 01 APR 1965 McCreadie, MO. Gold: 1952. Dan Pippin graduated from the University of Missouri in the late 40's and went on to become a star in the AAU basketball leagues with the Peoria Caterpillars. He was playing for Peoria when he made the 1952 Olympic team and he continued to play for them until the late 50's. He also left the employ of Peoria at that time to enter the insurance business.

PITTS, Robert C.

B. 23 JUN 1919 Pontotoc, MS. Gold: 1948. "R.C" Pitts played football and basketball at Arkansas, graduating in 1942, but he was with the Phillips 66ers when he made the 1948 Olympic team. At basketball he was all-Southwest Conference in 1942 and made the 1948 AAU all-America team. He spent over 20 years in the employ of Phillips before beginning his own company in specialized tank truck operations.

RAGLAND, Jack Williamson.

B. 09 OCT 1913 Hutchinson, KS. Gold: 1936. Jack Ragland played for the Wichita University basketball team until 1934, along with his future Olympic teammate, Frank Johnson. He later went on to play four years in the AAU leagues, at first with the Globe Refiners, with whom he made the 1936 Olympic team, and later with the Phillips 66ers. He started his business career with Phillips but later moved on into his business, working as a land agent.

RATLEFF, Edward.

B. 29 MAR 1950 Bellefontaine, OH. Silver: 1972. At Long Beach State in the early 70's, Ed Ratleff was one of the top guards in the nation, earning several all-America honors. He averaged almost 40 points per game in freshman ball, and over 20 points per game as a three-year varsity starter, including an amazing high game of 68 vs. San Diego State in 1970. After the Olympics and his senior year of college, Ratleff was drafted first by the Houston Rockets. He was 6'-6" tall and was very big for a guard but seemed to have all the attributes to be one of the greats at the position. However he played only five years in the NBA, never quite reaching the stardom predicted for him.

RENICK, Jesse Bernard.

B. 29 SEP 1917 Abner, OK. Gold: 1948. Jesse "Cab" Renick was a full-blooded Choctaw Indian who attended Oklahoma A&M Univ.—now Oklahoma State. Playing forward, Renick led the team to a 26-3 mark in 1940, and 12-0 in conference play. In both 1939 and 1940 he was named all-Missouri Valley and all-America. He continued to play basketball, twice being named AAU all-America, until he made the 1948 Olympic team, then retired to go into AAU coaching. His greatest fame as a coach came in 1950 when he led the Phillips 66ers to the AAU national title.

ROBERTSON, Oscar Palmer.

B. 24 NOV 1938 Charlotte, TN. Gold: 1960. Many people feel Oscar Robertson, "the big O," is the greatest guard to ever play basketball. A few will go even further and designate him the greatest basketball player—period. Robertson started his road to stardom at Crispus Attucks High School in Indianapolis and then took his show to the University of Cincinnati. For three consecutive years he led the NCAA in scoring, made first-team all-America, and was named collegiate Player of the Year. In his junior year, he broke the NCAA career scoring mark which had been set in a four-year career.

Robertson was 6'-5" tall and was a natural guard, though he was probably the biggest man to ever play that position at the time. At Rome in 1960 he often played forward because of his size and jumping ability. After the Olympics, Robertson joined the Cincinnati Royals with whom he stayed until 1970 when he was traded to the Milwaukee Bucks. It was while playing with the Bucks in 1971 that he finally played on an NBA champion.

In his 14-year pro career, Robertson rewrote the record book. He was 10 times named to first team all-NBA and twice, in the twilight of his career, was named to the second team. He was Rookie of the Year in 1961 and MVP in 1964—rare feats for a guard. His greatest honor probably came in 1980 when he was named to the NBA's 35th anniversary All-Time team. Perhaps the best measure of his dominance is the triple-double, a new term coined to describe the exploits of Magic Johnson, and which refers to a game in which a player scores in double figures in points, rebounds, and assists. It was not until the seventh year of his career that Robertson's career averages fell below a triple-double standard.

ROBINSON, Robert Jackson.

B. 26 APR 1927 Fort Worth, TX. Gold: 1948. "Jackie" Robinson graduated from Baylor University in 1949 but while there he made the 1948 Olympic team. He has since gone on to become an ordained Baptist minister which he has made his life's work.

ROLLINS, Kenneth Herman.

B. 14 SEP 1923. Gold: 1948. Kenny Rollins was a smooth play-making guard who began his collegiate career before World War II at the University of Kentucky. War intervened, however, and Rollins played one year with the famed Great Lakes Training Station outfit after joining the service. After the war, he returned to Kentucky and played on the NCAA champions of 1947 and 1948, serving as captain both years. Unlike the other Kentucky stars, he did not play for the Indianapolis Olympians, but instead joined the Chicago Stags. He played two years for them before joining the Boston Celtics for a few final years in the NBA.

RUSSELL, William Fenton.

B. 12 FEB 1934 Monroe, LA. Gold: 1956. Perhaps he was the greatest basketball players ever, perhaps only its greatest champion, but it matters little, for Bill Russell forever changed the shape of professional basketball. He turned it into the consummate team game, where defensive ability, rebounding and hustle were as important as great offensive skills.

Bill Russell played for the University of San Francisco, the 1956 Olympic team, and the Boston Celtics. But one rarely finds Russell's name in the record book as most of the records were set by his arch-rival, Wilt Chamberlain. However, when it counted, Russell's character refused to allow his team to lose. In 16 attempts to win championships with these clubs, he succeeded 13 times—and one loss occurred when he was injured in the NBA championship finals. Besides his gold medal, he played on two NCAA championship teams, and 10 NBA champs with the Celtics—eight of those in succession.

Russell was five times the NBA's Most Valuable Player, and was virtually always first or second-team all-NBA, often alternating the honor with Chamberlain. He was named *The Sporting News'* Athlete of the Decade in 1970, and also was named Sportsman of the Year by *Sports Illustrated*. After his retirement he was named to the NBA's 25th and 35th Anniversary All-Time Teams, was elected to the Basketball Hall of Fame in 1974 and, in perhaps his greatest honor, was named the NBA's greatest player ever in a poll of basketball writers.

Russell also coached in the NBA, but with mixed success. He twice led the Celtics to NBA titles as a player-coach, but later could do little to help the Seattle

The basketball player who won more championships than any other man, Bill Russell, 1956 Olympic gold medalist.

Courtesy Boston Celtics

Supersonics. He now works as a basketball commentator for CBS Sports, as well as serving as a spokesman for several companies in television commercials.

SAULTERS, Glynn.

B. 10 FEB 1945 Minden, LA. Gold: 1968. Glynn Saulters played for Northeast Louisiana State, graduating in 1968 and twice making small college all-America teams. In his last year he averaged 31 points per game, with a high of 51. After winning a gold medal at Mexico City in 1968, he joined the New Orleans Buccaneers of the ABA and played part of one season for them.

SCHMIDT, Willard Theodore.

B. 14 FEB 1910 Swanton, NB. D. 13 APR 1965 Coffeyville, KS. Gold: 1936. Willard Schmidt was a 6'-10" center from Creighton University who played for the

McPherson Globe Oilers in the mid 30's. He was primarily a back-up center in 1936 when McPherson lost in the finals of the Olympic Trials and so was not named to the original team. However he was later added to the team and played well in Berlin for the Olympic team.

SCOTT, Charles Thomas.
B. 15 DEC 1948 New York, NY. Gold: 1968. Charlie Scott was one of the reasons the 1968 US Olympic team won the gold medal. Lightly regarded before the Olympics, Scott, Spencer Haywood, and Jo Jo White were the big stars of that team which brought the U.S. the gold medal.

Scott starred for the University of North Carolina both before and after the Olympics. While there he helped the team make the NCAA finals in 1968, before losing, as everyone did in those years, to UCLA. After leaving Chapel Hill in 1970, Scott signed with the Virginia Squires of the ABA, with whom he had two brilliant years, being named Rookie of the Year in 1971, and leading the league in scoring in 1972. Scott then signed with the Phoenix Suns of the NBA and went on to a good career, but he never quite repeated his college or ABA heroics. His best years were his first few with Phoenix, though he later played for Boston, Los Angeles, and Denver.

SHEPPARD, Steven.
B. 21 MAR 1954 New York, NY. Gold: 1976. Steve Sheppard played his high school basketball at DeWitt Clinton High School in New York, where he was a teammate of 1972 Olympian, Tom Henderson, and also did well enough to be named New York City Player of the Year. He then went to the University of Maryland where academic problems kept him ineligible for one semester, but he became an immediate starter once eligible the next year. In a preview of international play he led his Maryland team to a victory over the Soviet Union by scoring 22 points and pulling down 15 rebounds. After leaving Maryland in 1977, Steve Sheppard played two years of basketball in the NBA, first with Chicago, then Detroit.

SHIPP, Jerry Franklin.
B. 27 SEP 1935 Shreveport, LA. Gold: 1964. Jerry Shipp attended Southeast Louisiana State College but his best days as a basketball player came in the AAU leagues. After college he played for the Phillips 66ers and helped them win several national AAU championships. It was while a member of the 66ers that he was named to the 1964 Olympic team. Shipp also began a career with the Phillips Company in the sales training program.

SHY, Carl.
B. 13 SEP 1908. Gold: 1936. Carl Shy attended UCLA but continued to play basketball after his graduation with the Universal Studios team. He played for Universal in 1934, 1935, and 1936, making the Olympic team in the last year. Shy later became a police officer with the Los Angeles Police Department, eventually reaching detective before retiring.

SILLIMAN, Michael Barnwell.
B. 05 MAY 1944 Louisville, KY. Gold: 1968. After receiving honorable mention for all three years of his basketball career at the U.S. Military Academy, Mike Silliman began serving his military obligation. But while in the service he found time to play on both the 1967 Pan-American and 1968 Olympic gold medalists for the United States. He also played AAU basketball from 1967 through 1970 with the Armed Forces team. While in the service he eventually achieved a rank of captain and served with the adjutant general corps in Korea.

After his military career ended Mike Silliman played one abbreviated year of pro basketball with the Buffalo Braves, appearing in only 36 games. He then settled back in his home of Kentucky where he first worked as a real estate broker but has since become a very successful mortgage banker.

SMITH, Adrian Howard.
B. 05 OCT 1936. Gold: 1960. From the University of Kentucky and an NCAA championship in 1958, Adrian "Odie" Smith went on to play on our 1960 Olympic team and had a successful 11-year pro career. Most of his NBA career was spent with the Cincinnati Royals where he played alongside Olympic teammate, Oscar Robertson. His greatest years came from 1965-1968 when he averaged over 15 points for four straight years. In 1966 the NBA All-Star game added a new innovation wherein the MVP of the game would be given a new automobile. That was the only time Odie Smith played in the NBA All-Star game and, by scoring 24 points in 26 minutes of

court time, he was voted MVP and made off with a brand new Ford Galaxie 500.

After one season in 1972 in the ABA, Smith left pro basketball and started working for a bank in Cincinnati where he has done quite well. He still owns the Galaxie, and though he has thought about selling it, decided that he couldn't part with what the car stands for.

SPAIN, Kenneth.
B. 06 OCT 1946 Houston, TX. Gold: 1968. Ken Spain lived in Houston all his early life, including his college days at the University of Houston. At Houston he played on the great team that in early 1968 beat the UCLA Bruins of Lew Alcindor (nka Kareem Abdul-Jabbar), Lucius Allen and "Hill Street Blues" star Mike Warren. Later that year UCLA avenged their loss to Houston, and Spain had to settle for only being an NCAA semi-finalist. After graduating from Houston, Spain played a few games in 1971 with the Pittsburgh Condors of the ABA.

SWANSON, Duane Alex.
B. 23 AUG 1913. Gold: 1936. Duane Swanson played for UCLA in the early 30's and later moved on to AAU basketball with the Universal Studios team which made up one-half of the 1936 Olympic team.

TOMSIC, Ronald Paul.
B. 03 APR 1933 Oakland, CA. Gold: 1956. Ron Tomsic was one of Stanford's greatest hoopsters. While in college he set school marks for single game scoring (40) and career scoring (1,600 points) He was twice MVP of the team, twice all-Pacific Coast, and twice honorable mention all-American. After graduation he was playing AAU ball when he made the 1956 Olympic team. He continued to play AAU basketball, mainly with the San Francisco Olympic Club, eventually making the Helms Amateur Basketball Hall of Fame. He was a three-time AAU all-America and played on one AAU national champion.

WALSH, James Patrick.
B. 29 AUG 1930 San Francisco, CA. D. 04 MAR 1976 San Francisco, CA. Gold: 1956. A 1952 graduate of Stanford, Jim Walsh went on to be a star on the service teams while a Marine stationed in Quantico, Virginia. He then went on to play with the Phillips teams in 1955

Gold medalist from the 1960 Olympics, Jerry West, as he looks today as the general manager of the Los Angeles Lakers.

Courtesy Los Angeles Lakers

and 1956, during which time he was named AAU Player of the Year, and made the Olympic team. The lure of pro basketball finally caught him, however, and he played 10 games in 1957-1958 with the Philadelphia Warriors. He briefly went on to coach in AAU basketball before beginning a career in the San Francisco area as a tax assessor.

WEST, Jerry Alan.
B. 28 MAY 1938 Cheylan, WV. Gold: 1960. In the 1960 Olympics, Jerry West teamed with Oscar Robertson to form the greatest guard tandem to ever play on a basketball team—amateur or pro. Though most people will say Robertson is the greatest guard to ever play basketball, a few will opt for West, and most basketball experts, if pressed to name their all-time, all-everything team, would start these same two guards.

Jerry West came from West Virginia University where he starred on an NCAA runner-up, being named the NCAA Tournament's MVP. For 14 years, he performed his magic with the Los Angeles Lakers, where he became known as "Mr. Clutch." In the last few seconds, if the game was close, the Laker's main play was "Give the ball to Jerry!"

West was 11 times NBA All-Star first-team, and twice second-team. He holds NBA playoff records for field goals made, field goals attempted, free throws made, assists, and scoring average. His career playoff average was 29 points and in 1965, he set the single season playoff record by averaging 40.6 points for 11 games.

After retiring as a player, West did some coaching for the Lakers. He was the head coach for three seasons, and later filled in briefly as an interim coach during a coaching shake-up. West has since settled into an executive position with the Lakers.

WHEATLEY, William John.
B. 05 JUL 1909 Gypsum, KS. Gold: 1936. Bill Wheatley never played college basketball but went right into the AAU leagues while in his early 20's. He was working for the Globe Oil & Refining Co. when they formed an AAU basketball team for which he would star. He made the 1936 Olympic team when his team finished second in the Olympic trials and, in Berlin, Bill Wheatley had the honor of mounting the victory podium to receive the wreath and gold medal at the awards ceremony. He then continued to play AAU basketball until 1941.

After 1941 Wheatley stayed involved in basketball both as a referee and a coach. His best team was the 1947 Oakland Bittners which he took to the finals of the AAU National Championship before losing to the Phillips 66ers. From 1948 through 1968, Bill Wheatley left coaching and worked as a superintendent on several construction crews. However in 1963, acting as coach and director, he took an AAU team on a 10-week tour of Africa. In his own words, in 1968, Bill Wheatley, "Got tired and retired!"

WHITE, Joseph Henry.
B. 16 NOV 1946 St. Louis, MO. Gold: 1968. A member of a Pan-American gold medalist in 1967, an Olympic gold medalist in 1968, and an NBA champion in 1974 and 1976, "JoJo" White missed only an NCAA title to add to his trophies. But he tried, as he was the top player at

Kansas in the late 60's, twice being named all-America and MVP of the Big Eight Conference. In 1969, he was drafted first by the Boston Celtics with whom he played for 10 seasons. He had an excellent career as a pro, quarterbacking the Celtics to two NBA titles. He also was named to the All-Rookie team in 1970, and was twice named NBA All-Star second team. He was named to play in seven consecutive NBA All-Star games, from 1971 through 1977. JoJo finished out his career with two seasons with Golden State and Kansas City before retiring in 1981. He has since gone into college coaching, starting out with his alma mater, the Kansas Jayhawks.

WILLIAMS, Howard Earl.
B. 29 OCT 1927 New Ross, IN. Gold: 1952. Howie Williams was a four-time letterman while at Purdue in the late 40's. He then went on to the AAU leagues, where he played mainly with the Peoria Caterpillars. He was a member of two AAU national champions (1951, 1952) and from 1951-1953 was named AAU all-America. It was while with the Cats that he was named to the 1952 Olympic team. He was also offered a chance to play with the Minneapolis Lakers but turned it down.

WILSON, George.
B. 09 MAY 1942 Meridian, MS. Gold: 1964. A 6'-8" power forward, George Wilson was the star of the Cincinnati team after Oscar Robertson left. He received all-America mention in both his junior and senior years, and after graduating in 1964, he was drafted in the first round by the Cincinnati Royals, where he again joined Robertson. Wilson played seven years as a pro, with fair success. He was never a great scorer, but played tough defense and rebounded well. He played for the Royals for three years, then hopped around the league with five other teams before ending his career in 1971 in Buffalo.

WOMEN

Women's basketball was first held as an Olympic sport in 1976 and the United States won a silver medal in its only Olympic appearance to date.

OUTSTANDING PERFORMANCES

Oldest Medalist
    24y43d Pat Head
Youngest Medalist
    18y18d Nancy Lieberman

BROGDON, Cynthia Jane.
B. 25 FEB 1957 Buford, GA. Silver: 1976. Cindy Brogdon attended Mercer University and made all-America while playing there in 1976. In her junior and senior years she averaged 30 points per game and scored over 20 points in 59 of 60 games. After playing on the Olympic team, she spent one year in the Women's Basketball League, playing for the New Orleans Pride, averaging 15 points per game and making second-team all-WBL. She now teaches physical education and coaches girl's basketball and track.

DUNKLE, Nancy Lynn.
B. 10 JAN 1955 Bainbridge, MD. Silver: 1976. A 6'-2" forward, Nancy Dunkle attended Cal State (Fullerton) and set every school record for scoring and rebounding. She was a two-time all-American (1975-76) and also played on the 1973 World University Games team which won a silver medal as well as the gold medal winning team at the 1975 Pan-American Games.

HARRIS, Lusia Mae.
B. 10 FEB 1955 Minter City, MS. Silver: 1976. Lucy Harris was one of the first great female centers in this country. She attended Delta State University, where she was a consensus All-American in her junior and senior years (1975-76), and led her team to three straight AIAW national championships. In her senior year she averaged 31 points and 15 rebounds a game, including a high of 58 points vs. Tennessee Tech. Combining beauty with athletic skill, she also was named homecoming queen at Delta State in 1975.

    Lucy Harris played on the 1975 Pan-American Games and World University Games team in addition to the Olympic team. After graduating from college, she was drafted by the New Orleans Jazz of the NBA, although she did not make a serious effort to make the team. She played one year of pro basketball in the WBL but her career was interrupted by pregnancy. Today, as Mrs. George Stewart, she is an admissions counselor and assistant basketball coach at Delta State and is working towards a masters degree in health, recreation and physical education.

HEAD, Patricia Sue.
B. 14 JUN 1952 Clarksville, TN. Silver: 1976. Pat Head played her collegiate basketball at the University of Tennessee at Martin. She was MVP of her team but did not have the college record held by some of her 1976 teammates. However she co-captained the 1973 World University Games silver medalists, played for the U.S. team at the 1975 World's Championship, and won a gold medal at the 1975 PanAmerican Games.

    Since retiring as a player, Pat Head has made her mark as one of the top coaches in the game. Now Mrs. R. B. Summitt, she is head coach and assistant athletic director at the University of Tennessee (Knoxville). She was the coach of the U.S. teams which won gold medals in the 1979 Pan-American Games and the World Championships, and was the assistant coach for the 1980 Olympic team which did not compete at Moscow. She has also been named to coach the 1984 U.S. Olympic women's basketball team at Los Angeles.

LEWIS, Charlotte.
B. 10 SEP 1955 Chicago, IL. Silver: 1976. Charlotte Lewis was a 6'-2" center who played college basketball at Illinois State. In 1975 and 1976 she received all-America mention and in 1975 she also played on the Pan-American Games gold medalists. She did not graduate from Illinois State but left school to play pro basketball with the Iowa Coronets of the now defunct Women's Basketball League.

LIEBERMAN, Nancy I.
B. 01 JUL 1958 Brooklyn, NY. Silver: 1976. Some people think Nancy Lieberman is the greatest women's basketball player the United States has ever produced. When only 17 years old, as a high school junior, she played on the 1975 Pan-American Games gold medal team and later played on the 1976 Olympic team. Highly recruited, she took her talents to Old Dominion University

Courtesy Pat Head Summitt

Pat Head, our 1984 Olympic women's basketball coach, as she appeared when she won a silver medal in basketball at the 1976 Olympics.

where she was all-everything for four years. She led her team to two national championships and also won the Wade Trophy as the outstanding women's intercollegiate player.

After her college days were over, Nancy Lieberman expected to play in the 1980 Olympics, but the boycott ended those hopes. After competing in several non-Olympic events as a member of the team, she signed the largest contract in the history of the Women's Basketball League. Unfortunately, the league, never financially stable, soon folded. Nancy Lieberman today makes most of her headlines as the trainer and manager of tennis superstar, Martina Navratilova.

MARQUIS, Gail.
B. 18 NOV 1956 New York, NY. Silver: 1976. Gail Marquis played for tiny Queen's College in New York and twice received all-America mention while playing there.

MEYERS, Ann Elizabeth.
B. 26 MAR 1955 San Diego, CA. Silver: 1976. Ann Meyers made headlines when she became the first woman to sign an NBA contract. The team was the Indiana Pacers and Meyers went to training camp but failed to make the team cuts.

Ann Meyers attended UCLA, as had her brother, Dave, who played for the men's basketball team, and later played in the NBA. She was a four-time basketball all-American at UCLA and also played two years of volleyball and track. At a school known as the greatest basketball power ever, Ann Meyers scored more points in school history than any other player—male or female. In 1978 she won the Broderick Award both as the outstanding collegiate basketball player and the outstanding female athlete.

Internationally, Meyers also had extensive experience. Besides the 1976 Olympics, she played on the 1975 Pan-American Games and World Championships teams, 1977 World University Games team, and the 1979 Pan-American Games and World Championships teams. She was also elected to carry the U.S. flag at the 1979 Pan-Am opening ceremonies.

In 1979-80 Ann Meyers played with the New Jersey Gems of the Women's Basketball League and was voted the league's co-MVP. Since the league folded she has worked mostly as a color commentator for women's basketball on television.

O'CONNOR, Mary Anne.
B. 01 OCT 1953 Bridgeport, CT. Silver: 1976. Mary Anne O'Connor first gained international experience playing on the U.S. national team which toured Russia in 1974. She also won a gold medal in the 1975 Pan-American Games. O'Connor attended Southern Connecticut State and after the Olympics, took a job there as a physical education teacher.

ROBERTS, Patricia.
B. 14 JUN 1955 Monroe, GA. Silver: 1976. At 6'-1", Pat Roberts could play either forward or center. In college, at Kansas State at Emporia, she usually played center and while there she averaged over 22 points and 13 rebounds a game.

ROJCEWICZ, Susan Marie.
B. 29 MAY 1953 Worcester, MA. Silver: 1976. Sue Rojcewicz was a 5'-7" guard who played college ball at Southern Connecticut. While there she made the Kodak all-America team in 1975 and was the team MVP in 1974 and 1975. She also played three years of collegiate softball and field hockey. In addition to her Olympic experience, Rojcewicz also played on the 1975 World Championships team, and won a gold medal as part of the 1975 Pan-American Games team.

   After her 1975 college graduation, Sue Rojcewicz took a job as a physical education teacher and assistant basketball coach at Penn State. She later moved to Stanford as assistant coach, and in 1982 was appointed head basketball coach at the Univ. of San Francisco. While at Stanford she supplemented her B.A. degree by earning a master's degree in education.

SIMPSON, Julienne Brazinski.
B. 20 JAN 1953 Elizabeth, NJ. Silver: 1976. Julienne Simpson attended John F. Kennedy College but she learned most of her basketball in the women's AAU leagues. In 1971 and 1975 she was named AAU all-America and in 1973 was the MVP of the national championship tournament. From 1970 to 1974 she was named to the National Girls' Traveling League All-League Team. In 1975 she played for the U.S. team which won a silver medal at the Pan-American Games and in 1976 made the Olympic team. She is now women's basketball coach at Arizona State University.

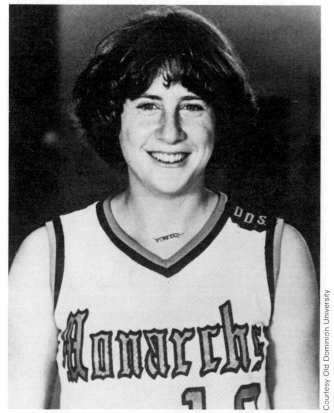

Courtesy Old Dominion University

Nancy Leiberman competed in the 1976 Olympics as a high school senior. She is considered by some to be the greatest women's basketball player in U.S. history.

BOBSLEDDING

Bobsledding has been held at every Olympic Winter Games, with the exception of 1960 in Squaw Valley. The United States did not participate in 1924 but starting in 1928 became one of the top nations in bobsledding until 1956. However since that time we have not won a medal in a sport now totally dominated by the Swiss and East Germans. Our best finishes since were achieved at Lake Placid in 1980, when our two-man teams finished fifth and sixth. Perhaps the bobsleigh gods have inveighed against our sledders for the Squaw Valley Organizing Committee's refusal to build a bobsled course. A better explanation is simply that the rest of the world caught up and surpassed the American sledders as there is only one bobsled course in North America—the one at Lake Placid—and it is far from a well-known sport in this country.

OUTSTANDING PERFORMANCES

Most Gold Medals
2 Billy Fiske, Clifford Gray
Most Medals
3 Pat Martin, John Heaton
Most Appearances
4 Jim Bickford
Oldest Gold Medalist
43y58d Frank Tyler
Youngest Gold Medalist
16y259d Billy Fiske
Youngest Medalist
15y129d Tom Doe

ATKINSON, James Neil.
B. 10 JAN 1929. Silver: 1952 4-man. Jim Atkinson can lay claim to many bobsled titles in addition to his Olympic silver medal. In 1950 at the World Championships, he teamed up with Stan Benham, Pat Martin and Bill D'Amico to win the 4-man title. This is one of only three times that the United States has won a world championship outside of Olympic competition.

Atkinson represented both the Lake Placid Bobsled Club and the Sno Birds of Lake Placid. Sledding for these clubs, he also was on three North American 4-man champions (1948, 1951 and 1953), and in those same years he slid on the AAU 4-man champion teams.

BENHAM, Stanley David.
B. 21 DEC 1913 Lake Placid, NY. D. 22 APR 1970 Florida. Silver(2): 1952 4-man, 1952 2-man. Stan Benham is probably the most titled man in American bobsledding, even though his best years came at the end of America's great success in the sport. In 1949 and 1950 he drove the 4-man sled that won the world title for the United States, the first two times this had been done. His other titles include the North American 2-man (1951, 1954, and 1956) and 4-man (1948, 1951, 1953, and 1956), and the AAU 2-man (1954, and 1956-57) and 4-man (1948, 1951, 1953-54 and 1956-57). He was renowned as a driver and drove with various partners, while representing the Lake Placid Bobsled Club.

Benham lived in Lake Placid most of his life, where he was the manager of the extensive park district and chief of the volunteer fire department. In the 60's he also did some commentary for televised bobsled competition.

BICKFORD, James John.
B. 02 NOV 1912 Lake Placid, NY. Bronze: 1948 4-man. Jim Bickford is one of only two Americans to compete in four Olympic Winter Games 1936, 1948, 1952 and 1956. In addition to his bobsled titles, he was honored for his contributions to American winter sports by being chosen to carry the United States flag at the opening ceremonies in both 1952 and 1956.

Bickford had a long career, winning his first big title in 1934 when he slid on the North American 4-man champions. His last national championship came in 1954 when he and Stan Benham took the AAU 2-man. He has lived near Lake Placid his entire life and worked for many years as a forest ranger.

BROWN, Ivan Elmore.
B. 17 APR 1908 Keene Valley, NY. D. 22 MAY 1963 Connecticut. Gold: 1936 2-man. Ivan Brown represented the Keene Valley Athletic Club and, together with his partner, Al Washbond, made up a great 2-man team. They won the 1936 Olympic title, as well as the North American championships of 1935 and 1938-39, and the AAU titles in 1934 and 1938-39. Brown eventually moved to Hartford where he worked as a machinist for many years.

BRYANT, Percy D.

B. 12 JUN 1899 Saranac Lake, NY. Silver: 1932 4-man. Percy Bryant represented the Saranac Lake Sports Association as a sledder. This club's team of Bryant, Henry Homburger, Paul Stevens, and Ed Horton won the North American and AAU 4-man titles in 1931 and 1932. It was this same team which took the silver medal at the 1932 Olympics.

BUTLER, Charles Thomas.

B. 11 JUN 1932 Saranac Lake, NY. Bronze: 1956 4-man. Tom Butler slid for the Adirondack Bobsled Club. Although he won a bronze medal in 1956, his first big championship did not come until 1958 when he slid on the AAU 4-man champions. In 1959 he became one of the few Americans to ride on a non-Olympic world champion sled, when he, Art Tyler, Gary Sheffield and Parker Voorix captured the 4-man championship at St. Moritz. Butler also rode sleds to two third-place finishes and one second-place finish at the World Championships.

Butler was a 1955 graduate of Brown where he also played the line on the football team. He formed there the first ever intercollegiate bobsled club with he and his buddies making weekend trips to Mt. Van Hoevenburg in an old Model A.

CARRON, Schuyler Anthony.

B. 20 AUG 1921 Lyon Mountain, NY. D. 15 JUN 1964 AuSable Forks, NY. Bronze: 1948 2-man. Other than the bronze medal in 1948, Sky Carron's biggest achievement in sledding came in 1947 when he and his Olympic partner, Fred Fortune, won the North American 2-man title.

COLGATE, Gilbert Bayard, Jr.

B. 21 DEC 1899 New York, NY. D. 09 OCT 1965 New York, NY. Bronze: 1936 2-man. Great-grandson of the founder of the Colgate-Palmolive Company, Gil Colgate graduated from Yale in 1922. He became an avid sportsman, winning many sailing trophies as well as competing as a sledder. Other than his Olympic appearance his only bobsled title was the 1934 North American 2-man championship with Olympic teammate, Richard Lawrence.

Colgate went on to become a director of the Colgate company and helped manage the family's in-vestments. He was also chairman and president of Colgate-Larsen Aircraft Co., which manufactured airplane parts. Aside from his business interests, Gil Colgate was a pioneer in the fight against the population explosion, as in 1938 he founded the Citizens Committee for Planned Parenthood and was the first treasurer of the Planned Parenthood Federation.

CROSSET, Howard Wallace, Jr.

B. 22 JUL 1918 Lake Placid, NY. Silver: 1952 4-man. Howard Crosset's biggest year in sledding came in 1951 when he slid on the North American and AAU 4-man champions with his Sno Birds of Lake Placid team. Crosset lived most of his life in Lake Placid where he was a policeman, but later moved to New Hampshire.

D'AMICO, William John.

B. 03 OCT 1910 Utica, NY. Gold: 1948 4-man. Bill D'Amico was one of the Lake Placid area's best athletes. He skiied, speed skated, played football and was a one-handicap golfer. But he was best known as a sledder. D'Amico is one of only three Americans (Stan Benham, Jim Atkinson) to have slid on two non-Olympic world championship teams, this coming in 1949 and 1950. In addition, he was on the winning teams at the 1941 AAU 4-man event and the 1942 North American 2-man championship.

DODGE, William Longstreth.

B. 07 JAN 1925. Bronze: 1956 4-man. In addition to his bronze medal at the Olympics, Bill Dodge also won the North American 2-man championship, sledding with Steve Phillips. Dodge was a 1955 graduate of Yale.

DOE, Thomas Bartwell, Jr.

B. 12 OCT 1912 Tacoma, WA. D. 19 JUL 1969 Charlotte, NC. Silver: 1928 5-man. Tom Doe lived in Europe during the 1920's and was in St. Moritz in 1928. The U.S. had no bobsled runs at that time so a team was recruited among Americans in Europe and Doe was selected to participate, even though he was only 15 years old at the time.

Tom Doe was the son of a former president of the Sperry Corporation. His father later took over the Vickers Corporation and it was this company that Tom Doe, Jr. eventually took over and made his life's work. He retired to a dairy farm in Asheville, NC.

DUPREE, Donald Victor.
B. 10 FEB 1919 Saranac Lake, NY. Bronze: 1948 4-man. At Lake Placid HS, Don Dupree was a great football player and he went to Colorado State University on a football scholarship. He also played baseball and ran track in college but an injury put an end to those endeavours, so when he returned to Saranac Lake he joined his five brothers and became a bobsledder. His biggest moment was his Olympic bronze medal as he never managed to ride on a national or North American champion.

Dupree has lived in Saranac Lake all his life where he has most recently worked as director of building and grounds for North Country Community College.

DUPREE, William Francis.
B. 07 JUN 1909 Saranac Lake, NY. D. 25 FEB 1955 Bound Brook, NJ. Bronze: 1948 4-man. Like his younger brother, Don, Bill Dupree was a football player in high school but he never played on the college level. He became interested in bobsledding when the Olympic track was built for the 1932 Olympics. He later would be part of the winning team in the 1947 AAU 4-man championships as well as winning an Olympic medal. Dupree worked in the family construction business most of his life, but moved to New Jersey four years before his death.

EAGAN, Edward Patrick Francis.
B. 26 APR 1897 Denver, CO. D. 14 JUN 1967 New York, NY. Gold(2): 1932 4-man, 1920 Welterweight Boxing. See the boxing section for the biography.

FISKE, William Mead Lindsley, III.
B. 04 JUN 1911 New York, NY. D. 17 AUG 1940 Chichester, England. Gold(2): 1928 5-man, 1932 4-man. From a wealthy banking family, Billy Fiske has been described as the quintessential amateur. He was educated in Europe where he played various sports and was one of the Americans chosen in 1928 to form a bobsled team. Fiske became famous as the driver of the two gold medal sleds. Later, on the toboggan run at St. Moritz, he became known as perhaps the greatest Cresta rider of all time. On the Cresta run, he took the Grand National title in 1936 and 1938 and won the Curzon Cup in 1935 and 1937.

Fiske worked in this country, for a time, as an executive with a motion picture company. But he spent much of his time in Europe and Britain, where in 1938 he married the Countess of Warwick. Billy Fiske had many British friends and when war broke out, he felt it only right to fight alongside them. He joined the Royal Air Force in 1939, the first American to do so. In June 1941, on returning from a mission, he was shot but landed his plane, only to die a few hours later. In his honor, the National AAU 4-man bobsled trophy was named the Billy Fiske Memorial Trophy.

FORTUNE, Frederick J., Jr.
B. 04 JAN 1921 Lake Placid, NY. Bronze: 1948 2-man. In addition to bobsledding, Fred Fortune was a fine skier and he served during World War II in the 10th Mountain Division Ski Troops, during which time he earned a Bronze Star. After the war, he returned to Lake Placid where he won the 1947 North American 2-man title with his Olympic partner, Sky Carron.

Fortune's basic occupation was as a contractor. He founded and built two towns—North Pole, New York and North Pole, Colorado (on Pike's Peak)—both Santa Claus Children's Villages.

GRANGER, David.
B. 26 JUN 1903 New York, NY. Silver: 1928 5-man. As there was no bobsled run in the United States in 1928, the U.S. team was made up of Americans who were in Europe at the time of the 1928 Olympics. Granger was one of those selected and he rode on the second-place sled.

Granger prepped at Phillips Exeter before attending Yale. He graduated from there in 1924 and did a year of post-graduate work at Christ's College, Cambridge. He later went on to become head of his own stock brokerage company in New York City and has held a seat on the New York Stock Exchange since 1926. He also has been a trustee and director of several companies.

GRAY, Clifford B.
B. 29 JAN 1892. Gold(2): 1928 5-man, 1932 4-man. Like David Granger, Cliff Gray was in St. Moritz in 1928 when he was selected for the bobsled team. But Gray later went on to win a second gold medal in 1932, joining Billy

Fiske as the only American sledders to win two golds. Clifford Gray also served as an alternate to the 1936 bobsled team, although he did not compete. Gray attended Cornell University and later became a professional songwriter.

HEATON, Jennison.

B. 16 APR 1903. D. 06 AUG 1971. Gold: 1928 Skeleton; Silver: 1928 5-man. Jennison Heaton was one of three brothers from a wealthy New Haven, Connecticut family who spent much of their time in Europe. The brothers, Jennison, Jack, and the non-Olympian, Trowbridge, were enthusiastic supporters of bobsledding and of the Cresta Run in particular. In the 1930-31 season they donated the Heaton Cup which is one of the most sought after trophies of the St. Moritz Tobogganing Club.

Although Jennison was not considered to be as accomplished a rider as younger brother, Jack, it was Jennison who won the 1928 Olympic title with Jack taking the silver medal. Jennison Heaton later married Beulah Fiske, becoming the brother-in-law of Olympic sledder Billy Fiske.

HEATON, John R.

B. 09 SEP 1908. Silver(2): 1928 Skeleton, 1948 Skeleton; Bronze: 1932 2-man. Together with Billy Fiske, Jack Heaton is rated as the most brilliant of all American riders on the Cresta Run. He won the Grand National in 1927 and 1929, the Curzon Cup in 1930 and 1933, the Bott Cup in 1929 and 1933 (from a scratch handicap), and the Carlton Challenge Cup in 1929 and 1933. Perhaps his greatest ride came in February 1929 when he lowered the record from the top, his record of 58.0 seconds remaining unbeaten for seven years.

Heaton is the only man to have won medals in the Olympic Winter Games 20 years apart and together with Pat Martin, he is second to Eric Heiden among Americans in number of medals won at the Winter Games. Jack Heaton eventually settled in Britain where he has lived for many years.

HICKS, Thomas.

B. 01 JUN 1918. Bronze: 1948 4-man. Tom Hicks represented the Lyon Mountain Miners Bobsled Club, which later changed its name to the Republic Miners Bobsled Club. While sledding for them he was on the winning

---

LAKE PLACID—AN AMAZING LITTLE VILLAGE

Lake Placid is a small village in upstate New York which is actually incorporated in the town of North Elba. Nestled midst the Adirondacks it attracts very little attention except during the Winter Olympic Games, when it becomes a very big town, indeed.

Twice, Lake Placid has hosted the Olympic Winter Games, in 1932 and 1980. This is despite the fact that the village population in 1980 was about 2,700 people, and the number of athletes competing that year was just over 1,400. For an accurate comparison, the 1984 Winter site, Sarajevo, has a population of 450,000 and will support only about the same number of competitors.

But the most amazing thing about Lake Placid is its habit of turning out Olympians and Olympic medalists. At every Olympic Winter Games, the United States team has had at least two athletes from the village of Lake Placid. They have turned out 38 competitors in the Winter Olympics, and 16 of these won medals of some sort! All this from a little village of less than 3,000 inhabitants.

---

teams in 1946 at both the AAU and the North American 4-man championships.

HINE, Lyman Northrop.

B. 22 JUN 1888. D. 05 MAR 1930 Paris, France. Silver: 1928 5-man. Lyman Hine was one of the Americans in Europe in 1928 who were selected to compete in the 1928 Olympic bobsled trials. He made the team and won a silver medal. While still a young man, Hine was killed in a terrible automobile accident.

HOMBURGER, Henry Anton.

B. 11 DEC 1902 Saranac Lake, NY. D. c1949 California. Silver: 1932 4-man. Henry Homburger attended college in Indiana where he studied engineering. He came back to Lake Placid and worked for many years as a civil engineer. Homburger was instrumental in helping design and then redesign the Mt. Von Hoevenburg bobsled run in Lake Placid. He put his knowledge of the course to good use at the 1932 Olympics to win a silver medal. He also slid on the winning 4-man team at the 1931 and 1932 North American and AAU Championships.

HORTON, Edmund Carlton.

B. 25 MAR 1896 Saranac Lake, NY. D. 26 MAY 1944 Saranac Lake, NY. Silver: 1932 4-man. Ed Horton was a member of the Saranac Lake Red Devils which won the 1931 and 1932 North American and AAU 4-man championships. This same team of Horton, Percy Bryant, Henry Homburger and Paul Stevens also won the silver medal at the 1932 Olympics. Horton studied at Cornell and lived all his life in Saranac Lake where he was a greenhouse proprietor and florist. In his youth he was also an outstanding speed skater.

LAMY, James Ernest.

B. 30 MAY 1928 Saranac Lake, NY. Bronze: 1956 4-man. In the first decade of this century, Ed Lamy was the greatest speed skater in the United States. His son, Jim Lamy, tried speed skating for a short time but went on to become one of the most titled men in American bobsledding. Lamy represented the Saranac Lake Bobsled Club and, in addition to his Olympic medal, he won the following titles: North American 4-man (1957, 1959 and 1962), AAU 2-man (1962 and 1963), and AAU 4-man (1955 and 1961-62).

Lamy worked for many years in sales with the Swift Co. near Lake Placid. Today he is the manager of the Mt. Van Hoevenburg bobsled facility.

LAWRENCE, Richard W.

B. 22 JUL 1906. Bronze: 1936 2-man. Dick Lawrence competed in both bobsled events at the 1936 Olympics and although he won a medal in the "boblet," he was a hero in the 4-man. The 4-man sled, driven by Frank Tyler, began to gain too much speed for one turn and his brakeman, Jim Bickford, was thrown backwards, was half out of the sled and was being dangerously dragged along. Although he could also have fallen out, Lawrence leaned backwards, grabbed Bickford, and pulled him back into the sled. They finished the run.

In addition to the 1936 Olympic bronze medal, Lawrence also partnered Gil Colgate to the 1934 North American 2-man championship.

MARTIN, Patrick Henry.

B. 19 AUG 1923 Louisville, NY. Gold: 1948 4-man; Silver(2): 1952 2-man, 1952 4-man. Among Americans, only Eric Heiden has won more medals in the Winter Olympics than the three owned by Pat Martin. Besides his Olympic medals, he can count among his bobsled trophies two North American 2-man titles (1951 and 1956), three North American 4-man titles (1951, 1953 and 1956), three AAU 2-man championships (1955-57), and six AAU 4-man championships (1940, 1941, 1953-54 and 1956-57). Martin won all his titles representing the Sno Birds of Lake Placid. One of his teammates on the 1940 AAU 4-man sled was Katharine Dewey, the only time a woman has won a major national sledding title. Pat Martin later went on to become a policeman in his hometown of Messena, New York.

MASON, Geoffrey Travers.

B. 13 MAY 1902 Philadelphia, PA. Gold: 1928 5-man. Geoffrey Mason attended Bowdoin College where he played football for four years and was the second best hammer thrower on the track team. The top hammer thrower at Bowdoin was Fred Tootell who would win an Olympic gold medal in that discipline, and later would name his son Geoffrey, after Geoffrey Mason.

After graduation in 1923, Geoff Mason did graduate work in literature at the University of Freiburg in Germany. While there he saw an ad in the Paris *Herald* which asked American athletes in Europe to come to St. Moritz and try out for the 1928 bobsled team. Mason did, made the team and won a gold medal in a sport in which his career was one month long—he never again slid after the Olympics.

Mason returned to the United States and became a Latin and German teacher, first at Bowdoin, but primarily in secondary schools. He was also a coach, and at one time coached seven different sports.

MINTON, Robert Henry.

B. 13 JUL 1904. D. 02 SEP 1974 New York, NY. Bronze: 1932 2-man. Bob Minton was a 1926 graduate of Dartmouth College. His star quickly rose on the New York Stock Exchange and by 1929 he was a partner in the firm of Laucheim, Minton & Co. He remained a stock broker until his retirement in 1967.

Minton was on the third place 4-man team at the Lake Placid Olympics but he never won a national title as a bobsledder.

O'BRIEN, J. Jay.
B. 22 FEB 1883 New York, NY. D. 05 APR 1940 Palm Beach, FL. Gold: 1932 4-man; Silver: 1928 5-man. In 1928 Jay O'Brien was head of the bobsled committee which was asked to select a team to compete at St. Moritz. O'Brien was faced with the problem of having no course in the United States on which to hold the tryouts so he selected the team among Americans who were in Europe at the time. O'Brien himself rode as a brakeman on the second place sled that year and returned four years later to add a gold medal.

O'Brien was an an investment banker and real estate broker, with holdings in both New York and Palm Beach. He was married three times, once to Mae Murray, silent screen star; next to Irene Fenwick, another well-known actress; and lastly to Julie Fleischmann, heir to the Fleischmann Company fortune.

PARKE, Richard Averell.
B. 1894. D. 23 AUG 1950 St. Moritz, Switzerland. Gold: 1928 5-man. Dick Parke graduated from Cornell in 1916 but spent much of his later life in Europe. He first visited St. Moritz after World War I, in which he served as an infantry officer in France. He then vacationed yearly in St. Moritz and while there in 1928 was selected for the U.S. Olympic bobsled team. He later went on to become president of a ski club and active in various St. Moritz civic groups.

RIMKUS, Edward William.
B. 10 AUG 1913 Schenectady, NY. Gold: 1948 4-man. Ed Rimkus probably had the shortest career of any American Olympic bobsledder. He slid for only two years—1947 and 1948—but during that time he managed to place second at the 1947 AAU and North American 4-man championships, which served as the trials for the 1948 Olympic team. A year later, his sled had improved sufficiently to take the gold medal.

Rimkus went to St. Lawrence College where he played football and ran track. He graduated in 1938 with a physics major, and later went to work in field engineering for General Electric.

STEVENS, Curtis Paul.
B. 01 JUN 1898 Lake Placid, NY. D. 15 May 1979 Saranac Lake, NY. Gold: 1932 2-man. Curtis Stevens slid with his youngest brother, Hubert, to win the 1932 2-man gold medal at Lake Placid. The elder Stevens also won several national titles and one North American title on the 4-man bobsled. Curtis Stevens spent much of his life running the family business, the Stevens Hotel in Lake Placid, but he also had a fuel and oil dealership in Lake Placid. A graduate of Rensselaer Polytech, Stevens was also an accomplished motorboat racer, having won many races in that sport, including an international regatta in Cuba in 1929.

STEVENS, Francis Paul.
B. 16 OCT 1889 Lake Placid, NY. D. 17 MAR 1949 Schenectady, NY. Silver: 1932 4-man. Paul Stevens slid for the Saranac Lake Sports Association in 1932 and he accompanied fellow team members, Henry Homburger, Ed Horton, and Percy Bryant, to the 1932 silver medal. With the same team, he also won the 1931 and 1932 North American and AAU 4-man titles. A few years later, after Curtis had retired from sledding, Paul joined brother Hubert to win the AAU 2-man championship in 1935.

Paul Stevens served as a lieutenant commander in both world wars. Between wars, he helped out with the family hotel business and also managed an auto business near the Lake Placid area. Stevens was a noted auto mechanic, having been a crew member with Ralph Mulford's car racing team in 1920's.

STEVENS, John Hubert.
B. 07 MAR 1890 Lake Placid, NY. D. 26 NOV 1950 Lake Placid, NY. Gold: 1932 2-man. Hubert Stevens must be considered, with Billy Fiske and Stan Benham, one of the greatest bobsled drivers in American history. In addition to the 1932 Olympic gold medal, he won three North American and three national championships as a sledder.

Courtesy Mrs. Mary MacKenzie

The three great bobsledding brothers, the Stevens, take the woman responsible for it all — their mother — for a sled ride. (L-R) — Curtis Stevens, F. Paul Stevens, Mrs. Frances Stevens, and Hubert Stevens.

Stevens was a well-known athlete growing up in Lake Placid, as he played hockey and golf. He went to Renssellaer Polytech, obtained an engineering degree, and served as a machinist and pilot in World War I. After the war he helped run the family hotel in Lake Placid, but he also served as superintendent of the Whiteface Mountain Highway Authority and was chairman of the Whiteface Mountain Commission for improving ski conditions in the area.

TUCKER, Nion Robert.
B. 21 AUG 1885 Suisan, CA. D. 22 APR 1950 San Francisco, CA. Gold: 1928 5-man. Nion Tucker graduated from the University of California in 1909 and shortly thereafter went into the investment brokerage business. By 1920 he was directing manager of the brokerage firm of Bond, Goodwin & Tucker. He later went on to have a leading role in the formation of United Airlines through the merger of a group of smaller airlines, and also sat on the board of directors of the San Francisco Chronicle Publishing Company.

In 1946 he retired to his ranch where he raised purebred Hereford cattle. He became involved in the organization of horse and livestock shows and was instrumental in making San Francisco's Cow Palace a leading site for those events. Later he headed a group which lobbied for permission to hold professional and amateur sporting events at the Cow Palace.

TYLER, Arthur Walter.
B. 26 JUL 1915 Utica, NY. Bronze: 1956 4-man. For many years, Art Tyler and his partner, Ed Seymour, probably made up the most erudite 2-man bobsled pairing ever. Seymour had a Ph.D. in engineering and Tyler had earned a Ph.D. in physics from the University of Michigan. They both worked in Rochester for Eastman Kodak and together twice won the North American and the National 2-man championships.

After his bronze medal performance in the 1956 Olympics, Art Tyler also was a part of the last American team to win a World Championship. This was the Adirondack Bobsled Club which took the 1959 World 4-man title at St. Moritz. Tyler is probably known as the most scientific of all American sledders. He designed many changes in his sleds, testing them in wind tunnels, and putting his physics background to use to arrive at the best combinations of aerodynamic factors.

Tyler eventually left Eastman Kodak and founded several electronic firms of his own. He lived for awhile in a Boston suburb but retired to the Philippines.

TYLER, Francis W.
B. 11 DEC 1904 Lake Placid, NY. D. 11 APR 1956 Lake Placid, NY. Gold: 1948 4-man. A member of the Sno Birds of Lake Placid, Frank Tyler's only national championship came on a 4-man sled at the 1941 AAU's. On that team was Bill D'Amico, and seven years later, Tyler and D'Amico were accompanied by Pat Martin and Ed Rimkus as they won the 4-man gold medal.

Tyler worked in Lake Placid until the 40's as a policeman and then became an insurance adjuster. In 1952 he lost his amateur status because he had sponsored an advertised product so instead he went to the 1952 Olympics as the bobsled coach. In 1956 at Cortina, he was the U.S. bobsled team's manager but was ill during most of the Games with a terrible flu and less than two months after the Olympics, he was dead of a heart attack.

WASHBOND, Alan M.
B. 12 OCT 1899 Keene Valley, NY. D. 30 JUL 1965 Plattsburgh, NY. Gold: 1936 2-man. Al Washbond started sledding with his brother, Bud, but it was with Ivan Brown that he formed one of this country's top 2-man teams ever. Together they won both the AAU and the North American championships in 1935, 1938 and 1939. Washbond lived most of his life in Keene Valley where he worked as the caretaker of several tourist camps.

BOXING

The United States has always been one of the top, if not the top, nations in Olympic boxing. There have been years when the Russians, the Cubans, or the Italians would win more medals, but since 1904, when boxing became an Olympic sport, the United States has won more medals (80, USSR second with 43) and more gold medals (36, USSR 14, Italy 13, Cuba and Great Britain 12) than any other country.

Our two greatest years have been 1952 and 1976 when, in both years, U.S. boxers won five gold medals. World champions to come from these two squads include Floyd Patterson, Davey Moore, Sugar Ray Leonard, and Michael Spinks.

OUTSTANDING PERFORMANCES

Most Gold Medals
  2 Oliver Kirk
Most Medals
  2 Jack Eagan, George Finnegan, Oliver Kirk, Charles Mayer, Harry Spanger
Most Appearances
  2 Eddie Eagan, Davey Armstrong
Oldest Gold Medalist
  31y139d Eddie Crook
Youngest Gold Medalist
  16y157d Jackie Fields

ADKINS, Charles.
B. 27 APR 1932. Gold: 1952 Light-Welterweight. Chuck Adkins won the AAU lightweight title in 1949 for his only national championship. In the 1952 Olympic trials he lost a decision in the finals to Joe Reynolds, but proved stronger than Reynolds in pre-Olympic training and the coaches elected to use Adkins in the Games. It was a good decision as he won the gold medal in Helsinki rather easily.

After the Olympics, Adkins turned pro and fought for five years as a lightweight. His main problem was that he was easily knocked out, losing several fights in that manner. In 1958, Eddie Perkins knocked him out in the first round, and he retired from boxing with a pro record of 16 wins and 5 losses.

ALI, Muhammed. (see Cassius Clay)

BALDWIN, John.
B. 26 AUG 1949 Detroit, MI. Bronze: 1968 Light-Middleweight (tied). Johnny Baldwin's top victories as an amateur came in the Michigan AAU championships in 1966 and 1968. He also was a runner-up in the National AAU in 1968. In that year he went to the semi-finals of the Olympics where he lost a close decision to Ricardo Garbey of Cuba.

Baldwin began fighting as a pro in 1970 and ran up a good record. Through 1976, in 32 fights as a middle-weight he lost only once, that to Marvelous Marvin Hagler, the future middleweight champ, by a 10-round decision. Inexplicably he was never given a title shot.

BARTH, Carmen.
B. 13 SEP 1912. Gold: 1932 Middleweight. Never a national champion, Carmen Barth surprised the experts by easily winning the middleweight gold medal at Los Angeles. After the Games, he turned pro but had a rather checkered career. In 1942 he was called into the service by the navy and never fought again professionally. His final professional record was 17 wins, 2 draws, and 11 losses.

BERGER, Samuel.
B. 25 DEC 1884 Chicago, IL. D. 23 FEB 1925. Gold: 1904 Heavyweight. A member of the Olympic Club of San Francisco, Sam Berger defeated William Michaels in the semi-finals and Charles Mayer, the middleweight champion, in the finals to win the heavyweight title in the 1904 Olympics. Berger then turned professional. He was expected to be a promising candidate for the heavyweight title but experts claimed he lacked the killer instinct necessary for survival in the ring. His last fight was in 1906 when he lost a 10-round decision to Al Kaufman.

Berger later served as a sparring partner and manager to Jim Jeffries when Jeffries made a comeback late in his career. Berger lived in San Francisco and eventually opened and ran a clothing store in that town.

BOR, Nathan.
B. 01 MAR 1913 Fall River, MA. D. 1973 New Bedford, MA. Bronze: 1932 Lightweight. Nat Bor was the Bay State's top amateur boxer in 1932 when he won the state title and the national AAU championship as a

lightweight. That year he also won his bronze medal in the Olympics.

After the Olympics, Bor stayed in Los Angeles and fought for eight years as a professional with marginal success. He joined the marines during World War II and served as a boxing coach stationed at Paris Island. After the war, he returned to Massachusetts where he opened the Olympic Dry Cleaners in his hometown of New Bedford.

BOYD, James Felton.
B. 30 NOV 1930 Rocky Mount, NC. Gold: 1956 Light-heavyweight. Although never a national amateur titlist, Jim Boyd was all-army and all-service champion in both 1955 and 1956 and he had no difficulty winning the gold medal at Melbourne. After the Games, he continued serving in the army until 1959 when he turned pro. However he fought only a few times in four years and never contended for a title.

BOYLSTEIN, Frederick.
B. 15 MAR 1904 Ford City, PA. D. 28 FEB 1972 Kittanning, PA. Bronze: 1924 Lightweight. Fred Boylstein won the AAU lightweight title in 1924 in addition to winning a bronze medal in the Olympic Games. In winning his AAU title that year he was forced to fight, and win, eight bouts in one night, which he did. He turned professional after the 1924 Olympics and fought until 1934, winning almost all of his fights, but never receiving a chance to fight for a championship. He worked most of his life in his hometown of Kittanning, Pennsylvania, as a police officer, eventually rising to captain. He also worked as a boxing coach at the local gym.

BROOKS, Nathan Eugene.
B. 04 AUG 1933. Gold: 1952 Flyweight. From Cleveland, Nate Brooks went on to have a fine career as a professional after his Olympic triumph. He fought as a professional and in 1953 chalked up seven victories against one defeat. On 8 February 1954 he won the North American bantamweight championship by KO-'ing Billy Peacock in the eighth round. He defended the title twice before losing it. This defeat led to a string of losses, and he retired from the ring after 1954.

Boxing medalist from the 1932 Olympics, Nat Bor.

Courtesy John Mallon

BROWN, Charles.
B. 28 FEB 1939 Cincinnati, OH. Bronze: 1964 Feather-weight (tied). Charlie Brown of Cincinnati had a fine year in 1964. He won the AAU title and the final Olympic trials before moving on to Tokyo. In the Olympics he won three decisions before losing a 4-1 decision to the Filipino, Anthony Villanueva, in the semi-finals.

BURKE, Miles J.
Silver: 1904 Flyweight. Miles Burke of St. Louis lost his only match in the flyweight division in 1904 but still won a silver medal. Burke weighed 107 + lbs, over the weight limit for the class, but there were only two entrants so he was permitted to box. Burke worked for one of the St. Louis newspapers at the time.

CARMODY, Robert John.
B. 04 SEP 1938 Brooklyn, NY. Bronze: 1964 Flyweight (tied). In 1964, Bob Carmody was a sergeant in the Army when he won the U.S. Olympic trials. At Tokyo he won his bronze medal by winning two matches, after one bye, and then losing a 4-1 decision in the semi-finals to Fernando Aztori of Italy.

CARRERAS, Ricardo Luis.
B. 08 DEC 1949 New York, NY. Bronze: 1972 Bantam-weight (tied). Ricardo Carreras first made headlines as a boxer in 1966 when he won the New York Golden Gloves. It was the first of many amateur victories. In 1971 he won a bronze medal in the Pan-American Games as well as winning the AAU championship. Three times, in 1969, 1971, and 1972, he was interser-vice champion while serving in the air force. He took an amateur record of 73 and 8 to Munich where he made it to the semi-finals to win a bronze medal.

CLAY, Cassius Marcellus (nka Muhammed Ali).
B. 17 JAN 1942 Louisville, KY. Gold: 1960 Light-heavyweight. He was born Cassius Marcellus Clay, the son of Odessa and Marcellus Clay, but he would not keep the name. He preferred instead a name which dignified the black man, and he wore it well as the most famous athlete of his time.

His story began as a reed-thin middleweight when he won the 1959 Golden Gloves championship. He repeated that victory in 1960, adding to it the AAU title

and the Olympic light-heavyweight crown. Thus was born the saga of "The Greatest."

Clay turned pro right after the Rome Olympics and fought his first fight against Tunney Hunsaker. He won easily and continued to win as he worked his way up the heavyweight ranks. He punctuated his pugilistic abili-ties by composing doggerel verse to predict the out-come of his fights—"Float like a butterfly, sting like a bee, his hands can't hit, what his eyes can't see."

Clay was the fastest heavyweight anybody had ever seen but few gave him a chance against "the Big Bear," Sonny Liston, when they met for the heavy-weight title on 25 February 1964. But Clay disarmed the menacing Liston, winning by a TKO in seven, and after-wards told the world he had embraced the Black Mus-lim faith and taken the name Muhammed Ali.

The Muhammed Ali of the late 60's was an awe-some fighting machine. With great speed, deceptive power, and an unequaled ability to take a punch, he was never beaten, never even seriously challenged. But the courts took away the title that other boxers could not. He refused induction into the U.S. Army, claiming a conscientious objection because of his faith, so he was stripped of his titles and a conviction was sought.

The attempted conviction was overturned. Ali was vindicated and allowed to fight again but he had lost three years of his prime. He made a comeback, losing to then undefeated champion and former Olympian, Joe Frazier, in a 15-round decision. However, Ali would later win back the heavyweight title by defeating George Foreman, another Olympic champion. He would eventually lose the title again, and regain it again, against 1976 Olympian Leon Spinks. But he was never the same fighter after his three-year exile.

In the late 70's, Ali attempted to regain the title again, but he was overweight and out of shape. A mere caricature of the once great fighter, he was punished by heavyweight champion Larry Holmes. Ali finally was convinced to retire but not before he had made his mark on the world of sport—as The Greatest.

COLBERG, Frederick William.
Bronze: 1920 Welterweight. Fred Colberg won two matches at the 1920 Olympics before losing in the semi-finals to the eventual champion.

CROOK, Edward.

B. 19 APR 1929 Detroit, MI. Gold: 1960 Middleweight. Eddie Crook lost in the finals of the Olympic trials in 1956 to Jose Torres, future world light-heavyweight champion, but in 1960 he had vastly improved as a fighter. By then he had won two Golden Gloves championships and an Eastern Regional AAU title and was considered a favorite to make the Olympic team. He did not disappoint and Crook was barely tested at Rome. He knocked out three of his first four opponents, before winning a 3-1-1 decision in the finals over Tadeusz Walasek of Poland.

DALEY, John Lawrence.

B. 16 AUG 1909 Newton, MA. D. 07 FEB 1963 El Paso, TX. Silver: 1928 Bantamweight. In 1928 John Daley had quite a year. He won the Massachusetts, New England and National AAU titles and went to the finals of the Olympic bantamweight championship. In the semifinals it appeared Daley was finished as the referee gave the fight to his opponent, Harry Isaacs, of South Africa. But the crowd raised such a ruckus over this decision that it was reversed and Daley was advanced to the finals. The same thing happened in the finals but this time Daley's victory was reversed and given to the Italian, Vittorio Tamagnini.

After the Olympics, Daley turned pro but fought only four times. He quit boxing when he realized it was less than financially rewarding. Daley took a job as a stock and bond broker and went on to become quite successful.

DANIELS, Quincey.

B. 04 AUG 1941 Biloxi, MS. Bronze: 1960 Light-welterweight. Quincey Daniels was 1959 AAU lightweight champion and Golden Gloves champion of the Western Regional in 1959 and 1960. He turned professional several years after the Olympics, but had only moderate success.

DAVIS, Howard Edward, Jr.

B. 14 FEB 1956 Glen Cove, NY. Gold: 1976 Lightweight. Howard Davis had a distinguished amateur career. In 1973 he won the AAU featherweight crown, and in 1974, at the first World's Amateur Boxing Championships, he became the first to win the featherweight title. He also won four Golden Gloves titles, and in 1976

BOXING TRIVIA TIME

Most people know that several U.S. Olympic boxers have gone on to win the world's professional championship, but do you have any idea how many did it? If that's too easy, try naming them all.

Fifteen — Cassius Clay (Muhammed Ali), Jackie Fields, George Foreman, Joe Frazier, Frankie Genaro, Marvin Johnson, Fidel LaBarba, Sugar Ray Leonard, Davey Moore, Floyd Patterson, Louis Salica, Leon Spinks, Michael Spinks, John Tate, and Jose Torres. All but Davey Moore won an Olympic medal and more information on their careers may be found under their biography.

Davey Moore competed as a bantamweight in the 1952 Olympics at Helsinki, losing in the second round of competition. In 1959 he won the world featherweight championship by knocking out Kid Bassey in the 13th round. He successfully defended the title four times before he fought Sugar Ramos on 21 March 1963. On that night Ramos defeated Moore and so severely injured him that Moore died a few hours after the fight.

Paul Berlenbach was an alternate to the 1920 Olympic wrestling team, but he never competed in the Olympics. He later became more famous as a boxer, winning the light-heavyweight world championship in 1923.

added the AAU lightweight title before taking the Olympic trials. At Montreal he won his gold medals with classy technical skills and speed.

Since 1976 Davis has fought as a professional and quite successfully. His record through early 1983 was 22 wins and one loss. He has yet to win a world championship but many observers think he will. Some, however, counter that Davis needs to become more aggressive in the ring if he is ever to become a professional champion.

DEVINE, Harold George.

B. 18 MAY 1909 New Haven, CT. Bronze: 1928 Featherweight. Harry Devine began fighting at 14 and five years later, really hit his stride. In 1928 he won both the AAU title and the Olympic trials before going to the Olympic Games. There he won two bouts before losing in the semi-finals. Devine, although fighting with a broken knuckle, earned his bronze medal by decisioning Lucien Biquet of Belgium for third place. After the Olympics, Devine fought professionally for seven years, without great distinction. Retiring in the 30's, he has spent almost 50 years working in the fur business in his hometown of Worcester, Massachusetts.

EAGAN, Edward Patrick Francis.
B. 26 APR 1898 Denver, CO. D. 14 JUN 1967 New York, NY. Gold(2): 1920 Light-heavyweight; 1932 4-man (Bobsledding). As the only person to win a gold medal at both the Winter and Summer Games, Eddie Eagan holds a unique place in Olympic history. In 1920 at Antwerp, Eagan beat Holstock (SAF), then H. Franks (GBR), and in the final Sverre Sorsdal of Norway to win the gold medal in the light-heavyweight division. After the Olympics, Eagan returned to Yale Law School. He left there in 1922 to become a Rhodes Scholar at Oxford where he soon made his mark in British amateur boxing circles. At the 1924 Olympics, Eagan chose not to defend his light-heavyweight title but instead weighed in as a heavyweight. He met first the Englishman, A. J. Clifton, who had replaced Eagan as British ABA champion. After a grueling three rounds Clifton got the verdict but in doing so, so severely injured his hands that he could not come forward for his second round match.

After competing twice in the summer Games, Eagan made his debut at the Olympic Winter Games in Lake Placid. It was here that he made Olympic history when, as a member of the 4-man bobsled team, he added a gold medal to the one he had won at the summer Games twelve years earlier.

Eagan obtained a B.A. degree from Oxford in 1928 and in 1932 was admitted to the U.S. Bar. He practiced law until the outbreak of World War II when he rejoined the armed forces. Colonel Eagan served with distinction throughout the period of hostilities and was awarded ribbons for combat in all three theatres of operations.

EAGAN, Jack.
Silver: 1904 Lightweight; Bronze: 1904 Welterweight. Jack Eagan was from Philadelphia in 1904. As a light-

weight, he won two decisions before losing in the finals to Harry Spanger. He was denied his chance for a rematch with Spanger when Al Young beat him in the semi-finals of the welterweight class.

FEARY, Frederick.
B. 10 APR 1912. Bronze: 1932 Heavyweight. In addition to winning a bronze medal at the Los Angeles Olympics, Fred Feary was also 1932 AAU heavyweight champion.

FEE, Raymond.
B. 12 JAN 1904. Bronze: 1924 Flyweight. Ray Fee, of San Francisco's Olympic Club, was probably a great poker player—he won his bronze medal on a bluff. In the 1924 Olympics he was beaten soundly in the semi-finals by Jim MacKenzie of Great Britain, and in the process, so severely injured his arm that he couldn't possibly box in the bout for third place. But he knew his opponent, Renaldo Castellenghi of Italy, was also injured, so Fee dressed for the fight, entered the ring and tried to look as fit as possible. Castellenghi looked at him, fell for the bluff and withdrew—giving Fee his bronze medal.

FIELDS, Jackie (né Jacob Finkelstein).
B. 09 FEB 1908 Chicago, IL. Gold: 1924 Featherweight. Jacob Finkelstein began boxing as a youth of 14 in Chicago. He was trained by a former fighter, Marty Fields, and he shortly adopted Fields' name as his own. Jackie Fields was a fine amateur, winning 51 of 54 bouts in addition to to his Olympic glory.

Jackie Fields' Olympic featherweight title was only the prelude to a great career. He turned professional shortly after returning from Paris and went on to twice become world welterweight champion. He first won the National Boxing Association version of the title on 25 March 1929, when he beat Young Jack Thompson in 10 rounds. On 25 July 1929 he laid claim to the undisputed title by winning on a second-round foul from Joe Dundee. Fields later lost his title to Thompson in 1930 but he regained it in 1932 by defeating Lou Brouillard in 10 rounds. After losing the title in 1933 to Young Corbett III, Fields fought only one more time and then retired.

FINNEGAN, George V.
Gold: 1904 Flyweight; Silver: 1904 Bantamweight. George Finnegan is one of only five men (all from 1904) to have won two boxing medals in the same year. Representing the Olympic Club of San Francisco, Finnegan defeated Miles Burke to win the flyweight division, but lost to Oliver Kirk in the bantamweight class. There were only two fighters in both classes.

FLYNN, Edward L.
B. 25 OCT 1909 New Orleans, LA. D. 1982 Tampa, FL. Gold: 1932 Welterweight. A fantastic amateur boxer, Eddie Flynn was National AAU champion in 1931 and 1932 in addition to winning the Olympic welterweight championship. His overall amateur record was 144 wins and no losses. After the Olympics he turned professional, and fought well for three years, losing only one fight in 15. But he was drafted in 1935 and served through World War II, never again fighting professionally. Flynn attended Loyola (New Orleans), graduating in 1936 with a degree in dentistry, at which he made his career.

FOREMAN, George.
B. 10 JAN 1949 Houston, TX. Gold: 1968 Heavyweight. George Foreman is one of the most powerful punchers who has ever fought. He had little experience in 1968 when he won the AAU title, the Olympic trials and the Olympic Games. At Mexico City he became famous when, after winning the final bout, he took a small American flag and waved it to the four corners of the auditorium. It was especially significant given the tenor of the times and the protests of blacks, Tommie Smith and John Carlos, on the Olympic victory platform.

Foreman quickly turned professional and began knocking out fighters left and right. In 1973 he fought Joe Frazier for the heavyweight title and punished him—flooring him seven times in the second round before the fight was stopped. Foreman defended the title twice but on 30 October 1974, Muhammed Ali stopped him in eight rounds.

Foreman was never a championship factor again. He fought for two more years, and although he never lost, he made few serious attempts to get a title shot. Foreman's professional record was 44 wins and only one loss. He retired to enter a completely different field—that of religion. George Foreman, the man with

Joe Frazier, 1964 gold medalist, later to become one of the greatest heavyweight champions of them all.

thunder in his fists but love in his heart, is today a practicing minister in Texas.

FRAZIER, Joseph.
B. 12 JAN 1944 Beaufort, SC. Gold: 1964 Heavyweight. Joe Frazier had no business winning a gold medal in the 1964 Olympics. He had been beaten in the Olympic trials by Buster Mathis, a fighter with a far better amateur record. But Mathis broke his thumb while training for the Olympics and Frazier got his chance. It was ironic because in the Olympic semi-finals, Joe Frazier broke his own thumb. But "Smokin' Joe" Frazier was not a man to be denied. He had the thumb taped, basically fought with one hand in the finals and won the gold medal. It was typical of this gutsy fighter.

Joe Frazier is one of the great heavyweight champions of all time. It is sad that he fought in the same era as Muhammed Ali because he did not get the acclaim

Ali did, and it was acclaim Frazier deserved. Frazier first won the heavyweight world championship in 1970 by stopping Jimmy Ellis in five rounds. He defended the title several times before being knocked out by former Olympian George Foreman. Frazier fought three tremendous battles with Ali. The first, in 1971, was the fight of the century, a battle of undefeated heavyweight champions, and Frazier won by a decision in 15. Frazier was on the losing end in the next two fights, but all three were great, great spectacles.

Frazier was very short for a heavyweight, and he made no pretense of backpedaling. He always came at you like a Sherman tank, willing to trade three punches to land one pulverizing blow. After losing his heavyweight title, he continued to fight for a few years before retiring in the mid 70's. He sang with a group called "The Knockouts" and made some television commercials. He fought once in 1981 in a comeback attempt but is now retired and managing his son, Marvis Frazier, a heavyweight contender himself.

HALLER, Frank.
Silver: 1904 Featherweight. Representing the Cincinnati Athletic Club and Gymnasium, Frank Haller defeated Fred Gilmore in the semi-finals in 1904, before losing a decision to Oliver Kirk in the finals of the featherweight class.

HARRIS, Ronald Allen.
B. 08 FEB 1947 Detroit, MI. Bronze: 1964 Lightweight. In addition to winning a bronze medal in the 1964 Olympics, Ronnie Harris won the National AAU title in that same year.

HARRIS, Ronald W.
B. 03 SEP 1948 Canton, OH. Gold: 1968 Lightweight. No relation to the above, Ronnie Harris also fought as a lightweight, and achieved the rare feat of winning the National AAU title three consecutive years—1966-1968. Harris twice won the Golden Gloves title and was a bronze medalist at the 1967 Pan-American Games. Harris attended Kent State University for a brief time but after the Olympics he turned professional and fought until 1976, with a good record, but not against well known fighters.

HERRING, Horace.
B. 19 JUN 1922. Silver: 1948 Welterweight. After winning four bouts by decision, Horace "Hank" Herring lost a decision to Julius Torma of Czechoslovakia in the finals of the 1948 Olympics. Herring fought professionally for two years after the Olympics but with minimal success.

JOHNSON, Marvin L.
B. 12 APR 1954 Indianapolis, IN. Bronze: 1972 Middleweight (tied). Marvin Johnson won the 1971 and 1972 AAU championships and the 1971 Golden Gloves crown. Then in 1972 he took the Olympic trials before losing in the semi-finals at Munich.

After the Olympics, Johnson turned professional and has done better as a pro than as an amateur. He has fought mostly as a light-heavyweight and has been able to win the championship of both the WBC (1978-1979) and the WBA (1979-1980).

GENARO, Frankie (né Frank DiGennara).
B. 26 AUG 1901 New York, NY. D. 26 DEC 1966 New York, NY. Gold: 1920 Flyweight. At 5'-2" and 112 lbs., Frankie Genaro originally wanted to be a jockey. But he became one of the greatest flyweights to ever live. Genaro's victory in the flyweight class at the 1920 Olympics was only the start. He turned professional shortly thereafter and won his first fight from Joe Coletti. Just over two years later, in 1923, Frankie Genaro decisioned all-time flyweight great, Pancho Villa, to win the world flyweight crown.

Genaro was not long recognized as the champion. Jimmy Wilde, the English champion, fought Villa and was strangely claimed to be the title-holder. In 1925, Genaro was beaten by 1924 Olympic champion, Fidel La Barba, but La Barba retired shortly thereafter to enter college. In 1928 Genaro won a version of the world title, and in 1930 laid claim to the unified title by defeating Willie La Morte. In 1931 he was KO'ed in a title defense but continued to fight until 1934, retiring after 128 bouts. Famous boxing expert, Nat Fleischer, ranked Genaro the third greatest flyweight of all-time, behind Wilde and Villa.

GILMORE, Fred.
Bronze: 1904 Featherweight. Fred Gilmore fought once, and lost, in the 1904 featherweight tournament. He was from Chicago.

HALAIKO, Stephen Michael.
B. 27 DEC 1908 Auburn, NY. Silver: 1928 Lightweight. The winner of 115 out of 116 amateur fights, Steve Halaiko won the National AAU title in 1928 before going on to his Olympic success. Halaiko repeated his AAU championship in 1929 and then turned professional. Halaiko had a long career as a professional, fighting through 1942, but it was not terribly successful. His career professional record was 57 wins, 40 losses, and 10 draws, and he ended his career fighting under the pseudonym of Frank Wint.

JONES, Alfred.
B. 01 OCT 1946 Detroit, MI. Bronze: 1968 Middleweight (tied). The 1965 Golden Gloves championship was the first breakthrough for young Al Jones, but he continued to win, later capturing the 1968 AAU title and winning the middleweight division of the Olympic trials. After a close loss in the semi-finals of the Olympics to eventual champion, Chris Finnegan of Britain, Jones turned professional. Inexplicably he fought for only two years although he lost no fights during that time.

KIRK, Oliver L.
Gold(2): 1904 Bantamweight, 1904 Featherweight. Oliver Kirk is the only boxer in Olympic history to win two weight classes in the same year. He first knocked out George Finnegan, the only other competitor, to win the bantamweight division. It appears then that he was not entered in the featherweight class, but after only two boxers entered, the crowd wanted to see Kirk fight the winner, Frank Haller. Kirk, from the Business Men's Gym in St. Louis, did so and won by decision.

La BARBA, Fidel.
B. 29 SEP 1905 New York, NY. D. 02 OCT 1981 Los Angeles, CA. Gold: 1924 Flyweight. Outstanding as an amateur, Fidel La Barba went on to even greater success as a professional. After winning the 1924 Olympic flyweight championship, La Barba won the world professional championship from another Olympian, Frankie Genaro, in 1925. La Barba never defended his

title and retired only a few months later to enter Stanford University and major in journalism. He stated that he had already made over $400,000 in the ring, but the stock market crash and depression depleted most of that. He returned to the ring in 1929, first as a bantamweight and eventually moving up to the featherweight class. Although he eventually had some title fights in the heavier classes, he was never the fighter he was as a flyweight. Nat Fleischer, well-known boxing expert, rated La Barba the fourth best flyweight of all-time, behind Genaro, Jimmy Wilde and Pancho Villa.

After retiring as a fighter in 1933, La Barba became a journalist, writing for boxing newspapers and magazines. He also served as a boxing advisor in Hollywood.

LAURIA, Louis Daniel.
B. 19 NOV 1919. Bronze: 1936 Flyweight. Louis Lauria was not well-known at all as an amateur fighter in 1936 but although he finished only third in the flyweight class, he won the Val Barker Trophy as the best technical boxer at the Olympics.

LEE, Norvel LaFollette Ray.
B. 22 SEP 1924. Gold: 1952 Light-heavyweight. Norvel Lee first came to boxing prominence in 1948 when he

lost in the finals of the Olympic trials to heavyweight Jay Lambert. Lee went to London with the Olympic team but did not compete. In the interim between Olympics he won the AAU championship in 1950 and 1951. At the 1952 Olympic trials Lee again lost in the finals of the heavyweight division, losing to Eddie Sanders. However, Lee was small for a heavyweight and the team's coaches felt he could make the light-heavyweight limit and asked him to do so. He managed to lose the weight and outshone Charles Spieser in training, so Lee was entered in the light-heavyweight division. Not only did he win the gold medal, but Lee won the Val Barker Trophy, an award given at the Olympics to the best boxer in any division.

Between the two Olympics, Lee made headlines of a different sort. In late 1948, in his hometown of Covington, Kentucky, Lee became one of the first blacks to defy the law which required blacks to sit in a separate section of local buses. Lee was arrested and fined, but appealed the ruling. Though he did not win that fight, the years have proven him a winner—in all ways.

LEONARD, Ray Charles.
B. 17 MAY 1956 Wilmington, DE. Gold: 1976 Light-welterweight. Sugar Ray Leonard was one of the most popular fighters of our time. He was christened Ray Charles Leonard, because, he explains, "I was supposed to be a singer." But he turned out to be quite a boxer.

Sugar Ray held numerous titles by the time he made it to the Olympics. He was twice (1974-75) North American amateur champion, twice (1973-74) Golden Gloves champion, twice (1974-75) AAU champion, and he won a gold medal at the 1975 Pan-American Games. He won his gold in Montreal rather easily.

Leonard originally stated he would not turn pro, but instead accept a scholarship to attend the University of Maryland. But the financial lure of professional boxing was too much and he turned pro in 1977. Leonard immediately became one of the top welterweights and a media favorite with his good looks, quick smile, and pleasant personality. In 1979 Ray Leonard won his first world title by defeating Wilfred Benitez for the WBA version of the welterweight championship. He lost the title in 1980 to Roberto Duran in what would prove to be his only loss as a professional. In a re-match

later in 1980, Leonard regained the title from Duran by a TKO in the eighth round. In 1981 Leonard fought Tommy Hearns to take the WBC version of the welterweight crown and unify the title. He won the fight and realized the largest payday ever for a professional athlete when he took home an estimated $10 million. Leonard later also won the light middleweight title in 1981 by defeating Ayub Kalule.

Leonard fought his last fight in early 1982. While training for a subsequent fight he noticed vision problems and his doctors diagnosed a detached retina. Surgery corrected this problem but rather than risk future damage, Sugar Ray retired from the ring. Today he works as a boxing commentator for television.

LYDON, Joseph Patrick.
B. 02 FEB 1878 Swinford, County Mayo, Ireland. D. 19 AUG 1937 St. Louis, MO. Silver: 1904 Soccer; Bronze: 1904 Welterweight. See the soccer section for the biography.

MARBLEY, Harlan J.
B. 11 OCT 1943 White Oak, MD Bronze: 1968 Light-flyweight (tied). Prior to the Olympics, Harlan Marbley had finished third at the 1967 Pan-American Games as well as winning the National AAU title in 1968. At Mexico City he lost in the semi-finals to eventual champion, Francisco Rodriquez of Venezuela.

MAYER, Charles.
Gold: 1904 Middleweight; Silver: 1904 Heavyweight. Charles Mayer is the only boxer from the 1904 Olympics to have won a U.S. national championship in another year. After winning the Olympic middleweight championship in 1904, he added the 1905 AAU middleweight championship. Mayer fought in the heavyweight division in 1904 only to appease the crowd who wanted to see him fight the heavyweight champion, Sam Berger. Though outweighed by 22 lbs. (180—158), Mayer put up a good fight but lost by decision.

McCLURE, Wilbert James.
B. 29 OCT 1938 Toledo, OH. Gold: 1960 Light-middleweight. Wilbert McClure had won the 1959 Pan-American Games gold medal as well as the 1959 and 1960 National AAU championships by the time he went

to Rome in 1960. At Rome he won four straight decisions but was never seriously challenged.

McClure turned professional shortly after the Olympics. He fought for seven years as a pro, compiling a lifetime record of 23 wins, seven losses and one draw. Wilbert McClure always stood on the edge of greatness as a pro. Several times he had fights which, had he won, probably would have brought him a title shot, but he could never quite break through. Among these were two losses by decision in late 1963 to recently dethroned middleweight champion, Luis Rodriguez; a loss in May 1964 to future light-heavyweight champion (and former Olympian), Jose Torres; and a loss and a draw in early 1966 to middleweight contender, Rubin 'Hurricane' Carter.

MICHAELS, William M.
Bronze: 1904 Heavyweight. Bill Michaels lost to Sam Berger in the first round of the 1904 heavyweight championship. Michaels was from St. Louis.

MOONEY, Charles Michael.
B. 27 JAN 1951 Washington, DC. Silver: 1976 Bantamweight. Charlie Mooney compiled most of his amateur record while in the service and he was an army and inter-service champion in 1976 when he made the Olympic team. Stationed at Fayetteville, NC in 1976, Mooney was a sergeant when he won his bronze medal.

MOSBERG, Samuel A.
B. 14 JUN 1896 Austria. D. 30 AUG 1967 Brooklyn, NY. Gold: 1920 Lightweight. Sammy Mosberg began to box with the Pastime Athletic Club in 1912. During World War I he served as a boxing instructor and won his base championship. At the Olympic trials in 1920 Mosberg lost but was allowed to go to Belgium as an alternate. He defeated one of the men chosen above him and was selected to fight in Antwerp. He justified the decision by winning the gold medal, and en route, scored the quickest knockout in Olympic boxing history.

Mosberg turned professional when he returned to the United States and fought for three years. He had 57 career fights without distinction. After retiring from boxing he entered the family furniture business and later became a real estate broker. In 1953 he served as the coach for the U.S. Maccabiah Games boxing team.

PROFESSIONAL BUT NOT OLYMPIC BOXERS

Four American Olympians have had professional boxing careers who competed in other sports in the Olympics, but none of them did very well. Jack Torrance was a shot-putter who had one fight and lost. Dan Hodge was a wrestler who fought nine professional bouts, winning only four. Bill Nieder was the Olympic shot put champion in 1960, but was knocked out in one round of his only professional prizefight. The fourth Olympian who boxed professionally was actually the first to do so. That was Fred Hird, who competed as a shooter in the 1912 and 1920 Olympics, but had several prize fights in the early 1900's.

One Olympic wrestling alternate did pretty well in the ring. That was Paul Berlenbach, who was on the 1920 wrestling team, but never got to compete. Berlenbach turned to pro boxing and in 1923 won the world's professional light-heavyweight championship.

PATTERSON, Floyd.
B. 04 JAN 1935 Waco, NC. Gold: 1952 Middleweight. Floyd Patterson took an excellent amateur record to the 1952 Olympics, as in 1951-52 he had won six major amateur titles, including the National AAU and New York Golden Gloves championships. His gold medal was easily won with a first round knockout over Romanian, Vasile Tita. Less than a month after the Olympics, Patterson fought his first professional fight against Eddie Godbold and knocked him out in four rounds.

Patterson grew out of the middleweight class, and although light for a heavyweight, on 30 November 1956, he defeated light-heavyweight champion, Archie Moore, for the vacant heavyweight title. In the next two years, Patterson defended the title four times and also fought several exhibitions. In 1959 he lost his title to Ingemar Johansson when Johansson knocked Patterson out in three rounds. On 20 June 1960, Floyd Patterson became the first man to regain the heavyweight title when he KO'ed Johansson in the fifth round.

Patterson defended the title twice before losing by KO in the first to Sonny Liston. Patterson twice more fought for the title, against Liston and then Muhammed Ali, but he was knocked out both times. In 1967 Patterson retired from the ring with a career record of 44 wins and five losses. Today Patterson works as chairman of the New York State Athletic Commission.

RADEMACHER, Thomas Peter.
B. 20 NOV 1928 Tieton, WA. Gold: 1956 Heavyweight. Pete Rademacher eventually fought professionally but his amateur record was far more impressive. Rademacher won several Golden Gloves titles in the Seattle area before entering Washington State University, which made him ineligible for NCAA boxing. Instead, Rademacher lettered for two years in football and played baseball in college. He continued to fight as an amateur and piled up championship after championship. In 1956 he won his gold medal by three consecutive knockouts, a true rarity in Olympic boxing, where the bouts are only three rounds long. He was then selected to carry the U.S. flag at the 1956 closing ceremonies.

After the Olympics, Rademacher turned pro, and fought his first fight against Floyd Patterson—for the heavyweight championship. He floored Patterson in round two, but Patterson got up and eventually knocked Rademacher down seven times, winning by a KO in six. Rademacher fought until 1962 as a pro, winning 17 and losing six, but he never again fought for the title.

Pete Rademacher has gone on to a very successful career as a salesman. He has also patented several inventions. One company of which he eventually became president, Kiefer-McNeil, was started by another Olympian, swimmer Adolph Kiefer.

RANDOLPH, Leo.
B. 27 FEB 1958 Tacoma, WA. Gold: 1976 Flyweight. Leo Randolph won four major amateur titles in 1976—the Golden Gloves Association of America, the National AAU, the final Olympic trials, and the Olympic Games. After the Olympics he turned professional but has had only moderate success to date.

ROBINSON, Albert.
B. 18 JUN 1947 Paris, TX. D. 25 JAN 1974 Oakland, CA. Silver: 1968 Featherweight. Al Robinson had no luck. In the 1968 Olympic final against Antonio Roldan of Mexico, Robinson appeared to be in complete control when the bout was stopped in the second round. But, amazingly, the referee gave the verdict to Roldan, disqualifying Robinson for head butts. Films of the fight failed to show the infraction, and Robinson was allowed to keep the silver medal, unusual for a disqualified fighter.

Shortly after the Olympics, Al Robinson began a pro career which was progressing nicely until 30 April 1971, when he collapsed during a workout. He never regained consciousness, dying three years later.

SALAS, Joseph.
B. 28 DEC 1905. Silver: 1924 Featherweight. Joe Salas won the National AAU title in 1924, which also served as the Olympic trials. Also chosen to represent the U.S. as a featherweight was Salas' good friend, and Los Angeles AC clubmate, Jackie Fields. At the Paris Olympics both Fields and Salas won their preliminary matches easily and met in the finals. It was a very close fight, but Fields was given the decision in three rounds. After the verdict was given the two fighters embraced in the ring while two American flags were raised.

Back in the United States public interest demanded another fight between the two friends. Again Fields defeated Salas in their last amateur fight. They turned professional and debuted against one another in late 1924—with Fields again winning, this time a 10-round decision. Joe Salas continued to fight professionally for several years but he never lived up to his initial promise.

SALICA, Louis.
B. 26 JUL 1913. Bronze: 1932 Flyweight. Lou Salica won the AAU title in 1932 but at the Olympic Games he was defeated in the semi-finals by Istvan Enekes of Hungary. Salica later won a bout for the bronze medal.

Salica fought as a professional in the bantamweight division and went on to greater success as a pro than he had as an amateur. In 1935 he claimed the vacant bantamweight championship by outpointing Sixto Escobar in 15 rounds. Escobar won a re-match later in the year. However in 1940, Escobar retired and Salica was recognized as champion by the New York Commission, while the National Boxing Association recognized George Pace. In 1941 Salica claimed both titles by winning a decision over Pace in 10 rounds. In

August of 1942 Salica lost the crown to Manuel Ortiz by a decision. Salica fought for a few more years before retiring.

SANDERS, Hayes Edward.
B. 24 MAR 1930 Los Angeles, CA. D. 12 DEC 1954 Boston, MA. Gold: 1952 Heavyweight. Ed Sanders was not a well-known boxer in 1952. He had attended Idaho State University, played football there, and competed in the decathlon—coached by former Olympian, Ken Carpenter. But he also took up boxing in college, as Idaho State had one of the top teams in the country.

Sanders learned quickly and, in the 1952 Olympics, knocked out several opponents en route to the final. There, his opponent was so terrified of Sanders' KO punch that he was disqualified for lack of aggressiveness. That opponent would do better as a professional, as Ingemar Johansson later became world heavyweight champion. After winning the 1952 heavyweight gold medal, Eddie Sanders served two years in the Navy and then turned professional, basing himself in Boston. Sanders won seven of his first eight fights, avenging his one loss with a later knockout. On 11 December 1954, he faced Willie James for the New England heavyweight title. James knocked out Sanders in the 11th round and Sanders had to be carried from the ring. He never regained consciousness and died 18 hours later.

SEALES, Ray.
B. 04 SEP 1952 St. Croix, Virgin Islands. Gold: 1972 Light-welterweight. Sugar Ray Seales took a 92 and nine record to the 1972 Olympics. His amateur titles included the 1971 AAU and North American championships and numerous Golden Gloves championships in the Pacific Northwest. To win his gold medal, Seales had to fight five times and won all his bouts by decisions.

Seales turned pro shortly thereafter and has fought mostly as a middleweight. He won his first 20 fights and it looked like he was headed for a title shot. But in August 1974 he was defeated by Marvin Hagler, and later fought a draw with Hagler. Seales came back and started winning again, but was KO'ed in 1976 by Alan Minter. Seales has recently retired, and is almost blind in both eyes, the result of detached retinae he has suffered during his fighting career.

SPANGER, Harry J.
Gold: 1904 Lightweight; Silver: 1904 Welterweight. From the National Turnverein in Newark, NJ, Harry Spanger defeated Joseph Lydon by decision before losing in the 1904 welterweight finals to Al Young, also by decision. In the lightweight division, he defeated, in succession, Ken Jewett (KO-2), Russell van Horn (by decision), and Jack Eagan (by decision).

SPINKS, Leon.
B. 11 JUL 1953 St. Louis, MO. Gold: 1976 Light-heavyweight. By the 1976 Olympics, Leon Spinks had already had 135 amateur bouts, but few would call him an accomplished boxer. Spinks was a brawler from the word go. He had won the 1975 AAU title and lost in the finals of the 1975 Pan-American Games. At the Montreal Olympics he seemed awkward in comparison to the polished Europeans and Cubans, but he won all his bouts with ease, knocking out the Cuban world champion, Sixto Soria, in the finals.

Spinks turned pro as soon as he returned to the United States. He put on a few pounds and began fighting aa a heavyweight. On 15 February 1978, after only seven pro fights, he took on Muhammed Ali for the heavyweight title, and upset him. In September of 1978, Ali again fought Spinks and regained the title, but in a close, controversial decision. Spinks' reign as heavyweight champion was the shortest in history—212 days.

Leon Spinks was small for a heavyweight. In the late 70's a new class was formed for fighters like him—the cruiserweight division. Leon Spinks has continued to box professionally and made an attempt to win the cruiserweight championship, but he has never matched his early professional success.

SPINKS, Michael.
B. 22 JUL 1956 St. Louis, MO. Gold: 1976 Middleweight. Michael Spinks was not nearly so well known in 1976 as his older brother, Leon. Michael had only one title to his name, 1976 Golden Gloves Association of America champion. But he joined his brother on the victory platform at Montreal by also winning a gold medal.

Since turning professional, Michael Spinks has gone on to a more successful career than his brother. Early in his career he won all his bouts but some said he didn't fight enough to make real progress. However he

Courtesy Butch Lewis Productions

The undisputed world light-heavyweight champion
through 1983 — 1976 Olympian, Michael Spinks.

won the WBA light-heavyweight championship in 1981 by defeating Eddie Mustafa Muhammed and in early 1983 he won a much ballyhooed unification title fight with WBC champion, Dwight Braxton, after which his career record stood at 23 wins and no losses.

SPRADLEY, Benjamin.
Silver: 1904 Middleweight. Ben Spradley fought only one bout in the 1904 Olympics. He lost by a TKO in the third to middleweight champion, Charles Mayer. Spradley represented the Business Men's Gymnasium in St. Louis.

TATE, John.
B. 29 JAN 1955 Marion City, AK. Bronze: 1976 Heavyweight (tied). As an amateur, Johnny Tate never quite seemed able to win the big title, although he was always close. He was runner-up in the 1975 Golden Gloves and the 1975 Pan-American Games. At the Olympics in 1976, he fought Teofilio Stevenson in the semi-finals and the great Cuban heavyweight knocked him out.

Johnny Tate has had a very mixed career as a professional. In 1979, by defeating Ken Norton, he laid claim to the WBA heavyweight title after Muhammed Ali retired. But Tate held the title only one year before losing to Mike Weaver in a 15th-round knockout. In addition, Larry Holmes was the WBC champion at the time and considered by everybody as the real heavyweight champion. Tate has not had a title fight since losing his championship.

TORRES, José Luis.
B. 03 MAY 1936 Playa Ponce, Puerto Rico. Silver: 1956 Light-middleweight. Jose Torres fought in the 1956 Olympics while he was serving in the Army. His only amateur titles had come in army and inter-service championships, several of which he had won. But he was a fine boxer and it was ill fortune that he was in the same class in the Olympics as the Hungarian, Laszlo Papp. Papp defeated Torres in the finals for his third consecutive Olympic boxing title.

While in the army, Torres fought for two more years as an amateur and managed to win the 1958 AAU championship. He then turned professional. He had a good career as a pro, climaxed when he won the light-heavyweight world title in 1965 by KO'ing Willie Pastrano in nine rounds. Torres defended the title four times before losing a 15 round decision to Dick Tiger in December 1966. After retiring from boxing, Torres co-authored one of the best biographies of Muhammed Ali.

TRIPOLI, Salvatore.
B. 12 NOV 1904. Silver: 1924 Bantamweight. From Yonkers, New York, Salvatore "Jack" Tripoli won the 1924 AAU championship in addition to gaining a silver medal at the 1924 Olympics.

VALDEZ, Jesse.
B. 12 JUL 1947 Houston, TX. Bronze: 1972 Welterweight (tied). Jesse Valdez was a classic stylist who was a top amateur fighter, although he never turned professional. By the time of Munich Olympics, his career record was 227 wins and 12 losses, and included two AAU titles, two National Golden Gloves titles, three inter-service championships, and a bronze at the 1967 Pan-American Games.

Valdez had attended Howard Payne College and then joined the air force. He was a staff sergeant in 1972 when he lost in the semi-finals to eventual champion, Emilio Correa of Cuba. Valdez retired after the Olympics but has remained in the air force.

Van HORN, Russell.
Bronze: 1904 Lightweight. Russell van Horn's one victory in the 1904 Olympics was over Art Seward, who was disqualified for lack of aggressiveness. Van Horn, from the South Broadway Athletic Club in St. Louis, then lost by decision to eventual champion Harry Spanger.

WALLINGTON, James R., Jr.
B. 28 JUL 1944 Philadelphia, PA. Bronze: 1968 Light-welterweight (tied). As an amateur boxer, Jim Wallington took the brilliant record of 76 and two to the Mexico City Olympics. His record in the three years before the Olympics was amazing. He had won three National AAU titles (1966-1968), three inter-service championships (1966-1968), three Golden Gloves titles (1966-1968) and the 1967 Pan-American Games gold medal. At the Olympics, however, he lost in the semi-finals to Enrique Regueiferos of Cuba by a decision.

WILSON, Jack.
B. 17 JAN 1918 Spencer, NC. D. 10 MAR 1956 Cleveland, OH. Silver: 1936 Bantamweight. As an amateur, Jackie Wilson lost one fight—in the finals of the Olympic Games. Later in 1936, however, he avenged that defeat to Ulderico Sergo of Italy and left the amateur ranks with a record of 50 wins and one loss. His titles had included Golden Gloves championships in New York, Chicago, and Cleveland, and the 1936 AAU flyweight crown.

As a professional Jackie Wilson fought for 13 years with moderate success. He took on most of the great fighters of his day, Ray Robinson and Jake La-Motta among them, but he never fought for a championship, and he retired in 1949 with a final record of 69 wins, 19 losses, and five draws.

YOUNG, Albert.
Gold: 1904 Welterweight. Al Young was from San Francisco's Olympic Club when he won the 1904 welterweight gold medal by defeating Jack Eagan in the semi-finals, and Harry Spanger in the finals.

CANOE & KAYAKING

MEN

The United States has never been one of the top countries in canoeing events. Between 1948 and 1956, we won several medals but since that time have been virtually shut out. Our one medal since came in 1972 in a canoe slalom event—an event which has been discontinued.

The two types of events are Canadian—in which the canoeist kneels and uses a single bladed oar, and kayak—in which the kayaker sits and uses a double bladed oar. The Canadian canoe is the classic Indian-style canoe while a kayak resembles an enclosed shell.

OUTSTANDING PERFORMANCES

Most Medals
　　2 Frank Havens, Steve Lysak, Steve Macknowski
Most Appearances
　　4 Frank Havens, Andras Toro*
Oldest Gold Medalist
　　33y361d Steve Lysak
Oldest Medalist
　　5y25d Ernie Riedel
Youngest Gold Medalist
　　26y177d Steve Macknowski
Youngest Medalist
　　19y332d Jamie McEwan

*competed twice for Hungary (1960 and 1964)

HAVENS, Frank Benjamin.

B. 01 AUG 1924 Arlington, VA. Gold: 1952 10,000 meter Canadian singles; Silver: 1948 10,000 meter Canadian singles. Frank Havens is our top individual medal winner among Olympic canoeists. His specialty was distance races—now no longer on the Olympic program. In addition to the two medal winning performances, Havens competed in the shorter Canadian singles events in 1948, 1952, 1956 and 1960. Havens won 10 National Championships, winning the Canadian singles championship in 1950-52, 1954, 1956-57, and 1961, as well as participating on several of the winning Canadian pairs and fours teams.

Havens has lived most of his life in the Washington, DC area where he paddled for the Washington Canoe Club. His career has been in insurance as an auto appraiser.

LYSAK, Stephen J.

B. 16 AUG 1914. Gold: 1948 10,000 meter Canadian pairs; Silver: 1948 1,000 meter Canadian pairs. Steve Lysak had a very long and varied career as a canoeist. His greatest success came in team events, either pairs or fours. He had many partners, but it was with Steve Macknowski that he reached his highest achievements. Together they won the U.S. title in 1948 in Canadian pairs as well as taking a gold and silver medal at the London Olympics of that year. Lysak and Macknowski also were on three national championship Canadian fours teams. Lysak also managed one national title at C-1.

Lysak was from the New York area and represented the Yonkers Canoe Club all his career. He designed and built the canoe that he and Macknowski used in the Olympics.

MACKNOWSKI, Stephen Albert.

B. 16 FEB 1922 Yonkers, NY. Gold: 1948 10,000 meter Canadian pairs; Silver: 1948 1,000 meter Canadian pairs. In addition to the two Olympic medals, Steve Macknowski won four national championships—one in C-2 in 1948 with Steve Lysak, and three C-4 titles in 1946-48.

Macknowski attended Columbia University. He went on to become an insurance agent and did so well that he eventually was able to open his own agency. He still passes time with his old sport as his favorite hobbies are canoe camping and rafting dangerous rivers.

McEWAN, James Patrick.

B. 24 SEP 1952 Olney, MD. Bronze: 1972 Canadian singles—slalom. Jamie McEwan was a student at Yale when he competed in the Olympics. He was our top U.S. hope in the new Olympic event of canoe slalom, having won the 1972 National Championships and competed at the 1971 World Championships. He took the bronze medal at Munich but hopes of further Olympic triumphs were dashed when the event was dropped from the 1976 and 1980 Olympic programs. McEwan graduated from Yale in 1975 as a literature major.

RIEDEL, Ernest.

B. 13 JUL 1901. Bronze: 1936 10,000 meter Kayak singles. Ernie Riedel is probably the greatest kayaker the United States has yet produced. But canoeing did not become an Olympic sport until 1936 and when the war intervened in 1940 and 1944, Riedel missed what might have been his best Olympic years. Still, his bronze medal is the only medal won by an American in kayak events.

Riedel's canoeing victories are too numerous to fully enumerate. Briefly, he won 33 national championships, mostly in kayak, although he occasionally raced in the Canadian events. In a yearly international race held against Canada, Riedel won 18 times between 1923 and 1947. Although by then he was 47 years old, he also raced in the 1948 Olympics.

TÖRÖ, András Istvan.

B. 10 JUL 1940 Budapest, Hungary. Bronze: 1960 1,000 meter Canadian pairs (competed for Hungary). András Törö competed in the 1960 and 1964 Olympics while he was a Hungarian citizen, and won his Olympic medal while competing for that country. In 1962 he also won a World Championship in the C-1 10,000 meter event.

But Törö defected from Hungary while at the 1964 Olympics and took up residence in Michigan. He earned a degree from the University of Michigan and began working as a naval architect and marine engineering consultant. He also began competing in canoe races in this country and when his citizenship came through in 1971, he was then eligible to compete for the United States Olympic team, which he has done twice—in 1972 and 1976. Törö has also won four U.S. Championships, the C-1 in 1969 and C-2 in 1969-71.

WOMEN

Though usually called the women's canoe & kayak events, women compete in the Olympics only in kayak. Women's kayaking first became an Olympic sport in 1948 but the United States did not enter any women until 1960. In the 60's we managed three medalists, quite respectable considering the number of women kayakers in this country. In the 70's we were shut out, but lately our women kayakers have shown improved form internationally.

OUTSTANDING PERFORMANCE

Most Appearances
　3 Marcia Jones Smoke

FOX, Francine Anne.

B. 16 MAR 1949 Washington, DC. Silver: 1964 500 meter Kayak pairs. Francine Fox had a relatively short career but a highly successful one. Her first national championship came in 1962 when she won the K-1 event, aged only 13 years. But most of her successes came in the pairs and fours events, partnered by Gloria Perrier. With Perrier she won the U.S. title in the K-2 from 1963 until 1965 and paddled with her in a K-4 boat to win the 1965 title in that discipline.

At the 1964 Olympics, Francine Fox and Gloria Perrier paddled to a silver medal, trailing a German pair by two seconds. The pairing was interesting for the disparity in ages, as, in 1964, Fox was a 15-year-old high school student, while Perrier was 20 years older.

JONES, Marcia. (see Marcia Jones Smoke)

PERRIER, Glorianne Aurore.

B. 21 MAR 1929 Lewiston, ME. Silver: 1964 500 meter Kayak pairs. In 1960, Gloria Perrier won the first U.S. National Championship in kayaking. She repeated as K-1 champion in 1961 but then turned to the team events. She paddled behind her stroke, Francine Fox, in the 1964 Olympics as well as in four National Championships—K-2 in 1963-65, and K-4 in 1965.

Perrier was a graduate of George Washington University. She remained in Washington where she worked as an administrative clerk for the government.

Courtesy Marcia Jones Smoke

America's greatest female canoeist — Marcia Jones Smoke.

SMOKE, Marcia Ingram Jones.

B. 18 JUL 1941 Oklahoma City, OK. Bronze: 1964 500 meter Kayak singles. Marcia Jones Smoke is easily the United States' greatest woman kayaker. She graduated from Michigan State in 1963 and had already won several national championships as Marcia Jones. She remained Marcia Jones through the 1964 Olympics where she won her bronze medal. Though she was beaten fairly decisively by the Russian gold medalist, she narrowly missed the silver medal.

She competed in two more Olympics as Marcia Smoke, just missing another bronze in 1968 when she finished fourth in the K-1 event. In 1976 Marcia Smoke was a member of the K-4 National Champions and this gave her 34 Senior National Championships, surpassing the U.S. canoeing record of 33 held by Ernie Riedel. Amazingly she returned in 1981 to win another national title, this one in the K-4 5000 meter event, giving her 35 in all. She has also won 24 North American Championships and at the 1967 Pan-American Games, she won three gold medals—in K-1, K-2, and K-4. The only American who ever defeated Marcia Smoke in her prime was her sister, Olympian Sperry Jones Rademaker.

CYCLING

The United States has never done very well in cycling. The last time an American won an Olympic medal was 1912 and since then our best finish has been a sixth place in the 1976 road race by George Mount.

The 1904 Olympic cycling events are considered by many to be unofficial, the arguments usually being raised that

- professionals competed;
- it was only the U.S. national championships;
- there were no foreign entries.

All of these are false. Professionals competed in separate races, although there was a professional program held on the same days in St. Louis. The U.S. championships that year were held in Vailsburg, NJ. Finally, the Germans entered a team of riders from the Deutsche Radfahrerbund, but they did not show up in St. Louis. Therefore we include the 1904 cycling medalists below, although little is known about many of the riders.

OUTSTANDING PERFORMANCES

Most Gold Medals
   4 Marcus Hurley
Most Medals
   6 Burton Downing
Most Appearances
   3 Dick Cortright, Jack Disney, John Howard,
      Tom Montemage, Jack Simes

ANDREWS, A. F.
Silver: 1904 25 miles; Bronze: 1904 5 miles. A. F. Andrews was from Indianapolis and was best known as a distance rider. In the 25 mile race, he took the lead with two laps to go, but could not hold it and was outsprinted on the last straight. Andrews also competed in the 1/4 mile and the 1/2 mile races, being eliminated both times in the heats.

BILLINGTON, Edwin.
Silver: 1904 1/2 mile; Bronze(3): 1904 1/4 mile, 1904 1/3 mile, 1904 1 mile. 'Teddy' Billington was from the hotbed of American cycling at the turn of this century—Vailsburg, New Jersey. Billington's silver medal in the 1/2 mile was remarkable his bike had not yet arrived by train so he borrowed another machine and rode to a second place behind Marcus Hurley.

DOWNING, Burton Cecil.
B. 05 FEB 1885 San Jose, CA. D. 01 JAN 1929 Red Bank, NJ. Gold(2): 1904 2 miles, 1904 25 miles; Silver(3): 1904 1/4 mile, 1904 1/3 mile, 1904 1 mile; Bronze: 1904 1/2 mile. With six medals at the 1904 Olympics, Burton Downing is surpassed by only three Americans for most medals at one celebration. Downing was from California and was not well-known by the Eastern riders; consequently, he surprised a lot of people by beating out Teddy Billington race after race.

The trip to St. Louis was part of a longer one which took Downing to the New York area where he settled. He joined up with a contracting firm, the Spearin Co., and by 1909, had become the president of that firm. He was later president of the New York Contracting Dock Builders Association.

GOERKE, Oscar.
Silver: 1904 2 miles. Brooklyn's Oscar Goerke competed in all seven cycling events at the 1904 Olympics, but his only medal came in the one mile race where he trailed Marcus Hurley. In that race, Goerke led at the start of the bell lap, but was no match for Hurley's finishing sprint.

HURLEY, Marcus Latimer.
B. 1885 New York, NY. D. 28 MAR 1941 New York, NY. Gold(4): 1904 1/4 mile, 1904 1/3 mile, 1904 1/2 mile; 1904 1 mile; Bronze: 1904 2 miles. With four individual gold medals in the 1904 Olympic cycling events, Marcus Hurley tied a record for individual golds at one Games which stood until Eric Heiden's domination of the 1980 speed skating events. Hurley was the greatest American amateur racer of the time. He won the U.S. amateur sprint championship from 1901 until 1904 and was world amateur sprint champion in 1904, as well.

Hurley is in a hall of fame—the College Basketball Hall of Fame. He played for Columbia, captained them in his senior year (1908), and was named all-America from 1905 through 1908. He also captained the New York AC team which won the Metropolitan championship in 1905. Hurley went on to a career as a consulting engineer.

KRUSCHEL, Albert.
B. 21 OCT 1889 Buffalo, NY. Bronze: 1912 Team Road Race. Albert Kruschel was from Buffalo and repre-

sented the Alma Athletic Club. He was one of the last qualifiers for the 1912 U.S. cycling squad, finishing 10th in the trials. However, at Stockholm, he finished 13th overall and third among the U.S. riders with a time of 11 hrs., 17:30.2 for the 200 mile course.

LAKE, John Henry.
B. 1878. Bronze: 1900 Match Sprint. John Lake was from New York and a member of the Harlem Wheelmen in 1900. In addition to his third-place Olympic finish, he also finished third that year in the World Championships.

LOFTES, Alvin Hjalmar.
B. 01 JAN 1891 Providence, RI. Bronze: 1912 Team Road Race. Al Loftes was from Providence in 1912. He was one of the last Americans to make the U.S. team as he finished 11th in the final trials. However at Stockholm he finished 11th overall and second among the U.S. riders. Loftes later moved to Newark, New Jersey, where he rode professionally for several years.

MARTIN, Walter C.
B. 28 SEP 1891 Grayville, IL. Bronze: 1912 Team Road Race. Walter Martin was one of the top riders in the United States in 1912. He was from St. Louis where he rode for the St. Louis Cycling Club and he had several times been a contender for the national championship. At the 1912 final trials Martin finished second behind Carl Schutte, easily making the U.S. team, although he had beaten Schutte in earlier winning the Western trials. At the Olympics he finished 17th overall to help the U.S. team earn a bronze medal.

SCHLEE, Charles.
Gold: 1904 5 miles. Charles Schlee was from Newark, New Jersey, and did most of his riding at the Vailsburg track. He entered six of the seven 1904 races, but had success only in the five mile. In that race there was a terrible crash, taking five riders out of the race, including Hurley, Downing and Billington. But Schlee was riding at the back of the pack, as was his custom, and avoided the melee. He trailed George Wiley going into the last turn of the race but overhauled him in the straight to win by five lengths.

SCHUTTE, Carl Otto.
B. 05 OCT 1887 Kansas City, MO. Bronze(2): 1912 Individual Road Race, 1912 Team Road Race. Although Carl Schutte never won a national championship, he deserves acclaim among American cyclists as being our only individual cycling medalist who raced against foreign competition.

A small, very thin rider, Schutte was from Kansas City but he represented the St. Louis Cycling Club. He won the final Olympic trials by three minutes over Walter Martin after having trailed Martin at the Western regionals. At the Olympics, Schutte never led and as early as the 120 km. mark he was 13 minutes behind eventual winner, Rudy Lewis of South Africa. However he never was worse than sixth at any check point, and with only 55 km. remaining, he was second. But he was passed by one rider near the end and his time of 10 hrs., 52:38.8 for 200 miles gave him third place individually and led the U.S. to the team bronze.

WILEY, George E.
B. 1882. D. 03 MAR 1954 Little Falls, NY. Silver: 1904 5 miles; Bronze: 1904 25 miles. At the 1904 Olympics, George Wiley led both the two distance races for the better part of each race, but both times he was overhauled by superior sprinters. Wiley went on to become one of the United States' premier distance riders. He won the U.S. professional motor-paced championship five times (1912-13, 1915, and 1917-18) and was also world champion in that event in 1912—the last American (male) to win a world cycling championship. Wiley had a professional riding career which lasted over 25 years. He later became a trainer for the Utica Braves minor league baseball team.

DIVING

MEN

The United States has consistently been the outstanding country in Olympic diving. U.S. divers have posted an especially amazing record in springboard competition, winning 12 of the 16 gold medals, and 33 of the 48 medals which have been awarded in Olympic competition. Between the 1920 and 1968 Olympics, inclusive, Americans won all 11 golds and 29 of the 33 springboard medals awarded, including seven medal sweeps. In platform diving, the other countries fare better, but we have still won 10 of the 18 competitions and received 26 of the 54 medals given.

OUTSTANDING PERFORMANCES

Most Gold Medals
2 "Pete" Desjardins, Sammy Lee,
  Bob Webster, Al White
Most Medals
4 "Mickey" Galitzen, "Bud" Pinkston
Most Appearances
2 Record shared by 12 men.
Winning Both Events, Same Year
Al White (1924), "Pete" Desjardins (1928)
Consecutive Victories, Same Event
Sammy Lee (1948-52 Platform),
Bob Webster (1960-64 Platform)
Oldest Gold Medalist
32y Sammy Lee (on his birthday)
Youngest Gold Medalist
21y120d "Pete" Desjardins
Youngest Medalist
17y98d "Pete" Desjardins

ANDERSON, Miller Altman.
B. 27 DEC 1922. D. 29 OCT 1965 Columbus, OH. Silver(2): 1948 Springboard, 1952 Springboard. Miller Anderson was a highly decorated army air corps officer in World War II and, when he was forced to bail out on his 112th mission, his left leg was so severely damaged that it was thought it might have to be amputated and his career as a top-class diver undoubtedly seemed over. The knee was saved only when doctors inserted a silver plate into the knee area, but he was forced to learn to dive all over again.

Anderson won his first AAU championship in 1943, when he took the highboard title. After the war he attended Ohio State and, despite his injuries, won the AAU indoor titles off both the 1m and 3m boards in 1946, 1947 and 1948, and was the NCAA 3m champion in those same three years. He was also noted as an innovative diver, originating the forward one-and-a-half somersault with two twists and the backward one-and-a-half with one twist.

ANDREASON, Larry Edwin.
B. 13 NOV 1945 Long Beach, CA. Bronze: 1964 Springboard. Larry Andreason, who competed for the Cerritos Jr. College and the Commerce SC, won one major title in his career when he took the AAU springboard championship in 1963.

BALBACH, Louis J.
Ddi. Bronze: 1920 Springboard. Louis Balbach, a New Yorker, placed sixth on the platform at the 1920 Olympics in addition to taking the bronze medal in the springboard.

BOGGS, Philip George.
B. 29 DEC 1949 Akron, OH. Gold: 1976 Springboard. After graduating from Florida State in 1971, Phil Boggs joined the Air Force and at the time of the 1976 Olympics he held the rank of captain. He is the only man to have won the springboard at the World Championships three times (1973, 1975 and 1978). Additionally Boggs was five times an AAU champion and won the NCAA in 1971.

Boggs left the service in 1976 and attended the University of Michigan Law School. Today he is often heard as a color commentator for televised diving competitions.

BROWNING, David Greig, Jr.
B. 05 JUN 1931. D. 14 MAR 1956 Kansas. Gold: 1952 Springboard. While attending the University of Texas, "Skippy" Browning won four NCAA titles and between 1949 and 1954 he won six AAU indoor and two outdoor championships. Browning won his Olympic gold medal with an outstanding series of dives. He never scored less than seven points on any of his dives and nine of his 12 dives averaged over eight points. Browning was

killed in a Navy jet crash on the Kansas plains two weeks before his 1956 Olympic training was due to begin.

CLOTWORTHY, Robert Lynn.

B. 08 MAY 1931 Newark, NJ. Gold: 1956 Springboard; Bronze: 1952 Springboard. After graduating from Ohio State, Bob Clotworthy competed for the New York AC. He was NCAA springboard champion in 1952 and won three AAU outdoor titles and two indoors. He later became an outstanding coach and produced winning teams at West Point, Dartmouth, Princeton, Arizona State and Texas. Clotworthy married Cynthia Gill, whom he met at the 1955 Pan-American Games where she won a bronze medal in the backstroke.

CONNOR, Richard Carroll.

B. 25 MAR 1934 Pueblo, CO. Bronze: 1956 Platform. As a student at Southern Cal, Dick Connor was undefeated in three years of Pacific Coast collegiate competition. At the Melbourne Olympics, Connor was in the lead after the qualifying round but eventually finished in third place.

DEGENER, Richard Kempster.

B. 14 MAR 1912. Gold: 1936 Springboard; Bronze: 1932 Springboard. Before turning professional in 1937, Dick Degener won a total of 12 AAU titles, including five straight wins in the indoor springboard, beginning in 1932. After graduating from the University of Michigan, where he won two NCAA championships, Degener represented the Detroit AC.

DESJARDINS, Ulise Joseph.

B. 10 APR 1907 St. Pierre, Manitoba, Canada. Gold(2): 1928 Platform, 1928 Springboard; Silver: 1924 Springboard. "Pete" DesJardins' family moved from Canada to Miami Beach when he was a small boy and it was there that he took up diving. Having become an American citizen, he qualified for the U.S. Olympic team in 1924, winning a silver medal in the springboard and placing sixth in the plain highboard event.

In 1928 he retained both Olympic diving titles for Stanford by matching Al White's double victory of 1924. At the Olympics, DesJardins was at his best in the springboard, being awarded a perfect 10 for two of his dives, but he was rather more fortunate to take the platform title. Initially the verdict went to Farid Simiaka, an Egyptian studying at UCLA, and the victory ceremony was actually underway with the Egyptian national anthem being played, when the decision was reversed. Although Simiaka had accumulated more points than DesJardins, four out of five judges had placed DesJardins ahead of the Egyptian and, under the rules in force at the time, the gold medal went to DesJardins.

Pete DesJardins won a total of 13 AAU titles, with nine of the victories coming while he was still a high school student. He was an economics graduate of Stanford, and after the 1928 Olympics he was declared a professional for appearing in a Miami water show with Johnny Weissmuller, Martha Norelius and Helen Meany. He continued to appear in Billy Rose's Aquacades until the outbreak of World War II and was still featured in diving shows until the 1960's.

FALL, David Athelstane.

B. 04 DEC 1902 Fairland, OK. D. 09 NOV 1964 San Bernadino, CA. Silver: 1924 Springboard. After winning the 1924 National Junior Championships off the 1m board, Dave Fall never succeeded in winning a senior title, although he was the runner-up on numerous occasions. After attending Oregon State, he went on to Stanford and graduated in 1924, being captain of the swim team in his last year. Fall made his living as an attorney, specializing in maritime law. Shortly before his death, he had been appointed a judge at a district court in California.

GAIDZIK, George William.

B. 22 FEB 1885. Ddi. Bronze: 1908 Springboard (tied). By sharing third place in the 1908 Olympic springboard event, George Gaidzik, of the Chicago AA, prevented the Germans from making a clean sweep of the medals. He also placed fifth in the platform in 1908 and competed in all three diving events at the 1912 Olympics but failed to place in any of them. Gaidzik won the AAU outdoor platform title from 1909-1911 and was the indoor champion in 1910 and 1912.

GALITZEN, Michael Riley.

B. 06 SEP 1909. D. 09 JUN 1959. Gold: 1932 Springboard; Silver(2): 1928 Springboard, 1932 Platform; Bronze: 1928 Platform. Michael Galitzen only used that name early in his career, preferring his nickname of

"Mickey Riley." He competed in four Olympic diving events and won a medal in each. While at Southern Cal he was twice the NCAA springboard champion and indoors and outdoors won a total of 10 AAU titles. Like his brother, John, also an AAU diving champion, Mickey competed for the Los Angeles AC.

GOMPF, Thomas Eugene.
B. 17 MAR 1939 Dayton, OH. Bronze: 1964 Springboard. After attending Ohio State, Tom Gompf served as a lieutenant in the U.S. Air Force and later became a pilot with National Airlines. The major victory of his career was in winning the 1963 AAU platform title. After retiring from competition he retained an active interest in the sport as coach of the University of Miami diving teams. He also served as a judge at the 1972 Olympics.

GORMAN, Francis Xavier.
B. 11 NOV 1937 New York, NY. Silver: 1964 Springboard. With two dives remaining, Frank Gorman held a seemingly unassailable lead in the springboard at the Tokyo Olympics. He then missed his 10th dive so badly that he dropped to second place, and although he was the top scorer on the 10th and final dive, he failed to recover sufficient ground on Ken Sitzberger to take the gold medal.

Of the many Harvard Olympians, Gorman is the only one to have won an Olympic diving medal. After the Olympics he became an investment broker but has recently moved into the telecommunications field.

GREENE, Al.
B. 29 AUG 1911. Bronze: 1936 Springboard. Al Greene, of the Lake Shore AC in Detroit, began the 1936 Olympic season on a high note by defeating Dick Degener and Marshall Wayne in April to take the AAU title indoor off the three ft. springboard. In June he finished second to Dick Degener in the AAU outdoor ten ft. board event and at the Final Trials he was again runner-up to Degener in the springboard with Marshall Wayne finishing in third place. At the Olympics, Dick Degener took the gold medal but Marshall Wayne reversed the result of the trials by edging Greene for the silver medal.

HALL, Sam Nesley.
B. 10 MAR 1937 Dayton, OH. Silver: 1960 Springboard. While at Ohio State, Sam Hall won the NCAA 3m spring-

board championship in 1959 and 1960. He also won two AAU outdoor titles and one indoors.

HARLAN, Bruce Ira.
B. 02 JAN 1926. D. 22 JUN 1959 Norwalk, CT. Gold: 1948 Springboard; Silver: 1948 Platform. Bruce Harlan joined the Navy in 1944 and, while serving at the Naval Training Center in Jacksonville in 1947, won the first of his eight AAU titles. He later enrolled at Ohio State and won five NCAA championships.

Harlan became one of the nation's leading diving coaches and took up an appointment at the University of Michigan in 1954. He was killed after a diving exhibition in Connecticut when he fell from a diving tower while dismantling the scaffolding.

HARPER, Donald De Wayne.
B. 04 JUN 1932 Redwood City, CA. Silver: 1956 Springboard. Like many top-class divers, Don Harper was also an accomplished gymnast, being the 1955 Pan-American Games trampoline champion and earning all-America gymnastics honors that year. He also won the NCAA trampoline championship in 1956 while at Ohio State. As a diver, Harper won the AAU 3m outdoor title in 1955 and in 1956 he was the AAU indoor and the NCAA outdoor champion.

HENRY, James Edward.
B. 04 SEP 1948 San Antonio, TX. Bronze: 1968 Springboard. Jim Henry followed Ken Sitzberger as Indiana University's leading diver. Sitzberger won the NCAA springboard title from 1965-1967 and Henry continued the streak by winning the next three titles. However, he could not retain Sitzberger's Olympic championship for Indiana and, after being in the lead in Mexico with three dives remaining, he finally finished in third place.

KEHOE, Frank.
Bronze: 1904 High Diving. Initially Frank Kehoe, of the Chicago AA, tied for third place with the German, Alfred Braunschweiger, in the diving event at the 1904 Olympics. Braunschweiger refused to take part in a dive-off and the bronze medal was awarded to Kehoe. The protests of the Germans were, at first, overruled, but following further German protests, the official result was announced, two years later, as a tie for third place.

Diver Lou Kuehn, a gold medalist at the 1920 Olympics.

Kehoe also played in the unofficial 1904 water polo tournament as a member of the Chicago AA.

KUEHN, Louis Edward.
B. 02 APR 1901 Portland, OR. D. 30 MAR 1981 West Linn, OR. Gold: 1920 Springboard. Lou "Hap" Kuehn was from Portland where he was a member of the Multnomah AC. He became the first American to win the Olympic springboard title when he upset the favorite, Bud Pinkston, at Antwerp. Prior to that, Kuehn's biggest victory had been the 1919 National Junior title,

although he had finished second at the 1920 AAU championships.

Kuehn attended Oregon State and Northwestern Law School and practiced law in Oregon. He was a part-time coach of the Oregon State divers and also served 30 years as clerk of the Multnomah County Circuit Court before his retirement.

KURTZ, Frank A.
B. 09 SEP 1911. Bronze: 1932 Springboard. After winning an Olympic bronze medal in 1932, Frank Kurtz, of the Los Angeles AC, placed fifth at the 1936 Games. He also won the AAU platform title in 1933.

During World War II, as the senior air aide to General George Brett, Major Frank Kurtz was the pilot of the historic plane "The Swoose," which is now on display in the Smithsonian. As pilot of The Swoose, Kurtz set a new flying record in 1942 when he took the plane from Brisbane, Australia to San Francisco in 36 hours and 10 minutes. For his efforts during the war, Frank Kurtz eventually reached the rank of colonel and was awarded the Distinguished Flying Cross with an Oak Leaf Cluster.

LEE, Samuel.
B. 01 AUG 1920 Fresno, CA. Gold(2): 1948 Platform, 1952 Platform; Silver: 1948 Springboard. After attending Occidental College, Sammy Lee entered medical school at Southern Cal. Lee, who was of Korean parentage, won his first AAU title in 1942 and then retired to concentrate on his medical career, but he made a comeback in 1946 when he was again AAU highboard champion.

Dr. Lee was the first man to retain an Olympic platform title and when he finally retired from competition, he established a reputation as an outstanding coach, counting among his pupils the next man to win back-to-back golds in the platform, Bob Webster. Lee was in charge of the U.S. diving team at the 1960 Olympics and still judges diving competitions. In his medical career he specializes in diseases of the ear.

LINCOLN, Craig Howard.
B. 07 OCT 1950 Minneapolis, MN. Bronze: 1972 Springboard. Craig Lincoln won his first national championship in 1970 when he took the AAU outdoor 3m title. The following year he won the AAU indoor off the 1m board

and took the silver medal in the springboard at the Pan-American Games. In 1972, his last year as a psychology student at the University of Minnesota, Lincoln finally won an NCAA title when he took the 3m championship.

LOUGANIS, Gregory.

B. 29 JAN 1960 San Diego, CA. Silver: 1976 Springboard. As a 16-year-old high school student in El Cajon, California, Greg Louganis won a silver medal in the highboard at the Montreal Olympics and also placed sixth in springboard.

Since the 1976 Olympics, Louganis has enrolled at the University of Miami and has developed into what many experts consider to be the most technically accomplished diver of all time. He won both springboard and platform at the 1979 Pan-American Games and repeated that feat at the 1982 World Championships. He has won 22 national championships (through 1982), more than any other American, and numerous international titles, but it is the manner in which he wins that stuns the fans and impresses the judges. At the 1982 Worlds, performing an inward two-and-one-half pike, he became the first diver in international competition to be awarded a perfect 10 from all seven judges. Later in that competition, his front three-and-one-half pike received the highest score ever awarded a single dive with 92.07 points. He performs these feats by combining great athletic ability with unusual grace honed by many years of classical dance training.

PINKSTON, Clarence Elmer.

B. 02 FEB 1900 Wichita, KS. D. 18 NOV 1961 Detroit, MI. Gold: 1920 Platform; Silver: 1920 Springboard; Bronze(2): 1924 Springboard, 1924 Platform. Among Americans, only Mickey Riley (Galitzen) has matched "Bud"Pinkston's record of winning four Olympic diving medals. Pinkston won the AAU outdoor for five straight years from 1920 and won two AAU springboard titles—one indoors and one outdoors. Pinkston was from the great school of divers who were coached by Ernst Brandsten at Stanford; at the 1924 Olympics, Stanford divers made a sweep of the medals in both the springboard and the platform.

Pinkston married Betty Becker, the 1924 Olympic platform champion, and coached her to her second

Dr. Sammy Lee, now an otolaryngologist, showing the form that made him the first diver to defend the Olympic platform diving championship.

gold medal in 1928. After retiring from competition he became a coach and athletic director for the Detroit AC.

PRIESTE, Harry.

Bronze: 1920 Platform. Harry Prieste was from Long Beach and represented the Los Angeles AC. He never won a major title.

ROOT, Elbert Alonzo.

B. 20 JUL 1915. Silver: 1936 Springboard. After winning the 1936 U.S. Olympic platform trials, Elbert Root took the silver medal at the Berlin Games, finishing second to Marshall Wayne, who had only placed third at the try-outs. Root, who competed for the Detroit AC, won the AAU highboard in 1937 and 1938.

RYDZE, Richard Anthony.
B. 15 MAR 1950 Pittsburgh, PA. Silver: 1972 Platform. Dick Rydze won the AAU platform, both indoors and outdoors, in 1969 and 1971 and he won the indoor title for the third time in 1972. He was also a silver medalist at the 1971 Pan-American Games. At the Munich Olympics he moved from fifth place into second on his final three dives.

Rydze graduated from the University of Michigan in 1971, having studied zoology and later attended the University of Pittsburgh School of Medicine. He now is a doctor practicing internal medicine.

SHELDON, George Herbert.
B. 17 MAY 1874. D. 25 NOV 1907 St. Louis, MO. Gold: 1904 Plain High Diving. Dr. George Sheldon of the Muegge Institute, St. Louis, had some anxious moments before being declared the winner of the 1904 diving event. He was initially announced as the winner but the Germans protested the judges' verdict, as they had done when Frank Kehoe was awarded equal third place, and the trophy was withheld from Sheldon while the protest was considered. One week after the competition, Games director James E. Sullivan rejected the protest and Sheldon, who studied medicine at the now defunct Barnes Medical College in St. Louis, was declared the winner.

SITZBERGER, Kenneth Robert.
B. 13 FEB 1945 Cedar Rapids, IA. Gold: 1964 Springboard. In 1964, Ken Sitzberger took the Olympic springboard title to give the U.S. their 10th successive victory in this event. Sitzberger came through to take the gold medal after his teammate, Frank Gorman, dropped his ninth dive.

After his Olympic victory, Ken Sitzberger enrolled at Indiana University where he won five NCAA titles and was three times the AAU indoor champion. He married Jeanne Collier, who won the silver medal in the women's springboard event at the 1964 Olympics.

SMITH, Harold.
B. 19 FEB 1909. D. 1958. Gold: 1932 Springboard; Silver: 1932 Platform. "Dutch" Smith of the Los Angeles AC made his Olympic debut in 1928 when he placed fourth in the springboard. Although his Olympic title was off the platform, all his AAU titles were in the springboard event, winning the 1m in 1928 and 1930 and the 3m crown in 1930 and 1931.

After his Olympic successes he turned pro and appeared in various aquacades in addition to coaching at the New York AC and Yale. He was also appointed coach to the 1936 German Olympic diving team. After serving as a captain in the marines in World War II, Smith worked for a time as a pool manager at luxury hotels in Palm Springs and Santa Barbara.

TOBIAN, Gary Milburn.
B. 14 AUG 1935 Detroit, MI. Gold: 1960 Springboard; Silver(2): 1956 Platform, 1960 Platform. At the Rome Olympics, Gary Tobian gave the U.S. their ninth straight victory on the springboard with a victory over his teammate, Sam Hall. In 1959 Tobian, of the Los Angeles AC and Southern Cal, was the Pan-American Games springboard champion and in 1960 he took the AAU platform title for the sixth straight year. He also won the AAU springboard, both indoors and out, in 1958.

WAYNE, Marshall.
B. 25 MAY 1912. Gold: 1936 Platform; Silver: 1936 Springboard. Marshall Wayne was the only double medalist in the men's diving events at the 1936 Olympics. A member of the Biltmore AC in Miami, he was the AAU outdoor platform champion in 1934 and 1936. Following the Olympics he turned professional and joined Billy Rose's Aquacades. After World War II he served as a Pan-Am pilot for 27 years.

WEBSTER, Robert David.
B. 25 OCT 1938 Berkeley, CA. Gold(2): 1960 Platform, 1964 Platform. Bob Webster won his first collegiate diving competition representing Santa Clara Jr. College, even though the school had no pool in which Webster could train. He transferred to Michigan where he came under the influence of the great coaches, Bruce Harlan and Dick Kimball. Webster was also coached by Sammy Lee and in 1964 he matched Dr. Lee's record of successfully defending an Olympic platform title.

After placing third in the platform at the 1959 Pan-American Games he became the first American to win that title four years later. Webster won two AAU outdoor platform titles and was the indoor springboard champion in 1962. He later became a coach at Minnesota, Princeton and, of late, at the University of Alabama. He was also the U.S. diving coach at the 1971 Pan-Am Games.

WHITE, Albert Cosad.
B. 14 MAY 1895 Oakland, CA. D. 08 JUL 1982 Richmond, CA. Gold(2): 1924 Springboard, 1924 Platform. As a serviceman in World War I, Al White toured Europe with a U.S. basketball team and after the war enrolled at Stanford and was on their gymnastics team which won the Pacific Coast Conference championship in 1921. He had an outstanding record as a diver, being the first man to win both diving titles at the same Olympics and winning, in all, 10 AAU championships. He was never beaten in lowboard 1m competition.

Al White served as a lieutenant colonel in World War II and later became city engineer in Richmond, California. He also served as AAU diving commissioner for the Pacific Coast.

WRIGHTSON, Bernard Charles.
B. 25 JUN 1944 Phoenix, AZ. Gold: 1968 Springboard. In 1967 Bernie Wrightson won the springboard at the Pan-American Games and the following year, prior to winning his Olympic gold medal, he equalled Gary Tobian's record of seven AAU outdoor diving championships. Wrightson attended Arizona State and in his senior year (1966), won the NCAA springboard. At the time of his Olympic victory, he was serving as an enlisted man in the Navy.

YOUNG, Edwin Frank.
B. 29 SEP 1947 Phoenix, AZ. Bronze: 1968 Platform. After winning the platform at the 1967 Pan-American Games, "Win" Young of Indiana University was the AAU outdoor platform champion in 1967. He never won an NCAA championship, his best finish being second in 1968.

MOST SPORTS IN WHICH PARTICIPATED

Have any Americans participated in more than one sport in the Olympic Games? Of course. This group is led by Frank Kungler who, at the 1904 Olympics, participated in heavyweight wrestling, the weightlifting events (open class) and pulled on a tug-of-war team—then considered part of the track & field program. Kungler thus competed in three sports, but even more impressive is the fact that he also won medals in all three.

Charles Sands also competed in three sports. He won the 1900 golf tournament for men and also played Olympic lawn tennis that year. In 1908 he returned to the Olympics to participate in his main sport, jeu de paume, known in the United States as court tennis.

In addition, 38 men and five women have participated in two sports. Not including the somewhat artificial division of swimming and diving, 26 men and one woman have competed in two sports. The woman was Jean Gaertner in 1960 track & field (high jump) and 1964 volleyball. Two men have competed in two sports in the Olympic Winter Games, Laurence Damon and Peter Lahdenpera, both doubling in the biathlon and nordic skiing.

WOMEN

Diving is the sport at which the United States' women have enjoyed their greatest success in the Olympic Games. Like the men, it is a sport they have totally dominated since they first entered competition in 1920. In springboard diving they have won 11 of the 14 titles and 30 of the 42 medals awarded. Similar to the men, they have had less success from the platform, but still have won eight of 14 titles and 21 of 45 medals (omitting 1912, when no U.S. women divers competed). Those figures become even more impressive if one omits the 1980 Olympics, at which our divers were also absent.

OUTSTANDING PERFORMANCES

Most Gold Medals
    4 Pat McCormick
Most Medals
    4 Georgia Coleman, Pat McCormick,
       Dorothy Poynton-Hill
Most Appearances
    4 Juno Stover-Irwin
Winning Both Events, Same Year
    Vicki Draves (1948), Pat McCormick (2)
    (1952 and 1956)
Consecutive Victories, Same Event
    Dorothy Poynton-Hill (1932-36 Platform),
    Pat McCormick (2) (1952-56 Springboard
    and Platform)
Oldest Gold Medalist
    26y209d Pat McCormick
Oldest Medalist
    28y15d Juno Stover-Irwin
Youngest Gold Medalist
    13y268d Marjorie Gestring
Youngest Medalist
    13y23d Dorothy Poynton (-Hill)

BECKER, Elizabeth Anna. (see Elizabeth Pinkston)

BUSH, Lesley Leigh.
B. 17 SEP 1947 Orange, NJ. Gold: 1964 Platform. Lesley Bush, a 16-year-old student at Princeton High School, was the surprise of the women's diving events at the Tokyo Olympics. In the platform she went into the lead in the first round and maintained her advantage to the end of the competition to finish 1.35 points ahead of the defending champion, Ingrid Engel-Kramer of East Germany. Lesley Bush then won the platform title at the 1967 Pan-American Games but when she defended her Olympic title in Mexico she had a poor first dive and finally finished in 19th place. In all, Miss Bush won five AAU titles. Lesley Bush married Olympic swimmer Charles Hickcox, though they were later divorced.

CHANDLER, Jennifer Bellomy.
B. 13 JUN 1959 Langdale, AL. Gold: 1976 Springboard. In 1975 Jennifer Chandler of Anniston Academy won the AAU indoor springboard title and the gold medal at the Pan-American Games. At the Olympics the following year she took the lead over the 1973 world champion, Christine Kohler of East Germany, and on every dive, except the ninth, Chandler increased her lead to give the U.S. their third successive victory in the women's Olympic springboard event.

After the Olympics, Miss Chandler attended the University of Alabama. She retired from competition after a series of debilitating injuries and has done some work as a television commentator.

COLEMAN, Georgia.
B. 23 JAN 1912 St. Maries, ID. D. 14 SEP 1940 Los Angeles, CA. Gold: 1932 Springboard; Silver(2): 1928 Platform, 1932 Platform; Bronze: 1928 Springboard. Georgia Coleman had only been diving for six months when, as a 16-year-old, she made the 1928 Olympic team. In Amsterdam she won medals in both diving events and in 1932 she again won two medals with a gold in the springboard and a second silver in the platform. During the Los Angeles Games, she announced her engagement to Micky Galitzen, who also won four Olympic diving medals, but they never married.

Coleman was the first woman to perform a two-and-one-half forward somersault in competition and in 1929 she won every U.S. national title and was only beaten once in the next four years. Competing for the Los Angeles AC, she won a total of 11 AAU championships. In 1937 she contracted polio but learned to swim again before her death at the tragically early age of 28.

COLLIER, Jeanne Ellen.
B. 15 MAY 1946 Indianapolis, IN. Silver: 1964 Springboard. Although Jeanne Collier never won an AAU title

she was the leading U.S. springboard diver at the Tokyo Olympics, finishing in second place behind the defending champion, Ingrid Engel-Kramer of East Germany. Collier was a student at Xavier High School in Phoenix and also represented the Dick Smith Swim Gym. She later married 1964 men's springboard gold medalist, Ken Sitzberger.

DRAVES, Victoria Manalo.

B. 31 DEC 1924 San Francisco, CA. Gold(2): 1948 Platform, 1948 Springboard. Born a twin daughter of an English mother and a Filipino father, Vicki Draves was obliged to use her mother's maiden name to gain entry to the then racially conscious swimming clubs in the San Francisco area.

She won the first of her four AAU titles in 1946 and at the 1948 Games she became the first woman to win both diving events at the same Olympics. After the war she married her coach, Lyle Draves.

DUNN, Velmy Clancy.

B. 09 OCT 1918. Silver: 1936 Platform. When Dorothy Poynton-Hill retained her Olympic platform title in 1936, Velma Dunn, a 17-year-old from Monrovia, California, took second place, finishing only 0.3 points behind the defending champion.

ELSENER, Patricia Anne.

B. 22 OCT 1929. Silver: 1948 Platform; Bronze: 1948 Springboard. Apart from Vicki Draves, who won two gold medals, Patsy Elsener of the Crystal Plunge Club, San Francisco, was the leading U.S. woman diver at the 1948 Olympics. She won the AAU indoor 3m title in 1946 and 1947.

FAUNTZ, Jane.

B. 19 DEC 1910. Bronze: 1932 Springboard. Jane Fauntz of the Illinois Women's AC made her Olympic debut as a breaststroke swimmer in 1928 when she was eliminated in the semi-finals of the 200m event in Amsterdam. After deciding to specialize in diving she won the AAU indoor title off the 1m board in 1929 and 1930. However, she never completely deserted swimming for diving and in 1929 she won the AAU outdoor 100y breaststroke.

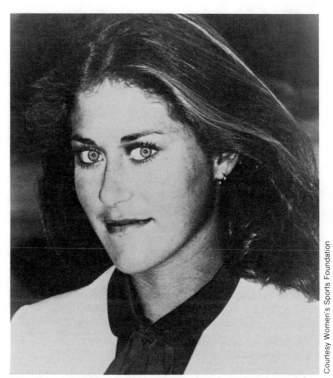

Courtesy Women's Sports Foundation

After winning her AAU indoor springboard title and her first-place finish at the Pan-American games, Jennifer Chandler captured gold at the 1976 Olympics.

FLETCHER, Caroline.

B. 22 NOV 1906. Bronze: 1924 Springboard. Carol Fletcher, a 17-year-old from Pasadena, completed the sweep of medals for the U.S. in the 1924 Olympic springboard by taking third place behind Betty Becker and Aileen Riggin. She also won the AAU indoor 3m title in 1924.

GESTRING, Marjorie.

B. 18 NOV 1922 Los Angeles, CA. Gold: 1936 Springboard. At the age of 13 years 267 days, Marjorie Gestring won the springboard title at the 1936 Berlin Games to become the youngest-ever woman Olympic champion. At the 1936 U.S. Trials, Gestring placed second behind Katherine Rawls, but in the Berlin pool she beat both Rawls and the defending champion, Dorothy Poynton-Hill, to take the gold medal. She won a total of eight AAU titles between 1936 and 1940 and in 1948, still aged only 25, she made a comeback. Placing fourth at the 1948 Final Trials, she barely missed making the

Courtesy U.S. Air Force

After competing in the Olympics while a member of the U.S. Air Force, Captain Micki King became the first woman member of the faculty at a military academy in the United States.

Olympic team for a second time. Marjorie Gestring, who usually competed for the Los Angeles AC, is now Mrs. Richard Redlick.

GOSSICK, Sue.
B. 12 NOV 1947 Chicago, IL. Gold: 1968 Springboard. Although born in Chicago, Sue Gossick learned her diving at a California high school. In 1964 she placed fourth in the Olympic springboard and, after finishing only third at the 1968 U.S. Trials, she was a surprise winner of the gold medal in Mexico. Miss Gossick won three AAU titles and was the Pan-American Games champion in 1967.

HILL, Dorothy Poynton.
B. 17 JUL 1915 Salt Lake City, UT. Gold(2): 1932 Platform, 1936 Platform; Silver: 1928 Springboard; Bronze: 1936 Springboard. When Dorothy Poynton won the silver medal in the 1928 Olympic springboard, she had barely passed her 13th birthday and set the record of being the youngest U.S. Olympic medalist in history. In 1932 she won the Olympic highboard and in 1936, as Mrs. Hill, she became the first woman to defend an Olympic highboard title and also won a bronze medal in the springboard.

Among U.S. women divers only Georgia Coleman and Pat McCormick have equalled Dorothy Poynton-Hill's record of winning four Olympic medals and only Paula Myers-Pope has matched her performance of winning medals at three different Olympics. Poynton-Hill made several television commercials, won seven AAU titles and, after her competitive retirement, operated her own aquatic club in Los Angeles.

IRWIN, Juno Roslays Stover.
B. 22 NOV 1928 Los Angeles, CA. Silver: 1956 Platform; Bronze: 1952 Platform. Juno Stover placed fifth in the 1948 Olympic platform, but as Mrs. Irwin she won medals in both 1952 and 1956. Her bronze medal in the 1952 platform was won while she was three-and-one-half months pregnant with her second child. Representing the Los Angeles AC, she won her second AAU platform title in 1960, and in that year became the first U.S. diver to compete in four Olympics.

After retiring from active competition, Mrs. Irwin coached both men's and women's diving for a junior college and then became women's diving coach at Cal/Berkeley.

JENSEN, Zoe Ann Olsen.
B. 11 FEB 1931. Silver: 1948 Springboard; Bronze: 1952 Springboard. Zoe Ann Olsen from the Athens AC in Oakland, California won the first of her 12 AAU diving titles as a 14-year-old in 1945. She was the only woman diver to win medals at both the 1948 and 1952 Olympics.

Between those two Olympics, Zoe Ann Olsen met and married Jackie Jensen. Olsen was a beautiful blonde, and Jensen was a handsome, muscular football and baseball player from Cal/Berkeley who would later play with both the New York Yankees and Boston Red

Sox. Theirs was thought to be a match made in heaven but like so many of those, it lasted only a short time.

KING, Maxine Joyce.
B. 26 JUL 1944 Pontiac, MI. Gold: 1972 Springboard. After graduating from the University of Michigan in 1966, Micki King joined the U.S. Air Force and, at the time of winning her Olympic gold medal in 1972, she held the rank of captain.

Micki King made her Olympic debut in 1968 and was lying third in the springboard when she hit the board and fractured her wrist on the penultimate dive, slipping to fourth place in the final rankings. At the 1972 Olympics she scored a spectacular victory in the springboard, moving from third to first place with her last three dives. She won eight AAU titles, four Canadian national titles and, while at Michigan, she was twice goalkeeper on the Ann Arbor team which won the Women's National AAU water polo championship.

Early in 1973, Miss King was appointed diving coach at the U.S. Air Force Academy, becoming the first woman ever to be a faculty member at a military academy in the United States. In the summer of 1976 she married Lt. Jim Hayne, who was captain of the swim team at the academy.

McCORMICK, Patricia Joan Keller.
B. 12 MAY 1930 Seal Beach, CA. Gold(4): 1952 Platform, 1952 Springboard, 1956 Platform, 1956 Springboard. Pat McCormick the world of women's diving to an extent that has never been matched. In 1956, only five months after the birth of her son, she successfully defended both her Olympic diving titles to become the only person in Olympic diving history to score a "double-double." Mrs. McCormick also won three gold and two silver medals at the Pan-American Games and 27 national championships.

She attended Long Beach State and later represented the Los Angeles AC, where her husband was a part-time coach. Their daughter, Kelly McCormick, is now an accomplished diver who made the 1983 Pan-American Games team.

McINGVALE, Cynthia Ann Potter.
B. 27 AUG 1950 Houston, TX. Bronze: 1976 Springboard. As the top-ranked American female diver at the 1972 Olympics, Cindy Potter was confidently expected to be among the medals but suffered a severe foot injury during a practice session in Munich and finished seventh in the springboard and only 21st in the platform. In 1976, as Mrs. McIngvale, she competed only in the springboard and took the bronze medal.

She was a prodigious performer in the AAU championships, equalling Pat McCormick's record of 27 titles in 1977 and eventually winning another to break the record. Cynthia Potter graduated from Indiana in 1973.

MEANY, Helen.
B. 15 DEC 1904. Gold: 1928 Springboard. After failing to place in the platform at the 1920 and 1924 Olympics, Helen Meany won the platform in 1928. She was the first U.S. woman diver to compete at three Olympics.

She competed for the Women's Swimming Association and won 13 AAU titles before her amateur career ended when she appeared in an unsanctioned water show in Miami Beach with Martha Norelius, Pete DesJardins and Johnny Weissmuller.

MYERS, Paula Jean. (see Paula Jean Pope)

OLSEN, Zoe Ann. (see Zoe Ann Jensen)

O'SULLIVAN, Keala.
B. 03 NOV 1950 Honolulu, HI. Bronze: 1968 Springboard. Apart from her bronze medal at the 1968 Olympics, Keala O'Sullivan's most notable feat was to win the 1968 AAU 1m title. She competed for the Punahou Swim Club in Hawaii.

PAYNE, Thelma R.
B. 18 JUL 1896. Bronze: 1920 Springboard. Competing for the Multnomah AC in Portland, Oregon, Thelma Payne won the AAU indoor springboard title for three straight years from 1918.

PETERSON, Ann.
B. 16 JUN 1947 Kansas City, MO. Bronze: 1968 Platform. After placing third at the 1967 Pan-American Games, Ann Peterson won the platform title at the 1968 AAU Championships. She then went on to win the Final Trials and was the leading American in the highboard at the Mexico Olympics. Ann Peterson competed for the Dick Smith Swim Gym and graduated from Arizona State in 1970.

Courtesy Aileen Riggin

The smallest of all U.S. Olympians, Aileen Riggin, was only 4'-8" tall and 70 lbs. when she competed in diving at the 1920 Olympics.

PINKSTON, Elizabeth Anna Becker.

B. 06 MAR 1903 Philadelphia, PA. Gold(2): 1924 Springboard, 1928 Platform; Silver: 1924 Platform. Betty Becker took up swimming as a child as therapy after a serious illness. She then turned to competitive diving and, after narrowly missing selection for the 1920 Olympics, won a gold and a silver medal at the 1924 Games. After the Paris Olympics she married Clarence Pinkston, winner of the platform title in 1920. Betty Pinkston gave birth to twins in 1926 but, coached by her husband, won her second gold medal on 11 August 1928, the second birthday of her twins. In addition to her Olympic feats, she also won six AAU titles.

POPE, Paula Jean Myers.

B. 11 NOV 1934 La Verne, CA. Silver(3): 1952 Platform, 1960 Platform, 1960 Springboard; Bronze: 1956 Platform. After winning medals at the 1952 and 1956 Olympics as Paula Myers, Mrs. Myers-Pope won two more Olympic medals in 1960 when she finished as runner-up to the East German, Ingrid Kramer, in both the springboard and the platform.

Paula Myers-Pope was a fine all-round diver, winning 11 AAU titles, and she was a double champion at the 1959 Pan-American Games. She graduated from Southern Cal in 1957 and later trained at the Sammy Lee Swim Club. She and her husband now run the Ojai Valley Racquet Club.

POTTER, Cynthia. (see Cynthia McIngvale)

POYNTON, Dorothy. (see Dorothy Hill)

RAWLS, Katherine Louise.

B. 14 JUN 1918. D. 08 APR 1982. Silver(2): 1932 Springboard, 1936 Springboard; Bronze: 1936 4x100 meter freestyle relay (Swimming). "Peggy" Rawls showed a rare versatility in the pool, winning a record number of 33 AAU titles (recently broken by Tracy Caulkins) in such diversified events as freestyle, breaststroke, individual medley and diving. She was undefeated in the individual medley for eight years and had it been on the Olympic program in 1932 or 1936 she would almost certainly have added an Olympic gold medal to her championship honors. She was the first American woman to win four national championships at a single meet, which she did by taking the 440y, 880y, and one-mile freestyle and the individual medley at the 1937 AAU Championships. She repeated this feat in 1938.

Peggy Rawls came from a dedicated swimming family in Fort Lauderdale and her sisters, Dorothy and Evelyn, both won national honors in relay events. She retired after the 1938 nationals and later, as Mrs. Thompson, became a top pilot in World War II, being one of the original 25 women who ferried planes to combat zones for air transport command.

RIGGIN, Aileen M.

B. 02 MAY 1906 Newport, RI. Gold: 1920 Springboard; Silver: 1924 Springboard; Bronze: 100 meter backstroke (Swimming). Aileen Riggin won the first Olympic springboard title in 1920 when she had just passed her 14th birthday and she was, at the time, the youngest-ever woman Olympic champion. She lost her record to another U.S. diver, Marjorie Gestring, at the 1936 Olympics.

Riggin won three AAU outdoor and one indoor springboard titles and was twice a member of the Women's Swimming Association team which won the AAU relay. In 1926 she turned professional, having earlier made the first underwater films and the first slow motion coaching films for Grantland Rice. As a pro she toured the world giving exhibitions, and helped organize Billy Rose's first Aquacade at the 1937 Cleveland Exposition. She made several films in Hollywood, was a successful journalist and later married, becoming Mrs. Howard Soule.

ROPER, Marion Dale.

Bronze: 1932 Platform. In front of her hometown crowd, Marion Roper placed third in the platform at the Los Angeles Olympics to complete a clean sweep of the medals for the United States.

SMITH, Caroline.

B. 21 JUL 1906 Cairo, IL. Gold: 1924 Platform. Caroline Smith, from Cairo, Illinois, was the first U.S. woman to win the Olympic platform title.

STOVER, Juno Roslays. (see Juno Irwin)

STUNYO, Jeanne Georgetta.

B. 11 APR 1936 Gary, IN. Silver: 1956 Springboard. Jeanne Stunyo came close to making the 1952 Olympic team when she placed fourth at the U.S. Trials. Although she never won an AAU title, she won silver medals in the springboard at both the 1955 Pan-American Games and the 1956 Olympics. On both occasions it was Pat McCormick who took the gold medal. Stunyo competed for the Detroit AC and the University of Detroit and now, as Mrs. Korpak, is a low-handicap golfer.

WAINWRIGHT, Helen E.

B. 15 MAR 1906. Silver: 1920 Springboard; Bronze: 1924 400 meter freestyle (Swimming). Helen Wainwright is one of only three American women who have won Olympic medals for swimming and diving. Representing the Women's Swimming Association of New York, she won 17 AAU swimming championships and two indoor AAU diving championships and during World War II turned over all her trophies to the government for the metal drive. She later turned professional and toured the country with several aquacades, playing the theaters with a portable tank. She married a career military man, Lt. Cree Stelling.

WILLARD, Mary Patricia.

B. 18 MAY 1941 Phoenix, AZ. Bronze: 1964 Springboard. Patsy Willard of Arizona State finished fourth in the springboard at the 1960 Olympics, improving to third at the 1963 Pan-American Games, a position she repeated at the Tokyo Olympics. Miss Willard won five AAU titles.

WILSON, Deborah Keplar.

B. 05 NOV 1955 Columbus, OH. Bronze: 1976 Platform. Debbie Wilson won the 1973 AAU outdoor platform as Debbie Keplar, and after she had married, she won the 1976 U.S. Trials. At the Montreal Games, she confirmed her form at the Trials by finishing as the leading American. After graduating from high school in her native Columbus, she competed for the Ron O'Brien Diving School.

EQUESTRIAN EVENTS

The United States has always done fairly well in the equestrian events. In the early Olympic years of the sport, it was limited to military personnel, and only commissioned officers, at that. In fact, in 1948, it was discovered that one of the Swedish riders was not an officer, and the team gold medal was taken away from the Swedes. In those early years, Sweden was easily the top riding nation, followed by the United States. Today it is difficult to call any nation dominant in this sport. Great Britain, West Germany, Switzerland and Italy all do well, as does the United States.

Since 1952, when the restriction against military personnel was lifted, women and men have competed on equal grounds in this sport. Four U.S. women have won medals and, since they competed with the men, they are not listed separately, but will be found below.

OUTSTANDING PERFORMANCES

Most Gold Medals
 2 Tad Coffin, Earl Thomson
Most Medals
 5 Michael Plumb, Earl Thomson
 4 Bill Steinkraus
Most Appearances (Men)
 6 Frank Chapot
 5 Bill Steinkraus, Michael Plumb
Most Appearances (Women)
 3 Kathy Kusner, Edith Master
Oldest Gold Medalist
 47y364d Earl Thomson
Oldest Medalist
 49y232d Hiram Tuttle
Youngest Gold Medalist
 21y75d 'Tad' Coffin
Youngest Medalist
 16y144d Michael Plumb
Oldest Medalist (Women)
 43y339d Edith Master
Youngest Medalist (Women)
 23y213d Dorothy Morkis

ANDERSON, Charles Howard.
B. 24 OCT 1914 California. Gold: 1948 Three Day Event—Team. Lt. Col. Charles Anderson was lying second in the individual competition after two days but dropped to fourth in the individual placings.

Anderson was a graduate of West Point, class of '38, and later became a career army officer, retiring in 1966, as a full colonel. He served with the Airborne Division during World War II.

ARGO, Edward Yancey.
B. 22 SEP 1895. Ddi. Gold: 1932 Three Day Event—Team. At the 1932 Olympics, Capt. Ed Argo won the jumping discipline and placed second in the dressage phase but fared badly in the cross-country event and finished eighth in the overall individual placings.

Argo was a West Point graduate, class of '18, who served as a lieutenant during the First World War. He was a career officer, retiring in 1944 as a colonel.

BORG, Robert John.
B. 27 MAY 1913. Silver: 1948 Dressage Team. Lt. Bob Borg placed fourth in the 1948 Olympic individual dressage competition, leading the U.S. to the silver medals in the team event, and he was desparately unlucky not to win the individual gold medal. After an almost faultless round which would have given him the Olympic title, one judge placed him first, and another equal second but a third placed him ninth—and awarded the first three places to riders from his own country.

Borg also competed in the Olympic dressage in 1952 and 1956, finishing 11th and 17th, respectively. He trained the U.S. Three Day Team from 1951 until 1956, but in 1960 he met with a riding accident which left him partially paralyzed. However, he was able to continue his activities at his farm in Michigan, working from a special platform he had devised.

CHAMBERLIN, Harry Dwight.
B. 19 MAY 1887 Elgin, IL. D. 29 SEP 1944 Monterey, CA. Gold: 1932 Three Day Event—Team; Silver: 1932 Show Jumping. For Major Harry Chamberlin, the Los Angeles Games were his third Olympics, having previously competed in 1920 and 1928. By finishing second in the show jumping in 1932, he became the first American to win an Olympic medal in this event.

Prior to graduating from the U.S. Military Academy in 1910, Chamberlin had attended Elgin Academy. While at West Point he had an outstanding athletic record and, with only a few minutes remaining in the 1909 game against Navy, he ran 95 yards for a touchdown to win the game for Army.

Harry Chamberlin went on to a brilliant military career, rising to the rank of brigadier general in 1941 and, in 1942, he commanded the combined services task force which captured the New Hebrides. As his Olympic medals in two different events indicate, Chamberlin was a versatile horseman and he captained the Army polo team for many years.

CHAPOT, Frank Davis.
B. 24 FEB 1932 Camden, NJ. Silver(2): 1960 Show Jumping—Team, 1972 Show Jumping—Team. Frank Chapot competed in Olympic show jumping six times, winning two silver medals in the team event, and having a highest individual placing of fourth in 1968. He is one of only four Americans to compete in six Olympic Games.

At the Pan-American Games he won two gold and one silver medal in the show jumping event and, in 1966, he placed second in the European Show Jumping championship to become the first American medalist in this event.

In 1965 Frank Chapot, a Penn graduate, married Mary Mairs, twice his Olympic teammate, and they currently farm in New Jersey.

COFFIN, Edmund.
B. 09 MAY 1955 Toledo, OH. Gold(2): 1976 Three Day Event, 1976 Three Day Event—Team. "Tad" Coffin is the first American to win the individual Olympic Three Day Event title. On his Olympic horse, Ballycon, he had previously won the individual competition at the 1975 Pan-American Games and led the U.S. to victory in the team event.

DAVIDSON, Bruce O.
B. 31 DEC 1949 Newburgh, NY. Gold: 1976 Three Day Event—Team; Silver: 1972 Three Day Event—Team. Bruce Davidson, who attended Iowa State, was one of the great American eventers. At the 1974 World Championships, he became the only American rider to win an individual title, and he won a gold medal in the team event. He repeated his individual victory at the 1978 Worlds. At the Pan-American Games in 1975 he was a member of the winning team and took the silver medal in the individual event.

Davidson is married to the former Carol Hannum, one of the top U.S. eventers.

DOAK, Sloan.
B. 28 JAN 1886 Taylor, TX. D. 10 AUG 1965 Ruxton, MD. Bronze: 1924 Three Day Event. After graduating from West Point in 1907, Sloan Doak spent the greater part of his service career as an instructor at the cavalry school at Fort Riley, Kansas. While at the Fort, he played polo extensively and was a member of the team which won the Western Circuit Championship in 1915. He retired from the army in 1936 at which time he held the rank of colonel.

Doak made the first of his three Olympic appearances in 1920 and in 1924 he won the bronze medal in the Three Day Event. At the 1928 Olympics, when he placed 17th, he was the captain of the U.S. equestrian team. Four years later, in Los Angeles, Sloan Doak served as the Chairman of the Olympic Equestrian Jury and was the first American to be honored with this exacting duty.

FREEMAN, Kevin John.
B. 21 OCT 1941 Portland, OR. Silver(2): 1964 Three Day Event—Team, 1972 Three Day Event—Team. Growing up in the American Northwest, Kevin Freeman had to travel to Canada or California to find competition in Three Day Events. His first international success came in 1963 when he won a gold medal in the team event at the Pan-American Games, and he won a second gold medal in the same event four years later. Between his two Olympic medals he was a reserve for the 1968 Olympics.

Freeman, who has worked in the family farm machinery manufacturing business, was educated at Cornell.

GURNEY, Hilda Carolyn.
B. 10 SEP 1943 Los Angeles, CA. Bronze: 1976 Dressage—Team. Prior to winning her Olympic medal in 1976, Hilda Gurney had finished second in the individual dressage and won a gold medal in the team event at the 1975 Pan-American Games.

After graduating from Cal State (Northridge) in 1966, Miss Gurney became a teacher of educationally handicapped children.

HENRY, Frank Sherman.
B. 15 DEC 1909 Cambridge, NY. Gold: 1948 Three Day Event—Team; Silver(2): 1948 Three Day Event, 1948

Dressage—Team. Frank Henry was selected as a member of the 1940 Olympic team, but following their cancellation he had to wait until 1948 to make his Olympic debut. He then enjoyed a highly successful Games in London and became the only U.S. equestrian to win three medals at one Olympic Games.

Henry graduated from West Point in 1933 and worked as an instructor at various military installations. During World War II he was on the War Department's General Staff. He retired from the army as a brigadier general.

HENRY, Guy Vernor, Jr.
B. 28 JAN 1875 Fort Robinson, NE. D. 29 NOV 1967 Chevy Chase, MD. Bronze: 1912 Three Day Event Team. At the 1912 Olympics, Guy Henry competed in all three equestrian events but only achieved success in the Three Day Event where he placed 10th individually and was a member of the team which won the bronze medals.

After graduating from West Point he enjoyed a distinguished military career, rising to the rank of major general. He also took a leading role in the administration of equestrianism in America and served as Equestrian Committee chairman of the USOC.

HOUGH, Charles Gordon, Jr.
B. 03 MAY 1934. Bronze: 1952 Three Day Event—Team. Charles Hough was the leading American eventer at the 1952 Olympics, placing ninth in the individual event.

KITTS, Isaac L.
B. 15 JAN 1896. Bronze: 1932 Dressage—Team. Capt. Isaac Kitts placed sixth in the individual dressage event at the 1932 Olympics and was the second scoring member of the team which won the bronze medals. He competed again at the 1936 Olympics and finished 25th in the individual event as the U.S. placed ninth and last in the team competition.

KUSNER, Kathryn Hallowell.
B. 21 MAR 1940 Gainesville, FL. Silver: 1972 Show Jumping—Team. Having finished 13th at the 1964 Olympics and 21st in 1968, Miss Kusner placed 10th in 1972 and won a silver medal in the team event. She is

the only U.S. woman to have won an Olympic medal in show jumping.

Kathy Kusner joined the U.S. Equestrian Team in 1962 and remained a member for many years. She won a gold medal in the team event at the 1963 Pan-American Games, finished as runner-up at the first World Championships in 1965 and, two years later, won the Ladies' European Championship.

Kusner is also licensed to ride in flat races which she has done with success in both the U.S. and South Africa. She is a vice president of the Alpha Instrument Co.

LEAR, Ben, Jr.
B. 12 MAY 1879 Hamilton, Ontario, Canada. D. 01 NOV 1966 Memphis, TN. Bronze: 1912 Three Day Event. At the age of 19, Ben Lear joined the Colorado National Guard and soon saw service in the Spanish-American War and in the Philippines. He rose through the ranks to become a lieutenant general and earned the reputation of being a reserved officer and a harsh disciplinarian. Questions were asked in Congress about his ordering a regiment of citizen-soldiers on a 15-mile disciplinary march but the controversy was forgotten when the Japanese attacked Pearl Harbor five months later.

Lear was the leading U.S. rider in the 1912 Olympic Three Day Event, finishing in seventh place. He was also a member of the team which placed fourth in the Show Jumping and Lear himself finished 12th in the field of 21 riders.

MASTER, Edith Louise.
B. 25 AUG 1932 New York, NY. Bronze: 1976 Dressage—Team. In her third Olympics, Mrs. Master, at slightly more than 43 years of age, became the second oldest U.S. woman to win an Olympic medal in any sport. In her previous Olympic appearances she had finished 23rd in 1968 and 18th in 1972. She was educated at Cornell and NYU and lived in Germany for a number of years, studying dressage under the great teacher, Heinz Lammers.

McCASHIN, Arthur John.
B. 05 MAY 1909. Bronze: 1952 Show Jumping—Team. A highly successful rider before the War, Arthur McCashin became the first riding captain of the U.S. Equestrian Team jumping squad. After retiring from

competitive riding he became a well-known course designer and planned the circuit at the New York's National Horse Show for many years.

MONTGOMERY, John Carter.
B. 22 NOV 1881 Kentucky. D. 07 JUN 1948 Washington, DC. Bronze(2): 1912 Three Day Event Team, 1920 Polo. The 1912 Olympics was a testing time for many horses and Lt. Jack Montgomery rode the same horse, Deceive, in the Three Day Event, the show jumping and the dressage competitions. He fared best in the Three Day Event, finishing eighth in the individual competition, and winning a bronze medal in the team event. Montgomery also won a bronze medal as a member of the polo team in 1920.

Montgomery served in World War I and was accorded the only battlefield promotion made by General Pershing during the entire war. The promotion took him to colonel, at which he remained until he retired in 1926 on the grounds of ill health. He then joined the First Boston Corporation and later became a director of the firm which grew to be the largest investment bank in America.

MOORE, Alvin H.
B. 11 NOV 1891. Bronze: 1932 Dressage—Team. In 1932 Sgt. Alvin Moore was a riding instructor at the army's Ft. Riley Cavalry School. At the Olympics, of the 10 competitors in the dressage event, Moore placed seventh and was the last scoring member of the U.S. squad which took the bronze medals in a three-team contest.

MORKIS, Dorothy.
B. 29 DEC 1942 Boston, MA. Bronze: 1976 Dressage—Team. Mrs. Morkis was a member of the winning team and won a bronze medal in the individual event at the 1975 Pan-American Games. At the 1976 Olympics she was the best placed of the American individuals, finishing in fifth place and winning a bronze medal in the team event.

MORRIS, George Hayes.
B. 26 FEB 1938 New York, NY. Silver: 1960 Show Jumping—Team. At the age of 22, George Morris, of the University of Virginia, was the youngest member of the U.S. show jumping team which won the silver med-

als at the Rome Olympics. Individually, he placed 10th.

After the 1960 Olympics, Morris retired from competition and had a brief fling at an acting career, but he was soon back with the horses and has achieved considerable success as an instructor.

PAGE, Michael Owen.
B. 23 SEP 1938 New York, NY. Silver(2): 1964 Three Day Event—Team, 1968 Three Day Event—Team; Bronze: 1968 Three Day Event. Michael Page was educated at the Briar Cliff High School (New York) and L'Ecole de Commerce in Neuchâtel, Switzerland. His first international Three Day Event was the 1959 Pan-American Games when he won the individual event and led the U.S. to the silver medals in the team event. He made his Olympic debut in 1960 when he placed a disappointing 17th but, before his second Olympic appearance, he again won the Pan-American title (1963) and was a member of the team which took the gold medals in the team competition.

At the 1964 Olympics, Page placed fourth in the individual competition and won a silver medal in the team event. At his third Pan-American Games in 1967, Michael Page again won a gold medal in the team event and placed third individually. On his third, and final, Olympic appearance in 1968, he won a silver medal in the team event and a bronze in the individual.

Today he has little time to spare from his New York business interests, but after retirement from active eventing he continued in competition as a show jumper and coached the 1976 Canadian Olympic Three Day Event team.

PLUMB, John Michael.
B. 28 MAR 1940 Islip, NY. Gold: 1976 Three Day Event—Team; Silver(4): 1964 Three Day Event—Team, 1968 Three Day Event—Team, 1972 Three Day Event—Team, 1976 Three Day Event. After being a member of the Three Day Event team which won the silver medals at three successive Olympics, Michael Plumb won a team gold and an individual silver at the 1976 Games. His total of five Olympic medals equalled Earl Thomson's record for a U.S. equestrian. Apart from his Olympic successes he won two team and one individual gold medal at the Pan-American Games and he was a member of the winning team at the 1974

World Championships, where he won the silver medal in the individual competition.

Michael Plumb graduated from the University of Delaware in 1972 and now farms in Maryland where he lives with his wife, the former Donnan Sharp, a well-known equestrienne, and their three children.

RUSSELL, John William.
B. 02 FEB 1920. Bronze: 1952 Show Jumping—Team. After competing in the 1948 and 1956 Olympics, Capt. John Russell retired from active competition and devoted himself to coaching the modern pentathlon. He coached four U.S. Olympic teams and today lives in San Antonio where he still advises pentathletes at Fort Sam Houston.

SHAPIRO, Neal.
B. 22 JUL 1945 Brooklyn, NY. Silver: 1972 Show Jumping—Team; Bronze: 1972 Show Jumping. Neal Shapiro began riding at the age of five and joined the U.S. international team in 1965. In 1972 he became only the third U.S. rider to win an individual medal in an Olympic show jumping event. Today Shapiro and his wife, Suzy, live on Long Island, where he is a well-known owner, trainer, and driver of trotting horses.

STALEY, Walter Goodwin, Jr.
B. 20 OCT 1932 St. Louis, MO. Bronze: 1952 Three Day Event—Team. Walter Staley made the first of his three Olympic appearances in 1952 when he placed 18th in the individual competition and won a bronze medal in the team event. In both the 1956 and 1960 Olympics, Staley failed to finish, as on both occasions his horses sustained injuries which prevented them from completing the courses.

Staley attended the University of Missouri where he earned a Ph.D. and then joined the family business.

STEINKRAUS, William Clark.
B. 12 OCT 1925 Cleveland, OH. Gold: 1968 Show Jumping; Silver(2): 1960 Show Jumping—Team, 1972 Show Jumping—Team; Bronze: 1952 Show Jumping—Team. Bill Steinkraus was one of the first members of the American Pony Club before he took up show jumping in 1938. He first joined the U.S. Equestrian Team (USET) in 1951 and won a bronze medal in his Olympic debut the following year. He was appointed captain of the USET in 1955 and held the post until his retirement in 1972. He later became president of the USET.

His successes around the world are too numerous to itemize in full, but apart from his Olympic medals he twice won gold medals in the team event at the Pan-American Games. His greatest achievement came in 1968 when he made history by becoming the first U.S. competitor to win an individual gold medal in an Olympic equestrian event. In all, he competed at five Olympic Games and was prevented from making a sixth appearance when his horse went lame at the last minute in Tokyo in 1964.

Steinkraus is an accomplished amateur musician and works as a book editor. He graduated from Yale ('48) and now lives with his wife in Connecticut where their three sons are continuing the family equestrian tradition.

TAUSKEY, Mary Anne.
B. 03 DEC 1955 Suffern, NY. Gold: 1976 Three Day Event—Team. In the Three Day Event at the 1976 Olympics, Mary Tauskey placed 20th and, as the high scorer on the U.S. team, her result was not taken into account when calculating the team scores. Riding Marcus-Aurelius, Miss Tauskey had fared reasonably well in the dressage and endurance phases, but two refusals in the show jumping phase dropped her well down the field in the final placings.

Mary Tauskey graduated from Ursuline Academy in Dallas in 1973 and was a member of the winning Three Day Event team at the 1975 Pan-American Games.

THOMSON, Earl Foster.
B. 14 AUG 1900 Ohio. D. 05 JUL 1971 Santa Barbara, CA. Gold(2): 1932 Three Day Event—Team, 1948 Three Day Event—Team; Silver(2): 1932 Three Day Event, 1936 Three Day Event; Bronze: 1948 Dressage. Earl Thomson's record of five Olympic medals is matched only by Michael Plumb among American Olympic equestrians. Thomson also holds the record of being the oldest American to win an Olympic equestrian gold medal.

Thomson was a West Point graduate who served as chief of staff for the 10th Mountain Division during World War II. After the war, he served in Europe for several years before retiring in 1954 as as full colonel.

TUTTLE, Hiram E.

B. 22 DEC 1882 Dexter, ME. D. 11 NOV 1956 Fort Riley, KS. Bronze(2): 1932 Dressage, 1932 Dressage—Team. In 1932 Major Hiram Tuttle became the first U.S. rider to win an individual medal in an Olympic dressage event. He also led his team to third place in the team competition but failed to meet with similar success on his second Olympic appearance in 1936. In Berlin he finished 27th out of the 29 competitors in the individual event and the U.S. finished last of the nine entries in the team event.

Tuttle was commissioned into the army in 1917 and in 1930 was posted to the Cavalry School at Fort Riley. Tuttle remained there until his retirement in 1944 at which time he held the rank of colonel.

WOFFORD, James Cunningham.

B. 03 NOV 1944 Junction City, KS. Silver(2): 1968 Three Day Event—Team, 1972 Three Day Event Team. Jimmy Wofford is a member of the well-known American equestrian family. In his Olympic debut in 1968 he was within reach of the individual gold medal when he met a freak accident on the flat during the show jumping phase. Despite this incident he still placed sixth. At the 1972 Olympics he individually finished back in 30th place but he again won a silver medal in the team event, although as a nonscoring member of the U.S. team.

Wofford, who was educated at the Culver Military Academy, also won a gold medal in the team event at the 1967 Pan-American Games, and placed third at the 1970 World Championships.

WOFFORD, John Edwin Brown.

B. 11 APR 1931. Bronze: 1952 Three Day Event—Team. John Wofford finished 31st in the individual Three Day Event at the 1952 Olympics and was the last scoring member of the U.S. team which took the bronze medals. He was the son of "Gyp" Wofford who, after missing the 1940 Olympics, played a vital part in ensuring that the U.S. equestrian team was properly represented at the first two post-war Olympics. In Helsinki, John Wofford rode his father's horse, Benny Grimes.

Courtesy United States Military Academy

Earl Thompson is the co-holder of the record for most medals won by an American Olympic equestrian.

FENCING

The United States has never been known as a fencing power. The sport has been dominated by the Italians, the French, and the Hungarians. Since 1952, the USSR has also produced top fencers. The United States has won a few medals in team events, mostly bronze. However, with the exception of the 1904 Olympics, when most of the competitors were American, we have managed to win only two individual medals. Our last Olympic fencing medal came in 1960.

OUTSTANDING PERFORMANCES

Most Gold Medals
  2 Albertson Van Zo Post
Most Medals
  4 Albertson Van Zo Post
  3 George Calnan, Charles Tatham
Most Appearances
  6 Norman Armitage
  5 Albert Axelrod
  4 Daniel Bukantz, George Calnan,
    Alfonso Morales, Tibor Nyilas, George Worth
Oldest Medalist
  c51y Charles Tatham
Youngest Medalist
  23y138d Richard Steere

ALESSANDRONI, Hugh Vincent.
B. 15 JAN 1908 New York, NY. Bronze: 1932 Team Foil. At the 1932 Olympics, Hugh Alessandroni was a member of the highly successful U.S. foil team which defeated France, throwing the final into a three-way tie between France, Italy and the U.S. that was decided by a series of barrage matches. Alessandroni later won the American Fencer's League of America championship in foil individual in 1934 and 1936. A graduate of Columbia, he later represented the New York Fencers Club and shared in seven team national championships, six with the foil and one in three-weapon.

ARMITAGE, Norman Cudworth (né Norman Cudworth Cohn).
B. 01 JAN 1907 Albany, NY. D. 14 MAR 1972 New York, NY. Bronze: 1948 Team Sabre. Norman Armitage took up fencing while a student at Columbia and, in 1928, won the IFA sabre individual championships and a

berth on the Olympic team. He made six Olympic teams in all, through 1956, equal best of any American, but his span of 28 years between appearances is unmatched among U.S. Olympic athletes.

At the 1948 Olympics, Armitage was the cornerstone of the sabre team that won the bronze medal. Also in 1948 he was part of the three-man color guard that carried the U.S. flag in the opening ceremonies. At the 1952 and 1956 Olympics, Armitage was standard bearer himself.

Armitage's record domestically is as lengthy as his Olympic record. In 25 years he placed in the first three in the sabre individual 22 times, winning on 10 occasions. He also won seven outdoor sabre individual titles and was a member of six national championship teams.

Armitage spent his business career first as a chemical engineer, then briefly as a patent lawyer before returning to chemical research. In a chemical accident in January 1936, he was the victim of third-degree burns on his right hand and arm. He was not expected to be able to fence again, but through exercise and determination he strengthened the arm sufficiently to make the 1936 Olympic team.

AXELROD, Albert.
B. 12 FEB 1921 New York, NY. Bronze: 1960 Individual Foil. Albert Axelrod, America's only individual medalist in fencing since 1960, began the sport at New York's Stuyvesant High School and continued at CCNY. While there he won the IFA and NCAA foil individual titles.

Axelrod won the AFLA National Championship in foil four times and was second on nine other occasions, and representing various clubs he was a member of 11 national championship teams. Internationally, besides his Olympic bronze, Axelrod finished fifth at the 1958 World Championships, which is the only time an American foilist has reached the finals in that event. He was a member of four Pan-American teams, winning a silver medal each time in the individual foil.

BRECKINRIDGE, Henry Cabell.
B. 25 MAY 1886 Chicago, IL. D. 02 MAY 1960 New York, NY. Bronze: 1920 Team Foil. Henry Breckinridge was a member of both the foil and epee team at the 1920 Olympics. At foil, he won the deciding bout that gave the U.S. a victory over Great Britain, and with it, the bronze

Albert Axelrod.

Norman Cudworth Armitage — U.S. standard bearer, 1952.

Norman Cudworth Armitage — U.S. standard bearer, 1956.

Courtesy Jeffrey Tishman

George Calnan, one of America's greatest epee fencers.

George C. Calnan — Olympic Oath of Participation, 1932.

medal. Breckinridge won only one AFLA national individual championship, that in outdoor epee in 1924, but he was a member of nine national championship teams, while representing either the Washington Fencers Club or the New York Fencers Club.

Breckinridge achieved prominence early in life. At 27 he was asked to join President Wilson's first cabinet as the assistant secretary of war, and he served in that post from 1913 until 1916. He then fought in World War I, commanding a battalion and seeing action at Vosges, St. Mihiel, and the Meuse Argonne, leaving the service as a lieutenant colonel.

Breckinridge, a Princeton grad who went on to Harvard Law, then took up the practice of law in New York. His most famous client was Charles Lindbergh and when Lindbergh's infant son was kidnapped in 1932, Breckinridge, acting as both friend and counsel, was responsible for the conduct of the lengthy and futile ransom negotiations and the widespread attempts to make contact with the kidnapper.

In 1934 Breckinridge ran for the U.S. Senate from New York but was defeated. In 1936 he entered several Democratic Presidential primaries, but with little success and he dropped out of contention for the nomination. He then returned to his law practice.

CALNAN, George Charles.
B. 18 JAN 1900 Boston, MA. D. 04 APR 1933 off Barnegat, NJ. Bronze(3): 1928 Team Epee, 1932 Team Epee, 1932 Team Sabre. Generally considered the first American fencer of international calibre, George Calnan began fencing at the U.S. Naval Academy. While there he was captain of the varsity and brigade champion, but never, surprisingly, intercollegiate champion.

At the 1928 Olympics, Calnan passed through three rounds into the epee final, where he placed third and entered a direct-elimination super-final of four. Calnan lost, 13-11, to George Buchard of France, the three-time world champion, but he defeated Tom, of Belgium, to win the bronze medal. At the 1932 Olympics, Calnan anchored two medal winning teams and again reached the final in epee individual, finishing seventh. Calnan also captained the U.S. fencing team in Los Angeles and took the oath of participation on behalf of the athletes of all nations. Calnan won nine AFLA national championships, and was a member of

13 national championship teams for the New York Fencer's Club. In 1925, he was a member of four national championship teams, a yet to be equalled feat.

A career naval officer, Calnan perished in the crash of the dirigible Akron. The year after he died, the AFLA established the George C. Calnan Memorial Trophy for the national three-weapon team championship.

deCAPRILES, Miguel Angel.
B. 30 NOV 1906 Mexico City, Mexico. D. 24 MAY 1981 San Francisco, CA. Bronze(2): 1932 Team Epee, 1948 Team Sabre. Miguel deCapriles' renown comes principally from his being the leading administrator of fencing in the U.S. for half a century. Emigrating to the States from Mexico in 1920, he began fencing while a student at NYU, but only achieved success after his 1927 graduation. Starting in 1930 he won 10 individual national titles and was a member of 12 national championship teams.

Besides his Olympic medals, deCapriles had the distinction of being the first American to preside at an Olympic final when he was the president of jury at the individual sabre final at Berlin in 1936. He held a variety of AFLA posts until 1949, when he was elected president of that organization, holding office until 1953. In 1960 he was elected president of the Federacion International d'Escrime (FIE), becoming the first non-European to hold that post. In 1975, for his many contributions to amateur sport, he was named a recipient of the newly created Olympic Order.

Miguel deCapriles spent nearly his entire professional career as a faculty member and administrator at New York University. Beginning as a professor of economics, he was later a law professor, dean of the law school, and eventually vice-president of the university. In 1975 he retired but then joined the faculty at Hastings College of Law in San Francisco.

CETRULO, Dean Victor.
B. 24 FEB 1919 Newark, NJ. Bronze: 1948 Team Sabre. Scion of one of the most illustrious families in American fencing history, Dean Cetrulo began fencing at the age of 10, taking instruction from his father, Gerardo Cetrulo, an Italian fencing master and longtime coach at Dartmouth. A champion in high school, he attended Seton Hall University, where he was coached by his older brother, and won the Eastern Intercollegiates in

foil and sabre in 1940 and 1941. In 1941, aged 22, he became the youngest national champion to that time by winning a four-way barrage for the foil individual title. He repeated as foil champion in 1947 and added the sabre individual title in 1948. Cetrulo, who represented the Salle Santelli, was a member of five national championship teams.

At the 1948 Olympics, Cetrulo fenced two weapons, the only U.S. fencer to do so. Besides the bronze medal in team sabre, he was a member of the fourth place foil team, and made the semi-finals in sabre individual and foil individual; in the latter case, failing to make the final on a barrage.

During World War II, Cetrulo was a first lieutenant in the U.S. Army air force, and was shot down over Italy. After being captured by the Germans and imprisoned in a POW camp, he made a successful escape. He was hidden by an Italian family in a small town north of Naples, until the Allies liberated that city and he could be repatriated.

EVERY, Dernell.
B. 18 AUG 1906 Athens, NY. Bronze: 1948 Team Foil. Dernell Every is one of the living legends of American fencing, having established a record as a competitor, sportsman, and administrator that is nearly without peer. Every began fencing at Yale when it was the powerhouse of U.S. collegiate fencing. He became the first fencer to win two successive and unshared IFA titles, capturing the foil in 1927 and 1928, and in 1926 he helped Yale win outright all four team championships, a feat equalled since only by NYU in 1971.

After college, Every was named to the 1928, 1932, 1936 and 1948 Olympic teams, although in 1936 he was forced to withdraw because of business obligations. Besides his 1932 bronze medal, in 1948 he was a member of the foil team which finished fourth. Every won three individual national titles, and representing either the New York Fencer's Club or the New York AC, he was a member of 15 national championship teams.

Dernell Every was secretary of the AFLA from 1940 to 1944 and again from 1948 to 1952, and was president of the league between those two terms. He was also the wartime editor of *The Riposte*, the league's publication. Every's administrative ability is generally credited with being one of the principal reasons that fencing survived the war in this country.

FLYNN, James Hummitzsch.
B. 08 AUG 1907 Paterson, NJ. Bronze: 1948 Team Sabre. James Flynn began fencing in a Boy Scout troop where one of his coaches was U.S. Olympian, Warren Dow. After attending the Ohio College of Chiropody, he returned east to commence his medical practice and organized the first of four fencing clubs he would eventually establish in New Jersey. He later became an AFLA vice-president and an internationally rated president of jury.

Flynn's competitive record includes winning the 1947 AFLA National Championship in sabre individual—at age 40. Representing the New York AC, he was a member of four national championship teams.

FOX, Arthur G.
Silver: 1904 Team Foil. Arthur Fox was probably fortunate that only two teams entered the 1904 team foil event, as in both his two individual events, foil and sabre, he failed to win a bout. Fox was from Chicago.

GREBE, William.
Silver: 1904 Individual Sabre; Bronze: 1904 Single-Sticks. Chicago's William Grebe won his Olympic silver medal in a fence-off with Albertson Van Zo Post, after they were both defeated by the Harvard-trained Cuban, Manual Diaz. In addition to his medal events, Grebe competed in individual foil at the 1904 Olympics, but was eliminated in a semi-final pool, losing every bout. He was also AFLA national champion in epee individual, while representing the Chicago Fencers Club.

HAMORI, Eugene Arhand (né Jenö Arhand Hámori).
B. 27 AUG 1933 Gyor, Hungary. Gold: 1956 Team Sabre (competed for Hungary). Gene Hámori was a Hungarian who fenced for their victorious sabre team at the Melbourne Olympics, even though his country fielded a smaller team than usual because of the recent Soviet invasion. Shortly after the 1956 Olympics, Hámori defected to the United States and became a well-known fencer in this country as well.

Hámori studied at the University of Budapest and then did graduate work at the University of Pennsylvania. He has won four U.S. national titles, all from 1960 to 1964. He is currently a research scientist.

The bronze-medal-winning U.S. Olympic sabre team of 1948 (L-R) — George Worth, Dean Cetrulo, Dr. Miguel deCapriles, Dr. Norman Armitage, Dr. Tibor Nyilas, Dr. James Flynn.

HEISS, Gustave Marinius.
B. 04 NOV 1906 Meridian, MS. D. 07 JUN 1982
Arlington, VA. Bronze: 1932 Team Epee. Epee, the most
inconsistent of the three weapons, generally produces
a new champion every year, and often a completely
new final round. But Gustave Heiss was an extremely
consistent fencer in this most inconsistent of disciplines. Introduced to fencing at West Point, Heiss won
the 1931 IFA epee individual title. After graduation, he
fenced for the New York Fencers Club, and won the
AFLA national title in epee individual four times, outdoor
epee twice, and was a member of seven national championship teams—all before 1941. Thus, in a 10-year
career, Gustave Heiss won six titles in this unpredictable event.

Heiss became a career military officer after graduating West Point. During World War II, he was with the
First Army, the Third Army and the 87th Division. On 2
January 1945, at the Battle of the Bulge, he triggered a
German "booby trap" that nearly killed him, left him
hospitalized for two years, and ended his military and
athletic careers. He went on to take up positions in
government civil service.

HONEYCUTT, Francis Webster.
B. 26 MAY 1883 California. D. 20 SEP 1940 Woodbine,
GA. Bronze: 1920 Team Foil. Francis Honeycutt won
the IFA foil individual championship in 1903 and 1904,
and was a member of Army's championship foil team
both those years as well. In 1905, just a year out of West
Point, he was second in the AFLA national championship in foil individual, an exceptional result for someone
of that age in that era. In 1921, representing the Washington Fencers Club, Honeycutt won the AFLA national
championship in foil individual, and was on the winning
team in both foil and epee. At the 1920 Olympics,
besides the bronze in foil team, he reached the semi-
finals of the foil individual.

Honeycutt spent his entire military career in the
field artillery, eventually attaining the rank of brigadier
general.

JAECKEL, Tracy.
B. 06 FEB 1905 New York, NY. D. 06 AUG 1969 Fire
Island, NY. Bronze: 1932 Team Epee. Tracy Jaeckel won
the 1928 IFA epee individual championship while a
student at Princeton. After graduation he never man-

aged to win a national individual title, but became primarily known as a great team fencer, sharing in seven
national epee team titles, and two national three-
weapon team titles.

Jaeckel graduated Princeton in 1928 and joined
the family business, Jaeckel, Inc., a well-known furrier.
It later merged to become Gunther-Jaeckel, and shortly
thereafter, Tracy Jaeckel left the company, moving to
the Virgin Islands, where he ran an exclusive men's
haberdashery.

KERESZTES, Attila.
B. 18 JAN 1928 Budapest, Hungary. Gold: 1956 Team
Sabre (competed for Hungary). Attila Keresztes was a
member of the 1956 Hungarian sabre team which, led
by the great Rudolf Karpati and Aladar Gerevich, won
the gold medal. With Gene Hámori, Keresztes defected
after the Olympics and made our Olympic team in 1964.
In this country he represented the New York AC in
competition, and won or shared three national championships, the 1962 sabre team, and the 1964 sabre
individual and team three-weapon.

LEVIS, Joseph L.
B. 20 JUL 1905 Boston, MA. Silver: 1932 Individual Foil;
Bronze: 1932 Team Foil. Joseph Levis was introduced
to fencing at MIT, where he became its first intercollegiate champion by winning the IFA foil individual in 1926.
In 1928, at his first Olympics, he became the first
American to advance to the final round in foil individual,
but in 1932, Levis was to very nearly reach the pinnacle
of success. He finished second in the foil individual,
generally acknowledged to be the finest result ever
attained by an American fencer in international competition.

Levis won nine AFLA national championships, six
in foil individual, two in outdoor foil, and one in three-
weapon individual. He was also a member of four
national championship teams. During the 1940's, in an
effort to maintain the team at his alma mater, he turned
professional and started coaching at MIT. In 1954, he
requested reinstatement as an amateur and that year
won the metropolitan and national championships after
a layoff of 13 years.

LYON, Arthur St. Clair.

B. 01 AUG 1876. D. 13 JUN 1952 Santa Monica, CA. Bronze: 1920 Team Foil. Arthur Lyon fenced all three weapons at the 1920 Olympics, the last American ever to do so. In the sabre team event, he defeated A. E. W. de Jong of the Netherlands, third in the sabre individual that year, and later, a world champion. Lyon was a member of the New York Fencer's Club and the New York AC. He won the AFLA national championship in sabre individual in 1917 and 1919 and was a member of three national championship teams.

In 1923, Robert H. E. Grasson presented twin cups to the Intercollegiate Fencing Association (IFA) for the epee team and sabre team championships. The sabre team cup carries a relief of Lyon, with the legend "Arthur S. Lyon—America's Greatest Sabre Fencer."

NYILAS, Tibor Andrew.

B. 03 JUN 1914 Budapest. Hungary. Bronze: 1948 Team Sabre. Tibor Nyilas began fencing as a youth at the Salle Santelli, the salle d'armes of Italo Santelli, the preeminent sabre coach of all-time. Because of the unstable political climate in Hungary in 1939, Nyilas decided to emigrate to the United States. A 1937 graduate of a Hungarian medical college, he first took up an appointment in St. Louis, but soon moved to New York where he became a general practitioner.

Nyilas was a member of four U.S. Olympic teams consecutively from 1948. His best individual finish was seventh in sabre in 1948. At the 1960 Olympics, he won all four of his bouts in the sabre team semi-final match against the Soviets, enabling the U.S. to advance to the final and place fourth, the last time we have done so well.

Nyilas won the AFLA national championship seven times in individual sabre and once in three-weapon. He was also a member of 12 national championship teams, fencing for either Salle Santelli or the New York AC. At the 1951 Pan-American Games, he won three gold medals—in sabre individual, sabre team, and foil team.

O'CONNOR, William Scott.

D. 16 JAN 1939. Silver: 1904 Single-Sticks. Along with Graeme Hammond, W. Scott O'Connor co-founded the Amateur Fencers League of America in 1891, and served as its secretary from its inception until 1925. He

FOREIGNERS HELPING OUT

There are several examples of a foreign athlete competing for another country in the Olympics, and then gaining U.S. citizenship, and competing for the U.S. at the Olympics. In fact, it has happened six times.

The first example was Dan Carroll, who competed in rugby for Australia in 1908 and for the United States in 1920, winning medals both times.

The next example, Olga Fikotova Connolly, became an American by marriage. As Olga Fikotova she won a gold medal in the discus throw for Czechoslovakia in 1956, but while at those Games, she met and fell in love with American hammer thrower, Hal Connolly. Overcoming mountains of red tape, they were married and Olga Connolly competed for the U.S. at the 1960 Olympics, and also at the next three Olympics.

In 1964 three Hungarians competed for the United States after defecting from their country shortly after the 1956 Russian invasion. These were fencers Eugene Hámori and Attila Keresztes, and rower Bob Zimonyi. All had won medals in the Olympics for Hungary—Hámori and Keresztes in 1956 in team sabre, and Zimonyi in 1948 in coxed pairs. Zimonyi also won a gold medal for the United States when he coxed the 1964 Vesper eight to a gold medal.

In 1972, Andras Törö repeated the feat of competing for Hungary and the United States. He had been a canoeist for Hungary at the 1960 and 1964 Olympics but emigrated to the United States and paddled for our team in the 1972 and 1976 Olympics.

was the first AFLA champion in foil individual in 1892 and added the epee title in 1905. A long-time member of the New York Fencers Club, he was a member of the AFLA national championship epee team in 1908. In 1940, the AFLA dedicated the new national trophy in epee individual to W. Scott O'Connor; a twin to the cup offered in honor of Graeme Hammond for sabre individual.

Fencers Club — AFLA foil team champions, 1891.
(L-R) — Charles Tatham, Albertson Van Zo Post, Charles
C. Nadal. Seated — William Scott O'Connor.

RAYNER, Harold Marvin.

B. 27 JUL 1888 Glen Ridge, NJ. D. 08 DEC 1954
Montrose, NY. Bronze: 1920 Team Foil. One of the most
versatile yet unsung of the early U.S. Olympians, Harold
Rayner began his fencing career at the U.S. Military
Academy, where he won the IFA foil individual title in
1912. He also made the 1912 Olympic team, but it was
at the 1920 Olympics where he attained his greatest
success. Rayner was the leader of the foil team that
won the bronze medal; he took part in the epee team
event and finished sixth in the modern pentathlon.

Rayner won the AFLA national championship in
foil individual in 1922, was second in 1921, and third in
1920. In 1921, representing the Washington Fencers
Club, he was a member of the team which won both the
national foil team and epee team championships.

Rayner's entire military career was spent in the
cavalry. He served at different times as an aide-de-
camp to Presidents Wilson and Harding, and to General
of the Armies John J. Pershing. Rayner retired in 1946,
having achieved the rank of colonel.

RIGHEIMER, Frank Stahl, Jr.

B. 28 FEB 1909 Chicago, IL. Bronze(2): 1932 Team Foil,
1932 Team Epee. Frank Righeimer began fencing at
Yale, where he became the first of only three fencers to
win two individual titles in a single IFA championship,
capturing the foil and epee in 1929. He was undefeated
in both weapons and untouched in epee. The same
year he became one of the very few undergraduates to
win a national championship, taking the title in epee as
well as third place in foil. He also won the outdoor epee
individual title in 1929 and 1933.

After graduating from Yale, Righeimer attended
Harvard Law School and is now a successful attorney
with offices in Chicago and Palm Beach.

SEARS, Robert.

B. 30 NOV 1884 Portland, OR. D. 09 JAN 1979 Atlanta,
GA. Bronze: 1920 Team Foil. The versatile Robert Sears
excelled in every sport he tried—boxing, fencing,
swimming, track and marksmanship. At West Point, he
was captain of the army team that won the IFA foil team
title in 1908 and 1909, and in the latter year, shared
individual honors with his teammate, Reginald Cocroft.

At the 1936 Olympics, Sears was 36 years old, but
still won a bronze medal in foil team, participated in the

epee team event, and finished eighth in modern pentathlon.

Sears spent most of his military career with the ordnance department. In World War II, he commanded the 35th Infantry during its sweep through France, despite the fact that at 60, he was the oldest combat soldier in the European theatre. He retired in 1946 with the rank of colonel.

SHEARS, Curtis Charles.

B. 04 JUL 1901 Omaha, NE. Bronze: 1932 Team Foil. Curtis Shears began fencing at the Naval Academy, where he won the IFA championship in foil individual and was a member of the championship foil team. He also won the AFLA national championship in outdoor epee individual in 1923.

Shears earned a J.D. degree from NYU in 1932 and became an assistant U.S. Attorney in New York City. He was one of the founders of the Big Brother organization, and is an authority on nutrition, having authored three books on the subject.

STEERE, Richard Clarke.

B. 15 MAR 1909 Kansas City, MO. Bronze: 1932 Team Foil. Richard Steere began fencing at the Naval Academy where he was the varsity captain in his senior year. At the 1932 Olympics the foil team, of which he was a member, defeated the French and threw the final into a series of barrage matches. This resulted in a change in the rules the following year, calling for a count of bouts in the event of a tie.

Steere became a career naval officer and an expert in meteorology. As a lieutenant commander during World War II he was principally responsible for determining weather conditions and their impact on amphibious landings. He served in the North Atlantic and Mediterranean and participated in the decisions to land troops at Casablanca, Sicily, Salerno, and Normandy. He retired in 1961 with the rank of captain.

Capt. Steere remains an active competitor and participated in the 1982 AFLA National Championships at the age of 73!

TATHAM, Charles T.

B. c1853 New York, NY. D. 24 SEP 1939 New York, NY. Silver(2): 1904 Individual Epee, 1904 Team Foil; Bronze: 1904 Individual Foil. For many years, the 1904 Olympic accomplishments of Charles Tatham were considered to have been done as a Cuban citizen. In fact, Tatham came from an old family with roots in New York and Philadelphia. His grandfather, Benjamin Tatham, founded the lead manufacturing concern in Philadelphia, Tatham Bros., for which Charles Tatham worked his entire business life.

Tatham won the AFLA national title in epee individual for three consecutive years from 1901, the first of only three fencers to accomplish this feat. In 1901 he won the foil individual as well. Tatham was the long-time treasurer of the New York Fencer's Club and was a member of their national championship epee team in 1908.

TOWNSEND, Charles Fitzhugh.

D. 11 DEC 1906 New York, NY. Silver: 1904 Team Foil. Fitzhugh Townsend is best remembered as the co-founder and first champion, in 1894, of the Intercollegiate Fencing Association (IFA). He repeated as champion in 1896. After college, Townsend represented the New York Fencers Club and won the AFLA national championship in foil individual in 1900 and 1903.

Townsend was an electrical engineering instructor at Columbia from 1897 until his death in 1906 from typhoid fever. He was the co-author, with Prof. George F. Sever, of *Laboratory and Factory Tests in Electrical Engineering*. Townsend was the inventor of an improved railway signal device, involving a number of ingenious features, that was under consideration by the New York Central and other railroads at the time of his death.

VAN Zo POST, Albertson.

B. c1866 New York, NY. D. 23 JAN 1938 New York, NY. Gold(2): 1904 Single-Sticks, 1904 Team Foil; Silver: 1904 Individual Foil; Bronze: 1904 Individual Epee, 1904 Individual Sabre. To Albertson Van Zo Post belongs the distinction of being the only American ever to win an Olympic championship in fencing. This is a credit long denied him because there has been a popular misconception for some years that he was a member of the Cuban team at the 1904 Olympics. In fact, he belonged to an old New York family. His father, Col. Henry V. Post, fought for the Union Army in the Civil War and was wounded seriously at Antietam.

Post represented the New York Fencers Club and won the AFLA national championship in foil individual in 1895, epee individual in 1896 and 1912, and sabre individual in 1902 and 1903. He is one of the very few fencers to win the national championship in all three weapons. At the 1904 Olympics, aided by a sparse turnout, Post took a medal in each of the four events he entered, including a gold in single-sticks, an event that was never again contested at the Olympics. Post fenced all three weapons in the 1912 Olympics, and with a larger and stronger field, Post's second-round elimination in all three weapons is probably a better indicator of his true ability.

Albertson Post had two careers. Although he trained as a civil engineer and entered that profession, he switched to writing novels, producing *Retz* and *Diana Ardway*.

WORTH, George Vitez (né György Vitez).

B. 01 APR 1915 Budapest, Hungary. Bronze: 1948 Team Sabre. George Worth began fencing while a youth in Hungary at the Salle Santelli, the salle d'armes of Italo Santelli, the preeminent sabre coach of all-time and the father of George Santelli, five-time U.S. Olympic coach. Because of the unstable political climate in Hungary in 1937, Worth decided to emigrate to the United States but was unable to do so directly. He spent two years in Cuba where he won the Cuban national sabre championships and fenced frequently with Cmdte. Ramon Fonst, the Olympic champion of 1900 and 1904.

Worth was a member of the U.S. Olympic teams in 1948, 1952, 1956 and 1960. In 1948, besides the team bronze medal, he finished fifth in the sabre individual, and this is regarded as the outstanding accomplishment of an American sabreur internationally. Worth won the AFLA National Championship in sabre individual in 1954 and was a member of 14 national championship teams, representing the Salle Santelli his entire career. He was also a member of three Pan-American teams, winning a gold medal for sabre team in 1951, 1955 and 1959. At the 1959 Pan-Am Games he spoke the Oath of Participation on behalf of all athletes in both English and Spanish.

FIELD HOCKEY

It seems rather unusual to be writing about United States field hockey medalists, since the United States has never won a game in Olympic field hockey competition. We have entered teams only in 1932, 1936, 1948 and 1956, and their combined record now stands at zero wins and eleven losses, with five goals for, and 91 goals against. However, in 1932, the long distance to Los Angeles from Europe, and the Depression, prevented many teams from attending the Olympics. There were, consequently, only three teams entered in field hockey. Thus, despite a 24-1 loss to India, and a 9-2 loss to Japan, the U.S. team finished third to win the bronze medals.

In fairness to U.S. field hockey players, it must be stated that field hockey is almost never played by men in this country. It tends to be a women's sport in the United States and, as a consequence, the U.S. Olympic field hockey teams have usually been made of athletes from other sports—often lacrosse and soccer.

OUTSTANDING PERFORMANCES

Oldest Medalist
  32y305d Henry Kirk Greer
Youngest Medalist
  21y256d Bill Boddington

BODDINGTON, William Westcott.
B. 22 NOV 1910. Bronze: 1932. Bill Boddington was from Glen Ridge, New York, in 1932 and represented the Germantown Cricket Club. He was a forward for the 1932 team and later played the same position at the 1936 Olympics. Boddington went on to become president of his own company, the Boddington Lumber Company in Colorado. He also coached soccer for a time at Colorado College.

BREWSTER, Harold S.
B. 02 MAY 1903. Bronze: 1932. From Rye, New York, "Mouse" Brewster played for the Rye Field Hockey Club in 1932. He was a Williams graduate who had played goalie for the Williams ice hockey teams and he filled the same slot for the 1932 field hockey team. Brewster also played amateur hockey for several years after college, as a goalie with the well-known St. Nicholas (Ice) Hockey Club.

DEACON, Amos R. Little.
B. 28 MAY 1904. Bronze: 1932. Amos Deacon was a forward from Germantown, Pennsylvania, who represented the Germantown Cricket Club. He played for the United States at both the 1932 and 1936 Olympics.

DISSTON, Horace Cumberland.
B. 07 JAN 1907 Philadelphia, PA. Bronze: 1932. Horace Disston went to Princeton where he played varsity football and ice hockey. For the 1932 field hockey team he played halfback and he also played for the 1936 Olympic field hockey club. Although originally from Philadelphia, he later moved to Maine where he started his own business.

EWING, Samuel Evans.
B. 27 JUL 1906 Bryn Mawr, PA. D. 06 APR 1981 Delray Beach, FL. Bronze: 1932. Sam Ewing was from Philadelphia and a member of the Merion Cricket Club in 1932 when he played fullback for the Olympic field hockey team. Ewing was a Princeton graduate, class of '27, who later attended Penn Law School. He was a well-known soccer, tennis and squash player on the East Coast and while at Princeton he quarterbacked the football team for two years, as well as playing on the tennis team for four years and the basketball team for one year.

Ewing practiced law until the outbreak of World War II, at which time he enlisted as a private. He eventually rose to the rank of major and received five campaign stars and the Bronze Star medal for his service. After the war, Ewing became associated with RCA, with whom he remained as an executive for many years. He also became influential in Philadelphia politics.

GENTLE, James Cuthbert.
B. 21 JUL 1904 Dorchester, MA. Bronze: 1932. Representing Philadelphia Cricket Club in 1932, Jimmy Gentle was another example of a U.S. field hockey player coming to the team from another sport. He attended the University of Pennsylvania and played on the soccer team there for three years, being named all-America in his last two years and leading his school to the 1924 intercollegiate championship. Gentle was recruited to play by several professional soccer clubs but

remained an amateur and played for the United States in the 1930 and 1931 World Championships.

In addition to soccer, Gentle also played football and ran track at Penn. He was a halfback on the 1932 field hockey team and also played on the 1936 team. He went to a very successful career as an insurance salesman, being named to the Million Dollar Round Table.

GREER, Henry Kirk.
B. 11 OCT 1899 New York, NY. D. 20 JUL 1978 Hyannis, MA. Bronze: 1932. "Heine" Greer graduated from Williams in 1922 and went on to Harvard Law School, from which he graduated in 1925. He went on to be very successful as a corporate lawyer in New York. However, he became better known as an amateur musician who played tenor banjo with the Bobby Condon and Eddie Hackett orchestras, and later founded the Cape Cod Jazz Society.

Greer was also responsible for the United States having a field hockey team at the 1932 Olympics. In 1931 he founded the Field Hockey Association of the United States of America and remained as its president for almost 30 years. He also served during that time on the U.S. Olympic Committee and was chairman of the U.S. Olympic Field Hockey Committee at all four of the Olympics at which a United States team participated.

KNAPP, Laurence A.
B. 30 MAY 1905. Bronze: 1932. Larry Knapp was a winger who played for both the 1932 and 1936 Olympic field hockey teams. He was from Yankton, South Dakota in 1932 and later went on to become an attorney.

McMULLIN, David, III.
B. 30 JUN 1908 Gwynedd Valley, PA. Bronze: 1932. Dave McMullin went to Princeton, where he played on the freshman tennis and soccer teams, but was primarily known as a squash racquets player. At that sport, he partnered Stanley Pearson to the United States and Canadian doubles championship in 1947. McMullin also served the U.S. Squash Racquets Association as its secretary in 1937-38.

After college, Dave McMullin entered the investment business in which he remained for four years before transferring to the John Wanamaker Co. in Philadelphia. He went on to become a top executive with that company before retiring in 1974. One of his duties with Wanamaker was as president of the Millrose Athletic Association which ran the well-known indoor track meet, the Millrose Games.

O'BRIEN, Leonard Francis.
B. 20 JAN 1904 North Adams, MA. D. 30 MAR 1939 Boston, MA. Bronze: 1932. "Mike" O'Brien graduated from Williams College in 1925 after having played on the baseball team there for four years. He was captain of the team in his senior year. O'Brien should have graduated in 1924 but missed an entire year with a severe case of typhoid fever. After college he became a bonds and securities broker, first in New York, later nearer his home in Boston. Besides his bronze medal winning performance as a fullback in 1932, O'Brien also played on the 1936 Olympic field hockey team.

SCHEAFFER, Charles Miller, Jr.
B. 06 DEC 1904. Bronze: 1932. Charles Scheaffer was from Merion, Pennsylvania, and represented the Merion Cricket Club at the 1932 Olympics. A forward on the field hockey team, he also played in 1936. He attended the University of Pennsylvania and, after graduation, became an insurance salesman.

WOLTERS, Frederick.
B. 14 JUN 1904. Bronze: 1932. Fred Wolters was a fullback on the 1932 Olympic field hockey team. He was from New York City.

FIGURE SKATING

MEN

Prior to World War II, United States men had very little success in figure skating. But starting with Dick Button in 1948, an American won the men's individual title at four consecutive Olympics. However, on 15 February 1961, the plane carrying the United States figure skating team to the world championships in Brussels crashed, killing all aboard. It took several years for U.S. figure skating to recover from the loss and, although we have had a few medalists since 1964, the men have yet to win another gold medal.

Men skate individually in the Olympics, but also skate in the dance event (since 1976) and pairs event with women. Americans have had much more success in the individual contests than in these combined events have been, of late, dominated by the Soviet teams.

OUTSTANDING PERFORMANCES

Most Gold Medals
  2 Dick Button
Most Medals
  2 Dick Button, David Jenkins
Most Appearances
  3 Nathaniel Niles
Oldest Medalist
  30y167d Sherwin Badger
Youngest Medalist
  15y5d Scott Allen

ALLEN, Scott Ethan.
B. 08 FEB 1949 Newark, NJ. Bronze: 1964 Individual. After the terrible plane crash of 1961 the United States had slim expectations for the 1964 Innsbruck Olympics. But they did not count on a young man with the wonderfully patriotic name of Scott Ethan Allen. He burst on the scene in 1964 by winning the U.S. National Championships and qualifying for the Olympic team. At Innsbruck he was always in the medal chase and pulled it off with a fine free skating performance. Big things were expected in the next few years, but Allen, though extremely charismatic and loved by the fans, never really improved. He finished second in the 1965 U.S. championships but won the title again in 1966. He never won a world championship and in 1968 failed in a second effort to make the U.S. Olympic team.

BADGER, Sherwin Campbell.
B. 29 AUG 1901 Boston, MA. D. 08 APR 1972 Sherborn, MA. Silver: 1932 Pairs. Sherwin Badger was the first great American skater. He was a five-time U.S. individual champion—all in succession (1920-24) and in 1923 won the first North American championship. But his Olympic success came in pairs skating when, in 1932, he partnered Beatrix Loughran to a silver medal.

Badger had studied at Harvard, graduating in 1923. His business career began that year with United Fruit Co., but in 1925 he joined Dow-Jones Publications as banking editor of the *Wall Street Journal* and *Barron's*. In 1940 he joined the New England Mutual Life Insurance Co., and remained with that firm, serving eventually as a senior vice-president and director until his retirement in 1972. Badger was also president of the U.S. National Figure Skating Assoc. in the 30's.

BUTTON, Richard Totten.
B. 18 JUL 1929 Englewood, NJ. Gold(2): 1948 Individual, 1952 Individual. Before World War II, figure skating was simply that cutting pretty figures on the ice. But with his bold jumps and spins, Dick Button ushered in a newer, modern era of athleticism on ice. His record clearly makes him the most dominant figure skater—male or female—of this modern school.

Dick Button won the U.S. men's title from 1946 through 1952, the world title from 1948 until 1952, and two Olympic gold medals. In 1948 he became the first American to win the European championship, and it was promptly changed to a closed event. From 1946 on, he was beaten only once, in a highly controversial decision at the 1947 world championships, where he outscored the Swiss skater Hans Gerschwiler but was relegated to second place by ordinal scores. So dominant was Button that at the 1952 Olympics, he became the first, and so far, only, individual to be placed first by every Olympic judge—in every phase of the competition. Button was the first skater to perform several risky jumps in competition, among them the double axel and triple toe loop. In 1949 he won the Sullivan Award, emblematic of the outstanding amateur athlete in the country—the only winter athlete to be so honored.

Button graduated Harvard in 1952 and finished law school there in 1956. He has gone on to become well known as an announcer for televised figure skating

Dick Button, noted television figure-skating announcer, during his competitive days, which earned him two gold medals.

events but he has also formed his own company which, among other things, has sponsored several professional skating competitions.

GROGAN, James David.

B. 07 DEC 1931. Bronze: 1952 Individual. Jim Grogan first made headlines nationally at the 1946 U.S. championships where he finished second to Dick Button. It was a role he would come to know well. Grogan remained a top skater for many years but was unable to ever win a major title, because of the presence of Button and later Hayes Alan Jenkins. He would repeat his runner-up finish at the Nationals for the next four years and also finish second at the 1951, 1952, 1953 and 1954 Worlds. At the 1952 Olympics he had the second highest point total, behind Button, but his ordinal placings relegated him to the bronze medal.

Grogan served in the army after the 1952 Olympics and skated as an amateur for two more years before skating for a while with the Ice Capades. He later married, and then divorced, Barbara Wagner, the Canadian who paired with Bob Paul to win the 1960 Olympic pairs championship.

JENKINS, David Wilkinson.

B. 29 JUN 1936 Akron, OH. Gold: 1960 Individual; Bronze: 1956 Individual. David Jenkins was the younger brother of Hayes Alan Jenkins, 1956 Olympic men's champion. That year, David was third behind his brother and Ronnie Robertson, but in 1957 he took over control of men's figure skating for himself. He won the U.S., North American and World title in that year, and would keep all three championships through 1959. In 1960 he won the gold medal, as well as defending his U.S. and North American championships, but faltered at the Worlds to finish second.

Jenkins trained in Colorado Springs,Colorado, and while there, attended Colorado College. From there he attended Case Western Reserve Medical School and now is a practicing physician, specializing in internal medicine.

JENKINS, Hayes Alan.

B. 23 MAR 1933 Akron, OH. Gold: 1956 Individual. Sixth in the 1949 World's championship was a 16-year-old named Hayes Alan Jenkins. Jenkins served his apprenticeship behind Dick Button for several years, but with

Button's retirement became the world's top male skater. From 1953 through 1956 he was never beaten. He was not a flashy free skater, but usually built a lead in the compulsories and would hold it with slightly conservative, but exquisitely done free skating performances.

Jenkins was a Phi Beta Kappa graduate of Colorado College who eschewed the world of professional ice shows to attend Harvard Law School. He later worked as an international lawyer for the Goodyear Company. Jenkins married Carol Heiss, the 1960 women's gold medalist.

KENNEDY, Michael Edward, III.

B. 04 SEP 1927 Olympia, WA. Silver: 1952 Pairs. When born, he was christened Michael Edward Kennedy, but a relative took one look at him, said, "That's a Peter!" and he has been called Peter since. Peter Kennedy and his sister, Karol, have the best record in world competition of any American pairs skaters. In 1950 they became the first Americans to win the world pairs title, after second place finishes in 1947 and 1949. They also finished second in the World's in 1951 and 1952 as well as at the Oslo Olympics. They were United States champions from 1947 until 1952.

Peter Kennedy retired from competitive skating after the 1952 Olympics and took up skiing. He went to the Olympic trials at that sport in 1956 but just missed the team. This led to a career for him, however, as he became a consultant and representative to several firms in the skiing industry.

LUDINGTON, Ronald Edmund.

B. 04 SEP 1934 Boston, MA. Bronze: 1960 Pairs. In 1957 Ron Ludington paired with Nancy Rouillard to win the National Pairs Championship. Later that year they married, and as Nancy and Ron Ludington they went on to win the U.S. championship for three more years. Their best world finish was a third place, which they equalled at the 1960 Olympics.

Ron Ludington is one of the very few skaters to have competed in the National Championships, and placed in all three disciplines, singles, pairs, and dance. This was in 1958 when his dance partner was Judy Lamarr. After his competitive days were over, Ron Ludington went on to become a very well known figure skating coach, numbering among his pupils Cynthia and Ron Kaufman and currently, Kitty and Peter Carruthers. He and Nancy have since divorced.

MILLNS, James G., Jr.

B. 13 JAN 1949 Toledo, OH. Bronze: 1976 Dance. At the first Olympic ice dancing competition in 1976, Jim Millns and his partner, Colleen O'Connor, finished third and upheld their position of the two previous years as the top U.S. dance pair. They began skating together in 1971 and trained for a while in England under former World Champion Bernard Ford. After one year with him they finished seventh in the U.S. national championships and then moved back to Colorado Springs where they changed coaches and quickly improved. They were U.S. champions from 1974-76 and at the 1975 Worlds, were leading after the set pattern, although they finished second. Millns was a graduate of the University of Illinois in park administration and was an avid outdoorsman.

ROBERTSON, Ronald F.

B. 25 SEP 1937. Silver: 1956 Individual. Ronnie Robertson was called the world's greatest spinner but he was also a tremendous jumper and, in all, was an outstanding free skater. His first title came at the 1952 U.S. championships where he won the men's junior title. Advancing to the seniors, he finished second in the 1953 Nationals. In the next few years, he had many battles with Hayes Alan Jenkins but he always came up short. He was second again at the 1954 and 1955 Worlds as well as the 1956 Nationals and Olympics. At the 1956 Nationals, Jenkins defeated Robertson in free skating, the only time Robertson ever lost the free skating phase of the competition.

Robertson turned pro after the 1956 Nationals, signing a two-year contract with the Ice Capades for a rumored $100,000 per year. He remained with them for many years. In 1973 he won the International Skating Festival in Tokyo, Japan, one of the first professional competitions.

TICKNER, Charles.

B. 13 NOV 1953 Lafayette, CA. Bronze: 1980 Individual. Charlie Tickner is one of the oldest American men to have competed individually in Olympic figure skating. Unlike most skaters, he started competing seriously at the relatively ancient age of 18. But it took him only a few years to become one of the top skaters in the United States.

In 1974 Tickner finished third at the U.S. Nationals and repeated that performance the next year. He was favored to earn a spot on the 1976 Olympic team but skated terribly in the Nationals—also the Olympic trials that year. However, it spurred him into working even harder. In 1977 he won the U.S. championship and placed fifth at his first World Championship. In 1978 he repeated the national title and became the first American since Tim Wood to be named world champion. But he never hit that peak again. He finished fourth at the 1979 worlds and third at both the 1980 Olympics and World Championships. After the Olympics, Tickner signed to skate professionally with the Ice Capades.

WOOD, Timothy Lyle.

B. 21 JUN 1948 Highland Park, MI. Silver: 1968 Individual. Although Tim Wood won an Olympic silver medal, he really hit his peak between Olympic years, which probably cost him a certain gold.

Wood's first big title was the U.S. Junior Men's which he won in 1964. Moving up to the seniors in 1965, he took third in the Nationals, fifth at the North Americans, and 13th in Worlds. He improved steadily over the next two years, but was unable to win any of the big senior championships, his best finish internationally being his silver at Grenoble. In 1969, however, Tim Wood reached the heights by winning both the U.S. and World titles—events which he would defend in the next year. With two years to go, he was now the top skater in the world, but he had had a long career and Sapporo seemed so far away. Wood decided to forego any more amateur competition and turned pro with the Ice Capades.

WOMEN

American women have always done well in figure skating. Since 1948, four women have won the individual title—Tenley Albright, Carol Heiss, Peggy Fleming, and Dorothy Hamill. However, several other United States women have also won medals in the individual.

In ice dancing (held only since 1976) and pairs, events skated by men and women together, the United States has not done as well. We have won only a few medals, none of them gold, in these events now dominated by the Russians.

OUTSTANDING PERFORMANCES

Most Medals
  3 Beatrix Loughran
  2 Tenley Albright, Carol Heiss
Most Appearances
  3 Beatrix Loughran, Theresa Weld Blanchard,
    Maribel Vinson
Oldest Medalist
  31y227d Beatrix Loughran
Youngest Medalist
  16y11d Carol Heiss

ALBRIGHT, Tenley Emma.

B. 18 JUL 1935 Newton Centre, MA. Gold: 1956 Individual; Silver: 1952 Individual. At the age of 12, Tenley Albright contracted a mild form of polio but was told to continue skating to help her minimize the loss of any leg muscles. The therapy apparently worked well because only five months later she won the Eastern Juvenile title, the first of many victories.

Tenley Albright won her first of five consecutive national titles in 1952. She was also world champion in 1953 and 1955. At the 1956 Olympics, she was hoping to better her 1952 silver medal performance but suffered a large gash in one leg while training. Despite the pain, she continued training and defeated arch-rival Carol Heiss for the gold.

Albright attended Radcliffe and then Harvard Medical School and has gone on to become a general surgeon. In 1982 she became a vice president of the U.S. Olympic Committee. She has been twice married, the first to Tudor Gardiner, the son of a former Maine governor.

BLANCHARD, Theresa Weld.

B. 21 AUG 1893 Brookline, MA. D. 12 MAR 1978. Bronze: 1920 Individual. Theresa Weld won the U.S. women's title in 1914 and 1920 and partnered Nathaniel Niles to the U.S. pairs championship in 1918 and 1920. In 1920 she married Charles Blanchard and, skating under that name, won the U.S. women's from 1921-1924 and the U.S. pairs from 1921-27 (with Niles). She was also the first North American champion (1923) and she and Niles won that pairs title in 1925. Her other titles include the 1931 U.S. dance championship and the 1934 U.S. fours.

Theresa Blanchard went on to become a great supporter of figure skating. She founded *Skating* magazine in 1923 and edited it from then until 1963, at which time she became editor emeritus. She served on various committees of the U.S. Figure Skating Assoc. until 1963, at which time she was elected an honorary life member.

FLEMING, Peggy Gale.

B. 27 JUL 1948 San Jose, CA. Gold: 1968 Individual. Sixth at the 1964 Olympics, Peggy Fleming vowed she would return in 1968 to win the gold medal. She did and has since gone on to become one of the most popular professional skaters ever.

Peggy Fleming first won at the 1960 Pacific Championships and her first National Senior title was in 1964. She defended that championship every year until through 1968 and won the World Championship in 1966, 1967 and 1968. After 1965, she was never again defeated. After the 1968 Olympics, silver medalist Gabrielle Seyfert described her as a skater without weaknesses . . . a pure ballerina.

Fleming has toured professionally with the Ice Follies, Holiday on Ice, and as a special star performer with the Ice Capades. She has made six television specials, has worked as a special commentator for televised skating competitions, and has made many commercials as a spokeswoman for various products. In addition, she has been on the President's Council for Physical Fitness and was 1972 National Chairperson for Easter Seals. Peggy Fleming is married to Dr. Gregory Jenkins, a dermatologist, by whom she has had one son.

FRATIANNE, Linda Sue.

B. 02 AUG 1960 Los Angeles, CA. Silver: 1980 Individual. When only 16 years old, Linda Fratianne was already an accomplished skater, finishing eighth in the 1976 Olympics as well as being the runner-up that year in the U.S. championships. But in the next few years she wore well the crown of America's new figure skating queen.

From 1977 until 1980, Linda Fratianne won the U.S. championships and never finished lower than second in the world championships. In 1977 and 1979 she would win the world title, but arch-rival Annett Poetzsch of East Germany defeated her in the 1978 and 1980 worlds as well as at the Lake Placid Olympics.

Fratianne was a spectacular skater known for great jumping ability but possessed of all-round skills. One of her trademarks was the stunning outfits she wore while competing. After the Olympics, Linda Fratianne turned professional, signing a huge contract with the Ice Follies and eventually skating for them in their show, Walt Disney's World on Ice.

HAMILL, Dorothy Stuart.

B. 26 JUL 1956 Chicago, IL. Gold: 1976 Individual. At the 1976 Innsbruck Olympics, Dorothy Hamill became America's darling with her beautiful skating, her new hairdo, and her button-cute squint as she tried to read her scores. The hairdo was a new creation and made a household word as women everywhere asked for a "Hamill Cut." The squint was the result of not wearing her glasses or contact lenses while skating.

The skating, however, was the result of many years of hard work, usually up to seven hours a day on the ice. Her first U.S. title came at the 1969 Novice Championship but she later won the Senior title in 1974, 1975 and 1976. She was not favored at the 1976 Olympics, as she had never won the World Championships, but her best-ever school figures and a steady free skating performance enabled her to defeat Dianne de Leeuw for the gold.

Immediately after the Olympics, Hamill signed a lucrative professional contract with the Ice Capades. She has also been seen regularly on television, in specials, in commercials, and professional skating competitions. She is now married to Dean-Paul Martin, the son of Dean Martin.

HEISS, Carol Elizabeth.

B. 20 JAN 1940 New York, NY. Gold: 1960 Individual; Silver: 1956 Individual. Carol Heiss can boast of the best competitive record in international competition for any American woman. She first competed in the World Championships in 1953, aged only 13, and finished fourth. In 1955 she was runner-up to Tenley Albright, but from 1956 until 1960 she was World Champion.

Heiss finished second to Albright at the 1956 Olympics, but defeated her at the Worlds only a few weeks later. She never again lost, adding the U.S. title in 1957-60 and the North American title in 1957 and 1959. At Squaw Valley she was chosen to speak the oath of the athlete's at the opening ceremonies. Her victory that year was a foregone conclusion and shortly thereafter, she retired from amateur skating.

Heiss was one of the prettiest of figure skaters, and it was thought she would be a big draw in a professional ice show. But she had delayed the move to keep a promise to her mother, who had died in October 1956. Before her death, she made Carol promise not to turn professional until she won the Olympic gold medal. That accomplished, she took her talents to ice shows and also made a movie, appearing as Snow White in an icy adaptation of that classic, but her professional career was relatively short. In 1961 she married 1956 gold medalist Hayes Alan Jenkins.

KENNEDY, Karol Estelle.

B. 14 FEB 1932 Shelton, WA. Silver: 1952 Pairs. Karol Kennedy partnered her brother, Peter, in two Olympics. They finished sixth at St. Moritz in 1948 but improved to the silver medal at Oslo four years later. In 1950 they became the first Americans to win the World Pairs Championship.

The sixth place finish at St. Moritz was perhaps Karol Kennedy's most amazing feat. She was having severe back pains, radiating down a leg and causing some loss of control over the muscles in that leg. It required disc surgery later in the year and doctors wondered in amazement how she could have even walked, much less skated in the Olympics.

Peter Kennedy once joked that his sister's goal in life was to be married and have six children. She has succeeded.

LOUGHRAN, Beatrix S.

B. 30 JUN 1900. Silver(2): 1924 Individual, 1932 Pairs; Bronze: 1928 Individual. Beatrix Loughran is the only American to have won three medals in figure skating. In addition she was U.S. women's champion in 1925, 1926 and 1927 and won the U.S. pairs title from 1930 until 1932, partnering Sherwin Badger. It was with Badger that she won the 1932 pairs silver medal.

LUDINGTON, Nancy Irene Rouillard.

B. 25 JUL 1939 Stoneham, MA. Bronze: 1960 Pairs. Nancy Rouillard was 1957 U.S. champion in the pairs with Ron Ludington. She married Ludington later that year and together they won three more U.S. pairs championships. The Ludingtons managed a third place finish at the 1960 World Championships as well as the 1960 Olympics for their top international performance ever.

Nancy Ludington later became a figure skating coach, as did her husband. They eventually divorced.

LYNN, Janet (née Janet Lynn Nowicki).

B. 06 APR 1953. Bronze: 1972 Individual. When she began winning figure skating championships, the Nowicki family figured that dropping the last name would give Janet Lynn better marquee value. As Janet Lynn, she went on to become one of the world's most popular free skaters—one with an up and down career.

Janet Lynn had no peer as a free skater. But in her competitive days, school figures were so heavily weighted that her weak performance in those always kept her from winning a world championship. She did manage five U.S. (1969-73) titles, but when her free skating routines drove crowds into frenzies, the figure skating authorities decided it was time to change the rules. They did, but too late for Janet who by then had turned professional.

In 1973 Janet Lynn signed a huge contract with the Ice Follies but her career was a short one. She began to have poorly explained respiratory problems and would be unable to finish her routines, forcing her retirement. In 1975 she married and had children, but in 1980 judged a professional skating show. Her problem was diagnosed as allergies—now under better control—and she was inspired to try again. She has returned to professional ice shows and competitions.

Glamorous figure skater Peggy Fleming, who competed at both the 1964 and 1968 Olympics, winning a gold medal in 1968.

Courtesy Peggy Fleming

O'CONNOR, Colleen.

B. 17 DEC 1951 Chicago, IL. Bronze: 1976 Dance. Colleen O'Connor began her skating career as a roller skater and competed in the national championships in that sport when she was 15. O'Connor then turned to ice skating where she skated briefly individually before turning to dance competitions. She and partner Jim Millns first skated at the U.S. championships in 1972, where they finished seventh. They quickly improved, however, and won the U.S. title in 1974, 1975 and 1976. They finished third at the 1975 World Championships before winning the bronze medal at the 1976 Olympics. After the Olympics, O'Connor turned professional and skated with the Ice Follies and Holiday on Ice.

ROLES, Barbara Ann.
B. 06 APR 1941 San Mateo, CA. Bronze: 1960 Individual. In the late 50's, Barbara Roles was a perennial runner-up to Carol Heiss at the U.S. national championships. After her bronze medal performance in the 1960 Olympics she retired and was soon to become Mrs. Barbara Pursley. After the 1961 airplane crash which killed the American figure skating team, Barbara Roles Pursley came out of retirement—both to give the U.S. an experienced competitor at the 1962 Worlds and to act as a stabilizing influence on the young skaters who were thrust into international competition at an earlier age than they normally would have been. In that year she won the U.S. title and finished third at the World Championships.

Barbara Roles Pursley later skated with the Ice Capades for a short time. She eventually divorced and has become a well-known coach under the name Roles, numbering among her pupils Lisa-Marie Allen and 1983 World Champion Rosalynn Sumners.

VINSON, Maribel Y.
B. 12 OCT 1911 Winchester, MA. D. 15 FEB 1961 Brussels, Belgium. Bronze: 1932 Individual. Maribel Vinson was a nine-time U.S. women's champion, and a four-time U.S. pairs champion (with George Hill). A three-time Olympic competitor, she placed fifth, third, and second individually.

In 1937 Maribel Vinson turned professional and toured the country in her own ice show. She later became Maribel Vinson Owen and taught, as well as authored two books about, figure skating. Maribel Owen also became the first woman sportswriter for the *New York Times* when she wrote on major skating competitions.

Maribel Vinson Owen had two very successful skating daughters. Laurie Owen won the 1961 U.S. women's championship, and Maribel Owen partnered Dudley Richards to the 1961 pairs championships. On their way to the 1961 World Championships in Brussels, Mrs. Owen and her two daughters were killed in the airplane crash which took the lives of all the American figure skaters.

WELD, Theresa. (see Theresa Weld Blanchard)

GOLF

MEN

Golf has twice been an Olympic sport—in 1900 and 1904. In 1900 there was an individual 36-hole stroke play event for men, as well as a 9-hole women's tournament. In 1904 there was play only for men—a match play individual event and a team stroke play event. In 1904, of the 73 entrants in the individual, 70 were American, and all 30 competitors in the team contest were from the United States. There were three teams composed of 10 players each, so all players in this event received an Olympic medal.

OUTSTANDING PERFORMANCES

Most Medals
  2 Chandler Egan, Frank Newton,
    Burt McKinnie
Most Appearances
  2 Albert Lambert

CADWALADER, Douglas P.

Bronze: 1904 Team. Doug Cadwalader was from Springfield, Illinois, and played his golf at the Springfield Country Club. In the 1905 team golf event, there were six entrants, but only two teams showed up. Several of the players on hand that day decided to form a team, which, since they were all from USGA member clubs, loosely represented the United States Golf Association. Cadwalader organized this team and was its captain, and, with 84-84, had the second low score individually in the team event.

CADY, John Deere.

B. 26 JAN 1866 New York, NY. D. 12 NOV 1933 Chicago, II. Silver: 1904 Team. John Cady came from a very famous family. He was the great-grandson of Merton Yale Cady, inventor of the famed Yale Lock, and was also the grandson of John Deere, the founder of the farm equipment company.

Cady lived most of his life in Moline, Illinois, although he attended prep school at Andover. He was the founder of the Rock Island Arsenal Golf Club, near Moline, a club he represented at the Olympics in 1904. Six times he won the championship of that club. His biggest golfing achievement, however, came in 1914 when he won the Trans-Mississippi Amateur cham-

pionship. He also twice made it to the match play portion of the U.S. Amateur, surviving until the quarterfinals in 1903. In 1912 and 1913 he served a term as president of the Western Golf Association.

While in Moline, Cady operated the family stone quarry until 1920, when he moved to Chicago. There he was in the brokerage business until his death.

CARLETON, Jesse L.

B. 20 AUG 1862 Cumberland, MD. D. 06 DEC 1921 St. Louis, MO. Bronze: 1904 Team. Jesse Carleton was a member of the Glen Echo Country Club in St. Louis, which was the site of the 1904 Olympic golf events. He was expected to do well in the 1904 Olympics, as earlier in the year he had won the amateur golf championship of St. Louis. Although he qualified for the match play at the Olympics, he lost his first round match to Ned Sawyer by 8 & 7. His greatest achievement in golf came in 1914 when he was the runner-up in the Missouri Amateur championship.

CUMMINS, Edward M.

Gold: 1904 Team. "Ned" Cummins was the nephew of Albert Cummins, governor and senator from Iowa, and the son of Benjamin Franklin Cummins, prominent Chicago lawyer and president of the Western Golf Association in 1904. Ned Cummins played out of the Exmoor Country Club in Chicago, as did several other members of the Western Golf Association team which won the 1904 team gold medal. Cummins did not have a great golf record, his only notable achievement being one appearance in the U.S. Amateur—in 1902.

EDWARDS, Kenneth Paine.

B. 09 MAR 1886. Gold: 1904 Team. A member of the Exmoor CC in Chicago, Ken Edwards played for the Western GA team in the 1904 team event. Edwards was a good amateur player, but just a notch away from being top ranked nationally. He three times played in the match play portion of the U.S. Amateur, winning only one match—that in 1908. But he twice finished 72 holes in the U.S. Open, finishing 26th in 1904, and 33rd in 1914. In addition he was medalist at the Western Amateur in 1907 and 1908 and was runner-up in that tournament in 1917—to Francis Ouimet.

EGAN, Henry Chandler.
B. 21 AUG 1884 Chicago, IL. D. 05 APR 1936 Monterey, CA. Gold: 1904 Team; Silver: 1904 Individual. Prior to the emergence of Walter Travis and Jerry Travers, Chandler Egan was probably this country's greatest amateur golfer. He played in the 1904 Olympic tournament as the heavy favorite to win the individual title, having in that year already won both the U.S. and Western Amateurs. But he lost in the finals to the Canadian, George Lyon. Egan was also low man for the Western GA team which won the team event.

In 1905, Egan repeated as U.S. Amateur champion. He would play in that tournament until 1910 when he moved to the west coast, but he returned to competition after World War I and continued playing in the Amateur until 1935—33 years after his first appearance. His last shot at winning came in 1929 when he went to the semi-finals before losing. In 1934, he was named to the Walker Cup team and remains the oldest American to ever play in that event. Among Egan's other titles can be counted the 1902 NCAA Championship (team and individual) while at Harvard, four Western Amateurs, two California Amateurs, five Pacific Northwest Amateurs, and he was twice low amateur in the U.S. Open—in 1904 and 1906 (when he finished eighth overall).

Egan moved to Oregon in 1910 where he ran an orchard business. However, his hobby became his main career—golf course architecture. He went into partnership with the famed architect Alistair Mackenzie, with whom he helped design and redesign several courses. Egan also assisted Jack Neville with some of the design of the Pebble Beach Golf Links.

EGAN, Walter Eugene.
B. 02 JUN 1881 Chicago, IL. D. 12 SEP 1971 Monterey, CA. Gold: 1904 Team. Walter Egan was the older brother of the more renowned Chandler Egan. But Walter was quite a golfer in his own right. Egan first played in the U.S. Amateur in 1899, losing in the first round. In his next appearance he made it to the finals where he was slated to play Walter Travis. But the finals were postponed for a weeek due to the assassination of President McKinley. Egan, a Harvard student, had to return to Cambridge to take some exams, did not play for an entire week, and lost to Travis in the finals, 5 & 4.

In that tournament, Egan played the new, wound Haskell ball, one of the first players to use the ball which quickly replaced the old gutta percha models.

Walter Egan was frustrated by his brother in many attempts to win major titles. But in 1903, Walter beat Chandler to win the Western Amateur championship. Walter Egan also lost in the finals of that event in 1902 and 1905—to Chandler Egan.

Egan eventually joined his brother in Monterey, California, where they both played their golf at Cypress Point Golf Club.

FRASER, Harold D.
Bronze: 1904 Team. A member of the Inverness Club in Toledo, Ohio, Harry Fraser joined up with the make shift team which finished third in the 1904 Olympic team golf event. In addition, Fraser qualified for the match play in the individual event, but lost in the first round to Chandler Egan. His only other appearance in a major event was the 1907 U.S. Amateur, where he lost in the second round after defeating Olympian Walter Egan in round one.

HUNTER, Robert Edward.
B. 20 NOV 1886 Chicago, IL. D. 28 MAR 1971 Santa Barbara, CA. Gold: 1904 Team. From Chicago, Bob Hunter went to Yale, where in addition to golf, he rowed crew for the Bulldogs. In 1910, Hunter won the NCAA golf championship individually and led Yale to the team title.

Bob Hunter had a fine golf record. In addition to his Olympic gold medal, he played in seven U.S. Amateurs, and he twice made the cut in the U.S. Open (1904 and 1906). In 1911 he lost in the finals of the North & South Amateur to Chick Evans. A few years later, Hunter moved to California but he continued to play, losing in the finals of the 1922 California Amateur.

After Yale, Bob Hunter attended L'Ecole des Beaux Arts in Paris where he studied architecture, a field in which he went on to make his living.

HUSSEY, Arthur D.
Bronze: 1904 Team. Art Hussey was a member of the Inverness Club in Toledo, Ohio, and played for the third-place team in the 1904 Olympic team event. He shot 89-98 in the team event, and in the individual competition, shot 93-98, which did not qualify for match play.

JONES, Orus W.

Bronze: 1904 Team. Orus Jones was a dentist from Toledo, Ohio who played golf at the Inverness Club in that city. He was on the third-place team at the 1904 Olympics and also qualified for match play as an individual, but lost in the first round to Nat Moore. In addition to his Olympic golf appearance he also played in the 1907 U.S. Amateur, losing in the first round.

LAMBERT, Albert Bond.

B. 06 DEC 1875 St. Louis, MO. D. 12 NOV 1946 St. Louis, MO. Silver: 1904 Team. Although little known, Al Lambert is one of the most distinguished of U.S. Olympians, and the reason the 1904 Olympics had a golf tournament.

Lambert played in the 1900 Olympic golf event in Compiegne, France—finishing eighth. When plans were being made for the 1904 Olympics in St. Louis, Lambert and his father-in-law, Col. George McGrew, were instrumental in bringing golf to their own Glen Echo CC. Lambert, a left-handed golfer, played again and made it to the quarter-finals individually in addition to playing on the second-place team. Lambert's most notable achievement in golf was winning the 1907 Missouri Amateur.

In 1896, Lambert had taken over the family business, the Lambert Pharmacal Co. This later became Warner-Lambert, which markets Listerine, invented by Al Lambert's father. Lambert was also a pioneer in aviation in this country. In 1920 he purchased some land near St. Louis and converted it into a flying field. This one-time cornfield is now the Lambert International Airport, St. Louis' main airport. In 1927, when Charles Lindbergh made his trans-Atlantic flight, he was sponsored by a group of St. Louis businessmen. The group was started, and headed, by Albert Lambert. He was known in St. Louis as the "Dean of Aviation."

LARD, Allen E.

Bronze: 1904 Team. From Columbia Country Club in suburban Washington, Allen Lard joined several others to form the third place golf team in the 1904 Olympics. Lard also competed as an individual, winning one match before losing in the second round. He had two quite important wins in his career, however, winning, in 1907 and 1908, the North & South Amateur championship.

Lard was head of a manufacturing company in Washington and was instrumental in getting the company to manufacture steel golf shafts in the late 20's—one of the first companies which offered this new innovation to the public.

MAXWELL, John R.

B. 16 JUL 1871 Olena, IL. D. 03 JUN 1906 Keokuk, IA. Silver: 1904 Team. The Olympic team golf event was held on a Sunday, and Dr. John Maxwell played with the Trans-Mississippi team. He did not compete individually bcause he had to return to a busy medical practice. At the Keokuk Medical College, Maxwell was a professor of anatomy and surgery, and was one of the first specialists in proctology. He had come to Keokuk as a medical student after his undergraduate days at the University of Illinois, where he had played on the football and baseball teams.

Maxwell died very young, from kidney failure, but he had won several golf titles by that time. Among them were the 1900 Iowa State Amateur and the 1903 Trans-Mississippi Amateur.

McKINNIE, Burt P.

Silver: 1904 Team; Bronze: 1904 Individual (tied). Burt McKinnie lost in the semi-finals of the Olympic tournament to eventual runner-up, Chandler Egan. It came a few days after he had played for the second-place Trans-Miss GA in the team event. McKinnie was not a well-known golfer. He played once in the U.S. Amateur, in 1904, but he was best known as a professional musician.

McKITTRICK, Ralph.

B. 17 AUG 1877 St. Louis, MO. D. 04 MAY 1923 St. Louis, MO. Silver: 1904 Team. Ralph McKittrick was well known in St. Louis as both a golf and a tennis player. In the 1904 Olympics he competed in both sports, and although he had little success individually, winning one match in both, he did win a silver medal in the team golf.

McKittrick won several local titles in tennis, but was probably slightly better in golf. He was Missouri Amateur Champion in 1910 and won the St. Louis CC club championship three times. After his 1899 graduation from Harvard, he made his living in the wholesale dry goods business.

MOORE, Nathaniel Fish, II.

Gold: 1904 Team. Nat Moore was the grandson of his namesake, who had been president of Columbia University in the 1840's. In 1904, Nat Moore lived in Lake Geneva, Wisconsin, where he was a member of the local country club. The club was a member of the Western Golf Association and Moore was able to play on the team which won the Olympic gold medal. Moore also won a first round match individually at the Olympics before losing, 7 & 6, to Chandler Egan.

Moore later moved to California where, in 1906 and 1908, he was the runner-up in the Southern California Amateur.

NEWTON, Francis Clement.

B. 03 JAN 1874 Washington, DC. D. 03 AUG 1946 Greenwich, CT. Silver: 1904 Team; Bronze: 1904 Individual (tied). Frank Newton attended George Washington University and later Johns Hopkins. He worked as a chemist for several firms, but eventually took over as general manager of the Frink Corp., a lighting fixture company. He went on to become president and chairman of the board of Frink, and later served on the board of several of its subsidiaries.

Newton had an excellent career and it was one of the longest competitive careers of any of the 1904 Olympians. He moved to California in 1905 and in 1910 won the California Amateur as well as the Pacific Northwest Amateur. In 1915 he moved east, to Massachusetts, where he went on to win the 1923 North & South Amateur, the 1925 Mid-South Amateur, and the 1926 New England Amateur. In addition to golf, Newton was known as an expert tennis player.

OLIVER, George C.

Bronze: 1904 Team. George Oliver was from Alabama and a member of the Birmingham CC in 1904. He played on the third place team in the Olympic team event, but it is difficult to say he helped them much, as he failed to break 100 in either of the two rounds. However there were only three teams, so Oliver is considered a bronze medalist. Oliver's golf later improved and in 1909 he was the runner-up in the Southern Amateur championship.

PHELPS, Mason Elliott.

B. 07 DEC 1885 Chicago, IL. D. 02 SEP 1945 Lake Forest, IL. Gold: 1904 Team. From a wealthy Chicago family, Mason Phelps went to Yale where he played golf for three years and captained the team in his senior year. He first became known as a golfer in 1904 when he finished 43rd in the U.S. Open, and later in the year, played for the Western GA team which won the Olympic gold medal. In addition, Phelps went to the quarter-finals individually at the Olympic golf tournament.

Phelps went on to have a fine golf career. He was a prominent player in the U.S. Amateur from 1907 until 1912. In 1909 he lost in the semi-finals to Robert Gardner (three-time champion as well as a future world record holder in the pole vault) and in 1912 he lost in the quarter-finals to Jerry Travers. Phelps also lost in the first round in 1911 to Fred Kammer, whose son, Fred, Jr., played on the 1936 U.S. Olympic ice hockey team. Phelps did not always lose, however. His biggest victories came in 1908 and 1910 when he won the Western Amateur crown.

After his 1906 graduation from Yale, Mason Phelps traveled a bit and then became interested in an invention useful in manufacturing electrical supplies. The invention was successful and he formed the Pheoll Manufacturing Co., of which he served as president from 1908 until his death.

POTTER, Henry.

B. 04 OCT 1881 St. Louis, MO. D. 24 JAN 1955 New York, NY. Silver: 1904 Team. In addition to golf, Henry (or Harry—he answered to both) Potter played hockey while he was a student at Yale. He graduated in 1906 and returned to St. Louis, where he was a member of the St. Louis Country Club. Other than his Olympic silver medal, Potter's biggest achievement in golf was a runner-up finish in the 1907 Missouri Amateur—losing to Olympian Albert Lambert.

Potter later moved to New York, where he worked for a law firm for several years.

PRICE, Simeon Taylor, Jr.

Bronze: 1904 Team. Sim Price was the son of a famous lawyer and judge in St. Louis. He was not known at all as a golfer and his biggest achievement is probably his 1904 bronze medal from the team golf event. He also qualified for the individual match play event, but went out, 8 & 7, in the first round. One of his distant relatives would achieve fame as an actor—Vincent Price.

RAHM, John.

Bronze: 1904 Team. John Rahm was from Omaha and the Omaha Country Club. In addition to his Olympic bronze medal, he also played in the match play portion of the 1902 U.S. Amateur, although he lost in the first round.

SANDS, Charles Edward.

B. 22 DEC 1865. D. 09 AUG 1945 Brookville, NY. Gold: 1900 Individual. Charles Sands is one of only two Americans to have competed in three different Olympic sports—all of which are no longer held. (The other is Frank Kungler—see TAF, WLT, WRE.) In October 1900, Sands shot rounds of 81-84 to win the first Olympic golf championship. He probably didn't care as golf was not his favorite, or best, sport, even though he had finished second in the first U.S. Amateur ever held—in 1895.

Charles Sands was primarily a court tennis player. He was the only American to win the Racquette d'Or, which he received at the Tuileries Gardens in Paris in 1899 and 1900. In 1905 he won his only American championship in court tennis, although by then he was a three-time winner of the Gold Racquet tennis championships. In 1908, court tennis was an Olympic sport, under the original French name of jeu de paume. Sands played, but lost in the first round. It was not his first appearance in Olympic tennis. In 1900, while he had been in Paris for the Racquette d'Or competition, he had played in the Olympic lawn tennis event, but lost in the early rounds.

SAWYER, Daniel Edward.

D. 06 JUL 1937 Chicago, IL. Gold: 1904 Team. In this century's first decade, "Ned" Sawyer was a golfing Alydar to Chandler Egan's Affirmed. Sawyer was one of the top golfers in the country but he always seemed to run afoul of Egan, who usually beat him in the top tournaments. Still, Sawyer was not without his titles. As a member of the Chicago Golf Club he played for the Western GA team which took the 1904 Olympic gold medal. He also won the 1906 Western Amateur and the 1920 Metropolitan Amateur.

In the U.S. Amateur, Sawyer had an enviable record but could never quite pull off the victory. He lost in the finals in 1905 to Egan, lost in the quarter-finals in 1907, lost again to Egan in the 1909 quarter-finals, and later would lose to the likes of Chick Evans, Bob Gardner, and Jess Sweetser. Ned Sawyer also finished second once in the Western Amateur—in 1904—to Chandler Egan.

Sawyer later moved to New York where he represented the Siwanoy Country Club and worked for a large manufacturing company.

SEMPLE, Frederick Humphrey.

B. 24 DEC 1872 St. Louis, MO. D. 21 DEC 1927 St. Louis, MO. Silver: 1904 Team. In addition to golf, Fred Semple also played in the 1904 Olympic tennis tournament. He played on the second-place team in the Olympic golf event and also qualified for the individual match play, although he lost in round one to Mason Phelps. He played both singles and doubles in the Olympic tennis competition, defeating his doubles partner, George Stadel, in the first round of the singles before losing in round two. He and Stadel lost in the first round of the doubles. Semple was a well-known stock broker in St. Louis who founded his own company, Semple, Jacobs & Co.

SMOOT, Clement E.

Gold: 1904 Team. Clement Smoot was from the Exmoor Country Club in Chicago when he played for the Western GA team in the 1904 Olympics. Smoot also competed individually, losing in the first round after qualifying scores of 91-87. He played in the 1905 U.S. Amateur, but lost in the first round.

STICKNEY, Stuart Grosvenor.

B. 09 MAR 1877 St. Louis, MO. D. 24 SEP 1932 St. Louis, MO. Silver: 1904 Team. Stu Stickney was a member of the St. Louis Country Club and played for the Trans-Mississippi team which finished second in the Olympic team golf event. It was thought he could contend for the individual Olympic title, but Stickney ran afoul of George Lyon, the eventual champion, in the second round. He was a noted local amateur player, but attempts to compete nationally were not as successful, as he four times lost in the first round of the U.S. Amateur. He did, however, win the 1912 Missouri Amateur and the 1913 Trans-Mississippi Amateur.

STICKNEY, William Arthur.

B. 25 MAY 1879 St. Louis, MO. D. 12 SEP 1944 St. Louis, MO. Silver: 1904 Team. Like his brother, Art Stickney was a member of the St. Louis Country Club in 1904. The Olympic silver medal for team golf was probably his greatest achievement in golf although he did compete in two U.S. Amateurs, losing both times in the first round.

Stickney graduated from Yale and later went into partnership with his brother, Stuart, as stock brokers in St. Louis.

WEBER, Harold.

Bronze: 1904 Team. Harry Weber was probably Ohio's greatest amateur golfer in the early part of this century and his competitive career, at the top levels, spanned almost 25 years.

Weber was from the Inverness Club in Toledo in 1904 and remained a member there for many years. His first appearance in the U.S. Amateur occurred in 1902 when he lost in the first round. Weber played in the National Amateur almost every year, and in 1923 he qualified for the match play, again losing in the first round. In the interim, however, he fared better, making it to the 1905 semi-finals and the 1910 quarter-finals. Weber four times was amateur champion of Ohio—in 1907, 1912, 1920, and 1921.

WOOD, Warren K.

Gold: 1904 Team. A member of the Homewood (now Flossmoor) Country Club in Chicago, Warren Wood was on the Western GA team which won the gold medal at the 1904 Olympics. Individually he lost his first round match, a big upset, but his golf career was only starting.

Wood's first big year was 1906, when he won the North & South Amateur, finished 31st in the U.S. Open, and was runner-up in the Western Amateur to Ned Sawyer. The next year he went to the quarter-finals of the U.S. Amateur, losing to the redoubtable Jerry Travers. In 1910 he made it to the finals of the U.S. Amateur, but was beaten by Bill Fownes. However, in 1912, he got revenge on Fownes by beating him in the second round of the National Championship, only to lose in the semi-finals to Chick Evans. Warren Wood finally won another major title in 1913 when he took the Western Amateur.

WOMEN

A nine-hole stroke play golf event for women was contested at the 1900 Olympics. It was held at the Compiegne Club, north of Paris, and it is the only time women's golf has graced the Olympic program. The American women did quite well, winning all the medals.

ABBOTT, Margaret Ives.

B. 15 JUN 1878 Calcutta, India. D. 10 JUN 1955 Greenwich, CT. Gold: 1900. With a nine-hole score of 47, Margaret Abbott gained a measure of renown by becoming the first American woman, and second overall, to win an Olympic gold medal. Miss Abbott was from Chicago, but had traveled to France with her mother to study art and music. While there she learned of the Olympic golf event and, already an accomplished golfer, entered. Her mother also played, finishing eighth.

Margaret Abbott had learned her golf at the Chicago Golf Club, schooled by Charles Blair MacDonald and H. J. Whigham, two of the top American amateurs. Although she never played in a major tournament in this country, she was probably Chicago's top woman player in 1900, winning many of the local events.

While in Paris, Margaret Abbott studied art under Degas and Rodin, but while there she met Finley Peter Dunne, who would later become a noted American humorist. She and Dunne were married in 1902 and lived in New York for many years.

PRATT, Daria Pankhurst Wright.

B. 1861 Cleveland, OH. D. 26 JUN 1938 Cannes, France. Bronze: 1900. Daria, or more properly Mrs. Thomas Huger Pratt, won her bronze medal in 1900 by shooting 53 for nine holes. Mrs. Pratt would probably have preferred the proper title, for she travelled in the highest social circles.

Daria Pankhurst of New York first married William Wright and lived in Cleveland for several years. Her second husband was Thomas Huger Pratt, who suffered an early death several years after the Olympics. Pratt was quite wealthy and the couple spent much of their time in Europe, often socializing with royalty. In 1913, Daria Pratt herself became a member of the titled class, when she married Prince Alexis Karageorgevitch of Serbia. She remained a princess until her death.

WHITTIER, Pauline.
B. 1877 Boston, MA. D. 03 MAR 1946 New York, NY. "Polly" Whittier was a member of the Massachusetts Whittier family from which the well-known poet John Greenleaf Whittier was also descended. At 10 she moved to New York but shortly thereafter was sent to Europe, where she was educated. At the time of the 1900 Olympic golf event, she was living in Switzerland and playing her golf at the St. Moritz Golf Club. Her score of 49 in the Olympics trailed only Margaret Abbott.

Returning to America, Polly Whittier was married in 1904 to Ernest Iselin, who sat on the board of many different companies. Always interested in philanthropy, his wealth enabled Mrs. Iselin to establish in 1933 the Generosity Thrift Shop, which sold various gifts to aid many needy organizations, including the City Hospital, the Children's Aid Society, the Harlem Hospital and the Manhattan Girl Scouts.

GYMNASTICS

MEN

The United States men have fared very poorly in Olympic gymnastic competition. Only twice have we been a top nation at the Olympics and both times were in unusual circumstances.

In 1904 the Olympics were held in St. Louis and almost all the gymnasts represented American gymnastic clubs/turnvereins. The only foreign country entered was Germany, who sent eight gymnasts ("turners"). Consequently a great many "Americans" won medals. We must put Americans in quotes because gymnastics, or turning, in 1904 was a German and Swedish creation. Many of the American gymnasts were recent European immigrants who probably did not have American citizenship but still competed for American turnvereins. This has been shown to be true in the case of the Julius Lenhart, the overall champion who represented the Philadelphia Turngemeinde, although still an Austrian citizen. Given the names of many of the gymnasts, it is likely that a number of them were in a similar situation.

Because of the transitory nature of many of the 1904 gymnasts (Lenhart moved back to Austria in 1906), we have many gaps in our knowledge of them. In those cases where we have no biographical data, we list only the club represented and that athlete's medals.

In 1932 the Depression and long distance from Europe caused the Olympic entry list to be much smaller than usual. In addition, the events were held in a highly "American" manner, rather than the international style usually used. Specialists were allowed to compete on a single apparatus, which had not been permitted before, and several events rarely seen in Europe were on the program—club swinging, tumbling, and rope climbing. The smaller entry and the Americanized program put our gymnasts at a great advantage and they capitalized by winning several medals.

Since 1932, faced with the international style of competition, and fuller entry fields, the United States men have managed only one medal, that in 1972. But the 1980 boycott may have struck men's gymnastics in this country the gravest blow of all. At the 1979 World Championships, Kurt Thomas (1976 Olympian) finished second in the all-around and he and Bart Connor (1976 Olympian) each won an apparatus final. Our team placed third overall, and great things were expected at the 1980 Olympics. But it was not to be.

OUTSTANDING PERFORMANCES

Most Gold Medals
   5 Anton Heida
Most Medals
   6 Anton Heida, George Eyser
Most Appearances
   4 Alfred Jochim

BASS, Raymond Henry.
B. 15 JAN 1910 Ellis City, AK. Gold: 1932 Rope Climb. "Benny" Bass was only 5'-6" tall and 130 lbs., but competing as both a boxer and a wrestler at the U.S. Naval Academy enabled him to develop an impressive pair of shoulders. One of his training exercises was climbing a rope and the Annapolis gym coach spotted him doing that one day and recruited him for the team. It led to a gold medal in the Olympics in his only serious year of competition in the sport.

After his Naval Academy graduation in 1931, Benny Bass served in the navy until 1959, eventually achieving a rank of rear admiral.
During World War II he was a submarine commander throughout, one of only two naval officers to hold that position, and live to tell of it, throughout the war. After the Japanese surrender, Bass led 12 submarines, dubbed "Benny's Peacemakers," into Tokyo Bay.

Since his naval retirement, Benny Bass worked for the Bendix Corporation as a consultant, and today is a real estate broker.

BEYER, Emil.
B. 1876. D. 15 OCT 1934 Rockville Centre, NY. Silver: 1904 Team. Emil Beyer represented the New York Turnverein at the 1904 Olympics and helped them win a silver medal. Beyer entered the United States Military Academy in 1897, with the class of 1901, but never graduated. He lived most of his life in Brooklyn, where he eventually ran a drugstore.

BISSINGER, John F.
B. 1869. Silver: 1904 Team. John Bissinger was a member of the New York Turnverein in 1904 and was one of its top gymnasts. His best finish individually at the Olympics was fifth in the triathlon. Bissinger won several National Championships, including the 1901 and 1903

all-around title; the horse vault in 1898, 1900-01, and 1903; the pommeled horse in 1899-1901 and 1903, and the 1901 horizontal bar championship.

BIXLER, Dallas Denver.

B. 17 FEB 1910 Hutchinson, KS. Gold: 1932 Horizontal Bar. Dallas Bixler was a specialist on the horizontal bar in 1932, the only time specialists have been allowed to compete in the Olympics. He made the most of the opportunity, winning the gold medal rather easily. Bixler eventually moved into all-around competition, but was hurt shortly before the trials for the 1936 Olympics, and retired from the sport.

Bixler went on to a career as a banker. He has remained active in the Olympic Movement, serving as president of the Southern California chapter of the U.S. Olympians, and assisting the 1984 Los Angeles Olympic Organizing Committee.

CARMICHAEL, Edward.

B. 02 JAN 1907. D. 1960 Los Angeles, CA. Bronze: 1932 Horse Vault. Ed Carmichael was a member of the Los Angeles Athletic Club when he won his bronze medal in 1932.

CONNOLLY, Thomas Francis.

B. 24 OCT 1909 St. Paul, MN. Bronze: 1932 Rope Climb. Tom Connolly began his education at UCLA but in 1929 received an appointment to the United States Naval Academy. It was while he was a midshipman that he won the 1932 bronze medal. He would later receive a master's degree from MIT.

Connolly went on to become a test pilot for the navy and during the war he commanded Patrol Squadron 13 for which he was awarded the DFC and Air Medals, both with two Gold Stars. He eventually rose to the rank of vice admiral and, for a short time in the 60's, was commander of the Pacific Fleet. Connolly retired from the navy in 1971 and has gone on to do consulting work on national defense matters with industry.

CUMISKEY, Frank.

B. 06 SEP 1912. Silver: 1932 Team. Frank Cumiskey was one of the greatest gymnasts this country has ever produced. He won 22 National Championships including five all-around titles. He competed on three Olympic teams—those of 1932, 1936 and 1948—and surely would have been named to the Olympic teams during the war years. At the 1948 Olympics he was given the honor of accompanying the United States flag bearer, Ralph Craig, as part of an honor guard at the opening ceremonies. Cumiskey has gone on to become the leading American historian of gymnastics.

DENTON, William Thomas.

B. 01 FEB 1911 Texas. D. 08 MAR 1946. Silver: 1932 Rings. Bill Denton was a midshipman at the U.S. Naval Academy in 1932. In addition to his Olympic silver medal, he won the 1932 National title on the rings.

DUHA, John.

Bronze(2): 1904 Team, 1904 Parallel Bars. New York Turnverein.

EMMERICH, Max.

Gold: 1904 Triathlon. From Indianapolis, Max Emmerich competed in two sports at the 1904 Olympics. Besides the gymnastics events he entered the all-around competition in track & field. At that sport, however, his participation lasted only a few seconds; as in the first event—the 100 yard dash—he pulled up lame after only a few yards. Emmerich won the triathlon in the gymnastics program, but it was really a track & field competition. It consisted of the 100 yard dash, long jump, and shot put, and was a part of the 12 event all-around competition.

ERENBERG, Philip Richard.

B. 16 MAR 1909 Russia. Silver: 1932 Club Swinging. Phil Erenberg was 1932 National Champion at Indian Club Swinging as well as winning a silver medal in the event at the 1932 Olympics. He later earned an M.D. degree from the University of California at Irvine and become a practicing doctor.

EYSER, George.

B. 1871. Gold(3): 1904 Parallel Bars, 1904 Horse Vault (tied), 1904 Rope Climb; Silver(2): 1904 Pommeled Horse, 1904 All-Around (4 events); Bronze: 1904 Horizontal Bar. George Eyser was a member of the Concordia Turnverein in 1904 and is probably one of the most amazing stories to emerge from any Olympic Games. In the 12-event All-Around competition he placed 71st individually, despite having finished 10th in the nine-event all-around. In the other three events the triathlon of 100 yard dash, long jump and shot put—he finished last, pulled down mostly by his 13' long jump and 15.4 time for the dash.

But those marks don't look so bad in another context, for George Eyser competed with a wooden leg. Unfortunately, little is known of his life and nothing of the circumstances of the loss of his limb. He was a member of the Concordia team which won an international meet in Frankfurt, Germany in 1908, and also won the National Turnfest in Cincinnati in 1909.

GALBRAITH, William Jackson.
B. 15 SEP 1906 Knoxville, TN. Silver: 1932 Rope Climb. Jack Galbraith started his academic career at the University of Tennessee, but earned his B.A. from the U.S. Naval Academy in 1929. During his collegiate days he won the Eastern Intercollegiate rope climbing title in 1929. He would later rank high in that event nationally, without winning the U.S. Championship, and won his silver medal in the rope climb.

From 1929 until 1959, Galbraith served in the navy, reaching the rank of rear admiral when he retired. His experiences included three-and-one-half years as a Japanese prisoner of war after his ship, the U.S.S. Houston, was sunk. He eventually received a Silver Star, a Bronze Star, a Purple Heart, and a Presidential Unit Citation.

In 1960, Jack Galbraith received a master's degree from Duke University and worked there for two years as a math professor. He left to teach math at Mary Baldwin College until 1974, where he now serves as professor emeritus.

GLASS, Herman T.
B. 1879 Chicago, IL. D. 1961. Gold: 1904 Rings. Herman Glass represented the Richmond YMCA at the 1904 Olympics. He started gymnastics in 1896 in Chicago upon a doctor's advice and continued the sport when his family moved to Los Angeles a few years later. He moved to Richmond in 1903 and shortly thereafter injured his hand severely. This caused him to give up all other events and specialize only on the rings.

GRIEB, John.
Gold: 1904 Team; Silver: 1904 Triathlon. Like Max Emmerich, the winner of the triathlon, John Grieb also competed in the all-around championship in track & field. After four events he was placed last with 2,199 points, but he then had no mark in the hammer throw and the pole vault and withdrew from the competition. Grieb represented the Philadelphia Turngemeinde in 1904.

GROSS, Edward.
Silver: 1932 Tumbling. Ed Gross was from the state of Washington, but represented the Los Angeles Athletic Club at the 1932 Olympics. In addition to his Olympic medal, he won the 1933 National Championship in tumbling.

GULACK, George Julius.
B. 12 MAY 1905 Riga, Latvia. Gold: 1932 Rings. As a youth in Latvia, George Gulack divided his time between pole vaulting and gymnastics, but when he came to America in 1922 he was purely a competitive gymnast. His best event was the rings, on which he won his gold medal and also two national titles—in 1928 and 1935.

Gulack has become one of the top administrators in gymnastics. In 1948 he helped the AAU design a new set of rules to conform to international standards. He has been manager of Olympic gymnastic teams, an international judge, and is now honorary vice-president of the International Gymnastic Federation.

HAUBOLD, Frank Otto.
B. 24 MAR 1906 Union City, NJ. Silver: 1932 Team; Bronze: 1932 Pommeled Horse. From the Swiss Turnverein in Union City, Frank Haubold was the top American in the all-around event at the 1932 Olympics. He had been National Champion in the all-around in 1931-32 and also won national titles on the pommeled horse (his best event) and the parallel bars.

Haubold spent many years as president of his club, the Swiss Turnverein. He also spent 46 years with the same firm—as a textile salesman.

HEIDA, Anton.
B. 1878. Gold(5): 1904 Team, 1904 All-Around (4 events), 1904 Pommeled Horse, 1904 Horse Vault, 1904 Horizontal Bar (tied); Silver: 1904 Parallel Bars. In 1904, Anton Heida won six medals, a record bettered by only three Americans. Representing the Philadelphia

Turngemeinde in 1904, his victories in the four-event all-around and the apparatus finals were also considered National Championships. His only other national title came in the 1902 horse vault.

HENNIG, Edward A.
B. 1880 Cleveland, OH. D. 28 AUG 1960 Cleveland, OH. Gold(2): 1904 Club Swinging, 1904 Horizontal Bar (tied). It is possible that Ed Hennig can boast of a longer competitive career in sports than perhaps any other athlete. His 1904 Indian club swinging gold medal also counted as the 1904 national title and he would win that championship 12 more times—the last two in 1950 and 1951 (at age 71!).

Like many of the earliest gymnasts, Hennig took up the sport on a doctor's advice, as he was a sickly youngster. He became outstanding at club swinging, but also was a top-notch horizontal bar performer, winning that National Championship in 1911, in addition to his Olympic success. In 1942, at 62 years old, Hennig won another national title in club swinging and was third that year in the voting for the Sullivan Award, given to the nation's top amateur athlete.

HERRMANN, William John.
B. 11 JAN 1912 Philadelphia, PA. Bronze: 1932 Tumbling. Bill Herrmann's father owned one of the top physical training institutes in Philadelphia. Under his father's eye he turned out to be an excellent tumbler. Herrmann won the U.S. tumbling championship in 1928, 1929 and 1931 and was Middle Atlantic champion 10 times. In addition to gymnastics, Herrmann became an outstanding fencer, and won several local championships in foil. He later taught fencing at the Drexel Institute. After his father's death, Herrmann took over the gymnasium as its manager and has continued in that profession since.

HESS, Max.
B. Schwetzingen, Germany. Gold: 1904 Team. Max Hess came over from Germany in 1897 with his brother, Charles, and started a dry goods store in Allentown, Pennsylvania. Although the store did well, Max Hess's son, Max, Jr., became much better known as the owner of Hess Brothers Department Store, the largest such store in Allentown.

JOCHIM, Alfred A.
B. 12 Jun 1902. D. c1981. Silver(2): 1932 Team, 1932 Horse Vault. Al Jochim has won more national championships than any other American gymnast. He six times won the all-around title from 1925 until 1930 and again in 1939, but he won at least one national title on each apparatus, something no other American can claim. Overall he won 34 National Championships, eight of them in his best event, floor exercise. Jochim worked with the New York Telephone Co. for many years.

KASSELL, Phillipp.
B. 1876. Gold: 1904 Team. Philadelphia Turngemeind.

KORMANN, Peter Martin.
B. 21 JUN 1955 Braintree, MA. Bronze: 1976 Floor Exercise. Peter Kormann's bronze medal in floor exercise at Montreal was the first Olympic medal won by an American male gymnast against foreign competition and using international rules.

Kormann went to Southern Connecticut State where he was coached by former Olympian Abe Grossfeld. He had quite a year in 1976, winning the U.S. Gymnastic Federation's first Gymnast of the Year Award, winning the NCAA Division I and Division II titles (the only time one gymnast has won two divisions), and taking his Olympic medal.

Kormann has since gone into coaching. Until 1979 he coached at his alma mater but then moved on to become a coach at the U.S. Naval Academy. He has also done some work as a gymnastics judge and as a color commentator for CBS Sports.

KRAUSE, Charles.
Silver: 1904 Rope Climb; Bronze: 1904 Team. Chicago Central Turnverein.

KRIZ, Frank J.
B. 26 MAR 1894. D. c1970. Gold: 1924 Horse Vault. Frank Kriz was from California and was one of our country's greatest gymnasts in the 20's. His gold medal in the horse vault was won in slightly unusual circumstances, as the event was not held according to strict international rules, but more closely resembled a high jump competition. In addition to his Olympic medal, Kriz

won five National Championships—all-around in 1922 and 1924, floor exercises in 1924, horse vault in 1922, and parallel bars in 1922.

KUHLEMEIER, William.
B. 1908. Bronze: 1932 Club Swinging. Bill Kuhlemeier represented the Los Angeles Athletic Club at the 1932 Olympics.

MAYER, George.
Bronze: 1904 Team. Chicago Central Turnverein.

MAYSACK, Robert E.
Bronze: 1904 Team. Chicago Central Turnverein.

MERZ, William A.
Silver: 1904 Rings; Bronze(4): 1904 All-Around (4 events), 1904 Triathlon, 1904 Horse Vault, 1904 Pommeled Horse. Concordia Turnverein, St. Louis.

MEYER, Frederick H.
B. 09 AUG 1910. Silver: 1932 Team. For many years, Fred Meyer was a member of the Swiss Turnverein in Union City, New Jersey. He never managed to win a national all-around title but in 1935 was national champion on the parallel bars and horse vault, and in 1936 won the floor exercise title.

RECKEWEG, Ernst.
Gold: 1904 Team. Philadelphia Turngemeinde.

ROSENKAMPFF, Arthur H.
B. 03 NOV 1884. D. 06 NOV 1952 Newark, NJ. Silver: 1904 Team. Art Rosenkampff represented the New York Turnverein at the 1904 Olympics. He made his living as an accountant.

ROTH, George Helm.
B. 25 APR 1911 Los Angeles, CA. Gold: 1932 Club Swinging. George Roth attended Southern Cal, earning a B.S. degree in geology. He was a member of the Los Angeles Athletic Club and won many gymnastic events in California, although he never won a national title. Roth eventually put his college degree to very good use—he became a petroleum engineer and consulting geologist.

SCHMITZ, Julian.
Silver: 1904 Team. New York Turnverein.

SCHUSTER, Philip.
Bronze: 1904 Team. Chicago Central Turnverein.

SIEGLER, Edward.
Bronze: 1904 Team. Chicago Central Turnverein.

STEFFEN, Otto I.
B. 09 AUG 1874 Oberstein, Germany. Silver: 1904 Team. Otto Steffen represented the New York Turnverein at the 1904 Olympics although he had recently moved to Maryland. Steffen was one of the top American gymnasts in the 1890's. He was national all-around champion from 1898-1900, and won national titles on the following apparatus events: horse vault (1899), parallel bars (1897-1900), and pommelled horse (1898).

Steffen's move to Maryland was so he could take up a position as a gymnastics instructor at the U.S. Naval Academy, where he remained until 1911.

VOIGT, Emil.
D. Detroit, MI. Silver: 1904 Club Swinging; Bronze(2): 1904 Rings, 1904 Rope Climb. Emil Voigt was from the Concordia Turnverein in St. Louis in 1904, but he later moved to Detroit where he became a gymnastics coach and dance instructor. He attended the Normal College in Indianapolis.

WILSON, Ralph.
Bronze: 1904 Club Swinging. National Turnverein, Newark, New Jersey.

WOLF, Max.
Silver: 1904 Team. New York Turnverein.

WOLFE, Rowland.
B. 08 OCT 1914. Gold: 1932 Tumbling. Rowland Wolfe was a member of the Dallas Athletic Club in 1932. He won the 1932 national championship in tumbling, as well as the Olympic gold medal.

WOMEN

American women have competed since 1936 in Olympic gymnastics events and have managed to win a medal only in 1948. However that was the team event; consequently, eight American women have earned a bronze medal in Olympic gymnastics. It is also significant that although the 1948 Olympic gymnastic competition may have been slightly weakened by the after-effects of the war, the U.S. women competed against all the top nations at London that year.

OUTSTANDING PERFORMANCES

Most Appearances
  3 Linda Metheny, Muriel Davis Grossfeld
Oldest Medalist
  29y323d Consetta Caruccio Lenz
Youngest Medalist
  22y163d Anita Simonis

BAKANIC, Ladislava A.
B. 03 MAY 1924. Bronze: 1948 Team. Laddie Bakanic was a member of the New York Turnverein in 1948. However, she was not from the Turnverein school of gymnastics, instead having learned from a teacher of the Czechoslovakian Sokol movement.

BARONE, Marian Emma Twining.
B. 18 MAR 1924 Philadelphia, PA. Bronze: 1948 Team. In 1945, Marian Twining won her first National Championships in gymnastics—on the horse vault and uneven bars. But in 1941 she won her first national championship—in the basketball throw event at the women's indoor track & field championships, a feat she repeated in 1945, 1946 and 1951. In 1947 she married, becoming Mrs. Barone, but continued to compete as a gymnast. Like all the 1948 team members, she worked during the day and trained at night. After her 1948 success, she won two more U.S. titles, again on the horse vault and uneven bars, and also competed at the 1952 Olympics.

Marian Barone attended Temple University at night and taught physical education there for several years. She went on to earn a graduate degree at Marshall University and taught there in the mid 60's, before returning to Temple.

CARRUCCIO, Consetta Anne. (see Consetta Caruccio Lenz)

DALTON, Dorothy C.
B. 01 AUG 1922. D. 09 MAY 1973. Bronze: 1948 Team. Dorothy Dalton was from the Chicago Turnverein in 1948. She trained at night and worked during the days as a secretary with the Westinghouse Corp. She was never able to win an individual National Championship.

ELSTE, Meta Neumann.
B. 16 OCT 1921 Bremen, Germany. Bronze: 1948 Team. Meta Neumann immigrated to Chicago when she was only three-years-old, and began her gymnastics career at age six. She was chosen nine times for AAU all-America honors as a gymnast and managed three national titles, the uneven parallel bars in 1947, floor exercise in 1949, and in 1952, she won the balance beam, breaking Clara Schroth Lomady's string of 11 straight titles in this event.

LENZ, Consetta Anne Carrucio.
B. 26 SEP 1918. D. 02 JUL 1980 Cambridge, MD. Bronze: 1948 Team. As Connie Carrucio she was one of the youngest women gymnasts at the Berlin Olympics, but she continued to compete and, despite having two children in the interim, made the 1948 Olympic team as Connie Lenz. Her best years, however, were before the war, when she won eight national titles—two in the all-around, three in floor exercises, and one each on the other apparatuses.

After her competitive days ended, Mrs. Lenz served on the U.S. Olympic Gymnastic Committee until 1960 and served as a judge at all levels of competition.

LOMADY, Clara Marie Schroth.
B. 05 OCT 1920 Philadelphia, PA. Bronze: 1948 Team. Clara Schroth Lomady has dominated United States women's gymnastics like no one else. She won 39 national titles between 1941 and 1952, including an amazing 11 straight (1941-1951) on the balance beam. She won six all-around titles, won championships on all four standard apparatuses, and won five U.S. championships on the flying rings, an event no longer contested by women. For variety, she also won a silver medal in the long jump at the 1945 AAU Women's Track & Field Championships.

Clara Schroth worked during her competitive years as a secretary, trained at night, and won her Olympic medal under that name. In 1951 she married Wendell Lomady and has since spent the bulk of her time raising a family. She has also been active with the U.S. Gymnastics Federation.

SCHIFANO, Helen.

B. 13 APR 1922. Bronze: 1948 Team. Helen Schifano had a noteworthy career as a competitor, but in the world of gymnastics she is best known today for her contributions to the administrative and coaching aspects of the sport. She won seven national championships between 1939 and 1948, including the all-around title in 1947 and 1948.

Since her competitive retirement, Helen Schifano Sjursen has written 10 books on the sport, been a frequent contributor to *Gymnast* magazine (now *International Gymnast*), and issued correspondence course material for judging. She has served as a coach and teacher at camps, clinics and schools mostly in the New Jersey area. However as a judge she has worked many national competitions. She has also coached the U.S. national team in several international events.

SCHROTH, Clara Marie. (see Clara Schroth Lomady)

SIMONIS, Anita A.

B. 02 MAR 1926. Bronze: 1948 Team. Anita Simonis was a member of the Chicago Turnverein in 1948 when she won her bronze medal.

MOST SPORTS IN WHICH MEDALLED

Several Americans have won medals in more than one sport. Foremost among these athletes is Frank Kungler who won medals in 1904 in track & field (tug-of-war), wrestling, and weightlifting. This feat is unique among Olympic athletes of all nations.

It's not quite as rare for athletes to medal in two sports. Among U.S. Olympians, this has been done by eight men and three women, as follows:

Austin Clapp (1928 SWI, 1932 WAP)
Eddie Eagan (1920 BOX, 1932 BOB)
Conn Findlay (1956/60/64 ROW, 1976 YAC)
Morris Kirksey (1920 RUG/TAF)
Joseph Lydon (1904 BOX/SOC)
John Montgomery (1912 EQU, 1920 POL)
Wally O'Connor (1924 SWI, 1924/32 WAP)
Kathy Rawls (1932/36 DIV, 1936 SWI)
Aileen Riggin (1920/24 DIV, 1924 SWI)
Helen Wainwright (1920 DIV, 1924 SWI)
Johnny Weissmuller (1920/24/28 SWI, 1924 WAP)

Neglecting the slightly artificial separations of swimming, diving, and water polo, which did not exist until more recent years, five American men have won medals in distinctly different sports. Among the Olympians from other countries, this has been performed by twenty-three men and one woman (Roswitha Krause of the German Democratic Republic—swimming and team handball).

Only four people have ever won gold medals in two Olympic sports and two of those are United States athletes. Eddie Eagan is one, having won gold medals in boxing and bobsledding. The other American is Morris Marshall Kirksey who won gold medals at the 1920 Olympics as a member of the rugby team and as a sprinter on the 4 × 100 meter relay team in track & field. The foreign athletes who have won gold in two sports were Daniel Norling of Sweden in gymnastics and the equestrian events, and Carl Schuhmann of Germany in gymnastics and wrestling.

ICE HOCKEY

The United States has never been the dominant nation in Olympic ice hockey. In the early years Canada virtually always won the gold medal, and in recent years the Soviet Union has been the big power. However the United States twice won the gold medal in Olympic ice hockey.

In 1960 the Olympic Winter Games were held in Squaw Valley, California, and the defending champion Russians were expected to win the ice hockey championship easily. The United States was given little, if any chance. But the U.S. won their first three games 6-3 over Sweden, 9-1 over Germany, and 2-1 over Canada. Then, on 27 February, they faced the mighty Soviets. The U.S. took an early lead on a goal by Bill Cleary but the Russians soon tied the score, then moved ahead by a goal. Midway through the second period, Billy Christian, on an assist from his brother, Roger, tied the score. At 14:59 of the last period, Billy Christian, on another pass from Roger, beat Russian goalie, Nikolai Puchkov, to put the Americans ahead to stay, 3-2.

The next day, the U.S. faced Czechoslovakia and was behind 4-3 after two periods. In the dressing room between periods, Nikolai Sologubov, Russian captain and star defenseman, came into the locker room and suggested the Americans take oxygen to regain their energy. It was a gesture showing all the good that can come from international sport and it worked. The Americans recovered to beat the Czechs and win the gold medal.

By 1980, the Russian ice hockey machine had become legendary with several wins over the mighty National Hockey League. If the 1960 team had little chance to win the title, the 1980 team had no chance. The week before the Olympics, they played the Russians in an exhibition and were destroyed, 10-3. But this was a team that would not quit. They tied Sweden in their first game on a last second goal. Big underdogs in game two, they beat Czechoslovakia, 7-3. Norway . . . Romania . . . West Germany . . . all were beaten as the U.S. kids looked next towards the big Russian bear. After one period, the score was tied, 2-2. After two periods, the Russians had moved ahead, 3-2. Then, at 8:39, Mark Johnson tied the game on a power play. Only moments later, Mark Pavelich battled for the puck on the boards, and kicked it out to Mike Eruzione, who whistled a wrist shot past Vladimir Myskin. U.S.A. 4, USSR 3. Then they waited out the clock. With only

seconds left, ABC television announcer, Al Michaels, echoed all our thoughts when he asked, "Do you believe in miracles?" We all do now, thanks to the 1980 U.S. Olympic ice hockey team.

OUTSTANDING PERFORMANCES

Most Medals
2 Bill Cleary, John Mayasich, Richard Meredith, Weldon Olson, Dick Rodenhiser, Herb Drury, Frank Synott, Gordon Smith
Oldest Gold Medalist
29y192d John Kirrane
Oldest Medalist
36y332d Allen Van
Youngest Gold Medalist
19y71d Mike Ramsey
Youngest Medalist
16y319d Mark Howe

ABEL, Clarence John.
B. 28 MAY 1900 Sault Ste. Marie, MI. D. 01 AUG 1964. Silver: 1924. "Taffy" Abel first played amateur hockey with the Fields Nationals in 1919. The next year, he joined the St. Paul AC and played with them until he joined the 1924 U.S. Olympic team. At Chamonix in 1924, he became the first American to carry the U.S. flag in the opening ceremonies of an Olympic Winter Games.

In 1926, Taffy Abel joined the New York Rangers. He played for eight years in the NHL as a defenseman, the last five of which were spent with the Chicago Black Hawks. With the Rangers in 1927, Abel became the first American Olympian to play on a Stanley Cup champion.

AHEARN, Kevin Joseph.
B. 20 JUN 1948 Milton, MA. Silver: 1972. Kevin Ahearn was a left wing at Boston College who was drafted by the Montreal Canadiens. After the 1972 Olympics he joined their farm club, the Nova Scotia Voyageurs. At the end of the season he was drafted by the New England Whalers of the WHA, for whom he played regularly in the next season, scoring 42 points. But Ahearn was slowed the next season by a broken ankle and was sent down to the minors. He spent a few more

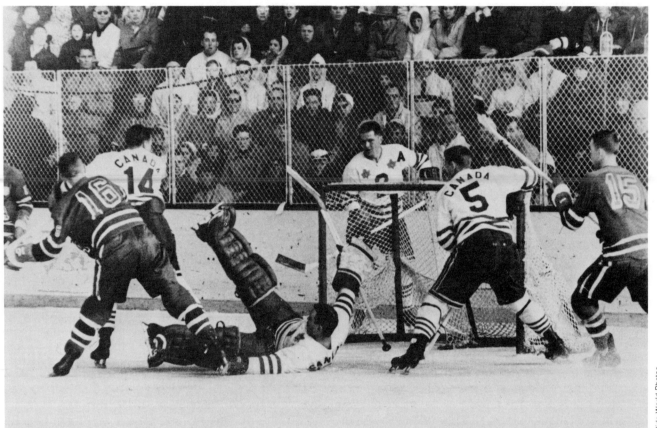

Wide World Photos

Center Paul Johnson (15) of the United States scored the winning goal against Canada in the 1960 Winter Olympic upset at Squaw Valley, California. The puck can be seen at the end of goalie Don Head's stick. Other players are left wing Weldon Olsen (16) of the U.S., and wing Fred Etcher (14), right defense Harry Sinden (2), and left defense Jack Douglas (5). The Americans eventually beat Czechoslovakia to win its first gold medal in hockey.

Members of the 1980 USA Olympic ice hockey team whooped it up on the ice at the arena in Lake Placid with American flags after defeating Finland 4-2 to take a gold medal for the first time since 1960 in the sport. Several fans joined in the celebration.

years bouncing around the minor leagues before retiring. He later began work as a real estate broker on Cape Cod.

ANDERSON, Osborne.
B. 15 OCT 1908 Norway. Silver: 1932. "Ty" Anderson was from Swampscott, Massachusetts, and played amateur hockey with the Boston Olympics. In addition to playing in the 1932 Olympics, he was a member of the U.S. National team which won a silver medal at the 1931 World Championships.

Anderson played minor league pro hockey for over a decade with the Atlantic City Seagulls and the Boston Olympics. He later became a high school hockey coach and worked during the summers as a golf professional.

ANDERSON, Wendell Richard.
B. 01 FEB 1933 St. Paul, MN. Silver: 1956. Wendell Anderson played for the University of Minnesota, graduating in 1954, and won a silver medal in the 1956 Olympics, but his greatest fame has come outside of sports.

After the Olympics, Anderson entered the army where he spent the next two years. After his discharge he entered the University of Minnesota Law School, receiving an LL.B. in 1960. From then until 1970 he had a busy law practice in Minnesota, but he also became active in politics. In 1962 he was elected to the Minnesota Senate, and served until 1970. On 3 November 1970, Anderson was elected governor of Minnesota by a comfortable margin. He was reelected governor in 1974 in a landslide victory. While in office, he expressed his concern for the environment and the family farmer by his support for new laws. He also signed into law several bills concerning judicial reform, and bills reforming existing laws on alcohol and drug use. With the election of Walter Mondale as vice president in 1976, Governor Anderson resigned to replace Mondale in the United States Senate. He served in the Senate until 29 December 1978, when he returned to the practice of law in Minnesota.

BAKER, William Robert.
B. 29 NOV 1956 Grand Rapids, MN. Gold: 1980. Bill Baker played collegiate hockey at the University of Minnesota and, while there, played for two NCAA champions—1976 and 1979. He was an excellent student in college, taking a predental course load, and was accepted at dental school but deferred it to play for the 1980 Olympic team.

After the Olympics, Bill Baker was signed by the Montreal Canadiens, but played mostly with their farm club, the Nova Scotia Voyageurs. In the middle of the 1980-81 season he was traded to the Colorado Rockies, then at the end of the year was traded to the St. Louis Blues. Late in 1981 he was picked up by the New York Rangers, where he has been reunited with Olympic coach, Herb Brooks.

BENT, John Peale.
B. 05 AUG 1908 Eagles Mere, PA. Silver: 1932. Johnny Bent went to Harrisburg Academy and the Kent School before he matriculated at Yale in 1926. He played three years of varsity hockey for Yale and one year of varsity baseball. After graduation in 1930, he played amateur hockey until he joined the 1932 Olympic team, after which he hung up the skates.

During the war, Bent served as a lieutenant for 15 months on aircraft carriers in the Atlantic. He received both a Bronze Star and a Purple Heart for his service. His business career has been as head of a financial lending institution.

BJORKMAN, Reuben Eugene.
B. 27 FEB 1929. Silver: 1952. Reuben Bjorkman sandwiched his Minnesota college career between two appearances on the Olympic team, in 1948 and 1952. The 1952 experience was far more successful and Bjorkman received a silver medal for his efforts. In 1955 he again played for the U.S. National team, this time at the World Championships. Bjorkman has gone on to a career as a college hockey coach, notably at the University of North Dakota.

BONNEY, Raymond Lenroy.
B. 1892. Silver: 1920. Bonney was from New York but represented the St. Paul AC when he made the 1920 Olympic team. Bonney was the starting goalie on that team.

BOUCHA, Henry Charles.
B. 01 JUN 1951 Warroad, MN. Silver: 1972. A full-blooded Chippewa Indian, Henry Boucha was such a

star in Minnesota high school hockey that he skipped college and went straight to Junior A hockey in Canada. He played in 1969-70 for the Winnipeg Jets before joining the U.S. National team. He represented the country at the 1970 and 1971 World Championships as well as the 1972 Olympics. Boucha was signed by the Detroit Red Wings after the Olympics and he played quite well for them for most of three seasons. In 1974 Boucha was signed by the Minnesota North Stars but missed half of the season due to an eye injury which required surgery. The eye injury hampered his effectiveness and he retired shortly thereafter.

BROTEN, Neal LaMoy.
B. 29 NOV 1959 Roseau, MN. Gold: 1980. Neal Broten was only a sophomore at the University of Minnesota when he played for the 1980 Olympic team. Minnesota and Olympic coach, Herb Brooks, called Broten, "The best freshman to ever play for the Gophers"—quite an accolade in view of their hockey tradition. After the Olympics, Broten played only one more year of college hockey, but in that year he was named first-team all-America, all-NCAA Tournament, and was the first winner of the Hobey Baker Trophy, ice hockey's equivalent of the Heisman Trophy. After that year, Broten signed with the Minnesota North Stars and had a great rookie year. His 98-point season was the third highest total ever by an NHL rookie and, in addition, he set an NHL record for the most goals scored by an American-born player with 38.

BROWN, Charles Erwin.
B. 26 OCT 1947. Silver: 1972. Before making the 1972 Olympic team, Charles Brown played college hockey at Bemidji State. He also played for the U.S. at the 1970 and 1973 World Championships.

BURTNETT, Wellington Parkner, Jr.
B. 26 AUG 1930 Somerville, MA. Silver: 1956. Wellington Burtnett was from Cambridge, Massachusetts, and attended Boston College, making all-America there in 1952 and 1953. The 1956 Olympic Winter Games were his only international experience. Burtnett still plays hockey in several old-timer hockey leagues in the Boston area.

CAMPBELL, Eugene Edward.
B. 17 AUG 1932. Silver: 1956. A Minnesota Gopher hockey star of the early 50's, Gene Campbell earned his college degree in business administration. He later put that degree to good use as a health administrator at the famous Mayo Clinic in Rochester, Minnesota.

CEGLARSKI, Leonard Stanley.
B. 27 JUN 1926. Silver: 1952. Lenny Ceglarski was from East Walpole, Massachusetts, and played his college hockey at Boston College. He played for the 1952 U.S. Olympic team in his only international appearance. Ceglarski never played professional hockey but since the Olympics has become a successful college hockey coach. He coached for several years at Clarkson, a team he led to the finals of the 1970 NCAA championships, where they lost to Cornell. Ceglarski is now the head hockey coach at his alma mater.

CHASE, John Peirce.
B. 12 JUN 1906 Milton, MA. Silver: 1932. A baseball player and hockey star at Harvard in the 20's, John Chase also was quite a horseman. In 1926 he finished third in the Bronco Riding division of the World Rodeo Championships. But it was as a hockey player that he was best known. After captaining the Harvard team in his senior year, Chase turned down pro offers but continued to play as an amateur. He played in the next few years with the Boston AA, the Boston University Club, and the Brae Burn Hockey Club. In 1932 he captained the U.S. Olympic team as it won a silver medal.

Chase later became a hockey coach, leading the Harvard Crimson from 1941 until 1951. But it was only an avocation for him; he had by then become a very successful investment counselor, a career which enabled him to set up his own company of which he remains chief executive officer and chairman of the board.

CHRISTIAN, David William.
B. 12 MAY 1959 Warroad, MN. Gold: 1980. As the son of 1960 gold medalist, Bill Christian, the nephew of 1960 gold medalist, Roger Christian, and the nephew of 1956 silver medalist, Gordon Christian, Dave Christian grew up in a very hockey-oriented environment. After making all-state in high school—where he also played football, baseball, and track—he went to the University

FAMILY AFFAIRS

It can hardly be called uncommon anymore for relatives to compete for the United States in the Olympics. But with anything that happens a lot, somebody had to be there first or with the most.

MOST MEMBERS OF ONE FAMILY—4 The Christians in ice hockey (David, Gordon, Roger and William) and the Cochrans in alpine skiing (Barbara, Linda, Marilyn, and Robert).

MOST GENERATIONS—3 The Nelsens in cycling (Chester 1928, Chester, Jr. in 1948 and Donald in 1964 father/son/grandson).

MOST AT ONE OLYMPICS—3 The Tritschlers in gymnastics (Edward, Richard and William in 1904), the Stevens in bobsledding (Curtis, Paul and Hubert in 1932), and the Hortons in yachting (Joyce, William and William, Jr. in 1952).

FIRST RELATIVES—1896 Frank Lane and Albert Tyler—cousins (both track & field).

FIRST BROTHERS—1896 John and Sumner Paine (both shooting).

FIRST SISTERS—1900 Marion and Georgina Jones (both tennis).

FIRST TWINS—1952 Edgar and Sumner White (both yachting).

FIRST BROTHER/SISTER—1936 James and Grace Madden (pairs figure skating).

FIRST OLYMPIC MARRIAGE—Richmond Wilcox (TAF) and Alice Lord (SWI) met on the boat to Antwerp in 1920 and later married.

FIRST HUSBAND/WIFE TO COMPETE, SAME OLYMPICS—Andrea Mead-Lawrence and her husband, David, both competed in alpine skiing in 1952. (The first in the Summer Olympics were Hal and Olga Connolly at the 1960 Rome Olympics.)

FIRST HUSBAND/WIFE TO COMPETE WHILE MARRIED—Frances Schroth who swam in 1920, and her husband, George Schroth, who played water polo in 1924.

FIRST OLYMPIC DIVORCE—Frances and George Schroth, who were divorced in 1925.

FIRST FATHER/SON—Chester Nelsen and Chester Nelsen, Jr. (1928 and 1948 cycling), and Paul and Hilary Smart, who were the first to compete at the same Olympics, and won gold medals in doing so.

FIRST MOTHER/DAUGHTER—Mary Abbott and her daughter, Margaret, competed together in 1900 golf. Through 1980, this has been repeated only by the figure skater, Maribel Vinson, and her figure skating daughters, Laurie and Maribel Owen.

FIRST MOTHER/SON—Alice Arden (1936 track & field) and her son, Russ Hodge (1964 track & field).

of North Dakota, where he played two years at right wing. He left college right after the Olympics to play with the Winnipeg Jets. In his first two full seasons in the NHL, he scored 71 and 76 points, good performances considering the Jets were a weak team in both of those years.

CHRISTIAN, Gordon Gene.
B. 21 NOV 1927 Warroad, MN. Silver: 1956. The oldest of the three Christian brothers, Gordy played collegiately at the University of North Dakota. He also played on two other international teams for the U.S.— at the 1955 and 1958 World's Championship. Since retiring as a player, Christian has joined the family business, Christian Brothers Stick Co., which manufactures hockey sticks.

CHRISTIAN, Roger Allen.
B. 01 DEC 1935 Warroad, MN. Gold: 1960. Roger Christian played amateur hockey in his hometown with the Warroad Lakers. He is best known for the two assists he handed to younger brother, Billy, which helped the United States defeat the Russians in the 1960 Olympics. Besides the 1960 Olympics, Roger Christian also played at Innsbruck in 1964 and played on three World Championship teams for the United States. With Billy and Gordy, he today is involved in running the family hockey stick business.

CHRISTIAN, William David.
B. 29 JAN 1938 Warroad, MN. Gold: 1960. Billy Christian scored two decisive goals against the Soviet Union in the 1960 Olympics, which enabled the United States to win that game. Christian never played collegiately, instead starring for the local amateur team, the Warroad Lakers. As did his older brother, Roger, he played on two Olympic teams and three World Championship teams. He is also involved in the family hockey stick business and is the father of 1980 Olympic gold medalist, Dave Christian.

CHRISTIANSEN, Keith R.
B. 14 JUL 1944 International Falls, MN. Silver: 1972. Keith Christiansen played college hockey for the University of Minnesota at Duluth (UMD). While there he set school records for career points, career assists, and points in a season. After his senior year at UMD, he

played for four consecutive years on the U.S. National team, representing the U.S. in three World Championships and one Olympics.

CHRISTOFF, Steve.
B. 23 JAN 1958 Springfield, IL. Gold: 1980. Another Minnesota Gopher, Steve Christoff was the top American in the NHL's 1978 draft, going in the second round to the Minnesota North Stars. But he stayed in school one more year, playing for an NCAA champion, and then joined the U.S. Olympic team. Immediately after the Olympics, he joined the North Stars and set a rookie record (since broken) by scoring eight goals in the Stanley Cup playoffs. His first full year in the pros was hampered by a broken collarbone suffered in training camp which forced him to miss 24 games, and at the end of that season he was traded to Calgary.

CLEARY, Robert Barry.
B. 21 APR 1936 Cambridge, MA. Gold: 1960. From 1955 through 1958, Bobby Cleary played hockey for Harvard and broke the school scoring record, set by his older brother, Billy. It is a record which still stands. He led the nation in scoring in both his junior and senior years, and captained the team as a senior. In addition he played three years of varsity baseball, also captaining that team in his senior year.

   After leaving college, Cleary played for the 1960 gold medalists, went into the insurance business, and also set up a casualty and property company with his older brother. He is a life member of the Million Dollar Round Table.

CLEARY, William John, Jr.
B. 19 AUG 1934 Cambridge, MA. Gold: 1960; Silver: 1956. Billy Cleary played for Harvard from 1953 to 1955 and set school records for scoring, which were later broken by his brother, Bobby. But he also set national records in 1955 for: points in a season (89); goals in a season (42); goals in a game (6); and assists in a game (8). He led his Harvard team to a third place finish in the NCAA tournament in that year. Cleary represented the United States four times internationally at the 1956 and 1960 Olympics, and at the 1957 and 1959 World Championships.

Bill Cleary has also been very successful in business, setting up a casualty and property company with his brother. In addition, since 1971 he has served as Harvard hockey coach, with his latest success coming when he took the team to a runner-up finish in the 1983 NCAA tournament. Cleary was named by hockey historian, Kip Farrington, as the top center in Harvard hockey between 1946 and 1970.

CONROY, Anthony J.

B. 19 OCT 1895 St. Paul, MN. D. 1977. Silver: 1920. After playing top-flight amateur hockey while still in high school, Tony Conroy joined the St. Paul Athletic Club and helped them win the McNaughton Trophy in 1916-17. St. Paul then took on Lachine, Quebec, for the Ross International Cup and won, despite being forced to play six-man hockey for the first time (hockey started as a seven-man sport). Conroy played for the 1920 Olympic team and still holds the Olympic record for most goals scored in one game—10 against Switzerland in a 29-0 rout. In 1925 the St. Paul Club turned professional and became the St. Paul Saints. Conroy stayed with them until 1929, despite offers to join the NHL.

COOKMAN, John Emory.

B. 02 SEP 1909 Englewood, NJ. D. 19 AUG 1982 Plattsburgh, NY. Silver: 1932. Johnny Cookman prepared for college at Phillips Exeter and went from there to Yale. While at Yale he played on the hockey team, the football team, and the tennis team. After his 1931 graduation he was selected to play on the 1932 Olympic team. Cookman later went on to become chief executive officer of Philip Morris, Inc.

CRAIG, James Downey.

B. 31 MAY 1957 North Easton, MA. Gold: 1980. It appeared that Jim Craig's story would be one of the happiest to come out of the 1980 Olympics. Craig was a star goalie at Boston University before he made the Olympic team, and he was one of the primary reasons the United States won the 1980 gold medal. After the final game, the television cameras caught him on the ice, with an American flag draped over his shoulders, plaintively looking into the stands, and asking, "Where's my father?", hoping to share the moment with him. He quickly signed with the Atlanta Flames and he (and his

father) made several television commercials. It seemed Jim Craig had it all.

But hard times hit Craig. First, he had difficulty as a pro netminder and suffered some bad games. Then he was beset by a succession of injuries which hampered a comeback. He was eventually traded to his hometown Boston Bruins. With the Bruins, however, injuries continued to haunt him, and he was shipped down to the minor leagues. Through this, Craig also began to get what some people claimed was "bad press." Craig has recently rejoined the U.S. National team and, due to new international rules, will again be eligible to play for the U.S. in the Olympics and world championships.

CURRAN, Michael Vincent.

B. 14 APR 1944 International Falls, MN. Silver: 1972. Mike Curran was a goaltender at the University of North Dakota from 1965 until 1968. After college he played both professional and amateur hockey and six times played internationally for the United States. In addition to the 1972 Olympics he was on the 1969-71 and 1976 and 1977 World's Championship teams.

Curran's first postcollege team had been the Green Bay Bobcats of the U.S. Hockey League with whom he played for three years. After the 1972 Olympics, however, he signed with the Minnesota Fighting Saints of the WHA, for whom he played for three years before returning to the amateur ranks.

CZARNOTA, Joseph John.

B. 25 MAR 1925 Wakefield, MA. D. 09 OCT 1968 Wakefield, MA. Silver: 1952. After graduating from high school, "Red" Czarnota enlisted in the marines to fight in World War II. After the war, he prepped at Brewster Academy and then went to Boston University where he played football as well as hockey. Czarnota was a legend as the enforcer for the BU hockey team, and he also served that role for the 1952 Olympic team. As a junior at BU, Czarnota was the most penalized player in the New England Intercollegiate Hockey League, and while touring Europe with the Olympic team, he was referred to by the press as the "Little Giant," and the "Bad Boy" of the American team.

Czarnota was an active supporter of youth hockey programs in his hometown of Wakefield. After his untimely death from a heart attack, a trophy was named in his honor which is given annually to the outstanding youth hockey player in Wakefield.

DESMOND, Richard Joseph.
B. 02 MAR 1927 Medford, MA. Silver: 1952. Many people consider Dick Desmond the greatest goaltender in Dartmouth College history. He minded the nets for Dartmouth from 1945 until 1949, during which time Dartmouth had its greatest hockey success ever, as they twice went to the finals of the NCAA tournament, although they came up short both times. However, at the 1949 NCAA's, Desmond was voted the tournament's MVP. Desmond had a career goals against average of less than three per game.

DOUGHERTY, Richard L.
B. 05 AUG 1932 International Falls, MN. Silver: 1956. Dick Dougherty played hockey at Minnesota from 1952 until 1954. After graduation he played on three U.S. National teams—the 1955 and 1957 World Championship teams, and the 1956 Olympic team. He has gone on to a career as a salesman in Green Bay, Wisconsin.

DRURY, Herbert John.
B. 1894 Midland, Ontario, Canada. Silver(2): 1920, 1924. Though Herb Drury was Canadian, in the strange rules of the early Olympic Games, he was allowed to play for the United States in two Olympic ice hockey tournaments. Drury managed his American association because he played club hockey for the Pittsburgh AA team. Drury was a right wing and in the 1924 Olympics he led all U.S. hockey players by scoring 22 goals in the five games the Americans played. Drury then played for six years in the NHL with the Pittsburgh Pirates and the Philadelphia Quakers.

ERUZIONE, Michael Anthony.
B. 25 OCT 1954 Boston, MA. Gold: 1980. The captain of the 1980 hockey team, Mike Eruzione is the man who scored the goal that beat the Russians. Eruzione came to the 1980 team from the Toledo Goaldiggers of the International Hockey League, a team he joined after playing four years at Boston University. While at BU, he played on four ECAC champions and later, with the Goaldiggers, he was the IHL American Rookie of the Year.

Courtesy Mike Eruzione

The man who scored the goal that beat the Russians — Mike Eruzione, captain of the 1980 Olympic ice hockey team.

Mike Eruzione retired from hockey after the Olympic Games. He said that he wanted to go out on top, as the captain of the gold medalists. Still, he has remained one of the most visible of the 1980 players. He was in great demand after the Games as a public speaker. He was also a consultant to the TV movie, "Miracle on Ice," which was made about the 1980 Olympic team. His main job is now as a hockey broadcaster for the USA cable television network.

Courtesy Doug Everett

Dartmouth's Doug Everett, who played for the 1936 Olympic ice hockey team.

EVERETT, Douglas Newton.

B. 03 APR 1905 Cambridge, MA. Silver: 1932. Doug Everett was one of the great defensemen in Dartmouth history. He graduated from the New Hampshire school in 1926 and played as an amateur with the Boston University Club and the Concord (NH) Hockey Club before joining the 1932 Olympic team.

By the time of the 1932 Olympics, Everett had already begun his career as a banker. He continued this after the Olympics and was quite successful, serving as chairman of the board of Merrill & Everett, Inc., and the New Hampshire Savings Bank until the late 70's.

FARRELL, Franklin, III.

B. 23 MAR 1908 Ansonia, CT. Silver: 1932. Frank Farrell attended Yale where he played on the hockey team for four years, but also played some soccer and lacrosse. The sports were suited to him for he played goalie at all three. Farrell never played professional hockey but instead spent several years with the St. Nicholas Hockey Club as their goalie.

Frank Farrell eventually took over the family business, the Farrell Corporation. He became president of that company in 1955, after working his way up, and in 1969 became an executive vice president of the USM Corporation.

FITZGERALD, John Edward.

B. 1891. Silver: 1920. Ed Fitzgerald was from St. Paul and played amateur hockey with the famed St. Paul Athletic Club team. Fitzgerald was a defenseman.

FITZGERALD, Joseph Francis.

B. 10 OCT 1904 Brighton, MA. Silver: 1932. Joe Fitzgerald learned his hockey on the ponds near Boston and went from there to play at Boston College. At BC, he played football and baseball as well as hockey before graduating in 1928. He then went on to play amateur hockey for several years with the University Club of Boston. At the same time he began a career as a teacher and coach at Reading High School in Massachusetts. After the 1932 Olympics, Fitzgerald was approached by the NHL to take a shot at pro hockey but declined. In 1937, he earned a master's degree in education at Boston College while continuing to teach and coach football and baseball. He stayed at Reading for 28 years, eventually being named mathematics chairman and assistant principal. In 1956 he moved to Wellesley High School where he taught math until he retired in 1970.

FRAZIER, Edwin Hartwell.

B. 21 JAN 1907 Stoneham, MA. D. 02 NOV 1971 Wilmington, MA. Silver: 1932. At Stoneham High School, Ted Frazier was a star at baseball as well as hockey. But it was as a hockey player that he made his mark in the Boston area, mainly as an amateur playing for the Boston Olympics. In addition to playing for the 1932 Olympic team, he made the 1931 national team which was the first U.S. team to compete at an ice hockey world's championship. Frazier was a mechanic by trade.

FTOREK, Robert Brian.
B. 02 JAN 1952 Needham, MA. Silver: 1972. In high school, Robbie Ftorek was all-state in soccer but it was hockey for which he was best known. He broke the state scoring record as a freshman, and then broke his own record every year until he graduated. Eschewing college hockey, Ftorek was so talented that he was given the chance to play Junior A in Canada, a chance he accepted.

After a year with the Halifax Atlantics, and his Olympic exposure, Ftorek was signed by the Detroit Red Wings. He played little for them in two years, spending most of his time with their minor league club. However, in 1974, he was signed by the Phoenix Roadrunners of the WHA, and it was in that league that Ftorek began to fulfill his potential. With Phoenix for three years, and the Cincinnati Stingers for two, he made all-WHA twice, second team all-WHA twice, was the league MVP in 1977, and voted the league's Player of the Year by *The Sporting News* in 1979. When the WHA disbanded in 1979, Ftorek signed with the Quebec Nordiques and, after two years, was traded to the New York Rangers. Through 1982 he had scored 216 goals and 523 points in professional hockey, both records for a U.S. Olympian.

GAMBUCCI, Andre Peter.
B. 12 NOV 1928 Eveleth, MN. Silver: 1952. From the Eveleth goldmine of hockey talent, Andy Gambucci took his skates to Colorado Springs, where he played college hockey for Colorado College. While there he made the U.S. Olympic hockey team which won the 1952 silver medal. After college he remained in Colorado Springs and became a referee for the Western Collegiate Hockey Asssociation, but the bulk of his time has been spent building up a very successful insurance business.

GARRISON, John Bright.
B. 13 FEB 1909 West Newton, MA. Silver: 1932; Bronze: 1936. John Garrison was one of the finest

Robbie Ftorek, from the 1972 U.S. ice hockey team, is the U.S. Olympian who has scored the most points in professional hockey.

Courtesy Quebec Nordiques

THE STANLEY CUP

It is no longer uncommon for American Olympic hockey players to go on to play in the NHL, although it once was. As a result only one U.S. ice hockey player can claim to have played for both an Olympic and a Stanley Cup champion. That one person is Ken Morrow who joined the New York Islanders shortly after the 1980 Olympics and has participated on four straight Cup champions.

The only other U.S. Olympian to play for a Stanley Cup winner was Clarence "Taffy" Abel, who played on the 1924 ice hockey squad and was a member of the New York Rangers when they won the Stanley Cup in 1928.

amateur hockey players of the 1930's. In addition to his two Olympic successes, he played on the 1933 U.S. National team which won the World Championships in Prague, Czechoslovakia. It was his unassisted overtime goal which brought the U.S. a victory over Canada in the final game.

Garrison had prepared for international play at Harvard where he played from 1928 through 1932, both as a forward and a defenseman. After his playing days were over, he continued in business but found time to coach the 1948 U.S. Olympic hockey team.

GERAN, George Pierce.
B. 03 AUG 1896 Holyoke, MA. D. 1968. Silver: 1920. Dartmouth's Jerry Geran has the unusual distinction of having played in the NHL twice—both before his Olympic appearance and after it. In 1918, he played four games with the old Montreal Wanderers club, while still an amateur. He then returned to Boston and rejoined his Boston Athletic Association amateur team. He continued to play with them until 1925 when he played in 33 games for the Boston Bruins.

GOHEEN, Frank Xavier.
B. 09 FEB 1894 White Bear Lake, MN. D. 13 NOV 1979. Silver: 1920. "Moose" Goheen is one of only three Americans to have been elected to the Hockey Hall of Fame. An outstanding football and baseball player as a youngster, he learned his hockey on the outdoor rinks of White Bear Lake and nearby St. Paul. In 1915 he joined the St. Paul AC before leaving to serve in World War I. After the war he returned to the St. Paul team and played for the 1920 U.S. Olympic team. He played the rover position for the Olympic team, as the 1920 ice hockey tournament was played as a seven-man game for the only time in Olympic history.

In 1925, St. Paul and its league turned professional and Moose did also, remaining with the team until 1932. Moose Goheen, one of the first players to ever wear a helmet, spurned several offers to play in the NHL, notably two by the Bruins and the Maple Leafs. He spent a good part of his life working with the Northern States Power Company.

GRAZIA, Eugene.
B. 29 JUL 1934 West Springfield, MA. Gold: 1960. Although Gene Grazia was from Massachusetts, he chose to play his college hockey at Michigan State. Grazia played on the U.S. National team at the 1959 World Championships in addition to his Olympic appearance. Grazia later played minor league professional hockey in Toledo for 10 years and then became a hockey coach.

HALLOCK, Gerard, III.
B. 04 JUN 1905 Pottstown, PA. Silver: 1932. "Buzz" Hallock learned his hockey at Princeton, where he played defense for four years until he graduated in 1926. After graduation he continued to play amateur hockey (with the famous St. Nicholas Hockey Club) and wrote a book in 1931 about the game of ice hockey. He also served as Chairman of the Hockey Advisory Committee at his alma mater.

Buzz Hallock served in World War II, entering as a first lieutenant although he eventually rose to the rank of major. He served in seven European theater campaigns and his outfit received a Presidential Unit Citation with an Oak Leaf Cluster. After the war he made his career as a banker.

HARRINGTON, John.
B. 24 MAY 1957. Gold: 1980. John Harrington was one of the less bally-hooed 1980 Olympians, having been a

walk-on in college at the relatively small school, University of Minnesota at Duluth. While in college he was known as a top penalty killer and was voted the school's top student-athlete. Prior to the Olympics he had not been drafted by the NHL, but he signed shortly after the Games with the Buffalo Sabres, who sent him to their farm club, the Rochester Americans. Harrington played part of a season with Rochester despite suffering a severe injury in one game. He then joined his old college and Olympic teammate, Mark Pavelich, and played a year in a Swiss league in Lugano. After returning to the United States, he coached a high school club for a year, and is now again playing for the U.S. National team.

HARRISON, Clifford.
B. 30 OCT 1927 Walpole, MA. Silver: 1952. Cliff Harrison went from Walpole High School to Dartmouth, graduating in 1951. His only international appearance came on the 1952 Olympic team.

HOWE, Mark Steven.
B. 28 MAY 1955 Detroit, MI. Silver: 1972. As a child, Mark Howe had little difficulty finding someone to teach him to play hockey. Howe is the son of Gordie Howe, the grand old man of hockey, whom some consider the greatest player of all time. Mark Howe prepped for pro hockey by playing in the Canadian Junior A leagues and then with the 1972 Olympic team. His first pro team was the Houston Aeros, and two of his teammates at Houston were father Gordie, and his brother, Marty Howe. In his first season with the Aeros, 1973-74, Mark Howe scored 38 goals and 79 points, and was voted the league's Rookie of the Year.

Mark Howe has gone on to have a very fine professional career. He played with Houston until 1977 when he and his father joined the New England (later Hartford) Whalers. He continued to be a fine player but from 1980 through 1982 his scoring fell off and many experts considered him almost finished as a player. However in 1982 he was picked up by the Philadelphia Flyers, for whom he had a very good year in 1982-83.

IKOLA, Willard John.
B. 28 JUL 1932 Eveleth, MN. Silver: 1956. Willard Ikola is usually considered the greatest goalie in Minnesota high school history—no small accomplishment in a

state where hockey is the number one high school sport. He led his Eveleth High School team to 50 straight victories in the 1940's, including three state championships. In four appearances at the state tournament, he had five shutouts—a mark which still stands.

After high school, Willard Ikola attended the University of Michigan and repeated his success there, starring on three straight NCAA championship teams. After college, while in the army, Ikola played for the U.S. National team at the 1956 Olympics, and again at the 1957 and 1958 World's Championships. Ikola has since become the hockey coach at Edina High School, in a suburb of Minneapolis, and has led the school to several state championships.

IRVING, Stuart K.
B. 02 FEB 1949 Beverly, MA. Silver: 1972. Stu Irving was from Beverly, Massachusetts, and never played hockey collegiately. But he made the 1972 Olympic team and also the 1973 U.S. National team which played at the World Championships (B Division). In addition, Irving labored for several years in the minor professional leagues. He started out with the Jacksonville Barons of the American Hockey League, but played from 1972 until 1979 with the Saginaw Gears of the International Hockey League.

JOHNSON, Mark Einar.
B. 22 SEP 1957 Madison, WI. Gold: 1980. Mark Johnson was the sparkplug of the 1980 Olympic team. He came to them from the University of Wisconsin, where he played on the 1977 NCAA champions, and was known as the top collegiate forward in the country. He was an all-American twice and was named college player of the year in 1979. Although small at 5'-10" and 170 lbs., he was highly sought by the Pittsburgh Penguins, whom he joined shortly after the Olympics. Late in the 1981-82 season he was traded to Minnesota, and before the next season began, he joined Hartford. Though he had fairly good seasons in his first two years, his last year with Hartford began to show the promise of his collegiate and Olympic days.

JOHNSON, Paul Herbert.
B. 18 MAY 1936 West St. Paul, MN. Gold: 1960. Paul Johnson never played college hockey but he has an extensive amateur and international record. Johnson played for several amateur hockey clubs in Minnesota, among them the Green Bay Bobcats, but he is best known for his many years starring with the Rochester Mustangs. In addition to his 1960 gold medal appearance, Johnson played on the 1964 Olympic team and represented the United States at the World's Championships in 1958, 1959, and 1961.

KAMMER, August Frederick, Jr.
B. 03 JUN 1912 Brooklyn, NY. Bronze: 1936. A 1934 graduate of Princeton, Fred Kammer played hockey (all four years), baseball (all four years), and golf (two years). He is known as one of Princeton's greatest right wings ever. After the 1936 Olympics, although he continued to play amateur hockey with the St. Nick Hockey Club, he became best known as a golfer.

Kammer became one of the top amateur golfers in the United States. He played in the United States Amateur championship for the first time in 1935 and last appeared in it in 1960—an impressive span of 25 years. His best finish in that event came in 1946 when he lost in the semi-finals to Smiley Quick, after defeating future pro great, Cary Middlecoff, in the quarter-finals. In 1947 Kammer was honored by being selected to play on the U.S. Walker Cup squad which played Great Britain at the Royal & Ancient Golf Club of St. Andrews.

As a businessman Kammer was also very successful. He has been a top executive with an electrical equipment manufacturing firm, which supplied most of the electrical systems to the Ford Motor Co.

KILMARTIN, Gerald Walsh.
B. 07 JUL 1926 Providence, RI. D. 16 JUN 1970 Newport, RI. Silver: 1952. "Killy" Kilmartin attended Bryant College where he played on the hockey team. He never played professionally but instead was with several amateur clubs in the Boston area. In addition to playing at the 1952 Olympics he was on the U.S. National team which competed at the 1947 and 1949 World Championships. He later became a salesman which led to the establishment of his own company, International Packaging, in Providence.

KIRRANE, John Joseph.
B. 20 AUG 1930 Brookline, MA. Gold: 1960. Jack Kirrane holds the record for the longest span of time between appearances on U.S. Olympic ice hockey teams. He played in 1948 as a member of the team which was eventually disqualified from the Olympics. He had been playing amateur hockey for the Boston Olympics and, after the Olympics, he had some feelers from the Bruins, but Uncle Sam quickly put an end to thoughts of a pro career. Kirrane sat out the next two Olympics, but did play on the 1957 U.S. national team at the World Championships. In 1960 he again made the Olympic team—12 years after his first appearance. He also was able to play for the 1963 U.S. team at the World Championships which was his last fling with competitive hockey. Jack Kirrane has worked for many years with the Brookline Fire Department.

LaBATTE, Philip William.
B. 05 JUL 1911 St. Paul, MN. Bronze: 1936. Phil LaBatte was really the first of the great college hockey players to come out of the University of Minnesota. He led his Gopher teams to three straight Western Conference championships and was captain of the team in 1934. He also played baseball while in college.

After his 1934 graduation, LaBatte played on the 1936 Olympic team and then played some professional hockey in Chicago, Portland (OR), and Baltimore, although he never played in the NHL. He went on to officiate hockey for a few years; however, his main job was with the U.S government, working for several years in the interior department and later serving as chief of special services with the U.S. Veterans Administration. He now calls himself semiretired, but dabbles in sales in home improvement.

LaCROIX, Alphonse A.
B. 21 OCT 1900. Silver: 1924. Alphonse LaCroix was a goalie from Newton, Massachusetts, and played his amateur hockey with the Boston Athletic Association club. After the Olympics he had a brief fling in pro hockey, playing in four games with the Montreal Canadiens.

LANGLEY, John Arthur.

B. 25 JUN 1896. Silver: 1924. Art Langley was from Melrose, Massachusetts, when he made the 1924 Olympic team.

LAX, John Charles.

B. 05 JUL 1911 Arlington, MA. Bronze: 1936. John Lax played both hockey and football at Boston University. It was as a senior at BU that Lax made the 1936 Olympic team. Lax earned a degree in education in college and has worked as a high school teacher since graduation, except for a break during the war when he served in the air force.

LIVINGSTON, Robert Cambridge.

B. 03 NOV 1908. D. 02 APR 1974 New Canaan, CT. Silver: 1932. Bob Livingston played college hockey as a defenseman at Princeton, graduating in 1931. After graduation he joined the U.S. Olympic team and won a silver medal in 1932. He then became a representative of the Grace Line in Peru for 12 years before serving in World War II as a lieutenant commander in the navy.

After World War II, Bob Livingston eventually rose to the presidency of International Instruments, Inc., a company which manufactured electronic components. He relinquished that position in 1969 when the company was sold although he remained on the board of directors.

LYONS, John Sharkey.

B. 04 APR 1899 Arlington, MA. D. 15 JAN 1971 Arlington, MA. Silver: 1924. John Lyons played amateur hockey for many years with the Boston AA club. It was while he was playing for this club that he made the 1924 Olympic team.

MATCHEFTS, John Peter.

B. 18 JUN 1931 Eveleth, MN. Silver: 1956. John Matchefts played on the Eveleth High School teams which won three straight Minnesota high school tournaments in the late 40's. He was a center with great speed and was highly recruited. He eventually went to the University of Michigan, where he helped that school also win three straight championships—this time of the NCAA version. In his last NCAA appearance, in 1953, Matchefts was voted the tournament's MVP.

After graduation in 1953, Matchefts served in the marines as a commissioned officer until 1956. He played on the 1955 and 1957 U.S. World Championship teams in addition to his Olympic participation. In 1956 he took a job as a high school hockey coach at Thief River, Minnesota, which lasted until 1958. He then took over his old high school's hockey team until 1966 at which time he was named head coach at Colorado College.

MAYASICH, John E.

B. 22 MAY 1933 Eveleth, MN. Gold: 1960; Silver: 1956. John Mayasich is one of the greatest hockey players to ever play for the Minnesota Gophers. He played from 1952 through 1955 and made all-America for three straight years, capturing the Western Collegiate Hockey Association scoring title in both of his last two years. In addition, he still holds the NCAA tournament record for the most points scored in one game—seven against Boston College in 1954. His career after leaving college was also distinguished. He declined several professional offers to continue playing amateur hockey, mainly with the Green Bay Bobcats. He played internationally for the United States more than any other man—playing on the 1956 and 1960 Olympic teams, and on the World Championship teams of 1957, 1958, 1961, 1962, 1966, and 1969.

John Mayasich is remembered at his college by the annual presentation of the Mayasich Award, given to the best student-athlete on the hockey team. He has gone on to work in the Twin Cities area for a local radio and television station.

McCARTAN, John William.

B. 05 AUG 1935 St. Paul, MN. Gold: 1960. From the University of Minnesota, Jack McCartan was the most famous of the 1960 Olympians. He was the goalie who seemingly stopped every shot thrown at him. After the Olympics he was in great demand to play professional hockey—quite a rarity for an American in 1960. He signed with the Rangers and played in four games in the 1959-60 season, and eight more in the next year, but he never again played in the NHL.

McCARTHY, Justin Jeremiah.

B. 25 JAN 1899 Charleston, MA. D. 08 APR 1976 Centerville, MA. Silver: 1924. Justin McCarthy was from

Arlington, Massachusetts, and attended the University of Massachusetts, graduating in 1921. He became an accountant, working for Monsanto Chemical and Acton Cross Co.

McCLANAHAN, Robert B.

B. 09 JAN 1958 St. Paul, MN. Gold: 1980. "Mac" played for the Minnesota Gophers in college, where he was known as one of the fastest skaters in college hockey. Signed by the Buffalo Sabres immediately after the Olympics, he played two years for them and their farm club in Rochester. In 1981 he was claimed on waivers by Hartford and spent most of the next season playing for their minor league teams. In February of 1982, he was traded to the New York Rangers, rejoining Olympic coach Herb Brooks, where he has been more successful.

McCORMICK, Joseph W.

B. 1891. Silver: 1920. Joe McCormick and his brother, Larry, were actually Canadians, both hailing from Buckingham, Quebec. However they played for the United States in 1920 because they represented the Pittsburgh AA team. Joe McCormick was a left wing who captained the 1920 ice hockey team.

McCORMICK, Lawrence J.

B. 1893. Silver: 1920. Larry McCormick was from Buckingham, Quebec, but played for the United States at the 1920 Olympics. He was a member of the Pittsburgh AA team which won the McNaughton Cup, given to the U.S. national amateur champions, in both 1918 and 1920.

McELMURY, James Donald.

B. 03 OCT 1949 St. Paul, MN. Silver: 1972. While in college at Bemidji State, Jim McElmury made the 1970 and 1971 U.S. National teams. After his graduataion in 1971, he also made the 1972 Olympic team and would later play for the U.S. in the 1976 and 1977 World Championships, giving him five international appearances in all.

McElmury, a defenseman, also played pro hockey from 1972 until 1978. He was signed by the Minnesota North Stars after the Olympics but played mostly with their farm clubs. In 1974 he was picked up by the NHL's Kansas City Scouts, for whom he played in 78 games

that year, his finest NHL season. Until 1978 he played for Kansas City and later the Colorado Rockies and their farm clubs. In that year he tore ligaments in his right knee, ending his career.

McGLYNN, Richard Anthony.

B. 19 JUN 1948 Medford, MA. Silver: 1972. Dick McGlynn played for the Massachusetts high school hockey power, Catholic Memorial, until 1966. He then went to Colgate University where he became one of that school's greatest hockey players ever. After college he played for the 1971 U.S. National team at the World Championships before making the 1972 Olympic team.

Upon his return to the United States, Dick McGlynn was able to play pro hockey with the Chicago Cougars of the fledgling World Hockey Association. He retired after one year to become a coach with the North Shore Red Wings of the North East Junior A Hockey League.

McKINNON, Daniel Duncan.

B. 21 APR 1922 Williams, MN. Silver: 1956. In addition to his role on the 1956 Olympic team, Dan McKinnon also represented the United States at the 1955 and 1958 World's Championships. He had started playing big time hockey at the University of North Dakota, which he attended from 1947 through 1950.

McVEY, Robert Patrick.

B. 14 MAR 1936 Hartford, CT. Gold: 1960. Bob McVey attended Harvard and played left wing on their hockey team. His biggest honor in college came in 1958 when he was awarded the John Tudor Memorial Cup as the MVP of the Harvard hockey team. In addition to playing on the 1960 Olympic champions, McVey represented the United States at the 1959 World's Championships. After the Olympics, McVey returned to his home in Connecticut where he had set up his own insurance business, which still occupies much of his time.

MELLOR, Thomas Robert.

B. 27 JAN 1950 Cranston, RI. Silver: 1972. Tom Mellor was a 6'-1", 185 lb. defenseman who attended Boston College. During his time in school in played for the 1972 Olympic team and the 1971 and 1973 U.S. National teams at the World's Championship. In his senior season he was voted first team all-East.

Mellor then went on to have a short career in the NHL. He was signed by the Detroit Red Wings, but spent most of his time with their minor league club, the Virginia Wings. He also spent part of the 1973-74 season playing in a British hockey league with the London Lions.

MEREDITH, Richard O.

B. 22 DEC 1932 South Bend, IN. Gold: 1960; Silver: 1956. Dick Meredith attended the University of Minnesota where he played forward on their hockey team all four years and made the 1956 Olympic team as a junior. He graduated in 1957 but continued to play amateur hockey, representing the United States at the 1958 and 1959 World Championships and then at the 1960 Olympics.

Meredith has remained in hockey. Since the formation of the Minnesota North Stars NHL club, he has been in the front office, serving as both a sales and a community relations director.

MOON, Thomas Henry.

B. 06 NOV 1908 Ottawa, Ontario, Canada. Bronze: 1936. Tom Moon was born in Canada but grew up near Boston, and attended school in the area. He never played college hockey but was a star with the Boston Olympics, helping win the U.S. Amateur Championship in 1935, 1937, and 1939. He has remained in the Boston area as a sales manager for a large metal company.

MORROW, Kenneth.

B. 17 OCT 1956 Flint, MI. Gold: 1980. At 6'-4" and 210 lbs., Ken Morrow is the prototype of an NHL defenseman. He was a star at Bowling Green University, where he was that school's first hockey all-American, and named the Central Collegiate Hockey Association's Player of the Year. But he was coveted by the New York Islanders who waited patiently while he played with the Olympic team.

Morrow joined the Islanders immediately after the Olympics and made history. The Islanders won the Stanley Cup in 1980 and Ken Morrow became the first American to play for an Olympic champion and a Stanley Cup champion. Morrow has skated a regular shift with the Islanders now for three-and-one-half years as they have continued to win, having now played on four consecutive Stanley Cup championship teams.

MULHERN, John Francis.

B. 18 JUL 1927. Silver: 1952. John Mulhern was a Boston College graduate who competed for the 1952 Olympic team in his only international appearance.

NASLUND, Ronald Alan.

B. 28 FEB 1943. Silver: 1972. Ron Naslund was from Minneapolis but he went to Denver University. After graduation he continued to play amateur hockey in Minneapolis, notably with the Rochester Mustangs. He represented the United States at three World Championships (1966, '67, and '69) as well as at the 1972 Olympics.

NELSON, Francis Augustus, Jr.

B. 24 JAN 1910 New York, NY. D. 09 MAR 1973 Upper Montclair, NJ. Silver: 1932. Frank Nelson went to Yale and was a great all-round athlete for the Elis. At Yale, in addition to playing hockey for four years, Nelson played soccer, baseball, and rowed for the crew team. After his 1931 graduation he immediately went into the insurance business, interrupting it briefly to make the 1932 Olympic team. He did quite well as an insurance broker and remained in that profession all his life.

NOAH, John Michael.

B. 21 NOV 1927 Crookston, MN. Silver: 1952. John Noah played collegiately at the University of North Dakota from 1947 until 1951. After graduation he played club hockey until he made the 1952 Olympic team, his only international appearance.

O'CALLAHAN, John.

B. 24 JUL 1957 Charlestown, MA. Gold: 1980. Jack O'Callahan played at Boston University and was on the 1978 NCAA championship team. In that year he was named the team's MVP and the school's Athlete of the Year. O'Callahan graduated from BU in 1979 with plans to eventually enter law school. But he would defer those plans to play first with the Olympic team and then in the NHL.

After the Olympics, Jack O'Callahan signed with the Chicago Black Hawks. Hampered by a knee injury and eventual surgery, he played little in the NHL for two years, playing mainly with the New Brunswick and Springfield farm clubs. However in late 1982 he was called up to the Chicago team and spent most of the next season on their roster.

OLDS, Walter Raymond.
B. 17 AUG 1949 Warroad, MN. Silver: 1972. At 6'-2" and 200 lbs., Wally Olds certainly was the right size for a defenseman. He played that position at every level of hockey, starting with the University of Minnesota, where he made all-western all-America in 1970. After graduation in 1971 he spent a year with the U.S. National team during which time he played in the Olympics.

Olds was signed by the Detroit Red Wings of the NHL and later the Chicago Cougars of the WHA. However he never played hockey in either major league. Instead he bounced around the minors with such teams as the Long Island Ducks, the New York Raiders, and the Oklahoma City Blazers. His best year in pro hockey was probably 1975 when, as a member of the Hampton Gulls, he was voted co-MVP of the Southern Hockey League. After leaving pro hockey, Olds played with the 1977 and 1979 U.S. National teams at the World Championships.

OLSON, Weldon Howard.
B. 12 NOV 1932 Marquette, MI. Gold: 1960; Silver: 1956. Weldy Olson was from Marquette, Michigan, and played college hockey at Michigan State. He represented the United States internationally for five straight years, sandwiching three world championship appearances in between his two Olympic medals.

OSS, Arnold Carl, Jr.
B. 18 APR 1928 Minneapolis, MN. Silver: 1952. As the son of a member of the Basketball Hall of Fame, Arnie Oss was probably destined for athletic greatness, though few could have predicted it to be as a hockey player. Oss was probably the greatest defenseman to ever play for Dartmouth. He played on the great Big Green teams of the late 40's which twice finished second in the NCAA tournament. As a sophomore and senior, he had great years, scoring 39 and 55 points, including 36 goals in his senior year. However he totalled "only" 98 points for his career because of injuries in his junior year which kept him out most of the year. The 1952 Olympics were his only international appearance.

OWEN, Edwyn Robert.
B. 08 JUN 1936 Minneapolis, MN. Gold: 1960. A Harvard graduate, class of '58, Bob Owen was a member of the great Harvard class which included Bob McVey and Bobby Cleary. Still, in 1957 he was voted by his teammates the Donald Angier Trophy, given to the Harvard hockey player who shows the greatest improvement over the course of a season. After graduation, Owen played hockey for two more years, during which time he made the 1960 Olympic team.

Owen eventually attended Stanford Business School, obtaining an M.B.A. in 1964. He later became a professor of business at Washburn University in Topeka, Kansas.

PAAVOLA, Rodney E.
B. 21 AUG 1939 Hancock, MI. Gold: 1960. Rod Paavola was from Hancock, Michigan, and played most of his hockey with the Portage Lake Pioneers. His only international appearance came at the 1960 Olympics when he and Bob Owen skated a shift together as defensemen.

PALMER, Laurence James.
B. 07 JAN 1938 Malden, MA. Gold: 1960. Larry Palmer received a commission to the U.S. Military Academy from which he graduated in 1959. After leaving West Point, he put in his required five years in the service, but found time to play on the 1960 Olympic team as well as the 1961 World Championship team. Palmer left the army in 1964 and has gone on to a very successful career as an investment banker and counselor.

PALMER, Winthrop Hale, Jr.
B. 05 DEC 1905 Summit, NJ. D. 04 FEB 1970 Madison, CT. Silver: 1932. In addition to his Olympic silver medal, "Ding" Palmer played on the 1933 U.S. National team which remains the only American team to have ever won the World's Championship in ice hockey. Palmer prepared for his international exploits while at Yale where he played on the hockey team for four years. In the 1927-28 season he scored an amazing 41 goals, including seven in one game against New Hampshire. He ended up setting the Yale record for career points scored and led the team to a 17-1-1 record in 1930, when they were called the greatest amateur hockey team in history.

After college he played amateur hockey for several years with the St. Nicholas Hockey Club. He eventually settled in Connecticut, where he lived all his life and made his living as a stockbroker in New Haven.

PAVELICH, Mark.

B. 28 FEB 1958 Eveleth, MN. Gold: 1980. A teammate of John Harrington's at Minnesota-Duluth, Mark Pavelich was not drafted by the NHL but hoped his Olympic experience would get him a shot at the bigs. After the Olympics he went to Lugano, Switzerland, and played for a year in the European leagues. In 1981 he was given his chance when he signed with the New York Rangers, and he did not disappoint them, scoring 76 points in 1981-82. In his next season he set an NHL record for most goals in one game (five) by an American-born player.

PETROSKE, John Edward.

B. 06 AUG 1934 Hibbing, MN. Silver: 1956. John Petroske was not originally selected to play on the 1956 Olympic team, failing to survive the final cut. However an injury to Frank O'Grady opened up a spot on the team and Petroske was able to play at Cortina. Petroske was a college junior at the University of Minnesota at the time. He played hockey all four years at Minnesota, and also represented the U.S. at the 1958 World Championships after graduation in 1957.

PURPUR, Kenneth Richard.

B. 01 MAR 1932 Grand Forks, ND. Silver: 1956. Ken Purpur played college hockey at his homestate school, the University of North Dakota, from 1951 through 1954. His only international experience came in 1956 when he helped the United States win the silver medal at Cortina. Purpur has since gone on to become a school teacher.

RAMSEY, Michael Allen.

B. 03 DEC 1960 Minneapolis, MN. Gold: 1980. In high school, Mike Ramsey was heavily recruited as a hockey player, but he also played a pretty fair game of tennis. He was third in the Minnesota state championships in tennis, and seventh in the Midwest 16-and-under tournament. But his size, 6'-3" and 190 lbs., made him a natural defenseman and he accepted a hockey scholarship to the University of Minnesota.

HERBERT PAUL BROOKS

While a student at the University of Minnesota, Herb Brooks was the last player cut from the 1960 U.S. Olympic ice hockey team, which went on to win the gold medal. Brooks thus did not get his gold medal and 20 years later, he would again be denied that honor because the coaches do not receive medals. But Brooks certainly gained a measure of pride in leading the 1980 U.S. ice hockey team to the Olympic gold medal.

Herb Brooks was born in St. Paul on 5 August 1937. Small at 5'-11" and 168 lbs., he played hockey for four years at Minnesota. Although cut from the 1960 Olympic team, he played on both the 1964 and 1968 U.S. Olympic teams, but neither team won a medal. Brooks also represented the United States four other times in international competition.

Brooks became the coach at his alma mater in the early 70's and led the Minnesota hockey powerhouse to several NCAA championships. After his Olympic success, he was courted by several NHL clubs but turned them all down to coach with a Swiss team in a European league. But Brooks has now returned to the United States to coach the NHL New York Rangers, with whom he has continued to have success.

However, after his freshman year at Minnesota, he joined the Olympic team, and after the Olympics, he turned pro with the Buffalo Sabres of the NHL. Ramsey has been one of the best pros of the 1980 Olympians. He has skated a regular shift with the Sabres since 1980 and, in 1983, was named to the All-Star game squad.

RICE, Willard Wadsworth.

B. 21 APR 1895 Newtonville, MA. D. 21 JUL 1967 Weston, MA. Silver: 1924. Willard Rice went to Harvard and graduated in 1918. After graduation he continued to play hockey with the Boston Athletic Association and made the 1924 Olympic team while playing for that club. Rice went on to a career as a soap manufacturer.

RIGAZIO, Donald Edmond.
B. 03 JUL 1934 Cambridge, MA. Silver: 1956. Don Rigazio accepted a hockey scholarship to Boston University but did not finish school, leaving to play Jr. A hockey in Canada. He represented the United States on four consecutive international teams, the World Championship teams of 1955, 1957, and 1958, and the 1956 Olympic team. He then turned pro and played in the minors for two years.

RODENHISER, Richard.
B. 17 OCT 1932 Malden, MA. Gold: 1960; Silver: 1956. Dick Rodenhiser was from Malden, Massachusetts,and played collegiately for the Boston University Terriers. In addition to winning medals at both the 1956 and 1960 Olympics, he represented the United States on the 1955 and 1957 National teams. Today he is the manager of a large ice rink in the suburban Boston area.

ROMPRE, Robert Edward.
B. 11 APR 1929. Silver: 1952. Bob Rompre was from International Falls, Minnesota, and played college hockey at Colorado College. His only international experience came at the 1956 Olympics.

ROSS, Elbridge Baker, Jr.
B. 02 AUG 1909 Boston, MA. Bronze: 1936. Elbridge Ross attended Colby College where he played both hockey and baseball. After graduating with a B.S. degree from Colby, Ross played amateur hockey before being selected for the 1936 Olympic team. Ross made his career as an equipment engineer with the New England Telephone & Telegraph Company for 36 years. He is now retired and spends his time with his hobbies of fishing and photography.

ROWE, Paul Edward.
B. 05 MAY 1914 Somerville, MA. Bronze: 1936. In addition to playing hockey at Boston University, Paul Rowe played golf and captained that team in his senior year. After his 1935 graduation he made the Olympic team in 1936. He went on to become an executive with an advertising firm, and worked with a prominent insurance company.

SAMPSON, Edward H.
B. 23 DEC 1921. Silver: 1956. Ed Sampson was from International Falls, Minnesota. He never played collegiately but played in many of the Minnesota amateur hockey leagues. The 1956 Olympics were his only international appearance.

SANDERS, Franklynn B.
B. 08 MAR 1949. Silver: 1972. Frank Sanders won varsity letters in hockey at Minnesota in 1969, 1970, and 1971 before making the 1972 Olympic team.

SARNER, Craig Brian.
B. 20 JUN 1949 St. Paul, MN. Silver: 1972. Craig Sarner played for the Minnesota Gophers from 1969 until 1971. The year after graduation he played club hockey in Minnesota and then made the U.S. Olympic team in 1972. He signed a pro contract in 1972 but played almost exclusively in the minor leagues. His one NHL stint came in 1975 when he appeared in seven games for the Boston Bruins. After leaving pro hockey he continued to play club hockey and represented the United States at the 1976 and 1979 World's Championships.

SCHNEIDER, William C.
B. 14 SEP 1954 Grand Rapids, MN. Gold: 1980. "Buzz" Schneider went to the University of Minnesota where he played hockey. He had also hoped to play baseball in college and even considered a pro career in that sport, but hockey took up all of his time. Buzz has been a regular on U.S. National teams since 1974. He played on the 1976 Olympic team and on the U.S. world's teams from 1974 through 1977. Starting in 1978 he played in the International Hockey League, before making the 1980 U.S. Olympic team. After the Olympics, Schneider played for Bern in the Swiss leagues for two years before rejoining the U.S. National team. However his latest efforts to make another Olympic team have been sidelined by back surgery.

SEARS, Gordon Peter.
B. 14 MAR 1947. Silver: 1972. Gordy Sears was from Lake Placid and played college hockey at Oswego State. The 1972 Olympics were his only international exposure.

SEDIN, James Walter.
B. 25 JUN 1930. Silver: 1952. A major in physics at the University of Minnesota did not prevent Jim Sedin from earning two varsity letters in hockey. After graduation, this St. Paul native played for the 1952 U.S. Olympic team.

SHAUGHNESSY, Francis John, Jr.
B. 21 JUN 1911 Roanoke, VA. D. 12 JUN 1982 Montreal, Canada. Bronze: 1936. Frank Shaughnessy was the son of "Shag" Shaughnessy, one of the legendary figures in Canadian athletics, and a two-time captain of the Notre Dame football team. Frank himself went on to become a legend in Canadian sports.

Shaughnessy attended McGill University where he played hockey, but was better known as an all-star halfback on the football team. Although he was really Canadian, he was able to play on the U.S. Olympic team because he carried a dual citizenship, having been born in Virginia. His career after the Olympics began with Bell Telephone and he remained with them until 1973.

It was as a sports administrator that Shaughnessy is best known. He was active for many years in the Canadian Olympic Association, serving as *chef de mission* at five Olympic Winter Games for the Canadian team. He was vice president of that organization from 1957 through 1975, and served on the Organizing Committee of the Montreal Olympic Games. In addition he was active as an administrator in both the Canadian Ski Association and the Canadian and Quebec Golf Associations.

SHEEHY, Timothy Kane.
B. 03 SEP 1948 Ft. Frances, ONT, Canada. Silver: 1972. Tim Sheehy had one of the most successful pro hockey careers of any U.S. Olympian. After the 1972 Olympics he was signed by the New England Whalers of the WHA. As a right wing he totaled 33 and 29 goals, and 71 and 58 points in his first two pro seasons. However he slumped a bit in 1974-75 and was traded to the Edmonton Oilers. With the Oilers he also played three years, his best one being 1975-76 when he had 34 goals and 65 points. Sheehy later played for the Birmingham Bulls of the WHA and the Detroit Red Wings in the NHL before finishing up his career where it started—with a last season with the New England Whalers.

SILK, David.
B. 01 JAN 1958 Scituate, MA. Gold: 1980. Dave Silk comes from a strong athletic background, counting among his relatives, cousin Mike Milbury of the Bruins and grandfather Hal Janvrin of the Red Sox. But Silk followed Milbury to the hockey rinks. He was a star forward for three years at Boston University where he played for an NCAA champion, two ECAC champions, and helped BU win two Beanpot Trophies, as the best Boston-area college hockey team. After the Olympics, Silk left school to play pro hockey. His first year was spent mostly in the American Hockey League, but he played most of 1980-82 with the New York Rangers. He had some problems starting the 1982-83 season and played only a brief time with the Rangers before being sent down.

SMALL, Irving Wheeler.
B. 29 JUL 1891 Cambridge, MA. D. 12 DEC 1925 Monrovia, CA. Silver: 1924. Irv Small was brought up in Massachusetts and played amateur hockey as a member of the Boston AA team. In 1913, however, he moved to California, but came east to play hockey during the winters. He made the 1924 ice hockey team while still a member of the BAA.

SMITH, Gordon.
B. 14 FEB 1908 Winchester, MA. Silver: 1932; Bronze: 1936. Although he attended Boston University briefly, Gordon Smith played most of his amateur hockey with the Boston Hockey Club and the Boston Olympics. In addition to his silver medals, he was on the U.S. National team that competed at the 1931 World Championships. Smith later became very successful as an investment counselor with Standish, Ayer & Wood in Boston.

SPAIN, Francis Jones.
B. 17 FEB 1909 Quitman, GA. D. 23 JUN 1977 Rochester, NY. Bronze: 1936. Frank Spain was born on an ancestral plantation in Georgia but later moved to Waban, Massachusetts, where he learned to play hockey. He attended Phillips Exeter prep school and then Dartmouth, where he majored in philosophy and played hockey and baseball. After college he played for an amateur team, the Boston Olympics, and also toured Europe for several years. Following his 1941 marriage,

Spain moved to Rochester, NY, where he began a career in the abrasive business, eventually forming his own company, Grinding Supply, Inc.

STROBEL, Eric Martin.
B. 05 JUN 1958. Gold: 1980. With a father who played for the New York Rangers, it was only natural that Eric Strobel would become a hockey player. Strobel went to the University of Minnesota where he played on the 1979 NCAA champions. He signed with the Buffalo Sabres shortly after the Olympics. He was sent to the Rochester Americans where he played for one month before breaking an ankle. He returned the next year to play briefly in Baltimore before retiring. Strobel returned to college to get his degree.

STUBBS, Frank Raymond, Jr.
B. 12 JUL 1909 South Wellfleet, MA. Bronze: 1936. Frank Stubbs played hockey at Harvard for two years, during which time he was coached by his father. He did not graduate from Harvard but continued to play amateur hockey and made the 1936 Olympic team while playing for the Boston Olympics. He retired from the Olympics in 1940 due to problems with his legs.

Stubbs entered the service at the outbreak of World War II, and served with distinction. He fought in Europe as an infantryman, was wounded several times, earning a Purple Heart, a Bronze Service Arrowhead, a Presidential Unit Badge, a Victory Medal, and an ETO Ribbon with the four stars of Normandy, Northern France, the Rhineland, and the Ardennes. After the war he returned to Massachusetts where he had been active in the insurance business.

SUTER, Robert Alan.
B. 16 MAY 1957. Gold: 1980. While Bob Suter was at the University of Wisconsin, he was known as somebody who liked to mix it up and was seen frequently in the penalty box. While in college he played for the 1977 NCAA champions. Unlike most of the Olympians, Suter made little effort to play pro hockey after Lake Placid. He returned to his hometown of Madison, Wisconsin, where he opened a sporting goods store. But in 1981 he signed with the Minnesota North Stars who shipped him to their Nashville farm club. He never played in the NHL, and after one season in the minors, retired from hockey to return to the store.

SYNOTT, Francis Allen.
B. 28 JAN 1889 Chatham, New Brunswick, Canada. D. 12 OCT 1945 Boston, MA. Silver(2): 1920, 1924. Though born in Canada, "Red" Synott came to America as a young man and fought with the U.S. Navy in World War I. He had by then become a well-known hockey star, playing with the Boston Maples, the Arena Hockey Club, and the Boston AA team. After retiring from hockey he became a referee in local college games and also for the Canadian-American Hockey League. Synott worked as a printer for the *Boston Herald* newspaper for most of his life.

TUCK, Leon Parker.
B. 02 JAN 1890. D. 02 SEP 1953. Silver: 1920. Leon Tuck went to Dartmouth, playing for three years, captaining the team as a senior, and graduating in 1915. After his college days he continued to play amateur hockey, mostly in Massachusetts. When he made the Olympic team he was a member of the Boston AA. Tuck made his living as the manager of an ice cream company.

VAN, Allen Alfred.
B. 30 MAR 1915. Silver: 1952. Allen Van is the oldest American to ever win a medal in Olympic hockey. With a 1945 letter in hockey from Minnesota, he also is that school's oldest hockey letterman.

Van had one of the longest amateur careers ever. He first played for the U.S. National team at the 1938 World Championships and repeated on the team in the following year. He would eventually represent the United States seven times internationally—a mark bettered only by John Mayasich, and matched only by 1980 Olympic coach, Herb Brooks. One of Van's international appearances was at St. Moritz in 1948 as a member of the AAU team which did not actually participate in the Olympics.

VERCHOTA, Philip J.
B. 28 DEC 1956. Gold: 1980. At Duluth East High School, Phil Verchota was a fine all-around athlete. He made all-state in both hockey and football (tight end and linebacker), and threw the discus for the track team. But at the University of Minnesota he played only hockey and helped the Gophers win two national titles, in 1976 and 1979. He was also an excellent student,

twice winning the Mayasich Award, given to the school's top student-athlete. After the Olympics, Verchota signed with Jokerit of the Finnish elite league and played for one year in Finland. He then returned to Minnesota to finish his degree requirements and has since rejoined the U.S. National team.

WEIDENBORNER, Cyril.
B. 1895. Silver: 1920. Cy Weidenborner was from St. Paul and played for the famous St. Paul AC hockey team, a team coached by his father. Weidenborner was the back-up goalie for the 1920 Olympic team.

WELLS, Mark Ronald.
B. 18 SEP 1957 Detroit, MI. Gold: 1980. Mark Wells attended Bowling Green University where he starred for several years prior to the 1980 Olympics. After Lake Placid he signed with the New York Rangers but really had very little success in pro hockey. He bumped around the minor leagues for two years, playing with New Haven, Flint, Fort Wayne, and Oklahoma City before deciding to retire from professional hockey. He then rejoined the U.S. National team for the 1983 World's Championship but did not survive the final cuts to make the team.

WHISTON, Donald Francis.
B. 19 JUN 1927 Lynn, MA. Silver: 1952. Don Whiston went to Brown, playing varsity baseball and hockey, and is undoubtedly the greatest goalie the Brown hockey team has ever had. In fact, his college career goals against average of 1.6 per game is among the lowest in college history. In 1951, he led his school to the NCAA finals, where they lost to Michigan; however, Whiston was voted the tournament's MVP for his performance.

After his Olympic appearance in 1952, Don Whiston returned to Boston where he built a brokerage business. He has continued in that business but found time in the early 60's to coach hockey at Brown for three years.

WILLIAMS, Thomas Mark.
B. 17 APR 1940 Duluth, MN. Gold: 1960. Tom Williams has had one of the greatest NHL careers of any United States Olympic hockey player. Williams never played college hockey but was a terror on amateur teams in the Duluth area. After the Olympics he signed with the Boston Bruins and played with them for eight years. He was a regular forward for the Bruins for many of those years. In 1969 the Bruins traded him to Minnesota where he finished his career, ending up with 111 goals and 299 points.

YACKEL, Kenneth James.
B. 05 MAR 1932 St. Paul, MN. Silver: 1952. Ken Yackel played for the Minnesota Gophers from 1953 until 1956. While in college he also lettered in baseball (three times) and football (twice). Yackel was very young in 1952, just out of high school, but he helped the U.S. win the silver medal in Oslo. Oddly, he never again played on a U.S. National team.

In 1959, Ken Yackel played six games with the Boston Bruins for his only NHL experience. Since retiring as a player he has gone on to become an insurance agent.

JEU DE PAUME

Jeu de paume is the French name for court or real tennis. It is the original form of tennis, played indoors. It appeared on the Olympic program only once, in 1908, and under its French name.

GOULD, Jay, Jr.
B. 1880. D. 26 JAN 1935 Margaretville, NY. Gold: 1908 Individual. As the son of a railroad multimillionaire, Jay Gould was able to add virtually unlimited financial resources to his considerable natural ability and he developed into the finest court tennis player in the world. In 1900 a private court was built at the family's palatial residence at Lakewood, New Jersey, and apart from retaining Frank Forester as his personal professional until 1915, Jay Gould also engaged many other professionals to provide both tutoring and competition.

When only 17, Gould won the U.S. Amateur Championship and held the title until his retirement from singles play in 1926. He was also the first amateur ever to win the World Championship (in 1914) and in 1908 Jay Gould won the Olympic jeu de paume competition without the loss of a set. Gould was equally outstanding as a doubles player, winning eight U.S. titles with W. T. H. Huhn and a further six titles with Joseph Wear, the 1904 Olympic tennis bronze medalist. Throughout his career, Gould lost only once in both singles and doubles. Gould was also a very capable squash racquets player.

Gould never had to work, but did manage the family fortune and real estate interests from offices in New York City—into which he had a court tennis dedans built.

JUDO

Judo first became an Olympic sport in 1964, and although it was dropped from the 1968 Olympics, it has been contested continuously since 1972. The top country in judo has been, to no one's surprise, the Japanese. The United States has not fared well, winning only two medals, both bronze, to date.

BREGMAN, James Steven.
B. 17 NOV 1941 Washington, DC. Bronze: 1964 Middleweight (tied). Jim Bregman started his judo career when only 12 but he quickly became very interested in the sport. In fact, after high school he went to college in Japan, at Sophia University of Tokyo, in order to study judo. Bregman returned to the United States just before the 1964 AAU Championships, where he defeated the Brazilian Pan-American champion to win the middleweight crown. Bregman also won the 1964 Olympic trials with ease, before taking his bronze medal at Tokyo. At the time of the Tokyo Olympics, Bregman was a third degree black belt.

COAGE, Allen James.
B. 22 OCT 1942 New York, NY. Bronze: 1976 Heavyweight (tied). Allen Coage started his judo career very late—when he was 22. But only two years later he won the AAU heavyweight championship. He repeated as AAU heavyweight champion in 1968, 1969, 1970 and 1975; and in 1970 he won the open division at that tournament. In addition to national titles, Coage won gold medals at both the 1967 and 1975 Pan-American Games. With his bronze medal at Montreal, Coage, a fifth dan black belt, became the first American black to win an individual medal in a sport other than track & field or boxing. Coage has spent some time as a professional bodyguard for singer Aretha Franklin.

MINORITIES — IN NUMBERS ONLY

With a black man and a Jew having won the only two judo medals for Americans, it seems appropriate here to reflect on the contributions made to the U.S. Olympic teams by various minority groups — other than male WASPs.

Women first competed at the 1900 Olympic Games in both golf and tennis. The first Americans to compete were two tennis-playing sisters, Marion and Georgina Jones. Marion Jones was the first American female medalist with a bronze in both the singles and the mixed doubles. The first American female to win a gold medal was Margaret Abbott in the 1900 gold event for women.

A Jewish athlete first appeared on the U.S. Olympic team in 1900. It was Meyer Prinstein and he was able to win a gold and silver medal, to become the first of his religious persuasion to medal. Prinstein also competed in 1904, as did marathon runner, Michael Spring, and since that time many Jews have been on U.S. Olympic teams, the most successful being Mark Spitz. A very complete synopsis of their contribution can be found in the book, *Encyclopedia of Jews in Sports*.

In 1904 Frank C. Pierce, of the Pastime AC in New York, became the first American Indian to compete in the Olympic Games when he ran in the marathon. In 1908, at London, he was joined by Frank Mt. Pleasant of the Carlisle Indian School. Although neither won a medal, four years later, two of Mt. Pleasant's Carlisle teammates did. One was Lewis Tewanima, of the Hopi tribe and a bronze medalist in the 10,000 meter run. The other was probably the greatest athlete of all time — Jim Thorpe, who was born Wa-tho-huck, a Sac and Fox Indian name meaning "Bright Path." Not many Indians have competed since for the United States in the Olympics, but three recent medalists were Jesse "Cab" Renick of the 1948 basketball team, Billy Mills, winner of the 1964 10,000 meter run, and Henry Boucha of the 1972 silver medal winning ice hockey team. Mills is usually described as being 7/16th Sioux, while Boucha was a full-blooded Chippewa.

Among minority groups, the black man has made by far the greatest contributions to our Olympic efforts. The first black man to compete in the Olympic Games, for the United States or any country, was George Coleman Poage who, on 31 August 1904, ran in a heat of the 60 meter dash. Poage may also have been the first black medalist. But Joseph Stadler was the second American black at the 1904 Olympics and he won a silver medal in the standing long jump on the same day that Poage won a silver medal in the 400 meter hurdles. Records of the exact time at which the events were held do not exist, so we can only speculate as to who was actually the first black medalist. *(Continued on next page)*

The first black to win a gold medal is well known, however. That was John Baxter Taylor, who was on the winning 1600 metre relay team at London in 1908. Taylor tragically died only a few months after the Olympics. The first individual gold medal won by a black was won in 1924 by William DeHart Hubbard in the long jump. In the movie, "Chariots of Fire," Hubbard is probably portrayed in a scene showing the American team training. They show a black man long jumping, but it could have been the 1924 silver medalist, Edward Gourdin, also a black.

All of the above athletes competed in track & field. But black men and women have also competed for the U.S. in other sports. Listed below are the first blacks to compete for the U.S. in each sport, as well as the first U.S. black to win a medal in that sport (if any), designated by an asterisk (*).

TRACK & FIELD (Men)—*George Poage (1904), *Joseph Stadler(1904)
TRACK & FIELD (Women)—Louise Stokes (1936), *Alice Coachman (1948) (Stokes and Tidye Pickett were on the 1932 U.S. Olympic squad, but they did not compete)
BOXING—Art Oliver, *Jackie Wilson (1936) (Benjamin Ponteau was on the 1920 U.S. Olympic squad, but did not compete)

WEIGHTLIFTING—John Terry (1936), *John Davis (1948)
BASKETBALL (Men)—*Don Barksdale (1948)
CYCLING—Herbert Francis (1960) (only black to date in cycling)
WRESTLING—Bobby Douglas, Robert Pickens, Charles Tribble (1964), *Lloyd Keaser (1976)
JUDO—George Harris (1964), *Allen Coage (1976)
VOLLEYBALL (Women)—Verneda Thomas (1964)
FENCING (Men)—Uriah Jones (1968)
FENCING (Women)—Ruth White (1968)
HANDBALL (Men)—Fletcher Abrams, Matt Matthews (1972)
ROWING (Women)—*Anita DeFrantz (1976)
BASKETBALL (Women)—*Lusia Harris, *Charlotte Lewis, *Gail Marquis, *Pat Roberts (1976)

To date there have also been two blacks to compete in the Winter Olympics—Willie Davenport and Jeff Gadley in the 1980 bobsled events. (It could be argued that Tai Babilonia in 1976, with a Filipino father and Afro-American mother, should also be included.) Had the United States gone to the 1980 Moscow Olympics, the color line would have been broken in two other sports—gymnastics with Ron Galimore, and soccer with Darryl Gee.

LACROSSE

Lacrosse has twice been an official Olympic sport, in 1904 and 1908, but only in 1904 did the United States enter a team. In three other years the sport has had demonstration status and the U.S. has sent college teams as representatives—Johns Hopkins (1928 and 1932) and Rensselaer Polytechnic (1948).

In 1904 the United States team consisted of 12 men from the St. Louis Amateur Athletic Association—known as the Triple A, for short. They first played a team of Mohawk Indians from Ontario, Canada, and won a closely fought game, 2-0. The other semi-final was to pair the Shamrock Lacrosse Team of Winnipeg, Canada, with the other United States entry, the Brooklyn Crescents, but the Crescents did not appear. The Shamrocks and the Triple A were then to play a two-game series to determine the champion. In the first scheduled game the Shamrocks exploded for seven goals in the second half to break open a tight match and win, 8-2. The second game was rained out and never rescheduled so the Shamrocks were declared Olympic champions with the silver medal going to the Triple A club.

Nothing is known about the lives of the St. Louis players. The Triple A's clubhouse was destroyed by fire a few years after the Olympics and all the club's records of the players were lost. Their names, as best we know them, are as follows:

DOWLING, J. W.
GIBSON
GROGAN, Patrick
HUNTER
MURPHY
PARTRIDGE
PASSMORE, George
PASSMORE, William
ROSS
SULLIVAN
VENN, A. H.
WOODS

MODERN PENTATHLON

Modern pentathlon is better termed the military pentathlon, because it consists of the skills a military man once needed in combat—running, swimming, riding, shooting, and fencing. The United States has a fair record in this sport, winning several team medals. But our competitors have yet to win an individual gold medal and have been just a cut below the competitors from the USSR, Sweden, and Hungary.

OUTSTANDING PERFORMANCES

Most Medals
2 Robert Beck, Jack Daniels, George Lambert
Most Appearances
2 Robert Beck, Jack Daniels, Jack Fitzgerald,
George Lambert, Richard Mayo, James Moore
Oldest Medalist
31y365d George Lambert
Youngest Medalist
23y161d Charles Leonard

ANDRE, William Jules.

B. 23 SEP 1931 Montclair, NJ. Silver: 1956 Team. Bill Andre fenced while a high school student, and this interest, combined with cross-country experience while at Dartmouth, led him to the modern pentathlon. Although he failed to make the 1952 Olympic team, he improved quickly, making the first U.S. World Championship team in 1953. There he finished third individually, and might have finished second had his swimming been better. This was his top individual performance ever in international competition, but his seventh place at Melbourne in 1956 helped the U.S. to the silver medals.

In 1956, Andre was second in the national championships. The leading fencer among the pentathletes, he also finished second in the 1956 AFLA epee individual competition and third in that event in 1958, and was a member of the winning three-weapon team that year as well. Andre is now a practicing attorney.

BECK, Robert Lee.

B. 30 DEC 1936 San Diego, CA. Bronze(2): 1960 Individual, 1960 Team. One of only three U.S. pentathletes to win two Olympic medals, Bob Beck finished third individually in 1960 by taking third in fencing, third in shoot-

ing, and fourth in swimming. A disastrous effort in riding, due to a balky horse, cost him the individual championship by only 43 points.

Beck also competed at the 1968 Olympics in both pentathlon and fencing. A strong epeeist, he was the AFLA national champion in 1961 and finished second in 1971. Strangely, he never won a national title in modern pentathlon, although he finished second five times between 1960 and 1970. Beck attended the University of Virginia, and then Harvard Medical School, and is now a surgeon.

DANIELS, Jack Tupper.

B. 26 APR 1933 Detroit, MI. Silver: 1956 Team; Bronze: 1960 Team. Jack Daniels is one of the three U.S. pentathletes to win two Olympic medals, both in the team event. In 1956 he finished 13th individually, based on the strength of a second in riding. In 1960 he was eighth individually, with a third place in swimming.

Daniels won the 1958 National Championships, was second in that event in 1957 and 1962, and third in 1960. He had a career in the army, but is now an exercise physiologist, working with the well-known Athletics West track club in Eugene, Oregon.

KIRKWOOD, David Archer.

B. 20 SEP 1935 Jackson, MS. Silver: 1964 Team. At Tokyo, besides the silver medal in the team event, Dave Kirkwood finished in ninth place in the individual competition. His best domestic finish came in 1964 when he was third in our national meet. He has since become a career officer in the U.S. Air Force.

LAMBERT, George Howard.

B. 01 SEP 1928 Hardin Cty., IA. Silver: 1956 Team; Bronze: 1960 Team. George Lambert won two medals in the team event, but in 1960 at Rome, he came close to an individual medal with a fifth place finish when he won the riding and placed fourth in shooting. In 1956 he fared less well, finishing 18th individually and second in the riding.

Lambert won the 1960 National Championship, was second in 1959, and third in 1956. He served for many years in the U.S. Army, but then entered government work and is now an escort officer for the State Department.

LEONARD, Charles Frederick, Jr.

B. 23 FEB 1913 Ft. Snelling, MN. Silver: 1936 Individual. While at West Point, Charles Leonard was a swimmer and runner. This, combined with his marksmanship training, led him to the pentathlon. At the 1936 Olympics, Leonard won the silver by taking a seventh place in running, a sixth in swimming, and a first in shooting with a perfect score—the only time this has ever occurred in international competition. Had there been a team event in 1936, Leonard, with Al Starbird and Fred Weber, would have won that competition.

Leonard spent his entire military career in the infantry. He taught military science and tactics at West Point before retiring from the army in 1967 as a major general. His decorations included the Distinguished Service Medal and the Legion of Merit.

MAYO, Richard Walden.

B. 12 JUN 1902 Boston, MA. Bronze: 1932 Individual. Richard Mayo was introduced to the modern pentathlon by Maj. William Rose, one of the sport's earliest administrators and proponents in this country. Mayo was a cross-country runner and captain of the fencing team at West Point, when Rose spotted his potential for this diverse event.

At the 1928 Olympics, Mayo finished a disappointing 19th, largely because he was 37th, and last, in riding. In 1931, as part of his training for the 1932 Olympics, he spent the entire year at the Cavalry School at Ft. Riley, Kansas. This dedication paid off with a second place in riding at Los Angeles and put him in the lead after four events, but a pulled Achilles tendon caused him to finish 17th in running and dropped him to the bronze medal, overall.

Mayo became a career military officer, commanding the 15th Army in France and Germany during World War II. He retired in 1956, having achieved the rank of brigadier general.

MOORE, George Bissland.

B. 06 OCT 1919 St. Louis, MO. Silver: 1948 Individual. George Moore entered pentathlon after a track career at West Point. At the 1948 Olympics, his silver medal came after a second place in riding and a third place in fencing.

Moore was in the U.S. Army in airborne and artillery during World War II, participating in the North African and Italian campaigns. His decorations included two Bronze Stars, the Purple Heart and the Legion of Merit. After the war, he taught at West Point before retiring in 1965, as a colonel, to enter the computer management field. He has since returned to education as an administrator, and is currently the business manager of his alma mater, the Lawrenceville School.

MOORE, James Warren.

B. 20 FEB 1935 Erie, PA. Silver: 1964 Team. James W. Moore, whose second place in the 4,000 meter run enabled the U.S. to capture the silver medal in the team event at Tokyo, is one of America's most consistent pentathlon performers ever. He was the first pentathlete to capture three U.S. Modern Pentathlon Association national titles (1963, 1964, 1968). At the Tokyo Olympics he finished sixth in the individual and in 1968, he was 11th.

Moore was a career officer in the army, attaining the rank of colonel before retiring in 1982. In Vietnam, he received four Bronze Stars. He is currently a teacher in a Christian religious school in Texas.

PESTHY, Paul Karoly.

B. 25 MAR 1938 Budapest, Hungary. Silver: 1964 Team. Paul Pesthy started in pentathlon as a teenager in Hungary, before emigrating to the United States in 1958. Pesthy competed in pentathlon only at the 1964 Olympics, but was a member of the U.S. Olympic fencing team in 1964, 1968, and 1976, and is a leading candidate for the 1984 team.

While at Rutgers, Pesthy won the IFA epee individual in 1964, and the NCAA epee individual in 1964 and 1965. He was also a member of the only championship team Rutgers has ever fielded, in epee at the 1964 IFA's. Pesthy won the U.S. modern pentathlon championship three times and is an outstanding fencer—and not merely among pentathletes. He has won the AFLA national title in epee individual five times, only one short of the record. Representing the New York AC, he has been a member of many national championship epee teams. Pesthy is today a faculty member in physical education at San Antonio College.

Courtesy West Point Archives

A career officer, Colonel James Moore was the first pent-athlete to capture three U.S. Modern Pentathlon Association national titles.

GEORGE SMITH PATTON, JR.

In 1912, while only a lieutenant in the army, George Patton became the first American to compete in the modern pentathlon at the Olympic Games. Patton did very well, finishing fifth overall, but came very close to winning the event. In four of the five events—swimming, running, fencing and riding—Patton did superbly and had the best overall score for those events. But Patton's shooting score brought him so far down that he fell to fifth place overall. On twenty shots with his pistol, Patton fired nineteen bulls-eyes and missed the target once completely, giving him a 190. Patton claimed he had not missed the target, but had, in fact, shot a double—two shots through the same hole. If this were true, he would have scored a perfect 200, finished first in the shooting, and finished first overall.

George Smith Patton was born on 11 November 1885 and would later study at the Virginia Military Institute before graduating from West Point in 1909. During World War I he served with Gen. John Pershing but it was his exploits during the Second World War that made him famous.

Patton's heroics began in November 1942 when he was sent to North Africa. Shortly after the American defeat at Kasserine Pass he was given command of the I Corps, later redesignated the Seventh Army. With the Seventh Army he was a leader in the invasion of Sicily, being the first Allied commander to reach Messina.

Patton was later given command of the Third Army in Europe. With that group he was credited with one of the most remarkable maneuvers in military history when he turned the Third Army northward to support the Allies' southern flank during the Battle of the Bulge.

Known as "Old Blood and Guts" for his colorful manner and great courage, Patton's life has been retold in many biographies and captured on film in the Academy Award winning movie, "Patton." George Smith Patton, Jr.—valiant soldier and U.S. Olympian—died on 21 December 1945.

NORDIC SKIING

Until very recently, the United States has had minimal success in nordic skiing disciplines. Once, at the 1954 World Championships, the officials began gathering up the course markers, assuming that all the competitors must have finished, only to find one U.S. skiier still out on the trails. Our Olympic nordic teams have not fared much better, winning only two medals. However, in the late 70's, the U.S. began to improve in nordic skiing; several of our skiiers have contended for major titles and one, Bill Koch, has won several of those titles.

HAUGEN, Anders.

B. 1888. Bronze: 1924 Special Jumping. It took longer for Anders Haugen to win his medal than any athlete in Olympic history. At the 1924 Olympics, Haugen was placed fourth—just behind Norway's Thorleif Haug, who had won three gold medals in other events. The result was accepted without argument.

In 1974, at the 50th reunion of the 1924 Norwegian team, Norwegian sports historian Jacob Vaage was going over the results when he noticed an error. Haugen had correctly been given 17.916 points, but Haug's scores added up to 17.821, not the 18.000 with which he had been credited. The IOC was notified and at a special ceremony in Oslo, on 12 September 1974, 86-year-old Anders Haugen was given his bronze medal by Haug's daughter—more than 50 years after the competition.

Haugen and his brother, Lars, were the first great American ski jumpers. Anders won four national ski jumping championships, while Lars took seven. But Anders also set three American records, the first in 1911 at Ironwood, Michigan, and the last in 1920 at Dillon, Colorado. That mark, 214 feet, would not be bettered by an American for 12 years.

Anders Haugen settled in California and coached skiing for many years. At the age of 75 he was still directing a junior alpine program for youngsters.

KOCH, William.

B. 07 JUN 1955 Brattleboro, VT. Silver: 1976 30 km. Bill Koch started out as a nordic combined competitor, but he was so much better at the cross-country portion of the event that he eventually dropped jumping altogether. Internationally, Koch first burst on the scene by finishing third at the 1974 European Junior Championships, the first medal for an American in top-level cross-country competition.

At the 1976 Olympics, Koch put on an amazing display. Besides his silver medal, he had the fastest leg in the relay, pulling the Americans from eighth to third; was sixth in the 15 km. race; and actually led the 50 km. at the halfway point, before fading to 13th. It was an unparalleled performance for an American at that level of competition.

Koch had some tough years after the Olympics. He was not prepared for the celebrity thrust upon him and skiied poorly for several years. He also continued to have problems with exercise-induced asthma, but refused to blame that for the trouble. At the 1980 Olympics, Koch was America's best skiier, but his performances lacked the luster of four years earlier.

After 1980, however, Bill Koch changed his training methods, began skiing longer marathon races, and developed a technique similar to skating with his skis. It enabled him to become the world's top cross-country skiier. In 1982 he won the individual Nordic World Cup, emblematic of the top skiier for the season. He led the same competition for much of 1983 but fell off at the end to finish third, still by far the top American ever.

OTHER SPORTS

There are several sports in which the United States has never won an Olympic medal. These are listed below along with a brief synopsis of our Olympic performances.

Biathlon

Biathlon, a sport which combines cross-country skiing with shooting, was held for the first time at Squaw Valley in 1960. The U.S. record in this event is far from outstanding. Our best individual finish occurred that first year when John Burritt finished 14th. Probably our top performance in biathlon occurred in 1972 when our relay team of Peter Karns, Dexter Morse, Dennis Donahue, and Jay Bowerman finished sixth out of ten teams.

Fencing — Women

Women's fencing first appeared in the Olympics in 1924 and one of the United States' competitors that year was Adeline Gehrig, the sister of Lou Gehrig. U.S. women have never won a medal but they have come very close three times. In 1948, Maria Cerra finished in a tie for second place at the end of the final pool. In a series of barrage matches with two other women, she lost out to finish fourth. Four years later, Janice-Lee York tied for third with three other women, including the United States' Maxine Mitchell. After a fence-off, York ended up fourth, with Mitchell fifth. Then in 1956, as Janice-Lee Romary, she finished outright fourth. Since that time, no U.S. woman has reached the finals in Olympic fencing.

Women also fence in team foil at the Olympics, but no U.S. team has ever made the finals in that event.

Handball — Team

Team handball, a sport which combines the best of basketball, soccer and lacrosse, was virtually unknown in this country until recently. It has been held in the Olympics since 1972, although a slightly different version was contested in 1936. In 1936 the game, similar to soccer but played with the hands, was held outdoors with 11 men to a team. Since 1972 the teams have been seven men and the game is now played indoors.

The United States has had virtually no success in Olympic competition in this sport. In 1936 they finished sixth of six teams, losing two games—to Germany and Hungary. In 1972 the U.S. was 14th of 16 teams, losing in the main pool to Japan, Hungary, and Yugoslavia. In the play-off pool for positions 13 through 16, the U.S. defeated Spain 22-20 when Bob Sparks broke a 20-20 deadlock by scoring two goals in the closing minutes. In 1976 we were again unable to win a game, losing five in succession, and finishing last among ten teams.

In 1976 and 1980, women also competed in Olympic team handball, but the United States has yet to enter a team.

Luge — Men and Women

The United States has had Olympic lugers since the sport's inception in 1964, but none have won medals and, in fact, Americans have yet to crack the top 10 in this sport. It was not until 1976—our fourth Olympic luge team—that every American finished all four of their runs.

The best U.S. men's finish in luge occurred in 1980 at Lake Placid when Jeff Tucker finished 12th in singles, and Ty Danco and Rich Healey were 11th in the doubles. Kathy Homstad Roberts has three times led the American women at the Olympics with a best finish of 14th in 1968.

Nordic Skiing — Women

American women have never won a medal in nordic skiing events. Our best individual finishes came in 1972 when Martha Rockwell finished 18th in the 5 km. event and 16th in the 10 km. event. Though she fared slightly less well in 1976, she also topped our American women in both events that year. In 1980 the nordic relay team of Alison Owen Spencer, Beth Paxson, Leslie Bancroft, and Margaret Spencer finished seventh, but out of only eight teams.

Volleyball — Men and Women

First held as an Olympic sport in 1964, the United States has not qualified for the Olympics since 1968 in either men's or women's volleyball. In 1964 and 1968 both teams failed to win any of the medals.

The high point of United States Olympic volleyball history occurred in 1968 when the U.S. men handed the champion Soviet team their only defeat of the tournament, 3-2. In their two appearances the U.S. women were able to boast of only one victory. It was highly unfortunate that the U.S. women's volleyball team was not able to compete at Moscow in 1980, for not only had they qualified for the tournament but, by the late 70's,

AREN'T THEY IN THE WRONG SPORT?

It's very common for American Olympic basketball players to go on to a career in the NBA; nowadays almost all of them play professionally for at least a few years. But two U.S. Olympic athletes played professional basketball in the NBA without playing on the Olympic basketball team. And they were both quite good. Any ideas who they were? The first was Walter "Buddy" Davis, the 1952 Olympic high jump champion, who went on to play in the 50's for six years with the Philadelphia Warriors. Davis was 6'-7" tall and, not surprisingly, a great leaper, and he backed up Wilt Chamberlain at center for a brief period.

The second was Keith Erickson who played on the 1964 Olympic volleyball team, but was much better known as a solid forward with the Los Angeles Lakers. Erickson actually played in the NBA for parts of 13 years, with San Francisco, Chicago and Phoenix, in addition to the Lakers. He has since become the announcer for the Lakers' games on radio in Los Angeles.

they were one of the top two or three teams in the world and would have been contenders for a gold medal.

Sports With No American Entries

There have been a very few official sports in which no U.S. athletes have taken part. Among discontinued sports, these include cricket (1900), croquet (1900), motorboating (1908), and racquets (1908).

Among sports currently on the Olympic program, the United States has yet to enter a women's team in team handball. It first appeared in the Olympics in 1976 and there was no U.S. entry, nor was there one, of course, in 1980. The only other sport in this category is field hockey for women but this first appeared as an Olympic sport in 1980 at Moscow when no American team competed.

New Olympic Sports

At 1984 in Los Angeles, several new sports will grace the Olympic program for the first time. The new sports will be women's synchronized swimming, men's and women's boardsailing, women's rhythmic gymnastics, and women's cycling. In addition, women will compete for the first time in several new track & field events, the most exciting one of which will be the first women's Olympic marathon.

In 1988 a very popular sport will return to the Olympic program when tennis will be held for the first time since 1924. Tennis was held at every Olympic Games from 1896 until 1924, but dropped off the program at that time due to disputes over amateur status and frequent conflicts with the scheduling of the Wimbledon fortnight.

Demonstration Sports

At every Olympic Games, the host country has the option of holding two demonstration sports. These are not official and the winners do not receive the same medals as competitors in official sports. It often happens that one sport is chosen which may soon appear on the Olympic program officially, and that the other selection is a sport indigenous to the host country but not widely practiced elsewhere. At 1984 in Los Angeles, the two demonstration sports will be tennis, to be an official sport in 1988, and baseball, a sport played in only a few countries outside of the United States.

The following are the demonstration sports in which Americans have participated: American Football (1932); Baseball (1912, 1936, 1956, 1964); Lacrosse (1928, 1932, 1948); Pelota Basque (1968); Sled Dog Racing (1932 Winter); Women's Speed Skating (1932 Winter); Tennis (1968); and Water Skiing (1972).

POLO

Polo has been an Olympic sport five times but the United States has only entered a team in 1920 and 1924, winning medals in both years. In 1900, several Americans also competed for a British team but are not included in our list of medalists (see the index).

OUTSTANDING PERFORMANCES

Oldest Medalist
41y63d Nelson Margetts
Youngest Medalist
19y230d Frederick Roe

ALLEN, Terry de la Mesa.
B. 01 APR 1883. D. 12 SEP 1969 El Paso, TX. Bronze: 1920. Terry Allen captained the 1920 U.S. Olympic polo team which, after losing 13-3 to Spain, beat Belgium by an identical score to take the bronze medal.

Not only was Terry Allen an outstanding polo player he was one of the army's greatest generals. Retiring in 1946 with the rank of major general, his decorations included the Distinguished Service Cross, the Distinguished Service Medal, the Legion of Merit, the Bronze Star, and the Purple Heart. He was also awarded high honors by the British and French governments. The British Field Marshall, Sir Harold Alexander, described Allen as "the finest division commander he had seen in two World Wars." Devotees of the movie "Patton" may remember George Scott, playing the former Olympian, mentioning Allen's name several times during one of the conferences.

BOESEKE, Elmer J., Jr.
Silver: 1924. Elmer Boeseke played most of his polo in Santa Barbara and he represented the West Coast against the East Coast in 1933 and 1934. He was a member of the Aurora team which won the National Open Championship and the Monty Waterbury Memorial Cup in 1933. Boeseke was also on the winning team for the Waterbury Memorial in 1929. In 1934 he became only the 11th player in U.S. polo history to be given a 10-goal handicap rating.

HARRIS, Arthur Ringland.
B. 01 AUG 1890 New Brunswick, Canada. D. 20 MAR 1968 New York, NY. Bronze: 1920. Like all his colleagues on the 1920 Olympic polo team, Arthur Harris

enjoyed a distinguished military career after graduating from West Point. He retired from the army in 1948 with the rank of brigadier general, having previously commanded the 1st Army (1941-43) and served as military attache in Mexico and Argentina.

HITCHCOCK, Thomas, Jr.
B. 11 FEB 1900 Aiken, SC. D. 19 APR 1944 Salisbury, England. Silver: 1924. Schooled in the sport from a very early age by an enthusiastic mother and a father who played in the first Westchester Cup match in 1886, Tommy Hitchcock was perhaps the greatest polo player ever. He was an aggressive rather than a particularly skillful rider, but he was a long and accurate striker of the ball. Hitchcock played for the U.S. in every international match between 1920 and 1940, with only two exceptions. During this period he was on the winning team in every match except the Cup of the Americas in 1936.

Courtesy Steven Feldman

America's greatest polo player and a 1924 Olympian, Tommy Hitchcock.

As a 17-year-old at St. Paul's school he tried to enlist in the Aviation Section of the Army Signal Corps for service in World War I. Having been rejected on the grounds of his youth, he enlisted with the French forces and went overseas, later transferring to the U.S. Air Service.

Hitchcock was shot down over enemy lines while flying a mission for the famous Lafayette Escadrille and spent a number of months in hospitals and prison camps. While being transferred between camps he jumped from a train as it was crossing a river and, although still wounded and walking only at nights, he covered the 100 miles to the Swiss border in just eight days.

After the war, Hitchcock was educated at Harvard and Oxford. Substantial family interests enabled him to devote much of his time to polo and he maintained a 10-goal handicap for 18 years.

At the outbreak of World War II he rejoined the Army Air Corps and served as assistant air attache to the embassy in London. His adventurous life came to an end when he was killed in an army airplane crash in England.

MARGETTS, Nelson E.

B. 27 MAY 1879 Salt Lake City, UT. D. 17 APR 1932 San Francisco, CA. Bronze: 1920. Nelson Margetts graduated from the mounted services school in 1909 and his military career advanced to his being appointed, in 1918, as a colonel of field artillery, after having served in 1916-17 as aide-de-camp to General John Pershing. He served in the Inspectors General Department from 1927-29 and was granted an honorable discharge from the army in 1930.

MONTGOMERY, John Carter.

B. 22 NOV 1881 Kentucky. D. 07 JUN 1948 Washington, DC. Bronze(2): 1912 Three Day Event (Equestrian), 1920 Polo. See the equestrian section for his biography.

ROE, Frederick.

B. 11 NOV 1904 Chicago, IL. D. 20 AUG 1965 Chicago, IL. Silver: 1924. Educated at Yale and the Harvard Business School, Roe was a founder and senior partner of the investment counselors Stein, Roe, & Farnham.

WANAMAKER, Rodman.

B. 1898. D. 03 FEB 1976 Southhampton, NY. Silver: 1924. Rod Wanamaker was the grandson of the founder of the department store chain which bears the family name. He was educated at Haverford School in Pennsylvania, and later studied abroad.

Wanamaker was largely responsible for the introduction of the use of helicopters by the New York police force. Serving as an aviation aide, with the title of deputy police commissioner, he convinced Mayor La Guardia of the value of helicopters to the city. Wanamaker had been a pilot in World War I, later ran a flying school for policemen, and in World War II handled a number of assignments as a navy commander.

As a polo player he rated a seven-goal handicap and was a member of the Great Neck team which won the National Open Championship in 1921.

ROQUE

Roque is a variant of croquet whose name was derived by dropping the "c" and "t" from the word, croquet. It appeared on the Olympic program for the only time in 1904 and all four entrants were from the United States. Croquet has also been an Olympic sport, in 1900 at Paris, but the United States had no entrants.

BROWN, Charles.
B. 12 MAR 1867 Onarga, IL. D. 07 JUN 1937 Onarga, IL. Bronze: 1904. Charles Brown won two matches and lost four to earn his 1904 bronze medal. He made his living as a veterinarian.

JACOBUS, Charles.
B. 28 JUN 1859. D. 07 DEC 1929. Gold: 1904. Charles Jacobus was known as the father of American roque, although he won only one national title in the sport—that in 1885. But he was editor, for many years, of Spalding's annual roque guide, and he was responsible for organizing the 1904 Olympic roque tournament. Jacobus was from Springfield, Massachusetts.

STREETER, Smith O.
B. JUL 1851 Canada. D. 1931 Thawville, IL. Silver: 1904. Smith Streeter had a 4-2 record to earn his silver medal and was the only roquist to defeat Charles Jacobus. Streeter was originally from Canada but in 1884 moved to the tiny village of Thawville where he owned a large farm. He later donated the land on which Thawville's Congregational Church was built.

ROWING

MEN

Men's rowing has been a part of the Olympic program at every celebration of the Games except the first, in 1896. The United States has had varied success in rowing. In recent years, we have not done well, as the German Democratic Republic (East Germany) now boasts of the world's best rowers, by far.

Prior to 1968 our rowers did as well as any country's, and before the appearance of the USSR at Helsinki in 1952, we were the top rowing nation in the world. Still, our success has always been a bit less in the small boats—pairs, fours, and the single and double sculls. In the eights, for many years we were unchallenged, winning the gold medal for eight consecutive Olympiads, from 1920 until 1956.

Through 1980 the U.S. has still won more medals and golds than any country but, as stated, this lead is based on older performances. The United States has currently won 27 gold medals, with East Germany second with 17, and Great Britain and Germany third with 14. In total medals, our rowers lead with 57, Great Britain second with 34, followed by Germany (32), the Soviet Union (29), and East Germany (28).

OUTSTANDING PERFORMANCES

Most Gold Medals
 3 Paul Costello, John Kelly, Sr.
Most Medals
 3 Paul Costello, John Kelly, Sr.,
   Conn Findlay, Ken Myers
Most Appearances
 4 John Kelly, Jr.
Consecutive Victories, Same Event
 3 Paul Costello (1920/24/28 Double Sculls)
 2 Louis Abell and John Exley (1900/04 Eights),
   John Kelly, Sr. (1920/24 Double Sculls)
Oldest Gold Medalist (cox)
 46y180d Robert Zimonyi Oldest
Gold Medalist (oarsman)
 37y179d W. Garrett Gilmore
Youngest Gold Medalist (cox)
 c16y Louis Abell
Youngest Gold Medalist (oarsman)
 19y53d Tom Price

ABELL, Louis G.
B. c1884. D. 25 OCT 1962 Elizabeth, NJ. Gold(2): 1900 Eights, 1904 Eights. Lou Abell coxed the Vesper Boat Club eight which won the gold medal at both the 1900 and the 1904 Olympics. He won another national title in 1902 when he coxed the same Vesper crew that had won at Paris in 1900. He later moved to Elizabeth, New Jersey, where he worked for the board of health for 40 years.

ADAM, Gordon Belgum.
B. 26 MAY 1915 Seattle, WA. Gold: 1936 Eights. Gordon Adam attended the University of Washington where he rowed crew all four years. He rowed on the freshman eights in 1935, which won the Pacific Coast and National Championships. In 1936 and 1937, the varsity eights took the same titles for varsity crews and, in 1936, this same crew took the gold medal at Berlin. Adam graduated in 1938, captaining the Huskie crew team in his last year. He went on to work with the Boeing Company for many years, before his recent retirement.

AHLGREN, George Lewis.
B. 16 AUG 1928. D. 30 DEC 1951 Arizona. Gold: 1948 Eights. While at Cal/Berkeley, George Ahlgren rowed all four years. In 1948 the Berkeley eight-oared crew lost twice to the team from the University of Washington, once in the finals of the Intercollegiate Rowing Association (IRA) regatta. However, in the semi-finals of the Olympic Trials, they heaped revenge on the crew from Seattle and went on to defeat a Harvard eight in the finals, thereby earning an Olympic berth and, eventually, a gold medal.

In Ahlgren's last two years in school, Cal had a bit more success with Washington, defeating them at the 1949 IRA's, but Washington again won that title in 1950, with Cal second. After college, George Ahlgren joined the U.S. Air Force but was killed shortly thereafter in a plane crash in Arizona.

AMAN, Charles.
Silver: 1904 Fours without. Charles Aman rowed the three-oar for the Mound City RC of St. Louis, which lost out by two lengths to St. Louis' Century BC in the coxless fours.

AMLONG, Joseph Brian.
B. 17 DEC 1936 Haines, AK. Gold: 1964 Eights. Joe Amlong came from a military family and began rowing in Belgium while his father was stationed there. He attended West Point, graduating in 1961. His rowing was done mainly in the company of his brother, Tom, and together they helped win the 1961 Canadian fours, finished second as a pair at Henley in 1963, and won the 1964 U.S. pair championship. Joe Amlong joined the Vesper BC in 1960 and was a member of the crew which won the U.S. eights in 1964 and then upset the favored Germans at Tokyo. He later spent 20 years in the U.S. Air Force, retiring as a captain.

AMLONG, Thomas Kennedy.
B. 15 JUN 1939 Ft. Knox, KY. Gold: 1964 Eights. Born in the land of gold, Ft. Knox, Kentucky, it was appropriate that Tom Amlong would win a gold medal in Tokyo. It came as a member of the eight-oared Vesper BC crew for whom he had been rowing for four years.

Amlong graduated from the University of Virginia and, like his brother, began a military career, which continues to this day. With his brother he won several national championships.

ARMSTRONG, Charles E.
Gold: 1904 Eights. Charles Armstrong rowed the five-oar for the Vesper BC eight which won the gold medal at St. Louis. The Olympic regatta doubled that year as the national championship, this provided Armstrong with his only national title.

AYRAULT, Arthur DeLancey, Jr.
B. 21 JAN 1935 Long Beach, CA. Gold(2): 1956 Pairs with, 1960 Fours without. "Dan" Ayrault rowed in the bow, pairing with Conn Findlay to win the 1956 pairs with a gold medal at Melbourne. Ayrault, a Stanford grad ('56), came back in 1960 as a member of the Lake Washington RC four which won the gold medal at Rome.

Ayrault captained the Stanford crew team in his last year and won one other national title—that the pairs in 1958 as a member of the Washington AC. He later earned a master's degree in education from Harvard and has become an educator and school administrator.

BARROW, Daniel Hubert, Jr.
B. 22 JUL 1909 Lansdowne, PA. Bronze: 1936 Single Sculls. Dan Barrow began rowing while at West Philly's Catholic High School, and sat in a combined Philadelphia high school eight which won the 1927 national prep crown. It was the first of many national titles for Barrow who did most of his rowing for the Penn AC. Early in his career, as a sweeper, he helped the eight-oared shell from that club win the World Championships at Belgium in 1930. Though world records are not recognized in rowing, due to the variability in courses, the time set that year by the Penn AC rowers is still mentioned in the Guinness Book as the fastest time ever for a 2,000 meter course.

In 1933, Dan Barrow switched over to sculling and won the 1934 and 1935 national titles in the doubles. He also was on the 1935 quads national champion and, in a rarely held event, the 1936 octuple sculls national champion. His only singles championships came in 1936, which qualified him for his only Olympic appearance.

BAYER, Ernest Henry.
B. 27 SEP 1904 Philadelphia, PA. Silver: 1928 Fours without. Ernest Bayer rowed for the Penn Barge Club for many years. He won his first national title stroking the junior eights and junior fours from that club at the 1924 national regatta. In 1925 he moved up to the seniors and was joined by Bill Miller and Charles Karle, who would row with him in the fours at Amsterdam when they won a silver medal.

Bayer retired in 1928 and spent a few years coaching, although he made a short-lived comeback to row in the 1936 Olympic Trials. He later became very active in rowing administration, serving as a treasurer, vice president and president of the National Association of Amateur Oarsmen. He made his career as a banker in Philadelphia before his retirement.

BECKLEAN, William Russell.
B. 23 JUN 1936 Kansas City, MO. Gold: 1956 Eights. William Becklean, known as "Beck" to his teammates, coxed the Yale crews for four years, graduating in 1958. The Eli's biggest wins behind Beck came in 1957 when they won the Eastern Sprints and also beat Harvard.

Courtesy Ted Nash

Watching the Stars and Stripes being raised while receiving their gold medals in rowing are (L-R) — John Sayre, Rusty Wailes, Ted Nash, and Dan Ayrault.

Becklean had prepared at Phillips Exeter, where he wrestled and coxed their prep crews. While at Yale he spent one year on the boxing team.

BEER, Donald Andrew Eilers.
B. 31 MAY 1935 New York, NY. Gold: 1956 Eights. Don Beer was an elelctrical engineering major at Yale, where he captained the freshman crew, and after his 1956 Olympic appearance, captained the varsity crew in 1957-58. For Yale, he was a member of two Eastern Sprint champions, those in 1957 and 1958.

At the Melbourne Olympics, the Yale eight, for which he sat in the fourth seat, had the sobering experience of being the first American eight to ever lose a race, finishing third in the first heat behind Canada and Australia. They came back with a decisive victory in the repechage, and then beat Canada by two seconds in the finals to win the gold medal.

BEGLEY, Michael.
Silver: 1904 Fours without. Mike Begley rowed the stroke-oar for the Mound City Rowing Club four at St. Louis.

BLAIR, James Howard.
B. 28 OCT 1909. Gold: 1932 Eights. Jim Blair went to Cal/Berkeley. In 1928 he rowed for their crew which won the IRA Regatta and, after graduation, was on their eight-oared shell which won the gold at the Los Angeles Olympics.

BLESSING, Donald F.
B. 26 DEC 1905 Hollister, CA. Gold: 1928 Eights. At 5'-7½", 120 lb., Don Blessing was the coxswain for the 1928 Cal/Berkeley boat which won the IRA championship, the Olympic Trials and the gold medal at Amsterdam. Blessing later became an investment banker in Piedmont, California.

BRINCK, John Manning.
B. 16 SEP 1908 Winters, CA. D. 1934. Gold: 1928 Eights. John Brinck sat in the second seat for the Cal eight that won the 1928 gold medal.

BROWN, David Preston.
B. 16 MAY 1928 Walnut Creek, CA. Gold: 1948 Eights. In 1947, Dave Brown was on the junior varsity boat for Cal which won the j.v. race at the IRA's in Poughkeepsie. After losing the 1948 IRA varsity race to Washington, his boat came back to defeat the Huskies at the Olympic Trials and went on to win the Olympics quite easily.

After earning an associate's degree from Cal, Brown finished up at Stanford and then attended med school at Palo Alto. He is today a practicing physician, specializing in family and emergency medicine.

BUDD, Harold Boyce, Jr.
B. 04 JAN 1939 Summit, NJ. Gold: 1964 Eights. A 1961 graduate of Yale, Boyce Budd then joined the Vesper BC and sat in the sixth seat of their eight that won the Tokyo gold medal. Budd also won national championships for Vesper in the pair, four, and eight in 1964 and 1965, and won a bronze medal in the 1965 European championships. After graduating Yale, he studied at Cambridge University, England, for a year, and was a member of their winning eight at Henley in 1962, also seated sixth. In addition he shared the pairs title at Henley in 1962.

BUERGER, John Joseph.
B. 19 SEP 1870. D. 1951. Bronze: 1904 Pairs without. Joe Buerger was a St. Louis blacksmith and rowed for the Western Rowing Club. He rowed stroke and was partnered by John Joachim at the 1904 Olympics.

BUTLER, Leon E.
B. 02 DEC 1892 Grand Rapids, MI. D. 18 JUN 1973. Bronze: 1924 Pairs with. Rowing for the Penn Barge Club in 1924, Leon Butler joined up with a pair-oared shell when, at the last minute, the United States decided to enter a boat in this event at the Olympics. Despite the inexperience of his team, seated in the bow, he helped them to a bronze medal, finishing behind Switzerland and Italy.

BUTLER, Lloyd LeMarr.
B. 11 NOV 1924. Gold: 1948 Eights. Lloyd Butler attended Cal/Berkeley, graduating in 1950. While a member of their eight-oared crew, he won the 1949 IRA Regatta, and finished second to Washington in that race in both 1948 and 1950. He is now an executive with Standard Oil.

CALDWELL, Hubert Augustus.
B. 26 DEC 1907 Oakland, CA. D. 09 AUG 1972. Gold: 1928 Eights. At 6'-2½", 185 lbs., Hubert Caldwell sat in the seventh seat for the Cal/Berkeley eight that won the IRA Regatta, the Olympic Trials, and the 1928 Olympic gold medal. Caldwell later became a well-known engineer in Piedmont, California.

CARPENTER, Leonard Griswold.
B. 28 JUL 1902 Minneapolis, MN. Gold: 1924 Eights. Leonard Carpenter took the bow seat for the Yale eight in 1924. He rowed for Yale all four years there, graduating shortly before he won his gold medal. After the Olympics he began a career in the lumber business, eventually becoming president of a large lumber company in Minnesota.

CARR, William J.
Gold: 1900 Eights. Bill Carr was a member of the Vesper Boat Club. His only national title came in 1900 with the eight-oared crew, which then went to Paris for the Olympics.

CHANDLER, Charles.
B. 22 JUL 1911. Gold: 1932 Eights. Charles Chandler went to college at Cal/Berkeley and helped their eight to the 1932 IRA championships as well as the Olympic gold medal.

CHARLTON, Thomas Jackson, Jr.
B. 12 JUL 1934 Savannah, GA. Gold: 1956 Eights. One of the smaller members of the 1956 Yale eight, at 6'-0" and 178 lbs., Tom Charlton rowed varsity at Yale for three years. He was the captain of their 1956 Olympic squad which won the gold medal.

CLAPP, Eugene Howard, IV.
B. 19 NOV 1949 Brookline, MA. Silver: 1972 Eights. Gene Clapp began rowing at summer camp when he was only 12 years old. He later rowed for Penn, helping their eight to the 1972 IRA championship, and the 1969 freshman intercollegiate title. His biggest title came in the 1971 World Championships when he was on the U.S. eight that captured the championship. Clapp was also accomplished in smaller boats, helping win the 1971 American Henley and national title in the fours. In the Olympic year, he was the captain of the Penn crew team.

CLARK, Emory Wendell, II.
B. 23 MAR 1938 Detroit, MI. Gold: 1964 Eights. While at Yale, Emory Clark captained the crew team in 1960, but won no major championships. His big titles came later, as he joined the Vesper BC and was a member of the 1964 pairs with national champion.

Clark later went to law school, earning a J.D. from Michigan in 1971, and now practices as an attorney. He still rows, winning a gold medal at an international masters' regatta in Heidelberg, West Germany, in 1981.

CLARK, Sherman Rockwell.
B. 16 NOV 1899 Baltimore, MD. D. 08 NOV 1980 Annapolis, MD. Gold: 1920 Eights; Silver: 1920 Fours with. Sherm Clark is the only American to ever cox two medal-winning boats at one Olympics. Clark went to the Naval Academy, graduating in 1922. At the 1920 Olympics he coxed the U.S. Naval Academy eight and filled in as a cox for the Penn Barge Club four. He made his career as a naval officer, retiring in 1971 as a rear admiral.

COFFEY, Calvin Thomas.
B. 27 JAN 1951 Norwich, CT. Silver: 1976 Pairs without. By the time of the 1976 Olympics, Calvin Coffey had a great deal of international experience. He had won a bronze medal in 1971 with the coxless pairs at the Pan-American Games and was on the U.S. team at the 1973 and 1975 World Championships. In 1973, while at Northeastern, he sat in the eight which won the Eastern Sprints. At the Montreal Olympics, he paired with Michael Staines and only the East Germans were able to get rid of the Coffey-Staines.

COOKE, John Patrick.
B. 09 APR 1937 Derby, CT. Gold: 1956 Eights. John Cooke played football in high school, but took up rowing after matriculating at Yale. He graduated in 1959, after rowing in the sixth seat for the 1956 gold medalists, and then went to law school.

COSTELLO, Bernard Patrick, Jr.
B. 12 MAR 1929 Detroit, MI. Silver: 1956 Double Sculls. Although no relation to the three-time gold medalist, Paul Costello, Pat Costello won almost as many titles. He attended his hometown college, Detroit, graduating in 1954, but his first national title had come years

before, in the 1948 intermediate eights. Costello did all his rowing for the Detroit BC and, between 1951 and 1958, won national titles as both a sweeper and a sculler, both here and in Canada. At the 1956 Olympics he was partnered by Jim Gardiner and, although they won their heat rather easily, they came upon a great Soviet pair in the finals and were beaten decisively.

COSTELLO, Paul Vincent.
B. 27 DEC 1894 Philadelphia, PA. Gold(3): 1920 Double Sculls, 1924 Double Sculls, 1928 Double Sculls. Paul Costello was the first Olympic rower to win three consecutive gold medals in the same event, a feat matched only by the USSR's Vyacheslav Ivanov in the single sculls.

Costello won two national titles in the single sculls, those in 1919 and 1922, but he was best known as a double sculler. In that boat, partnered mostly by John Kelly and later by Charles McIlvaine, he won innumerable national titles, both in the U.S. and Canada.

CRESSER, Frederick.
Gold: 1904 Eights. Fred Cresser was a member of the Vesper Boat Club eight and rowed the bow-oar for them at the 1904 Olympics.

CROMWELL, Seymour Legrand, II.
B. 17 FEB 1934 New York, NY. D. 02 MAY 1977 Cambridge, MA. Silver: 1964 Double Sculls. "Cy" Cromwell was a great rower and all-round sportsman who was tragically taken early by cancer. Cromwell went to Princeton, graduating in 1956, and later studied at MIT and Harvard. He had a brief career as a naval architect, but then went into teaching.

In 1964, Cromwell became won of the few Americans to win the Diamond Sculls at the Henley Regatta. He won seven national championships in the single sculls and several more in the doubles, in addition to winning the 1963 Pan-American Games gold medal in the singles. He made only one Olympic team, partnering Jim Storm in the 1964 doubles, but he was a life-long rower, finishing third in the 1976 Olympic Trials. In addition he was an avid mountain climber, both in the U.S. and in Europe. In 1964 he was a member of the crew of the boat, "Nefertiti," at the America's Cup Trials. Using his skills as a naval architect, he had also helped design the boat, which was not chosen to defend the Cup.

CWIKLINSKI, Stanley Francis.
B. 25 JUL 1943 New Orleans, LA. Gold: 1964 Eights. Stan Cwiklinski attended LaSalle College, majoring in zoology and rowing for both the frosh and varsity crews. He began club rowing with the Fairmount Rowing Association, but joined the Vesper BC in 1963. He sat in the third seat for the Vesper eight which won the gold medal. He has since gone on to a career as a naval officer.

DALLY, William Morris.
B. 22 FEB 1908 Elmira, CA. Gold: 1928 Eights. Bill Dally was in the fifth seat for the Cal/Berkeley eight at the 1928 Olympics. The Cal crew had also won the IRA Regatta earlier in the year. Dally later became a rancher in his hometown of Elmira.

DAY, Charles Ward.
B. 19 OCT 1916. Gold: 1936 Eights. Charles Day was a member of the University of Washington eight which won the IRA's in both 1936 and 1937, after having finished second the previous two years.

DeBAECKE, Harry Leopold.
B. 09 JUN 1879 Philadelphia, PA. D. 06 NOV 1961 Philadelphia, PA. Gold: 1900 Eights. Harry DeBaecke was the stroke oar for the Vesper eight which won the first Olympic eight-oared gold medal. In 1900 he also won the single sculls championship at the Schuylkill Navy Regatta. In the first decade of the century he was several times a national champion in a very long career. In 1910 he bridged two generations of American rowers when he sat in the seat behind John Kelly (Sr.) for the Vesper eight that finished third at the nationals.

DEMPSEY, Joseph F.
B. 27 SEP 1872. D. 09 OCT 1930 Germantown, PA. Gold: 1904 Eights. Joe Dempsey was one of three famous rowing brothers and, in fact, the 1904 Vesper eight was coached by his oldest brother, Jim. Both Joe and Jim Dempsey began rowing with the Penn Barge Club, but later switched to Vesper.

DETWEILER, Robert Milan.
B. 20 JUL 1930 Centralia, IL. Gold: 1952 Eights. Bob Detweiler attended the Naval Academy and was in the fifth seat on their eight-oared crew which won the 1952

Olympic gold medal. Detweiler graduated from the Academy in 1953 but while there rowed on the boats that won the 1952 and 1953 IRA Regatta and the Eastern Sprints. He has remained a career naval officer, specializing as a scientist in solid state physics.

DIETZ, George.
B. 1880. D. 1965. Gold: 1904 Fours without. George Dietz, of the Century Boat Club, was the manager of the Shardell Hotel in St. Louis for many years.

DONLON, Peter Dwight.
B. 16 DEC 1906 Hueneme, CA. D. 14 DEC 1979 Napa, CA. Gold: 1928 Eights. Peter Donlon took the stroke-oar for the Cal/Berkeley eight that won the IRA's, the Olympic Trials, and the Olympic Games in 1928. In 1932 he helped coach the Cal crew that again won the gold medal at the Olympics.

Donlon was from a California family who were pioneers in citrus farming in Northern California. He started out in the family business but later became a contractor, owning his own tile company.

DRAEGER, Richard Arthur.
B. 22 SEP 1937 Pasadena, CA. Bronze: 1960 Pairs with. Dick Draeger rowed for Stanford and the Lake Washington RC. He and Conn Findlay, both at 6'-6", made a giant pair at the 1960 Olympics en route to their bronze medal. Draeger's one national title came in the 1960 Olympic trials in this event, which doubled as the National Championship regatta.

DUMMERTH, Frank.
Bronze: 1904 Fours without. Frank Dummerth had the stroke-oar for the Western Rowing Club four at the 1904 Olympics. In 1902, Dummerth, rowing with Gustav Voerg and Lou Helm, two of his Olympic partners, won a national title in the fours without.

DUNBAR, James Ralph.
B. 11 JUL 1930. Gold: 1952 Eights. Jim Dunbar was in the third seat for the Naval Academy eight which won the 1952 Olympic gold medal. He attended Purdue briefly, but graduated from the Academy in 1955, but before leaving Annapolis, added three consecutive IRA and Eastern Sprint titles to his collection.

Dunbar became a career officer in the air force, distinguishing himself as an F-105 Thunderchief pilot in Southeast Asia. He flew over 100 successful missions in Vietnam, winning the Distinguished Flying Cross and more than 10 Air Medals.

DUNLAP, David Coombs.
B. 19 NOV 1910. Gold: 1932 Eights. Rowing for Cal/Berkeley until his graduation in 1932, Dave Dunlap won an Olympic gold medal and was on the winning team at the 1932 IRA Regatta. After college, Dunlap earned an LL.B. degree from the law school at Berkeley.

ERKER, August Casimir.
B. 1879 Wiesenwiesbach, Germany. D. 29 NOV 1951 St. Louis, MO. Gold: 1904 Fours without. Gus Erker came to the United States from Germany when he was 13 years old. He rowed in many regattas, both in the United States and Europe, primarily as a member of St. Louis' Century Boat Club. Erker overcame the handicap of having only one eye, which caused a lack of depth perception.

ESSELSTYN, Caldwell Blakeman, Jr.
B. 12 DEC 1933 New York, NY. Gold: 1956 Eights. From a longtime Yale family, "Es" Esselstyn won the university handball championship, in both singles and doubles, while a student in New Haven. He also was a member of the crew team for four years. After college, Esselstyn went to Case Western Reserve Medical School, earning his M.D. degree, and eventually practicing as a general surgeon.

EXLEY, John Onins, Jr.
B. 23 MAY 1867 Philadelphia, PA. D. 26 JUL 1938 Milford, DL. Gold(2): 1900 Eights, 1904 Eights. John Exley was born in Philadelphia but grew up on the prairie and formed his own cattle buying company. Working with livestock developed his physique and, after moving back to Philadelphia, a local coach spotted him one day, noting his massive arms and vascularity. Exley took up rowing on the coach's advice and became known as "The Iron Man" of rowing in Philadelphia. He was the stroke-oar on both of the Vesper Boat Club's championship eights in 1900 and 1904, in addition to winning several other major titles.

He continued rowing until 1912, at which time he took up coaching as a hobby, all the while running a farm and building supply company at the present site of the Philadelphia airport.

FARNAM, Robert.

Gold: 1904 Pairs without. Bob Farnam was from Brooklyn and rowed for the Seawanhaka Boat Club at the 1904 Olympics. In 1905, he and Olympic partner, Joe Ryan, added a national title in the fours, recruiting Jim McLoughlin from the Ravenswood BC to join them. McLoughlin had rowed on the boat which finished second in 1904 to Farnam and Ryan.

FEDERSCHMIDT, Erich H.

B. 14 JUN 1895 Philadelphia, PA. Ddi. Silver: 1920 Fours with. The 6'-3" Erich Federschmidt began rowing in 1916 with the Penn Barge Club. World War I intervened and he did not row at all for the next three years, serving in the medical corps in the army. He began rowing again in 1920, qualifying for the Olympic team. After the Olympics he jumped to the Undine Barge Club, but retired shortly thereafter.

FEDERSCHMIDT, Franz H.

B. 21 FEB 1894 Philadelphia, PA. Ddi. Silver: 1920 Fours with. The smaller yet older of the two brothers, Franz Federschmidt started out rowing with his brother for Penn Barge in 1916. He began again after the war and joined his brother at the Undine Barge Club.

FERRY, Edward Payson.

B. 18 JUN 1941 Seattle, WA. Gold: 1964 Pairs with. Ed Ferry joined up with Conn Findlay to form one of America's greatest ever pair-oared boats. They won the national title in that event in 1961, 1962, and 1964, and were Pan-American Games champions in 1963, in addition to winning their gold medal at Tokyo in 1964. Ferry went to Stanford but was an ensign in the navy at the time of his Olympic performance.

FIELDS, William Beauford.

B. 06 AUG 1929. Gold: 1952 Eights. Bill Fields was in the second seat for the great Navy crews which won so many titles. Fields graduated from the Academy in 1954, but was on three consecutive winning shells at

the IRA's and two consecutive champions at the Eastern Sprints. Fields became a career naval officer, retiring as a commander in 1977.

FIFER, James Thomas.

B. 14 JUL 1930 Tacoma, WA. Gold: 1956 Pairs without. In 1952, Jim Fifer and Duvall Hecht rowed the coxed pairs for the United States at the Olympics, without much success. In 1956 they decided to go it without a coxswain and qualified for the Olympic team in the pairs without by defeating the defending Olympic champions, Chuck Price and Tom Logg, in the Final Trials. At the Olympics, Fifer and Hecht won every race decisively, despite consistently understroking the opposition.

FINDLAY, Conn Francis.

B. 24 APR 1930 Stockton, CA. Gold(2): 1956 Pairs with, 1964 Pairs with; Bronze(2): 1960 Pairs with, 1976 Tempest Class (Yachting). Conn Findlay graduated from Cal/Berkeley in 1956 and has spent many years at sport's highest levels. He started as a rower for Cal and was partnered by Stanford's Dan Ayrault and coxswain, Kurt Seiffert, at the 1956 Olympics. After a losing effort in Rome in 1960, partnered by stroke-oar Dick Draeger, he reached the highest step of the victory platform with Ed Ferry and coxswain, Kent Mitchell, at the 1964 Olympics. Findlay and Ferry also won two national titles in the pairs with, as well as the 1963 Pan-Am gold medal in that event.

In 1974 Findlay was a crew member with Dennis Conner on the boat, "Mariner," at the America's Cup trials. Though "Mariner" was not chosen to defend the Cup, Conner picked Findlay to join him in 1976 and together they won a bronze medal in Tempest class yachting. Conn Findlay achieved yachting's ultimate in 1977, however, when he served as the mast man on Ted Turner's "Courageous," which defended the America's Cup. In 1983 he is again serving as a crew member on "Courageous" in the Cup Trials, this time for skipper John Kolius.

FLANAGAN, James Showers.

B. c1884. D. 28 MAR 1937 Philadelphia, PA. Gold: 1904 Eights. Jim Flanagan was in the fourth seat on the Vesper eight at the 1904 Olympics. Flanagan had a very long rowing career, winning several national titles for Vesper, almost always accompanied by his closest rowing companion, Harry DeBaecke.

FOLEY, Hugh Miller.
B. 03 MAR 1944 Seattle, WA. Gold: 1964 Eights. Hugh Foley began rowing for Loyola University in Los Angeles, but transferred to LaSalle, graduating from there in 1966 with a degree in accounting. Rowing for Vesper BC, Foley won six U.S. championships, either in the eights or the fours with. He also won several international regattas in Britain, Europe, and Australia, and at the 1967 Pan-American Games was joined by his 1964 Olympic teammates, Bill Stowe and Bob Zimonyi, to take a gold medal in the fours with.

Hugh Foley remained active in rowing when he coached the crew teams at Boston University for most of the 70's, but he is now again working as a programmer/accountant.

FREDERICK, Francis Harland.
B. 28 FEB 1907 Alameda, CA. D. 1968. Gold: 1928 Eights. Frank Frederick was known as the sparkplug of the 1928 Cal crew, mostly for his enthusiasm and optimistic attitude. He graduated from Cal in 1930 and became a noted geologist in the northern California area.

FREITAG, John.
Bronze: 1904 Fours without. John Freitag was from St. Louis and took the two-oar for the Western Rowing Club four at the 1904 Olympics.

FROMANACK, Martin.
Silver: 1904 Fours without. Martin Fromanack rowed for the Mound City RC in St. Louis. He was in the second seat in their four at the 1904 Olympics.

FRYE, Wayne Thomas.
B. 30 NOV 1930 Trinity, KY. Gold: 1952 Eights. Graduating from the Naval Academy in 1954, Wayne Frye was on the winning eight at the Olympic Games, three IRA Regattas, and two Eastern Sprints. Unlike many U.S. Naval Academy rowers, he went on to win other titles after graduation, taking national titles in both the association single sculls and the quad sculls while rowing for the Potomac BC.

Frye became a career officer in the air force. During the Vietnam War, he flew 266 combat missions, earning two Silver Stars, five Distinguished Flying Crosses, 15 Air Medals, and the Purple Heart. He retired from the navy air force as a colonel and has gone into aerospace management.

GALLAGHER, Vincent Joseph, Jr.
B. 30 APR 1899 Brooklyn, NY. Gold: 1920 Eights. Vince Gallagher started college at Rutgers but received an appointment to the Naval Academy and began there in 1919. He had no rowing experience but learned quickly and was on Navy boats which won the IRA Regatta in 1921 and 1922, as well as winning the Olympic gold medal. Gallagher became a career officer in the navy, retiring in 1957 as a commander.

GARDINER, James Arthur.
B. 25 OCT 1930 Detroit, MI. Silver: 1956 Double Sculls. Jim Gardiner teamed with Pat Costello to take the silver medal in double sculls at the 1956 Olympics. Gardiner was a many-titled sculler, having won the Pan-Am doubles in 1955, U.S. titles in the doubles in 1954 and 1956 and in the quads in 1953, and Canadian championships in the doubles in 1956. He also won Canadian national titles as a sweeper in the fours with and without in 1952.

Gardiner attended Wayne State, graduating in 1954, and representing the Detroit BC as a rower. He now is a college art professor, but continues to compete in masters' rowing events.

GATES, Gregory Crozier.
B. 28 APR 1926 Montclair, NJ. Bronze: 1948 Fours without. Greg Gates rowed for Yale, graduating from the New Haven school in 1950. While he was there, Eli eight-oared fortunes were down a bit, necessitating Gates to go to a smaller boat to make the Olympic team. In 1948, Gates rowed on the Yale crew that finished second to Harvard at the Eastern Sprints and in their match race. However, in 1949, Yale, and Gates, gained a measure of revenge by defeating Harvard in their match race.

GEIGER, John E.
Gold: 1900 Eights. John Geiger represented the Vesper Boat Club, rowing in their eight that won the Olympic gold medal at Paris.

The gold-medal-winning, eight-oared crew at the 1948 Olympics. (L-R) — Ralph Purchase, Ian Turner, Dave Turner, Jim Hardy, George Ahlgren, Lloyd Butler, Dave Brown, Justus Smith, John Stack.

GERHARDT, Robert Buchanan.
B. 03 OCT 1903 Baltimore, MD. Bronze: 1924 Fours with. Bob Gerhardt had a very short rowing career, lasting only two years. He started out rowing in a four-oared gig for the Arundel BC in Baltimore. His family moved to Philadelphia, and he joined the Bachelor's Barge Club, moving into their four-oared shell when one of their sweepers decided to take up sculling exclusively. Gerhardt made his living in the insurance and brokerage business.

GILMORE, William Evans Garrett.
B. 16 FEB 1895 Wayne, PA. D. 05 DEC 1969 Philadelphia, PA. Gold: 1932 Double Sculls; Silver: 1924 Single Sculls. Garrett Gilmore started rowing in 1919 when he joined the Bachelor's Barge Club. His first national titles came the following year when he won in some junior and intermediate shells. But Gilmore won many titles as a senior, including five national senior titles in the single sculls and several more in the doubles. At the 1924 Olympics he was beaten by the great British oarsman, Jack Beresford, but at the 1932 Olympics he teamed with Ken Myers to take the gold medal. Gilmore's career was as a real estate broker.

GIOVANELLI, Gordon S.
B. 11 APR 1925. Gold: 1948 Fours with. Gordy Giovanelli sat in the bow seat for the University of Washington four, which won all its races easily, both at the U.S. Final Trials and the London Olympic Games. Though the varsity eight did not fare so well during Giovanelli's stay at Washington, in 1949 he was on the junior varsity eight that won the IRA j.v. title.

GLEASON, Michael D.
D. 11 JAN 1923 Philadelphia, PA. Gold: 1904 Eights. Mike Gleason was a member of the Vesper BC eight which won the 1904 Olympics and then traveled to England and won the 1905 Henley Regatta. Gleason was a long-time police officer in Philadelphia.

GRAHAM, Norris James.
B. 25 JAN 1906. Gold: 1932 Eights. Norris Graham attended Cal/Berkeley. He also rowed for their boat that won the IRA Regatta in 1932.

GRAVES, Edwin Darius, Jr.
B. 10 JUL 1897 Maryland. Gold: 1920 Eights. Ed Graves was the captain of the U.S. Naval Academy crew which won the 1920 Olympic gold medal. He graduated from the Academy in June, 1920, but remained in Annapolis to train with the eight. Graves became a career officer in the naval air force, retiring in 1950 as a captain.

GREER, Frank B.
B. 1879 D. 07 MAY 1943 Winthrop, MA. Gold: 1904 Single Sculls. Frank Greer lived most of his life in Boston and his entire rowing career was spent as a sculler. He won the National Championships both in the United States and Canada for three consecutive years, beginning in 1903. He also added another U.S. single sculls championship in 1908. After his competitive retirement he coached for several years at the Detroit AC, but returned to Boston where he was the sheriff of the Suffolk County Jail for many years.

GREGG, Duncan Smith.
B. 28 FEB 1910. Gold: 1932 Eights. Graduating from Cal in 1934, Duncan Smith had a chance to row on championship boats at the IRA's in both 1932 and 1934, as well as the gold medal winning eight at the Los Angeles Olympics.

GRIFFING, Stuart Lane.
B. 09 NOV 1926 New Haven, CT. Bronze: 1948 Fours without. Before entering Yale, Stu Griffing joined the service and served out the last days of World War II. Upon returning to New Haven, he joined the Yale crew team, rowing for all four years. He was on the Yale varsity eight which lost to Harvard both at the Eastern Sprints and the Harvard-Yale Regatta in 1948, but the next year the tables were turned as Yale beat Harvard in their classic race.

GRIMES, Charles Livingston.
B. 09 JUL 1935 Washington, DC. Gold: 1956 Eights. At 6'-7", Charles Grimes played football for two years at Yale, as well as playing on the freshman basketball team and rowing for his entire college stay. In 1956 the Yale eight beat Harvard, but lost the Eastern Sprints.

Despite this setback they persevered to win the Olympic Trials and take the Olympic gold medal without the loss of a race. Grimes entered law school after his 1957 graduation from Yale.

HALL, Winslow William.

B. 15 MAY 1912 Oakland, CA. Gold: 1932 Eights. An Eagle Scout with two silver palms, Winslow Hall attended the University of California, graduating in 1933 with a degree in economics. He began working soon after, but was called to service during the war and won five battle stars before being discharged from the navy as a lieutenant commander. Upon returning to California, he went into the food and grain business and has become quite well known in that business. In addition, Hall is noted for his community service, having served on countless committees and councils in his hometown in Northern California.

HARDY, James Herbert.

B. 15 JAN 1923 San Francisco, CA. Gold: 1948 Eights. Jim Hardy began rowing in high school, helping Balboa High to the San Francisco city championship in 1940. He then served in the army medical corps during World War II, leaving as a second lieutenant in 1946, and matriculating at the University of California. Hardy graduated from Cal in 1949 with a degree in civil engineering, and has made his career as a traffic engineer in California. Hardy rowed the six-oar for the Cal eight at the Olympics.

HEALIS, George A.

B. 03 JUN 1906 Philadelphia, PA. Silver: 1928 Fours without. George Healis of the Penn Barge Club had a very short competitive rowing career. He never won a national title but rowed the two-seat at the 1928 Olympics to win a silver medal. He made his living as an architect.

HECHT, Duvall Young.

B. 23 APR 1930 Los Angeles, CA. Gold: 1956 Pairs without. Duvall Hecht rowed in the 1952 Olympic pairs with while still a student at Stanford. He then joined the marines and continued to row, teaming up with 1952 teammate, Jim Fifer, to make the Olympic team. At the 1956 Olympic Trials, Hecht and Fifer beat the defending Olympic champions, Tom Logg and Charles Price, to win their spot on the team.

Hecht graduated from Stanford in 1952, but returned there to take an M.A. degree in journalism in 1960. He is now the president of Books on Tape, Inc.

HEDLEY, Edwin.

B. c1864. D. 22 MAY 1947 Philadelphia, PA. Gold: 1900 Eights. At 36 years, Ed Hedley was one of the older members of the Vesper BC eight at the Paris Olympics. Hedley had been rowing a long time by then, having won the Canadian single sculls title in 1892. He also won the single sculls championship of the Schuylkill Navy five times between 1891 and 1899. Hedley won several U.S. national championships, including the 1902 coxswainless pairs.

HELM, Louis G.

Bronze: 1904 Fours without. Lou Helm rowed for the Western Rowing Club of St. Louis at the 1904 Olympics. Though they managed only a bronze medal, three of the four members of that shell, including Helm, had rowed together to win a national title in 1902.

HOBBS, Franklin Warren, IV.

B. 30 JUL 1947 Manchester, MA. Silver: 1972 Eights. "Fritz" Hobbs rowed in the Olympics in both 1968 and 1972, both times as a member of the eight-oared shell. He had a bit more success in 1972. Hobbs was a Harvard grad in that year, class of '69, and had played on the Harvard squash team, being named to the 1968 national collegiate squash team. He graduated magna cum laude in history and later became an investment banker in New York.

Hobbs rowed for Harvard in 1967 when they won their fourth straight title at the Eastern Sprints and defeated Yale in their big race. He also rowed on the U.S. National eight which won the 1967 Pan-American Games gold medal and finished second at the European championships.

HOBBS, William Barton Rogers.

B. 30 JUL 1949 Ponce, Puerto Rico. Silver: 1972 Eights. In high school, Bill Hobbs attended Milton Academy where he was named the fullback on the all-New England prep team. After his freshman year at Harvard he made the 1968 Olympic team, stroking the pair-oared shell that finished fifth at Mexico City. While at Harvard he rowed in the eights that won the 1969 and 1970 Eastern Sprints.

After college, Bill Hobbs took an M.B.A. from Harvard and today works as a corporate planner.

HOBEN, John Grey.
B. c1884 Greenpoint, NY. D. 06 JUL 1915 Long Island City, NY. Silver: 1904 Double Sculls. John Hoben was one of the better-known oarsmen in New York, rowing out of the Ravenswood BC at the 1904 Olympics. Hoben worked as a civil engineer.

HOFFMAN, Paul.
B. 21 APR 1946 New York, NY. Silver: 1972 Eights. Paul Hoffmann had a long career as a top-flight coxswain. He prepped at Phillips Andover and Bryanston in England, and coxed boats from those prep schools at the Henley Regatta in 1962 and 1964. In both 1968 and 1972 he was the cox for the U.S. eight at the Olympics, leading them to a silver medal in 1972. He also won a gold medal with the eight at the 1967 Pan-American Games and coxed Harvard to four straight wins at the Eastern Sprints, starting from 1965.

Hoffman served in the Peace Corps for a time after college, but returned to Harvard to earn a J.D. degree in 1974 and has worked mostly as a lawyer since. He also helped coach the U.S. team at the 1977 World Championships in Amsterdam.

HOUGH, Lawrence Alan.
B. 04 APR 1944 Janesville, WI. Silver: 1968 Pairs without. Larry Hough graduated from Stanford in 1966 and then teamed with Phil Johnson to have an outstanding year in 1967. Rowing a pair together, they won the U.S., North American, Pan-American, and European championships in that year. They repeated their national success in 1968 in both the pairs with and without, but lost a bow-baller at the 1968 Olympics to an East German pair.

HUME, Donald Bruce.
B. 25 JUL 1915. Gold: 1936 Eights. Don Hume attended the University of Washington and was the stroke-oar for their eight that won the IRA Regatta, the Olympic Trials, and the Olympic Games in 1936.

HUNT, George Elwood, Jr.
B. 01 AUG 1916. Gold: 1936 Eights. Rowing out of the sixth seat for the University of Washington eight, George Hunt shared in victories in 1936 at the IRA's, and the Olympic Games.

JACOMINI, Virgil Victor.
B. 30 MAY 1899 Washington, DC. Gold: 1920 Eights. Graduating from the Naval Academy in 1920, Virgil Jacomini rowed on their eight that decimated the opposition at Antwerp to win the Olympic gold medal. Jacomini only remained in the navy for a short time because after World War I the military was trying to decrease its numbers and graduating midshipmen were then given the option of resigning their commission. Jacomini took up this option in 1923 and became an engineer.

JASTRAM, Burton Albert.
B. 05 JUN 1910 San Francisco, CA. Gold: 1932 Eights. Burt Jastram went to the University of California, graduating in the Olympic year, but he later did some graduate work at Berkeley in architecture. It served him well for Jastram became a well-known architect, one of his creations being named by *Fortune* magazine as one of the 10 best U.S. buildings.

Jastram rowed for Cal both at the 1932 Olympics and on the eight that won the 1932 IRA Regatta in Poughkeepsie, New York.

JELINEK, Sidney.
B. 18 MAR 1899 Wilmington, DE. D. 09 MAR 1979 Philadelphia, PA. Bronze: 1924 Fours with. Sid Jelinek got his start rowing on the lightweight crew for Penn in 1920. By the following year he had moved up to the big boat and sat in the seventh seat on their eight for three years. He also played on the Penn water polo team. At the 1924 Olympic Trials, the Penn eight failed to defeat Yale for the Olympic berth, but Jelinek made the team in the fours with, rowing for the Bachelor's Barge Club. Jelinek later became an architect in his hometown of Philadelphia.

JENNINGS, Edward F.
B. 09 APR 1898 Philadelphia, PA. Ddi. Gold: 1932 Pairs with; Bronze: 1924 Pairs with. At 5'-2" and 97 lbs., Ed Jennings was the perfect size for a coxswain and he

coxed several Penn Barge Club boats to national championships. In the 1924 Olympics his oarsmen were Leon Butler and Harold Wilson, but he had more success in 1932, coxing Joe Schauers and Charlie Kieffer to a gold medal at Los Angeles.

JOACHIM, John L.
Bronze: 1904 Pairs without. John Joachim represented the Western RC of St. Louis and rowed the bow oar with Joe Buerger at the 1904 Olympics.

JOHNSON, Philip Anthony.
B. 16 NOV 1940 Washington, DC. Silver: 1968 Pairs without. Tony Johnson was one-half of what may be America's greatest ever pair without. In 1967, together with Larry Hough, he won the Pan-American Games, the National Championship, the North American Championship, and the European Championship. Johnson also won U.S. championships in the pairs without in 1963, 1965, and 1968, in the pairs with in 1967 and, rowing for the Potomac BC, in the 1965 eight-oared shell. He competed in the 1964 Olympics in the coxless pairs with Jim Edmonds, but they failed to make the finals. At Mexico City in 1968, Johnson and Hough were thought to have a good shot at a gold medal, but lost by inches to an East German pair.

Johnson graduated from Syracuse University and since 1970 has been the head crew coach at Yale.

JOHNSTON, Donald Hendrie.
B. 30 SEP 1899 Albany, NY. Gold: 1920 Eights. At 6'-2" and 190 lbs., Don Johnston was perfectly suited for the "engine room" and rowed the six oar for the Naval Academy eight at the 1920 Olympics. He developed into a top-flight oarsman very quickly—he had been rowing for only one year by the time of the 1920 Olympics. Johnston became a career officer in the U.S. Air Force, retiring in 1952 as a captain.

JORDAN, William Conrad.
B. 25 JUN 1898 Cleveland, OH. D. 13 JUL 1968 Springfield, OH. Gold: 1920 Eights. Bill Jordan was a 1922 Naval Academy graduate who rowed on their championship eight at the 1921 and 1922 IRA Regattas as well as at the 1920 Olympic Games. Jordan resigned his Naval commission in 1923 and became an industrialist.

He was a general manager for Curtiss-Wright Corporation's local plant in Columbus, Ohio, when he was named president of that company in 1948. He held that post until 1954, when he was named president and general manager of Hughes Aircraft.

JUVENAL, James B.
B. 12 JAN 1874 Philadelphia, PA. D. 02 SEP 1942 Philadelphia, PA. Gold: 1900 Eights; Silver: 1904 Single Sculls. Jim Juvenal was one of the most well known of the Philadelphia rowers at the turn of the century. In 1893 he won the Middle States regatta near Scranton, Pennsylvania, rowing in an aluminum shell, said to be the first time such a boat was used in competition. Between 1893 and 1906 he won over 100 races, including the 1902 National Association single sculls championship and six consecutive championships of the Schuylkill Navy.

In 1906, Juvenal turned professional to become a rowing coach, first with the Malta BC and later with Penn Barge. He also spent a short stint as the national coach in Cuba. Juvenal studied at the Drexel Institute and was employed for 40 years by the Philadelphia Electric Co.

KARLE, Charles G.
B. 15 MAY 1898 Philadelphia, PA. D. c1935 Philadelphia, PA. Silver: 1928 Fours without. Charles Karle's father was German-born and taught his son the exercises he had learned in a German turnverein. It helped him develop very strong muscles and Karle became an excellent athlete, excelling in cycling, speed skating, and gymnastics in addition to rowing. As a rower, Karle represented the Penn Barge Club, winning several national titles in the fours, accompanied by Bill Miller and Ernest Bayer. The sport of cycling unfortunately contributed to Karle's death—he was hit by a car while training one day in Philadelphia and died as a result.

KELLY, John Brenden.
B. 04 OCT 1889 Philadelphia, PA. D. 26 JUN 1960 Philadelphia, PA. Gold(3): 1920 Single Sculls, 1920 Double Sculls, 1924 Double Sculls. John Kelly is probably the greatest sculler the United States has ever produced. Kelly began rowing in 1908 with the Chamounix and Montrose Boat Clubs, but joined Vesper the following year. Between 1909 and his competitive retirement

Courtesy John Kelly, Jr.

John Kelly, Jr. stands beside a statue of his famous father, John Kelly (Sr.). Both won medals in Olympic rowing.

after the 1924 Olympics, Kelly won every sculling title available to him, including the World Championship in both singles and doubles, the Olympics in single and doubles, and many national titles in both boats.

Available to him is an important term; Kelly never won the Diamond Sculls at the Henley Regatta because he was denied entry. This was based on the fact that Kelly was a bricklayer, to the British a mere common laborer, and not worthy of competing with the gentlemen amateurs at the Henley. Kelly would certainly have won that title had he been allowed to compete and in later years had the last laugh on the British when his "bricklaying" led to a lucrative business as a contractor in Philadelphia. Kelly fathered two very famous children—John Kelly, Jr., another Olympic rower, and the late Grace Kelly, the American movie star who later became Princess Grace of Monaco.

KELLY, John Brenden, Jr.
B. 24 MAY 1927 Philadelphia, PA. Bronze: 1956 Single Sculls. John Kelly, Jr. never quite enjoyed the great Olympic success of his father, but surely one of his most satisfying victories had to be in 1947 when he won the Diamond Sculls at the Henley Regatta, finally bringing that title to the Kelly family (see above). It was one of only many championships that he won, and included eight U.S. National single sculls titles, six Canadian single sculls championships, and two gold medals at the Pan-American Games. Kelly, Jr. won the Diamond Sculls again in 1949, and was world singles champion in that year.

At the Olympics, John, Jr. was not quite able to grab the gold ring, but at the 1956 Olympics, though probably a bit past his peak as a single sculler, he put on an outstanding performance to take the bronze behind Russia's Vyacheslav Ivanov, and Australia's Stu Mackenzie.

John Kelly, Jr. has been very active in sports administration, especially in rowing. He has served as a president of the AAU, vice president of the USOC, and is currently president of the International Swimming Hall of Fame. His business is as chairman of the board of John B. Kelly, Inc., a masonry contracting company.

KENNEDY, John G.
B. 19 MAY 1900. Ddi. Bronze: 1924 Fours with. John Kennedy coxed the Bachelor's Barge four to a bronze medal at the 1924 Olympics. Before joining Bachelor's, he attended the University of Pennsylvania and coxed their lightweight and junior varsity crews.

KIEFFER, Charles M.
B. 11 AUG 1910. Gold: 1932 Pairs with. Charlie Kieffer won his first national title as a member of the all-Philadelphia prep eight which took the National High School Championship in 1927. He rowed for several more years, mostly with the Penn AC, and was a member of their eight which won the World Championships in Belgium in 1930, setting a still-standing record for the fastest time over a 2,000 meter course. At the 1932 Olympics, Kieffer was partnered by Joe Schauers and coxed by Ed Jennings en route to the gold medal.

KING, Clyde Whitlock.
B. 06 SEP 1898 Montezuma, IA. D. 20 AUG 1982 Mill Valley, CA. Gold: 1920 Eights. In 1919, Clyde King was only rowing for the plebe crew at the Naval Academy and was much better known as a football player for the Middies. But because of his outstanding strength and endurance he was taught to row from the port side and stroked the Annapolis eight at the 1920 Olympics. King graduated in 1922, but not before helping their football team defeat Army in 1919 by scoring all of Navy's points with two field goals in a 6-0 victory.

He resigned his commission in 1922, but was called to active service during World War II. He remained an active officer until 1958, retiring as a rear admiral. He then spent his civilian life in the glass business, but was very active in promoting sports through membership in many clubs and organizations.

KINGSBURY, Frederick John, IV.
B. 20 MAY 1927 Fredericksburg, VA. Bronze: 1948 Fours without. Fred Kingsbury went to Yale, graduating in 1950 with a degree in engineering. He continued on at the New Haven school to take a master's degree in engineering and returned there in the late 60's to receive a doctorate. As a rower, his two biggest moments came in 1948 when he was on the Yale four that won the National Championship and went on to take the bronze medal at London.

KINGSBURY, Howard Thayer, Jr.
B. 11 SEP 1904 New York, NY. Gold: 1924 Eights. The six-oar of the Yale eight in 1924, Howard Kingsbury also played football for the Elis. Graduating in 1926, Kingsbury took up civil engineering for a time, but left shortly thereafter to study at Oxford. He eventually became an educator.

KLOSE, Carl Otto.
B. 05 DEC 1891 Philadelphia, PA. Ddi. Silver: 1920 Fours with. Carl Klose began rowing in 1916 with the Penn Barge Club but was called away by World War I, during which time he served in the ambulance corps. He only returned to rowing three months before the Antwerp Olympics, but partnered the Federschmidt brothers and Ken Myers to a silver medal in the four.

KNECHT, William Joseph.
B. 10 MAR 1930 Camden, NJ. Gold: 1964 Eights. Short and stocky at 6'-0" and 200 lbs., Bill Knecht started rowing at LaSalle High School and later went to Villanova. He first joined the Vesper BC in 1946 and won many national titles with them. In addition to his Olympic gold medal in 1964, he stroked the Vesper eight to a gold medal at the 1955 Pan-American Games and won two more Pan-Am golds—in the 1959 and 1963 double sculls. His partner in 1959 was John Kelly, Jr., with whom he won several national double scull championships and also competed in the 1960 Olympics.

LEANDERSON, Matt Fillip.
B. 11 MAR 1931. Bronze: 1952 Fours with. Matt Leanderson rowed the stroke oar for the University of Washington four at the 1952 Olympics. Their boat qualified easily for the finals but was then beaten decisively by the Czech shell, although they narrowly lost the silver medals to a Swiss crew.

LINDLEY, Alfred Damon.
B. 20 JAN 1904 Minneapolis, MN. Gold: 1924 Eights. Al Lindley stroked the great Yale eight to the 1924 Olympic gold medal. Lindley spent three years at Yale on the varsity crew after having learned to row at Phillips Andover prep school. Lindley graduated from Yale in 1925 and became a lawyer.

LIVINGSTON, John Cleve.
B. 24 MAY 1947 Los Angeles, CA. Silver: 1972 Eights. Cleve Livingston was a member of some of the great Harvard eights of the late 60's. He helped Harvard to three straight victories at the Eastern Sprints (1966-68) and won a gold medal at the 1967 Pan-American Games in the eight-oared shell. He participated in two Olympics, the eight finishing sixth in 1968 but coming through for a silver medal in 1972.

LIVINGSTON, Michael Kent.
B. 21 SEP 1948 Denver, CO. Silver: 1972 Eights. Mike Livingston was only a spare at the 1968 Olympics and did not get to row, but before the next Olympics, he added plenty of hardware to his trophy case, helping Harvard to continue their mastery of the Eastern Sprints and over Yale.

After college, Mike Livingston earned a law degree and worked for several years with the American Civil Liberties Union. He then lived in Guatemala for two years but has returned to the states where he is now the head crew coach at Cal/Berkeley.

LOCKWOOD, Roscoe C.
B. c1874. D. 24 NOV 1960 Moorestown, NJ. Gold: 1900 Eights. Rowing for the Vesper BC, Roscoe Lockwood won his gold medal at Paris in 1900. He later became chief investigator for the division of Alcoholic Beverage Control in Moorestown, New Jersey.

LOGG, Charles Paul, Jr.
B. 24 FEB 1931 Princeton, NJ. Gold: 1952 Pairs without. In 1952, Charlie Logg was a junior at Rutgers with only three years of rowing experience and had never sat in a pair-oared shell until three months before the Olympics. Worse yet, his Olympic crewmate, Tom Price, had never rowed until the Olympic year. So at the Olympics, Logg and Price predictably finished dead last in their first heat behind boats from Switzerland, Britain, and Belgium. But Logg and Price came through the repechage and defeated those same three shells in the finals to win a gold medal, and earn the sobriquet, "The Cinderella Kids," in the process.

Logg served in the U.S. Army for six years after the Olympics and, after winning a Pan-Am gold with Price in 1955, they made an abortive attempt to qualify together for the 1956 U.S. Olympic team. Through the 1960's he was involved in several companies in the helicopter industry but left that in 1971 to start his own farming operation in Florida.

LOTT, Harry Hunter.
B. c1880. D. 05 FEB 1949 Lake Worth, FL. Gold: 1904 Eights. Hunter Lott rowed for the Vesper eight while he was a medical student at the Jefferson Medical College in Philadelphia. Shortly after the Olympics he earned his M.D. degree and practiced in Philadelphia as an otolaryngologist. He eventually became a professor at Jefferson, specializing in diseases of the ear.

LOVSTED, Carl Martin.
B. 04 APR 1930. Bronze: 1952 Fours with. Carl Lovsted made the 1952 Olympic team as a member of the University of Washington four. While rowing for the Huskies, he was on the 1950 eight that won the IRA Regatta, and the 1951 crew that finished second to Cal at the same race.

LYON, Richard Avery.
B. 07 SEP 1939 San Fernando, CA. Bronze: 1964 Fours without. A Stanford graduate, class of 1961, Dick Lyon rowed for the United States in two Olympic Games. In 1964 he had the two-oar for the Lake Washington RC four that took a bronze medal in Tokyo. In 1966 Lyon rowed for both a national and a world champion in that same event. In 1972 he again qualified for the Olympic team, this time in the coxless pairs with Larry Hough, but they failed to make the finals.

Lyon was a mechanical engineering major at Stanford, and makes his living as an engineer. He used those talents to help design the ergometer testing technique which is used by all major crews to help test the efficiency of their rowers.

MAHER, William Patrick.
B. 25 JUN 1946 Detroit, MI. Bronze: 1968 Double Sculls. Rowing for Northeastern University and the Detroit BC, Bill Maher was a four-time national champion in the single sculls, and helped win a national championship in the eights, that in 1963. At the 1968 Olympics, Maher was partnered by John Nunn in the double sculls.

MANRING, Charles David.
B. 18 AUG 1929 Cleveland, OH. Gold: 1952 Eights. Charley Manring started out at Rutgers but received a commission to the Naval Academy and left the New Jersey school after one year. Manring was the coxswain on the Annapolis shell that won the Olympics and the IRA Regatta and the stern Sprints in 1952. He later became a career naval officer.

MARSH, Edward.
B. 12 FEB 1874 Philadelphia, PA. Gold: 1900 Eights. An 1894 graduate of Lehigh, Ed Marsh did all his rowing for the Vesper Boat Club. With them he won six U.S. and two Canadian national titles, all prior to 1902. He later did some coaching, mostly with the West Philadelphia BC, but he had one year as an assistant at the University of Pennsylvania.

MARTIN, Robert.

B. 19 JUN 1925. Gold: 1948 Fours with. Bob Martin attended the University of Washington and had the three-oar for their gold medal-winning four at the London Olympics.

McDOWELL, Paul L.

B. 17 JAN 1905 Philadelphia, PA. Bronze: 1928 Pairs without. Paul McDowell was a member of the Penn Barge Club and was partnered by John Schmitt at the 1928 Olympics.

McILVAINE, Charles Joseph.

B. 16 AUG 1904 Philadelphia, PA. D. 1976. Gold: 1928 Double Sculls. Charley McIlvaine rowed for the Penn Athletic Club after graduating from Penn. He was partnered in the doubles by Paul Costello in 1928 and together they won several national championships. McIlvaine's son, Charles, Jr., also became an excellent oarsman, winning a gold medal in the eights at the 1955 Pan-American Games.

McINTOSH, James Stuart.

B. 09 AUG 1930 Detroit, MI. Silver: 1956 Fours without. Jim McIntosh attended his hometown school, the University of Detroit, and rowed for the Detroit BC. He was the stroke-oar for their club crew at the 1956 Olympics. He continued to compete after the Olympics, winning a national title in 1959 in the pairs with.

McKINLAY, Arthur Frank.

B. 20 JAN 1932 Detroit, MI. Silver: 1956 Fours without. Art McKinlay and his brother, John, became the second set of twin brothers to compete for the United States in the Olympics—after the White brothers in 1952 yachting. Together they had won three national titles for the Detroit BC, in the 1951 fours without, and the 1953 fours with and pairs with. Their 1956 Olympic Trials victory counted as another national championship and in 1957 they again won the U.S. title in the fours with.

McKINLAY, John Dickinson.

B. 20 JAN 1932 Detroit, MI. Silver: 1956 Fours without. John McKinlay attended Boston University and rowed on their varsity crew team in 1954 and 1955. His club team was the Detroit BC and he won several national titles in the company of his twin brother (see above). At the Olympics, their four-oared shell won their heat and semi-final easily, but they were beaten decisively in the final by a Canadian crew.

McLOUGHLIN, James.

B. 1885. D. 01 APR 1946. Silver: 1904 Double Sculls. Jim McLoughlin rowed for the Ravenswood BC at the 1904 Olympics and partnered John Hoben in the double sculls.

McMILLIN, James Burge.

B. 08 MAR 1914. Gold: 1936 Eights. Jim McMillin sat in the fifth seat for the University of Washington eight at the 1936 Olympics. Off to a poor start in the Olympic final, the Huskies gradually crept up on the leaders, Germany and Italy, and won the gold medal in the closest finish ever in the Olympic eights—less than a seat separated the first three boats.

MICKELSON, Timothy Carl.

B. 12 NOV 1948 Madison, WI. Silver: 1972 Eights. Tim Mickelson is the only male Olympic rower to have come out of the University of Wisconsin. He graduated from there in 1971 but did his club rowing for the Potomac BC in 1972 when he represented the United States in the Olympics. He continued to row and won a gold medal in the eights at the 1975 Pan-American Games.

MILLER, John Lester.

B. 05 JUN 1903 Brooklyn, NY. D. 01 AUG 1965 New York, NY. Gold: 1924 Eights. John Miller was on the football, water polo, and crew teams while a student at Yale, but it was at rowing that he achieved his greatest success. After graduating in 1924 Miller went into building construction and real estate.

MILLER, William G.

B. 16 MAR 1905 Philadelphia, PA. Silver(2): 1928 Fours without, 1932 Single Sculls. Bill Miller started rowing with the Penn Barge Club and helped them win a silver medal in the fours in 1928. After those Olympics, however, he joined the Penn AC and began sculling full-time. He was national champion for four straight years in the single sculls, starting in 1930.

MITCHELL, Edward P., Jr.
B. 23 JUL 1901 Philadelphia, PA. Ddi. Bronze: 1924
Fours with. Ed Mitchell rowed for Penn, graduating in
1923, and then joined the Bachelor's Barge Club. He
was a construction engineer.

MITCHELL, Henry Kent, II.
B. 29 MAR 1939 Albany, NY. Gold: 1964 Pairs with;
Bronze: 1960 Pairs with. One of only three Americans to
cox two crews to Olympic medals, Kent Mitchell earned
that first medal while a student at Stanford. He returned
to the Olympics in 1964 while a law student at Cal/
Berkeley and again coxed the Stanford Crew Association pair to a medal—this time gold. In non-Olympic
years, Mitchell also won two national championships, in
1961 and 1962, both in the pairs with. In 1960 his
oarsmen were Conn Findlay and Dick Draeger, but Ed
Ferry replaced Draeger for the other championships.

    Mitchell graduated from law school in 1964 and is
today a practicing attorney with his own law firm.

MITTET, Theodore Peder.
B. 23 DEC 1941 Seattle, WA. Bronze: 1964 Fours with-
out. From the University of Washington and the Lake
Washington RC, Ted Mittet had the bow-oar for the
American four that won the bronze medal at Tokyo.

MOCH, Robert Gaston.
B. 20 JUN 1914 Montesano, WA. Gold: 1936 Eights.
Graduating in the Olympic year of 1936, Bob Moch
coxed the University of Washington eight to the Olympic gold medal at Berlin. Moch was also calling cadence when the Huskies won the IRA Regatta that
same year. After college he went to Harvard Law
School and has practiced since 1941 as an attorney. He
also coached crew briefly, from 1936 to 1939 as an
assistant at Washington and as the head coach at MIT
from 1939 until 1944.

MOORE, Edward Peerman.
B. 20 OCT 1897 Ringgold, VA. D. 09 FEB 1968 Washington, DC. Gold: 1920 Eights. Before the Olympic year of
1920, Ed Moore had never sat in a shell. And a few
weeks before the 1920 Olympic Trials, he was only a
junior varsity oarsman for the Naval Academy. But, by
sheer hard work, he improved rapidly and was moved
to the big boat for the Henley Regatta. Moore so impressed the midshipmen that he was elected captain of
the crew team for the following year. He also played
football at Annapolis before his 1921 graduation.

    Ed Moore was a career naval officer who retired
as a rear admiral in 1945. First, though, he served with
valor in World War II, being the chief of staff to the
commander of the Pacific Task Force. For his efforts he
was awarded the Legion of Merit and two Presidential
Unit Citations.

MOREY, Robert Willis, Jr.
B. 23 AUG 1936 Cleveland, OH. Gold: 1956 Eights.
"Jack" Morey attended Yale, class of 1958, and was the
stroke-oar for their victorious Olympic eight in 1956.

MORGAN, Allan Jerome.
B. 16 JUL 1925. Gold: 1948 Fours without. Allan
Morgan was the coxswain of the 1948 Washington four
which took the gold medal at London.

MORRIS, Herbert Roger.
B. 16 JUL 1915. Gold: 1936 Eights. From the University
of Washington, Herb Morris was in the bow seat for
their eight which won the Olympic gold medal and won
the IRA Regatta in both 1936 and 1937.

MULCAHY, John J. F.
B. 1875. D. 19 NOV 1942. Gold: 1904 Double Sculls;
Silver: 1904 Pairs without. John Mulcahy was the first
U.S. Olympic rower to win a national title, having taken
the double sculls in 1891 with M. F. Monahan. Rowing
for the Atalanta BC in New York, he added another in
1904, partnered by Bill Varley in the doubles.

MURPHY, Richard Frederick.
B. 14 NOV 1931 New Jersey. Gold: 1952 Eights. Dick
Murphy was a member of the great Naval Academy
eight which won the IRA Regatta, the Eastern Sprints,
the Olympic Trials, and the Olympic Games in 1952. He
rowed for two more years, adding two more titles at the
IRA's and the Easterns. After graduation from Annapolis
in 1954 he spent his required time in the service, but
retired immediately thereafter as a first lieutenant.

MYERS, Kenneth.

B. 10 AUG 1896 Norristown, PA. Ddi. Gold: 1932 Double Sculls; Silver(2): 1920 Fours with, 1928 Single Sculls. With Paul Costello, John Kelly, Sr., and Conn Findlay, Ken Myers is one of only four Americans to have won three rowing medals. The first came as a member of the Penn Barge four in 1920, partnered by the Federschmidt brothers and Carl Klose, with the Naval Academy coxswain, Sherm Clark, filling in at the rudder. Myers won two national single scull championships, both in 1929.

NASH, Ted Allison, II.

B. 29 OCT 1932 Melrose, MA. Gold: 1960 Fours without; Bronze: 1964 Fours without. Ted Nash was the only man to row on both the U.S. coxless four shells that won medals at the 1960 and 1964 Olympics. The gold in 1960 was probably the highlight of a distinguished rowing career, both as an oarsman and a coach. Nash won over a dozen national titles, both in the United States and Canada, and won gold medals at both the 1959 and 1963 Pan-American Games. Though he started out at Boston University, most of his rowing was done either for the University of Washington or the Lake Washington RC.

As great a competitor as he was, it is probably surpassed by his career as a coach. He started with the freshman crew at Penn in 1965 and moved to the varsity job in 1969. Also coaching the Penn Elite Crew, he has produced 32 rowers who made Olympic teams, and coached nine boats in either Olympic or Pan-American competition. Twice he has led Penn to unbeaten seasons. Nash has also been active as an administrator; he is a founder and past president of the National Women's Rowing Association and is a member of the U.S. Olympic Rowing Committee for Women.

NASSE, Albert F.

B. 02 JUL 1878. D. 21 NOV 1910. Gold: 1904 Fours without. Al Nasse rowed the stroke-oar for the Century BC four which won the 1904 gold medal.

NUNN, John Hamann.

B. 12 OCT 1942 Terre Haute, IN. Bronze: 1968 Double Sculls. John Nunn graduated from Cornell, rowing on a winning junior varsity eight at the Eastern Sprints while there, but it was after college that he really blossomed as a rower. In 1967 Nunn won the national association single sculls and took a silver medal in that event at the Pan-American Games. The following year he teamed with Bill Maher to win the Olympic bronze at Mexico City. In 1971 he again rowed in the doubles, this time with Tom McKibbon at the Pan-Am Games, and they won a bronze medal together.

After college, John Nunn earned an M.B.A. at Michigan and he has since been very active in the business world, setting up his own business, which sells fabricated metals and packaged products to the aerospace industry.

PEREW, Robert S.

B. 05 AUG 1923. Bronze: 1948 Fours without. Bob Perew was a Yale student in 1948 when he had the bow seat in their four at the Olympic Games. The year 1948 was a difficult one for Perew because he had to suffer through the Elis losing to Harvard both in their match race and at the Eastern Sprints.

PICARD, Geoffrey William.

B. 20 MAR 1943 Oakland, CA. Bronze: 1964 Fours without. Geoffrey Picard was only selected as an alternate to the 1964 rowing team but he was moved into the four shell when Phil Durbrow became ill and collapsed after the first heat. Picard, rowing with a completely new crew and in a completely different style, adapted well enough to help the four win a bronze medal.

Picard was a student at Harvard in 1964 and eventually earned an M.B.A. from that school. While there he rowed all four years, helping the Crimson win the Eastern Sprints in 1964 and 1965 and beating Yale every year. After earning his M.B.A. he joined the investment banking world with the firm of Morgan Stanley & Co., and remains with that company to this day as a vice president.

PRICE, Thomas Steele.

B. 28 MAY 1933. Gold: 1952 Pairs without. Tom Price began rowing only six months before the 1952 Olympics and first sat in a pair-oared shell only two months before the Helsinki Games. At the time he was a freshman at Rutgers and his partner was also a Rutgers student, Charles Logg. Together they were soundly beaten in the first heat of the Olympics, finishing last. However they came through the repechages to the final where they met the same three boats who had beaten them in the first round. In the finals they reversed the decision to take the gold medal, being dubbed the "Cinderella Kids" in the process.

PROCTOR, Henry Arthur.
B. 19 OCT 1929 Kansas. Gold: 1952 Eights. Henry Proctor rowed for the great Naval Academy eight which won the IRA Regatta, the Eastern Sprints, the Olympic Trials and the Olympic Games in 1952. After graduating from Annapolis in 1954 he joined the U.S. Air Force, rising to colonel before his retirement in 1971.

PURCHASE, Ralph Kenneth.
B. 11 JUL 1916. Gold: 1948 Eights. Ralph Purchase was the coxswain for the Cal/Berkeley eight at the 1948 Olympics. Though Cal had had an indifferent season, losing twice to Washington during the year, they defeated the Huskies in the semi-finals of the Olympic Trials and won the gold medal in London without losing a race. Purchase later became a high-ranking executive with the Zellerbach Corp.

RANTZ, Joseph Harry.
B. 31 MAR 1914. Gold: 1936 Eights. Joe Rantz attended the University of Washington. He rowed the seven-oar for their eight that won the Olympic Games in 1936 and the IRA Regatta in 1936 and 1937.

RAVANACK, Joseph.
Bronze: 1904 Double Sculls. Joe Ravanack was from New Orleans and, together with John Wells, rowed for the Independent RC at the 1904 Olympics.

RAYMOND, Peter Harlow.
B. 21 JAN 1947 Princeton, NJ. Silver: 1972 Eights. In 1968, Pete Raymond was the first rower from Princeton to make the U.S. Olympic team (in the fours), and he repeated the feat in 1972 with a bit more success. After his graduation in 1968, Raymond rowed with the Union Boat Club, and made the U.S. National team as a spare in both 1970 and 1971. At the 1972 Olympics he had the third oar for the eight. Raymond later taught at a prep school near Boston and coached the Harvard lightweight and junior varsity crews.

ROCKEFELLER, James Stillman.
B. 08 JUN 1902 New York, NY. Gold: 1924 Eights. While at Yale, "Babe" Rockefeller earned both a major "Y" for his participation in crew, and a Phi Beta Kappa key for his scholarship. He went into banking almost immediately after graduation and remained in that business for many years, eventually becoming president of the National City Bank in New York as well as serving on the boards of several other businesses.

ROSSI, Albert.
B. 20 JUN 1931. Bronze: 1952 Fours with. Al Rossi was the coxswain for the University of Washington four at the 1952 Olympics. The boat won a close race in the first round over Great Britain, but won the semi-finals easily. However, in the finals, there was nothing Rossi could do with the cadence—they were beaten decisively by a Czech team and nosed out of second by the Swiss.

RYAN, Joseph.
Gold: 1904 Pairs without. Joe Ryan had the stroke-oar for the Seawanhaka Boat Club of New York at the 1904 Olympics. His bowman was Bob Farnam.

SALISBURY, Edwin Lyle.
B. 31 MAY 1910. Gold: 1932 Eights. Ed Salisbury was on the Cal eight which won the IRA Regatta as well as the Olympic Games in 1932.

SANBORN, Alden Ream.
B. 22 MAY 1899 Jefferson, WI. Gold: 1920 Eights. Al Sanborn started at Beloit College but earned an appointment to the Naval Academy in 1918. He was the strongest man on the 1920 Navy eight, and sat in the "engine room" at number five. Graduating in 1922, Sanborn earned an M.S. degree from MIT in 1928 in engineering, but remained a career naval officer, retiring in 1951 as a captain. He then worked as a sales engineer for the Wright Aeronautical Corp.

SAYRE, John Anthony.
B. 01 APR 1936 Tacoma, WA. Gold: 1960 Fours without. At the 1959 Pan-American Games, the Lake Washington RC four of John Sayre, Ted Nash, "Rusty" Wailes, and Jay Hall easily won a gold medal. At the 1960 Olympics in Rome, Sayre was in almost the same boat,

with "Dan" Ayrault replacing Hall, and the result was the same—they beat an Italian crew by almost three seconds to win the gold. John Sayre was a graduate of the University of Washington.

SCHAUERS, Joseph A.
B. 27 MAY 1909. Gold: 1932 Pairs with. Joe Schauers did his rowing for the Penn Barge Club. At the 1932 Olympics he was partnered by Charlie Kieffer and coxed by Ed Jennings.

SCHELL, Frank Reamer.
B. c1884. D. 05 DEC 1959 New Rochelle, NY. Gold: 1904 Eights. Frank Schell rowed for the Vesper BC for several years and had their three-oar at the 1904 Olympics. He later became a career officer in the U.S. Army.

SCHMITT, John V.
B. 23 DEC 1901 Philadelphia, PA. Bronze: 1928 Pairs without. At only 5'-7½" and 165 lbs., John Schmitt is one of the smallest U.S. Olympic rowers ever. In 1928 he represented the Penn Barge Club and partnered Paul McDowell at the Olympic Games.

SEIFFERT, Armin Kurt.
B. 21 DEC 1935 Detroit, MI. Gold: 1956 Pairs with. Kurt Seiffert coxed the Stanford crews from 1955 until 1957. After graduation he took a few years off from school and was a cox for the Lake Washington RC. He called cadence for U.S. boats at both the 1956 and 1960 Olympics and in 1956 he coxed his oarsmen, Conn Findlay and Dan Ayrault, to a gold medal. In 1960 he was with the fours with shell that did not reach the finals.

After the 1960 Olympics, Seiffert returned to school and earned an M.D. from Michigan in 1964. Since 1968 he has practiced as a neurologist.

SHAKESPEARE, Frank Bradford.
B. 31 MAY 1930 Philadelphia, PA. Gold: 1952 Eights. Frank Shakespeare was in the bow seat for the Naval Academy eight at the 1952 Olympics. He also rowed on winning eights at both the 1952 and 1953 IRA Regattas and Eastern Sprints. After graduating in 1953 he began a career as a naval officer.

SHEFFIELD, Frederick.
B. 26 FEB 1902 New York, NY. D. 08 MAY 1971 Wilton, CT. Gold: 1924 Eights. Fred Sheffield played freshman football at Yale, but crew was his only varsity sport. He obviously did well, making the varsity eight that won the 1924 gold medal. Sheffield graduated from Yale in 1924 and then went on to Yale Law School, finishing that in 1927.

Sheffield became a very famous corporation lawyer in New York and a partner in his own firm. He was known for his philanthropic pursuits and served from 1966 until 1971 as board chairman of the Carnegie Corporation. He also served as U.S. Commissioner to the 1940 New York World's Fair.

SMITH, Justus Ketcham.
B. 28 MAR 1922 Spokane, WA. Gold: 1948 Eights. A student at Cal/Berkeley in 1948, Justus Smith sat in the second seat on their eight at the Olympic Games. His college degree was in landscape architecture and he has since used it to become a consultant to regional planners in the western United States.

SPOCK, Benjamin McLane.
B. 02 MAY 1903 New Haven, CT. Gold: 1924 Eights. Ben Spock ran track for one year at Yale and rowed crew for four years, but his college career pales beside his accomplishments afterwards. After college he started med school at Yale, then transferred to Columbia, where he earned his M.D. and became a pediatrician.

As the author of *Baby and Child Care*, Dr. Spock is a name known to millions of parents in this country. The book was written while Spock practiced pediatrics in New York and sold over 25,000,000 copies. He also wrote five other books on child care.

During the 60's, Dr. Benjamin Spock was in the news for other reasons. He took a strong stand against nuclear proliferation and participated in several protests against military escalation in Vietnam. In 1972, Ben Spock became the only former U.S. Olympic athlete to run for the United States presidency. He ran on the People's Party ticket, espousing radical political action and severe reduction of the military, but received no electoral votes. He is now retired but does some occasional public speaking, usually at universities or for the benefit of peace groups.

STACK, John Charles.
B. 22 MAR 1924 Camden, NJ. Gold: 1948 Eights. John Stack attended the University of California and had the bow seat on their eight at the 1948 Olympics. That was the year that Cal pulled a big upset at the Olympic Trials by defeating a Washington crew that had beaten them twice earlier in the year. After college, Stack became an engineer, specializing in X-ray technology.

STAINES, Michael Laurence.
B. 30 MAY 1949 Guilford, England. Silver: 1976 Pairs without. Mike Staines had his first big year in 1971 when he rowed in the Pan-American Games and helped his Cornell eight to a victory at the IRA Regatta. He then competed in the 1972 Olympics, in the pairs with, but he and partner Luther Jones finished only eleventh. At the 1976 Olympics he and Calvin Coffey beat all but the East German pair to win the silver medal. Staines' wife, the former Laura Terdoslavich, was a member of the women's rowing team at the 1976 Olympics—in the pairs without.

STALDER, Marvin Frederick.
B. 09 DEC 1905 Riverside, CA. Gold: 1928 Eights. A 6'-1", 170 lb., bow-oarsman from the University of California, Marvin Stalder also rowed on the eight that won the IRA Regatta in 1928.

STEVENS, Edward Glenister, Jr.
B. 15 SEP 1932 St. Louis, MO. Gold: 1952 Eights. Appointed to the Naval Academy from Missouri, Ed Stevens was the stroke-oar for their eight at the Olympic Games. He also rowed that oar in leading Annapolis to three straight wins at the IRA's and Eastern Sprints, starting in 1952. After graduation he became a career naval officer and also did some graduate study in nuclear engineering at MIT.

STOCKHOFF, Arthur M.
B. 19 NOV 1879. D. 20 OCT 1934 St. Louis, MO. Bronze: 1904 Fours without. Dr. Arthur Stockhoff was a dentist in St. Louis who did his rowing for the Century Boat Club.

STODDARD, Laurence Ralph.
B. 22 DEC 1903 New York, NY. Gold: 1924 Eights. "Chick" Stoddard was the coxswain of the 1924 Yale eight. While a student in New Haven, he coxed the varsity crew in his sophomore and junior years and was a varsity swimmer those same years. After college he went into the shipping business with the West India Shipping Company.

STORM, James Eugene.
B. 12 FEB 1941 San Diego, CA. Silver: 1964 Double Sculls. At 6'-7½", Jim Storm is the tallest U.S. Olympian who did not play on the basketball team. He was the stroke in a double with "Cy" Cromwell at the 1964 Olympics where they lost by several seconds to a Soviet crew. Storm had attended Pomona College but was rowing for the San Diego RC in 1964. In 1967 he finally won a gold medal, again in the double sculls, but this time at the Pan-American Games. He graduated in 1971 from the University of California Medical School and became a practicing psychiatrist.

STOWE, William Arthur.
B. 23 MAR 1940 Oak Park, IL. Gold: 1964 Eights. Bill Stowe won many championships as a stroke-oar. He began rowing at the Kent School and then went to college at Cornell. As a freshman he stroked the Cornell freshman eight to a victory at the IRA's, and repeated that victory with the varsity in both 1961 and 1962. In 1963 he had an unusual club affiliation, rowing for the Club de Nautique de Saigon at the Hong Kong Regatta, while a lieutenant in the navy. Upon returning home in 1963 he joined the Vesper BC and again was the stroke-oar for their Olympic eight in 1964. At the 1967 Pan-American Games he also won a gold medal, this time in the fours. Two of his teammates in that boat were from the 1964 Vesper Olympic eight, Hugh Foley and coxswain Bob Zimonyi.

SUERIG, Frederick.
Silver: 1904 Fours without. Fred Suerig, a minister from St. Louis, rowed for the Mound City Rowing Club at the Olympics.

TERRY, Lawrence, Jr.
B. 12 APR 1946 Concord, MA. Silver: 1972 Eights. Lawrence Terry rowed in the fours without at the 1968 Olympics, finishing fifth. Before the next Olympics he won two national titles, in the 1970 pairs with and the 1971 pairs without. He was the stroke-oar on the 1972

Olympic eight which was beaten only by the New Zealand crew.

THOMPSON, William G.
B. 19 JUL 1908 Napa, CA. D. 1956. Gold: 1928 Eights. At 6'-3" and 190 lbs., Bill Thompson was the muscleman of the 1928 Cal eight. He graduated from the Berkeley college in 1931.

TITUS, Constance Sutton.
B. c1873 Pass Christian, MS. D. 24 AUG 1967 Bronxville, NY. Bronze: 1904 Single Sculls. While a youth in Mississippi, the first water sport in which Constance Titus participated was alligator hunting. Presumably he learned to row to get away from the alligators quickly.

Titus later moved to New York where he represented the Atalanta Boat Club. He won three national titles in the single sculls and one in the doubles, all in the first decade of the century. He spent a few years as crew coach at Princeton, but made his living for over 50 years as an insurance broker.

TOWER, Harold.
B. 17 JUL 1911. Gold: 1932 Eights. Harold Tower rowed on the Cal eight that won the Olympic Games and the IRA Regatta in 1932.

TURNER, David Lindsay.
B. 23 SEP 1923. Gold: 1948 Eights. Dave Turner rowed the seven-oar for Cal/Berkeley at the 1948 Olympics. The Cal team that year had lost twice to Washington but turned the tables at the U.S. Final Trials. Turner graduated in 1949 and rowed in the Cal boat which gained more revenge by defeating the Huskies at the IRA Regatta, thereby revenging their 1948 defeat in that race. He has since become a career officer in the U.S. Air Force.

TURNER, Ian Gordon.
B. 11 MAY 1925. Gold: 1948 Eights. Ian Turner sat behind his brother, David, in the stroke seat at the 1948 Olympics. He was a 1951 graduate of the University of California.

ULBRICKSON, Alvin Edmund, Jr.
B. 10 OCT 1930. Bronze: 1952 Fours with. Al Ulbrickson rowed for the University of Washington four at the 1952

Olympics. Though they won their heat and semi rather easily, the boat was beaten decisively by a Czech crew in the finals.

VARLEY, William P.
Gold: 1904 Double Sculls; Silver: 1904 Pairs without. Bill Varley competed in the above two events at the 1904 Olympics. A member of the Atalanta Boat Club, in both races he was the stroke-oar and was partnered by John Mulcahy.

VOERG, Gustav.
B. 07 JUN 1870 Germany. D. 21 APR 1944 St. Louis, MO. Bronze: 1904 Fours without. Gustav Voerg rowed for the Western RC of St. Louis. Though finishing only third at the 1904 Olympics, Voerg and his Olympic teammates, Lou Helm and Frank Dummerth, had rowed a four in 1902 which won the national championship. Voerg was well known locally as a competitive swimmer and later became an excellent bowler, having to his credit several 300 games.

WAHLSTROM, Richard Wayne.
B. 08 NOV 1931. Bronze: 1952 Fours with. Richard Wahlstrom attended the University of Washington. He was the three-oar on their 1952 Olympic eight.

WAILES, Richard Donald.
B. 21 MAR 1936 Seattle, WA. Gold(2): 1956 Eights, 1960 Fours without. "Rusty" Wailes is one of the few American rowers to have won two gold medals. The first came in 1956 when he rowed on the Yale eight that won the Olympic Games. He graduated from Yale in 1958, but helped their varsity eight to victories in 1957 and 1958 both at the Eastern Sprints and at the Harvard-Yale Regatta. In 1959, rowing for the Lake Washington RC, he teamed up with Ted Nash, John Sayre, and Jay Hall to win a gold medal in the fours without at the Pan-American Games. The following year, at the Rome Olympics, Dan Ayrault replaced Hall in the four, but they again won a gold medal.

WELCHLI, John Richard.
B. 06 MAR 1929 Detroit, MI. Silver: 1956 Fours without. John Welchli graduated from Brown in 1950 and was a fine all-round athlete for the Providence school. He competed for all four years on the swim, crew, and track

teams, and ran cross-country for two years. Welchli was rather small for a world-class rower, only 160 lbs., and he won numerous national championships in light-weight boats. Rowing for the Detroit BC, he was partnered at the Olympics by the McKinlay twins and Jim McIntosh. Welchli still rows and competes in masters' rowing events.

WELLS, John.
Bronze: 1904 Double Sculls. John Wells was from New Orleans and rowed for the Independent Rowing Club.

WELSFORD, Henry Reed.
B. 14 JUN 1900. Bronze: 1924 Fours with. Henry Welsford started rowing on the plebe crew at the U.S. Naval Academy in 1920, although he left school before graduating. He then joined the Malta Boat Club in 1921 and rowed for them until 1924 when he was recruited by the Bachelor's Barge Club to make up a four-oared shell for the 1924 Olympic Trials.

WESTLUND, Warren DeHaven.
B. 20 AUG 1926. Gold: 1948 Fours with. Warren Westlund attended the University of Washington. He rowed the stroke-oar for their 1948 Olympic four, which won every race easily at the Olympic Trials and the Olympics.

WHITE, John Galbraith.
B. 16 MAY 1916 Seattle, WA. Gold: 1936 Eights. John White rowed for the University of Washington freshman eight that won the IRA Regatta in 1935, and the next two years he moved up to their varsity boat, which also dominated the IRA's. He graduated with a degree in metallurgical engineering and later worked for Bethlehem Steel in sales.

WIGHT, David Henry.
B. 28 JUL 1934 London, England. Gold: 1956 Eights. Tall and lean at 6'-6" and 175 lbs., Dave Wight was in the second seat for the Yale eight at the 1956 Olympics. He later attended graduate school at Yale in architecture and became an architect.

WILL, Robert Ide.
B. 20 APR 1925. Gold: 1948 Fours with. Bob Will attended the University of Washington and rowed for their

four at the 1948 Olympics. He had also rowed on their eight that won the 1948 IRA Regatta.

WILSON, Alfred Mayo.
B. 31 DEC 1903 Minneapolis, MN. Gold: 1924 Eights. From Yale, class of 1925, Al Wilson rowed crew for all four years and was the captain of the crew team in his last year. After college he worked in Boston for a time, but returned to Minnesota during the war and worked there the rest of his life with the Honeywell Corp.

WILSON, Harold C.
B. 25 JAN 1903 Washington, PA. Bronze: 1924 Pairs with. Harold Wilson only started rowing in 1922 when he joined the Penn Barge Club. At the 1924 Olympics he partnered Leon Butler and was coxed by Ed Jennings.

WORKMAN, James Theodore.
B. 30 APR 1908 Woodward, OK. Gold: 1928 Eights. Jim Workman attended the University of California and rowed for their eight that won the 1928 IRA Regatta and the Olympic Games gold medal. He later became a career officer in the U.S. Air Force, eventually retiring as a lieutenant colonel.

ZIMONYI, Robert.
B. 18 APR 1918 Sarvar, Hungary. Gold: 1964 Eights; Bronze: 1948 Pairs with (competed for Hungary). Bob Zimonyi grew up in Hungary and was a noted coxswain in that country. At the 1948 Olympics he coxed Antal Szenday and Bela Zsitnik to a bronze medal in the pairs, and coxed the Hungarian eight at the 1952 Olympics. Zimonyi would have been on the 1956 Olympic team, but when the Russians invaded Hungary, that country sent only a few competitors to Melbourne.

Shortly after that episode, Zimonyi defected to the United States and joined the Vesper Boat Club as a coxswain. When he became a U.S. citizen he was eligible to compete for our team and, in addition to his Olympic gold medal, he won two gold medals at the Pan-American Games and coxed numerous Vesper crews to national championships.

WOMEN

Women's rowing became an Olympic sport in 1976 at Montreal. In two Olympic appearances, the women of the German Democratic Republic (East Germany) have made a shambles of the competition, winning eight of a possible 12 gold medals. The United States competed only in 1976 and won two medals, in the singles sculls and the eights.

OUTSTANDING PERFORMANCES

Oldest Medalist
27y46d Jacqueline Zoch
Youngest Medalist (coxswain)
17y91d Lynn Silliman
Youngest Medalist (oarswoman)
20y145d Peggy McCarthy

BROWN, Carol Page.
B. 19 APR 1953 Oak Park, IL. Bronze: 1976 Eights. While a student at Princeton, Carol Brown captained the women's swim team in addition to rowing crew for four years. Her first international appearance came at the 1974 World Championships when she finished fifth in a pair. The next year Brown took a silver at the Worlds in the eights. After the 1976 Olympics she continued to compete, winning a silver and a bronze at the FISA World Championships in 1978 and 1979. She made the 1980 Olympic team, again in the eight, rowing for the team that won the Lucerne Regatta over the East German Olympic champions.

In 1981, Carol Brown was part of history when she won a gold medal as a member of the U.S. coxed four at the Henley Royal Regatta, the first year that women were allowed to compete in the Henley. Brown works as a vice president for the ALPAC Corp., in Seattle, and is still training with an eye towards 1984.

DeFRANTZ, Anita Luceete.
B. 04 OCT 1952 Philadelphia, PA. Bronze: 1976 Eights. Anita DeFrantz continues to carve niches for herself in Olympic history. A 1974 graduate of Connecticut College, she went on to earn an LL.B. from Penn in 1977. While a law student she made the U.S. Olympic eight and became the first black to compete for the United States in Olympic rowing. Before the 1980 Olympics

she distinguished herself by winning six different national titles and sharing a silver medal at the 1978 World Championships in the coxed four. She then made the 1980 Olympic team, but the boycott dashed those hopes.

DeFrantz was an outspoken critic of the boycott and with her law background was an eloquent spokesperson for the athletes. Though it changed nothing, one congressman commented that he was highly impressed by her presentation and would welcome her in any law firm. For her support of the Olympic movement, in 1980 she became only the second American athlete to receive the Bronze Medal of the Olympic Order from the International Olympic Committee. Miss DeFrantz is a member of the President's Council on Physical Fitness, a trustee of Connecticut College, on the Executive Board of the USOC, is vice chair for the Athletes' Advisory Council of the USOC, and currently works as an assistant vice president for the Los Angeles Olympic Organizing Committee.

GRAVES, Carie Brand.
B. 27 JUN 1953 Madison, WI. Bronze: 1976 Eights. A University of Wisconsin graduate, Carie Graves' first international success came in 1975 when she won a silver medal in the eight-oared shell at the World Championships. She then made the 1976 Olympic team in the eight, adding an Olympic bronze. But she continued to row and made the 1980 Olympic team, rowing on the eight that won the Lucerne Regatta over East Germany. In 1981 she had the six-oar for the women's eight that finished second at the World Championships in Munich, but her big moment that year came at the Henley Royal Regatta when she was a member of the winning fours with crew in the first year that women were admitted to the Henley. Graves is now the women's crew coach at Harvard.

GREIG, Marion Ethel.
B. 22 FEB 1954 Hudson, NY. Bronze: 1976 Eights. Marion Greig was from Red Hook, New Jersey, and was a Cornell graduate. She rowed in the third seat on the women's eight at Montreal.

LIND, Joan Louise.

B. 26 SEP 1952 Long Beach, CA. Silver: 1976 Single Sculls. The greatest female sculler America has yet produced, Joan Lind began rowing in 1971, her freshman year at Long Beach State. She started out in doubles and quads but moved into the singles in 1973. She competed at the next two World Championships, gradually improving, and at the 1976 Olympics she lost by only 65/100th's of a second to East Germany's Christine Schleiblich. Lind has continued to scull, winning many national titles, and made the 1980 Olympic team. Though she could not compete in the 1980 Olympics, she won two silver medals at the Lucerne and Amsterdam Regattas.

Joan Lind later earned a master's degree from St. Thomas College and today teaches and coaches.

McCARTHY, Peggy Anne.

B. 01 MAR 1956 Urbana, IL. Bronze: 1976 Eights. The youngest oarswoman on the 1976 Olympic eight, Peggy McCarthy was then a student at the University of Wisconsin. Two of her biggest moments have come since then. McCarthy made the 1980 Olympic team, which did not compete, but was in the eight at the Lucerne Regatta that scored an historic victory over the East German Olympic champions. In 1981 she joined four other 1980 Olympians to form a coxed four which won the Henley Royal Regatta in the first year women were allowed at Henley since the races began in 1839.

Peggy McCarthy graduated with a degree in civil engineering and today works with a large engineering firm in the Boston area.

RICKETSON, Gail Susan.

B. 12 SEP 1953 Plattsburgh, NY. Bronze: 1976 Eights. Both a sculler and sweeper, Gail Ricketson also skiied while at the University of New Hampshire, making the All-East Collegiate Ski Team. She has won three national championships—two U.S. and one West German—and was a winner at the 1978 National Sports Festival. Although she went to the 1980 Olympic Trials, it was as a sculler and she failed to be selected for the team.

Ricketson rowed for the College Boat Club in Philadelphia and is a sculling coach at that club as well as the assistant women's crew coach at Penn. She has

worked as a medical lab technician, using her undergraduate degree in microbiology.

SILLIMAN, Lynn.

B. 24 APR 1959 Watsonville, CA. Bronze: 1976 Eights. Lynn Silliman was only a high school junior when she coxed the 1976 Olympic eight. She had earlier won a silver medal at the 1975 World Championships as a coxswain for the U.S. eight-oared boat. In high school, she played varsity tennis her last three years.

WARNER, Anne Elizabeth.

B. 29 AUG 1954 Boston, MA. Bronze: 1976 Eights. Anne Warner was a student at Yale in 1976 when she rowed the four-oar for the U.S. eight at the Olympics. She was also in the U.S. eight that finished second at the 1975 World Championships. While at Yale she was the conductor of the Yale Slavic Chorus.

After college, Warner started law school at Harvard, but took some time off to row. She made the 1980 Olympic team and was on the eight that won the Lucerne International Regatta by defeating the eight from the German Democratic Republic.

ZOCH, Jacqueline Jean.

B. 08 JUN 1949 Madison, WI. Bronze: 1976 Eights. Jackie Zoch was the six-oar for the U.S. women's eight at the 1976 Olympics. At the time she was a teacher, having graduated from the University of Wisconsin the year before. In 1975 she had been a member of the U.S. National Championship eight which finished second at the Worlds.

RUGBY FOOTBALL

Rugby football has appeared on four Olympic programs—those of 1900, 1908, 1920 and 1924. The United States did not have teams entered in 1900 or 1908, but the next two times the sport was held we managed to win the gold medals. Both titles were earned with victories over France in the decisive matches.

OUTSTANDING PERFORMANCES

Most Gold Medals
2 Charles Doe, John O'Neil, Jack Patrick, Rudy Scholz, Colby Slater
(see also Daniel Carroll)
Oldest Gold Medalist
31y224d Alan Williams
Youngest Gold Medalist
20y231d Heaton Wrenn

CARROLL, Daniel Brendan.
B. 17 FEB 1892 Melbourne, Australia. D. 05 AUG 1956 New Orleans, LA. Gold(2): 1908 (competed for Australia), 1920. When Dan Carroll played on the winning Australian team at the 1908 Olympics he set a record, which has not yet been broken, of being the youngest player ever to win international honors at rugby football.

In 1909, Carroll first visited America with the Australian rugby team and, when the Australians visited the West Coast again in 1912, Carroll stayed on in California and enrolled at Stanford. He was on the Stanford rugby team for four years and also played on the soccer team but, although he had been an outstanding sprinter at home, he did not make the Stanford track team. At the 1908 Olympics the Australians utilized his speed by playing him in the center, but at the 1920 Olympics Carroll himself decided, as player-coach, to play in the scrum-half position where his tactical knowledge could be put to its best use.

After Stanford, Carroll furthered his education at Oxford and the Royal School of Mines in England. In 1921 he took up an appointment with Standard Oil and remained with the company until his retirement. During World War I he served as a captain in the U.S. Infantry and was awarded the Distinguished Service Cross.

CLARK, Philip Corriston.
B. 1898. Gold: 1924. Like many of his teammates, Phil Clark was a Stanford grad and a member of the Olympic Club of San Francisco. He later became a geologist and petroleum engineer.

CLEAVELAND, Norman.
B. 04 APR 1901 Oakland, CA. Gold: 1924. Norman Cleaveland attended Stanford and played rugby for four years as well as playing on the football team for three years. After graduating in 1924, Cleaveland spent 22 years in Malaysia supervising the tin dredging operations for a British company, a profession at which he continued to make his living after returning to America. He wrote a book about his experiences in Malaysia during the "Communist Troubles," entitled *Bang Bang in Ampang*, and he had earlier written a well-reviewed biography of his grandparents, the Morleys, a legendary family in the 19th century history of New Mexico.

DeGROOT, Dudley Sargeant.
B. 20 NOV 1899 Chicago, IL. D. 05 MAY 1970 El Cajon, CA. Gold: 1924. Apart from being an outstanding football player at Stanford, Dudley DeGroot was also on the basketball, swimming, and water polo teams, and was the IC4A backstroke champion in 1923 and 1924.

After graduating, DeGroot became quite famous as a football coach, which led to his eventual induction into the College Football Hall of Fame. He began his coaching career as an assistant at Cal/Santa Barbara in 1926. He 1933 he started at San Jose State under the fabled coach Pop Warner and remained there until 1939. DeGroot's first head coaching position was at the University of Rochester in 1940, and in 1944 he became the head coach of the NFL's Washington Redskins. In 1945 he led the 'Skins to the Eastern Conference title, but lost in the championship game to the Cleveland Rams, 15–14. DeGroot was then lured to the new All-American Football Conference where he coached the Los Angeles Dons for two years. He returned to the college ranks, finishing out at West Virginia and New Mexico and ending up with a career head coaching mark of 134 wins, 74 losses and 12 ties.

DEVEREAUX, Robert H. Coleman.
B. 1898. D. c1975. Gold: 1924. Bob Devereaux was from San Francisco and represented both Stanford and the Olympic Club as an athlete. He later became an insurance agent.

DIXON, George Martin.
B. 1902. Gold: 1924. George Dixon came from Vallejo, California, and attended Cal/Berkeley. His best sport at Cal was basketball, in which he was the team star. After graduation he went into the oil business until World War II when he served as a navy pilot. This led to a career as a commercial pilot and for several years he was the private pilot for the Hearst family.

DOE, Charles Webster, Jr.
B. 04 SEP 1898 San Francisco, CA. Gold(2): 1920, 1924. Charlie Doe, from Lowell High School (CA) and Stanford, was one of five players to win golds in both 1920 and 1924. While at Stanford he had played both basketball and rugby and after graduation he continued playing both sports with the Olympic Club of San Francisco. He made his living in the family lumber business.

FARRISH, Linn Markley.
B. 03 OCT 1901 Rumsey, CA. D. 11 SEP 1943 Yugoslavia. Gold: 1924. Linn Farrish attended Stanford where he played football and rugby, and studied geology. After graduation he became a top geologist and petroleum consultant, but he became famous for his war exploits.

As an engineer and expert pilot, Farrish was sent into Yugoslavia as a secret agent. He mapped out the area and located many areas which, although dangerous, could be used as landing strips. He then flew in and out of Yugoslavia, rescuing hundreds of fliers who had bailed out of crippled planes in the Balkans. He spent three 90-day periods in Yugoslavia, each time parachuting in, and then surveying the area by plane, looking for appropriate landing strips. On the third of these trips, his plane crashed in the Balkan Mountains. He was given the Distinguished Service Cross and the government's code of secrecy towards the actions of secret agents was broken, so that his name could be released as a military hero.

FISH, George Winthrop.
B. 1895 Los Angeles, CA. D. 22 FEB 1977 East Hampton, NY. Gold: 1920. George Fish was a graduate of Cal/Berkeley and subsequently Columbia Medical School. He later became a noted urologist and headed many professional organizations. One of Dr. Fish's closest friends was Frederick Schuller, a prolific writer who penned the "Dr. Kildare" stories. Schuller started writing the stories in 1937 based on anecdotes related to him by George Fish, and Dr. Kildare was, in fact, modelled on the Olympic rugby gold medalist.

FITZPATRICK, James P.
Gold: 1920. Jim Fitzpatrick went to college at Santa Clara University and played rugby for San Francisco's Olympic Club.

GRAFF, Edward.
B. 1897. Ddi. Gold: 1924. Ed Graff came from San Francisco and attended Cal/Berkeley. He played the position of hooker on the 1924 Olympic rugby team. In 1932 he was instrumental in convincing his old school to revive rugby as a varsity sport, and Graff took over as the coach in the first years of its revival.

HUNTER, Joseph Garvin.
Ddi. Gold: 1920. In addition to winning a gold medal in 1920, "Lou" Hunter was an alternate on the 1924 team. He was from Mountain View, California, and attended Santa Clara University.

HYLAND, Richard Frank (né Frank William Hyland).
B. 26 JUL 1900 San Francisco, CA. D. 16 JUL 1981 Wawona, CA. Gold: 1924. While attending Stanford, Dick Hyland showed a fine all-round sporting talent and was on the football, track and baseball teams. It was, however, at football that he starred and became known as "Tricky Dicky" because of his open field running. In 1926 against Cal, on the first play from scrimmage, he raced 48 yards for a touchdown, which triggered Stanford to a 41–6 upset victory. He played in both the 1927 and 1928 Rose Bowl Games, and was elected to the Stanford Hall of Fame in 1961.

Hyland later became very well known as a sports writer for the *Los Angeles Times* and did some work as a motion picture director.

KIRKSEY, Morris Marshall.
B. 13 SEP 1895 Waxahachie, TX. D. 25 NOV 1981 Stanford, CA. Gold(2): 1920 Rugby Football, 1920 4 × 100 meter relay (Track & Field); Silver: 1920 100 meters (Track & Field). After graduating from Stanford, Morris Kirksey earned his medical degree from St. Louis Medical College. He later served for 25 years as a staff psychiatrist for the State Department of Corrections, working at San Quentin and Folsom prisons.

Kirksey was known mostly as a sprinter on the track team while at Stanford. He won the IC4A 100y in 1922 and in 1923, scored a sprint double at both the New Zealand and Hawaiian championships. Apart from his medals in the 100m and relay, Kirksey also competed in the 200m at Antwerp, but was eliminated in the heats. He is one of only four men (two Americans) to have won gold medals in two different Olympics sports.

MANELLI, Caeser.
B. 1897. Ddi. Gold: 1924. Caeser Manelli was from San Francisco and attended Santa Clara University. He was a good rugbyist and an excellent basketball player, but baseball was his best sport. He had a tryout with the minor league Oakland Oaks, but it was several years after his competitive prime and many people thought he could have played major league ball, had he started earlier. Manelli later worked for the city of San Francisco as an engineer.

MEHAN, Charles Thomas.
Ddi. Gold: 1920. Charles Mehan was from Alameda, California, and attended Cal/Berkeley.

MULDOON, John, Jr.
B. 02 MAR 1896 Ione, CA. D. c1945. Gold: 1920. John Muldoon graduated from Santa Clara in 1919. In 1920 he, John O'Neil, Jim Fitzpatrick, and Rudy Scholz became the first alums from that school to win an Olympic gold medal.

O'NEIL, John T.
B. 1897. D. 26 MAR 1950 Los Angeles, CA. Gold(2): 1920, 1924. John O'Neil was from a wealthy Texas oil family and attended Santa Clara University, where he learned his rugby. He was one of the organizers and provided much of the finance for the U.S. rugby tours of Europe in 1920 and 1924 and on both occasions he was rewarded with a gold medal.

At the Paris Olympics, O'Neil had recently undergone an operation for appendicitis and early in the game, a kick in the stomach opened the scar from his operation. No substitutions were allowed and O'Neil knew that to come out would leave the U.S. a man short, so he courageously played the entire game.

PATRICK, John Clarence.
B. 25 NOV 1898 Palo Alto, CA. D. 31 MAY 1959 San Francisco, CA. Gold(2): 1920, 1924. Jack Patrick played fullback for the Stanford football team for three years and in his last year (1921) he captained the team. He was also president of the class of '21. Patrick later became a San Francisco insurance broker and was vice-president of Insurance Securities Factors, Inc.

RIGHTER, Cornelius Erwin.
B. 07 MAR 1897 Campbell, CA. Gold: 1920. "Swede" Righter was a football and basketball star at Stanford and also played on the rugby team in 1917. Football was undoubtedly his major sport and he received honorable mention in the 1920 all-America selections.

After graduating in 1921 he became football, basketball, and track coach at the College of the Pacific for 12 years. He later served as a coach at several small Northern California colleges and high schools until his retirement in 1962.

ROGERS, William Lister.
B. 06 FEB 1902 Ventura, CA. Gold: 1924. "Lefty" Rogers was an outstanding basketball player at Stanford and he continued to serve the University throughout his life. He graduated in 1923 and took an M.D. degree from Stanford in 1926. Dr. Rogers served as professor of clinical surgery at Stanford Medical School. He started out as a general surgeon but became interested in the new field of thoracic surgery and was one of the founding members of the American Board of Thoracic Surgery. Rogers was also President of the Stanford Alumni Association and in 1966 he was elected to the Board of Trustees, replacing the well-known shot putter Otis Chandler.

SCHOLZ, Rudolph John.
B. 17 JUN 1896 Kewanee, IL. D. 09 DEC 1981 Palo Alto, CA. Gold(2): 1920, 1924. Rudy Scholz was a law graduate of Santa Clara University and practiced in San Francisco for many years. He also served in the army during both world wars, winning a Bronze Star in Okinawa and retiring with the rank of colonel.

He was remarkable for his longevity as an active rugby player. Scholz first played for Santa Clara at scrum-half in 1913 and in 1979, at the age of 83, he played his last game against the Irish side, Instonians. To mark his services to the sport, a "Rudy Scholz Day" was held at Stanford in 1981 and a plaque of appreciation was presented to him on the rugby field.

SLATER, Colby Edward.
B. 30 APR 1896 Berkeley, CA. D. 30 JAN 1965 Clarksburg, CA. Gold: 1924. "Babe" Slater came from northern California and went to school at "Cal Aggie," now known as the University of California at Davis. While in school he played mostly basketball, but played enough rugby to make two Olympic teams, although he did not play in the 1920 Olympic tourney. After graduating from Cal Aggie, he became a rancher in the Sacramento Delta, interrupted only by his infantry service in Europe during the second World War. He returned to his hometown of Clarksburg and farmed there the rest of his life.

SLATER, Norman Bernard.
B. 23 JAN 1894 Berkeley, CA. D. MAR 1979 Clarksburg, CA. Gold: 1924. Norm Slater was the older of the two Slater brothers to play on the 1924 Olympic team. He never attended college but was still known as a good soccer and basketball player, mostly with the Olympic Club of San Francisco. Like his brother, he became a farmer in Clarksburg, California.

TEMPLETON, Richard Lyman.
B. 27 MAY 1897 Helena, MT. D. 07 AUG 1962 Palo Alto, CA. Gold: 1920. "Dink" Templeton was a rugby, track and football star at Stanford, but his greatest influence at "The Farm" was as a coach. After graduating in 1921 he was immediately appointed track coach at the age of 24. He remained in the post until 1939 and developed many world record breakers and winning teams. Templeton also earned a law degree and, in addition to his duties at Stanford, was a broadcaster and journalist

and coached at the Olympic Club. His overall influence on the development of California sports was immeasurable.

At the 1920 Olympics, Dink placed fourth in the long jump in track and field in addition to his rugby exploits. In the match against France he clinched the rugby gold medal for the U.S. with a 55 yard drop goal.

TILDEN, Charles Lee, Jr.
B. 04 JUN 1894. D. NOV 1968. Gold: 1920. Charles Tilden attended Cal/Berkeley and was captain of the 1920 Olympic rugby team.

TURKINGTON, Edward L.
B. 10 JAN 1899 San Francisco, CA. Gold: 1924. Ed Turkington graduated from Cal/Berkeley and then established his own business as a grain broker. After service in World War II he attended the Industrial College of the Armed Forces and later held an appointment as Regional Director for the Small Business Administration. From 1944 to 1945 he was the police commissioner for San Francisco and then became the security chief for the UNO Offices in the U.S.

VALENTINE, Alan Chester.
B. 23 FEB 1901 Glen Cove, NY. D. 14 JUL 1980 Rockland, ME. Gold: 1924. After graduating from Swarthmore and earning a master's at Penn, Alan Valentine went to Oxford on a Rhodes Scholarship. While at Oxford he became the first American ever to win a rugby "blue" playing in the match against Cambridge three times.

Valentine, who earned a reputation in British rugby circles as a devastating tackler, was one of the organizers of the U.S. team for the 1924 Olympics. The gold medal he won literally proved to be "tarnished." When Valentine tried to turn it over to the Roosevelt Government in answer to an appeal during the depression, it was rejected as being "only lead, washed with gold."

After leaving Oxford, Alan Valentine held many academic appointments and until 1935, while he was at Yale, he was professor of history, arts and letters; chairman of the board of admissions; and Master of Pierson College. In 1935, he became president of the University of Rochester, at 34 one of the youngest men to ever head a major university. In 1948 and 1949 Valentine headed the Netherlands Mission of the Economic Stabilization Agency—better known as the Marshall Plan. In 1950, President Truman named him chief administrator of this plan. Valentine also wrote numerous books and held several honorary degrees.

WILLIAMS, Alan Frank.

B. 07 OCT 1893 West Orange, NJ. Ddi. Gold: 1924. Alan Williams started college at Cal/Berkeley in 1911 but later transferred to Cornell and remained there from 1912 until 1915, studying civil engineering. He later returned to the West Coast and played rugby with the Olympic Club of San Francisco. He worked as an engineer, mostly with the Northwestern Pacific and Western Pacific Railway Companies, and with the engineer corps during the First World War. He was also instrumental in forming the San Francisco Old-Timers Athletic Association.

WRENN, Heaton Luse.

B. 18 JAN 1900 San Francisco, CA. D. 16 JAN 1978 Honolulu, HA. Gold: 1920. Heaton Wrenn was from Burlingame and attended Stanford, earning an A.B. in 1922 and a J.D. in 1924. In 1924 he was first admitted to the California Bar, but he moved that year to Hawaii where he set up a lucrative practice. He was one of the two founders of Anderson, Wrenn & Jenks and became president of the Bar Association of Hawaii in 1945–46. In 1945 he was approved to practice before the United States Supreme Court, which he did several times.

SCHOLAR-OLYMPIANS

Seven United States Olympic athletes have earned one of the highest academic accolades—a Rhodes Scholarship to study at Oxford University in England. They are as follows:

Bill Bradley (1964 BAS)
John Carleton (1924 NSK)
Eddie Eagan (1920/24 BOX and 1932 BOB)
Tom McMillen (1972 BAS)
Bill Stevenson (1924 TAF)
Norman Taber (1912 TAF)
Alan Valentine (1924 RUG)

Coincidentally, Carleton, Eagan, Stevenson and Valentine all received their scholarship in 1922.

SHOOTING

The United States has had very varied performances in Olympic shooting. In 1896 the Paine brothers won everything they entered, but the U.S. did not again have Olympic shooters until 1908. From 1908 until 1924, the Olympic shooting program was massive, consisting of all manner of events, many of which were contested both for individuals and teams. During this period the U.S. was the dominant nation, along with the Swedes in some years. There was no Olympic shooting in 1928 and some changes in the amateur rules made ineligible virtually all the U.S. shooters for 1932 and 1936. Consequently our Olympic competitors in those years were inexperienced and won no medals. After the war, the USSR became the top country in shooting, but beginning with 1964 the United States began a resurgence in certain events which has continued to this day. While our pistol, trap, and skeet shooters are usually less than top caliber, our rifle shooters are now the equal of any nation's.

OUTSTANDING PERFORMANCES

Most Gold Medals
    5 Carl Osburn, Willis Lee, Alfred Lane,
        Morris Fisher
Most Medals
    11 Carl Osburn
    7 Willis Lee, Lloyd Spooner
    6 Alfred Lane
Most Gold Medals (Games)
    5 Willis Lee
    4 Carl Osburn, Lloyd Spooner
Most Medals (Games)
    7 Willis Lee, Lloyd Spooner
    6 Carl Osburn (twice)
Most Appearances
    6 Bill McMillan
Oldest Gold Medalist
    56y97d Walter Winans
Oldest Medalist
    60y90d Walter Winans
Youngest Gold Medalist
    c20y Joseph Crockett
    20y137d Arthur Cook
Youngest Medalist
    17y301d Marcus Dinwiddie

ADAMS, Harry Loren.
B. 01 OCT 1880 West Medway, MA. D. 16 FEB 1960 Bronxville, NY. Gold: 1912 Military Rifle—team. Harry Adams was a sergeant in the U.S. Cavalry when he competed in the 1912 Olympics. He was the second highest U.S. scorer in the military rifle—team event, but, although he entered three individual events, the best he could do in those was a pair of 12th places.

ANDERSON, Gary Lee.
B. 08 OCT 1939 Holdredge, NB. Gold(2): 1964 Free Rifle, 1968 Free Rifle. As the world's top rifle shooter in the 1960's, Gary Anderson is one of the shooters most responsible for our resurgence in international rifle shooting. In addition to his Olympic performances, Anderson won seven individual World Championships, set six individual world records, won 11 National Championships, and won 11 gold medals at the Pan-American Games. In addition he was a team member of several world record and world championship shoots. Anderson graduated from Hastings College in Nebraska and then studied for the seminary in San Francisco. Instead he entered local politics in Nebraska, eventually rising to become a Nebraska state senator. For the last several years he has been the executive director of the National Rifle Association.

ARIE, Mark Peter.
B. 27 MAR 1882 Thomasboro, IL. D. 19 NOV 1958 Champaign, IL. Gold(2): 1920 Clay Pigeon, 1920 Clay Pigeon—team. Mark Arie was one of the most colorful and popular trapshooters in American history. He began shooting in 1905 and competed at the Grand American Handicap (GAH) for over 30 years. He was the first Grand Doubles Champion in 1912 and 22 years later, in 1934, he took his second Grand Doubles crown. He tied for the 1917 GAH title only to lose the shoot-off. But in 1923 he became the first maximum-yardage shooter (23 yards) to ever win the GAH. He again won the singles title in 1928 and was high-over-all leader at the Grand seven times. He was a six-time member of the All-American Trapshooting squad, including the first four years of its existence—from 1927 through 1930.

AUER, Victor Lee.
B. 24 MAR 1937 Santa Ana, CA. Silver: 1972 Smallbore Rifle, prone. Vic Auer's specialty was the English

Courtesy Sidney Hinds

The 1924 Olympic Rifle Team. Standing (L-R) — Joe Crockett, Bud Fisher, Sid Hinds, L. W. T. Waller (captain), J. J. Dooley (spotter), C. E. Stodter (coach). Kneeling (L-R) — Dennis Fenton, Ray Coulter, Walter Stokes, and Cy Osburn.

match—the smallbore rifle, prone competition. The UCLA grad won his Olympic medal in this event, added three gold medals (two individual) at the 1971 and 1975 Pan-American Games in the English match, and won two national titles at this event. Auer makes his living as a scriptwriter for television.

AXTELL, Charles Sumner.
B. c1859. D. 24 NOV 1932 Springfield, MA. Gold: 1908 Rapid-Fire Pistol—team. Charles Axtell was one of the greats in the early days of competitive shooting in this country. He was also active as an administrator in the sport, being one of the founders of the U.S. Revolver Association and serving as its president from 1911 until 1913. Besides his team Olympic gold medal, Axtell competed individually in free pistol, just missing the medals with a fourth-place finish. Axtell also competed at some shooting events in 1900 connected with the Paris Exposition. Which events were and were not on the Olympic program in that year is not known, so it is possible that Axtell also competed in the 1900 Olympics.

BAILEY, Henry Marvin.
B. 24 APR 1893 Waterboro, SC. Gold: 1924 Rapid-Fire Pistol. The career marine, Henry Bailey, was a gunnery sergeant during the 1924 Olympics but rose to the rank of chief warrant officer before his marine retirement in 1947. He enlisted in the marines in 1910 and immediately established himself as one of their top marksmen. He was awarded the U.S. Marine Corps Distinguished Pistol Shooting award in 1921 and Distinguished Marksman award in 1929. Several times he competed on marine shooting teams which won national championships.

At the 1924 Olympics, Bailey won his gold with a display of steel nerves. He tied for first place with Wilhelm Carlberg of Sweden and neither missed a shot through six shoot-off strings. On his seventh string, Bailey's pistol jammed but with an instant reaction he reached for the slide with his free hand, cleared the jam, and fired off five perfect shots—all within eight seconds. This performance so unnerved Carlberg that the Swede missed two shots and Bailey had his gold medal.

BASSHAM, Lanny Robert.
B. 21 JAN 1947 Comanche, TX. Gold: 1976 Smallbore Rifle, 3 positions; Silver: 1972 Smallbore Rifle, 3 positions. Lanny Bassham served his apprenticeship at the 1972 Olympics when he took the silver medal behind fellow American, John Writer. But at Montreal in 1976 he won his gold medal only after he tied for first place with the United State's Margaret Murdock. Bassham graciously asked the Union Internationale de Tir that two gold medals be awarded but the rules stated that an examination of the targets was in order and it gave Bassham sole possession of the gold medal. At the awards ceremony, he refused to stand on the top step by himself and had Mrs. Murdock accompany him there while the U.S. flag was raised and our national anthem played in the background.

Bassham was not an undeserving champion. He was a world champion in both 1974 and 1978, won three gold medals at the Pan-American Games, won 22 national championships and has set 33 national or world shooting records. Lanny Bassham is now director of shooting for the U.S. Olympic shooting team and teaches courses in mental management for athletes and businessman. As a hobby, he also raises registered quarter horses.

BENEDICT, Charles Sumner.
B. c1857 New York, NY. D. 15 APR 1937 New Rochelle, NY. Gold: 1908 Military Rifle—team. Charles Benedict was a captain in the 7th Ohio Infantry when he competed in the 1908 Olympics. Besides his team gold medal, he also competed in the individual prone free rifle event, finishing 15th.

BENNER, Huelet Leo.
B. 01 NOV 1917 Jonesboro, AK. Gold: 1952 Free Pistol. "Joe" Benner can claim the top competitive record internationally of any American pistol shooter. In addition to his Olympic gold medal, he won three World Championships (1949, 1952, 1954), six National Championships, and won six gold medals at the Pan-American Games—five of those in 1955 alone. Benner also coached the sport for 10 years at the U.S. Military Academy, leading the cadets to an intercollegiate title during his tenure there.

Joe Benner competed in two other Olympics, though not with the success he had in 1952. At the 1948

Olympics, he finished fourth in the free pistol event, despite having had troubles with his equipment in training. A week before the Olympics he was loaned a pistol by the manager of the U.S. team, Karl Frederick, and Benner used it in the Olympics. Though Benner was an Olympic neophyte in 1948, the gun was a veteran, having been used by Frederick in 1920 to win a gold medal.

BILLINGS, Charles W.
B. 26 NOV 1886. D. 13 DEC 1928 Deal, NJ. Gold: 1912 Clay Pigeon. Charles Billings of Glen Ridge, New Jersey, was on the first trapshooting squad the U.S. ever entered in the Olympics. Though he was high man for the U.S. in the team match, he had difficulty in the individual event, finishing 42nd overall. From 1920 until his death in 1928, Billings was the mayor of Oceanside, New Jersey.

BOLES, John Keith.
B. 31 NOV 1888 Fort Smith, AK. D. 1952. Gold: 1924 Running Deer; Bronze: 1924 Running Deer—team. A major in the army in 1924, John Boles is the only American trained in this country to ever have any success in the running deer event. Boles was a career army officer, joining in 1912 after serving in the Arkansas National Guard for several years. Boles served for several years in the Philippine Islands and had his first experiences there hunting big game, which became his hobby. Boles eventually reached the rank of colonel, although his son, John, Jr., would become a famous full general officer.

BONSER, Horace R.
B. 27 MAR 1882 Cincinnati, OH. D. 07 JUN 1934 Cincinnati, OH. Gold: 1920 Clay Pigeon—team. Horace Bonser lived in Cincinnati all his life and was known as the top trapshooter in the southern Ohio area. He was equal second among the U.S. trapshooters in the team clay pigeon event and in the individual Olympic competition, he placed fifth.

BRACKEN, Raymond C.
B. 08 JAN 1891. D. 1963. Gold: 1920 Free Pistol—team; Silver: 1920 Rapid-Fire Pistol. Ray Bracken was from Columbus, Ohio in 1920. In addition to his medal-

winning Olympic performances he placed fifth in the individual free pistol event.

BRIGGS, Allan Lindsay.
B. 14 FEB 1873 Bridgeport, CT. Gold: 1912 Military Rifle—team. Capt. Allan Briggs of the U.S. Infantry was the second leading American in the military rifle-team event, at the 1912 Olympics. Briggs also competed in two individual events, not faring nearly as well, as he finished 25th and 35th in those.

BROWN, Thomas Cole.
B. 04 OCT 1879 Knox Cty., TN. Silver: 1920 Military Rifle—team; Bronze: 1920 Running Deer—team. At the time of the 1920 Olympics, Tom Brown was a first lieutenant in the 41st Infantry with the U.S. Army. In the running deer team event he was the top American shooter; he brought up the rear of the team members in the military rifle event. Brown was promoted to captain in 1925.

BURDETTE, Cornelius L.
B. 06 NOV 1878 Sandstone, WV. Gold: 1912 Military Rifle—team. Cornelius Burdette competed in three individual events at the 1912 Olympics, with a best finish in those of eighth. In the team military event, however, the West Virginia National Guardsman led the American shooters with the top individual score in that match.

CALKINS, Irving Romaro.
B. 31 OCT 1875. D. 26 AUG 1958 Springfield, MA. Gold: 1908 Rapid-Fire Pistol—team. Irving Calkins was a man of many talents. Besides his obvious ability as a pistol shooter he served the sport as president of U.S. Revolver Association. Calkins' career, however, was as a doctor and he practiced as a surgeon in his hometown of Springfield for over 50years. In addition, Irv Calkins spent much of his free time with his hobby, magic, and served a term as president of the American Society of Magicians.

CASEY, Kellogg Kennon Venable.
B. 17 SEP 1877 New York, NY. D. 18 OCT 1938 Wilmington, DE. Gold: 1908 Military Rifle—team; Silver: 1908 Free Rifle, prone. Kellogg Casey was one of the greatest long range shots in American shooting

history. In the 1908 free rifle event, shot prone at 1,000 yards, Casey shot a two (of five) early in his string that seemed to put him out of contention, but he came through beautifully near the end to finish second over-all. Three times Casey won the Wimbledon Cup, given to the American champion in long range shooting.

Besides his competitive shooting, Casey also fought in the Spanish-American War as a member of the 71st U.S. Infantry. His career was as director of military sales for the DuPont Company for whom he worked for over 30 years.

CLARK, Jay, Jr.
B. 25 JAN 1880 Newton, IA. D. 06 FEB 1948 Worcester, MA. Gold: 1920 Clay Pigeon—team. Team clay pigeon shooting was the only event that Jay Clark competed in at the 1920 Olympics. He was well known as a shooter, having won the Westy Hogan Trapshoot at Atlantic City in 1913, but he was better known as a race car driver in Massachusetts. He competed in hill climbs and dirt track races all over New England and set a record at a Worcester track which was broken only by Barney Oldfield.

Clark attended Grinnell College in Iowa and Harvard Law School and made his living practicing law in Worcester.

COOK, Arthur Edwin.
B. 19 MAR 1928. Gold: 1948 Smallbore Rifle, prone. Art "Cookie" Cook began shooting at a 1939 Boy Scout camp and later took his shooting skills to the University of Maryland. At the 1948 Olympics he became the youngest American to ever win a gold medal in shooting by winning the English match. His gold was won only after a target check as he tied for first place with fellow American, Walter Tomsen, with 599 of a possible 600, which was a world record at the time. Cookie had also won the U.S. English match title in 1948 and he later won two golds and one silver medal in Pan-American Games competition.

COULTER, Raymond Orville.
B. 24 SEP 1901 Hadley, IL. Gold: 1924 Free Rifle—team; Bronze: 1924 Running Deer—team. Ray Coulter was a career marine corpsman, and was a gunnery sergeant at the time of the 1924 Olympics. Enlisting in 1917, he had earned his distinguished marksman

badge from the corps in 1919. In 1918, 1919, 1922, and 1923 he was a member of the marine team which won the NRA rapid-fire rifle team event. He also competed internationally several times in addition to the Olympics, notably at the 1924 Pan-American Matches, and the Internationals of 1924, 1925, and 1927.

CROCKETT, Joseph W.
B. 1904. Gold: 1924 Free Rifle—team. Joe Crockett was from Falls Church, Virginia. He had the fourth best total among the five U.S. shooters in the free rifle-team match.

DIETZ, John A.
B. 24 NOV 1870 Germany. D. 11 OCT 1939 New York, NY. Gold(2); 1908 Rapid-Fire Pistol—team, 1912 Free Pistol—team. Lt. John Dietz competed in several individual Olympic events, in addition to his team successes, but his best finish in those was fourth in the 1912 rapid-fire pistol event. Dietz spent most of his life-long army career as armorer and superintendent of the 71st Regimental Armory in the Bronx. He did serve with the 71st in both the 1914 Mexican border skirmish and in World War I. For a short time, he also assisted the army as a shooting instructor at both Camp Perry, Ohio, and Fort Benning, Georgia.

DINWIDDIE, Marcus William.
B. 27 AUG 1907 Washington, DC. D. 20 AUG 1951 Oak Ridge, TN. Silver: 1924 Smallbore Rifle, prone. Marcus Dinwiddie is the youngest person to ever win a medal in Olympic shooting. He began shooting at the District of Columbia National Guard rifle range after they changed the regulations to allow civilians to use the facilities. After the 1924 Olympics, Dinwiddie enrolled at the University of Virginia and continued shooting as a member of the Monticello National Guard, with whose team he competed at several national championships. His only international honor, apart from his Olympic medal, came at the 1925 Internationals at Rheims, France when he won the English match.

DOLFEN, Peter J.
B. 21 MAY 1880 Hartford, CT. Gold: 1912 Free Pistol—team; Silver: 1912 Free Pistol. In 1912, Peter Dolfen was from the hotbed of American pistol shooting, Springfield, Massachusetts. Besides his two medal-

FAMOUS FAMILIES

Many Olympians have been related to rather famous non-Olympians. Following is a partial list:

SYBIL BAUER (SWI)—Bauer never quite became related to a famous person. She died of cancer before she was able to marry her fiance, sportswriter Ed Sullivan, who later hosted the well-known variety show on television.

HALE BAUGH (MOP)—Baugh had two children who became professional golfers. Beau Baugh played on the men's PGA Tour, but his sister, Laura Baugh Cole, won the U.S. Women's Amateur and was one of the most glamorous players on the LPGA Tour.

RALPH BEARD (BAS)—One of Ralph Beard's hobbies is golf, and he gets very good lessons from his brother, PGA Tour professional, Frank Beard.

ROSIE BONDS (TAF)—Bonds' brother is Bobby Bonds, who has been quite a well-known baseball player.

JAY BOWERMAN (BIA)—Bowerman's dad was Bill Bowerman, the famous track coach, who also coached several U.S. Olympic teams.

JOHN CADY (GOL)—John Deere Cady was the grandson of John Deere, who founded the famous farm equipment company.

ADELINE GEHRIG (FEN)—Adeline Gehrig had a brother who was a pretty fair first baseman for the Yankees, the Iron Horse, Lou Gehrig.

ALEX GROZA (BAS)—Alex Groza had a brother who became the leading all-time scorer in the NFL as a kicker, Lou Groza.

DOROTHY HAMILL (FSK)—Hamill married into a famous family with her marriage to Dean-Paul Martin, an actor and occasional pro tennis player, who is the son of singer/actor, Dean Martin.

ELEANOR HOLM (SWI)—Eleanor Holm married the famous big band leader of the 30's, Art Jarrett.

JACK KELLY and **JACK KELLY, JR.** (ROW)—The Kellys were the father and brother, respectively, of the late Princess Grace of Monaco.

WILLIS LEE (SHO)—Willis Lee was a descendant of Gen. Robert E. Lee, and also of Charles Lee, the third attorney general of the United States.

ANN MEYERS (BAS)—Ann Meyers' brother, Dave Meyers, also played basketball and made All-American at UCLA before going on to a career in the NBA.

ZOE ANN OLSEN (DIV)—Zoe Ann Olsen became Zoe Ann Olsen-Jensen when she married Jackie Jensen, an outfielder for the Yankees and Red Sox. Jensen is also one of only two men to have played in the Rose Bowl and a World Series.

JOHN and **SUMNER PAINE** (SHO)—The Paines' father, General John Paine, defended the America's Cup three times in the late 1880's. More distant relatives were Robert Treat Paine, a signer of the Declaration of Independence, and Thomas Paine, author of the pamphlet, *Common Sense*, during the revolutionary era.

SIM PRICE (GOL)—One of Simeon Price's distant descendants became the well-known actor Vincent Price.

MACK ROBINSON (TAF)—Mack Robinson's brother was a long jumper at UCLA. Oh, and Jackie Robinson also played major league baseball.

HENK SCHENK (WRE)—Schenk's cousin was an Olympian for the Netherlands. Before Eric Heiden came along, many people considered Ard Schenk the greatest speed skater of all time.

JO JO STARBUCK (FSK)—Jo Jo Starbuck married the great professional football quarterback Terry Bradshaw, although they later divorced.

TAUNA VANDEWEGHE (SWI)—Tauna Vandeweghe's father, Ernie, played in the NBA, but did not achieve the fame of her brother, Kiki, who played for UCLA and now is with the Denver Nuggets.

MILDRED WILEY (TAF)—As Mrs. Dee, Mildred Wiley gave birth to Bob Dee who played pro football with the Boston Patriots in the 60's.

EDWARD WILLKIE (WRE)—Ed Willkie had a brother, Wendell, who ran against Franklin Delano Roosevelt for president in 1940.

winning performances at the Olympics, Dolfen finished 16th in the rapid-fire pistol event.

EASTMAN, Ivan L.

Gold: 1908 Military Rifle—team. Corporal Ivan Eastman was a member of the 2nd Ohio Infantry in 1908. He was fourth of the five members of the U.S. team in military rifle event, and individually, finished 14th in the free rifle event.

ETCHEN, Fred R.

B. c1884 Coffeyville, KS. D. 06 NOV 1961 Phoenix, AZ. Gold: 1924 Clay Pigeon—team. Fred Etchen was the captain of the 1924 U.S. Olympic trapshooting team. While overseas with the team he won the British Open Trapshoot with a perfect score of 200, and later won the 1926 World Championship at Live Bird Shooting. Etchen competed for many years at the Grand American Handicap, winning the Doubles Championship in 1938. He won 17 Kansas state titles from 1925 until 1939—three singles, one handicap, seven doubles, and six all-round.

Etchen was also active in promoting shooting. He wrote a well-known book on the subject, *How to Be an Expert at Shotgun Shooting*, and helped form the American Trapshooting Association. After his retirement from the automotive business he spent several years training instructors for gunnery schools during the second World War.

FENTON, Dennis.

B. 1888. Gold(3): 1920 Free Rifle—team, 1920 Military Rifle, 600m—team, 1920 Smallbore Rifle—team; Bronze(2): 1920 Smallbore Rifle, 1924 Running Deer, single shot—team. At the 1920 and 1924 Olympics, Sgt. Dennis Fenton of the U.S. Army was a very busy man, competing in nine different shooting events. He won five medals, as given above, and finished fifth in the team match at running deer, double shot. His three other individual placings were 12th, 24th, and 27th.

FISHER, Morris.

B. 04 MAY 1890 Youngstown, OH. D. 23 MAY 1968 Honolulu, HA. Gold(5): 1920 Free Rifle, 1920 Free Rifle—team, 1920 Military Rifle, 300 m, prone—team, 1924 Free Rifle, 1924 Free Rifle—team. "Bud" Fisher enlisted in the Marines in 1911 and was awarded the

distinguished marksman badge in 1916. He went on to become the greatest rifle shot in Marine Corps history. In addition to his Olympic successes, Fisher was a holder of five internationally recognized world records and was a six-time world champion. He won many national open and national military championships before his competitive retirement in 1934. After that time he coached the marine shooters and spent time in Toledo, Ohio, training the police department there as shooters. Fisher retired as a gunnery sergeant in 1941 but was recalled to active duty as a shooting instructor during World War II.

FREDERICK, Karl Telford.

B. 02 FEB 1881 Chateaugay, NY. D. 11 FEB 1963 Rye, NY. Gold(3): 1920 Free Pistol, 1920 Free Pistol—team, 1920 Rapid-Fire Pistol—team. Besides his competitive accomplishments at the 1920 Olympics, Karl Frederick captained the U.S. Olympic shooting team in 1948. He later became president of the National Rifle Association and a vice-president of the U.S. Revolver Association.

Frederick attended Princeton, graduating in 1903, and then entered Harvard Law School, from which he earned an LL.B. in 1908. He made his career as a practicing lawyer in New York City for many years. He was also active in environmental causes, serving as chairman and president of the New York State Conservation Council and as a senior board member and vice-chairman of the executive committee of the American Forestry Association.

GARRIGUS, Thomas Irvin.

B. 09 NOV 1946 Hillsboro, OR. Silver: 1968 Clay Pigeon, trap. At the 1968 Olympics, Tom Garrigus had the dubious distinction of being the first shooter to miss a bird. He missed a second shortly thereafter, but overcame this poor start to take the silver medal. Garrigus was used to winning medals—between 1962 and 1982 he won 27 various national titles and 53 various state championships in Oregon, Idaho and Montana. In 1980 he was given the second highest handicap ever awarded in the history of the American Trapshooting Association—9,515.

GLEASON, Edward Francis.

B. 09 NOV 1869 Hyannis, MA. D. 09 APR 1944 Hyannis, MA. Gold: 1912 Clay Pigeon—team. Edward Gleason was a well-known trapshooter on Cape Cod, but he was better known as one of the area's top surgeons. He attended the University of Vermont Medical School, after which he interned at Boston City Hospital and then studied surgery in Europe at the University of Vienna. He returned to practice in Boston for a short time but later settled in his hometown of Hyannis.

GORMAN, James Edward.
B. 30 JAN 1859. Gold: 1908 Rapid-Fire Pistol—team; Bronze: 1908 Rapid-Fire Pistol. Jim Gorman was from San Francisco and was the top American pistol shooter in the 1908 rapid-fire pistol team match, as evidenced by his bronze medal winning performance in the individual event. His third-place finish there was disputed, however, because he was declared to have completely missed one target. Gorman protested that it was a "double"—two shots through the same hole—and was worth nine points. The protest was overruled, though, and the loss of nine points dropped him from first to third.

GRAHAM, James R.
B. 12 FEB 1873 Long Lake, IL. D. 18 FEB 1950. Gold(2): 1912 Clay Pigeon, 1912 Clay Pigeon—team. Although shooting under international conditions which were strange to him, Jim Graham won two gold medals in trapshooting at the 1912 Olympics—to nobody's surprise on the American team. He was the top American trapshooter of the time, having only a few years before run 432 birds straight. Graham turned professional shortly after the 1912 Olympics.

GREEN, Franklin C.
B. 05 MAY 1933 Chicago, IL. Silver: 1964 Free Pistol. Frank Green's first big championships were won at the 1963 Pan-American Games when he took two gold medals in pistol shooting. He won another Pan-Am gold in 1967 as a member of the team which won the free pistol-team match. He was also U.S. free pistol champion in 1968.

Green today owns his own company involved in shooting sport. Frank Green Enterprises manufactures the Green Free-Pistol, and does research and development work on electronic triggers.

GUNNARSSON, Martine Ingemar.
B. 30 MAR 1927 Fredsburg, Sweden. Bronze: 1964 Free Rifle. Martin Gunnarsson is the only armed force's enlisted man to have ever won medals in shooting at the Olympics, the Pan-American Games and the world championships. His Pan-American medals were both gold and were won in team events at the 1959 and 1963 Pan-Am Games—in the English match and free rifle event, respectively. At the 1966 World Championships in Wiesbaden, West Germany, he also won a gold medal in the free rifle-team event. In addition, both free rifle team performances (in 1963 and 1966) earned him a share of the world record. The second of these, 4,602 points in 1966, still stands today as the top performance of all time.

HALDEMAN, Donald S.
B. 29 MAY 1947 Sellersville, PA. Gold: 1976 Clay Pigeon, trap. Don Haldeman finished only 17th in trapshooting at the 1972 Olympics, but by 1976 he had improved all the way to first. His other successes in trapshooting include a team gold and individual silver at the 1975 Pan-American Games, a 1975 National Championship, and the 1972 Inter-Service Championship. Haldeman was a machinist and gunsmith in the army and designed the gunstock that was used at the 1976 Olympics by both himself and teammate, Charvin Dixon.

HALL, Frank.
B. 08 JUL 1865 Woodside, NJ. Gold: 1912 Clay Pigeon—team. Frank Hall of Ridgefield Park, New Jersey finished 15th in the individual clay pigeon event at the 1912 Olympics. In the team event he had the fourth best total of the five team members.

HARANT, Louis J.
B. 20 NOV 1892 Maryland. Gold: 1920 Rapid-Fire Pistol—team. In 1920, Louis Harant was a first lieutenant in the U.S. Army, stationed in Washington, D.C. Though he finished well back in the individual rapid-fire pistol event, he had the top score for the Americans in the team event.

Courtesy Sidney Hinds

Lt. Sidney Hinds, 1924 Olympian, as he looked preparing for the 1928 Olympic shooting events — which were never held.

HENDRICKSON, John H.
B. 25 FEB 1871 Long Island City, NY. Gold: 1912 Clay Pigeon—team. John Hendrickson was from New York City and finished 44th in the 1912 Olympic individual trapshooting event.

HILL, James E.
B. 30 OCT 1929 Chicago, IL. Silver: 1960 Smallbore Rifle, prone. By 1960, Gunnery Sergeant Jim Hill was a well-known shooter in the U.S. Marine Corps. He had earned the distinguished marksman badge in 1956 and

won the National Service Rifle Championship in that year. In 1957 he won the Pershing Trophy at the NRA Championships, given for the high individual in the free rifle team match.

HINDS, Sidney Rae.
B. 14 MAY 1900 Newton, IL. Gold: 1924 Free Rifle—team. A 1920 graduate of the U.S. Military Academy, Lt. Sid Hinds got the 1924 free rifle team off to a great start by shooting a 50 × 50 possible on his first string. This was done despite the fact that before the Games, at an international meeting in Rheims, France, Hinds had been shooting next to a Belgian who was constantly bickering with the officials. During one argument he knocked over his rifle and shot Hinds in the foot! Because of this, after his possible on the first string, U.S. team captain "Tubby" Waller threatened to shoot Hinds in the other foot!

Hinds became a career army officer, eventually reaching the rank of brigadier general before his retirement in 1947 due to war wounds. He had served in World War II in eight campaigns and three invasions and was awarded the Distinguished Service Medal, four Silver Stars, three Bronze Stars, four Army Citations, and a Purple Heart.

HIRD, Frederick S.
B. 06 DEC 1879 New Diggins, WI. D. 27 SEP 1952 Des Moines, IA. Gold: 1912 Smallbore Rifle, any position; Bronze(2): 1912 Smallbore Rifle, prone—team, 1912 Smallbore Rifle, disappearing target—team. In his youth, Fred Hird was a top athlete, playing semi-pro baseball and boxing professionally. In 1900 he joined the Iowa National Guard as a private, and rose through the army ranks until he retired as a lieutenant colonel in 1943. He was a veteran of the Mexican border campaign of 1914 and the first World War. From 1928 until 1936 he served two terms as U.S. marshall for southern Iowa and later served as a special agent for the Iowa attorney general's office.

HUGHES, Frank H.
B. 1881. Gold: 1924 Clay Pigeon—team. Bronze: 1924 Clay Pigeon. Frank Hughes was from Mobridge, South Dakota, when he competed in the 1924 Olympics. He had the high average in the U.S. that year, with 98.3% on 1,000 targets, and led the U.S. team members in the

Olympic team match. Hughes ran his first 70 birds in the individual match, but resumed shooting the next day in a bad downpour and missed two birds. The weather broke, but a later miss dropped him from a tie for first to a 97 and third place.

JACKSON, Arthur Charles.
B. 15 MAY 1918 Brooklyn, NY. Bronze: 1952 Smallbore Rifle, prone. At the 1949 World Championships in Buenos Aires and the 1952 Worlds in Oslo, Art Jackson won the English match by shooting a new world record both times. He was thus one of the favorites in 1952, but one miss out of 400 cost him the gold medal and he finished third. Jackson had an excellent record at the 1951 and 1955 Pan-American Games, winning eight gold medals (four individual) and one bronze.

JACKSON, John E.
B. 14 FEB 1885 Lincoln, IL. Gold: 1912 Military Rifle—team; Bronze: 1912 Military Rifle, 600m, prone. Sgt. John Jackson was a member of the Iowa National Guard in 1912. He had the fourth best score (of six) among the U.S. military rifle team members, but improved to take a bronze medal in the 600 meter prone event.

JACKSON, Joseph.
B. 23 SEP 1880 St. Louis, MO. Gold(3): 1920 Military Rifle, 300m, prone—team, 1920 Military Rifle, 300 + 600m, prone—team, 1920 Military Rifle, 600m, prone—team. Joe Jackson entered the U.S. Marine Corps in 1901 as an enlisted man, won the distinguished marksman badge in 1913, and was promoted to an officer in 1917. Jackson was the first great internationally known shooter produced by the marines. He won innumerable national, marine, and service titles and competed internationally for the United States in 1920, 1922, 1923, and 1924. He later became a captain and coach for the marine shooters before retiring from the service in January 1932.

KELLY, Michael.
Gold(2): 1920 Rapid-Fire Pistol—team, 1920 Free Pistol—team. In 1920, Mike Kelly was a sergeant in the U.S. Army Engineer Corps when he competed in the two team pistol events at the Olympics.

LANE, Alfred P.
B. 26 SEP 1891 New York, NY. Gold(5): 1912 Free Pistol, 1912 Free Pistol—team, 1912 Rapid-Fire Pistol, 1920 Free Pistol—team, 1912 Rapid-Fire Pistol—team; Bronze: 1920 Free Pistol. Al Lane began his shooting career with the Manhattan Rifle and Revolver Association in New York. He was known as the boy wonder, having won several U.S. Revolver Association (USRA) championships in 1911 when aged only 19. After the 1912 Olympics, he was USRA Champion for three consecutive years. He later worked in the ad department of the Remington Company before leaving to become the head of the photographic department for a magazine publisher.

LEE, Willis Augustus, Jr.
B. 11 MAY 1888 Natlee, KY. D. 25 AUG 1945 Portland, ME. Gold(5): 1920 Free Rifle—team, 1920 Military Rifle, 300m, prone—team, 1920 Military Rifle, 600m, prone—team, 1920 Military Rifle, 300 + 600m, prone—team, 1920 Smallbore Rifle, standing—team; Silver: 1920 Military Rifle, 300m, standing—team; Bronze: 1920 Running Deer, single shot—team. Willis Lee was a distant relative of Gen. Robert E. Lee and the great-great-grandson of the third Attorney General of the United States, Charles Lee. With that background, Lee headed to the U.S. Naval Academy, from which he graduated in 1908. While a midshipman in 1907, he became the only person to win the national championship in rifle and pistol shooting in the same year. He was a member of the navy rifle teams of 1908, 1909, 1913, 1919, and 1930.

Lee served during World War I but rose to the top of the navy cream during the second World War. In 1941 he was appointed assistant chief of staff to the U.S. fleet commander-in-chief and later served as commander of battleships for the Pacific fleet. With the exception of the Battle of Midway Island, he participated in all the major naval engagements in the Pacific during World War II. He commanded the task force which defeated the Japanese on Guadalcanal in 1942, a victory which was termed pivotal in the Pacific war. At the time of his death he was a vice-admiral.

LEUSCHNER, William D. F.
B. 27 NOV 1863 Cookstown, Ontario, Canada. D. 25 OCT 1935 Buffalo, NY. Gold: 1908 Military Rifle—team;

Silver: 1912 Running Deer, single shot—team; Bronze(2): 1912 Smallbore Rifle, prone—team, 1912 Smallbore Rifle, disappearing target—team. Bill Leuschner was a sergeant at the 1908 Olympics, but during a 50-year career with the New York National Guard and Army Reserve, he rose to become a lieutenant colonel. He served mostly in the Buffalo area and for 16 years was superintendent and armorer of the 174th Armory in Buffalo, New York. He also fought as an enlisted man in the Mexican border dispute of 1914 and the first World War.

LIBBEY, William A.
B. 27 MAR 1855 Jersey City, NJ. Silver: 1912 Running Deer, single shot—team. At 57 years, Bill Libbey is one of the older Americans to have won a medal in the Olympics, which he did in the only event he shot in, in 1912. Libbey was a lieutenant colonel in the New Jersey National Guard and also served the U.S. Olympic shooters as adjutant in 1912 and liaison officer in 1920.

MARTIN, William Franklin.
B. 19 JUL 1863 Ohio. Gold: 1908 Military Rifle—team. Maj. William Martin, of the 2nd New Jersey Infantry, competed in only one event at the 1908 Olympics, but he made the most of it—he had the top score among the American rifle shooters and led them to a team gold medal.

McDONELL, William Neil.
B. 15 JUL 1876. Silver: 1912 Running Deer, single shot—team; Bronze: 1912 Smallbore Rifle, disappearing target—team. Dr. Neil McDonnell was the medical officer for the U.S. Olympic shooters in both 1912 and 1920, and he competed in six events in 1912. Individually he did little, and in the running deer event—which he had never shot before—if anything, he cost the U.S. team the gold medal by a very poor performance. But in the smallbore rifle team match he shot very well to help the Americans win a bronze medal.

McMILLAN, William Willard.
B. 29 JAN 1929 Frostburg, MD. Gold: 1960 Rapid-Fire Pistol. Retired Marine Lt. Col. Bill McMillan has competed in six Olympic Games, a mark equalled by only three other Americans. The only Olympics he missed between 1952 and 1976 was in 1956 when his pistol misfired, costing him a spot on the team. McMillan has competed only in rapid-fire pistol in the Olympics, winning it in 1960 and with his next best finish being seventh in 1952. He has won two world championships in free pistol and five golds at the Pan-American Games in various events, as well as four national titles at rapid-fire pistol and one at free pistol. He currently works as a sheriff for San Diego County, C A.

McNEIR, Forest W.
B. c1876. D. 09 MAY 1957 Houston, TX. Gold: 1920 Clay Pigeon—team. Forest McNeir competed 47 times in the Grand American Handicap at Vandalia, Ohio, despite many physical problems of his own. In 1910, McNeir received the Carnegie Hero Award Gold Medal for his efforts in freeing a trapped city fireman. The fireman was caught on a ladder, opposite a window from which flames and smoke were billowing. An electric wire was touching the ladder and had repelled previous attempts at rescue, but McNeir jumped onto the ladder, knocking the wire loose and freeing the fireman's foot. McNeir was knocked unconscious and was disabled for weeks with scalp wounds and burns on his hands and face.

McNeir went on to become one of the greatest American trapshooters ever, breaking the third-high score on the 1920 Olympic trapshooting team. He won many titles through 1936 when, at his job as a building contractor, he fell from a third-floor framework, crushing his left hand and all his wrist bones. After major surgery he continued to shoot with a friend loading the gun for him and in 1937 he earned the 18-yard trophy at the Grand American Handicap.

MORRIS, William Clifton, III.
B. 27 JUN 1939 Fairfax, OK. Bronze: 1964 Clay Pigeon. Bill Morris won his first big title in 1956 when he took the U.S. Junior Trapshooting All-Around Championship. He continued to win state titles, but never managed another national crown until 1963 when he won the U.S. international-style championship in skeet shooting. A year later he won his Olympic bronze medal in a shoot-off for second place with Italy's Ennio Mattarelli and Russia's Pavel Senichev. Senichev shot a clean round for second place, but Morris' total of 24 × 25 was good for the bronze over the Italian's 23 × 25.

Morris, who graduated from Oklahoma as a finance major, is now an independent oil producer and farmer in Oklahoma.

MURDOCK, Margaret L. Thompson.
B. 25 AUG 1942 Topeka, KS. Silver: 1976 Smallbore Rifle, 3 positions. Margaret Murdock is one of the most amazing women athletes ever. She has competed on equal terms with men, and won, for many years now. Her first titles came as Margaret Thompson at the 1967 Pan-American Games, with two golds in smallbore shooting. Her 391 total that year in the kneeling position was a new world record—for men or women—the first time any woman had set an internationally recognized world record above the men's mark—in any sport. Margaret Thompson Murdock continued to win titles and set records, but did not make an Olympic team until 1976.

At the 1976 Olympics she tied for first place with Lanny Bassham in the smallbore, three position event. But on the examination of the targets, Bassham was awarded first place and Mrs. Murdock was relegated to the silver medal. Bassham gallantly asked Margaret Murdock to share the victory platform with him as the flag was raised and the anthem played—and rightly so.

Margaret Murdock graduated from Kansas State in 1965 and Washburn University School of Nursing in 1977. She is now a registered nurse and registered nurse anaesthetist in addition to being a competitive shooter, housewife, and mother.

NUESSLEIN, Lawrence Adam.
B. 16 MAY 1895 Ridgefield Park, NJ. D. 10 MAY 1971 Allentown, PA. Gold(2): 1920 Smallbore Rifle, standing; 1920 Smallbore Rifle, standing—team; Silver: 1920 Military Rifle, standing—team; Bronze(2): 1920 Military Rifle, standing, 1920 Running Deer, single shot—team. Besides his five Olympic medals, Larry Nuesslein was twice a world champion—in 1923 with the free rifle and in 1927 with the smallbore rifle. In addition he competed internationally for the United States every year from 1922 through 1927.

Nuesslein lived most of his life in Allentown, Pennsylvania, where he was manager of the Sears, Roebuck & Co. store for 22 years. He was also very active in civic affairs in Allentown.

OSBURN, Carl Townsend.
B. 05 MAY 1884 Jacksontown, OH. D. 28 DEC 1966 Helena, CA. Gold(5): 1912 Military Rifle—team, 1920 Free Rifle—team, 1920 Military Rifle, standing, 1920 Military Rifle, 300m, prone—team, 1920 Military Rifle, 300 + 600m, prone—team; Silver(4): 1912 Military Rifle, any position, 1912 Military Rifle, 3 positions, 1920 Military Rifle, standing—team, 1924 Free Rifle; Bronze(2): 1912 Smallbore Rifle, prone—team, 1912 Running Deer, single shot—team. Only Mark Spitz has won as many Olympic medals as Carl Osburn. And only Spitz and fellow shooter Lloyd Spooner have won more medals at one Olympics than the six Osburn won at two separate Olympics—those of 1912 and 1920.

Osburn attended the U.S. Naval Academy, graduating in 1906. He then launched a career as a career officer in the navy, which eventually saw him reach the rank of commander before retiring. Besides his Olympic shooting success, he competed internationally for the United States at the World Championships of 1921, 1922, 1923, and 1924, and at the Pan-American matches of 1913.

PAINE, John Bryant.
B. 08 APR 1870 Moline, IL. D. 02 AUG 1951 Weston, MA. Gold: 1896 Military Pistol. John Paine and his brother, Sumner, came from a notable sporting family. Their father, Gen. John Paine had thrice defended the America's Cup for the United States—in 1885, 1886, and 1887. In 1896 Lt. John Paine was a member of the Boston Athletic Association, which was sending several track & field athletes to the Olympic Games. Paine decided to go over to Athens and on the way, stopped in Paris to meet his brother, who was working at the Gastin-Renette Galleries. John convinced Sumner to join him in Paris and, once there, John easily won the first competition, the military pistol event, over his brother. So easily did he win, in fact, that John thought it unsporting to enter any further events and withdrew from the remaining pistol event.

John Paine returned to Boston after the Olympics, but left again in 1898 to fight in the Spanish-American War. He later settled in a suburb of Boston, where he became a wealthy investment banker.

PAINE, Sumner.
B. 13 MAY 1868 Moline, IL. D. 18 APR 1904 Boston, MA. Gold: 1896 Free Pistol; Silver: 1896 Military Pistol. Sumner Paine was descended from the same stock as his brother, John, which in addition to their yachtsman-father, included Robert Treat Paine, one of the signers of the Declaration of Independence. Sumner attended Harvard briefly in the 1890's, but finished up at the University of Colorado Medical School, where he earned an M.D. He never practiced, however, leaving immediately to work in Paris as a gunsmith. When John Paine arrived in 1896 to take Sumner to Paris, Sumner immediately rounded up a stock of the best pistols he had, and 3,500 rounds of ammunition—more than enough, as they used up only 96 rounds. In Athens, Sumner lost the military pistol event to his brother, but with John not entering the free pistol match, Sumner won easily.

PINION, Offutt.
B. 23 MAR 1910 Floyd County, KY. D. c1975. Bronze: 1956 Free Pistol. Offutt Pinion was a navy shooter in 1956 and contended with some horrible conditions to win the bronze medal in free pistol. The day of the event was very cold, with winds gusting up to 30 miles per hour. However, Pinion used some great wind doping to overcome one bad string of 88 and win the bronze medal. This was in his first international competition, although he had been all-navy champion in 1956 and northwest regional champion in 1951 and 1952.

POOL, Tommy Gayle.
B. 10 FEB 1935 Bowie, TX. Bronze: 1964 Smallbore Rifle, prone. Tommy Pool's first international experience came at the 1959 Pan-American Games when he won a gold, three silvers, and one bronze medal. After that he became U.S. champion in the English match in 1961 and 1962. At the 1964 Olympics, Pool competed in both smallbore events and, besides winning a bronze in the English match, he was doing well in the 3-position match until his standing scores pulled him down out of medal contention.

ROBINSON, Crittenden.
Bronze: 1900 Live Pigeon (tied). Crit Robinson was from San Francisco when he tied for third in the 1900 live pigeon shooting event.

ROTHROCK, Arthur D.
B. 07 JAN 1886 Ohio. Gold: 1920 Smallbore Rifle, standing—team; Silver: 1920 Smallbore Rifle, standing. Capt. Arthur Rothrock of the U.S. Army's 29th Infantry won the U.S. free rifle championship in 1908. At the 1920 Olympics, he was edged for the smallbore-standing title by teammate Larry Nuesslein, with another American, Dennis Fenton, in third. Using those scores for the team event, the U.S. easily won the team gold medal in smallbore rifle, standing position.

SCHRIVER, Ollie Martin.
B. 17 DEC 1879 Washington, DC. D. 28 JUN 1947 Washington, DC. Gold(3): 1920 Military Rifle, 300 + 600m, prone—team, 1920 Military Rifle, 600m, prone—team, 1920 Smallbore Rifle, standing—team. Ollie Schriver was a gunnery sergeant in the marines in 1920. In 1905 he became the first marine to earn the distinguished marksman badge. He competed for several marine teams that won NRA championships and competed internationally for the U.S. in 1912 and 1913 at the Pan-American matches, as well as at the 1920 Olympics. At the 1924 DeWar Cup Match vs. Great Britain, Schriver led the U.S. to victory as the high man on the squad.

Schriver was a career Marine Corpsman and served as his company's trumpeteer as well as coaching the Corps' shooters in the late 20's. He retired from the Marine Corps in May 1929, and took up a position as the official scorer for the National Rifle Association.

SEARS, Henry Francis.
B. 08 JAN 1862 Boston, MA. D. 01 JAN 1942 Boston, MA. Gold: 1912 Free Pistol—team. Henry Sears was from a very wealthy family, which gave him plenty of time to practice his shooting. He attended Harvard and then spent one year at Harvard Law School before deciding upon medicine. He received an M.D. degree from Harvard in 1884 and took up a position as a pathologist at Boston City Hospital, but held the position for only a few years. In 1899 he was elected a member of the Boston Music Hall Association and supported this organization for many years, financially and otherwise. His main hobby seemed to be philanthropy—he gave several gifts to Harvard and local charitable organizations.

SHARMAN, Samuel H.
B. 1878. Gold: 1924 Clay Pigeon—team. Sam Sharman was from Salt Lake City and was high individual for the United States in the 1924 Olympic team clay pigeon event. He also finished sixth in the individual clay pigeon event at the 1924 Olympics.

SILKWORTH, William Sylvester.
B. 28 OCT 1884 Williamsburg, CA. Gold: 1924 Clay Pigeon—team. Bill Silkworth was a member of the 1924 U.S. team which won the gold in the clay pigeon event. It was remarkable that he could concentrate on his shooting, given the events of his recent past.

In 1918 Silkworth was elected president of the Consolidated Stock Exchange of New York. In 1923 he was forced to resign as president when questions were raised about his bank deposits of $123,000 on a salary of $10,000. On 28 May 1924 he was charged with defrauding investors in stocks and bonds, only two days before he left for Paris with the U.S. Olympic team. He was put on trial, with several of his cohorts, after his return from Paris, and on 29 November 1929, he was found guilty of using the mails to defraud and was sentenced to a short jail term and fined several thousand dollars.

SIMON, Harry E.
Silver: 1908 Free Rifle. Harry Simon was a lieutenant in the 6th Ohio Infantry in 1908. The 1908 free rifle event was shot at three positions, almost unknown in the United States, where it was only shot prone or kneeling. Thus, the U.S. was not expected to fare well in the event, but Harry Simon put on a tremendous show to win the silver medal. He was the high man in the prone and kneeling phases of the competition, being pushed down to second only by his standing score.

SNOOK, James Howard.
B. 1880. D. 28 FEB 1930 Columbus, OH. Gold(2): 1920 Free Pistol—team, 1920 Rapid-Fire Pistol—team. James Snook made national headlines in 1929 and 1930, but not for anything to do with his shooting ability. Snook was a 1908 graduate of the Ohio State Veterinary School and in 1920 was a professor of veterinary medicine at Ohio State. In June 1929 he was practicing at the Ohio State rifle range when he was arrested and accused of the murder of Theora K. Hix, a medical student at Ohio State.

It turned out that Snook and Hix had posed as man and wife for three years, sharing an apartment near the school's campus. On 13 June 1929, Snook claimed that Hix asked him to divorce his wife and marry her, threatening to kill his wife and child if she was refused. Snook confessed to then beating Hix several times with a hammer before severing her jugular vein with a pocketknife to "relieve her suffering." On 14 August 1929 a jury deliberated only 28 minutes before finding Snook guilty of first-degree murder. A week later he was sentenced to be put to death, and at 7:10 p.m. on 28 February 1930, he died in the electric chair at the Ohio State Penitentiary.

SPOONER, Lloyd S.
B. 06 OCT 1884 Washington State. Gold(4): 1920 Free Rifle—team, 1920 Military Rifle, 300m, prone—team, 1920 Military Rifle, 600m, prone—team, 1920 Military Rifle, 300 + 600m, prone—team; Silver: 1920 Military Rifle, 300m, standing—team; Bronze(2): 1920 Military Rifle, 600m, prone, 1920 Running Deer, single shot—team. In 1920, First Lieutenant Lloyd Spooner of the U.S. Army's 47th Infantry competed in 12 events at the Antwerp Olympic Games—an absolute record for the most events participated in at one Olympics. As above, he won seven medals in these events, which also stood as a record until the 1980 Olympics when the USSR's Alexander Ditiatin won eight gymnastics medals. It remains an American record, tied in 1972 by Mark Spitz. Spooner was a career army officer who was promoted to captain in 1924.

SPOTTS, Ralph Lewis.
B. 14 JUN 1875. D. 17 APR 1924 New York, NY. Gold: 1912 Clay Pigeon—team. Tenth individually in trapshooting at the 1912 Olympics, Ralph Spotts broke the third-high number of birds among the six U.S. members in the team event. Spotts was a three-time American trapshooting champion and was the chairman of the New York AC trapshooting committee for many years. He made his living as a real estate broker in New York City.

Courtesy Sidney Hinds

Walter Stokes, a U.S. Naval Officer who won two gold medals in shooting at the 1924 Olympics.

SPROUT, Warren A.
B. 03 FEB 1874 Picture Rocks, PA. D. 23 AUG 1945 Westfield, NJ. Gold: 1912 Military Rifle—team; Bronze(2): 1912 Smallbore Rifle, prone—team; 1912 Smallbore Rifle, disappearing target—team. Warren Sprout, a career navy officer, was a hospital steward at the time of the 1912 Olympics. Besides his three team medals, he competed in five individual events at the Olympics, but failed to crack the top 10 in any of them.

STOKES, Walter Raymond.
B. 23 MAY 1898 Mohawk, FL. Gold: 1924 Free Rifle—team; Bronze: 1924 Running Deer, single shot—team. Walter Stokes graduated from the U.S. Naval Academy in 1918 and then went on to earn both an LL.B. and an M.D. degree, one of only two American Olympians to do so (fencer Graeme Hammond being the other). Both professional degrees came from George Washington University and, while he was in school, Stokes coached the school's rifle team to intercollegiate championships in 1924, 1927, and 1928.

As a competitor himself, Stokes was on the rifle, swimming and wrestling teams at Annapolis. He competed internationally for the U.S. as a rifle shooter from 1919 until 1923, at which time he entered medical school. At the 1921 World Championships in Lyon, France he was a member of the free rifle team which won four titles—prone, kneeling, standing, and 3-position.

TOMSEN, Walter.
B. 04 MAR 1917. Silver: 1948 Smallbore Rifle, prone. From Flushing, New York, Walter Tomsen shot a Winchester Model 52 rifle at the 1948 Olympics. He used it well to take the silver medal with a score of 599 of a possible 600, missing only once—that on the third string of six.

TROEH, Frank M.
B. c1882 North Dakota. D. 24 DEC 1968. Gold: 1920 Clay Pigeon—team; Silver: 1920 Clay Pigeon. Frank Troeh did not begin trapshooting until he was 31 years old but he learned quickly. His first title was the Washington State Singles in 1914 and he won several more before leading the U.S. shooters in average in 1918 (.9722), 1920 (.9752), and 1922 (.9838—the highest recorded to that date). From 1926 until 1930 he won 10 major titles at the Grand American Handicap, including the All-Around from 1926 to 1929, and the high-overall in 1926 and again in 1929 and 1930. Troeh was captain of the All-American Trapshooting team from 1927 through 1930 and a team member again in 1931, 1933-36, 1938, and 1940. During his lifetime he shot at 109,015 registered targets with a career average of .9751.

WIGGER, Lones Wesley, Jr.

B. 25 AUG 1937 Great Falls, MT. Gold(2): 1972 Free Rifle, 1964 Smallbore Rifle, 3 positions; Silver: 1964 Smallbore Rifle, prone. Little argument can be given to the statement that Lones Wigger is the greatest competitive rifle shooter yet produced in the United States. Leaving aside his Olympic record, which includes making the team in 1968 and 1980, he has held or co-held 27 world records—14 team and 13 individual. He has won 58 National Championships of almost every variety since 1963. He has been a member of 16 major U.S. international teams, starting with the 1963 Pan-American Games and his record includes: 22 World Championships (two individual, 20 team); seven Pan-American titles; 18 victories in the Championship of the Americas meet; 16 victories in the Council Internationale Sport du Militaire meet; and in those four meets, plus the Olympics, he has won 108 medals. For his rivals the worst news is that Wigger is still shooting and still competing very successfully, as witnessed by four individual world records in 1981.

WINANS, Walter.

B. 05 APR 1852 St. Petersburg, Russia. D. 12 AUG 1920 Barking, Essex, England. Gold: 1908 Running Deer, double shot; Silver: 1912 Running Deer, single shot—team. After settling in America in the late 17th century, the Wynants family changed their Dutch name to Winans and prospered with the development of the railroads. Walter Winans' father was one of two brothers who went to Russia to direct the building of the national railway system and the future Olympic champion was born and educated in St. Petersburg. Winans eventually settled in England and showed immense talent in many fields. Apart from his Olympic rifle successes, he was a noted pistol shot and a renowned equestrian sculptor, exhibiting 14 times at the British Royal Academy. In this field he won a second Olympic gold medal in the Arts Competition at Stockholm in 1912—the only American to win medals both in the art and sport phases of Olympic competition.

At the 1908 Olympics, there was a question raised about Winans' eligibility because he had never set foot in America and he was required to swear his allegiance to the U.S. Consul General in order to participate in the Olympics. But he died before he ever visited the United States. Trotting, another of his interests, led to his death.

While driving in a race in England, he suffered a heart attack, fell, and broke his skull, dying instantly.

WINDER, Charles B.

Gold: 1908 Military Rifle—team. Maj. Charles Winder had the second-best score among the U.S. team members in the 1908 military rifle event. In the individual free rifle event, shot prone at 1,000 yards, Winder finished 16th.

WRIGHT, Frank S.

B. 26 DEC 1878. Gold: 1920 Clay Pigeon—team; Bronze: 1920 Clay Pigeon. Frank Wright was from Kenmore, New York, and competed at the 1920 Olympics only in the two events in which he won medals.

WRITER, John Henry.

B. 17 SEP 1944 Chicago, IL. Gold: 1972 Smallbore Rifle, 3 positions; Silver: 1968 Smallbore Rifle, 3 positions. John Writer's first big titles came when he won the intercollegiate championship in 1964, 1965, and 1966 for West Virginia. He added the 1967 U.S. title in smallbore position shooting before winning his silver medal at the 1968 Olympics. Before the next Olympics, Writer stamped himself as the man to beat with his performance at the 1970 World Championships, when he won the smallbore title, was second with the free rifle, and third in the standard rifle at 300 meters. At Munich he dominated the smallbore position event, setting a new world record of 1,166, which included a world record of 381 for the standing phase. Writer has also won three gold medals in the Pan-American Games, all in the smallbore position match.

SOCCER (Association Football)

The United States has had very little success in Olympic soccer. With the exception of 1972, our teams have not qualified for the Olympics since 1956. Although in 1972 we managed a scoreless tie with Morocco, the last time a United States team won a game in the Olympics was 1924, when we defeated Estonia, 11–2.

In 1904, there were only three entrants: a Canadian team—the Galt Football Club of Toronto, and two club teams from St. Louis, representing Christian Brothers' College (CBC) and St. Rose Parish. Consequently, both the CBC and the St. Rose team won medals, although the Canadian team took the gold. Both CBC and St. Rose lost to Galt and then played each other on 18 September for second place. The game went three overtimes and ended in a scoreless tie, so they played again on 23 September, CBC winning this time, 2–0.

Very little is known about the players from the CBC team and almost nothing is known about the players from St. Rose, including, in many cases, their complete names. Biographies are supplied below, therefore, only for the players about whom something is known. Otherwise we list only the name, medal won, club represented, and position played.

BARTLIFF, Charles Albert.
D. Akron, OH. Silver: 1904. Christian Brothers' College. Forward.

BRADY, Joseph J.
Bronze: 1904. St. Rose. Halfback.

BRITTINGHAM, Warren G.
Silver: 1904. Christian Brothers' College. Forward. Warren Brittingham was from Chihuahua, Mexico, and attended Christian Brothers' College as a boarder with his brother, Juan.

BROCKMEYER, Oscar B.
B. 14 NOV 1883. D. 10 JAN 1954. Silver: 1904. Christian Brothers' College. Forward/Fullback. Oscar Brockmeyer played fullback in the first game, against Galt, but in the games against St. Rose he reversed positions with Joe Lydon and played forward. Brockmeyer was one of the best athletes in the school and also captained the football team.

COOKE, George Edwin.
B. 17 FEB 1883 St. Louis, MO. D. 03 JUN 1969 St. Louis, MO. Bronze: 1904. St. Rose. Fullback. George Cooke was the brother of Tom Cooke, who also played for St. Rose. Cooke later went to work as a supervisor for the Liggett & Meyers Co., with whom he remained for 50 years.

COOKE, Thomas J.
B. AUG 1885 St. Louis, MO. Bronze: 1904. St. Rose. Left Wing. Tom Cooke played against Galt and started the first game against CBC. But in that game he broke his leg, had to be taken from the field, and could play no more.

COSGROVE, Cormic F.
Bronze: 1904. St. Rose. Right Wing.

CUDMORE, Alexander.
B. St. Louis, MO. Silver: 1904. Christian Brothers' College. Forward.

DIERKES.
Bronze: 1904. St. Rose. Halfback.

DOOLING, Martin T.
Bronze: 1904. St. Rose. Halfback.

FROST, Frank.
Bronze: 1904. St. Rose. Goalie.

JAMESON, Claude Stanley.
B. c1883. Bronze: 1904. St. Rose. Center Forward.

JAMESON, Henry Wood.
B. c1885. Bronze: 1904. St. Rose. Fullback.

JANUARY, Charles James, Jr.
B. 01 FEB 1888 St. Louis, MO. D. c1975 Los Angeles, CA. Silver: 1904. Christian Brothers' College. Halfback. One of the January brothers, "Hicks" January eventually moved to California, where he had a daughter, Lois January, who became a motion picture actress.

JANUARY, John Hartnett.
B. 06 MAR 1882 St. Louis, MO. D. 01 DEC 1917 St. Louis, MO. Silver: 1904. Christian Brothers' College.

Halfback. John January was one of three brothers who played for Christian Brothers' College.

JANUARY, Thomas Thurston.
B. 08 JAN 1886 St. Louis, MO. D. 25 JAN 1957 St. Louis, MO. Silver: 1904. Christian Brothers' College. Fullback. Tom January was the best known soccer player of the three January brothers, and was voted captain of the CBC team. He also played football for CBC. On 10 January 1911, he married Margaret McCarthy, by whom he had four children.

JOHNSON.
Bronze: 1904. St. Rose. Left Wing. Johnson did not play in the game against Galt, but he did play against CBC when he replaced Tom Cooke after Cooke broke his leg.

LAWLOR, Raymond E.
Silver: 1904. Christian Brothers' College. Forward. Ray Lawlor was originally from St. Louis.

LYDON, Joseph Patrick.
B. 02 FEB 1878 Swinford, County Mayo, Ireland. D. 19 AUG 1937 St. Louis, MO. Silver: 1904 Soccer; Bronze: 1904 Welterweight (Boxing). Christian Brothers' College. Fullback/Forward. Joe Lydon is distinguished among American Olympians as having won Olympic medals in two truly disparate sports.

Lydon was probably the outstanding athlete at the CBC school in 1904 and when an Olympic soccer tournament was scheduled, school officials approached him about organizing a soccer team, which he did. But in addition, Lydon boxed in the Olympics, losing in the welterweight semi-finals to Harry Spanger. Besides boxing and soccer, Lydon was an outstanding track star. He was primarily a sprinter, with a best time of 49.0 in the 440 yds.—heady stuff for 1904.

Lydon began his business career as a whiskey salesman before prohibition hit the country. He also served as superintendent of St. Louis streets from 1901 until 1909. From 1918 until his death, Joe Lydon ran his own company, the Joseph P. Lydon Oil Company. However, a hobby took up much of his time. He raised beagles and was a charter member of the St. Louis AKC Beagle Club.

Joe Lydon, who in 1904 performed the rare feat of winning medals in two sports — soccer and boxing.

Courtesy Mary Margaret Sullivan

MENGES, Louis John.
B. 30 OCT 1888. D. 10 MAR 1961. Silver: 1904. Christian Brothers' College. Goalie. "Turk" Menges was originally from East St. Louis, Illinois. He later became a State Senator in Illinois.

O'CONNELL.
Bronze: 1904. St. Rose. Right Wing.

RATICAN, Peter Joseph.
B. 1887. D. 20 NOV 1922 St. Louis, MO. Silver: 1904. Christian Brothers' College. Halfback. Peter Ratican started one of the most famous soccer families in St. Louis. He went on to become the owner-manager of Ben Miller's soccer franchise and both he and his brother, Harry, have been inducted into the Soccer Hall of Fame.

TATE, Harry.
Bronze: 1904. St. Rose. Left Wing.

SPEED SKATING

MEN

Bobsledding produced many medals for the United States through the 1956 Olympic Winter Games, but for overall consistency, speed skating must rate as our top sport at the Winter Olympics. This is despite the fact that the international style of skating was rarely used in this country until very recently. Most of the United States' successes have come in the shorter races, although at Lake Placid in 1932 and 1980 the United States swept all the speed skating events. There were extenuating circumstances in both cases, however. In 1932, the races were skated pack style and several Europeans declined to compete. In 1980 the extenuating circumstance was the greatest speed skater of all time, Eric Heiden.

OUTSTANDING PERFORMANCES

Most Gold Medals
    5 Eric Heiden
    2 Irving Jaffee, Jack Shea
Most Appearances
    3 Ken Henry, Terry McDermott
Oldest Gold Medalist
    25y146d Irving Jaffee
Oldest Medalist
    27y355d Ken Bartholomew
Youngest Gold Medalist
    21y151d Jack Shea
Youngest Medalist
    20y4d Leo Freisinger

BARTHOLOMEW, Kenneth Eldred.

B. 10 FEB 1920. Silver: 1948 500 meters. Ken Bartholomew has won more speed skating championships than any other American—including Eric Heiden. He was the United States' National Outdoor Champion 14 times—in 1939, 1941, 1942, 1947, 1950-57, 1959, and 1960. He also won the North American Outdoor Championship in 1941, 1942, and 1956. In 1948, he and teammate Bobby Fitzgerald tied for the silver medal in the 500m with a time of 43.2 seconds. After retiring from competition, Bartholomew promoted youth programs in speed skating.

DISNEY, William Dale.

B. 03 APR 1932 Topeka, KS. Silver: 1960 500 meters. Bill Disney never won a major outdoor title at pack style speed skating, but he was the U.S. National and North American Indoor champion in 1955. Almost exclusively a sprinter, Bill Disney skated an excellent time of 40.3 seconds at Squaw Valley to finish second to the Russian great, Evgeni Grishin. Although it was never recognized by the International Skating Union, only a few weeks before the Olympics, Disney had skated 500 meters in 40.1 seconds to break Grishin's world mark.

In 1964 Bill Disney was given the honor of carrying the United States flag into the stadium at the opening ceremonies of the Innsbruck Winter Olympics. Disney, like most speed skaters, also competed as a cyclist, but not with the success of his brother, Jack, who made the U.S. Olympic team three times in that sport. Following his competitive days, Bill Disney has coached many top U.S. speed skaters.

FARRELL, John O'Neill.

B. 28 AUG 1906. Bronze: 1928 500 meters (tied). O'Neill Farrell won his only major championship in 1926, taking the International Outdoor Championship at pack style skating. After winning his bronze medal in 1928 he continued to compete and skated in the 500m in the 1932 Olympics. Farrell also coached the 1936 Olympic speed skating team.

FITZGERALD, Robert Emmett.

B. 03 OCT 1923 Silver: 1948 500 meters (tied). Bobby Fitzgerald never won a national speed skating title because they were dominated by Ken Bartholomew. However, in 1948 he tied Bartholomew in the 500m at the St. Moritz Olympics, and they shared the silver medal. Fitzgerald also competed on the 1952 Olympic team. During his career, he set three national records.

FREISINGER, Leonard.

B. 07 FEB 1916 Chicago, IL. Bronze: 1936 500 meters. The 1936 bronze medal was really the first major breakthrough for Leo Freisinger. Only 19 when he won the medal, his greatest years came after the Garmisch Olympics. In 1937 and 1938 he was U.S. National Indoor champion and in 1940 he was National and North American Outdoor champion. Also in 1938, at a meet in Davos, Switzerland, Freisinger broke the world record for 500 meters then held by the Norwegian, Hans Engnestangen. The record was not ratified because, skating in the next pair, Engnestangen beat Freisinger's time to regain the record. Leo Freisinger was also selected to represent the United States in the 1940 Olympics—which were never held.

For a speed skater, Freisinger had a very unusual career—he became a figure skater in professional ice shows, although he also did some barrel jumping. Freisinger was later head coach of the 1964 Olympic speed skating team.

HEIDEN, Eric Arthur.

B. 14 JUN 1958 Madison, WI. Gold(5): 1980 500 meters, 1980 1,000 meters, 1980 1,500 meters, 1980 5,000 meters, 1980 10,000 meters. Eric Heiden is the greatest speed skater of all time and his utter domination of the sport in the late 70's warrants him a place among the greatest athletes of all time.

Heiden competed at the 1976 Olympics where his best finish was seventh in the 1,500 meters. But at the world championships after the Olympics, he gave a hint of things to come when he won the 500m title. In 1977 he won the World Junior All-round, the World Senior Sprints and became the first American to win the World Senior All-round. In 1978 he defended all three titles. Too old for the juniors in 1979, he won the sprints and the all-around for the third straight year, and did what no man had done outright since 1912—win all four titles at the World Championships.

Heiden, whose sister Beth also won world championships at both speed skating and cycling, was a tireless worker. His training routines were legend, and enabled him to develop massive thighs. Heiden was a freak in that he was dominant both at the longer distances and the sprints. During his career he set nine world records, a mark which surely would have been higher had he ever been allowed to compete (in his prime) at the record factory of Alma Ata in the USSR.

At the 1980 Olympics, Heiden won five individual gold medals—an absolute record for the Olympic Games. His closing act came in the 10,000 meters, where he broke the world record to win easily. After the Olympics he competed in the World Championships, and lost for the first time since 1977. He then retired from speed skating, contemplating a future career as an orthopaedic surgeon. He has gone on to finish his pre-medical studies, finishing up at Stanford, and now competes as a professional bike racer.

HENRY, Kenneth Charles.

B. 07 JAN 1929. Gold: 1952 500 meters. Among Americans, only Eric Heiden has done what Ken Henry did—win an Olympic and a World Championship in speed skating. Henry actually twice won the World 500 meter championship, in 1949 and 1952, placing fourth in the overall championship in both years. In 1952 he also added his Olympic gold medal in the short sprint. Henry also competed in the 1948 and 1956 Olympics without winning a medal.

Ken Henry holds the distinction of being the only American Olympic athlete to carry the Olympic torch into the stadium at the opening ceremonies. This occurred in 1960 at Squaw Valley when he was handed the torch by skiing gold medalist, Andrea Mead Lawrence. Henry circled the ice rink before lighting the Olympic flame.

In 1968, Henry's Olympic connection continued when he was the head coach of the U.S. speed skating team. Henry is still much involved in sports with his job—for many years he has been a golf professional at a club in a Chicago suburb.

IMMERFALL, Daniel James.

B. 14 DEC 1955 Madison, WI. Bronze: 1976 500 meters. In high school, Dan Immerfall was a track star; he was easily the top sprinter in Madison and one of the best in the state. But by then he had also begun to be known as a top speed skater the sport at which he achieved his greatest fame. Immerfall won a bronze medal in the 1976 Olympics 500 meter event by a margin of only .02 seconds. Although he usually finished in the top 10 in the world sprint events, this was his highest finish ever internationally.

Immerfall was a music major at the University of Wisconsin, and he is an accomplished clarinetist. He supported himself as a music teacher during his racing career.

JAFFEE, Irving W.

B. 15 SEP 1906 New York, NY. D. 20 MAR 1981. Gold(2): 1932 5,000 meters, 1932 10,000 meters. Irv Jaffee's first important title was the Silver Skates two-mile in 1926. On the strength of this, and several American records in 1927, he was considered an excellent prospect for a medal at the 1928 Olympics in St. Moritz. Jaffee finished fourth that year in the 5,000 meters, but his best chance was thought to be in the 10,000. Paired with 1927 world champion Bernt Evensen, Jaffee matched his strides for six miles and then outkicked him to take the lead in the event. But the weather was warm, and the outdoor rink was beginning to soften and gradually melt. A few pairs later, the event was called off, the results voided, and Jaffee was denied any medal—although several skaters, including Evensen, protested to the officials that Jaffee should be declared the champion.

In 1932 Jaffee qualified again for the Olympic team and this time fared much better. Skating in the more familiar American pack style, Jaffee outkicked the field twice to win the 5,000 and 10,000 meter titles. Jaffee later went on to become winter sports director at the Grossinger resort in New York and also coached several U.S. Olympic speed skaters.

JEWTRAW, Charles.

B. 05 MAY 1900 Lake Placid, NY. Gold: 1924 500 meters. On 26 January 1924, Charley Jewtraw wrote his name indelibly into the Olympic record book. On that date he won the 500 meter speed skating event to become the first gold medalist ever at the Olympic Winter Games.

Jewtraw was no fluke as a champion. He had been United States champion in both 1921 and 1923 and was a renowned sprinter, holding the American record for 100 yards on skates (9.4 seconds). After his Olympic victory, Jewtraw left Lake Placid and moved to New York, where he became a sporting goods representative, starting with the Spalding company.

McDERMOTT, Donald Joseph.

B. 07 DEC 1929 Bronx, NY. Silver: 1952 500 meters. Like many other American speed skaters of the 40's and 50's, Don McDermott never won a national title, because they were totally monopolized by Ken Bartholomew. But McDermott won his share of races. His first big title came at the 1949 Silver Skates in Madison Square Garden, and in the next two years he won several other invitational races and the Chicago Silver Skates. At the 1952 Olympics, he finished second behind fellow American Ken Henry.

McDermott also competed in the 1956 Olympics, but without much success. After his Oslo silver medal, his biggest competitive moment came in the 1955 World Championships, when he finished third in the 500 meters. At the 1960 Olympics, McDermott was chosen by the U.S. team to carry the flag into the stadium at the opening ceremonies. McDermott's career has been with the U.S. Postal Service, for whom he has held various management positions.

McDERMOTT, Richard Terrance.

B. 20 SEP 1940 Essexville, MI. Gold: 1964 500 meters; Silver: 1968 500 meters (tied). In 1964 they called him the Essexville barber, and he was all we had that year, as Terry McDermott won the only United States gold medal at the 1964 Olympic Winter Games. McDermott was well known as a sprinter in the United States, having won the National Indoor title in 1960 and the North American indoor in 1961.

McDermott continued to be a force in the sprints through 1968. He set an American record in the 220 yards which stood for many years, and in 1968, he was again a favorite to take the gold in the 500 meters at Grenoble. But on that day, Terry McDermott skated late in the field, well after the ice had started to soften, and he had little chance. Amazingly, he finished in 40.5 to share the silver medal only 2/10 out of first. Winner Erhard Keller graciously conceded that McDermott had had the best race of the day, given the conditions under which he had skated.

From 1963 until 1967, Terry McDermott was a barber. In that year, however, he took a job as a manufacturer's representative in the Detroit area, and has remained at the job since. He has also served as a speed skating official and at the 1980 Olympics spoke the official's oath at the opening ceremonies of the Winter Games.

MUELLER, Peter.

B. 27 JUL 1954 Madison, WI. Gold: 1976 1,000 meters. Peter Mueller is one of the top sprinters American speed skating has ever produced. Exclusively a sprinter, he competed in the World Sprints in 1974 and 1975 and did well, but gave no hint he could win the gold medal in 1976 in the first ever Olympic 1,000 meter competition. Although overshadowed by Eric Heiden, between 1976 and 1980 Mueller proved himself one of the top sprinters in the world, finishing second in the 1977 World Sprints and fourth in the 1979 World Sprints. It was thought he could win another medal at Lake Placid, but he finished fifth in his specialty, the 1,000 meters.

In September 1977, Mueller married Leah Poulos, a three-time Olympic speed skating medalist.

MURPHY, Edward L.
B. 01 FEB 1905. D. 1973. Silver: 1932 5,000 meters. Ed Murphy competed at both the 1928 and 1932 Olympics. He was primarily a distance skater and the 1932 Olympic medal was the highlight of his career.

SHEA, John Amos.
B. 07 SEP 1910 Lake Placid, NY. Gold(2): 1932 500 meters, 1932 1,500 meters. Taking time off from his senior year at Dartmouth College to compete in the Olympics, Jack Shea came home to a hero's welcome in his hometown of Lake Placid. The local fans were expecting big things from Shea and he would not disappoint them. Shortly after the opening ceremonies, the heats of the 500 meters began and Shea easily qualified for the final. He won that final and the next day, 5 February, he added a second gold medal when he took the 1,500 meter event.

Jack Shea was no stranger to winning speed skating races. He had been 1929 U.S. National and 1930 North American champion. Still, he competed very little after the Olympics and it remains his finest moment in sports.

Shea settled in his hometown of Lake Placid. He went on to become town manager and when the tiny hamlet again was awarded the Olympic Winter Games, Jack Shea helped out and served as a key figure on the organizing committee for the 1980 Games.

Courtesy Jack Shea

The first American to win two gold medals in Olympic speed skating, Jack Shea.

WOMEN

The United States women have been very successful in Olympic speed skating since its inception in 1960. That year, Jeanne Ashworth won a bronze medal in the 500 meters, starting a trend of American successes in the sprints. However, in recent years our distance skaters have also done well. To date, nine women have won 15 medals for the United States in speed skating.

OUTSTANDING PERFORMANCES

Most Medals
   4 Dianne Holum
   3 Leah Poulos Mueller, Sheila Young
Most Appearances
   3 Jeanne Ashworth, Jeanne Omelenchuk,
      Leah Poulos Mueller
Oldest Gold Medalist
   26y115d Sheila Young
Oldest Medalist
   28y135d Leah Poulos Mueller
Youngest Gold Medalist
   16y158d Anne Henning

ASHWORTH, Jeanne Chesley.
B. 01 JUL 1938 Burlington, VT. Bronze: 1960 500 meters. In the first official Olympic speed skating for women, Jeanne Ashworth finished behind a German and a Russian to take a bronze medal. In the late 50's and early 60's, Ashworth and the other Jeanne, Omelenchuk, monopolized American speed skating— Ashworth winning 11 national championships and Omelenchuk eight.

Jeanne Ashworth was also an excellent softball player, and she competed in that sport on a national level. In 1960 she received a B.S. degree in physical therapy from an affiliate school of Tufts. Today she lives near Lake Placid,where she helps run the family toy and candy company.

FISH, Jennifer Lee.
B. 17 MAY 1949 Strongsville, OH. Silver: 1968 500 meters (tied). At the 1968 Olympics, Jennifer Fish was one of the American women who amazingly finished in a three-way tie for second in the 500 meters. In Fish's case, this was a bit of an upset, as her international experience was minimal. However she had, at one time, held eight U.S. national speed skating records.

Jennifer Fish majored in health and physical education at Baldwin-Wallace College and went on to receive a master's in education at Kent State. She became a physical education teacher.

HEIDEN, Elizabeth Lee.
B. 27 SEP 1959 Madison, WI. Bronze: 1980 3,000 meters. Beth Heiden is one of the world's most amazing women athletes. In high school she played tennis and soccer, but also ran track, setting a national age-group record for the mile. She went on to an outstanding career as a speed skater, becoming in 1979 the first American to win the Women's World Championship's. She finished second in that event in 1980, was second in the 1978 and 1979 World Sprints, and was expected to join her brother, Eric, in picking up a slew of medals at Lake Placid. But an ankle injury hounded her, and the press's expectations bothered her, as she was not the dominant force that Eric was. She came away with a bronze medal in her best event, the 3,000.

Heiden has not skated competitively since the 1980 season. However, she has kept in shape. Later in 1980, she became the first American to win the cycling road race at the Women's World Championships, and for awhile it seemed cycling had become her primary sport.

Beth Heiden had attended the University of Wisconsin as a physics major. But in 1981 she transferred to the University of Vermont where she tried a completely new sport—cross-country skiing. Amazingly, only one year after taking up the sport, in 1983, she won the NCAA Women's championship in cross-country skiing.

HENNING, Anne.
B. 06 SEP 1955 Raleigh, NC. Gold: 1972 500 meters; Bronze: 1972 1,000 meters. Although only 16, Anne Henning was a favorite to win the two shortest speed skating races at the 1972 Olympics. By then she had been second in the World Championships—at all-around. She had also set three official and two unofficial world records in the 500, and one official world record in the 1,000.

In the 1972 Olympic 500, Anne Henning skated a fine time, despite being interfered with by her pair partner on the cross-over. She was offered a re-skate, and took the opportunity. It was probably a mistake, for although she bettered her time, her initial 500 time would also have taken the gold medal. The next day, in the 1,000, she could manage only a bronze—she described her legs as being "dead."

HOLUM, Dianne Mary.

B. 19 MAY 1951 Chicago, IL. Gold: 1972 1,500 meters; Silver(2): 1968 500 meters, 1972 3,000 meters; Bronze: 1968 1,000 meters. In 1966, Dianne Holum became the youngest person to ever compete in the World Championships. It was the start of a distinguished speed skating career which saw her win more medals than any U.S. woman in Winter Games history.

The 1967 Worlds were the first top international finish for Holum, as she finished third overall. She went on to win two medals at the 1968 Games, and in the interval between Olympics, became less of a sprinter and more of a distance skater. In 1970 and 1971 she was fourth in the Worlds overall, winning the 1,000 meters in 1971. She also had two top 10 finishes at the World Sprints. In 1972 she finally got a gold medal and added a fourth medal with a second place in the Olympic 3,000 meters.

Since retiring as a competitor, Dianne Holum has become a well-known coach. At the 1976 Olympics, she became the first woman to coach the women speed skaters. She has numbered among her many pupils two kids from Madison, Wisconsin, named Heiden.

MEYERS, Mary Margaret.

B. 10 FEB 1946 St. Paul, MN. Silver: 1968 500 meter (tied). Mary Meyers was part of the U.S. three-way tie in the 1968 500 meters. For her, it was probably a bit of a disappointment; in the 1967 World Championships she had won the 500 meter event, and was expected to be a top contender for the gold. Meyers attended the University of Minnesota, from which she graduated in 1969.

MUELLER, Leah Jean Poulos.

B. 05 OCT 1951 Berwyn, IL. Silver(3): 1976 1,000 meters, 1980 500 meters, 1980 1,000 meters. As Miss Poulos, Leah Mueller competed in the 1972 and 1976 Olympics, winning a silver in the 1000 meters at Innsbruck and narrowly missing a bronze in the 500 meters. In September 1977, she married U.S. speed

skating team member, Peter Mueller, and won two more medals under her married name at Lake Placid.

Besides her Olympic successes, Leah Poulos Mueller was twice World Sprint champion—in 1974 and 1979—and twice second in that event—in 1976 and 1977. She competed in the longer distances only early in her career because it was apparent that she was a pure sprinter. She retired in 1978 to travel with her husband and watch him compete, but quickly became bored with that and returned to competition the next year. She was coached early in her career by her father and three-time world champion, John Werket, but her husband and Peter Schotting took over those duties in preparation for Lake Placid.

POULOS, Leah. (see Leah Poulos Mueller)

COMPETING IN WINTER AND SUMMER OLYMPICS

Four Americans have competed in both the Olympic Games and the Olympic Winter Games. They are:

Eddie Eagan (1920–1924 BOX, 1932 BOB)
Arthur Longsjo (1956 CYC & SSK)
Arnold Uhrlass (1960 SSK, 1964 CYC)
Willie Davenport (1964–1976 TAF, 1980 BOB)

Among these four, Longsjo and Uhrlass failed to win a medal in either sport. Davenport won two medals as a hurdler in track & field, but failed to medal in the bobsled events. Eddie Eagan, however, not only won medals in both sports, but he won gold medals as a light-heavyweight boxer in 1920 and in the four-man bobsled in 1932.

Eagan's feat is unique in Olympic history. In fact, only one other man, Jacob Tullin Thams of Norway, has won medals in both the Winter and Summer Games. Thams won a gold medal in ski jumping in 1924 and a silver medal in yachting in 1936.

Courtesy Women's Sports Foundation

More than twenty years after competing in her first Olympics, Sheila Young is still competing internationally.

YOUNG, Sheila.

B. 14 OCT 1950 Detroit, MI. Gold: 1976 500 meters; Silver: 1976 1,500 meters; Bronze: 1976 1,000 meters. Sheila Young first competed in the U.S. National Championships in 1964. Twenty years later, she is still competing. Her first Olympics were in 1972, when she managed a fourth place in the 500 meters. In 1973 she performed the astounding feat of winning world sprint championships in both cycling and speed skating. She continued to be a top sprinter internationally in both sports. Through the 1976 Winter Olympics, she lost only two major 500 meter sprints and in 1976 won three medals at Innsbruck. In addition, later in 1976 she repeated her cycling world championship after a third place in 1975. As a speed skater, she also set three world records in the 500 meters, the last one of which, 40.68, set in 1976, lasted until 1982.

After 1976, Sheila Young retired from competition and married U.S. Olympic cyclist Jim Ochowicz. However they divorced a few years later and Sheila Young began to get the urge to compete again. After the 1980 Olympics she laced up the skates and began to compete again internationally. While not yet regaining a world championship, she has finished among the top again at both sports and is expected to be a contender at the 1984 Winter Olympics in Sarajevo.

SWIMMING

MEN

Overall, the United States' men swimmers have had overwhelming success at the Olympic Games. There have been a few years where the Australians, Japanese, or Swedes may have had one great Olympics, but no country approaches our record in this sport.

The U.S. has won 74 gold medals, only seven shy of 50% of all those offered, and more than the seven next best countries combined. They have won 180 medals, more than the total of the four next best nations. In every event on the current program, the U.S. male swimmers have won the most medals and gold medals of any country. In 10 of the current 15 events, Americans have won over 50% of the gold medals, and in five of those, over 50% of the total medals. Quite a record.

ADAMS, Edgar H.
Silver: 1904 Plunge for distance. The first three places in the 1904 plunge event went to members of the New York AC with Edgar Adams taking the silver medal. Adams also competed in the 220y and 880y freestyle and the relay, finishing fourth in each event.

AUSTIN, Michael MacKay.
B. 26 AUG 1943 West Orange, NJ. Gold: 1964 4 × 100 meter freestyle relay. After placing sixth in the individual 100m freestyle, Mike Austin won a gold medal in the relay. He was one of three Yale men on that world record breaking relay squad. Austin won the NCAA 50y freestyle in 1964.

BABASHOFF, Jack, Jr.
B. 13 JUL 1955 Whittier, CA. Silver: 1976 100 meter freestyle. Jack and Shirley Babashoff are one of the few American brother-sister combos to have won Olympic medals. Jack attended the University of Alabama and he was at his best at the 1975 Pan-American Games when he won two relay golds and an individual silver in the 100m freestyle.

BACKHAUS, Robin.
B. 12 FEB 1955 Lincoln, NE. Bronze: 1972 200 meter butterfly. While attending the University of Washington, Robin Backhaus won two NCAA titles. He was also a three-time winner at the AAU championships, but the highlight of his career came in 1973 when he took the gold medal in the 200m butterfly at the World Championships.

OUTSTANDING PERFORMANCES

Most Gold Medals
   9 Mark Spitz
   5 Charles Daniels, Don Schollander
   4 John Naber
Most Medals
   11 Mark Spitz
   8 Charles Daniels
   6 Don Schollander
Most Golds (Games)
   7 Mark Spitz
   4 John Naber, Don Schollander
Most Medals (Games)
   7 Mark Spitz
   5 Charles Daniels, John Naber
Most Silver Medals
   3 Tim McKee
Most Bronze Medals
   3 George Breen
Most Appearances
   3 Charles Daniels, Gary Hall,
      Duke Kahanamoku
Most Years Between Appearances
   12 Duke Kahanamoku
Consecutive Victories, Same Event
   2 Mike Burton (1968-72 1500 m. free), Charles Daniels (1906-08 100 m. free), Duke Kahanamoku (1912-20 100 m. free), Jim McLane (1948-52 800 m. freestyle), Don Schollander (1964-68 800 m. free relay), Mark Spitz (2) (1964-68 400 m. and 800 m. free relay), Johnny Weissmuller (2) (1920-24 100 m. free and 800 m. free relay)
Oldest Gold Medalist
   30y206d Louis Handley
Oldest Medalist
   33y331d Duke Kahanamoku
Youngest Gold Medalist
   16y173d Warren Kealoha
Youngest Medalist
   16y61d John Kinsella

BENNETT, Robert Earl.
B. 23 MAY 1943 Los Angeles, CA. Bronze(2): 1960 100 meter backstroke, 1964 200 meter backstroke. Bob Bennett took the NCAA 100y backstroke title for Southern Cal in 1963 and 1964, and was the AAU indoor champion in 1964. In 1961, he set a world record for the 100m backstroke. In addition to his individual Olympic events, he swam in the heats of the medley relay at both Rome and Tokyo, and in 1960 was a member of the relay team which set a world record in the heats before a completely different U.S. foursome bettered the record in the final.

BLICK, Richard Adolph.
B. 29 JUL 1940 Los Angeles, CA. Gold: 1960 4 × 200 meter freestyle relay. Prior to winning the Olympic gold in Rome with a new world record, Dick Blick, of North Central College in California, had won a gold medal in the 800m freestyle relay at the 1959 Pan-American Games. He later became a swim coach and physical education teacher.

BOOTH, Frank Ewen.
D. 1980. Silver: 1932 4 × 200 meter freestyle. Although he never won an individual AAU title, Frank Booth was a member of the Hollywood AC team which won the AAU freestyle relay in 1929 and 1931.

BOTTOM, Joseph Stuart.
B. 18 APR 1955 Santa Clara, CA. Silver: 1976 100 meter butterfly. While at Southern Cal, Joe Bottom won three NCAA freestyle titles and placed sixth in the 100m free at the 1976 Olympics. Despite winning a silver at the 1973 Pan-Am Games and the '76 Olympics, Bottom never won a major domestic championship.

BREEN, George Thomas.
B. 19 JUL 1935 Buffalo, NY. Silver: 1956 4 × 200 meter freestyle relay; Bronze(3): 1956 400 meter freestyle, 1956 1,500 meter freestyle, 1960 1,500 meter freestyle. George Breen first took up swimming seriously at the relatively late age of 17, but he went on to win 22 AAU championships and set six world records. His greatest performance came at the 1956 Olympics, where he lowered the world 1,500 freestyle record by 13 seconds. Unfortunately this was in the heats and he could not repeat this form in the final, where he finished third.

Breen attended Cortland State and later did graduate work at Indiana. He is now the head swim coach at Penn.

BREYER, Ralph.
B. 24 FEB 1904. Gold: 1924 4 × 200 meter freestyle relay. After winning his heat of the 400m freestyle at the Paris Olympics, Ralph Breyer withdrew from the semifinals but won a gold medal, later in the Games, as a member of the world record breaking relay team. Breyer attended Northwestern and won two freestyle titles at the inaugural NCAA championships in 1924. He added a third NCAA championship in 1925.

BRUCE, Thomas Edwin.
B. 17 APR 1952 Red Bluff, CA. Gold: 1972 4 × 100 meter medley relay; Silver: 1972 100 meter breaststroke. Tom Bruce of UCLA won the NCAA 100y backstroke in 1972, but he never won an AAU title. The 1972 Olympic medley relay team, on which Bruce swam the backstroke leg, set a new world record in taking the gold medals.

BRUNER, Michael Lee.
B. 23 JUL 1956 Omaha, NE. Gold(2): 1976 200 meter butterfly, 1976 4 × 200 meter freestyle relay. While at Stanford, Mike Bruner won the NCAA 1,500m freestyle in 1975. He proved his versatility at the 1974 AAU's by winning the indoor 1,650y freestyle and the outdoor 200m fly. Bruner continued to swim after 1976 and would have been one of the favorites at Moscow had we competed. One of his more amazing accomplishments came in a fund-raising drive for his club, DeAnza of Cupertino, California. He swam 10,000m in 1 hour, 39:18.59 (short-course), which netted over $43,000 for the club.

BUCKINGHAM, Gregory F.
B. 29 JUL 1945 Riverside, CA. Silver: 1968 200 meter individual medley. In addition to his Olympic silver in 1968, Greg Buckingham placed fourth in the 400m individual medley (IM). Buckingham attended Stanford and won one NCAA championships and four AAU titles in both the freestyle and IM events.

BURTON, Michael Jay.
B. 03 JUN 1947 Des Moines, IA. Gold(3): 1968 400 meter freestyle, 1968 1,500 meter freestyle, 1972 1,500 meter freestyle. Although severely injured at the age of 12 when struck by a truck while riding a bicycle, Mike Burton recovered sufficiently to become one of the great distance freestylers ever. He set seven world and 16 U.S. records, won 10 AAU titles, and while at UCLA he was five times an NCAA champion.

Burton was the first man to break 16 minutes for the 1,650y free and the first to swim 800m under 8:30. He was also the first to follow the now standard training regimen of mega-mileage. The only man to win two Olympic 1,500m freestyle titles, between those championships he needed further surgery on his knee, a residual of his old injury.

CARTER, Keith E.
B. 30 AUG 1924. Silver: 1948 200 meter breaststroke. Keith Carter attended Purdue and won the NCAA 200y butterfly in 1949. He finished second to Joe Verdeur at the 1948 U.S. Final Trials and it was Verdeur who again beat him at the Olympics.

CLAPP, Austin Rhone.
B. 08 NOV 1910. D. 22 DEC 1971. Gold: 1928 4 × 200 meter freestyle relay; Bronze: 1932 Water Polo. Apart from his gold medal in the relay, Austin Clapp also competed in the 400m and 1,500m freestyle events at the 1928 Olympics, his best finish in those being fifth in the 400m. Clapp won one NCAA and one AAU indoor title and was one of the five Stanford men on the 1932 Olympic water polo team. A poly sci major as an undergrad, Clapp also attended Stanford Law School and became a prominent attorney in Northern California.

CLARK, Stephen Edward.
B. 17 JUN 1943 Oakland, CA. Gold(3): 1964 4 × 100 meter freestyle relay, 1964 4 x 200 meter freestyle relay, 1964 4 × 100 meter medley relay. In 1960, while still attending Los Altos High School, Steve Clark made the Olympic team and swam in the heats of both relay events. He then attended Yale, and while there won five NCAA titles and took six individual and five AAU relay championships for the Santa Clara SC. A short-course specialist noted for his split-second turns, Clark set nine

world records, but was deprived of many more because short-course marks could not be accepted for world records.

Clark was suffering from shoulder tendinitis at the 1964 U.S. Trials and only made the Tokyo team as a member of the relays, but did quite well in those, helping win three golds and set three world records. After Yale, Clark attended Harvard Law School and wrote a best-selling book on competitive swimming.

COLELLA, Richard Phillip, Jr.
B. 14 DEC 1951 Seattle, WA. Bronze: 1976 200 meter breaststroke. Rick Colella graduated from the University of Washington and later competed for the Totem Lake SC. He won the 200m breaststroke at the 1971 Pan-Am Games and both the breaststroke events at the 1975 Pan-Ams. Colella also won three AAU titles, but his Olympic bronze fell short of the efforts of his sister, Lynn, who brought home a silver in women's swimming.

COWELL, Robert Elmer.
B. 12 JUN 1924 Pennsylvania. D. 11 JAN 1960 Athens, GA. Silver: 1948 100 meter backstroke. At both the Final Trials and the 1948 Olympics, Bob Cowell, a U.S. Navy ensign, finished second to Alan Stack in the backstroke event. Cowell won the 1946 NCAA 100y backstroke for the Naval Academy and was the AAU champ in the 100m outdoor in 1945 and the 150y indoors in 1947. He became a career naval officer before his early passing.

CRABBE, Clarence Linden.
B. 07 FEB 1910 Oakland, CA. D. 23 APR 1983 Scottsdale, AZ. Gold: 1932 400 meter freestyle; Bronze: 1928 1,500 meter freestyle. "Buster" Crabbe moved to Hawaii as a 2-year-old when his father took a job as an overseer on a pineapple plantation. But he returned to the mainland to attend Southern Cal as an undergrad and a law student and, although he won only one NCAA title, he went on to win 18 AAU championships and set 16 world records. At the 1932 Olympics he was the only U.S. gold medalist in men's swimming and after the Games, he was signed by Paramount, who was looking for a rival to Johnny Weissmuller's Tarzan at MGM. The first of Crabbe's 175 movies was "King of the Jungle" in which he played the role of Kasta, the Lion Man. Al-

though he played Tarzan only once, as the star of "B" movies he was never short of work, playing the title role in Flash Gordon and Buck Rogers films in addition to appearing in 65 westerns.

Crabbe was a life-long advocate of physical fitness, conducted televised physical fitness programs and in 1971, aged 63, he set a world age group record for the 400m freestyle. He had extensive business interests, including Buster Crabbe Swim Pools.

CRAIG, William Norval.
B. 16 JAN 1945 Culver City, CA. Gold: 1964 4 × 100 meter medley relay. Although Bill Craig was rather below his best on the breaststroke stage of the medley relay final at the 1964 Olympics, the U.S. still became the first team ever to beat four minutes for the event. Craig, who attended Southern Cal, won three AAU and three NCAA titles. He also won a gold medal at the 1963 Pan-American Games as a member of the medley relay team.

CRISTY, James Crapo, Jr.
B. 22 JAN 1913 Detroit, MI. Bronze: 1932 1,500 meter freestyle. Jim Cristy won his Olympic bronze while he was attending the University of Michigan. In 1936, representing the Lake Shore AC of Chicago, he placed third in the 1,500m free at the U.S. Trials, but was eliminated in the semi-finals in Berlin.

DANIELS, Charles Meldrum.
B. 24 MAR 1885. D. 09 AUG 1973 Carmel Valley, CA. Gold(5): 1904 220 yard freestyle, 1904 440 yard freestyle, 1904 4 × 50 yard freestyle relay, 1906 100 meter freestyle, 1908 100 meter freestyle; Silver: 1904 100 yard freestyle; Bronze(2): 1904 50 yard freestyle, 1908 4 × 200 meter freestyle relay. Charlie Daniels was a major influence on the development of American swimming. He perfected the Australian crawl, changing it slightly to be renamed the American crawl, and using it to win a record 31 AAU individual championships. He set world freestyle records at every distance from 25y to one mile and in 1905, he posted 14 world records within a period of four days. His tally of eight Olympic medals has only been beaten by Mark Spitz among American swimmers. In addition to his outstanding abili-

ties in the pool, Daniels was also the bridge and squash champion of the New York AC and later became a top amateur golfer.

DICKEY, William Paul.
B. 13 OCT 1883. D. 17 FEB 1950. Gold: 1904 Plunge for distance. Bill Dickey was a member of the New York AC and won his Olympic gold with a plunge of 62'6".

DILLEY, Gary J.
B. 15 JAN 1945 Washington, DC. Silver: 1964 200 meter backstroke. Gary Dilley set a new Olympic record in the heats and semi-finals of the 200m backstroke at the 1964 Olympics, but Jed Graef improved on the records in the second semi-final and the final. While at Michigan State, Dilley won the NCAA outdoor backstroke double in 1965 and 1966.

EDGAR, David Holmes.
B. 27 MAR 1950 Fort Lauderdale, FL. Gold: 1972 4 × 100 meter freestyle relay. Dave Edgar was known primarily as a short-course sprinter with amazing turns. Besides his Olympic gold, he was on a winning relay team at the 1971 Pan-American Games. He won the AAU 100y indoor freestyle in 1970 and the same event at the NCAA for Tennessee in 1970, 1971, and 1972. In addition, Edgar was a world-ranked butterflyer and placed fifth in the 100m fly at Munich.

EVANS, Gwynne.
B. 03 SEP 1880. D. 12 JAN 1965. Bronze: 1904 4 × 50 yard freestyle relay. Gwynne Evans competed in no individual swimming events at the 1904 Olympics, but was a member of the Missouri AC team which played in the non-Olympic water polo tournament, finishing third.

FARRELL, Felix Jeffrey.
B. 28 FEB 1937 Detroit, MI. Gold(2): 1960 4 × 200 meter freestyle relay, 1960 4 × 100 meter medley relay. Jeff Farrell started out at the University of Oklahoma but transferred to Yale, where his swim career was haunted by injury and illness. He swam on the 1960 U.S. Trials only six days after an appendectomy, graciously having declined an offer made by U.S. officials to allow him to try to qualify, based on time, a few weeks

later. Though he would have been the favorite in the 100m free, he finished fourth at the Trials, and made only the relay teams. But by the time of the Olympics, he had recovered sufficiently to anchor the U.S. teams to world records in both events.

Farrell won five AAU titles and was the 100m freestyle champion at the 1959 Pan-American Games.

FERRIS, John Edward.
B. 24 JUL 1949 Sacramento, CA. Bronze(2): 1968 200 meter butterfly, 1968 200 meter individual medley. John Ferris scored his first major victory in 1967 when he won the 200 fly at the World University Games with a new world record. At the 1970 University Games, he won both butterfly events, while at home he took the NCAA 200m fly for Stanford in 1969.

FISSLER, George.
B. 13 OCT 1906. Silver: 1932 4 x 200 freestyle relay. George Fissler of the New York AC won the 200m freestyle at the 1932 Final Trials which earned him a spot on the relay team, as there was no individual 200m Olympic event at that time. He swam the second leg at the Olympics, where the U.S. was well beaten by the Japanese. Fissler won his only AAU title in 1933 when he took the indoor 220y freestyle.

FLANAGAN, Ralph Drew.
B. 14 DEC 1918. Silver: 1936 4 × 200 meter freestyle relay. Ralph Flanagan, who swam for the Miami SC and the Miami Biltmore Aquatic Club, made his Olympic debut in 1932 when he was eliminated in the semi-finals of the 1,500m freestyle. In 1936 he was a finalist in both the 400m and 1,500m free, but won his only medal in the relay. Flanagan won 20 AAU titles and set 26 U.S. and two world records and at one time held every U.S. freestyle record from 220y to one mile. After his retirement he stayed in swimming as a Red Cross professional and more recently was the director of safety programs for Los Angeles.

FORD, Alan Robert.
B. 07 DEC 1923. Silver: 1948 100 meter freestyle. Alan Ford came from the Canal Zone, and after attending Mercersburg Academy, went to Yale. The first of the many highlights of his swim career came in 1943 when he broke Johnny Weissmuller's 17-year-old world re-

cord for the 100y freestyle. The following year he became the first man to swim that distance under 50 seconds, and it was eight years before Dick Cleveland became the second man under that barrier.

Ford also broke the 100m freestyle world record twice, won two AAU titles and, after service in the navy, made a comeback to win a silver medal at the 1948 Olympics. In 1944 he became only the third man in history to win three NCAA individual titles in one year.

FORRESTER, William.
B. 18 DEC 1957 Darby, PA. Bronze: 1976 200 meter butterfly. At the 1975 World Championships, Bill Forrester took the gold medal in the 200m butterfly and the bronze in the 100m. He also won the AAU 200m butterfly in 1976. Forrester graduated from Auburn in 1980.

FURNISS, Bruce MacFarlane.
B. 27 MAY 1957 Fresno, CA. Gold(2): 1976 200 meter freestyle, 1976 4 × 200 meter freestyle relay. Bruce Furniss was the younger of two extremely talented brothers from Southern Cal. Bruce emerged as a top-class swimmer in 1975 when he finished second in the 200m and 400m freestyle and won a gold medal in the relay at the World Championships. He also set his first world record that year when he posted a new best for the 200m freestyle twice in one day during June. He made a further improvement in August and two days later deprived his brother of the world 200m IM record. At the Olympics, Furniss won both his gold medals with new world records. He won nine AAU titles and six NCAA championships during his career.

Furniss now works in marketing and public relations. He also does public speaking and is a columnist for *Swimmer's World* magazine.

FURNISS, Steven Charles.
B. 21 DEC 1952 Madison, WI. Bronze: 1972 200 meter individual medley. Steve Furniss was an IM specialist, winning the 200m and 400m IM at both the 1971 and 1975 Pan-American Games. In 1974 he tied David Wilkie's world record before brother Bruce took over as record holder in 1975. Apart from his Olympic bronze medal at 200m, Steve Furniss swam in the 400IM at the 1972 and 1976 Olympics and was a finalist on both occasions.

Furniss studied dentistry for a short time at Southern Cal but now works in public relations for the swimwear company Arena.

GAILEY, Francis.
Silver(3): 1904 220 yard freestyle, 1904 440 yard freestyle, 1904 880 yard freestyle; Bronze: 1904 one mile freestyle. Frank Gailey of San Francisco's Olympic Club was unlucky to be matched against Charlie Daniels, Germany's Emil Rausch, and Hungary's Geza Kiss at the 1904 Olympics. Though Gailey swam well, those three prevented him from winning a gold medal.

GENTER, Steven.
B. 04 JAN 1951 Rural Artesia, CA. Gold: 1972 4 × 200 meter freestyle relay; Silver(2): 1972 400 meter freestyle, 1972 200 meter freestyle. Before enrolling at UCLA, Steve Genter was a high school all-American at both swimming and water polo. At the 1972 Olympics, Genter suffered a collapsed lung only days before his event. Though his doctors advised him against it, he swam despite the handicap, finishing second to Mark Spitz in the 200 and being moved up to third in the 400 after the disqualification of Rick DeMont for using an illegal asthma medication. Genter was known for shaving his head completely, earning him the nickname "Curly." His only AAU championship came in the indoor 200y free in 1972.

GILLANDERS, John David.
B. 18 MAY 1939 Schenectady, NY. Bronze: 1960 200 meter butterfly. In 1959, Dave Gillanders beat Mike Troy for the 200m butterfly title at the Pan-American Games, but it was Troy who won the Olympic title the following year, with Gillanders in third. Gillanders swam for Michigan and the Detroit AC and won the NCAA 200y fly in 1959 and 1961.

GLANCY, Harrison S.
B. 17 SEP 1904 Bens Run, WV. Gold: 1924 4 × 200 meter freestyle relay. Harry Glancy was attending Mercersburg Academy when he swam on the relay team which took the gold medals at the Paris Olympics. Glancy, who later competed for the Penn AC, won two AAU freestyle titles and one in the IM.

GOETZ, Hugo L.
Silver: 1904 4 × 50 yard freestyle relay. In his Olympic appearance, Hugo Goetz helped his Chicago AA relay team to a silver medal.

GOODELL, Brian Stuart.
B. 02 APR 1959 Stockton, CA. Gold(2): 1976 400 meter freestyle, 1976 1,500 meter freestyle. Among American swimmers of the late 70's, Brian Goodell was a legend for his long-distance workouts and tireless capacity for work. En route to his two gold medals, Goodell broke both world records at the U.S. Trials and then rebroke his own marks at the Olympics. He was attending Mission Viejo HS in California at the time, but he later went to UCLA. He made the 1980 Olympic team but unfortunately, what would have been the swimming battle of the Olympics—Goodell vs. Russian great Vladimir Salnikov—failed to materialize.

GOODWIN, Leo G.
B. 13 NOV 1883. D. 25 MAY 1957. Gold: 1904 4 × 50 yard freestyle relay; Bronze(2): 1904 Plunge for distance, 1908 4 × 200 meter freestyle relay. "Budd" Goodwin of the New York AC won numerous championships during a long career, but his days as an active swimmer were nearly ended in 1906 when he almost lost an arm following a severe case of blood poisoning. At the 1904 Olympics he also swam in three individual freestyle events, but failed to place in any of them.

GRAEF, Jed Richard.
B. 01 MAY 1942 Montclair, NJ. Gold: 1964 200 meter backstroke. When Jed Graef won the 200m backstroke with a new world record at the Tokyo Games, he became the first Princetonian to win an Olympic gold medal for swimming. This proved to be by far the most significant victory of his career; the only other major title he won was the NCAA 200y backstroke in 1964.

Graef has since earned a Ph.D. in psychology and works in the emerging field of sports psychology.

GREGG, Steven Garrett.
B. 03 NOV 1955 Wilmington, DE. Silver: 1976 200 meter butterfly. Steve Gregg attended North Carolina State and won the 1976 NCAA 200y butterfly. He also won the AAU indoor 100m butterfly in 1976 and, at both the 1975 Pan-American Games and the 1976 Olympics, he

took the silver medal in the 200 fly. Gregg was never known as much of a sprinter, but few flyers could finish the 200 race like he could.

HACKETT, Robert William.
B. 15 AUG 1959 Yonkers, NY. Silver: 1976 1,500 meter freestyle. Though a tireless worker, Bobby Hackett was frustrated throughout his career by his inability to defeat Brian Goodell. Hackett did win the Pan-American and AAU 1,500m freestyle in 1975, but Goodell beat him at Montreal in that race, en route to a world record. Hackett competed in the Olympics while a student at Fordham Prep, but later attended Harvard.

HAIT, Paul William.
B. 25 MAY 1940 Pasadena, CA. Gold: 1960 4 × 100 meter medley relay. Paul Hait was a finalist in the 200m breaststroke at the Olympics, in addition to his performance on the relay team that won and set world records in both the heats and finals. Hait swam for the Santa Clara SC.

HALL, Gary Wayne.
B. 07 AUG 1951 Fayetteville, AK. Silver(2): 1968 400 meter individual medley, 1972 200 meter butterfly; Bronze: 1976 100 meter butterfly. Although Gary Hall's three Olympic medals came in the butterfly, he was, without doubt, at his absolute best in the IM. A graduate of Indiana, Hall set 10 world records, of which eight were set in IM events and one each in the fly and backstroke, and he was the first man to break four minutes for the 400m IM. He won 23 AAU and seven NCAA championships and posted 23 U.S. records.

Hall carried the U.S. flag at the 1976 opening ceremonies. He was by then a medical student at the University of Cincinnati and today is a practicing ophthalmologist.

HAMMOND, David.
Silver: 1904 4 × 50 yard freestyle relay. Apart from being on the second-placed relay team, David Hammond of the Chicago AA also competed in the 100y free and the 100y backstroke, but was not a threat to the medalists in either event.

HANDLEY, Louis de Breda.
B. 14 FEB 1874 Rome, Italy. D. 28 DEC 1956 New York, NY. Gold: 1904 4 × 50 yard freestyle relay. Lou Handley came to New York from his native Italy as a 22-year-old and set up business as an importer. He joined the New York AC, where he was active in many sports and his multiple talents were seen to advantage when he won a "medley" race which consisted of successive quarter-miles of walking, running, horseback riding, cycling, rowing, and swimming. In second place in this bizarre competition was Joe Ruddy, who was a teammate of Handley's on the winning 1904 Olympic relay team.

Lou Handley was also an outstanding water polo player and was on the New York AC team which won all but one of the AAU titles — both indoors and outdoors — between 1898 and 1911. When the U.S. "softball" rules were dropped in 1911 in favor of international regulations, Handley retired from water polo but continued his sporting interests as a yachtsman and field dog trainer.

He later became a noted coach and journalist. He was the first official coach to a women's U.S. Olympic swim team and, in addition to publishing five books on the sport, he contributed the swimming section to the *Encyclopaedia Brittanica*.

HANDY, Henry Jamison.
B. 06 MAR 1886. 1904 440 yard breaststroke. "Jam" Handy retired after he had won the AAU long distance swim for three years straight from 1907, but after a considerable interval, he began a second sporting career and made the 1924 Olympic team as an alternate on the water polo squad.

Handy competed for the Chicago AA and the Illinois AC; working for *The Chicago Tribune*, he was forced to do most of his training at 3:00 AM, after the newspaper had been put to bed. Handy was an innovative swimmer and would have won more championships had all his ideas stood the test of competition. However, in many fields he was years ahead of his time; he was, for example, the first to use the alternate arm style in the backstroke. He also pioneered underwater photography for stroke analysis and in his later years, he set up the Jam Handy Corporation, which specialized in motivational training. As of July 1983, Jam Handy is the oldest living American Olympic medalist.

HANLEY, Richard Dennis.
B. 19 FEB 1936 Evanston, IL. Silver: 1956 4 × 200 meter freestyle relay. Dick Hanley attended the University of Michigan, and although he won two AAU titles, he never succeeded in winning an NCAA championship. The 100m freestyle final at the 1956 Olympics was dominated by the Australians and the Americans, and as Australia swept the medals, the U.S. filled the next three places, with Dick Hanley finishing fifth. After their success in the individual sprint, the Australian victory in the relay came as no surprise, but Dick Hanley swam the lead-off leg for the U.S. team which took the silver medals.

HARRIGAN, Daniel Lee.
B. 29 OCT 1955 South Bend, IN. Bronze: 1976 200 meter backstroke. Dan Harrigan's first international exposure came at the age of 10, when he competed in a U.S.-Canada dual meet. Ten years later, in 1975, he won the 200m backstroke at the Pan-American Games, and although he improved on his winning Pan-Am time by almost five seconds at the 1976 Olympics, he still finished third behind teammates John Naber and Peter Rocca. Harrigan was a dean's list student in architecture at North Carolina State.

HARRIS, William W., Jr.
B. 26 OCT 1897. Bronze: 1920 100 meter freestyle. The 100m freestyle final at the 1920 Olympics was swum twice because the Australian, Bill Herald, claimed that Norman Ross had fouled him in the first race. Bill Harris, from the Outrigger Canoe Club in Hawaii, finished third in each race. He was also a finalist in the 400m free but failed to finish the race.

HARRISON, George Prifold.
B. 09 APR 1939 Berkeley, CA. Gold: 1960 4 × 200 meter freestyle relay. George Harrison, of Stanford and the Santa Clara SC, won the AAU indoor IM for three straight years from 1958 and set a new U.S. short-course record on each occasion. Outdoors, he was the AAU champion in 1955 and set two world records for the 400 IM in 1960. As this event was not included in the Olympic program until 1964, Harrison was forced to turn to another event in search of Olympic honors in Rome, and after winning the 200m free at the Final

Trials, he swam the lead-off stage for the relay team which set a new world record at the 1960 Olympics.

HEBNER, Harry J.
B. 15 JUN 1891. D. 12 OCT 1968. Gold: 1912 100 meter backstroke; Silver: 1912 4 × 200 meter freestyle relay; Bronze: 1908 4 × 200 meter freestyle relay. From 1910 to 1917, Harry Hebner held all the world backstroke records. He won 35 AAU titles in freestyle and backstroke events, including the 150y backstroke for seven straight years from 1910. Hebner was also a fine water polo player and was a member of the Illinois AC team which won the AAU title seven times between 1914 and 1924. He made a third Olympic appearance in 1920 as a member of the water polo team and was the standard bearer for the U.S. team at the Antwerp opening ceremonies.

HEIDENREICH, Jerry Alan.
B. 04 FEB 1950 Tulsa, OK. Gold(2): 1972 4 × 100 meter freestyle relay, 1972 4 × 100 meter medley relay; Silver: 1972 100 meter freestyle; Bronze: 1972 100 meter butterfly. The U.S. won all three relays at the 1972 Olympics, each with a new world record, and Jerry Heidenreich was a member of two of the winning teams. He also won three gold and one silver at the 1971 Pan-American Games. Heidenreich attended Southern Methodist and won the NCAA 220y freestyle in 1972.

HENCKEN, John Frederick.
B. 29 MAY 1954 Culver City, CA. Gold(3): 1972 200 meter breaststroke, 1976 100 meter breaststroke, 1976 4 × 100 meter medley relay; Silver: 1976 200 meter breaststroke; Bronze: 1972 100 meter breaststroke. John Hencken began swimming as therapy to recover from an operation which removed a growth behind his knee. He ended up setting six world records in the 100m breaststroke and five in the 200m, and both his individual Olympic titles were won with new world records. Another of his world records came in the 1975 World Championships where he won the 100m breaststroke. Hencken, who attended Stanford and also swam for the Santa Clara SC, won 10 AAU titles between 1972 and 1976.

At The Movies

Many American Olympians have appeared on the silver screen. The most famous roles they have played have been in multiple Tarzan pictures. Five American Olympians have played the jungle hero in the movies.

Johnny Weissmuller was the first and most famous. He starred in "Tarzan the Ape Man" in 1932 and made twelve Tarzan pictures, the last being "Tarzan and the Mermaids" in 1948. Shot putter Herman Brix, who later acted under the name Bruce Bennett, is the only other Olympian to appear as Tarzan more than once. In 1938 he played the jungle hero three times, in "The New Adventures of Tarzan," "Tarzan and the Green Goddess," and "Tarzan in Guatemala." Buster Crabbe was more famous for his movie roles of Flash Gordon and Buck Rogers, but he played Tarzan in 1933 in "Tarzan the Fearless." Glenn Morris played in "Tarzan's Revenge" in 1938, opposite an Olympian co-star of Eleanor Holm. Lastly, in 1964, Don Bragg filmed "Tarzan and the Jewels of Opar" in Jamaica, but the movie was never released.

Weissmuller is not the Olympian with the most movie credits. That would either be Buster Crabbe, who made about 150 movies, or wrestler Nat Pendleton, who is credited with over 100 movie roles. Brix, as Bruce Bennett, also appeared in dozens of movies.

No American Olympian has ever won an Oscar for his acting efforts—not too surprisingly. But a movie about an American Olympian won the Oscar for Best Movie—"Patton," about the 1912 modern pentathlete, George Smith Patton, Jr. And did you know that the Oscar itself was formerly manufactured by Dodge, Inc., founded and owned by Olympic runner Ray Dodge? And George Patton is not the only U.S. Olympian who had a movie made about him—Jim Thorpe, Bob Mathias and Cassius Clay (Muhammed Ali) have also been so honored.

Following is a list of American Olympians and their film credits, partial in some cases:

Muhammed Ali (BOX)—"The Greatest," "Freedom Road"

John Anderson (TAF)—"Search for Beauty"
Lee Barnes (TAF)—stand-in for Buster Keaton in several
Don Bragg (TAF)—"Tarzan and the Jewels of Opar"
Herman Brix (Bruce Bennett) (TAF)—many
Georgia Coleman (DIV)—"The Beachcomber"
Buster Crabbe (SWI)—many
Pat Donnolly (TAF)—"Personal Best"
Gertrude Ederle (SWI)—"Swim, Girl, Swim"
Joe Frazier (BOX)—"Rocky"
Carol Heiss (FSK)—"Snow White and the Three Stooges"
Eleanor Holm (SWI)—"Tarzan's Revenge"
Bruce Jenner (TAF)—"Can't Stop the Music"
Rafer Johnson (TAF)—many
Duke Kahanamoku (DIV/WAP)—many
Helene Madison (SWI)—"The Warrior's Husband"
Bob Mathias (TAF)—"It Happened in Athens"
Josephine McKim (SWI)—"Lady, Be Careful"
Kenny Moore (TAF)—"Personal Best"
Glenn Morris (TAF)—"Tarzan's Revenge"
George Morris (EQU)—"Anna's Sin"
Charles Paddock (TAF)—"Nine and Three-Fifths Seconds"
Nat Pendleton (WRE)—many
Harold Sakata (WLT)—"Goldfinger" and others
Floyd Simmons (TAF)—many
Harold Smallwood (TAF)—stand-in for Robert Taylor in several
Dean Smith (TAF)—many as a stuntman
Jim Thorpe (TAF)—many as an extra
Johnny Weissmuller (SWI/WAP)—many

In addition we should probably include the entire cast of the movie, "Personal Best," which was filmed at the 1980 Olympic track & field trials and concerned track & field athletes. Pat Donnolly and Kenny Moore, who had prominent roles, are included above, but among the U.S. Olympians who appeared in that movie were: Earl Bell, Al Feurbach, Cindy Gilbert, Debby LaPlante, Maren Seidler, Patty Van Wolvelaere Johnson, Martha Watson, and Mac Wilkins.

HICKCOX, Charles Buchanan.
B. 06 FEB 1947 Phoenix, AZ. Gold(3): 1968 200 meter individual medley, 1968 400 meter individual medley, 1968 4×100 meter medley relay; Silver: 1968 100 meter backstroke. Charlie Hickcox had an outstanding record in the IM and backstroke at every level of competition. He held seven NCAA individual titles, led Indiana to two team championships, won nine AAU titles, and was twice a gold medalist at the Pan-American Games. Hickcox also set eight world records. He has since become a coach and occasional television announcer. Hickcox married U.S. Olympic diver Lesley Bush, though they have since divorced.

HORSLEY, Jack.
B. 25 SEP 1951 Salt Lake City, UT. Bronze: 1968 200 meter backstroke. Although born in Utah, Jack Horsley went to high school in Seattle where he swam for the Red Shield Triton SC. Horsley won the AAU 200m backstroke in 1968.

HUSZAGH, Kenneth Arthur.
B. 03 SEP 1891 Chicago, IL. D. 11 JAN 1950 Delray Beach, FL. Silver: 1912 4×200 meter freestyle relay; Bronze: 1912 100 meter freestyle. Ken Huszagh represented the Illinois AC at the 1912 Stockholm Olympics. He later became an executive with the American Mineral Spirits Co. of New York and rose to president of that company before retiring.

ILMAN, Gary Steven.
B. 13 AUG 1943 Glendale, CA. Gold(2): 1964 4×100 meter freestyle relay, 1964 4×200 meter freestyle relay. Apart from being a member of the teams that set new world records in both freestyle relays at the Tokyo Olympics, Gary Ilman also placed fourth in the individual 100m freestyle after setting new Olympic records in the heats and semi-finals. Ilman, who represented the Santa Clara SC, was also a member of the team that won the 800m free relay at the 1963 Pan-American Games.

IVEY, Mitchell.
B. 02 FEB 1949 San Jose, CA. Silver: 1968 200 meter backstroke; Bronze: 1972 200 meter backstroke. Mitch Ivey started college at Stanford, but transferred to Long Beach State and graduated from there in 1972. In his Olympic debut in 1968, Ivey took the silver medal in the 200m backstroke behind Roland Matthes of East Germany; in 1972, Matthes repeated his victory as Ivey dropped to third place. At the 1972 Olympics, Ivey also placed fourth in the 100m back and swam in the heats of the medley relay. Representing the Santa Clara SC, he won three AAU titles.

JASTREMSKI, Chester Andrew.
B. 12 JAN 1941 Toledo, OH. Bronze: 1964 200 meter breaststroke. Chet Jastremski went to Indiana University as a butterfly specialist, but soon developed into the world's leading breaststroke swimmer. In individual events he set nine world records, 17 U.S. records, and won 12 AAU titles, in addition to his numerous records and championship honors in relays. He is also noted as the first man to break one minute for the 100 yard breaststroke.

Despite these successes, Jastremski had a checkered career at the Olympics. In 1956 he won his heat of the 200 breast at the Final Trials but was disqualified for using an illegal kick. In 1960 he finished second at the Final Trials but the coach took him off the Olympic team, and after his bronze medal in 1964, he made the 1968 Olympic team but swam only in the heats of the medley relay. Chet Jastremski has become a doctor, specializing in family medicine, and was a member of the U.S. Olympic medical team at the 1976 Olympics.

JOB, Brian Gregory.
B. 29 NOV 1951 Warren, OH. Bronze: 1968 200 meter breaststroke. Brian Job was an engineering graduate from Stanford and he swam for the Santa Clara SC. He won 14 AAU titles. In addition to his bronze medal in 1968, he also swam in the 200m breaststroke at the 1972 Olympics, but was eliminated in the heats.

KAHANAMOKU, Duke Paoa Kahinu Makoe Hulikohoa.
B. 24 AUG 1890 Honolulu, HA. D. 22 JAN 1968 Honolulu, HA. Gold(3): 1912 100 meter freestyle, 1920 100 meter freestyle, 1920 4×200 meter freestyle; Silver(2): 1912 4×200 meter freestyle, 1924 100 meter freestyle. Duke Kahanamoku, who was named after the Duke of Edinburgh, was the first of the truly great Hawaiian swimmers. In 1911, swimming in the open

sea but without any tidal advantage, he bettered the world 100y record by almost five seconds. Not surprisingly, this, and some of his other marks, were viewed with skepticism by the AAU.

However, after Duke had competed on the mainland and then in Europe, the world was left with no doubt that a genuine new swimming talent had arrived. He went on to set numerous world records and only Johnny Weissmuller prevented him from winning an unprecedented hat trick of Olympic 100 free titles. Kahanamoku won his second Olympic title in 1920 on his 30th birthday, but his Olympic career was far from over. He won a silver medal in 1924, was an alternate on the 1928 team and in 1932, after 10 years in Hollywood, was an alternate to the water polo team.

KAHANAMOKU, Samuel.
B. 04 NOV 1904 Honolulu, HA. Bronze: 1924 100 meter freestyle. The younger brother of the Duke, Sam Kahanamoku took the bronze medal in the 1924 Olympics behind quite a pairing—his brother and Johnny Weissmuller. Overshadowed by their great abilities, Sam Kahanamoku was never able to win a major title.

KALILI, Maiola.
B. 19 FEB 1909. Silver: 1932 4 × 200 meter freestyle relay. At the 1932 AAU indoor championships, Maiola Kalili, a Hawaiian who swam for the Los Angeles AC, scored a notable double by taking the 100y and 220y freestyle titles.

KALILI, Manuella.
Silver: 1932 4 × 200 meter freestyle relay. Like his brother, Manuella Kalili also represented the Los Angeles AC when not competing in his native Hawaii. In addition to a silver medal in the Olympic relay, Kalili placed fourth in the 100m free. His only AAU championship came in 1931 when he won the outdoor 100m freestyle.

KEALOHA, Pua Kele.
B. 14 NOV 1902. D. 1973. Gold: 1920 4 × 200 meter freestyle relay; Silver: 1920 100 meter freestyle. Between the Kahanamoku and the Kalili brothers, the Kealoha brothers dominated Hawaiian swimming. The older of the brothers, Pua Kealoha, finished second to his fellow Hawaiian, the Duke, in the 100m freestyle at

the 1920 Olympics and then joined Kahanamoku on the world record breaking relay team. Pua Kealoha won his only AAU championship in 1921 when the 100y event was held in Honolulu harbor. His only competition was his brother, and Pua's time of 53.0 equalled the world record.

KEALOHA, Warren Paoa.
B. 03 MAR 1904. D. 08 SEP 1972. Gold(2): 1920 100 meter backstroke, 1924 100 meter backstroke. At the age of 16, Warren Kealoha of Hawaii won his first Olympic title and four years later became the first man to win two Olympic backstroke gold medals. He held the world 100m backstroke record for six years, setting his first world record in winning the Olympic title in 1920 and his fourth world record in Honolulu in 1926. This final record was short-lived—the following day, Walter Laufer, who was on a European tour, bettered Kealoha's mark. Warren Kealoha later became a successful rancher.

KEGERIS, Ray.
B. 10 SEP 1901. Silver: 1920 100 meter backstroke. Ray Kegeris swam for the Los Angeles AC and won the AAU indoor 150y backstroke title in 1921 and 1922.

KIEFER, Adolph Gustav.
B. 27 JUN 1918 Chicago, IL. Gold: 1936 100 meter backstroke. Adolph Kiefer of the Lake Shore AC in Chicago was the first man to swim the 100y backstroke in under one minute. He set 17 world records between 1935 and 1944 and none of his backstroke records were broken until 1950, four years after he had retired from competitive swimming. Indoors and outdoors he won a total of 18 AAU titles in the backstroke, the freestyle, and the IM, but the backstroke was clearly his forte.

During World War II, Kiefer conducted a survery of shipwrecks and documented the toll of GI deaths from drowning. As a result, Lt. Kiefer was put in charge of swimming instruction for the entire U.S. Navy. He later formed his own company, with various subsidiaries, all involved in the manufacture of swimming pool accessories and swim-related items.

KINSELLA, John Pitann.
B. 26 AUG 1952 Oak Park, IL. Gold: 1972 4 × 200 meter freestyle relay; Silver: 1968 1,500 meter freestyle. After winning his Olympic silver medal in 1968, John Kinsella set a world 1,500m freestyle record in 1970 and won the Sullivan Award that year as the top amateur athlete in the United States. Kinsella won a total of six NCAA titles for Indiana and won four AAU championships. Considering all these races were 500 yards plus, Kinsella showed a surprising turn of speed in qualifying for the relay team at the 1972 Olympics. Kinsella was known for doing very high mileage in his workouts, which has obviously helped—he is now a professional long distance swimmer.

KIRSCHBAUM, William.
B. 05 NOV 1902. Bronze: 1924 200 meter breaststroke. Bill Kirschbaum was from Hawaii. The high point of his career was his Olympic bronze medal; he never managed to win a major title.

KOJAC, George Harold.
B. 02 MAR 1910 New York, NY. Gold(2): 1928 100 meter backstroke, 1928 4 × 200 meter freestyle relay. George Kojac was the son of Ukranian immigrants, and while attending DeWitt Clinton High School, he learned to swim in New York's East River. He set the first of his 23 world records while still in high school and won AAU titles in both freestyle and backstroke events. Kojac attended Rutgers and never lost a race while there, but he missed the 1932 Olympics because of his studies at Columbia Law School. However the Olympic backstroke record he set at the 1928 Games was the only Olympic record to survive the 1932 Games.

KONNO, Ford Hiroshi.
B. 01 JAN 1933 Honolulu, HA. Gold(2): 1952 1,500 meter freestyle, 1952 4 × 200 meter freestyle relay; Silver(2): 1952 400 meter freestyle, 1956 4 × 200 meter freestyle relay. At Ohio State, Ford Konno won six NCAA titles and during his career, which took off shortly after World War II, he won 12 AAU individual titles. He set his first world record at the 800m freestyle in 1951 and that record remained on the books for five years. In 1954 he added the world 400m freestyle record to his list of

successes and it was almost three years before the great Murray Rose replaced Konno as the world record holder.

After his college graduation, Konno married Olympic bronze medalist Evelyn Kawamoto, and he is now a coach and teacher in Hawaii.

LANGER, Ludy.
B. 22 JAN 1893. Silver: 1920 400 meter freestyle. Ludy Langer was one of six Hawaii-based swimmers on the men's Olympic team in 1920. Between them, they won a total of seven medals. He had earned his place on the team for Antwerp when he won the Western Olympic Trials at Alameda, California. Langer scored a triple victory at the AAU championships of 1915 and 1916, winning the 440y, 880y and one mile freestyle in both years. In 1921 he won his seventh AAU title when he beat Johnny Weissmuller in the 440y freestyle, thus contradicting the legend that Weissmuller was unbeaten throughout his career.

LARSON, Lance Melvin.
B. 03 JUL 1940 Monterey Park, CA. Gold: 1960 4 × 100 meter freestyle relay; Silver: 1960 100 meter freestyle. In the most controversial Olympic swim race ever, Lance Larson received a silver medal for his gold medal efforts. Swimming in the 100m free against Australia's John Devitt, Larson and Devitt touched almost simultaneously. The six finish judges were split in their opinion, but all three watches had Larson timed faster (55.1, 55.1, 55.0 vs. 55.2 for Devitt on all three). The back-up electric timer also had Larson timed faster, but the president of the International Swimming Federation gave the nod to Devitt, even though the rules did not give him a vote in the matter. Protests were made ad nauseam, but to no avail. Larson did manage to strike gold in the relay, however.

Lance Larson, who attended Southern Cal, was a superb all-round swimmer and was the first man to break one minute for the 100m butterfly. He won AAU titles in the freestyle, fly, and IM events, and set five world and 12 U.S. records. Larson is now a successful dentist in California and is a prolific record breaker in master's swimming competition.

LAUFER, Walter.
B. 05 JUL 1906. Gold: 1928 4 × 200 meter freestyle relay; Silver: 1928 100 meter backstroke. Walter Laufer, of the Cincinnati Central YMCA and the Lake Shore AC of Chicago, was one of the more versatile swimmers of his generation. He won 10 AAU indoor titles in three different styles—freestyle, backstroke and IM—and also won the AAU outdoor 220y backstroke title in 1925. At the 1928 Olympics he also finished fifth in the 100m freestyle.

Laufer was a prodigious competitor and, during a European tour in 1926, he competed in 21 cities in 23 days and lost only one race. During the course of the tour he set one world record for the 100m backstroke and three for the 200m backstroke.

LEARY, J. Scott.
Silver: 1904 50 yard freestyle; Bronze: 100 yard freestyle. The 1904 Olympics were a year early for Scott Leary. In 1905, Leary became a pupil of Australian coach Syd Cavill, who taught him the Australian crawl. He was the first American to abandon the Trudgeon stroke for the revolutionary crawl and Leary dominated American sprinting with it in 1905 and 1906, before Charlie Daniels picked it up and regained his spot as America's top swimmer. But on 18 July 1905, in Portland, Oregon, J. Scott Leary, of San Francisco's Olympic Club, made swimming history when he became the first person to swim 100 yards in 60 seconds flat—even time for the classic sprint.

MACIONIS, John Joseph.
B. 27 MAY 1916 Philadelphia, PA. Silver: 1936 4 × 200 meter freestyle relay. In addition to his silver medal in the relay at the 1936 Olympics, John Macionis of Yale also swam in the 400m freestyle in Berlin, but as the slowest of the eight semi-finalists, he failed to qualify for the final. His greatest moment came at the 1935 AAU outdoor championships when he won the 440y free, beating such luminaries as Jack Medica, Ralph Flanagan and James Gilhula, all of whom were world record holders at varying freestyle distances.

MANN, Harold Thompson.
B. 01 DEC 1942 Norfolk, VA. Gold: 1964 4 × 100 meter medley relay. After clocking exactly 60.0 sec. for the 100m backstroke in September 1964, Thompson Mann, of the University of North Carolina, became the first person to break the one-minute barrier when he clocked 59.6 on the opening leg of the 1964 Olympic medley relay final. Representing the North Carolina AC, Mann won all four AAU backstroke titles in 1965.

McBREEN, Thomas Sean.
B. 31 AUG 1952 Spokane, WA. Bronze: 1972 400 meter freestyle. After winning a gold medal in the 1,500m freestyle at the 1971 Pan-American Games, Tom McBreen set a world record in the 400m free later in the month. He was also a member of two world record breaking teams in the 800m freestyle relay. McBreen, who swam for Southern Cal and the Golden Gate SC, won the AAU outdoor 400m freestyle in 1971 and 1972. All his records and championships were won despite being legally blind in both eyes, and having suffered several minor injuries—all to his right side—during his swim career. McBreen later went to medical school and now specializes in family medicine.

McGILLIVRAY, Perry.
B. 05 AUG 1893. D. 27 JUL 1944. Gold: 1920 4 × 200 meter freestyle relay; Silver: 1912 4 × 200 meter freestyle relay. Perry McGillivray was a top-class swimmer and water polo player for 20 years. Between 1908 and 1927 he won 16 AAU individual titles, was on 13 winning relay teams, and was seven times a member of the Illinois AC team that won the AAU water polo championship. He played water polo at the 1920 Olympics and was coach to the U.S. water polo team at the 1928 Games. McGillivray invented the lob shot, and with Harry Hebner, did much to revolutionize the game. Although Perry McGillivray was always more concerned with winning than with fast times, he set nine U.S. records and, when he won his Olympic gold medal in 1920, he shared in a new world relay record.

McKEE, Alexander Timothy.
B. 14 MAR 1953 Ardmore, PA. Silver(3): 1972 200 meter individual medley, 1972 400 meter individual medley, 1976 400 meter individual medley. Tim McKee missed a gold medal by the smallest margin in Olympic history. In the 400 IM, he and Sweden's Gunnar Larsson apparently tied for first when the electronic timing clocked them both at 4:31.98 secs. But the timing was sensitive enough to measure to thousandths of a second and

Larsson's 4:31.981 defeated McKee's 4:31.983—a margin of 2/1,000th's of a second. This episode caused a change in international rules, as McKee's defeat was by less than the amount a fingernail grows over several weeks. In fact, it was determined that McKee could actually have lost had the paint on the wall in his lane been applied slightly too thin!

In addition to his three Olympic silver medals, Tim McKee, who attended the University of Florida, won a silver medal in the 200m backstroke at the 1971 Pan-American Games.

McKENZIE, Donald Ward, Jr.
B. 11 MAY 1947 Hollywood, CA. Gold(2): 1968 100 meter breaststroke, 1968 4 × 100 meter medley relay. Although he was an Olympic gold medalist in an individual event, Don McKenzie surprisingly never won an AAU title. His major domestic victory came in 1969 when he won the NCAA 100y backstroke for Indiana University.

McKINNEY, Frank Edward, Jr.
B. 03 NOV 1938 Indianapolis, IN. Gold: 1960 4 × 100 meter medley relay; Silver: 1960 100 meter backstroke; Bronze: 1956 100 meter backstroke. As a 16-year-old, Frank McKinney won the 100m backstroke at the Pan-American Games and was the youngest member of the team that set a new world record in the medley relay. He again won gold medals in both events at the 1959 Games.

McKinney won 14 AAU titles and took two NCAA championships for Indiana University In 1959 he twice set a world record for the 200m backstroke and in 1960 he was a member, on two occasions, of teams which posted new world records in the medley relay.

After two years as an army intelligence officer, Frank McKinney became a banker and served as president and chairman of the board of the American Fletcher National Bank in Indianapolis.

McLANE, James Price, Jr.
B. 13 SEP 1930. Gold(3): 1948 1,500 meter freestyle, 1948 4 × 200 meter freestyle relay, 1952 4 × 200 meter freestyle relay; Silver: 1948 400 meter freestyle. In 1944, Jimmy McLane became the youngest-ever men's AAU swimming champion by winning the long distance event at the age of 13. In a long career, which ended with his retirement in 1955, McLane won, in addition to his four Olympic medals, three golds at the 1955 Pan-American Games, 21 AAU titles and, while attending Yale, he won two NCAA championships in 1953.

MEDICA, Jack C.
B. 05 OCT 1914. Gold: 1936 400 meter freestyle; Silver(2): 1936 1,500 meter freestyle, 1936 4 × 200 meter freestyle relay. While at the University of Washington, Jack Medica ran up a phenomenal record at the NCAA championships. He won three individual events (the maximum allowed) three years in a row, and as a one-man team, he placed Washington third behind the big squads from Michigan and Iowa. One year he was awarded a Michigan varsity letter because, although he never attended Michigan, he took enough points away from Yale and Iowa that Michigan was able to win the team championship, and the Michigan coach, Matt Mann, sent Medica a letter sweater.

Jack Medica won 10 AAU individual titles and set 11 world records. His 1935 200m freestyle record was unbeaten for nine years, his 400m freestyle record, set in 1934, stood for seven years; and in a sport of frequent record breaking, the length of time for which his records stood gives an indication of the stature of his performances. After retiring from competition, Jack Medica coached at Columbia and Penn.

MILLS, Ronald P.
B. 25 FEB 1951 Fort Worth, TX. Bronze: 1968 100 meter backstroke. After attending Arlington Heights High School, Ronnie Mills competed for the Burford SC of Fort Worth. His Olympic bronze was the high point of a short career, as he never won a major title.

MONTGOMERY, James Paul.
B. 24 JAN 1955 Madison, WI. Gold(3): 1976 100 meter freestyle, 1976 4 × 200 meter freestyle relay, 1976 4 × 100 meter medley relay; Bronze: 1976 200 freestyle. With two individual golds and three more in the relays, Jim Montgomery was the star swimmer of the 1973 World Championships. He attended Indiana, where he won the NCAA 200y free before going on to win four AAU titles. Montgomery set two world records for the 100m freestyle in 1975 and improved his world record twice at the Montreal Olympics. There he broke a barrier as, with his time in the finals of 49.99, he became

the first man to swim 100 meters in under 50 seconds. Between 1973 and 1976, Montgomery was also a member of five world record breaking relay teams.

MOORE, Wayne Richard.
B. 30 NOV 1931. Gold: 1952 4 × 200 medley relay. In 1952, Wayne Moore was a member of the team from Yale that set a new world record in the 800m freestyle relay. While at Yale, Moore won two individual NCAA individual titles and was a two-time winner at the AAU outdoor championships. Among his other successes were a silver in the 400m freestyle and a gold in the relay at the 1955 Pan-American Games. At the 1952 Olympics, Moore placed sixth in the 400m free in addition to his gold in the relay.

MULLIKEN, William Danforth.
B. 27 AUG 1939 Urbana, IL. Gold: 1960 200 meter breaststroke. Inspired by a motivational talk he heard from Olympic pole vaulting gold medalist Bob Richards, Bill Mulliken vowed he would win a gold medal at the 1960 Olympics. After winning gold at the 1959 Pan-American Games, Mulliken did just that. Mulliken, who attended Miami (Ohio), won his only major domestic championship in 1960 at the AAU indoor meet when he took the 220y freestyle.

MURPHY, John Joseph.
B. 19 JUL 1953 Chicago, IL. Gold: 1972 4 × 100 meter freestyle relay; Bronze: 1972 100 meter backstroke. After his bronze in the 100m backstroke, John Murphy finished fourth in the 100m freestyle at the 1972 Games, narrowly missing the distinction of winning Olympic individual medals in two very different styles of swimming. Murphy attended Indiana University and won silver medals in the 100m backstroke at the 1971 Pan-American Games and the 1975 World Championships.

NABER, John Phillips.
B. 20 JAN 1956 Evanston, IL. Gold(4): 1976 100 meter backstroke, 1976 200 meter backstroke, 1976 4 × 200 meter freestyle relay, 1976 4 × 100 meter medley relay; Silver: 1976 200 meter freestyle. With four gold medals, all in world-record time, and one silver, John Naber was the outstanding swimmer of the Montreal Olympics. His record at every other major championship was equally impressive.

At the NCAA's, Naber won 10 individual and five relay titles and at the AAU's, he won 18 individual and seven relay titles. He won three golds at the 1977 Pan-American Games and ran up a fine record as a "barrier breaker" in the backstroke. Naber was the first man to beat 50 seconds for 100y, the first under 56 seconds for 100m, the first to better 1:50 for 200y, and the first man to break the two-minute barrier for the 200m. Such was the quality of his records that his world records, set in winning both backstroke events at Montreal, lasted until August 1983.

Prior to attending Southern Cal, John Naber's early education was in Italy and England, where his father worked as a management consultant. He is currently involved as an active member of the Organizing Committee for the Los Angeles Olympics.

NELSON, John Mauer.
B. 08 JUN 1948 Chicago, IL. Gold: 1968 4 × 200 meter freestyle relay; Silver: 1964 1,500 meter freestyle; Bronze: 1968 200 meter freestyle. After winning his first Olympic medal in 1964, John Nelson of Yale won his only AAU title in 1965 and set a world record for the 400m freestyle the following year. Apart from his three Olympic medals, John Nelson was an Olympic finalist in the 400m freestyle in 1964 and 1968, and in 1968 he was a finalist in the 1,500m freestyle.

NORTHWAY, Douglas Dale.
B. 28 APR 1955 Ontario, CA. Bronze: 1972 1,500 meter freestyle. At the time he won his Olympic medal, Doug Northway was a high school student in Tucson, Arizona. He improved rapidly, dropping his 1,500 time by 45 seconds between the 1971 AAU and the 1972 Olympic Trials. Although he never won an AAU title, Northway won the 400m freestyle at the 1975 Pan-American Games.

O'CONNOR, James Wallace.
B. 25 APR 1905. D. 11 JAN 1950 Los Angeles, CA. Gold: 1924 4 × 200 meter freestyle relay; Bronze(2): 1924 Water Polo, 1932 Water Polo. A four-time Olympian, Wally O'Connor is rated as the greatest U.S. water polo

Courtesy Steven Feldman

Double 1968 swim gold medalist, Dr. Steve Rerych, as he appears today in his physiology research lab at Duke University.

player of all time. Although he was a water polo specialist, his Olympic gold came as a swimmer when the U.S. won the relay in 1924 with a new world record. O'Connor was, in fact, an outstanding swimmer and won the 220y and 440y freestyle for Stanford at the 1926 NCAA championships. Most of his water polo was played for the Los Angeles AC, and at his fourth Olympics in Berlin, Wally O'Connor accompanied the U.S. flag bearer at the opening ceremonies as a member of the color guard. O'Connor made a fifth Olympic team in 1940, but the war in Europe prevented those Games from being held.

ORTHWEIN, William Robert.
B. 16 OCT 1881. D. 02 OCT 1955 St. Louis, MO. Bronze: 1904 4 × 50 yard freestyle relay. Bill Orthwein was the first of many Yale graduates to win an Olympic swimming medal. At the 1904 Olympics he represented the Missouri AC and, in addition to his relay medal, he placed fourth in the 100m freestyle. Orthwein later

attended Washington University Law School and became a prominent attorney in St. Louis. He also entered politics, once running for governor of Missouri, although he was defeated in that attempt.

OYAKAWA, Yoshinobu.
B. 09 AUG 1933 Hawaii. Gold: 1952 100 meter backstroke. In winning the 100m backstroke at the Helsinki Games, Oyakawa beat Adolph Kiefer's Olympic record which had stood since 1936. Oyakawa could not repeat his Helsinki form at the 1956 Olympics and finished in last place in the Melbourne final.

Oyakawa won six AAU titles, including the backstroke double in 1953 and 1955, and scored a double for Ohio State at the NCAA's of 1953, 1954, and 1955. He set world records at 100y and 100m for the straight-arm backstroke style. Oyakawa later settled in Cincinnati, became a swim coach, and, in 1972, was named Ohio High School Coach of the Year.

RERYCH, Stephen Karl.
B. 14 MAY 1946 Philadelphia, PA. Gold(2): 1968 4 × 100 meter freestyle relay, 1968 4 × 200 meter freestyle relay. After being forced to withdraw from the final of the individual 200m freestyle because of illness, Steve Rerych won a gold medal in both freestyle relays. Rerych, who attended North Carolina State, won his only AAU title when he took the indoor 100y freestyle in 1966. He later attended medical school at Columbia and is currently a thoracic surgeon at Duke University.

REYBURN, Amedee V.
Bronze: 1904 4 × 50 yard freestyle relay. Amedee Reyburn represented the Missouri AC at the 1904 Olympics. Although he won a bronze medal in the relay, he did not compete in any of the individual events.

RICH, Leslie George.
B. 29 DEC 1886. Bronze: 1908 4 × 200 meter freestyle relay. Apart from his bronze medal in the relay, Leslie Rich also placed fourth in the 100m freestyle at the 1908 Olympics.

RIS, Walter Steve.
B. 04 JAN 1924. Gold(2): 1948 100 meter freestyle, 1948 4 × 200 meter freestyle relay. Wally Ris was a a member of the Great Lakes Navy team which set a

world record for the 400y freestyle relay during the war. After the war he entered the University of Iowa, winning the AAU outdoor 100m freestyle and the NCAA 100y freestyle titles in both 1947 and 1948. His most successful meet was the AAU indoor championships where he won the 100y freestyle for five straight years from 1945.

ROBIE, Carl Joseph, III.
B. 12 MAY 1945 Darby, PA. Gold: 1968 200 meter butterfly; Silver: 1964 200 meter butterfly. At the 1964 Olympics, Carl Robie was the fastest qualifier in both the 200 butterfly and the 400 IM, but in the finals he only placed second in the fly and fourth in the IM. It was thought at the time that Robie had missed his chance of top Olympic honors, but he made a surprising comeback to win the 200m butterfly at the 1968 Games.

Robie won a total of nine AAU championships, including five straight wins in the outdoor 200m butterfly from 1961, and he won a gold medal in this event at the 1963 Pan-American Games. He won two NCAA titles for the University of Michigan, and after graduation he attended Dickinson Law School. Robie set four world records in the 200m butterfly and two of them came in separate races on the same day in August 1962.

ROCCA, Peter.
B. 27 JUL 1957 Oakland, CA. Silver(2): 1976 100 meter backstroke, 1976 200 meter backstroke. Peter Rocca, of Cal/Berkeley, had the misfortune of being a top backstroker in the eras of Roland Matthes and John Naber, and he finished second to Naber in both backstroke events at the 1976 Olympics. At the 1975 Pan-American Games, Rocca won gold medals in the 100m backstroke and the medley relay, but he never won an AAU title. He continued to swim after Montreal, making the 1980 Olympic team.

ROSS, Norman DeMille.
B. 02 MAY 1896 Portland, OR. D. 19 JUN 1953 Evanston, IL. Gold(3): 1920 400 meter freestyle, 1920 1,500 meter freestyle, 1920 4 × 200 meter freestyle. After winning five events at the Inter-Allied Games in Paris in 1919, Norman Ross took three gold medals at the 1920 Olympics. He set 12 world records at international distances and won 18 AAU championships. He swam

---

PRETTY HEALTHY

It is well known that Olympic athletes are among the best conditioned and healthiest of people. But exactly how healthy are they? One measure doctors use is known as the cardiac output, which measures the amount of blood the heart is able to pump through the body in one minute. For a normal male the average is 5 liters/minute. But the record during exercise is held by a former U.S. Olympic swimmer, Steve Gregg, who won a silver medal in the 1976 200 meter butterfly.

In 1977 Gregg was asked to come to the Duke University Hospital to participate in an experiment which would measure his maximum cardiac output. The experiment was performed by Steve Rerych, a thoracic surgeon and research physiologist at Duke, and himself a double swimming gold medalist at the 1968 Olympics. During this experiment, Gregg raised his cardiac output to the astounding figure of 56.6 liters/minute, the highest ever recorded.

---

for Stanford and later attended Northwestern Law School.

During a swim meet in Honolulu, Ross met and later married a Hawaiian princess. After giving up competition, he went into the music business and became the country's first classical disc jockey, known to millions as "Uncle Normie." His son followed him on the airwaves, becoming a familiar voice on radio and television in the Chicago area. Norman Ross was decorated by Gen. Pershing during World War I, and served as an aide to Gen. Doolittle in World War II.

ROTH, Richard William.
B. 26 SEP 1947 Palo Alto, CA. Gold: 1964 400 meter individual medley. The night before the 1964 Olympic individual medley final, Dick Roth was stricken by an attack of appendicitis, but he refused an operation. He insisted the surgeons delay to allow him to swim in the final, and his courage was rewarded with an Olympic gold medal. Roth, who attended Stanford, won six outdoor AAU IM titles before retiring at the early age of 19.

RUDDY, Joseph A.
B. 1878. D. 11 NOV 1962. Gold: 1904 4 × 50 yard freestyle relay. Joe Ruddy was best known as a water polo player and was a member of the New York AC team that won the tournament held in conjunction with the St. Louis Games. Two of his sons, Ray and Steve, later competed for the United States in Olympic swimming.

RUSSELL, Douglas A.
B. 20 FEB 1946 New York, NY. Gold(2): 1968 100 meter butterfly, 1968 4 × 100 meter medley relay. Doug Russell was very busy in 1967, winning two golds at the Pan-American Games. At one meet in Tokyo, he set world records in the 100m backstroke, the 100m butterfly, and the medley relay. He earned a share of a second world medley relay record at the Olympics the following year. Russell attended the University of Texas at Arlington, and won the AAU outdoor 100m butterfly in 1969.

SAARI, Roy Allen.
B. 26 FEB 1945 Buffalo, NY. Gold: 1964 4 × 200 meter freestyle relay; Silver: 1964 400 meter freestyle. Roy Saari won the first of his 17 AAU titles in 1959 when he won the long distance swim at the age of 13, equalling Jimmy McLane's record of being the youngest ever AAU swimming champion. While at Southern Cal, Saari matched Jack Medica's NCAA record of winning nine individual events—three events for three consecutive years—and was on two winning NCAA relay teams. At the 1964 U.S. Trials, Saari became the first man to break 17 minutes for the 1,500m freestyle, but at the Olympics, he could place no better than seventh, some 30 seconds outside his best.

Saari was from a famous swimming family. His father, Urho "Whitey" Saari coached the 1964 Olympic water polo team, which included his son, and Roy's brother, Robert.

SCHMIDT, Frederick Weber.
B. 23 OCT 1943 Evanston, IL. Gold: 1964 4 × 100 meter medley relay; Bronze: 1964 200 meter butterfly. Fred Schmidt set the only individual world record of his career when he won the AAU outdoor 100m butterfly in 1961. This was to be the only AAU outdoor title of his career, although he was twice a winner at the indoor

championships, and he won three NCAA titles for Indiana University. Schmidt claimed a share in a second world record at the Tokyo Olympics when the U.S. became the first team to beat four minutes for the 400m medley relay.

SCHOLES, Clarke Currie.
B. 25 NOV 1930. Gold: 1952 100 meter freestyle. After his Olympic victory, Clarke Scholes won two golds at the 1955 Pan-American Games. At home, he won two AAU indoor championships and five NCAA titles for Michigan State.

SCHOLLANDER, Donald Arthur.
B. 30 APR 1946 Charlotte, NC. Gold(5): 1964 100 meter freestyle, 1964 400 meter freestyle, 1964 4 × 100 meter freestyle relay, 1964 4 × 200 meter freestyle relay, 1968 4 × 200 meter freestyle relay; Silver: 1968 200 meter freestyle. Don Schollander was the first swimmer to win four golds at one Olympics and he would almost certainly have won a fifth had the 200m freestyle been included in the 1964 Olympic program. In this event, Schollander set nine world records between 1963 and 1968, and was the first man to break two minutes for that distance. Schollander was also denied a fifth gold when he was left off the medley relay team—the U.S. already had plenty of firepower in that event.

Schollander also posted eight world records for the 400m freestyle and was a member of eight world record breaking relay teams. In addition to winning 16 AAU titles, Schollander, a Yale graduate, won two gold medals at the 1967 Pan-American Games.

SCHWARTZ, Albert.
B. 18 DEC 1908 Chicago, IL. Bronze: 1932 100 meter freestyle. After narrowly failing to make the 1928 Olympic team, Albert Schwartz won a bronze medal four years later. While attending Northwestern, he became the first swimmer to score a triple victory at the NCAA championships when he took three freestyle titles at the 1930 indoor meet. Playing for the Illinois AC, Schwartz was on six winning teams at the AAU water polo championships. After graduating from Northwestern, Schwartz attended law school at the University of Chicago and later practiced law in California.

SCHWARZ, Marquard J.

B. 30 JUL 1887 St. Louis, MO. D. 17 FEB 1968 Santa Monica, CA. Bronze: 1904 4 × 50 yard freestyle relay. Marquard Schwarz was a member of the Missouri AC. After winning a bronze medal in the relay in 1904, he competed again at the 1906 Olympics. In Athens he was a member of the team which placed fourth in the relay. and he also competed in the 100m freestyle.

SHAW, Timothy Andrew.

B. 08 NOV 1957 Long Beach, CA. Silver: 1976 400 meter freestyle. For Tim Shaw, it was unfortunate that the Olympics were not held in 1974 or 1975. He was unbeatable in those years, becoming in 1974 only the second man to hold world records in the 200m, 400m, and 1,500m freestyle events. He accomplished this feat when only 16 years old, and in the space of four days. In 1975, he set five more individual world records, won five gold medals at the World Championships, and received the Sullivan Award, emblematic of the top amateur athlete in the United States.

SKELTON, Robert D.

B. 26 JUN 1903. Gold: 1924 200 meter breaststroke. Bob Skelton, of the Illinois AC, won two indoor and two outdoor AAU titles. In 1924 he became the first American to set a world record for the 200m breaststroke.

SMITH, William, Jr.

B. 16 MAY 1924 Hawaii. Gold(2): 1948 400 meter freestyle, 1948 4 × 200 meter freestyle relay. Bill Smith learned his swimming in an irrigation ditch on a sugar plantation in Hawaii. He later attended Ohio State, but although his stay was interrupted by the war, between 1943 and 1949 he won seven NCAA individual titles and was a member of the winning relay team in 1947.

Smith won a total of 15 AAU championships and his greatest year was 1942,when he won three outdoor freestyle events and set one world record and two U.S. records. In all, he set seven world records in 1941 and 1942. Bill Smith was at one time captain of the surf guards at Waikiki Beach, and later served as water safety director for the department of parks and recreation in Honolulu.

SOHL, Robert Raymond.

B. 28 MAR 1928. Bronze: 1948 200 meter breaststroke. The 1948 Olympic breaststroke final proved to be a repeat of the U.S. Olympic Trials. In both races, Joe Verdeur was the winner, Keith Carter finished second, and Bob Sohl of the University of Michigan finished third.

SPITZ, Mark Andrew.

B. 10 FEB 1950. Gold(9): 1968 4 × 100 meter freestyle relay, 1968 4 × 200 meter freestyle relay, 1972 100 meter freestyle, 1972 200. meter freestyle, 1972 100 meter butterfly, 1972 200 meter butterfly, 1972 4 × 100 meter freestyle relay, 1972 4 × 200 meter freestyle relay, 1972 4 × 100 meter medley relay; Silver: 1968 100 meter butterfly; Bronze: 1968 100 meter freestyle. After five gold medals at the 1967 Pan-American Games, great things were expected of Mark Spitz at the 1968 Olympics, but he surprisingly failed to win an individual event. Before the 1972 Olympics, however, Spitz became undoubtedly the world's greatest swimmer, and perhaps the greatest ever. In 1971 he became the first swimmer to win four individual AAU titles at one meet, setting three world records in the process. The next week, at a meet in East Germany, he won all four events again, this time breaking all four world records.

At the 1972 Olympics, Spitz set a not-soon-to-be-matched Olympic record by winning seven gold medals, all of them in world-record time. The performance made him an overwhelming choice for the 1972 Sullivan Award. Overall, he won 24 AAU championships, eight NCAA titles (Indiana University), and set 32 world records. Since the 1972 Olympics he has capitalized on his fame through various commercial interests, and is seen occasionally as an announcer for televised swim meets.

STACK, Allen McIntyre.

B. 23 JAN 1928. Gold: 1948 100 meter backstroke. In 1948, Allen Stack finally removed Adolph Kiefer's 12-year-old 200m backstroke world record from the books. Stack set a total of six world records, won 10 AAU titles, and was a double gold medal winner at the 1951 Pan-American Games. After Yale, he attended Columbia Law School and now practices law in Honolulu.

STAMM, Michael Eugene.
B. 06 AUG 1952 San Pedro, CA. Gold: 1972 4 × 100 meter medley relay; Silver(2): 1972 100 meter backstroke, 1972 200 meter backstroke. Had it not been for the East German great Roland Matthes, Mike Stamm would have won three major international titles; Stamm finished second to Matthes in both of his Olympic races and in the 100m back at the 1973 World Championships. In 1970, however, Stamm did break Matthes' world 200m backstroke record, only to have the East German recapture it three weeks later. Stamm attended Indiana University and won one NCAA and eight AAU individual titles.

STASSFORTH, Bowen D.
B. 07 AUG 1926. Silver: 1952 200 meter breaststroke. Bowen Stassforth, of the University of Iowa, won a bronze medal in the 100m backstroke and a gold in the medley relay at the 1951 Pan-American Games. He won his only AAU title in 1952.

STRACHAN, Rodney.
B. 16 OCT 1955 Santa Monica, CA. Gold: 1976 400 meter individual medley. Rod Strachan of Southern Cal won the 400m IM at the Final Trials with a new U.S. record, then went on to set a new world record in winning the Olympic title. In college, Strachan had a 3.96 grade point average, which helped earn him admission to Southern Cal's medical school. He is now a doctor, specializing in internal medicine.

TAYLOR, Jack G. N.
B. 31 JAN 1931. Bronze: 1952 100 meter backstroke. After graduating from Ohio State, Jack Taylor swam for the Navy Olympics. Before specializing in the backstroke, he won the AAU 1,500m freestyle, both indoor and outdoor, in 1948.

THORNE, Raymond.
Silver: 1904 4 × 50 yard freestyle relay. Ray Thorne was a member of the Chicago AA.

TROY, Michael Francis.
B. 03 OCT 1940 Indianapolis, IN. Gold(2): 1960 200 meter butterfly, 1960 4 × 200 meter freestyle relay. Mike Troy began his competitive swimming career in the Indianapolis park district program, but joined the Indianapolis AC before enrolling at Indiana University At the 1959 Pan-American Games, he finished second to Dave Gillanders in the 200m butterfly, but gained his revenge at the 1960 Olympics, where Troy took the gold medal and Gillanders placed third. At both the 1959 Pan-Am Games and the 1960 Olympics, Troy was a member of the winning freestyle relay team. He was a prolific record breaker in both freestyle and butterfly events, but surprisingly won only two AAU outdoor titles.

Mike Troy was decorated for valor while serving with the navy in Vietnam. He is now involved in real estate brokerage in California.

TUTTLE, William.
Silver: 1904 4 × 50 yard freestyle relay. Bill Tuttle was a member of the Chicago AA in 1904.

TYLER, Frederick Daniel.
B. 15 MAR 1954 Orlando, CA. Gold: 1972 4 × 200 meter freestyle relay. Apart from being a member of the 1972 Olympic relay team, Fred Tyler was also a finalist in the 200m freestyle in Munich. He won his only major title when he took the NCAA 200 IM for Indiana in 1975.

Vande WEGHE, Albert.
B. 28 JUL 1916 New York, NY. Silver: 1936 100 meter backstroke. Al Vande Weghe, of the Newark AC, set world records for the 100m and 200m backstroke. After winning his Olympic silver in Berlin he entered Princeton and, in 1938, became the first man to break one minute for the 100y backstroke. Vande Weghe won three consecutive NCAA titles and at the AAU's he won two indoor and one outdoor title. He made his career as a chemical engineer with the DuPont Co. for over 35 years.

VERDEUR, Joseph Thomas.
B. 07 MAR 1926 Philadelphia, PA. Gold: 1948 200 meter breaststroke. Between 1948 and 1950, Joe Verdeur set 12 world records in butterfly events, and at the AAU championships he won 19 titles in the breaststroke and IM. While attending LaSalle College, Verdeur was a four-time NCAA champion and worked his way through school as a night stoker at the famous Turner's Building.

After graduation, the Kirk Douglas look-alike had aspirations of adding his name to the role of Olympic champions who have played Tarzan in the movies, but his dreams of Hollywood fame were not to be fulfilled.

VOGEL, Matt.

B. 03 JUN 1957 Fort Wayne, IN. Gold(2): 1976 100 meter butterfly, 1976 4 × 100 meter medley relay. Although Matt Vogel placed only third at the 1976 Final Trials, he came through to win the 100m butterfly title in Montreal. However, he failed to dislodge Mark Spitz's world record and this was the only event on the men's swimming program at Montreal which failed to produce a new world record. Vogel is a graduate of the University of Tennessee.

WALES, Ross Elliot.

B. 17 OCT 1947 Youngstown, OH. Bronze: 1968 100 meter butterfly. Princeton's Ross Wales won his first major title in 1966 when he took the AAU indoor championship. In 1967 he won a silver medal at the Pan-American Games and was the NCAA champion.

Wales retired from competition after the 1968 Olympics, enrolling in law school at the University of Virginia. He was called to action in Vietnam, however, but later returned to complete his law studies at the Charlottesville campus. He is now a lawyer in Cincinnati and serves as the current president of the U.S. Swimming Federation.

WALSH, Kenneth M.

B. 11 FEB 1945 Orange, NJ. Gold(2): 1968 4 × 100 meter freestyle relay, 1968 4 × 100 meter medley relay; Silver: 1968 100 meter freestyle. In 1967 and 1968, a U.S. foursome made three improvements on the world record for the 400m freestyle relay, and Ken Walsh and Zac Zorn were the only swimmers to be members of all three teams. Walsh was an outstanding relay swimmer, and in addition to his two Olympic golds, was on two winning relay teams at the 1967 Pan-American Games and set a new world record for the 100m on the opening leg of the freestyle relay. In individual events, his only major victory came in 1967 when he won the NCAA 100y freestyle for Michigan State.

WEISSMULLER, Peter John.

B. 02 JUN 1904 Windber, PA. Gold(5): 1924 100 meter freestyle, 1924 400 meter freestyle, 1924 4 × 200 meter freestyle relay, 1928 100 meter freestyle, 1928 4 × 200 meter freestyle relay; Bronze: 1924 Water Polo. Although his records have long since been surpassed, and although others have won more Olympic medals, Johnny Weissmuller remains the best known swimmer of all time.

Weissmuller set the first of his many world records as a 17-year-old in 1922 and experts considered his 100y freestyle record of 51.0 in 1927 to be the greatest of all his achievements. This remained a world record for 17 years, although Weissmuller himself swam 48.5, as a 36-year-old, after he had joined the professional ranks. He was the first man to better one minute for the 100m freestyle, the first man under five minutes for the 440y freestyle, and he won a total of 51 AAU championships. After a loss in the 1921 AAU 440y freestyle to Ludy Langer, there is no record of his ever losing another race.

Weissmuller later became the best known of the screen Tarzans and involvement in a number of successful aquatic related businesses enabled him to lead a prosperous life. He has been married six times, and sadly, has been in rather poor health in recent years.

WOLF, Paul.

B. 06 OCT 1916. Silver: 1936 4 × 200 meter freestyle relay. Two years after winning his Olympic silver medal, Paul Wolf of the Los Angeles AC returned to the Berlin pool as a member of the U.S. team that set a world record in the 800m freestyle relay.

WOLF, Wallace Perry.

B. 02 OCT 1930 Los Angeles, CA. Gold: 1948 4 × 200 meter freestyle relay. After attending Southern Cal, Wally Wolf swam for the Navy Olympics. At the 1952 Final Trials he was the top man in the 200m freestyle, but surprisingly only swam in the relay heats in Helsinki. He played on the water polo team at the 1956 and 1960 Games, becoming only the second U.S. swimmer/water poloist to have competed in four Olympics. Wolf is now a successful attorney in Los Angeles and, at one time, numbered among his clients Johnny Carson, who, to the best of our knowledge, never competed in the Olympics.

WOOLSEY, William Tripp.

B. 13 SEP 1934 Honolulu, HA. Gold: 1952 4 × 200 meter freestyle relay; Silver: 1956 4 × 200 meter freestyle relay. Apart from winning two Olympic relay medals, Bill Woolsey was a finalist in the 1,500m freestyle in the 1952 Olympics, and the 100m freestyle in the 1956 Olympics. While at Indiana University he was twice an NCAA champion and he won four AAU titles.

WYATT, Paul.

B. 27 FEB 1907. Silver: 1924 100 meter backstroke; Bronze: 1928 100 meter backstroke. Between winning his two Olympic medals, Paul Wyatt won the AAU indoor backstroke title in 1925 and was AAU outdoor champion the following year. He represented the Uniontown YMCA of Pennsylvania.

YORZYK, William Albert.

B. 29 MAY 1933 Northampton, PA. Gold: 1956 200 meter butterfly. Bill Yorzyk was the first Olympic champion in a butterfly event, setting a world record in the heats and final of the 200m fly at Melbourne. He was a fine all-round swimmer and won AAU titles in the fly and IM, as well as a gold medal in the freestyle relay at the 1955 Pan-American Games.

After graduating from Springfield College, Yorzyk attended medical school at the University of Toronto and won the university's Bickler Prize as the top scholar-athlete in 1958 and 1959. He became an anesthesiologist, later serving as a captain in the U.S. Air Force medical corps and as an associate physician to the U.S. Olympic team in 1964.

ZORN, Zachary.

B. 10 MAR 1947 Dayton, OH. Gold: 1968 4 × 100 meter freestyle relay. Zac Zorn won his only major individual title when he took the 1968 NCAA 100m freestyle for UCLA. He went to the 1968 Olympics as the world record holder in that event, but poor pace judgment ruined his chances for a medal and he finished eighth, and last, in the final. Zorn set one individual world record and was a member of three world record breaking relay teams.

WOMEN

Women's swimming became an Olympic sport in 1912 with the United States' first appearance occurring in 1920. Since that time we have been the top nation in the world in this sport. There have been pretenders to the throne, notably Sweden in the early days of the sport and Australia shortly after World War II. The biggest challenge has recently come from the women of the German Democratic Republic (GDR)—East Germany. In fact, many people now consider their female swimmers the best in the world and their performances at the 1976 Olympics certainly lend credence to that hypothesis. However, the United States began a resurgence after 1976 and was very successful at the 1978 World Championships. The boycott in 1980 has put a damper on our recent success and it is difficult to assess our current status vis-a-vis that of the GDR. Still, swimming has been the sport in which American women have had the most Olympic success.

American women have won 48 gold medals and 113 medals, more than the next three countries (East Germany, Australia, and Holland) combined. They have won the most medals and golds in every stroke, except for the breaststroke, at which, for some reason, the U.S. women have never done very well.

ALDERSON, Joan.

B. 05 MAR 1935. Bronze: 1952 4 × 100 meter freestyle relay. Jody Alderson of the Chicago Town Club won the 100m freestyle at the 1952 Final Trials and went on to place fifth in the Olympic final and win a bronze medal in the relay. She won her only national titles in 1954 by capturing the AAU 100y/100m championships, both indoors and outdoors.

ATWOOD, Susan Jean.

B. 05 JUN 1953 Long Beach, CA. Silver: 1972 200 meter backstroke; Bronze: 1972 100 meter backstroke. Susie Atwood made her Olympic debut in 1968 when she was eliminated in the heats of the 200m backstroke. In 1972 she improved to take two backstroke medals and competed in the heats of the medley relay. She won a total of 18 AAU titles and set 12 American and four world records in the 200m backstroke and 400m medley relay.

Atwood attended both Long Beach City College and the University of Hawaii, but finally graduated from

OUTSTANDING PERFORMANCES

Most Gold Medals
  3 Melissa Belote, Ethelda Bleibtrey, Helene Madison, Debbie Meyer, Sandy Neilson, Martha Norelius, Sharon Stouder, Chris Von Saltza
Most Medals
  8 Shirley Babashoff
  4 Ellie Daniel, Kathy Ellis, Jan Henne, Sue Pederson, Eleanor Garatti-Saville, Sharon Stouder, Chris Von Saltza
Most Golds (Games)
  3 Melissa Belote, Ethelda Bleibtrey, Helene Madison, Debbie Meyer, Sandy Neilson, Sharon Stouder, Chris Von Saltza
Most Medals (Games)
  5 Shirley Babashoff
  4 Kathy Ellis, Jan Henne, Sue Pederson, Sharon Stouder, Chris Von Saltza
Most Appearances
  2 Record shared by 20 women
Consecutive Victories, Same Event
  2 Shirley Babashoff (1972-76 400 m. free relay), Jane Barkman (1972-76 400 m. free relay), Martha Norelius (1924-28 400 m. free), Eleanor Saville-Garatti (1928-32 400 m. free relay)
Most Silver Medals
  6 Shirley Babashoff
Most Bronze Medals
  2 Ellie Daniel, Kathy Ellis, Evelyn Kawamoto, Frances Schroth
Oldest Gold Medalist
  27y140d Frances Schroth
Youngest Gold Medalist
  14y96d "Pokey" Watson

Whittier College in 1977 with a physical education degree. From 1977 to 1980 she was the women's swim coach at Ohio State, but today she works in public relations and promotions with Arena USA.

BABASHOFF, Shirley.

B. 31 JAN 1957 Whittier, CA. Gold(2): 1972 4 × 100 meter freestyle relay, 1976 4 × 100 meter freestyle relay; Silver(6): 1972 100 meter freestyle, 1972 200 meter freestyle, 1976 200 meter freestyle, 1976 400 meter freestyle, 1976 800 meter freestyle, 1976 4 × 100 meter medley relay. With a total of eight Olympic medals, Shirley Babashoff is the most successful U.S. woman Olympian of all time. Although she never won an individual Olympic title she is recognized as one of the greatest of all freestyle swimmers.

Babashoff set six world records in individual events and shared in a further five in relays. She also set 37 U.S. records (17 individual and 20 relay) and at one time held the U.S. freestyle record at every distance from 100m to 800m.

Apart from her record-breaking ability, Shirley Babashoff had a fine competitive record in major championships, winning—including relays—27 AAU titles in addition to taking the 200m and 400m individual gold medals at the 1975 World Championships. Her greatest performance ever came at the 1976 Olympic Trials when she won every freestyle event and the 400m individual medley. She set three U.S. records in the heats, three more in the finals, and broke the world record in the 800m freestyle. Not only was this her greatest performance ever, but it ranks among the great swimming feats of all time.

BALL, Catherine.
B. 30 SEP 1951 Jacksonville, FL. Gold: 1968 4 × 100 meter medley relay. At the start of the 1968 Olympics, Catie Ball held all four world records for the breaststroke and seemed a certainty for the gold medals in Mexico. But during the Games, she contracted a virus infection and only managed fifth place in the 100m and was too ill to start in the heats of the 200m. However she recovered in time to compete in the medley relay and swam the breaststroke leg on the winning team. Ball did win both breaststroke events at the 1967 Pan-American Games, as well as setting 13 world records and winning nine AAU titles.

BARKMAN, Jane Louise.
B. 20 SEP 1951 Bryn Mawr, PA. Gold(2): 1968 4 × 100 meter freestyle relay, 1972 4 × 100 meter freestyle relay; 1968 200 meter freestyle. After winning a gold and silver medal at the 1968 Olympics, Jane Barkman retired from competition. However she made a comeback for the 1972 Olympics and was the only member of the 1968 freestyle relay team to win a second gold in that event in 1972. Barkman had won three AAU titles

during her competitive days. She is now the women's swim coach at Princeton.

BAUER, Sybil.
B. 18 SEP 1903 Chicago, IL. D. 31 JAN 1927 Chicago, IL. Gold: 1924 100 meter backstroke. Sybil Bauer, the daughter of Norwegian parents living in Chicago, was the first great woman backstroker. Perhaps her finest achievement came in Bermuda in 1922 when she was clocked at 6:24.8 for the 440y backstroke, which represented a four-second improvement on "Stubby" Kruger's world record for men! Bauer won the 1924 Olympic title by a massive margin, set 23 world records, and won six successive AAU 100y backstroke championships from 1921.

Sybil Bauer attended Northwestern and was on the basketball and field hockey teams, in addition to the swim team. She was a leader in the campaign to get full competitive programs into women's university sports, but became ill early in 1927. She died from cancer in her senior year of college without seeing her wish fulfilled. Bauer also missed her chance to marry her fiance, Ed Sullivan, who at the time was a Chicago sportswriter but later became the well-known host of his own television variety show.

BELOTE, Melissa.
B. 10 OCT 1956 Washington, DC. Gold(3): 1972 100 meter backstroke, 1972 200 meter backstroke, 1972 4 × 100 meter medley relay. Apart from Shane Gould, the 15-year-old Melissa Belote was the only woman swimmer to win more than one individual title in Munich. She went to the U.S. Final Trials as a little-known outsider, but beat the U.S. record holder, Susie Atwood, in the 100m backstroke and then took the 200m after setting a world record in the heats. At the 1972 Olympics she again set a world record in the 200m and the following year she won the 200m backstroke at the World Championships. In 1976 she made the Olympic team for the second time and placed fifth in the 200m.

In her collegiate career at Arizona State, Belote collected four AIAW titles. After graduating with a degree in communications she returned to Virginia, where she had swum for the Solotar Swim Team, and as Mrs. Hamlin took the post of assistant head coach at Solotar.

BLEIBTREY, Ethelda M.

B. 27 FEB 1902 Waterford, NY. D. 06 MAY 1978 West Palm Beach, FL. Gold(3): 1920 100 meter freestyle, 1920 300 meter freestyle, 1920 4 × 100 meter freestyle relay. Ethelda Bleibtrey was the first American woman to win an Olympic swimming title and also the first woman, from any country, to win three gold medals. In each of her Olympic victories in Antwerp, she set a new world record; had there been a backstroke event on the program she almost certainly would have won a fourth gold medal because she was a world record holder in the backstroke at the time.

Bleibtrey had a brief career as an amateur before turning pro in 1922, but between 1920 and 1922 she was undefeated and won an AAU title at every distance from 50y to the long distance event. She was often in the news for incidents related to swimming and in 1919 only public opinion prevented her from being jailed for swimming "nude." She had merely removed her stockings before going for a swim at Manhattan Beach, but in 1919 this was considered "nudity." In 1928 she did spend a night in jail after swimming in the Central Park Reservoir, but Mayor Jimmy Walker quickly intervened and New York got its first large swimming pool, which was the original object of the publicity stunt.

Bleibtrey had a successful career as a pro swimmer, then became a well-known coach in New York and Atlantic City, and later was a nurse in Palm Beach.

BOGLIOLI, Wendy Lansbach.

B. 06 MAR 1955 Merrill, WI. Gold: 1976 4 × 100 freestyle relay; Bronze: 1976 100 meter butterfly. Mrs. Wendy Boglioli won her only AAU title when she took the 1976 100m butterfly, but she was also a good freestyler and fourth place in the 100m at the 1976 Final Trials earned her a place on the Olympic relay team. The relay gold was the only one earned by the U.S. women at Montreal and one of only two which eluded the East Germans.

Boglioli graduated from Monmouth College and then worked for a short time as an assistant coach for her club team, the Central Jersey Aquatic Club. She married Bernie Boglioli in August 1975.

BRIDGES, Alice W.

B. 19 JUL 1916 Oakland, ME. Bronze: 1936 100 meter backstroke. Alice Bridges was a student at the Posse School of Physical Education in Uxbridge, Massachusetts when she won her bronze medal at the 1936 Olympics. She had earlier won the AAU 220y backstroke title in 1934 and at the 1936 U.S. Trials she finished third behind Eleanor Holm-Jarrett and Edith Motridge. Jarrett did not compete in Berlin, due to disciplinary reasons, and Bridges reversed the results of the U.S. Trials by narrowly beating Motridge for the Olympic bronze medal.

After the Olympics, Alice Bridges retired from competitive swimming and worked in New Jersey as a swimming instructor. She has since become Mrs. Joseph Roche.

BURKE, Lynn Edythe.

B. 22 MAR 1943 New York, NY. Gold(2): 1960 100 meter backstroke, 1960 4 × 100 meter medley relay. After an interval of 28 years, Lynn Burke of the Santa Clara Swim Club brought the women's Olympic 100m backstroke title back to America. Her many other interests restricted her career as a top-flight swimmer, but she won four AAU individual titles and two in the relays. In 1960 she lowered the world 100m backstroke record four times within the space of three months.

Lynn Burke later became a successful New York model, author, and business woman, and has raised three children.

CARR, Catherine.

B. 27 MAY 1924 Albuquerque, NM. Gold(2): 1972 100 meter breaststroke, 1972 4 × 100 meter medley relay. Cathy Carr, an 18-year-old from Highlan High School in Albuquerque, won the 1972 AAU 100m breaststroke and then took the Olympic title by defeating the veteran 1964 champion, Galina Stepanova of the USSR. Carr set a world record of 1:13.58 to better Catie Ball's four-year-old world best of 1:14.2 and earned a share of a second world record as a member of the winning medley relay team. Carr trained for the Olympics at the Coronado Swim Club under former men's gold medalist, Mike Troy.

COLELLA, Lynn Ann.

B. 13 JUN 1950 Seattle, WA. Silver: 1972 200 meter butterfly. Lynn Colella started competitive swimming at the age of 10 and her first international success came in 1971 when she won two golds and a bronze at the

Pan-American Games. After her silver medal at the Olympics she placed third in both the 200m breast-stroke and 200m butterfly at the 1973 World Championships.

Her younger brother, Rick, won four Pan-American Games gold medals and joined his sister on the 1972 Olympic team. Aided by a scholarship from the Phillips Petroleum Co., Lynn earned a degree in electrical engineering from the University of Washington, where she later pursued postgraduate studies.

CONE, Carin Alice.
B. 18 APR 1940 Huntington, NY. Silver: 1956 100 meter backstroke. Carin Cone set six U.S. records in the 50m pool and many others in short course events. During the period 1955-59 she won 16 AAU titles and took two gold medals at the 1959 Pan-American Games. Her eight AAU backstroke titles bettered Suzanne Zimmerman's record of seven.

After attending school in Ridgewood, New Jersey, Cone attended the University of Houston and later represented the Shamrock SC. Cone attempted to qualify for the 1960 Olympic team but missed out at the Final Trials. Today, as Mrs. Vanderbush, she competes actively in master's swimming competition.

CORRIDON, Marie Louise.
B. 05 FEB 1930 Norwalk, CT. Gold: 1948 4 × 100 meter freestyle relay. Although a gold medal winner in the relay at the 1948 Olympics, Marie Corridon, of the Women's Swimming Association of New York, was eliminated in the semi-finals of the individual 100m freestyle. Her only AAU title came in the 1948 100y freestyle.

Corridon is today Mrs. William Mortell and the mother of seven children. Five girls are competitive swimmers and, in 1983, two competed at the NCAA Div. I Championships and one competed at the NCAA Div. II Championships.

CURTIS, Ann Elisabeth.
B. 06 MAR 1926. Gold(2): 1948 400 meter freestyle, 1948 4 × 100 meter freestyle relay; Silver: 1948 100 meter freestyle. With three Olympic medals, Ann Curtis of the Crystal Plunge Club in San Francisco was the most successful woman swimmer of the 1948 Games. During her career Miss Curtis won an incredible 34

AAU titles (including eight relays), but surprisingly she set only two world records, posting a new long course best for the 880y freestyle in 1944 and a new 440y record, in a 25-yard pool, in 1947.

Ann Curtis was one of the best known sportswomen of her time and was the first woman to win the Sullivan Award. She was a cover girl on the front of *Colliers, Newsweek*, and many other magazines. Now, as Mrs. Gordon Cuneo, she lives in California and runs the Ann Curtis School of Swimming.

DANIEL, Eleanor Suzanne.
B. 11 JUN 1950 Philadelphia, PA. Gold: 1968 4 × 100 meter medley relay; Silver: 1968 100 meter butterfly; Bronze(2): 1968 200 meter butterfly, 1972 200 meter butterfly. Ellie Daniel began swimming with the Vesper Boat Club and was coached for a time by Mary Kelly, wife of Olympic rower, Jack Kelly, Jr. She first broke through internationally with a gold in the 100m butterfly at the 1967 Pan-American Games, and after winning a set of medals at Mexico City, she enrolled at Penn. She trained with the men's team at Penn under Olympic gold medalist, George Breen. After two years, she moved to California to train in preparation for the Munich Olympics, after which she retired from swimming and returned to Penn, graduating in 1974.

DEARDURFF, Deena Diana.
B. 08 MAY 1957 Cincinnati, OH. Gold: 1972 4 × 100 meter butterfly. In 1971, Deena Deardurff won the 100m butterfly at the Pan-American Games and won both the indoor and the outdoor title at the AAU's. At the Munich Olympics she missed out on a bronze medal in the 100m butterfly by a narrow margin, but won a gold medal and a share of a world record in the medley relay.

Today, as Mrs. Robert Schmidt, she coaches age group swimmers in San Diego and still competes in master's events.

De VARONA, Donna Elizabeth.
B. 26 APR 1947 San Diego, CA. Gold(2): 1964 400 meter individual medley, 1964 4 × 100 meter medley relay. At only 13 years old, Donna DeVarona was the youngest member of the 1960 Olympic swim team, but she competed only in the relay heats. By the 1964 Olympics, however, she had become the best known woman swimmer in the world—she had set 18 world

records in the interim and won innumerable titles. She was voted by both AP and UPI as the top female athlete of 1964, but her success did not end with the Tokyo Olympics.

Miss DeVarona made the cover of several national magazines in 1964. She used her fame to launch a career in sportscasting, first with ABC and, in more recent years, with NBC. She was the first female sportscaster in the United States and the first to cover the Olympics for television, which she did in 1968, 1972, and 1976. She has also been very active in promoting women's sports, and amateur sports in general. Her activities include being a member of the Women's Sports Hall of Fame, the President's Commission on Olympic Sports, and a founding member and past president of the Women's Sports Foundation.

DONNOLLY, Euphrasia.
B. 06 JUN 1906. Ddi. Gold: 1924 4 × 100 meter freestyle relay. Three of the four members of the winning U.S. relay team in 1924 also won medals in individual events, but Euphrasia Donnolly competed only in the relay where the U.S. beat Great Britain by almost 20 seconds to set a new world record. Miss Donnolly was from Indianapolis and never won an AAU title.

DUENKEL, Virginia Ruth.
B. 07 MAR 1947 Orange, NJ. Gold: 1964 400 meter freestyle; Bronze: 1964 100 meter backstroke. Having set a world 100m backstroke record 18 days earlier, Ginny Duenkel was one of six world-record holders in the 1964 Olympic final. In a desperately close finish, she placed third behind Cathy Ferguson, the holder of the 200m world record, and France's "Kiki" Caron, a former holder of the 100m record.

Ginny Duenkel then went into the 400m freestyle as the American third-string. She reversed the results of the U.S. trials by taking the gold medal, but missed the world record held by her teammate, Marilyn Ramenofsky, who finished second.

EDERLE, Gertrude Caroline.
B. 23 OCT 1906 New York, NY. Gold: 1924 4 × 100 meter freestyle relay: Bronze(2): 1924 100 meter freestyle, 1924 400 meter freestyle. Although she won three Olympic medals, "Trudy" Ederle will also be remembered for other outstanding swimming feats. In August

At the tender age of 12 years 298 days, Gertrude Ederle became the youngest woman to set a world swimming record.

1919 in Indianapolis, at the age of 12 years 298 days, she became the youngest woman ever to set a world swimming record when she posted a new best for the 880y freestyle. She set a total of nine world records and seven of them came during the course of a 500m swim at Brighton Beach, New York, in 1922. She turned professional in 1925; the following year she became the first woman to swim the English Channel. Her time of 14 hr., 34 min. broke the men's record for the crossing.

ELLIS, Kathleen.
B. 28 NOV 1946 Indianapolis, IN. Gold(2): 1964 4 × 100 meter freestyle relay, 1964 4 × 100 meter medley relay; Bronze(2): 1964 100 meter freestyle, 1964 100 meter butterfly. Kathy Ellis swam in four events at the 1964 Olympics and won a medal in each. She won a gold and a share of the world record in both relays and her two bronze medals came in individual events. In the 100m freestyle she was only the seventh fastest qualifier, but still took third place from an outside lane.

FERGUSON, Cathy Jean.
B. 17 JUL 1948 Stockton, CA. Gold(2): 1964 100 meter backstroke, 1964 4 × 100 meter medley relay. Cathy Ferguson was one of six world record holders in the 100m backstroke final at the 1964 Olympics. She proved to be the best of this distinguished field by taking the gold medal with a new record of 1:07.7. Having set a world record over 200m the previous month, she thus became the record holder at both backstroke distances. She also set two world records in the medley relay, the second of these coming at the Tokyo Olympics where she was a member of the winning U.S. team.

Miss Ferguson swam for the Los Angeles AC, setting seven U.S. records in addition to her four world bests and winning 10 AAU titles. She is now Mrs. Larry Brennan and, in addition to raising three children, coaches swimming at the high school and club level in California.

FINNERAN, Sharon Evans.
B. 04 FEB 1946 Rockville Center, NY. Silver: 1964 400 meter individual medley. Sharon Finneran was a member of a well-known swimming family. Her brother, Mike, was a diver on the 1972 Olympics team and her mother was a team official at the 1976 Games. Sharon swam for Santa Clara High School and the Los Angeles AC and was a truly versatile competitor. In 1962 she won the AAU titles both indoors and out in her Olympic event (400 IM), she twice won the AAU 200m butterfly outdoors, and was a good enough distance freestyler to win the AAU indoor title over 1,650y in 1964. In addition to winning these national titles she was the 400m freestyle champion at the 1963 Pan-American Games.

FREEMAN, Mavis Ann.
B. 07 NOV 1948. Bronze: 1936 4 × 100 meter freestyle relay. Mavis Freeman placed fourth in the 100m and 400m at the 1936 U.S. Trials and earned a place on the relay team for the Berlin Olympics. She swam the third leg for the team which took the bronze medals. Mavis Freeman represented the Women's Swimming Association of New York and won the AAU long distance title in 1936 and 1937.

GARATTI, Eleanor A. (see Eleanor Saville)

GERAGHTY, Agnes.
B. 26 NOV 1907. D. 01 MAR 1974 Oceanside, NY. Silver: 1924 200 meter breaststroke. After winning a silver medal in the breaststroke at the 1924 Olympics, Agnes Geraghty of the Women's Swimming Association of New York competed again at the 1928 Olympics. Although she made a substantial improvement on her time in Paris, she was eliminated in the semi-finals. Geraghty won a total of 10 AAU breaststroke titles and between 1924 and 1930 set world breaststroke records at every distance between 50 yards and 400 meters.

As Mrs. Felix McAndrews, Geraghty later turned to coaching swimming, first at Jones Park and then for the South Shore Yacht Club in Freeport, Long Island.

GOYETTE, Cynthia Lee.
B. 13 AUG 1946 Detroit, MI. Gold: 1964 4 × 100 meter medley relay. Cynthia Goyette of Wayne State and the Golden Lions SC swam the breaststroke stage on the team that set a new world record in winning the medley relay at the 1964 Olympics. Although she never won an AAU outdoor title, she was five times a winner at the indoor championships.

GUEST, Irene.
B. 22 JUL 1900. D. 1979. Gold: 1920 4 × 100 meter freestyle relay; Silver: 1920 100 meter freestyle. Representing the Meadowbrook Club of Philadelphia, Irene Guest placed third in the 100m freestyle at the U.S. Olympic Trials in 1920. At the Games she won her heat in 1:18.8 and, although she made a nearly two-second improvement in the final, she could not match Ethelda Bleibtrey's new world record of 1:13.6. Four days later, Guest joined with Bleibtrey, Fran Schroth and Peggy Woodbridge to win the relay with a new world record.

GUSTAVSON, Linda Lee.
B. 30 NOV 1949 Santa Cruz, CA. Gold: 1968 4 × 100 meter freestyle relay; Silver: 1968 400 meter freestyle; Bronze: 1968 100 meter freestyle. At the 1967 World University Games, Linda Gustavson of Cabrillo College was a medalist in the 100m and 200m freestyle and in both relays. The following year she added to her collection by winning a complete set of medals at the Mexico Olympics. She also won a gold in the freestyle relay at the 1967 Pan-American Games, but despite these manifold successes she managed only one victory at the AAU Championships, when she won the indoor 200y freestyle for the Santa Clara SC in 1969.

HALL, Kaye.
B. 15 MAY 1951 Tacoma, WA. Gold(2): 1968 100 meter backstroke, 1968 4 × 100 meter medley relay; Bronze: 1968 200 meter backstroke. After winning a bronze medal behind Canada's Elaine Tanner in the 100m backstroke at the 1967 Pan-American Games, Kaye Hall gained her revenge at the next year's Olympics by beating Tanner for the title and setting a new world record. Hall also claimed a share in a second world record as a member of the winning medley relay team. At the 1969 Canadian championships she won five gold medals and, representing the Tacoma SC, she won three AAU titles and retired after taking three golds at the 1970 World University Games.

HELSER, Brenda Mersereau.
B. 26 MAY 1926. Gold: 1948 4 × 100 meter freestyle relay. Prior to winning a gold with a new Olympic record in the freestyle relay at the 1948 Games, Brenda Helser swam in both the freestyle individual events. In the 100m she was eliminated in the semi-finals and in the 400m she placed fifth in the final.

Having won the first of her eight AAU titles in 1940, and having qualified for that year's Olympic team, which did not compete, Brenda Helser was one of the veterans on the women's swim team at the London Olympics. In the early part of her career she represented the Multnomah AC in Portland, Oregon, but later swam for the Los Angeles AC. She later became, by marriage, the Countess de Morelos.

HENNE, Jan Margo.
B. 11 AUG 1947 Oakland, CA. Gold(2): 1968 100 meter freestyle, 1968 4 × 100 meter freestyle relay; Silver: 1968 200 meter freestyle; Bronze: 1968 200 meter individual medley. Jan Henne turned from a mediocre breaststroke swimmer into an Olympic freestyle champion, although she never won a U.S. national title at freestyle.

Apart from the four events in which she won medals at the 1968 Olympics, she also swam in the heats of the medley relay. She won nine AAU titles, set eight U.S. records and, while attending Arizona State, won four events at the 1970 AIAW championships.

HOLM, Eleanor.
B. 06 DEC 1913 Brooklyn, NY. Gold: 1932 100 meter backstroke. As a 14-year-old, Eleanor Holm finished fifth in the 100m backstroke in the 1928 Olympics. Four years later she won a gold medal at the Los Angeles Games. She made the Olympic team for a third time in 1936 as a married woman, having married the crooner, Art Jarrett, in 1933. But on the boat trip to Europe, the behavior of the attractive and vivacious reigning champion did not meet with the approval of the USOC officials and she was banned from the team—ostensibly for drinking champagne while in training. However, Holm-Jarrett stayed on in Berlin and reported the Games for the International News Service. On her return home she turned professional and her second marriage was to Billy Rose, the promoter of the aquacades in which she starred. She also appeared in one movie, a Tarzan flick which starred Olympic decathlete Glenn Morris.

Despite the publicity she generated away from the pool, the current Eleanor Holm-Jarrett-Rose-Walker was undoubtedly a highly talented swimmer, having won a total of 29 AAU titles, nine of which came in the individual medley, and setting seven world backstroke records.

JEZEK, Linda Louise.
B. 10 MAR 1960 Palo Alto, CA. Silver: 1976 4 × 100 meter medley relay. After winning the AAU 100m backstroke in 1975 and 1976, Linda Jezek of the Santa Clara SC won the same event at the 1976 Final Trials. At the trials she also placed third in the 200m backstroke, but

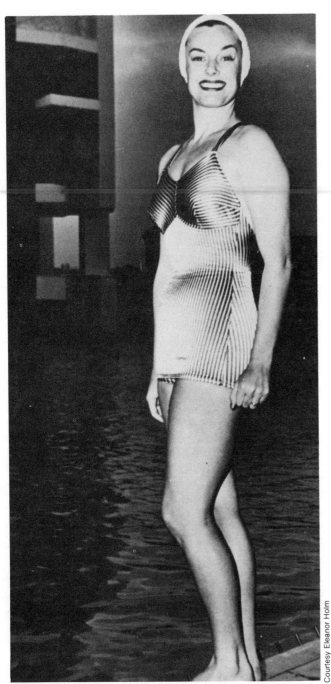

Courtesy Eleanor Holm

Eleanor Holm as she appeared when she made three Olympic swim teams and won one gold medal in the backstroke.

swam only in the 100m at Montreal. After being eliminated in the Olympic semi-finals in that event, she won a silver medal in the medley relay.

JOHNS, Helen Eileen.
B. 25 SEP 1914 East Boston, MA. Gold: 1932 4 × 100 meter freestyle relay. Helen Johns swam for the Brookline Women's Swimming Association and won the 1932 AAU junior indoor 100y freestyle title. Although she did not make the 1932 Olympic team in the individual events, she picked up a gold medal and a share of the world record in the relay.

Johns later became a swim coach and special education teacher and, as Mrs. Eugene Carroll, had two children—both girls.

KALAMA, Thelma.
B. 24 MAR 1931 Hawaii. Gold: 1948 4 × 100 meter freestyle relay. Thelma Kalama got to the 1948 Olympic Trials because Hawaiian beach boys took up a collection among the bathers so she could afford the trip. She placed fourth at both the 100m and 400m freestyle events at the trials, which earned her a relay spot at the Olympics. She won three AAU titles and set one American record for the 400m freestyle.

Thelma Kalama later joined the marines, eventually becoming a sergeant. She also attended college at Miami of Ohio and was married for a short time.

KAWAMOTO, Evelyn Tokue.
B. 17 SEP 1933. Bronze(2): 1952 400 meter freestyle, 1952 4 × 100 meter freestyle relay. In June 1952, Evelyn Kawamoto of the Hawaiian SC bettered her own U.S. 400m freestyle record and the following month she won this event at the Final Trials by a margin of more than five seconds. At the Olympics she took third place behind two Hungarians and won a second bronze medal in the relay.

Kawamoto married her fellow Olympian from Hawaii, Ford Konno, who won four medals at the 1952 Games.

KEMP, Jennifer Jo.
B. 28 MAY 1955 Cincinnati, OH. Gold: 1972 4 × 100 meter freestyle relay. Jenny Kemp was a backstroker until 1971, when she told her coach she was simply

bored with backstroke training and wished to try something else. The something else was freestyle and earned her a berth on the Olympic team. After being eliminated in the semi-finals of the individual 100m freestyle at the 1972 Olympics, Kemp won a gold medal and a share of a new world record in the freestyle relay. Swimming for the Cincinnati Pepsi Marlins, she won her only AAU title in 1972 in the 100m free.

KEMPNER, Patty.

B. 24 AUG 1942 Augusta, GA. Gold: 1960 4 × 100 meter medley relay. As a 13-year-old, Patty Kempner placed fifth in the 200m breaststroke at the 1956 Final Trials. Four years later she improved to take second place at the Trials and finished seventh in the Olympic final in Rome. Kempner, a student at Arizona, swam the breaststroke stage in the medley relay at the Olympics when the U.S. set a world record and beat the more fancied Australians by a comfortable margin. She won the AAU indoor 100y breaststroke title in 1957 and 1958.

KIGHT, Lenore. (see Lenore Wingard)

KOLB, Claudia Ann.

B. 19 DEC 1949 Hayward, CA. Gold(2): 1968 200 meter individual medley, 1968 400 meter individual medley; Silver: 1964 200 meter breaststroke. At the 1964 Olympics, Claudia Kolb, a 14-year-old from the Santa Clara SC, won an unexpected silver medal in the 200m breaststroke. She had only made the Tokyo final as the fifth fastest qualifier, but a brilliant finish took her from fourth to second place in the last 25 meters. After the 1964 Olympics, Kolb concentrated on the individual medley and set the inaugural official world record at 200m in 1966. At the Mexico Olympics she won both individual medley events by incredible margins, and during her six-year career she set a total of 23 world records. In all she won 25 AAU titles and at the 1967 Pan-American Games she won both individual medley events and the 200m butterfly in addition to placing second in the 200m breaststroke.

KRUSE, Pamela.

B. 03 JUN 1950 Miami, FL. Silver: 1968 800 meter freestyle. At the 1967 Pan-American Games, Pam Kruse won the 200m freestyle, placed second in the

400m, and picked up a second gold in the freestyle relay. The following year she concentrated on the longer distances and, after placing third in both the 400m and 800m freestyle at the U.S. Final Trials, won a silver medal in the 800m and placed fourth in the 400m at the Mexico Olympics.

Pam Kruse graduated from Marymount College in Florida and competed for the Fort Lauderdale Swimming Association. She won two AAU indoor titles and one outdoors.

LACKIE, Ethel.

B. 10 FEB 1907. Ddi. Gold(2): 1924 100 meter freestyle, 1924 4 × 100 meter freestyle relay. Ethel Lackie grew up in California, where she had learned to swim by the time she was three. She later lived near Lake Michigan and represented the Illinois AC in competition. Lackie set numerous U.S. and world records and was the first woman to break 60 seconds for the 100y freestyle and the first to clock 1:10.0 for the 100m freestyle. After her retirement she married Bill Watkins, a well-known rowing champion in the Santa Monica area.

LAMBERT, Adelaide T.

B. 27 OCT 1907. Gold: 1928 4 × 100 meter freestyle relay. Although Adelaide Lambert of the Women's Swimming Association of New York placed third in the 100m backstroke at the 1928 Final Trials, she did not take part in this event at the Olympics and competed only in the relay. She won AAU titles in freestyle, backstroke, and individual medley.

LAPP, Bernice Ruth.

B. 11 SEP 1917. Bronze: 1936 4 × 100 meter freestyle relay. After finishing second to Kathy Rawls in the 100m freestyle at the U.S. Final Trials, Bernice Lapp reached the semi-finals at the Berlin Olympics. Although she finished fourth, she failed to make the final because her time was inferior to that of the fourth-place swimmer in the other semi-final. Lapp competed for the Newark Women's AC.

LaVINE, Jacqueline Carol.

B. 04 OCT 1929. Bronze: 1952 4 × 100 meter freestyle relay. Jackie LaVine of the Chicago Town Club placed fifth in the 100m at the 1952 U.S. Final Trials and swam the lead-off leg for the freestyle relay team which won

Courtesy Women's Sports Foundation

Debbie Meyer was the first woman to win three individual gold medals at a single Olympics.

west High School Championship in 1928. In the early 1930's she dominated women's freestyling to an extent that is rarely seen at the highest levels. Swimming for the Washington AC, she won every AAU freestyle title in 1930, 1931, and 1932 with the solitary exception of the 1932 100m, in which she did not compete. She set a total of 26 world records, three of which came at the 1932 Olympics, and although she retired after the Los Angeles Games, many of her records remained on the books for years to come.

After giving up amateur swimming, Helene Madison had a brief fling at a Hollywood career, playing a minor role in the film, "The Warrior's Husband." She had a similar lack of success as a nightclub entertainer and, after the failure of three marriages, she lived alone in Seattle and in her later years particularly regretted that she had not succeeded in her ambition to become a registered nurse.

MANN, Shelly I.

B. 15 OCT 1937 New York, NY. Gold: 1956 100 meter butterfly; Silver: 1956 4 × 100 meter freestyle relay. Two years after taking up competitive swimming at the age of 12, Shelly Mann won the first of her 24 AAU titles. She won national championships in the freestyle, breast-stroke, butterfly, and individual medley events. Apart from her two medals at the 1956 Olympics, she also swam in the 100m freestyle in Melbourne, placing sixth in the final. The versatile Miss Mann set world records in the butterfly (100m and 200m) and the individual medley, and in the heats of the 1956 U.S. Trials, she equalled the world record for the 100m freestyle.

Mann was a student at American University and a member of the Walter Reed Swim Club, where she was coached by Jim Campbell. She trained at daybreak in a hospital pool before it was needed by the patients who were swimming for rehabilitative purposes.

McKEAN, Olive Mary.

B. 10 AUG 1915. Bronze: 1936 4 × 100 meter freestyle relay. After placing third in the 100m freestyle at the 1936 U.S. Final Trials, Olive McKean of the Washington AC placed fifth in the Olympic final in Berlin. She later won a bronze medal with the freestyle relay team. McKean was the AAU outdoor 100m freestyle cham-pion in 1934 and 1935, and indoors she won the AAU 100y title in 1934.

the bronze medals at the Helsinki Olympics. Four years earlier, she had also finished fifth in the 100m freestyle at the Final Trials and went to London as an alternate to the relay team, but did not get to compete. Between the two Olympics, however, she won five AAU titles.

MADISON, Helene E.

B. 19 JUN 1913 Madison, WI. D. 27 NOV 1970 Seattle, WA. Gold(3): 1932 100 meter freestyle, 1932 400 meter freestyle, 1932 4 × 100 meter freestyle relay. Helene Madison was born in Wisconsin but, while still a child, her family moved to Seattle where she had her first success as a competitive swimmer, winning the North-

McKIM, Josephine E.

B. 04 JAN 1910. Gold: 1932 4 × 100 meter freestyle relay; Bronze: 1928 400 meter freestyle. Initially, Josephine McKim represented the Carnegie Library Club of Homestead, Pennsylvania, but she later moved to the Canal Zone and competed as an unattached swimmer. She originally specialized in the longer distances and won the AAU 440y in 1929 and the one mile in 1928 and 1929. Following these successes, her second place in the 100m freestyle at the 1932 U.S. Final Trials caused a major surprise; she swam to a creditable fourth place at the Los Angeles Games before winning a gold medal and a share in a new world record in the Olympic freestyle relay. She later had a brief acting career.

MEYER, Deborah.

B. 14 AUG 1952 Annapolis, MD. Gold(3): 1968 200 meter freestyle, 1968 400 meter freestyle, 1968 800 meter freestyle. Although handicapped by a stomach infection in Mexico, Debbie Meyer of the Arden Hills SC became the first woman swimmer to win three individual gold medals at a single Olympics.

The previous year she had won two golds at the Pan-American Games, and in 1967 she took over as the undisputed freestyle queen. She won the AAU 400m and 1,500m four years straight from 1967, and in 1969 she won the 400m individual medley. She won 10 AAU titles indoors and was a prolific record breaker, setting 27 U.S. records (including three relays) and 15 individual world records including, at the 1968 Final Trials, new world bests at each of the three distances at which she was to win top Olympic honors. In addition, she won the 1968 Sullivan Award as the nation's top amateur athlete.

MOE, Karen Patricia. (see Karen Thornton)

NEILSON, Sandra.

B. 20 MAR 1956 Burbank, CA. Gold(3): 1972 100 meter freestyle, 1972 4 × 100 meter freestyle relay, 1972 4 x 100 meter medley relay. Although she finished only third in the U.S. Final Trials and third in the Olympic semifinal, 16-year-old Sandy Neilson was a surprise winner of the 100m freestyle at the Munich Olympics. She also won a gold medal in both relays, the U.S. posting a new world record in each.

Neilson, from El Monte, California, won her only AAU title in 1971 when she won the 100y indoor championship. She also won the Pan-American Games 100m freestyle in the same year.

NORELIUS, Martha.

B. 20 JAN 1908 Stockholm, Sweden. D. 23 SEP 1955. Gold(3): 1924 400 meter freestyle, 1928 400 meter freestyle, 1928 4 × 100 meter freestyle relay. Martha Norelius was originally coached by her father, who swam for Sweden at the 1906 Olympics, but on emigrating to America, Louis de B. Handley took over as her coach and Martha soon made an impact in U.S. swimming circles. During her career she won 16 AAU titles, set 29 world records, and became the first woman ever to defend an individual Olympic swimming title.

In 1929 she was suspended by the AAU for giving an exhibition in the same pool as some professionals. She therefore decided to turn pro herself and won the $10,000 Wrigley Marathon in Toronto. While there she met Joe Wright, who had won an Olympic silver medal for Canada in the 1928 double sculls, and whom she subsequently married.

OSIPOWICH, Albina Lucy Charlotte.

B. 26 FEB 1911 Worcester, MA. D. 06 JUN 1964. Gold(2): 1928 100 meter freestyle, 1928 4 × 100 meter freestyle relay. Worcester's Albina Osipowich placed only third in the 100m freestyle at the 1928 Final Trials, but she went on to win a gold medal in Amsterdam with a new world record. She also won a gold medal in the relay when the U.S. bettered the world record.

After the Olympics, Miss Osipowich won two AAU titles indoors and set a national and world record for the 100m freestyle. She attended Pembroke College of Brown University, where she played field hockey and continued to swim as a hobby. After college she worked briefly as a buyer for a department store before marrying Brown basketball star, Harrison Van Aken.

PEDERSON, Susan Jane.

B. 16 OCT 1953 Sacramento, CA. Gold(2): 1968 4 × 100 meter freestyle relay, 1968 4 × 100 meter medley relay; Silver(2): 1968 100 meter freestyle, 1968 200 meter individual medley. Sue Pederson won a gold medal in both relays at the Mexico Games as the U.S. set a new

Olympic record in each. Additionally, she won two silvers in individual events and placed fourth in the 100m freestyle. She competed for the Arden Hills SC and, in addition to winning three silver medals at the 1967 Pan-American Games, won four AAU titles.

PEYTON, Kim Maurie.
B. 26 JAN 1957 Hood River, OR. Gold: 1976 4 × 100 meter freestyle relay. Kim Peyton made her Olympic debut in 1972 when she swam in the heats of the freestyle relay. Four years later, in Montreal, she won a gold medal in this event in addition to placing fourth in the 100m freestyle. For Kim Peyton, then an incoming freshman at Stanford, the 1976 Olympic relay was the highlight of her career. After a series of losses to the East Germans, the freestyle relay was America's last chance for a gold medal in women's swimming at the Montreal Games; with Peyton swimming the lead-off stage, the U.S. at last defeated the East Germans and took a full three seconds off the world record.

At the Pan-American Games, she won the 100m and 200m freestyle in 1971 and, after defending her 200m title in 1975, won two more Pan-American golds as a member of the two relay teams. Peyton also won four AAU titles.

RAMENOFSKY, Marilyn.
B. 20 AUG 1946 Phoenix, AZ. Silver: 1964 400 meter freestyle. In July and August 1964, Marilyn Ramenofsky broke the 400m freestyle world record three times, but failed in her bid for the Olympic title. At Tokyo, the favored Ramenofsky lost to her teammate, Ginny Duenkel, but her world record remained intact.

Marilyn Ramenofsky attended Pomona College, where she trained with the men's swim team because there was no team for women. After college she earned a Ph.D. from the University of Washington in the field of ecology and ethnology. She married, becoming Mrs. Wingfield, and then did postdoctoral study on the behavior of birds.

RAMEY, Nancy Jane.
B. 29 JUN 1940 Seattle, WA. Silver: 1956 100 meter butterfly. At the time she won her Olympic medal, Nancy Ramey was a 16-year-old student at Mercer Island High School in Washington. She was disappointed at the Melbourne Olympics when she was denied her chance to compete against the great Dutch butterfly swimmers, when the Netherlands boycotted the 1956 Olympics in protest of Russia's invasion of Hungary. In 1958 she set world records for the 100m butterfly (twice) and for the 200m fly (once) and won six national titles (five U.S., one Canadian).

Nancy Ramey later graduated from the University of Washington and then earned an M.A. and a Ph.D. degree from the University of Wisconsin. She put her degrees to use in the 70's as an assistant professor of religious studies at Stanford. As Mrs. Jim Lethcoe, she and her husband today organize and lead Alaskan wilderness safaris.

RANDALL, Martha Irene.
B. 12 JUN 1948 Chicago, IL. Bronze: 1964 400 meter individual medley. Martha Randall competed for the Vesper Boat Club of Philadelphia. Although her Olympic medal came in the individual medley, her five individual AAU titles came in freestyle events. She also won three AAU championships in the relay events.

RAWLS, Katherine Louise.
B. 14 JUN 1918. D. 08 APR 1982. Silver(2): 1932 Springboard (Diving), 1936 Springboard (Diving); Bronze: 1936 4 × 100 meter freestyle relay. See the diving section for the biography.

RIGGIN, Aileen M.
B. 02 MAY 1906. Gold: 1920 Springboard (Diving); Silver: 1924 Springboard (Diving); Bronze: 1924 100 meter backstroke. See the diving section for the biography.

ROSAZZA, Joan Ann.
B. 19 MAY 1937 Torrington, CT. Silver: 1956 4 × 100 meter freestyle. In 1956, Joan Rosazza was a student at Purdue and, in noncollegiate competition, she represented the Lafayette Swim Club. At the 1956 Olympics she finished fourth in the 100m freestyle behind three Australians, all of whom were members of the team which beat the U.S. out of the gold medals in the freestyle relay.

ROTHHAMMER, Keena Ruth.

B. 26 FEB 1957 Little Rock, AR. Gold: 1972 800 meter freestyle; Bronze: 1972 200 meter freestyle. Keena Rothhammer was a highly talented and versatile swimmer, but one who was also rather inconsistent. She went to the Munich Olympics as the U.S. third-string for the 800m freestyle, but won the gold medal with a new world record; she had been top U.S. qualifier for the 400m free but finished only in sixth place; and only in the 200m freestyle, where she finished as second American, did she confirm her form of the U.S. Trials.

Rothhammer proved to be equally unpredictable at the 1973 World Championships. Although she was the reigning Olympic champion, she failed to win a medal in the 800m; in the 200m she was the U.S. second choice, but won the World Championship; and in the 400m, in which she was the current world record holder, she lost to her teammate, Heather Greenwood.

Rothhammer retired after that year and attended Southern Cal. She has since competed in the Women's Superstars on ABC Television and done color commentary at swim meets for CBS.

RUUSKA, Sylvia Eliina.

B. 04 JUL 1942 Berkeley, CA. Silver: 1956 4 × 100 meter freestyle relay; Bronze: 1956 400 meter freestyle. Sylvia Ruuska developed through the age-group swim program and, together with her younger sister Pat, was a star performer on her father's Berkeley YMCA team that twice won the AAU national team championship. She set five world records and won 20 AAU titles, including the 400y individual medley for five straight years from 1956.

She was aged only 14 when she won her two medals at the 1956 Games. On her second Olympic appearance in 1960 at Rome, she was appointed captain of the women's swim team, but swam only the heats of the freestyle relay.

SAVILLE, Eleanor A. Garatti.

B. 12 JUN 1909. Gold(2): 1928 4 × 100 meter freestyle relay, 1932 4 × 100 meter freestyle relay; Silver: 1928 100 meter freestyle; Bronze: 1932 100 meter freestyle. Competing in 1928 as Miss Eleanor Garatti, and in 1932 as Mrs. Saville, she was the only U.S. swimmer to be on the winning relay teams at both the Amsterdam and Los Angeles Olympics. On both occasions she helped the U.S. to new world records.

In the 100m freestyle, Saville-Garatti bettered the Olympic record in the heats in both 1928 and 1932, but failed to win either final. However she had the distinction of becoming the first woman to win two individual Olympic medals in the shortest freestyle event. When she won the second of her two AAU 100m outdoor freestyle titles in 1929, she set a new world record, becoming the first woman to swim under 1:10 for the distance.

SCHOENFIELD, Dana Lee.

B. 13 AUG 1953 Harvey, IL. Silver: 1972 200 meter breaststroke. Dana Schoenfield won her only AAU championship in 1972, when she took the 200m breaststroke title. The AAU's also served as the Final Olympic Trials in 1972 and she confirmed her form by being the first American to finish in the 200m breaststroke at the Olympics.

Schoenfield went on to study communications at UCLA and has worked for several years in public relations with an advertising firm in California. While at UCLA she met her husband, Robert Reyes, who played football for UCLA in the 1976 Rose Bowl. Mrs. Dana Schoenfield Reyes has also begun a new career, studying dance and acting, and has recently appeared in a theatre production of the play "Pippin."

SCHROTH, Frances Cowells.

B. 11 APR 1893. Ddi. Gold: 1920 4 × 100 meter freestyle; Bronze(2): 1920 100 meter freestyle, 1920 300 meter freestyle. Mrs. Frances Schroth, from Oakland, California, shared with Ethelda Bleibtrey the distinction of winning three swimming medals at the 1920 Olympics. She was married to George Schroth, also a noted swimmer, who won a bronze medal as a member of the 1924 U.S. water polo team. They were divorced shortly after the 1924 Olympics.

SCHULER, Carolyn Jane.

B. 05 JAN 1943 San Francisco, CA. Gold(2): 1960 100 meter butterfly, 1960 4 × 100 meter medley relay. After placing second in the 100m butterfly at the 1960 U.S. Trials, Carolyn Schuler of the Berkeley YMCA competed in the individual event and swam the butterfly leg on the medley relay team at Rome. The winner of the butterfly in the U.S. Trials was Carolyn Wood, but Wood failed to finish at the Olympics when she swallowed water at the turn. This eliminated Schuler's main competition and she won rather easily. Her relay gold medal also brought her a share of a new world record.

SEARS, Mary Jane.
B. 10 MAY 1939 Plymouth, VA. Bronze: 1956 100 meter butterfly. Although Mary Sears was better known at home as a breaststroker, it was in the butterfly that she won her Olympic medal, after finishing no better than seventh in the 200m breaststroke in Melbourne. Sears, who competed for the Walter Reed SC, won four AAU titles indoors and four outdoors in breaststroke events, but she never won a national championship using the style that took her to an Olympic medal. Miss Sears later became Mrs. William Parks and, with her husband, has raised four children.

SHIELDS, Susan.
B. 03 FEB 1952 Erie, PA. Bronze: 1968 100 meter butterfly. Susie Shields swam for the Plantation SC in Louisville, Kentucky. After finishing second in the 100m fly at the 1968 AAU she confirmed her second ranking among Americans by taking the bronze medal in Mexico behind Lynnette McClements of Australia and her American teammate, Ellie Daniel.

SIERING, Lauri Gail.
B. 23 FEB 1957 Pomona, CA. Silver: 1976 4 × 100 meter medley relay. Lauri Siering was the breaststroke specialist on the medley relay team at the 1976 Olympics. She also competed in the two individual breaststroke events at Montreal, failing to survive the heats of the 200m and being eliminated in the semi-finals of the 100m. Siering overcame severe problems with asthma and hay fever to become a world-class swimmer. After difficult workouts she would often become ill because of problems getting a full breath, and for the Montreal Olympics she was at less than her best because her normal medication was banned by the IOC and she had to switch to a different drug.

Siering later attended Southern Cal, where she was coached by former Olympian "Pokey" Watson-Richardson.

SIMONS, Nancy Joan.
B. 20 MAY 1938 Oakland, CA. Silver: 1956 4 × 100 meter freestyle relay. Nancy Simons was a student at Northwestern and also competed for the Chicago Town Club. In the 1956 Olympics she was eliminated in the semi-finals of the individual 100m freestyle. She then joined the relay team that bettered the world record in the Olympic final, but still finished two seconds down to the Australian quartette. Although she never won an AAU title, she set a U.S. long-course record for the 400m freestyle in 1954. She is now Mrs. Peterson.

SPILLANE, Joan Arlene.
B. 31 JAN 1943 Glen Ridge, NJ. Gold: 1960 4 × 100 meter freestyle relay. After taking the silver medal in the 100m freestyle at the 1959 Pan-American Games, Joan Spillane placed third at the 1960 U.S. Final Trials but only swam in the relays at the Rome Olympics. She competed in the heats of the medley relay and the final of the freestyle relay where, swimming the first stage, she put the U.S. on their way to the gold medals and a new world record.

STEPAN, Marilee.
B. 02 FEB 1935. Bronze: 1952 4 × 100 meter freestyle relay. Swimming for the Lake Shore Club of Chicago, Marilee Stepan took third place at the 1952 Final Trials in the 100m freestyle and then placed seventh in the Olympic final. She later won a bronze medal in the relay; the only AAU title she won was the indoor 220y freestyle in 1952.

STERKEL, Jill.
B. 27 MAY 1961 Los Angeles, CA. Gold: 1976 4 × 100 meter freestyle relay. At the 1975 Pan-American Games, Jill Sterkel won a gold medal in the relay and a silver in the individual 100m freestyle. At the 1976 Olympics she again won a relay gold, but fared less well in the individual freestyle events, placing seventh in the 100m final and losing out in the heats of the 200m free.

Jill Sterkel won her only individual AAU title when she won the outdoor 100m freestyle in 1976, but she led her club to the AAU freestyle relay title, both indoors and out, that year. Sterkel swam for the El Monte AC with the same coach, Don LaMont, who trained Sandy Neilsen.

STICKLES, Terri Lee.

B. 11 MAY 1946 San Mateo, CA. Bronze: 1964 400 meter freestyle. In September 1964, Terri Stickles was a member of the U.S. team that set a new 400 meter freestyle relay record, but at the Tokyo Olympics the following month she swam only in the individual 400m freestyle, where she completed a medal sweep for the United States by taking the bronze medal behind Ginny Duenkel and Marilyn Ramenofsky. In 1963, Stickles won the 100m freestyle at the Pan-American Games. Swimming for the Santa Clara SC, she won four AAU indoor titles.

STOBS, Shirley Anne.

B. 20 MAY 1942 Miami, FL. Gold: 1960 4 × 100 meter freestyle relay. Prior to winning a gold in the Olympic relay in 1960, Shirley Stobs' greatest success had been a silver medal in the 200m freestyle at the 1959 Pan-American Games. She swam for the Miami Shores CC and won her only AAU title when she took the indoor 100y freestyle in 1959.

STOUDER, Sharon Marie.

B. 09 NOV 1948 Altadena, CA. Gold(3): 1964 100 meter butterfly, 1964 4 × 100 meter freestyle relay, 1964 4 × 100 meter medley relay; Silver: 1964 100 meter freestyle. Fifteen-year-old Sharon Stouder from Glendora High School in California was the surprise swimmer of the 1964 Olympics. She was the unexpected winner of the 100m butterfly, defeating the highly favored Ada Kok and depriving the Dutch girl of her world record in the bargain. In the 100m freestyle she nearly caused even a greater upset, finishing only 0.4 seconds down to the great Dawn Fraser. In taking the silver medal she became the second woman to break the one-minute barrier. She won two more golds in the relays, picking up world record shares in both events.

Her other successes included a gold medal in the medley relay at the 1963 Pan-American Games, and at the 1964 AAU outdoor championships she won the 100m freestyle and both butterfly events, bettering her own world record in the 200 fly.

SWAGERTY, Jane.

B. 30 JUL 1951 Oakdale, CA. Bronze: 1968 100 meter backstroke. At the 1968 Final Trials, Jane Swagerty finished second to Kaye Hall in the 100m backstroke. At

Courtesy Jane Swagerty Caldwell

Jane Swagerty, backstroke swimming bronze medalist at the 1968 Olympics.

the Olympics she again placed behind Miss Hall and with the favored Canadian, Elaine Tanner, also finishing ahead of her, she took the bronze medal. Jane Swagerty, who represented the Santa Clara AC and the University of the Pacific, also swam in the heats of the medley relay at the Mexico Olympics.

THORNTON, Karen Patricia Moe.

B. 22 JAN 1952 Del Monte, Philippines. Gold: 1972 200 meter butterfly. Born in the Philippines but educated at Santa Clara High School and UCLA, Karen Moe set her fourth and final 200m butterfly world record in winning the Olympic title in Munich. She also competed in the 100m backstroke at the 1972 Olympics, finishing fourth. After marrying Mike Thornton, she made a comeback in 1976 and again made the Olympic team, finishing fourth in the 200m butterfly at Montreal, but with a new American record.

Mrs. Thornton has served as head coach of the women's swim team at Cal/Berkeley since her retirement from competition.

VIDALI, Lynn Marie.

B. 26 MAY 1952 San Francisco, CA. Silver: 1968 400 meter individual medley; Bronze: 1972 200 meter individual medley. Between her two Olympic medals, Lynn Vidali won four AAU titles in the individual medley and one in the breaststroke. In addition to her bronze medal in the 200m IM in Munich, she swam in the 100m breaststroke but was eliminated in the heats. In the 400m IM she placed seventh as, for the first time, the U.S. failed to win a medal in this event.

Von SALTZA, Susan Christine.

B. 03 JAN 1944 San Francisco, CA. Gold(3): 1960 400 meter freestyle, 1960 4 × 100 meter freestyle relay, 1960 4 × 100 meter medley relay; Silver: 1960 100 meter freestyle. After winning five golds at the 1959 Pan-American Games, Chris Von Saltza lived up to her advance billing by taking three Olympic golds in 1960. Her 400m freestyle victory ended the long-standing Australian domination of this event, but her victory at Rome was not unexpected because at the U.S. Trials she had set a new world record of 4:44.5 to become the first American woman to break the five-minute barrier.

Von Saltza swam for the Santa Clara SC and led them to many team victories at the nationals, in addition to winning 19 individual AAU titles. After she retired from competitive swimming, she entered Stanford, where she majored in Asian history. She later served the U.S. women's swim team as an assistant coach/ chaperone at the 1968 Olympics. Miss Von Saltza was more properly the Baroness Von Saltza as her grandfather, Count Philip, came to America at the turn of the century, and she is still recognized by her titled name in the *Who's Who of Swedish Nobility*.

WAINWRIGHT, Helen E.

B. 15 MAR 1906. Silver: 1920 Springboard (Diving), 1924 400 meter freestyle. See the diving section for the biography.

WATSON, Lillian Debra.

B. 11 JUL 1950 Mineola, NY. Gold(2): 1964 4 × 100 meter freestyle relay, 1968 200 meter backstroke. "Pokey" Watson was yet another U.S. swimming star to come from the Santa Clara SC. After her relay gold medal in 1964 she won three AAU outdoor freestyle titles, but she went to Mexico without a national backstroke title to her credit and still won the Olympic title by a handsome margin. One of her three AAU freestyle championships came in 1966 when she set a world record for 200m. She later became women's swim coach at Southern Cal.

WEHSELAU, Mariechen.

B. 15 APR 1906 Germany. Gold: 1924 4 × 100 meter freestyle relay; Silver: 1924 100 meter freestyle. Mariechen Wehselau, whose first name means "Little Marie" in German, was born of German parents, but her family moved to Hawaii shortly after World War I. She was the first great woman swimmer from the island paradise. At the 1924 Olympics she set a world record of 1:12.2 in winning the first heat of the 100m freestyle, but could not quite repeat that form in the final and lost to Ethel Lackie, who won by a touch in 1:12.4. She set a second world record later in the Games as a member of the winning relay team. After the Games she returned to Hawaii, where she became a swim coach for several years.

WEINBERG, Wendy Farber.

B. 27 JUN 1958 Baltimore, MD. Bronze: 1976 800 meter freestyle. The University of Virginia's Wendy Weinberg's first international success came at the 1973 Maccabiah Games, where she won four gold and three silver medals. She then won the 800m free at the 1975 Pan-American Games before placing second to Shirley Babashoff in the same event at the 1976 Olympic Trials. At the Olympics she again finished behind Babashoff, but with the East German, Petra Thumer, beating both Americans, Weinberg took the bronze.

WICHMAN, Sharon.

B. 13 MAY 1952 Detroit, MI. Gold: 1968 200 meter breaststroke; Silver: 1968 100 meter breaststroke. At the 1968 Olympics three swimmers—Galina Prozumenshikova of the USSR, Djurdjica Bjedova of Yugoslavia, and Sharon Wichman—shared all six medals in the two breaststroke events. Wichman, who competed for the Club Olympia in Indianapolis, also won two AAU breaststroke titles in the indoor short-course championships, winning the 200y in 1968 and the 100y in 1969.

WINGARD, Lenore Kight.
B. 26 SEP 1911. Silver: 1932 400 meter freestyle; Bronze: 1936 400 meter freestyle. Lenore Kight, and from 1936, Mrs. Lenore Wingard, won 23 AAU titles at distances ranging from 100y to one mile. Competing for the Carnegie Library Club of Homestead, Pennsylvania, she set a total of seven world and 24 U.S. records before turning pro in 1937. Her biggest professional victory came that same year when she won the "marathon" at the Toronto Canadian Exhibition.

WOOD, Carolyn Virginia.
B. 18 DEC 1945 Portland, OR. Gold: 1960 4 × 100 meter freestyle relay. Carolyn Wood, who swam for the Multnomah AC in her home town of Portland, competed in four events at the 1960 Olympics, when still only 14 years old. In the 100m freestyle she placed fourth, but in the 100m butterfly final she was forced to give up when she swallowed water near the turn. She swam in the medley relay, though only in the heats, but in the freestyle relay she won a well-deserved gold medal.

WOODBRIDGE, Margaret.
B. 1902. Gold: 1920 4 × 100 meter freestyle relay; Silver: 1920 300 meter freestyle. At the 1920 U.S. Final Trials, Margaret Woodbridge of the Detroit AC finished fifth in the 100m freestyle and fourth in the 300m freestyle. At the Olympics she improved in the 300m event to beat Francis Schroth and Eleanor Uhl, who had finished ahead of her at the Trials. Miss Woodbridge's only AAU title came in the indoor 220y freestyle in 1921.

WRIGHT, Camille.
B. 05 MAR 1955 New Albany, IN. Silver: 1976 4 × 100 meter medley relay. Camille Wright, who attended the University of Hawaii, won gold medals in the 100m and 200m butterfly and the medley relay at the 1975 Pan-American Games, and swam in all three events at the Olympics in the following year. At the Montreal Games she placed fourth in the 100m butterfly, was eliminated in the heats of the 200m fly, but matched her Pan-Am performance with an Olympic gold in the medley relay.

ZIMMERMAN, Suzanne W.
B. 13 JUL 1925. Silver: 1948 100 meter backstroke. After winning the AAU 100m freestyle title in 1942, Suzanne Zimmerman won seven outdoor backstroke championships over the next six years, a record bettered only by Carin Cone with eight. Indoors, Zimmerman, who represented the Detroit AC, won one indoor freestyle title and six backstroke championships. As these 16 AAU titles came between the years 1942 and 1948, Miss Zimmerman was certainly deprived of further Olympic honors by the cancellation of the 1944 Games.

TENNIS

MEN

Tennis, then called lawn tennis, appeared on every Olympic program between 1896 and 1924. The United States had very spotty participation, with two men in 1900 and one man in 1912. In 1904 all but one competitor at St. Louis was from the United States, and in 1924 we entered a full team. In 1896, 1906, 1908, and 1920 we had no competitors.

OUTSTANDING PERFORMANCES

Most Gold Medals
2 Vincent Richards, Beals Wright
Most Medals
3 Vincent Richards
Oldest Gold Medalist
c40y Spalding de Garmendia
Oldest Medalist
33y174d Dick Williams
Youngest Gold Medalist
21y115d Vincent Richards
Youngest Medalist
19y204d Robert LeRoy

BELL, Alphonzo Edward.
B. 29 SEP 1875 Los Angeles, CA. D. 27 DEC 1947 Los Angeles, CA. Silver: 1904 Men's Doubles; Bronze: 1904 Men's Singles (tied). Alphonzo Bell graduated from Occidental College in Los Angeles in 1895 and then studied at the San Francisco Theological Seminary for two years. In 1897 he entered into the first of his many real estate deals and, as a result of oil being found on one of his properties in 1922, he became an immensely wealthy man.

He won the first of his three Southern California singles titles in 1900 and was on the winning doubles team three times. He was ranked nationally only once when, in 1904, he was placed ninth in the singles ratings.

At the Olympics he was awarded joint third place in the singles after losing to the eventual champion, Beals Wright, in the semi-finals. In the doubles, Bell, and Robert LeRoy of Columbia University, lost in straight sets in the final to the Harvard pair of Wright and Edgar Leonard.

GAMBLE, Clarence Oliver.
B. 16 AUG 1881 St. Louis, MO. D. 13 JUN 1952 St. Louis, MO. Bronze: 1904 Men's Doubles (tied). In the 1904 men's doubles, Clarence Gamble partnered Arthur Wear. Together they won two matches before coming upon the team of Beals Wright and Edgar Leonard, the eventual champions, to whom they succumbed quite easily.

Gamble was not well known as a tennis player, but he was recognized as an all-round athlete. He attended Washington University (St. Louis) where he played football, baseball, and golf. In later years Gamble became a successful stock broker in St. Louis, where he worked for the same firm as his partner Arthur Wear.

GARMENDIA, Basil Spalding de.
B. 1860 Baltimore, MD. D. 09 NOV 1932 St. Raphael, France. Silver: 1900 Men's Doubles. Spalding de Garmendia was best known as a racquets player, having been the U.S. champion in that sport for six years beginning with the first time it was held in 1890. He was from a wealthy family in Baltimore and spent much of his life in France. He was there in 1900 and decided to try his hand at a similar sport, lawn tennis.

De Garmendia teamed up that year with Max Decugis of France, the most successful Olympic tennis player ever. They played well enough to reach the finals but, like every other pairing of that time, they were no match for the great Doherty brothers from England and went down in straight sets. In the singles, de Garmendia lost early, to the younger of the Doherty brothers, Laurie.

Spalding de Garmendia was also an accomplished golfer and polo player and was a member of the Organizing Committee for the Yachting Regatta at the 1900 Olympics. In 1895 he entered the first U.S. Amateur golf tournament, but did not get by the first round. Due to his family's wealth he never had to work, but served during World War I as a special attache to the American Embassy in Paris.

HUNTER, Francis Townsend.
B. 28 JUN 1894 New York, NY. D. 02 DEC 1981 Palm Beach, FL. Gold: 1924 Men's Doubles. In the days when lissome stroke players reigned supreme, Frank Hunter, a rugged former captain of the Cornell hockey team, was a noticeable figure on the tennis court. Hunter

went out of the 1924 Olympic singles in the third round. In the doubles he was joined by Vinnie Richards and after a five-setter in the semi-final against Jean Borotra and Rene Lacoste of France and a final, which also went the full distance, against two more Frenchmen—Jacques Brugnon and Henri Cochet—the U.S. pairing took the Olympic title.

Hunter and Richards had won the Wimbledon doubles earlier in the season and Hunter won again at Wimbledon in 1927 with Bill Tilden as his partner. Hunter and Tilden also won the U.S. doubles in 1927 and they played together in the Davis Cup in 1927 and 1928. Hunter won the mixed doubles at Wimbledon in 1927 and 1929 before turning professional in 1931.

In World War I he served as a lt. commander in the navy and was assigned to Admiral Beatty's flagship when the German fleet surrendered. He later wrote a book about his experience of serving under Beatty.

Frank Hunter ultimately prospered in the business world. After involvements in the coal industry and newspaper publishing he founded, in 1935, "21" Brands Inc., and later "21" Brands Distillers, and served as president of both corporations.

LEONARD, Edgar Welch.

B. 19 JUN 1881 West Newton, MA. D. 07 OCT 1948 New York, NY. Gold: 1904 Men's Doubles, Bronze: 1904 Men's Singles. Together with his Harvard classmate, Beals Wright, Edgar Leonard took the 1904 Olympic doubles title, losing only one set in the four matches they played. In the singles that year, Leonard lost in the semi-finals to the eventual runner-up, Robert LeRoy.

Leonard graduated Harvard in 1903 after having captained the tennis team and having shared the intercollegiate doubles title in 1902. He never won a national championship, but in 1903 he achieved his highest national ranking of eighth.

Leonard became a very successful businessman in a number of different fields. After college he helped his father run the family wool business, but in 1915 Leonard settled in New York, where he helped establish the brokerage firm of Moore, Leonard, & Lynch. This was his primary occupation for the rest of his life although he served on the board of several companies. During these years Leonard occupied his leisure hours with court tennis and polo.

LeROY, Robert.

B. 07 FEB 1885 New York, NY. D. 07 SEP 1946 New York, NY. Silver(2): 1904 Men's Singles, 1904 Men's Doubles. Apart from Beals Wright, Robert LeRoy was the most successful lawn tennis player at the 1904 Olympics, winning two silver medals. LeRoy played in the Olympic tennis event while a student at Columbia University, from which he graduated in 1905. He later went on to Columbia Law, earning his LL.B. in 1908. It was at law that LeRoy did his life's work, mainly with the firm of Cadwalader, Wickersham, and Taft on Wall Street.

LeRoy never won a national tennis championship, but was three times ranked among America's top ten players, reaching as high as fifth in 1907. His wife, née Grace Arnold Moore, was also a fine player, winning the women's championship several times at the West Side Tennis Club in Queens, NY.

Robert LeRoy was instrumental, in 1923, in establishing the Museum of the City of New York. He served as secretary and trustee of that institution until his death.

RICHARDS, Vincent.

B. 20 MAR 1903 New York, NY. D. 28 SEP 1959 New York, NY. Gold(2): 1924 Men's Singles, 1924 Men's Doubles; Silver: 1924 Mixed Doubles. In 1918, Vinnie Richards, at the age of 15 years 139 days, became the youngest player ever to win a U.S. national title when he won the men's doubles with Bill Tilden. He was a student at Fordham Prep at the time and later attended Fordham University and Columbia University. Richards went on to win four more U.S. men's doubles titles, and he won once at Wimbledon, once at the French championships, and took the U.S. mixed doubles twice.

Although he was the only triple medal winner in the 1924 Olympic lawn tennis events, he survived some desperately close matches. Of the five matches Richards played on the way to the singles title, three went to five sets and another to four sets. Both the semi-final and the final of the men's doubles went to five sets and, adding in his mixed doubles schedule, it is not surprising that Richards lost 18 lbs. during the tournament. After the Davis Cup matches of 1926, Vinnie Richards turned professional at the age of 23 and won the first U.S. pro singles title.

WEAR, Arthur Yancey.

B. 01 MAR 1880 St. Louis, MO. D. 06 NOV 1918 Pouilly, France. Bronze: 1904 Men's Doubles (tied). At Yale, Arthur Wear was a member of the freshman, college, and university baseball teams, but was not noted as a lawn tennis player. But for the doubles at the 1904 Olympics he teamed up with Clarence Gamble and they lost to the winners, Wright and Leonard, in the semi-finals.

After graduating from Yale, Wear joined the family dry goods business in St. Louis in 1903 and remained with the firm until the outbreak of the war. He commanded an infantry company in the battle of St. Mihiel and, although not actually wounded, his health suffered badly; as a result of refusing to obtain proper treatment for a probable perforated duodenal ulcer, he died, still commanding his battalion, during the Meuse-Argonne fighting. His older brother, Joseph Wear, also won a bronze medal at the 1904 Olympics.

WEAR, Joseph Walker.

B. 27 NOV 1876 St. Louis, MO. D. 04 JUN 1941 Philadelphia, PA. Bronze: 1904 Men's Doubles (tied). On graduating from Yale in 1899, Joseph Wear initially worked for the family dry goods business, but later became an investment banker and a partner in a brokerage firm in Philadelphia.

At the St. Louis Olympics, Allen West was Wear's partner in the doubles and they lost in the semi-finals to Alphonzo Bell and Robert LeRoy. Wear was the U.S. court tennis doubles champion five times (with Jay Gould) and won the racquet doubles championship three times. With his son, William, he won the now-defunct U.S. father and son lawn tennis championship in 1923. Joseph Wear continued to serve the sport of lawn tennis after his playing days were over. He was first vice president of the USLTA (1936-41), chairman of the Davis Cup committee (1928-1931), and nonplaying captain of the Davis Cup team in 1935.

Apart from their close connection with the Davis Cup, the Wear family also had an association with the Walker Cup—Joseph and Arthur's sister, Lucretia, married George Herbert Walker, the donor of the trophy which is played for by British and U.S. amateur golfers.

WEST, Allen Tarwater.

B. 1880 Mobile, AL. D. 1924. Bronze: 1904 Men's Doubles (tied). Allen West partnered Joseph Wear in the 1904 men's doubles and together they made it to the semi-finals before losing. This was West's most notable achievement in tennis. West was much better known as a golfer and in 1922 he won the prestigious Broadmoor Invitational in Colorado. Like many of the other tennis players in 1904, West's career was as a stock broker in St. Louis.

WILLIAMS, Richard Norris, III.

B. 29 JAN 1891 Geneva, Switzerland. D. 02 JUN 1968 Bryn Mawr, PA. Gold: 1924 Mixed Doubles. The early years of Dick Williams' life were spent in Lausanne where his father, a tennis enthusiast, was working; under his father's tutelage he won the Swiss Junior title at the age of 12. In 1912, Mr. Williams accompanied his son to America when Dick was accepted for Harvard. Tragically, they chose to travel aboard the ill-fated Titanic. Although his son survived the ordeal of spending more than an hour in the icy Atlantic, Mr. Williams, Sr. perished.

Dick Williams won the mixed doubles at the U.S. championships and the national clay court singles in his first American season (1912) and was ranked second nationally that year. In 1913, while still at Harvard, he began his Davis Cup career and in his eight single matches that year he lost only to James Parke, the Irish rugby football international, in the match against Great Britain. Williams was to remain a Davis Cup player until 1926 and in the intervening years he won the U.S. singles title twice and the men's doubles on two occasions.

Williams graduated from Harvard in 1916 and was soon with the armed forces. He saw active service as a captain of artillery and served as an aide to Major Gen. John Harbord, winning the Croix de Guerre and the Legion d'Honneur in the second battle of the Marne. After the war, Williams played his tennis at the Longwood Cricket Club and started his career as a stockbroker. In 1920 he teamed up with Charles Garland and they became the only Harvard/Yale combination to ever win the Wimbledon doubles. At the 1924 Olympics, Dick Williams went out to Henri Cochet in the quarter-finals of the singles; in the men's doubles, playing with his former Harvard teammate, Watson

Washburn, he again lost in the quarter-finals when the South Africans, Condon and Richardson, came back to win after trailing by two sets to one. However, in the mixed doubles, with Hazel Wightman as his partner, they scored a comfortable victory after disposing of the Wimbledon champions, Kitty McKane and John Gilbert of Great Britain, in the semi-finals.

WRIGHT, Beals Coleman.

B. 19 DEC 1879 Boston, MA. D. 23 AUG 1961. Gold(2): 1904 Men's Singles, 1904 Men's Doubles. In 1869, Harry Wright, the English-born son of a cricket professional, formed the first professional baseball team in America. Harry Wright was the player-manager of the Cincinnati Red Stockings and included on the team was his younger brother, George, who drew the then-record salary of $1,400 for the season. As the popularity of pro baseball increased, George Wright was to earn much more than this and prospered sufficiently to send his son, Beals, to Harvard.

Beals Wright was to become one of the leading players in the early days of lawn tennis in America, but surprisingly he never won his letter at Harvard. He was America's first Olympic lawn tennis champion, winning the singles and doubles (with Edgar Leonard) in 1904. These two Olympics titles came relatively early in his career although three years previously he had been runner-up in the U.S. singles. Beals Wright was destined to be runner-up on four other occasions, but in 1905 he took the national title by beating Holcombe Ward, a fellow Harvardian. Wright and Ward won the doubles for three straight years (1904-1906) and in 1910, at the age of 30, the left-handed Wright became the first American to reach the final of the All-Comer's singles at Wimbledon, where he lost to the New Zealander, Tony Wilding, who went on to win the Challenge Round.

Apart from these successes, Wright will also be remembered for his contribution to the Davis Cup squad. He was on the team in 1905, 1907, 1908, and 1911 and although the U.S. reached the Challenge Round in three of those years, they never succeeded in winning the Cup. They lost by only three matches to two in 1908 against Australasia in Melbourne, and Wright's magnificent victories over Tony Wilding and Norman Brooks put the U.S. within an ace of winning the tie. In his later years, Wright maintained his keen interest in the sport and served a term as president of the USLTA.

WOMEN

American women have competed in Olympic tennis only in 1900 and 1924. It was the sport in which women first competed in the Olympics and the first two female American Olympians were two sisters from the West Side Tennis Club, Marion and Georgina Jones, who competed in singles and mixed doubles at the 1900 Olympics.

OUTSTANDING PERFORMANCES

Most Gold Medals
   2 Hazel Wightman, Helen Wills
Most Medals
   2 Marion Jones, Hazel Wightman,
      Helen Wills
Oldest Gold Medalist
   37y214d Hazel Wightman
Youngest Gold Medalist
   18y281d Helen Wills

JESSUP, Marion Zinderstein.

B. 02 MAY 1897. Silver: 1924 Mixed Doubles. After being eliminated in the first round of the ladies' doubles and the quarter-finals of the singles, Marion Jessup reached the finals of the 1924 Olympic mixed doubles with Vinnie Richards as her partner. They lost the final to another U.S. pair, Hazel Wightman and Dick Williams, 2-6, 3-6.

Jessup reached the finals of the U.S. singles in 1919 and 1920 and won the ladies' doubles in 1918, 1919, and 1920 (as Miss Zinderstein) and again in 1922 (as Mrs. Jessup). She also won the mixed doubles in 1919 with her future Olympic partner, Vinnie Richards.

Marion Jessup was coached by Hazel Wightman and together they won four national indoor doubles championships between 1919 and 1927. More than two decades later they teamed up again and won the national veterans' doubles in 1948.

JONES, Marion.

B. 02 NOV 1879 Nevada. D. 14 MAR 1965 Los Angeles, CA. Bronze(2): 1900 Ladies' Singles (tied), 1900 Mixed Doubles (tied). Marion Jones deserves an exalted place among United States Olympians. She was the first American woman to win a medal at the Olympic Games when, on 9 July 1900, she won two bronze medals in tennis—one for the ladies' singles, one for the mixed doubles. In doubles she teamed with the great British star, Laurie Doherty, in an international pairing.

Jones was one of the top American tennis stars at the turn of the century. She and her sister, Georgina (who also competed in the 1900 Olympic tennis events) played at the West Side Tennis Club in New York. The practice enabled Marion to twice win the U.S. women's title (1899, 1902) and once win the U.S. mixed doubles title (1901). In addition, Miss Jones was the first non-British woman to ever play at Wimbledon, reaching the quarter-finals there in the 1900 ladies' singles.

Jones' family was from Nevada, where her father, John Percival Jones, was a five-time U.S. Senator. Jones eventually married Robert Farquhar, but they divorced shortly thereafter. From 1920 until 1961, Marion Jones Farquhar lived in Greenwich Village, where she was well known as a violinist and voice coach. She also translated opera librettos and for a short time was head of the New York Chamber Opera. In 1961 she moved to Los Angeles, where she lived until her death.

WIGHTMAN, Hazel Virginia Hotchkiss.

B. 20 DEC 1886 Healdbury, CA. D. 05 DEC 1974 Chestnut Hill, MA. Gold(2): 1924 Ladies' Doubles, 1924 Mixed Doubles. Multiple champion on all surfaces in all age groups, renowned coach and administrator, and donor of the Wightman Cup, Hazel Wightman was one of the legendary figures of lawn tennis.

In 1912, Hazel Hotchkiss married George Wightman, who later became the president of the USLTA, and although she gave birth to three children during the following seven years, she still won a total of 16 U.S. championships between 1909 and 1928. She would win 50 national titles in all. She donated the Wightman Cup as the trophy for an international team match between the best female amateurs of Britain and the U.S., and the first competition for the cup was held in 1923. Hazel not only was the donor of the cup that year, but she played on the U.S. team, a feat she repeated in 1924, 1927, 1929, and 1931. Though in recent years the competition has been rather one-sided, the Wightman Cup is still a coveted trophy.

In 1924, Hazel Wightman journeyed to Paris, where she opted not to play in the Olympic ladies' singles event. She saved her best for the ladies' and mixed doubles events and partnered Dick Williams and Helen Wills to comfortable victories in those events. Though in later years she continued to play tennis, and win championships, she also became a well-known coach, numbering among her pupils Marion Zinderstein Jessup and Helen Wills Moody. At the Jubilee Wightman Cup match at Boston in 1973, Hazel Wightman was accorded perhaps her greatest honor—an Honorary C.B.E.

WILLS, Helen Newington.

B. 06 OCT 1905 Berkeley, CA. Gold(2): 1924 Ladies' Singles, 1924 Ladies' Doubles. Rated by many authorities as the greatest woman player of all time, Helen Wills Moody won a total of 31 titles at Wimbledon and the U.S. and French championships. She came east from California while still a pigtailed teenager to win her first major title in 1922. She would eventually win eight Wimbledon and seven U.S. singles titles, with her last being the Wimbledon championship in 1938. This impressive total of victories was accomplished despite the fact that she did not play in the U.S. championships after 1933 because of an estrangement with the authorities.

Helen Wills won the Olympic singles in 1924 without the loss of a set and added a second gold medal by taking the doubles with her coach, Hazel Wightman, who was almost 20 years her senior.

Helen Wills was educated at the University of California (Berkeley). In 1929 she became Mrs. Moody and in 1939 she again married, this time Mr. A. Roark. Today, as Mrs. Helen Roark, she has retired to a quiet life in her native California.

TRACK & FIELD (Athletics)

MEN

The United States' domination of men's track & field is unparalleled among nonteam Olympic sports. And among team sports, only our domination of basketball, and India's field hockey supremacy, surpasses it. Numbers do not always tell the true story, but here they state our case powerfully. The United States has won 532 medals in men's track & field—which is more than the seven next best countries combined. We have won 225 gold medals—more than the 19 next best countries combined. At every Olympic Games, the U.S. has won the most gold medals in men's track & field, the most silver medals, and only three times has another country won the most bronze medals at any Olympics. The United States has won the most medals in every event except the 1,500, 5,000, 10,000, the walks, the steeple-chase, and triple jump; we have won the most gold medals in all events except for those and the javelin throw.

One often reads that we are no longer the world's top track & field power, having been surpassed by either the USSR or East Germany. This is untrue. *Track & Field News*, "The Bible of the Sport," publishes annual rankings and with these lists, the point leaders in the rankings, among nations, every year. The United States has never failed to finish first in these rankings and the discussion each year is usually how big was our lead. While true that we win fewer medals today than years ago, it is due as much to the appearance of many more competitive countries as to any one single threat to our dominance.

ABLOWICH, Edgar Allen.
B. 29 APR 1913. D. 1981 St. Petersburg, FL. Gold: 1932 4×400 meter relay. Fourth place at the Olympic Trials earned Ed Ablowich, the 19-year-old from Southern Cal, a place on the Olympic relay team. He ran a creditable second leg of 47.6 when hard pressed by Tom Hampson (GBR), the newly crowned 800 meter champion. Ablowich also finished second in the 1934 AAU 400 m. hurdles. His son, Ron, also a talented intermediate hurdler at Georgia Tech, ran in the 1960 Olympic Trials but failed to make the team for Rome.

ADAMS, Benjamin W.
B. 31 MAR 1890. D. 14 MAR 1961 Neptune, NJ. Silver: 1912 Standing High Jump; Bronze: 1912 Standing Long

OUTSTANDING PERFORMANCES

Most Gold Medals
10 Ray Ewry
5 Martin Sheridan
Most Medals
10 Ray Ewry
9 Martin Sheridan
6 Robert Garrett, Jim Lightbody, Ralph Rose
Most Gold Medals (Games)
4 Alvin Kraenzlein, Jesse Owens
Most Medals (Games)
5 Irving Baxter, Martin Sheridan, Walter Tewksbury
Most Silver Medals
3 Irving Baxter, Martin Sheridan
Most Bronze Medals
3 Robert Garrett
Consecutive Wins, Same Event
4 Al Oerter (1956/60/64/68 discus)
3 John Flanagan (1900/04/08 hammer), Frank Wykoff (1928/32/36 400 relay), Martin Sheridan (1904/06/08 discus)
Most Years Between Golds
12 Al Oerter (1956–1968)
Most Years Between Medals
16 Matt McGrath (1908–1924)
Most Years Between Appearances
16 Matt McGrath (1908–24), Clarence DeMar (1912–1928), George Crosbie (1932–48), Ron Laird (1960–76)
Most Appearances (track events)
4 George Bonhag, George Young, Willie Davenport, Ron Laird
Most Appearances (field events)
4 Ray Ewry, Matt McGrath, Parry O'Brien, Hal Connolly, Al Hall, Al Oerter, Jay Silvester
Oldest Gold Medalist
42y26d Patrick McDonald
Oldest Medalist
45y205d Matt McGrath
Youngest Gold Medalist
17y263d Bob Mathias

Jump. A stalwart of the New York AC team for many years, Ben Adams never won an AAU title because his older brother monopolized them at that time. His second place in the standing high jump was a notable moment in Olympic history because this is the only time that brothers have finished 1–2 in a track and field event.

ADAMS, Platt.

B. 23 MAR 1885 Belleville, NJ. D. 27 FEB 1961 Normandy Beach, NJ. Gold: 1912 Standing High Jump; Silver: 1912 Standing Long Jump. Platt Adams won the AAU junior long jump in 1907 and then took 20 senior titles while representing the New York AC. Apart from his prowess in the standing jumps he finished fifth in the Olympic triple jump in 1908 and 1912 and was the leading American on each occasion.

ALBRITTON, David Donald.

B. 13 APR 1913 Danville, AL. Silver: 1936 High Jump. Both Dave Albritton and "Corney" Johnson cleared 6'-9¾" at the 1936 Olympic Trials to become the first black athletes to hold the world high jump record. However, Albritton will be remembered best for his career's longevity. Apart from 1941 to 1943, when he was in the service, he competed in the AAU championship from 1936 through 1951. He finished first (or equal first) on five occasions, placed second once, and was third (or equal third) four times. Representing Ohio State he also finished first in the NCAA (1936-38) and was a notable performer on the indoor circuit, where his best mark was 6'-8", which he cleared in 1948 at the age of 34.

Albritton later went on to a career as a politician and in 1966 was elected to the Ohio House of Representatives.

ALDERMAN, Frederick Pitt.

B. 24 JUN 1905 East Lansing, MI. Gold: 1928 4 × 400 meter relay. After winning the Central Olympic Trials in a career best of 48.0, Alderman withdrew from the Final Trials but was selected for the relay squad in Amsterdam. He ran poorly in the Olympic final, with an estimated time of no better than 49.4 on the third leg, losing ground to both Storz (GER) and Rinkel (GBR). He won the IC4A 440y for Michigan State in 1927.

ANDERSON, John Franklin.

B. 04 JUL 1907 Cincinnati, OH. D. 11 JUL 1948 Nankek, AK. Gold: 1932 Discus Throw. After placing fifth in the 1928 discus, John Anderson improved to beat the world record holder, Paul Jessup, at the 1932 Final Trials. He then took the gold medal in Los Angeles with a new Olympic record. He won the AAU title in 1933 and in June 1936 he had the best throw of his career in winning the Eastern Olympic Trials—165'-9"—but he failed to make a third consecutive Olympic team. Anderson was also an above-average performer with the shot and won the 1929 IC4A indoor shot put title.

While at Cornell, Anderson played tackle on the football team for three years, was on the track team for three years, captaining it as a senior, and was president of the student council in his last year.

Anderson was thought by Hollywood to have "dazzling masculine beauty" and after the 1932 Olympics he stayed on in California to star in the film "Search for Beauty." Later, experience gained in the Pacific during the war as a lieutenant commander in the naval reserve led to his obtaining a post as chief navigator of a salmon fishing fleet. While on an expedition some 700 miles north of Anchorage, he suffered a brain hemorrhage and died immediately, aged only 41.

ANDERSON, Stephen Eugene.

B. 06 APR 1906. Silver: 1928 110 meter hurdles. Steve Anderson equalled the world record of 14.4 a total of five times, the last time being in 1930 when he won his third consecutive AAU title. This was the only clocking that received official IAAF recognition. He looked a likely winner of the 1928 Olympic crown when the South African, Weightman-Smith, hit the ninth hurdle and left Anderson with a narrow lead, but another South African, Atkinson, came through to reach the tape inches ahead.

Representing the University of Washington, he won the NCAA 220y hurdles in 1929 and the high hurdles in 1930.

ASHBURNER, Lesley.

B. 02 OCT 1883. D. 12 NOV 1950. Bronze: 1904 110 meter hurdles. Although not known as an outstanding athlete at Cornell, Lesley Ashburner reached the final of the hurdles at St. Louis and missed second place by inches.

ASHENFELTER, Horace, III.

B. 23 JAN 1923 Phoenixville, PA. Gold: 1952 3,000 meter steeplechase. "Nip" Ashenfelter won his first AAU title when he took the 10,000m in 1950. The following day he ran his first steeplechase and finished fifth. He won the AAU steeplechase in 1951 and at the 1952 Olympic Trials ran 9:06.4 to better Harold Manning's 16-year-old U.S. record. Ashenfelter further improved the record to 8:51.0 in the Olympic heats in Helsinki; in a classic Olympic final he defeated the much-vaunted Russian, Vladimir Kazantsev, and posted a new world record of 8:45.4. He competed again at Melbourne but could do no better than sixth in a heat of the steeplechase.

During a long career, Ashenfelter won three AAU outdoor titles, was the indoor two mile champion for five successive years (1952–56) and over the same five-year period he led the New York AC to victory in the cross-country team event. In three of those years (1954–56), he also won the individual cross-country title.

After leaving Penn State, Ashenfelter joined the FBI in November 1951, but when he retired from competition after the 1956 Olympics, he also resigned from the Bureau and took a post in business, as a salesman for various metallurgy firms.

ASHWORTH, Gerald Howard.

B. 01 MAY 1942 Haverhill, MA. Gold: 1964 4 × 100 meter relay. After winning the IC4A 100y title for Dartmouth in 1962, Gerry Ashworth never won another major title. Fourth place at the Olympic Trials won him a place on the relay team at Tokyo, where Bob Hayes took the Americans to the tape first in a new world record of 39.0.

BABCOCK, Harold Stoddard.

B. 15 DEC 1890 Pelham Manor, NY. D. 15 JUN 1965 Norwalk, CT. Gold: 1912 Pole Vault. Harry Babcock began his career as a long jumper, placing third at the IC4As in 1909. He won the AAU pole vault in 1910 and 1912 and the IC4A title in 1911. Marc Wright set a new world record of 13′-2¼″ at the 1912 Olympic Trials, but in Stockholm, Babcock was always in command. Frank Nelson, Wright, and Babcock were the only competitors to clear 12′-7½″ and Babcock was the only one over when the bar was raised to 12′-9½″. He then went

---

ANY OF YOU PITCHERS THROW THE JAVELIN?

Pro baseball and the Olympics is a combination that just doesn't seem to mix. In fact only three United States Olympians have ever played at all in the major leagues. The amazing Jim Thorpe was the last — he played from 1913–1919 with the New York Giants and the Cincinnati Reds. The first was an obscure sprinter at the 1900 Olympics, Edmund Joseph "Cotton" Minahan. Minahan attended Georgetown University after his Olympic competition but in 1907 he found time to pitch in two games for the Cincinnati Reds, losing both. The second also competed in 1900, as a shooter. This was Albert Goodwill Spalding who had played major league baseball from 1871 until 1878, later founded the Spalding sporting goods company, and was inducted into the Hall of Fame in 1939.

---

on to clear 12′-11½″ before failing three times at a new world record height of 13′-3¾″.

Babcock graduated from Columbia in 1912 with an engineering degree, but spent most of his business life as a salesman with a lumber company in Irvington, New York.

BABKA, Richard Aldrich.

B. 23 SEP 1936 Cheyenne, WY. Silver: 1960 Discus Throw. After winning the AAU discus in 1958, "Rink" Babka never again managed to win this particular title, although for the next 10 years he was never out of the first six, was runner-up on three occasions, and placed third three times.

Babka set a world record of 196′-6½″ in August 1960 before going to Rome where he placed second behind Al Oerter at the Olympics. Babka enjoyed a remarkably long career at the top and his best mark ever came in 1968 when, at the age of 32, he threw 209′-9″. A graduate of USC in industrial management, he went on to work in the electronics industry.

Courtesy Mrs. Sarah Babcock Shauer

The 1912 pole vault gold medalist, Harry Babcock, as he appeared preparing to vault during that competition.

BACON, Charles Joseph, Jr.

B. 09 JAN 1885. D. 15 NOV 1968 Florida. Gold: 1908 400 meter hurdles. A prominent member of the Irish-American AC, Charles Bacon set a new world record of 57.0 in the heats of the 400m hurdles at the 1908 Olympics. The defending champion, Harry Hillman, brought the record down to 56.4 in the second round but, in the final Bacon beat Hillman on the run-in and further reduced the record to 55.0. Bacon won the AAU junior 880y title in 1903 but never won a national championship in the senior ranks.

BAIRD, George Hetzel.

B. 05 MAR 1907 Grand Island, NB. Gold: 1928 4 × 400 meter relay. After being eliminated in the semi-finals at

the 1928 Final Trials, Baird earned his trip to Amsterdam by winning a special race to decide the last two places on the relay team. At the Olympics he put the U.S. into a three-meter lead with an opening leg of 48.8, which his teammates carried on to a new world record of 3:14.2. He was also a member of the team that set a new world record of 3:13.4 for the 4 × 440y relay in London one week after the Olympics.

After graduating from the University of Iowa, Baird had a number of jobs during the early depression years and for a while worked with his brother who ran a well-known troupe of marionettes. He finally became an assistant professor of education at NYU, where he also had earned a master's degree.

BAKER, Walter Thane.

B. 04 OCT 1931 Elkhart, KS. Gold: 1956 4 × 100 meter relay; Silver(2): 1952 200 meters, 1956 100 meters; Bronze: 1956 200 meters. Thane Baker won the NCAA 220y in 1953 and the AAU 200m in 1956. Because he was generally considered at his best over the longer sprint, his second place in the 1956 Olympic 100m was one of the surprises of the Games. Baker was usually overshadowed by the likes of Bobby Morrow and Andy Stanfield at the major championship meets, but when measured against the stopwatch he could claim a truly impressive list of marks: 100y (9.4), 100m (10.2), 200m (20.6), 220y straight (20.4), and in 1956 he set a world "record" of 29.4 for 300 yards.

Baker majored in economics education at Kansas State and after serving in the air force he went into the oil business, working as a purchasing manager for Mobil. One of his daughters, Cathy, followed in her father's footsteps by winning the 1981 women's collegiate (Div. II) title at 800 meters. Baker is still active in track, acting as a starter and official at various meets. Through 1982 he held the world's age group records at 100m for the 40–44 and 45–49 year age groups.

BARBUTI, Raymond J.

B. 12 JUN 1905 Brooklyn, NY. Gold(2): 1928 400 meter, 1928 4 × 400 meter relay. Barbuti won his only AAU title in 1928, when the 400m final was run in a gale force wind and Barbuti's rugged strength enabled him to win in a seemingly modest 51.8. He improved that to 47.8 at the Olympics when he was the only American to win an individual track title. He was brought onto the relay team at the last minute and led the U.S. to a new world record of 3:14.2. The following week he claimed a share in a second world record when the U.S. ran 3:13.4 for the 4 × 440y in London in the match against the British Empire team.

Barbuti captained both the football and track teams at Syracuse. During his war service he was awarded the Air Medal and the Bronze Star and left the army air corps as a major. He later became deputy director of the Civil Defense Commission for New York State and director of the New York State Office of Disaster Preparedness. After his competitive days were over he was more interested in football than track and he officiated at more than 500 intercollegiate games.

BARNARD, Arthur.

B. 10 MAR 1929 Seattle, WA. Bronze: 1952 110 meter hurdles. Competing in an era dominated by such great hurdlers as Jack Davis, Harrison Dillard, and Dick Attlesey, Art Barnard never really came close to winning a major championship. His highest placing was third in the 1951 NCAA while attending Southern Cal. After finishing fifth at the 1952 AAUs he surprisingly improved to third place at the Olympic Trials, beating both Anderson and Dixon, who had finished ahead of him at the AAUs. In Helsinki, after a poor start, he finished third behind Harrison Dillard and Jack Davis.

BARNES, Lee Stratford.

B. 16 JUL 1906 Salt Lake City, UT. D. 28 DEC 1970 Oxnard, CA. Gold: 1924 Pole Vault. As a 15-year-old schoolboy at Hollywood High School, Barnes was consistently capable of clearing 12 feet and one week before his 18th birthday he won the Olympic title in Paris after a jump-off with Glenn Graham. On entering Southern Cal he came under the tutelage of the great coach, Dean Cromwell, and won the AAU in 1927 and 1928. In April 1928 he set a world record of 14'-1½" but was below form at the Amsterdam Olympics and finished only fifth. Barnes is the youngest competitor to ever win the Olympic pole vault. He later went on to become the head of his own manufacturing company in Oxnard, California.

BARRON, Harold Earl.

B. 29 AUG 1894 Philadelphia, PA. Silver: 1920 110 meter hurdles. After winning the AAU high hurdles in 1917, Hal Barron repeated in 1920 and also won the NCAA title in 1922. Indoors, over the 70y hurdles he won the AAU in 1918, 1921, and 1922 and the IC4A in 1922. Barron took the 1920 Olympic Trials in 15.2 and then equalled the Olympic record of 15.0 in the semifinals at Antwerp, but in the finals could not match the pace of the Canadian from Dartmouth, Earl Thomson, and finished in second place. After graduating from Penn State, Barron coached briefly at Mercersburg Academy and Cascadilla School (NY) before taking up an appointment as head coach at Georgia Tech.

BATES, Alfred Hilborn.

B. 24 APR 1905 Philadelphia, PA. Bronze: 1928 Long Jump. Bates won the IC4A indoor and outdoor long

Jim Bausch, decathlon gold medalist and future pro football player.

Courtesy University of Kansas Sports Information Dept.

jump titles in 1927 and 1928, his winning mark of 24'-10⅜" in the 1928 outdoor meet being the best of his career, and still the Penn State record. Bates also won the AAU outdoor championship in 1930 and 1931, representing the Meadowbrook Club of Philadelphia. In Amsterdam, the Olympic title went to Ed Hamm, whom Bates had beaten at the Final Trials; the Haitian, Silvio Cator, also finished ahead of Bates.

After graduation from Penn State, Bates worked as a budget analyst for 40 years before retiring. He remembers his biggest Olympic thrill occurring on the trip to Holland, when, while going thru the Holland canal, a U.S. Navy cruiser passed the Olympic ship. The navy band broke into "The Star Spangled Banner" while all the sailors stood at attention in honor of the Olympic athletes.

BAUSCH, James Aloysius Bernard.
B. 29 MAR 1906 Marion Junction, SD. D. 09 JUL 1974 Hot Springs, AK. Gold: 1932 Decathlon. Jim Bausch was a letterman in basketball, football, and track during his brief stay at Wichita University (now Wichita State) and when he moved on to the University of Kansas, he became nationally known as an all-American football player. In 1931 he put his multiple talents as a track and field star together and won the AAU pentathlon and placed sixth in the decathlon. In 1932 he won the AAU decathlon, and in only his third try at the event, he won the Olympic gold medal. In Los Angeles, Bausch was in fifth place after the first day but on the second day he placed first in the discus, javelin, and pole vault to set a new world record of 8,462.235 points. His outstanding performance on the second day came in the pole vault when he cleared 13'-1½", which would have earned him fifth place in the individual pole vault.

Bausch had some difficult years after the Olympics. He played pro football briefly with the Cincinnati Reds (1933) and Chicago Cardinals (1934), but with little success. Even more dismal was his attempt to launch a career as a nightclub singer. Bausch finally had some luck as an insurance salesman but during World War II, while serving with the navy in the Pacific, he contracted osteomyelitis, which plagued him the rest of his life. The pain was severe and he eventually had some problems with alcohol abuse, but overcame them and spent his last years gallantly helping others with the same problem.

BAXTER, Irving Knott.

B. 25 MAR 1876 Utica, NY. D. 13 JUN 1957 Frankford, NY. Gold(2): 1900 High Jump, 1900 Pole Vault; Silver(3): 1900 Standing High Jump, 1900 Standing Long Jump, 1900 Standing Triple Jump. Irv Baxter finished equal second in the 1897 IC4A high jump while representing Trinity College and then won the title in 1899 while a student at Penn. He also won the AAU high jump and pole vault that year.

The American team for the Paris Olympics stopped off for the British AAA Championships and Baxter took the high jump at 6'-2". At the Paris Games he jumped marginally higher and won the Olympic gold medal at 6'-2½". Later the same day, he won the pole vault in somewhat bizarre circumstances. Daniel Horton and Bascom Johnson, who had both beaten Baxter at the British meet, were missing, as was Charles Dvorak, who would become Olympic champion in 1904. Johnson and Dvorak had left the grounds on being told that the pole vault had been postponed, and Horton declined to compete on sabbatical grounds. Notwithstanding the information given to Johnson and Dvorak, the event was held as scheduled and Baxter, who was still at the field after his high jump victory, registered as a last-minute entry and won his second Olympic title. The following day he finished second to Ray Ewry in all three standing jumps, thus winning a total of five Olympic medals in the space of two days.

In 1901, Baxter returned to England where he successfully defended his British high jump title but, as at the Olympics, he was involved in drama surrounding the pole vault. Baxter had arrived at the Championships without a pole and as the only other competitor refused to lend him his, Baxter uprooted a flagpole, cleared the same height as his rival, and shared the British championship.

Baxter was admitted to the New York State Bar in 1901 and in 1903 he was chosen as a special city judge on the Democratic ticket. Apart from a break during World War I, he continued in private law practice until 1921, when he was appointed Commissioner of the Northern District of New York. In 1925 he resigned and returned to private practice.

BEAMON, Robert.

B. 29 AUG 1946 Jamaica, NY. Gold: 1968 Long Jump. In winning the 1968 Olympic title Bob Beamon achieved

FRANCIS ADONIJAH LANE

It's safe to say that Frank Lane is unknown by today's generations of sports fans, but he has an exalted place among United States Olympians. Lane was a member of the first U.S. team that competed at the 1896 Olympics in Athens. On 6 April 1896, he toed the line in the first heat of the 100 meter dash, winning the heat, and becoming in the process the first American to compete in the modern Olympic Games. Lane went to the finals of the 100m but finished only fourth in his only Olympic event.

Frank Lane was born in Franklin, Ohio, in 1875. He competed in the first Olympics while in his junior year at Princeton. Of the four Princetonians on the first U.S. Olympic team, Lane was probably the one least well known athletically, as he never won any sort of major championship. After graduation in 1897 he went to medical school at Washington University in St. Louis. He practiced medicine as an ophthalmologist, becoming the head of that department at Rush Medical College and the Presbyterian and Illinois Central Hospitals in Chicago. Lane died in Chicago on 17 February 1927.

what is generally recognized as the outstanding single performance in track & field history. Showing perfect technique in ideal conditions, he not only became the first man to break the 28-foot barrier but also the 29-foot mark. More precisely, he cleared 29'-2½" (8.90 meters) and finished more than two feet ahead of his nearest rival. Prior to this amazing feat Beamon had set a national high school triple jump record in 1965 and in 1967 he won the AAU indoor long jump. In 1968 he won both the AAU and NCAA indoor long jump and triple jump titles, and won the AAU outdoor long jump that year. Due to injury he never again approached his 1968 Olympic form and he turned professional in 1973.

After first attending Adelphi, Beamon graduated from the University of Texas at El Paso in 1970, where he also briefly played basketball. Beamon had little success as a professional trackster and has spent most of his business career in social work.

BEARD, Percy Morris.

B. 26 JAN 1908 Hardinsburg, KY. Silver: 1932 110 meter hurdles. At the 1932 Olympics, Percy Beard was in the lead until he hit the sixth hurdle and ended up losing by a very narrow margin to George Saling. Beard had won the first of three AAU high hurdles titles in 1931, posting a new world record of 14.2 for 120 yards. Over the 110 meter distance, he equalled the world record of 14.4 in 1932 and during a European tour in 1934 he lowered the record to 14.3 and then to 14.2 After graduating from Auburn as a civil engineer, he ran four outdoor and five indoor seasons for the New York AC, losing only one race in all. He won the AAU indoor hurdles in 1931, 1932, 1933 and again in 1935.

Beard went on to earn a master's degree from Auburn and taught engineering there from 1929 to 1935. He then moved to the University of Florida as track coach and became athletic director before his retirement in 1973. The University of Florida track is named for Percy Beard.

BELL, Gregory Curtis.

B. 07 NOV 1930 Terre Haute, IN. Gold: 1956 Long Jump. As a freshman at Indiana University, Greg Bell won the 1955 AAU long jump. The following year he jumped 26'-6½", a mark which to then had been bettered only by Jesse Owens. Bell then went on to win the Olympic title, and won the NCAA long jump in 1956 and 1957 and the AAU indoors in 1958. He has gone on to a career in dentistry.

BENNETT, Basil B.

B. 30 NOV 1884. D. 19 SEP 1938. Bronze: 1920 Hammer Throw. Basil Bennett was ranked second nationally in 1917 and while attending the University of Illinois he was the leading collegiate hammer thrower that year. He was deprived of the 1917 IC4A title because the meet was cancelled, and he was out of competition for the next two years. However, he came back in 1920 and, as a member of the Chicago AA, placed fourth at the Final Trials. At the Olympics, he took third place with the best throw of his career and beat his teammates, Matt McGrath and James McEachern, both of whom had finished ahead of him at the U.S. Trials.

BENNETT, John Dale.

B. 14 NOV 1930 Grand Forks, ND. Silver: 1956 Long Jump. John Bennett of Marquette won the NCAA long jump in 1953 and the following year he scored a noteworthy triple by taking the AAU, NCAA and IC4A titles. In 1954 he also won the IC4A high jump. At the 1955 Pan-American Games he jumped 26'-3½" (8.01 meters) to become the first white athlete to go beyond the 26 foot (and 8 meter) mark, but this was only good for second place behind Ross Range.

Bennett also placed second at the 1956 Olympics and this time it was Greg Bell who defeated him. Bell beat Bennett again at the post-Olympic U.S. vs. British Empire meet. Although competing only occasionally in 1957, Bennett was runner-up in the AAU. He retired at the end of the 1958 season and today owns and operates a men's clothing store in Wisconsin.

BENNETT, Robert Howard.

B. 09 AUG 1919 Providence, RI. D. 13 DEC 1974 Cranston, RI. Bronze: 1948 Hammer Throw. One of a number of fine hammer throwers to come from the University of Maine, Bob Bennett won the IC4A in 1939 and 1940. He topped the National rankings in 1940 with a new collegiate record of 183'-10¾". Bennett missed the next five seasons (during the war), but made a comeback in 1946 and in 1947, by which time he was attending Brown and was again the top ranked thrower in the U.S. During his three years at Brown, Bennett won the AAU and IC4A in 1947 and the AAU again in 1948. He also won the IC4A 35 lb. weight throw in 1947. At the 1948 Olympics he edged Sam Felton, formerly of Harvard, out of third place by a mere three inches. Bennett coached at West Point for several years and then returned to Brown in 1954 as assistant track coach.

BERNA, Tell Schirnding.

B. 24 JUL 1891 Pelham Manor, NY. D. 05 APR 1975 Nantucket, MA. Gold: 1912 3,000 meter team race. While at Cornell, Tell Berna won the IC4A two miles title in 1910 and 1911 and the following year set a U.S. record of 9:17.8, which was to remain unbeaten for 20 years. After finishing a creditable fifth in the 5,000m at the Stockholm Olympics, Berna led the U.S. team to victory in the 3,000m team race by finishing in a dead-heat for first place with Thorid Ohlsson of Sweden.

After graduation, Tell Berna worked for a number of firms in the machine tool business and in 1937 he became general manager of the National Machine Tools Business Association. In that capacity he worked closely with the War Production Board during World War II to maximize production of munitions.

BIFFLE, Jerome Cousins.

B. 20 MAR 1928 Denver, CO. Gold: 1952 Long Jump. While attending the University of Denver, Jerome Biffle won the 1950 NCAA long jump title. In 1951 he joined the army and competed only in minor service meets, but in 1952, after being injured in the spring, he placed third in the AAU and then finished second to Meredith Gourdine at the Final Trials. In Helsinki, Biffle was lying second to Gourdine after two rounds, but moved into the lead with his third jump. Although his final three jumps were fouls, that third round effort of 24'-10" brought him the gold medal.

Biffle has worked for many years in the Denver school system and is today a college counselor at a Denver high school.

BILLER, John A.

B. 14 NOV 1879. Silver: 1908 Standing High Jump (tied); Bronze: 1904 Standing Long Jump. Apart from placing third in the 1904 standing long jump, John Biller, a member of the National Turnverein of Newark, NJ, placed fourth in the standing high jump and fifth in the discus. In 1908 he tied for second in the standing high jump and finished fourth in the standing long jump.

BLACK, Edmund Franklin.

B. 05 MAY 1905. Bronze: 1928 Hammer Throw. The top hammer thrower in 1928 was Frank Connor of Yale, but he only placed fourth at the Final Trials—Ed Black of the University of Maine, the Boston AA, and the Newark AC led the Americans in Amsterdam. After the qualifying round at the 1928 Olympics, Black was in second place, but he eventually finished third. He won the AAU in 1928 and the IC4A in 1929.

Black did not confine his athletic talents to the track. In high school he was an all-state fullback, and in 1970 he was the Maine state champion in bowling. He made his living as a lobsterman.

BLACK, Larry J.

B. 20 JUL 1951 Miami, FL. Gold: 1972 4 × 100 meters relay; Silver: 1972 200 meters. Larry Black twice ran 20.0 before the Munich Games, but lost the Olympic title to Valery Borzov of the USSR by two meters. He had a fine collegiate season for North Carolina Central in 1971, winning the NCAA, NAIA, and NCAA-College Division. A versatile all-round sprinter, Black led off the Olympic 4 × 100 meters relay team that posted a new world record and he ran a 440y relay leg in 43.8 at the 1972 Penn Relays.

Black was from Miami and still lives there, now as director of that city's parks and recreation department. Larry Black was a first cousin of fellow Olympian, Gerry Tinker.

BLAKE, Charles Arthur.

B. 26 JAN 1872 Boston, MA. D. 23 OCT 1944. Silver: 1896 1,500 meters. Indirectly, Arthur Blake played a major part in the American participation at the first Modern Olympic Games. After winning a 1,000y race at Mechanic's Hall in Boston in January 1896, he jokingly remarked, "Oh, I am too good for Boston. I ought to go over and run the marathon in Athens." The remark was overheard by a stockbroker, Arthur Burnham, who offered to finance the trip of the U.S. team to Greece. Burnham did not finance the whole trip, but a substantial portion of it, and Blake's remark was the impetus that brought him into the agreement.

In Athens, Blake placed second in the 1,500m with a time of 4:34.0, which was hardly comparable with his best times at home, where he held the Boston AA indoor record for the mile with 4:39.8. Blake, a Harvard grad ('93), also ran the marathon in Athens, but dropped out after 14 miles.

Arthur Blake settled in Dedham, Massachusetts, where he became a successful insurance salesman and a well-known golfer and sailor.

BONHAG, George V.

B. 31 JAN 1882 Boston, MA. D. 30 OCT 1960 New York, NY. Gold(2): 1906 1,500 meter walk, 1912 3,000 meter team race; Silver: 1908 3 mile team race. George Bonhag of the Irish-American AC won seven AAU indoor titles, but a national outdoor championship always eluded him. However, at the 1906 Olympics, disappointed with his fifth place in the 1,500m after leading entering the home stretch, Bonhag decided to enter the 1,500m walk at the last moment. This was the first walking race in which Bonhag had ever competed, and

after several better-known walkers had been disqualified, George Bonhag won the race and was crowned
the first Olympic walking champion.

At the 1908 Games, he finished sixth in the three
mile team race and was the second scoring individual
for the United States' second place team. Four years
later, in Stockholm, he placed fifth individually in the
3,000m team event when the U.S won the Olympic title.

BORAH, Charles Edward.

B. 11 NOV 1906 Fawfield, IL. D. 04 NOV 1980 Phoenix,
AZ. Gold: 1928 4 × 100 meter relay. Charley Borah won
the AAU 100y in 1926, but was narrowly defeated by
Chester Bowman the following year. However, he won
the AAU 200m in 1927 and took both sprints for Southern Cal at the IC4A meet. In 1928 he retained his AAU
200 title. Although a more notable performer in the
longer sprint, he won his gold medal by running the third
leg of the 4 × 100 relay after surprisingly being eliminated in the second round of the individual 200m. Borah
was a member of the USC team which set a world
record for the 4 × 220y relay in 1927. Charley Borah
also attended Southern Cal Dental School and later
practiced dentistry.

BOSTON, Ralph Harold.

B. 09 MAY 1939 Laurel, MS. Gold: 1960 Long Jump;
Silver: 1964 Long Jump; Bronze: 1968 Long Jump. Until
a few weeks before the 1960 Olympics, Ralph Boston
seemed no more than an average long jumper. But in
August he beat Jesse Owen's 25-year-old world record
with a mark of 26'-11¼" and went on to take the gold
medal. In 1961 he twice improved the record, becoming the first man to jump 27 feet, but then lost the record
to Igor Ter-Ovanesyan of the Soviet Union in 1962.
Boston equalled that mark in August 1964, broke it the
following month, and in May 1965, set his last world
record.

Boston won the AAU outdoor long jump for six
successive seasons (1961–1966) and the AAU indoor
in 1961. Competing for Tennessee State, he won the
NCAA outdoor title in 1960. Boston was also a gifted
performer in other events. In 1961 he was undefeated
in the high hurdles and won the AAU indoor in 1965. He
placed fourth in the 1963 Pan-American Games high
jump, and in that year headed the U.S. lists in the triple
jump.

Ralph Boston retired after the 1968 Olympics. He
currently is on the administrative staff of the University
of Tennessee and occasionally is heard as an announcer on televised track events.

BOURLAND, Clifford Frederick.

B. 01 JAN 1921 Los Angeles, CA. Gold: 1948 4 × 400
meter relay. After placing fifth in the 200m at the 1948
Olympics, Cliff Bourland confirmed that he was really at
his best over the full lap with a 47.3 second leg in the
4 × 400m relay, which put the U.S. into a winning lead.
Bourland had reached the peak of his career some
years earlier. In the 1941 AAU he finished third in the
400m in 46.1 and ran a sub-46-second relay leg when
Southern Cal finished second to Cal-Berkeley, with
both teams breaking the world record for the 4x400m
relay. Cliff Bourland also won the AAU and NCAA
400m in 1942 and 1943.

BRADLEY, Everett Lewis.

B. 19 MAY 1897 Cedar Rapids, IA. D. 25 JUL 1969
Wichita, KS. Silver: 1920 Pentathlon. After placing second in the decathlon and third in the pentathlon at the
1920 Olympic Trials, Everett Bradley surprisingly only
competed in the pentathlon at Antwerp. At the Games,
he finished second to Eero Lehtonen of Finland and
beat the two men, Brutus Hamilton and Bob LeGendre,
who had finished ahead of him at the U.S. Trials.

After graduating from the University of Kansas
with a geology degree, Bradley put it to good use with a
consulting and oil producing company. The company
eventually made him a wealthy man and allowed him to
spend his last years leisurely enjoying golf and flycast-
ing.

BRAGG, Donald George.

B. 15 MAY 1935 Penns Grove, NJ. Gold: 1960 Pole
Vault. Don Bragg was the last of the great prefiberglass
pole vaulters. He won the 1960 Final Trials with a new
world record of 15'-9¼" and this remains a world
"best" with a metal pole. Bragg had won the 1959 AAU
outdoor and, after sharing first place at the AAU indoor
in 1956 and 1958, he was an outright winner in 1959–
1961. While at Villanova, he won the NCAA in 1955 and
was IC4A champion—both indoors and out—for three
successive years (1955–57).

POLITICIANS, STATESMEN, ROYALTY

It is not uncommon for American Olympians to use their Olympic fame as a springboard to a political career. Many Olympians have served in state legislatures, Gary Anderson and Jim Beatty among them. However only four Olympians, all medalists, have served in the U.S. Congress, two in the House and two in the Senate:

Wendell Richard Anderson (Senate; Dec 1976-Dec 1978) (ICH)
William Warren Bradley (Senate; 1979-date) (BAS)
Robert Bruce Mathias (House; 1967-1975) (TAF)
Ralph Harold Metcalfe (House; 1971-Oct 1978 — deceased) (TAF)

Wendell Anderson is particularly interesting. He is also the only U.S. Olympic athlete who has served as a governor of a state. He was elected governor of Minnesota in 1970 and easily won re-election to a second term in 1974. When Jimmy Carter was elected president, Walter Mondale resigned his senate seat to serve as vice president. Anderson then resigned as governor to serve out Mondale's term in the Senate.

Has an American Olympian ever run for President? Certainly. In 1972 one of the candidates was Benjamin Spock, better known as the baby doctor and Vietnam pacifist, a gold-medal-winning rower in the 1924 Olympics. Spock ran as the candidate for the People's Party, receiving no electoral votes and less than 100,000 popular votes. He might have fared better had babies been given the vote.

An American Olympian has also served in the cabinet, although almost nobody knows he competed in the Olympics. That would be Dwight Filley Davis, who played tennis at St. Louis in 1904. Davis is much better known as the donor of the Davis Cup, but he was assistant secretary of war from 1923 until 1925, and secretary of war from 1925 until 1929.

Now about royalty and nobility. Two American Olympic swimmers were descended from royal blood, but the Baroness Susan Christine Von Saltza, descended from a Swedish Count, rarely mentioned the fact. On the other hand, it was quite well known that Duke Kahanamoku was descended from a Hawaiian king. Three other American women married into royalty, one of them competing in the Olympics under that name. That was Patricia Galvin, who competed under her maiden name in 1960, but in 1964 was the Princess Patricia Galvin de la Tour d'Auvergne. The others were Brenda Helser, who was a swimmer in the 1948 Olympics and by marriage became the Countess de Morelos, and Daria Pankston Wright Pratt, a 1900 golfer, who in 1913 became the Princess Daria Pankston Wright Pratt Karageorgevitch of Serbia.

Don Bragg earned the nickname "Tarzan" as a result of his life-long dream to play that role in the movies. After his Olympic victory, his plans were thwarted by injury, legal problems, and scandal.

After his dreams of movie stardom faded, Tarzan Bragg became athletic director at Stockton State (NJ) College and is the owner of a boys' summer camp near the school.

BRAUN, Max.
Silver: 1904 Tug-of-War. Max Braun was a member of the St. Louis Southwest Turnverein team which took second place in the 1904 tug-of-war.

BRAY, John.
B. 19 AUG 1875 Middleport, NY. D. 18 JUL 1945 San Francisco, CA. Bronze: 1900 1,500 meters. Third place in the 1,500m in 1900 gave John Bray the honor of being the first Olympic medalist from Williams College. He also qualified for the 800m final, but placed sixth.

Bray eventually settled in San Francisco where he worked for several electric companies and served on the board of directors of the San Francisco Board of Trade.

BREITKREUTZ, Emil William.
B. 16 NOV 1883 Wausau, WI. D. 03 MAY 1972 San Gabriel, CA. Bronze: 1904 800 meters. As an engineering graduate student at Southern Cal, Emil Breitkreutz was, as he subsequently admitted, more interested in the engineering exhibits at the 1904 St. Louis World's Fair than in the Olympic program—which was held concurrently. However, representing the Milwaukee AC, he performed creditably in the 800m, and after leading the field at the half-way mark in an adventurous 53.0, he faded badly in the closing stages but hung on to take third place.

In 1907 Breitkreutz served as the first head basketball coach at Southern Cal. He went on to an active career as a sports administrator, serving as an AAU official in track & field and on the AAU volleyball committee as chairman.

BRIX, Harold Herman.
B. 19 MAY 1906 Tacoma, WA. Silver: 1928 Shot Put. After winning the 1928 Final Trials, Herman Brix set a new Olympic record of 51'-8" on his first attempt in Amsterdam. However, he could not match the new world record of 52'-0¾" set by countryman John Kuck later in the competition.

Brix won the AAU for four years straight (1928–1931), the NCAA in 1927, and the AAU indoor in 1930 and 1932, his winning mark in 1930 of 51'-2½" being a new world indoor record. In 1932 he had a career best of 52'-8⅝" in May, but could not maintain his form and failed to make the team for the Los Angeles Games.

Herman Brix, a graduate of the University of Washington, later became a movie actor, changing his name to Bruce Bennett in 1940. He featured in the title role in several Tarzan films and was well known as the second lead in several well-known films, including "Mildred Pierce."

BROOKER, James Kent.
B. 12 AUG 1902. Bronze: 1924 Pole Vault. Jim Brooker, of the University of Michigan, was one of the athletes who finished in a four-way tie at 13'-0" at the 1924 Final Trials. None of the U.S. vaulters could match this height at Paris, although by finishing third to his teammates, Barnes and Graham, Brooker completed a clean sweep of the medals for the United States. In 1923 he tied for first place at the NCAA.

BROWN, Benjamin Gene.
B. 27 SEP 1953 San Francisco, CA. Gold: 1976 4 × 400 meter relay. Benny Brown of the Maccabi Track Club, and formerly of UCLA, finished in fourth place at the 1976 Final Trials. This earned him a spot on the 1,600m relay team and he ran the third leg in 44.6 in the Montreal final. Earlier in the season he had won the NCAA 400 meter championship.

BROWN, Horace Hallock.
B. 30 MAR 1898 Madison, NJ. Gold: 1920 3,000 meter team race. After winning the 5,000m at the Final Trials, Hal Brown reached the Olympic final at this distance but did not finish the race. Five days later, he led the field home in the 3,000m team event when the U.S., with three men in the first six, took the gold medals. He also won the IC4A 2 mile title in 1920.

Brown entered Williams College in 1915, but his studies were interrupted when he went to France in 1917 to serve in World War I. Serving initially as an ambulance driver, he later saw active service as a pilot and aerial gunner. He was commissioned in 1918, returned to Williams in 1919, and graduated with the Class of 1920. Brown was a seismologist and worked for many years with the Geotechnical Corp. of Dallas.

BROWN, Leroy Taylor.
B. 01 JAN 1902 New York, NY. D. 21 APR 1970 Sharon, CT. Silver: 1924 High Jump. Leroy Brown, from Dartmouth, won the AAU indoor high jump in 1922, the outdoor in 1923, and the IC4A indoor and outdoor in 1922 and 1923. His winning mark of 6'-5⅝" at the 1923 AAU outdoor was the best performance in the world that year. Earlier in the season he had tied for first place with Dick Landon, the 1920 Olympic champion, at the Millrose Games when both set a world indoor record of 6'-5¼". At the 1924 Olympics, Brown came close to repeating his 1923 form, but did not seriously threaten the winner, Harold Osborn.

BURKE, Thomas Edmund.
B. 15 JAN 1875. D. 14 FEB 1929 Boston, MA. Gold(2): 1896 100 meters, 1896 400 meters. Of the six Americans to win Olympic track and field titles in 1896, Tom Burke was perhaps the only one who would still have been crowned a champion if all the world's best athletes had been assembled in Athens. At the Athens

Courtesy Horace Hallock Brown

Hal Brown (left) during the 1920 3,000 meter team race, in which he nipped Sweden's Erik Backman to finish first individually and lead the U.S. to a gold medal in the team event.

Olympics, he completely dominated both sprints and was never seriously threatened in the heats or the final of either event.

Having won the AAU 440y in 1895, he was the only reigning American champion to compete in Athens. He won the AAU again in 1896 and 1897, and in 1898 took the 880y. His winning time of 48.8 in the 1896 440y had been bettered only by the legendary Lon Myers among Americans.

At the IC4A, Burke won the 440y in 1896 and 1897 for Boston University, and in 1899 he took the 880y when he was a graduate student at Harvard. He also represented the New York AC and in 1897 was a member of their relay team which won the first AAU championship.

Tom Burke set up a law practice in Boston and was also a journalist, writing first for the *Boston Journal* and later the *Boston Post*. He served briefly as track coach at Mercersburg Academy.

BUTTS, James A.

B. 09 MAY 1950 South Los Angeles, CA. Silver: 1976 Triple Jump. James Butts took the NCAA triple jump in 1972 while at UCLA, but did not win his first and only AAU title until 1978. In placing second at the Montreal Games he became the first U.S. athlete to win an Olympic triple jump medal since Levi Casey in 1928. Butts also narrowly missed making the Olympic team in 1972 and 1980 when he placed fourth in the Final Trials on both occasions. He also placed third in the 1979 Pan-American Games.

After graduation in 1974, Butts represented the Tobias Striders. While training for the Montreal Olympics, Butts worked two jobs to help support himself, his mother, and a sister, forcing him to do his daily workout at 5:00 AM.

BYRD, Richard Leslie.
B. 16 MAY 1892 Shiloh, ID. Silver: 1912 Discus Throw. Dick Byrd succeeded in beating the world record holder James Duncan in the 1912 Olympic discus, but was outclassed by Armas Taipale of Finland, who had a winning margin of almost ten feet. Captain R. L. Byrd, U.S. Marine Corps, won the discus at the Inter-Allied Games held at the Pershing Stadium, Paris, in 1919. Later in the year he finished second in the AAU.

CAGLE, Harold D.
B. 03 AUG 1913 Purcell, OK. Silver: 1936 4 × 400 meter relay. For the 1,600m relay in Berlin, the U.S. team managers decided to field a completely fresh team and not use the runners who had competed in the individual 400m. Thus Harold Cagle of Oklahoma Baptist, who had placed only sixth at the Final Trials, earned his Olympic selection. He ran the opening leg in the Olympic final in 48.7 Cagle graduated Oklahoma Baptist in 1939 and went on to teach and coach in Oklahoma. He is a member of the NAIA and the Oklahoma Baptist Athletic Halls of Fame.

CALHOUN, Lee Quency.
B. 23 FEB 1933 Laurel, MS. Gold(2): 1956 100 meters hurdles, 1960 110 meters hurdles. Lee Calhoun is the only man to have won two Olympic high hurdles titles. In 1956 he brought his best time down from 14.4 to 13.5 to win the first of his gold medals. In 1960, Calhoun improved to 13.4 and won his second Olympic title. Apart from these successes, he won the AAU (indoor and outdoor), the NAIA, and the NCAA in 1956 and successfully defended all four titles in 1957. He was suspended for the 1958 season for being married on television and receiving gifts after the ceremony. He came back in 1959 to win his third AAU outdoor championship as well as the Pan-American Games title. Shortly before winning his second Olympic crown he equalled the 110m world record with 13.2.

Calhoun graduated from North Carolina Central and, after coaching at Grambling, became the head track coach at Yale.

CAMPBELL, Milton Gray.
B. 09 DEC 1933 Plainfield, NJ. Gold: 1956 Decathlon; Silver: 1952 Decathlon. Milt Campbell was the first great black decathlete and the first to win the Olympic

decathlon. He won the AAU decathlon in 1953 and the AAU and NCAA high hurdles in 1955. In 1957 he set a world record of 13.4 for the 120y hurdles. While at Indiana University, Campbell won letters in both football and track. After graduation he had a fling with pro football, playing briefly in 1957 with the Cleveland Browns, but has since run programs in New Jersey for underprivileged children. He is also a well-known lecturer.

CARLOS, John Wesley.
B. 05 JUN 1945 New York, NY. Bronze: 1968 200 meters. After withdrawing from East Texas State, claiming racial prejudice, John Carlos enrolled at San Jose State. His finest performance was 19.7 for the 200 meters at the 1968 Final Trials which, although 3/10 of a second inside the world record, was never ratified because Carlos was wearing illegal brush spikes. During the Olympic medal presentation in Mexico City, Carlos and 200 meter winner, Tommie Smith, stood at attention, but raised black-gloved fists in the "Black Power" salute, hoping to call attention to the plight of the black man in America. For this, they were banned from the Olympic Village.

In 1969, Carlos won the AAU and NCAA 220y and equalled the world record for the indoor 60y and the outdoor 100y. He made several abortive efforts to play in the NFL and did play for a few years with the Montreal Alouettes of the Canadian Football League. Today Carlos works for the Los Angeles Olympic Organizing Committee.

CARNEY, Lester Nelson.
B. 21 MAR 1934 Bellaire, OH. Silver: 1960 200 meters. Although better known as a football player at Ohio University, Les Carney was a match for all but the very best of his contemporary sprinters. In 1959 he finished third in the AAU 200m and NCAA 220y and placed second in the Pan-American Games. In 1960, Carney took second place at the AAU and edged defending Olympic champion, Bobby Morrow, out of third place in the 200m at the Final Trials. In Rome, he took the silver medal, beating both of his teammates who had finished ahead of him at the Trials.

Carney was drafted by the Baltimore Colts in 1958 but never played pro football. He has spent most of his career in Akron, Ohio, as a buyer for a major sporting goods firm.

CARPENTER, William Kenneth.

B. 19 APR 1913 Compton, CA. Gold: 1936 Discus Throw. Southern Cal's Ken Carpenter won the AAU, NCAA, and IC4A discus titles in 1935. The following year he again took the AAU and NCAA, but only placed second to Gordon Dunn at the Final Trials. In Berlin, Dunn led the field after four rounds with Carpenter in third place, also behind Oberwerger of Italy. In the fifth round, Carpenter moved into the lead and, with both Dunn and Oberwerger fouling their last trial, Carpenter took the gold medal. After the Games, Carpenter came within one inch of Willy Schroder's (GER) world record in an international meet in Prague.

CARR, Henry.

B. 27 NOV 1942 Detroit, MI. Gold(2): 1964 200 meters, 1964 4 × 400 meter relay. While at Arizona State, Henry Carr won the NCAA 220y in 1963 and tied for first place in the AAU. The following year, as a member of the Phoenix Olympic Club, he won the AAU outright and lowered the world record for the furlong to 20.2, having himself set the previous record of 20.3 in 1963. At the Tokyo Olympics he won the 200m in a new Olympic record of 20.3 and ran a 44.5 anchor leg in the 1,600 meter relay to bring the U.S. home in a new world record of 3:00.7. In two seasons (1963–64), Carr lost only two races at 200m/220y.

Henry Carr went on to a good career in pro football as a defensive back with the New York Giants from 1965 through 1968. He has since become a devout Christian and works as a lay preacher.

CARR, Sabin William.

B. 04 SEP 1904 Dubuque, IA. D. 12 SEP 1983 Ventura, CA. Gold: 1928 Pole Vault. In 1927, Sabin Carr set new indoor and outdoor world records. In early February he took the indoor record up to 13'-7⅛", which he improved one week later to 13'-9¼". In May, at the IC4A outdoor, he became the first man to clear 14 feet, then in 1928, at the AAU indoor, he vaulted 14'-1" to become the first to clear 14 feet indoors. In 1928, Carr lost his world outdoor record to the 1924 Olympic champion, Lee Barnes, but at the Olympics, Carr got his revenge—he took the gold medal, with Barnes finishing fifth.

Carr, a Yale graduate, had a fine record in major championships, winning the AAU indoor twice, the

Pole vaulting gold medalist, Sabin Carr, in the classic fence picture taken of all captains of Yale sports.

Courtesy Yale University

IC4A outdoor three times, and the IC4A indoor twice. Oddly, he never placed better than third at the AAU outdoor meet. Carr eventually went into the lumber business in Oakland, California, and became president of the Sterling Lumber Co.

CARR, William Arthur.

B. 24 OCT 1909 Pine Bluff, AK. D: 14 JAN 1966 Tokyo, Japan. Gold(2): 1932 400 meters. 1932 4 × 400 meter relay. Bill Carr of Penn went to the the 1932 IC4A with a best time for the 440y of no better than 48.4, but at Berkeley he caused a major upset by beating the world record holder, Ben Eastman. He again beat Eastman at the AAU, which also served as the Final Trials that year, and crowned the season, which he had begun as an unknown, by winning the Olympic title. Once more the runner-up was Ben Eastman and this time Carr took Eastman's world record with a 46.2 clocking. Carr then anchored the winning U.S. 1,600 meter relay team to another world record of 3:08.2.

Soon after the Olympics, Bill Carr was seriously injured in an automobile accident and never ran again. Throughout his career, albeit a tragically brief one, Carr was never beaten over the one lap distance. He died of a heart attack while on vacation in Japan.

CARTMELL, Nathaniel John.

B. 13 JAN 1883 Union Town, KY. D. 23 AUG 1967 Forest Hills, NY. Gold: 1908 1,600 meter medley relay; Silver(2): 1904 100 meters, 1904 200 meters; Bronze: 1908 200 meters. Although Penn State's first Olympic champion, Nate Cartmell never won an AAU title. He did take the British AAA 220y crown in 1909 and was runner-up in the 100y to Reggie Walker, the reigning Olympic champion. After finishing a close second to Archie Hahn in both sprints at the 1904 Olympics, he took the sprint double at the IC4A for three successive years (1906–08). At the 1908 Games, Cartmell finished fourth in the 100m, third in the 200m, and his 200m leg for the winning medley relay team earned him an Olympic gold medal. At the end of the 1909 season, he joined the professional ranks and in his first race at Stoke-in-Trent, England, he set a new world professional record for 220y around a turn with 21.5, although the track was covered with snow.

Cartmell retired from competition in 1912 and devoted himself to coaching. He actually began coaching in 1910 at the University of North Carolina, and then coached winning teams at West Virginia and Lafayette before returning to Penn State. He had several run-ins with the football coach and athletic director, Hugo Bezdek, and was dismissed in 1933. He later coached at Princeton, Fordham, and West Point before retiring.

CARUTHERS, Edward J., Jr.

B. 13 APR 1945 Troy, AL. Silver: 1968 High Jump. After placing eighth in the 1964 Olympics, Caruthers developed into a great high jumper while attending Arizona State. In 1967 his only defeats were at the NCAA and the AAU and on both occasions he lost only on the count-back, never being outjumped. Among his victories that year were five international titles, including the Pan-American Games gold medal. At the 1968 Olympics, Caruthers cleared a personal best of 7'-3½" but had to settle for second best behind Dick Fosbury, who was using the then relatively unknown "flop" style, which he pioneered.

CASEY, Levi B.

B. 19 OCT 1902. Silver: 1928 Triple Jump. Levi Casey's triple jump silver medal was the only American Olympic medal in that event between 1906 and 1976. Casey, of Cal State (LA) and the Los Angeles AC, won the AAU three straight years starting in 1926. In 1930 he marginally improved his career best to 49'-9¾" in winning the Central Association Championships in Chicago and one week later, representing the Illinois AC, he won his fourth AAU title. At the 1932 Final Trials, Casey placed third, but was surprisingly not selected for the Olympic team.

CASSELL, Ollan Conn.

B. 05 OCT 1937 Norton, VA. Gold: 1964 4 × 400 meter relay. After being eliminated in the semi-finals of the individual 400m, Ollan Cassell picked up a gold medal and a share of a new world record as lead-off man in the 1,600m relay.

After graduation from the University of Houston, Cassell represented the Houston Track Club. He won the 200m at the 1963 Pan-Am Games and at the AAU he won the 220y in 1957 and the 440y in 1965. He is currently executive director of The Athletics Congress, track's governing body in the United States.

CASTLEMAN, Frank Riley.

B. 17 MAR 1877 Tracy Creek, OH. D. 09 OCT 1946 Columbus, OH. Silver: 1904 200 meter hurdles. Frank Castleman, of Colgate and the Greater New York Irish AA, gave Harry Hillman, one of the outstanding hurdlers of the time, a good race in the 200m hurdles at the Olympics. The event was run as a straight final with no heats, and Castleman, who would win the IC4A 220y hurdles in 1905–06, finished little more than a yard behind Hillman. Castleman also finished second in the IC4A 120y hurdles for three straight years (1904–06), losing each time to a different winner.

Castleman was a three-letter man at Colgate and was known as one of their greatest football players. After a short stint coaching at Colorado, he settled in Columbus, Ohio, where he became track coach and professor of physical education at Ohio State, from which he had obtained an M.D. degree in 1921.

CAWLEY, Warren Jay.
B. 06 JUL 1940 Detroit, MI. Gold: 1964 400 meter hurdles. At the 1959 AAU, "Rex" Cawley made track history by becoming the only athlete ever to place in the first six in all three hurdles events. The 18-year-old schoolboy finished fifth in the 110y, third in the 220y, and sixth in the 440y hurdles.

In the fall of 1959, Cawley entered Southern Cal. After failing to make the 1960 Olympic team, he had excellent seasons in 1961 and 1962 despite injury problems in those years. In 1963 he enjoyed a full season and won the AAU and NCAA 440y hurdles, also placing second in the open quarter at the NCAA with a career best of 46.0. In 1964, Cawley set a world record of 49.1 for the intermediate hurdles and went on to win the Olympic title. His last major championship came when he won the AAU in 1965.

CHILDS, Clarence Chester.
B. 24 JUL 1884 Wooster, OH. D. 16 SEP 1960. Bronze: 1912 Hammer Throw. Track was but one of three sports at which Clarence Childs excelled. He was on the football, wrestling, and track teams at Yale and 1912 was the only year that he treated hammer throwing with any degree of seriousness. Prior to placing second at the Final Trials that year, his best performance had been a third place at the IC4A in 1911. In Stockholm he finished more than 20 feet behind the winner, Matt McGrath, but came close to beating Duncan Gillis of Canada for the silver medal.

From 1914 to 1916, Childs was track and football coach at Indiana University and then saw service in France. Among other posts, he held that of athletic director at the Colombes Stadium in Paris. Leaving the army with the rank of major, he returned home and became an industrial engineer.

Ollan Cassell won a gold medal as the lead-off man in the 1,600m relay in 1964.

CLARK, Ellery Harding.
B. 13 MAR 1874 West Roxbury, MA. D. 27 JUL 1949 Boston, MA. Gold(2): 1896 High Jump, 1896 Long Jump. Ellery Clark holds the distinction of being the only man to win both the Olympic high jump and long jump. Clark, a 22-year-old Harvard grad, claimed this noteworthy double at the first Modern Olympics with marks of 5'-11½" and 20'-11". On his return from Greece, Clark developed into a highly versatile athlete, winning the National All-Around Championship in 1897 and

Courtesy Ed Kirwan Graphic Arts

Robert Clark's success as a decathlete was largely the result of his ability as a long jumper.

1903. In 1904, the American and Olympic All-Around Championship were one and the same event, but Clark was seriously weakened by bronchitis in St. Louis and in his second Olympic appearance he placed no better than fifth in the event that was the forerunner of the modern decathlon.

In his professional life, Ellery Clark showed all-round talents that even exceeded his sporting versatility. He wrote 19 books, ranging from the definitive work on railway accident law to a book on religious philosophy, and two of his novels were adapted for films by Hollywood. He was an alderman of the city of Boston, an assistant track coach at Harvard, a teacher of English composition at a Cambridge school, and a prominent lawyer in Boston.

CLARK, Robert Hyatt.
B. 28 JAN 1913 Covina, CA. Silver: 1936 Decathlon. Bob Clark's success as a decathlete was built on an outstanding talent as a long jumper. Apart from winning the AAU decathlon in 1934 and 1935, he won the IC4A long jump for Cal/Berkeley in 1934 and, in the 1936 AAU

decathlon, jumped 25'-11¼". This was the sixth best mark of all time. At the Berlin Olympics, Clark finished sixth in the individual long jump but another fine effort of 25'-0" in the decathlon enabled him to lead ultimate winner, Glenn Morris, by two points at the end of the first day. Clark eventually finished second with 7,601 points, a mark that had been bettered to that time by only Morris and Hans Sievert of Germany.

CLARKE, Louis Alfred.
B. 23 NOV 1901 Statesville, NC. D. 24 FEB 1977. Gold: 1924 4 × 100 meter relay. After winning the AAU Junior 220y in 1922, Louis Clarke enrolled at Johns Hopkins and finished second in the 100y and third in the 220y at the 1923 IC4A. In February 1924, he posted a world record of 9.8 for the 100y indoors and later in the year placed third on both sprints at the IC4A. At the 1924 Olympics, Clarke was a member of the sprint relay team which set three world records. In the first round they posted a new record of 41.6, brought this down to 41.0 in the second round, and matched that time in the final.

CLOUGHEN, Robert.

B. 26 JAN 1889 New York, NY. Silver: 1908 200 meters. Bobby Cloughen won the AAU indoor 60y in 1908 and 1910 and the AAU Junior 100y in 1908, all while representing the Irish-American AC. At the 1908 Games he lost the 100m title by only inches to the Irish-born Canadian, Robert Kerr.

COCHRAN, Commodore S.

B. 20 JAN 1902. D. c1969. Gold: 1924 4 × 400 meter relay. Commodore Cochran of Mississippi A&M won the NCAA 440y in 1922 and 1923. He ran the lead-off leg for the U.S. quartet which set a new world record in the 1,600m relay at the Paris Olympics. After graduation, he represented the Olympic Club of San Francisco. Twenty-four years later, his younger brother, Roy, won a gold medal in the same event, as well as one in the 400m hurdles.

COCHRAN, Leroy Braxton.

B. 06 JAN 1919 Richton, MS. D. 28 SEP 1981 Gig Harbor, WA. Gold(2): 1948 400 meter hurdles, 1948 4 × 400 meter hurdles. Roy Cochran won the 1939 AAU 400m hurdles and was one of the favorites for the 1940 Olympic title, but he had to wait eight years to fulfill that particular goal.

Coached at Indiana University by the great Billy Hayes, Cochran set world indoor records for 400m and 440y and a world outdoor record for the 440y hurdles in 1942, as well as winning the AAU indoor 600y that year. This was his last prewar season; after serving in the Pacific as a lieutenant in the navy, he returned home in 1946 and enrolled at Southern Cal to study for a master's in physiology. Although he was not considering a comeback, he was encouraged by his form in workouts and began to take the sport seriously once more.

In 1946, Cochran finished third in the AAU 400m flat in a career best of 46.7 and in 1947 he placed second in the AAU 400m hurdles. In the Olympic year he was supreme, winning his second AAU intermediate hurdles title before taking the gold medal in London in 51.1, the second fastest time ever, and contributing a 47.8 leg in the relay to win a second Olympic gold.

COCHRAN, Richard Lee.

B. 23 JUN 1938 Tulsa, OK. Bronze: 1960 Discus Throw. Dick Cochran, a student at the University of Missouri,

---

THE MEDAL WITHOUT THE ACCLAIM

U.S. runners have won the Olympics marathon three times—Tom Hicks in 1904, Johnny Hayes in 1908, and Frank Shorter in 1972. One other thing they share in common is that none of them were the first runner to enter the stadium when they won. In 1904 Fred Lorz, another American, was first into the stadium and first across the line but he was later disqualified when it was discovered that he had covered part of the course in an automobile. In 1908 Dorando Pietri of Italy was first into the stadium and also first across the line but he too was disqualified because he had received aid from the British officials in order to finish the race. In 1972 a noncompetitor jumped onto the race course just outside the stadium and posed as a competitor, which sent ABC television announcer Erich Segal into paroxysms of indignation. The imposter was a West German college student who did it as a prank. Though Segal's wish was that the imposter's name would forever remain anonymous, we'll reveal it here—Norbert Sudhaus.

---

first became a force on the national scene in 1959 when he won the NCAA discus, finished second in the Pan-American Games, and placed third in the AAU. In 1960 he again won the NCAA, and after finishing third at the Final Trials, he took third place at the Olympics as the U.S. made a clean sweep of the discus medals.

COE, William Wesley, Jr.

B. 08 MAY 1879 Boston, MA. D. 24 DEC 1926 Bozeman, MT. Silver: 1904 Shot Put. Competing regularly on both sides of the Atlantic, Wesley Coe was one of the better-known athletes of his time. In 1900 he won the first AAU Junior shot put title, and the following year began study at Oxford. While there he won the British AAA title in 1901 and 1902 and won both the shot and hammer in the annual match against Cambridge in 1902. On his return to the states, Coe entered Yale, but did not represent them at the major collegiate meets. After placing second in the 1904 Olympic shot, he won the AAU in 1905 with a new world record of 49'-6", repeating that title in 1906. At the 1908 Olympics he was out of form and only placed fourth with a modest throw.

Coe frequently traveled to England in later years; in 1912 he finished second in the shot at the AAA championships and in 1920 he won the 56 lb. weight event on the only occasion it was held at the British Championships. From a wealthy family, Coe never worked but tinkered with some minor inventions. He returned to America in 1926, settling in Montana for his health, but died six months later of Hodgkin's disease.

COLE, Gerrard Eugene.
B. 18 DEC 1928. Silver: 1952 4 × 400 meters relay. After he ran 48.0 for 440y in 1948 while in high school, no more was heard of Gene Cole for the next four years. During the interim he attended Ohio State, leaving track, but he decided to give it another try in 1952. After placing fifth in the AAU, Cole took second place at the Final Trials and at the Helsinki Games he ran 46.8 for fourth place in the semi-finals to become the first man in Olympic history to run a sub-47.0 400m and not make the final.

Running the second stage of the relay he clocked a remarkable 45.5, which gave some indication of what he might have accomplished had he chosen to spend more than one season in top-class track.

COLKET, Meredith Bright.
B. 19 NOV 1878 Philadelphia, PA. D. 07 JUN 1947 Philadelphia, PA. Silver: 1900 Pole Vault. When the 1900 U.S. Olympic team stopped over in London en route to Paris, Meredith Colket finished second to Bascom Johnson, a fellow student at Penn, in the pole vault at the British AAA championships. Colket then placed second in the Olympic pole vault to another Pennsylvanian, Irving Baxter.

Colket was better known athletically as a tennis player—he lettered for Penn for four years and later captained the Merion Cricket Club tennis team. He worked as an attorney in Philadelphia throughout his life.

COLLETT, Wayne Curtis.
B. 20 OCT 1949 Los Angeles, CA. Silver: 1972 400 meters. Wayne Collett of UCLA emerged as a world class one-lap runner in 1968 when he had five sub-46.0 marks. His fastest run of the year was in the quarter finals of the Final Trials, where he ran 44.9, but the effort of this run following a 45.6 heat led him to drop out in the semi-finals.

In 1972, Collett was a surprise winner of the Final Trials, beating John Smith, Vince Matthews, and Lee Evans in a new personal best of 44.1. Matthews took his revenge in the Olympic final and beat Collett to the tape by some two meters. At the awards ceremony, Collett and Matthews stood relaxed, arms akimbo, jackets disheveled and open, paying little heed to the national anthem. The IOC banned them for life from Olympic competition because of their behavior.

Collett earned an M.B.A. in 1973 and a J.D. degree in 1977—both from UCLA. Today he makes his living as a lawyer.

COLLIER, John Sheldon.
B. 26 SEP 1907 Buffalo, NY. D. 31 OCT 1974 Coronado, CA. Bronze: 1928 110 meter hurdles. John Collier attended Brown where his father, Prof. Theodore Collier, was chairman of the history department. At the 1928 Final Trials, Collier placed second to Steve Anderson; in Amsterdam, Anderson and the South African, Syd Atkinson, finished ahead of him. He won the 1929 IC4A high hurdles in 14.6, beating the 1928 champion, Ross Nichols of Stanford, who finished second. In 1929, Collier also won the IC4A indoor hurdles and set a world record of 7.6 for the 60y hurdles at the Millrose Games. Collier made a comeback in 1933 and the following year he equalled the indoor record for the 60y hurdles (five hurdles) three times before bringing the record down to 7.5 at the Millrose Games. He also won the AAU indoor in 1934 and set a new world record of 7.4 for the 60y hurdles (four hurdles). Like his father, John Collier became a teacher and for many years was science master and track coach at St. Paul's School.

CONNOLLY, Harold Vincent.
B. 01 AUG 1931 Somerville, MA. Gold: 1956 Hammer Throw. After winning the Olympic title in 1956, Connolly placed eighth in 1960, sixth in 1964, and in 1968 failed to qualify for the finals. In a 10-year span from 1956 to 1965, he raised the world record seven times, won a total of nine AAU hammer titles, and won the AAU indoor 35 lb. weight throw three times.

Connolly graduated from Boston College and became a teacher. In October 1957, he overcame oceans of political red tape to marry Olga Fikotova, the Czech Olympic discus champion, whom he had met at the 1956 Olympics. Best man at the ceremony was Czech distance running hero, Emil Zatopek. The Connollys were divorced in 1975 and Hal Connolly later married Pat Winslow, U.S. Olympic pentathlete in 1960, 1964, and 1968. He is now supervisor of secondary education in Santa Monica and director of a health club.

CONNOLLY, James Brendan.

B. 28 NOV 1865 South Boston, MA. D. 20 JAN 1957 Boston, MA. Gold: 1896 Triple Jump; Silver(2): 1896 High Jump (tied), 1900 Triple Jump; Bronze: 1896 Long Jump. For purely historical reasons, James Connolly must be considered the most distinguished of all United States Olympians because, on 6 April 1896, he became the first winner at the Modern Olympic Games and the first known Olympic champion since Varasdates in the 4th century, A.D. In addition to his triple jump crown, Connolly won medals in the high jump and long jump.

One can safely assume that this victory adequately compensated Connolly for the decision he had made at Boston some two months earlier. Connolly's dean at Harvard had counselled him not to make the trip to Athens because his low academic standing might prejudice his being readmitted to the university upon his return. Connolly, however, entertained no doubts as to his priorities and walked out of Harvard, not setting foot there until 50 years later when, as a well-known writer of Gloucester fishing stories, he was invited to speak on literature before the Harvard Union.

In 1898, Connolly was with the 9th Massachusetts Infantry at the Siege of Santiago, but in 1900 he again sought Olympic honors. He improved on his 1896 winning mark, but had to settle for second place behind Meyer Prinstein. Connolly missed the 1904 Olympics but competed in 1906, failing to make a valid jump in either the long or triple jump.

Connolly later served in the navy and in 1912 he ran for Congress as a Progressive, although he was defeated. Connolly covered Pershing's "punitive expedition" into Mexico for *Colliers* and in 1917 he became European naval correspondent for the magazine. He remained a writer for the rest of his life.

COOK, Edward Tiffin, Jr.

B. 27 NOV 1888 Chillicothe, OH. D. 18 OCT 1972. Gold: 1908 Pole Vault (tied). Ed Cook was a fine all-round jumper and hurdler. He won the IC4A long jump in 1908 and 1909, the AAU pole vault in 1907, and tied for first place in 1911. He had such marks to his credit as 21.6 for 220y, 6'-2" for the high jump, 23'-5½" for the long jump, 15.6 for the 120y hurdles, and 12'-4½" for the vault. At the 1908 Olympics he shared the title with Alfred Gilbert and this tie for first place in the pole vault remains unique in Olympic history.

Cook graduated from Cornell in 1910 and became a farmer and director of the First National Bank of Chillicothe (Ohio).

CORSON, James Hunt.

B. 14 JAN 1906 Modesto, CA. D. 12 NOV 1981 Burlingame, CA. Bronze: 1928 Discus Throw. Jim Corson, of the College of the Pacific and the Olympic Club of San Francisco, placed third in the 1928 Final Trials and went on to take the bronze medal in Amsterdam with a personal best of 154'-6". He also won the NCAA discus throw in 1927.

After graduating from Pacific, Corson earned a master's degree at Southern Cal and became a well-known educator. He later returned to Pacific as track and football coach, but was promoted almost annually, eventually becoming dean of the college. He later was president of Willamette College in Oregon and received honorary doctorates from both Pacific and Willamette.

COURTNEY, Thomas William.

B. 17 AUG 1933 Newark, NJ. Gold(2): 1956 800 meters, 1956 4 × 400 meter relay. As a 400/800m runner, Fordham's Tom Courtney was a worthy successor to Mal Whitfield for both speed and consistency. He won the NCAA 880y in 1955 and the AAU in 1957 and 1958. Courtney was also the top 400m man in the world in 1956 and won the AAU in 45.6. In 1957 he set a new world 880y record of 1:46.8 and the following year he came within one tenth of a second of the world 800m record. He won the 1956 Final Trials in a new American record of 1:46.4 and then went on to set a new Olympic record of 1:47.7 in winning the Melbourne final. Courtney won a second Olympic gold with a 45.7 anchor leg in the 1,600 meter relay. He was also a notable indoor performer and in 1957 he tied Whitfield's world record of 1:09.5 for 600y and set three world records for the 880y on a flat indoor track.

COX, William John.
B. 12 JUL 1904 Rochester, NY. Bronze: 1924 3,000 meter team race. Bill Cox was still attending Mercersburg Academy when he went to Paris for the 1924 Games and won his Olympic bronze medal the day after he had celebrated his 20th birthday. He later enrolled at Penn State and won nine IC4A titles. Cox won the cross-country individual title in 1926 and 1927 and Penn State won the team race in both those years and again in 1929. Cox also won the IC4A mile in 1927 and indoor mile in 1927-28.

At the Olympics, Bill Cox finished eighth in a field of 44 runners and was the second scoring man on the U.S. team which took third place. Cox had a best mile time of 4:18.6, which he posted in winning the 1927 IC4A indoor title. He also won the AAU Junior one mile in 1924.

CRAIG, Ralph Cook.
B. 21 JUN 1889 Detroit, MI. D. 21 JUL 1972 Lake George, NY. Gold(2): 1912 100 meters, 1912 200 meters. While attending the University of Michigan, Ralph Craig won the IC4A 220y in 1910 and 1911 and each time equalled the world record of 21.2 for a straightaway. In 1911 he also won the 100y in 9.8.

After his 1911 graduation, Craig represented the Detroit YMCA, and despite the lack of suitable training facilities available at the club, he made the 1912 Olympic team for Stockholm. Once in Sweden, Craig trained exceptionally hard and took first place in both Olympic sprints. This was virtually the end of his short but brilliant track career, but in his later years he took up yachting and was an alternate on the 1948 Olympic team. It is often written that Craig competed in 1948 at London, but this is not correct, although he was given the honor of carrying the U.S. flag in the opening ceremonies.

CREGAN, John Francis.
B. 29 JAN 1878 Schenectady, NY. D. 26 DEC 1965 Philadelphia, PA. Silver: 1900 800 meters. The Princetonian John Cregan won the AAU 880y in 1897, the one mile in 1897 and 1898, and at the IC4A he won the 880y

in 1898 and the mile for three successive years (1898–1900). This record clearly indicates Cregan's quality as a miler, but he withdrew from the 1,500m in the 1900 Olympics because the event was staged on a Sunday. When the U.S. team stopped over in London on their way to Paris, John Cregan took second place to Alfred Tysoe at the British AAA Championships. It was Tysoe who again beat him in the Olympic final.

CRONAN, Thomas F.
Bronze: 1906 Long Jump. Apart from taking the bronze medal in the long jump, Tom Cronan placed sixth in the long jump.

CUHEL, Frank Josef.
B. 23 SEP 1904. D. 22 FEB 1943 Spain. Silver: 1928 400 meter hurdles. After winning the 400m hurdles at the Midwestern Olympic Trials in 53.4, Frank Cuhel finished second to Morgan Taylor at the Final Trials when Taylor set a new world record of 52.0. Cuhel himself ran 52.2 behind Taylor and was also inside the previous world record. Neither of the Americans could repeat this form in Amsterdam and the Olympic title went to Lord Burghley (GBR) in 53.4.

Cuhel, a University of Iowa grad, became a newscaster for the Mutual Broadcasting System. During World War II he was being transferred to the North African war zone when his plane crashed on 22 February 1943. His body was not found until three weeks later.

CULBREATH, Joshua.
B. 14 SEP 1932 Norristown, PA. Bronze: 1956 400 meter hurdles. Josh Culbreath first took hurdling seriously when he was attending Morgan State and won the AAU in 1953, 1954, and 1955. In the 1956 Final Trials he brought his best time for the intermediate hurdles down to 50.1 behind Glenn Davis and Eddie Southern, and the Olympic final was a repeat of the U.S. Trials with these three sweeping the medals. Culbreath, who was the first great black intermediate hurdler, won at the Pan-Am Games in 1955 and 1959 and, at Oslo in 1957, he set a world record for the 440y hurdles of 50.5.

CUNNINGHAM, Glenn V.
B. 04 AUG 1909 Atlanta, KS. Silver: 1936 1500 meters. Severely injured as a child in a schoolhouse fire, in

which his brother perished, Glenn Cunningham developed into a tough and durable competitor and was a force to be reckoned with on the world miling scene for almost a decade. He was a prolific runner and fully justified the nickname, "The Iron Man of Kansas."

Cunningham won the NCAA 1,500m in 1932 and then finished third in the AAU before taking fourth place at the Olympics. In 1933 he won the NCAA mile and the AAU 1,500m. After losing the 1934 AAU to Bill Bonthron of Princeton, Glenn Cunningham took the title for the next four years (1935-1938). In 1934 he set a world mile record of 4:06.7 and two weeks after finishing second in the 1936 Olympic 1,500m he set a world record of 1:49.7 for 800m in Stockholm. Cunningham ran his fastest 1,500m in 1940 when he clocked 3:48.0 in finishing second to Walter Mehl in the AAU.

Cunningham earned degrees from Kansas, Iowa, and NYU. His life's work has been a youth ranch which houses needy and abused children.

CURTIS, Thomas Pelham.
B. 07 SEP 1870 Boston, MA. D. 23 MAY 1944 Nahant, MA. Gold: 1896 110 meter hurdles. Although Tom Curtis never won any major championship and was not even awarded his letter at Harvard, he is assured of a place in sporting history as the winner of the first Olympic hurdles title. In Athens, he narrowly defeated the Englishman, Grantley Goulding, and although Goulding was a superior hurdler, Curtis' speed on the flat took him to the tape a yard ahead of the only other finalist. Curtis also won a heat in the 100m at the Olympics, but did not contest the final. In World War I, Curtis commanded the Massachusetts ambulance corps and he later became an executive with the Lord Electric Company of Massachusetts.

CUSHMAN, Clifton Emmett.
B. 02 JUN 1938 Cedarville, MI. D. 25 SEP 1966 Vietnam. Silver: 1960 400 meter hurdles. Cliff Cushman was a remarkably versatile athlete whose talents ranged from a 4:11.6 mile to a sixth place in the 1959 NCAA triple jump. While attending the University of Kansas, Cushman won the 1960 NCAA 400m hurdles and finished third in the Final Trials. At the Olympics he turned the tables on Dick Howard, who had beaten him at the trials, and took second place with a career best of 49.6. In 1961, Cushman won the AAU intermediate hurdles.

AVERY BRUNDAGE

The Olympics were founded by a Frenchman, the Baron Pierre de Coubertin, but one other name is intimately associated with the Olympic Games—that of Avery Brundage. Brundage was initiated into the Olympic family when he competed in track & field in 1912 at Stockholm. He competed in the decathlon, where he withdrew before the last event; the pentathlon, in which he finished sixth; and the discus throw, in which he failed to qualify for the finals.

Avery Brundage was born in Detroit on 28 September 1887. He attended the University of Illinois, majoring in civil engineering and competing on the basketball and track teams. He became an excellent athlete, winning the AAU All-Around championship in 1914, 1916, and 1918. And in his later life he formed a construction company which made him a multi-millionaire. But it was as a sports administrator that he became best known.

Brundage became president of the AAU in 1928 and first made headlines for his autocratic stance insisting that the United States participate in the 1936 Berlin Olympics, despite Hitler's known anti-Semitic policies. Over the furor raised, an American member of the IOC was ousted and Brundage was elected in 1936 to serve on the International Olympic Committee.

In 1952, Brundage became president of the IOC, and would hold that post through 1972. He ruled with an iron hand, and was known as an almost anachronistic defender of amateurism. Among his actions for which he was censured are the ousting of Karl Schranz at the 1972 Winter Olympics for professionalism, the refusal to listen to proposals to return Jim Thorpe's medals, and the labeling of the African boycott of the 1972 Olympics as a tragedy equal to the massacre of the Israeli athletes. America's only IOC president was not a popular one. He died only a few years after his retirement from the IOC.

DAVENPORT, Ira Nelson.

B. 08 OCT 1887 Pond Creek, OK. D. 17 JUL 1941 Dubuque, IA. Bronze: 1912 800 meters. Before turning to the two-lap event, Ira Davenport ran 48.8 for 440y in 1910 which was the fastest time recorded in the world that year. Having graduated from the University of Chicago, he ran the 800m at the 1912 Olympics and, using his basic speed to good effect, closed rapidly on the leaders in the finals stages and failed to take the gold medal by less than one meter.

While at Chicago, Davenport played football from 1909 to 1911 and later became a football coach at Loras College in Dubuque, Iowa. He spent most of his life as the general manager of the Dubuque Boat and Boiler Works.

DAVENPORT, Willie D.

B. 08 JUN 1943 Troy, AL. Gold: 1968 110 meter hurdles; Bronze: 1976 110 meter hurdles. Willie Davenport, a 19-year-old army private, caused one of the sensations of the 1964 Final Trials when he won the high hurdles, finishing ahead of Hayes Jones and Blaine Lindgren. In Tokyo he sustained a thigh injury and was eliminated in the semi-finals, but fours years later, in Mexico City, Davenport took the gold medal. He also finished fourth in 1972 and third in 1976. After the 1964 Games he enrolled at Southern University and won the AAU outdoor title outright in 1965, 1966, and 1967, and tied for first place in 1969.

In 1980 he competed in the 4-man bobsled in the 1980 Winter Olympics, becoming only the fourth American to compete in both sets of Games. Davenport is employed by the city of Baton Rouge and also serves as an athlete's representative to the U.S. Olympic Committee.

DAVIS, Glenn Ashby.

B. 12 SEP 1934 Wellsburg, WV. Gold(3): 1956 400 meter hurdles, 1960 400 meter hurdles, 1960 4 × 400 meter relay. Glenn Davis ran his first intermediate hurdles race in April 1956, which he won in 54.4; within two months he had, incredibly, become the first man to break the 50-second barrier when he brought the world record down to 49.5 at the Final Trials. In Melbourne he won comfortably and defended that title in Rome, becoming the only man in history to win two Olympic 400m hurdle titles. Later in the 1960 Games, he won a

third gold when he contributed a 45.4 third stage to the new world record set by the 1,600m relay team.

Shortly after the Games, Davis signed a pro football contract and played with the Detroit Lions in 1960–61, but in the years between Olympics he had shown himself to be one of the great track talents of all time. He won the AAU 400m/440y hurdles four times and, on the flat, twice broke the world record for the open 440y; his best mark came at the 1958 NCAA where, representing Ohio State, he ran 45.7. He also set two more world records in the 400m/440y hurdles, leaving them at 49.2 and 49.9 respectively, as well as running a 22.5 world record for the 200m hurdles immediately prior to the 1960 Olympics.

DAVIS, Jack Wells.

B. 11 SEP 1930 Amarillo, TX. Silver(2): 1952 110 meter hurdles, 1956 110 meter hurdles. Considering his competitive record, Jack Davis is unfortunate to have never won an Olympic gold medal. He was virtually invincible in the years between his two Olympic appearances and at one stage of his career he won 37 consecutive high hurdle finals, including an unbeaten record in 1953 and 1954.

In 1952 he finished second to Harrison Dillard at both the AAU and the Final Trials and in Helsinki, Dillard beat him again, after Davis hit the ninth hurdle hard. Davis went to the Melbourne Games in 1956 as the firm favorite—he had had the best of his main rival, Lee Calhoun, all year. But Calhoun upset Davis in the Olympic final by a few inches.

Davis won the NCAA high hurdles in 1951, 1952, and 1953 and the low hurdles in 1953. At the AAU he won the highs in 1953 and 1954. Additionally he placed second in the 220y flat at the NCAA in 1952 and was Pan-Am high hurdles champion in 1955.

DAVIS, Otis Crandell.

B. 12 JUL 1932 Tuscaloosa, AL. Gold(2): 1960 400 meters, 1960 4 × 400 meter relay. Otis Davis started at the University of Oregon as a basketball player, taking up track in 1958 at the age of 26. The following year he ran 46.5 for 440y and finished third in the AAU, and in 1960 he won the AAU before going on to take the Olympic title with a new world record of 44.9. Davis also ran the anchor on the gold medal winning relay team, which also set a world record. After winning the 1961

AAU 440y, Davis retired, ending a brief but brilliant track career. He went into coaching and teaching until 1980 when he was appointed the Director of Recreation of the Sports Complex for the U.S. Military in Germany.

DAVIS, Walter Francis.
B. 05 JAN 1931 Beaumont, TX. Gold: 1952 High Jump. A severe attack of polio as a child took a heavy toll on "Buddy" Davis and it took seven years of continual exercise before he was able to walk properly. By the time he enrolled in 1948 at Texas A&M, much of the strength had returned to his legs and by 1951 he was a good enough high jumper to rank second in the world with a best of 6'-9". In 1952 he won the AAU at 6'-10½"—the second highest jump to that time—and then set a new Olympic record in taking the gold medal in Helsinki.

At 6'-8½" tall, Davis was an outstanding basketball player at Texas A&M and was much coveted by the pros. He was drafted and signed after the 1952 Olympics by the Philadelphia Warriors. He had a good pro basketball career, playing six years, backing up Wilt Chamberlain at center in his last years.

DELANEY, Francis James.
B. 01 MAR 1921. Silver: 1948 Shot Put. Jim Delaney of the Olympic Club in San Francisco, and formerly of Notre Dame, set a personal career best when he won the 1948 Final Trials at 55'-1¾". In London, Delaney bettered the previous Olympic record but he was decisively beaten by "Moose" Thompson. Delaney did edge out Jim Fuchs as the U.S. swept the shot put medals.

DELLINGER, William Solon.
B. 23 MAR 1934 Grants Pass, OR. Bronze: 1964 5,000 meters. Bill Dellinger of the University of Oregon won the 1954 NCAA mile, but subsequently concentrated on the 5,000m. In 1956 he won the NCAA title and then set a new U.S. record of 14:16.2 before leaving for Melbourne where, after qualifying comfortably, he failed to finish in the final.

In 1957, Dellinger posted a new U.S. 1,500m record of 3:41.5 while finishing third in a dual meet with Hungary. He won the 5,000m at the AAU and Pan-American Games in 1959 and he won the AAU again in 1960. However, as in 1956, he failed to show his true form at the Olympics and was eliminated in the heats.

At his third Olympics, Bill Dellinger finally came through and, on a rain-soaked track in Tokyo, he put in a devastating last lap to snatch third place from Michel Jazy of France. Dellinger's time of 13:49.8 was the fastest of his long career. He has since become the head coach at his alma mater, where he has numbered among his pupils Steve Prefontaine and Alberto Salazar.

DeMAR, Clarence Harrison.
B. 07 JUN 1888 Madeira, OH. D. 11 JUN 1958 Reading, MA. Bronze: 1924 Marathon. Known as Mr. De-Marathon, Clarence DeMar is a legendary figure in the annals of the Boston Marathon. On his first appearance in the race in 1910 he finished second and the following year he won the race, setting a course record in the process. DeMar, a printer by trade and a devoted lay preacher, then took a five-year break from competition. This decision was taken because a doctor, apparently little-versed in examining the well-conditioned athlete's heart, thought he had a heart condition. After his return to competition, DeMar's final Boston record read seven victories, three seconds, and two thirds. His last victory, in 1930, made DeMar, at 41, the oldest winner on record.

At the Olympics, DeMar finished 12th in 1912, third in 1924, and 27th in 1928. He was a graduate of the University of Vermont, and attended Harvard briefly as a graduate student.

DESCH, August George.
D. 1964. Bronze: 1920 400 meter hurdles. The 400m hurdles final at the 1920 Olympics proved to be a repeat of the U.S. Final Trials with Frank Loomis, John Norton, and Gus Desch finishing in the first three places, in that order, in both events.

In 1921 Desch won the 220y hurdles at the NCAA and the AAU 440y hurdles in 53.4. This was the fastest time of his career and relegated John Norton into second place.

A collegian at Notre Dame, Desch was also an outstanding football player. He later became a well-known football coach and authored several books about his coaching theories.

DeWITT, John Riegel.
B. 29 OCT 1881 Philipsburg, NJ. D. 28 JUL 1930 New York, NY. Silver: 1904 Hammer Throw. While at Princeton, John DeWitt played on the football team for three years (1901–03) and was captain in his last year. In 1902 and 1903 he was named to Walter Camp's All-American team as a guard. He was described by experts as one of the most versatile football players of his time—he played the line, kicked, and occasionally filled a backfield spot.

As a hammer thrower, DeWitt won the IC4A for four successive years (1901–04), setting a meet record of 164'-10" in 1902 which remained unsurpassed until 1915. Later in the season he had the best throw of his career and the best mark in the world in 1902 when he threw 168'-7" at Celtic Park to beat the great John Flanagan by almost six feet. In 1903, DeWitt again topped the world ranking lists.

DILLARD, William Harrison.
B. 08 JUL 1923 Cleveland, OH. Gold(4): 1948 100 meters, 1948 4 × 100 meter relay, 1952 110 meter hurdles, 1952 4 × 100 meter relay. "Bones" Dillard caused a major Olympic upset when he won the 100m in 1948. He went to the 1948 AAU with an unprecedented streak of 82 consecutive hurdle victories, but was surprisingly beaten by Bill Porter. A week later, at the Final Trials, Porter won again and Dillard failed to finish. But he made the Olympic team by placing third in the 100m and then took the Olympic title. Four years later he made no mistakes, winning the hurdles at Helsinki, and winning the gold on the sprint relay team for a second time.

Originally inspired by the victory parade in his native Cleveland for Jesse Owens after the 1936 Olympics, Dillard developed into one of the most consistent hurdlers the world has ever seen. Owens encouraged Dillard to take up hurdling and later gave him the spikes he had worn in Berlin. Dillard went on to win 14 AAU titles and six NCAA championships, as well as setting world records in both the high and low hurdles.

DILLION, James Leo.
B. 02 MAY 1929 Plain City, OK. Bronze: 1952 Discus Throw. After winning the 1951 NCAA discus title for Auburn, Jim Dillion took the 1952 AAU title, beating both Sim Iness and Fortune Gordien. The following week he finished third, behind those two, at the Finals Trials. At Helsinki, he beat Gordien, but Iness won the gold, and Adolpho Consolini of Italy edged Dillion for the silver.

DIXON, Craig Kline.
B. 03 MAR 1926 Los Angeles, CA. Bronze: 1948 110 meter hurdles. The 1948 Olympics arrived just a year too early for Craig Dixon. In 1949 he won the AAU and NCAA high hurdle titles for UCLA and began a winning streak of 59 consecutive hurdles races. Dixon put in a strong bid for a place on the 1952 Olympic team but, after winning his heat at the Final Trials, he fell at the eighth hurdle in the final.

DOHERTY, John Kenneth.
B. 16 MAY 1905 Detroit, MI. Bronze: 1928 Decathlon. The 1928 AAU decathlon was held over three days and also served as the Final Trials. Ken Doherty, later of the University of Michigan, won the event by a margin of less then 70 pts. and was not considered a likely Olympic medalist. But in Amsterdam he vastly improved his score with a total of 7,706 points to take third place behind two Finns.

Ken Doherty won his second AAU decathlon in 1929 and went on to become one of the world's most distinguished and respected coaches. He coached at Michigan from 1940 to 1948, and later at Penn. He has authored three editions of *Track and Field Omnibook*, recognized as one the top instructional books ever written on track & field.

DONAHUE, James J.
B. 20 APR 1886 Brooklyn, NY. D. 29 MAY 1937 Glen Rock, NJ. Silver (Bronze): 1912 Pentathlon. Apart from Jim Thorpe, Jim Donahue of the Los Angeles AC was the leading U.S. all-round athlete at the 1912 Olympics. After his second-place performance in the pentathlon, he placed fourth in the decathlon. (Actually third and fifth if Thorpe's scores are included.) Donahue spent most of his life as a treasurer for the Wright Aeronautical Corp. of Paterson, New Jersey.

DOUGLAS, Herbert Paul, Jr.
B. 09 MAR 1922. Bronze: 1948 Long Jump. Herb Douglas of the University of Pittsburgh won the AAU outdoor long jump in 1945 and the indoor title in 1947. At the IC4A he was the outdoor winner in 1946 and was

UNITED STATES COLLEGES AND THEIR OLYMPIANS

Since the first modern Olympic Games in 1896 the United States intercollegiate athletic system has been responsible for providing the bulk of our Olympic athletes. But exactly which colleges have had the most U.S. Olympians? To be included in our collegiate list we required that the athlete must have actually competed in an Olympic event, and he must have attended school — undergraduate, graduate or professional — at the college in question. A myriad of sources have been checked to compile this information — including the colleges themselves — but it is likely that errors exist. For that we apologize and welcome any known corrections.

Fifteen colleges have had 50 or more Olympic athletes (listed below) with Southern Cal leading the pack. Southern Cal has also contributed the most United States summer Olympians, with 113. Harvard University, however, has been the most constant in its Olympic participation. A Harvard athlete has competed in every summer Olympic Games in which the United States has participated, and every Olympic Winter Games save those of 1924, 1964 and 1972. Other schools with long-running streaks of participation in the summer Olympics include Yale, which missed only in 1896, and Penn, which was not represented only in 1896 and 1906.

The University of Minnesota has by far the most United States Winter Olympians, with 47 — the majority of these being ice hockey players. However they have not been represented at every Olympic Winter Games, nor has any American college. The best record in this category is held by Dartmouth, which failed to have a Winter Olympian only in 1964.

1.	Southern California	143
2.	Harvard	124
3.	Yale	118
4.	Stanford	109
5.	Pennsylvania	85
6.	California (Berkeley)	77
7.	United States Naval Academy	68
8.	California (Los Angeles)	65
9.	Minnesota	64
10.	Cornell	62
11.	United States Military Academy	61
12.	Dartmouth	58
13.	Michigan	57
14.	Princeton	54
15.	Indiana	52

the indoor champion three times. The best mark of his career came at the 1948 Final Trials when he jumped 25'-3" but he could not match this at the Olympics and finished one centimeter out of second.

DRAPER, Foy.

B. 26 NOV 1913 Georgetown, TX. D. FEB 1943. Gold: 1936 4 × 100 meter relay. After clocking a 9.6 100y in 1932 while attending Huntington Park High School in Los Angeles, Foy Draper enrolled at Southern Cal and won the 1935 IC4A 220y. He never bettered his high school mark for 100y, but he improved to a best of 20.8 for 220y, which he set in winning the Far Western AAU in 1934. He also clocked 10.3 for 100m when giving Jesse Owens a close run in the 1935 NCAA. Draper, who ran the third leg on the 1936 relay team, was killed in action during World War II.

DRAYTON, Otis Paul.

B. 08 MAY 1939 Glen Cove, NY. Gold: 1964 4 × 100 meter relay; Silver: 1920 200 meters. While at Villanova, Paul Drayton was a member of the U.S. relay team which set a world record of 39.1 for the 400m relay in the 1961 U.S.-USSR dual meet. Three years later, in Tokyo, he played a part in bringing that record down to 39.0 and was the only runner on both record-breaking teams.

He won the AAU 200m in 1961 and 1962, and tied with Henry Carr for the 1963 220y title. His winning time of 20.5 in 1962 equalled the world record. He defeated Carr, previously unbeaten that season, at the Final Trials, but it was Carr who took the Olympic title, with Drayton finishing second.

DRESSER, Ivan Chandler.
B. 03 JUL 1896 Burr Oak, MI. D. 27 DEC 1956 New York, NY. Gold: 1920 3,000 meter team race. Before becoming a track star ar Cornell, Ivan Dresser was an outstanding cross-country runner and, as captain of the varsity team in 1917, he was the individual winner of the IC4A race. At the 1920 Olympics, Dresser did not finish the 5,000m race, but a few days later joined Hal Brown, Mike Devaney, Arlie Schardt and Larry Shields in the 3,000m team event. Brown won the race, with Schardt third and, with three runners from each country to score, Dresser's sixth place assured the U.S. of the gold.

In 1925, Ivan Dresser joined General Motors and rose to become one of their top executives. He successively held posts as sales manager in Belgium, managing director in Mexico, and manager of the European-South African Region. At his death, he was special assistant to the general manager of General Motors. In 1955, King Baudouin of Belgium conferred the honor of Office of the Order of Leopold II on Ivan Dresser and, among his many civic commitments, he was a member of the board of governors of the New York City Symphony Orchestra.

DROEGEMULLER, William Herbert.
B. 07 OCT 1906 Chicago, IL. Silver: 1928 Pole Vault. Bill Droegemuller of Northwestern won the pole vault at the NCAA in 1927, but in 1928 he was destined to place second in the major meets. He finished as runner-up to Ward Edmonds of Stanford at the NCAA, then placed second to Lee Barnes at the AAU and took the Olympic silver medal behind the United States' Sabin Carr.

After graduation, Droegemuller attended Northwestern Medical School and then established himself as an ophthalmologist in Chicago before retiring to Arizona, where he continues to have a small practice.

DUMAS, Charles Everett.
B. 12 FEB 1937 Tulsa, OK. Gold: 1956 High Jump. As an 18-year-old schoolboy, Charley Dumas caused a sensation when he tied for first place in the 1955 AAU high jump. The following year he won the AAU and became the first man to break the seven-foot barrier when he cleared 7'-0⅝" at the Final Trials, going on to win the Olympic gold as well. Dumas won the AAU again in 1957, 1958 and 1959 but he never won the NCAA during his years at Southern Cal. In 1960 he placed sixth at the Olympics and then retired. In 1964 he attempted a comeback and, after clearing 7'-0¼" in April, finished second in the Coliseum Relays but did not finish the season.

DUNCAN, James Henry.
B. 25 SEP 1887. Bronze: 1912 Discus Throw. Jim Duncan of the Mohawk AC in New York was the first holder of the official world discus record. On 27 May 1912, he threw 156'-1⅜" at Celtic Park and this was recognized by the IAAF when they issued their inaugural list of records. On this form Duncan was the favorite for the 1912 Olympic title, but he only managed third place with a throw some 20 feet below his best. Although he never won an AAU title, he was again the top U.S. performer in 1918 with a mark of 149'-2½".

DUNN, Gordon Glover.
B. 16 APR 1912 Portland, OR. D. 1964. Silver: 1936 Discus Throw. "Slinger" Dunn was leading the 1936 Olympic discus competition until Ken Carpenter, whom Dunn had beaten at the Final Trials, got off the winning throw on his fifth trial. While at Stanford, Dunn had won the 1934 NCAA and IC4A titles and, competing for the Olympic Club of San Francisco, had the best mark of his career in 1936 when he threw 171'-5¼" at the Compton Invitation meet.

DVORAK, Charles Edward.
B. 27 NOV 1878 Chicago, IL. D. 18 DEC 1969. Gold: 1904 Pole Vault. From the University of Michigan, Charles Dvorak was unfortunate not to win an Olympic medal in 1900. He went to the field on the Sunday for which the event had been scheduled only to be told that, for sabattarian reasons, the event would not be held that day. It was held, however, and Irving Baxter won with a modest vault of 10'-10" after Dvorak and his two colleagues, Bascom Johnson and Daniel Horton, had left the scene. The following day a "consolation" event was held, which Horton won at 11'-3¾" with Dvorak second at 11'-1¾".

Four years later in St. Louis, under more organized circumstances, Dvorak won the gold medal with a new Olympic record of 11'-6" and had three failures at a new world record height of 12'-2". He also won the AAU in 1901 and 1903 and was in a six-way tie for first at the 1901 IC4A. He was the first vaulter to use a bamboo pole instead of the ash or hickory pole which had been in vogue for many years.

DYER, Hector Monroe.
B. 02 JUN 1910 Los Angeles, CA. Gold: 1932 4 × 100 meter relay. Hec Dyer of Stanford and the Los Angeles AC ran the third leg on the 1932 Olympic sprint relay team that set a new world record in both the heats and the final. His best mark for 100y was 9.6, when he won the dual meet against Southern Cal in April of 1930.

Dyer made his living as an oil leaser in California, Texas, North Dakota, and the Pacific Northwest.

EASTMAN, Benjamin Bangs.
B. 19 JUL 1911 Burlingame, CA. Silver: 1932 400 meters. In 1931 Ben Eastman helped Stanford set a world record for the 4 × 440y relay and eight days later equalled Ted Meredith's 15-year-old world record of 47.4 for the 440y. Early the following season, Eastman came up with what was probably the most impressive performance of an outstanding career. Running for Stanford against the Los Angeles AC on his home track at Palo Alto, he clocked 46.4 to clip exactly one second off the world 440y record, which he already shared. Later the same afternoon he ran a 45.9 relay leg. Eastman followed this in June with 1:50.9 for 880y, having been timed enroute at 1:50.0 for 800m—both world records.

On the advice of his coach, Dink Templeton, Eastman ran the 400m at the 1932 Olympics, but could not match the finishing speed of Bill Carr. Eastman continued to run for several years, mostly at longer distances. He set world records for 500m, 600y, 800m and 880y before he took off 20 months because of business commitments. After placing fifth in the 800m at the 1936 Olympic Trials, he retired.

EBY, Earl William.
B. 18 NOV 1894 Chicago, IL. D. 14 DEC 1970. Silver: 1920 800 meters. While serving in the infantry in France, Lt. Earl Eby won the 400m and placed second in the 800m at the Inter-Allied Games in Paris in 1919. After the war he returned to the University of Pennsylvania and won the AAU indoor 600y in 1920 and 1923, having first won this title in 1917 before departing for France.

In addition to his Olympic silver medal, in 1920 he won the IC4A 880y and in 1921 he took both the IC4A and NCAA titles. Earl Eby later became one of America's most distinguished track writers.

EISELE, John Lincoln.
B. 18 JAN 1884 Newark, NJ. D. 30 MAR 1933 Newark, NJ. Silver: 1908 3 mile team race; Bronze: 1908 3,200 meter steeplechase. While at Princeton, John Eisele enjoyed only limited success as an athlete. Later, representing the New York AC, he won the AAU 10-mile championship in 1908 and was the leading U.S. distance runner at the Olympics that year. Individually he placed fourth in the three mile team race—the first American to finish—and in the steeplechase he was the only U.S. runner to make the final.

After graduating Princeton in 1906, Eisele joined his father's stock brokerage firm, Eisele & King, in Newark, and did quite well for himself and his family. But the stock market crash affected many lives and Eisele died as the result of a self-inflicted gunshot wound.

ENCK, Schuyler Colfax.
B. 25 JAN 1900. D. NOV 1970. Bronze: 1924 800 meters. "Sky" Enck is best remembered for his Olympic bronze medal in the 1924 800m and for the part he played when Penn State set a new world record of 7:48.8 for the 4 × 880y relay in beating Oxford at the 1923 Penn Relays. However, his championship victories were at the mile and he won the NCAA in 1923 and the IC4A, both indoor and outdoor, the following year.

ENGLEHARDT, Frederick.
Silver: 1904 Triple Jump. On the same day at the 1904 Olympic, Fred Englehardt of New York's Mohawk AC placed second in the triple jump and fourth in the long jump.

EVANS, Dwayne Eugene.
B. 13 OCT 1958 Phoenix, AZ. Bronze: 1976 200 meters. An oustanding high school sprinter at South Mountain in Phoenix, Dwayne Evans went on to place second in the 1976 Final Trials and then finished third at the Olympics. He went on to the University of Arizona and has been unable to duplicate his early successes. He has suffered some injuries, retired once, come back, and to date his only major title has been the 1979 AAU 200m.

Courtesy San Jose State

Lee Evans, the winner of five AAU titles, won gold
medals in both the 400 meter and 4 X 400 meter relay
races.

EVANS, Lee Edward.

B. 25 FEB 1947 Madera, CA. Gold(2): 1968 400 meters,
1968 4 × 400 meter relay. In 1966, his first year out of
Overfelt High School, Lee Evans was undefeated and
won his first AAU title. In 1967 he won the 400m at the
Pan-Am Games and in 1968, while a junior at San Jose
State, he was NCAA champion. Evans then went on to
win the Final Trials with a world record of 44.0, which he
reduced to 43.86 in the Olympic final. He won a second
gold and another world record plaque in the 1,600m
relay.

Evans won the last of his five AAU titles in 1972
and, after placing fifth at the Final Trials, went to Munich
as a member of the 1,600m relay team. However,
because of the ouster of Vince Matthews and Wayne
Collett, and the injury to John Smith, the U.S. could not
field a team in this event. At the end of the 1972 season,
Evans joined the professional ranks. Through 1982, his
400m mark of 43.86 still stood as a world record.

EWELL, Harold Norwood.

B. 25 FEB 1918 Harrisburg, PA. Gold: 1948 4 × 100
meter relay; Silver(2): 1948 100 meters, 1948 200 meters. "Barney" Ewell of Penn State had a remarkable
career as a top-class sprinter. He began by winning the
AAU junior 100m in 1936 while a schoolboy in Lancaster, Pennsylvania, and finished 12 years later, at the age
of 30, with three medals at the 1948 Olympics. In the
intervening years he won 16 major outdoor titles, which
included sprint doubles at both the 1940 and 1941
NCAA and IC4A meets, with a repeat at the 1942 IC4A.

Ewell was also an outstanding long jumper and in
the three years he won the IC4A sprint double, he won
the long jump. He also won the AAU indoor long jump in
1944 and 1945 and the IC4A indoor long jump in 1940
and 1942.

After winning the 100m at the 1948 combined
AAU and Final Trials meet in a world record equalling
10.2, he lost the Olympic final by inches to the outsider
Harrison Dillard and in the 200m he was beaten by a
similar margin by Mel Patton. After the Olympics he lost
his amateur status for accepting an excessive amount
of gifts from his townsfolk, and then competed in Australia and New Zealand as a professional.

EWRY, Raymond Clarence.

B. 14 OCT 1873 Lafayette, IN. D. 29 SEP 1937 New
York, NY. Gold(10): 1900 Standing High Jump, 1900
Standing Long Jump, 1900 Standing Triple Jump, 1904
Standing High Jump, 1904 Standing Long Jump, 1904
Standing Triple Jump, 1908 Standing High Jump, 1908
Standing Long Jump. "Deac" Ewry was paralyzed by
polio as a child, but by dint of diligent exercising he
developed immense strength in his legs and became
the greatest exponent of the standing jumps that the
sport has ever seen.

He attended Purdue from 1890 to 1897, where he
captained the track team and also played football. After
gaining a graduate degree in mechanical engineering
he competed briefly for the Chicago AA before moving
to New York, where he worked for the city as an hydrau-
lics engineer and joined the New York AC.

He won the first of his 15 AAU titles in 1898 at the
age of 25 and the last in 1910. He was undoubtedly
deprived of many more titles when the standing jumps
were dropped from the AAU program from 1899 to

1905. He attempted a comeback in 1912 but, not surprisingly, some of the spring had gone from his legs as he approached his 40th birthday and he failed to make the Olympic team. Ewry's 10 gold medals is an absolute Olympic record.

FAGER, August.
B. 25 SEP 1891. Silver: 1924 Cross-Country team race. Although he finished third in the 10,000m at the Final Trials, Gus Fager of the Finnish-American AC did not compete in the track event at the Paris Games. Placing eighth in the cross-country race, he was the third scoring member of the U.S. team that took the silver medals.

FARRELL, Thomas Francis.
B. 18 JAN 1944 New York, NY. Bronze: 1968 800 meters. After placing fifth in the 800m at the Tokyo Olympics, Tom Farrell improved to take the bronze medal in Mexico with a career best of 1:45.4. While at St. John's he won the NCAA in 1964 and 1965 and the AAU title in 1966. He also won the British AAA 800m in 1965; he also set an indoor 880y record with 1:49.8 that year. Farrell is today an account executive with the Xerox Corp.

FEUERBACH, Leon E. J.
B. c1884. Bronze: 1904 Shot Put. Leon Feuerbach of NYU placed a distant third in the 1904 shot and was a member of the New York AC team that finished fourth in the tug-of-war. In 1903 he won both the junior and senior AAU shot put titles.

FITCH, Alfred Lord.
B. 01 DEC 1912. Silver: 1936 4 × 400 meter relay. Al Fitch of Southern Cal placed fourth at the 1936 Final Trials in a race in which the first five finishers were Californian athletes. At the Berlin Olympics he ran the anchor leg on the relay team that took the silver medals. His best mark at 400m was 47.1 behind Archie Williams' 47.0 at the 1936 NCAA and at 440y he had a best of 47.4 in finishing second in the Pacific Coast Conference meet at Berkeley in May 1936.

FITCH, Horatio May.
B. 06 DEC 1900. Silver: 1924 400 meters. Horatio Fitch of the Chicago AA, and formerly of the University of Illinois, set a new Olympic record and a career best of 47.8 in the first semi-final of the 400m at the Paris Games. He had finished second to Coard Taylor in the Final Trials and although Fitch soundly defeated Taylor in the Olympic final, he was beaten by Eric Liddell of Scotland. If you watched the movie "Chariots of Fire" closely, you will remember a runner asking his coach before the start of the 400 meters if Liddell was anything to worry about. The coach told him to disregard Liddell, but it was a mistake. The character, who was not identified, would have been Horatio Fitch.

FLANAGAN, John J.
B. 09 JAN 1873 Kilbreedy, County Limerick, Ireland. D. 04 JUN 1938 Ireland. Gold(3): 1900 Hammer Throw, 1904 Hammer Throw, 1908 Hammer Throw; Silver: 1904 56 lb. weight throw. Before emigrating to America in the autumn of 1896, John Flanagan won the British AAA title earlier that year and the previous season he had set the first of his numerous world records. After the nine foot circle and the stiff wooden-handled hammer to which he had been accustomed at home, Flanagan initially had some difficulty in adapting to the American seven foot circle and an implement with a pliable handle.

Once he mastered making three turns in the smaller circle, Flanagan was virtually invincible. During the 15 years he lived in America, he topped the world ranking list 12 times and set 13 world records, culminating with a throw of 184'-4" on July 24, 1909. For championships, Flanagan could count, besides his Olympic golds, seven AAU hammer titles and six with the 56 lb. weight. He also won a second British AAA title in 1900 en route to the Paris Olympics. He returned to Ireland in 1911 and made his final international appearance when he won the hammer throw for Ireland in their match against Scotland. His successes were not limited to the hammer and weight events. He placed fourth in the 1904 discus and surprisingly, for a man of his size, he finished second in both the high and long jumps and the all-around event at the 1895 Irish championships.

FLANAGAN, Patrick.
Gold: 1904 Tug-of-War. Pat Flanagan represented the Milwaukee AC in the 1904 tug-of-war event but, like all the members of that team, he was actually from Chicago.

FLYNN, Patrick J.

B. 1895 Bandon, Ireland. Silver: 1920 3,000 meters steeplechase. After emigrating from Ireland, Pat Flynn was considered no more than an average distance runner until his coach at the Paulist AC persuaded him to try the steeplechase. Shortly thereafter, he finished second to Mike Devaney in the 1919 AAU steeplechase. In his first attempt over the Olympic distance of 3,000m, Flynn won the 1920 AAU title with a new U.S. record of 9:58.2. At the Antwerp Olympics, Flynn won his heat comfortably but fell at the water jump in the final and eventually finished some 100 meters behind the winner, Percy Hodge (GBR). Considering Hodge's winning time was 10:00.4, there is little doubt that Flynn would have been in contention for the gold medal had he not fallen.

FORSHAW, Joseph, Jr.

B. 13 MAY 1880 St. Louis, MO. D. 26 NOV 1964 St. Louis, MO. Bronze: 1908 Marathon. Joe Forshaw of the Missouri AC was the first American to compete in three Olympic marathons. He placed 12th in 1906 and 10th in 1912, in addition to his bronze medal performance.

Forshaw was an amazing athlete. Besides distance running he was a champion cyclist and speed skater around St. Louis. He gave those sports up, but at the age of 50 took up figure skating, which he continued until his death. He also played hockey in St. Louis amateur leagues from 1907 until 1936—aged 55 years.

But Joe Forshaw was also a fine distance runner. Besides his marathon successes, he set a long-standing record in 1909 when he ran up Pike's Peak in 2 hrs., 41 minutes, finishing at 14,000 feet of altitude. Despite all this, Forshaw found time to run the family stove and outdoor equipment business.

FOSBURY, Richard Douglas.

B. 06 MAR 1947 Portland, OR. Gold: 1968 High Jump. Dick Fosbury will be remembered more for the high jump style he perfected than for his gold medal. With his "Fosbury Flop," he completely revolutionized the event. Though now often called simply the Flop, many Eastern European jumpers call this style of jumping the Fosbury.

While attending Oregon State he won the NCAA in 1968 and after his Olympic victory he won the title again in 1969. This was his only major post-Olympic victory

and Fosbury turned professional in 1973, with limited success.

FOSS, Frank Kent.

B. 09 MAY 1895. Gold: 1920 Pole Vault. Frank Foss of Cornell and the Chicago AA was the first man to win an Olympic pole vault gold medal with a new world record. At Antwerp he cleared 13'-5" to beat the unofficial world record of 13'-3½", which Foss had himself set the previous year. Foss also shared the 1915 IC4A title, won it outright in 1916, and was AAU champion in both 1919 and 1920.

FRANK, Daniel.

Silver: 1904 Long Jump. Dan Frank of the New Westside AC set a career best and scored a notable victory over Meyer Prinstein in winning the 1904 Metropolitan AAU Championships. Prinstein, however, gained ample revenge at the Olympics and beat Frank by a handsome margin.

FRANK, William G.

Bronze: 1906 Marathon. The New Yorker, William Frank, had a rather undistinguished record at home, but in Athens he was always up with the leaders and was in second place until he was passed a few miles from the stadium.

FRAZIER, Herman Ronald.

B. 29 OCT 1954 Philadelphia, PA. Gold: 1976 4 × 400 meter relay; Bronze: 1976 400 meters. After placing third at the Final Trials, Herman Frazier of Arizona State improved to become the second best American in Montreal by taking the bronze with a career best of 44.95. He also finished second in the NCAA in 1975 and 1976, winning that title in 1977. Frazier was a member of the winning relay team at the 1975 Pan-American Games in addition to running the opening stage on the team that won the 1976 Olympic title.

After 1976, Frazier continued to compete as a runner, but he also trained as a bobsledder in hopes of making the 1980 Winter Olympic team. His chances as a sledder looked good, but he became assistant athletic director at Arizona State and when the Frank Kush controversy erupted, Frazier was unable to train much for either sport, and missed out at both in the 1980 trials.

FREEMAN, Ronald J., II.

B. 12 JUN 1947 Elizabeth, NJ. Gold: 1968 4 × 400 meters relay; Bronze: 1968 400 meters. Ron Freeman's 43.2 lap on the second leg of the 1,600m relay in Mexico is the fastest 400m that has ever been run. Taking over the baton three meters down on Nyamau of Kenya, he put the U.S. into a 20-meter lead and on their way to a new world record of 2:56.1—which has stood through 1982.

In the individual 400m, Freeman, from Arizona State, took the bronze in 44.40 which was the fourth fastest 400m of all time. But he never won a major championship and never again matched the form he had shown in Mexico City.

FRIEDE, Oscar C.

Bronze: 1904 Tug-of-War. The Southwest Turnverein of St. Louis entered two teams in the 1904 tug-of-war and Oscar Friede was a member of the team which finished third.

FRIEND, Hugo Morris.

B. 21 JUL 1882 Prague, Czechoslovakia. D. 29 APR 1966 Chicago, IL. Bronze: 1906 Long Jump. Hugo Friend's parents emigrated to America when he was two years old and initially settled in Great Bend, Kansas, before moving to Chicago in 1890. Friend later enrolled at the University of Chicago and, in 1905, captained the first Chicago team to win the Big Ten Championship. Later in the season he scored a double in the long jump and the high hurdles at the AAU championships. After graduation, Friend joined the Chicago AA and at the 1906 Olympics, placed fourth in the hurdles in addition to his long jump bronze medal.

Friend practiced as a lawyer but was soon appointed to judge, and he was the presiding judge at baseball's most notorious trial, the Chicago Black Sox scandal of 1919. After the jury acquitted the accused players, Friend congratulated them for "a just verdict."

FUCHS, James Emanuel.

B. 06 DEC 1927 Chicago, IL. Bronze(2): 1948 Shot Put, 1952 Shot Put. While at Yale, Jim Fuchs won the NCAA and the AAU shot in 1949 and 1950. Between July 1949 and August 1950 he set four world records; his last mark of 58'-10¾" remained the world record for almost three years. He won the discus at the 1951 Pan-American Games and he was also a fine sprinter. After leaving Yale, where he was also a football star, he joined the New York AC and won three AAU indoor shot titles (1951–1953).

During his peak years, Fuchs was invincible and he had a winning streak of 88 shot put victories before losing to Parry O'Brien at the 1951 AAU outdoor meet.

FUQUA, Ivan William.

B. 09 AUG 1909 Decatur, IL. Gold: 1932 4 × 400 meter relay. Ivan Fuqua's first major competition at a national level was the 1929 AAU, in which he hitchhiked to Denver and got a job cleaning the stadium in preparation for the meet. He also got a nice sunburn and, not surprisingly, failed to show his true form when the competition began.

While at Indiana University, Fuqua won the AAU 400m in 1933 and 1934 and was a member of the team which won the AAU indoor relay in 1934. His best clockings were 47.3 for 440y in the 1933 NCAA (placing second) and 47.4 for 400m in winning the 1934 AAU title. A time of 46.6 often credited to him in Budapest in 1933 was actually a wire service error and was correctly 47.6.

After graduation, Ivan Fuqua was appointed track coach at Connecticut State (now the University of Conn.). He entered the navy during the War, was discharged in 1946 with the rank of lieutenant commander, and joined Brown as a coach. He stayed there as head coach from 1947 until 1973, when he retired. He is currently manager and co-owner of a beach club in Rhode Island.

GARRELLS, John Carlyle.

B. 18 NOV 1885 Bay City, MI. D. 21 OCT 1956 Grosse Ile, MI. Silver: 1908 110 meter hurdles; Bronze: 1908 Shot Put. In 1907, Johnny Garrells, of the University of Michigan, won both hurdle events and placed second in the shot at the IC4A. The following year he represented the U.S. in the high hurdles and the shot at the Olympics an unusual combination. He won a medal in both events and competed in both discus events at the 1908 Olympics.

GARRETT, Robert.

B. 24 JUN 1875 Baltimore Cty., MD. D. 25 APR 1961 Baltimore, MD. Gold(2): 1896 Shot Put, 1896 Discus

Throw; Silver(2): 1896 High Jump (tied), 1896 Long Jump; Bronze(2): 1900 Shot Put, 1900 Standing Triple Jump. Bob Garrett was captain of the Princeton track team when Prof. William Milligan Sloane, a future IOC member, suggested he try his hand at the discus throw at the revival of the Olympics. The event was unknown in America, but Sloane consulted the works of Lucian. Garrett, from a wealthy Baltimore banking family, hired a local blacksmith to construct an implement in accordance with the description of Lucian. The result of this weighed some 20 lbs. and Garrett quickly relinquished his interest in discus throwing.

At Athens, however, Garrett spotted the competition disc, took several throws with this vastly more manageable instrument, and decided to enter after all. He took the first Olympic discus title by upsetting local favorite Panagiotis Paraskevopoulos. The following day the long jump and shot put were held within half-an-hour of each other and Garrett finished as runner-up in the long jump, but claimed a second Olympic title in the shot put.

Bob Garrett won two more medals at the 1900 Olympics and in the intervening years he won the shot and finished second at the 1897 IC4A for Princeton; the following year, representing Johns Hopkins, he finished second in the shot.

With his six Olympic medals, Garrett is the most successful of all Princeton Olympians and in recognition of his accomplishments, the Garrett Memorial Track at Princeton is named after him. The discus which Garrett threw at Athens in 1896 is also on display at the Dillon Gymnasium.

GATHERS, James.
B. 17 JUN 1930 Sumter, SC. Bronze: 1952 200 meters. With Andy Stanfield and Thane Baker taking the first two places, Jim Gathers completed the medal sweep for the U.S. in the 1952 200m by finishing third.

Gathers, of the U.S. Air Force and formerly Tillotson College, officially placed equal third in the 100m at the 1952 Final Trials, but the selectors preferred Dean Smith as their Olympic choice and Gathers ran only the 200m in Helsinki.

GIFFIN, Merritt H.
Silver: 1908 Discus Throw. Merritt Giffin of the Chicago AA was leading the 1908 discus throw until Martin Sheridan moved into the lead on his final throw. Giffin won the AAU discus title in 1910.

GILBERT, Alfred Carleton.
B. 15 FEB 1884 Salem, OR. D. 24 JAN 1961 Boston, MA. Gold: 1908 Pole Vault (tied). After attending the College of the Pacific, Al Gilbert enrolled at Yale, where their reputation as a fine vaulting center was just being established. In 1907 he was in a four-way tie for the IC4A title and all four vaulters were from Yale. In June 1908, Gilbert set a world record of 12'-7½" only to lose the record six days later to Walter Dray, a fellow Eli. Gilbert won the AAU junior title in 1905 but never won the senior outdoor championship. At the 1908 Olympics, Gilbert tied for first place with Ed Cook of Cornell, the only time this has happened in Olympic pole vault history.

Besides vaulting, Gilbert finished second in the Yale gymnastics championships in 1905 and was intercollegiate wrestling champion in 1906. After his sporting days were over, he made a fortune as president of the toy company that bore his name and manufactured Erector Sets, American Flyer electric trains, and many other popular toys. Gilbert also earned an M.D. degree from Yale, but he never practiced medicine.

GLANCE, Harvey.
B. 28 MAR 1957 Phenix City, AL. Gold: 1976 4×100 meters relay. While at Auburn, Harvey Glance scored a sprint double at the 1976 NCAA and then took the 100m at the Final Trials. In the Olympic 100m he was the first American home (in fourth place) as, for the first time since 1928, the U.S. failed to medal in the short sprint.

Glance won the NCAA 100m again in 1977 and placed third in 1978 and 1979. In 1980 he again qualified for the Olympic team but, of course, did not compete. Glance was a fine relay runner and, apart from his Olympic gold medal, was on the team that won the 1979 Pan-American Games 400m relay.

GLOVER, Edward Chester.
B. 1885 Emsworth, PA. D. 02 NOV 1980 Crown Point, IN. Bronze: 1906 Pole Vault. Ed Glover entered Purdue in January 1903, but did not graduate. He later competed for the Chicago AA, winning the 1905 AAU pole vault. At the 1906 Olympics he could not repeat the form he had shown at home and placed third behind the

world record holder, Fernand Gonder (FRA), and Bruno Soderstrom of Sweden.

Glover later became a lawyer in Lake County, Indiana,and served two terms as mayor of Crown Point, Indiana.

GORDIEN, Fortune Everett.
B. 09 SEP 1922 Spokane, WA. Silver: 1956 Discus Throw. Bronze: 1948 Discus Throw. Fortune Gordien first topped the world ranking list in 1947 and although he never quite did himself justice at the Olympics, he remained a major force in the discus for more than a decade. He won six AAU titles and while at the University of Minnesota he was three times NCAA champion. He posted a new world record four times, finishing with a throw of 194'-6" at Pasadena in August 1953. This was the best mark of his career but in 1960, as a 38-year-old, he was still capable of 187'-10".

Gordien, who is now a cattle rancher in Oregon, was also an accomplished shot putter, placing second in the 1947 AAU and third in the NCAA with a mark of 54'-2¼", which was the fifth best mark in the world that year. Apart from his two Olympic medals he also placed fourth in the discus at the 1952 Games.

GORDON, Edward Lansing, Jr.
B. 01 JUL 1906 Jackson, MS. D. SEP 1971 Detroit, MI. Gold: 1932 Long Jump. After placing seventh in the 1928 Olympic long jump, Ed Gordon showed dramatic improvement to take the gold medal at Los Angeles four years later. Gordon also won the AAU in 1929 and 1932 and the NCAA for Iowa in 1929–31. He remained a top flight performer for many years and in 1938, representing the Grand Street Boys Club of New York, won the AAU indoor long jump, successfully defending that title in 1939. His career best of 25'-4⅜" came in winning the Kansas Relays in 1931.

GOURDIN, Edward Orval.
B. 10 AUG 1897 Jacksonville, FL. D. 21 JUL 1966 Quincy, MA. Silver: 1924 Long Jump. With the possible exception of Sol Butler, Ed Gourdin of Harvard was the first of the great black long jumpers. On July 23, 1921, at the Harvard/Yale vs. Oxford/Cambridge meet, he set a world record of 25'-3", defeating the British first string, Harold Abrahams, by the shattering margin of almost three feet. Gourdin was also an outstanding sprinter

and at the same meet defeated Abrahams, the future Olympic champion of "Chariots of Fire" fame, in the 100y. Gourdin won the AAU long jump in 1921, the pentathlon in 1921–22, and the IC4A long jump in 1921.

Gourdin, a lawyer, was admitted to the Massachusetts bar in 1925 and the Federal bar in 1931. He became a U.S. attorney in 1936 and in 1958 became the first black to become a member of the Massachusetts Supreme Court.

GOURDINE, Meredith C.
B. 26 SEP 1929 Newark, NJ. Silver: 1952 Long Jump. Meredith Gourdine of Cornell won the 1951 IC4A with a career best of 25'-9¾" and at the same meet won the 220y hurdles. In the Olympic year, Gourdine beat Jerome Biffle to win the Final Trials. One week earlier, at the AAU, he had also defeated Biffle, although finishing second to George Brown. However, Biffle won the one that mattered, finishing a bare four centimeters ahead of Gourdine in the Olympic final.

GRAHAM, Glenn.
B. 17 JAN 1904. Silver: 1924 Pole Vault. Glenn Graham of Cal Tech lost the Olympic pole vault after a jump-off with his fellow Californian, the 18-year-old schoolboy, Lee Barnes. His son, Jim Graham, made the 1956 U.S. Olympic team, also as a pole vaulter, but in a show of great magnanimity, relinquished his spot to Bob Gutowski who, as the Games approached, showed better form than Graham.

GREENE, Charles Edward.
B. 21 MAR 1945 Pine Bluff, AK. Gold: 1968 4×100 meters relay; Bronze: 1968 100 meters. Hampered by a muscle injury, Charlie Greene, a frosh at the University of Nebraska, finished sixth in the 100m at the 1964 Final Trials after he had seemed a virtual certainty to make the team. Four years later he placed second in the trials and in Tokyo he won a gold medal in the relay and a bronze in the 100m.

Greene won the NCAA 100 three times and the AAU twice; he also claimed three NCAA titles and two at the AAU indoors. In 1968 he had some memorable battles with Jim Hines, winning three of their six meetings, but losing the biggest one of all.

GROMAN, Herman Charles.
B. 18 AUG 1882 Odebolt, IA. D. 21 JUL 1954 Whitehall, MI. Bronze: 1904 400 meters. Herman Groman, a Yale grad, represented the Chicago AA at the 1904 Olympics. He was an early leader in the 400m but faded in the closing stages and eventually lost second place to Frank Waller by less than one meter.

After Yale, Groman attended Rush Medical College from which he earned his M.D. in 1907. He set up a practice in Hammond, Indiana, but he was also active in community affairs and was on the board of several local businesses.

GUNN, Adam B.
Silver: 1904 All-Around. Adam Gunn of the Buffalo YMCA won the AAU All-Around championship in 1901 and 1902. In the 1904 Olympic event he was leading the competition, a forerunner of the decathlon, after seven events but finally ended up 129 points behind the Irishman, Tom Kiely.

GUTOWSKI, Robert Allen.
B. 25 APR 1935 San Pedro, CA. D. 02 AUG 1960. Silver: 1956 Pole Vault. Bob Gutowski broke Dutch Warmerdam's world pole vault record of 15 years standing. In April 1957, Gutowski cleared 15'-8¼" to become the new world record holder, and later in the season he improved to 15'-9¾", but the height was not approved as a world record because the pole passed under the bar, in contravention of IAAF rules. Gutowski finished fourth at the 1956 Final Trials and only made the team after Jim Graham withdrew.

As a contemporary of Don Bragg and Bob Richards, Gutowski found championships hard to come by, but he tied Bragg for the 1958 AAU indoor title and while at Occidental he tied for the NCAA title in 1956, winning it outright in 1957. Gutowski was also a talented long jumper and his best mark of 24'-8¾" came in the 1960 AAU decathlon. This was to be his last competition—less than one month later, at the age of 25, he was killed in an automobile accident.

GUTTERSON, Albert Lovejoy.
B. 23 AUG 1887 Andover, VT. D. 07 APR 1965 Burlington, VT. Gold: 1912 Long Jump. Albert Gutterson of the University of Vermont showed the best form of his career when he won the 1912 Penn Relays with a jump of 24'-0⅝". He then added almost one foot to this mark in Stockholm and won the gold medal at 24'-11¼" which was only one-half inch behind Peter O'Connor's (Ireland) world record.

Gutterson became an engineer who eventually owned his own tool company. He was an active supporter of Vermont athletics and a leader of the New England chapter of the U.S. Olympians Society.

HABERKORN, Charles.
Bronze: 1904 Tug-of-War. Charles Haberkorn was a member of the St. Louis Southwest Turnverein #2 team which finished third in the 1904 tug-of-war. Haberkorn also competed in the lightweight class in wrestling, but was eliminated in his first bout.

HAHN, Archibald.
B. 14 SEP 1880 Dodgeville, WI. D. 21 JAN 1955 Charlottesville, VA. Gold(4): 1904 60 meters, 1904 100 meters, 1904 200 meters, 1906 100 meters. In 1904, Archie Hahn of the University of Michigan became the first man to win both the 100m and 200m at the Olympic Games, and he won the 60m, an event which has not been held in the Olympics since. By winning the 100m at Athens he became the first and, so far, only man to successfully defend the 100m title.

Hahn took both sprints at the U.S. and Canadian championships in 1903 and he again won the AAU 220y in 1905. His time of 21.6 in winning the 1904 Olympic 200m was a new world record and was not bettered at the Olympics until 1932, although it must be noted that the 1904 race was run on a straight course.

Archie Hahn later became a track coach, first at Princeton and then at the University of Virginia. He wrote one of the first definitive books on sprinting.

HALL, David Connolly.
B. 01 MAY 1875 Sherbrooke, Quebec, Canada. D. 27 MAY 1972 Seattle, WA. Bronze: 1900 800 meters. Although Dave Hall never won a national title, he was an outstanding performer at the New England Championships, winning the one mile twice, the 10 miles four times, and setting a new half-mile record. Hall, the first Olympian from Brown, was the fastest of the heat winners in the 1900 800m. In the final he was lying second at the halfway mark, at which point he lost a shoe; despite this handicap, he finished third while

retaining the Olympic record—the final was won in 2:01.2 compared with Hall's time of 1:59.0 in the first heat.

After graduating from Brown, David Hall took his Sc.M. from the University of Chicago in 1903 and his M.D. from Rush Medical College in 1907. He taught at the University of Oklahoma for two years and then went to the University of Washington as Professor of Hygiene. In 1918 he was a colonel in charge of the ambulance troops on the Italian front and was honored by the King of Italy for his services. Dr. Hall then returned to Washington and retired in 1947 after 39 years at the University.

HALL, Ervin.
B. 02 JUL 1947 Philadelphia, PA. Silver: 1968 110 meter hurdles. Erv Hall set an Olympic record of 13.3 in winning the first semi-final in Mexico, but in the final he could not match Willie Davenport's superb start, and Davenport went on to take the gold medal in a time which matched Hall's semi-final clocking. While attending Villanova, Hall won the IC4A title in 1968.

HAMILTON, Brutus Kerr.
B. 19 JUL 1900 Peculiar, MO. D. 28 DEC 1970 Berkeley, CA. Silver: 1920 Decathlon. As a student at the University of Missouri, Brutus Hamilton won both the 1920 AAU pentathlon and decathlon and at the Olympics placed sixth in the pentathlon and took the silver medal in the decathlon. In 1924 he competed in the Olympic pentathlon for a second time and placed seventh. Hamilton's greatest contribution to the sport was, however, as a coach. He was coach at Cal/Berkeley from 1932–65 and during that time his team won six NCAA championships and 14 NCAA individual titles. He was a greatly respected man and was assistant coach to the 1932 and 1936 Olympic teams and head coach for the 1952 team. In 1950 he was voted Missouri's Greatest Amateur Athlete.

HAMILTON, William Frank.
B. 1884. Gold: 1908 1600 meter medley relay. Representing the Chicago AA, Bill Hamilton won the 1908 AAU 100y and was selected for both sprints and the relay at the 1908 Olympics. After winning his heat of the 100m in London, he withdrew from the second round, and in the 200m he again won his heat but was elimina-

Courtesy Ed Kirwan Graphic Arts

Coach Brutus Hamilton's team at Cal-Berkeley won six NCAA Championships and fourteen individual titles during his thirty-four-year coaching career.

ted in the second round by the ultimate winner, Bobby Kerr of Canada.

Hamilton did, however, win a gold medal in the medley relay when he ran the opening 200m stage and put the U.S. team into a six-meter lead which each of his teammates improved upon, with the anchorman, Mel Sheppard, breaking the tape 25 meters ahead of the Germans.

HAMM, Edward Barton.

B. 13 APR 1906 Lonoke, AK. D. 25 JUN 1982. Gold: 1928 Long Jump. While attending Georgia Tech, Ed Hamm won the NCAA in 1927 and 1928 and then took the 1928 AAU long jump with a world record of 25'-11⅛". At the Olympics, Hamm scored a comfortable win over Silvio Cator of Haiti with a new Olympic record of 25'-4¼", but a mere nine days later, Cator took the world record with the first jump ever over 26 feet—26'-0½".

HAMPTON, Millard Frank.

B. 08 JUL 1956 Fresno, CA. Gold: 1976 4 × 100 meter relay; Silver: 1976 200 meters. Millard Hampton of UCLA set a career 200m best of 20.10 in winning the 1976 Final Trials. He had earlier won the AAU title and, apart from placing only fifth in the California Relays in May, his second place to Don Quarrie of Jamaica at the Olympics was Hampton's only defeat of the season. Hampton won a relay gold medal at Montreal and continued competing until 1980, when he placed second at the TAC championships.

HANSEN, Frederick Morgan.

B. 29 DEC 1940 Cuero, TX. Gold: 1964 Pole Vault. On 5 June 1964, Fred Hansen of Rice became the first man to ever clear 17 feet in the pole vault. His winning height that day in Houston was actually 17'-1" and eight days later at the San Diego Invitational he raised the record to 17'-2". He then won the AAU title at 17'-0" and in July, in the match against the USSR in Los Angeles, he pushed the world record up to 17'-4" and rounded off a memorable season by taking the Olympic gold medal.

Hansen is today a practicing dentist in Dallas. He is also an accomplished golfer—he played in the match play portion of the 1980 U.S. Amateur.

HARDIN, Glenn Foster.

B. 01 JUL 1910 Derma, MS. D. 06 MAR 1975 Baton Rouge, LA. Gold: 1936 400 meter hurdles; Silver: 1932 400 meter hurdles. Despite his Olympic successes, Glenn Hardin will be best remembered for his 50.6 400m hurdles in Stockholm in 1934 which stood as a world record for 19 years. He had two earlier world records to his credit, the first coming in the 1932 Olympic final when the winner, Bob Tisdall of Eire, was debarred from having his time of 51.7 recognized be-cause he knocked over the last hurdle and the record went to Hardin, who ran 52.0 in second place. This equalled Morgan Taylor's 1928 world record but Hardin made the record his own by winning the 1934 AAU in 51.8.

While at LSU, Hardin won the 440y flat and the low hurdles at the NCAA in 1933 and 1934; he also won the AAU intermediate hurdles in both those years. In 1936 he won his third AAU intermediate title then took the Olympic title and retired, having been unbeaten in the intermediates since the 1932 Olympic final. His son, Billy, carried on the family tradition by competing in the 400m hurdles in the 1964 Olympics.

HARE, Thomas Truxtun.

B. 12 OCT 1878 Philadelphia, PA. D. 02 FEB 1956 Radnor, PA. Silver: 1900 Hammer Throw; Bronze: 1904 All-Around. Better known as a four-time all-American guard on the Penn football team, track & field was a secondary sport to Truxtun Hare, who was considered by Walter Camp as one of the linemen on his all-time college football team from the turn of the century.

Hare's best performances in track athletics were saved for the Olympics; he never placed higher than second in the IC4A and his throw of 161'-2" in the 1900 hammer was, by 20 feet, his longest throw ever. He also competed in the 1900 Olympic discus event and in the 1904 All-Arounds, where he finished third after leading through five events.

Hare was an amazingly versatile person. He was an outstanding archer and was president of the United Bowmen of America. He became an attorney, specializing in corporate law until his 1951 retirement. He wrote poetry and published eight books of children's poems. In addition he was one of the civic leaders of Philadelphia, serving on several boards and betterment groups.

HARNDEN, Arthur H.

B. 20 MAY 1924. Gold: 1948 4 × 400 meter relay. Fourth place at the Final Trials earned Art Harnden of Texas A&M a place on the 1948 Olympic relay team. He ran a 48.0 opening leg in the final, which put the U.S. into a lead they held to the tape. Harnden had a career best of 47.3 for 400m in placing third in the 1948 NCAA.

HART, Eddie James.

B. 24 APR 1948 Martinez, CA. Gold: 1972 4 × 100

meter relay. After winning his heat in the 1972 Olympic 100m, Eddie Hart, together with Rey Robinson, failed to arrive at the start in time to compete in the second round. It was tragic, for Hart had equalled the world record of 9.9 in winning the Final Trials and had looked like a certain medalist and possible champion. He gained some consolation and revenge later in the Games when he ran the anchor leg, holding off 100m champion Valery Borzov of the USSR, on the relay team that set a new world record.

While at Cal/Berkeley, Hart won the 1970 NCAA 100y, but never figured prominently at the AAU meet, his best placing being sixth in 1969. He retired at the end of 1972 but made a comeback in 1978 and for two years was again ranked among the top U.S. sprinters.

HARTRANFT, Samuel Glenn.
B. 03 DEC 1901 Aberdeen, SD. D. 12 AUG 1970. Silver: 1924 Shot Put. Although his Olympic honors came in the shot, Glenn "Tiny" Hartranft was equally successful with the discus. While at Stanford he scored a shot/discus double at the IC4A in 1922 and 1924. In winning the 1924 discus he threw 158'-1⅛" which bettered the existing world record but was not ratified "because of a high wind." However, he set an official world record the following year of 157'-1⅛". In the 1924 Olympic discus he was completely out of form and only placed sixth with a throw some 20 feet below his best.

HATCH, Sydney H.
Silver: 1904 4 mile team race. Sydney Hatch was from River Forest, Illinois, and represented the Chicago AA team which took second place, out of only two teams, in the 4-mile team race at the 1904 Games. Individually, Hatch finished last of the 10-man field. He also competed in the marathon in 1904, finishing eighth, and placed 14th in the 1908 Olympic marathon.

Hatch won the Missouri AC marathon in 1906, 1907, and 1908, but he did not have any success at the Boston Marathon until almost a decade had passed. There, he finished third in 1915 and 1916, and achieved his best placing by finishing second in 1917.

HAWKINS, Martin W.
B. 20 FEB 1888 Sweden. D. 27 OCT 1959. Bronze: 1912 110 meter hurdles. The United States provided five of the six finalists for the high hurdles in the 1912 Olym-

pics. Martin Hawkins of the Multnomah AC of Portland, Oregon, barely edged John Case out of third place as the U.S. swept the first four places. Hawkins later became a lawyer, then a judge, and in 1940 was elected to the circuit court.

HAYES, John Joseph.
B. 10 APR 1886 New York, NY. D. 23 AUG 1965 Englewood, NJ. Gold: 1908 Marathon. The 1908 Olympic marathon is best remembered for the disqualification of Dorando Pietri, but this does less than justice to Johnny Hayes, who finished unaided only half a minute behind the Italian. Johnny Hayes was born in America soon after his parents emigrated from Ireland. He first took up running in 1905 and his initial success came when he took third place in the 1907 Boston Marathon. Later in the season he won the Yonkers Marathon then, by finishing second in the 1908 Boston race, Hayes won a spot on the Olympic team.

After his Olympic victory, Hayes paid a brief visit to his grandparents in Ireland and then returned to New York where Bloomingdale's had plastered their department store with photographs of Hayes and announced that their employee, who had been rumored to train on the store track on the roof, had been promoted to manager of sporting goods. Years later, Hayes laid to rest this oft-repeated bit of Olympic lore. He never did actually work at Bloomingdale's, or train on the roof. He drew a salary from Bloomingdale's but most of his time was spent training at a track outside Manhattan.

Hayes turned pro upon his return to America and four times met, and lost to, Dorando Pietri in professional marathon races. In 1912, Hayes coached the U.S. Olympic marathoners and later was cross-country coach at Columbia. After a brief spell as a vaudeville artist, Johnny Hayes settled in New York for a business career and became a successful food broker.

HAYES, Robert Lee.
B. 20 DEC 1942 Jacksonville, FL. Gold(2): 1964 100 meters, 1964 4 × 100 meters. Bob Hayes is arguably the fastest sprinter of all time. During his four years at Florida A&M, he lost only two of 62 finals at 100y or 100m. At 100m he had a best time of 10.05, which he clocked in the Olympic final on a cinder track after running a wind-assisted 9.91 in the semi-finals. Hayes

Courtesy Florida A&M

As the anchor of the 1964 Olympic relay team, Hayes (center) made up a four-meter deficit with a time estimates as low as 8.6 seconds for his 100 meter leg.

was the first runner to run 100y in 9.1, and the first man to better six seconds for 60y indoors.

Hayes won the AAU 100y for three straight years starting in 1962 and the NCAA 200m in 1964. His anchor leg in the 1964 Olympic relay, making up a four-meter deficit, was a fitting climax to a truly brilliant career. Estimates of his time range as low as 8.6 for the 100 meter leg, with an estimated 100y time of 7.7 seconds.

The relay was his final race and upon his return home, he signed a pro football contract with the Dallas Cowboys. As a wide receiver and punt returner he became one of the great players of the game and should be credited with revolutionizing pass defense. Man-to-man coverage was woefully inadequate in coping with his speed, and it ushered in the current era of zone defense in pass coverage. Hayes played pro football for 11 years—10 with Dallas and a final one with the San Francisco 49ers. Unfortunately, in later years he ran into trouble with the law and served a two-year jail term for possession and trafficking in illegal drugs.

HEARN, Lacey Ernest.
B. 03 MAR 1881 Portland, IN. D. 19 OCT 1969 Fort Wayne, IN. Silver: 1904 4 mile team race; Bronze: 1904 1500 meters. Lacey Hearn represented the Chicago AA at the 1904 Olympics, losing a close race to his teammates, Jim Lightbody and Frank Verner, in the 1,500m. All three were on the Chicago team that won the silver medals in the 4-mile team race. Hearn graduated from Purdue in 1905 with a degree in electrical engineering and later became a real estate broker.

HEDGES, Benjamin Van Doren, Jr.
B. 08 JUN 1907 Plainfield, NJ. D. 31 DEC 1969 New York, NY. Silver: 1928 High Jump. Prior to graduating from Princeton in 1930, Ben Hedges won the IC4A high jump in 1929. With his second place in the 1928 high jump, Hedges is the last Princetonian to have won an Olympic track & field medal.

In 1931, Hedges joined Bankers Trust Co. as a personnel administrator and later became executive vice-president of the Big Brother Movement. He was also a war hero, winning 13 Battle Stars and receiving a Presidential Unit Citation for his work in the Pacific as an air combat intelligence officer.

HELFFRICH, Alan Boone.
B. 07 AUG 1900 New York, NY. Gold: 1924 4 × 400 meter relay. Alan Helffrich of Penn State was primarily a half-miler and was an alternate on the 1920 Olympic team in the 800m. The following year he won his first AAU 880y title and was again champion in 1922 and 1925. He won the NCAA 880y in 1922 and again in 1923, and at the IC4A he was the 880y champion in 1923 and won the 440y in 1924.

Inexplicably, he lost his form in the 1924 Olympic Trials and after running 1:54.8 in the heats, failed to place in the first six in the final. However, he did place sixth in the 400m, which earned him a place on the relay team in Paris and he broke the tape for the U.S. in a new world record of 3:16.0. The previous year at the Penn Relays, he had run the anchor stage in another world record effort, this one the 4 × 880y relay as Penn State defeated visiting Oxford.

HICKS, Thomas J.
B. 07 JAN 1875 Birmingham, England. D. 02 DEC 1963. Gold: 1904 Marathon. The first two men to finish in the 1904 Olympic marathon were the English-born Tom Hicks and the French-born Albert Corey. Although they had a European birthplace in common, their occupations could hardly have been more divergent—Hicks was a clown by profession and Corey earned his living as a professional strike-breaker.

Tom Hicks had been around the American distance running scene for some years, having finished sixth in Boston in 1900, improving to fifth in 1901 and placing second in 1904. This experience was to stand him in good stead, considering the extreme conditions in which the 1904 Olympic marathon was run. The course was hilly, the temperature was 90° F., there were no watering stations apart from a well at the halfway mark, and the automobiles following the race churned up a great deal of dust. Only the fact that Hicks had been sustained by doses of brandy, egg white, and strychnine during the latter stages of the race enabled him to finish. But his dreams of being champion were shattered when he arrived at Francis Field only to see Fred Lorz being photographed, as the victor, with Alice Roosevelt, the daughter of the President Teddy Roosevelt. It later transpired that Lorz had covered much of the course in an automobile and then claimed that his Olympic "victory" was only a practical joke. The AAU did not share his sense of humor and they immediately banned him (he was later reinstated and won the 1905 Boston Marathon). No more was heard of Hicks as after his ordeal, both physical and mental, he retired on the spot.

HILL, Ralph Anthony.
B. 26 DEC 1908. Silver: 1932 5000 meters. In 1930, Ralph Hill of the University of Oregon surprised the track world by setting a new American mile record of 4:12.4 in Oregon's dual meet against Washington. By 1932, though, he had moved up to the 5,000m and took the AAU title in 14:55.7. Three weeks later the virtual unknown took on the recognized masters of distance running, the Finns. Hill matched strides with the great Lauri Lehtinen and Lauri Virtanen throughout the 1932 Olympic 5,000m, and although Virtanen was dropped in the closing laps, Hill waged a great battle with Lehtinen in the home straight. In the desperation of the struggle, Lehtinen changed course as the finish approached and impeded Hill. An official protest was overruled, although the decision was not unanimous, and Hill settled for the

silver medal. The uproar in the LA Coliseum over this prompted public address announcer Bill Henry to caution the crowd, "Please remember, these people are our guests!"

HILL, Thomas Lionel.

B. 17 NOV 1949 New Orleans, LA. Bronze: 1972 110 meter hurdles. After winning the Final Trials, Tom Hill confirmed his position as one of the favorites for the 1972 Olympic high hurdles title by winning the first semi-final at Munich. In the Olympic final he hit the fifth hurdle and only managed to take the bronze medal when Willie Davenport, who was in second place, hit the eighth hurdle.

While at Arkansas State, Hill's best placing at the NCAA was second in 1972, but he won three AAU titles and in 1977 he reached the AAU final for the sixth time.

HILLMAN, Harry Livingston, Jr.

B. 08 SEP 1881 Brooklyn, NY. D. 09 AUG 1945. Gold(3): 1904 400 meters, 1904 200 meter hurdles, 1904 400 meter hurdles; Silver: 1908 400 meter hurdles. Harry Hillman's first major titles came in the 1902 AAU junior and senior 220y hurdles, and the following year he added the AAU senior title in the open quarter. He won several more national championships, both U.S. and Canadian, although the fact that the 440y hurdles was not included in the AAU program until 1914, certainly deprived him of many more.

Hillman was one of three triple winners in track & field at the 1904 Olympics and his winning time of 53.0 in the 400m hurdles shattered the existing world record. However, he knocked over the eighth hurdle, which, in 1904, invalidated any record claim and, more importantly, the barriers were only 2'-6" in height instead of the regulation 3 feet.

After 1904, Harry Hillman competed at both the 1906 and 1908 Olympics, but with less success. At London in 1908, he concentrated on the 400m hurdles and, after setting a world record of 56.4 in the heats, improved to a career best of 55.3 in the final but still placed second to Charley Bacon. Harry Hillman went to Dartmouth as a coach in 1910 and remained there until his death, save for his World War I duty as a lieutenant in the aviation corps. Hillman was also on the Olympic coaching staff in 1924, 1928, and 1932. Harry Hillman is still listed in the *Guinness Book of World Records* as

coholder of one of the most unusual track records. He and Lawson Robertson still hold the record of 11.0 seconds for 100 yds—in a three-legged race.

HILLS, Ralph Gorman.

B. 19 JAN 1902 Washington, DC. D. 20 SEP 1978 Baltimore, MD. Bronze: 1924 Shot Put. While attending Princeton, Ralph Hills won the IC4A shot put in 1923, the AAU title in 1924, and the IC4A again in 1925. Indoors he won the AAU in 1922 and 1924 and the IC4A for three years, starting in 1923. At the 1924 Trials, Bud Houser, Tiny Hartranft, and Hills finished 1–2–3; they placed in the same order at the Olympics. In addition to track, Hills played three years of varsity football for Princeton and served as class president.

Hills graduated in 1925 and went to Johns Hopkins Medical School, from which he received his M.D. degree in 1929. He later became a professor of medicine at Hopkins.

HINES, James Ray.

B. 10 SEP 1946 Dumas, AK. Gold(2): 1968 100 meters, 1968 4 × 100 meter relay. Jim Hines, who was coached at Texas Southern by former Olympic champion, Bobby Morrow, made track history at the 1968 AAU when he became the first man to better 10 seconds for 100m. He clocked a windy 9.8 that day in the heats, but had a legal 9.9 in the semis before losing the final to Charlie Greene, both runners recording a windy 10.0.

In Mexico, Hines won the gold medal in 9.95 which, thru 1982, remains the world record on fully automatic timing. In the relay Hines took the baton in third place, but ran an outstanding anchor leg to give the U.S. a victory and another world record. After the 1968 Olympic season, Hines turned professional and had a brief career in pro football with the Miami Dolphins.

HOGENSEN, William P.

B. 1884. D. 14 OCT 1965. Silver: 1904 60 meters; Bronze(2): 1904 100 meters, 1904 200 meters. On leaving Lewis Institute, Bill Hogensen enrolled at the University of Chicago, and at the 1904 Olympics he represented the Chicago AA. In St. Louis, Hogensen finished third behind Archie Hahn and Nate Cartmell in both the 100m and 200m, but in the 60m, which Cartmell skipped, he moved up to take a silver medal.

HOLLAND, William Joseph.

B. 03 MAR 1874. D. 20 NOV 1930 Malden, MA. Silver: 1900 400 meters. The 1900 Olympic 400m final was reduced to three runners after the U.S. runners, Dixon Boardman, Fred Moloney, and Harry Lee, withdrew on religious grounds because the race was held on a Sunday. The depleted field should not, however, detract from Holland's second place, as he ran a commendable 49.6 and led the winner, Maxie Long, until the closing stages.

After the Olympics, Holland won the IC4A 440y for Georgetown in 1901 and 1902, his winning time of 49.6 in 1902 being the fastest time in the world that year. He was also a talented performer in other events and finished second in the New England All-Around championship in 1897. Holland eventually settled in Massachusetts, where he practiced medicine after his graduation from Georgetown Medical School.

HOOPER, Clarence Darrow.

B. 30 JAN 1932 Fort Worth, TX. Silver: 1952 Shot Put. Although Darrow Hooper was deprived of a single AAU title by contemporaries such as Parry O'Brien, he was one of the great shot putters of his time. He beat world record holder O'Brien and former record holder, Jim Fuchs, at the 1952 Final Trials, and only lost the Olympic title to O'Brien by a mere three-quarters of an inch.

His winning throw of 57'-1⅝" at the 1952 Trials was the best mark of his career and would have sufficed to win the Olympic gold medal had he been able to repeat the performance at Helsinki. Hooper continued to compete the season following the 1952 Olympics, and lost only three times in a busy season.

HORINE, George Leslie.

B. 03 FEB 1890 Escondido, CA. D. 29 NOV 1948 Modesto, CA. Bronze: 1912 High Jump. Inhibited by the backyard layout of a new family home, George Horine was forced to set the high jump standards for his practice sessions in such a manner that he had to approach the bar from the left instead of the right, which had been his former style. The new style, which Horine had adopted of necessity, was effectively the forerunner of the western roll technique. When Horine was a freshman at Stanford in 1910, his coach ordered him to abandon his new technique and adopt a more traditional style. Initially this paid dividends as, in 1911, Horine jumped 6'-4" to equal the 24-year-old collegiate record.

But in his junior year, Horine reverted, against his coach's wishes, to his roll technique and the results were startling. First he pushed up the collegiate record to 6'-4¾", then he broke the world record with 6'-6⅛", and a few weeks later, he became the first man to jump two meters, clearing 6'-7" (2.00 meters).

Horine could not maintain this early season form and managed only a bronze at the Olympics. But his world record stayed intact until 1914 and, in 1915, Horine won his only AAU title in the high jump.

HORR, Marquis Franklin.

B. 01 JUL 1880. D. 01 JUL 1955 Syracuse, NY. Silver: 1908 Discus Throw (Greek style); Bronze: 1908 Discus Throw. Apart from his two medals in the discus events, "Bill" Horr placed sixth in the hammer, seventh in the shot, and competed in the tug-of-war at the 1908 Olympics.

While at Syracuse University, Bill Horr won the IC4A hammer in 1906 and 1907, and later won the 1908 AAU title. Horr also played football at Syracuse and in 1908 made all-America on his way to becoming a member of the College Football Hall of Fame. He later attended Syracuse Law School and practiced as an attorney, after a short period as assistant football coach at Syracuse.

HOUSER, Lemuel Clarence.

B. 25 SEP 1901 Winnigan, MO. Gold(3): 1924 Shot Put, 1924 Discus Throw, 1928 Discus Throw. "Bud" Houser's double victory at the 1924 Games is the last time that anyone has succeeded in winning both the shot and discus at the same Olympics. He set an Olympic record in the discus, which he further improved when he won the title for a second time in 1928. Between Olympics, Houser set a world record for the discus with 158'-1¾" in 1926.

While he was at Southern Cal, Houser won the NCAA discus in 1926 and at the AAU he won the shot twice and the discus three times. After graduation, he became a dentist, practicing in Palm Springs.

HOWARD, Richard Wayne.

B. 22 AUG 1935 Oklahoma City, OK. D. 09 NOV 1967 Los Angeles, CA. Bronze: 1960 400 meter hurdles. Dick

Howard first took up track when in the service; after he had served his two years he ran the low hurdles for Compton College in 1957. The following season he placed fourth in the AAU 440y hurdles in June, after sustaining a serious back injury in an automobile accident in April. He then enrolled at the University of New Mexico and in 1959, Howard won the AAU and the NCAA, and finished second in the Pan-Am Games and in the meet against the USSR.

In the pre-Olympic meets in 1960, he finished second to Glenn Davis at both the AAU and the Final Trials and, although he brought his career best down to 49.7 at the Rome Games, he was beaten not only by Davis but also Cliff Cushman. Cushman and Howard both met tragic ends—Cushman was killed in Vietnam and Howard died from a heroin overdose.

HOYT, William Welles.
B. 07 MAY 1875 Glastonbury, CT. D. 01 DEC 1954 Berlin, NY. Gold: 1896 Pole Vault. The first Olympic pole vault competition only drew an entry of five competitors and after the early elimination of the three Greek entrants, it became a two-man contest between Bill Hoyt of Harvard and Albert Tyler of Princeton. Tyler had the early edge, clearing 10'-0" on his first attempt, while Hoyt had two misses at that height. But when the bar was set at 10'-10" only Hoyt was successful, which won him the gold medal.

Hoyt's Olympic victory was the only truly major success of his career. At home, he had placed second in the IC4A pole vault in 1895 and 1897, and he tied for first place in 1898 with Raymond Clapp of Yale.

After graduating Harvard in 1897, Hoyt entered their medical school, from which he graduated in 1901. Initially he practiced as a doctor in Chicago and was later commissioned into the 1st Illinois Field Hospital Company and served in France in 1918. After the war he tried to resume his Chicago practice, but soon returned to France as a surgeon with the foreign service of the U.S. Public Health Service, and he served overseas for many years. He finally settled in the small town of Berlin, New York, where he continued to practice medicine.

HUBBARD, William De Hart.
B. 25 NOV 1903 Cincinnati, OH. D. 23 JUN 1976 Cleveland, OH. Gold: 1924 Long Jump. De Hart Hubbard was the first black athlete to win an Olympic gold medal in an individual event. Hubbard studied at the University of Michigan starting in 1921, and the following year he won the first of six straight AAU long jump titles. He also won the AAU triple jump in 1922 and 1923 and at the NCAA he won the 100y in 1925 and the long jump in 1923. In 1925 he set a world record of 25'-10⁷⁄₈" when he took the NCAA title for a second time, and then in 1926 he confirmed his ability as a sprinter when he equalled the world record of 9.6 for 100y.

Although injured, De Hart Hubbard won the 1924 Olympic long jump comfortably; he was again injured at the 1928 when he finished 11th. Between these two appearances he had the best mark of his career in 1927 when he jumped 26'-2¹⁄₄", but the mark was not recognized as a world record, because the take-off board was one inch higher than the landing pit. In all, Hubbard beat 25 feet on eleven occasions and was undoubtedly the greatest jumper of the pre-Owens era.

HUSSEY, Francis Valentine Joseph.
B. 14 FEB 1905 New York, NY. D. 26 DEC 1974 Coxsackie, NY. Gold: 1924 4 × 100 meter relay. As an 18-year-old at Stuyvesant High School in New York, Frank Hussey ran 9.6 for 100y, but the mark was never ratified as equalling the world record. He later attended Boston College and Columbia. In 1924 he placed fourth at the Final Trials in the 100m, which put him on the relay team that set a world record in the heats, semi-final, and final.

Hussey's only AAU title came in 1925 when he beat the redoubtable Jackson Scholz over 100y, and the following day he ran the opening stage for the New York AC team that won the AAU 4 × 110y relay with a new world record of 41.4.

Frank Hussey worked most of his life as a salesman, but also taught in the New York State Prison System. He spent much of his free time as an official at local track meets.

INESS, Simeon Garland.
B. 09 JUL 1930 Keota, OK. Gold: 1952 Discus Throw. On his 18th birthday, Sim Iness placed sixth at the 1948 Final Trials, but four years later he won the Trials and went on to take the Olympic title, beating Consolini's Olympic record with all of his six throws.

While at Southern Cal, Iness won the NCAA in 1952 and 1953 and on the second occasion he became the first man in history to throw 190 feet when he took the title with a world record 190'-0⅞". After his active days were over, Iness became a football and track coach.

IRONS, Francis C.
B. 23 MAR 1886 Des Moines, IA. Gold: 1908 Long Jump. In winning the 1908 Olympic long jump, Frank Irons of the Chicago AA far exceeded any previous form he had shown and his winning jump of 24'-6½" placed him third on the all-time list behind O'Connor and Prinstein. In 1909 and 1910 he also won the AAU and topped the world ranking list in both years. Irons looked like a likely candidate to become the only man to defend an Olympic long jump title, but he was far from his best in Stockholm and finished in eighth place.

JACOBS, Charles Sherman.
B. 15 FEB 1872. D. FEB 1945. Bronze: 1908 Pole Vault (tied). After winning the Big Ten championship in 1908 with a career best of 12'-4", Jacobs was in a three-way tie for third at the London Olympics. Jacobs, who attended both Albion College and the University of Chicago, twice set world indoor records and had a best indoor vault of 12'-3".

JACOBS, Harry.
Bronze: 1904 Tug-of-War. Harry Jacobs was a member of the #2 team from the St. Louis Southwest Turnverein.

JAMES, George Lawrence.
B. 06 NOV 1947 Mount Pleasant, NJ. Gold: 1968 4 × 400 meter relay; Silver: 1968 400 meters. Prior to 1968, Larry James was known primarily as a hurdler and triple jumper, but in the Olympic year he concentrated on the one-lap event with astonishing success. Although he was beaten at the Final Trials and the Olympics by Lee Evans, his time of 43.97 at Mexico City still ranks as the second-fastest 400m of all time through 1982. Later in the Games, James ran a 43.8 relay leg when the U.S. bettered the world record by more than three seconds.

While at Villanova, James won the IC4A outdoor 440y and the NCAA indoor 440y for three straight years from 1968. Additionally he won the NCAA outdoor 440y in 1970.

JAMISON, Herbert Brotherson.
B. 17 SEP 1875 Peoria, IL. D. 22 JUN 1938 Peoria, IL. Silver: 1896 400 meters. Herbert Jamison was described by his contemporaries as an "above mediocre" sprinter. Because his favorite event, the 200m, was not on the program in Athens, he chose to run in the 400m, but he was no match for Tom Burke and finished some 10 meters behind the AAU champion.

After graduating from Princeton in 1897, Jamison entered the family business, which manufactured agricultural implements, but after seven years he established his own insurance agency in Peoria and remained in that business until his death.

JARVIS, Frank Washington.
B. 31 AUG 1878 California, PA. D. 02 JUN 1933 Sewickley, PA. Gold: 1900 100 meters. Apart from winning an Olympic gold medal, Frank Jarvis enjoyed the distinction of being a direct descendant of George Washington.

After Arthur Duffey, who had beaten Jarvis in the British Championships the previous week, broke down in the 1900 Olympic final, Jarvis came through to win an unexpected gold medal. He equalled the world record of 10.8 in the heats, but reports suggest that the leniency of the French starter made a significant contribution to this time.

Jarvis was on the Princeton track team for three years, winning the AAU 100y and the IC4A 440y in 1898 and the IC4A 220y in 1900. After graduating from Princeton, Frank Jarvis took a law degree at the University of Pittsburgh and practiced law in that city until shortly before his death.

JEFFERSON, George G.
B. 28 FEB 1910. Bronze: 1932 Pole Vault. At the 1932 Final Trials, George Jefferson of UCLA placed third with a career best of 13'-10". The winner on that occasion was Bill Graber, who posted a new world record of 14'-4¼", but Graber could not repeat that form at the Olympics and Jefferson pushed the world record holder back in to fourth place.

JENKINS, Charles Lamont.
B. 07 JAN 1934 New York, NY. Gold(2): 1956 400 meters, 1956 4 × 400 meter relay. After placing second in the 1956 IC4A and AAU 400m, and no better than third

at the 1956 NCAA and Olympic Trials, Charlie Jenkins was a surprise winner of the Olympic title. His winning time of 46.7 was the slowest since 1928, but he showed a truer indication of his abilities with a 45.5 relay leg which gave him a second gold medal. While at Villanova, Jenkins won the AAU in 1955 and the IC4A in 1955 and 1957. Indoors he won the AAU 600y three times and he set a world record for the 500y in 1956.

After his competitive days ended, Jenkins went into coaching and in 1981 he succeeded the legendary Jumbo Elliott as head coach at his alma mater.

JENNER, William Bruce.
B. 28 OCT 1949 Mt. Kisco, NY. Gold: 1976 Decathlon. While in high school, Bruce Jenner three times won the Eastern States water ski championship and placed well in the Connecticut State High School track & field meet, but he gave no indication that he would one day become the world's greatest athlete.

Jenner went to tiny Graceland College in Lamoni, Iowa, on a football scholarship, but shortly took up the decathlon and only one year later qualified for the 1972 Olympic team. After placing 10th in the 1972 Olympic decathlon, Jenner won the 1974 AAU title and in 1975 he was Pan-Am champion and set a world record in the triangular meet with the USSR and Poland. In 1976, Jenner won his second AAU title and crowned a brilliant career by taking the Olympic gold medal with a new world record of 8,618 points.

The charismatic Jenner became a television and movie personality as soon as his competitive days were over. After splitting with his first wife, he married Linda Thompson, who was Elvis Presley's girlfriend when that legend passed away in 1978.

JOHNSON, Carl Edward.
B. 21 MAY 1898 Genessee Cty., MI. D. 13 SEP 1932 Detroit, MI. Silver: 1920 Long Jump. Carl Johnson first attracted the attention of the sports world when, as a Spokane high school student in 1915, he competed in the National Interscholastics, and finished second by himself—in the team competition! Johnson then attended Michigan and headed the world long jump lists in 1918 and 1919, despite serving as president of the college student council and earning a Phi Beta Kappa key. In college, his all-round talents were shown best at the 1919 IC4A, where he placed second in the 100y and

tied for second in the high jump as well as winning the long jump.

Although he was sidelined for most of the 1920 college season, he was included on the Olympic team despite a poor performance at the Trials. Johnson justified the decision of the selectors by being the highest placed American in Antwerp when he finished second behind William Pettersson of Sweden.

JOHNSON, Cornelius Cooper.
B. 28 AUG 1913 Los Angeles, CA. D. 15 FEB 1946. Gold: 1936 High Jump. As an 18-year-old high school student, "Corny" Johnson tied for first place in the 1932 Olympic high jump, but was relegated to fourth place in the jump-off. Johnson then went to Compton Junior College and early in 1936 he set a world indoor record of 6'-8^{15}/$_{16}$". At the 1936 Final Trials he tied with Dave Albritton when both set a world record of 6'-9^{3}/$_{4}$" and he then took the Olympic title, clearing 6'-8" without a single failure before unsuccessfully attempting a new world record of 6'-10".

Johnson won or shared the AAU title five times and was AAU indoor champion three times—twice tied.

JOHNSON, Jan Eric.
B. 11 NOV 1950 Hammond, IN. Bronze: 1972 Pole Vault. While attending Kansas, Jan Johnson won the 1970 NCAA outdoor pole vault although the competition was concluded indoors in a nearby fieldhouse because of a cloudburst.

Johnson later enrolled at Alabama and claimed three major victories in 1971, winning the AAU outdoor, the NCAA Indoor, and the Pan-American Games. His career best of 18'-0½" came at the 1972 Final Trials when he placed third. Johnson took a Ph.D. in physical education at Southern Illinois and continued to compete sporadically for a number of seasons after the Olympics.

JOHNSON, Rafer Lewis.
B. 18 AUG 1934 Hillsboro, TX. Gold: 1960 Decathlon; Silver: 1960 Decathlon. Rafer Johnson made his decathlon debut in 1954 and the next year he won the Pan-American Games title and set the first of his three world decathlon records.

The world's greatest athlete, Bruce Jenner, exults as he crosses the finish line to officially earn that title.

Courtesy University of Texas

Johnny "Lam" Jones got his nickname from his home town of Lampases, Texas.

Johnson, who competed for UCLA and the Southern California Striders, won the AAU decathlon in 1956, 1958, and 1960 and after placing second to Milt Campbell at the 1956 Olympics, never lost another decathlon. He was injured at the 1956 Games, which forced him to withdraw from the Olympic long jump, for which he had also qualified. After his retirement in 1960 he acted in a few movies, and has served for many years as a commercial spokesman for many products.

The plaintiff cry moment's after Robert Kennedy's assassination was, "Get the gun, Rafer!", and it was Rafer Johnson to whom the voice beckoned. Johnson and football star Rosey Grier were rabid Kennedy supporters and were standing next to him that fateful night.

JOHNSON, Richard Earle.
B. 10 MAR 1891. Silver: 1924 Cross-Country team race; Bronze: 1924 Cross-Country. Earle Johnson was the first nationally prominent black distance runner. A member of the Thompson Steelworks AA, near Pittsburgh, he made his Olympic debut in 1920 when he was eliminated in the heats of the 10,000m. Four years later there were no heats for this event and Johnson placed eighth in a field of 43. In the cross-country event in Paris, Johnson finished third behind the redoubtable Finns, Paavo Nurmi and Wille Ritola, and led the U.S. to the silver medals in the team event.

He won the AAU cross-country title in 1921; on the track he was the AAU champion at five miles for three straight years from 1921 and in 1924 he won the AAU 10 miles.

JOHNSON, Sidney B.
Gold: 1904 Tug-of-War. Sid Johnson represented the Milwaukee AC on the winning tug-of-war team in 1904, but like all the members of that team, he was actually from Chicago.

JONES, Hayes Wendell.
B. 04 AUG 1938 Starksville,MS. Gold: 1964 110 meter hurdles; Bronze: 1960 110 meter hurdles. Although at 5'-11" Hayes Jones seemingly lacked the height for a world-class hurdler, he made up for this apparent handicap with an explosive start and blazing speed on the flat. On the indoor circuit his exceptional starting abilities put him on his way to six AAU titles and he won 55 consecutive indoor races from March 1959 through his retirement in 1964.

Jones' speed on the flat earned him a share in a world 4 × 100m relay record in 1961 and over the high hurdles he won the AAU title a record five times. He was also Pan-American Games and NCAA champion in 1959.

After his retirement he served as director of recreation for New York City for two years before returning to private business.

JONES, John Wesley.
B. 04 APR 1958 Lawton, OK. Gold: 1976 4 × 100 meter relay. "Lam" Jones earned his nickname as a wide receiver for the Texas Longhorns in the late 70's. A teammate's name was also Johnny Jones, so they were called by the names of their hometowns—"Ham" Jones and "Lam" Jones for Lampasas, Texas.

Before starting college, Lam Jones had placed fourth in the 100m at the 1976 Final Trials, but was nominated for the individual event in Montreal when Houston McTear withdrew because of injury. In the Olympic 100m, Jones finished sixth, but won a gold medal in the relay after running an outstanding second leg. Jones never won a major title, his best finish being second in the 1977 NCAA 100m.

Lam Jones has gone on to the pro football wars where, for several seasons now, he has been an outstanding wide receiver for the New York Jets.

JONES, Louis Woodard, III.
B. 15 JAN 1932 New Rochelle, NY. Gold: 1956 4 × 400 meter relay. After graduating from Manhattan College in 1954, Lou Jones set a world 400m record in winning the 1955 Pan-American Games. He improved the world mark to 45.2 at the 1956 Final Trials, but failed to show his true form at the Melbourne Olympics. In the individual 400m he ran no better than 48.1 for sixth place and in the relay he was clocked at a modest 47.1 as lead-off man in the final. After his brief career came to a close, Jones became a high school teacher in New York.

JONES, Samuel Symington.
B. 1879. D. 13 APR 1954. Gold: 1904 High Jump. Sam Jones won the IC4A high jump in 1900 and 1901 and the AAU title in 1901, 1903, and 1904. His winning jump of 5'-11" at the 1904 Olympics was well below his best of 6'-2" which he cleared at the 1901 AAU championships. Jones attended NYU and was the school's top all-round athlete. He played varsity football for four years, varsity gymnastics for three years, and captained the track team. After graduation, he made his career first as a civil engineer and eventually as a teacher.

KELLY, Daniel Joseph.
B. 01 SEP 1883. D. 09 APR 1920. Silver: 1908 Long Jump. Dan Kelly of the University of Oregon was one of the great sprinter/long jumpers of his time. In May 1906 he jumped 24'-2¼" to become only the third American to break the 24-foot barrier, and the following month in a meet in Spokane he equalled the world records for both the 100y (9.6) and 220y around a turn (21.2) in the same afternoon. Kelly won his only AAU title in the 1907 long jump.

KELLY, Frederick Warren.
B. 12 SEP 1891 Beaumont, CA. D. 07 MAY 1974 Medford, OR. Gold: 1912 110 meter hurdles."King" Kelly took the 1912 Olympic hurdles title after the prerace favorite and reigning AAU champion, John Nicholson, fell at the eighth hurdle. Shortly after the Games, Kelly suffered a surprise defeat in Rheims at the hands of Jim Thorpe, who equalled the world record of 15.0.

Kelly twice equalled that record in 1913 before winning his first and only AAU title later in the season. By 1916 the high hurdle record was 14.6 and Kelly equalled it for a third time, although none of his marks ever received official recognition. In 1919, seven years after his Olympic victory, he placed second to fellow Southern Cal alumnus Bob Simpson at the AAU championships and then retired.

Kelly became one of the pioneers of commercial aviation. In 1925 he joined Western Air Express (later Western Airlines) and when he retired in 1946 he was their chief pilot.

KERRIGAN, Herbert W.
D. 10 SEP 1959. Bronze: 1906 High Jump (tied). Due to an injury sustained during the sea voyage to Greece, Herbert Kerrigan of the Multnomah AC of Portland, Oregon, failed to do himself justice at the 1906 Olympics. He had won the 1905 AAU title at 6'-1½" but in Athens he could manage only 5'-8" to tie for third place. He also competed in the 1906 Olympic pole vault.

KIESEL, Robert Allan.
B. 30 AUG 1911 Sacramento, CA. Gold: 1932 4 × 100 meter relay. Bob Kiesel of the University of California never won a major title, but the fact that he won a place on an Olympic relay team during a golden age of American sprinting was testament in itself to his ability. Although championship honors eluded him, Kiesel was a match for the best sprinters around when measured against the stop watch. His 9.5 for 100y in 1932 was matched only by Ralph Metcalfe among world sprinters that year and in 1932 he also ran a windy 10.4 for 100m. At the longer sprint he could point to a 20.8 clocking for 220y in 1934.

After graduation Bob Kiesel worked for a paint manufacturing company until 1941 and after his war service he spent 23 years in the family real estate and investment business in Utah before moving to his farm in Idaho.

KING, Charles M.

Silver(2): 1904 Standing Long Jump, 1904 Standing Triple Jump. The legendary Ray Ewry deprived Charles King, from McKinney, Texas, of two gold medals by outjumping him at both standing jumps for distance at the 1904 Olympics.

KING, Leamon.

B. 13 FEB 1936 Tulare, CA. Gold: 1956 4 × 100 meter relay. After setting a world record of 9.3 for 100y in May 1956, Leamon King of the University of California placed fourth at the Final Trials and only made the Olympic team as a member of the relay squad. After the Melbourne team had been chosen, King twice equalled the world record of 10.1 for 100m and on both occasions he beat Bobby Morrow who went on to win the Olympic title. King won his only major championship when he took the AAU 100y in 1957.

KING, Robert Wade.

B. 20 JUN 1906 Los Angeles, CA. D. 29 JUL 1965 Walnut Creek, CA. Gold: 1928 High Jump. In a competition that lasted five hours, Bob King took the 1928 Olympic high jump at 6'-4¼". This was well below Harold Osborne's Olympic record, although by clearing 6'-6⅝" earlier in the season, King had shown that he was clearly the best high jumper in the world in 1928. While at Stanford, Bob King won the IC4A high jump in 1926; in 1927 he won the AAU; and in 1928 he won the IC4A, the NCAA, and tied for first place at the AAU.

After serving as president of his senior class at Stanford, King went to medical school and later became a well-known obstetrician.

KINSEY, Daniel Chapin.

B. 22 JAN 1902 St. Louis, MO. D. 27 JUN 1970 Richmond, IN. Gold: 1924 110 meter hurdles. Apart from winning the 1924 Olympic gold medal, Dan Kinsey's only major championship honors came at the 1924 IC4A when he won the high hurdles for Illinois. After graduating from Illinois, Kinsey received a master's degree from Oberlin and a Ph.D. from Michigan. He taught and coached at Oberlin for 31 years, then went to Earlham College in Indiana as director of physical education and later held a similar post at Delta College in Bay City, Michigan, until his 1967 retirement.

KIRBY, Edward Buckler.

B. 30 OCT 1901. D. 05 JUL 1968 West Orange, NJ. Bronze: 1924 3,000 meter team race. In 1923, Ed Kirby won the IC4A mile for Cornell in a career best of 4:17.9 and only Joie Ray among U.S. milers ran faster that year. The following year Kirby and Ray met in the 3,000m at the Final Trials; although Ray won comfortably, Kirby proved to be the better man at the Olympics and, finishing in sixth place, he led the U.S. team home in the team race. Kirby took his degree at Cornell in civil engineering and worked for several engineering companies before his retirement in 1958.

KIRKSEY, Morris Marshall.

B. 13 SEP 1895 Waxahachie, TX. D. 1982. Gold(2): 1920 4 × 100 meter relay, 1920 Rugby Football; Silver: 1920 100 meters. See the rugby football section for the biography.

KIVIAT, Abel Richard.

B. 23 JUN 1892 New York, NY. Silver: 1912 1500 meters. Born the son of a peddler in New York's lower East Side, Abel Kiviat took up track in 1909, his senior year at Curtis High School. That year, when barely 17, he won the Canadian mile championship in 4:23.2 and from then on his successes were legion.

Kiviat became one of the greatest indoor runners of all time and, despite his casual training methods and his inelegant bow-legged running style, he was also a record-breaker outdoors. Indoors, he won the AAU 600y twice and the 1,000y three times; at the outdoor championships he won the mile in 1911, 1912, and 1914. He also won the AAU cross-country title in 1913 when he led his Irish-American AC team to the team title.

During his build-up for the 1912 Olympics he set three 1,500m world records in three weeks, culminating with a mark of 3:55.8 at the Olympic Trials when he continued on to the mile post, where he was clocked in 4:15.6, which was only 0.2 seconds outside the world record. Kiviat arrived in Stockholm as the favorite for the 1,500m title, but he was surprised by the home stretch drive of Oxford undergraduate Arnold Jackson and he took second in a photo from his teammate Norman Taber. However, Kiviat's world record held and remained unbeaten for five more years.

Courtesy Desmond Koch

The U.S. Air Force Olympians at the 1956 Olympics. Top (L-R) — Lon Spurrier, Des Koch, Parry O'Brien, Thane Baker. Bottom (L-R) — Jesse Mortensen (coach), Bill Dellinger, Jim Lea, George Mattos.

After seeing front line service with the army in France, he continued his athletic career until 1925. He coached track briefly, but maintained a lifelong interest in the sport, officiating at major meets for more than 60 years and serving as chief press steward at the Penn Relays and many Madison Square Garden meets.

KOCH, Desmond Dalworth.
B. 10 MAY 1932 Lincoln, NE. Bronze: 1956 Discus Throw. Des Koch went to Southern Cal from Reed High School in Shelton, Washington, having been the nation's top prep discus thrower in 1950. He won the NCAA discus in 1955 and made the 1956 Olympic team after Ron Drummond withdrew because of academic commitments. Koch proved to be an adequate substitute, placing third in Melbourne as the U.S. swept the medals.

Des Koch was probably better known for his football prowess. With a 43.4 average he led the nation in punting in his junior year and in 1953, as a senior, he averaged 43.5 yards and had a 72-yarder in the Rose Bowl. He may be the last player to have drop-kicked a field goal in major college football. After college, Koch had a brief fling at pro football, trying out with Green Bay and San Diego, but he never played.

Koch, who married Mitzi Whitefeather, a seven-eighths Indian whom he met when she had an apartment next to Parry O'Brien, is now an executive with a plastics manufacturing plant.

KRAENZLEIN, Alvin Christian.

B. 12 DEC 1876 Milwaukee, WI. D. 06 JAN 1928 Wilkes Barre, PA. Gold(4): 1900 60 meters, 1900 110 meter hurdles, 1900 200 meter hurdles, 1900 Long Jump. With his four 1900 gold medals, Al Kraenzlein still holds the record for the most individual track & field victories at a single Olympic celebration.

Kraenzlein was educated at Wisconsin and Penn and was one of the great all-round athletes of the sport. He refined the straight lead-leg style of hurdling and in 1898 set a world record of 15.2 for the 120y hurdles. The previous month he had posted a world record of 23.6 for the 200m hurdles that would remain unbeaten for 25 years. Kraenzlein also twice improved the world long jump record in 1899. He scored a notable triple at the 1899 AAU championships, winning the 100y, the 120y hurdles and the long jump. He again won the 120y hurdles in 1899 and at the IC4A meet he won a total of eight events in three years.

Kraenzlein graduated from Penn in 1901 with a dental degree, but never practiced extensively. Instead he became a distinguished track coach and was appointed coach to the German team for the ill-fated 1916 Olympics. He later coached the University of Michigan and the Cuban National Team.

KUCK, John.

B. 27 APR 1905 Wilson, KS. Gold: 1928 Shot Put. John Kuck of Emporia State, and later of the Kansas AC and Los Angeles TC, improved the world shot put record three times in 1928. Only the third of these performances was officially recognized when he won the Olympic title with a mark of 52'-0¾". Kuck won the NCAA shot title in 1926 and was AAU champion the following year. In 1926 he set a U.S. javelin record of 214'-2⅛" and won the AAU javelin title that year.

KUNGLER, Frank.

Silver: 1904 Heavyweight (Wrestling); Bronze(3): 1904 Tug-of-War, 1904 Barbell Event (Weightlifting), 1904 Dumbbell Event (Weightlifting). Frank Kungler was a member of the St. Louis Southwest Turnverein team that finished third in the tug-of-war. He also medalled in weightlifting and wrestling, making him the only man to have ever won medals in three different sports at one Olympic Games.

LABORDE, Henri Jean.

B. 11 SEP 1909. Silver: 1932 Discus Throw. After placing second in the 1932 Olympic discus, Henri Laborde of Stanford took both the NCAA and the IC4A titles in 1933. Later that season, while on a European tour, he threw 165'-3½" in Dusseldorf, which was a career best for Laborde and the best throw in the world in 1933.

LANDON, Richmond Wilcox.

B. 20 NOV 1898 Richmond, CT. D. 13 JUN 1971 Lynbrook, NY. Gold: 1920 High Jump. After attending Hotchkiss, Dick Landon enrolled at Yale and won the IC4A high jump in 1919 and 1920. At the 1920 AAU championships, which doubled as the Final Trials, Landon placed second to John Murphy of Notre Dame, but at Antwerp, Landon took the title, with Murphy fifth. Landon achieved the best mark of his career in 1921 when he cleared 6'-6" to win the Harvard/Yale vs. Oxford/Cambridge dual meet. He was also an excellent indoor jumper and at the 1923 Millrose Games he tied with Leroy Brown of Dartmouth as both set a new world indoor record of 6'-5¼". Landon's only AAU title came at the 1921 indoor meet.

The gold medal was not the only piece of good fortune that came Dick Landon's way at the Olympics—on the boat going to Antwerp he met Alice Lord, a member of the diving team, and they were married in 1922.

LARRABEE, Michael Denny.

B. 02 DEC 1933 Los Angeles, CA. Gold(2): 1964 400 meters, 1964 4 × 400 meter relay. At the age of 30, Mike Larrabee is the oldest man to have won the Olympic 400m title. After ranking second in the world in 1957 he showed in-and-out form over the next six seasons, but in 1964 he was back at his best and, after winning the AAU 400m, he went on to become Olympic champion and won a second gold medal in the relay.

Larrabee, a Southern Cal graduate, later became a regional Coors distributor.

LAZ, Donald Robert.

B. 17 MAY 1929 Chicago, IL. Silver: 1952 Pole Vault. Don Laz of the University of Illinois won the NCAA pole vault in 1951 and tied George Mattos for the 1953 AAU title. These were his only major championship honors, but he came desperately close to winning the 1952 Olympic gold medal as Bob Richards cleared the winning height on his final attempt to eliminate the need for a jump-off.

At the Ohio Relays in 1954, Laz cleared 15'-2" to become the second-best vaulter of all time, behind only the legendary Warmerdam. However, the family record now stands to the credit of his son, Doug, who cleared 17'-4¾" in 1976.

In 1960, Laz sued CBS and the Ford Motor Co. for invasion of privacy after a film of him vaulting had been used in a TV commercial. The case was eventually settled out of court. Don Laz became an architect in Champaign, Illinois, but his career was tragically handicapped when he suffered a stroke, causing aphasia. He now has only limited use of one hand.

LEAVITT, Robert Grandison.

B. 20 SEP 1883 Dorchester, MA. D. 22 FEB 1954 South Hanover, MA. Gold: 1906 110 meter hurdles. Bob Leavitt attended Williams, but withdrew after his sophomore year and never graduated. While at Williams, he tied the college record of 15.8 for the 120y hurdles in May 1905, and although he failed to approach this time at the Athens Olympics, he succeeded in winning a close and exciting final.

After college, Leavitt initially joined New England Tel & Tel in Boston, but later worked for many years as treasurer of the Brighton Cooperative Bank.

LECONEY, Jeremiah Alfred.

B. 11 MAR 1901 Moorestown, NJ. D. 11 NOV 1959 Plainfield, NJ. Gold: 1924 4 × 100 meter relay. After finishing second in both sprints for Lafayette College at the 1922 IC4A, Al Leconey won both titles the following year and confirmed his ability at the longer sprint by also taking the AAU 220y in 1923.

On leaving college, Leconey represented the Meadowbrook Club of Philadelphia; at the 1924 Olympic Trials he placed fourth on both the 100m and the 200m and went to Paris as the anchor man on the relay team that took the gold medal in 41.0 to equal the world record they had set in the preliminaries.

Leconey began his career using his civil engineering degree but eventually became an insurance underwriter. He posed for the 1932 3 cent postage stamp, which was issued to help finance the Los Angeles

A 3¢ stamp issued for the 1932 Los Angeles Olympics. The model for the runner on it was 1924 Olympic sprinter, J. Alfred LeConey.

Courtesy United States Postal Service

Olympics, and is immortalized as the sprinter on that stamp.

LeGENDRE, Robert Lucien.

B. 07 JAN 1898 Lewiston, ME. D. 21 JAN 1931 Brooklyn, NY. Bronze: 1924 Pentathlon. After placing fourth in the 1920 Olympic pentathlon, Bob LeGendre improved to place third in 1924. The highlight of his career came in the long jump phase of the 1924 pentathlon when LeGendre, although he had not qualified for the U.S. team in the individual event, set a world record of 25'-5⅝", which was more than one foot further than De Hart Hubbard's winning mark in the long jump.

While at Georgetown, LeGendre briefly played football and baseball and won the IC4A long jump in 1922. He went on to earn Ph.D. and D.D.S. degrees from Georgetown and signed a Hollywood contract, but an acting career never materialized. At his death he was a store dentist for Hecht & Co. in Washington.

LIEB, Thomas John.

B. 20 OCT 1899. D. 30 APR 1962 Los Angeles, CA. Bronze: 1924 Discus Throw. Tom Lieb of Notre Dame won the NCAA discus in 1922 and 1923 and the AAU title in 1923 and 1924. After winning the Final Trials at 153'-6", Lieb could manage only third place at the Olympic with a throw of 147'-0" but two months after the Games he took the world record up to 156'-2½".

Lieb later became a football coach, coaching at Wisconsin, Florida, Alabama, and Notre Dame. He also wrote several books about line coaching techniques.

LIGHTBODY, James Davies.

B. 15 MAR 1882 Pittsburgh, PA. D. 02 MAR 1953 Charleston, SC. Gold(4): 1904 800 meters, 1904 1,500 meters, 1904 2,590 meter steeplechase, 1906 1,500 meters; Silver(2): 1904 4 mile team race, 1906 800 meters. With three gold medals, James Lightbody was the outstanding middle distance runner at the 1904 Olympics. Although his winning time of 4:05.4 in the 1,500m was said to be a new world record, it was vastly inferior in quality to Tom Conneff's amateur mile record of 4:15.6.

After an 880y/mile double at the 1905 AAU championships, Lightbody successfully defended his Olympic 1,500m title in 1906, but failed by a narrow margin to retain his 800m crown. In 1908 he made his third Olympic appearance, competing in the 800m, 1500m, and steeplechase, but he was eliminated in the heats of all three events. Lightbody attended the University of Chicago and later represented the Chicago AA.

LINDBERG, Edward Ferdinand Jacob.

B. 09 NOV 1887 Cherokee, IA. Gold: 1912 4 × 400 meter relay; Bronze: 1912 400 meters. Representing the Chicago AA, Ed Lindberg won the AAU 440y in 1909 and 1911. At the 1912 Olympics he set a career best of 48.4 in placing third in the 400m and was a member of the winning relay team that took almost two seconds off the world record. Lindberg attended the University of Illinois.

LINDGREN, Harold Blaine.

B. 26 JUN 1939 Salt Lake City, UT. Silver: 1964 110 meter hurdles. After winning the high hurdles at the Pan-American Games, Blaine Lindgren remained a top class hurdler for two more seasons although he never won another major title. He was often thwarted in his quest for championship honors by the great Hayes Jones, who beat Lindgren by inches in the 1964 AAU and at the Olympics.

Lindgren is a graduate of Utah and works for the sheriff's department in his hometown in that state.

LIPPINCOTT, Donald Fithian.

B. 16 NOV 1893 Philadelphia, PA. D. 10 JAN 1962 Philadelphia, PA. Silver: 1912 200 meters; Bronze: 1912 100 meters. After setting a world record of 10.6 in the heats of the 100m at Stockholm, Lippincott only managed to place third in the final. However, he went one better in the 200m and took the silver medal. The following year he again showed his strength over the longer sprint and set a world record of 21.2 in taking the IC4A 220y title on the straightaway track at Harvard.

Lippincott is reputed to have beaten 48.0 for the quarter-mile and while this remains a highly suspect claim, he was undoubtedly a talented performer over this distance and was a member of the Penn team which set a world record of 3:18.0 for the 4 × 440y relay in 1915.

After graduating from Penn in 1915, Lippincott saw war service as a lieutenant in the navy and later went into banking. He eventually became a broker, first with Bache, and later with Merrill Lynch.

LIVERSEDGE, Harry Bluett.

B. 21 SEP 1894 Volcano, CA. D. 25 NOV 1951. Bronze: 1920 Shot Put. While attending the University of California at Berkeley, Harry "The Horse" Liversedge won the shot put at the 1916 IC4A championships. His athletic career was interrupted when he joined the marines in May, 1917 and this led to him becoming a career marine corpsman.

In 1920, Liversedge finished third in the shot at the Antwerp Olympics and with two Finns taking the leading places this was the first time that an American did not win the event.

Liversedge resumed his marine career after the Olympics and achieved the rank of brigadier general. He is best remembered as the commander of the 28th Regiment, which raised the flag on Iwo Jima.

LONG, Dallas Crutcher, III.

B. 13 JUN 1940 Pine Bluff, AK. Gold: 1964 Shot Put; Silver: 1960 Shot Put. In March 1959 the 18-year-old Dallas Long equalled Parry O'Brien's world record of 63'-2"; between then and May 1964 he improved the world record six times officially and had two other marks that surpassed the existing record but which were not ratified. Long won the AAU title in 1961 and was NCAA champion for three years straight from 1960. His career closed with an Olympic victory in 1964 after he had trailed Randy Matson at the end of three rounds.

Long, who attended Southern Cal, was also an outstanding discus thrower and had a best mark of 172'-3½". He has since become a practicing dentist.

LONG, Maxwell Warburn.

B. 1878. D. 04 MAR 1959 New York, NY. Gold: 1900 400 meters. Although Maxie Long had won the AAU 440y in 1898 and 1899 and was to win his third successive title after the 1900 Olympics, he was soundly beaten at the 1900 IC4A championships by Dixon Boardman of Yale and Harry Lee of Syracuse. Boardman and Lee both qualified for the 400m final at the Paris Olympics but declined to run because the race was held on a Sunday; in their absence, Long had a comfortable victory. In Paris, Long ran in the blue and white stripe of his school, Columbia, which resembled to the colors of the Racing Club de Paris, and the uninitiated crowd cheered Long down the home straight under the impression that they were urging a local hero to victory.

After the Olympics, Long raced for a time in Britain, and on his return home at the end of the season, he was in outstanding form. In late September he ran 47.8 for 440y in a handicap event at Travers Island and five days later, again in a handicap race, he clocked 47 flat at the Guttenberg race track in New Jersey, by far the fastest quarter-mile up to that time. In addition to his three AAU titles at 440y, Long won the 100y in 1900 and the 220y in 1899, as well as the IC4A 440y in 1899.

LOOMIS, Frank J.

B. 22 AUG 1896. D. 03 NOV 1962. Gold: 1920 400 meter hurdles. While a senior at Oregon High School in Minneapolis, Frank Loomis equalled the national interscholastic record of 24.2 for the 220y hurdles and after joining the Chicago AA he won the AAU title over this distance in 1917 and 1918.

After winning the 440y hurdles at the Western Olympic Trials in a new world record of 54.2, John Norton looked a likely winner of the Olympic title, but Loomis beat him at the AAU and confirmed his superiority with a comfortable win over Norton at the Olympics with a new world record of 54.0.

Frank's brother, Jo Gilbert Loomis, was a talented high jumper, who also made the 1920 Olympic team as an alternate on the sprint squad.

LuVALLE, James Ellis.

B. 10 NOV 1912 San Antonio, TX. Bronze: 1936 400 meters. While at UCLA, Jimmy LuValle proved himself to be a great furlong runner. In 1934 he ran 20.8 for 220y on a straightaway and Bob Kiesel and Foy Draper were the only sprinters in the world to match LuValle's time that year.

In 1935, LuValle moved up to the quarter-mile and took the NCAA 440y in 47.7. In the Olympic year he brought his best 440y time down to 47.1 at the Princeton Invitational and two weeks later he won the 400m at the Western Olympic Trials in 46.3, which would remain the best mark of his career.

MacDONALD, J. Oliver.

B. 20 FEB 1904 Paterson, NJ. D. 14 APR 1973 Philadelphia, PA. Gold: 1924 4 × 400 meter relay. Oliver MacDonald, a freshman at Penn, finished fourth at the 1924 Olympic Trials and was selected as a member of the 4 × 400m relay team for the Paris Olympics. He ran the third leg as the U.S. posted a world record of 3:16.0 in the final.

MacDonald earned a D.D.S. degree from Penn in 1927 and returned to his native Paterson to practice dentistry. In 1959, he closed his practice, moved to Flemington, New Jersey, and started a real estate brokerage business.

MAGNUSSEN, Conrad.

Gold: 1904 Tug-of-War. Conrad Magnussen was a member of the Milwaukee AC team that won the 1904 tug-of-war although, like all the members of that team, he was actually from Chicago.

Courtesy Bob Mathias

Bob Mathias, the only two-time decathlon champion, as he looks today as head of the U.S. Olympic Training Center in Colorado Springs.

MANN, Ralph Vernon.
B. 16 JUN 1949 Long Beach, CA. Silver: 1972 400 meter hurdles. While at Brigham Young, Ralph Mann won both the NCAA and the AAU 440y hurdles in 1969, 1970, and 1971. In 1971 he also won the Pan-American

Games and in 1972, after setting a U.S. record of 48.4 at the Final Trials, he was beaten by Uganda's John Akii-Bua at the Olympics.

Mann won his fourth AAU title in 1975. In winning the 1970 NCAA title, he set a world record of 48.8 for the 440y hurdles and his best metric mark was 48.4 at the 1972 Final Trials.

MASHBURN, Jesse William.
B. 14 FEB 1933 Seminole, OK. Gold: 1956 4 × 400 meter relay. Jesse Mashburn of Oklahoma A&M placed fourth at the 1952 Final Trials and went to Helsinki as a member of the relay squad. He did not, however, compete in the Olympics because the U.S. brought hurdler Charlie Moore onto the relay team in a vain effort to counter the talented Jamaican foursome.

In 1956, Mashburn again placed fourth at the Final Trials, but this time he got a chance to show his paces on the relay team and came back from Melbourne with a gold medal. Mashburn also won the NCAA one-lap title in 1955 and 1956, and his best performance was a 46.2 clocking for 440y. Today he works in the real estate business in Oklahoma.

MATHIAS, Robert Bruce.
B. 17 NOV 1930 Tulare, CA. Gold(2): 1948 Decathlon, 1952 Decathlon. When, as a 17-year-old, Bob Mathias won the 1948 Olympic decathlon, he established a record, which still stands, as the youngest-ever winner of an Olympic track & field event.

Mathias won four AAU titles, set three world records, and was undefeated in the 11 decathlons in which he competed. His third world record came at the 1952 Olympics when he won his second gold medal. He was also an outstanding running back on the Stanford football team and in 1952 became the only man to compete in the Olympics and the Rose Bowl in the same year.

Mathias had a brief movie career and among the films he made was his life story. He later became a congressman representing California's 18th District, serving in the 91st, 92nd, and 93rd Congresses. As a congressman he served on the Agriculture Committee, the Foreign Affairs Committee, and as a delegate to the House NATO Conferences. He now works for the United States Olympic Committee as director of the Olympic Training Center.

MATSON, James Randel.

B. 05 MAR 1945 Kilgore, TX. Gold: 1968 Shot Put; Silver: 1964 Shot Put. After failing by a narrow margin to defeat Dallas Long at the 1964 Olympics, Randy Matson enjoyed a comfortable win at the 1968 Games. In 1964, as a freshman at Texas A&M, he also won the first of his six AAU shot titles and at the NCAA championships he scored a shot/discus double in 1966-67. He also won the shot at the 1965 NCAA indoor and the 1967 Pan-Am Games.

Matson improved the world shot record four times culminating with a mark of 71'-5½" in April 1967. Earlier in the month he threw the discus 213'-9" which was then only two and one-half inches off the world record. When Matson set his third world record of 70'-7¼" in May 1965, he became the first man to break the 70-foot barrier. Before retiring he came close to making the Olympic team for a third time when he placed fourth at the 1972 Final Trials.

MATSON, Oliver Adrian.

B. 01 MAY 1930 Trinity, TX. Silver: 1952 4 × 400 meter relay; Bronze: 1952 400 meters. In 1948, as an 18-year-old schoolboy, Ollie Matson competed in the 400m at the Final Trials, but failed to make the Olympic team. Four years later he won two medals at the Helsinki Olympics and signed a pro football contract immediately after the Olympics. While at the University of San Francisco, Matson was the top college runner in his senior year. He led the NCAA in scoring and rushing and was a first-team all-America selection.

Matson became one the best running backs in the NFL, playing for the Chicago Cardinals, Detroit Lions, Los Angeles Rams, and Philadelphia Eagles. He was an all-league selection in 1954–57 and was voted MVP of the 1955 Pro Bowl Game. When he retired in 1966, after 14 years in the NFL, he was second only to the legendary Jimmy Brown in combined rushing yardage. His heroics earned him a niche in the Pro Football Hall of Fame. After his pro career ended, he became a football coach.

MATTHEWS, Vincent Edward.

B. 16 DEC 1947 New York, NY. Gold(2): 1968 4 × 400 meter relay, 1972 400 meters. After an impressive 1967 season, which included a 45.0 for 400m, Vince Matthews set a world record of 44.4 in 1968 although the mark was never ratified because Matthews was wearing illegal brush spikes. Because he finished fourth at the 1968 Final Trials he only made the relay team for the Mexico Olympics, where the U.S. took the gold medals and set a world record of 2:56.1.

Matthews retired after the 1968 Olympics but made a comeback in 1972, and after finishing third at the Final Trials, pulled off a surprise win in the Olympic final. He missed a chance for another medal when the U.S. was unable to field a team for 4 × 400m after Matthews and Wayne Collett were banned from future Olympic competition for their behavior during the medal ceremony for the individual 400m. They refused to stand at attention during the national anthem and openly conversed as it played. They later stated they did it as a protest against the treatment of blacks in the United States.

MAY, William Lee.

B. 11 NOV 1936 Knoxville, AL. Silver: 1960 110 meter hurdles. As a senior at Indiana, Willie May placed second to Lee Calhoun at the 1960 Final Trials and it was Calhoun who again defeated May in the Olympic final. Although he never won a major title, May had an impressive record of fast clockings with a career best of 13.4.

McCLUSKEY, Joseph Paul.

B. 02 JUN 1911. Bronze: 1932 3,000 meter steeplechase. Joe McCluskey must be rated as one of the greatest performers in the history of U.S. distance running. Between 1930 and 1943 he won the AAU steeplechase a record nine times and was three times a winner of a distance race on the flat. Indoors, he won the AAU steeplechase eight times and won the two miles on the flat in 1930. While at Fordham, he built up an impressive record at the IC4A championships, winning the outdoor two miles twice and the indoor title three times.

McCluskey was equally talented and durable as a cross-country runner. He won the individual AAU title in 1930 and was a scoring member of the New York AC team which won the AAU team title in 1941, 1946, and 1947.

A two-time Olympian, Joe McCluskey was unlucky not to win a silver medal in 1932. At the 3,000m mark he was in second place, but due to an error on the part of the officials, an extra lap was run during which

McCluskey dropped back to third place. In 1936 he finished 10th and in 1948 he failed to make the Olympic team for a third time when, at the age of 37, he finished a commendable fifth at the Final Trials.

McCRACKEN, Josiah Calvin, Jr.

B. 30 MAR 1874. D. 15 FEB 1962 Chestnut Hill, PA. Silver: 1900 Shot Put; Bronze: 1900 Hammer Throw. Josiah McCracken was a useful all-round performer in the weight events, taking the shot/hammer double at the IC4A championships in 1898 and 1899. By international standards he was perhaps a better performer in the hammer and his career best of 153'-8" in 1898 ranked him second in the world that year.

Despite his Olympic successes, track & field was only a secondary sport for McCracken as, at Penn, he was better known as a footballer and was on Walter Camp's All-American team in 1899. The silver medalist in the 1900 Olympic hammer throw, Truxtun Hare, was also an All-American football player at Penn and it was only the Irish immigrant John Flanagan who prevented the two Penn footballers from taking top Olympic honors at Paris.

McCracken earned an M.D. degree from Penn and later served as a medical missionary in China for 50 years.

McDONALD, Patrick Joseph (né Patrick Joseph McDonnell).

B. 29 JUL 1878 County Clare, Ireland. D. 16 MAY 1954. Gold(2): 1912 Shot Put, 1920 56 lb. weight throw; Silver: 1912 Shot Put (two-hand aggregate). When Pat McDonnell's sister landed at Ellis Island after her sea voyage from Ireland, immigration officials pinned a name tag on her and spelled the name McDonald. She was taking no chances of being deported so she, and all the McDonnells who came after her, accepted the name McDonald.

Inspired by the feats of his countrymen John Flanagan, Matt McGrath, and Martin Sheridan, Pat McDonald initially had aspirations of becoming a hammer thrower, but he showed more aptitude as a shot putter. After placing second to Ralph Rose at the AAU in 1909 and 1910, he took the title in Rose's absence in 1911 and defeated Rose at the 1912 championships as well as the 1912 Olympics.

McDonald won both the shot and the 56 lb. weight

event at the AAU championships in 1914, 1919, and 1920 and competed at both events at the Antwerp Olympics. He won the weight throw and placed fourth in the shot. McDonald's career was remarkable for its longevity. When he won his Olympic gold medal in 1920, he was aged 42, making him the oldest Olympic track & field champion ever. He is also the oldest AAU champion ever—he won the last of an amazing 16 titles in the 56 lb. weight throw in 1933, at 56 years old.

McGINNIS, Charles English.

B. 04 OCT 1906. Bronze: 1928 Pole Vault. At the Central Olympic Trials, Charles McGinnis of the Chicago AA won the high jump at 6'-5" and the pole vault at 13'-6". One week later at the Final Trials he matched these heights exactly in both events to place second in the high jump and fourth in the pole vault. He competed in both events at Amsterdam, placing seventh in the high jump and winning a bronze medal in the pole vault.

McGRATH, Matthew J.

B. 18 DEC 1878 Nenagh, County Tipperary, Ireland. D. 29 JAN 1941. Gold: 1912 Hammer Throw; Silver(2): 1908 Hammer Throw, 1924 Hammer Throw. Matt McGrath made his Olympic debut in 1908 at the age of 30 and in 1928, as a 50-year-old, he came within an ace of becoming the only U.S. track & field athlete to compete in five Olympic Games. After finishing second at the 1928 Eastern Olympic Trials, he had an off day at the Final Trials and finished in fifth place. Frank Connors and Ken Caskey, both of whom McGrath had beaten at the Eastern meet, finished ahead of him and made the Olympic team. There was a public outcry over McGrath's omission from the team and although he went to Amsterdam after a subscription fund had been raised to pay his fare, he was, not surprisingly, not allowed to compete.

Still, McGrath is remembered as one of the great hammer throwers of all time. He won seven AAU titles, set a world record in 1911, and his 1912 Olympic record was not beaten until 1936. He also won the AAU 56 lb. weight throw title seven times and, in addition to his three Olympic medals, placed fifth in the hammer in 1920, although he competed with a badly twisted knee.

McLEAN, John Frederick.

B. 10 JAN 1878 Menominee, MI. D. 04 JUN 1955. Silver: 1900 110 meter hurdles. In addition to placing second in the 110m hurdles at the 1900 Olympics, John McLean of the University of Michigan placed sixth in the long jump, and competed in the 200m hurdles and both the running and standing triple jumps.

McMILLEN, Robert Earl.

B. 05 MAR 1928. Silver: 1952 1,500 meters. After falling three times in the heats of the 1948 Olympic steeplechase, Bob McMillen wisely gave up the event and turned his attentions to miling. He won the NCAA 1,500m for Occidental in 1952 and, after winning the Final Trials, his devastating finishing burst narrowly failed to net him the Olympic gold.

McMillen's time of 3:45.2 in Helsinki was a new U.S. record and he had a best time for the mile of 4:07.8, which he clocked in finishing second to Jim Newcomb at the 1950 Southern Pacific AAU meet.

MEADOWS, Earle Elmer.

B. 29 JUN 1913 Corinth, MS. Gold: 1936 Pole Vault. Prior to the advent of Cornelius Warmerdam, Earle Meadows of Southern Cal could claim to be the greatest bamboo vaulter in history. He tied with his teammate from USC, Bill Sefton, for the 1935 AAU title and for the NCAA crown in 1935 and 1936, but he was a clear winner at the 1936 Final Trials and at the Olympics. Meadows again had some close contests with Sefton in 1937 and in May they both raised the world record to 14'-8½" and three weeks later, the "Heavenly Twins," as they were known, took the record up to 14'-11". The occasion was the Pacific Coast Conference Meet in Los Angeles and we might have seen history's first 15-foot vault that day but Meadows and Sefton were unable to continue the competition because the standards had been raised to their maximum and the bar could be raised no higher.

Meadows also had a fine record on the indoor circuit, winning the AAU three times, and in 1941 he twice set a world indoor record. In 1948 the veteran Meadows twice cleared 14'-6" indoors, but failed to maintain his form throughout the summer and missed a chance to defend his Olympic title when he only tied for sixth at the Final Trials. Meadows has since become the owner of a musical instrument business in Texas.

MEREDITH, James Edwin.

B. 14 NOV 1891 Chester Heights, PA. D. 02 NOV 1957.

Gold(2): 1912 800 meters, 1912 4 x 400 meter relay. Ted Meredith of Mercersburg Academy is still recognized as the greatest prep runner of all time. At Princeton in 1912 he took almost two seconds off the national interscholastic record with a 49.2 440y and he set a new 880y record of 1:55.0. Two weeks later he brought the 440y record down to 48.4, and after an impressive showing at the Finals Trials, was selected for three events at the Stockholm Olympics.

The 19-year-old schoolboy's Olympic career started auspiciously. He defeated the defending champion, Mel Sheppard, in the 800m in a new world record of 1:51.9, and continued on to the 880y mark, where he also posted a new world record of 1:52.5. In the 400m he misjudged the pace and finished fourth but he claimed a second gold in the 4x400m relay. On his return from Stockholm, Meredith enrolled at Penn, and at the 1916 IC4A he set a world record of 47.4 for 440y and won the 880y. He retired in 1918 as the holder of the interscholastic, Collegiate, American, and World Records for 400m, 400y, 800m, and 880y, and was a member of the relay world record holders for 1,600m and the mile. James Meredith attempted a comeback in 1920, but was eliminated in the semi-finals of the Olympic 400m. He then closed his career and became a real estate broker.

METCALFE, Ralph Harold.

B. 29 MAY 1910 Atlanta, GA. D. 10 OCT 1978 Chicago, IL. Gold: 1936 4 × 100 meter relay; Silver(2): 1932 100 meters, 1936 100 meters; Bronze: 1932 200 meters. Although some 50 years later Jesse Owens is remembered as the great sprinter of the 30's, Ralph Metcalfe was on many counts Owens' superior. Metcalfe was at his best between the 1932 and 1936 Olympics and he won both sprints at the AAU and NCAA for three straight years (1932–34) and won the AAU 200m in 1935–36 to give him a record of five straight wins in this event.

Metcalfe, who attended Marquette, equalled the world record of 10.3 for 100m eight times, but only three of those clockings reached the record books. In 1932 he ran a wind-assisted 19.8 for 220y on a straight track in Toronto to become the first man to break the 20-second barrier. In the 1932 Olympic 200m, Metcalfe may have been unfairly deprived of a gold medal when it was later shown that the lane in which he ran was about two meters longer than it should have been.

Metcalfe graciously declined a protest and a rerun because the American threesome of Eddie Tolan, George Simpson, and himself had swept the medals in the event.

Ralph Metcalfe later became well known in Chicago politics, serving on the city council under Mayor Daley for many years. In 1970, Metcalfe was elected to the U.S. Congress from the 1st District in Illinois, serving until his death. He also gave yeoman service to the USOC, being elected to their board of directors in 1969.

MEYER, Alvah T.

B. 18 JUL 1888 New York, NY. D. 1940. Silver: 1912 100 meters. After winning the AAU indoor 60y in 1911 and the 220y outdoor in 1912, Alvah Meyer of the Irish-American AC performed poorly at the 1912 Final Trials and was only included on the Stockholm team on the condition that he pay his own way. His parents provided the necessary funds and Meyer took the silver medal in the 100m but, although he was the reigning U.S. champion, he failed to make the final of the 200m. In 1914, Meyer set a world indoor record of 6.4 for 60y and the following year he posted an indoor record of 32.2 for 330y.

MILBURN, Rodney, Jr.

B. 18 MAY 1950 Opelousas, LA. Gold: 1972 110 meter hurdles. After winning 27 consecutive high hurdles finals, Rod Milburn of Southern University and the Baton Rouge TC came unstuck at the 1972 Final Trials when, after hitting the seventh and 10th hurdles, he finished in third place. He quickly made amends by taking the Olympic title with a new world record of 13.24 (fully automatic timing), and then ran up a further streak of 31 victories until he lost to Leon Coleman over 50m in a pro race in April 1975.

Milburn won the AAU and the NCAA title twice and was the Pan-American Games champion in 1971. Indoors, he won the AAU twice and set numerous records at varying distances. In winning the 1971 outdoor AAU he became the first man to officially run 13 seconds flat for the 120y hurdles, and one version of the automatic timing was 12.94 seconds.

MILLER, William Preston.

B. 22 FEB 1930 Lawnside, NJ. Silver: 1952 Javelin Throw. Although Bill Miller beat Cy Young three times in pre-Olympic meets, it was Young who took the gold medal in Helsinki, but with Miller placing second, this was the best showing ever by the U.S. in Olympic javelin competition.

Miller, an Annapolis grad, won the AAU in 1952 and in 1954 a technicality denied him the opportunity of becoming the only black athlete ever to hold the world javelin record. He had a mark of 266'-8½" but the throw was made with a javelin which had been broken and in repairing the implement the center of gravity had been moved out of the specified limits. After retiring from track, Miller spent a number of years in the Far East as coach to various national teams.

MILLER, William Waring.

B. 07 NOV 1912. Gold: 1932 Pole Vault. At the 1932 Final Trials, Bill Graber set a world record of 14'-4¼" with Bill Miller of Stanford finishing second at 14'-1¼". At the Olympics three weeks later, Graber could only manage fourth and Miller took the gold medal with a career best of 14'-1¾". This was to be the only major title that Bill Miller ever won outright although he was in a three-way tie for first place at the 1932 IC4A championships.

MILLS, William Mervin.

B. 30 JUN 1938 Pine Ridge, SD. Gold: 1964 10,000 meters. As a virtual unknown on the international track scene, Billy Mills caused one of the major upsets at the 1964 Games by becoming the first American to win the Olympic 10,000m. He also placed a creditable 14th in the marathon.

Mills later set a world six mile record at the 1965 AAU championships when he was given the same time as Gerry Lindgren, and later in the season he set a U.S. 10,000m record in the dual meet against West Germany. After graduating from Kansas, Mills served as a lieutenant in the marines and later worked for a life insurance company. Mills, who is 7/16th Sioux Indian, is active in Indian affairs and in 1983 a Canadian Indian tribe made a film of his life story.

MITCHEL, James Sarsfield.

B. 30 JAN 1864 County Limerick, Ireland. D. 03 JUL 1921 New York, NY. Bronze: 1904 56 lb. weight throw. Until the emergence of John Flanagan, Jim Mitchel was undoubtedly the greatest performer in the weight events that the sport had ever seen. He won a total of 76 national event championships (American, Canadian, English, and Irish) but when he made his Olympic debut he was 40 years old and rather past his prime. He was at his best as a hammer thrower and set four world records between 1886 and 1892.

In addition to competing in three weight events at St. Louis in 1904, Mitchel went to Athens for the 1906 Games, but was unable to compete because he was injured when the boat carrying the U.S. team ran into a severe storm and violent waves. Mitchel later became a well-known sportswriter in New York and an author of several books on polo and rowing.

MOLONEY, Frederick Graham.
B. 04 AUG 1880. Bronze: 1900 110 meter hurdles. Fred Moloney competed in the 100m and the 110m and 200m hurdles at the 1900 Olympics, but he qualified only for the final of the high hurdles, where he took the bronze medal. His brother, William Arthur, also competed in Paris, and qualified for the final of the 400m but did not contest it because it was held on a Sunday.

Fred Moloney registered at the University of Chicago various times between 1898 and 1907 but never completed work for a degree. He later became the vice president and general manager of the Helios Corp. in Ottawa, Illinois.

MOORE, Charles Hewes, Jr.
B. 12 AUG 1929 Coatesville, PA. Gold: 1952 400 meter hurdles; Silver: 1952 4 × 400 meter relay. As a high hurdler, Charles Moore, Sr. went to Paris in 1924 as an alternate on the Olympic team. In 1952, 28 years later, his son enjoyed far greater success at the Olympics when he won the 400m hurdles and ran a 46.3 relay leg for the team that took the silver medals behind Jamaica.

Moore won the NCAA 440y flat for Cornell in 1949 and the low hurdles in 1951. He won the AAU 440y hurdles four years straight from 1949 and was unbeaten in his 23 races as an intermediate hurdler. After the 1952 Olympics he twice posted a world record for the 440y hurdles during the space of five days at meets in London.

MORRIS, Glenn Edward.
B. 18 JUN 1912 Simla, CO. D. 31 JAN 1974 Burlingame,

CA. Gold: 1936 Decathlon. After graduating from Colorado State in 1934, Glenn Morris stayed on at Fort Collins and worked as a part-time assistant to football coach, Harry Hughes. This gave Morris the time and facilities to develop his talents as a decathlete and in April 1936 he broke the U.S. record in his first ever decathlon competition at the Kansas Relays. Two months later, he won the Final Trials with a new world record and in his third and final competition, Morris won the Olympic title, again with a new world record, after he had trailed teammate Bob Clark by two points after the first day.

In October 1936 Morris signed a contract with NBC as a radio announcer and in 1938 he had a brief career in movies, playing in three films, including the title role in "Tarzan's Revenge." He had a similarly brief career as a pro footballer with the Detroit Lions in 1940 and after being seriously wounded while serving as a naval office in the Pacific he found employment difficult to come by. Sadly for a man who had been a nationwide celebrity after his Olympic victory, he died in poor circumstances in a small desert town in California.

MORRIS, Ronald Hugh.
B. 27 APR 1935 Glendale, CA. Silver: 1960 Pole Vault. After setting a national high school record of 13′-11½″ in 1953, Ron Morris enrolled at USC and was AAU pole vault champion in 1958, 1961, and 1962. He set a career best of 16′-3¾″ during a 1963 European tour and after his competitive days were over he became head track coach at Los Angeles State.

MORROW, Bobby Joe.
B. 15 OCT 1935 Harlingen, TX. Gold(3): 1956 100 meters, 1956 200 meters, 1956 4 × 100 meter relay. Although other sprinters can claim faster times, Bobby Morrow has the finest competitive record of any man in the history of sprinting and is unquestionably the greatest white sprinter in history.

In his freshman year at Abilene Christian he lost only once; the following year he was undefeated at 220y and lost only once at 100y. Apart from his triple Olympic successes he equalled the world 220y turn record three times and matched the world 100m record three times. As a member of the winning Olympic relay team in 1956 he shared the world record of 39.5 and he twice helped Abilene Christian set a world record in the

$4 \times 110y$ relay. He was also a member of three teams which set world records for the $4 \times 220y$ relay. In addition he took the AAU 100 three times, the 220y once, and won the sprint double at the 1956–57 NCAA. Perhaps Morrow's greatest honor came in January 1957 when he was named Sportsman of the Year by *Sports Illustrated*.

MOSES, Edwin Corley.
B. 31 AUG 1955 Dayton, OH. Gold: 1976 400 meter hurdles. Ed Moses has dominated the intermediate hurdles to an extent that no man has ever achieved in this or any other event. At the end of the 1981 season he had won 72 consecutive 400m hurdle finals. He set a world record of 47.6 in winning the 1976 Olympic title and improved the record in 1977 before setting the current world record of 47.13 in 1980.

Moses, a Morehouse College '77 grad, won the AAU in 1977 and 1979 and the World Cup race in the same years. The 1980 boycott deprived him of an almost certain second gold medal. He has seldom run other races, but has clocked 45.60 for 400m (44.1 in a relay), 13.64 for the 110m hurdles, and has spoken in 1983 of beginning to run some 800m races.

MOULTON, Fay R.
B. 07 APR 1876 Marion, KS. D. 19 FEB 1945 Kansas City, MO. Silver: 1906 100 meters; Bronze: 1904 60 meters. Fay Moulton won the 1902 AAU and Canadian 440y championships and in 1903 he won the IC4A 100y and finished second in the 220y. At the 1904 Olympics he placed fourth in both the 100m and 200m in addition to his bronze medal performance. At the 1906 Olympics he placed sixth in the 400m.

After attending Kansas State, Fay Moulton entered Yale Law School and graduated in 1903. He later worked for United Clay Products Corp., serving for many years as secretary-treasurer. He also briefly practiced law in Kansas City.

MULLER, Harold Powers.
B. 12 JUN 1901. D. 17 MAY 1962 Berkeley, CA. Silver: 1920 High Jump. "Brick" Muller was best known at the University of California as an outstanding tailback on the football team and, after having been named third team in 1920, he was voted first-team all-America in 1920 and 1921. He was the star of the 1920 Cal football

Bobby Joe Morrow won three gold medals in sprinting at the 1956 Melbourne Olympics.

team—considered one of the greatest college football teams of all time.

Muller was an outstanding all-round athlete and at the 1920 Western Olympic Trials he not only won the high jump but also placed second in the long jump and triple jump. In 1921 he tied for first place in the IC4A high jump and in 1922 he finished second in the IC4A discus throw.

Muller earned an M.D. degree from Cal in 1924 and practiced medicine the rest of his life.

MUNSON, David Curtiss.

B. 19 MAY 1884 Medina, NY. D. 17 SEP 1953. Gold: 1904 4 mile team race. David Munson secured the New York State Cornell Scholarship for Orleans County while attending Medina High School and, after entering Cornell, soon proved himself to be a valuable member of the track team. In his sophomore year he won the IC4A mile in 4:25.6 and, after winning the AAU mile in the extraordinarily slow time of 4:41.2, he went to St. Louis for the Olympics. At the Games, Munson finished fourth in the 1,500m in addition to running for the winning New York AC team in the four mile team race.

In 1905, Munson again won the IC4A mile and set a new world indoor record for 1½ miles and a new Cornell record for the mile outdoors. In 1906 he captained the Cornell track and cross-country teams. On leaving Cornell, David Munson entered New York Law School and, after graduating in 1909, embarked on a distinguished career in law.

MURCHISON, Ira James.

B. 06 FEB 1933 Chicago, IL. Gold: 1956 4 × 100 meter relay. After attending Iowa and Western Michigan, Ira Murchison joined the army and took both sprints at the 1956 army championships. In June 1956 he twice equalled the world 100m record of 10.2 and then brought the record down to 10.1 in winning the International Military Championships in Berlin. At the 1956 Olympics he placed fourth in the 100m, but then won a gold medal as the lead-off man on the world record breaking relay team.

After his military service, Murchison returned to Western Michigan and finished second to Bobby Morrow in the 1957 NCAA 100y. Both men equalled the world record, but only Morrow had his time recognized by the IAAF. Murchison gained some consolation by winning the NCAA title in 1958. Standing only 5'-5" tall, Murchison was one of the smallest ever world class sprinters and was ideally suited to indoor competition. He won the AAU indoor 60y in 1957 and twice equalled the world record that year. He was ranked as the leading indoor sprinter in 1957 and 1959.

MURCHISON, Loren C.

B. 17 DEC 1898. D. 11 JUN 1979. Gold(2): 1920 4 × 100 meter relay, 1924 4 × 100 meter relay. Loren Murchison of the New York AC was one of the finest Olympic sprinters of all time. In addition to two relay gold medals he reached the individual sprint finals three times.

Murchison won his first AAU title in 1918 when he took the 220y and in 1923 he won the AAU sprint double, repeating that feat at the 1925 British championships. Indoors he won the AAU five times and set numerous world records at distances varying from 50m to 300y.

MURPHY, Frank Dwyer.

B. 21 SEP 1889 East Chicago, IL. Bronze: 1912 Pole Vault (tied). Frank Murphy, of the University of Illinois, was awarded a bronze medal in the 1912 pole vault although he only placed fourth. Frank Nelson and Marc Wright were tied for second place at 12'-7½" and the three athletes who cleared 12'-5½" were each awarded a bronze medal although they were beaten by three other athletes.

MURRAY, Frederick Seymour.

B. 15 MAY 1984 San Francisco, CA. Bronze: 1920 110 meter hurdles. Fred Murray was on the Stanford track team for three years and was captain in his senior year—1916. He entered the 1915 AAU as a member of the Olympic Club (San Francisco) and won the 110y and 220y hurdles. He won the low hurdles again the following year and won both IC4A hurdle titles. Murray later served with the American Expeditionary Forces in France and then joined the Metropolitan Newspaper Service as a sports cartoonist.

MYERS, Edwin Earl.

B. 18 DEC 1896. Bronze: 1920 Pole Vault. Ed Myers of Dartmouth College and the Chicago AA tied for the 1920 AAU pole vault title but lost on a jump-off and, after winning outright in 1923 and 1924, he again lost in a jump-off in 1926. He also won the IC4A in 1919 and 1920.

Myers was an alternate on the 1924 Olympic team and represented the U.S. in the post-Games meet against the British Empire. He later placed fourth in the 1927 AAU and was one of the top U.S. vaulters for almost a decade; a remarkable achievement during a period of very rapid development in the event.

NELSON, Frank Thayer.

B. 22 MAY 1887. D. 16 JUL 1970. Silver: 1912 Pole Vault (tied). In 1909 Frank Nelson and Charles Campbell of

Yale tied for first place at 12'-4" in the dual meet with Harvard and were the top-ranked vaulters in the world that year. Nelson lost to Campbell at the 1909 IC4A but he won the title in 1910 when he beat yet another fine Yale vaulter, Robert Gardner, who went on to set a world record in 1912 as well as win the U.S. Amateur Golf Championship three times. Gardner failed to make the Olympic team but the first three places in Stockholm still went to the Ivy League. Harry Babcock (Columbia) took the gold medal, and Marc Wright (Dartmouth) and Frank Nelson tied for second.

NEWHOUSE, Frederick Vaughn.
B. 08 NOV 1948 Haney Grove, TX. Gold: 1976 4 × 400 meter relay; Silver: 1976 400 meters. After running 44.2 in the semi-finals at the 1972 Final Trials, Fred Newhouse of Prairie View A&M faded badly in the final and failed to make the team for Munich. At the 1976 Trials, by which time he was representing the Baton Rouge Track Club, Newhouse qualified comfortably for the Montreal team by finishing second to Maxie Parks. Newhouse beat Parks at the Olympics but lost first place to the great Cuban, Alberto Juantorena. In the relay, Newhouse ran 43.8 on the third leg and lengthened the already-considerable lead of the U.S. team. Today he is an engineer with the Exxon Corp. in Baton Rouge.

NEWTON, Arthur Lewis.
B. 31 JAN 1883 Upton, MA. D. 19 JUL 1950 Worcester, MA. Gold: 1904 4 mile team race; Bronze(2): 1904 2590 meter steeplechase, 1904 Marathon. After finishing fourth in the steeplechase and fifth in the marathon at the 1900 Olympics, Arthur Newton fared much better at the St. Louis Games. He took the bronze medal in both the steeplechase and the marathon and led the New York AC team to a one-point victory over the Chicago AA in the 4-mile team race. Newton also won the AAU five mile title in 1900, the steeplechase in 1902 and the AAU junior mile in 1900.

NIEDER, William Henry.
B. 10 AUG 1933 Hempstead, NY. Gold: 1960 Shot Put; Silver: 1956 Shot Put. While at Kansas, Bill Nieder won the 1955 NCAA title and the following season he became the second man in history to beat 60 feet. The first man across that barrier was Parry O'Brien, and it was O'Brien who beat Nieder at the 1956 Olympics.

Nieder won his only AAU title in 1956 and, although often troubled by a knee injury, he was at his best in 1960 when he improved the world record three times and took the Olympic gold medal, having turned the tables on silver medalist O'Brien. Nieder was fortunate to make the 1960 Olympic team — he qualified only fourth, but was advanced to the team when alternate Dave Davis dropped out with an injury. Soon after the Rome Olympics, Bill Nieder launched a pro boxing career. It lasted one round—he was knocked out quickly in his only fight.

NORTON, Emerson Carlysle.
B. 16 NOV 1900 Kansas City, KS. Silver: 1924 Decathlon. Emerson Norton was overshadowed as a decathlete by Harold Osborn but, like Osborn, he was also a fine high jumper. His best performance in that event came at the 1923 Penn Relays when he tied Leroy Brown at 6'-3⅜" and then won the jump-off. He was a consistent performer on the indoor circuit, winning the IC4A high jump in 1925 and sharing the title in 1926. At the indoor AAU championships he was runner-up in 1927 and placed third in 1928. Surprisingly, Norton only competed in one AAU decathlon, placing third in 1923.

After obtaining degrees from Kansas and Georgetown, Emerson Norton worked as a lawyer for the Air Defense Command and the Department of Defense.

NORTON, John Kelley.
B. 16 APR 1893 Santa Clara, CA. D. 28 DEC 1979 New York, NY. Silver: 1920 400 meter hurdles. After setting a world record of 54.2 for the 440y hurdles in April 1920, John Norton finished second to Frank Loomis at the Final Trials in July. The following month he again placed second to Loomis in the Olympic final. Norton had attended Stanford and later represented the Olympic Club of San Francisco.

OBERST, Eugene G.
B. 23 JUL 1901. Bronze: 1924 Javelin Throw. Although he only placed fourth at the 1924 Final Trials, Gene Oberst of Notre Dame became the first U.S. athlete to win an Olympic medal in the javelin throw.

O'BRIEN, Edward T.
B. 14 SEP 1914. Silver: 1936 4 × 400 meter relay. Seventh place in the 400m at the 1936 Final Trials earned Eddie O'Brien a place on the Olympic relay team. Syra-

cuse's O'Brien was the fastest of the U.S. quartet in Berlin, running the third leg in 46.7. His best mark was 47.3 for 440y, which he clocked in winning the Princeton Invitational in 1935. O'Brien won the AAU outdoor 440y in 1935 and in 1936 he was unbeaten indoors, setting a world record for 600m in winning the AAU title. He won the AAU again in 1937 and lost only one race during the indoor season. In 1936 and 1937 he also won the IC4A indoor 600 and he set a world record of 57.8 when he won the Buremeyer 500 in 1936. He brought that record down to 57.6 when he scored a repeat win in 1937.

O'BRIEN, William Parry, Jr.
B. 28 JAN 1932 Santa Monica, CA. Gold(2): 1952 Shot Put, 1956 Shot Put; Silver: 1960 Shot Put. Although his records have now been surpassed, Parry O'Brien is, by the standards of his contemporaries, the greatest shot-putter of all time. Indoors and outdoors he won a total of 17 AAU titles and between July 1952 and June 1956 he ran up a winning streak of 116 consecutive victories. He broke the world record 16 times, although only 10 of these were ratified, and he was the first man to beat the 18-meter, 60-foot, and 19-meter barriers. O'Brien set his last world record in 1959, but he continued to improve and set a career best of 64'-7¼" in 1966, two years after his final Olympic appearance in Tokyo, where he placed fourth. O'Brien was Pan-American Games champion in 1955 and 1959 and, while at Southern Cal, he won the NCAA title in 1952 and 1953. He also added the 1955 AAU discus championship.

Apart from his multiple victories and records, Parry O'Brien made a significant contribution to the sport by pioneering a new style which was copied by many of those who followed him as world record holders. He now works in the banking and real estate business in Southern California.

OERTER, Alfred Adolph, Jr.
B. 19 SEP 1936 Astoria, NY. Gold(4): 1956 Discus Throw, 1960 Discus Throw, 1964 Discus Throw, 1968 Discus Throw. With four successive victories in one event, Al Oerter holds a unique place in Olympic history. A superb competitor in major meets, he did not set his first world record until 1962, when he became the first man to throw beyond 200 feet. He posted three more world records, but it was competition, not records, that motivated Al Oerter.

He won the AAU title six times and was NCAA champion in 1957, sharing that title in 1958. Oerter was never the favorite at any of his Olympic victories, nor was he the world record holder going into the meet, but such was his competitive greatness that at three of the four meets he responded with the longest throw of his career to win the gold. He walked out of the record books into legend at Tokyo in 1964 when he threw with torn rib muscles and a pinched cervical nerve that required a neck brace. On his fifth throw, he almost had to be carried from the field because of the pain, but that throw gave him the gold medal.

Oerter retired at the end of the 1969 season, but he made a comeback in 1977 and the following year set a personal best of 221'-4". Incredibly, in 1980 he placed fourth at the Olympic Trials, having earlier in the season, at the age of 43, raised his career best 227'-11". Oerter is a systems analyst and computer engineer for an electronics firm on Long Island, and since graduation from Kansas, he has competed for the New York AC. He is still training and looking for number five in 1984.

OLSON, Oscar G.
Gold: 1904 Tug-of-War. Apart from his gold medal in the tug-of-war, Oscar Olson, of Chicago and the Milwaukee AC, also placed fourth in the two-handed weightlifting event at the 1904 Olympics.

OSBORN, Harold Marion.
B. 13 APR 1899 Butler, IL. D. 05 APR 1975 Champaign, IL. Gold(2): 1924 High Jump, 1924 Decathlon. Harold Osborn is the only man to have won an individual Olympic event in addition to winning the decathlon. He is also the first man to have won the decathlon with a world-record score. Osborn won his first AAU decathlon on 1923; although the world record he established on that occasion was never ratified, his subsquent record at the AAU championships endorses what a truly versatile athlete he was. During his long career he won 35 AAU medals (including 18 victories) in nine different events. Apart from his decathlon records, he set a world high jump record of 6'-8¼" in 1924 and in 1936, at the age of 37, he set a world record of 5'-6" for the standing high jump. This mark was set indoors but it remained the world best—indoors or out—for many years.

Osborn was a graduate of the University of Illinois

PAYS MORE THAN RUNNING THE HURDLES

In 1982 Renaldo Nehemiah signed a contract to play pro football with the San Francisco 49ers. It's not uncommon for an American Olympic trackster to go on to play pro football. In fact, 22 have done it—mostly sprinters, a few decathletes, and a few others. Many more than the following have tried, but only these 22 ever were listed on the roster during an American regular season pro football game.

JAMES BAUSCH   1932 decathlete   running back
   1933 Cincinnati Reds and Chicago Cardinals
FRANK BUDD   1960 sprinter   running back
   1962 Philadelphia Eagles, 1963 Washington Redskins
LARRY BURTON   1972 sprinter   end
   1975–76 New Orleans Saints
SOL BUTLER   1920 long jumper   back
   1923–26 with the Rock Island Independents, Hammond
     Pros, Akron Pros, and Canton Bulldogs
MILT CAMPBELL   1952/56 decathlete running back
   1957 Cleveland Browns
HENRY CARR   1964 sprinter   defensive back
   1965–67 New York Giants
FRANK COYLE   1912 pole vaulter   end
   1924 Milwaukee Badgers, 1924–26 Rock Island
     Independents
GLENN DAVIS   1956/60 hurdler   end
   1960–61 Detroit Lions
BOB HAYES   1964 sprinter   end/flanker
   1965–74 Dallas Cowboys, 1975 San Francisco 49ers
JIM HINES   1968 sprinter   end/flanker
   1969 Miami Dolphins
TRENTON JACKSON 1964 sprinter   defensive back
   1966 Philadelphia Eagles, 1967 Washington Redskins

MORTON KAER   1924 pentathlete   quarterback
   1931 Frankford Yellowjackets
OLLIE MATSON   1952 sprinter   running back
   1952–66 with the Chicago Cardinals, Los Angeles Rams,
     Detroit Lions and Philadelphia Eagles
GLENN MORRIS   1936 decathlete   end
   1940 Detroit Lions
RAY NORTON   1960 sprinter   end/flanker
   1960–61 San Francisco 49ers
JAMES OWENS   1976 hurdler   end/flanker
   1978-date with the San Francisco 49ers and the Tampa
     Bay Buccaneers
BO ROBERSON   1960 long jumper   back
   1961–66 with the San Diego Chargers, Oakland Raiders,
     Buffalo Bills, and Miami Dolphins
JIM ROSENBERGER 1912 sprinter   tackle
   1921 Evansville Crimson Giants
CLYDE SCOTT   1948 hurdler   back
   1949–52 Philadelphia Eagles, 1952 Detroit Lions
TOMMY SMITH   1968 sprinter   end/flanker
   1969 Cincinnati Bengals
JIM THORPE   1912 decathlete   running back
   1919–25 with the Canton Bulldogs, Cleveland Indians,
     Oorang Indians, Toledo Maroons, Rock Island
     Independents, and New York Giants
JACK TORRANCE   1936 shot putter   tackle
   1939–40 Chicago Bears

The last two, Thorpe and Torrance, played two professional sports—Thorpe played major league baseball and Torrance had one professional prizefight.

Is that it? No way—take a look at the wrestling section.

and later became a well-known osteopath. He married the Canadian Ethel Calderwood, who won the 1928 Olympic high jump, but they were subsequently divorced.

OWENS, James Cleveland.
B. 12 SEP 1913 Danville, AL. D. 31 MAR 1980 Tucson, AZ. Gold(4): 1936 100 meters, 1936 200 meters, 1936 4 × 100 meters relay, 1936 Long Jump. By any definition, Jesse Owens was one of the greatest athletes of all time. Many outstanding sportsmen have been given that sobriquet, but Owens was one of the very few deserving of the title. Two feats in particular ensured his

place among sports immortals. At Ann Arbor, Michigan, on 25 May 1935, he set five world records and equalled another within the space of one hour! The occasion was the Big Ten Championships and Owens started with a record-equalling 9.4 in the 100y. Ten minutes later he took his only trial in the long jump and set a world record of 26'-8¼", which would remain unbeaten for 25 years. After another 10-minute break, Owens ran 20.3 for 220 yards on the straight. Fifteen minutes later, he clocked 22.6 for the 220y hurdles, again on the straightaway. Because the times for both the 220y flat race and hurdles bettered the existing records for the marginally shorter 200m distances,

Owens was also credited with the metric world records.

Owens' second great triumph came at the Berlin Olympics the following year, when he won four gold medals and set a world record of 20.7 for 200m around a turn and contributed to a second world record in the 4 × 100m relay. At Berlin he was the leader of what the Germans termed "America's Black Auxiliaries" and his dominance made a mockery of Hitler's theories of Aryan supremacy.

Jesse Owens was the second youngest of the 11 children of an impoverished Alabama sharecropper; when he was nine, the family moved to Cleveland. Owens first showed his outstanding sporting talent at East Tech High School in Cleveland and then attended Ohio State. In addition to his above triumphs, he won several AAU and NCAA championships while a student at Ohio State.

Shortly after the Berlin Olympics, Owens turned professional at the age of 23 and experienced many years of financial hardship and racial discrimination. Eventually his public relations firm prospered and his last years were spent as a successful businessman. He became a member of the USOC, was awarded the Presidential Medal of Freedom in 1976, and was a dedicated and much sought-after speaker for the causes of Olympism and racial harmony.

PADDOCK, Charles William.
B. 11 AUG 1900 Gainesville, TX. D. 21 JUL 1943 Sitka, AK. Gold(2): 1920 100 meters, 1920 4 × 100 meter relay; Silver(2): 1920 200 meters, 1924 200 meters. Although he had been the California sprint champion for the previous three years, Charlie Paddock first achieved international recognition with a double victory at the Inter-Allied Games in Paris in 1919. Paddock was a lieutenant in the artillery at the time, and when he returned home he became the most famous track athlete of the twenties. He had a bouncing stride, high knee action and a famous "jump finish." He always wore silk when he ran and, in addition to being a successful journalist, he was his own publicity manager. He thus presented an aura which endeared him to the sporting public and, to satisfy his admirers, he frequently set world records at a variety of odd and seldom contested distances.

Paddock had a wonderful record in more traditional competition, as well. He won five AAU titles and officially equalled the world 100y record of 9.6 five times before running the first official 9.5 in May 1926. Early in 1924 he ran 10.4 for 100m to equal the world record, but his finest performance came two months later when he clocked 10.2 for 110y (100.58m) although this was not accepted as a world record because he had run more than 100m.

Paddock was a Southern Cal graduate ('23) who appeared in several movies—usually playing himself. He was later portrayed in the Oscar-winning film, "Chariots of Fire," as the brash American—not totally untrue. Paddock was killed in an air crash over Alaska while serving as a captain in the marines.

PARKER, Jack.
B. 27 SEP 1915 Beaver, OK. Bronze: 1936 Decathlon. The 1936 Olympic decathlon proved to be a repeat of the 1936 AAU championships with Glenn Morris, Bob Clark, and Jack Parker filling the first three places, in that order, at both meets. Parker, from Sacramento Junior College, had set a career best with 7,290 at the AAU meet, but approached that with 7,275 at Berlin.

PARKS, Maxie Lander.
B. 09 JUL 1951 Arkansas, AR. Gold: 1976 4 × 400 meter relay. After winning both the AAU and Final Trials 400m in 1976, Maxie Parks placed no better than fifth at the Olympics. He made ample amends in the relay when his anchor leg of 45.0 clinched the gold medals for the United States.

Parks attended UCLA but was never a major force in the NCAA championships, his highest placing in the 440y being third in 1974. Parks continued to run after Montreal and made the 1979 World Cup team. At that meet, he was anchoring the 1,600m relay team to what appeared to be a runaway victory when he collapsed on the track with a severely pulled hamstring. He has not competed since.

PATTON, Melvin Emery.
B. 16 NOV 1924 Los Angeles, CA. Gold(2): 1948 200 meters, 1948 4 × 100 meter relay. During his three seasons of competition, Mel Patton was the undisputed king of American sprinters. A highly nervous runner, he never competed in the AAU championships, but he won the NCAA 100y in 1947 and took both sprints in 1948 and 1949.

Courtesy Mel Pender

Mel Pender, who competed as a sprinter at both the 1964 and 1968 Olympics.

After twice running 9.4 for 100y in 1947, Patton ran the first official 9.3 at the West Coast Relays in 1948. In 1949 he ran a wind-assisted 9.1 and at the same meet, when the wind had dropped, he ran a legal 20.2 for a new world 220y record. One of Patton's rare defeats came in the Olympic 100m final in 1948 when he placed fifth. His only other losses during his peak years came at the 1948 Final Trials when he lost to Harrison Dillard in the heats and to Barney Ewell in the final. Patton was also a fine relay runner who twice ran on world-record-setting 4 × 220y teams for Southern Cal.

After his retirement he ran a series of pro races in Australia. He then became manager of the Washington office of Sanders Associates, Inc., an electronics company.

PEARMAN, Joseph B.

B. 08 MAY 1892. Silver: 1920 10,000 meter walk. At the 1920 Olympics, Joe Pearman of the New York AC competed in both the 3,000m and 10,000m walks. At the shorter distance he was eliminated in the heats, but in the 10,000m he placed second to the Italian Ugo Frigerio in the heats and these two then took the gold and silver medals in the final. Pearman also won two AAU outdoor titles and one indoor championship. Pearman later became editor of *The Winged Foot*, the journal of the New York AC.

PENDER, Melvin.

B. 31 OCT 1937 Atlanta, GA. Gold: 1968 4 × 100 meter relay. Mel Pender made the final of the Olympic 100m in 1964 and 1968 and placed sixth each time, but in 1968 he helped win a gold medal in the relay. In 1972, at the age of 35, he tied the world indoor bests for 50y and 60y and, as a pro in 1973, he again tied the world indoor record for 60y.

Mel Pender, an Adelphi graduate, recently retired after 21 years as a career army officer, having achieved a rank of captain. He has also worked as a track shoe designer and marketing specialist, track coach at West Point, and most recently has been director of the Youth Development Program of the NFL Players' Association.

PILGRIM, Paul Harry.

B. 1883 New York, NY. D. 08 JAN 1958 White Plains, NY. Gold(3): 1904 4 mile team race, 1906 400 meters, 1906 800 meters. Although Paul Pilgrim was on the New York AC team that won the four mile team race at the 1904 Olympics, he will be best remembered for his double victory at Athens in 1906, a double only repeated by Alberto Juantorena at the 1976 Olympics.

Pilgrim was a last-minute choice for the 1906 Olympic team and owed his selection to the insistence of his trainer, Matt Halpin. Clearly he fully justified his inclusion on the team, but at his third Olympics in 1908 he was eliminated in the heats of the 400m. Pilgrim later served as Athletic Director of the New York AC from 1914 to 1953.

POAGE, George Coleman.
B. 06 NOV 1880 Hannibal, MO. D. 11 APR 1962. Bronze(2): 1904 200 meter hurdles, 1904 400 meter hurdles. As the first black competitor and medalist, George Poage has a special place in Olympic history.

When Poage was three years old his family moved to LaCrosse, Wisconsin, where his father obtained a position as coachman to a wealthy lumberman in that town. In 1899, George Poage became the first black student to graduate from LaCrosse High School, after which he entered the University of Wisconsin, graduating from there in 1904. While a senior at Wisconsin he set another first by being the first black athlete to be invited to become a member of the Milwaukee AC.

Poage was outstanding for Wisconsin in dual meets and set collegiate records of 49.0 for 440y and 25.0 for the 220y hurdles. At the 1904 Olympics, Poage was eliminated in the heats of the 60m dash before he won his two medals. But his participation in that race made him the first of his race to compete in the Olympic Games.

Immediately following the Games, Poage took up a teaching post at Charles Sumner High School in St. Louis and remained there until 1914, when he returned to Minnesota and purchased a quarter section, which he farmed until 1920. He then moved to Chicago, briefly worked in the restaurant business, and then was in the employ of the post office for 27 years before retiring.

POLLARD, Frederick Douglas, Jr.
B. 18 FEB 1915 Springfield, MA. Bronze: 1936 110 meter hurdles. "Fritz" Pollard, son of the Brown football immortal, attended the University of North Dakota and was a student there when he won his Olympic bronze medal in 1936. While at UND, Pollard played football, ran track, and was on the school boxing team. He later attended law school and began a career as a physical educator in Chicago. He was eventually appointed director of the U.S. State Department's Office of Equal Employment Opportunity.

POPE, Augustus Russell.
B. 29 NOV 1898. Bronze: 1920 Discus Throw. After placing third at the 1920 Olympics, Gus Pope topped the world discus rankings in 1921 with a throw of 152'-7". He won the AAU title three years straight from 1920

and, while attending the University of Washington, he was NCAA champion in both the shot and discus in 1921. Pope, who threw with a unique style that he had developed himself, made the Olympic team again in 1924 when he placed fourth.

PORTER, Harry Franklin.
B. 31 AUG 1882 Bridgeport, CT. Gold: 1908 High Jump. While at Cornell, Harry Porter was not rated as an outstanding high jumper and his best performance was to tie for second place at the 1905 IC4A championships. After graduation, Porter joined the Irish-American AC and after winning the 1908 AAU title he went on to take the Olympic gold medal. With a mark of 6'-4" he topped the world ranking lists in 1909, and in 1911 he tied for first place at the AAU.

PORTER, William Franklin, III.
B. 24 MAR 1926 Jackson, MI. Gold: 1948 110 meter hurdles. Bill Porter was enrolled at Western Michigan from July 1944 thru November 1945, when he transferred to Northwestern. At Northwestern, Porter made steady rather than spectacular progress and, after finishing second to Harrison Dillard in the 1947 NCAA high hurdles, he beat Dillard at the AAU and the Final Trials in 1948 and crowned a great season by taking the Olympic title with a new Games record of 13.9. Porter was also an accomplished low hurdler, having beaten Dillard in 22.7 in 1947 and, when Dillard won the 1947 NCAA championship with a new world record of 22.3, Porter, in second place, equalled the former record of 22.5.

POWELL, John Gates.
B. 25 JUN 1947 San Francisco, CA. Bronze: 1976 Discus Throw. John Powell began his career in modest fashion, placing no better than 11th in the NCAA and 16th in the AAU discus in 1968. After consistent improvement he placed fourth at the 1972 Olympics and won three AAU titles—most recently in 1983. The following year he was the Pan-American Games champion and set a world record. After his bronze medal at Montreal, he qualified for a third Olympics by finishing third at the 1980 Final Trials. Powell was, of course, deprived of the chance to add his name to the limited list of U.S. discus throwers who have competed in three Olympics.

PRINSTEIN, Meyer.
B. 1880. D. 10 MAR 1925. Gold(4): 1900 Triple Jump, 1904 Long Jump, 1904 Triple Jump, 1906 Long Jump; Silver: 1900 Long Jump. While attending Syracuse, Meyer Prinstein won the 1898 IC4A long jump with a new American record of 23'-7$^3/_8$" and two weeks later at the New York AC Games he posted a world record of 23'-8$^7/_8$". Prinstein's duals with Alvin Kraenzlein were the highlight of many track meets at the turn of the century and they met three times in major meets in 1900. Prinstein opened with a new world record of 24'-7$^1/_4$" at the Penn Relays, then Kraenzlein took the IC4A title and the Olympic gold medal, although that victory engendered considerable ill feeling between the two athletes. At the end of the qualifying round Prinstein held a narrow lead and he then declined to compete in the final because it was held on a Sunday. Prinstein claimed that he had an agreement with Kraenzlein that neither would compete in the final, but either Kraenzlein did not know this, or he reneged on the promise, because he returned to the Racing Club de Paris on that Sunday and beat Prinstein's mark by a mere quarter of an inch. It seems likely that Kraenzlein did, in fact, renege on an agreement—it is unlikely that Prinstein, a Jew, would refuse to compete on Sunday unless in support of his teammates' stand. Prinstein's response to Kraenzlein's actions was to take action of his own. He punched Kraenzlein, but they were quickly pulled apart before a fight ensued.

After graduating from Syracuse in 1901, Prinstein joined the Irish-American AC and at the 1904 Olympics became the only man to ever win the long jump and triple jump at the same Olympics. Besides his Olympic successes, Prinstein won the AAU long jump title four times between 1898 and 1906. Prinstein later practiced as a lawyer, but died rather young.

QUINN, James F.
B. 11 SEP 1906. Ddi. Gold: 1928 4 × 100 meter relay. Jimmy Quinn of Holy Cross and the New York AC had only a brief career as a top-class sprinter. After winning the 1928 IC4A 100y, he placed fifth in the 100m at the Final Trials and ran the second leg on the relay team that won the gold medals in Amsterdam.

RAMBO, John Barnett.
B. 09 AUG 1943 Atlanta, TX. Bronze: 1964 High Jump.

While at Long Beach State, John Rambo won the 1964 NCAA high jump and later won the AAU indoor title in 1967 and 1969. After graduation he represented the Southern Cal Striders and came close to making the Olympic team for a second time when he tied for fourth place at the 1968 Final Trials. In 1965, Rambo was drafted in the sixth round by the St. Louis Hawks of the NBA, but never actually played pro basketball.

RECTOR, James Alcorn.
B. 22 JUN 1884 Hot Springs, AR. D. 10 MAR 1949 Hot Springs, AR. Silver: 1908 100 meters. Although he never won a major championship at home, James Rector of the University of Virginia proved to be the fastest U.S. sprinter at the London Olympics, finishing only one meter behind the winner, Reggie Walker of South Africa, in the 100m. The week before the Olympics had seen Rector approached by the South African coach, who asked him to teach Walker the faster crouch start used by the Americans. In a great gesture of fair play, Rector did not hesitate but spent the next day tutoring his soon-to-be conqueror.

Earlier in 1908, Rector was clocked at 9.4 for 100y, but this rather dubious mark was never accorded record status because it was made in an unsanctioned meet.

REDD, Charles Lambert.
B. 18 FEB 1908 Grafton, IL. Silver: 1932 Long Jump. After winning the 1932 NCAA long jump with a career best of 25'-6$^1/_4$", Charles Redd of Bradley finished second to Ed Gordon at the Final Trials. Gordon again beat Redd at the Olympics, but in an extremely close finish—Redd only failed to take the gold by four centimeters.

REIDPATH, Charles Decker.
B. 20 SEP 1889 Buffalo, NY. D. 21 OCT 1975 Buffalo, NY. Gold(2): 1912 400 meters, 1912 4 × 400 meter relay. After winning the IC4A 440y in 1910, Reidpath missed the 1911 meet through injury, but he came back in 1912 to score a notable double with a 21.4 220y (straight) and a 48.0 440y which placed him second on the world all-time list.

Charles Reidpath was still in top form at the Olympics and, after running the fastest 400m semi-final (48.7), he took the gold medal with a new Olympic record of 48.2. He later ran the anchor leg on the relay team which set a new world record of 3:16.6. At Syracuse, Reidpath was on the football and track teams for three years and after graduation he entered the building trade. Apart from the years 1941 to 1946, when he was serving with the engineers corps in Europe, Charles Reidpath was the director of buildings for the city of Buffalo from 1937 until 1954.

REMER, Richard Frederick.
B. 21 JUN 1883 Brooklyn, NY. Bronze: 1920 3,000 meter walk. Richard Remer failed to place in the 3,000m walk at the Olympic Trials, but in Antwerp he proved to be the best of the Americans by taking the bronze medal. Between 1916 and 1921 he won three AAU outdoor championships and was once the indoor champion as well as setting numerous American records.

Remer was educated in the New York public school system and later worked for Manufacturer's Trust.

REMIGINO, Lindy John.
B. 03 JUN 1931 New York, NY. Gold(2): 1952 100 meters, 1952 4 × 100 meter relay. After finishing third in the IC4A 100y, fifth at the NCAA meet, and failing to qualify for the finals at the AAU championships, Lindy Remigino surprisingly finished second to Art Bragg at the 1952 Final Olympic Trials. Remigino, a junior at Manhattan, then pulled an even more startling upset by taking the Olympic 100m title from Jamaica's Herb McKenley in the closest race in Olympic sprint history. After winning a second gold medal in the relay, Remigino was not heard from again in top-class sprinting, but he maintained his interest in the sport and has become one of the country's most successful high school track coaches at Hartford High School in Connecticut.

RICHARDS, Alma Wilford.
B. 20 FEB 1890 Parowan, UT. D. 03 APR 1963. Gold: 1912 High Jump. After the failure of the world record holder, George Horine, to clear 6'-3¼", Alma Richards and the German, Hans Liesche, battled it out for the 1912 Olympic high jump title. Richards cleared 6'-4" on his final attempt and, with the German failing three times, the gold medal went to the 22-year-old Brigham

Young student. Richards' Olympic victory was, apart from the 1913 AAU title, his only major championship honor.

RICHARDS, Robert Eugene.
B. 20 FEB 1926 Champaign, IL. Gold(2): 1952 Pole Vault, 1956 Pole Vault; Bronze: 1948 Pole Vault. Bob Richards was the second man to vault 15 feet and, like the first man over this height, "Dutch" Warmerdam, he dominated the event for a number of years. Richards is the only man in history to win two Olympic gold medals in the pole vault, and these came after an Olympic bronze in 1948. Unlike many champions in this event, he was not an outstanding collegiate athlete, and while at Illinois, his best placing at the NCAA meet came in 1947 when he was in a six-way tie for first. However, he went on to win the AAU title a record nine times and won eight AAU indoor crowns. He was also Pan-American Games champion in 1951 and 1955.

Richards was also a fine decathlete, winning the AAU title three times and the All-Around Championship once. In 1956 he made the Olympic team in the decathlon but, hampered by an injury, placed only 12th.

Richards later became a familiar face on TV. He did sports commentary and was a commercial spokesman for Wheaties. He has gone on to form a company which specializes in motivational speaking and film producing. The Reverend Robert Richards, known as the "Vaulting Vicar," lost his family record of 15'-6" in the pole vault when his son, Bob, Jr., cleared 17'-6" in 1973.

RIDDICK, Steven Earl.
B. 18 SEP 1951 Newport News, VA. Gold: 1976 4 × 100 meter relay. Steve Riddick graduated from Norfolk State in 1974 and then ran for the Philadelphia Pioneers. After being eliminated in the semi-finals of the individual 100m in Montreal, he won a gold medal as the anchor man on the relay team. Riddick never featured in the major domestic championship meets; at the NCAA he was second in 1973 and third in 1974, and at the AAU he finished fourth four times.

RILEY, Ivan Harris.
B. 31 DEC 1900. D. 28 OCT 1943. Bronze: 1924 400 meter hurdles. While at Kansas State, Ivan Riley won the NCAA 120y hurdles and the AAU 440y hurdles in

1923 and the 120y hurdles in 1924. In May 1924, Riley set a world record 400m hurdles record of 52.1, but the mark never received official recognition and by the time of the Olympics came around in July he had lost some of his competitive edge—only took the bronze medal after his teammate, Charley Brookins, had been disqualified.

Riley graduated from college with a degree in architecture and became a well-known architect in the Midwest. His career was a short one; he died tragically early from brain cancer.

ROBERSON, Irvin.

B. 23 JUL 1935 Blakely, GA. Silver: 1960 Long Jump. In 1958, Cornell's "Bo" Roberson was ranked only 25th in the world as a long jumper with a mark of 24'-10½" when competing for the Cornell/Penn team against Oxford/Cambridge.

Roberson showed dramatic improvement in 1959 when he won the Pan-American Games with a wind-aided 26'-2" and had a legitimate mark of 26'-0". In 1960 he qualified for the Olympic team by pushing the defending champion, Greg Bell, back into fourth place, and at the Rome Games he came within one centimeter of matching Ralph Boston's winning jump. Had Roberson been able to equal Boston's 26'-7¾", he would have won the Olympic title by virtue of having a superior second longest jump.

In 1961, Roberson signed a pro football contract with the San Diego Chargers. He played defensive back in the AFL for six years, first with the Chargers, then four years with the Oakland Raiders, and finished up with a few games with the Buffalo Bills and Miami Dolphins. He later became the track coach at Cal/Irvine.

ROBERTS, David Luther.

B. 23 JUL 1951 Stillwater, OK. Bronze: 1976 Pole Vault. Rice's Dave Roberts placed sixth at the 1970 NCAA and then took the title for the next three years. He won the AAU in 1972 and 1974, and was runner-up in the 1971 Pan-American Games. Although he was the AAU champion, Roberts could only place fourth at the 1972 Final Trials. However, after setting a world record of 18'-6½" in 1975 he defeated a class field at the 1976 Final Trials, taking the world record up to 18'-8¼".

At the Montreal Olympics, Roberts took a calculated risk by passing at 18'-2½" and, after the two remaining competitors had failed at that height, Roberts himself missed three times at 18'-4½" and finished third on the countback.

After graduating from Rice in 1974, Dave Roberts enrolled at the University of Florida Medical School; he now practices as a surgeon.

ROBERTSON, Lawson N.

B. 24 SEP 1883 Aberdeen, Scotland. D. 22 JAN 1951 Philadelphia, PA. Silver: 1906 Standing High Jump (tied); Bronze(2): 1904 Standing High Jump, 1906 Standing Long Jump. After winning the AAU 100y in 1904 as a member of the Irish-American AC, Lawson Robertson was appointed coach of the club in 1909. Although he enjoyed moderate success as an athlete, Robertson will be best remembered as an outstanding coach. He remained as coach of the Irish-American club until 1916 when he took up an appointment at Penn. Robertson remained at Franklin Field for 31 years, except for a brief period during World War I, when he served as a lieutenant in the air service. Robertson was assistant coach to the U.S. Olympic teams in 1912 and 1920 and was head coach in 1924, 1928, 1932, and 1936.

ROBINSON, Clarence Earl, Jr.

B. 07 APR 1948 San Diego, CA. Gold: 1976 Long Jump; Silver: 1972 Long Jump. After taking the 1970 NCAA long jump while attending San Diego State, "Arnie" Robinson won many more major titles. Only De Hart Hubbard and Ralph Boston could match his record of six AAU titles, and Robinson won the Pan-Am title in 1971 as well as the first World Cup long jump championship in 1977. In winning the Olympic gold medal in 1976, Robinson set a career best of 27'-4¾" and he was still in the top flight of long jumpers in 1980 when he placed sixth at the Final Olympic Trials.

ROBINSON, Matthew Mack.

B. 18 JUL 1914 Cairo, CA. Silver: 1936 200 meters. Mack Robinson was a fine athlete, but he is best known as the brother of Jackie Robinson, the first black to play major league baseball in modern times.

In 1936, Mack Robinson was attending Pasadena Junior College, but he later enrolled at the University of Oregon and won the NCAA 220y in 1938. He also won the AAU 200m that year. Robinson had best marks of 9.5 (100y), 20.8 (200m-turn), and 25'-5½" in the long jump.

RODENBERG, August.
Silver: 1904 Tug-of-War. Gus Rodenberg was a member of the St. Louis Southwest Turnverein team that lost to the Milwaukee AC in the final of the 1904 tug-of-war.

ROSE, Charles.
Silver: 1904 Tug-of-War. Chuck Rose was a member of the St. Louis Southwest Turnverein team that lost to the Milwaukee AC in the final of the 1904 tug-of-war.

ROSE, Ralph Waldo.
B. 17 MAR 1885 Louisville, KY. D. 16 OCT 1913 San Francisco, CA. Gold(3): 1904 Shot Put, 1908 Shot Put, 1912 Shot Put (both hands); Silver(2): 1904 Discus Throw, 1912 Shot Put; Bronze: 1904 Hammer Throw. In 1904, 19-year-old Ralph Rose, a 6'-6", 235 lb. giant, won three Olympic medals. His best performance in St. Louis came in the shot put when, after trailing Wesley Coe, he came back to take the Olympic title with a new world record of 48'-7". Rose lost his world record to the Irishman, Dennis Horgan, later in the season, and Coe made a further improvement in 1905, but Rose recaptured the record in 1907 and beat both Horgan and Coe at the 1908 Olympics.

By 1909, Rose's weight had risen to a massive 286 lbs. and, in winning his third straight AAU title, he became the first man to break the 50-foot barrier. One week later Rose established the first official IAAF record, but his greatest day had come earlier in the season at Healdsburg, California, when he took the shot put at 5'-4" and threw the hammer 178'-5". Both marks bettered existing world records, but they were never ratified because they were made in an unsanctioned meet. The shot put mark would not be bettered, however, until 1934. Apart from his four AAU shot titles, Rose won the discus twice and was the inaugural AAU javelin champion in 1909.

Rose attended the University of Michigan and later studied law at Chicago. He was the flag-bearer in 1908 who refused to dip the flag as he walked past the English king, leading to the tradition which survives to this day.

ROTHERT, Harlow Phelps.
B. 01 APR 1908 Carthage, MO. Silver: 1932 Shot Put. Harlow Rothert was the outstanding sportsman of his generation at Stanford. In 1928, 1929, and 1930 he was on their track, football, and basketball teams and he was voted an all-America at basketball in 1930. In track, Rothert won the NCAA shot put for three years from 1928 and, after placing seventh at the 1928 Olympics, he improved to take the silver in 1932.

RUSSELL, Henry Argue.
B. 15 DEC 1904. Gold: 1928 4 × 100 meter relay. While at Cornell, "Honey" Russell won three IC4A sprint titles and in 1926 he had a double victory in the Princeton/Cornell vs. Oxford/Cambridge match. Although he was generally considered to be at his best over the longer sprint, he placed third in the 100m at the 1928 Final Trials. In Amsterdam, Russell was eliminated in the semi-finals of the 100m, but he ran a fine anchor leg in the relay to give the U.S. a narrow victory over the German quartet.

RYAN, Patrick James.
B. 04 JAN 1887 Pallasgreen, County Limerick, Ireland. D. 13 FEB 1964 County Limerick, Ireland. Gold: 1920 Hammer Throw; Silver: 1920 56 lb. weight throw. "Paddy" Ryan won his first Irish hammer title in 1902 when, as a virtual novice, he beat the great Tom Kiely for the championship. In 1910, Ryan emigrated to America and, after placing third in the hammer at the 1911 AAU meet, improved to take second place in 1912 before taking his first AAU title in 1913. Apart from 1918, when he was in France with the American Expeditionary Forces, he then won the hammer title up to 1921, when he retired. While in New York, Ryan worked as a labor foreman, but in 1924 he returned to Eire to take over the family farm and remained there until his death.

Ryan was not eligible to represent the U.S. at the 1912 Olympics, but the following year he showed what a threat he might have been in Stockholm. At the 1913 Eccentric Fireman's Games he set the first official IAAF world record with a throw of 189'-6½", which was to remain a world record for more than 25 years and was not beaten as a U.S. record until 1953. In 1920, Paddy Ryan won the Olympic title by the widest margin on record, beating Carl Lindh of Sweden by almost 15 feet.

RYUN, James Ronald.
B. 29 APR 1947 Wichita, KS. Silver: 1968 1,500 meters. Although undoubtedly the finest middle distance runner

of his time, Jim Ryun failed three times to add his name to the roll of Olympic champions. When the 17-year-old Ryun made his Olympic debut in 1964 he had already run the first sub-four minute mile by a schoolboy, but in Tokyo he disappointed by finishing last in his 1,500m semi-final.

By the time of the Mexico Games, Ryun held the world records at 880y, 1,500m, and the mile, but in the Olympic final he was outwitted and outrun by Kip Keino of Kenya. Such was Ryun's talent that the world records he had set in 1967 for 1,500m and the mile were still intact when he made his third Olympic appearance in 1972. Tragically, he was tripped in his 1,500m heat and his silver medal would remain his sole Olympic reward after dominating his specialty for many seasons.

Domestically, Ryun fared better, winning the AAU mile for three years straight from 1965 and the NCAA mile for Kansas in 1967. After his graduation, Ryun began a career as a photojournalist. He also conducts evangelical running camps.

SALING, George J.
B. 24 JUL 1909 Memphis, TN. D. 15 APR 1933. Gold: 1932 110 meter hurdles. George Saling of the University of Iowa won the 1932 NCAA 120y hurdles in 14.1, although this world record clocking was never officially ratified. At the 1932 Final Trials, Jack Keller beat Saling but at the Olympics it was Percy Beard who gave him the most trouble Saling just held him off in a close finish. Less than one year after his Olympic victory, George Saling was killed in an automobile accident.

SAMSE, Leroy Perry.
B. 1885. D. 01 MAY 1956 Sherman Oaks, CA. Silver: 1904 Pole Vault. Leroy Samse was a graduate of Indiana and took the silver medal in the 1904 Olympic pole vault after a jump-off with his teammate from the Chicago AA, Louis Wilkins. Samse was at his best in 1906 when he set a world record of 12'-4⁷⁄₈" and took the AAU title after a jump-off with H. L. Moore of the New York AC.

SCHARDT, Arlie Alfred.
B. 24 APR 1895 Milwaukee, WI. D. 03 FEB 1980. Gold: 1920 3,000 meter team race. After graduating from Wisconsin in 1917, Arlie Schardt served with the army in France as a lieutenant and placed second in the mile at the 1919 American Expeditionary Forces championships. The following year he returned to Europe as a member of the Olympic team and, finishing in third place, was the second scoring member of the team that took the gold medals in the 3,000m team event by a handsome margin. Arlie Schardt later coached at the South Division High School in his native Milwaukee.

SCHMIDT, William David.
B. 29 DEC 1947 Muse, PA. Bronze: 1972 Javelin Throw. With his third place in Munich, Bill Schmidt became the first U.S. athlete to win an Olympic medal in the javelin for 20 years. Schmidt, who had graduated from North Texas State in 1970, was serving as a private in the army at the time of the Olympics. He went to Munich with a personal best of 270'-6", but at the Games he improved to 276'-11½" to take the bronze medal.

In 1976, Schmidt won his only major championships when he took the AAU title and, after being on the coaching staff at the University of Tennessee, he recently served as sports director for the 1982 Knoxville World's Fair.

SCHOLZ, Jackson Volney.
B. 15 MAR 1897 Buchanan, MI. Gold(2): 1920 4 × 100 meter relay, 1924 200 meters; Silver: 1924 100 meters. Jackson Scholz was the first man to reach the final of an individual sprint event at three separate Olympic Games. In 1920 he was a finalist in the 100m, in 1924 he won the 200m and was second in the 100m, and in 1928 he made the final of the 200m, narrowly missing a fourth Olympic medal. Initially, Scholz was placed equal third with Helmut Kornig of Germany, but the judges ruled in favor of a run-off the next day. Scholz had already left the track and begun partying and the next day he was in no shape to run, so he declined the offer. The photo of the finish subsequently showed that this was, in fact, the correct decision.

Scholz, who attended Missouri, had a great competitive record and could claim victories over all the great sprinters of his era. In his 10 races with Charlie Paddock he won five and tied another, but the 220y in 1925 was, surprisingly, the only AAU title that he won. Scholz also laid claim to world records at 100y, 200m, and the 4 × 100m relay.

Jackson Scholz later became well known as a writer of pulp fiction. The movie, "Chariots of Fire," again made Scholz famous by portraying him as a leading character. Shortly after the movie, when asked how he would like to be remembered, he remarked, ". . . as a winner, a successful runner, a decent writer and a gentleman. And one other thing . . . I was fast. I hope they remember I was fast." He made it hard to forget.

SCHUL, Robert Keyser.
B. 28 SEP 1937 West Milton, OH. Gold: 1964 5,000 meters. A few days after Billy Mills had caused a major upset by winning the 10,000m at the Tokyo Games, Bob Schul took the gold medal in the 5,000m to complete an Olympic double unprecedented in the history of U.S. distance running.

Schul began his career as a miler, but on moving to the longer distances he set a world record for two miles and a U.S. 5,000m record. He was renowned for his devastating finishing kick and he turned on a 54.8 last lap in the Olympic 5,000m which none of the more fancied runners could match. Schul, a Miami (Ohio) graduate, won the AAU 5,000m in 1964 and the three miles in 1965.

SCHULE, Frederick William.
B. 27 SEP 1879. Ddi. Gold: 1904 110 meter hurdles. Having won the AAU high hurdles in 1903, Fred Schule, of the University of Michigan, took the Olympic gold the following year.

SCOTT, Clyde Louis.
B. 29 AUG 1924 Dixie, LA. Silver: 1948 110 meter hurdles. Clyde Scott of the University of Arkansas beat Bill Porter to take the 1948 NCAA 110m hurdles, but Porter won all their subsequent meetings that year, including the Olympic final.

SEAGREN, Robert Lloyd.
B. 17 OCT 1946 Pomona, CA. Gold: 1968 Pole Vault; Silver: 1972 Pole Vault. In addition to his two Olympic medals, Bob Seagren was the Pan-American Games champion in 1967 and, indoors and outdoors, he won a total of six AAU and four NCAA titles. He also broke the world outdoor record six times, finishing up with a vault of 18'-5¾" at the 1972 Final Trials, but in Munich he was handicapped by a last minute IAAF ruling which forced him to change his pole and he failed to retain his Olympic title. He was equally prolific as a record

breaker on the indoor circuit and broke the world record eight times between 1966 and 1969.

Seagren graduated from Southern Cal in 1968 and, after his outstanding amateur career, turned professional and won the first U.S. Superstars competition in 1973 and the first World Superstars title in 1977. He has since worked as an actor, but is now an executive with a major running shoe company.

SEILING, Henry.
Gold: 1904 Tug-of-War. Although a Chicago native, Henry Seiling was a member of the Milwaukee AC team that won the tug-of-war at the St. Louis Olympics.

SEILING, William Bernard.
B. 28 MAY 1863 St. Louis, MO. D. 05 JAN 1951 St. Louis, MO. Silver: 1904 Tug-of-War. William Seiling was a member of the #1 team from the St. Louis Southwest Turnverein that won the silver medals in the 1904 tug-of-war event. He was well known as a local strongman and from 1895 to 1905 he was undefeated in local beer barrell lifting contests. He later opened a successful furniture store in St. Louis.

SERVISS, Garrett Putnam, Jr.
D. 23 DEC 1908. Silver: 1904 High Jump. The son of a famous author, Garrett Serviss's first athletic success was in 1900 at the Caledonian Games when he won the high jump. He entered Princeton in 1899, but left in 1901 to enroll at Cornell. In 1900, representing Princeton, he tied for third in the IC4A high jump and in 1904 he was fourth in the same event for Cornell. At the 1904 Olympics, Serviss won a jump-off for second with the German, Paul Weinstein, and finished fourth in the triple jump.

SEXTON, Leo Joseph.
B. 27 AUG 1909 Danvers, MA. D. 05 SEP 1968 Perry, OK. Gold: 1932 Shot Put. Having twice set world indoor records early in 1932, Leo Sexton came within two inches of the outdoor record in winning the 1932 Olympic title. One month later he became the holder of both the indoor and outdoor records with a put of 53'-0½" at the Nassau Fireman's Games at Freeport, Long Island.

Sexton, a Georgetown grad, won the IC4A title in 1929 and to his 1932 AAU title he added two AAU indoor championships. As befitted his physique—he stood 6'-4" and weighed 240 lbs.—Sexton began his career as a weight thrower, winning three AAU outdoor titles and he was the AAU indoor 56 lb. weight champion in 1932. Despite his build, Sexton was a finely coordinated athlete and in 1929 he cleared 6'-4" in the high jump.

Leo Sexton later had a successful insurance career, eventually becoming vice-president of a company in his hometown of Perry, Oklahoma.

SEYMOUR, Stephen Andrew (né Seymour Cohen).

B. 04 OCT 1920 New York, NY. D. 18 JUN 1973 Los Angeles, CA. Silver: 1948 Javelin Throw. Steve Seymour's silver medal in 1948 was the best performance by a U.S. athlete in the Olympic javelin up to that time. He had a long career as a top-class performer. In 1941, as a senior at Franklin & Marshall College, when known as Seymour Cohen, he won the AAU junior title and placed fourth in the senior championships. In 1945 he set his first U.S. record with a throw of 235'-3" in Istanbul when he was serving with the army in the Middle East. This remained a U.S. record until Seymour himself improved the national best to 248'-10" in 1947 when he won the first of his three AAU titles.

Poor weather conditions hampered the throwers at the 1948 Olympics, where Seymour took second place with a modest performance. He took sixth place at the 1952 Final Trials and did not qualify for the 1956 Trials, but his best performance was yet to come. In 1958, 10 years after his Olympic success, he came up with a throw of 251'-1" to register the longest throw of his career.

Dr. Stephen Seymour completed his medical studies at the Los Angeles College of Osteopathic Physicians and Surgeons and practiced as an osteopath in addition to operating a clinic for alcoholics.

SHANKLE, Joel Warren.

B. 02 MAR 1933 Fines Creek, NC. Bronze: 1956 110 meter hurdles. In both the 1956 Final Trials and the Olympic Final, Joel Shankle finished third in the 110 meter hurdles behind Lee Calhoun and Jack Davis. Shankle was also a fine long jumper and decathlete, winning the 1955 NCAA long jump for Duke and placing third in the AAU decathlon that year. He is now a pilot for American Airlines.

SHAW, Arthur Briggs.

B. 28 APR 1886 Joliet, IL. D. 18 JUL 1955 Altadena, CA. Bronze: 1908 110 meter hurdles. After placing third in the 120y hurdles at the 1906 IC4A meet, Art Shaw of Dartmouth finished as runner-up in 1907 and then became the IC4A champion in 1908. He also won the AAU title in 1908, equalling the world record of 15.2. Then, in the Olympic final, in which Shaw placed third, Forrest Smithson set a new world record of 15.0, but Shaw equalled this time on his return home to again become coholder of the world record.

SHELDON, Lewis Pendleton.

B. 09 JUN 1874 Rutland, VT. D. 18 FEB 1960 Biarritz, France. Bronze(2): 1900 Standing High Jump, 1900 Triple Jump. Before graduating from Yale, Lewis Sheldon won the IC4A long jump in 1895 and 1896 although he did not compete in this event at the 1900 Olympics. In 1896, representing the New York AC, he also won the AAU All-Around title.

In 1906 he went to London as a representative for financial institutions. This led to many official connections with European governments and he later received official decorations from the governments of France, Italy, and Finland. He left France during World War II, but returned to his Biarritz estate after the German occupation ended.

SHELDON, Richard.

B. 09 JUL 1878 Rutland, VT. D. 23 JAN 1935 New York, NY. Gold: 1900 Shot Put; Bronze: 1900 Discus Throw. Like his older brother, Lewis, Dick Sheldon was an outstanding performer for both Yale and the New York AC. The first of his many successes came in 1896 when he won the IC4A shot. In 1897 he placed second in the shot and third in the hammer at the British championships and the following year he won the AAU shot and 56 lb. weight throw. In 1899, Sheldon confirmed his talents as an all-round weightman by taking a shot/discus double at the AAU championships and setting a world discus record of 122'-3½".

In 1900, Sheldon won the British shot title with a new championship record and then crossed the Channel to Paris where he improved his best to 46'-3¼" and became the youngest ever winner of the Olympic shot put title. Reports of his being the youngest champion in an Olympic weight event are unfounded; examination of his birth certificate shows him to be born in 1878, not in 1880 as usually quoted.

In addition to track, Dick Sheldon competed on the football team at Yale. After graduation he worked for the Cadillac Motor Co.

SHEPPARD, Melvin Winfield.
B. 05 SEP 1883 Almenesson, NJ. D. 04 JAN 1942 Queens, NY. Gold(4): 1908 800 meters, 1908 1,500 meters, 1908 1,600 meter medley relay, 1912 4 × 400 meter relay; Silver: 1912 800 meters. As a dedicated frontrunner, Mel Sheppard had a great influence on the development of middle distance running. In both his Olympic 800m finals he led the field at the half-way mark, running 53.0 in 1908 and 52.4 in 1912. In London a second 400m of 59.4 was good enough to take Sheppard to the Olympic gold medal in a new world record of 1:52.4, but in Stockholm his 59.6 second lap failed to match the finishing speed of Ted Meredith, who removed from Sheppard his Olympic title and world record. To his gold medal for the 800m in London, Sheppard added Olympic victories in the 1,500m and the medley relay, and won a fourth gold medal in 1912 as a member of the 1,600m relay team.

Mel Sheppard won the AAU 880y in 1906–08 and 1911–12, and was the Canadian 880y champion in those years. His record of five AAU titles has been equalled by Mel Whitfield and James Robinson, but stands through 1982. Sheppard was educated at Brown Prep School and, having been rejected by the New York police because of a weak heart(!), he entered the employ of John Wanamaker in 1913 and served as the recreational director of the Millrose AA for many years.

SHERIDAN, Martin Joseph.
B. 28 MAR 1881 Bohola, Cty. Mayo, Ireland. D. 27 MAR 1918 New York, NY. Gold(5): 1904 Discus Throw, 1906 Shot Put, 1906 Discus Throw, 1908 Discus Throw, 1908 Discus Throw (Greek style); Silver(3): 1906 Standing High Jump (tied), 1906 Standing Long Jump, 1906 Stone Throw; Bronze: 1908 Standing Long Jump. The Irish-born Martin Sheridan was the greatest all-round athlete of his time and his total of nine Olympic medals has been bettered by only three Americans. Inspired by his older brother, Richard, who won the AAU discus in 1901 and 1902, Martin himself won the title four times.

Discus thrower, Martin Sheridan — not well known, but one of the greatest athletes ever.

Courtesy Steven Feldman

He also won the AAU shot in 1904 and three times was the AAU All-Around champion, setting a new world record each time. Further proof of his versatility came at the 1908 Olympics when he placed ninth in the triple jump. The discus was undoubtedly his best event; in addition to his three Olympic titles and four AAU championships, he improved the world record six times between 1902 and 1909. Sheridan almost certainly missed another gold medal when he was forced to withdraw from the 1906 pentathlon due to injury.

Apart from his prowess as a competitor, Martin Sheridan has passed into Olympic lore with his remark to the press at the 1908 Olympics, where he was quoted as saying, "This flag dips to no earthly King!" after the Michigan weightman, Ralph Rose, refused to lower the American flag as he passed the Royal Box at the opening ceremony.

Like many of the great Irish-American athletes of the time, Sheridan was employed by the New York police and was the personal bodyguard of the New York governor whenever he visited the city. Sheridan, who had come to America in 1897, retired from active competition in 1911 and died of pneumonia at the early age of 37.

SHIDELER, Thaddeus Rutter.
B. 1884. D. 22 JUN 1966 Collbran, CO. Silver: 1904 110 meter hurdles. Thad Shideler of Indiana University and the Chicago AA placed second to the 1904 AAU champion, Frank Castleman of Colgate, in the heats of the 110m hurdles at the 1904 Olympics. In the final, Shideler beat Castleman but lost to the 1903 AAU champion, Fred Schule of the Michigan Wolverines.

SHIELDS, Marion Lawrence.
B. 05 MAR 1895 West Chester, PA. D. 19 FEB 1976 Rochester, MN. Bronze: 1920 1,500 meters. Larry Shields of Penn State won the IC4A mile in 1920 and 1922 and, in addition to his bronze medal in the Olympic 1,500m, was a nonscoring member of the U.S. team that won the 3,000m team race in Antwerp. In 1923 he began a 37-year-long career at Phillips Andover Academy as teacher, coach, alumni director and member of the Board of Trustees.

SHINE, Michael Lyle.
B. 19 SEP 1953 Warren, PA. Silver: 1976 400 meter hurdles. Mike Shine, a senior at Penn State, was a surprise silver medalist in the 400m hurdles at the Montreal Olympics. This matched Shine's highest placing at any major championship. He finished second at the 1976 NCAA, but never placed better than fourth at the AAU meet. After the Olympics, Shine went into the service, but returned to Penn State for a graduate degree, during which time he served as assistant track coach.

SHORTER, Frank Charles.
B. 31 OCT 1947 Munich, Germany. Gold: 1972 Marathon; Silver: 1976 Marathon. Frank Shorter is the only U.S. athlete to have won two Olympic medals in the marathon. He started as a long distance track runner, winning the NCAA six miles for Yale in 1969. Shorter went on to win five AAU titles at six miles/10,000m; he also won the AAU outdoor three miles in 1970 and the indoor title in 1971. He won the 1971 Pan-American Games 10,000m event and, at the 1972 Olympics, he set a U.S. record in the 10,000m heats, which he further improved by taking fifth place in the final.

Despite these track successes, Frank Shorter will be best remembered as a marathon runner. He made his marathon debut when he placed second to Kenny Moore in the 1971 AAU Championships. In his second race he won the Pan-Am Games title, and he rounded off his first season as a road runner with the first of his record number of four victories in the Fukuoka Marathon. In winning this Japanese classic for the second time in 1972, Shorter set his career best of 2-10:30.

Shorter is often described as being responsible for the late 70's running boom in the United States. He has become highly visible as a television announcer and commercial spokesman, and has started his own chain of running stores, based in Colorado, which markets his own brand of running apparel. Through 1983, Shorter is still a competitive road racer, but with far less success than he enjoyed in the early 70's.

SILVESTER, L. Jay.
B. 27 AUG 1937 Tremonton, UT. Silver: 1972 Discus Throw. Jay Silvester won five AAU discus titles and set four world records, but he was never at his best in his four Olympic appearances. In 1964 he placed fifth; he finished fourth in 1968; and, after his silver medal in 1972, he finished eighth in 1976. Silvester, who attended Utah State, was the greatest shot/discus performer on distance thrown until Mac Wilkins, and he won both events at the 1962 British championships. His best mark with the shot was 65'-7¾" and in the discus he had a best of 230'-11". He is today a professor of physical education at Brigham Young.

Yale's Dick Sheldon, a medal winner in the shot put at the 1900 Olympics.

Courtesy Duke University Sports Information Dept.

Silver medalist in the 1960 Olympic 100 meter dash, Dave Sime.

SIME, David William.
B. 25 JUL 1936 Paterson, NJ. Silver: 1960 100 meters. During an injury-plagued career, Duke's Dave Sime never won a major championship, but was undoubtedly one of the fastest sprinters of his time. He equalled the world record of 9.3 for 100y three times, set a world record of 20.0 for 220y straight, and equalled the world record of 22.2 for 220y hurdles. After a poor start in the 1960 Olympic 100m final, Dave Sime narrowly failed to catch world record holder, Armin Hary of West Germany, at the tape. He also ran a great anchor leg in the relay to make up a two meter-deficit on the West Germans, but although Sime broke the tape in a world record, the Americans were disqualified for a faulty change-over on the first pass.

After graduation, Sime turned down pro baseball offers in order to attend medical school. He is now a practicing ophthalmologist in Miami and he made headlines in the 70's for his successful treatment of Miami Dolphins quarterback, Bob Griese, for some vision problems.

SIMMONS, Floyd Macon, Jr.
B. 10 APR 1923 Charlotte, NC. Bronze(2): 1948 Decathlon, 1952 Decathlon. "Chunk" Simmons went to the University of North Carolina to play tailback on the football team but encountered an obstacle in the form of Tar Heel legend, Charlie "Choo Choo" Justice. Simmons graciously moved to fullback, but he may be Chapel Hill's greatest all-round athlete, as evidenced by his two decathlon medals. Even as an Olympian, though, Simmons was overshadowed by the great Bob Mathias, who beat him in both 1948 and 1952.

Simmons later had a moderately successful career as a film actor, first with Universal and then with MGM. He is now a professional photographer.

SIMPSON, George Sidney.
B. 21 SEP 1908 Columbus, OH. D. 02 DEC 1961 Columbus, OH. Silver: 1932 200 meters. George Simpson became the first man to run the 100y in 9.4 when he took the first leg of his sprint double at the 1929 NCAA championships. Although this was a valid clocking, the mark was not recognized as a world record because Simpson used starting blocks, which had not then been approved by the IAAF. Apart from his 1929 double, Ohio State's Simpson won both the AAU and NCAA 220y in

1930. Before winning his silver medal in the 200m at the 1932 Olympics, he placed fourth in the 100m.

SMITH, Finis Dean.
B. 15 JAN 1932 Breckenridge, TX. Gold: 1952 4 × 100 meter relay. Dean Smith of the University of Texas placed fourth in the 1952 Olympic 100m prior to winning a gold medal in the relay. Earlier in the season he won his only major championship when he took the AAU 100m. Smith later worked for many years as a film stuntman.

SMITH, Owen Guinn.
B. 02 MAY 1920 McKinney, TX. Gold: 1948 Pole Vault. Guinn Smith was the last man to win the Olympic pole vault title using a bamboo pole. He won the 1940 IC4A and tied for the NCAA title in 1941. After graduating from Cal/Berkeley in 1942 he was out of the sport for three years, during which time he won the Distinguished Flying Cross as a captain in the army air corps.

On his return to competition in 1947, Smith took the AAU indoor title and at the 1948 Final Trials he placed second with a career best of 14'-8⅛". At the Olympics he was trailing for much of the competition, but despite a painful knee injury, he was the only man to clear 14'-1¼", which he did on his last attempt.

SMITH, Ronald Ray.
B. 28 MAR 1949 Los Angeles, CA. Gold: 1968 4 × 100 meter relay. In the semi-finals of the 1968 AAU 100m, Jim Hines and Ronnie Ray Smith both ran 9.9 to set a new world record. At the Final Trials, Smith placed fourth in the 100m and ran only in the relay in Mexico, where the U.S. set a world record of 38.2. Smith was a graduate of San Jose State and later competed for the Southern California Striders.

SMITH, Tommie C.
B. 05 JUN 1944 Acworth, TX. Gold: 1968 200 meters. As an all-round sprinter, Tommie Smith was a worthy successor to the great Henry Carr. In 1966, Smith set four world records—200m and 220y straight and turn; in 1967 he posted world records at 400m and 440y; and he claimed his seventh individual world record when he won the 1968 Olympic 200m title. Smith also won the AAU and NCAA 220y in 1967 and the AAU 200m in 1968. He was also a member of the first team to run

under three minutes for the 4 × 400m relay when the U.S. clocked 2:59.6 in an international meet at Los Angeles in 1966.

During the victory ceremony in Munich, Smith gained much publicity when he and bronze medalist, John Carlos, made a protest for black power and unity and were expelled from the Olympic village. After graduating from San Jose State in 1969, Smith turned to professional track, and played pro football for three seasons with the Cincinnati Bengals. He later became a professor and athletic director at Oberlin College and now is a professor at a college in Los Angeles.

SMITHSON, Forrest Custer.
B. 26 SEP 1881 Portland, OR. D. 1963. Gold: 1908 110 meter hurdles. Forrest Smithson attended both Notre Dame and Oregon State, but did not graduate from either. He later became a Baptist minister and won the 1908 Olympic high hurdles carrying a Bible in his hand as a protest against Sunday competition.

Smithson won the AAU title in 1907 and 1909 and his winning time of 15.0 at the 1908 Olympic was recognized as the first official IAAF record.

SOUTHERN, Silas Edward.
B. 04 JAN 1938 Dallas, TX. Silver: 1956 400 meter hurdles. Eddie Southern set national prep records at 220y and 440y before taking up the hurdles. In finishing second to Glenn Davis at the 1956 Final Trials, he ran the second fastest 400m hurdles in history (49.7); he again lost to Davis at the Olympics. Southern graduated from the University of Texas in 1959 and he won the NCAA 440y flat that year.

SPENCER, Emerson Lane.
B. 14 OCT 1906 San Francisco, CA. Gold: 1928 4 × 400 meter relay. "Bud" Spencer's first major victory came at the 1926 AAU junior championships when he won the 440y hurdles. The following year he won the NCAA 440y flat and his time of 47.7 was the fastest clocking in the world that year. Spencer also topped the world lists in 1928 with a world record of 47.0 for 400m in May, but at the Final Trials he placed no better than fifth and ran only in the relay at Amsterdam. He ran the second leg for the U.S. team that set a new world record and one week later in London he took the anchor stage for the team that set a world record for the 4 × 440y relay.

Spencer was for many years the sports editor of the now defunct *San Francisco News* and after his retirement he served as assistant track coach at Stanford.

STADLER, Joseph F.
Silver: 1904 Standing High Jump; Bronze: 1904 Standing Long Jump. Joseph Stadler of the Franklin AC in Cleveland, was one of two black athletes to compete in the 1904 Olympics. This was only recently discovered and Stadler may have been the first black to win a medal. He won his first medal on the same day that George Poage won his first medal, but the order of the events is not known. Apart from his two medals, Stadler's athletic career was undistinguished.

STANFIELD, Andrew William.
B. 29 DEC 1927 Washington, DC. Gold(2): 1952 200 meters, 1952 4 × 100 meter relay; Silver: 1956 200 meters. Andy Stanfield graduated from Seton Hall in 1952 and then represented the New York Pioneer AC. He took the sprint double at the 1949 AAU and went on to win the 200m title in 1952 and the 220y in 1953. He won the AAU indoor long jump in 1951; was also a fine hurdler. At the IC4A championships he won the 100y for three straight years from 1949 and in 1951 he won the 220y. Indoors he was three times the IC4A 60y champion and he won the long jump in 1951. Stanfield also set a world record in the 220y with 20.6 in 1951—a mark he equalled the following year.

STANGLAND, Robert Sedgwick.
B. 1881 New York, NY. D. 15 DEC 1953 Nyack, NY. Bronze(2): 1904 Long Jump, 1904 Triple Jump. Robert Stangland of Columbia University won the 1904 IC4A long jump at 23'-6½", but he failed to repeat this form at the Olympics later in the season. In St. Louis he placed third in the long jump with a modest effort of 22'-7" and he placed third in the triple jump with a mark of 43'-10". While at Columbia, in addition to track he played football and rowed varsity crew. He made his career as a consulting engineer.

STANICH, George Anthony.
B. 04 NOV 1928. Bronze: 1948 High Jump. After placing seventh in the 1948 NCAA high jump and sixth at the AAU championships, George Stanich of UCLA seemed an unlikely candidate for the Olympic team. He then showed dramatic improvement at the Final Trials and cleared a personal best of 6'-8¼" to take second place after a countback with Verne McGrew of Rice. At the London Olympics, McGrew was surprisingly eliminated at 6'-2¾", but Stanich was one of four athletes to clear 6'-4¾" and was awarded the bronze medal on the fewer-misses rule.

STEBBINS, Richard Vaughn.
B. 14 JUN 1945 Los Angeles, CA. Gold: 1964 4 × 100 meter relay. In his first season as a 200m runner Dick Stebbins of Grambling placed second in the 1964 Final Trials, but in Tokyo he failed to fulfill expectations and finished seventh in the Olympic final. He was in better form in the relay when the U.S. took the gold medals with a new world record of 39.0. In 1967, Dick Stebbins tried pro football briefly, but never survived training camp to play in an NFL game.

At the 1948 Olympics, Steele was suffering from a variety of injuries. He won the gold medal with his first jump and after limping through a second trial, which still exceeded the best effort of the silver medalist, he retired from the competition. Had his career not been interrupted by war service and injury problems he would almost certainly have succeeded Owens as world record holder. He later played pro football briefly, but injuries continued to plague him, and his career with the LA Rams was undistinguished.

STEELE, William S.
B. 14 JUL 1923 Seeley, CA. Gold: 1948 Long Jump. In 1942 the 18-year-old Willie Steele won the AAU Junior long jump and had a best mark of 25'-7", which topped the world rankings that year. He then missed what might have been his best years because of service with the army in Italy and the Philippines and, after a three-year absence, he returned to serious competition and won the 1946 AAU title. The following year he again won the AAU and at the NCAA meet, representing San Jose State, he came close to Jesse Owens' world record with a jump of 26'-6". In 1948 he won his second NCAA title and, after skipping the AAU championships, he won the Final Trials at 26'-2" to become the first man in history—apart from Jesse Owens—to break the 26-foot barrier twice.

STEVENSON, William Edwards.

B. 25 OCT 1900 Chicago, IL. Gold: 1924 4 × 400 meter relay. After leaving Phillips Andover Academy, Bill Stevenson served in the Marine Corps, winning the Bronze Star, and then entered Princeton in 1920. The following year he was ranked as the top quarter-miler in America and won the AAU 440y in 48.6, which proved to be the best time of his career. Later in the season he beat the reigning Olympic champion, Bevil Rudd, in the dual meet between Princeton/Cornell and Oxford/Cambridge.

In 1923, Stevenson went to Oxford on a Rhodes Scholarship and placed second in the match against Cambridge before winning the British title. In the Olympic year he had a poor start to the season, finishing only third in the match against Cambridge and in the British championships, but he fully justified his selection for the Olympic relay team by turning a 2-meter deficit into a 5-meter advantage on the second leg. In 1925, his last year at Oxford, Stevenson finally won the quarter-mile against Cambridge and he closed his career back on American tracks with victories for the combined Oxford/Cambridge team against teams from Harvard/Yale and Princeton/Cornell.

Bill Stevenson, who also represented Oxford at lacrosse, was admitted as a barrister-at-law in England in 1925 and in 1927 he became a member of the New York Bar. He eventually became a partner in the law firm of Deboise, Stevenson, Plimpton and Tage, and from 1946 until 1959 he served as president of Oberlin College. He also held numerous civic and government posts, the most distinguished of these being his appointment as U.S. Ambassador to the Philippines from 1961 to 1964.

STONES, Dwight Edwin.

B. 06 DEC 1953 Los Angeles, CA. Bronze(2): 1972 High Jump, 1976 High Jump. After placing third at the 1972 Games, Dwight Stones was considered a certainty for the 1976 Olympic title, but his form went to pieces in the rainy conditions in Montreal and he again had to settle for a bronze medal.

Stones set three world records, his best of 7'-7¼" coming only four days after the 1976 Olympic final. He won five AAU outdoor and three indoor titles, and while at Long Beach State he was the NCAA indoor and outdoor champion in 1976. Stones missed the 1979 season after being suspended for receiving money in the Superstars competition, but he has since made a comeback. Stones has been known as one of the more outspoken personalities in track and, although he still competes, he puts that personality to good use as a television commentator for track meets.

STROBINO, Gaston M.

B. 23 AUG 1891 Bern, Switzerland. D. 30 MAR 1969 Downers Grove, IL. Bronze: 1912 Marathon. Gaston Strobino came to America from Italy as a young boy. In 1912 he represented the South Paterson AC in New Jersey, but did not qualify for the American Olympic team. He was only added to the team after paying his own expenses to Stockholm; he proved to be one of the surprises of the Games with his bronze medal. He made his living as a machinist.

STUDENROTH, Arthur Addison.

B. 09 OCT 1899. Silver: 1924 Cross-Country team race. In the 1923 AAU cross-country championships, Art Studenroth finished second to the great Finnish runner Wille Ritola, but Studenroth led his Meadowbrook Club of Philadelphia to the team title. Ritola and Studenroth met again over the country at the 1924 Olympics when Ritola placed second behind Paavo Nurmi. Running in extraordinary heat, Studenroth did well to finish sixth overall and was the second scoring member of the U.S. team that took the silver medals.

TABER, Norman Stephen.

B. 03 SEP 1891 Providence, RI. D. 15 JUL 1952 Orange, NJ. Gold: 1912 3,000 meter team race; Bronze: 1912 1,500 meters. Although better known as a miler, Norman Taber won his Olympic gold medal in the 3,000m team race in which he individually placed third. He finished third in the 1910 IC4A mile for Brown and, after giving track a miss in 1911, his early season form in 1912 augured well for his Olympic chances.

One week after dead-heating with John Paul Jones for the 1911 IC4A mile title, Taber pushed Abe Kiviat to a world 1,500m record at the Final Trials and, with an estimated 3:56.4, Taber was himself inside the old record. In the Olympic 1,500m the U.S. provided seven of the 14 finalists, but none of them could match the home stretch drive of Arnold Jackson of Britain and Taber lost second place to Kiviat in a photo-finish. At the

MOST UNITED STATES OLYMPIANS BY SPORTS

Certain colleges have outstanding teams, or produce outstanding athletes, in only certain sports. Following is a list of the colleges which have produced the most United States Olympians in each sport, as well as other colleges which have had many athletes in each particular sport.

By far the greatest domination of any one sport is that of the U.S. Military Academy (West Point) in modern pentathlon. With 19 athletes the Academy has contributed over one-half of the U.S. Olympians in that sport. Two other schools with impressive domination of a sport are the University of Minnesota in ice hockey (40 of 187 players), and Tennessee State in women's track and field (25 of 157 athletes).

Sports not listed have not had a school with at least eight athletes represented in that sport.

Alpine Skiing . . . . . . .Colorado (13), Dartmouth (8)
Basketball . . . . .Kansas (9), Kentucky (8)
Equestrian . . . . .USMA (19)
Fencing . . . . .NYU (15), Columbia (14), USNA (14), USMA (10)
Gymnastics . . . . . . .Penn State (8), Princeton (6)
Ice Hockey . . . . . . .Minnesota (40), Dartmouth (11), Harvard (11)

Modern Pentathlon . .USMA (19)
Nordic Skiing . . . . . .Colorado (8), Denver (8), Dartmouth (7)
Rowing (Men) . . . . . .Harvard (35), Washington (30), USNA (29), Cal (29), Yale (28), Penn (21), Stanford (11)
Rugby . . . . .Stanford (12)
Swimming & Diving (Men) . . . . .Indiana (29), Southern Cal (26), Stanford (25), Ohio State (19), Yale (19), Michigan (17)
Swimming & Diving (Women) . . . . .Southern Cal (14), Stanford (11), Arizona State (7)
Track & Field (Men) . . . . .Southern Cal (58), Penn (38), Cornell (34), Yale (31), Stanford (30), Michigan (24), Cal (22) Oregon (22), Chicago (21), Illinois (21), Harvard (21), Kansas (20), Princeton (18), Penn State (17), UCLA (17), Dartmouth (13), Syracuse (13), Villanova (13), San Jose State (12), Arizona State (11), Indiana (11), Iowa (10), Ohio State (10), Wisconsin (10)
Track & Field (Women) . . . . .Tennessee State (25)
Water Polo . . . . .Southern Cal (13), Stanford (10), UCLA (8)
Wrestling . . . . .Oklahoma State (16), USNA (10), Oklahoma (8)
Yachting . . . . .Harvard (11)

end of 1913, Taber went to Oxford on a Rhodes Scholarship, but failed to make any impact on the sport in Britain. He was, however, on the Oxford team for the 4 × one-mile relay at the 1914 Penn Relays where he ran a disastrous leg, having been up the previous night getting engaged.

Taber's final year in track was 1915 and in a paced trial at Harvard he ran the 1,500m in 3:55.0 and went on to reach the mile in 4:12.6. Both times were world records and his mile time beat Walter George's record of 4:12.75, which had been set five years before Taber was born. Despite objections to his use of pacemakers in the race, the IAAF ratified the time as the official mile record.

After graduation, Taber established himself as an expert on municipal finance and he formed his own company which specialized in this field. He later became a Life Trustee of Brown University.

TAYLOR, Frederick Morgan.
B. 17 APR 1903 Sioux City, IA. D. 16 FEB 1975 Rochester, NY. Gold: 1924 400 meter hurdles; Bronze(2): 1928 400 meter hurdles, 1932 400 meter hurdles. Morgan Taylor is the only athlete to have won three medals in the Olympic 400m hurdles. He won the 1924 Final Trials with a world best of 52.6, which became an American record but never received IAAF recognition as the world mark. Taylor matched the time at the Olympics

If it looks familiar, that's because it's an actual scene from the 1924 Olympics, a facsimile of which was used in the movie "Chariots of Fire." Crossing the finish line first in the 400 meter hurdles is American hurdler, Morgan Taylor.

but again did not receive official recognition because he knocked one hurdle over. In 1925 he bettered the world record for 440y hurdles with 53.8 in winning the second of four AAU titles, but once again the mark was not ratified. Finally, Taylor became an official world record holder when he won the 1928 Final Trials in 52.0.

While at Grinnell College, F. Morgan Taylor won the NCAA 220y hurdles in 1927 and in 1925 he finished second in the long jump, beaten only by De Hart Hub-

bard's world record. He was also a good quarter-miler, having run a best of 48.5. His son continued the family tradition, winning the IC4A long jump for Princeton in 1952 and 1953.

After leaving Grinnell, Taylor initially worked as an ad salesman for the *Chicago Tribune*. He later became a teacher and coach, but continued work in various forms of sales.

TAYLOR, John Baxter, Jr.

B. 03 NOV 1882 Washington, DC. D. 02 DEC 1908 Philadelphia, PA. Gold: 1908 1,600 meter medley relay. John Taylor was the first black Olympic gold medalist. While attending Penn he won three IC4A 440y titles, and his winning times in 1904 (49.2) and 1907 (48.8) were the fastest times recorded in the world in those years. He was also the AAU champion on 1907.

Taylor was a favorite at the 1908 Olympics in the 400m, but ran a poor race. The race, however, was marked by an incident involving Britain's Halswelle and America's Carpenter. It was claimed that Carpenter forced Halswelle to run wide in the stretch run, and he was disqualified and the race ordered rerun. The Americans were aghast at this decision because they felt no foul was committed and they, including Taylor, did not run in the second final.

Just before leaving for London, Taylor had earned a degree in veterinary medicine from Penn and planned to open a practice when he returned. But before the year was out, Taylor died of typhoid fever.

TAYLOR, Robert.

B. 14 SEP 1948 Tyler, TX. Gold: 1972 4 × 100 meter relay; Silver: 100 meters. Because Eddie Hart and Rey Robinson failed to make the start of the second-round races in Munich, Robert Taylor, who had placed only third at the Final Trials, was the solitary U.S. finalist in the 1972 Olympic 100m. Taylor finished one meter down on the Russian, Valeri Borzov, and later won a gold medal when the U.S. posted a world record in the relay. His only other major title came in the 1972 AAU 100m while he was a student at Texas Southern.

TEWANIMA, Louis.

B. 1888. D. 18 JAN 1969 Second Mesa, AZ. Silver: 1912 10,000 meters. Louis Tewanima was a Hopi Indian and a teammate of Jim Thorpe at the Carlisle Indian School. He finished ninth in the 1908 Olympic marathon and 16th in 1912, having earlier won the silver medal in the 10,000m. This was to remain the best performance by a U.S. athlete in this event until Billy Mills, also of Indian descent, won the 10,000 in 1964.

TEWKSBURY, John Walter Beardsley.

B. 21 MAR 1878 Ashley, PA. D. 24 APR 1968 Philadelphia, PA. Gold(2): 1900 200 meters, 1900 400 meter hurdles; Silver(2): 1900 60 meters, 1900 100 meters; Bronze: 1900 200 meter hurdles. Before graduating from Penn in 1899, Walter Tewksbury won both sprints at the IC4A meet in 1898 and 1899. He won a total of five medals at the 1900 Olympics, including a surprise victory over the French champion, Henri Tauzin, in the 400m hurdles. With hurdles fashioned out of telegraph poles and a 16-foot water jump before the finish, Tewksbury did well to clock 57.6.

Tewksbury earned a dental degree from Penn and practiced in his hometown of Tunkhannock. When he died in 1968 he was the last known survivor of the 1900 Olympic Games.

THIAS, Charles.

Bronze: 1904 Tug-of-War. Charles Thias was a member of the #2 team entered by the St. Louis Southwest Turnverein that took the bronze medals in the 1904 tug-of-war.

THOMAS, John Curtis.

B. 03 MAR 1941 Boston, MA. Silver: 1964 High Jump; Bronze: 1960 High Jump. As a 17-year-old freshman at Boston University, John Thomas set a world indoor high jump record of 7'-1¼" in 1959 that was, at that time, superior to the outdoor record. He missed the rest of the 1959 season due to injury, but came back to show the best form of his life in 1960. After raising the world indoor record to 7'-2½" he set an outdoor record of 7'-3¾" at the Final Trials.

At the Rome Olympics, Thomas was the heaviest of favorites, but he finished behind two Russians. Before the 1964 Olympics, one of them, Valeri Brumel, had usurped Thomas' title as the world's premier high jumper, and Brumel again beat Thomas at Tokyo.

Although Thomas did not succeed in winning an Olympic title, he had a fine competitive record. He won two AAU championships outdoors and five indoors, was twice NCAA champion, and for three years he won both the indoor and outdoor high jump at the IC4A meet. After retiring from active competition he took up a coaching appointment at Boston University, but is today a regional sales manager with New England Bell Telephone.

Courtesy Robert Wheeler and Dr. Florence Ridlon

The greatest athlete of all time — Jim Thorpe.

THOMPSON, Wilbur Marvin.

B. 06 APR 1921 Frankfort, SD. Gold: 1948 Shot Put. While attending high school in Modesto, "Moose" Thompson was a nationally ranked age-group shot putter in 1937 and 1938. He moved on to Modesto Junior College and won the National Junior College Title in 1939 and 1940, but on enrolling at Southern Cal success did not come immediately and it was not until 1946, after Thompson returned from war service, that he made any sort of impact in the senior ranks. In 1946 he placed second in the NCAA championships and, although he never won an AAU title, he was a comfortable winner at the 1948 Olympics. Three of his marks were superior to Jim Delaney's best effort in second place and Thompson's winning put of 56'-2" was an Olympic record and a career best.

THORPE, James Francis (né Wa-tho-huck).

B. 28 MAY 1888 Bellemont, OK. D. 28 MAR 1953 Lomita, CA. Gold(2): 1912 Decathlon, 1912 Pentathlon. Although Jim Thorpe was a laughingly easy winner of both all-round events at the 1912 Olympics and placed in the first six in both the long jump and high jump, he was not allowed to keep his Olympic medals. It was discovered that Thorpe had played semi-pro baseball in the summer of 1911 and, although his financial rewards had been minimal, he forfeited his amateur status and was stripped of his medals.

Thorpe is probably the greatest athlete of all time and although his track career was brief, he made a lasting impact. His 1912 Olympic decathlon mark was not bettered for 15 years and he was a world-class performer in many of the events which made up the decathlon. Shortly after the 1912 Olympics, he equalled the world 110m hurdles record of 15.0 and, although the mark was not officially recognized he beat Fred Kelly, the recently crowned Olympic hurdles champion, which confirmed his ability.

Thorpe was a Sac and Fox Indian whose name meant "Bright Path" and while at the Carlisle Indian School he was one of the greatest college football players of the early part of the 20th century. He became one of the first stars of pro football and, to capitalize on his name, he was appointed the first president of the NFL. Thorpe also played major league baseball with the New York Giants, Boston Braves, and Cincinnati Reds.

Thorpe worked for a while as a movie extra in Hollywood, but was a pauper much of his post-athletic life. In 1932 he could not afford the price of a single ticket to attend the Olympics, but Vice President Charles Curtis, himself of Indian origin, invited Thorpe to be his guest in the Presidential Box throughout the Games. Thorpe eventually died penniless only a few years after being voted by the nation's sportswriters as the greatest athlete of the first half of the 20th century. A movie, starring Burt Lancaster, was made of his life.

In 1973 the USOC restored Thorpe's amateur status and 10 years later the IOC followed suit and took the long overdue step of reinstating this great athlete to his rightful position of Olympic champion.

THURBER, Delos Packard.
B. 23 NOV 1916. Bronze: 1936 High Jump. Although Delos Thurber was a 6'-7½" high jumper, his performances tended to be overshadowed by the record-breaking feats of his contemporaries, Corny Johnson and Dave Albritton. He never won a major domestic championship, but placed third at the NCAA in 1937 and tied for third the following year. After his graduation from Southern Cal he became an airline pilot in the Philippines.

TIBBETTS, Willard Lewis, Jr.
B. 26 MAR 1903. Bronze: 1924 3,000 meter team race. While at Harvard, Willard Tibbetts won the IC4A two mile title, both indoors and outdoors, in 1926. He was also the IC4A cross-country champion in 1925. He earned his place on the 1924 Olympic team by finishing fourth in the 3,000m at the Final Trials and in Paris he placed 11th individually. Tibbets took up a career as an investment banker, working for the Boston firm of White, Wild & Co.

TINKER, Gerald.
B. 19 JAN 1951 Miami, FL. Gold: 1972 4 × 100 meter relay. After giving athletics a miss in 1971, Gerald Tinker of Kent State placed fourth in the 100m at the Final Trials and was selected for the relay squad in Munich. He ran a great third leg and made a vital contribution to the U.S. victory and to their world record.

TOLAN, Thomas Edward.
B. 29 SEP 1908 Denver, CO. D. 31 JAN 1967 Detroit, MI. Gold(2): 1932 100 meters, 1932 200 meters. Eddie Tolan, whose success was built on amazing leg speed, won both sprints at the 1927 National Interscholastic Championships and, although he qualified for the 1928 Final Olympic Trials, he was eliminated in the preliminaries of the both the 100m and 200m.

In 1929, Tolan ran the first official 9.5 for 100y and took his first major championship with a double victory in the AAU sprints. Apart from winning the AAU 100y he had a relatively poor season in 1930, but in 1931, while at the University of Michigan, he won the 220y at both the NCAA and IC4A championships. At the 1932 Final Trials, Tolan placed second to Ralph Metcalfe in both sprints, but he reversed the result at the Olympics and won two gold medals.

TOOMEY, William Anthony.
B. 10 JAN 1939 Philadelphia, PA. Gold: 1968 Decathlon. After graduating from the University of Colorado in 1962, Bill Toomey obtained a master's degree in education from Stanford. Although he was a promising all-round athlete while at Colorado, his performances there did not presage his future greatness.

He won the first of his four AAU pentathlon titles in 1960 and turned to the decathlon in 1963, placing fifth in the AAU. In 1964 he took fourth place at the Final Trials, only missing the Tokyo team by 109 points. Toomey's first major victory came in 1965 when he won the first of his record number of five AAU titles and in 1966 he set a world record of 8,234 points, although the mark was not ratified. In 1967 he was the Pan-Am Games champion and in 1968 he took the Olympic title after setting a record first day score of 4,499 points, which included a 45.6 400m. The following year, Toomey set an official world record of 8,417 points and one week later he married Mary Rand, Britain's 1964 Olympic long jump champion.

After a successful career as a television broadcaster and marketing consultant, Bill Toomey replaced Bo Roberson as coach at Cal/Irvine.

TOOTELL, Frederic Delmont.
B. 09 SEP 1902 Lawrence, MA. D. 29 SEP 1964. Gold: 1924 Hammer Throw. After five successive victories by Irish-born athletes representing the U.S., Fred Tootell was the first native-born American to win the Olympic hammer title.

As an 18-year-old, Tootell placed 10th in the 1921 national rankings, but by 1923 he was in a class by himself as he won the IC4A, NCAA, and AAU titles. His throw of 181'-6½" at the IC4A meet lasted as a championship record until 1954 and his 1923 NCAA record remained on the books until 1952.

After leaving Bowdoin, Tootell briefly attended medical school at Tufts, but trained at Bowdoin for the 1924 Olympics, where he duly took top honors by a margin of more than eight feet. He then launched a career as a coach which included over 30 years at the University of Rhode Island, beginning in 1925. He served as President of the Association of Track Coaches and at one time his team was undefeated in dual meets for 12 years. He remained at Rhode Island until his death at which time he was Chairman of the Physical Education Deptartment and, in recognition of his services to the University, their new $3 million sports complex was named after him.

TOPPINO, Martin Emmett.
B. 01 JUL 1909 New Orleans, LA. D. 08 SEP 1971 New Orleans, LA. Gold: 1932 4 × 100 meter relay. After graduating from Loyola (New Orleans) in 1931 with a B.S., Emmett Toppino stayed on a further year to take a master's degree in chemistry. After graduation he worked briefly for an oil company as a research chemist and then had a long career with the Freeman Shoe Corp.

As an athlete, Toppino placed third in the NCAA 100y in 1930 and 1931 and in the latter year he ran 9.5 in the heats, which was his fastest ever century. At the 1932 Final Trials he placed fourth in the 100m, narrowly missing selection for the 100m at the Olympics, but he

won a gold medal in the relay. Short in stature, Toppino was ideally suited to the indoor circuit. He was undefeated in the 1932 season, defeating Eddie Tolan in the AAU, and equalling the world 60y record no less than six times that year. He also set world records in the 50m and 60m.

TOWNS, Forrest Grady.
B. 06 FEB 1914 Fitzgerald, GA. Gold: 1936 110 meter hurdles. While in high school at Richmond Academy, "Spec" Towns was better known as a footballer, but in his senior year he cleared 6'-0" in the high jump to earn a track scholarship to Georgia. Towns took up hurdling in 1934 and ran a then-respectable 15.1, improving to 14.4 in 1935, and in 1936 he was invincible. He equalled the world record of 14.1 six times in 1936, although only two of the marks were officially recognized.

After winning the Olympic title in Berlin, Towns finished the 1936 season with one of the most memorable performances in track history. At a post-Olympic meet in Oslo, Towns was angry with the USOC officials for insisting that he remain in Europe rather than allowing him to return home for football practice; this ire spurred him to a world record of 13.7 that was to remain unbeaten for 11 years. Apart from his Olympic gold medal, Towns won the AAU in 1936, the NCAA in 1936 and 1937 and, although he didn't compete outdoors in 1938, he won the AAU indoor that year.

TRUBE, Herbert Lawrence.
B. 03 SEP 1886. D. 13 JUL 1959 Norwalk, CT. Silver: 1908 3 mile team race. Although he won the 1908 IC4A two mile title for Cornell, Herb Trube was primarily a one mile specialist and he won the 1908 AAU mile championship in highly unusual circumstances.

The 1908 AAU championships were held on a five-lap track in New York and the first race, which Trube won, was declared void as an official rang the bell after three laps. A rerun was held an hour later and again Trube won, but incredibly the officials made the same mistake and rang the bell prematurely. A third race was held the following Wednesday and Trube's winning time of 4:25.0 went into the record books as the official result.

In February 1909, Trube ran 4:19.8 to become the first man to beat 4:20 for an indoor mile. At the 1908 Olympics he placed ninth in the three mile event and was the third scoring member of the U.S. team which took the silver medals in the team race.

TYLER, Albert Clinton.

B. 04 JAN 1872 Glendale, OH. D. 25 JUL 1945 East Harpswell, ME. Silver: 1896 Pole Vault. Albert Tyler lettered in track, football, and baseball at Princeton, but he was primarily known as a pole vaulter. His best finish in a major meet was the Olympic silver; otherwise, he finished third in the 1897 IC4A championships.

He graduated from Princeton later in 1897 and became a school teacher and also a well-known football official. In 1945 he was teaching math in Philadelphia, but died of pneumonia while on vacation in Maine.

UNDERWOOD, George B.

B. 1884 Manchester, NH. D. 28 AUG 1943 Boston, MA. Gold: 1904 4 mile team race. After running in the 400m and 800m at the 1904 Olympics, George Underwood won a gold medal as a member of the New York AC team that won the four-mile team race. Individually, Underwood placed fifth in the 10-man field.

Underwood later became a well-known sportswriter. He was boxing editor of the *New York World*, sports editor of the *New York Morning Telegraph*, sports editor and columnist for the *Boston American*, and a news editor for the *Boston Globe*. He also served as publicity director for the Madison Square Garden.

UPSHAW, Orrin Thomas.

B. 1874. D. 1937. Silver: 1904 Tug-of-War. Orrin Upshaw was a member of the St. Louis Southwest Turnverein #1 team that finished second in the 1904 tug-of-war event. Upshaw was a doctor who practiced in St. Louis.

VALENTINE, Howard V.

B. 1881. D. 25 JUN 1932 New York, NY. Gold: 1904 4 mile team race; Silver: 1904 800 meters. In addition to his two medals at the 1904 Olympics, the New York AC's Howard Valentine placed seventh in the 1,500m and competed in the 400m. He was the AAU 880y champion in 1903 and 1904. Valentine's medals were not long for his sideboard, however; several years later his home was robbed and all his trophies and medals were taken.

Van OSDEL, Robert L.

B. 01 APR 1910. Silver: 1932 High Jump. The University of Southern California claimed the first two places in the 1932 Olympics high jump as Duncan McNaughton took the gold medal for Canada and his fellow Trojan, Bob Van Osdel, finished second. Van Osdel also tied with Bill O'Connor of Columbia for the 1932 IC4A title, and later in the season he was in a three-way tie for first place at the AAU. He was at his best in 1930 when, as a 19-year-old, he cleared 6'-7¼" for USC in a dual meet with Occidental, a mark which topped the world ranking lists that year.

VERNER, William Frank.

B. 24 JUN 1883 Grundy County, IL. D. JUL 1969. Silver(2): 1904 1,500 meters, 1904 4 mile team race. Bill Verner at one time held the Purdue records at 880y, one mile, and two miles, and the Indiana state records for 880y and the mile. In the 1904 Olympics 1,500m, Purdue took the second and third places with Verner winning the silver medal and Lacey Hearn the bronze. These two also ran well for the Chicago AA team in the four mile team race, finishing third and fourth respectively. Verner also placed fourth in the steeplechase and sixth in the 800m. He was offered a chance to go to Athens with the 1906 Olympic team, but preferred to stay behind and represent Purdue as their captain in his last year of collegiate eligibility.

Verner graduated with a B.S. in mechanical engineering in 1906 and for many years served as consulting engineer to the Washtenaw County Treasurer in Ann Arbor, Michigan.

WALLER, Frank Laird.

B. 1886. D. 29 NOV 1941. Silver(2): 400 meters, 400 meter hurdles. Frank Waller of the University of Wisconsin and the Chicago AA was unfortunate to encounter Harry Hillman at his best at the St. Louis Olympics. However, he gave Hillman a good race in the 400m and 400m hurdles and won a silver medal in both events. Waller, later representing the Milwaukee AC, also won the AAU junior 440y in 1903 and the senior title in 1905 and 1906, as well as the 1905 AAU 220y hurdles.

WARNER, Karl DeWitt.

B. 23 JUN 1908 Woodbury, CT. Gold: 1932 4×400 meter relay. Karl Warner of Yale ran the third leg on the

1932 Olympic relay team when the U.S. set a new world record of 3:08.2. His best performance had come earlier in the season when he ran 47.6 for 400m in June.

WEILL, David Lawson.
B. 25 OCT 1941 Berkeley, CA. Bronze: 1964 Discus Throw. It was generally Dave Weill's lot to finish third at important meets. He took that slot at the 1964 Final Trials, the 1964 Olympics, and three times at the AAU championships. He did win the 1962 and 1963 NCAA for Stanford, but his best performance came in 1967 when he threw 206'-7½" at the Sacramento Invitational Meet. He placed third.

WENDELL, James Isaac.
B. 03 SEP 1890 Schenectady, NY. D. 22 NOV 1958 Philadelphia, PA. Silver: 1912 110 meter hurdles. James Wendell won the 1912 IC4A 120y hurdles for Wesleyan; the following year he again took the high hurdles and won the 220y hurdles. After graduating in 1913, Wendell earned several honorary degrees as an educator. Most of his life was spent as the headmaster at The Hill School in Pottstown, Penn.

WHITFIELD, Malvin Groston.
B. 11 OCT 1924 Bay City, TX. Gold(3): 1948 800 meters, 1948 4 × 400 meter relay, 1952 800 meters; Silver: 1952 4 × 400 meter relay; Bronze: 1948 400 meters. Mal Whitfield was the finest 400/800m runner of his time. Between June 1948 and the end of the 1954 season he lost only three of his 69 races at 800m/880y, and during that period he won all his two-lap races in major championships, including five AAU wins—two at the NCAA, two Olympic, and one Pan-American Games gold medal. He also won the AAU 440y in 1952. Whitfield, who was an Ohio State Buckeye, set U.S. records at 400m and 440y and three world records— two at 880y and one at 1,000m. Indoors he won two AAU titles and set world records at three different distances.

In 1955 he tried unsuccessfully to move up to the mile, but he reverted to the 800m in 1956 and, after placing fifth at the Final Trials, he finally retired. Mal Whitfield then travelled the world working for the U.S. Intelligence Service and at one stage of his career lived in Africa for three years.

WHITNEY, Lawrence Atwood.
B. 02 FEB 1891 Millbury, MA. D. 24 APR 1941 Boston, MA. Bronze: 1912 Shot Put. Although he won a bronze medal in Stockholm, Larry Whitney had not quite reached his peak at the time of the 1912 Olympics. In 1913 he won both the IC4A and the AAU shot put titles, in 1914 he set a Dartmouth record of 48'-0½" and after winning the IC4A title again in 1915 he retired from competition. While at Dartmouth he also played halfback on the football team and won a varsity letter in basketball. As football and track captain he is one of only three men to captain two different sports at Dartmouth.

WIESNER, Kenneth George.
B. 17 FEB 1925 Milwaukee, WI. Silver: 1952 High Jump. While at Marquette, Ken Wiesner won the NCAA high jump three times (once tied), the IC4A title in 1946, and he tied for the AAU indoor crown in 1945. After the 1946 season, Ken Wiesner retired, but after a five-year break he made a highly successful comeback and the 27-year-old navy dentist won a silver medal at the 1952 Olympics. Continuing to improve, in 1953 he three times broke the world indoor high jump record before retiring.

WILKINS, Louis Gary.
B. 10 DEC 1882 Bourbon, IN. Bronze: 1904 Pole Vault. After a series of jump-offs, Lou Wilkins of the University of Chicago was finally awarded third place in the 1904 Olympic pole vault. Earlier in the season, the 1904 AAU championships had also been held in St. Louis and Wilkins lost the title to H. L. Gardner, again after a jump-off.

WILKINS, Maurice Mac.
B. 15 NOV 1950 Eugene, OR. Gold: 1976 Discus Throw. Mac Wilkins' greatest year was undoubtedly 1976. Apart from his Olympic gold medal he bettered the world record four times and three of those records came in one inspired competition. After setting a world record of 226'-11½" in April, he went to San Jose in May and, with each of his first three throws, progressively improved that record. Wilkins opened with 229'-0"; then threw 230'-5½", which, at 70.24 m., was the first-ever 70 meter throw; and on his third trial he took the record up to 232'-5½".

Track and Field News

Mac Wilkins bettered the world record four times and won his Olympic gold medal in 1976.

Wilkins has been called America's greatest all-round thrower, although this sobriquet omits such old-timers as Martin Sheridan and Ralph Rose. Still, Wilkins' versatility is impressive. He began as a javelin thrower for the Oregon track team, placing third in the 1973 NCAA and 1977 AAU indoor shot put events. He also threw the hammer, but all his big titles came with the disc. He took the AAU title six times, the NCAA championship in 1973, and won a Pan-American discus gold medal.

WILLIAMS, Archibald Franklin.
B. 01 MAY 1915 Oakland, CA. Gold: 1936 400 meters. Prior to 1936, Archie Williams was a virtual unknown in track circles, but he made astounding progress in the Olympic year. After running 47.4 for 440y in April, he clocked 46.8 in May and then, in a heat of the NCAA championships in June, he set a world 400m record of 46.1. At the Berlin Olympics he beat Britain's Godfrey Brown by inches and then disappeared from the track scene as quickly as he had arrived.

Williams, a graduate of Cal/Berkeley, became a schoolteacher in Marin County, California.

WILLIAMS, Randy Luvelle.
B. 23 AUG 1953 Fresno, CA. Gold: 1972 Long Jump; Silver: 1976 Long Jump. In 1972 the 19-year-old Randy Williams of Southern Cal became the youngest Olympic long jump champion in history. Four years later, he took the silver medal in Montreal and in 1980 he qualified for his third Olympics but, because of the boycott, was denied a chance at his third Olympic medal. Williams saved his best for the Olympics; his domestic accomplishments were less impressive. He won his only NCAA title in 1972 and was AAU champion in 1972 and 1973.

WILLIAMS, Ulis C.
B. 24 OCT 1941 Hollandale, MS. Gold: 1964 4 × 400 meter relay. Ulis Williams of Arizona State won the AAU 440y relay in 1962 and 1963 and, after winning the NCAA title in 1963, he tied for first place in 1964. His best marks seemed to come in races he lost. In 1963, Williams ran a 45.6 440y behind Adolph Plummer's world record 44.9 at the Western Athletic Conference Meet and his career best 400m also came finishing second to a world record. At the 1964 Final Trials, Mike Larrabee set that record with 44.9 and Williams was the runner-up in 45.0. At the Tokyo Olympics he was a bit disappointing with a fifth place finish in the individual 400m, but won the gold medal as a member of the world record breaking relay team. He later served as associate dean of Compton Community College and as a college professor.

WOHLHUTER, Richard Charles.
B. 23 DEC 1948 Geneva, IL. Bronze: 1976 800 meters. While at Notre Dame, Rick Wohlhuter won the 1971 IC4A 880y and in 1972, after placing second to Dave

THE ENCYCLOPEDIA OF AMERICAN OLYMPIANS

Wottle at both the AAU and the Final Trials, he seemed a certain Olympic finalist and possible medalist. Sadly, he fell in the 800m heats in Munich, but at the Montreal Games he won the bronze medal in the 800m and placed sixth in the 1,500m.

Between his two Olympic appearances, Wohlhuter set a U.S. 800m record of 1:43.9 in 1973 and, in that race, he continued to the 880y mark where he set a world record of 1:44.6. In 1974 he brought the world 880y record down to 1:44.1 and set a world 1,000m record. In both 1973 and 1974 he was the AAU champion and he won the AAU indoor 1000y for three years straight from 1974. After retiring from track in 1977, he contemplated a comeback in 1980, but the boycott dashed those hopes. He has begun a career as an insurance claims adjuster.

WOODRING, Allen.
B. 15 FEB 1898 Bethlehem, PA. Gold: 1920 200 meters. Although he failed to place at the 1920 Final Trials, Allen Woodring was surprisingly chosen for the 200m at the Antwerp Olympics. Equally surprisingly, Woodring won the Olympic title, edging Charlie Paddock at the tape. While at Syracuse, Woodring won the IC4A 220y in 1921 and the 440y in 1923. After graduation he worked for the Spalding company as a salesman.

WOODRUFF, John Youie.
B. 05 JUL 1915 Connellsville, PA. Gold: 1936 800 meters. John Woodruff's winning time of 1:52.9 in the Berlin 800m was the slowest winning Olympic time since 1920. The time was, however, not a true reflection of his abilities; he twice ran under 1:48.0 under conditions that were only marginally irregular, and he had a clocking of 1:47.7 in an 880y indoor race.

While at the University of Pittsburgh, Woodruff won the IC4A 440/880y double for three straight years (1937–39) and in those same three years, he won the NCAA 880y. Although he was supreme in collegiate competition, Woodruff won only one AAU title when he took the 880y championship in 1937. From July 1936, when he lost a badly judged race to Charlie Beetham at the AAU, Woodruff never lost another 800m/880y until he retired in 1940. He was, undoubtedly, one of the great unfulfilled talents of the sport; apart from his record in the two-lap event, he had such marks to his credit as a 46.8 400m and a 4:12.8 mile. John Woodruff later became a career officer in the army.

WOODS, George Roger.
B. 11 FEB 1943 Portagville, MO. Silver(2): 1968 Shot Put, 1972 Shot Put. While at Southern Illinois, George Woods' best placing at the NCAA was in 1964 when he finished second and, although during his long career he won the AAU indoor shot four times, he never succeeded in winning the outdoor title.

After placing second to Randy Matson at the 1968 Olympics he was desperately unlucky not to win the gold medal at Munich. Woods' final trial at the 1972 Games would almost certainly have exceeded Wladyslaw Komar's winning mark—albeit marginally—but the shot hit Komar's measuring peg and Woods lost the Olympic title by a mere centimeter. Woods made a third Olympic appearance in 1976 when he placed seventh. He tried for a fourth team in 1980, but placed only eleventh at the Final Trials. Woods had a career best of 72'-2¾" in 1974 which, bettered the current world record, but because it was indoors at the Los Angeles Times Games, it did not receive official approval.

WOTTLE, David James.
B. 07 AUG 1950 Canton, OH. Gold: 1972 800 meters. In 1970, Dave Wottle of Bowling Green placed second in the NCAA mile and, within the space of one week, brought his personal best for 880y down from 1:51.6 to 1:47.8. He was expected to have an outstanding year in 1971, but he missed the entire season due to injury.

Wottle did, however, fulfill his promise in 1972. He started by winning the NCAA indoor 880y and then, after winning the AAU 800m, he equalled the world record of 1:44.3 at the Final Trials. In the Olympic Final he was placed last in the eight-man field with 200m to go, but put on a devastating finish and won the gold medal by 3/100ths of a second. In 1972, Wottle also won the NCAA 1,500m and, by placing second at the Final Trials, he qualified for a second event at the Munich Games. In the Olympic 1,500m he was eliminated in the heats.

His major win in 1973 was the NCAA mile and at the end of the season, Wottle, who was easily identified on the track by his habit of running in a golf cap, turned professional. He later became track coach at Bethaney College in West Virginia.

WRIGHT, Lorenzo Christopher.
B. 09 DEC 1926 Detroit, MI. D. 27 MAR 1972 Detroit, MI. Gold: 1948 4 × 100 meter relay. In May 1948.

Courtesy Ed Kirwan Graphic Arts

Jack Yerman, a Cal-Berkeley graduate, was a member of the world record setting 4 X 400 relay team in the 1960 Olympics.

Lorenzo Wright of Wayne State set a career best in the long jump of 25'-11" but he could not reproduce this form at the Olympics and finished out of the medals in fourth place. He came onto the relay team as a substitute for Ed Conwell who was suffering from asthma and won the medal he had missed in his specialty event.

After earning a master's in education from Wayne State, he became supervisor of athletics for Detroit public schools. In 1972 he was stabbed to death in his home during a quarrel with his wife about a possible separation. In 1973 he was posthumously inducted into the Michigan Sports Hall of Fame.

WRIGHT, Marc Snowell.
B. 21 APR 1890 Chicago, IL. D. 05 AUG 1975 Reading, MA. Silver: 1912 Pole Vault (tied). At the 1912 Olympic trials, Marc Wright, a left-handed vaulter from Dartmouth, set a world record of 13'-2¼" (4.02 meters) to become the first 4-meter vaulter in history. He was well below his best in Stockholm and tied for second place at 12'-7½". Surprisingly, Wright, although he was a world record holder, never featured prominently at the IC4A championships, finishing equal fourth in 1912 and tied for second in 1913.

WYKOFF, Frank Clifford.
B. 29 OCT 1909 Des Moines, IA. D. 01 JAN 1980 Alhambra, CA. Gold(3): 1928 4 × 100 meter relay, 1932 4 × 100 meter relay, 1936 4 × 100 meter relay. Frank Wykoff is the only man to have won three Olympic relay medals, all of them gold and all world-record efforts.

Wykoff first astounded the track world as an 18-year-old at Glendale High School when he beat the great Charlie Paddock in both sprints at the Southwest Olympic Trials. He went on to make the Olympic team for Amsterdam, where he won the first of his gold medals. His 200m victory over Paddock at the Southwest Trials was Wykoff's only major win at this distance, although his time of 20.8 showed his potential in the longer sprint. Wykoff wisely chose to concentrate on the 100y/100m and in 1930 he ran the first official 9.4 for 100 yards.

While at Southern Cal, he won three IC4A, two NCAA, and two AAU dash titles. After graduation he served as director of special schools for Los Angeles County for many years.

YERMAN, Jack L.
B. 05 FEB 1939 Oroville, CA. Gold: 1960 4 × 400 meter relay. After some disappointing early season performances, Jack Yerman of Cal/Berkeley rounded into form for the Final Trials and, after setting a career best of 46.0 in the heats, he won the final later in the day in 46.3. In the individual 400m at the Rome Olympics, Yerman was eliminated in the semi-finals, but in the relay he set the U.S. on their way to the gold medals and a world record with an opening leg of 46.2.

YOUNG, Cyrus C., Jr.

B. 23 JUL 1928 Modesto, CA. Gold: 1952 Javelin Throw. Cy Young is the only U.S. athlete to have won the Olympic javelin title. In April 1956, Young had the best throw of his career with 259'-8½". Later in the season, he won his only AAU championship, but he failed to make a significant challenge in defense of his Olympic crown and finished 11th in Melbourne. Young graduated from UCLA in 1951 and became a rancher.

YOUNG, Earl Verdelle.

B. 14 FEB 1941 San Fernando, CA. Gold: 1960 4 × 400 meter relay. Earl Young took up quarter-miling in his freshman year (1959) at Abilene Christian. In his first season he ran 48.5 for 440y, but showed dramatic improvement in the Olympic year and ran 45.9 for sixth place in the Olympic final before contributing a 45.6 stage on the winning relay team.

YOUNG, George L.

B. 24 JUL 1937 Roswell, NM. Bronze: 1968 3,000 meter steeplechase. George Young was one of the gutsiest distance runners in the annals of U.S. track. In his Olympic debut he failed to survive the heats of the 1960 steeplechase but, in 1964, he placed fifth and improved to take the bronze medal in 1968. He also ran in the 1968 marathon, placing 16th, and in his fourth Olympics he ran only in the 5,000m and was eliminated in the heats.

Prior to becoming a school teacher, George Young attended, at various times, Northern Arizona, Western New Mexico, and Arizona. He won the AAU steeplechase three times, the three miles once, the marathon once, and he was twice the AAU indoor three mile champion.

YOUNG, Lawrence Dean.

B. 10 FEB 1943 Independence, MO. Bronze(2): 1968 50 kilometer walk, 1972 50 kilometer walk. Larry Young is America's most successful international walker ever. In addition to his two Olympic medals, he placed 10th in the Olympic 20km walk in 1972 and was Pan-American Games champion at 50km in 1967 and 1971.

After enlisting in the navy out of high school, Larry Young attended Columbia College (Missouri) on the only race-walking scholarship ever given in the United States. He has since become a metal sculptor.

Earl Young, who won a gold medal at the 1960 Olympics, as a member of the 1,600 meter relay team.

YOUNG, Robert Clark.

B. 15 JAN 1916. Silver: 1936 4 × 400 meter relay. The 20-year-old Bob Young of UCLA was the youngest member of the 1936 4 × 400m relay team. Young placed fifth at the Final Trials, having earlier set a personal best of 47.1 for 400m in finishing second to Jimmy LuValle at the Western Olympic Trials. In 1937 he posted his best mark for 440y when he ran 47.7.

ZAREMBA, Peter E.

B. 07 APR 1909. Bronze: 1932 Hammer Throw. In winning the IC4A title in 1932, Pete Zaremba of NYU set a career best of 170'-6⅝". He won the IC4A again in 1933 and, although he never won an AAU title, Zaremba was ranked in the top six hammer throwers from 1932 to 1935 and again in 1937. He had a poor season in 1936 and placed fifth at the Final Trials.

WOMEN

Women's track & field first appeared on the Olympic program in 1928 with only a few events being held. Gradually, the Olympic committee and IAAF have realized that women can compete successfully in any event and have added an event or two at almost every Olympics. The 1984 Olympics will see the addition of the 3,000 meter run, the 400 meter hurdles and, probably most keenly awaited, the women's marathon.

The United States has always been one of the top powers in Olympic track & field, but never truly has been the dominant nation. The United States women have won the most medals in track & field only once, in 1932. U.S. women have won more medals than any nation in just two events, the 100 meters and the 4 × 100 meter relay. We stand third on the overall medal list behind the Soviet Union and East Germany. Today the sport is dominated by those two nations, while several other Eastern Bloc nations figure prominently.

OUTSTANDING PERFORMANCES

Most Gold Medals
  3 Wilma Rudolph, Wyomia Tyus
Most Medals
  4 Wilma Rudolph, Wyomia Tyus
  3 Babe Didrikson, Betty Robinson
Consecutive Victories, Same Event
  2 Wyomia Tyus (1964/68 100m),
    Annette Rogers (1932/36 400m relay)
Most Appearances
  5 Willye White, Olga Connolly*
  4 Martha Watson
Oldest Gold Medalist
  27y251d Lillian Copeland
Youngest Gold Medalist
  15y123d Barbara Jones

*Includes one appearance as Miss Fikotová and representing Czechoslovakia.

BAILES, Margaret Johnson.
B. 23 JAN 1951 Bronx, NY. Gold: 1968 4 × 100 meter relay. The 16-year-old Mrs. Margaret Bailes of the Oregon Track Club began her career as one of the top U.S. sprinters with a fifth place in the 1967 AAU 200m. The following year she won the AAU 100m after equalling the world record of 11.1 in both the heats and the final. In the 200m at the AAU, Bailes finished second to Wyomia Tyus, but at the Final Trials a week later, the positions were reversed—Tyus took the 100m, while Bailes won the 200m with Tyus in second place.

At the 1968 Olympics, Bailes reached the finals of both sprints, finishing fifth in the 100m and seventh in the 200m. Margaret Bailes was a member of the relay team that set a new world record of 42.8 and at the end of the season she retired from the sport at the age of 17.

BLAND, Harriet Claiborne.
B. 13 FEB 1915 St. Louis, MO. Gold: 1936 4 × 100 meter relay. Although never placing better than third (1935–36) in an AAU individual sprint, Harriet Bland was a member of the St. Louis AC team that won the AAU relay in 1935. In Berlin she ran the first stage on the relay team that took the gold medals after the Germans, who had set a world record in the heats but dropped the baton on the last exchange. Harriet Bland, who attended the prestigious finishing school, Mary Institute, later became Mrs. William Green.

BROWN, Earlene Dennis.
B. 11 JUL 1935 Latexo, TX. Bronze: 1960 Shot Put. A three-time Olympian, Mrs. Earlene Brown, a 225 lb. black, is the only U.S. female to have ever won a medal in the Olympic shot put.

The former Miss Dennis won the first of her eight AAU shot put titles in 1956 with a new U.S. record and at the Final Trials she set new U.S. records in both the shot and the discus. At the 1956 Olympics she placed fourth in the discus and sixth in the shot and, four years later in Rome, she improved to take the bronze medal in the shot. At her last Olympics—Tokyo in 1964—she placed 12th in the shot.

Mrs. Brown, a Los Angeles housewife and mother, improved on the U.S. record in her two specialty events on numerous occasions, her best season being 1960 when she took the records up to 54'-9¼" and 176'-10". In three of the eight years when she won the AAU shot she also won the discus throw, and she won both events at the 1959 Pan-American Games.

BRYANT, Rosalyn Evette.
B. 07 JAN 1956 Chicago, IL. Silver: 1976 4 × 400 meter relay. After winning the AAU 100y outdoors and the

220y indoors in 1975, Rosalyn Bryant moved up to the one-lap event in the Olympic year. Although only placing third at the Final Trials, she proved to be the best of the Americans in Montreal. In the second semi-final she set a U.S. record of 50.62 and, with all three Americans reaching the final, Rosalyn Bryant was the first home in fifth place. She later ran a magnificent 49.7 anchor stage in the relay and brought the U.S. team home in second place behind the East Germans, with both teams inside the previous world record. Bryant, who attended Long Beach State, also won the AAU indoor 220y in 1977.

CAREW, Mary Louise.
B. 08 SEP 1913 Medford, MA. Gold: 1932 4 × 100 meter relay. An explosive start put the diminutive Mary Carew on her way to four straight wins (1929–32) in the AAU indoor 40y and her winning time of 5.2 in 1930 and 1931 equalled the world indoor record. She also won the AAU outdoor 50y in 1930 and, although tending to fade in the later stages at the standard sprint distances, she tied for third place at the 1932 Final Trials. Her starting ability made her a natural choice for the lead-off runner on the Olympic relay team that went on to beat the Canadians by a foot in a new world record of 46.9 although, by the rules in force at that time, both teams were given a new world record of 47.0. Mary Carew, who represented Medford Girls Club, retained her interest in track after her competitive days were over and, as Mrs. Mary Armstrong, served as secretary of the New England Chapter of the U.S. Olympians.

COACHMAN, Alice.
B. 09 NOV 1923 Albany, GA. Gold: 1948 High Jump. Alice Coachman became the first black woman to win an Olympic gold medal in any sport when she won the 1948 high jump title with a new Games record of 5'-6¼". She was also the only U.S. woman to win a track & field gold medal in 1948.

Alice Coachman still holds the record for the most victories in the AAU outdoor high jump with consecutive championships between 1939 and 1948, and in 1941–43, she also won the indoor title. Additionally, Alice Coachman won eight AAU sprint titles outdoors and two indoors. Before enrolling at Albany State, whom she represented for most of her career, she attended Tuskegee Institute and was twice on their

winning relay team at the AAU meet. She thus won a total of 25 AAU championships. As Mrs. Davis, she is today a teacher in Atlanta.

CONNOLLY, Olga Fikotová.
B. 13 NOV 1932 Prague, Czechoslovakia. Gold: 1956 Discus Throw (competed for Czechoslovakia). Olga Fikotová, a student at the Charles University of Medicine in Prague, took the Czech discus title in 1955 and 1956 and then went on to win the Olympic gold medal with a new Games record of 176'-1". Her much-publicized romance with Hal Connolly, who won the hammer throw for the U.S., captured more headlines than her Olympic victory. The two were subsequently married and, as an American citizen, she represented the U.S. at the next four Olympics.

Olga Connolly won five AAU titles between 1957 and 1968 and, at the Olympics, she finished seventh in 1960, 12th in 1964, and then sixth in 1968. Four years later, as a 39-year-old mother of four children, she came out of retirement and showed the best form of her long career.

After having a new U.S. record of 177'-5" disallowed on a technicality at the beginning of 1972, she officially beat Earlene Brown's 12-year-old record with a throw of 179'-2" in early May, and then improved the record to 185'-3" later in the month. At the 1972 Olympics, Olga Connolly did not maintain her early season form. She was selected to carry the U.S. flag at the opening ceremonies, however, and was preoccupied during those Games with promoting the Olympics as a forum for world peace. Erich Segal, the American author and television commentator during those Olympics, told her, "You may not have won as an athlete, but you've been a great success as a human being."

Olga and Hal Connolly were divorced in the mid-70's but one of their daughters is carrying on the family tradition and has a chance to make the 1984 Olympic volleyball team.

COPELAND, Lillian.
B. 25 NOV 1904 New York, NY. D. 07 FEB 1964. Gold: 1932 Discus Throw; Silver: 1928 Discus Throw. Lillian Copeland won a total of nine AAU titles between 1925 and 1932 in three different events—shot, discus, and javelin—and in 1926 she took all three championships setting a new U.S. record in each event. After the 1928

U.S. Competitors In Both The Winter And Summer Olympics

It's quite a rare feat for an American (or anyone, for that matter) to compete in both the Winter and Summer Olympics. In fact, only four U.S. competitors have pulled off this trick. Eddie Eagan was the first, and most successful —he won gold medals in boxing in 1920 and in bobsledding in 1932. In 1956, Art Longsjo became the only American to do so in the same year; he competed in both cycling and speed skating. The cycling/speed skating combo hit again with Arnold Uhrlass in 1960 and 1964. Finally, Willie Davenport won a gold medal in the 110 meter high hurdles in 1968 and then competed in 1980 as a bobsledder.

Olympics, Copeland entered Southern Cal Law School and did not compete seriously again until 1931. The following year she finished third in the discus at the Final Trials and barely made the Olympic team, but at the Games she came up with a new Olympic record of 133'-2" on her last throw and snatched the gold medal from Ruth Osborn, who had led the field going into the last round. The 27-year-old Copeland is the oldest U.S. woman to have won an Olympic gold medal in track & field events. In 1935 she came out of retirement and won three gold medals in her specialty events at the Second World Maccabiah Games in Palestine.

During the seasons 1926–28 Lillian Copeland broke the world javelin record three times and set three world records for the 8 lb. shot put. The javelin was not included in the women's program at the Games until 1948, which almost certainly deprived her of further Olympic honors. For a specialist in throwing events, she had a surprising turn of speed and in February 1928, she was a member of the team from the Pasadena A&CC that set a new U.S. record of 50.0 for the 440y relay.

Lillian Copeland worked for many years for the Los Angeles County Sheriff's Department in many capacities and was a juvenile officer for 24 years.

CROSS, Jessica.
B. 14 APR 1909. Silver: 1928 4 × 100 meter relay. Her best placing in an AAU individual event was second in the 100y in 1929 but Jessie Cross was on the winning relay team that year and again in 1930 when the Milrose AA set a new world record of 49.4. In Amsterdam she ran the second leg on the relay team that was soundly beaten by the Canadians, who included three finalists from the individual 100m on their team.

DANIELS, Isabelle Francis.
B. 31 JUL 1937 Jakin, GA. Bronze: 1956 4 × 100 meter relay. In 1955, Isabelle Daniels finished second in the 60m and was on the winning relay team at the Pan-American Games. Although she finished second to Mae Faggs in the 1956 AAU 100m, she reversed the decision at the Final Trials and went to Melbourne as the first-string U.S. sprinter. At the Games she was initially awarded third place in a desperately close finish, but after a reexamination of the photo finish she was placed fourth. In the relay she ran the anchor leg on the team that set a new U.S. record of 44.9 behind Australia and Great Britain, with all three teams bettering the previous world record.

Isabelle Daniels won five AAU sprint titles outdoors and seven indoors. She was also a member of the Tennessee State team that won the AAU relay for five years in a row.

DIDRIKSON, Mildred Ella.

B. 26 JUN 1914 Port Arthur, TX. D. 27 SEP 1956. Gold(2): 1932 80 meter hurdles, 1932 Javelin Throw; Silver: 1932 High Jump. One of seven children of Norwegian immigrants, "Babe" Didrikson is almost certainly the most versatile, and possibly greatest, woman athlete of all time. Her track career was brief but brilliant and her performance at the 1932 AAU meet remains among the greatest in sporting history.

In the space of two-and-one-half hours she competed in eight events, winning four of them outright and finishing equal first in another. As the only representative of her club, Employers Casualty AA of Dallas, she won the national team championship with the powerful Illinois Women's AC, who fielded more than 20 athletes, in second place. At the end of the day, the score was Didrikson—30 points, Illinois 22 points.

The Babe opened her Olympic campaign by winning the javelin on her first throw with a new Olympic record, then she equalled the world record (11.8) in the heats of the 80 meter hurdles and the following day brought the record down to 11.7 as she took her second gold medal. Finally, she placed second in the high jump after a controversial jump-off with Jean Shiley. The judges ruled that Didrikson had dived over the bar although she had been using the same style throughout the competition.

Prior to the Games the Babe had already been voted an all-American in basketball for three years and, as a 17-year-old, she twice broke the world javelin record in 1930. Babe forfeited her amateur status after the Olympics by allowing her name to be used in an automobile advertisement, so she then turned her attention to golf and was easily the greatest woman golfer of her era. In 1934 she won the first tournament she entered and, until cancer ended her career in 1955, she won 17 major titles, including the U.S. and British Amateur (the only person to ever win both of those championships) and, as a professional, the U.S. Open three times, once—in 1955, after recovering from an operation for the cancer. Better known professionally under her married name of Babe Zaharias, she lived but one more year before dying from cancer at the age of 42.

Courtesy Evelyn Hall

A dead heat? The disputed finish of the 1932 80 meter hurdles in which Babe Didrikson was given the nod over Evelyn Hall (no. 473).

FAGGS, Heriwentha Mae.

B. 10 APR 1932 Mays Landing, NJ. Gold: 1952 4 × 100 meter relay; Bronze: 1956 4 × 100 meter relay. After being eliminated in the semi-finals of the 200m in 1948, Mae Faggs placed sixth in the 100m in 1952 and failed to make the final of either of the individual sprints in 1956. However, she had a better record in the relays, winning a gold medal in 1952 and a bronze in 1956.

During the course of a long career, she won the AAU 200m in 1954 and, in 1955 and 1956, she took the sprint double at the AAU meet. Indoors she won the 100y in 1952 and claimed six victories in the 220y between 1949 and 1956. At the 1955 Pan-American Games she won a silver medal in the 200m and a gold in the relay. During her early days she represented the New York Police Athletic League, though she later attended, and represented, Tennessee State.

As Mrs. Starr she is now a teacher and very active in promoting youth programs in Cincinnati.

FERGUSON, Mable.

B. 18 JAN 1955 Los Angeles, CA. Silver: 1972 4 × 400 meter relay. After placing fifth in the individual 400m at the 1972 Olympics, the 17-year-old Mable Ferguson of Pomona High School and the West Coast Jets ran a 51.8 lead-off leg in the 1,600m relay. In addition to her Olympic success, she won the AAU 400m in 1971 and in 1973 she won both the 220y and 440y. Her sister, Willomae, was also a nationally ranked sprinter.

FERRELL, Barbara Ann.

B. 28 JUL 1947 Hattiesburg, MS. Gold: 1968 4 × 100 meter relay; Silver: 100 meters. Barbara Ferrell, a student at Los Angeles State and later a member of the Los Angeles Mercurettes, won the 100m at the Pan-American Games in 1967 and the following year, after winning both sprints at the Final Trials, she finished second in the 100m and fourth in the 200m at the Olympics. At the Munich Games four years later, she again reached the 100m final, placing seventh, but was eliminated in the semi-finals of the 200m.

Barbara Ferrell equalled the world record of 11.1 for 100m in winning the 1967 AAU and won the 220y in 1969. Indoors, she won the AAU 60y in 1968 and 1969, and the 240y (sic) in 1969.

FURTSCH, Evelyn.

B. 16 AUG 1911. Gold: 1932 4 × 100 meter relay. Because both Elizabeth Wilde and Louise Stokes, who finished ahead of her at the Final Trials, were not selected for the Olympics, Evelyn Furtsch of the Los Angeles AC was perhaps fortunate to have won a place on the relay team for the Los Angeles Games. The only time she placed in an AAU championship was in 1929, when she finished second in the 100y.

HALL, Evelyne Ruth.

B. 10 SEP 1909 Minneapolis, MN. Silver: 1932 80 meter hurdles. After leading the great Babe Didrikson over the final barrier in the 80 meter hurdles at the 1932 Olympics, Evelyne Hall lost out on the run-in, but she was given the same time as the winner and shared the new world record of 11.7.

She won only one AAU individual title outdoors (1930), but she was on the winning relay team three times (1931–33) and in 1932 the foursome from the Illinois Women's AC equalled the world record of 49.4 for the 440y relay. Indoors, Evelyn Hall won the AAU hurdles in 1931, 1933, and 1935, and in 1936 she placed fourth at the Final Trials to narrowly miss making the Olympic team for a second time.

After her competitive retirement, Evie Hall (and later as Evie Adams) stayed intimately involved in the sport. She was a coach and physical education instructor, coaching the first U.S. women's team at the 1951 Pan-American Games, and serving as chairman for U.S. Olympic women's track & field for several years. She also worked as a supervisor of the Glendale (California) parks and recreation department and served as president of the Southern Cal chapter of the U.S. Olympians.

HAMMOND, Kathleen.

B. 02 NOV 1951 Sacramento, CA. Silver: 1972 4 × 400 meter relay; Bronze: 1972 400 meters. Kathy Hammond won her first senior title as a 15-year-old when she took the AAU indoor 440y in 1967. She won again in 1970 and 1972, and was outdoors AAU champion in 1969 and 1972. The year 1969 was a truly outstanding one for Hammond—she lost only one race throughout an entire season and twice posted new U.S. records while on a European tour, her best mark being 52.1 for 400m in Warsaw. Kathy Hammond was handicapped by injury in 1970 and was suspended for much of the 1971 season, but in 1972 she was back at the top of her form and improved her own U.S. record to 51.64 in taking third place in the Olympic final. At the time many thought of her as a veteran but she was, in fact, still only 20 years old and, to add to her bronze in the individual event, she ran the anchor leg in the relay in close to 50 seconds to clinch the silver medals for the Americans.

HARDY, Catherine.
B. 08 FEB 1932. Gold: 1952 4 × 100 meter relay. Cathy Hardy of Fort Valley State in Georgia scored a sprint double at the 1952 AAU and at the Final Trials she ran 24.3 for 200m to break Helen Stephens' long-standing U.S. record. At the Helsinki Olympics she failed to reach the final of either of the individual sprints but she anchored the relay team that took the gold medals with a new world record. Apart from her AAU outdoor double in 1952, Cathy Hardy won the AAU indoor 50y in 1951.

HUDSON, Martha.
B. 21 MAR 1939 Eastman, GA. Gold: 1960 4 × 100 meter relay. Like all her teammates on the relay squad that won the 400m relay at the 1960 Olympics, Martha Hudson had attended Tennessee State. She finished last in her heat of the individual 100m in Rome and the only major title she won was the AAU indoor 100y in 1959.

INGRAM, Sheila Rena.
B. 23 MAR 1957 Washington, DC. Silver: 1976 4 × 400 meter relay. While attending Coolidge High School in her native Washington, Sheila Ingram set a U.S. junior record of 53.0 as a 17-year-old in 1974. Over the next two years her talent developed and in 1976 she finished second in the AAU 400m, won the Final Trials, and went to Montreal where she added the U.S. senior record to the junior record, that she still held. At the Olympics, Ingram set a new U.S. record of 51.31 in the quarter-finals only to lose it to Debra Sapenter (51.23) later in the same round. Sheila Ingram recaptured the record in the first semi-final with 50.90 but lost it again when Rosalyn Bryant ran 50.62 in the second semi-final. In the final, Ingram finished sixth and was later clocked in 50.0 when she ran the second stage for the relay team that took the silver medals.

JACKSON, Madeline Manning. (see MANNING, Madeline)

JILES, Pamela Theresa.
B. 10 JUL 1955 New Orleans, LA. Silver: 1976 4 × 400 meter relay. Better known as a 200m runner prior to the Olympics, Pam Jiles was a surprise choice for the 4 × 400m relay, but a 51.3 leg in the final fully justified her selection. She ran for Dillard University, the New Orleans Superdames, and later for LSU and, although she never won an AAU title, she was the 100m champion at the 1975 Pan-American Games where she also finished second in the 200m and was on the winning sprint relay team.

JONES, Barbara Pearl.
B. 26 MAR 1937 Chicago, IL. Gold(2): 1952 4 × 100 meter relay, 1960 4 × 100 meter relay. At the age of 15 years 123 days, Barbara Jones of the Chicago CYO is the youngest female of any nation to have won an Olympic gold medal in track & field. She missed the 1956 Games but in 1960, by which time she was attending Tennessee State, Barbara Jones won a second gold medal in the relay. In Rome she also ran in the 100m but was eliminated in the semi-finals. Between her two Olympic successes, Barbara Jones won the AAU 100m in 1953 and 1954, and the 100y in 1957.

MANNING, Madeline.
B. 11 JAN 1948 Cleveland, OH. Gold: 1968 800 meters; 1972 4 × 400 meter relay. Madeline Manning was the first U.S. 800m runner of truly world class. Her career at the top spanned 14 years and, despite the fact that she chose not to compete for six of those years, she won an Olympic and a Pan-American title, six AAU championships outdoors and three indoors, and won the 400m at the 1966 World University Games.

In 1968, while attending Tennessee State, she won the 800m gold medal in Mexico with a new Olympic record. Four years later in Munich, as Mrs. Madeline Manning-Jackson and representing the Cleveland Track Club, she was eliminated in the semi-finals of the Olympic 800m. In 1976 she again failed to make the finals, which seemed to indicate that her Olympic career was at an end. Although technically true, only the boycott prevented her from making a fourth Olympic appearance at Moscow. In 1980, now Mrs. Mimms, although competing again as Madeline Manning, the 32-year-old who is now a graduate student at Oral Roberts, won the "Olympic Trials" in 1:58.3, which was the second best mark of her life.

During the course of a long and distinguished career, Madeline ManningJackson-Mimms set numerous U.S. records and her 1:57.9 set in 1976 still stands (through 1983) as an American record.

MATTHEWS, Margaret Rejean.
B. 05 AUG 1935 Griffin, GA. Bronze: 1956 4 × 100 meter relay. Although primarily a long jumper, Margaret Matthews picked up an Olympic bronze medal in the relay after she had failed to qualify for the final in her specialty event. In the long jump, after setting a U.S. record of 19'-4" at the 1956 AAU, she improved to 19'-9¼" at the Final Trials but could not repeat this form in Melbourne. She won the AAU in 1957–59.

McDANIEL, Mildred Louise.
B. 04 NOV 1933 Atlanta, GA. Gold: 1956 High Jump. After winning the AAU outdoor high jump in 1953 and both the outdoor and indoor titles in 1955 and 1956, Millie McDaniel of Tuskegee Institute achieved the ultimate in track & field by winning an Olympic gold medal with a new world record performance. For good measure she also beat the former world record holder, Iolanda Balas of Romania. McDaniel later won the 1959 Pan-American Games high jump.

McGUIRE, Edith Marie.
B. 03 JUN 1944 Atlanta, GA. Gold: 1964 200 meters; Silver(2): 1964 100 meters, 4 × 100 meters relay. Although she won her Olympic title at 200m, Edith McGuire of Tennessee State was initially a better prospect at the shorter sprint and the long jump. In 1963 she won these two events at both the AAU indoor and outdoor meets and won the 100m at the Pan-American Games. In the Olympic year, she specialized in the longer sprint to good effect and was undefeated in major races over 200m throughout the season. Prior to her Olympic victory, Edith McGuire won the AAU 200m in 1964 and defended her title at 220y in 1965. Indoors she won the AAU 200y (sic) in 1965 and the 220y in the following year.

McGuire eventually married (Mrs. Duvall), became a teacher, and settled in Detroit, where she has worked with underprivileged children as part of a federal program.

McMILLAN, Kathy Laverne.
B. 07 NOV 1957 Raeford, NC. Silver: 1976 Long Jump. As an 18-year-old recent graduate of Hoke County High School in North Carolina, Kathy McMillan set a new U.S. record of 22'-3" in winning the 1976 AAU long jump. At the Montreal Olympics she had a marginal foul of 22'-4½", that would have won the gold, but McMillan had to settle for second place, that matched Willye White's performance of 20 years earlier as the best ever by a U.S. woman in the Olympic long jump.

After the Games, McMillan enrolled at Tennessee State and placed second in the AAU in 1977 and 1978. In 1979 she won the AAU and was the Pan-American Games champion. In 1980 she placed second in the "Olympic Trials," but was denied a trip to Moscow.

McNEIL, Loretta T.
B. 10 JAN 1907. Silver: 1928 4 × 100 meter relay. The Millrose AA team won the AAU outdoor relay in 1929 and 1930, setting a new world record in 1930 and the AAU indoor relay in 1930 and 1931. Loretta McNeil was a member of the winning team on all four occasions. Her best placing in an AAU individual event was her second place in the 100y in 1929. At the 1928 Final Trials she placed no better than seventh in the 100m, but was nominated for Amsterdam and eventually selected to run the third leg on the relay team.

MOREAU, Janet Theresa.
B. 26 OCT 1927. Gold: 1952 4 × 100 meter relay. Janet Moreau of the Red Diamond AC of Boston was the only white runner on the winning Olympic relay team in 1952 and, at the age of 24, she was the oldest member of the team. Although she never won an AAU title, she came close to making the 1948 Olympic team when she placed fourth in the 200m at the Final Trials.

NETTER, Mildrette.
B. 16 JUN 1948 Gunnison, MS. Gold: 1968 4 × 100 meter relay. Fourth place in both the 100m and the 200m at the 1968 Final Trials earned the virtually unknown Mildrette Netter of Alcorn A&M a place on the 1968 Olympic relay team. After the Trials she confirmed her form by taking third place in both sprints at the AAU

and then in Mexico won an Olympic gold medal and two world record plaques as the U.S. relay team beat the previous global best in both heats and the final. Four years later, in Munich, Netter was the only member of the 1968 team to compete again in the relay—this time the U.S. finished fourth.

OSBORN, Ruth.
B. 24 APR 1912. Silver: 1932 Discus Throw. After winning the AAU and Final Trials that were held as a combined meet in 1932, Ruth Osborn led the Olympic competition until Lillian Copeland's final throw of 133'-2" deprived her of the gold medal. Osborn threw 131'-7" to take second, short of her AAU/Final Trials mark of 133'-0¾". She later won another AAU title in 1933.

PATTERSON, Audrey Mickey.
B. 27 SEP 1926. Bronze: 1948 200 meters. Audrey Patterson of Tennessee State finished second in the 100m and won the 200m at the 1948 Final Trials and, although she failed to make the 100m final, she was a surprise winner of the bronze medal in the longer sprint. At the time that Patterson was at her best, the AAU sprints were dominated by Stella Walsh (née Stanislawa Walasiewiczowna), but Patterson did win the indoor 200m in 1948.

ROBINSON, Elizabeth.
B. 23 AUG 1911 Riverdale, IL. Gold(2): 1928 100 meters, 1936 4 × 100 meter relay; Silver: 1928 4 × 100 meter relay. "Babe" Robinson ran her first race on March 30, 1928, finishing second to the U.S. record holder, Helen Filkey. In her second race she equalled the world 100m record of 12.0 and then went to Newark for the Olympic Trials. At the Trials she finished second to Elta Cartwright and at the Olympics, which was only the fourth meet at which she had ever competed, she beat the highly favored Canadians to take the 100m title and become America's first woman track & field champion.

On her return home, Robinson set a world record of 11.0 for 100y at Chicago in September, then in 1929 she won the 50y and the 100y at the AAU, setting a world record in the shorter sprint. In March 1931, she set world records for 60y (6.9) and 70y (7.9), but was then severely injured in a plane crash. Out of competition for three-and-one-half years at the peak of her career, she made a brave comeback in 1936 and,

although the injuries she sustained forced her to make a standing start at the Final Trials, she made the Olympic relay team and won a second gold medal.

After her retirement she continued to take a keen interest in the sport and, as Mrs. Richard Schwartz, was an official AAU timekeeper for many years. She has also been active as a public speaker, and was the first woman ever awarded a varsity "N" by her college, Northwestern.

ROGERS, Annette Joan.
B. 22 OCT 1913 Chicago, IL. Gold(2): 1932 4 × 100 meter relay, 1936 4 × 100 meter relay. Annette Rogers was the only member of the 1932 relay team to win a second gold medal in 1936. In the intervening period she won the AAU 100y in 1933 and was a member of the winning relay team in 1931–33. Running the anchor leg for the Illinois Women's AC on each occasion, she broke the tape in 1932 in a world record equalling 49.4. Indoors, she scored a 200m/high jump double at the AAU meet in both 1933 and 1936. In the Olympic high jump she placed sixth in 1932 and fifth in 1936 and she placed fifth in the 1936 Olympic 100m.

Annette Rogers attended Northwestern and later, as Mrs. Peter Kelly, taught physical education in the Chicago area.

RUDOLPH, Wilma Glodean.
B. 23 JUN 1940 Clarksville, TX. Gold(3); 1960 100 meters, 1960 200 meters, 1960 4 × 100 meter relay; Bronze: 1956 4 × 100 meter relay. Wilma Rudolph overcame many obstacles to become the first U.S. woman to win the Olympic sprint double. As the 17th child in a family of 18, she contracted polio as an infant and was unable to walk properly until she was 11.

As a 16-year-old she went to the 1956 Olympics and, although eliminated in the preliminaries of the 200m, won a bronze medal in the relay. Over the next four years she developed into the world's fastest sprinter and in July 1960 she set a world record of 22.9 for 200m and added the 100m record in winning the Olympic title in 11.3. The following season she equalled her 100m record in Moscow and, four days later, in Stuttgart, lowered it to 11.2. Rudolph won the AAU 100m for four successive years from 1959 and in 1960 she added the 200m. She also won three AAU indoor titles.

Wilma Rudolph overcame a childhood bout with polio to win three gold medals at the 1960 Olympics.

Rudolph was known to the Europeans as "The Black Gazelle," both for her speed and her beauty. She has made a great impact on women's athletics in this country by both her performances and her promotional work on behalf of women's sports. She has formed her own company, the Wilma Rudolph Foundation, that works with underprivileged children and sponsors athletic competition for children in Indianapolis.

SAPENTER, Debra.

B. 27 FEB 1952 Prairie View, TX. Silver: 1976 4 × 400 meter relay. After graduating from Prairie View A&M in 1974, Debra Sapenter enrolled as a graduate student at Northwestern. At the 1976 Olympics she made the final of the 400m, finishing in eighth place, but got a well-deserved medal in the relay after a 51.8 lead-off stage. She won the AAU 440y in 1974, the 400m in 1975, and finished second in the 400m at the 1975 Pan-American Games.

SCHMIDT, Kathryn Joan.

B. 29 DEC 1953 Long Beach, CA. Bronze(2): 1972 Javelin Throw, 1976 Javelin Throw. Kate "The Great" Schmidt is undoubtedly the greatest U.S. female javelin thrower of all time. She won the AAU seven times between 1969 and 1979 and improved the U.S. record several times, finishing with a world record of 227'-5" in 1977. She attended UCLA and Long Beach State and qualified for her third Olympics in 1980 but, obviously, did not compete.

In recent years, Kate Schmidt has continued to compete, but less often. She now works as a technical consultant to shoe companies and is on the production staff of Trans World International.

SHILEY, Jean M.

B. 20 NOV 1911 Harrisburg, PA. Gold: 1932 High Jump. As a 16-year-old schoolgirl from Haverford High School, Jean Shiley placed fourth in the 1928 Olympic high jump. The following year she won both the AAU indoor and outdoor titles and repeated the double for the next three years, although she tied for the 1932 outdoor title with Babe Didrikson. She was destined to meet Didrikson again later in the season in a classic Olympic final. Both cleared 5'-5" for a new world record, and in the jump-off both were over at 5'-5¾", but the judges ruled that Didrikson had illegally dived over the bar and the gold medal went to Shiley. IAAF rules at the time prohibited world records being recognized if set in a jump-off, so both Shiley and Didrikson were credited with a new world record of 5'-5".

Jean Shiley, who joined the Meadowbrook Club of Philadelphia after leaving school, also set an unofficial world record of 5'-3½" at Boston in April 1930. As Mrs. Herman Newhouse, she now resides in Southern California.

Helen Stephens set an Olympic and world record in winning the 100 meter race at the 1934 Olympic Games.

Courtesy Helen Stephens

STEPHENS, Helen Herring.

B. 03 FEB 1918 Fulton, MO. Gold(2): 1936 100 meters, 1936 4 × 100 meter relay. In her very first race, just a few days after her 17th birthday, Helen Stephens of Fulton High School (Missouri) equalled the world indoor record for 50m and beat the reigning Olympic 100m champion, Stella Walsh. Following that auspicious start, Stephens was never defeated and, although her career lasted only some 30 months, it involved more than 100 races. Apart from her two Olympic gold medals, she won 14 AAU titles in the sprints, the shot put, discus throw, and the standing long jump. She also finished ninth in the discus at the 1936 Olympics.

In 1935 she set world records of 10.8 for 100y and 11.6 (twice) for 100m and shortly after the Berlin Games she ran 11.5 for 100m in Dresden, but none of these apparently accurate marks were ever recognized by the IAAF.

Helen Stephens later turned professional and ran a series of exhibition races against Jesse Owens and for seven years she toured with two professional basketball teams, the Professional Red Heads and the Olympic Coeds. She then joined the Federal Civil Service and worked for more than 25 years at the Defense Mapping Agency Aerospace Center in St. Louis. On her retirement, Stephens, who never married, returned to Florissant, Missouri, and helped coach at her alma mater, William Woods College. She has stayed in fairly good shape, however, as evidenced by seven medals at the 1980 Senior Olympics and seven gold and one bronze at the 1981 edition of that meet.

TOUISSANT, Cheryl.

B. 16 DEC 1952 Brooklyn, NY. Silver: 1972 4 × 400 meter relay. After winning the AAU 880y title in 1970 and 1971, Cheryl Touissant of NYU and the Atoms Track Club, lost her place as the U.S. "No. 1" in 1972. She finished second to Carol Hudson in the AAU and lost at the Final Trials to Madeline Manning. At the Olympics she was eliminated in the heats of the 800m, but her fifth place in the 400m at the Final Trials earned her a spot on the relay team where her 51.3 third leg made a significant contribution to the new U.S. record of 3:22.8. She won the AAU indoor 880y in 1972 and 1973.

TYUS, Wyomia.

B. 29 AUG 1945 Griffin, GA. Gold(3): 1964 100 meters, 1968 100 meters, 1968 4 × 100 meter relay; Silver: 1964 4 × 100 meter relay. With three golds and one silver medal, Wyomia Tyus of Tennessee State is the most successful of all U.S. women track & field athletes at the Olympics. She also has the distinction of being the only athlete—male or female—to successfully defend an Olympic 100m title.

She won the 100m title in 1964 with a new world record of 11.2 and in July 1965 brought the record down to 11.1, having two weeks earlier claimed a share of the 100y record with a 10.3 clocking. In 1968 she again won the Olympic 100m, again setting a world record (11.0) in doing so. Although she never posted a world record in the longer sprint, she won two AAU titles at 200m/220y to add to her three victories at 100m/100y. She also won the AAU indoor 60y three times and was the 200m champion at the 1967 Pan-American Games.

Von BREMEN, Wilhelmina.

B. 13 SEP 1909 San Francisco, CA. D. 16 JUL 1976 California. Gold: 1932 4 × 100 meter relay; Silver: 1932 100 meters. Although the 1932 AAU meet was combined with the Final Trials, Wilhelmina Von Bremen won the AAU title but did not finish first in the Trials. The reason for this apparently contradictory statement is that Ethel Harrington did not qualify for the 100m final but was permitted to run and, although she finished first, she could not be declared the AAU champion. Thus, Miss Von Bremen, a graduate of Western Women's College (Ohio), won the only AAU title of her career.

WASHBURN, Mary T.

B. 04 AUG 1907. Silver: 1928 4 × 100 meter relay. Mary Washburn of the Millrose AA finished fourth in the 100m at the 1928 Final Trials and was, somewhat surprisingly, selected for the Olympics over Anne Vrana, who had placed third at the Trials. Washburn was eliminated in the semi-finals in Amsterdam, but won a silver medal in the relay.

WHITE, Marilyn Elaine.

B. 17 OCT 1944 Los Angeles, CA. Silver: 1964 4 × 100 meter relay. The only AAU title that Marilyn White of UCLA won was the indoor 220y in 1963, but she was in the top flight of U.S. sprinters for a number of seasons.

She placed fourth in the 100m in Tokyo and ran the third leg on the relay team that took the silver medals.

WHITE, Willye B.

B. 01 JAN 1939 Money, MS. Silver(2): 1956 Long Jump, 1964 4 × 100 meter relay. "Red" White began her Olympic career in 1956 when she competed in the long jump and in Munich, 16 years later, she established a record of being the only woman track & field athlete to represent the U.S. in five Olympics.

During her long career she won the AAU outdoor long jump ten times and was the indoor champion in 1962. As her silver medal in the relay indicates, White was also an outstanding sprinter, winning the AAU indoor 50y three times. She also won the Pan-Am Games long jump in 1963 and was on the winning relay team that year. Willye White improved the U.S. long jump record numerous times, finally taking it up to 21'-6" in 1964.

After graduating from Tennessee State, she competed for the Mayor Daley Youth Foundation of Chicago and took up nursing as a career, although she has continued to be active as a coach for young women in Chicago.

WILEY, Mildred Olive.

B. 03 DEC 1901 Taunton, MA. Bronze: 1928 High Jump. After winning the 1928 Final Trials, the 27-year-old Mildred Wiley of the Boston Swimming Association tied for second at the Olympics, but lost a jump-off with Carolina Gisolf of Holland. She won the inaugural women's AAU indoor high jump in 1927 and was again indoor champion in 1928. She later became Mildred Dee, but did not compete again after her marriage. She and her husband had five children, one of whom, Bob Dee, played professional football for eight years with the Boston Patriots in the 60's.

WILLIAMS, Lucinda.

B. 10 AUG 1937 Savannah, GA. Gold: 1960 4 × 100 meter relay. Lucinda Williams of Tennessee State made her Olympic debut in 1956 and was eliminated in the heats of the 100m. Prior to making her second Olympic appearance in Rome, she took the sprint double at the

Willye White is the only woman track & field athlete to represent the U.S. in five Olympics.

1959 Pan-American Games. At the 1960 Olympics she ran in the 200m, but failed to make the final; however, she won a gold medal in the relay. Lucinda Williams won the AAU 220y in 1958 and the indoor title in 1957 and 1959.

WATER POLO

The United States has not produced many great water polo teams. Although it was actively played years ago in both Chicago and New York, the sport is not well known in this country today, except in California. To date, the United States water polo teams have won only three medals at the Olympics—all bronze—in the years 1924, 1932, and 1972.

OUTSTANDING PERFORMANCES

Most Medals
  2 Wally O'Connor
Most Appearances
  4 Wally O'Connor
  3 Stan Cole, Ron Crawford
Oldest Medalist
  33y16d Charles Finn
Youngest Medalist
  20y335d Eric Lindroth

ASCH, Peter Gregory.
B. 16 OCT 1948 Monterey, CA. Bronze: 1972. Peter Asch played on the U.S. team that won the 1971 Pan-American Games title and, after his bronze medal at the Munich Olympics, he won a silver at the 1975 Pan-Am Games.

Asch graduated from Cal/Berkeley in 1971, joined the Bank of America Corp., and is currently president of one of the group subsidiaries.

AUSTIN, Arthur.
B. 08 JUL 1902. Bronze: 1924. Art Austin was a member of the Olympic Club of San Francisco that boasted one of the best water polo teams in the country in the mid-20's.

BARNETT, Steven William.
B. 06 JUN 1943 Los Angeles, CA. Bronze: 1972. Steve Barnett made his Olympic debut in 1968 when the U.S. finished in fifth place. In 1972 he again played as goalkeeper and had an outstanding tournament as the Americans won their first Olympic water polo medals since 1932. Barnett also won a gold medal at the 1971 Pan-American Games. After graduating from Long Beach State in 1965 with a degree in physical education, he became a high school teacher.

BRADLEY, Myron Bruce.
B. 25 JAN 1947 Los Angeles, CA. Bronze: 1972. With six years on the national team, a total of 51 international matches to his credit, and a member of the 1968 Olympic team, Bruce Bradley was one of the most experienced members of the U.S. squad in Munich. Bradley graduated from UCLA with a degree in psychology in 1968.

CLAPP, Austin Rhone.
B. 08 NOV 1910. D. 22 DEC 1971. Gold: 1928 4 × 200 meter freestyle relay (Swimming); Bronze: 1932 Water Polo. See the swimming section for the biography.

COLE, Stanley Clark.
B. 12 OCT 1945 Dover, DE. Bronze: 1972. Stan Cole was the only member of the U.S. team in Munich who had also played in both the 1964 and 1968 Olympics. He won a gold medal at the 1971 Pan-American Games and, after graduating from UCLA in 1968, worked in the commercial construction business.

DAUBENSPECK, Philip Burton.
B. 28 OCT 1906. Bronze: 1932. Phil Daubenspeck of the Los Angeles AC was one of the four members of the 1932 medal-winning team who competed again, less successfully, in the 1936 Olympics.

FERGUSON, James Michael.
B. 27 APR 1949 Kokoma, IN. Bronze: 1972. Jim Ferguson, an economics student at UCLA, was one of the youngest members of the U.S. Olympic water polo team in 1972. Like five of his teammates in Munich, Ferguson also won a gold medal at the 1971 Pan-American Games.

FINN, Charles Thornton.
B. 28 JUL 1899. Bronze: 1932. By winning a bronze medal in 1932 at the age of 33, Charley Thornton of the Los Angeles AC became the oldest U.S. Olympic water polo medalist. Thornton competed again at the 1936 Games when, aged 37, he added to that record by becoming the oldest U.S. competitor ever in water polo.

HORN, Oliver H.
B. 22 JUN 1901. Bronze: 1924. Oliver Horn was a member of the Illinois AC team that won the AAU indoor championships in 1924, 1927 and 1930.

LAUER, Frederick.
B. 1898. Bronze: 1924. In addition to winning a bronze medal in 1924, Fred Lauer was an alternate on the 1928 team. Lauer played on the Illinois AC team that won the AAU indoor championships six times between 1924 and 1934.

LINDROTH, Eric Emil.
B. 12 SEP 1951 Huntington Beach, CA. Bronze: 1972. Eric Lindroth was a member of the UCLA team that took the NCAA title in 1969 and 1971. Between these two championships he made his international debut in 1970. Lindroth graduated from UCLA in 1973 with a degree in physical education. He was the youngest member of the 1972 U.S. water polo team and has continued to play competitive water polo, playing on the national team for many years, including 1983.

McCALLISTER, Charles Howard.
B. 10 OCT 1903. Bronze: 1932. At the 1932 Olympics, the United States was represented in the water polo tournament by a team from the Los Angeles AC. Charles McCallister played for that team; he also made the Olympic squad for a second time in 1936.

MITCHELL, George F.
B. 23 APR 1901. Bronze: 1924. George Mitchell was a member of the Olympic Club of San Francisco and played again at the Olympics in 1928.

NORTON, John D.
B. 27 NOV 1899. Bronze: 1924. John Norton was a member of the Chicago AA team that won the AAU indoor water polo championship in 1926 and 1928.

O'CONNOR, James Wallace.
B. 25 APR 1905. D. 11 JAN 1950 Los Angeles, CA. Gold: 1924 4 × 200 meter freestyle relay (Swimming); Bronze(2): 1924 Water Polo, 1932 Water Polo. See the swimming section for the biography.

PARKER, John Michael.
B. 13 SEP 1946 Newport, RI. Bronze: 1972. For John Parker, a graduate of both Stanford and Harvard (MBA), the Munich Games were his second Olympics, having previously played on the U.S. team that placed fifth at the 1968 Games. He also won a gold medal at the 1971 Pan-American Games. After finishing his studies, Parker established his own investment banking firm.

SCHROTH, George Edward.
B. 03 DEC 1899 Sacramento, CA. Bronze: 1924. George Schroth was outstanding both as a swimmer and water polo player for the Olympic Club of San Francisco. He was on the water polo team that won the AAU indoor title in 1925 and he was the Pacific Coast freestyle champion at distances ranging from 50 to 100 yards. Schroth, who also played on the 1928 Olympic water polo team, worked as a publicity officer.

SHEERER, Gary Peter.
B. 18 FEB 1947 Berkeley, CA. Bronze: 1972. Gary Sheerer won a gold medal at the 1967 Pan-American Games and played on the Olympic team the following year. He missed the 1971 Pan-Am Games, but won an Olympic bronze medal in Munich in 1972. Sheerer graduated from Stanford with a degree in engineering in 1969.

SLATTON, James Walter.
B. 30 JUL 1947 Los Angeles, CA. Bronze: 1972. As an outstanding goalkeeper, Jim Slatton played a major part in UCLA winning the NCAA championship in 1966 and 1967. After being chosen as an alternate on the Pan-American Games team in 1967 he did not play again internationally until the 1972 Olympics. After his college graduation in 1970 he worked as a securities analyst.

STRONG, Calvert.
B. 12 AUG 1907. Bronze: 1932. Calvert Strong was a member of the Los Angeles AC team that, after beating the powerful Illinois AC in the 1932 Olympic Trials, went on to represent the U.S. at the Los Angeles Games.

VOLLMER, Herbert Eberhard.
B. 15 FEB 1895. D. 08 NOV 1961 New York, NY. Bronze: 1924. Herb Vollmer was a stalwart of the New York AC team for many years. He was a member of the team

Courtesy Ed Kirwan Graphic Arts

Charles Weitzenberg was the most experienced player on the 1972 U.S. Olympic squad.

Vollmer started out as a swimmer, like most water poloists, and was the intercollegiate champion in 1915 and 1916 while a student at Columbia. His biggest day came on 17 February 1916 when he set three world indoor records en route to capturing the metropolitan 220y championship. Vollmer later became a wealthy real estate broker.

WEBB, Russell Irving.
B. 01 JUN 1945 Los Angeles, CA. Bronze: 1972. Russ Webb made his international debut as a swimmer, winning a gold medal in the medley relay and a silver in the 100m breaststroke at the 1967 Pan-American Games. The following year he competed at the Mexico Olympics as a water polo player and in 1972 he won an Olympic bronze medal. Webb graduated from UCLA in 1968.

WEISSMULLER, Peter John.
B. 02 JUN 1904. Gold(5): 1924 100 meter freestyle, 1924 400 meter freestyle, 1924 4 × 200 meter freestyle relay, 1928 400 meter freestyle, 1928 4 × 200 meter freestyle relay (all Swimming); Bronze: 1924 Water Polo. See the swimming section for the biography.

WEITZENBERG, Charles Barry.
B. 30 SEP 1946 Palo Alto, CA. Bronze: 1972. With 60 international matches to his credit, Barry Weitzenberger was the most experienced player on the 1972 U.S. Olympic squad. He had previously been a member of the 1968 Olympic team and won a gold medal at the 1967 Pan-American Games. Weitzenberger graduated from Cal/Berkeley in 1969 with a degree in industrial engineering.

WILDMAN, Herbert Henry.
B. 06 SEP 1912 Marion, OH. Bronze: 1932. Herb Wildman was the goalkeeper on the U.S. team at both the 1932 and 1936 Olympics. At the 1932 Games he stopped all eight free throws awarded against the U.S., and this proved to be a vital factor in the Americans taking the bronze medal. Wildman played for the Los Angeles AC for nine years and, before retiring from business, he owned and operated a garage and service station in Los Angeles.

that won the AAU outdoor title in 1929 and he played on the last of five AAU indoor championship teams in 1936 at the age of 41. Vollmer also played on the Olympic water polo team in 1920.

WEIGHTLIFTING

Overall, the United States trails only the Soviet Union in the number of medals and gold medals won in Olympic weightlifting, but that statistic is misleading today because all our success came years ago.

Oddly, after a few U.S. competitors appeared in the weightlifting events at St. Louis in 1904, no American weightlifters competed in the Olympics until 1932. After several years of competitive seasoning, however, and then through 1952, we were the top country in the world in this sport. In 1952 the USSR first competed in the Olympic Games and they have become the most powerful weightlifting nation in the world, with the Bulgarians now pushing them for supremacy. The United States has won only three medals in weightlifting, none of them gold, since the 1960 Olympics.

OUTSTANDING PERFORMANCES

Most Gold Medals
  2 John Davis, Tommy Kono, Chuck Vinci
Most Medals
  4 Norb Schemansky
  3 Isaac Berger, Peter George, Tommy Kono
Most Appearances
  4 Norb Schemansky
Oldest Gold Medalist
  34y62d Joe DePietro
Oldest Medalist
  40y141d Norb Schemansky
Youngest Gold Medalist
  23y27d Peter George
Youngest Medalist
  19y42d Peter George

ANDERSON, Paul Edward.
B. 17 OCT 1932 Toccoa, GA. Gold: 1956 Heavyweight. Many people think Paul Anderson is the strongest man who has ever lived. He had a short but meteoric career in Olympic-style lifting, winning the U.S. championship in the heavyweight class in 1955 and then, later in the year, taking the world title by a margin of 82 lbs.— unheard of in world competition. He won his gold medal at Melbourne in 1956, however, in a surprisingly close competition with Humberto Selvetti of Argentina. In fact, Selvetti and Anderson tied in poundage lifted, but Anderson was declared the winner because, at 310 lbs., he was the lighter of the two.

Anderson has set hundreds of records since as a powerlifter. He has bench-pressed 625 lbs., squatted with 1,200 lbs., dead-lifted 820 lbs., and done three repetitions in the squat with 900 lbs. In addition he performed a back-lift off trestles, supporting 6,270 lbs.—the greatest weight ever lifted by a human.

Paul Anderson is a devout Christian and is a well-known public speaker in support of his faith. He runs a Christian boys' home where he shares his principles. Sadly, in recent years he has had health problems, necessitating a kidney transplant.

BERGER, Isaac.
B. 16 NOV 1936 Jerusalem, Israel. Gold: 1956 Featherweight; Silver(2): 1960 Featherweight, 1964 Featherweight. Ike Berger became a naturalized American citizen in December 1955, and immediately began winning weightlifting crowns for the United States. In addition to his three Olympic medals, he was world featherweight champion in 1958 and 1961, and was the runner-up for that title in 1957, 1959, and 1963. His 1961 world championship victory revenged his 1960 Olympic defeat at the hands of the Soviet, Yevgeni Minayev. He also won two gold medals at the Pan-American Games in weightlifting and has been an eight-time national champion.

BRADFORD, James Edward.
B. 01 NOV 1928 Washington, DC. Silver(2): 1952 Heavyweight, 1960 Heavyweight. Jim Bradford won the AAU heavyweight title in both 1960 and 1961; they were his only major championships after winning the 1950 AAU Junior championship. But Bradford had the misfortune to be lifting against some of the greatest weightlifters in history and his record of second-place finishes is actually quite impressive when one considers his competition. At the 1952 Olympics and 1951 World Championships, he lost out to America's John Davis. At the 1954 Worlds he was second to Norb Schemansky, while Paul Anderson defeated him in 1955. In the 1959 World Championships and 1960 Olympics, the great Russian lifter, Yuri Vlasov, won both competitions over Bradford.

Courtesy Joe DePietro

Olympic weightlifter Joe DePietro shows off the muscles that earned him his bronze medal in 1948.

DAVIS, John Henry, Jr.

B. 12 JAN 1921 Smithtown, NY. Gold(2): 1948 Heavyweight, 1952 Heavyweight. Between 1938 and 1953, John Davis was never defeated. During that period, he won two Olympic gold medals, seven World Championships, 11 National Championships, and the 1951 Pan-American Games gold medal. He was the first lifter to clean and jerk over 400 lbs., and the second man to total over 1,000 lbs. for three lifts. His only defeat before his retirement came at the 1953 World Championships when he was hampered by a thigh injury.

Davis worked for many years with the New York City Department of Corrections before his recent retirement.

DePIETRO, Joseph Nicholas.

B. 08 JUN 1914 Paterson, NJ. Gold: 1948 Bantamweight. In addition to his Olympic gold medal, Joe DePietro won the 1947 World Championships, a 1951 Pan-American Games gold medal, and was a nine-time U.S. and North American champion. He also finished third at the 1949 World Championships.

DUBE, Joseph D.

B. 15 FEB 1944 Altha, FL. Bronze: 1968 Heavyweight. In 1967, Joe Dube won the heavyweight gold medal at the Pan-American Games, but he was not one of the favorites for a gold at the 1968 Olympics. It was expected that Leonid Zhabotinsky of the USSR and Serge Reding of Belgium would fight it out for the gold, with Dube given a possible chance to win the bronze. Zhabotinsky won easily, and Dube only lost the silver medal to Reding because he outweighed the Belgian—they lifted the same amount. This was the highlight of a rather short weightlifting career for Dube, who never won an AAU championship or a world championship medal.

DUEY, Henry.

B. 01 MAY 1908. Bronze: 1932 Light-heavyweight. Detroit's Henry Duey did not threaten the two leaders in the light-heavyweight division at the 1932 Olympics, but he rather easily won the bronze medal. It was the only medal he ever won in international competition.

GEORGE, James D.

B. 01 JUN 1935 Akron, OH. Silver: 1960 Light-heavyweight; Bronze: 1956 Light-heavyweight. Although not as well known as his older brother, Pete, Ohio State's Jim George was a very accomplished lifter in his own right. He was a four-time AAU champion in the light-heavyweight class and won that division at the 1959 Pan-American Games. He never won a world title, but had two second and two third place finishes at the World Championships.

GEORGE, Peter T.

B. 29 JUN 1929 Akron, OH. Gold: 1952 Middleweight; Silver(2): 1948 Middleweight, 1956 Middleweight. Between 1947 and 1956, Pete George ran up an impressive record in major competition. In addition to his Olympic record, he won five World Championships and was twice runner-up for that title. He also won two Pan-American Games gold medals and was a five-time national champion.

Pete George attended Kent State University and then went to dental school at Ohio State. He is now a practicing orthodontist in Hawaii, where he also serves as an assistant professor on the staff of the Medical College of the University of Hawaii and is a past president of the Hawaiian Dental Association.

JAMES, Lee R., Jr.

B. 30 OCT 1953 Gulfport, MS. Silver: 1976 Middle-heavyweight. Lee James was the top American hope for a medal at the 1976 Olympics, but he was still given only a slim chance. He came through with the best total of his life (by 17 lbs.) to capture a silver medal behind one of the greatest lifters of all time, David Rigert of the USSR. James had won only one national title before, in 1976, but in 1975 he had won a gold medal in the Pan-American Games.

KONO, Tommy Tamio.

B. 27 JUN 1930 Sacramento, CA. Gold(2): 1952 Light-weight, 1956 Light-heavyweight; Silver: 1960 Middleweight. Pound for pound, Tommy Kono is probably the greatest lifter the United States has yet produced. Between 1953 and 1959 he was undefeated in world and Olympic competition, adding six straight world titles to

Now a Hawaiian dentist, Pete George as he looked during his Olympic days when he won a gold and a silver medal.

his two Olympic gold medals. He also won three straight gold medals in the Pan-American Games, in 1955, 1959, and 1963.

Kono was capable of lifting well at almost any bodyweight, witnessed by his Olympic medals in three different classes. He is the only man to ever set world records in four different classes, and won 11 AAU championships—in three different weight classes.

KUNGLER, Frank.

Silver: 1904 Heavyweight (Wrestling); Bronze(3): 1904 Barbell Event, 1904 Dumbbell Event, 1904 Tug-of-War (Track & Field). See the track & field section for the biography.

OSTHOFF, Oscar Paul.

B. 23 MAR 1883 Milwaukee, WI. D. 1950. Gold: 1904 Dumbbell Event; Silver: 1904 Barbell Event. Although Oscar Osthoff won his Olympic medals in weightlifting, he was much better known as a swimmer. Osthoff swam for the Milwaukee AC and University of Wisconsin and was primarily a sprinter. In 1906 he set a central AAU record for 100 yards and in 1907 he broke the intercollegiate record for the same distance. Osthoff remained with the Milwaukee AC swim team until 1924 and as late as 1923 he was still winning titles, specifically the Wisconsin state diving championship. Osthoff was an excellent all-round athlete—he was also a member of the football, track, and gymnastics teams while in college.

After graduating from Wisconsin, Oscar Osthoff coached both football and track at Washington State University and then utilized his engineering major in a lifelong career as a consulting engineer.

SAKATA, Harold T.

B. 01 JUL 1920 Hawaii. D. 29 JUL 1982 Honolulu, HA. Silver: 1948 Light-heavyweight. Though his name is almost unknown, Harold Sakata is probably the best recognized Olympic weightlifter of all time, but not for his weightlifting. In 1949, Sakata began a career as a professional wrestler, under the name "Tosh Togo." In the early 60's a movie producer saw him perform and launched him on a career as an actor that would later include guest appearances on "Hawaii Five-O" and "Police Woman." Sakata's best remembered role, however, was as the evil villain, Oddjob, in the James Bond movie, "Goldfinger." During the filming of the movie, Sakata was once asked to put some realism into a karate chop and ended up putting star Sean Connery out of action for several days. Sakata himself suffered painful burns, but no permanent injuries, from the fireworks used to "electrocute" Oddjob at the end of the movie.

SCHEMANSKY, Norbert.

B. 30 MAY 1924 Detroit, MI. Gold: 1952 Middle-heavyweight; Silver: 1948 Heavyweight; Bronze(2): 1960 Heavyweight, 1964 Heavyweight. Norb Schemansky is the only man in history to win four medals in Olympic weightlifting. He first became prominent internationally when he finished second in the 1947 World Championships, behind John Davis. Though Schemansky had several second-place finishes, both at the Olympics and the worlds, he won one gold at the Olympics and three World Championships—in 1951, 1953, and 1954. He won his first national title in the 1949 AAU heavyweight division and would win eight more, ending up with the 1965 AAU heavyweight title. He also won the heavyweight gold medal at the 1955 Pan-American Games.

SHEPPARD, David Joseph.

B. 12 DEC 1931 New York, NY. Silver: 1956 Middle-heavyweight. Internationally, Dave Sheppard was a great lifter, but he was always a notch away from winning world titles. Besides his Olympic silver, he was a runner-up four times at the World Championships. One of those losses, in 1951 to Pete George, came about only because Sheppard outweighed George — they lifted an equal amount. Dave Sheppard did set three world records, however. In addition, he won the 1954 and 1955 AAU middle-heavyweight title and the 1955 Pan-American Games gold medal in the middle-heavyweight class.

SPELLMAN, Frank Isaac.

B. 17 SEP 1922 Paoli, PA. Gold: 1948 Middleweight. In 1946, Frank Spellman finished third in the World Championships, moving up to second in 1947 and finally winning at the 1948 Olympic Games. He had an unusually short career, it seemed, winning the 1946 and 1948 AAU title and then retiring after the Olympics with only three years at the top flight of weightlifters. However, in 1961 he came out of retirement and amazingly won another AAU championship. Spellman has made his living as a professional photographer.

STANCZYK, Stanley Anthony.

B. 10 MAY 1925 Armstrong, WI. Gold: 1948 Light-heavyweight; Silver: 1952 Light-heavyweight. Between 1946 and the 1952 Olympic Games, Stan Stanczyk was never defeated. He won five straight World Championships, in three different weight classes, and six straight national titles in addition to his 1948 Olympic gold medal. At the 1952 Olympics he was beaten by the Russian, Trofim Lomakin, by only six pounds. He won the 1953 AAU title, but finished third at the World Championships in both 1953 and 1954, after which he retired. He has since become a competitive bowler, having averaged over 190 for 25 consecutive years.

TERLAZZO, Anthony.

B. 28 JUL 1911 Sicily, Italy. D. 26 MAR 1966. Gold: 1936 Featherweight; Bronze: 1932 Featherweight. Though a naturalized citizen, Tony Terlazzo was the first American to win a gold medal in Olympic weightlifting against international competition. He also won two World Championships (1937–38) and 12 national titles, the most of any American lifter, with nine of those consecutive from 1937 until 1945.

TOM, Richard W. S.

B. 15 MAR 1923. Bronze: 1948 Bantamweight. Rich Tom finished second in the 1947 World Championships before taking his bronze medal at the 1948 Olympics. His only national title came in the 1952 AAU bantamweight division.

VINCI, Charles Thomas, Jr.

B. 28 FEB 1933 Cleveland, OH. Gold(2): 1956 Bantamweight, 1960 Bantamweight. Chuck Vinci is the last American to have won a gold medal in Olympic weightlifting to date. Besides his two Olympic golds, he also won two gold medals at the 1955 and 1959 Pan-American Games. He never managed to win a world title, but was the runner-up in both 1955 and 1958. He won seven National AAU titles, those of 1954–56, and 1958–61.

WINTERS, Frederick.

Silver: 1904 Dumbbell Event. Fred Winters of the New Westside AC in New York led the dumbbell event throughout most of the 1904 Olympic competition. The event consisted of 10 exercises with points awarded for

---

A ROSE BY ANY OTHER NAME

Let's play the name game here. What's the worst name of any United States' Olympian? That's hard to say, but certainly the most inappropriate name is that possessed by the 1964 water poloist, Dan Drown. The U.S. has not been too good in water polo, but we hope he didn't live up to his name! What's the most common surname among the Olympians? No surprises here—the top five, in order, are Smith, Johnson, Brown, Jones, and Davis.

Some Olympians don't like their names so they change them. Cassius Clay became Muhammed Ali. Walt Hazzard became Abdul Mahdi-Rahman. Michael Riley Galitzen hated his last name so he often competed under the name Mickey Riley. Janet Lynn was born Janet Lynn Nowicki but thought Janet Lynn had better marquee appeal.

The longest name of a competitor (multiple marriages after appearing in the Olympics don't count) would be that of Princess Patricia Galvin de la Tour d'Auvergne. But she has the advantage of a title and an extra name by being married. Limiting it to given names, the longest belongs to Duke Paoa Kahinu Makoe Hulikohoa Kahanamoku, but with Alexander Dalglish Neilson Breckinridge close behind. The shortest full name is that of 1936 basketball player, Carl Shy.

Alphabetically the U.S. Olympians range from David Abbott, the 1928 distance runner, to James Zylker, the 1972 soccer player.

---

each. Winters led through the first nine exercises, but the 10th exercise was an optional one with points awarded at the judges' discretion. Winters did six one-arm push-ups with 105 lbs. on his back, but the judges thought Oscar Osthoff's performance of putting up in a bridge six times, with 177 lbs. on his back, was worth sufficient points to put him ahead of Winters.

WRESTLING

There are two distinctly different styles of wrestling in the Olympics, freestyle and Greco-Roman. Greco-Roman is a form of wrestling that is almost never practiced in the United States and our Olympic record reflects this—no American has won a medal in Greco. The Soviets and other East European countries completely dominate this style of competition.

Freestyle wrestling is similar to the American collegiate folkstyle of wrestling, but the rules are slightly different. It is a derivative of the older form of catch-as-catch-can, which was a style used at several Olympics prior to its being replaced in 1924 by freestyle. In freestyle the United States has enjoyed much more success.

The top performances by U.S. wrestlers came at the 1972 Olympics when they won six medals—three golds, a silver, and two bronzes; and at the 1924 Olympics when they won four golds, a silver, and a bronze in only seven classes.

Following is a list of the top countries in freestyle wrestling, in terms of medals and gold medals won. But two things should be remembered: in 1904 all the competitors were American, and produced seven gold and 21 total medals for the United States; the USSR did not enter Olympic competition until 1952.

GOLD MEDALS		MEDALS	
1. U.S.A.	30	1. U.S.A.	74
2. USSR	23	2. USSR	45
3. Turkey	15	3. Turkey	28
4. Japan	13	4. Sweden	26
5. Sweden	8	5. Bulgaria	25

OUTSTANDING PERFORMANCES

Most Gold Medals
2 George Mehnert
Most Medals
2 George Mehnert, Ben Peterson, John Peterson, Rich Sanders, Henry Wittenberg
Most Appearances
3 Wayne Baughman, Bill Kerslake, Dick Wilson
Best Finish in Greco-Roman
4th Alexander Weyand (1920 Heavyweight), Brad Rheingans (1976 Heavyweight)
Competing Both Styles (Same Year)
Tom Evans, George Metropoulos, Nat Pendleton, Chris Taylor
Competing Both Styles (Different Years)
Tom Evans, Lee Allen, Isidor "Jack" Niflot, Henk Schenk
Oldest Gold Medalist
29y317d Henry Wittenberg
Oldest Medalist
33y309d Henry Wittenberg
Youngest Gold Medalist
22y17d Pete Mehringer
Youngest Medalist
18y261d John Hein

ACKERLY, Charles Edwin.
B. 03 JAN 1898. D. 1982. Gold: 1920 Featherweight. Charley Ackerly wrestled for Cornell University and won his only major title at the Eastern Intercollegiate Wrestling Association meet in 1919 by pinning Sam Gerson of Penn. In 1920 he lost to Gerson, but at the Olympics, Ackerly gained his revenge by beating Gerson in the finals to win the gold medal.

APPLETON, Lloyd Otto.
B. 01 FEB 1906. Silver: 1928 Welterweight. Lloyd Appleton attended Cornell College in Iowa where he was undefeated in four years of dual meet competition. His best year was easily the Olympic year of 1928, when he took the Midwest AAU and National AAU titles at 158 lbs. He continued to wrestle for several more years and competed at the 1932 Olympic Trials, but he made the team only as an alternate and did not wrestle.

Appleton later earned graduate degrees in education from Columbia and NYU and became an instructor for over 20 years at the U.S. Military Academy in West Point. While there he coached the wrestling team for 19 years and developed the physical aptitude examination required of all cadets. For his services to the Academy, in 1958 he was given the Civilian Service Decoration—the first time it was ever awarded.

BAUER, Gustav.

B. 04 APR 1884. Ddi. Silver: 1904 Flyweight. Gustav Bauer won one match at the 1904 Olympics and then lost the gold medal by a decision to George Mehnert. Mehnert and Bauer knew each other's moves quite well because they were both members of Newark's National Turnverein and were regular practice partners. Though Mehnert had much the better Olympic record, Bauer's record in national competition was quite impressive. Between 1905 and 1912 he won six AAU titles at either 115 or 125 lbs., and he was a three-time runner-up at the AAU, twice in the 105 lb. class.

BECKMANN, William.

Silver: 1904 Welterweight. From New York's New West Side AC, Bill Beckman won three matches by throws at the 1904 Olympics, but he lost a close decision in the finals to Charles Ericksen. Beckman was the defending national champion in 1904, having won his only AAU championship in 1903 at 158 lbs.

BEHM, Donald.

B. 13 FEB 1945 Vancouver, WA. Silver: 1968 Bantamweight. In 1971, Michigan State's Don Behm won the bantamweight gold medal at the Pan-American Games. He came close to duplicating the feat at Munich in 1972, but was outclassed by the great American-trained Japanese, Yojiro Uetake. Behm later won two AAU titles, in 1973 at 125 lbs. and in 1974 at 135 lbs. After retiring from competition he became a wrestling coach.

BLAIR, Peter Steele.

B. 14 FEB 1932 Cleveland, OH. Bronze: 1956 Lightheavyweight. Pete Blair attended the Naval Academy, graduating in 1955 and winning two NCAA crowns at 190 lbs. His greatest year was 1956 when he won the Eastern All-Navy heavyweight title, the all-navy title at 191 lbs., the 191 lb. class at the National AAU Championships, and then the Olympic Trials. After the Olympics he retired from wrestling and has become a career officer in the navy.

BLUBAUGH, Douglas Morton.

B. 31 DEC 1934 Ponca City, OK. Gold: 1960 Welterweight. Doug Blubaugh was a two-time AAU champion before he made the 1960 Olympic team. At Rome he

Three bespectacled U.S. wrestling gold medalists from the 1960 Olympics. (L-R) — Shelby Wilson, Terry McCann, Doug Blubaugh.

beat the supposedly unbeatable Iranian, Emamali Habibi, and then had a clear road to the gold medal. For his efforts, Blubaugh was named the World's Outstanding Wrestler in 1960.

Blubaugh has since become a wrestling coach at Indiana University and his son was a high school wrestler. In the late 70's, Habibi became embroiled in the political turmoil in Iran and, although he remained there, he arranged for his family to emigrate to the United States, settling in Indiana. In a high school wrestling match in 1980, the son's of Doug Blubaugh and Emamali Habibi competed for opposing teams, although they did not meet each other.

ISN'T IT THE SIZE OF THE FIGHT IN THE MAN THAT'S IMPORTANT

Olympic athletes come in all sizes. The following are the U.S. Olympian's "size" records.

HEAVIEST	—	Chris Taylor (1972 WRE)	about 410 lbs.
HEAVIEST FEMALE	—	Earlene Brown (1964 TAF)	250 lbs.
TALLEST	—	Tommy Burleson (1972 BAS)	7'-4"
TALLEST FEMALE	—	Gale Fitzgerald (1976 TAF)	6'-3"
LIGHTEST	—	Aileen Riggin (1920 DIV)	70 lbs.
LIGHTEST MALE	—	Tom Mack (1928 ROW)	90 lbs.
SHORTEST	—	Aileen Riggin (1920 DIV)	4'-8"
SHORTEST MALE	—	Joe DePietro (1948 WLT)	4'-8"

Several of the above competed in other years but these are their most extreme heights or weights. Taylor's weight was difficult to measure as most scales wouldn't go that high. He was actually light at the Olympics as he often wrestled in college at 450 + lbs. Sadly, he died from a condition relating to his excess weight.

It is now common for the superheavyweight wrestlers and weightlifters to weigh over 300 lbs. However, the first two American Olympians to excede that barrier were Paul Anderson in 1956 weightlifting and Bill Kerslake in 1956 wrestling. Only one other American woman has weighed in excess of 200 lbs. at the Olympics. This was Maren Seidler, who, like Earlene Brown, was a three-time Olympic shot putter.

Two other Olympians have taped out at 7 feet—both basketball players. Bob Kurland was 7 feet tall when he played in 1948 and 1952, and Mel Counts measured that height in 1964. For women the barrier was 6 feet and it was not until 1964 that it was broken by three volleyball players—Linda Murphy (6'-2"), Mary Jo Peppler (6'), and Verneda Thomas (6'). Since then, women over 6 feet tall have represented the U.S. in track & field, basketball, rowing, and swimming.

Had the U.S. competed in Moscow in 1980, Gale Fitzgerald would have lost her status as our tallest female Olympian as basketball player Anne Donovan was 6'-8" tall, and hoopster Cindy Noble and volleyballer "Flo" Hyman were both 6'-5". Given the current sizes of female basketball players, the 1984 Olympians will certainly revise those records officially, and Aileen Riggin's diminutive figures will also be threatened by several of the girl gymnasts.

BRADSHAW, Benjamin Joseph.

B. 15 AUG 1879 Brooklyn, NY. D. 19 APR 1960. Gold: 1904 Featherweight. Ben Bradshaw was the defending national champion at the 1904 Olympics and he won his first two matches quite easily. In the finals he had a difficult match with 1902 AAU champion, Ted McLear, but won by a decision after 15 minutes of wrestling. Bradshaw later won a second AAU Championship by winning the 135 lb. class in 1907.

BRAND, Daniel Oliver.

B. 04 AUG 1935 Lincoln, NB. Bronze: 1964 Middleweight. Dan Brand attended the University of Nebraska but he really didn't develop into a great wrestler until after college. He was coached at Nebraska by 1948 Olympian, Bill Smith, and after college he followed Smith to San Francisco's Olympic Club, where his potential began to come out. He made the 1960 Olympic team, placing fifth at Rome, and then finished third at the 1962 World Championships. In 1963 and 1964 he won the AAU freestyle title as a middleweight and the 1964 AAU title at Greco-Roman wrestling. After the Olympics, Brand retired from competition to devote full time to his career as an engineer.

BRAND, Glen.

B. 03 NOV 1923 Clarion, IA. Gold: 1948 Middleweight. While competing for Iowa State, Glen Brand won the 1948 NCAA title at 177 lbs. and then won the Olympic Trials. He was not a top pick to win a gold medal at that time, but after the trials he wrestled head-to-head with alternate Joe Scarpello, and the intense daily competition helped him so much that he came through to a victory.

CLAPPER, Charles E.

Bronze: 1904 Featherweight. Charles Clapper represented Chicago's Central YMCA at the 1904 Olympics. He won one match by a fall before being thrown by eventual champion, Ben Bradshaw, in the second round. In a match for third place, Clapper threw F. C. Ferguson in 54 seconds to win the bronze medal. Clapper also won the 1906 AAU title at 145 lbs.

CURRY, Robert.

Gold: 1904 Light-flyweight. The light-flyweight division was not held again in the Olympics until 1972, so it could be said that Bob Curry held his Olympic title for 68 years. He won it by taking both his matches by falls. Curry, who represented the St. George's AC of New York, won the 1903 AAU championship at 105 lbs. by defeating another Olympic medalist, Gustav Bauer.

DAVIS, Gene.

B. 17 NOV 1945 Missoula, MT. Bronze: 1976 Featherweight. Gene Davis wrestled in the 1972 Olympics but caught a terrible draw, losing to both the eventual winner and the eventual fourth-placer, which put him out in the third round. The 1966 NCAA champion while representing Oklahoma State, Davis continued training and won the 1974 and 1975 AAU titles, giving him three in all. His best international performance between Olympics came when he finished sixth as a lightweight at the 1974 World Championships. By dropping a weight, he improved markedly to move up to a medal at Montreal. After the 1976 Olympics, Davis retired from competition and now coaches the Athletes-in-Action wrestlers.

DOLE, George Stuart.

B. 30 JAN 1885 Ypsilanti, MI. D. 06 SEP 1928 Winthrop, ME. Gold: 1908 Featherweight. Although weighing only 130 lbs., the gritty George Dole played football at Yale as well as wrestling. He had a bit more success wrestling—he won the 1905 intercollegiate title, later taking the 1908 AAU championship at 135 lbs. Dole also earned a graduate degree in economics from Yale and became an economics professor as well as a football coach. Unfortunately he died rather young from heart failure.

Following his Olympic medal-winning performance, Stan Dziedzic won a World Championship in 1977.

DZIEDZIC, Stanley, Jr.

B. 05 NOV 1949 Allentown, PA. Bronze: 1976 Welterweight. Amazingly, Stan Dziedzic won his Olympic medal using American collegiate moves rather than adjusting to the international style. Dziedzic wrestled collegiately at Slippery Rock State, where he won the 1971 NCAA title at 150 lbs. He also won the 1974 and 1976 AAU championships and the 1975 World Cup, beating the favored Russian, Ruslan Ashuraliev. In 1977, Dziedzic performed the rare feat (for an American) of winning a non-Olympic World Championship. He has since gone into coaching and is now the U.S. National Team coach.

ERICKSEN, Charles F.
B. 1875. D. 23 FEB 1916 Brooklyn, NY. Gold: 1904 Welterweight. Charles Ericksen represented New York's Norwegian Turnverein at the 1904 Olympics and won the gold medal in a closely fought bout with Bill Beckmann. Ericksen became active in sports administration and at his death was the president of the Scandanavian-American Athletic League.

EVANS, Jay Thomas.
B. 21 JAN 1931 Tulsa, OK. Silver: 1952 Lightweight. Tommy Evans competed at two Olympic Games and is one of only seven Americans to have competed in both styles of Olympic wrestling. Obviously his success came in the freestyle, where he had a great career record. While a student at Oklahoma he won the 1952 and 1954 NCAA championship at 145 lbs., adding the 1954 AAU title at that weight. After graduation he took the gold medal at the 1955 Pan-American Games and added two more AAU trophies to his trophy case. He became the head wrestling coach at his alma mater after retiring from competition, but after several years of coaching he left that profession to become a commercial pilot—his current occupation.

FLOOD, Aaron Ross.
B. 28 DEC 1910 Braman, OK. Silver: 1936 Bantamweight. While in high school, both Ross Flood and his twin brother won state high school championships in wrestling. But it was Ross Flood that became the greater wrestler, and after enrolling at Oklahoma State he won the NCAA title three years straight from 1933. In 1935 and 1936 he added the AAU title at 123 lbs. before losing out at the Olympics to the Hungarian, Odon Zombori. Flood later coached for several years and then moved into the livestock business as an owner of a cattle auction.

GABLE, Danny Mack.
B. 25 OCT 1948 Waterloo, IA. Gold: 1972 Lightweight. Dan Gable is certainly America's best-known wrestler and some experts think he is the greatest wrestler yet produced in the United States. In high school and collegiate competition he never lost a match until his senior year when, in the final match of the 1970 NCAA tournament, he was beaten by Larry Owings.

Gable was already known as a workaholic and the most dedicated wrestler in a sport that requires dedication if one is to compete at the top levels, but the loss spurred him on to even greater efforts. He won the 1970 AAU title (his second) and the 1971 Pan-American Games as well as winning the 1971 World Championships. In a succession of international meets, he beat several Russians, and after Gable was named outstanding wrestler at a meet in Russia in 1972, the Soviet national coach vowed to an American present that, "Before the Olympics, we will find someone who can beat Gable." They never did.

Gable severely injured his knee shortly before the 1972 Olympics, but wrestled at Munich despite it. Gable performed the amazing feat of winning his gold medal by a shutout—no opponent scored a point off him in six matches. In 21 matches at the U.S. Trials and the Olympics, he gave up one point—wrestling basically on one leg.

After the Olympics, Gable competed sporadically but launched a coaching career. He retired in 1973, but came back in 1975 only to lose to Lee Kemp when he wrestled with a pinched nerve in his neck. At the University of Iowa, Gable has become America's top wrestling coach, leading his teams to five consecutive NCAA tournament victories.

GERSON, Samuel Norton.
B. 30 NOV 1895. D. 30 SEP 1972 Philadelphia, PA. Silver: 1920 Featherweight. In 1920, as a junior at Penn, Sam Norton won the Eastern Intercollegiates and the Middle Atlantic wrestling championships. They were the biggest titles of his short wrestling career.

Gerson later became a civil engineer, but a hobby occupied much of his time. He was the founder of the United States Olympian Society, an organization of former Olympic athletes. In addition he was instrumental in helping start a similar world-wide organization, Olympian International, for whom he served a term as president. Gerson also served as historian of the U.S. Olympians and spent much of his time collecting data on former athletes.

HANSEN, Bernhuff.
Gold: 1904 Heavyweight. Bernhuff Hansen won three matches at the 1904 Olympics, all by falls, the first of

America's greatest wrestler — Dan Gable — as he received his gold medal at the 1972 Olympics.

Russ Hellickson moved up to the heavyweight division for the 1976 Montreal Olympics and won a silver medal.

Courtesy of USA Wrestling

HEIN, John C.

B. 27 JAN 1886 New York, NY. D. 29 AUG 1963 New York, NY. Silver: 1904 Light-flyweight. John Hein wrestled for the Boy's Club of New York at the 1904 Olympics. Though Bob Curry threw him in the finals, Hein later won three AAU titles—in 1905, 1910, and 1913. After retiring from competition, Hein became a coach and trainer. During his own competitive days he had boxed often while training, and this helped him as one of the early trainers of Benny Leonard, world lightweight professional boxing champion.

HELLICKSON, Russell Owen.

B. 29 MAY 1948 Madison, WI. Silver: 1976 Heavyweight. Although Russ Hellickson won three AAU titles and three consecutive Pan-American Games gold medals (1971, 1975, 1979), he was never quite able to win the big international meets. Hellickson was expected to make the 1972 Olympic team easily but was upset by Ben Peterson, who went on to win a gold medal. Between 1972 and 1976, Hellickson was beaten five times by the Soviet great, Levan Tediashvili, at 198 lbs., so he elected to move up to his more natural weight of 220 lbs. for the Montreal Olympics. However, he could not overcome the defending Olympic champion, Russia's Ivan Yarygin.

Hellickson is now a coach, and has been quite successful at his alma mater, the University of Wisconsin. He has numbered among his pupils two-time world champion, Lee Kemp.

HENSON, Josiah.

B. 24 FEB 1922 Oklahoma. Bronze: 1952 Featherweight. Undefeated in dual meets while at the Naval Academy, Joe Henson won two Eastern Intercollegiate titles, but never managed an NCAA championship. In 1952, however, he won the AAU crown at 135 lbs., being named the tournament's outstanding wrestler. Later in the year he became the second oldest American wrestler to win an Olympic medal.

Henson served in the navy for several years, but has recently become very active in sports adiministration. For several years he was on the U.S. Olympic wrestling committee, chairing it in 1964–1968. He is the current president of the AAU.

which took him only 23 seconds. Hansen represented New York's Norwegian Turnverein at the Olympics, which doubled in 1904 as the AAU tournament. In 1905 he defended his AAU title for his only other national title.

HINES, Bryan.

B. 14 MAY 1896. Ddi. Bronze: 1924 Bantamweight. Bryan Hines attended Northwestern and won his only AAU title at 123 lbs. in 1924. He was expected to be a contender for the gold at the 1924 Olympics, but was overweight when he arrived in Paris and worked so hard to lose the weight that he was very weak for his matches. Still, he hung on to take a bronze medal behind two Finns.

HODGE, Daniel Allen.

B. 13 MAY 1932 Perry, OK. Silver: 1956 Middleweight. Dan Hodge was the first wrestler to grace the cover of *Sports Illustrated*. Renowned for his strength, he was wrestling's big attraction while a student at Oklahoma in the mid 50's, but he never managed to win the gold medal that was expected of him. He won three AAU freestyle titles, three NCAA titles, and one AAU Greco-Roman championship. In 1956 he won all three, recording 14 pins in 14 matches en route, but at the Olympic Trials he was beaten by 1952 gold medalist, Bill Smith. Hodge was taken to Melbourne as the Greco representative, but was moved back to freestyle when Smith was declared ineligible because of some coaching activities. At the Olympics, Hodge lost the gold medal when he was pinned by Bulgaria's Nikola Stanchev with only two seconds remaining in the match.

In 1958, Hodge embarked on a career in a new sport—boxing. He had seventeen amateur bouts, culminating with a victory in the 1959 National Golden Gloves Heavyweight division. He turned professional and had 10 fights as a heavyweight, winning eight before retiring in 1961. He has since become a very successful pro wrestler.

JOHNSON, Charles F.

B. 14 AUG 1896 Massachusetts. D. 15 FEB 1946 Massachusetts. Bronze: 1920 Middleweight. From Boston's Posse Gymnasium, Charley Johnson won four AAU titles in addition to his Olympic bronze medal. He had an exceptionally long career—his first AAU title was at 145 lbs. in 1909 and his last came at 158 lbs. in 1921.

KEASER, Lloyd Weldon.

B. 09 FEB 1950 Pumphrey, MD. Silver: 1976 Lightweight. Annapolis' "Butch" Keaser first came to national prominence with his AAU championship in 1973.

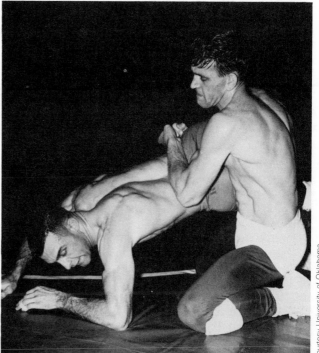

Dan Hodge (right) went undefeated during his college career at University of Oklahoma, but never succeeded in capturing the gold medal.

In 1975 he performed the unusual feat of winning the National Greco-Roman title and the Pan-American Games freestyle championship. Before the Montreal Olympics he won the AAU title again and was thought to be a favorite for the gold medal.

At the Olympics, Keaser established himself early as the best wrestler in his class. Going into his final match with arch-rival Pavel Pinigan of the Soviet Union, Keaser was leading the competition. International wrestling is scored on a demerit system where you earn points for a poor result. When a wrestler receives six penalty points, he is eliminated from the competition. Going into the final match, Keaser and his coaches determined that he could lose to Pinigan and still win the title, he merely had to avoid being pinned. Keaser wrestled with that end in mind and was beaten decisively on points. The Russians were jubilant because the American officials had miscalculated and Pinigan's victory by "majority decision" handed him the gold—a medal that should have belonged to Butch Keaser.

DANIEL VINCENT GALLERY

Dan Gallery was a wrestler on the 1920 Olympic team and was expecting to wrestle for the U.S. in the featherweight division of catch-as-catch-can. But he ate too much! Though he was beating America's featherweights, Charles Ackerly and Sam Gerson, in practice, he couldn't make weight and was forced to wrestle in the Greco-Roman division, a style completely foreign to him.

Dan Gallery was born in Chicago on 10 July 1901 and attended the U.S. Naval Academy. After graduating from Annapolis in 1920, he became a career naval officer and made history during World War II. Capt. Gallery took command of the carrier, Guadalcanal, in August 1943 and on 4 June 1944, encountered the submarine U-505 near the northwestern coast of Africa. They forced the sub to surface with depth charges, and then forced the crew to surrender under fire. Gallery then gave his order, "Away boarders." A boarding party from his ship boarded and secured the sub, the U.S. Navy's first capture of an enemy vessel on the high seas since the capture of the Nautilus by Capt. Warrington of the Peacock in 1815. The U-505 was towed to Bermuda, where it yielded valuable information that led to the cracking of several important enemy codes. codes.

Gallery was later promoted to rear admiral and served for five years as assistant chief of naval operations. He retired in 1960 and devoted his time to writing, authoring several books, one of which was *Clear the Decks!*, the story of the capture of the U-505. Daniel Gallery died in Bethesda, Maryland, on 16 January 1977.

KUNGLER, Frank.
Silver: 1904 Heavyweight; Bronze(3): 1904 Tug-of-War (Track & Field), 1904 Dumbbell Event (Weightlifting), 1904 Barbell Event (Weightlifting). See the track & field section for the biography.

LEEMAN, Gerald Grant.
B. 20 JUN 1922 Little Cedar, IA. Silver: 1948 Bantamweight. Gerry Leeman attended Iowa Teacher's College (now Northern Iowa). He won one AAU and one NCAA championship six years apart, but oddly the AAU title came first—in 1940. At the 1948 Olympics he was beaten only by the Turk, Nasuh Akar. Leeman then went into coaching and was the wrestling coach at Lehigh for many years before his recent retirement.

LEWIS, Frank Wyatt.
B. 06 DEC 1912 Coleman, TX. Gold: 1936 Welterweight. Frank Lewis was the only American to win a gold medal at the 1936 Olympics, but he did it in an odd manner. Due to the scoring system of demerits and the tournament format, which was not a round-robin, Lewis earned the gold medal over Sweden's Ture Andersson even though Andersson had pinned Lewis in their only match.

Lewis was a deserving champion, however. He had won two NCAA titles for Oklahoma State (1934–35) and was voted the outstanding wrestler at the 1935 AAU tournament when he won the 155 lb. division. Lewis has done quite well for himself as an independent oil producer in Oklahoma.

MAURER, Walter S.
Ddi. Bronze: 1920 Light-heavyweight. Representing the Chicago Hebrew Institute, Walter Maurer never won a major championship of any kind. His best finish before the Olympics came at the 1920 AAU meet when he lost to the New York AC's Eino Leino. Leino was a Finn and eventually won a complete set of medals, including a gold at the 1920 Olympics in the middleweight class. At Antwerp, Maurer won his bronze medal by defeating his teammate, John Redman, in the match for third place.

McCANN, Terrence John.
B. 23 MAR 1934 Chicago, IL. Gold: 1960 Bantamweight. While at the University of Iowa, Terry McCann won three consecutive NCAA crowns, starting with 1955. In 1957 he won the first of three consecutive AAU championships, these at 125 lbs. He was also undefeated in Russian dual meets prior to the 1960 Olympics, so McCann was expected to do well and he disappointed no one with a gold medal.

After the Olympics, McCann was recruited by Olympic pole vaulter, Bob Richards, to join his motivational organization as a public speaker. McCann left his job as a bookkeeper and began an outstanding career as a motivational speaker. Today he is the executive director of Toastmaster's International.

McLEAR, Theodore J.

B. 29 JUN 1879. Silver: 1904 Featherweight. From Newark, New Jersey, and the National Turnverein, Ted McLear never finished higher than second at a major meet. At the 1902 AAU meet he was thrown by Fred Cook in 25 seconds. He had improved by 1904, and at the Olympics he only lost in the final to Ben Bradshaw after 15 minutes of hard wrestling, which resulted in McLear receiving a bloody nose. McLear's only other important medal came at the 1908 AAU meet when he was beaten by Olympic gold medalist, George Dole.

MEHNERT, George Nicholas.

B. 03 NOV 1881 Newark, NJ. D. 08 JUL 1948. Gold(2): 1904 Flyweight, 1908 Bantamweight. George Mehnert is the only American to have won two gold medals in Olympic wrestling. In addition, he won six AAU championships between 1902 and 1908. At the 1908 Olympics in London it was said he "showed form quite above any other man in the whole contest, and undoubtedly was the most scientific, both in attack and defense, of any wrestler taking part in the Games." Throughout his entire career he lost only two matches, the only significant one being in the finals of the 1907 AAU meet when he was defeated by George Dole, who also won a gold medal in 1908.

Mehnert was a vegetarian, which probably helped him keep his weight down to less than 130 lbs. Despite being so small, he toured as a professional wrestler in 1909 and 1910. He later was active in sports administration, serving as president of his club, the National Turnverein in Newark, New Jersey, and acting as the chief clerk of the AAU wrestling committee.

MEHRINGER, Peter Joseph.

B. 15 JUL 1910. Gold: 1932 Light-heavyweight. Although he lost at the 1932 Olympic Trials as a heavyweight, Pete Mehringer was named to the team when he cut weight to wrestle as a light-heavyweight. Although Mehringer lost only twice in his entire career, he never won a national title. His best finish in major meets was second at the 1932 NCAA tournament.

Mehringer was much more interested in playing football at the University of Kansas, which he did well enough to be named All-Big Six as a tackle. After college he played pro football with the Chicago Cardinals and toured as a professional wrestler, mostly in New Zealand. Though he at one time wished to be a doctor, he opted instead for the life of a consulting engineer.

MERRILL, Leland Gilbert, Jr.

B. 04 OCT 1920 Danville, IL. Bronze: 1948 Welterweight (tied). In high school in West Virginia, Lee Merrill was coached by Ben Schwartzwalder, who later gained fame as the Syracuse football coach. Merrill took his talents to Michigan State, graduating from there in 1942. He went on to graduate school at Michigan State, although he pitched two years of semi-pro baseball in 1946 and 1947 and turned down several offers to turn pro.

Merrill earned an M.A. and a Ph.D. in entomology from Michigan State and, while a grad student, won his only national title, the 1948 AAU championships at 160 lbs. Today he enjoys a distinguished career as an educator at Rutgers.

MEYER, Fred Julius.

B. 17 MAY 1900 Chicago, IL. Bronze: 1920 Heavyweight (tied). Fred Meyer was a member of the Chicago Hebrew Institute in 1920, but he also attended DePaul. At the 1920 Olympics he tied for third with Ernst Nilsson of Sweden. In the wrestle-off for the bronze medals, they wrestled two 15-minute bouts before the match was called a draw and two medals were awarded. Meyer had an excellent record in American competition. He won six Central AAU and four National AAU titles, including winning both the 191 lb. and the heavyweight division at the 1922 National Championships. He later became very successful as a pro wrestler.

MILLARD, Francis Edward.

B. 31 MAY 1914 North Adams, MA. D. 14 JUL 1958 North Adams, MA. Silver: 1936 Featherweight. Frank Millard was a millworker from North Adams, Massachusetts, who was an entirely self-taught wrestler. Before the Olympics his biggest titles were two National YMCA crowns, but in 1938 he won his only National AAU championship, in the 135 lb. class.

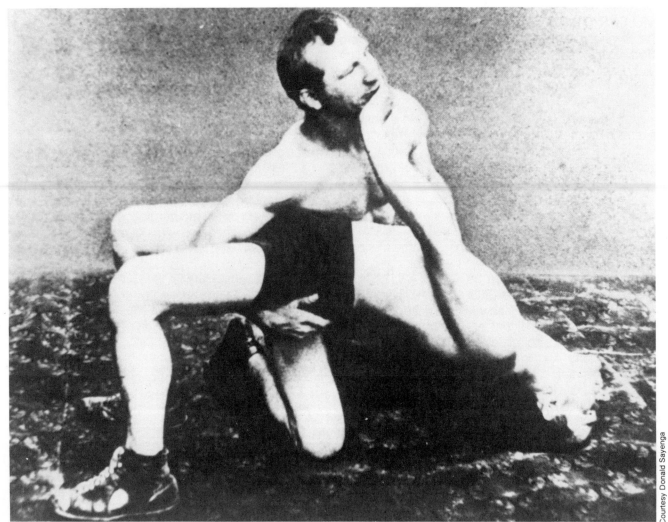

Courtesy Donald Sayenga

Two wrestlers from our 1904 Olympic team. George Mehnert attempts to pin Gustav Bauer, who avoids it by bridging.

MORRISON, Allie Roy.
B. 29 JUN 1904 Marshalltown, IA. D. 18 APR 1966 Omaha, NB. Gold: 1928 Featherweight. At the University of Illinois, Allie Morrison never lost a match in three seasons of wrestling, but he never won an NCAA title. He preferred to face the more strenuous competition of the AAU competitors, but it mattered little, for he won the 135 lb. class three years from 1926. He then went into coaching, both wrestling and football.

NELSON, William L.
Bronze: 1904 Flyweight. William Nelson won two National AAU titles. These came consecutively in 1899 and 1900, and the second one was earned with a victory over future Olympic champion, George Mehnert, in the finals. Four years later, Nelson was defeated at the Olympics by Mehnert's clubmate, Gustav Bauer, in the first round. It was an exceptionally close match that required three overtimes before

Bauer was declared the winner. Since there were only three wrestlers entered in the class, Nelson is considered a bronze medalist.

NEMIR, Edgar.
B. 23 JUL 1910. Silver: 1932 Featherweight. Ed Nemir did not take great credentials with him to the Olympics, his biggest championships having been the Pacific Coast South titles in 1929 and 1930. In Los Angeles, however, he pulled a surprise—only the Finn, Hermanni Pihlajamaki, was able to defeat him.

NEWTON, Chester Willard.
B. 18 SEP 1903. D SEP 1982. Silver: 1924 Featherweight. Representing Oregon State and the Multnomah AC, Chester Newton never won a national title. He was an arch-rival of Robin Reed, who took the 1924 featherweight gold medal away from Newton. At Oregon State, Reed coached Newton for a time, but his intense dislike of Newton caused to him concoct a scheme whereby Oregon State would share their wrestlers with other schools. In effect, Reed tried to "trade" Newton to another school, and it led to Reed's dismissal as coach.

NIFLOT, Isidor.
B. c1882. D. 29 MAY 1950 Long Eddy, NY. Gold: 1904 Bantamweight. "Jack" Niflot dominated the 1904 bantamweight division and easily won the gold medal with three straight falls, throwing August Wester in 1:58 in the finals. Niflot was the favorite; he had won four consecutive AAU championships and when he won the AAU featherweight division in 1905, it gave him six straight national championships.

PEARCE, Robert Edward.
B. 29 FEB 1908 Wyconda, MD. Gold: 1932 Bantamweight. In high school, Bob Pearce was coached by Oscar Berg, who also developed another American gold medalist, Jack VanBebber. Pearce then went to Oklahoma State, where he won two AAU titles. At the NCAA tournament, however, he lost in the finals in 1932 while attempting to defend the championship he had won the year before.

PENDLETON, Nathanael Greene.
B. 09 AUG 1899 Davenport, IA. D. 12 OCT 1967 San Diego, CA. Silver: 1920 Heavyweight. Nat Pendleton

An unknown quantity in the 1932 Olympics, Ed Nemir proved he belonged there by winning the silver medal.

Courtesy Ed Kirwan Graphic Arts

was a two-time AAU champion by the time he went to the 1920 Olympics. The American team expected him to bring back a gold medal, but he was beaten in the semi-finals by Switzerland's Robert Roth in a highly controversial decision. After the Olympics, he finished up at Columbia and then had a short career as a professional wrestler.

Nat Pendleton later became a famous character actor in motion pictures. He appeared in almost 100 different movies, numbering among his screen credits, "You Said a Mouthful," "The Great Ziegfield," "Young Doctor Kildare," "Northwest Passage," "Top Sergeant Mulligan," and "Death Valley."

Ben Peterson participated in three Olympic Games and won two medals—a gold in 1972 and a silver in 1976.

Courtesy of USA Wrestling

PETERSON, Benjamin Lee.

B. 27 JUN 1950 Cumberland, WI. Gold: 1972 Light-heavyweight; Silver: 1976 Light-heavyweight. Although Iowa State's Ben Peterson was the 1971–72 NCAA titlist, he pulled a major upset when he defeated Russ Hellickson to win the light-heavyweight berth on the Olympic team. Peterson proved himself quite a worthy competitor by sweeping the field to win the gold medal.

Before the next Olympics, Peterson won two AAU titles and finished third at the 1973 World Championships. He managed another win at the 1975 Pan-American Games, but lost four times during that period to the Russian, Levan Tediashvili, who eventually defeated him in Montreal for the gold medal. After the 1976 Olympics, Peterson continued to wrestle, winning two more AAU titles and making the 1980 Olympic team. He makes his living as an architect.

PETERSON, John Allan.

B. 22 OCT 1948 Cumberland, WI. Gold: 1976 Middleweight; Silver: 1972 Middleweight. John Peterson attended the small school, University of Wisconsin at Stout, graduating in 1972. At the 1972 Olympics he was defeated by the USSR's Levan Tediashvili, who would later defeat his brother, Ben, at the 1976 Olympics.

After college John Peterson competed for Athletes-in-Action and had his best years in 1975 and 1976. He won the AAU Championship in both years and was a champion in the Midlands Tournament in 1975. In Montreal he defeated another Russian, Viktor Novoschilov, to win the middleweight class. Peterson is now a coach with his old club, Athletes-in-Action.

REED, Robin.

B. 20 OCT 1899 Pettigrew, AK. D. 20 DEC 1978 Salem, OR. Gold: 1924 Featherweight. Robin Reed was America's greatest wrestler in the prewar era, and possibly the greatest ever. In a career that began in high school, and then at Oregon State, he was never defeated, winning three AAU titles in 1921, 1922, and 1924. He was not tremendously strong, but worked endlessly on improving his moves to better himself.

He was also a bit of a character. While hitchhiking his way across the country to join the 1924 U.S. Olympic team in New York, he stopped at Iowa State and asked the coach if he could work out when the team came to practice. When the coach refused, Reed asked if he could do so if he pinned every man on the team. He then stood in the doorway and grabbed each team member as he came to practice, pinning all of them in quick succession. Reed weighed only 135 lbs., but at the Paris Olympics he won a bet when he pinned Harry Steel, the American heavyweight gold medalist, five times within 15 minutes.

After retiring from a short, yet brilliant, competitive career, Reed went into coaching and had a short stay as a professional wrestler before becoming a land developer on the Oregon coast.

RILEY, John Horn.

B. 13 JUN 1909. Silver: 1932 Heavyweight. John Riley attended Northwestern and won back-to-back NCAA championships in wrestling. But wrestling was far from his only sport; he was also an excellent rower and he played football at Northwestern. In fact, after winning his silver medal at the 1932 Olympics, Riley played one year in the NFL with the old Boston Redskins. He later became the wrestling coach at his alma mater for many years.

ROEHM, Otto F.

B. 1882. D. 1958. Gold: 1904 Lightweight. After three straight pins, Otto Roehm met Rudolf Tesing in the lightweight finals at the 1904 Olympics. Though Roehm seemed to be the class of the division, he had a very difficult match with Tesing and was only awarded the victory on the basis of a decision, citing his superior aggressiveness.

SANDERS, Richard Joseph.

B. 20 JAN 1945 Lakeview, OR. D. 18 OCT 1972 Yugoslavia. Silver(2): 1968 Flyweight, 1972 Bantamweight. Unlike many wrestlers, Rich Sanders was not a terribly dedicated conditioner, but he still managed to have a very long career at the top levels of the sport. This was due to his technical ability—he possessed some of the best moves of any wrestler in the world.

Sanders went to Portland State, where he was twice NCAA 118 lb. champion in the university division and twice in the college division. His record in the World Championships while a college student is unparalleled among American wrestlers; he finished third in 1966, and second in 1967, 1968, and 1969. He also won four

Robin Reed, 1924 Olympic gold medalist, who never lost a match in his life.

FOOTBALL PLAYING WRESTLERS

OK, we told you earlier about all those runners and jumpers who played in the NFL. But there have been five U.S. Olympic wrestlers who played professional football in this country.

RAYMOND CLEMONS   1936 light-heavyweight   guard
   1937 Los Angeles Bulldogs (AFL), 1939 Detroit Lions
PETER MEHRINGER   1932 light-heavyweight   tackle
   1934–36 with the Chicago Cardinals and 1937 with the
   Los Angeles Bulldogs (AFL)
JOHN RILEY   1932 heavyweight   tackle
   1933 Boston Redskins
JOHN SPELLMAN   1924 light-heavyweight   end
   1925–32 with the Providence Steamrollers and the
   Boston Braves
CHARLES STRACK   1924 light-heavyweight   guard
   1928 Chicago Cardinals

AAU titles, the first, in 1965, while only a college freshman. His two Olympic appearances brought silver medals; both times he lost to a Japanese wrestler. Shortly after the Munich Olympics, he died in an auto accident while on vacation in Yugoslavia.

SMITH, William Thomas.
B. 17 SEP 1928 Portland, OR. Gold: 1952 Welterweight. While at Iowa Teacher's College (now Northern Iowa), Bill Smith won two NCAA championships in 1949 and 1950, and three straight AAU titles, starting in 1949. After winning his gold medal he continued to wrestle competitively, and at the 1956 Olympic Trials he became the only person to ever give Dan Hodge a decisive defeat. But Smith did not wrestle at Melbourne, because he was taken off the team when it was revealed that he had been paid to coach in an Illinois high school.

SPELLMAN, John Franklin.
B. 14 JUN 1899 Middletown, CT. D. 01 AUG 1966 Mangula, Southern Rhodesia. Gold: 1924 Light-heavyweight. Twice a National AAU champion while at Brown, John Spellman could not get permission from

the dean of students to attend the 1924 Olympic Trials. He went anyway and was refused permission to graduate with his class, although he had fulfilled all the requirements. Spellman was a noted athlete; he was a tackle on the football team, and captained both the football and wrestling squads in his senior year.

After graduation, Spellman became a professional wrestler and football player. He played for eight years in the NFL with the Providence Steamrollers, retiring in 1932, but then coaching the now-defunct NFL team, the Boston Redskins. In 1936, Spellman went on a world tour with his wrestling troupe and arrived in Africa in 1938. When World War II broke out, he was unable to return to the states, and he lived the rest of his life in Africa as a mining engineer.

STEEL, Harry Dwight.
B. 18 APR 1899. D. OCT 1971. Gold: 1924 Heavyweight. Ohio State's Harry Steel was a big ol' farm boy who had almost no coaching, but was as strong as the proverbial ox. He had no experience to speak of, his best finish against good competition having been third in the 1924 AAU tournament, but at the Paris Olympics he came under the tutelage of America's top wrestler, Robin Reed. Reed taught Steel some moves, notably a leg dive that he learned quickly and used throughout the competition. The new skills, combined with his natural strength, paid off — he won the gold medal.

STREBLER, Z. B.
Bronze: 1904 Bantamweight. Z. B. Strebler was from St. Louis and wrestled at the Olympics in both the featherweight and bantamweight divisions. He lost his first match in both, but because of the unusual rules in effect at the time, he was considered to have finished third in the bantamweight class.

TAYLOR, Chris J.
B. 13 JUN 1950 Dowagiac, MI. D. 30 JUN 1979 Story City, IA. Bronze: 1972 Super-heavyweight. Weighing over 400 lbs., Chris Taylor is the heaviest American Olympian of all time. Despite his weight he was a very good technical wrestler, possessed of surprising quickness. This enabled him to twice win the NCAA championship while at Iowa State, and he won national titles in Greco-Roman wrestling. At the Munich Olympics he competed in both styles, losing early in the Greco com-

petition. In freestyle, however, he was beaten only by Russia's awesome heavyweight, Alexander Medved, but in a highly controversial decision. It appeared Medved was stalling, but the referee awarded a point to the Russian, charging Taylor with a lack of action. Later admitting that he felt sorry for Medved because of Taylor's size, the referee was dismissed from the Olympic tournament and banned from international officiating.

Chris Taylor was a natural to go into professional wrestling and he signed a very lucrative pro contract shortly after the Olympics. However, after several successful years, he died in 1979 from complications of phlebitis and hepatitis.

TESING, Rudolph.
Silver: 1904 Lightweight. Rudolph Tesing wrestled for the St. George's AC in New York. At the 1904 Olympics he won several close decisions, but in the finals Otto Roehm was awarded the victory by a narrow margin. In 1905, Tesing won his only national title.

THIEFENTHALER, Gustav.
Bronze: 1904 Light-flyweight. From the South Broadway AC in St. Louis, Gus Thiefenthaler wrestled one bout at the Olympics, and lost, but earned a bronze medal for his efforts.

VanBEBBER, Jack Francis.
B. 27 JUL 1907 Perry, OK. Gold: 1932 Welterweight. Though Oklahoma State has produced many great wrestlers, Jack VanBebber was voted the greatest wrestler to ever take the mat for the Stillwater college. For his efforts he is now a member of the Helms Hall of Fame, the National Wrestling Hall of Fame, and the Jim Thorpe-Oklahoma Hall of Fame.

At the 1932 Olympics, VanBebber represented the Los Angeles AC when he won his gold medal, adding it to his collection of titles, which included three AAU and three NCAA championships. After the Olympics, VanBebber coached wrestling and taught economics briefly, but later made his living as an employee of the Phillips Co. in his native Oklahoma.

VIS, Russell John.
B. 22 JUN 1900 Grand Rapids, MI. Gold: 1924 Lightweight. Russ Vis spent his boyhood in Portland, Oregon,

Courtesy of USA Wrestling

Chris Taylor was the favorite in the super-heavyweight, but lost a controversial decision at the Munich Olympics.

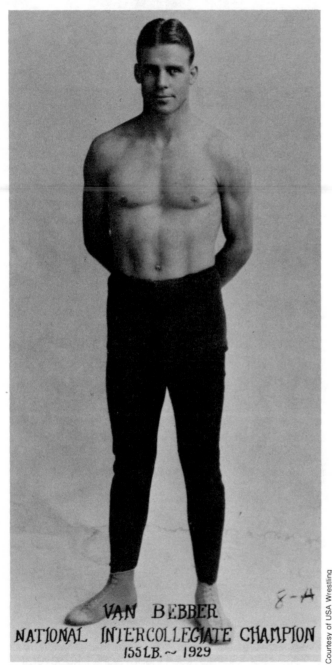

VAN BEBBER
NATIONAL INTERCOLLEGIATE CHAMPION
155 LB. ~ 1929

Jack VanBebber won three AAU titles, three NCAA championships, and an Olympic gold medal during his wrestling career.

Courtesy of USA Wrestling

where he started wrestling with the same instructor who taught the legendary Robin Reed. By the time he got to the 1924 Olympics he had established himself as one of our top wrestlers with four straight victories at the National AAU tournament. In Paris, he came through for the gold by defeating two Finns in the last rounds.

VOLIVA, Richard Lawrence.
B. 18 OCT 1912 Bloomington, IN. D. c1982. Silver: 1936 Middleweight. Although twice a national champion, Dick Voliva only made the 1936 Olympic team as an alternate. He moved up when his form improved in the pre-Olympic training camp, and at the Olympics he posted six straight victories before being pinned in the finals by Emile Poilve of France.

Voliva earned his degree from Indiana University and later coached football and track at Montclair State. He moved on to Rutgers in 1946, and coached wrestling, football, and track at the New Jersey school for over 30 years.

WARMBOLDT, Fred Charles.
Bronze: 1904 Heavyweight. Fred Warmboldt's Olympic career lasted 23 seconds; it took only that long for Bernhuff Hansen to throw him in the first match of the heavyweight division. Warmboldt was from St. Louis.

WELLS, Wayne Turner.
B. 29 SEP 1946 Abilene, TX. Gold: 1972 Welterweight. The University of Oklahoma's Wayne Wells wrestled at the 1968 Olympics and finished fourth. But in the next four years he became one of the world's great wrestlers. In the interim he won a Pan-American Games gold medal, two AAU titles, three U.S. Wrestling Federation championships, finished second at the 1969 World Championships, and moved up the following year to become a world champion. Thus he was a favorite at the Munich Olympics and he came through as expected to win the gold.

Wells graduated from college in 1968 and accomplished most of the above while a law student at the University of Oklahoma. He is now a practicing attorney in that state.

WESTER, August, Jr.
B. 12 FEB 1882. Silver: 1904 Bantamweight. Gus Wester was from the National Turnverein in Newark, where he frequently practiced with Olympians Gus Bauer and George Mehnert. In the 1902 AAU championships he lost in the finals to Mehnert at 115 lbs. This, and his Olympic second-place, were his best finishes in major tournaments.

WILSON, Shelby A.
B. 14 JUL 1937 Ponca City, OK. Gold: 1960 Lightweight. When Shelby Wilson first started school at Oklahoma State, he had trouble just making the wrestling team as they already had a national champion in his weight class. His college career was less than distinguished; twice an NCAA runner-up, his only title of consequence was a Big Eight championship. Wilson persevered, however, and continued to train after graduation. At Rome in 1960, it paid off when he defeated the Soviet, Vladimir Sinyavski, to win the gold. Wilson then spent a brief time as a clergyman before becoming a wrestling coach, now at the University of Colorado.

WINHOLTZ, Jerry E.
Bronze: 1904 Welterweight. Jerry Winholtz wrestled Charles Ericksen in the first round of the 1904 Olympics, and gave the eventual champion a good match before losing by decision. Records have not survived, but Winholtz probably wrestled at least another match to win his bronze medal because there were several losers eligible to compete for that place.

WITTENBERG, Henry.
B. 18 SEP 1918 Jersey City, NJ. Gold: 1948 Light-heavyweight; Silver: 1952 Light-heavyweight. For 13 years, Henry Wittenberg was never defeated in the AAU tournament, winning all seven times he entered. Wrestling at two Olympics, he lost only one match, and he finished his career with a record of over 400 wins and only four defeats.

Wittenberg earned degrees from both CCNY and Columbia. He became a professor of physical education at CCNY after working for a while with the New York police department. He also coached the U.S. Greco-Roman team at the 1968 Olympics.

Courtesy of USA Wrestling

Wayne Wells became one of the world's greatest wrestlers between finishing fourth at the 1968 Olympics and winning his gold medal in 1972.

ZIRKEL, Albert.
B. 23 OCT 1885. Bronze: 1904 Lightweight. Like several other wrestlers at the 1904 Olympics, Al Zirkel trained at the National Turnverein in Newark, New Jersey. He won one match at the 1904 Olympics before losing a hard-fought battle to Otto Roehm in the semi-finals.

YACHTING

The United States has always fared quite well in Olympic yachting and continues to do so today. The best countries in Olympic yachting have been the U.S., Great Britain, and the Scandanavian countries, but it is a difficult sport to evaluate overall because of the myriad of different events and formats used in Olympic competition. As a means of comparison, following is a list of the top countries in Olympic yachting in terms of medals and gold medals won.

GOLD MEDALS		MEDALS	
1. Norway	15	T1. Great Britain	28
2. Sweden	14	Sweden	28
3. Great Britain	13	3. U.S.A.	27
4. U.S.A.	11	4. Norway	26
5. France	8	5. France	22
6. Denmark	6	6. Denmark	17

OUTSTANDING PERFORMANCES

Most Gold Medals
2 Herman Whiton
Most Medals
2 Peter Barrett, Bill Bentsen,
"Buddy" Melges, Lowell North, Herman Whiton
Most Appearances
3 Peter Barrett, Owen Churchill,
Herman Whiton
Oldest Gold Medalist
59y112d Everard Endt
Youngest Gold Medalist
15y33d Don Douglas

ALLEN, William Charles.
B. 20 DEC 1947 Minneapolis, MN. Gold: 1972 Soling. Bill Allen was originally an alternate on the 1972 Olympic team, but at the Games he was chosen to join Bill Bentsen as crew for Buddy Melges and between them they won the Olympic Soling class by a handsome margin. Allen won a national title in the 1970 E Scow class and was 1972 National Champion in the Finn class. He graduated from Colorado College in 1971 with a degree in business administration.

ASHBROOK, Temple W.
B. 23 MAY 1896. Silver: 1932 6 meter. Temple Ashbrook represented the Los Angeles Yacht Club at the 1932 Olympics.

BARRETT, Peter Jones.
B. 20 FEB 1935 Madison, WI. Gold: 1968 Star; Silver: 1964 Finn Monotype. Peter Barrett made his Olympic debut in 1960 when he finished 11th in the Finn Class. In 1964 he improved to take the silver medal and four years later, with Lowell North, he won a gold medal.

Barrett won the 1970 World title in the 470 Class, was second in the 1967 Star World Championships, and was North American champion sailing a Finn in 1966. In 1962 he won the George O'Day Trophy as the North American Single-Handed Champion, and he won a silver medal in the Finns at the 1963 Pan-American Games. Peter Barrett was educated at Cornell and the University of Wisconsin Law School. After graduation he was initially an engineering teacher, but then went into business as a sailmaker.

BATCHELDER, Joseph Laws.
B. 24 AUG 1935 Brookline, MA. Bronze: 1964 5.5 meter. Dartmouth-educated Joe Batchelder joined two Harvard men, John McNamara and Frank Scully, to take a bronze medal at the 1964 Olympics. Batchelder was a member of many clubs, but most of his sailing was done from the Eastern YC.

BENTSEN, William Bruce.
B. 18 FEB 1930 Chicago, IL. Gold: 1972 Soling; Bronze: 1964 Flying Dutchman. Bill Bentsen won both his Olympic medals crewing for Buddy Melges, and they combined to win the Flying Dutchman class at the 1967 Pan-American Games.

Bentsen graduated from Denison, Wisconsin, and Minnesota and undertook post gradate studies at the London School of Economics, Yale, and the University of Chicago. He was later a faculty member at Beloit College for 10 years before becoming a full-time sports administrator with the U.S. Yacht Racing Union.

BIBY, John Edward, Jr.
B. 23 FEB 1912 Los Angeles, CA. Gold: 1932 8 meter. John Biby was a 20-year-old student at UCLA when, as a crew member for Owen Churchill, he won his Olympic

gold medal. After graduating in 1933, Biby joined the Douglas Aircraft Co. and worked for them for 37 years.

BURNAND, Alphonse A., Jr.
B. 21 JAN 1896. Gold: 1932 8 meter. Like his Olympic skipper, Owen Churchill, Alphonse Burnand attended Stanford. He graduated in 1914 and later started his own business as an investment broker. Burnand and Churchill were close friends and sailed together frequently. They went into business together as fruit and vegetable brokers in the San Joaquin Valley.

CARLSON, Robert.
B. 11 APR 1905. Silver: 1936 6 meter. Bob Carlson represented the Los Angeles Yacht Club at the 1932 Olympics.

CHANCE, Britton.
B. 24 JUL 1913 Wilkes Barre, PA. Gold: 1952 5.5 meter. After graduating from Penn, Britton Chance attended Cambridge and has subsequently received honorary doctorates from many other universities, both here and abroad. He is currently a professor of biochemistry at Penn, but is recognized as a distinguished academic in a variety of scientific fields. He is also a well-known boat designer and holds the patent on numerous automatic steering devices. For the 1974 America's Cup Trials, two of the contenders to defend the Cup for the United States were "Mariner" and "Valiant." Chance was the designer of "Mariner" and assisted in the design of "Valiant." At the 1952 Olympics, Britton Chance skippered his boat, "Complex II," to victory with the White twins, Edgar and Sumner, as his crew. Chance's son, Britton, Jr., was an alternate to the 1964 Olympic team.

CHURCHILL, Owen Porter.
B. 08 MAR 1896. Gold: 1932 8 meter. Owen Churchill has been a leading figure in U.S. yachting circles for more than 50 years. The son of a rich banker and oil man, his mother gave him a boat to try and dissuade him from his passion for flying. After graduating from Stanford in 1919, he won his first major race when he captured the San Diego Thomas Lipton trophy with his 53-foot sloop, "Galliano." From then on his successes were legion, but Churchill had to wait until 1928 for the United States to send yachtsmen to the Olympics. He competed in 1928, 1932, and 1936 to become the first American to compete in three Olympic regattas. In 1932, Churchill's boat, "Angelita," won the gold easily by sweeping the Canadian entry in four straight races. Churchill was the captain of the U.S. yachting team in all three of his Olympic appearances and he would later serve on the international jury at the 1952 Games.

After a disappointing performance at the 1936 Olympics, Owen Churchill leased a Tahitian island for two years and, while there, he was intrigued by the crudely fashioned fins which the natives used for diving. Churchill spotted the commercial possibilities of the swim fin and imported the idea to the states, where his "invention" was a huge commercial success.

Owen Churchill was a friend of sporting champions and film stars and married the former Norma Drew, who had appeared in the early Laurel and Hardy films.

COHAN, Donald Smith.
B. 24 FEB 1930 New York, NY. Bronze: 1972 Dragon. Don Cohan took up sailing relatively late in life, but he travelled the world in search of competition and experience and developed into one of America's leading yachtsmen, being on the U.S. team at the World Championships in 1969, 1970, and 1971.

Cohan graduated cum laude from Amherst and then obtained his law degree from Harvard. Initially he practiced law before establishing his own real estate business.

CONANT, Frederic Warren.
B. 08 FEB 1892. D. 24 MAR 1974 Hollywood, CA. Silver: 1932 6 meter. Ted Conant, who was from New Orleans, was the skipper of the yacht, "Gallant," which finished second to the Swedish boat in all six races of the 6m class at the 1932 Olympics. Conant's career was with the McDonnell-Douglas Corp. He eventually rose to be senior vice president and vice chairman of that company, and during World War II he was responsible for the almost immediate build-up that enabled McDonnell-Douglas to produce 30,000 aircraft for the war effort.

CONNER, Dennis W.
B. 16 SEP 1942 San Diego, CA. Bronze: 1976 Tempest. Known for his almost maniacal dedication to sailing sport, Dennis Conner, who attended San Diego State, was the helmsman of the U.S. pairing which took the

Courtesy Donald Cohan

Yachtsman Donald Cohan stands in front of the boat that helped him win a medal in 1972.

bronze medals in the Tempest class at the 1976 Olympics. He was twice a world champion in the Star class (1971 and 1977) and finished as runner-up in 1978.

Despite these small boat successes, Conner is much better known for his America's Cup exploits. At the 1974 trials, he served as helmsman for two boats (at separate times) in the defender trials. Neither boat was chosen, but in 1980, Conner skippered the boat "Freedom" as she defended the Cup by defeating the Australian challenger, winning four of five races. In 1983, Conner was again chosen to defend the Cup, this time skippering the boat "Liberty." Sadly, Conner suffered the ignominy of losing the Cup to a faster boat, "Australia II," for the first U.S. loss in the 132-year history of the event.

COOPER, William H.
B. 04 AUG 1910. Ddi. Gold: 1932 8 meter. Bill Cooper was a nephew of Owen Churchill and one of his sailing buddies. Cooper attended UCLA and later became an insurance agent.

DAVIS, Emmett S.
B. 28 FEB 1886. Silver: 1932 6 meter. Emmett Davis represented the Los Angeles Yacht Club at the 1932 Olympics.

DAVIS, Pierpont.
B. 27 DEC 1884 Baltimore, MD. D. 15 JUL 1953 Los Angeles, CA. Gold: 1932 8 meter. At the age of 47, Pierpont Davis was the oldest member of Owen Churchill's boat in the 1932 8m class. Davis was also well known in the sport as an administrator and served as a member of the international jury at the 1932 Games, in addition to competing.

Davis attended Baltimore City College and the Maryland Institute of Art and Design. Starting in 1910 he formed his own architectural firm and designed many famous buildings in the Los Angeles area. He also helped design the Pentagon in Washington.

DEAN, Peter Sweetser.
B. 06 MAR 1951 Boston, MA. Bronze: 1972 Tempest. Peter Dean sailed as crew to Glen Foster when they won the 1971 World Championships in the Tempest class in Kiel. Over the same course at the following year's Olympics, Dean and Foster placed third. Dean graduated from Milton Academy in Massachusetts and later attended Colby.

DEAVER, Richard Burke.
B. 07 FEB 1931 Huntington Park, CA. Bronze: 1964 Dragon. After graduating from Occidental, Dick Deaver sailed with the San Diego YC and was four times the Pacific Coast Champion.

DORSEY, Karl James.
B. 12 MAY 1894. Ddi. Gold: 1932 8 meter. Karl Dorsey was another of Owen Churchill's regular sailing partners. Dorsey was an insurance agent with Pacific Mutual.

DOUGLAS, Donald Wills, Jr.

B. 03 JUL 1917 Washington, DC. Silver: 1932 6 meter. Don Douglas is the youngest American male to win an Olympic medal in any sport. He was only in high school in 1932, but started at Stanford shortly thereafter. Soon after graduation in 1938, he began a career with Douglas Aircraft and the McDonnell-Douglas Corp., which has lasted over four decades. Douglas eventually became president and chief executive officer of that corporation and has been very active in setting up research and development programs in the aerospace field in southern California.

ENDT, Everard C.

B. 07 APR 1893. Ddi. Gold: 1952 6 meter. As one of the crew members on Herman Whiton's "Llanoria" at the 1952 Olympics, "Ducky" Endt became the oldest American to win a gold medal in yachting. He was known as an excellent all-round athlete who raced in all types of boats, but was especially known as an ocean racer.

EVANS, Ralph L., Jr.

B. 07 FEB 1924. Silver: 1948 Firefly. Ralph Evans was a graduate of MIT and sailed out of the Massachusetts Bay Area Club at the 1948 Olympics.

FINDLAY, Conn Francis.

B. 24 APR 1930 Stockton, CA. Gold(2): 1956 Pairs with (Rowing), 1964 Pairs with (Rowing); Bronze(2): 1960 Pairs with (Rowing), 1976 Tempest. See the rowing section for the biography.

FOSTER, Glen Seward, II.

B. 14 AUG 1930 Orange, NJ. Bronze: 1972 Tempest. After attending Phillips Academy and Brown University, Glen Foster took up a career as a stockbroker. Most of his sailing was done out of the Noroton YC, from which he was world champion in the Tempest class in 1971 and won two U.S. titles and one North American title in the Finn class. While at Brown he was elected as member of the Intercollegiate Sailing Hall of Fame.

FRIEDRICHS, George Shelby, Jr.

B. 15 FEB 1940 New Orleans, LA. Gold: 1968 Dragon. "Bud" Friedrichs attended Tulane in his native New Orleans, where he later became a partner in a stock-brokerage firm. Friedrichs won numerous national and international championships, mostly in the Dragon class. In that class he won the 1967 World Championship; the 1965, 1966, and 1967 North American titles; and the 1966 European Championship. At the 1968 Olympics, with his fellow Louisianans, Barton Jahncke and Gerry Schreck, as his crew, he outclassed the opposition with four first and two second places in the six counting races.

GLASGOW, Walter.

B. 19 APR 1957 Houston, TX. Silver: 1976 Soling. Walter Glasgow began competitive sailing at the age of 13 and he was a 19-year-old Houston high school student when he won his Olympic medal. The U.S. representatives in the Soling class in Kingston (Ontario) were all from Houston. Glasgow joined Dick Hoepfner as a crew member, supporting helmsman John Kolius.

GRAY, Gilbert T.

B. 01 JUN 1902. Gold: 1932 Star. Gilbert Gray was from New Orleans and, with Andrew Libano as his crew, he skippered "Jupiter" to a comfortable victory in the Star class at the 1932 Olympics. Winning five races out of seven, Gray's boat finished 11 points clear of the second-placed British entry.

HALPERIN, Robert Sherman.

B. 26 JAN 1908 Chicago, IL. Bronze: 1960 Star. Apart from his prowess as a yachtsman, Bob Halperin was well known as a football player at Notre Dame and the University of Wisconsin. At the 1960 Olympics he crewed for Bill Parks, a fellow member of the Chicago YC, and at the 1963 Pan-American Games, Halperin won a gold medal as crew to Dick Stearns.

Halperin enlisted in the navy at the outbreak of World War II and finished his service as a lieutenant commander. He saw action in the Pacific, North African, and European combat zones and was highly decorated for gallantry. Halperin was awarded the Navy Cross, the Silver Star, two Bronze Stars, and a Presidential Citation. He was also awarded the highest possible honor by the Nationalist Chinese government.

HOEPFNER, Richard H.

B. 14 NOV 1944 Houston, TX. Silver: 1976 Soling. Dick Hoepfner was a member of the all-Texan crew which took the silver medals in the Soling class at the 1976 Olympics. At the World Championships, he placed third in the Soling class in 1974 and fifth in 1975.

HORTER, Charles John.
B. 27 APR 1942 Philadelphia, PA. Bronze: 1972 Dragon. Charles Horter graduated from Drexel University in 1970 and took up a career in real estate management. He was one of America's most talented sailors in the Dragon class, winning the pre-Olympic regatta in Kiel in 1971 in addition to being the Atlantic Coast champion in 1970 and 1971, and the Pacific Coast champion in 1972.

HUNT, James Hawley.
B. 25 JUL 1936 Boston, MA. Gold: 1960 5.5 meter. Two years after graduating from Middlebury, Jim Hunt won an Olympic gold medal in Naples, Italy, sailing as crew with Dave Smith on the boat skippered by George O'Day. In 1968, Hunt won the Clifford D. Mallory Cup, symbolic of the North American Sailing Champion. He is currently president of a sailboat building company in Tampa, Florida.

JAHNCKE, Barton Williams Benedict.
B. 05 AUG 1939 New Orleans, LA. Gold: 1968 Dragon. Barton Jahncke was equally proficient as a helmsman or as crew, but at the 1968 Olympics he sailed as crew to the helmsman Bud Friedrichs who, like Jahncke, was a graduate of Tulane. After graduation, Jahncke worked for the Lykes Bros. Steamship Co. and was appointed as vice president in 1974.

KOLIUS, John Waldrip.
B. 01 APR 1951 Houston, TX. Silver: 1976 Soling. Together with his two fellow Texans, Walter Glasgow and Dick Hoepfner, John Kolius skippered his boat, "Good News," to the silver medals in the Soling class at the 1976 Olympics. Kolius, a graduate of Houston, went into business in his hometown as a sailmaker.

Kolius first became nationally prominent in 1968 when he won the Sears Cup, emblematic of the junior national sailing champion. In 1983 he achieved his greatest measure of fame—he was selected to skipper the boat "Courageous" in the America's Cup Trials. "Courageous" was the boat that defended the Cup in 1974 and 1977 but was not still expected to be a worthy challenger to the newer boats, "Liberty" and "Defender." However, "Challenger," under Kolius' rein, surpassed the performance of "Defender" and was narrowly beaten out by "Liberty" as the selection to defend the Cup in 1983.

LIBANO, Andrew J., Jr.
B. 19 JAN 1903. Gold: 1932 Star. Andrew Libano sailed as crew member to helmsman Gilbert Gray.

LOOMIS, Alfred Lee, Jr.
B. 15 APR 1913 Tuxedo Park, NY. Gold: 1948 6 meter. Lee Loomis was a 1935 graduate of Harvard who went on to Harvard law school. He then entered the navy and served as a personal assistant to Adm. John Towers throughout the war. Upon returning home he began as an investment banker, but switched to a partnership as an independent gas and oil producer.

Loomis was an avid yachtsman. In addition to his Olympic gold medal, he served as the manager for both "Courageous" and "Independence" during the 1977 America's Cup Trials. "Courageous" won the trials and easily won the Cup, so Loomis ended up as the victorious manager.

LOW, Lawrence Edgar.
B. 22 AUG 1920 Trenton, NJ. Gold: 1956 Star. Larry Low crewed for helmsman Bert Williams to win the 1956 Olympic Star class title. Low, who was a builder by trade, was a frequent winner of races in the Long Island area.

MARSHALL, John Knox.
B. 09 APR 1942 Santiago, Chile. Bronze: 1972 Dragon. John Marshall graduated from Harvard in 1963. He won the North American 505 championship in 1969 but three years were to pass before his Olympic success. At the 1972 Olympics he crewed with Charles Horter on the boat skippered by Don Cohan.

Marshall has also been very active in America's Cup sailing. In 1974 he sailed as a crew member on the "Intrepid" during the trials, although she was not chosen to defend. In 1977, Marshall crewed for Lowell North on the "Enterprise" although again the boat failed to be picked as the defender. In 1980, Marshall was a part of the successful crew aboard "Freedom." Marshall was in charge of the sail inventory and the trimming of the mainsail that year. As president of Lowell North's company, North Sails, it was a job for which he was well suited.

MARVIN, John.
B. 17 OCT 1927 Cambridge, MA. Bronze: 1956 Finn Monotype. While attending MIT, John Marvin was the national intercollegiate champion in 1946. At the U.S. Olympic Trials 10 years later, he tied with George O'Day in the Finn class, but under a tie-breaking rule involving superior secondary placings, Marvin was declared the winner and gained the place on the Olympic team.

McFAULL, David Rockwell.
B. 10 NOV 1948 Honolulu, HI. Silver: 1976 Tornado. David McFaull, a 1970 Cornell graduate, and his crew member, Mike Rothwell, did their sailing in Hawaii, where McFaull worked as a disc jockey.

McNAMARA, John Joseph, Jr.
B. 07 FEB 1932 Boston, MA. Bronze: 1964 5.5 meter. John McNamara was the skipper of "Bingo" in the 5.5m class at the 1964 Olympics, aided by a crew of Joe Batchelder and Frank Scully. After graduating from Harvard, McNamara became an investment broker, but then decided to merge business and pleasure as a ship broker. He is the author of two books, *White Sails, Black Clouds*, and *The Money Maker*.

MELGES, Harry Clemens, Jr.
B. 26 JAN 1930 Elkhorn, WI. Gold: 1972 Soling; Bronze: 1964 Flying Dutchman. "Buddy" Melges, a graduate of the University of Wisconsin, enjoyed his first major success in 1959 when he took the North American championship and went on to a long career as a top sailor. He has won innumerable races and is the only person to have won the Clifford D. Mallory Cup for three straight years (1959–1961). The Mallory Cup symbolizes the North American Sailing Championship.

At the 1964 Olympics he was joined by Bill Bentsen and they took the bronze medals in the Flying Dutchman class. At the 1972 Games, Melges again had Bill Bentsen as a partner and they were joined by third crew member, Bill Allen. With the experienced Melges as helmsman, the U.S. scored an overwhelming victory as, apart from the discard race (in which they finished fourth), they were in the top three in all six scoring races.

MOONEY, Michael.
B. 14 MAY 1930. Gold: 1948 6 meter. In 1948, Mike Mooney was from Oyster Bay, New York, and raced out of the Seawanhaka Corinthian YC. He served as a crew member to skipper Herman Whiton on the boat "Llanoria" at the 1948 Olympics.

MORGAN, John Adams.
B. 17 SEP 1930 Oyster Bay, NY. Gold: 1952 6 meter. A grandson of the wealthy industrial magnate, J. P. Morgan, John Morgan went to Yale, where he briefly played on the soccer team. He has gone on to a career in investment banking, but sails frequently, mostly in ocean racing. Much of his racing has been with 1952 crew member, Eric Ridder. At the 1952 Olympics, Morgan was a crew member for Herman Whiton aboard "Llanoria" and sailed in all the races save one, when he was indisposed and Whiton's wife, Emelyn, took over Morgan's place in the crew.

NORTH, Lowell Orton.
B. 02 DEC 1929 Springfield, MO. Gold: 1968 Star; Bronze: 1964 Dragon. In both the 1964 and 1968 Olympics, Lowell North was the helmsman on the medal-winning boats. In Tokyo Bay in 1964 he had Charles Rogers and Dick Deaver as his crew, while at Acapulco in 1968 he was partnered by Peter Barrett in the star class. Partly for the gold medal performance, North was voted the Martini & Rossi Award as 1968 Yachtsman of the Year.

North, a Cal/Berkeley graduate, was a four-time world champion in the Star class. The 1968 win was particularly satisfying because it came over the legendary Dane, Paul Elvstrom, who had beaten him at two previous World Championships. In 1977, North skippered the boat "Enterprise" at the America's Cup Trials, but failed to be chosen to defend. He is the owner of his own sailmaking company.

O'DAY, George Dwyer.
B. 19 MAY 1923 Brookline, MA. Gold: 1960 5.5 meter. Shortly after George O'Day, a former Harvard football player, had won the U.S. Olympic 5.5m Trials with "Wistful," the boat was badly damaged in a collision with a runaway cruiser. O'Day then purchased "Minotaur" which, coincidentally, had been designed by the father of his crew member, Jim Hunt. Despite this setback, O'Day won the Olympic title by a comfortable margin.

O'Day is one of the greatest of American sailors. He also won a Pan-American gold medal in 1959 and 12 World Championships in various classes. In 1960 he was given the Nathaniel G. Herreshoff trophy for his contributions to the sport of sailing during the past year. Two years later he donated the George O'Day Trophy to the North American Yacht Racing Union, to be given each year to the North American Single-Handed Champion.

PARKS, William Wilson.
B. 11 DEC 1921 Oak Park, IL. Bronze: 1960 Star. In the 1960 Olympics, Bill Parks skippered "Shrew II" with Bob Halperin, a fellow member of the Chicago YC, as his crew. Parks graduated from the Illinois Institute of Technology and took up engineering as a career. In the late 50's, however, he returned to school, earning an M.B.A. from the University of Chicago. He is now a corporate executive in that city and has served on the editorial board of the magazine, *One Design Yachtsman*.

PIRIE, Lockwood.
B. 25 APR 1904. D. 04 MAY 1965 Miami, FL. Bronze: 1948 Swallow. "Woody" Pirie was a member of the family that helped found Carson, Pirie & Scott, the large Chicago department store. He worked as an executive in the store and sailed with the Sheridan Shore YC and the Lake Michigan YC.

Pirie's main interest was ocean racing, but he also had considerable success in smaller boats. After taking the bronze medal at the 1948 Olympics with Owen Torrey as his crew, Pirie went to Portugal, where he won the World Star class title.

PRICE, John Wesley.
B. 19 JAN 1920. Silver: 1952 Star. Miami's John Price was the helmsman of "Comanche" and his crew member was John Reid. At the 1952 Olympics, Price led "Comanche" to four wins in seven races, but the Italian boat, "Merope," never finished worse than second in any race, and a seventh-place finish in the second race relegated Price and Reid to the silver medals.

REID, John S.
B. 27 NOV 1919. Silver: 1952 Star. John Reid sailed as a crew member to helmsman John Price. Reid was from Miami.

RIDDER, Eric.
B. 01 JAN 1918 Hewlett, NY. Gold: 1952 6 meter. Eric Ridder has done most of his sailing in large ocean racing. As a young man he attended Harvard but never graduated. He has spent his entire career in newspaper work, mainly as a publisher.

ROGERS, Charles Sinclair.
B. 01 JUN 1937 National City, CA. Bronze: 1964 Dragon. Charlie Rogers joined Dick Deaver as Lowell North's crew on "Tom Tom" to take third place in the Dragon class at the 1964 Olympics. Rogers was employed by a sailmaking firm in San Diego and he sailed for the San Diego YC.

ROOSEVELT, Julian Kean.
B. 14 NOV 1924 New York, NY. Gold: 1952 6 meter. Julie Roosevelt made his first Olympic appearance in 1948 when, as a 23-year-old Harvard student, he was a crew member on the U.S. entry in the Dragon class that finished 11th of 12 starters. His fortunes improved considerably at the 1952 Olympics and Roosevelt won a gold medal as a member of Herman Whiton's crew in the 6m class.

At the 1956 Olympics, Roosevelt was a reserve crew member in the Sharpie class in addition to being a member of the international jury and chairman of the 5.5m race committee. Roosevelt, who is an investment banker, has been very active in sports administration and, for his contributions to sailing, he was given the Nathaniel G. Herreshoff Trophy in 1962. He was also appointed treasurer of the USOC in 1965 and in 1975 he was elected as member of the International Olympic Committee.

ROTHWELL, Michael.
B. 30 JUN 1953 Honolulu, HI. Silver: 1976 Tornado. Mike Rothwell crewed for Dave McFaull aboard "Zomby Woof" at the 1976 Olympics. In 1974, Rothwell finished third in the Tornado class at the World Championships.

SCHRECK, Gerald Click.
B. 08 MAR 1939 Pensacola, FL. Gold: 1968 Dragon. Gerry Schreck graduated from high school in his native Pensacola and then moved to New Orleans, where he joined the Southern YC. He sailed with Barton Jahncke

as crew under helmsman George Friedrichs and this Louisiana trio won the North American Dragon class championship in 1965, 1966, and 1967 before taking the Olympic title in 1968. Schreck was in business as a sailmaker.

SCULLY, Francis Paul, Jr.

B. 14 JAN 1925 Boston, MA. Bronze: 1964 5.5 meter. While attending Harvard, Frank Scully won the intercollegiate Dinghy championship in 1948. At the 1959 Pan-American Games he won a gold medal in the 5.5m class, crewing for George O'Day, and it was again O'Day who took the role of helmsman when Scully won his Olympic bronze in 1964.

Scully works as a manufacturer, developing and selling ideas to the oil industry in the United States and Canada.

SMART, Hilary Hurlburt.

B. 29 JUL 1925 New York, NY. Gold: 1948 Star. As an undergraduate at Harvard, Hilary Smart won the intercollegiate Star class championship in 1946 and placed second in the world championships in that class in 1947. The following year he won the Olympic title, with his father crewing for him, a unique occurrence in Olympic history.

Although his business interests as vice president of Maridyne International Corp. make considerable demands on his time, Smart still sails occasionally and qualified for the 1981 World Championships.

SMART, Paul Hurlburt.

B. 13 JAN 1892 Yarmouth, Nova Scotia, Canada. D. 22 JUN 1979. Gold: 1948 Star. Paul Smart earned law degrees from both Harvard and Oxford, and while at Harvard he competed in the 1912 Olympic Trials as a pole vaulter. He won his "H" in hockey in 1913 and 1914, and was on the soccer team that won the IC4A championship in 1914.

In World War I, Smart served as a lieutenant in the artillery, winning the Silver Star, the Distinguished Service Cross, and the Purple Heart. After the war, he initially practiced as a lawyer, but later became an investment banker. He also served as president of the Newspaper Institute.

As a yachtsman, Smart won five world championships and a gold medal at the 1948 Olympics crewing

for his son, Hilary. He was an alternate crew member for the Star class at the 1952 Olympics, and at the 1968 and 1972 Games he was the manager of the U.S. yachting team. His greatest honor as a yachtsman came in 1969 when he was given the Nathaniel G. Herreshoff Trophy for his contributions to the sport of sailing.

SMITH, Charles E.

B. 21 OCT 1889. Silver: 1932 6 meter. Charles Smith represented the Los Angeles Yacht Club at the 1932 Olympics.

SMITH, David J.

B. 31 OCT 1925 Salem, MA. Gold: 1960 5.5 meter. Dave Smith was from Marblehead, Massachusetts, and joined Jim Hunt as a crew member under helmsman George O'Day at the 1960 Olympics. Smith graduated from the University of Massachusetts and became the president of Fife and Drum, Inc.

SMITH, James Hopkins, Jr.

B. 15 DEC 1909. Gold: 1948 6 meter. James Smith was from Oyster Bay, New York, and sailed for the Seawanhaka Corinthian Yacht Racing Association.

STEARNS, Richard Irving.

B. 04 SEP 1927 Evanston, IL. Silver: 1964 Star. Dick Stearns won gold medals in the Star class at the World Championships, the Pan-American Games, and the North American Championships. At the 1964 Olympics, the U.S. failed to win a yachting gold medal for the first time since 1936 and their two silvers came in the Star and Soling classes. As helmsman on the Star entry, Stearns had as his crew, Lynn Williams, who was a fellow member of the Chicago YC. Dick Stearns was a graduate of Drake and works in the sailmaking business. In 1968 he was assistant manager of the Olympic yachting team.

TORREY, Owen Cates, Jr.

B. 31 OCT 1925 New York, NY. Bronze: 1948 Swallow. After graduating from St. Paul's Prep in 1943, Owen Torrey enlisted in the army and was called to active duty in 1944. He was discharged in 1945 after being wounded in action in the European campaign. After his return home he graduated from Harvard in 1948 and

Courtesy Hilary Smart

The only father/son combination to win gold medals for the United States while competing together — Paul (left) and Hilary Smart, in 1948.

from Columbia Law School three years later. Initially he practiced admiralty law in New York for nine years, but then set up his own sailmaking business. The venture proved to be very successful and Torrey sold the business to Charles Ulmer, Inc., although he was retained by the owners as vice president and designer.

Because there were no Swallow class boats in the U.S. in 1948, the American entry for the Olympics was the runner-up boat in the Star class at the U.S. Trials. Despite their obvious unfamiliarity with the boat, Torrey and his crew member, Lockwood Pirie, surprisingly took

the bronze medals. Torrey continues to be active in sailing, both through his business and, in 1983, as a sail consultant to the America's Cup trial yacht, "Courageous."

Van BURGEN, Harry A.
Bronze: 1900 Open. The 1900 Olympic yachting races for the two larger classes of boats were held off Le Havre, France, and in the Open Class (over 20 tons), Harry Van Burgen sailed his 102-ton "Formosa" into third place over a course of 40 nautical miles.

WEEKES, James Higginson.

B. 11 SEP 1911. Gold: 1948 6 meter. Like the rest of the crew of Herman Whiton's "Llanoria" in 1948, Jim Weekes represented the Seawanhaka Corinthian Yacht Racing Association.

WHITE, Edgar Pardee Earle.

B. 17 NOV 1929 New York, NY. Gold: 1952 5.5 meter. Crewing for Britton Chance on "Complex II," Ed White was partnered by his twin brother, Sumner, and they became the first twin brothers to win gold medals for the U.S. at the Olympics. Ed White was a Harvard graduate (class of 1952) who, after graduation, initially did investigative work for the army. He has since gone into sales with a large commercial printing firm in New York.

WHITE, Sumner Wheeler, III.

B. 17 NOV 1929 New York, NY. Gold: 1952 5.5 meter. As did his twin brother, Edgar, Sumner White attended the Groton School before attending college. After Sumner White graduated from Harvard in 1952 he began a career as an investment banker.

WHITON, Herman Frasch.

B. 06 APR 1904 Cleveland, OH. D. 06 SEP 1967 New York, NY. Gold(2): 1948 6 meter, 1952 6 meter. Herman Whiton began sailing in 1920 when he was attending St. Paul's School and his love of the sport never deserted him. After attending Princeton and Harvard Law School he was, in 1928, a member of the first official U.S. Olympic yachting team.

In the 1928 Olympics, Whiton skippered his 6m yacht, "Frieda," which he named after his mother, the Countess Frieda Frasch. Whiton finished sixth out of 13 starters, and this was the best placing of any American boat in the 1928 Olympic sailing regatta. Twenty years later, Whiton won the gold medal at the 1948 Olympics, sailing "Llanoria," and in 1952 he again took "Llanoria" to Europe and successfully defended his Olympic title. In one race in 1952, his wife, Emelyn Whiton, filled in as a crew member when John Morgan was too ill to sail.

"Swede" Whiton graduated from Princeton in 1926 and later took postgraduate work at Harvard and Columbia's department of geology. He was president of the Union Sulphur & Oil Corp. and was generous in assisting those less well placed financially to take up the sport of sailing. On one occasion he purchased eight boats to endow a series of nautical summer courses.

WILLIAMS, Herbert Philip.

B. 24 JUL 1908 Hove, England. Gold: 1956 Star. The English-born Herb Williams later became an American citizen and attended DePaul and Northwestern. As helmsman at the 1956 Olympics he had Larry Low as his crew, and in winning the gold medals they beat the defending champions, Agostino Straulino and Nicolo Rode of Italy. Before his business retirement, Williams worked as an executive in the coal industry.

WILLIAMS, Lynn Alfred, III.

B. 29 JUN 1939 Evanston, IL. Silver: 1964 Star. Lynn Williams (crew) and Dick Stearns (helmsman) formed a pairing from the Chicago YC to take the silver medals in the Star class at the 1964 Olympics. Williams was a graduate of the University of Chicago and was an engineer by profession.

APPENDIX I–
OLYMPIC RECORDS

In the following we list the U.S. record or top performance, the second best, and other noteworthy performances. In addition, to show how the United States athletes have fared against the rest of the world, we list the absolute best Olympic performance if not already held by an American.

OVERALL

Most Appearances—Men

8 Raimondo d'Inzeo (EQU-ITA) 1948, 1952, 1956, 1960, 1964, 1968, 1972, 1976
6 Norman Armitage (FEN) 1928, 1932, 1936, 1948, 1952, 1956
  Frank Chapot (EQU) 1956, 1960, 1964, 1968, 1972, 1976
  Bill McMillan (SHO) 1952, 1960, 1964, 1968, 1972, 1976
5 Albert Axelrod (FEN) 1952, 1956, 1960, 1964, 1968
  Michael Plumb (EQU) 1960, 1964, 1968, 1972, 1976
  Bill Steinkraus (EQU) 1952, 1956, 1960, 1968, 1972
  Willie Davenport (TAF) 1964, 1968, 1972, 1976, (BOB) 1980

Most Appearances—Women

6 Janice-Lee Romary (FEN) 1948, 1952, 1956, 1960, 1964, 1968
  Lia Manoliu (TAF–ROM) 1952, 1956, 1960, 1964, 1968, 1972
5 Willye White (TAF) 1956, 1960, 1964, 1968, 1972
  Olga Connolly (TAF) 1956(CZE), 1960, 1964, 1968, 1972
4 Juno Stover Irwin (DIV) 1948, 1952, 1956, 1960
  Harriet King (FEN) 1960, 1964, 1968, 1972
  Maxine Mitchell (FEN) 1952, 1956, 1960, 1968
  Martha Watson (TAF) 1964, 1968, 1972, 1976

Most Appearances—Winter Games, Men

4 James Bickford (BOB) 1936, 1948, 1952, 1956
  Laurence Damon (NSK) 1956, 1964, 1968, (BIA) 1960
  Record shared with several non-Americans
3 Fourteen Americans tied

Most Appearances—Winter Games, Women

4 Sonja Henie (FSK-NOR) 1924, 1928, 1932, 1936
  Galina Koulakova (NSK-URS) 1968, 1972, 1976, 1980
3 Eight Americans tied

Most Years Between Appearances—Men

40 Ivan Ossier (FEN-DAN) 1908–1948
   Magnus Konow (YAC-NOR) 1908–1948
28 Norman Armitage (FEN) 1928–1956
24 Herman Whiton (YAC) 1928–1952
   Bill McMillan (SHO) 1952–1976

Note: Ralph Craig competed for the U.S. in 1912 in track and field. He also made the 1948 U.S. Olympic team as a yachtsman—a 36-year gap between his appearances on the team. However, in 1948 he served only as an alternate in the yachting events and did not compete.

Most Years Between Appearances—Women

24 Ellen Muller-Preiss (FEN-AUT) 1932–1956
20 Janice-Lee Romary (FEN) 1948–1968
16 Willye White (TAF) 1956–1972
   Olga Connolly (TAF) 1956–1972
   Maxine Mitchell (FEN) 1952–1968

Most Years Between Appearances—Winter Games, Men

20 James Bickford (BOB) 1936–1956
   John Heaton (BOB) 1928–1948
   Record shared with several non-Americans

Most Years Between Appearances—Winter Games, Women

12 Jeanne Omelenchuk (SSK) 1960–1972
   Sonja Henie (FSK-NOR) 1924–1936
   Galina Koulakova (NSK-URS) 1968–1980

OUTSTANDING PERFORMANCES: SUMMER OLYMPICS

Most Gold Medals—Total, Men
10 Ray Ewry (TAF)
 9 Mark Spitz (SWI)

Most Gold Medals—Total, Men, Individual
10 Ray Ewry (TAF)
 5 Martin Sheridan (TAF)

Most Gold Medals—Games, Men
 7 Mark Spitz (1972 SWI)
 5 Anton Heida (1904 GYM)
    Willis Lee (1920 SHO)

Most Gold Medals—Games, Men, Individual
 4 Nikolai Andrianov (1976 GYM-URS)
    Anton Heida (1904 GYM)
    Marcus Hurley (1904 CYC)
    Alvin Kraenzlein (1900 TAF)
    Mark Spitz (1972 SWI)

Most Gold Medals—Total, Women
 9 Larisa Latynina (GYM-URS)
 4 Pat McCormick (DIV)
 3 Ten Americans tied

Most Gold Medals—Total, Women, Individual
 7 Vera Caslavska (GYM-CZE)
 4 Patricia McCormick (DIV)
 3 Debbie Meyer (SWI)

Most Gold Medals—Games, Women
 4 Vera Caslavska (1968 GYM-CZE)
    Larisa Latynina (1956 GYM-URS)
    Agnes Keleti (1956 GYM-HUN)
    Kornelia Ender (1976 SWI-GDR)
    Fanny Blankers-Koen (1948 TAF-HOL)
 3 Melissa Belote (1972 SWI)
    Ethelda Bleibtrey (1920 SWI)
    Helen Madison (1932 SWI)
    Debbie Meyer (1968 SWI)
    Sandra Neilsen (1972 SWI)
    Wilma Rudolph (1960 TAF)

Sharon Stouder (1964 SWI)
Chris Von Saltza (1960 SWI)

Most Gold Medals—Games, Women, Individual
 4 Vera Caslavska (1968 GYM-CZE)
    Fanny Blankers-Koen (1948 TAF-HOL)
 3 Debbie Meyer (1968 SWI)
    Ethelda Bleibtrey (1920 SWI)
    "Babe" Didrikson (1932 TAF)
    Lida Scott Howell (1904 ARC)
    Claudia Kolb (1968 SWI)
    Helen Madison (1932 SWI)
    Pat McCormick (1952/56 DIV)
    Melissa Belote (1972 SWI)
    Wilma Rudolph (1960 TAF)

Most Medals—Total, Men
15 Nikolai Andrianov (GYM-URS)
11 Carl Osburn (SHO)
    Mark Spitz (SWI)

Most Medals—Total, Men, Individual
12 Nikolai Andrianov (GYM-URS)
10 Ray Ewry (TAF)
 9 Martin Sheridan (TAF)

Most Medals—Games, Men
 8 Alexander Ditiatin (1980 GYM-URS)
 7 Willis Lee (1920 SHO)
    Mark Spitz (1972 SWI)
    Lloyd Spooner (1920 SHO)

Most Medals—Games, Men, Individual
 7 Alexander Ditiatin (1980 GYM-URS)
 6 Burton Downing (1904 CYC)
    George Eyser (1904 GYM)
    Anton Heida (1904 GYM)

Most Medals—Total, Women
18 Larisa Latynina (GYM-URS)
 8 Shirley Babashoff (SWI)
 4 Twelve Americans tied

Most Medals—Total, Women, Individual
14 Larisa Latynina (GYM-URS)
 5 Shirley Babashoff (SWI)

4 Georgia Coleman (DIV)
  Pat McCormick (DIV)
  Paula Jean Myers-Pope (DIV)
  Dorothy Poynton-Hill (DIV)

Most Medals—Games, Women
7 Maria Gorochovskaya (1952 GYM-URS)
5 Shirley Babashoff (1976 SWI)
4 Kathy Ellis (1964 SWI)
  Jan Henne (1968 SWI)
  Sue Pederson (1968 SWI)
  Sharon Stouder (1964 SWI)
  Chris Von Saltza (1960 SWI)

Most Medals—Games, Women, Individual
5 Vera Caslavska (1968 GYM-CZE)
  Larisa Latynina (1956/60/64 GYM-URS)
  Maria Gorochovskaya (1952 GYM-URS)
3 Shirley Babashoff (1976 SWI)
  "Babe" Didrikson (1932 TAF)
  Jan Henne (1968 SWI)
  Debbie Meyer (1968 SWI)

Most Silver Medals—Total
6 Shirley Babashoff (SWI)
  Alexander Ditiatin (GYM-URS)
  Mikhail Voronin (GYM-URS)
4 Carl Osburn (SHO)
  J. Michael Plumb (EQU)

Most Bronze Medals—Total
6 Heikki Savolainen (GYM-FIN)
4 William Merz (GYM)
3 Teddy Billington (CYC)
  George Breen (SWI)
  George Calnan (FEN)
  Frank Kungler (TAF/WRE/WLT)

OUTSTANDING PERFORMANCES: WINTER OLYMPICS

Most Gold Medals—Total, Men
5 Eric Heiden (SSK)
  Clas Thunberg (SSK-FIN)
2 Dick Button (FSK)
  Billy Fiske (BOB)
  Clifford Gray (BOB)
  Irving Jaffee (SSK)
  Jack Shea (SSK)

Most Gold Medals—Total, Men, Individual
5 Eric Heiden (SSK)
  Clas Thunberg (SSK-FIN)
2 Dick Button (FSK)
  Jack Shea (SSK)
  Irving Jaffee (SSK)

Most Gold Medals—Games, Men
5 Eric Heiden (1980 SSK)
2 Irving Jaffee (1932 SSK)
  Jack Shea (1932 SSK)

Most Gold Medals—Games, Men, Individual
5 Eric Heiden (1980 SSK)
2 Irving Jaffee (1932 SSK)
  Jack Shea (1932 SSK)

Most Gold Medals—Total, Women
6 Lidia Skoblikova (SSK-URS)
2 Andrea Mead Lawrence (ASK)
1 Nine Americans tied

Most Gold Medals—Total, Women, Individual
6 Lidia Skoblikova (SSK-URS)
2 Andrea Mead Lawrence (ASK)
1 Nine Americans tied

Most Gold Medals—Games, Women
4 Lidia Skoblikova (1964 SSK-URS)
2 Andrea Mead Lawrence (1952 ASK)
1 Nine Americans tied

Most Gold Medals—Games, Women, Individual
    4 Lidia Skoblikova (1964 SSK-URS)
    2 Andrea Mead Lawrence (1952 ASK)
    1 Nine Americans tied

Most Medals—Total, Men
    9 Sixten Jernberg (NSK-SWE)
    5 Eric Heiden (SSK)
    3 John Heaton (BOB)
       Pat Martin (BOB)

Most Medals—Total, Men, Individual
    7 Ivar Ballangrud (SSK-NOR)
       Sixten Jernberg (NSK-SWE)
       Clas Thunberg (SSK-FIN)
    5 Eric Heiden (SSK)
    2 Eight Americans tied

Most Medals—Games, Men
    5 Eric Heiden (1980 SSK)
    2 Stanley Benham (1952 BOB)
       Irving Jaffee (1932 SSK)
       Pat Martin (1952 BOB)
       Jack Shea (1932 SSK)

Most Medals—Games, Men, Individual
    5 Eric Heiden (1980 SSK)
    2 Irving Jaffee (1932 SSK)
       Jack Shea (1932 SSK)

Most Medals—Total, Women
    8 Galina Koulakova (NSK-URS)
    4 Dianne Holum (SSK)
    3 Beatrix Loughran (FSK)
       Leah Poulos Mueller (SSK)
       Sheila Young (SSK)

Most Medals—Total, Women, Individual
    6 Lidia Skoblikova (SSK-URS)
    4 Dianne Holum (SSK)
    3 Leah Poulos-Mueller (SSK)

Most Medals—Games, Women
    4 Lidia Skoblikova (1964 SSK-URS)
       Tatiana Averina (1976 SSK-URS)
    3 Sheila Young (1976 SSK)
    2 Gretchen Fraser (1948 ASK)
       Anne Henning (1972 SSK)
       Dianne Holum (1972/76 SSK)
       Andrea Mead-Lawrence (1952 ASK)
       Penny Pitou (1960 ASK)
       Jean Saubert (1964 ASK)

Most Medals—Games, Women, Individual
    4 Lidia Skoblikova (1964 SSK-URS)
       Tatiana Averina (1976 SSK-URS)
    3 Sheila Young (1976 SSK)
    2 Gretchen Fraser (1948 ASK)
       Anne Henning (1972 SSK)
       Dianne Holum (1972/76 SSK)
       Andrea Mead-Lawrence (1952 ASK)
       Penny Pitou (1960 ASK)
       Jean Saubert (1964 ASK)

AGE RECORDS: SUMMER OLYMPICS

We again list the overall Olympic record first, followed by the top U.S. performance. For these records we list only the best U.S. performance, unless it is held by an archer from 1904—which occurs in several cases. For those marks we list a second best mark because some sources do not consider archery to have been an official Olympic event in 1904.

Youngest Gold Medalist—Men
   c8y Unknown French boy (1900 ROW)
        (coxed a Dutch crew)
   16y161d Jackie Fields (1924 BOX)

Oldest Gold Medalist—Men
   64y258d Oscar Swahn (1912 SHO-SWE)
   64y2d Galen Spencer (1904 ARC)
   59y112d Everard Endt (1952 YAC)

Youngest Gold Medalist—Women
   13y268d Marjorie Gestring (1936 DIV)

Oldest Gold Medalist—Women
45y13d Lis Linsenhoff (1972 EQU-FRG)
45y23d Lida Howell (1904 ARC)
42y40d Doreen Wilbur (1972 ARC)

Youngest Medalist—Men
c8y Unknown French boy (1900 ROW)
(coxed a Dutch crew)
15y40d Donald Douglas (1932 YAC)

Oldest Medalist—Men
72y280d Oscar Swahn (1920 SHO-SWE)
68y194d Samuel Duvall (1904 ARC)
60y90d Walter Winans (1912 SHO)

Youngest Medalist—Women
12y24d Inge Sorensen (1936 SWI-DAN)
13y23d Dorothy Poynton (1936 DIV)

Oldest Medalist—Women
46y258d Maud von Rosen (1972 EQU-SWE)
45y23d Lida Howell (1904 ARC)
43y339d Edith Master (1976 EQU)

Youngest Participant—Men
c8y Unknown French boy (1900 ROW)
(coxed a Dutch crew)
13y56d William Horton, Jr. (1952 YAC)

Oldest Participant—Men
72y280d Oscar Swahn (1920 SHO-SWE)
68y194d Samuel Duvall (1904 ARC)
61y152d Henry Allen (1920 EQU)

Youngest Participant—Women
11y328d Liana Vicens (1968 SWI-PUR)
13y23d Dorothy Poynton (1936 DIV)

Oldest Participant—Women
70y5d Hilda Johnstone (1972 EQU-GBR)
55y289d Kyra Downton (1968 EQU)

AGE RECORDS:
WINTER OLYMPICS

Youngest Gold Medalist—Men
16y260d Billy Fiske (1928 BOB)

Oldest Gold Medalist—Men
47y218d Giacomo Conti (1956 BOB-ITA)
43y58d Francis Tyler (1948 BOB)

Youngest Gold Medalist—Women
15y128d Maxi Herber (1936 FSK-GER)
16y177d Anne Henning (1972 SSK)

Oldest Gold Medalist—Women
35y276d Ludovika Jakobsson (1920 FSK-FIN)
28y359d Gretchen Fraser (1948 ASK)

Youngest Medalist—Men
14y363d Scott Allen (1964 FSK)

Oldest Medalist—Men
47y218d Giacomo Conti (1956 BOB-ITA)
43y58d Francis Tyler (1948 BOB)

Youngest Medalist—Women
15y79d Cecilia Colledge (1936 FSK-GBR)
16y13d Carol Heiss (1956 FSK)

Oldest Medalist—Women
39y190d Ludovika Jakobsson (1924 FSK-FIN)
31y227d Beatrix Loughran (1932 FSK)

Youngest Participant—Men
12y161d Alain Giletti (1952 FSK-FRA)
14y363d Scott Allen (1964 FSK)

Oldest Participant—Men
52y144d Joseph Savage (1932 FSK)

Youngest Participant—Women
11y74d Cecilia Colledge (1932 FSK-GBR)
14y309d Janet Lynn (1968 FSK)

Oldest Participant—Women
43y209d Ludovika Jakobsson (1928 FSK-FIN)
35y182d Theresa Blanchard (1928 FSK)

APPENDIX II – HONOR ROLL OF UNITED STATES OLYMPIANS

Following are the United States athletes who have won a minimum of three gold medals or five medals, total, in the Olympic Games.

	G	S	B	T		G	S	B	T
Ray Ewry (TAF)	10			10	Sharon Stouder (SWI)	3	1		4
Mark Spitz (SWI)	9	1	1	11	Wyomia Tyus (TAF)	3	1		4
Carl Osburn (SHO)	5	4	2	11	Chris Von Saltza (SWI)	3	1		4
Martin Sheridan (TAF)	5	3	1	9	Dennis Fenton (SHO)	3		2	5
Charles Daniels (SWI)	5	1	2	8	Jim Montgomery (SWI)	3		1	4
Willis Lee (SHO)	5	1	1	7	Wilma Rudolph (TAF)	3		1	4
Anton Heida (GYM)	5	1		6	Melissa Belote (SWI)	3			3
Don Schollander (SWI)	5	1		6	Ethelda Bleibtrey (SWI)	3			3
Alfred Lane (SHO)	5		1	6	Mike Burton (SWI)	3			3
Johnny Weissmuller (SWI/WAP)	5		1	6	Steve Clark (SWI)	3			3
Morris Fisher (SHO)	5			5	Paul Costello (ROW)	3			3
Eric Heiden (SSK)	5			5	Glenn Davis (TAF)	3			3
James Lightbody (TAF)	4	2		6	Karl Frederick (SHO)	3			3
Lloyd Spooner (SHO)	4	1	2	7	Clarence Houser (DIV)	3			3
John Naber (SWI)	4	1		5	Joseph Jackson (SHO)	3			3
Meyer Prinstein (TAF)	4	1		5	John Kelly (ROW)	3			3
Mel Sheppard (TAF)	4	1		5	Helene Madison (SWI)	3			3
Marcus Hurley (CYC)	4		1	5	Debbie Meyer (SWI)	3			3
Harrison Dillard (TAF)	4			4	Bobby Joe Morro (TAF)	3			3
Archie Hahn (TAF)	4			4	Sandra Neilson (SWI)	3			3
Alvin Kraenzlein (TAF)	4			4	Martha Norelius (SWI)	3			3
Pat McCormick (DIV)	4			4	Paul Pilgrim (TAF)	3			3
Al Oerter (TAF)	4			4	Norman Ross (SWI)	3			3
Jesse Owens (TAF)	4			4	Frank Wykoff (TAF)	3			3
George Eyser (GYM)	3	2	1	6	Shirley Babashoff (SWI)	2	6		8
Ralph Rose (TAF)	3	2	1	6	Burton Downing (CYC)	2	3	1	6
Duke Kahanamoku (SWI)	3	2		5	Irving Baxter (TAF)	2	3		5
John Hencken (SWI)	3	1	1	5	Earl Thomson (EQU)	2	3		5
Mal Whitfield (TAF)	3	1	1	5	Robert Garrett (TAF)	2	2	2	6
John Flanagan (TAF)	3	1		4	J. W. B. Tewskbury (TAF)	2	2	1	5
Charles Hickcox (SWI)	3	1		4	Lawrence Nuesslein (SHO)	2	1	2	5
Harry Hillman (TAF)	3	1		4	William Merz (GYM)		1	4	5
Jim McLane (SWI)	3	1		4	Michael Plumb (EQU)		1	4	5

APPENDIX III –
CEREMONIES AND AWARDS

U. S. PARTICIPATION OLYMPIC GAMES OPENING CEREMONIES

Torch Bearers
1960 Squaw Valley	Ken Henry (passed from Andrea Mead Lawrence)
1980 Lake Placid	Charles Morgan Kerr, M.D.

Participant in the Torch Ceremony
1972 Munich	Jim Ryun (accompanied torch bearer Günter Zahn as part of a color guard representing the five continents)

Speakers of the Oath
1932 Lake Placid	Jack Shea
1932 Los Angeles	George Calnan
1960 Squaw Valley	Carol Heiss
1980 Lake Placid	Eric Heiden (athlete's), Terry McDermott (official's)

FLAG BEARERS

Summer Games
1906 Athens	Matthew Halpin
1908 London	Ralph Rose
1912 Stockholm	George Bonhag (name standard borne by Joseph Forshaw)
1920 Antwerp	Pat McDonald (name standard borne by Harry Hebner)
1924 Paris	Pat McDonald (name standard borne by Matt McGrath)
1928 Amsterdam	L. Clarence "Bud" Houser (name standard borne by John Weissmuller)
1932 Los Angeles	F. Morgan Taylor
1936 Berlin	Alfred Jochim (color guard of Wally O'Connor and Fred Lauer)
1948 London	Ralph Craig (color guard of Norman Armitage and Frank Cumiskey)
1952 Helsinki	Norman Armitage
1956 Melbourne	Norman Armitage
1960 Rome	Rafer Johnson
1964 Tokyo	Parry O'Brien
1968 Mexico City	Janice Romary
1972 Munich	Olga Connolly
1976 Montreal	Gary Hall

Equestrian Games
1956 Stockholm	Warren B. Wofford

Winter Games
1924 Chamonix	Clarence "Taffy" Abel
1928 St. Moritz	Godfrey Dewey, M.D.
1932 Lake Placid	Billy Fiske
1936 Garmisch	Rolf Monsen
1948 St. Moritz	John Heaton
1952 Oslo	James Bickford
1956 Cortina d'Ampezzo	James Bickford
1960 Squaw Valley	Don McDermott
1964 Innsbruck	Bill Disney
1968 Grenoble	Terry McDermott
1972 Sapporo	Dianne Holum
1976 Innsbruck	Cindy Nelson
1980 Lake Placid	Scott Hamilton

ART COMPETITIONS

The founder of the modern Olympic Games, Baron Pierre de Coubertin, had a fervent wish that the Olympics would become a great cultural as well as athletic event. To this end, he instituted a series of art competitions which accompanied the Olympic Games from 1912 through 1948. Competitions were held in various categories and the winners in each category were awarded gold, silver and bronze medals, exactly similar to those of the athletes. The competitions were discontinued after 1948 because of the problem of professionalism among the artists. The following Americans, however, won Olympic medals in the art competitions.

BLAIR, Lee—1932—Gold in Drawings and Water Colors for "Rodeo."

CROSBY, Percy—1932—Silver in Drawings and Water Colors for "Jackknife."

GOLINKIN, Joseph Webster—1932—Gold in Graphics for "Leg Scissors."

LAY, Charles Downing—1936—Silver in Architecture for "Marine Park in Brooklyn."

MacMONNIES, Frederick William—1932—Gold in Medals for "Lindbergh Medal."

MILLER, Ruth —1932—Silver in Paintings for "Struggle."

POPE, John Russell—1932—Silver in Architectural Designs for "Design for the Payne Whitney Gymnasium in New Haven."

WINANS, Walter—1912—Gold in Sculpture for "An American Trotter."

YOUNG, Mahonri Mackintosh—1932—Gold in Sculpture for "Knockout."

The Olympic Order

The Olympic Order is an award bestowed by the IOC in honor of meritorious service to the Olympic Movement. It is currently the only award the IOC bestows upon individuals.

Gold: 1975 Avery Brundage
Silver: 1975 Miguel de Capriles
          1976 Dan Ferris
                Jesse Owens
Bronze: 1978 Al Oerter
          1981 Anita DeFrantz
          1983 Clarence F. Johnson
          1983 Robert Kane

APPENDIX IV –
TABLES OF U.S. COMPETITORS

The following tables contain the number of United States athletes who have competed at each of the celebrations of the Olympiad. Please note that totals may not always appear to add up because of the cases where people have competed in multiple sports at one Olympics.

SUMMER GAMES

Men

	1896	1900	1904	1906	1908	1912	1920	1924	1928	1932	1936	1948	1952	1956	1960	1964	1968	1972	1976	TOTAL
Archery	–	0	23	–	1	–	0	–	–	–	–	–	–	–	–	–	–	3	2	28
Basketball	–	–	*	–	–	–	–	–	–	–	14	14	14	12	12	12	12	12	12	111
Boxing	–	–	18	–	0	–	16	16	8	8	8	8	10	8	10	10	11	11	11	151
Canoe/Kayak	–	–	–	–	–	–	–	–	–	–	10	7	9	12	10	8	10	20	13	78
Cycling	0	1	18	0	2	9	10	5	3	12	6	9	9	9	14	16	14	14	13	137
Diving	–	–	2	1	2	2	4	5	4	4	5	3	6	6	3	6	5	5	5	56
Equestrian	–	1	–	–	–	4	8	5	5	8	8	7	8	7	8	4	6	8	8	59
Fencing	0	2	8	0	0	14	17	19	14	18	19	17	17	15	16	13	15	14	13	150
Field Hockey	–	–	–	–	0	0	0	0	0	12	14	14	0	13	0	0	0	0	0	40
Golf	–	3	74	–	–	–	–	–	–	–	–	–	–	–	–	–	–	–	–	76
Gymnastics	0	0	112	0	0	0	4	8	8	20	8	8	8	6	6	6	6	6	6	188
Handball (Team)	–	–	–	–	–	–	–	–	–	–	13	–	–	–	–	–	–	15	14	35
Jeu de Paume	–	–	–	–	2	–	–	–	–	–	–	–	–	–	–	–	–	–	–	2
Judo	–	–	–	–	–	–	–	–	–	–	–	–	–	–	–	4	–	6	6	14
Lacrosse	–	12	0	–	–	–	–	–	–	–	–	–	–	–	–	–	–	–	–	12
Mod. Pentathlon	–	–	–	–	–	1	2	4	3	3	3	3	3	3	3	3	3	3	3	34
Polo	–	*	–	–	0	–	4	4	–	–	0	–	–	–	–	–	–	–	–	8
Roque	–	–	4	–	–	–	–	–	–	–	–	–	–	–	–	–	–	–	–	4
Rowing	–	9	35	0	0	0	15	20	26	26	26	26	26	26	26	27	26	26	30	326
Rugby Football	–	–	–	–	–	–	15	19	–	–	–	–	–	–	–	–	–	–	–	30
Shooting	2	6	–	0	17	26	29	21	–	6	6	12	6	8	9	10	12	14	13	166
Soccer	–	0	23	0	0	0	0	13	11	–	11	11	11	11	0	0	0	19	0	103
Swimming	1	2	25	4	8	7	14	14	10	17	16	17	16	15	17	27	30	24	27	248
Tennis	0	3	35	0	0	1	0	4	–	–	–	–	–	–	–	–	–	–	–	43
Track & Field	10	45	104	33	80	108	95	96	81	67	64	64	62	62	63	66	66	64	61	1,069
Volleyball	–	–	–	–	–	–	–	–	–	–	–	–	–	–	–	12	12	0	0	22
Water Polo	–	0	*	–	0	0	12	9	9	7	8	8	10	10	10	10	11	11	0	83
Weightlifting	0	–	4	0	0	0	0	0	0	10	10	12	7	7	7	7	7	9	9	65
Wrestling	0	–	41	2	6	2	18	14	7	7	7	8	8	15	16	16	16	18	20	195
Yachting	–	2	–	–	0	0	0	0	10	20	13	13	14	11	11	11	11	13	12	129
MEN'S TOTALS	13	85	516	37	118	173	256	274	197	245	268	261	244	255	241	267	272	315	278	3,629

*Both basketball and water polo were held in 1904 but their Olympic status is rather doubtful. We are not including them as official sports but, for the record, there were 40 and 21 competitors respectively in the two sports.

In 1900 polo, the United States had three polo players who competed for Great Britain and won medals.

Women

	1900	1904	1906	1908	1912	1920	1924	1928	1932	1936	1948	1952	1956	1960	1964	1968	1972	1976	TOTAL
Archery	–	6	–	0	–	–	–	–	–	–	–	–	–	–	–	–	3	2	10
Basketball	–	–	–	–	–	–	–	–	–	–	–	–	–	–	–	–	–	12	12
Canoe/Kayak	–	–	–	–	–	–	–	–	–	–	0	0	0	3	3	2	6	3	13
Diving	–	–	–	–	0	7	5	5	5	5	4	5	5	3	6	6	3	6	43
+ Equestrian	–	–	–	–	–	–	–	–	–	–	–	1	1	2	6	5	3	4	15
Fencing	–	–	–	–	–	–	2	2	3	3	3	3	3	5	5	5	5	5	26
Field Hockey	–	–	–	–	–	–	–	–	–	–	–	–	–	–	–	–	–	–	0
Golf	4	–	–	–	–	–	–	–	–	–	–	–	–	–	–	–	–	–	4
Gymnastics	–	–	–	–	–	–	–	0	–	8	8	8	6	6	6	6	6	6	48
Handball (Team)	–	–	–	–	–	–	–	–	–	–	–	–	–	–	–	–	–	0	0
Rowing	–	–	–	–	–	–	–	–	–	–	–	–	–	–	–	–	–	24	24
+ Shooting	–	–	–	–	–	–	–	–	–	–	–	–	–	–	–	0	0	1	1
Swimming	–	–	–	–	0	7	11	12	11	11	11	12	14	14	21	22	27	24	178
Tennis	2	–	0	0	0	0	5	–	–	–	–	–	–	–	–	–	–	–	7
Track & Field	–	–	–	–	–	–	–	17	15	13	12	9	19	18	20	25	33	30	157
Volleyball	–	–	–	–	–	–	–	–	–	–	–	–	–	–	12	12	0	0	19
+ Yachting	0	–	–	0	0	0	0	0	0	1	0	2	0	0	0	0	0	0	3
WOMEN'S TOTALS	6	6	0	0	0	14	22	36	34	40	38	40	48	51	79	83	86	117	554
OVERALL TOTALS	91	520	37	118	173	270	296	233	279	308	299	284	303	292	346	355	401	395	4,183

+ Women now compete in equestrian sports, shooting, and yachting on an equal basis with men and have done so in the years shown above which do not have a "–" given.

WINTER GAMES

Men

	1908	1920	1924	1928	1932	1936	1948	1952	1956	1960	1964	1968	1972	1976	1980	TOTAL
Alpine Ski	–	–	–	–	–	4	7	7	6	8	6	5	7	8	7	49
Biathlon	–	–	–	–	–	–	–	–	–	4	4	5	4	5	6	24
Bobsledding	–	–	–	11	12	11	16	10	11	–	9	10	9	9	9	94
Figure Skating	1	1	1	3	6	4	5	5	5	6	6	6	5	7	7	54
Ice Hockey	–	11	10	0	14	11	15	15	17	17	17	18	17	19	19	181
Luge	–	–	–	–	–	–	–	–	–	–	8	4	8	6	7	26
Nordic Ski	–	–	6	3	14	11	8	12	10	17	11	14	18	16	14	113
Speed Skating	–	–	6	4	12	5	9	7	8	9	9	9	9	7	7	66
MEN'S TOTALS	1	12	23	21	58	46	60	56	57	61	70	71	77	77	76	605

Women

	1908	1920	1924	1928	1932	1936	1948	1952	1956	1960	1964	1968	1972	1976	1980	TOTAL
Alpine Ski	–	–	–	–	–	4	6	5	4	6	6	6	6	6	6	48
Figure Skating	0	1	2	3	5	5	5	5	5	6	6	6	6	7	7	54
Luge	–	–	–	–	–	–	–	–	–	–	0	3	2	3	3	9
Nordic Ski	–	–	–	–	–	–	–	–	–	–	0	0	5	6	5	12
Speed Skating	–	–	–	–	–	–	–	–	–	6	6	6	7	7	4	26
WOMEN'S TOTALS	0	1	2	3	5	9	11	10	9	18	18	21	26	29	25	149
OVERALL	1	13	25	24	63	55	71	66	66	79	88	92	103	106	101	754

TOTALS

	Summer	Winter	Total
Men	3,629	605	4,230
Women	554	149	703
Overall	4,183	754	4,933

APPENDIX V–
The 1940 And 1980 Teams

Although the 1940 Olympics were cancelled because of the war in Europe, the United States still selected an Olympic team in certain sports. The following athletes were members of the 1940 team that was unable to compete in the Olympics.

Winter, 1940

Merrill Barber—Nordic Skiing
James John Bickford—Bobsledding
Walter Isaac Bietila—Nordic Skiing
Robert Blatt, Jr.—Alpine Skiing
Ivan Elmore Brown—Bobsledding
Hannah Locke Caldwell—Alpine Skiing
Howard Chivers—Nordic Skiing
Warren H. Chivers—Nordic Skiing
Angus W. Clain—Bobsledding
Wendall Cram—Alpine Skiing
William John D'Amico—Bobsledding
Richard Durrance—Alpine Skiing
Alf Engen—Nordic Skiing
M. Bernard Fox—Figure Skating
Sverre Fredheim—Nordic Skiing
Leonard Freisinger—Speed Skating
Peter Garrett—Alpine Skiing
Oliver Haupt, Jr.—Figure Skating
Harry L. Hillman, Jr.—Alpine Skiing
Robert Heckenbach—Speed Skating
Arthur Keysor—Bobsledding
Al Kucera—Speed Skating
Delbert Thomas Lamb—Speed Skating
Robin Lee—Figure Skating
Charles Leighton—Speed Skating
Grace Carter Lindley—Alpine Skiing
Robert Linney—Bobsledding
John Litchfield—Nordic Skiing
Robert Martin—Bobsledding
Marion McKean—Alpine Skiing
Richard Mitchell—Alpine Skiing
Matt Monahan, Jr.—Bobsledding
Audrey Peppe—Figure Skating
Nancy Reynolds—Alpine Skiing
Edward J. Schroeder—Speed Skating
George Shimek—Speed Skating
William Stacavich—Bobsledding
Curtis Paul Stevens—Bobsledding
John Hubert Stevens—Bobsledding

Joan Tozzer—Figure Skating
Francis W. Tyler—Bobsledding
Hugh Varno—Bobsledding
George Wallace—Speed Skating
Alan M. Washbond—Bobsledding
Aubrey Wells—Bobsledding
Elizabeth D. Woolsey—Alpine Skiing

Summer, 1940

Louis Abele—Weightlifting
Norman Cudworth Armitage—Fencing
Patty Aspinwall—Swimming
Beverley Beck—Diving
Theodore Blackman—Canoe & Kayaking
Doris Brennan—Swimming
James Burk—Rowing
Joseph Burk—Rowing
Gloria Callen—Swimming
Jose Raoul deCapriles—Fencing
Miguel Angel deCapriles—Fencing
Stanley Cimokowski—Canoe & Kayaking
William Collis—Canoe & Kayaking
Shirley Condit—Diving
Edward Crafagno—Fencing
Helen Crlenkovich—Diving
John Henry Davis—Weightlifting
Robert DeClercq—Rowing
Warren Alvin Dow—Fencing
Royce A. Drake—Equestrian
Claudia Eckert—Swimming
Frank English—Rowing
Dernell Every—Fencing
Marion Falconer—Swimming
William Gaehler—Canoe & Kayking
Arthur A. Gallagher—Rowing
Marjorie Gestring—Diving
Steve Gob—Weightlifting
Ann Hardin—Swimming
William A. Harris—Equestrian
William Havens, Jr.—Canoe & Kayaking
Don Heinicke—Track & Field
Brenda Mersereau Helser—Swimming
Frank Sherman Henry—Equestrian
John Randolph Huffman—Fencing
Fujike Katsutani—Swimming
John Adelbert Kelley—Track & Field

Casimir Klosiewitz—Weightlifting
Frank Joseph Krick—Canoe & Kayaking
Dorothy Leonard—Swimming
Norman Lewis—Fencing
James Lyons—Rowing
John Lyons—Rowing
Joyce Macrae—Swimming
Ralph Marson—Fencing
Hugh McCaffrey—Rowing
Howard McGillin—Rowing
William McNaughton—Rowing
Helena Mroczkowska—Fencing
Robert B. Neely—Equestrian
Eugene O'Brien—Rowing
Leslie S. Pawson—Track & Field
Helen Perry—Swimming
Carl William Albert Raguse—Equestrian
Margaret Reinhold—Swimming
Ernest Riedel—Canoe & Kayaking
Mary M. Ryan—Swimming
Marilyn Sahner—Swimming
Scott M. Sanford—Equestrian
Ralph Scull—Weightlifting
Fred Siebert—Fencing
Alfred Skrobisch—Fencing
Steve Stanko—Weightlifting
Mildred Stewart—Fencing
John Terlazzo—Weightlifting
Anthony Terlazzo—Weightlifting
John Basil Terpak—Weightlifting
John F. Terry—Weightlifting
Loyal Tingley—Fencing
Edward J. Trilling—Canoe & Kayaking
Hiram E. Tuttle—Equestrian
Ralph Vigliott—Rowing
Franklin Fearing Wing Jr.—Equestrian
John William Wofford—Equestrian

The only time the United States did not compete in the Olympics was in 1980, when President Carter ordered a boycott in protest of the invasion of Afghanistan. Nonetheless, Olympic trials were held in all sports and teams were selected. This book is dedicated to those athletes who were denied their chance at Olympic competition. Their names and the teams they were selected for follow.

Summer, 1980

Randolph Phillip William Ableman—Diving
Mark Aguirre—Basketball
Christopher Alsopp—Rowing
Charles Altekruse—Rowing
Elizabeth Anders—Field Hockey
Colin Anderson—Track & Field
Jodi Anderson—Track & Field
Lynne Winbigler Anderson—Track & Field
Ron Anderson—Yachting
Terence M. Anderson—Shooting
Jana Marie Angelakis—Fencing
Peter Arnautoff—Soccer
Duncan Atwood—Track & Field
John Azevedo—Wrestling
Janet Baier—Volleyball
Willie Banks—Track & Field
Valerie Barber—Rowing
Leslie J. Barczewski—Cycling
Hope Barnes—Rowing
Stephen Barnicoat—Swimming
William Barrett—Swimming
Bruce Barton—Canoeing
Gregory Mark Barton—Canoeing
Terry Baxter—Swimming
Jackie Beard—Boxing
Craig Beardsley—Swimming
Carolyn Marie Becker—Volleyball
Elizabeth Beglin—Field Hockey
William T. Belden—Rowing
Roberta Belle—Track & Field
Tony Bellinger—Soccer
Stephen D. Benjamin—Yachting
Andy Francis Bessette—Track & Field
Washington D. Bishop, III—Equestrian
Rolando Blackman—Basketball
Jeffrey C. Blatnick—Wrestling
Carol Blazejowski—Basketball
Jeanette Bolden—Track & Field
Earl Frederick Borchelt—Rowing
Mark R. Borchelt—Rowing
Henry Peter Bossett—Yachting
Michael Bottom—Swimming
Carol Ann Bower—Rowing
Sam Bowie—Basketball
Laurel Kaye Brassey—Volleyball
Willie Broad—Boxing

Michael Brooks—Basketball
Alice Brown—Track & Field
Carol Page Brown—Rowing
Douglas C. Brown—Track & Field
Julie Brown—Track & Field
Michael Lee Bruner—Swimming
William Buchanan—Yachting
Richard T. Buerkle—Track & Field
Lisa Buese—Swimming
Johnny Bumphus—Boxing
Brian Bungum—Diving
David Burgering—Diving
Michael E. Burley—Modern Pentathlon
James Butler—Track & Field
Phil Cahoy—Gymnastics
Gregory Caldwell—Track & Field
Mark Cameron—Weightlifting
Anthony Campbell—Track & Field
Christopher Campbell—Wrestling
Robin Campbell—Track & Field
John P. Carababas—Rowing
Rick Carey—Swimming
Kimberly Carlisle—Swimming
Guy A. Carlton—Weightliftng
Willie Carter—Boxing
Richard Marshall Cashin—Rowing
Tracy Caulkins—Swimming
Christopher Cavanaugh—Swimming
Matthew Centrowitz—Track & Field
Daniel Christie Chandler—Wrestling
John Chatzky—Rowing
Chandra Danette Cheeseborough—Track & Field
Gwen Cheeseman—Field Hockey
Sepven E. Christensen—Rowing
Dean O. Clark—Shooting
Timothy Clark—Soccer
Paul Coffee—Soccer
Bob Coffman—Track & Field
Michael M. Cohen—Weightlifting
Sean P. Colgan—Rowing
Luci Collins—Gymnastics
Steven K. Collins—Shooting
Bart Connor—Gymnastics
Robert Cook—Cycling
    In Memoriam: October 30, 1957–March 9, 1981
Dedy Cooper—Track & Field
Rita Louise Crockett—Volleyball

Denise Curry—Basketball
Don Curry—Boxing
James Curry—Weightlifting
Christina Cruz—Rowing
Sharon Dabney—Track & Field
Thomas W. Darling—Rowing
Gay Kristine D'Asaro—Fencing
Rod David—Yachting
Mary Decker—Track & Field
Anita Luceete DeFrantz—Rowing
Norman DelloJoio—Equestrian
Brian Derwin—Weightlifting
Denise DeSautels—Field Hockey
Angelo DiBernardo—Soccer
James W. Dietz—Rowing
Theresa DiMarino—Canoeing
Frederick Dixon—Track & Field
Boris Dov Djerassi—Track & Field
Bruce M. Donaghy—Cycling
Anne Donovan—Basketball
Chris Dorst—Water Polo
Thomas N. Doughty—Cycling
Patricia Dowdell—Volleyball
Linda Murray Dragan—Canoeing
Karla Hull Drewsen—Rowing
Matthew A. Dryke—Shooting
John Marshall Duane—Yachting
Benji Ray Durden—Track & Field
Michael K. Durkin—Track & Field
Donald Ebert—Soccer
Martin Edmondson—Shooting
Stephanie Elkins—Swimming
Bruce E. Epke—Rowing
Brent Robert Emery—Cycling
Robert D. Espeseth—Rowing
John Gardner Everett—Rowing
Marco Evoniuk—Track & Field
Rod Ewaliko—Track & Field
Allan Dean Feuerbach—Track & Field
Benjamin F. Fields—Track & Field
Gary Figueroa—Water Polo
Andy Fisher—Rowing
Benita Fitzgerald—Track & Field
John David Fitzgerald—Modern Pentathlon
Roderick M. Fitz-Randolph, Jr.—Shooting
Lauie Jean Flachmeier—Volleyball
Jeanne Flanagan—Rowing

Jeffrey Float—Swimming
Stanley Floyd—Track & Field
William Forrester—Swimming
Neal Lawrence Fowler—Yachting
Nikki V. Tomlinson Franke—Fencing
Herman Ronald Frazier—Track & Field
Marcia Frederick—Gymnastics
Gregory Fredericks—Track & Field
Mark Albert Fuller—Wrestling
Albrose "Rowdy" Gaines—Swimming
Ron Galimore—Gymnastics
Gwen Gardner—Track & Field
Willie Gault—Track & Field
Darryl Lester Gee—Soccer
Charlotte Geer—Rowing
Julia Hand Geer—Rowing
Larry Gerard—Gymnastics
Virginia Gilder—Rowing
David R. Gilman—Canoeing
Bob Giordano—Weightlifting
Paula Girven—Track & Field
Harvey Glance—Track & Field
Timothy C. Glass—Fencing
Dean W. Glenesk—Modern Pentathlon
Boyd D. Goldsby—Rowing
Jesse H. Goldstein—Judo
Brian Stuart Goodell—Swimming
Mark Brian Gorski—Cycling
Jill Evans Grant—Field Hockey
Carie Brand Graves—Rowing
Lendon Fentress Gray—Equestrian
Bill Green—Track & Field
Debbie Green—Volleyball
Pamela Greene—Track & Field
John Gregorek—Track & Field
Matt Gribble—Swimming
Lorna Griffin—Track & Field
David Grylls—Cycling
Brian B. Gust—Wrestling
Robert Bentley Haines—Yachting
Steve Hamann—Water Polo
Donald Hamilton—Shooting
Jerome Hannan—Weightlifting
Bill Hanzlik—Basketball
James Hartung—Gymnastics
Janet Harville—Rowing
Hollis Straley Hatton—Rowing

Karen Hawkins—Track & Field
John Patrick Hayes—Soccer
Thomas Hazeltine—Rowing
Kyle Heffner—Track & Field
James A. Heiring—Track & Field
Tara Heiss—Basketball
Russell Owen Hellickson—Wrestling
John Hencken—Swimming
Stephanie Hightower—Track & Field
Elizabeth Dorrepaal Hills—Rowing
Thomas Hintnaus—Track & Field
Nancy Hogshead—Swimming
Conrad Holmfield—Equestrian
Denean Howard—Track & Field
James Allen Howard—Track & Field
Sherri Howard—Track & Field
Terry M. Howard—Shooting
Thomas A. Howes—Rowing
Thomas W. Hull—Rowing
Flora Jean Hyman—Volleyball
Bruce Ibbetson—Rowing
Elaine Ingram-Cheris—Fencing
Robert Jackson—Swimming
Robert Jaugstetter—Rowing
Linda Louise Jezek—Swimming
Kathy Johnson—Gymnastics
Mark Anthony Johnson—Wrestling
Sheryl Ann Johnson—Field Hockey
Stacey R. Johnson—Fencing
Paul Jordan—Track & Field
Michael Karchut—Weightlifting
Jay T. Kearney—Canoeing
Kathryn Keeler—Rowing
David Kehoe—Rowing
Stephen P. Kelly—Canoeing
Lee Kemp—Wrestling
Bruce Kennedy—Track & Field
Elizabeth Kent—Rowing
Jeff Kent—Yachting
Ty Keough—Soccer
Stephen Kiesling—Rowing
David William Kimes—Shooting
Elizabeth Kinkhead—Swimming
Kris Kirchner—Basketball
Kris Kirchner—Swimming
Luke David Klaja—Weightlifting
Leslie Klein—Canoeing

Beth Kline—Gymnastics
Amy Koopman—Gymnastics
Karin LaBerge—Swimming
Stephen M. Lacy—Track & Field
Debra Lynn Landreth—Volleyball
Francina Larrieu—Track & Field
Christine Larson—Field Hockey
David Larson—Swimming
Mel Lattany—Track & Field
Adolphus Lawson—Soccer
David Kenneth Lee—Track & Field
Stanley V. Lekach—Fencing
Greg J. LeMond—Cycling
Bradley Lewis—Rowing
Carol LeGrant Lewis—Track & Field
Frederick Carleton Lewis—Track & Field
Randall Scott Lewis—Wrestling
Kimberley Linehan—Swimming
Joan Louise Lind—Rowing
Eric Emil Lindroth—Water Polo
Marybeth Linzmeier—Swimming
Alton Lister—Basketball
Michael Leshine Loeb—Yachting
Thomas John Losonczy—Fencing
Gregory Louganis—Diving
Walter H. Lubsen, Jr.—Rowing
Stephen Lundquist—Swimming
Charles Lyda—Canoeing
Kevin Machemer—Diving
Joseph Manley—Boxing
Madeline Manning—Track & Field
Susan Marcellus—Field Hockey
Anne Marden—Rowing
Henry Dinwoody Marsh—Track & Field
Tommy Martin—Judo
Michael A. Marx—Fencing
Gregory D. Massialas—Fencing
John Matthews—Wrestling
John McArdle—Track & Field
Peggy Ann McCarthy—Rowing
Valerie McClain—Rowing
Diane Elizabeth McCormick—Volleyball
Walter McCoy—Track & Field
Rodney McCray—Basketball
William McChesney—Track & Field
Andrew McDonald—Water Polo
Amy McGrath—Diving

William McKeon—Soccer
Kathy Laverne McMillan—Track & Field
Julianne McNamara—Gymnastics
Mary Terstigge Meagher—Swimming
Daniel Alan Mello—Wrestling
Anita C. Miller—Field Hockey
Debra Miller—Basketball
Gene Mills—Wrestling
Glenn Mills—Swimming
Leslie Woods Milne—Field Hockey
Thomas Austin Minkel—Wrestling
John Moffet—Swimming
Katherine Morgan Monahan—Equestrian
Brenda Morehead—Track & Field
Charlene Morett—Field Hockey
Angus G. Morrison—Canoeing
Joseph Morrone—Soccer
Edwin Corley Moses—Track & Field
Diane Marie Moyer—Field Hockey
Roland P. Muhlen—Canoeing
Lee Roy Murphy—Boxing
Larry Ellwyne Myricks—Track & Field
Keith Nakasone—Judo
Louis Nanchoff—Soccer
Ernest W. Neel—Shooting
Renaldo Nehemiah—Track & Field
Ron Neugent—Swimming
Megan Neyer—Diving
Robert Lee Nieman—Fencing/Modern Pentathlon
Leonard Harvey Nitz—Cycling
Cindy Noble—Basketball
John Michael Nonna—Fencing
Kristine Lee Norelius—Rowing
Mark E. O'Brien—Rowing
Daniel O'Connor—Track & Field
Mary O'Connor—Rowing
Alex Orban—Fencing
Mary T. Osborne—Track & Field
Nathaniel Page—Track & Field
Don Paige—Track & Field
Jan Louise Palchikoff—Rowing
Lee Palles—Track & Field
William Paulus—Swimming
Joan Pennington—Swimming
Njego Pesa—Soccer
Paul Karoly Pesthy—Fencing
Benjamin Lee Peterson—Wrestling

Terry Ann Place—Volleyball
John Robert Plankenhorn—Canoeing
Ben Plucknett—Track & Field
John Michael Plumb—Equestrian
Lataunya Pollard—Basketball
Cynthia Potter—Diving
John Powell—Track & Field
Paul Prioleau—Rowing
Joseph Robert Puleo—Weightlifting
William Purdy—Rowing
Jill Rankin—Basketball
Susan Rapp—Swimming
Phillip Reilly—Fencing
Steve F. Reiter—Shooting
Brad Bert Rheingans—Wrestling
Kelly Rickon—Rowing
Dan Ripley—Track & Field
Louise Ritter—Track & Field
Kevin Robertson—Water Polo
James Robinson, Jr.—Track & Field
Peter Rocca—Swimming
Brian Roney—Swimming
Teresa Lee Rudd—Equestrian
Alberto Salazar—Track & Field
Daniel Salvemini—Soccer
Anthony Sandoval—Track & Field
Richard Sandoval—Boxing
Mitch Santa Maria—Judo
Daniel Sayner—Rowing
Cal Schake—Weightlifting
Kathryn Joan Schmidt—Track & Field
Peter Schnugg—Water Polo
Terry Schroeder—Water Polo
Carl F. Schueler—Track & Field
Thomas J. Schuler—Cycling
Steven Michael Scott—Track & Field
Clark Todd Scully—Track & Field
Peter Schmock—Track & Field
Steven Seck—Judo
Maren Elizabeth Seidler—Track & Field
Kurt Setterberg—Weightlifting
Chris Seufert—Diving
Robert Shannon—Boxing
Douglas Craig Shapiro—Cycling
Karen Christina Shelton—Field Hockey
James Shuler—Boxing
John Siman—Water Polo

David Sims—Swimming
Karen Kiefer Smith—Track & Field
Mark J. T. Smith—Fencing
Melanie Ainsworth Smith—Equestrian
Willie Smith, III—Track & Field
Kurt Somerville—Rowing
Pamela Ann Spencer—Track & Field
Patricia Spratlen—Rowing
Julie Ann Staver—Field Hocker
Philip Stekl—Rowing
Jill Sterkel—Swimming
Dale Emery Stetina—Cycling
Wayne Douglas Stetina—Cycling
Randy W. Stewart—Shooting
Karen E. Stives—Equestrian
Thomas Stock—Weightlifting
Gwen Elaine Stockebrand—Equestrian
Nancy Storrs—Rowing
Terry Mathew Streib—Canoeing
Judith Ann Strong—Field Hockey
Jon Svendsen—Water Polo
Michael Lee Swain—Judo
Tracee Talavera—Gymnastics
Bernard Taylor—Boxing
Frederick G. Taylor—Track & Field
John Terwilliger—Rowing
Cathleen Thaxton—Rowing
Susan Thayer—Swimming
Isiah Thomas—Basketball
Bruce Thompson—Wrestling
Richard Thornton—Swimming
Edward Norman Trevelyan—Yachting
Miguel A. Tudela—Judo
Michael Tully—Track & Field
Mary Ann Turbyne—Track & Field
Ann Turner—Canoeing
Susan E. Tuttle—Rowing
Darnell Valentine—Basketball
John Van Blom—Rowing
Jonathan Edward Van Cleave—Canoeing
Perry Van der Beck—Soccer
Danny F. Van Haute—Cycling
Joseph Vargas—Water Polo
Jesse Vassallo—Swimming
Nancy Vespoli—Rowing
Peter Vidmar—Gymnastics
Greg Villa—Soccer

Craig Steven Virgin—Track & Field
Danny Vranes—Basketball
James Walker—Track & Field
Rosie Walker—Basketball
Larry A. Walker—Track & Field
Susan Walsh—Swimming
Holly Warlick—Basketball
Anne Elizabeth Warner—Rowing
Torrance Watkins—Equestrian
Andrew T. Weaver—Cycling
Bob Weaver—Wrestling
Andreas J. Weigand—Canoeing
Barbara Weinstein—Diving
Christopher Wells—Rowing
Peter Westbrook—Fencing
Nancy Pitkin White—Field Hockey
Terry White—Canoeing
Lones Wesley Wigger, Jr.—Shooting
Clifford Wiley—Track & Field
Mac Maurice Wilkins—Track & Field
Barton Williams—Track & Field
Buck Williams—Basketball
Diane Williams—Track & Field
Randy Luvelle Williams—Track & Field
Mike Wilson—Gymnastics
Randy Wilson—Track & Field
John Windfield Winnett, Jr.—Equestrian
James Cunningham Wofford—Equestrian
Gregory Wojciechowski—Wrestling
Al Wood—Basketball
Christopher Wood—Rowing
Lynette Woodard—Basketball
Cynthia "Sippy" Woodhead—Swimming
Thomas Woodman—Rowing
Susan Jean Woodstra—Volleyball
Charles E. Yagla—Wrestling
Nicholas Yonezuka—Judo
Canzetta Young—Track & Field
Linda Goad Zang—Equestrian

APPENDIX VI–
INDEX OF COMPETITORS

This is an index, by sport, of every American athlete who has competed in the Olympic Games. The years and events in which each athlete participated follow the athlete's name. We have included only those athletes who actually competed at some time, even in team sports. All but a very few of the earliest U.S. Olympic team members who were not well known have been uncovered by extensive research.

The index is completely cross-referenced. Athletes who competed under more than one name (mainly women, using married names) or in more than one sport are listed in both places, with a reference to the other listing. When an athlete competed under more than one name, the sports and events information is given only with the name under which that person last competed. We have used the most complete name known, giving the nickname if not merely a diminution of the given name. Name changes after the athlete's Olympic participation ended are not included (with one very famous exception).

Four symbols often precede the athlete's names:

*—athlete won a medal in the sport listed
@—athlete won a medal in another sport (or sports)
&—athlete won medals in two (or three) sports
#—athlete is a woman who competed on equal terms
   with men in equestrian, shooting, or yachting

In the cases where an athlete won a medal in a sport other than the one listed, the cross-reference will indicate which sport.

In each sport's index, preceding the athlete's names will be found the number of U.S. competitors in that sport (next to the name of the sport), a short synopsis of our Olympic participation in that sport, and a list of codes used for the various events.

ALPINE SKIING (Men) (49)
Men first competed in alpine skiing at the 1936 Olympic Winter Games. The United States has never failed to be represented.

AC = Alpine combined	DH = Downhill
GS = Giant slalom	SL = Slalom

ADGATE, Cary Glen   1976 SL, GS
    1980 GS

ANDERSON, Karl	1976 DH
	1980 DH
BARRIER, James M.	1960 SL, GS
BECK, William LeBaron	1952 DH
	1956 DH
BLATT, Robert, Jr.	1948 SL, DH, AC
BROWN, Frank E.	1960 SL
BRUCE, Geoff	1976 SL
BUEK, Richard Carl	1952 DH
CHAFFEE, Frederick Stoddard, II	1968 SL, GS
	1972 SL, GS
COCHRAN, Robert	1972 SL, GS, DH
CORCORAN, Thomas Armstrong	1956 SL, GS
	1960 SL, GS
CURRIER, David Henry	1972 GS, DH
DODGE, Joseph Brooks, Jr.	1952 SL, GS, DH
	1956 SL, GS
DURRANCE, Richard Henry, Jr.	1936 AC
EATON, Gordon Ladd	1960 DH
FERRIES, Charles Thompson	1960 SL
	1964 SL, DH
GORSUCH, Scott David	1960 GS, DH
*HEUGA, James Frederic	1964 SL, GS
	1968 SL, GS
JENNINGS, H. Devereaux	1948 DH
JONES, Greg	1976 SL, GS, DH
KASHIWA, Henry Charles	1972 GS, DH
*KIDD, William Winston	1964 SL, GS, DH
	1968 SL, GS, DH
KNOWLTON, Stephen P.	1948 SL, DH, AC
LAFFERTY, Michael	1972 DH
LAWRENCE, David Judah	1952 GS
LIVERMORE, Robert, Jr.	1936 AC
*MAHRE, Phil	1976 SL, GS
	1980 SL, GS, DH
MAHRE, Steve	1976 GS
	1980 SL, GS
MAROLT, Max S.	1960 GS, DH
MAROLT, William Charles	1964 GS
McCOY, Dennis Marshall	1968 DH
McLEAN, Robert L.	1948 SL, DH, AC
MELVILLE, Marvin Alton	1956 DH
	1960 DH
MILL, Andy	1976 DH
	1980 DH
MILLER, Ralph English	1956 SL, GS, DH
MOVITZ, Richard David	1948 DH
NAGEL, Jack Edward	1952 SL, GS
ORSI, Annibale John "Ni," Jr.	1964 DH
PAGE, George Hugh	1936 AC
PALMER, Reuben Tyler	1972 SL
PALMER, Terry	1972 SL
PATTERSON, Pete	1976 DH
	1980 SL, GS, DH
REDDISH, Jack Nichols	1948 SL, DH, AC
	1952 SL, GS, DH

ROBISON, Darrell Donald	1952 SL
SABICH, Vladimir Peter "Spider"	1968 SL, GS
STEWART, Colin Campbell	1948 SL
TAYLOR, William	1980 SL
WASHBURN, Albert Lincoln	1936 AC
WERNER, Wallace J. "Buddy"	1956 SL, GS, DH
	1964 SL, GS, DH

ALPINE SKIING (Women) (48)

Alpine skiing for women first appeared in the Olympic Winter Games in 1936 and the United States women have always fielded a team.

AC = Alpine combined	DH = Downhill
GS = Giant slalom	SL = Slalom

ALLEN, Wendy	1968 SL, GS
ANDERSON, Beverley Marie	1960 SL, GS
BIRD, Mary Elizabeth	1936 AC
BOUGHTON-LEIGH, Helen Bendelari	1936 AC
BOYDSTUN, Patricia	1972 SL
BUDGE, Karen	1972 GS, DH
BURR, Jannette Weston	1952 SL, GS, DH
CHAFFEE, Suzanne Stevia	1968 SL, GS
*COCHRAN, Barbara Ann	1972 GS, DH
COCHRAN, Linda	1976 SL, GS
COCHRAN, Marilyn	1972 SL, GS, DH
COOPER, Christin	1980 SL, GS
*CORROCK, Susan	1972 SL, DH
COX, Renie K.	1960 SL
CREMER, Rebecca Fraser	1948 SL, DH, AC
CUTTER, Christina "Kiki"	1968 SL, GS, DH
FERRIES, Barbara Hale	1964 SL, GS
FISHER, Abbi	1976 SL
	1980 SL
FLANDERS, Holly Beth	1980 DH
FORTNA, Rosie	1968 SL
*FRASER, Gretchen Kunigk	1948 SL, DH, AC
GRASMOEN, Brynhild	1948 SL, DH
HANNAH, Joan Lee	1960 DH
	1964 SL, GS, DH
HEATH, Clarita	1936 AC
KANN, Paula	1948 SL, DH
*LAWRENCE, Andrea B. Mead	1948 SL, DH, AC
(as Miss Mead in 1948)	1952 SL, GS, DH
	1956 SL, GS, DH
McKINNEY, Tamara	1980 SL, GS
*MEAD, Andrea B.	
MEYERS, Linda	1960 GS, DH
	1964 SL, GS
NAGEL, Judy Ann	1968 SL, GS
*NELSON, Cynthia	1976 SL, GS, DH
	1980 SL, GS, DH
OPTON, Imogene Anna	1952 SL, GS
PATTERSON, Susan	1976 DH

*PITOU, Penelope Theresa	1956 SL, GS, DH
	1960 SL, GS, DH
POULSEN, Sandra	1972 GS, DH
PREUSS, Heidi	1980 GS, DH
RODOLPH, Catherine L.	1952 SL, GS, DH
*SAUBERT, Jean Marlene	1964 SL, GS, DH
SEATON, Mary	1976 SL, GS
SHELLWORTH, Sandra W.	1968 DH
SMITH, Leslie Lelete	1976 SL, DH
*SNITE, Betsy B.	1960 SL, GS, DH
STEWART, Ruth-Marie	1948 SL, DH, AC
SURGENOR, Dorothy L.	1956 SL, DH
WALTERS, Margo Lee	1964 DH
WALTON, Starr	1964 DH
WEIR, Betty Ellen	1952 DH
WERNER, Gladys M.	1956 GS, DH
WOOLSEY, Elizabeth D.	1936 AC

ARCHERY (Men) (28)

Archery was held as a men's sport in the Olympics in 1900, 1904, 1908, and 1920 and then was not held again until 1972. It has been on every Olympic program since. The United States had no competitors in 1900 or 1920.

Y = Double York Round	
A = Double American Round	
F = Double FITA Round	T = Team Round
Y1 = Single York Round	C = Continental Round

BRUCE, Edward M.	1904 Y, A, T
*BRYANT, George Phillip	1904 Y, A, T
*BRYANT, Wallace	1904 Y, A, T
CASSELMAN, Amos B.	1904 A
*CLARK, William A.	1904 A, T
*DALLIN, Cyrus Edwin	1904 Y, A, T
*DUVALL, Samuel Harding	1904 A, T
ELIASON, Edwin	1972 F
FRENTZ, Edward	1904 Y, A
*HUBBARD, Charles R.	1904 A, T
KEYS, Benjamin	1904 Y, A, T
*MAXSON, Lewis W.	1904 Y, A, T
McCOMAK, Dennis	1972 F
McGOWAN, D. F.	1904 Y
McKINNEY, Richard Lee	1976 F
*PACE, Darrell Owen	1976 F
*RICHARDSON, Henry Barber	1904 Y, A, T
	1908 Y1, C
SCOTT, Thomas F.	1904 Y, A
*SPENCER, Galen Carter	1904 A, T
TAYLOR, Homer S.	1904 Y, A, T
TAYLOR, Ralph B.	1904 Y, A
*THOMPSON, William Henry	1904 Y, A, T
VALENTINE, W. G.	1904 A

WESTON, E. H.	1904 A
WESTON, Edward Bruce	1904 Y, A, T
*WILLIAMS, John Chester	1972 F
*WILLIAMS, Robert W., Jr.	1904 Y, A, T
*WOODRUFF, C. S.	1904 Y, A, T

ARCHERY (Women) (10)

American women competed in Olympic archery in 1904. Women's archery was held in 1908, although no Americans competed. Beginning in 1972 it has now become a regular sport on the Olympic program.

C = Double Columbia Round   F = Double FITA Round
N = Double National Round

BECHDOLT, Maureen	1972 F
*COOKE, Emma C.	1904 N, C
*HOWELL, Lida Scott	1904 N, C
MYERS, Linda Ann	1972 F
	1976 F
*POLLACK, Jessie	1904 N, C
*RYON, Luann	1976 F
TAYLOR, Louise	1904 N, C
TAYLOR, Mabel	1904 N, C
*WILBER, Doreen Viola Hansen	1972 F
WOODRUFF, Laura	1904 N, C

BASKETBALL (Men) (111)

Basketball became an official Olympic sport in 1936 although a basketball tournament was held at the 1904 Olympics. That event is of marginal Olympic caliber because it was actually the United States AAU championship for 1904 and there were no foreign entries, much less actual competing teams. Those players have not been included in the main body of players but do merit a special list at the end.

*ARMSTRONG, Michael Taylor "Tate"	1976
*ARNETTE, Jay Hoyland	1960
*BALTER, Samuel J., Jr.	1936
*BANTOM, Michael Allen	1972
*BARKER, Clifford Eugene	1948
*BARKSDALE, Donald Argee	1948
*BARNES, James	1964
*BARRETT, Michael	1968
*BEARD, Ralph Milton, Jr.	1948
*BECK, Louis W., Jr.	1948
*BELLAMY, Walter Jones, Jr.	1960
*BISHOP, Ralph English	1936
*BONTEMPS, Ronald Yngve	1952
*BOOZER, Robert Lewis	1960
*BORYLA, Vincent Joseph	1948

*BOUSHKA, Richard James	1956
*BRADLEY, William Warren	1964
*BREWER, James Turner	1972
*BROWN, Lawrence Harvey	1964
*BUCKNER, William Quinn	1976
*BURLESON, Tommy Loren	1972
*CAIN, Carl Cecil	1956
*CALDWELL, Joe Louis	1964
*CARPENTER, Gordon	1948
*CARR, Kenneth Alan	1976
*CLAWSON, John Richard	1968
*COLLINS, Paul Douglas	1972
*COUNTS, Mel Grant	1964
*DANTLEY, Adrian Delano	1976
*DARLING, Charles Frick	1956
*DAVIES, Richard Allen	1964
*DAVIS, Kenneth Bryan	1972
*DAVIS, Walter Paul	1976
*DEE, Donald F.	1968
*DISCHINGER, Terry Gilbert	1960
*EVANS, William Best	1956
*FORBES, James	1972
*FORD, Gilbert	1956
*FORD, Phil Jackson, Jr.	1976
*FORTENBERRY, Joseph Cephis	1936
*FOWLER, Calvin	1968
*FRIEBERGER, Marcus Ross	1952
*GIBBONS, John Haskell	1936
*GLASGOW, Victor Wayne	1952
*GROZA, Alexander John	1948
*GRUNFELD, Ernest	1976
*HALDORSON, Burdette Eliele	1956
	1960
*HAYWOOD, Spencer	1968
*HAZZARD, Walter Raphael	1964
*HENDERSON, Thomas Edward	1972
*HOAG, Charles Monroe	1952
*HOSKETT, Wilmer Frederick	1968
*HOUGLAND, William Marion	1952
*HUBBARD, Phillip Gregory	1976
*IMHOFF, Darrell T.	1960
*JACKSON, Lucius Brown	1964
*JEANGERARD, Robert Eugene	1956
*JOHNSON, Francis Lee	1936
*JONES, Dwight Elmo	1972
*JONES, K. C.	1956
*JONES, Robert Clyde	1972
*JONES, Wallace Clayton	1948
*JOYCE, Kevin Francis	1972
*KELLER, John Frederick	1952
*KELLEY, Earl Allen	1960
*KELLEY, Melvin Dean	1952
*KENNEY, Robert Earl	1952
*KING, James	1968
*KNOWLES, Carl Stanley	1936
*KUPCHAK, Mitchell	1976

*KURLAND, Robert Albert	1948
	1952
*LaGARDE, Thomas Joseph	1976
*LANE, Lester E.	1960
*LIENHARD, William Barner	1952
*LOVELETTE, Clyde Edward	1952
*LUBIN, Frank John	1936
*LUCAS, Jerry Ray	1960
*LUMPP, Raymond G.	1948
*MAY, Scott Glenn	1976
*McCABE, Frank Reilly	1952
*McCAFFREY, John Paul	1964
*McMILLEN, Charles Thomas	1972
*MOLLNER, Arthur Owen	1936
*MULLINS, Jeffry Vincent	1964
*PIPER, Donald Arthur	1936
*PIPPIN, Daniel Luther	1952
*PITTS, Robert C.	1948
*RAGLAND, Jack Williamson	1936
*RATLEFF, Edward	1972
*RENICK, Jesse Bernard	1948
*ROBERTSON, Oscar Palmer	1960
*ROBINSON, Robert Jackson	1948
*ROLLINS, Kenneth Herman	1948
*RUSSELL, William Fenton	1956
*SAULTERS, Glynn	1968
*SCHMIDT, Willard Theodore	1936
*SCOTT, Charles Thomas	1968
*SHEPPARD, Steven	1976
*SHIPP, Jerry Franklin	1964
*SHY, Carl	1936
*SILLIMAN, Michael Barnwell	1968
*SMITH, Adrian Howard	1960
*SPAIN, Kenneth	1968
*SWANSON, Duane Alex	1936
*TOMSIC, Ronald Paul	1956
*WALSH, James Patrick	1956
*WEST, Jerry Alan	1960
*WHEATLEY, William John	1936
*WHITE, Joseph Henry "JoJo"	1968
*WILLIAMS, Howard Earl	1952
*WILSON, George	1964

1904 "Olympic" Teams

Buffalo German YMCA Alfred A. HEERDT, Albert W. MANWEILER, Charles MONAHAN, Edward MILLER, George REDLEIN, William RHODE.

Chicago Central YMCA W. K. ARMSTRONG, Axel BERGGREN, Seth COLLINS, Melvin B. IDARIUS, J. A. JARDINE, John J. SCHOMMER, Carl WATSON, W. A. WILLIAMS.

Missouri AC Martin ARHELGER, William BUSCH, Harvey KIENER, William NEWMAN, Robert RAUSCHER, H. C. WALDMAN.

St. Louis Central YMCA Harold J. BARKER, Tracy FARNHAM, L. N. FORBES, William HARDIN, John McKNIGHT, LaRue WEBER.

Turner Tigers (Los Angeles) Frank BEEBE, Arba W. CUNNINGHAM, Henry HINCKE, J. HOLDEN, George KARSTENS, Thomas KEATING.

Xavier AC (New York) Charles B. CLEVELAND, Frank CRAVEN, James DONOVAN, W. HERSCHEL, James KENNY, Julius LEITZ, E. J. ROACH, J. S. SMITH.

BASKETBALL (Women) (12)
Women's basketball first appeared on the Olympic program in 1976.

*BROGDON, Cynthia Jane	1976
*DUNKLE, Nancy Lynn	1976
*HARRIS, Lusia Mae	1976
*HEAD, Patricia Sue	1976
*LEWIS, Charlotte	1976
*LIEBERMAN, Nancy I.	1976
*MARQUIS, Gail	1976
*MEYERS, Ann Elizabeth	1976
*O'CONNOR, Mary Anne	1976
*ROBERRR,AH0,TS, Patricia	1976
*ROJCEWICZ, Susan Marie	1976
*SIMPSON, Julienne Brazinski	1976

BIATHLON (24)
Biathlon, a sport combining cross-country skiing and shooting skills, became an Olympic sport in 1960. Prior to 1980 there was only one individual event, one of 20 kilometers, but in 1980 a second individual race of 10 kilometers was added.

I = Individual (20 km. prior to 1980)	R = 4 × 7.5 km. relay
	20 = 20 km. individual event
0 = 10 km. individual event	

AKERS, Charles Arthur	1964 I
BOWERMAN, William Jay, Jr.	1972 I, R
BURRITT, John C.	1960 I
CHAFFEE, Jonathan Knowlton	1968 I
DAMON, Laurence Snow (see also Nordic Skiing)	1960 I
DASCOULIAS, Peter George	1976 I, R
DONAHUE, Dennis Anthony	1972 I, R
	1976 R
EHRENSBECK, John Robert	1968 R

HAGEN, Martin Olaf	1976 I
	1980 20, R
HANSON, Gustave	1960 I
HOAG, Peter Coffin	1980 10, R
JOBE, Glenn Rea, Jr.	1980 20
KARNS, Peter Van	1972 I, R
LAHDENPERA, Peter Juhani	1964 I
(see also Nordic Skiing)	
MIZE, Richard	1960 I
MORSE, Dexter Terrance	1972 I, R
MORTON, John Michael	1976 R
NELSON, Lyle Barber	1976 I, R
	1980 10, R
NIELSEN, Donald M., Jr.	1980 10, R
RENNE, Paul Wisner	1964 I
RUGER, John W., II	1980 20
SPENCER, William Allen	1964 I
	1968 I, R
WAKELY, Ralph C.	1968 I, R
WILLIAMS, Edward Gustave	1968 I, R

BOBSLEDDING (94)

Bobsledding has been held at every Olympic Winter Games except for the 1960 Games in Squaw Valley. The United States entered no teams at Chamonix in 1924, but has had sledders at every Olympic Winter Games since.

2 = 2-man sled	4 = 4-man sled
5 = 5-man sled	S = Skeleton

*ATKINSON, James Neil	1952 4
BAUMGARTNER, Floyd Joseph "Mike"	1964 4
BECKER, Thomas M.	1972 2, 4
	1976 2, 4
BENHAM, Reginald Joseph	1964 4
*BENHAM, Stanley David	1952 2, 4
*BICKFORD, James John	1936 4
	1948 4
	1952 4
	1956 4
BIESIADECKI, Patrick Walter	1956 2
BLY, Max T.	1936 4
BRENNAN, Peter John	1976 4
BRIDGES, James	1972 4
*BROWN, Ivan Elmore	1936 2
*BRYANT, Percy D.	1932 4
*BUTLER, Charles Thomas	1956 4
*CARRON, Schuyler Anthony	1948 2
CLIFTON, Howard	1968 2, 4
*COLGATE, Gilbert Bayard, Jr.	1936 2
COPLEY, John	1972 4
*CROSSET, Howard Wallace	1952 4
CROWLEY, Robert	1968 4

*D'AMICO, William John	1948 4
@DAVENPORT, Willie D.	1980 4
(see also Track & Field)	
*DODGE, William Longstreth	1956 4
*DOE, Thomas Bartwell, Jr.	1928 5
DUNDON, William Frederick	1964 4
DUNN, David Kircher	1968 4
*DUPREE, Donald Victor	1948 4
*DUPREE, William Francis	1948 4
DUPREY, Philip M.	1968 4
	1972 4
	1976 4
* EAGAN, Edward Patrick Francis	1932 4
(see also Boxing)	
*FISKE, William Mead Lindsley, III	1928 5
	1932 4
*FORTUNE, Frederick J., Jr.	1948 2
	1952 2
FRISBIE, Earl Peter	1976 4
FRITSCH, Frederick W.	1976 4
GADLEY, Jeffrey	1980 4
*GRANGER, David	1928 5
*GRAY, Clifford B.	1928 5
	1932 4
*HEATON, Jennison	1928 5, S
*HEATON, John R.	1928 S
	1932 2
	1948 S
HELMER, John Leslie	1952 2
HICKEY, James John, Jr.	1972 4
HICKEY, Robert	1980 4
HICKEY, William David	1964 4
	1968 4
*HICKS, Thomas	1948 4
*HINE, Lyman Northrop	1928 5
HOLLROCK, William, III	1976 4
*HOMBURGER, Henry Anton	1932 4
*HORTON, Edmund Carlton	1932 4
HUSCHER, Robert W.	1968 2
JACQUES, Donald C., Jr.	1956 4
JOHNSON, C. William	1948 S
JORDAN, Jeff	1980 4
JOST, Jeffrey William	1980 4
LAMEY, Paul E.	1968 2
	1972 2
*LAMY, James Ernest	1956 4
	1964 2, 4
LATOUR, Tuffield A.	1948 2
*LAWRENCE, Richard W.	1936 2, 4
LUCE, Michael L.	1968 2, 4
MacCARTHY, Fairchilds	1948 S
MARTIN, Leo J.	1948 2
*MARTIN, Patrick Henry	1948 4
	1952 2, 4
MARTIN, Robert P.	1936 4
MARTIN, William L.	1948 S

*MASON, Geoffrey Travers	1928 5
McDONALD, Charles	1964 2
McKILLIP, Lawrence R.	1956 4
	1964 2, 4
MERKEL, Crawford C.	1936 4
MILLER, Hubert G.	1952 4
	1956 4
*MINTON, Robert Henry	1932 2
MORGAN, James Patrick	1976 2, 4
MORRIS, Kenneth J.	1972 4
NALLEY, Dick	1980 2, 4
*O'BRIEN, J. Jay	1928 5
	1932 4
PANDOLPH, Charles William	1964 2, 4
*PARKE, Richard Averell	1928 5
PROCTOR, John R.	1976 2, 4
*RIMKUS, Edward William	1948 4
ROGERS, Neil Robert	1964 4
RUSHLAW, Brent Donald	1976 2
	1980 2
SAID, Boris Robert, Jr.	1968 4
	1972 2, 4
SAVAGE, Paul Dillon	1968 4
SCOTT, Robert Joseph	1952 4
SEVERINO, Maurice Richard	1952 4
SEYMOUR, Edgar Duff	1956 2
SHENE, John J.	1936 4
SILER, Howard B.	1972 2, 4
	1980 2, 4
*STEVENS, Curtis Paul	1932 2
*STEVENS, Francis Paul	1932 4
*STEVENS, John Hubert	1932 2
	1936 4
*TUCKER, Nion Robert	1928 5
*TYLER, Arthur Walter	1956 2, 4
*TYLER, Francis W.	1936 4
	1948 4
TYLER, Joseph William	1980 2, 4
*WASHBOND, Alan M.	1936 2
WASHBOND, Waightman A. "Bud"	1956 2

BOXING (151)

Boxing has been contested at all but four of the Olympic Games—1896, 1900, 1906, and 1912. (In 1912 it could not be contested because the Games were held in Stockholm and boxing was then illegal in Sweden.) No United States boxers competed in 1908, but we have otherwise sent boxers every time the sport has been held.

Classes are listed by their names because the weight limits have undergone frequent changes.

B = Bantamweight	LH = Light-heavyweight
FE = Featherweight	LM = Light-middleweight
FL = Flyweight	LW = Light-welterweight
H = Heavyweight	M = Middleweight
L = Lightweight	W = Welterweight
LF = Light-flyweight	

*ADKINS, Charles	1952 LW
*ALI, Muhammed (see Cassius Clay)	
ARMSTRONG, David Lee	1972 LF
	1976 FE
ARMSTRONG, Jerry Lee	1960 B
ATKINSON, James Clark	1936 M
BALDWIN, A. Phil	1960 W
*BALDWIN, John	1968 LM
BARRERA, Humberto O.	1960 FL
*BARTH, Carmen	1932 M
*BERGER, Samuel	1904 H
BICKLE, Robert L.	1952 L
BOBICK, Duane David	1972 H
BOLLINGER	1904 L
*BOR, Nathan	1932 L
BOSSIO, William	1948 B
*BOYD, James Felton	1956 LH
*BOYLSTEIN, Frederick	1924 L
*BROOKS, Nathan Eugene	1952 FL
*BROWN, Charles	1964 FE
BROWN, Edson	1952 FE
*BURKE, Miles J.	1904 FL
BUSCEME, James Anthony, Jr.	1972 L
CAMPBELL, Harry	1960 L
*CARMODY, Robert John	1964 FL
*CARRERAS, Ricardo Luis	1972 B
CASSIDY, Frank	1920 L
CHRISTOPHERSON, Robert H.	1964 LH
CLARK, William (né William Oistacher)	1920 W
*CLAY, Cassius Marcellus (nka Muhammed Ali)	1960 LH
*COLBERG, Frederick William	1920 W
CRANSTON, Joseph Alfred	1920 M
*CROOK, Edward	1960 M
CURTIS, Louis	1976 LF
*DALEY, John Lawrence	1928 B
*DANIELS, Quincey	1960 LW
*DAVIS, Howard Edward, Jr.	1976 L
DEMENT, Timothy Lee	1972 FL
*DEVINE, Harold George	1928 FE
*EAGAN, Edward Patrick Francis (see also Bobsledding)	1920 LH
	1924 H
*EAGAN, Jack	1904 L, W
ELLIS, Charles Ray	1964 LW
ETZELL, George D.	1920 FE
*FEARY, Frederick	1932 H

*FEE, Raymond	1924 FL	MELLO, Alfons	1924 W
*FIELDS, Jackie	1924 FE	(né Alfons Mello Tavares)	
(né Jacob Finkelstein)		*MICHAELS, William M.	1904 H
*FINNEGAN, George V.	1904 FL, B	MILER, John	1932 LH
*FLYNN, Edward L.	1932 W	MILLER, Hyman	1928 FL
*FOREMAN, George	1968 H	MOLINA, Louis	1956 L
*FRAZIER, Joseph	1964 H	*MOONEY, Charles Michael	1976 B
FRILOT, Maurice Emmett	1964 W	MOORE, David	1952 B
FUNK, Benjamin Franklin	1924 M	*MOSBERG, Samuel A.	1920 L
GAGE, Louis A.	1952 W	MULHOLLAND, George	1924 LH
*GENARO, Frankie	1920 FL	MUNIZ, Armando	1968 W
(né Frank DiGennara)		OLIVER, Arthur	1936 H
GIBSON, Tolman, Jr.	1964 LM	*PATTERSON, Floyd	1952 M
*GILMORE, Fred	1904 FE	PEREZ, Ray	1956 FL
GOSS, Samuel	1968 B	PRICE, Percy J., Jr.	1960 H
GREATHOUSE, Edward Guy	1924 H	*RADEMACHER, Thomas Peter	1956 H
HAGGERTY, Hugh	1924 W	*RANDOLPH, Leo	1976 FL
*HALAIKO, Stephen Michael	1928 L	REDDEN, Arthur G.	1968 LH
*HALLER, Frank	1904 FE	*ROBINSON, Albert	1968 FE
*HARRIS, Ronald Allen	1964 L	ROSETTE, James Columbus	1964 M
*HARRIS, Ronald W.	1968 L	ROTHWELL, Benjamin, Jr.	1924 L
HARTMAN, Edward Earl	1920 B	ROUSE, Roger Wilson	1956 M
HENDERSON, Harry Havelock	1928 M	RUSSELL, Raymond N.	1972 LH
*HERRING, Horace	1948 W	RUTECKI, Chester	1936 W
HERSCHMAN, Maurice N.	1920 B	*SALAS, Joseph	1924 FE
HINES, John	1932 FE	*SALICA, Louis	1932 FL
JACKSON, Clinton	1976 W	*SANDERS, Hayes Edward	1952 H
JEWETT, Kenneth	1904 L	SCHELL, Edwin Wright	1920 LH
JOHNSON, Edward	1948 FE	SCRIVANI, Andrew	1936 L
JOHNSON, Louis Henry	1964 B	*SEALES, Ray	1972 LW
*JOHNSON, Marvin L.	1972 M	SELF, Louis Henry	1972 FE
*JONES, Alfred	1968 M	SEWARD, Arthur	1904 L
JONES, Reginald	1972 LM	SHAW, Joseph	1956 LW
JONES, Washington	1948 M	SMITH, Wallace	1948 L
KALETCHETZ, Al	1928 H	SODANO, Frank J.	1948 FL
KARA, Theodore Ernst	1936 FE	SPANAKOS, Nikos Michalis	1960 FE
KIRBY, Thomas Joseph	1924 LH	*SPANGER, Harry J.	1904 L, W
*KIRK, Oliver L.	1904 B, FE	SPIEZER, Charles W.	1948 LH
*La BARBA, Fidel	1924 FL	SPENGLER, William	1920 H
LAGONIA, Sam	1920 M	*SPINKS, Leon	1976 LH
LAMBERT, Jay	1948 H	*SPINKS, Michael	1976 M
LANE, Pearce Allen	1956 W	*SPRADLEY, Benjamin	1904 M
LANG, Joseph	1932 B	STEWART, Samuel G.	1920 H
*LAURIA, Louis Daniel	1936 FL	STURHOLDT, Peter	1904 L
LAZARUS, Joseph A.	1924 B	*TATE, John	1976 H
*LEE, Norvel LaFollette Ray	1952 LH	*TORRES, José Luis	1956 LM
LEFKOWITCH, Adolph	1924 M	*TRIPOLI, Salvatore	1924 B
*LEONARD, Ray Charles	1976 LW	*VALDEZ, Jesse	1972 W
LOWN, Thomas	1928 W	*Van HORN, Russell	1904 L
LUCAS, Leon	1928 LH	VASQUEZ, David	1968 FL
*LYDON, Joseph Patrick	1904 L, W	VINCIQUERRA, Carl	1936 LH
(see also Soccer)		WALKER, Charles Dexter, Jr.	1976 LM
*MARBLEY, Harlan J.	1968 LF	*WALLINGTON, James R., Jr.	1968 LW
*MAYER, Charles	1904 M, H	WEBB, Ellsworth	1952 LM
*McCLURE, Wilbert James	1960 LM	*WILSON, Jack	1936 B
		*YOUNG, Albert	1904 W

| ZIVIC, Jack A. | 1920 FE |
| ZIVIC, Peter P. | 1920 FL |

CANOE & KAYAKING (Men) (78)

Men's canoe & kayak events first appeared at the Olympics as a demonstration sport in 1924, but it became an official sport in 1936. The United States has always had a canoe team at the Olympics. The races have usually been of 1,000 meters, but events of 10,000 and 500 meters have been held. If no distance follows the event code, then that event was held at only one distance that year—1,000 meters.

5 = 500 meters	F1 = Folding kayak singles, 10,000 meters
10 = 1,000 meters	F2 = Folding kayak pairs, 10,000 meters
10k = 10,000 meters	R = 4 × 500 meters kayak singles relay
K1 = Kayak singles	C1 = Canadian singles
K2 = Kayak pairs	C2 = Canadian pairs
K4 = Kayak fours	K1S = Kayak singles slalom
C1S = Canadian singles slalom	C2S = Canadian pairs slalom

ANDERSON, John J.	1952 K2–10k
BARTON, Bruce	1976 K4, K2–10
BEACHAM, Paul John	1960 K1
	1968 K2
BOCHNEWICH, Paul	1952 K2–10k
BROSSIUS, John T., III	1972 K2
BUDROCK, Michael N.	1952 K1–10
BURTON, John Gamble	1972 C2S
BYERS, George Albert	1956 C2–10
CAMPBELL, Dwight Douglas	1972 K1S
CLARK, Raymond G., Jr.	1948 K2–10, K2–10k
CUTLER, Lester Edward	1968 K4
DEMUS, Arnold W.	1960 C2
DERMOND, Russell C.	1956 K2–10
	1960 R
DEYO, Peter Wallace	1976 K2–10, K4
DRONZEK, Joseph Francis	1964 C2
EISEMAN, John H.	1948 K2–10, K2–10k
	1952 K2–10
EVANS, Eric Maxfield	1972 K1S
EVANS, John Richard	1972 C2S
FOLKS, Burr	1936 K2–10, F1
GAEHLER, William	1936 K2–10k
GATES, William J.	1968 C2
GILMAN, David R.	1976 K1–10
GLAIR, John	1968 K1

GRAF, Robert J.	1936 C2–10
GRIGOLEIT, Gert Rudolf	1964 K2
HAAS, John Able	1952 C2–10, C2–10k
	1956 C2–10k
HASENFUS, Joseph Louis	1936 C1–10, C2–10k
HASENFUS, William Martin	1936 C2–10
*HAVENS, Frank Benjamin	1948 C1–10, C1–10k
	1952 C1–10, C1–10k
	1956 C1–10k
	1960 C1
HEINCKE, Ernest A.	1968 K4
HICKOX, Malcolm M.	1968 K4
HOLLAND, John Adams	1972 K1S
HORTON, Thomas F.	1948 K1–10
	1952 K2–10
HOUSTON, Edward Francis, Jr.	1956 K2–10k
JEWELL, William Harvey	1964 K4
JOHNSON, Michael A.	1976 K2–5
KELLY, Stephen A.	1972 K4
	1976 K4
KRAWCZYK, Henry	1976 K1–5
KRICK, Frank Joseph	1952 C2–10, C2–10k
	1956 C2–10k
LARSON, Mervil C.	1968 K4
LEACH, William	1976 K2–5
LOFGREN, William	1936 K2–10k
LUNDMARK, Charles M.	1960 R
LYDA, Charles	1976 C2–10
LYSAK, John	1936 F2
*LYSAK, Stephen J.	1948 C2–10, C2–10k
*MACKNOWSKI, Stephen Albert	1948 C2–10, C2–10k
*McEWAN, James Patrick	1972 C1S
McNUTT, Clarence Russell	1936 C2–10
MERWIN, David Pemberton	1956 K1–10
MITCHELL, Robert C.	1972 K1
MORAN, Richard L.	1956 C2–10
	1960 C2
MORRISON, Angus G.	1972 C1S
	1976 C1–5, C1–10
MUHLEN, Roland P.	1972 C2
	1976 C2–5
NICHOLS, Clayton Russell	1972 C2S
O'BRIEN, Robert William	1956 K1–10K
	1960 R
O'ROURKE, James J.	1936 F2
O'ROURKE, James J., Jr.	1964 C2
PAGKOS, John Cyril	1956 K2–10
	1960 R
PICKETT, John R.	1968 K4
RALPHS, Anthony W.	1964 K1, K2, K4
RICHARDS, Walter Charles, III	1964 K4
*RIEDEL, Ernest	1936 K1–10, K1–10k, K2–10
	1948 K1–10k
ROGOSHESKE, Philip Roy	1972 K4

SCHUETTE, William Henry	1952 K1–10k
	1956 C1–10
SMOKE, William Archibald	1964 K4
SOUTHWORTH, Thomas Roy	1972 C2S
*TORO, Andras Istvan	1960 C2
(competed for Hungary	1964 C1
in 1960 and 1964)	1972 C1
	1976 C2–10
TURNER, Brent	1976 K4
Van DYKE, John L.	1972 K4
Van VALKENBURGH, Dennis A.	1964 C1
WALKER, Wickliffe	1972 C1S
WEIGAND, Andreas J.	1968 C1
	1972 C2
	1976 C2–5
WEIGAND, Peter M.	1968 K2
WELBOURN, Jerry Lowell	1972 K4
WHITNEY, Alan Lawrence	1972 K2
WILSON, Kenneth James	1956 K2–10k
	1960 K2
WOLTERS, John A.	1960 K2

CANOE & KAYAKING (Women) (13)

Women's canoe & kayaking is a bit of a misnomer since in the Olympic Games women compete only in kayak events. Women's kayak events first appeared on the Olympic program in 1948, but the United States women first competed in 1960.

| 1 = Kayak singles | 4 = Kayak fours |
| 2 = Kayak pairs | S = Kayak slalom |

ASHTON, Caroline L.	1972 S
DRAGON, Linda J. Murray	1972 2
(as Miss Murray in 1972)	1976 2
DuCHAI, Mary Ann	1960 2
*FOX, Francine Anne	1964 2
GOODWIN, Cynthia Annice	1972 S
HOLCOMBE, Louise	1972 S
JEROME, Diane Irene	1960 2
*JONES, Marcia	
(see Marcia Smoke)	
LEACH, Julia Marie Jones	1976 1
MURRAY, Linda	
(see Linda Dragon)	
*PERRIER, Glorianne Aurore	1960 1
	1964 2
PURVIS, Nancy C.	1972 2
RADEMAKER, Sperry Joanna Jones	1968 2
*SMOKE, Marcia Ingram Jones	1964 1
(as Miss Jones in 1964)	1968 1, 2
	1972 1
TURNER, Ann Clare	1976 2

CYCLING (137)

Cycling is one of the few sports that has been included in every Olympic program, with the United States failing to have entrants only in 1896. The events have varied a great deal in distances, but the code below groups the events according to their type, such as the match sprint, which has been held at several distances (now always 1,000 meters). Until 1960 there was only one road race event, and the times or places for the individual team members determined the team placing as well. In 1960 a separate team road race event, the 100km team time trial, was instituted.

K = 1,000 meter time trial	50k = 50 km. tracrace
MS = Match sprint	20k = 20 km. track race
R = Road race (individual, since 1960)	1/4 = 1/4 mile track race
RI = Road race (individual, before 1960)	1/3 = 1/3 mile track race
RIT = Road race, individual and team	660 = 660 yard track race
T = Tandem match sprint (usually 2,000 m.)	1/2 = 1/2 mile track race
4kT = 4,000 meter team pursuit	M = 1 mile track race
4kI = 4,000 meter individual pursuit	2M = 2 mile track race
100T = 100 km. team time trial	5M = 5 mile track race
100k = 100 km. track race	25M = 25 mile track race

ADE, Harold	1932 4kT
ALLEN, Michael Gary	1964 100T
ALLEN, Russell	1932 4kT
ALLIS, John Cotton	1964 R, 100T
	1968 100T
*ANDREWS, A. F.	1904 1/4, 1/2, 5M, 25M
BALL, Richard Neal	1972 100T
BARCZEWSKI, Leigh Francis	1976 MS
BECHT, John	1912 RI
BECK, William H.	1920 4kT, MS, 50k
BECKER, Joseph Harry	1956 RIT
BELL, Allen Charles	1956 K, 4kT
	1960 K
BERTI, Ruggero	1932 4kT
*BILLINGTON, Edwin	1904 1/4, 1/3, 1/2, M, 2M, 5M, 25M
BIZZONI, Frank	1904 1/4
BOLL, David Lofgren	1976 R

BOULICAULT, John	1924 RIT
BRILANDO, Frank Peter	1948 RIT
	1952 K, T
BRINK, David L.	1968 4kI
BUTLER, Daniel	1968 R
BYRD, Albert	1936 4kT, RIT
CAMERON, George G.	1908 660, MS, 20k
CASTILLOUX, J. Raymond	1964 R
CHAUNER, David M.	1968 R, 4kT
	1972 4kT
CHOWEN, Wesley John	1960 R, 100T
	1964 100T
CONNELL, Frank	1932 RIT
CORTRIGHT, Richard Willis	1952 T
	1956 4kT
	1960 4kT
CUTTING, Harry Warren, III "Skip"	1964 4kI
	1968 4kT
DEEM, Paul Thomas	1976 4kT
DISNEY, Jack Wayne	1956 MS
	1964 T
	1968 T
DOTTERWEICH, Christopher	1920 4kT, MS, 50k
*DOWNING, Burton Cecil	1904 1/4, 1/3, 1/2, M, 2M, 5M, 25M
FENN, William S., Jr.	1924 MS, 50k
FERGUSON, Donald	1956 T
FRANCIS, Herbert N.	1960 MS
FREEMAN, James B.	1920 RIT
FREUND, William R.	1960 100T
FRITZ, Aime L. G.	1904 1/2
*GOERKE, Oscar	1904 1/4, 1/3, 1/2, M, 2M, 5M, 25M
GRIECO, Alan	1964 MS
GRINHAM, Fred	1904 1/4, 1/3, 1/2
GRONKOWSKI, Ignatius	1924 RIT, 50k
HARTMANN, Jack Ernest	1960 T
HEID, John S.	1948 K, MS
HENTSCHEL, Augustus	1924 RIT
HEWITT, Charles Noyes	1960 4kT
HILTNER, Michael Beckwith	1960 R, 100T
	1964 R, 100T
HOPKINS, Victor	1924 RIT
HOWARD, John Kennedy	1968 R, 100T
	1972 R, 100T
	1976 R, 100T
HROMJAK, Steve E.	1952 MS, 4kT
*HURLEY, Marcus Latimer	1904 1/4, 1/3, 1/2, M, 2M, 5M
INGHAM, Reydens	1932 T
KINGSBERRY, Alan	1976 100T
KOCKLER, Ernest T.	1920 RIT
KOPSKY, Joseph G.	1912 RI
*KRUSCHEL, Albert	1912 RIT
KUND, William	1964 K
*LAKE, John Henry	1900 MS
LARSEN, Leo	1904 1/2
LAUF, James George	1952 4kT
LaVOICE, Samuel	1904 25M
*LOFTES, Alvin Hjalmar	1912 RIT
LOGAN, William	1936 4kT, T
LONGSJO, Arthur Matthew (see also Speed Skating)	1956 RIT, 4kT
LUEDEKE, Otto	1932 RIT
LYNCH, Edward Arnold	1948 RIT
MAARANEN, Steven	1968 4kT
MAMMES, Bernard	1932 K
MARTIN, Oliver, Jr.	1964 4kT
	1968 100T
*MARTIN, Walter C.	1912 RIT
McCREA, Joel Nash	1904 M, 5M
MEISSNER, Frank August	1912 RI
MONTALDI, Frank	1904 1/4
MONTEMAGE, Thomas Ronald	1948 4kT
	1952 4kT
	1964 R
MORTON, Charles	1936 4kT, RIT
MOUNT, George L.	1976 R
MOUNTFORD, Timothy Howard	1964 T
	1968 MS
MULLICA, David	1972 4kT
NEEL, Michael	1976 R
NELSEN, Chester Alfred, Jr.	1948 RIT
NELSEN, Chester Alfred	1928 RIT
NELSEN, Donald Robert	1964 4kT
NEUMANN, Erhard M.	1956 RIT
NITZ, Leonard Harvey	1976 4kI, 4kT
NIXON, Paul E.	1936 RIT
NOGARA, August J.	1920 RIT
O'BRIEN, Henry, Jr.	1928 RIT
	1932 RIT
OCHOWICZ, James Lionel	1972 4kT
O'ROURKE, Thomas Charles	1952 RIT
OTTO, John	1920 RIT
PFARR, Robert M.	1960 4kT
PIKE, Jesse R.	1912 RI
PRANKE, Charles William	1968 T
RHOADS, David Stewart	1952 RIT
	1956 RIT
RHOADS, Ronald D.	1952 RIT
ROLLINS, Wendell L.	1948 RIT
ROSSI, James Joseph	1956 4kT, T
	1960 4kT
SCHAEFER, Julius	1904 5M, 25M
*SCHLEE, Charles	1904 1/3, 1/2, M, 2M, 5M, 25M
SCHNEIDER, Robert Roy	1972 R
*SCHUTTE, Carl Otto	1912 RIT
SCHWAB, Oscar	1904 1/4
SELLINGER, Albert	1936 MS, K, T
SHARP, David	1960 T
SHELDON, Donald Thomas	1952 4kT, RIT

SIMES, John Weston, III	1960 MS
	1964 MS
	1968 MS, K
SINIBALDI, John	1932 RIT
	1936 4kT, RIT
SKARIN, Ronald Philip	1972 100T
	1976 4kT
SMALL, Frank J.	1920 50k
SMESSAERT, Peter	1928 RIT
SMITH, Theodore Richard	1948 4kT
SPENCER, Jeffrey Eric	1972 MS, T
STEINERT, Jerome	1912 RI
STETINA, Wayne Douglas	1972 100T
	1976 100T
STILLER, Alfred William	1948 T, 4kT
STOCKHOLM, Carl G.	1920 RIT
TAYLOR, Fred	1920 4kT, MS, 50k
TESTA, Edward	1932 4kT
TESTA, Frank	1932 T
TETZLAFF, Robert P.	1960 R
THERRIO, Ralph P.	1972 T
	1976 4kT
THOMAS, Robert	1932 MS
THOMPSON, Marc	1976 100T
THOMSON, Marvin George	1948 T
UHRLASS, Arnold H.	1964 4kT
(see also Speed Skating)	
Van BOVEN, James W.	1968 100T
Vande VELDE, John C.	1968 4kT
	1972 4kI, 4kT
VEHE, Robert Ernest	1976 K
WALDETEUFEL, Emile	1972 R
WEINTZ, Louis J.	1908 MS, 20k, 100k
*WILEY, George E.	1904 1/2, M, 5M, 25M
WILLIAMSON, Anthony	1904 1/4, 1/2, M, 25M
WITTMAN, Henry	1904 1/4, 1/2
WOLF, Hans Joachim	1964 4kT
WOZNICK, Steven J.	1972 K
YOUNG, Anthony P.	1920 4kT, MS, 50k
YOUNG, Roger George	1972 MS
ZEBROSKI, E. Lars	1960 R

DIVING (Men) (56)

Diving events have been on the Olympic program at every Olympics except 1896 and 1900. The United States has been represented at all competitions.

SD = Springboard diving	HD = High (platform) diving
PHD = Plain high diving	D = Diving

*ANDERSON, Miller Altman	1948 SD
	1952 SD
*ANDREASON, Larry Edwin	1964 SD
*BALBACH, Louis J.	1920 SD, HD

*BOGGS, Philip George	1976 SD
BORNAMANN, Frank A.	1906 HD
(see also Swimming)	
*BROWNING, David Greig, Jr.	1952 SD
BUSH, Donald David	1972 SD
CALHOUN, John Collier	1952 HD
*CLOTWORTHY, Robert Lynn	1952 SD
	1956 SD
COLBATH, Walter Newell	1928 HD
*CONNOR, Richard Carroll	1956 HD
CRAGG, Robert Lewis, Jr.	1976 SD
*DEGENER, Richard Kempster	1932 SD
	1936 SD
*DesJARDINS, Ulise Joseph "Peter"	1924 SD, PHD
	1928 SD, HD
EARLEY, Richard Douglas	1972 HD
*FALL, David Athelstane	1924 HD
FARRELL, William Cesar	1956 HD
FINNERAN, Michael Holman	1972 SD, HD
*GAIDZIK, George William	1908 SD, HD
	1912 SD, HD, PHD
*GALITZEN, Michael Riley	1928 SD, HD
	1932 SD, HD
GILBERT, Richard Walter	1968 HD
*GOMPF, Thomas Eugene	1964 HD
*GORMAN, Francis Xavier	1964 SD
*GREENE, Al	1936 SD
GROTE, H. C.	1908 SD, HD
*HALL, Sam Nesley	1960 SD
*HARLAN, Bruce Ira	1948 SD, HD
*HARPER, Donald De Wayne	1956 SD
*HENRY, James Edward	1968 SD
*KEHOE, Frank	1904 D
*KUEHN, Louis Edward	1920 SD
*KURTZ, Frank A.	1932 HD
	1936 HD
*LEE, Samuel	1948 SD, HD
	1952 HD
*LINCOLN, Craig Howard	1972 SD
*LOUGANIS, Gregory	1976 SD, HD
McALEENAN, Arthur, Jr.	1912 SD, PHD
McCORMACK, John William	1952 HD
MOORE, Timothy David	1976 HD
*PINKSTON, Clarence Elmer	1920 SD, HD
	1924 SD, HD, PHD
*PRIESTE, Harry	1920 HD
*ROOT, Elbert Alonzo	1936 HD
RUSSELL, John Keith	1968 SD, HD
*RYDZE, Richard Anthony	1972 HD
*SHELDON, George Herbert	1904 D
*SITZBERGER, Kenneth Robert	1964 SD
*SMITH, Harold	1928 SD
	1932 SD, HD
THRASH, Ben	1924 PHD
*TOBIAN, Gary Milburn	1956 HD
	1960 SD, HD

VITUCCI, Louis Vincent	1964 HD
VOSLER, Kent Douglas	1976 HD
*WAYNE, Marshall	1936 SD, HD
*WEBSTER, Robert David	1960 HD
	1964 HD
*WHITE, Albert Cosad	1924 SD, HD
WHITTEN, Glen Allen	1956 SD
*WRIGHTSON, Bernard Charles	1968 SD
*YOUNG, Edwin Frank	1968 HD

DIVING (Women) (43)

Women's diving events first appeared in the Olympics in 1912, although the United States did not enter any female divers until the Antwerp Olympics in 1920. We have been represented without exception since that time.

SD = Springboard diving   HD = High (platform) diving

ALLEN, Aileen	1920 SD
*BECKER, Elizabeth Anna	
(see Elizabeth Pinkston)	
BRILEY, Melissa	1976 HD
*BUSH, Lesley Leigh	1964 HD
	1968 HD
*CHANDLER, Jennifer Bellomy	1976 SD
*COLEMAN, Georgia	1928 SD, HD
	1932 SD, HD
*COLLIER, Jeanne Ellen	1964 SD
COOPER, Linda Lee	1964 HD
*DRAVES, Victoria Manalo	1948 SD, HD
*DUNN, Velma Clancy	1936 HD
*ELSENER, Patricia Anne	1948 SD, HD
ELY, Janet	1972 SD, HD
	1976 HD
*FAUNTZ, Jane	1932 SD
(see also Swimming)	
*FLETCHER, Caroline	1924 SD
FRICK, Carol Helen	1952 SD
*GESTRING, Marjorie	1936 SD
GILDERS, Barbara Sue	1956 SD
GILLISEN, Cornelia	1936 HD
*GOSSICK, Sue	1964 SD
	1968 SD
GRIMES, Betty	1920 HD
*HILL, Dorothy Poynton	1928 SD
(as Miss Poynton in 1928	1932 HD
and 1932)	1936 SD, HD
HUNSBERGER, Clarita	1928 HD
*IRWIN, Juno Roslays Stover	1948 HD
(as Miss Stover in 1948)	1952 HD
	1956 HD
	1960 HD

*JENSEN, Zoe Ann Olsen	1948 SD
(as Miss Olsen in 1948)	1952 SD
*KING, Maxine Joyce "Micki"	1968 SD
	1972 SD, HD
LORD, Alice Harlekinden	1920 HD
*McCORMICK, Patricia Joan Keller	1952 SD, HD
	1956 SD, HD
*McINGVALE, Cynthia Ann Potter	1972 SD, HD
(as Miss Potter in 1972)	1976 SD
*MEANY, Helen	1920 HD
	1924 HD
	1928 SD
*MYERS, Paula Jean	
(see Paula Jean Pope)	
NEJMAN, Barbara Shaefer	1976 SD
*OLSEN, Zoe Ann	
(see Zoe Ann Jensen)	
*O'SULLIVAN, Keala	1968 SD
*PAYNE, Thelma R.	1920 SD
*PETERSON, Ann	1968 HD
*PINKSTON, Elizabeth Anna Becker	1924 SD, HD
(as Miss Becker in 1924)	1928 HD
*POPE, Paula Jean Myers	1952 HD
(as Miss Myers in 1952	1956 HD
and 1956)	1960 SD, HD
*POTTER, Cynthia	
(see Cynthia McIngvale)	
*POYNTON, Dorothy	
(see Dorothy Hill)	
&RAWLS, Katherine Louise	1932 SD
(see also Swimming)	1936 SD
&RIGGIN, Aileen M.	1920 SD, HD
(see also Swimming)	1924 SD
*ROPER, Marion Dale	1932 HD
*SMITH, Caroline	1924 HD
*STOVER, Juno Roslays	
(see Juno Irwin)	
*STUNYO, Jeanne Georgetta	1956 SD
TALMAGE, Barbara Ellen McAlister	1964 HD
	1968 HD
&WAINWRIGHT, Helen E.	1920 SD
(see also Swimming)	
*WILLARD, Mary Patricia	1960 SD
	1964 SD
*WILSON, Deborah Keplar	1976 HD

EQUESTRIAN EVENTS (74: 59 Men, 15 Women)

Women and men have competed against one another in equestrian events since 1952, prior to which time women were not allowed as competitors. Consequently we have not included a separate list for the women, but have included them below. They can be easily found by the "#" preceding their name.

A team event for dressage was first introduced in 1928 and, although scoring methods have differed, the team event has always been decided by the performance of the riders in the individual event. No differentiation between team and individual events is therefore necessary—with the exception of 1960 (when team scores were not officially calculated), a rider automatically competed in both events.

In the 3-day event, team placings have always been decided on the collective performances of the riders in the individual events so, again, no separate notations are necessary.

In 1912, 1920, 1960, and from 1968 onwards separate individual and team events were held in show jumping. From 1924 to 1956 and again in 1964, team placings were decided by the performances of the team members in the individual events.

3 = 3-day event (team and individual)	D = Dressage (team and individual)
J = Jumping (team and individual)	JI = Jumping (individual)
	HJ = High jump
JT = Jumping (team)	LJ = Long jump

ALLEN, Henry Tureman, Jr.	1920 JI
*ANDERSON, Charles Howard	1948 3
*ARGO, Edwin Yancey	1932 3
BABCOCK, Conrad Stanton	1936 D
BARRY, John Burke Alexander	1920 3, D
	1924 J, 3
BONTECAU, Frederic H.	1924 J
*BORG, Robert John	1948 D
	1952 D
	1956 D
BRADFORD, William B.	1932 J
	1936 J
BROWN, William	1976 JI
BURTON, Johnathan Rowell	1956 3
CARR, Frank Leslie	1924 3
	1928 J, 3
*CHAMBERLIN, Harry Dwight	1920 JT, 3, D
	1928 J
	1932 J, 3
*CHAPOT, Frank Davis	1956 J
	1960 JT
	1964 J
	1968 J
	1972 JT
	1976 J
#CHAPOT, Mary Wendy Mairs	1964 J
(as Miss Mairs in 1964)	1968 JT
*COFFIN, Edmund "Tad"	1976 3

*DAVIDSON, Bruce O.	1972 3
	1976 3
*DOAK, Sloan	1920 JT, 3, D
	1924 J, 3
	1928 3
DOWNER, John W.	1920 JI
#DOWNTON, Kyra G.	1968 D
DUFFY, Frank Hopkins	1956 3
#DuPONT, Helena Allaire	1964 3
ERWIN, Vincent P.	1920 JT
*FREEMAN, Kevin John	1964 3
	1968 3
	1972 3
FRIERSON, Andrew Allison	1948 J
#GALVIN, Patricia	
(see Princess de la Tour d'Auvergne)	
GEORGE, Charles P.	1928 3
GRAHAM, Ephraim Foster	1912 3
GREENWALD, Karl Chris	1920 JT
*#GURNEY, Hilda Carolyn	1976 D
#HAINES, Marjorie Benzet	1952 D
*HENRY, Frank Sherman	1948 3, D
*HENRY, Guy Vernor, Jr.	1912 JT, 3, D
*HOUGH, Charles Gordon, Jr.	1952 3
JADWIN, Cornelius Comegys, Jr.	1936 J
*KITTS, Isaac L.	1932 D
	1936 D
*#KUSNER, Kathryn Hallowell	1964 J
	1968 J
	1972 J
*LEAR, Ben, Jr.	1912 JT, 3
LURIE, David V.	1960 3
#MAIRS, Mary Wendy	
(see Mary Chapot)	
MANDL, Hermann John	1900 JI, HJ, LJ
*#MASTER, Edith Louise	1968 D
	1972 D
	1976 D
MATZ, Michael	1976 JT
*McCASHIN, Arthur John	1952 J
#McINTOSH, Karen Stuart	1964 D
&MONTGOMERY, John Carter	1912 JT, 3, D
(see also Polo)	
*MOORE, Alvin H.	1932 D
*#MORKIS, Dorothy	1976 D
*MORRIS, George Hayes	1960 J
MURPHY, William Dennis	1976 J
#NEWBERRY, Anne Jessica	1960 D
	1964 D
PADGETT, Vernon L.	1924 J, 3
*PAGE, Michael Owen	1960 3
	1964 3
	1968 3
PAULY, Hartmann Heinrick	1952 D
#PLUMB, Donnan Sharp	1968 D

*PLUMB, John Michael	1960 3
	1964 3
	1968 3
	1972 3
	1976 3
RAGUSE, Carl William Albert	1936 J, 3
RIDLAND, Robert Alexander	1976 JT
ROFFE, Adolphus Worrell	1928 J
*RUSSELL, John William	1948 J
	1952 J
*SHAPIRO, Neal	1972 J
*STALEY, Walter Goodwin, Jr.	1952 3
	1956 3
	1960 3
*STEINKRAUS, William Clark	1952 J
	1956 J
	1960 J
	1968 JI
	1972 J
#STEPHENS, Lois	1972 D
*#TAUSKEY, Mary Anne	1976 3
*THOMSON, Earl Foster	1932 3
	1936 3
	1948 3, D
#TOUR d'AUVERGNE, Princess	1960 D
Patricia Galvin de la	1964 D
(as Miss Patricia Galvin in 1960)	
*TUTTLE, Hiram E.	1932 D
	1936 D
#WATT, Elaine Shirley	1956 D
WEST, William Whitehead, Jr.	1920 JI, 3
WILEY, Hugh	1956 J
	1960 JI
WILLEMS, John Murphy	1936 3
WING, Franklin Fearing, Jr.	1948 J
WINNETT, John Windfield, Jr.	1972 D
*WOFFORD, James Cunningham	1968 3
	1972 3
*WOFFORD, John Edwin Brown	1952 3
WOFFORD, John William	1932 3

FENCING (Men) (150)

Fencing has been part of every Olympic program. The United States, however, had no fencers in 1896, 1906, and 1908.

EI = Epee, individual	ET = Epee, team
FI = Foil, individual	FT = Foil, team
SI = Sabre, individual	ST = Sabre, team
SS = Single-sticks	SM = Sabre for masters
	(professionals)

ACEL, Ervin S.	1928 ST

*ALESSANDRONI, Hugh Vincent	1932 FT
	1936 FI, FT
ALLISON, Philip Whalley	1924 FT
ANASTASI, Lawrence Joseph	1964 FT, ET
	1968 FI, FT
ANGER, Frank David	1964 EI, ET
APOSTOL, Paul	1972 SI, ST
	1976 SI, ST
*ARMITAGE, Norman Cudworth	1928 SI, ST
(né Norman Cudworth Cohn)	1932 SI, ST
(as Norman Cohn in 1928)	1936 SI, ST
	1948 ST
	1952 ST
	1956 ST
*AXELROD, Albert	1952 FI, FT
	1956 FI, FT
	1960 FI, FT
	1964 FI, FT
	1968 FT
BALLA, J. Thomas	1968 ST
BALLINGER, Edward	1976 FI, FT
BARNETT, Edward W.	1928 EI, ET
@BECK, Robert Lee	1968 ET
(see also Modern Pentathlon)	
BLOOMER, Harold Franklin	1924 FI, FT
BLOOMER, Millard J., Jr.	1920 FI
BLUM, Robert Max	1964 ST
	1968 ST
BORACK, Carl	1972 FI, FT
BOWMAN, Roscoe Leroy	1920 ST
BOWMAN, William Lawrence	1912 EI, FI, ET
BOYCE, Burke	1924 FI, FT
BOYD, Andrew L.	1936 ET
	1948 ET
BOZEK, Edward Scott	1972 ET
	1976 EI, ET
*BRECKINRIDGE, Henry Cabell	1920 EI, ET, FI, FT
	1924 ET
	1928 ET, FT
BRECKINRIDGE, Scott Dudley	1912 EI, FI, ET
BREED, George Horace	1912 EI, FI, ET
	1924 EI, ET, FT
BRUDER, Peter W.	1932 SI, ST
	1936 SI, ST
BUKANTZ, Daniel B.	1948 FT
	1952 FI, FT
	1956 FT
	1960 FT
*CALNAN, George Charles	1920 FI
	1924 EI, FI, FT
	1928 EI, ET, FI, FT
	1932 EI, ET, FT
CANTILLON, Daniel J.	1968 ET
deCAPRILES, Jose Raoul	1936 ET
	1948 EI, ET
	1952 ET, SI, ST

*deCAPRILES, Miguel Angel	1932 ET
	1936 ST
	1948 ST
CARSTENS, Theodore	1904 FI, SI
CASTNER, Lawrence Varsi	1924 SI, ST
*CETRULO, Dean Victor	1948 FI, FT, SI, ST
CHECKES, Jeffrey Alan	1968 FI, FT
COHEN, Abram Dreyer	1956 ET, ST
COHEN, Herbert Morris	1964 FI, FT
	1968 FI, FT
*COHN, Norman Cudworth	
(see Norman Armitage)	
CORBIN, Harold A.	1932 EI
CUNNINGHAM, Frederick John	1920 SI, ST
D'ASARO, Michael Anthony	1960 SI, ST
(né Michael Dasaro)	
DAVIS, Martin Jay	1972 FT
DIMOND, John William	1920 EI, ET, SI, ST
DONOFRIO, Edward Joseph	1976 FI, FT
DOW, Robert Stanley	1972 ST
DOW, Warren Alvin	1936 FT
DUTCHER, Ray W.	1920 EI, ET
DYER, Rex Richard	1956 ST
	1960 ST
*EVERY, Dernell	1928 FI, FT
	1932 FI, FT
	1948 FT
FAULKNER, Ralph Bearce	1932 ST
*FLYNN, James Hummitzsch	1948 ST
*FOX, Arthur G.	1904 FI, FT, SI
FRALEY, C. Bradford	1920 ST
FREEMAN, Joseph Bertham	1972 FI, FT
FULLINWIDER, Edwin Gaines	1920 SI, ST
	1924 ST
GIGNOUX, John Ernest	1912 EI, FI
	1924 SI, ST
GIOLITO, Silvio Louis	1948 FI, FT
	1952 FT
GLAZER, Eugene Gerson	1960 FI, FT
	1964 FT
GOLDSMITH, Harold David	1952 FT
	1956 FI, FT
	1960 FT
GOLDSTEIN, Ralph Myer	1948 ET
	1956 ET
*GREBE, William	1904 FI, SI, SS
HALL, Sherman	1912 EI, ET, FI
HAMMOND, Graeme Monroe	1912 EI, FI
*HAMORI, Eugene Arhand	1956 ST
(né Jenö Hámori)	1964 SI, ST
(competed for Hungary and	
as Jenö Hámori in 1956)	
*HEISS, Gustave Marinius	1932 EI, ET
	1936 EI, ET
HOITSMA, Kinmont Trefry	1956 EI, ET
HOLROYD, Wilfred G.	1904 FI

*HONEYCUTT, Francis Webster	1920 FI, FT
HUFFMAN, John Randolph	1928 SI, ST
	1932 SI, ST
	1936 SI, ST
HURD, John Gavin	1936 FT
*JAECKEL, Tracy	1932 ET
	1936 ET
JETER, Thomas Powers	1924 FI, FT
JONES, Uriah	1968 FT
KAPLAN, Stephen	1976 SI, ST
KEANE, Anthony John	1968 SI, ST
*KERESZTES, Attila	1956 ST
(competed for Hungary	1964 SI, ST
in 1956)	
KOLOWRAT, Henry, Jr.	1960 ET
KRIEGER, Byron L.	1952 FT
	1956 FI, FT
KWARTLER, Allan Sidney	1952 SI, ST
	1956 SI, ST
	1960 SI, ST
LANG, Martin	1976 FI, FT
LARIMER, Marc Winthrop	1912 EI, FI
*LEVIS, Joseph L.	1928 FI, FT
	1932 FI, FT
	1936 FI, FT
LEWIS, Norman	1948 EI, ET
LORBER, Theodore	1932 FI
LOSONCZY, Thomas John	1976 ST
LUBELL, Nathaniel	1948 FI, FT
	1952 FI, FT
	1956 FT
*LYON, Arthur St. Clair	1920 ET, FT, SI, ST
	1924 EI, ET, FT, SI, ST
	1928 ET, ST
MacLAUGHLIN, John Andrews	1912 EI, ET, FI
MAKLER, Brooke Adrian	1976 EI, ET
MAKLER, Paul Todd	1952 EI, ET
MAKLER, Paul Todd, Jr.	1972 ET
MARGOLIS, James Arthur	1960 EI, ET
MASIN, George Gabriel	1972 EI, ET
	1976 EI, ET
McPHERSON, Chauncey Ryder	1924 SI, ST
MELCHER, James Laurence	1972 EI, ET
MICAHNIK, David Morris	1960 EI, ET
	1964 EI, ET
	1968 EI, ET
MILNER, Allan B.	1924 EI, ET
	1928 EI, ET
MOORE, James Merriam	1912 EI
MORALES, Alfonso Hector	1960 SI, ST
	1964 ST
	1968 SI, ST
	1972 SI, ST
MURAY, Nickolas	1928 SI, ST
	1932 ST

deNAGY, Bela Tibor	1936 ST
NETBURN, Stephen Jeffrey	1968 EI, ET
	1972 EI, ET
NONNA, John Michael	1972 FI, FT
*NYILAS, Tibor Andrew	1948 SI, ST
	1952 ST
	1956 SI, ST
	1960 ST
*O'CONNOR, William Scott	1904 SS
ORBAN, Alex	1968 SI, ST
	1972 SI, ST
	1976 ST
ORLEANS, N.	1900 SM
ORLEY, Szaboles Thomas	1964 SI, ST
PALETTA, Joseph, Jr.	1960 FI, FT
PARKER, Joseph Brooks Bloodgood	1920 FI, SI, ST
	1924 ST
PATTON, George Smith, Jr.	1912 SI
(see also Modern Pentathlon)	
PECORA, William T., II	1936 FI, FT
PEROY, René	1928 FT
@PESTHY, Paul Karoly	1964 EI, ET
(see also Modern Pentathlon)	1968 EI, ET
	1976 ET
PEW, Richard Worden	1956 EI, ET
POTTER, John Ferdinand	1936 FT
PROKOP, Austin Martin	1948 FT
*RAYNER, Harold Marvin	1912 FI
(see also Modern Pentathlon)	1920 ET, FT
	1928 ET, FT
RICHARDS, Edwin Allan	1964 FI, FT
*RIGHEIMER, Frank Stahl, Jr.	1932 ET, FT
	1936 EI, ET
RUSSELL, William H.	1920 EI, ET
	1924 ET
SANDS, Thomas Jahn	1936 ET
SAUER, Alfred Ernest	1912 EI, FI, SI
SCHENCK, Fredric	1912 EI
SCHOONMAKER, Leon Monroe	1920 EI, FI
*SEARS, Robert	1920 ET, FT
(see also Modern Pentathlon)	
*SHEARS, Curtis Charles	1932 ET
SHORE, Leon	1924 ET
SHURTZ, Sewall	1956 EI, ET, FT
SIMMONS, Tyrone	1972 FT
SKROBISCH, Alfred	1952 EI, ET
SPINELLA, Ralph	1960 EI, ET
*STEERE, Richard Clarke	1932 FT
STEWART, Samuel Thompson, Jr.	1936 ST
STRAUCH, James	1952 ET
STRAUSS, Albert	1924 ST
*TATHAM, Charles T.	1904 EI, FI, FT
THOMPSON, Donald Gilkey	1948 ET
*TOWNSEND, Charles Fitzhugh	1904 EI, FI, FT
TREVES, Alessandro Emanuele	1952 ST

Van BUSKIRK, Harold	1924 ST
	1928 ST
	1932 ST
*Van Zo POST, Albertson	1904 EI, FI, FT, SI, SS
	1912 EI, ET, FI, SI
VEBELL, Edward Thomas	1952 EI, ET
WALDHAUS, Donald	1924 ET
WALKER, Claiborne Jay	1920 SI, ST
WEBER, Fredrick Reginia	1936 EI
(see also Modern Pentathlon)	
WEILL	1900 FI
WESTBROOK, Peter	1976 SI, ST
WOLFF, Albert	1948 EI, ET
	1952 ET
WOMMACK, Roland Raymond	1960 ET
*WORTH, George Vitez	1948 SI, ST
(né György Vitez)	1952 SI, ST
	1956 SI, ST
	1960 ST
WRIGHT, Edward	1976 FT

FENCING (Women) (26)
Fencing for women was first on the Olympic program in 1924. The United States has entered women fencers for every Olympic tournament. Women compete only in the foil in the Olympics in an individual and a team event.

I = Individual	T = Team

ADAMOVICH, Tatyana P.	1972 T
ANGELL, Tommy Ferrell	1964 I, T
ARMSTRONG, Sheila Dorothy	1976 I, T
CERRA, Maria del Pilar	1948 I
CLOVIS, Natalia	1972 T
CRAUS, Polly	1952 I
D'ASARO, Gay Kristine Jacobson	1976 T
DOW, Helena Mroczkowska	1948 I
DRUNGIS, Anne Mary	1964 T
FRANKE, Nikki V. Tomlinson	1976 I, T
GEHRIG, Adeline	1924 I
GOODRICH, Judy Kay	1956 I
	1960 T
GUGGOLZ, Muriel	1932 I
HOPPER, Irma	1924 I
	1928 I
KING, Harriet	1960 I, T
	1964 I, T
	1968 I, T
	1972 I, T
LLOYD, Marion	1928 I
	1932 I
	1936 I

LOCKE, Dorothy Brown	1932 I
	1936 I
MITCHELL, Maxine Elizabeth	1952 I
	1956 I
	1960 T
	1968 T
O'CONNOR, Denise Catherine	1964 T
	1976 T
O'DONNELL, Ann Patricia	1972 I, T
	1976 I, T
PECHINSKY, Sally	1968 T
ROMARY, Janice-Lee York	1948 I
(as Miss York in 1948	1952 I
and 1952)	1956 I
	1960 I, T
	1964 I, T
	1968 I, T
SMITH, Veronica Cserepfalvi	1968 I, T
TERHUNE, Evelyn F.	1960 I, T
deTUSCAN, Joanna Savich	1936 I
WHITE, Ruth C.	1972 I, T
YORK, Janice-Lee	
(see Janice Romary)	

FIELD HOCKEY (40)

Men's field hockey has been part of the Olympic program since 1908, although not continuously. The United States has entered teams only in 1932, 1936, 1948, and 1956.

In 1980 at Moscow, women competed in a field hockey tournament in the Olympics for the first time. Of course the United States was not represented. Field hockey for women is also on the 1984 Olympic program and it is expected that the United States will make its Olympic debut in the sport at that time.

BLACK, Edgar Newbold, IV	1956
*BODDINGTON, William Westcott	1932
	1936
*BREWSTER, Harold S.	1932
BUCK, Donald E.	1948
BUCK, Lanphear	1936
CLIFFORD, Henry Charles	1956
*DEACON, Amos R. Little	1932
	1936
*DISSTON, Horace Cumberland	1932
	1936
*EWING, Samuel Evans	1932
	1936
FENTRESS, Paul Lyon	1936
*GENTLE, James Cuthbert	1932
	1936

GERSON, Claus O.	1948
GODFREY, Ellwood Watson	1936
GOODE, Henry Russell	1948
*GREER, Henry Kirk	1932
HARRIS, Stanley James, Jr.	1956
HEWITT, Frederic M.	1948
JONGENEEL, James Cornelius	1956
*KNAPP, Laurence A.	1932
	1936
KRUIZE, Gerrit	1956
KURTZ, William L.	1948
LEEGSTRA, Tjerk Hidde	1956
LUBBERS, Henrik M.	1948
MARCOPLOS, Harry Byron	1948
	1956
*McMULLIN, David, III	1932
	1936
*O'BRIEN, Leonard Francis	1932
	1936
ORBAN, Kurt	1948
	1956
RENWICK, John P., Jr.	1948
ROTE, John	1956
*SHEAFFER, Charles Miller, Jr.	1932
	1936
SIMS, Sanders S.	1948
SLADE, John H.	1948
(né John Schlessinger)	
STUDE, Walter William	1948
	1956
TURNBULL, John Iglehart	1936
THOMPSON, Alexis	1936
UCKO, Felix Alfred	1948
	1956
UCKO, Kurt Joseph	1956
WILSON, William A.	1948
WITTELSBERGER, Raymond Charles	1956
*WOLTERS, Frederick	1932

FIGURE SKATING (Men) (54)

Figure skating has been held at every celebration of the Olympic Winter Games. In addition, special figure skating competitions were held as part of the Summer Games in 1908 and 1920. The United States has been represented every time the sport has been held.

S = Men's singles	P = Pairs
D = Ice dancing	

*ALLEN, Scott Ethan	1964 S
*BADGER, Sherwin Campbell	1928 S, P
	1932 P
BERNDT, Douglas Brian	1972 S
BORDEN, Gail, II	1932 S

BOTTICELLI, Michael	1980 P
BREWER, Robert L.	1960 S
BROKAW, Isaac Irving	1908 S
BROWN, Timothy T.	1960 S
*BUTTON, Richard Totten	1948 S
	1952 S
CARRUTHERS, Peter	1980 P
FAUVER, William Benjamin	1976 P
FOTHERINGILL, Jerry Joseph	1964 P
GARDNER, Randy	1976 P
GREINER, Robin Lewis	1956 P
*GROGAN, James David	1948 S
	1952 S
HADLEY, Ray E., Jr.	1960 P
HAMILTON, Scott	1980 S
HILL, George Edward Bellows	1936 S, P
HOYT, Monty	1964 S
*JENKINS, David Wilkinson	1956 S
	1960 S
*JENKINS, Hayes Alan	1952 S
	1956 S
JOSEPH, Ronald Bert	1964 P
KAUFFMAN, Ronald Lee	1964 P
	1968 P
*KENNEDY, Michael Edward, III	1948 P
	1952 P
KOTHMAN, Sully	1956 P
KUBICKA, Terry Paul	1976 S
LEE, Robin	1936 S
LETTENGARVER, John	1948 S
LITZ, Thomas Jeffry	1964 S
*LUDINGTON, Ronald Edmund	1960 P
MADDEN, James L.	1932 S
	1936 P
McKELLEN, Gordon Riley, Jr.	1972 S
MILITANO, Mark	1972 P
*MILLNS, James G., Jr.	1976 D
NAGLE, William J.	1932 S
NIGHTINGALE, John Sheridan	1952 P
NILES, Nathaniel William	1920 S, P
	1924 S, P
	1928 S, P
PETKEVICH, John Misha	1968 S
	1972 S
REITER, Erle	1936 S
RICHARDS, Dudley Shaw	1960 P
*ROBERTSON, Ronald F.	1956 S
SANTEE, David Neil	1976 S
	1980 S
SAVAGE, Joseph Knebel	1932 P
(né Joseph Knebel Staples)	
SEIBERT, Michael	1980 D
SHELLEY, Kenneth	1968 P
	1972 S, P
STROUKOFF, Andrew	1976 D
SUMMERS, John	1980 D

SWENNING, Robert J.	1948 P
*TICKNER, Charles	1980 S
TURNER, Roger F.	1928 S
	1932 S
VISCONTI, Gary	1968 S
WAGELEIN, Roy	1968 P
WEIGLE, Douglas Kent	1976 D
*WOOD, Timothy Lyle	1968 S

FIGURE SKATING (Women) (54)

Like the men, women have participated in Olympic figure skating competitions since 1908, although the U.S. had no entrants in 1908.

Since 1920, United States women have been represented at every Olympic figure skating tournament.

S = Women's singles   P = Pairs
D = Ice dancing

*ALBRIGHT, Tenley Emma	1952 S
	1956 S
ALLEN, Lisa-Marie	1980 S
ASH, Lucille Mary	1956 P
BABILONIA, Tai Reina	1976 P
BAXTER, Virginia D.	1952 S
BENNETT, Margaret	1932 S
*BLANCHARD, Theresa Weld	1920 S, P
(as Miss Weld in 1920)	1924 S, P
	1928 S, P
BLUMBERG, Judy	1980 D
BROWN, Barbara	1972 P
BURGE, Wendy Lee	1976 S
CARRUTHERS, Caitlin "Kitty"	1980 P
COOK, Alice Maxine	1976 P
DAVIS, Suzanne	1932 S
*FLEMING, Peggy Gale	1964 S
	1968 S
FOTHERINGILL, Judianne	1964 P
FRANKS, Sheryl	1980 P
*FRATIANNE, Linda Sue	1980 S
GENOVESI, Judi	1976 P
GERHAUSER, Janet Jean	1952 P
HADLEY, Ila Ray	1960 P
HAIGLER, Christine	1964 S
*HAMILL, Dorothy Stuart	1976 S
*HEISS, Carol Elizabeth	1956 S
	1960 S
HOLMES, Julie Lynn	1972 S
JOSEPH, Vivian Laureen	1964 P
KAUFFMAN, Cynthia Diane	1964 P
	1968 P
KELLEY, Susan	1976 D

*KENNEDY, Karol Estelle	1948 P	BURTON, William W.	1904 I
	1952 P	*CADWALADER, Douglas P.	1904 I, T
KLOPFER, Sonya Helen	1952 S	*CADY, John Deere	1904 I, T
LENZ, Sandra	1980 S	*CARLETON, Jesse L.	1904 I, T
*LOUGHRAN, Beatrix S.	1924 S	CARLETON, Murray	1904 I
	1928 S, P	CASE, Henry L.	1904 I
	1932 P	CORY, Charles B.	1904 I
*LUDINGTON, Nancy Irene Rouillard	1960 P	*CUMMINS, Edward M. "Ned"	1904 I, T
*LYNN, Janet	1968 S	DAVIS, E. M.	1904 I
(née Janet Lynn Nowicki)	1972 S	EDMUNDS, E. C.	1904 I
MACHADO, Catherine Louise	1956 S	*EDWARDS, Kenneth Paine	1904 T
MADDEN, Grace E.	1936 P	*EGAN, Henry Chandler	1904 I, T
MEREDITH, Gertrude	1932 P	*EGAN, Walter Eugene	1904 I, T
MERRILL, Gretchen van Zandt	1948 S	FLACK, R. H.	1904 I
MILITANO, Melissa	1972 P	FOULIS, Simpson	1904 I
MURRAY, Suna	1972 S	*FRASER, Harold D.	1904 I, T
NOYES, Albertina Natalie	1964 S	GOULD, Edward	1904 I
	1968 S	GROSECLOSE, William B.	1904 I
*O'CONNOR, Colleen	1976 D	HARBAUGH, Simon James	1904 I
ORMACA, Carole Anne	1956 P	HAVEMEYER, Arthur	1904 I
OWEN, Laurence R.	1960 S	HAVEMEYER, Raymond	1904 I
OWEN, Maribel Y.	1960 P	HAZLETON, L. J.	1904 I
PEPPE, Audrey	1936 S	HERSEY, W. A.	1904 I
*ROLES, Barbara Ann	1960 S	HOWARD, J. J.	1904 I
SEIGH, Eileen	1948 S	HUNT, Jarvis	1904 I
SHERMAN, Yvonne	1948 S, P	HUNTER, Edwin L.	1904 I
SMITH, Stacey	1980 D	*HUNTER, Robert Edward	1904 I, T
STARBUCK, Alicia "JoJo"	1968 P	*HUSSEY, Arthur D.	1904 I, T
	1972 P	JONES, E. Lee	1904 I
SWEITZER, Sandi Sue	1968 P	*JONES, Orus W.	1904 I, T
*VINSON, Maribel Y.	1928 S	*LAMBERT, Albert Bond	1900 I
	1932 S		1904 I, T
	1936 S, P	LANSING, E. W.	1904 I
WEIGEL, Estelle D.	1936 S	*LARD, Allen E.	1904 I, T
WEIGEL, Louise E.	1932 S	MACKINTOSH, Alexander	1904 I
	1936 S	*MAXWELL, John R.	1904 T
*WELD, Theresa		*McKINNIE, Burt P.	1904 I, T
(see Theresa Blanchard)		*McKITTRICK, Ralph	1904 I, T
		(see also Tennis)	

GOLF (Men) (76)

An Olympic golf championship was held on an individual basis for men in 1900. At the 1904 Olympics, there was an individual and team championship held for men.

I = Individual event	T = Team event	*MOORE, Nathaniel Fish, II	1904 I, T
		NEWBERY, Frederick Ernest	1904 I
		*NEWTON, Francis Clement	1904 I, T
ADAMS, Bart	1904 I	*OLIVER, George C.	1904 I, T
ALLEN, Harry W.	1904 I	*PHELPS, Mason Elliott	1904 I, T
ALLIS, Louis	1904 I	POTTER, Charles	1904 I
ANGIER, Clarence	1904 I	*POTTER, Henry	1904 I, T
ANNAN, A. H.	1904 I	POWELL, George	1904 I
BOYD, Louis	1904 I	*PRICE, Simeon Taylor, Jr.	1904 I, T
BRANDT, J. S.	1904 I	*RAHM, John B.	1904 I, T
BROWN, E. Campbell	1904 I	*SANDS, Charles Edward	1900 I
		(see also Tennis and Jeu de Paume)	
		*SAWYER, Daniel Edward "Ned"	1904 I, T
		SCUDDER, Charles White	1904 I
		*SEMPLE, Frederick Humphrey	1904 I, T
		(see also Tennis)	
		SHAW, Wallace F.	1904 I

SIMKINS, Harold W.	1904 I
SMITH, William Poultney	1904 I
*SMOOT, Clement E.	1904 I, T
STACK, J. L.	1904 I
*STICKNEY, Stuart Grosvenor	1904 I, T
*STICKNEY, William Arthur	1904 I, T
SUMNEY, Herbert Clayton	1904 I
TAYLOR, Frederick W.	1900 I
THOMAS, George A.	1904 I
VICKERY, Abner C.	1904 I
WATSON, John T.	1904 I
*WEBER, Harold	1904 I, T
WILLARD, C. E.	1904 I
WITHERS, William T.	1904 I
*WOOD, Warren K.	1904 I, T
YATES, Mead W.	1904 I

GOLF (Women) (4)

Golf appeared on the Olympic program twice, in 1900 and 1904, but only in 1900 did women compete. There was an individual event only.

*ABBOTT, Margaret Ives	1900
ABBOTT, Mary Perkins Ives	1900
*PRATT, Daria Pankhurst Wright	1900
*WHITTIER, Pauline "Polly"	1900

GYMNASTICS (Men) (188)

Gymnastics has been on the program of every modern Olympic Games. Americans competed for the first time at St. Louis in 1904, making up virtually the entire entry list, but they did not appear again until 1920. Since 1920 the U.S. has entered male gymnasts at every celebration.

In 1904 the gymnastics events were held in July, although a much smaller set of events was also held in October. (The October events are of marginal Olympic caliber.) In the July events all gymnasts competed on three apparatuses, performing three exercises on each. In addition they competed in three track & field events—shot put, 100 yard dash, and long jump. There were four championships contested: a triathlon consisting of scores from the three track & field events; all-around (12 events), consisting of adjusted triathlon scores and scores from the nine performances on the three apparatuses; all-around (nine events), consisting of scores from the nine performances on the three apparatuses; and a team event based on adjusted total scores made by team members in the all-around (12 events). In the October events that year there was another all-around championship consisting of four events—horizontal bar, horse vaulting, pommelled horse, and parallel bars.

In 1920 there was an individual and a team all-around event. There was no American team in the team event, but several of our gymnasts entered the individual all-around, consisting of parallel bars, horizontal bars, pommelled horse, and rings. There were no individual apparatus championships.

In 1924 and 1928 there were five individual apparatus championships based on scores made in the individual all-around. Team all-around was also based on the individual scores. Thus all competitors competed in every event. There was also a rope climb in 1924 that was part of the all-around competition.

In 1932 the individual all-around consisted of five events—horizontal bar, parallel bars, pommelled horse, horse vaulting, and rings. Individual apparatus finals were held in these events, separate from the all-around; they were also offered in floor exercise, club swinging, rope climbing and tumbling. There was a team all-around that was based on the scores made in the individual all-around competition.

From 1936 through 1956 all competitors competed on six apparatuses—floor exercises, horizontal bar, parallel bar, pommelled horse, horse vaulting, and rings. Scores on these were used to determine individual apparatus champions, then totaled to determine individual all-around champions, and the team members' scores determined team all-around placings. Thus all team members automatically competed in all eight events.

Since 1960 the situation has varied slightly, but all team members now compete automatically only in the team all-around. Their scores in that event determine qualifiers for the individual all-around, but not all competitors qualify for this event. Scores made in the individual all-around then determine qualifiers for the individual apparatus finals—but again not all individual all-around competitors qualify for this section of the program.

AI = All-around, individual (since 1920)	P = Parallel bars
	PH = Pommelled horse
AT = All-around, team	
AIT = All-around, individual & team (since 1920)	V = Vaulting horse
12 = All-around, 12 events (1904)	F = Floor exercises
9 = All-around, 9 events (1904)	R = Rings
4 = All-around, 4 events (1904)	RC = Rope climbing
3 = Triathlon (1904)	C = Club swinging
H = Horizontal bar	T = Tumbling

ALLEN, Kanati	1968 AIT
ANDELFINGER, William	1904 3, 9, 12
ASCHENBRENER, George	1904 3, 9, 12, AT
AVENER, Marshall	1972 AT
	1976 AT
BANNER, Larry Shyres	1960 AIT
	1964 AIT
BARAK, Ronald S.	1964 AIT
BARRY, M.	1904 3, 9, 12
BASCHER, M.	1904 3, 9, 12, AT
*BASS, Raymond Henry	1932 RC
BEACH, Thomas	1976 AT
BECKNER, John Gilbert	1952 AIT
	1956 AIT
	1960 AIT
BECKNER, Richard Andrew	1956 AIT
BEREWALD, William	1904 3, 9, 12, AT
BERG, Bernard	1904 3, 9, 12, AT
BERG, Ragnar	1904 3, 9, 12, AT
BERRY, Glenn H.	1928 AIT
*BEYER, Emil	1904 3, 9, 12, AT
BISHOP, Richard Alfred	1932 R
*BISSINGER, John F.	1904 3, 9, 12, AT
*BIXLER, Dallas Denver	1932 H
BLATTMAN, Walter Conrad	1952 AIT
BOHNKE, Otto	1904 3, 9, 12
BONSALL, William Alfred	1948 AIT
BORDO, Louis John (did not compete in horse vaulting)	1948 AIT
*CARMICHAEL, Edward	1932 V
CHIMBEROFF, Barney	1904 3, 9, 12
COHEN, Steven Robert	1968 AIT
*CONNOLLY, Thomas Francis	1932 RC
CONNOR, Bart	1976 AT
CROSBY, John George, Jr.	1972 AT
CULHANE, James Patrick, Jr.	1972 AT
*CUMISKEY, Frank	1932 AIT, PH
	1936 AIT
	1948 AIT
D'AUTORIO, Vincent	1948 AIT
	1952 AIT
DELLERT, Charles	1904 3, 9, 12
DELLERT, John	1904 3, 9, 12, AT
*DENTON, William Thomas	1932 R
DEUBLER, Christian	1904 3, 9, 12, AT
*DUHA, John	1904 3, 4, 9, 12, AT
DWYER, James	1904 3, 9, 12, AT
*EMMERICH, Max (see also Track & Field)	1904 3, 9, 12
*ERENBERG, Philip Richard	1932 C
*EYSER, George	1904 3, 4, 9, 12, AT, RC
FEYDER, Otto	1904 3, 9, 12, AT
FISCHER, M.	1904 3, 9, 12, AT
FREUDENSTEIN, Sidney	1968 AIT
FRIEDRICH, William	1904 3, 9, 12, AT
*GALBRAITH, William Jackson	1932 RC
*GLASS, Hermann T.	1904 R
GLEYRE, Marcel	1932 V
GREENFIELD, George H.	1972 AT
*GRIEB, John (see also Track & Field)	1904 3, 9, 12, AT
GRIFFIN, Kenneth	1936 AIT
*GROSS, Edward	1932 T
GROSS, Theodore	1904 3, 9, 12, AT
GROSSFELD, Abraham Israel	1956 AIT
	1960 AIT
GUERNER, L.	1904 3, 9, 12
*GULACK, George Julius	1932 R
GUSSMAN, P.	1904 3, 9, 12, AT
HANSEN, Harry	1904 3, 9, 12, AT
*HAUBOLD, Frank Otto	1928 AIT
	1932 AIT, P, PH
	1936 AIT
*HEIDA, Anton	1904 3, 4, 9, 12, AT
*HENNIG, Edward A.	1904 3, 4, 9, 12, AT, C
*HERMANN, William John	1932 T
HERMERRLING, G.	1904 3, 9, 12, AT
HERRMANN, Robert	1904 3, 9, 12, AT
HERTENBAHN, Jacob	1904 3, 9, 12, AT
HERZOG, William	1904 3, 9, 12
*HESS, Max	1904 3, 9, 12, AT
HOLDER, Donald Joseph	1952 AIT
HORSCHKE, William	1904 3, 9, 12, AT
HUNGER, L.	1904 3, 9, 12, AT
HUG, Steven Keith	1968 AIT
	1972 AIT
JAHNKE, Anthony	1904 3, 9, 12
*JOCHIM, Alfred A.	1924 AIT
	1928 AIT
	1932 AIT, P, V, H, PH
	1936 AIT

JORGENSEN, Bjorne	1920 AI
*KASSELL, Phillipp	1904 3, 9, 12, AT
KEIM, Leander	1904 3, 9, 12, AT
KEMPF, Andreas	1904 3, 9, 12
KIDDINGTON, Clarence	1904 3, 9, 12, AT
KNERR, Otto	1904 3, 9, 12
KNIEP, Louis	1904 3, 9, 12
KOEDER, Henry	1904 3, 9, 12, AT
*KORMANN, Peter Martin	1976 AIT, F
KOTYS, Joseph	1948 AIT
KRAFT, Henry	1904 3, 9, 12, AT
*KRAUSE, Charles	1904 3, 9, 12, AT, RC
KREMPEL, Paul W.	1920 AI
	1928 AIT
KRITSCHMANN, Alvin	1904 3, 9, 12, AT
*KRIZ, Frank J.	1920 AI
	1924 AIT
	1928 AIT
KRUPITZER, Rudolph	1904 3, 9, 12, AT
KRUPPINGER, William	1904 3, 9, 12
*KUHLEMEIER, William	1932 C
LANDNES, Oluf	1904 3, 9, 12, AT
LANG, Michael	1904 3, 9, 12, AT
LEICHINGER, John	1904 3, 9, 12, AT
LUDWIG, Martin	1904 3, 9, 12
MAIS, John D.	1920 AI
	1924 AIT
MASTROVICH, George	1904 3, 9, 12
*MAYER, George	1904 3, 9, 12, AT
*MAYSACK, Robert E.	1904 3, 9, 12, AT
*MERZ, William A.	1904 3, 4, 9, 12, AT, R
MESSELL, John	1904 3, 9, 12, AT
*MEYER, Frederick H.	1932 AIT
	1936 AIT
MEYLAND, Hy	1904 3, 9, 12, AT
MITCHELL, Russell Duncan	1964 AIT
MUELLER, Gustav	1904 3, 9, 12
NEIMAND, Otto	1904 3, 9, 12, AT
NEU, Andrew	1904 3, 9, 12, AT
NEWHART, Harold Guthrie	1928 AIT
NILSEN, Bergin	1904 3, 9, 12, AT
NOVAK, Rudolph	1924 AIT
OLSEN, Oliver	1904 3, 9, 12, AT
O'QUINN, Garland Deloid, Jr.	1960 AIT
ORLOFSKY, Frederick C.	1960 AIT
PEARSON, John Bartling, Jr.	1924 AIT
	1928 AIT
PHILLIPS, Chester W.	1936 AIT
PITT, Arthur E.	1936 AIT
PLACKE, August	1904 3, 9, 12, AT
PRINZLER, Henry	1904 3, 9, 12
PUESCHELL, Edward	1904 3, 9, 12
RAAD, Frank	1904 3, 9, 12
RATHKE, L.	1904 3, 9, 12, AT
REAL, Walter	1904 3, 9, 12, AT
*RECKEWEG, Ernst	1904 3, 9, 12, AT

REYNOLDS, Robert	1904 3, 9, 12, AT
RITTER, P.	1904 3, 9, 12, AT
ROEDEK, K.	1904 3, 9, 12, AT
ROETHLISBERGER, Frederick	1968 AIT
ROETZHEIM, William Henry, Jr.	1948 AIT
	1952 AIT
ROISSNER, Otto	1904 3, 9, 12, AT
*ROSENKAMPFF, Arthur H.	1904 3, 9, 12, AT
*ROTH, George Helm	1932 C
ROTHE, Emil	1904 3, 9, 12, AT
ROTTMAN, Curtis	1924 AIT
SAFANDRA, Frank	1924 AIT
SAKOMOTO, Makoto Douglas	1964 AIT
	1972 AT
SCHICKE, Frank	1904 3, 9, 12, AT
SCHMIND, Fred	1904 3, 9, 12,
*SCHMITZ, Julian	1904 3, 9, 12, AT
SCHRADER, Rudolph	1904 3, 9, 12, AT
SCHRADER, Willard	1904 3, 9, 12
SCHROEDER, George	1904 3, 9, 12
SCHULER, Michael	1932 AIT, P, H
*SCHUSTER, Philip	1904 3, 9, 12, AT
SCHWARTZ, Charles	1904 3, 9, 12
SCHWEGLER, Emil	1904 3, 9, 12
SCROBE, Edward J.	1948 AIT
	1952 AIT
SHURLOCK, Arthur David	1964 AIT
*SIEGLER, Edward	1904 3, 9, 12, AT
SIMMS, Charles Otto	1952 AIT
	1956 AIT
SONTAG, Phillip	1904 3, 9, 12, AT
SORENSEN, Raymond Stephen	1948 AIT
SORUM, Charles	1904 3, 9, 12, AT
SPANN, Lorenz	1904 3, 9, 12
SPERL, Christian	1904 3, 9, 12, AT
STAPF, George	1904 3, 9, 12, AT
*STEFFEN, Otto I.	1904 3, 9, 12, AT
STOUT, Robert H.	1952 AIT
STUDEL, Paul	1904 3, 9, 12, AT
STUDLER, Theodore	1904 9, 12, AT
SUNDBYE, Arthur	1904 3, 9, 12
THOMAS, Kurt Bitteraux	1976 AIT
THOMAS, Max	1904 3, 9, 12
THOMSEN, Otto	1904 3, 9, 12
THOR, David B.	1968 AIT
TOM, William	1956 AIT
TONRY, Donald Robert	1960 AIT
TRABAND, William	1904 3, 9, 12
TRITSCHLER, Edward	1904 3, 9, 12, AT
TRITSCHLER, Richard	1904 3, 9, 12
TRITSCHLER, William	1904 3, 9, 12, AT
UMBS, Charles	1904 3, 9, 12, AT
VEGA, Jose Armando	1956 AIT
*VOIGT, Emil	1904 3, 9, 12, AT, R, RC, C
WAGNER, Reinhard	1904 3, 9, 12, AT
WANDRER, Max	1924 AIT

WARNKEN, Harry	1904 3, 9, 12, AT
WASSOW, J.	1904 3, 9, 12, AT
WEISS, Gregor Richard	1964 AIT
WHEELER, George Edward	1936 AIT
*WILSON, Ralph	1904 C
WITZIG, Herman, Jr.	1928 AIT
WOERNER, K.	1904 3, 9, 12
WOLF, John	1904 3, 9, 12
*WOLF, Max	1904 3, 9, 12, AT
*WOLFE, Rowland	1932 T
YOUNG, Wayne	1976 AIT
ZABEL, Wilhelm	1904 3, 9, 12

GYMNASTICS (Women) (48)

Women's gymnastics first appeared on the Olympic program in 1928. It was not held in 1932, but returned in 1936, when United States women made their first appearance.

In 1936 all women competed on three apparatuses—uneven parallel bars, balance beam, and vaulting horse. The totals for each team member were then added to determine team all-around placings. There was no individual all-around event, nor were there individual apparatus championships. The same situation held true in 1948.

In 1952 a new event was added—floor exercise; an individual all-around was also added. Women again competed in every event; their apparatus scores were added to give individual all-around placings and the totals were added to give team placings. This was also true in 1956.

In 1960 a new format appeared and has been in use until today with only minor variations. Team competition was held first and all competitors competed on all apparatuses. Individual all-around scores were also determined (now only in part) by this segment. Separate championships were then held for each apparatus and only six women competed on each—those with the six best scores for that event in the all-around championship. Thus women no longer necessarily compete in every event—in fact, since 1964, the United States has advanced only one woman (Linda Metheny—1968 balance beam) to an apparatus final.

6 = All six events (team and individual all-around, uneven parallel bars, balance beam, vaulting horse, and floor exercise) in 1952 or 1956
AIT = All-around (individual and team) since 1960
AT = All-around (team only)
BB = Balance beam
Pt = Combined exercises, portable apparatus, team

*BAKANIC, Ladislava A.	1948 AT
*BARONE, Marian Emma Twining	1948 AT
	1952 6
CAPUTO, Jennifer	1936 AT
*CARRUCCIO, Consetta Anne (see Consetta Lenz)	
CASEY, Colleen	1976 AIT
CHACE, Kimberly Ann	1972 AIT
	1976 AIT
CLUFF, Wendy	1968 AIT
CORRIGAN, Kathleen Margaret	1964 AIT
*DALTON, Dorothy C.	1948 AT
	1952 6
DAVIS, Muriel Evelyn (see Muriel Grossfeld)	
DUFF, Margaret	1936 AT
*ELSTE, Meta Neumann	1948 AT
	1952 6
ENGLERT, Carrie	1976 AIT
FUCHS, Doris Gudrun	1956 6, Pt
	1960 AIT
GLEASON, Kathy	1968 AIT
GROSSFELD, Muriel Evelyn Davis (as Miss Davis in 1956)	1956 6, Pt
	1960 AIT
	1964 AIT
GRULKOWSKI, Ruth C.	1952 6
HAUBOLD, Irma Pezzia	1936 AT
HOESLY, Marie M.	1952 6, Pt
HOWARD, Kathy	1976 AIT
HOWE, Judith Ann Hult	1956 6, Pt
KIBLER, Marie Martin	1936 AT
KIRKMAN, Doris A.	1952 6
KLEIN, Jacquelyn Joyce	1956 6, Pt
*LENZ, Consetta Anne Carruccio (as Miss Carruccio in 1936)	1936 AT
	1948 AT
*LOMADY, Clara Marie Schroth (as Miss Schroth in 1948)	1948 AT
	1952 6
LUNARDONI, Ada	1936 AT
MAYCOCK, Betty Jean	1960 AIT
McCLEMENTS, Dale Elizabeth	1964 AIT
METHENY, Linda Jo	1964 AIT
	1968 AIT, BB
	1972 AIT
MEYER, Adelaide	1936 AT
MONTEFUSCO, Theresa Marie	1960 AIT
MOORE, Joan	1972 AIT

MULVIHILL, Colleen	1968 AIT
PIERCE, Roxanne	1972 AIT
RACEK, Joyce May	1956 6, Pt
RICHARDSON, Sharon Lee	1960 AIT
RIGBY, Catherine	1968 AIT
	1972 AIT
RUDDICK, Sandra Marlene	1956 6, Pt
*SCHIFANO, Helen	1948 AT
*SCHROTH, Clara Marie (see Clara Lomady)	
*SIMONIS, Anita A.	1948 AT
SONTGERATH, Gail E.	1960 AIT
SPEAKS, Janie Lee	1964 AIT
TANAC, Joyce Eileen	1968 AIT
THIES, Nancy	1972 AT
TOPALIAN, Ruth E.	1952 6
WALTHER, Marie Sue	1964 AIT
WILLCOX, Debra Ann	1976 AIT
WOLFSBERGER, Leslie Ann	1976 AIT
WRIGHT, Mary F.	1936 AT

HANDBALL (Team) (35)

Team handball, a game similar to soccer but played entirely with the hands, has been contested in two different forms in the Olympics. In 1936 it was held outdoors with 11 men to a team. It then appeared again as an indoor sport at Munich in 1972 with seven men to a side, and this format has been used since. The United States has had a team in 1936, 1972, and 1976.

ABRAHAMSON, Richard Neal	1972
	1976
ABRAM, Fletcher, Jr.	1972
AHLEMEYER, William Alexander	1936
BAKER, Roger Lewis	1972
	1976
BERKHOLTZ, Dennis Lee	1972
BOWDEN, Walter	1936
BUEHNING, Peter, Jr.	1976
CATON, Larry R.	1972
DAUNER, Charles C.	1936
DEAN, Randolph	1976
DEAN, Robert	1976
DiCALOGERO, Vincent J.	1972
	1976
EDES, Elmer	1972
GLANTZ, Ezra	1976
HAGEN, Edward John	1936
HARDIMAN, Thomas J.	1972
JOHNSON, William	1976
KAYLOR, Joseph	1936
LEINWEBER, Fred	1936
MATTHEWS, Rudolph "Matt"	1972
OEHLER, Henry	1936

OEHLER, Otto	1936
OEHMICHEN, Herbert Karl	1936
O'NEILL, Patrick	1976
RENZ, Willy K.	1936
RIVNYAK, Sandor	1972
	1976
ROGERS, James Galvin	1972
	1976
ROSESCO, Alfred	1936
SCHALLENBERG, Edmund	1936
SCHLESINGER, Richard Bradley, Jr.	1972
SERRAPEDE, Kevin J.	1972
	1976
SPARKS, Robert B.	1972
	1976
VOELKERT, Joel R.	1972
WINKLER, Harry W., Jr.	1976
YANTZ, Gerard	1936

ICE HOCKEY (181)

Ice hockey first appeared as a sport in the 1920 Olympic Games (summer) at Antwerp. It has since appeared on the program of every Olympic Winter Games. The United States has sent a team to every Olympic ice hockey tournament except for 1928.

In 1948 there were two different teams that attempted to represent the United States at St. Moritz. One was a team representing the AAU, which, before the war, had complete control of amateur ice hockey in the U.S. However, after the war a new organization, the Amateur Hockey Association of the United States (AHAUS), came into being and was recognized as the national governing body by the International Ice Hockey Federation. The U.S. Olympic Committee continued to recognize the AAU as the governing body and there the dispute arose. The USOC wanted the AAU team to represent the United States but the IOC was bound by the rules of the International Ice Hockey Federation to accept only the AHAUS entry. Eventually the AHAUS team was entered, played, and finished fourth. However, soon after the Olympics the team was disqualified because several of the players were declared to be professionals.

The USOC records still list only the members of the AAU team as being Olympians in 1948. Because only Olympic participants are included herein, we list the AHAUS team below and include a special listing for the AAU team at the end of the ice hockey index.

*ABEL, Clarence John	1924
*AHEARN, Kevin Joseph	1972
ALLEY, Steven James	1976
*ANDERSON, Osborne	1932
*ANDERSON, Wendell Richard	1956
BAKER, Robert	1948
*BAKER, William Robert	1980
*BENT, John Peale	1932
*BJORKMAN, Reuben Eugene	1948
	1952
BOESER, Robert	1948
BOLDUC, Daniel George	1976
*BONNEY, Raymond Lenroy	1920
*BOUCHA, Henry Charles	1972
BROOKS, David Alan	1964
BROOKS, Herbert Paul	1964
	1968
*BROTEN, Neal LaMoy	1980
*BROWN, Charles Erwin	1972
*BURTNETT, Wellington Parkner, Jr.	1956
*CAMPBELL, Eugene Edward	1956
*CEGLARSKI, Leonard Stanley	1952
*CHASE, John Peirce	1932
*CHRISTIAN, David William	1980
*CHRISTIAN, Gordon Gene	1956
*CHRISTIAN, Roger Allen	1960
	1964
*CHRISTIAN, William David	1960
	1964
*CHRISTIANSEN, Keith R.	1972
*CHRISTOFF, Steve	1980
*CLEARY, Robert Barry	1960
*CLEARY, William John, Jr.	1956
	1960
COMSTOCK, Blaine	1976
*CONROY, Anthony J.	1920
*COOKMAN, John Emory	1932
COPPO, Paul Francis	1964
*CRAIG, James Downey	1980
CUNLIFFE, Bruce Fergusson	1948
CUNNIFF, John Paul	1968
*CURRAN, Michael Vincent	1972
*CZARNOTA, Joseph John	1952
DALE, John Byron	1968
*DESMOND, Richard Joseph	1952
DILWORTH, Daniel Joseph	1964
DOBEK, Robert Andrew	1976
*DOUGHERTY, Richard L.	1956
*DRURY, Herbert John	1920
	1924
*ERUZIONE, Michael Anthony	1980
*EVERETT, Douglas Newton	1932
FALKMAN, Craig D.	1968
*FARRELL, Franklin, III	1932
*FITZGERALD, John Edward	1920
*FITZGERALD, Joseph Francis	1932

*FRAZIER, Edwin Hartwell	1932
FRYBERGER, Dates Featherstone	1964
*FTOREK, Robert Brian	1972
*GAMBUCCI, Andre Peter	1952
*GARRISON, John Bright	1932
	1936
GARRITY, John Paul	1948
GAUDREAU, Robert Rene	1968
GEARY, Donald	1948
*GERAN, George Pierce	1920
	1924
*GOHEEN, Frank Xavier	1920
*GRAZIA, Eugene	1960
*HALLOCK, Gerard, III	1932
HARDING, Goodwin	1948
*HARRINGTON, John	1980
HARRIS, Robert Barton	1976
*HARRISON, Clifford	1952
*HOWE, Mark Steven	1972
HURLEY, Paul M.	1968
HURLEY, Thomas F.	1968
HYMANSON, Jeffrey D.	1976
*IKOLA, Willard John	1956
*IRVING, Stuart K.	1972
JENSEN, Paul Richard	1976
JENSEN, Steven Alan	1976
*JOHNSON, Mark Einar	1980
*JOHNSON, Paul Herbert	1960
	1964
*KAMMER, August Frederick, Jr.	1936
*KILMARTIN, Gerald Walsh	1952
*KIRRANE, John Joseph	1948
	1960
*LaBATTE, Philip William	1936
*LaCROIX, Alphonse A.	1924
LAMBY, Richard A.	1976
*LANGLEY, John Arthur	1924
*LAX, John Charles	1936
LILYHOLM, Leonard P.	1968
*LIVINGSTON, Robert Cambridge	1932
LOGUE, James Brian	1968
LUNDEEN, Robert Michael	1976
*LYONS, John Sharkey	1924
MARTIN, Thomas Joseph	1964
*MATCHEFTS, John Peter	1956
MATHER, Bruce Ellery	1948
*MAYASICH, John E.	1956
	1960
*McCARTAN, John William	1960
*McCARTHY, Justin Jeremiah	1924
*McCLANAHAN, Robert B.	1980
*McCORMICK, Joseph W.	1920
*McCORMICK, Lawrence J.	1920
McCOY, Thomas James	1964
*McELMURY, James Donald	1972
*McGLYNN, Richard Anthony	1972

*McKINNON, Daniel Duncan	1956
*McVEY, Robert Patrick	1960
*MELLOR, Thomas Robert	1972
*MEREDITH, Richard O.	1956
	1960
MEREDITH, Wayne Brent	1964
MILLER, Robert Michael	1976
*MOON, Thomas Henry	1936
MORRISON, John Lewis	1968
*MORROW, Kenneth	1980
*MULHERN, John Francis	1952
NANNE, Louis Vincent	1968
*NASLUND, Ronald Alan	1972
*NELSON, Francis Augustus, Jr.	1932
*NOAH, John Michael	1952
*O'CALLAHAN, John	1980
*OLDS, Walter Raymond	1972
*OLSON, Weldon Howard	1956
	1960
OPSAHL, Allan W.	1948
*OSS, Arnold Carl, Jr.	1952
*OWEN, Edwyn Robert	1960
*PAAVOLA, Rodney E.	1960
*PALMER, Laurence James	1960
*PALMER, Winthrop Hale, Jr.	1932
PARADISE, Robert Harvey	1968
*PAVELICH, Mark	1980
PEARSON, Frederick Gordon Neil	1948
*PETROSKE, John Edward	1956
PLEAU, Lawrence Winslow	1968
PRIDDY, Stanton Bliss	1948
*PURPUR, Kenneth Richard	1956
*RAMSEY, Michael Allen	1980
RANDOLPH, Michael D.	1976
REICHART, Frank William	1964
*RICE, Willard Wadsworth	1924
*RIGAZIO, Donald Edmund	1956
RILEY, John Patrick, Jr.	1948
RIUTTA, Bruce Henry	1968
*RODENHISER, Richard	1956
	1960
*ROMPRE, Robert Edward	1952
ROSS, Donald Francis	1964
	1968
ROSS, Douglas George	1976
*ROSS, Elbridge Baker, Jr.	1936
ROSS, Gary	1976
*ROWE, Paul Edward	1936
RUPP, Patrick Lloyd	1964
	1968
*SAMPSON, Edward H.	1956
*SANDERS, Franklynn B.	1972
*SARNER, Craig Brian	1972
SCHMALZBAUER, Gary Owen	1964
*SCHNEIDER, William C. "Buzz"	1976
	1980

*SEARS, Gordon Peter	1972
*SEDIN, James Walter	1952
SERTICH, Stephen J.	1976
*SHAUGHNESSY, Francis John	1936
*SHEEHY, Timothy Kane	1972
*SILK, David	1980
*SMALL, Irving Wheeler	1924
*SMITH, Gordon	1932
	1936
*SPAIN, Francis Jones	1936
STORDAHL, Larry D.	1968
*STROBEL, Eric Martin	1980
*STUBBS, Frank Raymond, Jr.	1936
*SUTER, Robert Allen	1980
*SYNOTT, Francis Allen	1920
	1924
TAFT, John Philip	1976
THORNDIKE, Theodore Baker	1976
*TUCK, Leon Parker	1920
*VAN, Allen Alfred	1952
Van INGEN, Herbert Terrell, Jr.	1948
*VERCHOTA, Philip J.	1980
VOLMAR, Douglas Steven	1968
WARBURTON, Ralph	1948
WARDEN, James Brian	1976
*WEIDENBORNER, Cyril	1920
*WELLS, Mark Ronald	1980
WESTBY, James Allen	1964
*WHISTON, Donald Francis	1952
*WILLIAMS, Thomas Mark	1960
*YACKEL, Kenneth James	1952
YURKOVICH, Thomas Michael	1964

1948 AAU Team

William BRIELL, Crawford Murray CAMPBELL, Neil R. CEELEY, Edward Francis CROWLEY, Thomas Roswell DOCKRELL, George Francis DONAHUE, Bruce David GARDNER, Milton Roy IKOLA, Lewis Thompson PRESTON, George Simpson PULLIAM, Joseph Augustus RILEY, Christopher Raymond Perry RODGERS, James Ross SLOANE, Allen Alfred VAN (see above index), Paul R. WILD.

JEU DE PAUME (2)

Jeu de paume is the French name for court or real tennis, the original form of the game of tennis. It appeared on the Olympic program in 1908 only.

*GOULD, Jay	1908
@SANDS, Charles Edward	1908
(see also Golf and Tennis)	

JUDO (14)

Judo first became an Olympic sport in 1964, but was not on the program in 1968. It returned in 1972 and has been on the Olympic program since.

The United States has always had judoka entered.

L = Lightweight	W = Welterweight
M = Middleweight	LH = Light-heavyweight
H = Heavyweight	U = Unlimited

BOST, Joseph R.	1976 L
*BREGMAN, James Steven	1964 M
BURRIS, Patrick Mitsugi	1972 W
	1976 W
CAMPBELL, Benjamin M.	1964 U
*COAGE, Allen James	1976 H
COHEN, Irwin Lee	1972 M
HARRIS, George Lee	1964 H
JONSTON-ONO, Telmoc	1976 M
MARTIN, Tommy Gerard	1976 LH
MARUYAMA, Paul Kuniaki	1964 L
NELSON, Douglas	1972 H
OKADA, Kenneth	1972 L
WATTS, Johnny	1972 U
WOOLEY, James Ralph	1972 LH
	1976 U

LACROSSE (12)

Lacrosse has been a demonstration sport several times, but only in 1904 and 1908 did it have official status on the Olympic program. The U.S. did not send a team in 1908, but in 1904 a team from St. Louis competed in the three-team tournament. The team members' names are not fully known.

*DOWLING, J. W.	1904
*GIBSON	1904
*GROGAN, Patrick	1904
*HUNTER	1904
*MURPHY	1904
*PARTRIDGE	1904
*PASSMORE, George	1904
*PASSMORE, William	1904
*ROSS	1904
*SULLIVAN	1904
*VENN, A. H.	1904
*WOODS	1904

LUGE (Men) (26)

Luge became an Olympic sport for men in 1964 and the United States has since fielded competitors at every Games. Men compete in singles and doubles in the Olympics.

1 = Singles	2 = Doubles

BATEMAN, Raymond Henry	1980 2
BERKLEY, Robert Olen, Jr.	1972 2
	1976 2
CAVANAUGH, Richard Price	1972 2
	1976 2
DANCO, Walter TenEyck "Ty"	1980 2
ELDER, Jack	1972 2
FALES, Raymond Lawrence	1964 2
FARMER, George Robert	1964 1
FEE, John Richard	1976 2
	1980 1
FELTMAN, Francis Lloyd "Buddy"	1964 1
HAVENS, Ralph C.	1972 1
HEALEY, Richard	1980 2
HESSEL, John Michael	1964 1
	1968 1
HIGGINS, James Jeremiah	1964 2
JONES, Frank	1972 2
LAYTON, Kim Alfred	1968 1
MASLEY, Francis	1980 2
MASTROMATTEO, Nicholas Paul	1964 2
MORIARTY, James W.	1976 2
MURRAY, James D.	1968 1
	1972 1
	1976 1
NEELY, Robert Thomas	1964 1
O'BRIEN, Terrence William	1972 1
	1976 1
PARTCH, Robin T.	1968 1
ROCK, Robert S., Jr.	1972 1
STITHEM, Richard A.	1980 1
TUCKER, Jeffrey Paul	1980 1
WALTERS, Ronnie D.	1964 2

LUGE (Women) (9)

Luge became an Olympic sport for men and women in 1964, but U.S. women first participated in 1968. (Although two women were entered in 1964, they did not compete). Women compete only in singles in the Olympics.

BURKE, Donna Margaret	1980
CHARLESWORTH, Susan	1980
FRAIR, Margaret Ann	1972
GENOVESE, Debra Kay	1980

HAPONSKI, Maura Jo	1976
HOMSTAD, Kathleen Ann Roberts	1968
(as Miss Roberts in 1968)	1972
	1976
JOHANSEN, Sheila M.	1968
ROBERTS, Karen Lee	1976
ROBERTS, Kathleen Ann	
(see Kathleen Homstad)	
WILLIAMS, Ellen	1968

MODERN PENTATHLON (34)

The modern pentathlon was an invention of Baron Pierre de Coubertin, the founder of the modern Olympic Games. It was intended to be a test of the skills necessary for the military athlete—running, swimming, fencing, shooting, and equestrian skill. It was first held at the 1912 Olympics as an individual event and has been held at every Olympics since, with a team event being added in 1952. The U.S. has had competitors at every celebration. No listing of events is given below (i.e., individual or team) because before 1952 athletes competed only as individuals and since 1952 all individual competitors from a country make up that country's team score, necessarily competing in both events.

*ANDRE, William Jules	1956
BARE, George Huston	1924
BAUGH, Hale	1948
*BECK, Robert Lee	1960
(see also Fencing)	1968
BRADY, Brookner West	1932
BURLEY, Michael E.	1976
*DANIELS, Jack Tupper	1956
	1960
DENMAN, Frederick Lockwood	1952
FITZGERALD, John David	1972
	1976
GRUENTHER, Richard Louis	1948
HAINS, Peter Conover, III	1928
HARMON, Ernest Nason	1924
*KIRKWOOD, David Archer	1964
*LAMBERT, George Howard	1956
	1960
*LEONARD, Charles Frederick, Jr.	1936
LOUGH, Maurice Thomas	1968
MacARTHUR, W. Thad	1952
MANSFIELD, Clayton John	1932
*MAYO, Richard Walden	1928
	1932
*MOORE, George Bissland	1948
*MOORE, James Warren	1964
	1968
NEWMANN, Aubrey Strode	1928

NIEMAN, Robert Lee	1976
PATTON, George Smith, Jr.	1912
(see also Fencing)	
*PESTHY, Paul Karoly	1964
(see also Fencing)	
PITTS, Frederick Robert	1924
@RAYNER, Harold Marvin	1920
(see also Fencing)	
RICHARDS, Charles Leonard	1972
SCOTT, Donald	1924
@SEARS, Robert	1920
(see also Fencing)	
STARBIRD, Alfred Dodd	1936
TAYLOR, Scott Lee	1972
TROY, Guy Kent	1952
WEBER, Frederick Reginia	1936
(see also Fencing)	

NORDIC SKIING (Men) (113)

Nordic skiing has been included in every Olympic Winter Games and the United States has been represented at all celebrations. Included in this list are ski jumping and nordic combined events. Biathlon is listed as a separate sport.

Through 1960 there was only one ski jumping event. Since 1964, however, there have been two jumping events—one on a 70-meter hill and one on a 90-meter hill.

15 = 15 km. cross-country	J = Ski jumping (through 1960)
18 = 18 km. cross-country	70J = 70 m. ski jump (since 1964)
30 = 30 km. cross-country	90J = 90 m. ski jump (since 1964)
50 = 50 km. cross-country	NC = Nordic combined (jumping and cross-country)
R = 4 x 10 km. cross-country relay	

AKERS, Charles Arthur	1960 15
ANDERSEN, Erling N.	1932 18
BACKSTROM, Nils	1932 50
	1936 50
BAKKE, William	1968 70J, 90J
BALFANZ, John Carlyle	1964 70J, 90J
	1968 70J, 90J
BATSON, Lemoine	1924 J
BERRY, William Scott	1972 70J, 90J
BIETILA, Walter Isaac	1936 J
	1948 J

BILLINGS, Norton R.	1932 50
BLOOD, Edward J.	1932 NC
	1936 NC
BODNAR, Bela Andrew	1976 30
BOHLIN, Karl Anders	1960 R
	1964 15
BOWER, John Ford	1964 R, NC
	1968 R, NC
BROOMHALL, Wendall W.	1948 18
	1952 18, R
BURTON, John Cotton	1952 18, R
CALDWELL, John Homer	1952 18, NC
CALDWELL, Timothy	1972 15, R
	1976 15, 30, 50, R
	1980 15, R
CARLETON, John Porter	1924 18, NC
CHIVERS, Warren H.	1936 18, R
CRAWFORD, Gary	1980 NC
CRAWFORD, Marvin Leaman	1956 NC, R
CRESS, John Robert	1960 NC
DAMON, Lawrence Snow	1956 15, R
(see also Biathlon)	1964 30, 50
	1968 15, 50
DAVIS, Jeff	1980 70J, 90J
DENDAHL, John Hoge	1960 R
DENNEY, James Jay	1976 70J, 90J
	1980 70J, 90J
DEVECKA, Michael Alan	1972 NC
	1976 NC
	1980 NC
DEVLIN, Arthur Donovan	1952 J
	1956 J
DUNKLEE, Everett	1972 15, 50
DUNKLEE, Stanley Richard	1976 50
	1980 15, 30, 50, R
ELLINGSON, Lloyd C.	1932 NC
ELLIOTT, Michael Wordsworth	1964 15, 30, R
	1968 15, 30, 50, R
	1972 30, R
ENGEN, Corey	1948 18, NC
ERICKSEN, John M.	1932 NC
FALSTAD, Pedar	1932 J
FARWELL, Theodore Austin, Jr.	1952 18, NC, R
	1956 NC, R
	1960 50, NC
FREDHEIM, Sverre	1936 J
	1948 J
GALANES, James	1976 NC
	1980 15, 30, R
GALLAGHER, Michael Donald	1964 15, R
	1968 15, 30, 50, R
	1972 30, R
GRAY, Robert Hawkes	1968 15, R
	1972 30, 50
HAINES, Christopher Borne	1976 30, 50
*HAUGEN, Anders	1924 18, J, NC
	1928 18, J, NC
HICKS, David Anthony	1964 70J, 90J
HIRVONEN, Olavi E.	1960 15, 50
HOVLAND, George J., Jr.	1952 18, R
JACOBS, Thomas Michael	1952 18, NC
JOHANSON, Sven J.	1960 30
JOHNSON, Donald	1948 18, NC
KELLOGG, Charles Wetmore, II	1968 30, 50
KENDALL, Robert C.	1972 NC
KERN, Terry	1976 90J
*KOCH, William	1976 15, 30, 50, R
	1980 15, 30, 50, R
KOTLAREK, Eugene Robert	1960 J
	1964 70J, 90J
KROG, Georg Richard P.	1968 NC
LAHDENPERA, Peter Juhani	1960 15, R
(see also Biathlon)	
LEVY, Lynn Thurber	1956 30, NC
LIEN, Harry	1924 J
LUFKIN, Jon Alton	1968 30
LUSSI, Craig Maurice	1960 NC
LYNCH, Kerry	1980 NC
MAKI, James	1976 90J
	1980 70J
MALMQUIST, Walter August, II	1976 NC
	1980 NC, 90J
MARTIN, Jay Warren	1968 90J
MARTIN, Jerry K.	1972 70J, 90J
	1976 70J, 90J
MARTIN, Larry	1972 15, R
MASSA, Leo E.	1960 30, 50
MATIS, Clark Arvo	1972 30
McNEILL, Chris	1980 70J
McNULTY, Joseph Turner	1972 50
MIKKELSEN, Roy Johan	1932 J
	1936 J
MILLER, Andrew Mack	1956 15, 30, R
	1960 15, 30, 50, R
MILLER, James George	1968 NC
	1972 NC
MONSEN, Rolf B.	1928 18, J
	1932 18, NC
MORGAN, Gene	1972 50
OIMON, Caspar	1932 J
	1936 J
OLSON, Willis Stuart	1952 J
	1956 J
OMTVEDT, Ragnar	1924 18, NC
OVERBYE, Sigurd	1924 18, NC
PARSONS, Richard E.	1932 18, 50
	1936 18, 50, R
PERRAULT, Paul Joseph	1948 J
PETERSON, Douglas	1976 15, R
	1980 30, 50
PIDACKS, Robert Walter	1952 18

PROCTOR, Charles N.	1928 18, J, NC
RAHOI, Richard Allen	1956 J
RAND, Jay J., II	1968 70J, 90J
REID, Robert H.	1932 50
St. ANDRE, Jon J.	1960 J
SAMUELSTEN, Ansten	1960 J
	1964 70J, 90J
SATRE, Karl Magnus	1936 18, 50, NC, R
SATRE, Paul Ottar	1936 NC
SHEA, James Edmund	1964 30, NC, R
SHERWOOD, Roy	1956 J
STEELE, John D.	1932 J
STEELE, Ron	1972 70J, 90J
SUNDGAARD, Kip	1976 70J
SWOR, Gregory	1972 70J, 90J
TAYLOR, Richard William	1964 15, 30, 50
TOKLE, Arthur Emil	1952 J
TORRISSEN, Berger	1936 18, 50, NC, R
TOWNSEND, Ralph Joseph, Jr.	1948 18, NC
TREMBLAY, Charles N.	1956 NC
UPHAM, Thomas Ferguson	1968 NC
VINCELETTE, Alfred Leo, Jr.	1960 NC
WEDIN, Robert Carl	1960 J
WEED, Walker Ten Eyck, III	1972 NC
WEGEMAN, Alvin Paul	1952 NC
WEGEMAN, Keith Richard	1952 J
WILSON, Joseph Peter	1960 30
WINDSPERGER, Gregory Lee	1976 70J
WREN, Gordon L.	1948 18, J, NC
YEAGER, Ronald P.	1972 15
	1976 15, R
ZETTERSTROM, Olle	1932 18
ZUEHLKE, Reed	1980 90J

NORDIC SKIING (Women) (12)

Nordic skiing events for women were first held in 1964 at Innsbruck; however, the United States did not enter any women in these events until 1972.

5 = 5 km. individual	10 = 10 km. individual
R = 3 × 5 km. relay (1972); 4 × 5 km. relay (since 1976)	

BANCROFT, Leslie	1980 5, 10, R
BRITCH, Barbara Ann	1972 5, R
HAINES, Betsy	1980 5
HINKLE, Twila	1976 10, R
HLAVATY, Jana	1976 5, 10, R
HOSMER, Trina Arlene Barton	1972 10
MAHONEY, Marguerite	1972 5, 10
	1976 10
OWEN, Alison	
(see Alison Spencer)	
PAXSON, Elizabeth	1980 R
PORTER, Terry Blackall	1976 5, R

ROCKWELL, Martha	1972 5, 10, R
	1976 5, 10
SPENCER, Alison Owen	1972 5, 10, R
(as Miss Owen in 1972)	1980 5, 10, R
SPENCER, Margaret Lynn	1976 5
(as Mrs. M. Lynn S. Von	1980 10, R
der Heide in 1976)	
Von der HEIDE, Margaret Lynn Spencer	
(see Margaret Spencer)	

POLO (8)

Polo has been on the Olympic program in 1900, 1908, 1920, and 1924, but the United States fielded a team only in 1920 and 1924. In 1900 three Americans competed with several British and Spanish players on two different mixed international teams (listed separately below). In addition there was a 1900 team that is usually listed as from North America, but all the players have been shown to have been Mexican.

*ALLEN, Terry de la Mesa	1920
*BOESEKE, Elmer J., Jr.	1924
*HARRIS, Arthur Ringland	1920
*HITCHCOCK, Thomas, Jr.	1924
*MARGETTS, Nelson E.	1920
@&MONTGOMERY, John Carter	1920
(see also Equestrian)	
*ROE, Frederick	1924
*WANAMAKER, Rodman	1924

1900 International Teams Foxhall Parker KEENE (Foxhunter's), Frank Jay MACKEY (Foxhunter's), Walter Adolphe McCREERY (Rugby).

ROQUE (4)

Roque, a variant of croquet, was on the Olympic program for the only time in 1904. The only entries were the following four Americans.

*BROWN, Charles	1904
CHALFANT, William A.	1904
*JACOBUS, Charles	1904
*STREETER, Smith O.	1904

ROWING (Men) (326)

Rowing has been held at every Olympic Games except the first, in 1896. American rowers have competed at every Olympics since except for 1906, 1908, and 1912.

SS = Single sculls	2w = Pairs with coxswain
DS = Double sculls	4 = Fours without coxswain
QS = Quadruple sculls	4w = Fours with coxswain
2 = Pairs without coxswain	8 = Eights with coxswain

*ABELL, Louis G.	1900 8
	1904 8
*ADAM, Gordon Belgum	1936 8
*AHLGREN, George Lewis	1948 8
ALM, Charles Pheiffer	1960 4w
*AMAN, Charles	1904 4
*AMLONG, Joseph Brian	1964 8
*AMLONG, Thomas Kennedy	1964 8
ANGYAL, Joseph	1948 DS
*ARMSTRONG, Charles E.	1904 8
AUSTIN, John Paul	1936 4w
*AYRAULT, Arthur DeLancey, Jr.	1956 2w
	1960 4
BALDWIN, Joseph Anthony	1960 8
*BARROW, Daniel Hubert, Jr.	1936 SS
*BAYER, Ernest Henry	1928 4
*BECKLEAN, William Russell	1956 8
*BEER, Donald Andrew Eilers	1956 8
BEGGS, James Judson	1952 2w
*BEGLEY, Michael	1904 4
BELDEN, William T.	1976 DS
BELISLE, Eugene Louis	1928 4w
BENNETT, Edward Howard, Jr.	1936 4w
*BLAIR, James Howard	1932 8
*BLESSING, Donald F.	1928 8
BORCHELT, Earl Frederick	1976 4w
BOS, Peter George	1960 8
*BRINCK, John Manning	1928 8
BROOKS, Anthony Dean	1976 4
BROOKS, Stephen Harrington	1968 8
*BROWN, David Preston	1948 8
*BUDD, Harold Boyce, Jr.	1964 8
*BUERGER, Joseph	1904 2
*BUTLER, Leon E.	1924 2w
*BUTLER, Lloyd LeMarr	1948 8
CADWALADER, Aspinwall Gardner	1968 4w
*CALDWELL, Hubert Augustus	1928 8
CANNING, Curtis Ray	1968 8
CARDWELL, Ronald Edmund	1956 4w
*CARPENTER, Leonard Griswold	1924 8
*CARR, William J.	1900 8
CASHIN, Richard Marshall	1976 8
*CHANDLER, Charles	1932 8

*CHARLTON, Thomas Jackson Jr.	1956 8
CHRISTIANSEN, Steven E.	1976 8
*CLAPP, Eugene Howard, IV	1972 8
*CLARK, Emory Wendell, II	1964 8
CLARK, Eugene	1932 2
*CLARK, Sherman Rockwell	1920 4w, 8
CLARK, Thomas	1932 2
*COFFEY, Calvin Thomas	1976 2
*COOKE, John Patrick	1956 8
CORTES, Peter Michael	1976 QS
*COSTELLO, Bernard Patrick, Jr.	1952 DS
	1956 DS
*COSTELLO, Paul Vincent	1920 DS
	1924 DS
	1928 DS
*CRESSER, Frederick	1904 8
*CROMWELL, Seymour Legrand, II	1964 DS
CURRAN, Thomas A.	1936 2w
CUSHMAN, Allerton	1928 4w
CUTLER, Robert Bradley	1936 4w
CUTLER, Roger Wilson, Jr.	1936 4w
*CWIKLINSKI, Stanley Francis	1964 8
DAHM, George Lewis, Jr.	1936 2
*DALLY, William Morris	1928 8
DAVIS, John Bonthron	1952 4
*DAY, Charles Ward	1936 8
*De BAECKE, Harry Leopold	1900 8
DEENEY, J. Vincent	1948 2w
*DEMPSEY, Joseph F.	1904 8
*DETWEILER, Robert Milan	1952 8
*DIETZ, George	1904 4
DIETZ, James W.	1972 SS
	1976 SS
*DONLON, Peter Dwight	1928 8
DOUGHERTY, Joseph Michael	1928 2w
	1936 2w
*DRAEGER, Richard Arthur	1960 2w
DREISSIGACKER, Richard	1972 4
DREYFUSS, Kenneth Benoit	1976 2w
DRUEDING, Charles	1932 4w
DUFFIELD, David	1904 SS
DUGAN, William	1936 DS
*DUMMERTH, Frank	1904 4
*DUNBAR, James Ralph	1952 8
*DUNLAP, David Coombs	1932 8
DURBROW, Philip Marshall	1964 4
EDMONDS, James Stuart	1964 2
EDMUNDS, Richard Roland	1968 2w
ENGLISH, Francis	1932 4w
*ERKER, August Casimir	1904 4
*ESSELSTYN, Caldwell Blakeman, Jr.	1956 8
EVERETT, John Gardner	1976 8
*EXLEY, John Onins, Jr.	1900 8
	1904 8
*FARNAM, Robert	1904 2
*FEDERSCHMIDT, Erich H.	1920 4w

*FEDERSCHMIDT, Franz H.	1920 4w
FELLOWS, David Munro	1976 8
*FERRY, Edward Payson	1964 2w
FIECHTER, Jacques Poindexter	1968 8
*FIELDS, William Beauford	1952 8
*FIFER, James Thomas	1952 2w
	1956 2
&FINDLAY, Conn Francis	1956 2w
(see also Yachting)	1960 2w
	1964 2w
*FLANAGAN, James Showers	1904 8
*FOLEY, Hugh Miller	1964 8
FOOTE, Kenneth Glen	1976 QS
*FREDERICK, Francis Harland	1928 8
*FREITAG, John	1904 4
*FROMANACK, Martin	1904 4
FROST, Theodore Strathy	1960 2
FRUEHAUF, Eugene Joseph, Jr.	1936 4
*FRYE, Wayne Thomas	1952 8
GALLAGHER, Arthur A.	1948 DS
*GALLAGHER, Vincent Joseph, Jr.	1920 8
*GARDINER, James Arthur	1956 DS
*GATES, Gregory Crozier	1948 4
*GEIGER, John E.	1900 8
*GERHARDT, Robert Buchanan	1924 4w
*GILMORE, William Evans Garrett	1924 SS
	1932 DS
*GIOVANELLI, Gordon S.	1948 4w
*GLEASON, Michael D.	1904 8
GOETZ, Augustus Shaw	1928 2w
*GRAHAM, Norris James	1932 8
*GRAVES, Edwin Darius, Jr.	1920 8
*GREER, Frank B.	1904 SS
*GREGG, Duncan Smith	1932 8
*GRIFFING, Stuart Lane	1948 4
*GRIMES, Charles Livingston	1956 8
GROSSMILLER, Harry	1932 4w
GUNDERSON, Paul Einar	1964 4w
HAGUE, George Turner	1936 4
*HALL, Winslow William	1932 8
HALLEEN, Neil Carl	1976 QS
HAMLIN, Charles Borden	1968 4
*HARDY, James Herbert	1948 8
HARTIGAN, John DeStefani	1968 4w
	1976 4w
HASKINS, William Chandler	1936 4w
HAYES, Patrick A.	1976 4w
*HEALIS, George A.	1928 4
*HECHT, Duvall Young	1952 2w
	1956 2
*HEDLEY, Edwin	1900 8
*HELM, Louis G.	1904 4
HERMAN, Aaron Benjamin	1972 2w
HESS, Michael	1976 8
HEWITT, Charles Colby, III	1972 4
HIGGINS, David D.	1968 8

*HOBBS, Franklin Warren, IV	1968 8
	1972 8
*HOBBS, William Barton Rogers	1968 2w
	1972 8
*HOBEN, John Grey	1904 DS
*HOFFMAN, Paul	1968 8
	1972 8
HOOVER, Walter McCall, Jr.	1952 DS
*HOUGH, Lawrence Alan	1968 2
	1972 2
HOUSER, John William	1936 DS
HUBBARD, James de Wolf	1928 4w
*HUME, Donald Bruce	1936 8
*HUNT, George Elwood, Jr.	1936 8
JACKSON, Dempster McKee	1952 4
*JACOMINI, Virgil Victor	1920 8
*JASTRAM, Burton Albert	1932 8
*JELINEK, Sidney	1924 4w
*JENNINGS, Edward F.	1924 2w
	1932 2w
*JOACHIM, John L.	1904 2
*JOHNSON, Philip Anthony	1964 2
	1968 2
JOHNSON, W. Edgar	1932 4
*JOHNSTON, Donald Hendrie	1920 8
JONES, Luther Hio, III	1968 4w
	1972 2w
*JORDAN, William Conrad	1920 8
*JUVENAL, James B.	1900 8
	1904 SS
*KARLE, Charles G.	1928 4
*KELLY, John Brenden	1920 SS,
	1924 DS
*KELLY, John Brenden, Jr.	1948 SS
	1952 SS
	1956 SS
	1960 DS
*KENNEDY, John G.	1924 4w
*KIEFFER, Charles M.	1932 2w
*KING, Clyde Whitlock	1920 8
*KINGSBURY, Frederick John, IV	1948 4
*KINGSBURY, Howard Thayer, Jr.	1924 8
KLECATSKY, Lawrence Joseph	1976 DS
*KLOSE, Carl Otto	1920 4w
*KNECHT, William Joseph	1960 DS
	1964 8
LARKIN, Andrew	1968 8
LAWRENCE, James, Jr.	1928 4w
*LEANDERSON, Matt Fillip	1952 4w
*LINDLEY, Alfred Damon	1924 8
*LIVINGSTON, John Cleve	1968 8
	1972 8
*LIVINGSTON, Michael Kent	1972 8
*LOCKWOOD, Roscoe C.	1900 8
*LOGG, Charles Paul, Jr.	1952 2
LONG, William Camielle	1960 8

*LOTT, Harry Hunter	1904 8
LOVELESS, George Gilbert	1936 2w
*LOVSTED, Carl Martin	1952 4w
LUBSEN, Walter A., Jr.	1976 8
*LYON, Richard Avery	1964 4
	1972 2
MacDONALD, Stewart Gray	1968 2w
	1972 4w
MACK, Thomas P., Jr.	1928 2w
	1932 4w
*MAHER, William Patrick	1968 DS
*MANRING, Charles David	1952 8
*MARSH, Edward	1900 8
MARSHALL, Edward	1932 4w
MARTIN, Anthony Edward, III	1968 4w
*MARTIN, Robert	1948 4w
MASON, Charles Ellis, Jr.	1928 4w
MASTERSON, Edward Anthony	1956 4w
MATTHEWS, John	1976 2w
MATTSON, George A.	1932 4
McCOSKER, John	1932 4
*McDOWELL, Paul L.	1928 2
*McILVAINE, Charles Joseph	1928 DS
*McINTOSH, James Stuart	1956 4
McINTYRE, John V.	1948 2w
McKIBBON, Thomas D.	1972 DS
*McKINLEY, Arthur Frank	1956 4
*McKINLEY, John Dickinson	1956 4
*McLOUGHLIN, James	1904 DS
McMILLAN, Louis Kelly, Jr.	1952 4
*McMILLIN, James Burge	1936 8
McMULLEN, James Arthur	1956 4w
*MICKELSON, Timothy Carl	1972 8
*MILLER, John Lester	1924 8
MILLER, William	1972 4
*MILLER, William G.	1928 4
	1932 SS
*MITCHELL, Edward P., Jr.	1924 4w
*MITCHELL, Henry Kent, II	1960 2w
	1964 2w
*MITTET, Theodore Peder	1964 4w
*MOCH, Robert Gaston	1936 8
*MOORE, Edward Peerman	1920 8
MOORE, Mark Wendell	1960 8
*MOREY, Robert Willis, Jr.	1956 8
*MORGAN, Allan Jerome	1948 4w
MORONEY, James Edmond, III	1972 4
	1976 4
*MORRIS, Herbert Roger	1936 8
*MULCAHY, John J. F.	1904 DS, 2
*MURPHY, Richard Frederick	1952 8
*MYERS, Kenneth	1920 4w
	1928 SS
	1932 DS
*NASH, Ted Allison, II	1960 4
	1964 4

*NASSE, Albert F.	1904 4
NORELIUS, Mark Alan	1976 8
*NUNN, John Hamann	1968 DS
PARKER, Harry Lambert	1960 SS
*PEREW, Robert S.	1948 4
PERRY, Lyman Spencer Abson	1960 8
PIANTEDOSI, Gary Gennaro	1976 4
*PICARD, Geoffrey William	1964 4
PIERIE, Thomas Williams	1932 4
PLUMB, Michael A.	1976 4w
POLLOCK, Harry Winslow	1964 4w
POLLOCK, Thomas Elmer, III	1964 4w
*PRICE, Thomas Steele	1952 2
*PROCTOR, Henry Arthur	1952 8
*PURCHASE, Ralph Kenneth	1948 8
PURDY, William Kimball	1968 4w
*RANTZ, Joseph Harry	1936 8
*RAVANACK, Joseph	1904 DS
*RAYMOND, Peter Harlow	1968 4
	1972 8
*ROCKEFELLER, James Stillman	1924 8
ROGERS, Robert Peck	1960 2
*ROSSI, Albert	1952 4w
RUBIN, Roy John	1960 4w
RUDOLPH, Chadwick Stanley	1972 4w
RUTHFORD, Charles Eric	1972 4w
*RYAN, Joseph	1904 2
*SALISBURY, Edwin Lyle	1932 8
*SANBORN, Alden Ream	1920 8
SAPECKY, Alfred James	1936 4
SAWYIER, David Robert	1972 4w
*SAYRE, John Anthony	1960 4
*SCHAUERS, Joseph A.	1932 2w
*SCHELL, Frank Reamer	1904 8
*SCHMITT, John V.	1928 2
*SEIFFERT, Armin Kurt	1956 2w
	1960 4w
*SHAKESPEARE, Frank Bradford	1952 8
SHARKEY, Harry James	1936 2
SHEALY, Alan Wardwell	1976 8
*SHEFFIELD, Frederick	1924 8
*SMITH, Justus Ketcham	1948 8
SPERO, Donald M.	1964 SS
*SPOCK, Benjamin McLane	1924 8
*STACK, John Charles	1948 8
*STAINES, Michael Laurence	1972 2w
	1976 2
*STALDER, Marvin Frederick	1928 8
STEKETEE, Scott Nelson	1968 8
STEPHAN, Ralph William, Jr.	1948 2
*STEVENS, Edward Glenister, Jr.	1952 8
STEVENSON, Chris Hugh	1976 4
STOCKER, Alfred Edward, Jr.	1960 4w
*STOCKHOFF, Arthur M.	1904 4
*STODDARD, Laurence Ralph	1924 8
*STORM, James Eugene	1964 DS

*STOWE, William Arthur	1964 8
*SUERIG, Frederick	1904 4
SWEETSER, Warren Edward, III	1960 8
*TERRY, Lawrence, Jr.	1968 4
	1972 8
TEW, James Dinsmore, III	1964 4w
THOMPSON, Gayle Robert	1960 8
THOMPSON, James	1936 4
*THOMPSON, William G.	1928 8
*TITUS, Constance Sutton	1904 SS
TOLAND, Joseph S.	1948 2w
*TOWER, Harold	1932 8
*TURNER, David Lindsay	1948 8
TURNER, Douglas Laird	1956 4w
*TURNER, Ian Gordon	1948 8
*ULBRICKSON, Alvin Edmund, Jr.	1952 4w
Van BLOM, John	1968 SS
	1972 DS
	1976 QS
*VARLEY, William P.	1904 DS, 2
VESPOLI, Michael L.	1972 4w
*VOERG, Gustav	1904 4
VREUGDENHIL, Darrell	1976 2w
WADE, Festus John, III	1948 2
*WAHLSTROM, Richard Wayne	1952 4w
*WAILES, Richard Donald	1956 8
	1960 4
WASHBURN, Edward Hall	1964 4w
WEINBERG, David Bruce	1976 8
*WELCHLI, John Richard	1956 8
*WELLS, John	1904 DS
*WELSFORD, Henry Reed	1924 4w
WELSH, James Carter	1952 4
*WESTLUND, Warren DeHaven	1948 4w
*WHITE, John Galbraith	1936 8
*WIGHT, David Henry	1956 8
*WILL, Robert Ide	1948 4w
*WILSON, Alfred Mayo	1924 8
*WILSON, Harold C.	1924 2w
WILSON, Robert Bruce	1960 8
WINFREE, Howard Thomas	1960 8
*WORKMAN, James Theodore	1928 8
WRIGHT, Raymond Garfield, II	1968 4
WYNNE, James Michael	1956 4w
YONKER, Michael Alan	1960 4w
ZAGUNIS, Robert Frank	1976 4w
*ZIMONYI, Robert	1948 2w
(competed for Hungary in 1948	1952 8
and 1952)	1964 8

ROWING (Women) (24)

Women's rowing first appeared as an Olympic sport in 1976.

S = Single sculls	2 = Pairs without coxswain	
D = Double sculls	4 = Fours with coxswain	
Q = Quadruple sculls with coxswain	8 = Eights with coxswain	

BEHRENS, Pamela J.	1976 4
BRACELAND, Diane	1976 D
*BROWN, Carol Page	1976 8
*DeFRANTZ, Anita Luceete	1976 8
GEER, Julia Hand	1976 4
*GRAVES, Carie Brand	1976 8
*GREIG, Marion Ethel	1976 8
HANSEN, Lisa	1976 Q
HILLS, Elizabeth Dorrepaal	1976 Q
KELLOGG, Mary Louise	1976 4
*LIND, Joan Louise	1976 S
*McCARTHY, Peggy Anne	1976 8
McCLOSKEY, Karen Lynn	1976 Q
MENGES, Catherine Ann	1976 4
MORENO, Irene J.	1976 Q
MORGAN, Susan	1976 2
PALCHIKOFF, Jan Louise	1976 D
*RICKETSON, Gail Susan	1976 8
SCHNEIDER, Claudia A.	1976 Q
*SILLIMAN, Lynn	1976 8
STAINES, Laura Catherine Terdoslavich	1976 2
STORRS, Nancy	1976 4
*WARNER, Anne Elizabeth	1976 8
*ZOCH, Jacqueline Jean	1976 8

RUGBY (UNION) FOOTBALL (30)

Rugby (union) football has graced the Olympic festival four times—in 1900, 1908, 1920, and 1924. The United States has competed twice, and quite nobly both times, winning the gold medal in 1920 and 1924.

*CARROLL, Daniel Brendan	1908
(competed for Australia in 1908)	1920
*CLARK, Philip Corriston	1924
*CLEAVELAND, Norman	1924
*DeGROOT, Dudley Sargeant	1924
*DEVEREAUX, Robert H. Coleman	1924
*DIXON, George Martin	1924
*DOE, Charles Webster, Jr.	1920
	1924
*FARRISH, Linn Markley	1924
*FISH, George Winthrop	1920
*FITZPATRICK, James P.	1920
*GRAFF, Edward	1924
*HUNTER, Joseph Garvin	1920
*HYLAND, Richard Frank	1924
(né Frank William Hyland)	
&KIRKSEY, Morris Marshall	1920
(see also Track & Field)	

*MANELLI, Caeser	1924
*MEHAN, Charles Thomas	1920
*MULDOON, John, Jr.	1920
*O'NEIL, John T.	1920
	1924
*PATRICK, John Clarence	1920
	1924
*RIGHTER, Cornelius Erwin	1920
*ROGERS, William Lister	1924
*SCHOLZ, Rudolph John	1920
	1924
*SLATER, Colby Edward	1924
*SLATER, Norman Bernard	1924
*TEMPLETON, Robert Lyman	1920
(see also Track & Field)	
*TILDEN, Charles Lee, Jr.	1920
*TURKINGTON, Edward L.	1924
*VALENTINE, Alan Chester	1924
*WILLIAMS, Alan Frank	1924
*WRENN, Heaton Luse	1920

SHOOTING (167: 166 Men, 1 Women)

Shooting events have been held at the Olympics except in 1904 and 1928, and the United States has failed to be represented only once, that in 1906. The shooting program has varied widely, especially in the early years; consequently there have been many, many different events.

In the following, only sufficient information is given to identify an event. For example, distances are not given unless there was more than one event of exactly similar conditions, except for the distance. The names of the events, in many cases, are slightly different from the name used on the official program during the year of competition, in order to facilitate a more orderly grouping of the events.

Since 1968 women have been allowed to compete in the shooting events and have competed against the men on equal terms. The United States has had only one woman on their shooting teams, Margaret Murdock, and she is listed herein.

CP = Clay pigeon
CPt = Clay pigeon, team
CS = Clay pigeon, skeet
CT = Clay pigeon, trap
FP = Free pistol
FPt = Free pistol, team
FR = Free rifle
FRp = Free rifle, prone
FRt = Free rifle, team
LP = Live pigeon shooting
MP = Military pistol
MRa = Military rifle, any position
MR3 = Military rifle, 3 positions
MRs = Military rifle, standing
MRst = Military rifle, standing, team
MRt = Military rifle, team
MR300p = Military rifle, 300 meters, prone
MR600p = Military rifle, 600 meters, prone
MR300pt = Military rifle, 300 meters, prone, team
MR600pt = Military rifle, 600 meters, prone, team
MR3 + 6pt = Military rifle, 300 and 600 meters, prone, team
RDss = Running deer, single shot
RDds = Running deer, double shot
RDsd = Running deer, single and double shot
RDsst = Running deer, single shot, team
RDdst = Running deer, double shot, team
RF = Rapid-fire pistol
RFt = Rapid-fire pistol, team
SBa = Small-bore rifle, any position
SB3 = Small-bore rifle, 3 positions
SBp = Small-bore rifle, prone
SBs = Small-bore rifle, standing
SBdt = Small-bore rifle, disappearing target
SBmt = Small-bore rifle, moving target
SBpt = Small-bore rifle, prone, team
SBst = Small-bore rifle, standing, team
SBdtt = Small-bore rifle, disappearing target, team
WB = Running wild boar

*ADAMS, Harry Loren	1912 MRt, MRa, MR3, FR
	1920 MR300p
ANDERSON, Edwin L.	1912 SBa, SBdt
*ANDERSON, Gary Lee	1964 FR
	1968 FR, SBp
ANDERSON, Hershel	1972 FP
	1976 FP
*ARIE, Mark Peter	1920 CP, CPt
*AUER, Victor Lee	1972 SBp
	1976 SBp
*AXTELL, Charles Sumner	1908 RF, RFt
*BAILEY, Henry Marvin	1924 RF
BARTLETT, Harold Terry	1912 MR3, MRa, FR
*BASSHAM, Lanny Robert	1972 SB3, FR
	1976 SB3
BAYLES, Howard Alfred	1920 FP, RF
BEAUMONT, John H., Jr.	1956 RF

*BENEDICT, Charles Sumner	1908 MRt, FRp
*BENNER, Huelet Leo	1948 FP
	1952 RF, FP
	1956 FP
BETKE, George Bernard	1924 RF
*BILLINGS, Charles W.	1912 CP, CPt
*BOLES, John Keith	1924 SBp, RDss, RDds, RDsst, RDdst
*BONSER, Horace R.	1920 CP, CPt
*BRACKEN, Raymond C.	1920 FP, FPt, RF
*BRIGGS, Allan Lindsay	1912 MRt, MR3, MRa, FR
BROOKS, Quentin Thomas	1948 FP
*BROWN, Thomas Cole	1920 RDss, RDds, RDsst, RDdst, MRst
*BURDETTE, Cornelius L.	1912 MRt, MRa, MR3, FR
CAIL, Harry Vaughn	1948 SBp
*CALKINS, Irving Romaro	1908 RF, RFt
CARR, Thomas M.	1932 RF
*CASEY, Kellogg Kennon Venable	1908 MRt, FRp
CHOW, Frank Robert	1948 RF
CLARK, James R.	1960 CP
*CLARK, Jay, Jr.	1920 CPt
*COOK, Arthur Edwin	1948 SBp
*COULTER, Raymond Orville	1924 FRt, RDss, RDds, RDsst, RDdst
CRAWFORD, Richard	1976 FP
*CROCKETT, Joseph W.	1924 FRt
DAVIS, Charles D.	1972 WB
*DIETZ, John A.	1908 RF, RFt
	1912 FP, RF, FPt, RFt
*DINWIDDIE, Marcus William	1924 SBp
DIXON, Charvin	1976 CT
*DOLFEN, Peter J.	1912 FP, RF, FPt
DOOB, Morris A.	1936 RF
DORSEY, Jimmie	1972 FP
*EASTMAN, Ivan L.	1908 MRt, FRp
EDMONDSON, Martin	1976 WB
ERSKINE, F.	1900 LP
*ETCHEN, Fred R.	1924 CP, CPt
FAWCETT, Wilford H.	1924 CP
*FENTON, Dennis	1920 FRt, MR600pt, SBs, SBst
	1924 FR, RDss, RDds, RDsst, RDdst
FISHER, Clarence Ingals	1936 RF
*FISHER, Morris	1920 MR300pt, FR, FRt
	1924 FR, FRt
FISKE, George Foster, Jr.	1920 FP
FORMAN, John Charles	1956 RF
FOSTER, John Robert	1960 FR
	1968 FR, SB3
FRAZER, Willard D.	1924 RF
*FREDERICK, Karl Telford	1920 RF, RFt, FP, FPt

*GARRIGUS, Thomas Irvin	1968 CT
*GLEASON, Edward Francis	1912 CP, CPt
*GORMAN, James Edward	1908 RF, RFt
*GRAHAM, James R.	1912 CP, CPt
*GREEN, Franklin C.	1964 FP
GREENE, Edward Alonzo	1908 FR, FRp
GRIER, John B.	1924 SBp
*GUNNARSSON, Martine Ingemar	1964 FR
*HALDEMAN, Donald S.	1972 CT
	1976 CT
*HALL, Frank	1912 CP, CPt
HAMILTON, Donald Leslie	1968 FP
*HARANT, Louis J.	1920 RF, RFt
HARDING, William Wadley	1932 SBp
*HENDRICKSON, John H.	1912 CP, CPt
HERRING, Earl Francis	1968 CS
HESSIAN, John W.	1908 FR, FRp
*HILL, James E.	1960 SB3, SBp
*HINDS, Sidney Rae	1924 FRt
*HIRD, Frederick S.	1912 MRa, MR3, FR, SBa, SBpt, SBdt, SBdtt
	1920 MR300p
HUDNUTT, Dean	1936 RF
*HUGHES, Frank H.	1924 CP, CPt
HURST, John W.	1960 FP
*JACKSON, Arthur Charles	1948 FR
	1952 SBp, SB3
	1956 SBp, SB3
*JACKSON, John E.	1912 MRa, MR3, MRt
*JACKSON, Joseph	1920 RDss, RDds, MR300p, MR300pt, MR600p, MR600pt, MR3 + 6pt
JEFFERS, Charles J.	1908 FRp
JOHNSON, John Edward	1972 CS
JONES, Elliott	1936 FP
*KELLY, Michael	1920 FPt, RFt
*LANE, Alfred P.	1912 FP, RF, FPt, RFt
	1920 FP, RF, FPt, RFt
LAWLESS, Joseph T.	1920 MR600p
LAYTON, John B.	1948 RF
LeBOUTILLIER, Thomas, II	1908 RF
*LEE, Willis Augustus, Jr.	1920 RDss, RDds, RDsst, RDdst, MRs, MRst, MR300p, MR300pt, MR600p, MR600pt, MR3 + 6pt, FRt, SBst, SBs
*LEUSCHNER, William D. F.	1908 FRp, MRt
	1912 SBa, SBpt, SBdt, SBdtt, RDss, RDds, RDsst

*WINDER, Charles B.	1908 MRt, FRp
*WRIGHT, Frank S.	1920 CP, CPt
WRIGHT, Verle Franklin, Jr.	1956 SBp, SB3
*WRITER, John Henry	1968 SB3
	1972 SB3

SOCCER (Association Football) (103)

With the exception of 1896 and 1932, soccer (known throughout the rest of the world as association football, or more simply, football) has always been on the Olympic program. However, American representation has been sparse, due to a lack of interest in the sport in the early years and qualifying strictures in recent years. The United States has had teams entered in the following years: 1904 (two teams—Christian Brothers' College and St. Rose, both of St. Louis), 1924, 1928, 1936, 1948, 1952, 1956, and 1972.

AITKEN, Robert, Jr.	1928
ALTEMOSE, Charles William	1936
BAHR, Walter Alfred	1948
BAHR, Walter Alfred, Jr.	1972
BARTKUS, Francis Anthony	1936
*BARTLIFF, Charles Albert	1904
BECKMAN, Raymond Paul	1948
BERTANI, William Joseph	1948
BOCWINSKI, John	1972
*BRADY, Joseph J.	1904
*BRITTINGHAM, Warren G.	1904
BRIX, Aage Emil	1924
*BROCKMEYER, Oscar B.	1904
BURKHARD, Robert L.	1952
CARENZA, John	1972
COLUMBO, Charles Martin	1948
	1952
CONTERIO, William Amedeo	1956
COOK, Ellwood Eugene	1952
*COOKE, George Edwin	1904
*COOKE, Thomas J.	1904
COOPER, Albert, Jr.	1928
*COSGROVE, Cormic F.	1904
COSTA, Joseph Rego	1948
CROCKETT, James	1936
*CUDMORE, Alexander	1904
DALRYMPLE, Samuel Hugh	1924
DAVIS, Irving Cyril	1924
DEAL, John J.	1928
DEMLING, Arthur	1972
*DIERKES	1904
*DOOLING, Martin T.	1904
DORRIAN, James Patrick	1956
DOUGLAS, James Edward	1924
DUFFY, John J.	1928

ENGEDAL, Svend R. H.	1956
FARRELL, Henry Charles	1924
FERREIRA, Joseph	1948
FIEDLER, William John	1936
FINDLAY, William	1924
	1928
FLATER, Michael Harold	1972
*FROST, Frank	1904
GAJDA, Andrew	1936
GALLAGHER, James A.	1928
GAY, Robert Steven	1972
GREINART, Frank	1936
HAMM, Joseph P.	1972
HERNANDEZ, Manuel Fonseca	1972
HORNBERGER, Raymond A.	1924
IVANOW, Michael	1972
*JAMESON, Claude Stanley	1904
*JAMESON, Henry Wood	1904
*JANUARY, Charles James, Jr.	1904
*JANUARY, John Hartnett	1904
*JANUARY, Thomas Thurston	1904
*JOHNSON	1904
JOHNSON, Carl W. F.	1924
JONES, F. Burkhart	1924
KEOUGH, Harry Joseph	1952
	1956
KUNTNER, Rudolph F.	1928
*LAWLOR, Raymond E.	1904
LOOBY, William Edward	1956
LUTKEFEDDER, Fred	1936
&LYDON, Joseph Patrick	1904
(see also Boxing)	
LYONS, John P.	1928
MARGULIS, Michael	1972
MARTIN, Manuel Oliveira	1948
McHUGH, Edward J., Jr.	1952
McLAUGHLIN, Bernard Joseph	1948
MENDOZA, Ruben Michael	1952
	1956
*MENGES, Louis John	1904
MESSING, Shep Norman	1972
MONSEN, Lloyd	1952
	1956
MURPHY, Edward John	1956
NEMCHIK, George	1936
O'CARROLL, Henry C.	1928
*O'CONNELL	1904
O'CONNOR, Frederick E.	1924
PIETRAS, Peter P.	1936
ROBOOSTOFF, Alex Archie	1972
*RATICAN, Peter Joseph	1904
RUDD, Arthur George	1924
RYAN, Francis J.	1928
	1936
SALCEDO, Hugo	1972
SCHALLER, Willy	1952

SEEREY, Michael Kevin	1972
SHEPPELL, William Rose	1952
SMITH, Harry J.	1928
SNYLYK, Zenon	1956
SOUZA, Edward Neto	1948
SOUZA, John	1948
	1952
STAM, Neil Joseph	1972
STEMKE, Horst	1972
STRADEN, Andrew John	1924
STRIMEL, Archie L.	1948
SUROCK, Lawrence Carmen	1952
*TATE, Harry	1904
TROST, Alan Philip	1972
WECKE, Herman William	1956
WELLS, Herbert	1924
ZBIKOWSKI, Ferdinand J.	1936
ZERHUSEN, Albert Ferdinand	1956
ZIAJA, Walter	1972
ZYLKER, James	1972

SPEED SKATING (Men) (66)

Speed skating has been held at every Olympic Winter Games and the United States has fielded a team at every celebration.

5 = 500 meters	5K = 5,000 meters
10 = 1,000 meters	10K = 10,000 meters
15 = 1,500 meters	

*BARTHOLOMEW, Kenneth Eldred	1948 5
BEDBURY, Floyd Curtis	1960 15, 5K
	1964 15
BIALAS, Valentine	1924 5K, 10K
	1928 5, 15, 5K, 10K
	1932 10K
BLATCHFORD, Nathaniel H., IV "Neil"	1968 5
	1972 5
BLUM, Raymond Edward	1948 15, 5K
BROADHURST, Alfred George	1952 5K, 10K
BURKE, Charles William	1952 5K, 10K
	1956 5K
CAMPBELL, Howard Wayne	1964 15
CAPAN, Roger	1968 15
CAROW, William Ambrose	1956 5
	1960 5
CARROLL, Daniel Joseph, III	1972 15, 5K, 10K
	1976 10, 15, 5K, 10K
CHAPIN, James	1976 5
	1980 5
COX, William	1968 5K, 10K

*DISNEY, William Dale	1960 5
	1964 5
DONOVAN, Richard	1924 5K, 10K
EBERLING, Peter	1972 5
FAIL, Stanley Clair	1964 5K
*FARRELL, John O'Neill	1928 5, 15, 5K
	1932 5
*FITZGERALD, Robert Emmett	1948 5, 15
	1952 5
*FREISINGER, Leonard	1936 5, 15
GILMORE, Charles	1972 5K
	1976 10K
GRAY, Thomas James	1964 5
	1968 5
GUENTHER, Lloyd W.	1932 15
*HEIDEN, Eric Arthur	1976 15, 5K
	1980 5, 10, 15, 5K, 10K
*HENRY, Kenneth Charles	1948 5, 15, 5K
	1952 5, 15, 5K
	1956 5
HUNT, Richard Howard	1960 15, 5K
	1964 15, 5K
*IMMERFALL, Daniel James	1976 5, 10
	1980 5
*JAFFEE, Irving W.	1928 5, 15, 5K, 10K
	1932 5K, 10K
*JEWTRAW, Charles	1924 5, 15, 5K
JONLAND, Gary	1972 15
KASKEY, Harry H.	1924 5, 15, 10K
KING, Clark David	1972 15, 5K, 10K
KRESSLER, Craig	1980 10, 15, 5K, 10K
LAMB, Delbert Thomas	1936 5
	1948 5
LANIGAN, William Thomas	1968 15, 5K, 10K
	1972 15
LeBOMBARD, Wayne Arthur	1964 5K, 10K
	1968 15, 5K
LONGSJO, Arthur Matthew (see also Cycling)	1956 5K
LYMAN, Gregory G.	1972 5
*McDERMOTT, Donald Joseph	1952 5, 15
	1956 5, 15
*McDERMOTT, Richard Terrance	1960 5
	1964 5
	1968 5
McNAMARA, Matthew Patrick Francis	1952 15, 5K, 10K
	1956 15, 5K, 10K
MEYER, Keith E.	1960 15
MOORE, Joseph J.	1924 5, 15, 10K
*MUELLER, Peter	1976 5, 10
	1980 10
*MURPHY, Edward L.	1928 5, 15, 5K
	1932 5K

MURRAY, Raymond V.	1932 5, 15
PETERSEN, Robert G.	1936 5, 15, 5K, 10K
PLANT, Thomas	1980 15
POTTS, Allan W.	1932 5
	1936 5, 15
RUDOLPH, Edward John	1960 5, 15
	1964 5, 15
RUPPRECHT, Louis	1948 5K, 10K
SANDVIG, Eugene Myron	1956 15, 5K
SCHROEDER, Edward J.	1932 10K
	1936 15, 5K, 10K
SEAMAN, Arthur Francis	1948 10K
*SHEA, John Amos	1932 5, 15
SOLEM, Richard Earl	1948 5K, 10K
SPRINGER, Carl F.	1932 5K
STEINMETZ, William E.	1924 5, 15, 5K
TAYLOR, Herbert B.	1932 15, 5K
UHRLASS, Arnold H.	1960 5K, 10K
(see also Cycling)	
WEDGE, Edwin	1932 10K
WERKET, John Roland	1948 15, 10K
	1952 5, 15, 10K
	1956 5, 15
WOODS, Michael Paul	1976 15, 5K, 10K
	1980 5K, 10K
WURSTER, John	1968 5
	1972 5
WURSTER, Richard	1968 15
ZUCCO, Ross B.	1960 10K

SPEED SKATING (Women) (26)

Speed skating for women first appeared on the Olympic program as an exhibition at the 1932 Olympic Winter Games. Its next appearance was as an official sport in 1960 and it has been held quadrennially since. The United States women have always entered a team.

5 = 500 meters	10 = 1,000 meters
15 = 1,500 meters	30 = 3,000 meters

*ASHWORTH, Jeanne Chesley	1960 5, 10, 15, 30
	1964 5, 10, 30
	1968 10, 15, 30
BUHR, Beverly J.	1960 30
CARPENTER, Connie	1972 15
CROWE, Peggy	1976 10
DOCTER, Mary	1980 15, 30
DOCTER, Sarah	1980 5, 10, 15, 30
DORGAN, Toy Joan	1968 30
*FISH, Jennifer Lee	1968 5, 10
HARRINGTON, Cornelia K.	1960 30

*HEIDEN, Elizabeth Lee	1976 30
	1980 5, 10, 15, 30
*HENNING, Anne	1972 5, 10
*HOLUM, Dianne Mary	1968 5, 10, 15
	1972 10, 15, 30
LAWLER, Janice Marie	1964 5, 15
LOCKHART, Barbara Day	1960 15
	1964 10, 30
LUNDA, Kay	1972 5
*MEYERS, Mary Margaret	1968 5
MONK, Lori Jeanne	1976 5
MORSTEIN, Judith Helen	1964 15
*MUELLER, Leah Jean Poulos	1972 15, 30
(as Miss Poulos in 1972	1976 5, 10, 15
and 1976)	1980 5, 10
MULHOLLAND, Kathleen F.	1960 5
OMELENCHUK, Jeanne Marie Robinson	1960 5, 10, 15
	1968 15, 30
	1972 30
*POULOS, Leah	
(see Leah Mueller)	
SEIKKULA, Cindy	1976 15, 30
SMITH, Janice Marie	1964 5, 10, 15
SWIDER, Nancy Louise	1976 30
WHITE, Sylvia Josephine	1964 30
*YOUNG, Sheila	1972 5, 10
	1976 5, 10, 15

SWIMMING (Men) (248)

Swimming has been on the program of every Olympic Games. The United States has been represented at each swimming program, but our information on the two swimmers who represented the U.S. in 1900 is very scanty.

Olympic swimming rules allow for substitutions in relay heats, so some of the swimmers listed below for relays actually swam only in the heats.

In the following, all numbers indicate the distance in meters, unless followed by "y" for a yard race. If no letter code follows a distance, the event is a freestyle event. Other codes are as follows:

BF = Butterfly	MR = Medley relay
BK = Backstroke	IM = Individual medley
BS = Breaststroke	y = Yards
FR = Freestyle relay	P = Plunge for distance

*ADAMS, Edgar H.	1904 220y, 880y, Mile, 200yFR, P
ANDERSON, Wayne Robert	1964 200BS
*AUSTIN, Michael MacKay	1964 100, 400FR
*BABASHOFF, Jack, Jr.	1976 100, MR

*BACKHAUS, Robin	1972 200BF
BARBIERE, Lawrence Edward	1968 100BK
*BENNETT, Robert Earl	1960 100BK, MR
	1964 200BK, MR
BERK, Brent Thales	1968 400
BLANKENBERG, Thomas	1928 200BS
*BLICK, Richard Adolph	1960 800FR
BOLDEN, Eugene T.	1920 1500
*BOOTH, Frank Ewen	1932 800FR
BORNAMANN, Frank A.	1906 1000FR
(see also Diving)	
*BOTTOM, Joseph Stuart	1976 100, 100BF, MR
BRATTON, David H.	1904 200yFR
*BREEN, George Thomas	1956 400, 1500, 800FR
	1960 1500
*BREYER, Ralph	1924 400, 800FR
*BRUCE, Thomas Edwin	1972 100BS, MR
*BRUNER, Michael Lee	1976 200BF, 800FR
*BUCKINGHAM, Gregory F.	1968 200IM, 400IM
*BURTON, Michael Jay	1968 400, 1500
	1972 1500, 800FR
*CARTER, Keith E.	1948 100, 200BS
CHALMERS, Gordon	1932 100BK
CHATFIELD, Mark Webster	1972 100BS
&CLAPP, Austin Rhone	1928 400, 1500, 800FR
(see also Water Polo)	
*CLARK, Stephen Edward	1960 800FR, MR
	1964 400FR, 800FR, MR
CLEVELAND, Richard Fitch	1952 100
*COLELLA, Richard Phillip, Jr.	1972 200BS
	1976 200BS
CONELLY, Gary Robert	1972 400FR, 800FR
CONVERSE, Keith "Casey"	1976 400
*COWELL, Robert Elmer	1948 100BK
*CRABBE, Clarence Linden "Buster"	1928 400, 1500
	1932 400, 1500
*CRAIG, William Norval	1964 MR
*CRISTY, James Crapo, Jr.	1932 1500
	1936 1500
*DANIELS, Charles Meldrum	1904 50y, 100y, 220y, 440y, 200yFR
	1906 100, 1000FR
	1908 100, 800FR
DARNTON, William Thomas	1960 800FR
De MONT, Richard James	1972 400, 1500
*DICKEY, William Paul	1904 P
*DILLEY, Gary J.	1964 200BK
DOOLEY, Frank Martin	1952 800FR
DOWLER, Lawrence	1976 100BS
DRYSDALE, Taylor	1936 100BK
DUDLEY, William H., III	1948 800FR
*EDGAR, David Holmes	1972 100BF, 400FR

*EVANS, Gwynne	1904 200yFR
FAIRBANK, David	1972 400FR, MR
FARLEY, William Winfield	1964 1500
*FARRELL, Felix Jeffrey	1960 800FR, MR
*FERRIS, John Edward	1968 200BF, 200IM
FICK, Peter Joseph	1936 100
*FISSLER, George	1932 800FR
*FLANAGAN, Ralph Drew	1932 1500
	1936 400, 1500, 800FR
*FORD, Alan Robert	1948 100
FOREGGER, Richard V.	1900
*FORRESTER, William	1976 200BF
FOSTER, Robert B.	1908 100
FRANCIS, Basil H.	1932 200BS
*FURNISS, Bruce MacFarlane	1976 200, 800FR
*FURNISS, Steven Charles	1972 200IM, 400IM
	1976 400IM
*GAILEY, Francis	1904 220y, 440y, 880y, Mile
GAUL, David	1904 50y, 100y
*GENTER, Steven	1972 200, 400, 800FR
GIBE, Robert	1948 800FR
GILBERT, Edwin Fisher	1948 800FR
GILHULA, James R.	1932 400
*GILLANDERS, John David	1960 200BF, MR
GILMAN, Ralph	1936 800FR
*GLANCY, Harrison S.	1924 800FR
GOESSLING, Augustus M.	1908 100BK, 200BS
*GOETZ, Hugo L.	1904 200yFR
*GOODELL, Brian Stuart	1976 400, 1500
*GOODWIN, Leo G. "Budd"	1904 50y, 100y, 440y, 200yFR, P
	1908 400, 800FR
GORA, Ronald Francis	1952 100
*GRAEF, Jed Richard	1964 200BK
GREEN, James B.	1908 1500
*GREGG, Steven Garrett	1976 200BF
*HACKETT, Robert William	1976 1500
*HAIT, Paul William	1960 200BS, MR
*HALL, Gary Wayne	1968 200BK, 400IM
	1972 200BF, 200IM, 400IM, MR
	1976 100BF
*HAMMOND, David	1904 100y, 100yBK, 200yFR
*HANDLEY, Louis de Breda	1904 Mile, 200yFR
*HANDY, Henry Jamison	1904 880y, 440yBS
*HANLEY, Richard Dennis	1956 100, 800FR
*HARRIGAN, Daniel Lee	1976 200BK
*HARRIS, William W., Jr.	1920 100, 400
*HARRISON, George Prifold	1960 800FR
HARTLOFF, Paul Michael	1976 1500

*HEBNER, Harry J.	1908 100, 800FR
(see also Water Polo)	1912 100, 100BK, 800FR
*HEIDENREICH, Jerry Alan	1972 100, 100BF, 400FR, MR
*HENCKEN, John Frederick	1972 100BS, 200BS, MR
	1976 100BS, 200BS, MR
HENDSCHEL	1900
HESSER, David	1904 200yFR
HEUSNER, William W.	1948 400, 1500
*HICKCOX, Charles Buchanan	1968 100BK, 200IM, 400IM, MR
HIGGINS, John Herbert	1936 200BS
HIGHLAND, Arthur Raymond	1936 100
HOLAN, Gerald Ray	1952 200BS
*HORSLEY, Jack	1968 200BK
HOWELL, Jack	1920 200BS, 400BS
HOWELL, Richard	1924 1500, 800FR
HUGHES, Robert Earl	1956 200BS
(see also Water Polo)	
HUNTER, Richard Bruce	1960 100
*HUSZAGH, Kenneth Arthur	1912 100, 800FR
HUTTER, Charles George, Jr.	1936 800FR
*ILMAN, Gary Steven	1964 100, 400FR, 800FR
*IVEY, Mitchell	1968 200BK
	1972 100BK, 200BK, MR
JACKSON, Robert Scott	1976 100BK
*JASTREMSKI, Chester Andrew	1964 200BS
	1968 MR
JECKO, Perry Timothy	1956 800FR
*JOB, Brian Gregory	1968 200BS
	1972 200BS
JOHNSON, David Charles	1968 400FR, 800FR
JOHNSON, William R.	1968 400FR, 800FR
JONES, Burwell Otis	1952 800FR
*KAHANAMOKU, Duke Paoa Kahinu	
Makoe Hulikohoa	1912 100, 800FR
(see also Water Polo)	1920 100, 800FR
	1924 100
*KAHANAMOKU, Samuel	1924 100
KAHELE, Fred K.	1920 400, 1500
*KALILI, Maiola	1932 800FR
*KALILI, Manuella	1932 100, 800FR
KASLEY, Jack Hare	1936 200BS
KAYE, Ray	1936 200BS
*KEALOHA, Pua Kele	1920 100, 800FR
*KEALOHA, Warren Paoa	1920 100BK
	1924 100BK
KEATING, Charles Humphrey	1976 200BS
*KEGERIS, Ray	1920 100BK
KERBER, Robert	1932 100BK
*KIEFER, Adolph Gustav	1936 100BK

*KINSELLA, John Pitann	1968 1500
	1972 800FR
*KIRSCHBAUM, William	1924 200BS
*KOJAC, George Harold	1928 100, 100BK, 800FR
*KONNO, Ford Hiroshi	1952 400, 1500, 800FR
	1956 800FR
KRUGER, Harold H.	1920 100BK
*LANGER, Ludy	1920 400, 1500
*LARSON, Lance Melvin	1960 100, MR
*LAUFER, Walter	1928 100, 100BK, 800FR
*LEARY, J. Scott	1904 50y, 100y
LENZ, Eugene Carl	1960 400
LINDEGREN, Arthur	1936 100
LONG, Philip Edward	1968 200BS
LUKEN, Virgil W.	1964 MR
LUNING, Henry	1924 100BK
LYONS, David Chandler	1964 800FR
*MACIONIS, John Joseph	1936 400, 800FR
*MANN, Harold Thompson	1964 MR
*McBREEN, Thomas Sean	1972 400, 800FR
McDERMOTT, Michael J.	1912 200BS, 400BS
(see also Water Polo)	1920 200BS, 400BS
McGEAGH, Richard Michael	1964 MR
*McGILLIVRAY, Perry	1912 100, 800FR
(see also Water Polo)	1920 100BK, 800FR
*McKEE, Alexander Timothy	1972 200BK, 200IM, 400IM
	1976 400IM
*McKENZIE, Donald Ward, Jr.	1968 100BS, MR
*McKINNEY, Frank Edward, Jr.	1956 100BK
	1960 100BK, MR
*McLANE, James Price, Jr.	1948 400, 1500, 800FR
	1952 400, 1500, 800FR
*MEDICA, Jack C.	1936 400, 1500, 800FR
MERTEN, Kenneth	1968 100BS, 200BS
METTLER, William Roy	1964 800FR
MEYERS, John	1904 Mile
*MILLS, Ronald P.	1968 100BK, MR
MOLES, Edwin Janney	1932 200BS
*MONTGOMERY, James Paul	1976 100, 200, 800FR, MR
*MOORE, Wayne Richard	1952 400, 800FR
*MULLIKEN, William Danforth	1960 200BS
*MURPHY, John Joseph	1972 100, 100BK, 400FR
*NABER, John Phillips	1976 200, 100BK, 200BK, 800FR, MR
NELSON, Jack Weyman	1956 200BF

*WOOLSEY, William Tripp	1952 1500, 800FR
	1956 100, 400, 800FR
*WYATT, Paul	1924 100BK
	1928 100BK
*YORZYK, William Albert	1956 200BF
YOUNG, David K.	1928 800FR
ZEHR, Robert Dan	1932 100BK
*ZORN, Zachary	1968 100, 400FR

SWIMMING (Women) (178)

Women first competed in Olympic swimming competition in 1912. The United States had no competitors that year, but has had women swimmers at every Olympics since.

In Olympic swimming relays, the team for the heats may be different from that for the finals. Consequently not all the people listed as relay competitors necessarily swam in the finals.

In the following, all numbers indicate the distance in meters. If no letter code follows a distance, the event is a freestyle event. Other codes are as follows:

BF = Butterfly	FR = 4 × 100 meter freestyle relay
BK = Backstroke	MR = 4 × 100 meter medley relay
BS = Breaststroke	IM = Individual medley

*ALDERSON, Joan	1952 100, FR
ALLSUP, Lynn Marie	1964 FR
*ATWOOD, Susan Jean	1968 200BK
	1972 100BK, 200BK, MR
*BABASHOFF, Shirley	1972 100, 200, 400, FR, MR
	1976 100, 200, 400, 800, FR, MR
*BALL, Catherine	1968 100BS, MR
*BARKMAN, Jane Louise	1968 200, FR
	1972 FR
BARTZ, Jennifer	1972 200IM, 400IM
*BAUER, Sybil	1924 100BK
*BELOTE, Melissa	1972 100BK, 200BK, MR
	1976 200BK
*BLEIBTREY, Ethelda M.	1920 100, 300, FR
*BOGLIOLI, Wendy Lansbach	1976 100BF, FR, MR
BORGH, Brenda	1976 400
BOTKIN, Molly Ray	1960 FR
BOYLE, Charlotte	1920 100
BREY, Betty Mullen	1956 FR

BRICKER, Erika Eloise	1964 FR
*BRIDGES, Alice W.	1936 100BK
*BURKE, Lynn Edythe	1960 100BK, MR
CADWELL, Jane	1932 200BS
CARETTO, Patty	1968 800
*CARR, Catherine	1972 100BS, MR
CHAMBERS, Florence	1924 100BK
CLEVENGER, Claudia	1972 200BS
*COLELLA, Lynn Ann	1972 200BF
COLEMAN, Eleanor	1924 200BS
*CONE, Carin Alice	1956 100BK
CORNELL, Julia M.	1952 200BS
*CORRIDON, Marie Louise	1948 100, FR
CUMMINGS, Iris	1936 200BS
*CURTIS, Ann Elisabeth	1948 100, 400, FR
*DANIEL, Eleanor Suzanne	1968 100BF, 200BF, MR
	1972 100BF, 200BF
*DEARDURFF, Deena Diana	1972 100BF, MR
*De VARONA, Donna Elizabeth	1960 FR
	1964 100BF, 400IM, FR
DOERR, Susan Elizabeth	1960 FR
*DONNOLLY, Euphrasia	1924 FR
*DUENKEL, Virginia Ruth	1964 100BK, 400
*EDERLE, Gertrude Caroline	1924 100, 400, FR
*ELLIS, Kathleen	1964 100, 100BF, FR, MR
@FAUNTZ, Jane	1928 200BS
(see also Diving)	
*FERGUSON, Cathy Jean	1964 100BK, MR
*FINNERAN, Sharon Evans	1964 400IM
FONOIMOANA, Lelei	1976 100BF, MR
FORBES, Norene	1932 400
FREEMAN, Mary	1952 100BK
*FREEMAN, Mavis Ann	1936 FR
*GARATTI, Eleanor A.	
(see Eleanor Saville)	
*GERAGHTY, Agnes	1924 200BS
	1928 200BS
GIEBEL, Diane	1968 200BF
GILMAN, Marion	1928 100BK
GOVEDNICK, Ann B.	1932 200BS
*GOYETTE, Cynthia Lee	1964 MR
GRAHAM, Maryanne	1976 200BK
GRAY, Susan Douglas	1956 400
GREEN, Carolyn Virginia	1952 400
*GUEST, Irene	1920 100, FR
*GUSTAVSON, Linda Lee	1968 100, 400, FR
*HALL, Kaye	1968 100BK, 200BK, MR
HALLOCK, Jeanne Courtney	1964 100, FR
HANEY, Jeanne Marie	1976 400IM
HAPE, Janis Lynn	1976 200BS
HARMER, Nina Adams	1960 100BK
	1964 100BK, MR

*STOBS, Shirley Anne	1960 FR
*STOUDER, Sharon Marie	1964 100, 100BF, FR, MR
*SWAGERTY, Jane	1968 100BK, MR
*THORNTON, Karen Patricia Moe	1972 100BK, 200BF
(as Miss Moe in 1972)	1976 200BF
UHL, Eleanor	1920 300
VANDEWEGHE, Tauna Kay	1976 100BK
*VIDALI, Lynn Marie	1968 400IM
	1972 100BS, 200IM, 400IM
*Von SALTZA, Susan Christine	1960 100, 400, FR, MR
&WAINWRIGHT, Helen E.	1924 400
(see also Diving)	
WARNER, Anna Kindel	1960 200BS, MR
*WATSON, Lillian Debra "Pokey"	1964 FR, MR
	1968 200BK
*WEHSELAU, Mariechen	1924 100, FR
*WEINBERG, Wendy Farber	1976 800
WENNERSTROM, Donna Lee	1976 200BF, 400IM
*WICHMAN, Sharon	1968 100BS, 200BS
WILSON, Jeanne Elizabeth	1948 200BS
*WINGARD, Lenore Kight	1932 400
(as Miss Kight in 1932)	1936 400
*WOOD, Carolyn Virginia	1960 100, 100BF, FR, MR
*WOODBRIDGE, Margaret	1920 300, FR
WOODS, Carolyn	1972 200IM
*WRIGHT, Camille	1976 100BF, 200BF, MR
WYLIE, Jennifer Susan	1972 400
*ZIMMERMAN, Suzanne W.	100BK

TENNIS (Men) (43)
Tennis, then called lawn tennis, was held in every Olympics from 1896 through 1924 and has been a demonstration sport several times since, including 1984. The U.S. had players in 1900, 1904 (all but one player was American), 1912, and 1924. In 1908 and 1912 there were also indoor tennis events but no American competed in them. Tennis returns to the Olympic program as an official sport in 1988.

S = Singles	D = Doubles	M = Mixed Doubles

*BELL, Alphonzo Edward	1904 S, D
BLATHERWICK, W. E.	1904 S, D
CHARLES, Joseph C.	1904 S, D
CRESSON, Charles C., Jr.	1904 S, D
CUNNINGHAM, J.	1904 S
DAVIS, Dwight Filley	1904 S, D
DREW, Andrew	1904 S, D
EASTON, William	1904 S
FELTSHANS, F. R.	1904 S

FORNEY, Chris	1904 S
*GAMBLE, Clarence Oliver	1904 D
*GARMENDIA, Basil Spalding de	1900 S, D
(played doubles with a French partner)	
GLEASON, Paul	1904 D
(played doubles with a German partner)	
HUNTER	1904 D
*HUNTER, Francis Townsend	1924 S, D
JONES, Hugh McKittrick	1904 S, D
KAUFFMAN, Harold Meredith	1904 D
*LEONARD, Edgar Welch	1904 S, D
*LeROY, Robert	1904 S, D
MacDONALD, Malcolm C.	1904 S, D
@McKITTRICK, Ralph	1904 S, D
(see also Golf)	
MONTGOMERY, Forest H.	1904 S, D
NEELY, John C.	1904 S
PELL, Theodore Roosevelt	1912 S
*RICHARDS, Vincent	1924 S, D, M
RUSS, Semp	1904 S, D
SANDERSON, Fred R.	1904 S
@SANDS, Charles Edward	1900 S, D, M
(played doubles with a British partner)	
(see also Golf and Jeu de Paume)	
@SEMPLE, Frederick Humphrey	1904 D
(see also Golf)	
SEMPLE, Nathaniel Meacon	1904 S, D
SMITH, N. M.	1904 S, D
STADEL, George H.	1904 S, D
TRITLE, J. Stewart	1904 S, D
TURNER, Douglass	1904 S, D
VERNON, Orien V.	1904 S, D
VOIGHT, Charles A.	1900 S
WASHBURN, Watson McLeay	1924 S, D
*WEAR, Arthur Yancey	1904 D
*WEAR, Joseph Walker	1904 D
*WEST, Allen Tarwater	1904 D
WHEATON, Frank	1904 S, D
*WILLIAMS, Richard Norris, III	1924 S, D, M
*WRIGHT, Beals Coleman	1904 S, D

TENNIS (Women) (7)
In 1900 tennis became the first sport in which women participated in the Olympic Games, and two American women, the Jones sisters, competed. Tennis for women was again held in 1906, 1908, 1912, 1920, and 1924, but American women did not return to the Olympic courts until 1924.

S = Women's singles	D = Women's doubles
M = Mixed doubles	

GOSS, Eleanor	1924 S, D
*JESSUP, Marion Zinderstein	1924 S, D, M

JONES, Georgina Frances	1900 S, M
*JONES, Marion	1900 S, M
(played doubles with a British partner)	
SCHARMAN, Lillian	1924 S
*WIGHTMAN, Hazel Virginia Hotchkiss	1924 D, M
*WILLS, Helen Newington	1924 S, D

TRACK & FIELD (Athletics) (Men) (1,069)

Track & field, called athletics by most of the world, has been on the program at every Olympic Games. The United States has never failed to be represented in the track & field program.

All numbers below indicate distances in meters, unless followed by a large "M," which indicates miles.

b = Both hands	PV = Pole vault
DT = Discus throw	R = Relay
g = Greek style	s = Standing
h = Hurdles	SP = Shot put
HJ = High jump	S = Steeplechase
HT = Hammer throw	TJ = Triple jump
JT = Javelin throw	TW = Tug-of-War
LJ = Long jump	5k = 5,000 meters
10k = 10,000 meters	20k = 20,000 meters
50k = 50,000 meters	Mar = Marathon
Dec = Decathlon	Pen = Pentathlon
AA1 = All-around	M = Miles
T = Team event	XC = Cross-country
W = Walking event	MR = Medley relay
56 = 56 lb. weight throw	ST = Stone throw

ABBOTT, David	1928 5k
*ABLOWICH, Edgar Allen	1932 1600R
*ADAMS, Benjamin W.	1912 sHJ, sLJ
*ADAMS, Platt	1908 sHJ, sLJ, TJ
	1912 sHJ, sLJ, TJ
AGEE, William	1928 Mar
AHEARN, Daniel F.	1920 TJ
(né Daniel Ahearne)	
ALBANS, William Everett	1948 TJ
*ALBRITTON, David Donald	1936 HJ
*ALDERMAN, Frederick Pitt	1928 1600R
ALLEN, Claude Arthur	1904 PV
ALLEN, Fred Harold	1912 LJ
ALLEN, John W.	1960 50kW
ALLEY, Francis William	1960 JT
*ANDERSON, John Franklin	1928 DT
	1932 DT
ANDERSON, Jon Peter	1972 10k
ANDERSON, Karl Walter	1924 110h
ANDERSON, Lewis Robbins	1912 1500

ANDERSON, Norman Fred	1924 SP
ANDERSON, Otto Kenneth	1924 Dec
*ANDERSON, Stephen Eugene	1928 110h
ANGIER, Milton Sanford	1920 JT
ARGUE, John Clifford	1924 Pen
ASHBAUGH, Walter S.	1952 TJ
*ASHBURNER, Lesley	1904 110h
*ASHENFELTER, Horace, III	1952 3000S
	1956 3000S
ASHENFELTER, William Nyman	1952 3000S
*ASHWORTH, Gerald Howard	1964 400R
ATLEE, John Cox	1908 400
AULT, Richard Francis	1948 400h
*BABCOCK, Harold Stoddard	1912 PV, Dec
*BABKA, Richard Aldrich	1960 DT
BACHELER, John Stangl	1968 5k
	1972 Mar
BACKUS, Robert Hudson	1952 HT
*BACON, Charles Joseph, Jr.	1904 1500
	1906 400, 800
	1908 400h
BAGDONAS, Edward	1960 HT
*BAIRD, George Hetzel	1928 1600R
*BAKER, Walter Thane	1952 200
	1956 100, 200, 400R
BANNISTER, Jeffrey Granville	1972 Dec
BANTUM, Kenneth Owens	1956 SP
BARBER, Richard Alvah	1932 LJ
*BARBUTI, Raymond J.	1928 400, 1600R
BARKER, Ervin Jerold	1904 HJ
*BARNARD, Arthur	1952 110h
BARNES, John Baird	1952 800
*BARNES, Lee Stratford	1924 PV
	1928 PV
BARRINEAU, James Archibald, Jr.	1976 HJ
*BARRON, Harold Earl	1920 110h
BARTEN, Herbert Otto	1948 800
BARTLETT, Lee Marion	1928 JT
	1932 JT
	1936 JT
BARTLETT, William Kenneth	1920 DT
*BATES, Alfred Hilborn	1928 LJ
*BAUSCH, James Aloysius Bernard	1932 Dec
*BAXTER, Irving Knott	1900 HJ, PV, sHJ, sLJ, sTJ
*BEAMON, Robert	1968 LJ
BEARD, Clarke Briar	1908 800
*BEARD, Percy Morris	1932 110h
BEATTY, James Tully	1960 5k
BECKUS, Robert J.	1948 TJ
BELL, Earl Holmes	1976 PV
*BELL, Gregory Curtis	1956 LJ
BELL, C. Wade	1968 800
BELLAH, Samuel Harrison	1908 LJ, TJ, PV
	1912 PV
BELLARS, Frederick G.	1908 5M

BELOTE, Frank V.	1912 100, 400R, sHJ
*BENNETT, Basil B.	1920 HT
BENNETT, Jefferson Taft	1972 Dec
*BENNETT, John Dale	1956 LJ
*BENNETT, Robert Howard	1948 HT
BERLINGER, Bernard Ernst	1928 Dec
*BERNA, Tell Schirnding	1912 3000T, 5k
BETTON, Arnold	1952 HJ
BEUCHER, Terence Eugene	1960 JT
*BIFFLE, Jerome Cousins	1952 LJ
BIHLMAN, George H.	1920 SP
BILES, Martin Broomall	1948 JT
*BILLER, John A.	1904 sHJ, sLJ, DT
	1908 sHJ, sLJ
BJORKLUND, Garry Brian	1976 10k
*BLACK, Edmund Franklin	1928 HT
*BLACK, Larry J.	1972 200, 400R
BLACKMAN, Roland	1952 400h
BLAIR, Clyde Amel	1904 60, 100, 400
*BLAKE, Charles Arthur	1896 1500, Mar
BLANCHARD, Vaughn Seavy	1912 110h
BOARDMAN, Dixon	1900 100, 400
BOHLAND, Max	1920 XC
BOLEN, David Benjamin	1948 400
*BONHAG, George V.	1904 800
	1906 1500, 5M, 1500W
	1908 3200S, 3MT
	1912 3000T, 5k
BOOTH, Verne Hobson	1924 10k, XC, XCt
*BORAH, Charles Edward	1928 200, 400R
*BOSTON, Ralph Harold	1960 LJ
	1964 LJ
	1968 LJ
BOURGEOIS, Lloyd Henry	1928 TJ
*BOURLAND, Clifford Frederick	1948 200, 1600R
BOWDEN, Donald Paul	1956 1500
BOWMAN, Chester	1924 100
BOWMAN, Sidney Howard	1928 TJ
	1932 TJ
BRACEY, Claude Odell	1928 100
*BRADLEY, Everett Lewis	1920 Pen
BRAGG, Arthur George	1952 100
*BRAGG, Donald George	1960 PV
*BRAUN, Max	1904 TW
BRAWLEY, Henry A.	1904 Mar
*BRAY, John	1900 800, 1500
BRECKENRIDGE, Alexander Dalglish Neilson	1960 Mar
*BREITKREUTZ, Emil William	1904 800
BRENNAN, John Joseph	1908 LJ, TJ
BRETNALL, George Stuart	1920 1600R
BRICKLEY, Charles Edward	1912 TJ
*BRIX, Harold Herman	1928 SP
BRODIE, Michael Warren	1964 50kW
BROMILOW, Joseph, Jr.	1908 800

*BROOKER, James Kent	1924 PV
BROOKINS, Charles Robert	1924 400h
BROOKS, John William	1936 LJ
BROSIUS, Carlton L.	1920 TW
*BROWN, Benjamin Gene	1976 1600R
BROWN, Douglas Charles	1972 3000S
	1976 3000S
BROWN, Ellison Myers "Tarzan"	1936 Mar
BROWN, George Henry, Jr.	1952 LJ
*BROWN, Horace Hallock	1920 3000T, 5k
*BROWN, Leroy Taylor	1924 HJ
BROWN, Reynaldo	1968 HJ
BROWN, William	1936 TJ
BRUGGEMAN, Richard John	1972 400h
BRUNDAGE, Avery	1912 DT, Pen, Dec
BUDD, Francis Joseph	1960 100, 400R
BUERKLE, Richard T.	1976 5k
BUKER, Raymond Bates	1924 1500
BURDICK, Jervis Watson	1912 HJ
BURKE, Edward Andrew	1964 HT
	1968 HT
*BURKE, Thomas Edmund	1896 100, 400
BURLESON, Dyrol Jay	1960 1500
	1964 1500
BURROUGHS, Charles Lindsey	1900 100
BURROUGHS, Wilbur Gordon	1908 SP, DT, DTg, TW
BURTON, Lawrence Godfrey	1972 200
BURTON, William E.	1948 DT
BUSHNELL, Edward Rogers	1900 800
BUTLER, Edward Solomon	1920 LJ
*BUTTS, James A.	1976 TJ
*BYRD, Richard Leslie	1912 sHJ, sLJ, DT, DTb
*CAGLE, Harold D.	1936 1600R
CALDWELL, David Story	1912 800
*CALHOUN, Lee Quency	1956 110h
	1960 110h
*CAMPBELL, Milton Gray	1952 Dec
	1956 Dec
CAMPBELL, Thomas	1920 800
CANN, Howard Gardsell	1920 SP
CANTELLO, Albert Anthony	1960 JT
CAPOZZOLI, Charles Joseph	1952 5k
*CARLOS, John Wesley	1968 200
CARLSEN, Gary	1968 DT
*CARNEY, Lester Nelson	1960 200
CARPENTER, John Conduit	1908 400
*CARPENTER, William Kenneth	1936 DT
CARR, Edward P.	1904 Mar
	1908 3200S, 5M
*CARR, Henry	1964 200, 1600R
*CARR, Sabin William	1928 PV
*CARR, William Arthur	1932 400, 1600R
CARRIGAN, Casey D.	1968 PV
CARRINGTON, Preston Morrand	1972 LJ
CARROLL, Walter Cockrill	1900 HJ

Name	Events
CARTER, Ernest Nicholas	1928 1500
*CARTMELL, Nathaniel John	1904 60, 100, 200
	1908 100, 200, MR
*CARUTHERS, Edward J., Jr.	1964 HJ
	1968 HJ
CASE, John Ruggles	1912 110h
*CASEY, Levi B.	1928 TJ
CASKEY, Kenneth Harry	1928 HT
*CASSELL, Ollan Conn	1964 400, 1600R
*CASTLEMAN, Frank Riley	1904 60, 100, 110h, 200h
*CAWLEY, Warren Jay "Rex"	1964 400h
CENTROWITZ, Matthew	1976 1500
CHADWICK, Charles	1904 SP, HT, 56, TW
CHAMBERS, Robert David	1948 800
CHARLES, Wilson David	1932 Dec
*CHILDS, Clarence Chester	1912 HT
CHISHOLM, George Alpin	1912 110h
CHISHOLM, William Hugh	1932 50kW
CHURCHILL, Kenneth Maurice	1932 JT
CHURCHILL, Thomas Ralph	1928 Dec
CHURCHILL, William J.	1924 Mar
CLARK, David Eugene	1960 PV
*CLARK, Ellery Harding	1896 HJ, LJ
	1904 AA
*CLARK, Robert Hyatt	1936 LJ, Dec
*CLARKE, Louis Alfred	1924 400R
CLOSE, Peter Michael	1960 1500
*CLOUGHEN, Robert	1908 100, 200
*COCHRAN, Commodore S.	1924 1600R
*COCHRAN, Leroy Braxton	1948 400h, 1600R
*COCHRAN, Richard Lee	1960 DT
COE, Harry Lee	1908 800, 1500, 400h
*COE, William Wesley, Jr.	1904 SP
	1908 SP, TW
COFFMAN, Clifford Clyde	1932 Dec
COHN, Harvey W.	1904 800, 1500, 2590S
	1906 1500, 5M
	1908 3MT
*COLE, Gerrard Eugene	1952 400, 1600R
COLEMAN, Leon	1968 110h
COLEMAN, Philip Yates	1956 3000S
	1960 3000S
*COLKET, Meredith Bright	1900 PV
*COLLETT, Wayne Curtis	1972 400
*COLLIER, John Sheldon	1928 110h
COLSON, Samuel Linn	1976 JT
COMINS, William Albert	1924 LJ
CONGER, Raymond Milton	1928 1500
CONLEY, Philip R.	1956 JT
CONNOLLY, Francis	1906 LJ, TJ
*CONNOLLY, Harold Vincent	1956 HT
	1960 HT
	1964 HT
	1968 HT
*CONNOLLY, James Brendan	1896 HJ, LJ, TJ
	1900 TJ
	1906 LJ, TJ
CONNOLLY, James Joseph	1920 1500
	1924 3000T
CONNOR, Frank Norris	1928 HT
	1932 HT
*COOK, Edward Tiffin, Jr.	1908 LJ, PV
COOKE, Carl Clement	1912 200, 400R
CORBITT, Theodore	1952 Mar
CORNETTA, George	1920 10k
*CORSON, James Hunt	1928 DT
COSTES, Nicholas	1956 Mar
COULTER, Chan Frank	1924 400h
COURTNEY, J. Ira	1912 100, 200, 400R
*COURTNEY, Thomas William	1956 800, 1600R
COVELLI, Frank George	1964 JT
	1968 JT
*COX, William John	1924 3000T
COYLE, Frank James	1912 PV
CRAFT, John Melvin	1972 TJ
*CRAIG, Ralph Cook	1912 100, 200
CRAWFORD, Robert	1920 XC
*CREGAN, John Francis	1900 800
*CRONAN, Thomas F.	1906 LJ, TJ
CROSBIE, George William Ernest	1932 50kW
	1936 50kW
	1948 50kW
CROWLEY, Francis Arthur	1932 1500
*CUHEL, Frank Josef	1928 400h
*CULBREATH, Joshua	1956 400h
CUMMINGS, Henry H., Jr.	1928 200
CUNLIFFE, William Ernest	1960 800
*CUNNINGHAM, Glenn V.	1932 1500
	1936 1500
CURTIS, Edward Burnam	1920 1500
*CURTIS, Thomas Pelham	1896 100, 110h
*CUSHMAN, Clifton Emmett	1960 400h
DAGGS, Charles Daniel	1920 400h
DALTON, Melvin J.	1928 3000S
*DAVENPORT, Ira Nelson	1912 400, 800
*DAVENPORT, Willie D.	1964 110h
(see also Bobsledding)	1968 110h
	1972 110h
	1976 110h
*DAVIS, Glenn Ashby	1956 400h
	1960 400h, 1600R
DAVIS, Ira Sylvester	1956 TJ
	1960 TJ
	1964 TJ
*DAVIS, Jack Wells	1952 110h
	1956 110h
*DAVIS, Otis Crandall	1960 400, 1600R
*DAVIS, Walter Francis	1952 HJ
DAWS, Ronald H.	1968 Mar

DAWSON, Glenn Wilson	1932 3000S
	1936 3000S
DAY, Robert Winston	1968 5k
DEAN, Daniel Ely	1932 5k
DEARBORN, Arthur Kent	1908 DT, DTg, TW
DECKARD, Thomas Marshall	1936 5k
*DELANEY, Francis James	1948 SP
*DELLINGER, William Solon	1956 5k
	1960 5k
	1964 5k
*DeMAR, Clarence Harrison	1912 Mar
	1924 Mar
	1928 Mar
DENI, John Michael	1948 50kW
	1952 50kW
DENMAN, Elliott	1956 50kW
*DESCH, August George	1920 400h
DEVANEY, Michael A.	1920 3000S, 3000T
	1924 3000S
DEVLIN, F. P.	1904 Mar
*De WITT, John Riegel	1904 HT
DIEGES, Charles J.	1904 TW
*DILLARD, William Harrison	1948 100, 400R
	1952 110h, 400R
*DILLION, James Leo	1952 DT
*DIXON, Craig Kline	1948 110h
DIXON, Frederick	1976 Dec
DODGE, Ray E.	1924 800
*DOHERTY, John Kenneth	1928 Dec
*DONAHUE, James J.	1912 Pen, Dec
DOOLEY, Thomas Robert	1968 20kW
	1972 20kW
DOOLITTLE, Eastman Rilus	1924 5k
*DOUGLAS, Herbert Paul, Jr.	1948 LJ
*DRAPER, Foy	1936 400R
DRAY, Walter Remy	1904 PV
*DRAYTON, Otis Paul	1964 200, 400R
*DRESSER, Ivan Chandler	1920 3000T, 5k
DREW, Howard Porter	1912 100
DREYER, Henry Francis	1936 HT
	1948 HT
*DROEGEMULLER, William Herbert	1928 PV
DRUETZLER, Warren Oliver	1952 1500
DRUMHELLER, Walter Edwin	1900 400, 800
DUFFEY, Arthur Francis	1900 100
DUKES, Gordon Bennett	1912 PV
DULL, Gale Albert	1908 3200S, 3MT
*DUMAS, Charles Everett	1956 HJ
	1960 HJ
*DUNCAN, James Henry	1912 DT, DTb
DUNN, Christopher Williams	1972 HJ
*DUNN, Gordon Glover	1936 DT
DUNNE, Robert Jerome	1920 Pen
DUPREE, Rayfield, Jr.	1976 TJ
DURKIN, Michael Kevin	1976 1500
*DVORAK, Charles Edward	1904 PV
DYE, Leighton William	1928 110h
*DYER, Hector Monroe	1932 400R
DYRGALL, Victor J.	1952 Mar
*EASTMAN, Benjamin Bangs	1932 400
EATON, William David	1906 100
*EBY, Earl William	1920 800
EDELEN, Leonard Graves "Buddy"	1964 Mar
EDGREN, Robert W.	1906 SP, DT
EDDLEMAN, Thomas Dwight	1948 HJ
EDMUNDSON, Clarence Sinclair	1912 400, 800
EDSTROM, David Allan	1960 Dec
EISCHEN, Clement George	1948 1500
*EISELE, John Lincoln	1908 3200S, 3MT
ELLER, John J., Jr.	1912 110h, Pen
ELLIS, Everett Ralph	1920 Dec
EMBERGER, Richard John	1964 Dec
EMERY, Robert Simpson	1920 400
@EMMERICH, Max	1904 AA
(see also Gymnastics)	
*ENCK, Schuyler Colfax	1924 800
ENGEL, Martin Stephen	1952 HT
*ENGLEHARDT, Frederick	1904 LJ, TJ
ENRIGHT, Harold Bradford	1912 HJ
ENYEART, Mark Bruce	1976 800
ERICKSON, Egon R.	1912 HJ
ERXLEBEN, Joseph	1912 Mar
*EVANS, Dwayne Eugene	1976 200
*EVANS, Lee Edward	1968 400, 1600R
*EWELL, Harold Norwood "Barney"	1948 100, 200, 400R
*EWRY, Raymond Clarence	1900 sHJ, sLJ, sTJ
	1904 sHJ, sLJ, sTJ
	1906 sHJ, sLJ
	1908 sHJ, sLJ
*FAGER, August	1924 XC, XCt
FALLER, Frederick W.	1920 10k, XC
FARRELL, Edward Leo	1912 LJ, TJ
*FARRELL, Thomas Francis	1964 800
	1968 800
FAUST, Joseph Patrick	1960 HJ
FAVOR, Donald Emerson	1936 HT
FELTON, Samuel Morse, Jr.	1948 HT
	1952 HT
*FEUERBACH, Leon E. J.	1904 SP, TW
FEURBACH, Allan Dean	1972 SP
	1976 SP
FIELD, Henry W.	1904 sLJ
FIELDS, Stephen C.	1920 TW
FISHBACK, Jeffrey Mason	1964 3000S
*FITCH, Alfred Lord	1936 1600R
*FITCH, Horatio May	1924 400
FITZGERALD, Edward John	1912 5k
*FLANAGAN, John J.	1900 DT, HT
	1904 DT, HT, 56
	1908 DT, HT, TW
*FLANAGAN, Patrick	1904 TW
FLEMING, Joseph J.	1904 400

FLETCHER, Forest	1912 sHJ, sLJ
FLOERKE, Kent Lee	1964 TJ
*FLYNN, Patrick J.	1920 3000S, XC
*FORSHAW, Joseph, Jr.	1906 Mar
	1908 Mar
	1912 Mar
*FOSBURY, Richard Douglas	1968 HJ
*FOSS, Frank Kent	1920 PV
FOSTER, Charles H.	1924 10kW
FOSTER, Charles Wayne	1976 110h
FOWLER, Robert J.	1904 Mar
	1906 Mar
FOY, John J.	1904 Mar
FRANCIS, Harrison Samuel	1936 SP
*FRANK, Daniel	1904 LJ
FRANK, Victor Harry, Jr.	1948 DT
*FRANK, William G.	1906 5M, Mar
*FRAZIER, Herman Ronald	1976 400, 1600R
*FREEMAN, Ronald John, II	1968 400, 1600R
FRENCH, Charles Martin	1908 800
FRENN, George	1972 HT
FREYMARK, Emil	1904 HJ
FRICK, Harvey	1928 Mar
FRIEDA, Harry Gaylord	1924 Dec
*FRIEDE, Oscar C.	1904 TW
*FRIEND, Hugo Morris	1906 110h, LJ, sLJ
FRITZ, William Howard, Jr.	1912 PV
*FUCHS, James Emanuel	1948 SP
	1952 SP
FUHLER, John W.	1904 TJ
FULLER, Earl	1928 800
*FUQUA, Ivan William	1932 1600R
FURLA, John	1904 Mar
FURNAS, Clifford Cook	1920 5k
FURTH, Solomon H.	1932 TJ
GAGE, Thomas Lewis	1972 HT
GALLAGHER, John James, Jr.	1912 Mar
GALLOWAY, John Franks "Jeff"	1972 10k
GARCIA, Benjamin Benito	1956 JT
GARCIA, William R.	1904 Mar
*GARRELLS, John Carlyle	1908 110h, SP, DT, DTg
*GARRETT, Robert	1896 HJ, LJ, SP, DT
	1900 sTJ, SP, DT
*GATHERS, James	1952 200
GEGAN, Walter T.	1928 3000S
GEHRMANN, Donald Arthur	1948 1500
GEIS, Paul Geoffrey	1976 5k
GEIST, Kaufman	1920 TJ
GENUNG, Edwin Bernard	1932 800
GEORGE, Richard Lloyd	1976 JT
GERHARDT, James	1952 TJ
GERHARDT, Peter C.	1912 100, 200
GIBSON, John J.	1928 400h
GIDNEY, Herbert Alfred	1908 HJ
*GIFFIN, Merritt H.	1908 DT
*GILBERT, Alfred Carleton	1908 PV
GILLIS, Simon Patrick	1908 DT, HT
*GLANCE, Harvey	1976 100, 400R
*GLOVER, Edward Chester	1906 PV
GOEHRING, Leo	1912 sHJ, sLJ
GOELITZ, Harry G.	1920 Dec
GOFFBERG, Herman	1948 10k
*GORDIEN, Fortune Everett	1948 DT
	1952 DT
	1956 DT
*GORDON, Edward Lansing, Jr.	1928 LJ
	1932 LJ
GORDON, James Allen	1932 400
*GOURDIN, Edward Orval	1924 LJ
*GOURDINE, Meredith C.	1952 LJ
GRABER, William Noe	1932 PV
	1936 PV
*GRAHAM, Glenn	1924 PV
GRAHAM, Merwin B.	1924 TJ
GRANROSE, Sylvester	1920 TW
GRANT, Alexander	1900 800, 4000S
GRANT, Dick	1900 Mar
GRAY, John J.	1924 10k, XC, XCt
GRAY, Nelson Alexander	1932 SP
*GREENE, Charles Edward	1968 100, 400R
GREGORY, Louis P.	1932 10k
GRELLE, James Edward	1960 1500
@GRIEB, John	1904 AA
(see also Gymnastics)	
*GROMAN, Herman Charles	1904 400
GROTH, Morgan Dustin	1964 800
GRUMPELT, Harry John	1912 HJ
GUIDA, George J.	1948 400
GUINEY, John C.	1904 SP
*GUNN, Adam B.	1904 AA
GUTHRIE, George Phineas, Jr.	1924 110h
*GUTOWSKI, Robert Allen	1956 PV
*GUTTERSON, Albert Lovejoy	1912 LJ
GWINN, Donald S.	1928 HT
*HABERKORN, Charles	1904 TW
(see also Wrestling)	
HAFF, Carroll Barse	1912 400
HAGERMAN, John Percival	1904 LJ, TJ
*HAHN, Archibald	1904 60, 100, 200
	1906 100
HAHN, Lloyd	1924 1500
	1928 800, 1500
HALL, Albert William	1956 HT
	1960 HT
	1964 HT
	1968 HT
HALL, Anthony	1976 JT
HALL, Charles Lincoln	1908 3200S, 5M
*HALL, David Connolly	1900 800, 1500
*HALL, Ervin	1968 110h
HALLOWELL, Norwood Penrose	1932 1500

HALPIN, Thomas J.	1912 800	HINKEL, Harvey Robert	1924 10kW
HALSTEAD, John Preston	1908 800, 1500		1932 50kW
HALUZA, Rudolph John	1960 20kW	HODGE, Russell Arden	1964 Dec
	1968 20kW	*HOGENSON, William P.	1904 60, 100, 200
*HAMILTON, Brutus Kerr	1920 Pen, Dec	HOLDEN, Harland Ware	1912 800
	1924 Pen	*HOLLAND, William Joseph	1900 60, 200, 400
*HAMILTON, William Frank	1908 100, 200, MR	HOLMES, Francis Leroy	1908 sHJ, sLJ
*HAMM, Edward Barton	1928 LJ	*HOOPER, Clarence Darrow	1952 SP
*HAMPTON, Millard Frank	1976 200, 400R	HOPKINS, Gayle Patrick	1964 LJ
*HANSEN, Frederick Morgan	1964 PV	*HORINE, George Leslie	1912 HJ
*HARDIN, Glenn Foster	1932 400h	HORNBOSTEL, Charles Christian	1932 800
	1936 400h		1936 800
HARDIN, William Foster	1964 400h	*HORR, Marquis Franklin "Bill"	1908 SP, DT, DTg, HT, TW
*HARE, Thomas Truxtun	1900 DT, HT		
	1904 AA	HORTON, Daniel Slawson	1900 TJ, sTJ
HARLOW, Charles Vendale	1928 JT	*HOUSER, Lemuel Clarence	1924 SP, DT
*HARNDEN, Arthur H.	1948 1600R		1928 DT
*HART, Eddie James	1972 100, 400R	*HOWARD, Richard Wayne	1960 400h
HART, Lawrence Thomas	1976 HT	HOWE, Leonard Vernon	1908 110h
HART, Richard Lewis	1956 10k	*HOYT, William Welles	1896 110h, PV
*HARTRANFT, Samuel Glenn	1924 SP, DT	*HUBBARD, William De Hart	1924 LJ, TJ
*HATCH, Sidney H.	1904 4MT, Mar		1928 LJ
	1908 Mar	HUFF, Harold J.	1908 100, 200
*HAWKINS, Martin W.	1912 110h	HULSEBOCH, Albert Joseph	1920 3000S
HAWORTH, Charles	1928 5k	HUNTER, Charles F.	1920 5k
HAYDEN, Steven Roy	1972 50kW	HUNTER, William B.	1904 60
HAYES, Howard Wood	1900 800	*HUSSEY, Francis Valentine Joseph	1924 400R
*HAYES, John Joseph	1908 Mar	*INESS, Simeon Garland	1952 DT
*HAYES, Robert Lee	1964 100, 400R	*IRONS, Francis C.	1908 LJ, TJ, sHJ, sLJ
HAYNES, Thomas	1976 TJ		1912 LJ
HEALEY, Joseph F.	1932 400h	JACKSON, Trenton	1964 100
*HEARN, Lacey Ernest	1904 800, 1500, 4MT	*JACOBS, Charles Sherman	1908 PV
HECKWOLF, Frederick	1904 100	*JACOBS, Harry	1904 TW
*HEDGES, Benjamin van Doren, Jr.	1928 HJ	*JAMES, George Lawrence	1968 400, 1600R
HEDLUND, Oscar Frederick	1912 1500	*JAMISON, Herbert Brotherson	1896 400
HEILAND, Harold William	1912 100, 200	JANKUNIS, William	1976 HJ
HELD, Franklin Wesley	1952 JT	JAQUITH, Clarence E.	1920 TJ
*HELFFRICH, Alan Boone	1924 1600R	*JARVIS, Frank Washington	1900 100, TJ, sTJ
HELLAWELL, Harry Hallas	1912 10k, XC	*JEFFERSON, George G.	1932 PV
HENIGAN, James P.	1924 XC, XCt	*JENKINS, Charles Lamont	1956 400, 1600R
	1928 Mar	JENNE, Eldon Irl	1920 PV
	1932 Mar	*JENNER, William Bruce	1972 Dec
HENNEMANN, Charles H.	1904 56		1976 Dec
HERMAN, Paul Irvin	1964 Dec	JESSUP, Paul Boulet	1932 DT
HEWSON, James Edward	1956 20kW	JOHNSON, Albert A.	1904 SP, HT
*HICKS, Thomas J.	1904 Mar	*JOHNSON, Carl Edward	1920 LJ
HILL, George Leroy	1924 200	*JOHNSON, Cornelius Cooper	1932 HJ
*HILL, Ralph Anthony	1932 5k		1936 HJ
*HILL, Thomas Lionel	1972 110h	JOHNSON, Franklin Picther	1924 110h
*HILLMAN, Harry Livingston, Jr.	1904 400, 200h, 400h	*JOHNSON, Jan Eric	1972 PV
	1906 400, 110h	*JOHNSON, Rafer Lewis	1956 Dec
	1908 400h		1960 Dec
*HILLS, Ralph Gorman	1924 SP	JOHNSON, Richard Earle	1920 10k
HILTON, Leonard Lane	1972 5k		1924 10k, XC, XCt
HINES, Creth B.	1928 JT	*JOHNSON, Sidney B.	1904 TW
*HINES, James Ray	1968 100, 400R	JOHNSON, Stone Edward	1960 200, 400R

Name	Events
JOHNSON, Wayne	1924 10k
JOHNSTONE, John Oliver	1912 HJ
JONES, Charles Nicholas	1956 3000S
	1960 3000S
*JONES, Hayes Wendell	1960 110h
	1964 110h
JONES, John Paul	1912 800, 1500
*JONES, John Wesley	1976 100, 400R
JONES, Lloyd Peniston	1908 800
*JONES, Louis Woodard, III	1956 400, 1600R
*JONES, Samuel Symington	1904 HJ, TJ, TW
JONES, Thomas M.	1952 Mar
JOURDAN, Ronnie Lee	1972 HJ
JOYCE, John	1904 800
JUDAY, Robert L.	1924 HJ
KAER, Morton Armour	1924 Pen
KAISER, Frederick Henry	1912 10kW
KARDONG, Donald F.	1976 Mar
KELLER, John Alton Claude	1932 110h
KELLEY, John Adelbert	1936 Mar
	1948 Mar
KELLEY, John Joseph	1956 Mar
	1960 Mar
KELLEY, Robert Matthew	1928 TJ
*KELLY, Daniel Joseph	1908 LJ
*KELLY, Frederick Warren	1912 110h
KELSEY, Floyd A.	1920 TW
KENNEDY, Thomas J.	1904 Mar
*KERRIGAN, Herbert W.	1906 HJ, sLJ, PV
*KIESEL, Robert Allan	1932 400R
*KING, Charles M.	1904 sLJ, sTJ
*KING, Leamon	1956 400R
*KING, Robert Wade	1928 HJ
KING, Sloss Price, Jr.	1952 10kW
*KINSEY, Daniel Chapin	1924 110h
KIRALFY, Edgar Graham	1908 100
*KIRBY, Edward Buckler	1924 3000T
KIRK, Jeffery L.	1948 400h
&KIRKSEY, Morris Marshall	1920 100, 200, 400R
(see also Rugby Football)	
*KIVIAT, Abel Richard	1912 1500, 3000T
KLOPFER, Goetz Heinrich	1968 50kW
	1972 20kW
KNEELAND, David J.	1904 Mar
KNOUREK, Edward Emil	1920 PV
*KOCH, Desmond Dalworth	1956 DT
KOEHLER, Ernest	1936 50kW
KOUTONEN, Erik	1948 TJ
*KRAENZLEIN, Alvin Christian	1900 60, 110h, 200h, LJ
KRAMER, William J.	1912 10k
KRENZ, Eric Christian William	1928 SP
*KUCK, John	1928 SP
&KUNGLER, Frank	1904 TW
(see also Weightlifting and Wrestling)	
KSZYCZEWISKI, Joseph	1920 TW
KUTSCHINSKI, Ronald Craig	1968 800
*LaBORDE, Henri Jean	1932 DT
LAIRD, Ronald Owen	1960 50kW
	1964 20kW
	1968 20kW
	1976 20kW
LANDERS, Sherman George	1920 TJ
*LANDON, Richmond Wilcox	1920 HJ
LANE, Francis Adonijah	1896 100
LARIS, Thomas Constantine	1968 10k
*LARRABEE, Michael Denny	1964 400, 1600R
LARRIEU, Gilbert Ronald	1964 10k
LARRIVEE, Leo Edward	1924 3000T
LASH, Donald Ray	1936 5k, 10k
LASKAU, Henry Helmut	1948 10kW
	1952 10kW
	1956 20kW
*LAZ, Donald Robert	1952 PV
LEA, James Gilbert, Jr.	1956 400
*LEAVITT, Robert Grandison	1906 110h
*LeCONEY, Jeremiah Alfred	1924 400R
LEE, Harry Glover	1900 400
*LeGENDRE, Robert Lucien	1920 Pen
	1924 Pen
LEIBLEE, Clark Moses	1900 100
LERMOND, George William	1924 5k
LERMOND, Leo	1928 5k
LEWIS, William Fraser	1900 110h, 200h, 400h
*LIEB, Thomas John	1924 DT
*LIGHTBODY, James Davies	1904 800, 1500, 2590S, 4MT
	1906 400, 800, 1500
	1908 800, 1500, 3200S
LIKENS, Robert W.	1948 JT
LILLEY, Thomas H.	1912 Mar
LINCOLN, James C., Jr.	1920 JT
*LINDBERG, Edward Ferdinand Jacob	1912 400, 1600R
LINDER, Carl W. A.	1920 Mar
LINDGREN, Gerald Paul	1964 10k
*LINDGREN, Harold Blaine	1964 110h
*LIPPINCOTT, Donald Fithian	1912 100, 200
LIQUORI, Martin William	1968 1500
*LIVERSEDGE, Harry Bluett	1920 SP
*LONG, Dallas Crutcher, III	1960 SP
	1964 SP
*LONG, Maxwell Warburn	1900 400
*LOOMIS, Frank J.	1920 400h
LORD, Harvey Hurd	1900 400, 800
LORDON, John C.	1904 Mar
LORZ, Fred	1904 Mar
LUCK, James Edward	1964 400h
LUKE, Frederick Allen	1972 JT
LUTZ, Mark Edward	1976 200
*LuVALLE, James Ellis	1936 400

MacDONALD, Bruce Duncan	1956 20kW
	1960 50kW
	1964 50kW
*MacDONALD, J. Oliver	1924 1600R
MacDONALD, Ronald John	1900 Mar
MacDOUGALL, Grant	1932 HT
MADEIRA, Louis Childs, III	1912 1500
MAGGARD, David	1968 SP
*MAGNUSSON, Conrad	1904 TW
MAGUIRE, Hugh Francis	1912 10k
MAHAN, Jack H.	1920 JT
MANGAN, Albert J.	1936 50kW
MANLEY, Peter Michael	1972 3000S
*MANN, Ralph Vernon	1972 400h
MANNINEN, A. Olavi	1948 Mar
MANNING, Harold W.	1936 3000S
MARONEY, Thomas A.	1920 3000W, 10kW
MARSH, Henry Dinwoody	1976 3000S
*MASHBURN, Jesse William	1956 1600R
*MATHIAS, Robert Bruce	1948 Dec
	1952 Dec
*MATSON, James Randel	1964 SP
	1968 SP
*MATSON, Oliver Adrian	1952 400, 1600R
*MATTHEWS, Vincent Edward	1968 1600R
	1972 400
MATTOS, George Frank	1952 PV
	1956 PV
MAXWELL, Robert	1928 400h
*MAY, William Lee	1960 110h
MAY, William Wyman	1908 100, 200
MAYS, Charles	1968 LJ
McALLISTER, Robert F.	1928 100
McARDLE, Peter Joseph	1964 Mar
McCARTHY, Christopher	1964 50kW
McCLAIN, Thaddeus Brew	1900 100, 200h, LJ,
	4000S
McCLURE, Walter Rayburn	1912 800, 1500
*McCLUSKEY, Joseph Paul	1932 3000S
	1936 3000S
*McCRACKEN, Josiah Calvin, Jr.	1900 SP, DT, HT
McCURDY, Wallace Macafee	1912 5k
McDONALD, Duncan E.	1976 5k
*McDONALD, Patrick Joseph	1912 SP, SPb
(né Patrick Joseph McDonnell)	1920 SP, 56
McEACHERN, James M.	1920 HT, 56
	1924 HT
*McGINNIS, Charles English	1928 HJ, PV
*McGRATH, Matthew J.	1908 HT, TW
	1912 HT
	1920 HT
	1924 HT
McGREW, Vernon Vorhees	1948 HJ
McKENZIE, Gordon Edmund	1956 10k
	1960 Mar
McLANAHAN, Craig Ward	1904 110h, PV
*McLEAN, John Frederick	1900 110h, LJ, TJ, sTJ
McMAHON, William Francis	1936 Mar
*McMILLEN, Robert Earl	1948 3000S
	1952 1500
*MEADOWS, Earle Elmer	1936 PV
MECHLING, Edward Anthony	1900 800
MELLOR, Charles L.	1920 Mar
	1924 Mar
MELLOR, Samuel A., Jr.	1904 Mar
MENAUL, James Austin	1912 Pen
MENDOZA, Edward Eugene	1976 10k
MERCER, Eugene Leroy	1912 LJ, Dec
MERCHANT, John William	1920 LJ
	1924 HT
*MEREDITH, James Edwin	1912 400, 800, 1600R
	1920 400, 1600R
MERRIAM, Ned Alvin	1908 400
METCALF, Malcolm Ward	1932 JT
	936 JT
*METCALFE, Ralph Harold	1932 100, 200
	1936 100, 400R
*MEYER, Alvah T.	1912 100, 200
MICHELSEN, Albert Richard	1928 Mar
	1932 Mar
*MILBURN, Rodney, Jr.	1972 110h
*MILLER, William Preston	1952 JT
*MILLER, William Waring	1932 PV
*MILLS, William Mervin	1964 10k, Mar
MIMM, Robert F.	1960 20kW
MINAHAN, Edmund Joseph	1900 60
*MITCHEL, James Sarsfield	1904 DT, HT, 56, TW
MOFFITT, Thomas Robinson	1908 HJ
*MOLONEY, Frederick Graham	1900 100, 110h, 200h
MOLONEY, William Arthur	1900 400
MONDSCHEIN, Irving	1948 Dec
MONTEZ, Javier	1952 1500
MONTGOMERY, Jesse Langford	1928 3000S
*MOORE, Charles Hewes, Jr.	1952 400h, 1600R
MOORE, Kenneth Clark	1968 Mar
	1972 Mar
MOORE, Oscar W., Jr.	1964 5k
MORCOM, Albert Richmond "Boo"	1948 PV
*MORRIS, Glenn Edward	1936 Dec
*MORRIS, Ronald Hugh	1960 PV
MORRISSEY, Thomas P.	1908 Mar
*MORROW, Bobby Joe	1956 100, 200, 400R
MORTLAND, John Eggart	1964 20kW
*MOSES, Edwin Corley	1976 400h
*MOULTON, Fay R.	1904 60, 100, 200
	1906 100, 400
MOUNT PLEASANT, Frank	1908 LJ, TJ
MUCKS, Arlie Max	1912 DT, DTb
MUENZ, Sigmund	1908 sLJ
MULKEY, Philip R.	1960 Dec
MULLER, Emil Joseph	1912 DT, DTb
*MULLER, Harold Powers	1920 HJ
*MUNSON, David Curtiss	1904 1500, 2590S, 4MT
*MURCHISON, Ira James	1956 100, 400R

*MURCHISON, Loren C.	1920 100, 200, 400R	PARSONS, Eli Burton	1906 400, 800
	1924 100, 400R	PATASONI, Amisoli	1920 10k
*MURPHY, Frank Dwyer	1912 PV	PATTERSON, John Norman	1908 HJ
MURPHY, John Leonard	1920 HJ	PATTERSON, Joseph Hester	1936 400h
MURPHY, Thomas Joseph	1960 800	PATTERSON, Norman James	1912 1500
*MURRAY, Frederick Seymour	1920 110h	*PATTON, Melvin Emery	1948 100, 200, 400R
MURRO, Mark Paul	1968 JT	PAYNE, C. Russell	1924 3000S
*MYERS, Edwin Earl	1920 PV	*PEARMAN, Joseph B.	1920 3000W, 10kW
MYRICKS, Larry Ellwyne	1976 LJ	PEARMAN, Reginald B., III	1952 800
*NELSON, Frank Thayer	1912 PV	PEMELTON, Billy Gene	1964 PV
NELSON, Van Arthur	1968 10k	*PENDER, Melvin	1964 100
NEUFELD, William	1924 JT		1968 100, 400R
*NEWHOUSE, Frederick Vaughn	1976 400, 1600R	PENN, William	1920 TW
*NEWTON, Arthur Lewis	1900 2500S, Mar	PENNELL, John Thomas	1964 PV
	1904 2590S, Mar, 4MT		1968 PV
NICHOLSON, John Patrick	1912 110h	PENTTI, Eino Walter	1932 10k
*NIEDER, William Henry	1956 SP		1936 10k
	1960 SP	PHELPS, Harold Roy	1924 5k
NIGHTINGALE, Conrad K.	1968 3000S	PHILBROOK, George Warren	1912 SP, DT, Dec
NORTON, Bayes Marshall	1924 200	PHILLIPS, Herman Edgar	1928 400
*NORTON, Emerson Carlysle	1924 Dec	PIERCE, Frank C.	1904 Mar
*NORTON, John Kelley	1920 400h	PIGGOTT, Richard Francis	1912 Mar
NORTON, Otis Ray	1960 100, 200, 400R	*PILGRIM, Paul Harry	1904 400, 800, 4MT
*OBERST, Eugene G.	1924 JT		1906 400, 800
*O'BRIEN, Edward T.	1936 1600R		1908 400
*O'BRIEN, William Parry, Jr.	1952 SP	PLANT, William	1920 10kW
	1956 SP	*POAGE, George Coleman	1904 60, 400, 200h,
	1960 SP		400h
	1964 SP	*POLLARD, Frederick Douglas, Jr.	1936 110h
O'CONNELL, John F.	1908 LJ	POOR, Thomas Woodson	1924 HJ
*OERTER, Alfred Adolph	1956 DT	*POPE, Augustus Russell	1920 DT
	1960 DT		1924 DT
	1964 DT	PORTER, Guy J.	1904 Mar
	1968 DT	*PORTER, Harry Franklin	1908 HJ
O'HARA, Thomas Martin	1964 1500	PORTER, Terry Lynn	1976 PV
OLDAG, Hans	1932 Mar	*PORTER, William Franklin, III	1948 110h
OLDFIELD, Brian Ray	1972 SP	*POWELL, John Gates	1972 DT
OLER, Wesley Marion, Jr.	1912 HJ		1976 DT
*OLSON, Oscar G.	1904 TW	PREFONTAINE, Steven Roland	1972 5k
(see also Weightlifting)		PRIESTER, Lee Bryan, Jr.	1924 JT
ORGAN, Joseph LeRoy	1920 Mar	*PRINSTEIN, Meyer	1900 LJ, TJ
*OSBORN, Harold Marion	1924 HJ, Dec		1904 60, 100, 400, LJ,
	1928 HJ		TJ
O'TOOLE, Edward D.	1948 10k		1906 100, LJ, TJ
OTTEY, Thomas Charles	1932 10k	PRITCHARD, Edwin M.	1912 110h
OVERTON, William O.	1948 3000S	PRITCHARD, Walter Herbert	1932 3000S
*OWENS, James Cleveland "Jesse"	1936 100, 200, 400R, LJ	PROUT, William Christopher	1908 400
		PUTNAM, Herbert Nathan	1912 800, 1500
OWENS, James Earl	1976 110h	QUESTAD, Larry Ronald	1968 200
OXLEY, John Taylor	1904 LJ	QUEYROUZE, George Hamilton	1906 400
PACKARD, Robert R.	1936 200	*QUINN, James F.	1928 400R
*PADDOCK, Charles William	1920 100, 200, 400R	*RAMBO, John Barnett	1964 HJ
	1924 100, 200	RAMEY, Horace Patton	1908 400, 800
	1928 200	RAND, William McNear	1908 110h
*PARKER, Jack	1936 Dec		
*PARKS, Maxie Lander	1976 400, 1600R		

RAY, Joie W.	1920 1500
	1924 3000T
	1928 10k, Mar
REAVIS, Philip Martin	1956 HJ
RECKERS, Paul E.	1932 5k
*RECTOR, James Alcorn	1908 100
RED, Walter Edward	1964 JT
*REDD, Charles Lambert	1932 LJ
*REIDPATH, Charles Decker	1912 200, 400, 1600R
REILLY, William L.	1968 3000S
*REMER, Richard Frederick	1920 3000W
*REMIGINO, Lindy John	1952 100, 400R
REMINGTON, William Proctor	1900 110h, 200h, LJ
RENZ, Edward	1912 10kW
REYNOLDS, John James	1912 Mar
*RICHARDS, Alma Wilford	1912 HJ
*RICHARDS, Robert Eugene	1948 PV
	1952 PV
	1956 PV, Dec
RICHARDSON, William Hord	1924 800
RICK, Edwin Marvin	1924 3000S
*RIDDICK, Steven Earl	1976 100, 400R
RILEY, Frank N.	1908 1500
*RILEY, Ivan Harris	1924 400h
RING, Carl	1928 110h
ROBBINS, William Corbett	1908 400
*ROBERSON, Irvin "Bo"	1960 LJ
*ROBERTS, David Luther	1976 PV
*ROBERTSON, Lawson N.	1904 60, 100, sHJ
	1906 100, 400, sHJ, sLJ, Pen
	1908 100, 200, sHJ
ROBERTSON, Raymond A.	1924 400
*ROBINSON, Clarence Earl, Jr. "Arnie"	1972 LJ
	1976 LJ
ROBINSON, James, Jr.	1976 800
*ROBINSON, Matthew Mack	1936 200
ROBINSON, Reynaud Syverne	1972 100
ROBINSON, Sidney	1928 1500
ROBISON, Clarence F.	1948 1500
ROCHE, Miquel Santiago	1976 3000S
*RODENBERG, August	1904 TW
RODGERS, William Henry	1976 Mar
ROELKER, William J.	1920 3000W, 10kW
ROMANSKY, David	1968 50kW
ROMERO, Rolland Lee	1932 TJ
	1936 TJ
ROMIG, John Luther	1924 5k
	1928 10k
ROND, Joseph A.	1920 TW
ROSE, Albert Edward	1924 LJ
*ROSE, Charles	1904 TW
*ROSE, Ralph Waldo	1904 SP, DT, HT, 56
	1908 SP, DTg, TW
	1912 SP, SPb, DT, HT
ROSENBERGER, James Maher	1912 400
ROSS, Harris Browning	1948 3000S
	1952 3000S
ROTH, Arthur V.	1920 Mar
*ROTHERT, Harlow Phelps	1928 SP
	1932 SP
ROWE, William John Alfred	1936 HT
*RUSSELL, Henry Argue	1928 100, 400R
RYAN, Michael J.	1908 Mar
	1912 Mar
*RYAN, Patrick James	1920 HT, 56
*RYUN, James Ronald	1964 1500
	1968 1500
	1972 1500
SAGER, Arthur Woodbury	1928 JT
*SALING, George J.	1932 110h
SAMARA, Frederick Ameen	1976 Dec
*SAMSE, Leroy Perry	1904 PV
SANFORD, Richard L.	1904 2590S
San ROMANI, Archie J.	1936 1500
SANTEE, David Wesley	1952 5k
SAVAGE, Stephen Read	1972 3000S
*SCHARDT, Arlie Alfred	1920 3000T
SCHICK, William Anthony	1906 100
SCHILLER, George S.	1920 400, 1600R
*SCHMIDT, William David	1972 JT
SCHMOCK, Peter	1976 SP
SCHOFIELD, M. Dale	1936 400h
*SCHOLZ, Jackson Volney	1920 100, 400R
	1924 100, 200
	1928 200
SCHOTERMAN, Albert Edward	1972 HT
*SCHUL, Robert Keyser	1964 5k
*SCHULE, Frederick William	1904 110h, 200h
SCHWARTZ, Samuel	1912 10kW
*SCOTT, Clyde Louis	1948 110h
SCOTT, Donald M.	1920 800
SCOTT, Henry Louis	1912 5k, 10k, 3000T, XC
SCOTT, Louis Cohn	1968 5k
SCRAFFORD, Justus Moak	1900 800
SCULLY, Clark Todd	1976 20kW
*SEAGREN, Robert Lloyd	1968 PV
	1972 PV
SEFTON, William Healy	1936 PV
*SEILING, Henry	1904 TW
*SEILING, William Bernard	1904 TW
SELDING, Frederick Monroe de	1908 400
*SERVISS, Garrett Putnam, Jr.	1904 HJ, sTJ
*SEXTON, Leo Joseph	1932 SP
SEYMOUR, James	1972 400h
*SEYMOUR, Stephen Andrew (né Seymour Cohen)	1948 JT
*SHANKLE, Joel Warren	1956 110h
SHARAGE, Frederick	1948 10kW

SHARPE, William John	1956 TJ
	1960 TJ
	1964 TJ
*SHAW, Arthur Briggs	1908 110h
SHAW, George Donald	1952 TJ
	1956 TJ
SHEA, Frank J.	1920 400, 1600R
SHEEHAN, Francis Patrick	1908 800
*SHELDON, Lewis Pendelton	1900 sHJ, sLJ, sTJ, TJ
*SHELDON, Richard	1900 SP, DT
*SHEPPARD, Melvin Winfield	1908 800, 1500, MR
	1912 400, 800, 1500,
	1600R
*SHERIDAN, Martin Joseph	1904 SP, DT
	1906 sHJ, sLJ, SP, DT,
	DTg, Pen, ST
	1908 sHJ, sLJ, TJ, SP,
	DT, DTg
SHERMAN, Benjamin Franklin	1912 HT
SHERMAN, Nathaniel Alden	1908 100, 200, TJ
*SHIDELER, Thaddeus Rutter	1904 110h
*SHIELDS, Marion Lawrence	1920 1500, 3000T
*SHINE, Michael Lyle	1976 400h
SHINNICK, Phillip Kent	1964 LJ
*SHORTER, Frank Charles	1972 10k, Mar
	1976 Mar
SIEBERT, Jerome Francis	1960 800
	1964 800
*SILVESTER, L. Jay	1964 DT
	1968 DT
	1972 DT
	1976 DT
*SIME, David William	1960 100, 400R
*SIMMONS, Floyd Macon, Jr.	1948 Dec
	1952 Dec
*SIMPSON, George Sidney	1932 100, 200
SINK, Ronald Eugene	1948 1500
SITTIG, John Franz	1928 800
SJOGREN, Leo Allen	1952 50kW
	1956 50kW
SLACK, Henry Berry	1900 100, 400
SLOAN, Richard Donald	1968 Dec
SMALLWOOD, Robert Harold	1936 400
SMITH, Charles Kenneth	1972 200
SMITH, David	1968 TJ
	1972 TJ
*SMITH, Finis Dean	1952 100, 400R
SMITH, Harrison Preserved	1900 800
SMITH, Harry J.	1912 Mar
SMITH, John Macauley Letchworth	1928 5k, 10k
SMITH, John Walton	1972 400
*SMITH, Owen Guinn	1948 PV
*SMITH, Ronald Ray	1968 400R
SMITH, Steven Norwood	1972 PV
*SMITH, Tommie C.	1968 200
SMITH, Tracey Evans	1968 10k
SMITH, Walker	1920 110h
*SMITHSON, Forrest Custer	1908 110h
SNIDER, Emil	1928 400
SOCKALEXIS, Andrew	1912 Mar
SONSKY, Milton Barry	1972 JT
SOTH, Robert Charles	1960 5k
*SOUTHERN, Silas Edward	1956 400h
SOWELL, Arnold M.	1956 800
SPEAROW, Albert Ralph	1924 PV
*SPENCER, Emerson Lane	1928 1600R
SPENCER, William Octavius	1924 1500
	1928 3000S
SPITZ, George Burton	1932 HJ
SPITZER, Roger Adelbert	1908 3200S
SPRING, Michael	1904 Mar
	1906 Mar
SPROTT, Bryan Albert	1920 800
SPURRIER, Lonnie Vernon	1956 800
*STADLER, Joseph F.	1904 sHJ, sTJ
STALEY, Roy Mason	1936 110h
*STANFIELD, Andrew William	1952 200, 400R
	1956 200
*STANGLAND, Robert Sedgwick	1904 LJ, TJ
*STANICH, George Anthony	1948 HJ
*STEBBINS, Richard Vaughn	1964 200, 400R
*STEELE, William S.	1948 LJ
STENLUND, Gary Michael	1968 JT
STEVENS, Lester Barber	1908 100
*STEVENSON, William Edwards	1924 1600R
STEWART, James Daniel	1928 Dec
STOKES, Herman Ray	1960 TJ
STONE, Curtis Charles	1948 5k
	1952 5k, 10k
	1956 5k
*STONES, Dwight Edwin	1972 HJ
	1976 HJ
*STROBINO, Gaston M.	1912 Mar
*STUDENROTH, Arthur Addison	1924 XC, XCt
SULLIVAN, Daniel Albert	1906 Pen
(see also Wrestling)	
SULLIVAN, James P.	1906 800, 1500
	1908 1500
SWENSON, Kenneth Lloyd	1972 800
*TABER, Norman Stephen	1912 1500, 3000T
TALBOT, Leander James, Jr.	1908 SP, DT, DTg, HT,
	TW
(see also Wrestling)	
TATE, Norman	1968 TJ
*TAYLOR, Frederick Morgan	1924 400h
	1928 400h
*TAYLOR, John Baxter, Jr.	1908 400, MR
TAYLOR, John Coard	1924 400
*TAYLOR, Robert	1972 100, 400R
@TEMPLETON, Robert Lyman	1920 LJ
(see also Rugby Football)	
TERRY, Floy Alton	1936 JT

*TEWANIMA, Lewis	1908 Mar
	1912 10k, Mar
*TEWKSBURY, John Walter Beardsley	1900 60, 100, 200,
	200h, 400h
THACKWRAY, Dean Allan	1956 Mar
*THIAS, Charles	1904 TW
*THOMAS, John Curtis	1960 HJ
	1964 HJ
THOMAS, Rupert Broas, Jr.	1912 100
THOMPSON, Jerald Stillwell	1948 5k
*THOMPSON, Wilbur Marvin	1948 SP
*THORPE, James Francis	1912 HJ, LJ, Dec, Pen
(né Wa-tho-huck—meaning	
"Bright Path")	
*THURBER, Delos Packard	1936 HJ
*TIBBETTS, Willard Lewis, Jr.	1924 3000T
TIERNEY, Joseph Paul	1928 400
*TINKER, Gerald	1972 400R
TIPTON, Leslie Eugene	1964 JT
*TOLAN, Thomas Edward	1932 100, 200
*TOOMEY, William Anthony	1968 Dec
*TOOTELL, Frederic Delmont	1924 HT
*TOPPINO, Martin Emmett	1932 400R
TORRANCE, John	1936 SP
*TOWNS, Forrest Grady	1936 110h
*TRUBE, Herbert Lawrence	1908 3MT
TRUEX, Max Edwin	1956 10k
	1960 10k
TUCK, Arthur M.	1920 JT
TURNER, Edwin Thomas	1932 800
*TYLER, Albert Clinton	1896 PV
*UNDERWOOD, George B.	1904 400, 800, 4MT
*UPSHAW, Orrin Thomas	1904 TW
*VALENTINE, Howard V.	1904 400, 800, 1500,
	4MT
	1906 400, 800
Van CLEAF, George A.	1904 LJ, TJ
(see also Swimming)	
VANDERSTOCK, Geoffrey Peter	1968 400h
*Van OSDEL, Robert L.	1932 HJ
VARNELL, George Marshall	1904 200h, 400h
VENZKE, Eugene George	1936 1500
*VERNER, William Frank	1904 800, 1500,
	2590S, 4MT
VIDAL, Eugene Luther	1920 Dec
VIRGIN, Craig Steven	1976 10k
VOELLMEKE, Alfred	1912 10kW
VOGEL, Theodore John	1948 Mar
VOLLMER, Timothy William	1972 DT
Von RUDEN, Thomas	1968 1500
WADDELL, Thomas Flubacher	1968 Dec
WALKER, Arthur Franklin	1968 TJ
	1972 TJ
WALKER, Larry A.	1976 20kW
*WALLER, Frank Laird	1904 400, 400h
WALTERS, Jerome Douglas	1956 1500

*WARNER, Karl DeWitt	1932 1600R
WATSON, Anthony Lamar	1960 LJ
WATSON, Ray Bates	1920 3000S, XC
	1924 1500
	1928 800
WATTERS, John Nockerson	1924 800
WEBBER, Ernest	1948 10kW
WEIGLE, William Franklin	1972 50kW
*WEILL, David Lawson	1964 DT
WEINACKER, Adolf J.	1948 50kW
	1952 50kW
	1956 50kW
WELCHEL, Homer	1924 JT
WELTON, Alton Roy	1908 Mar
*WENDELL, James Isaac	1912 110h
WENDLING, Frank E.	1924 Mar
WHALEN, Walter Leo	1920 HJ
WHEELER, Quentin David	1976 400h
WHEELER, Robert Tomlinson, III	1972 1500
WHEELER, Theodore Stanley	
Richardson	1956 1500
*WHITFIELD, Malvin Groston	1948 400, 800, 1600R
	1952 400, 800, 1600R
*WHITNEY, Lawrence Atwood	1912 SP, SPb, DT
WHITNEY, Ronald Howard	1968 400h
WIECKER, Frederick E.	1928 DT
*WIESNER, Kenneth George	1952 HJ
WIKOFF, Garnett Merrill	1912 5k
WILKINS, Dudley Griffin	1936 TJ
*WILKINS, Louis Gary	1904 PV
*WILKINS, Mac Maurice	1976 DT
*WILLIAMS, Archibald Franklin	1936 400
WILLIAMS, Ralph A.	1924 Mar
*WILLIAMS, Randy Luvelle	1972 LJ
	1976 LJ
*WILLIAMS, Ulis C.	1964 400, 1600R
WILLIAMSON, Harry Webb	1936 800
WILSON, Clement Pierce	1912 100, 200, 400R
WILSON, Eric Colquhoun	1924 400
WILSON, Richard Earle	1924 TJ
WILSON, Vernon Troylee	1956 HJ
WILT, Frederick Loren	1948 10k
	1952 10k
WINSTON, Joseph	1920 TW
*WOHLHUTER, Richard Charles	1972 800
	1976 800, 1500
WOOD, Walter Dongan	1936 DT
*WOODRING, Allen	1920 200
*WOODRUFF, John Youie	1936 800
*WOODS, George Roger	1968 SP
	1972 SP
	1976 SP
WORTHINGTON, Harry Thomas	1912 LJ
*WOTTLE, David James	1972 800, 1500
*WRIGHT, Lorenzo Christopher	1948 400R, LJ
*WRIGHT, Marc Snowell	1912 PV

WUDYKA, Stanley J.	1936 10k
*WYKOFF, Frank Clifford	1928 100, 400R
	1932 400R
	1936 100, 400R
*YERMAN, Jack L.	1960 400, 1600R
YODER, Dewie Lee	1952 400h
*YOUNG, Cy C., Jr.	1952 JT
	1956 JT
YOUNG, Donnell Brooks	1912 200, 400
*YOUNG, Earl Verdelle	1960 400, 1600R
*YOUNG, George L.	1960 3000S
	1964 3000S
	1968 3000S, Mar
	1972 5k
*YOUNG, Lawrence Dean	1968 50kW
	1972 20kW, 50kW
*YOUNG, Robert Clark	1936 1600R
YOUNT, William Joseph	1920 110h
ZAITZ, Dimitri Nickitovitch	1936 SP
ZAMPERINI, Louis S.	1936 5k
*ZAREMBA, Peter E.	1932 HT
ZINN, Ronald Lloyd	1960 20kW
	1964 20kW
ZUNA, Frank T.	1924 Mar
ZWOLAK, Victor A.	1964 3000S

TRACK & FIELD (Athletics) (Women) (157)

Track & field athletics for women first appeared in the Olympic Games in 1928 and has been held ever since. The United States has always had a team in this sport.

All numbers below indicate distances in meters.

DT = Discus throw	LJ = Long jump
h = Hurdles	SP = Shot put
HJ = High jump	R = Relay
JT = Javelin throw	Pen = Pentathlon

ANDERSON, Karen Linnea (see Karen Oldham)	
ARDEN, Alice Jean	1936 HJ
ARMSTRONG, Debra Sue Edwards	1972 400
(as Miss Edwards in 1972)	1976 200, 400R
ASHFORD, Evelyn	1976 100, 400R
ATTLESLEY, Kim	1972 LJ
*BAILES, Margaret Johnson	1968 100, 200, 400R
BAIR, RaNae Jean	1964 JT
	1968 JT
BASKERVILLE, Estelle	1964 HJ
	1968 HJ
*BLAND, Harriet Claiborne	1936 100, 400R
BOECKMAN, Dolores Halpin "Dee"	1928 800
BONDS, Rosalyn L.	1964 80h
BRADY, Rhonda	1976 100h

BROWN, Barbara A.	1960 HJ
BROWN, Doris Elaine Severtsen	1968 800
*BROWN, Earlene Dennis	1956 SP, DT
	1960 SP, DT
	1964 SP
BROWN, Roberta	1972 JT
BROWN, Terrezene	1964 HJ
BROWN, Vivian Dolores	1964 200
*BRYANT, Rosalyn Evette	1976 400, 1600R
BURCH, Elizabeth L.	1936 JT
CALLAHAN, Sharon	1968 HJ
CALVERT, Sharon Lynn	1972 JT
	1976 JT
*CAREW, Mary Louise	1932 400R
CARTWRIGHT, Elta	1928 100
CHEESEBOROUGH, Chandra Danette	1976 100, 200, 400R
*COACHMAN, Alice	1948 HJ
*CONNOLLY, Olga Fikotová	1956 DT
(competed for Czechoslovakia	1960 DT
and as Miss Fikotová	1964 DT
in 1956)	1968 DT
	1972 DT
*COPELAND, Lillian	1928 DT
	1932 DT
*CROSS, Jessica	1928 400R
CROWDER, Shirley	1960 80h
DANIELS, Billee Patricia (see Billee Winslow)	
*DANIELS, Isabelle Francis	1956 100, 400R
DARNOWSKI, Constance Stella	1952 80h
	1956 80h
DAVIS, Iris LaVerne	1972 100, 400R
DEUBEL, Paula Phillips	1956 SP
DICKS, Janet	1952 SP
*DIDRIKSON, Mildred Ella "Babe"	1932 80h, HJ, JT
DODSON, Dorothy L.	1948 SP, DT, JT
DONNOLLY, Patricia	1976 100h
DRINKWATER, Lois Anne	1968 400
DWYER, Dolores Ann	1952 200
DYER, Julia Marie	1968 80h
EDWARDS, Debra Sue (see Debra Armstrong)	
ELLIS, Meredith Lorraine	1956 200
*FAGGS, Heriwentha Mae	1948 200
	1952 100, 200, 400R
	1956 100, 200, 400R
*FERGERSON, Mabel	1972 400, 1600R
FERRARA, Evelyn Lucy	1936 DT
*FERRELL, Barbara Ann	1968 100, 200, 400R
	1972 100, 200
*FIKOTOVA, Olga (see Olga Connolly)	
FITZGERALD, Gale	1972 Pen
	1976 Pen
FLYNN, Ann Marie	1956 HJ

FREDERICK, Jane Wardell	1972 Pen
	1976 Pen
FRIEDRICH, Barbara Ann	1968 JT
*FURTSCH, Evelyn	1932 400R
GAERTNER, Jean Kay	1960 HJ
(see also Volleyball)	
GILBERT, Cindy	1972 HJ
GINDELE, Nan	1932 JT
GIRVEN, Paula Darcel	1976 HJ
GOLDSBERRY, Sandi	1972 HJ
GREENE, Pamela	1972 200
GRISSON, Jo Ann Terry	1960 80h
(as Miss Terry in 1960)	1964 LJ
*HALL, Evelyne Ruth	1932 80h
HAMBLIN, Cathy Louise	1968 Pen
*HAMMOND, Kathleen	1972 400, 1600R
*HARDY, Catherine	1952 100, 200, 400R
HARRINGTON, Ethel	1932 100
HOLLEY, Marion	1928 HJ
*HUDSON, Martha	1960 100, 400R
HUNTLEY, Joni Luann	1976 HJ
*INGRAM, Sheila Rena	1976 400, 1600R
*JACKSON, Madeline Manning	1968 800
(as Miss Manning in	1972 800, 1600R
1968 and 1972)	1976 800
JACKSON, Nell Cecelia	1948 200, 400R
JENKINS, Margaret	1928 DT
	1932 DT
*JILES, Pamela Theresa	1976 1600R
JOHNSON, Francea Norma Kraker	1968 800
(as Miss Kraker in 1968)	1972 1500
JOHNSON, Patricia Jean Van	
Wolvelaere	1968 80h
(as Miss Van Wolvelaere in 1968)	1972 100h
*JONES, Barbara Pearl	1952 400R
	1960 100, 400R
KASZUBSKI, Frances T. Gorn	1948 DT, SP
KELLY, Kathlyn	1936 HJ
KING, Marilyn	1976 Pen
KNOTT, Sandra Phyllis	1964 800
KNUDSON, Wendy Carol Koenig	1972 800
(as Miss Koenig in 1972)	1976 800
KOENIG, Wendy	
(see Wendy Knudson)	
KRAKER, Francea	
(see Francea Johnson)	
KURRELL, Pamela Joan	1956 DT
	1960 DT
LANDRY, Mabel M.	1952 LJ
LaPLANTE, Deborah Lansky	1976 100h
LARNEY, Marjorie Lea	1952 JT
	1956 DT, JT
LARRIEU, Francina	1972 1500
	1976 1500
MAGUIRE, Catherine	1928 HJ

*MANNING, Madeline	
(see Madeline Jackson)	
MANUEL, Theresa A.	1948 80h, 400R, JT
*MATTHEWS, Margaret Rejean	1956 400R, LJ
*McDANIEL, Mildred Louise	1956 HJ
McDONALD, Florence	1928 800
McDONALD, Rena	1928 DT
*McGUIRE, Edith Marie	1964 100, 200, 400R
*McMILLAN, Kathy Laverne	1976 LJ
*McNEIL, Loretta T.	1928 400R
MERRILL, Janice	1976 1500
MONTGOMERY, Eleanor Inez	1964 HJ
	1968 HJ
*MOREAU, Janet Theresa	1952 100, 400R
MOREHEAD, Brenda Louise	1976 100
MOSEKE, Carol Jean	1968 DT
MUELLER, Barbara Ann	1956 80h
*NETTER, Mildrette	1968 400R
	1972 400R
O'BRIEN, Anne Vrana	1928 100
(as Miss Vrana in 1928)	1936 80h
OLDHAM, Karen Linnea Anderson	1956 JT
(as Miss Anderson in 1956)	1960 JT
O'NEAL, Leahseneth	1964 80h
	1972 100h
*OSBURN, Ruth	1932 DT
*PATTERSON, Audrey Mickey	1948 100, 200, 400R
PICKETT, Tidye Anne	1936 80h
POLLARDS, Ernestine	1960 200
POOR, Cynthia	1976 1500
RALLINS, Mamie	1968 80h
	1972 100h
REED, Emma	1948 HJ, LJ
REICHARDT, Maybelle	1928 DT
RENDER, Mattiline	1972 100, 400R
ROBERTSON, Irene Rose	1956 80h
	1960 80h
ROBINSON, Cynthia Bernice	1948 80h, HJ
*ROBINSON, Elizabeth	1928 100, 400R
	1936 400R
*ROGERS, Annette Joan	1932 400R, HJ
	1936 100, 400R, HJ
ROGERS, Naomi	1960 HJ
*RUDOLPH, Wilma Glodean	1956 200, 400R
	1960 100, 200, 400R
RUSSELL, Gloria	1932 JT
*SAPENTER, Debra	1976 400, 1600R
SCHALLER, Simone E.	1932 80h
	1936 80h
*SCHMIDT, Kathryn Joan	1972 JT
	1976 JT
SCOTT, Jarvis	1968 400
SEIDLER, Maren Elizabeth	1968 SP
	1972 SP
	1976 SP
SHERRARD, Cherrie Mae Parish	1964 80h

*SHILEY, Jean M.	1928 HJ
	1932 HJ
SMITH, Ann Lois	1960 LJ
SMITH, Janell L.	1964 400
SMITH, Karin Kiefer	1976 JT
SPENCER, Pamela Ann	1976 HJ
*STEPHENS, Helen Herring	1936 100, 400R, JT
STROY, Esther	1968 400
SVENDSON, Jan	1972 SP
TERRY, Jo Ann	
(see Jo Ann Grisson)	
TESTA, Lois Ann	1956 SP
THOMPSON, Deborah Ann	1964 200
THOMPSON, Jacqueline	1972 200
*TOUISSANT, Cheryl	1972 1600R
*TYUS, Wyomia	1964 100, 400R
	1968 100, 200, 400R
Van WOLVELAERE, Patricia Jean	
(see Patricia Johnson)	
*Von BREMEN, Wilhelmina	1932 100, 400R
VRANA, Anne	
(see Anne O'Brien)	
WALKER, Mabel E.	1948 100, 400R
WALKER, Sharon Elaine	1976 LJ
WALRAVEN, Jean	1948 80h, J
*WASHBURN, Mary T.	1928 100, 400R
WATSON, Martha Rae	1964 LJ
	1968 LJ
	1972 400R, LJ
	1976 400R, LJ
WERSHOVEN, Amelia	1956 JT
WESTON, Kathleen Stella	1976 800
*WHITE, Marilyn Elaine	1964 100, 400R
*WHITE, Willye B.	1956 LJ
	1960 LJ
	1964 400R, LJ
	1968 LJ
	1972 LJ
WILDE, Elizabeth	1932 100
*WILEY, Mildred Olive	1928 HJ
WILHELMSEN, Gertrude	1936 DT, T
*WILLIAMS, Lucinda	1956 100
	1960 200, 400R
WILSON, Deanne	1972 HJ
WILSON, Rayma B.	1928 800
WINBIGLER, Margrethe Lynne	1976 DT
WINSLOW, Billee Patricia Daniels	1960 800
(as Miss Daniels in 1960)	1964 Pen
	1968 Pen
WORST, Martha Virginia	1936 DT
YOUNG, Lillian	1948 100, LJ

VOLLEYBALL (Men) (22)

Volleyball became an Olympic sport in 1964, but the United States has not been able to qualify a team for Olympic competition since 1968.

ALSTROM, John Kirby	1968
BRIGHT, David Michael	1964
	1968
BROWN, Barry Ross	1964
DAVENPORT, Winthrop, Jr.	1968
DUKE, Horace Smith	1968
ERICKSON, Keith Raymond	1964
GRIEBENOW, William Earl	1964
HAINE, Thomas A.	1968
HAMMER, Richard Bernarr	1964
HENN, John T.	1968
HIGHLAND, Jacob Alapaki	1964
LANG, Ronald Dwayne	1964
MAY, Robert Stanley, Jr.	1968
NELSON, Charles Tomlinson	1964
O'HARA, Michael Futch	1964
PATTERSON, Daniel E.	1968
RUNDLE, Larry Dean	1968
STANLEY, Jon C.	1968
SUWARA, Ernest Emil, Jr.	1964
SUWARA, Rudy	1968
TAYLOR, John Franklin	1964
VELASCO, Pedro, Jr.	1964
	1968

VOLLEYBALL (Women) (19)

Women's volleyball was first held in the Olympics at Tokyo in 1964. The U.S. had a team entered in 1964 and 1968, but has not been able to qualify since.

BRIGHT, Patricia Ann Lucas	1964
	1968
GAERTNER, Jean Kay	1964
(see also Track & Field)	
GALLOWAY, Lou Sara Clark	1964
HARWERTH, Barbara Jean	1964
HECK, Kathryn Ann	1968
HOPEAU, Fanny R.	1968
JORGENSEN, Ninja Louise	1968
LEWIS, Laurie Ann	1968
McFADDEN, Barbara Briggs "Micki"	1968
McREAVY, Marilyn Louise	1968
MURPHY, Linda Kathleen	1964
O'ROURKE, Gail Patricia	1964
OWEN, Nancy Lee	1964
	1968
PEPPLER, Mary Joan	1964
PERRY, Barbara Beverly	1968

PERRY, Mary Margaret	1964
	1968
PETERSON, Sharon Roberta	1964
	1968
THOMAS, Verneda Estella	1964
WARD, Jane Lois	1964
	1968

WATER POLO (83)

Water polo has been held at all but the two Athens Olympic Games—those of 1896 and 1906. The United States contributed all (three) of the teams in 1904 but did not participate again until 1920. After that they competed at every Olympics until 1976, when they did not qualify for the Olympic competition.

The 1904 teams are not included in the following list because the 1904 tournament was of marginal Olympic caliber. They are instead included in a special list at the end.

*ASCH, Peter Gregory	1972
ASHLEIGH, David Michael	1964
	1968
*AUSTIN, Arthur	1924
*BARNETT, Steven William	1968
	1972
BECK, Kenneth Melvyn	1936
	1948
BISBEY, Harry Arthur	1952
BITTICK, Charles Greene	1960
*BRADLEY, Myron Bruce	1968
	1972
BRAY, Rutledge	1948
BROWN, Clement	1920
BUDELMAN, Ralph N.	1948
BURNS, Marvin Duane "Ace"	1952
	1960
CARDSON, James G.	1920
CASE, Lemoine Spencer	1948
CHRISTENSEN, Devere W.	1948
&CLAPP, Austin Rhone	1932
(see also Swimming)	
*COLE, Stanley Clark	1964
	1968
	1972
CRAWFORD, Ronald Emerson	1960
	1964
	1968
DANIELS, Harry C.	1928
DASH, Harold N.	1948
*DAUBENSPECK, Philip Burton	1932
	1936
DORNBLASSER, Norman W.	1952
DROWN, Daniel Hannon	1964

*FERGUSON, James Michael	1972
*FINN, Charles Thornton	1932
	1936
FISKE, Dixon	1936
	1948
FROJEN, Robert Charles	1956
GAUGHRAN, James Alan	1956
GRAHAM, Frank Charles	1936
GREENBERG, Richard J.	1928
GRELLER, Samuel Joseph	1928
HAHN, Kenneth Al	1956
HALL, Gordon R.	1960
@HEBNER, Harry J.	1920
(see also Swimming)	
*HORN, Oliver H.	1924
HORN, Robert Martin	1956
	1960
HUGHES, Robert Earl	1952
(see also Swimming)	1956
JAWORSKI, Edward Lawrence	1952
JENSEN, Sophus C.	1920
@KAHANAMOKU, Duke Paoa Kahinu Makoe Hulikohoa	1920
(see also Swimming)	
KNOX, Edwin B.	1948
KOOISTRA, Samuel Gene	1956
	1956
LAKE, Norman Ezra	1952
*LAUER, Frederick	1924
*LINDROTH, Eric Emil	1972
*McCALLISTER, Charles Harold	1932
	1936
McDERMOTT, Michael J.	1920
(see also Swimming)	
@McGILLIVRAY, Perry	1920
(see also Swimming)	
McILROY, Charles Raymond	1960
	1964
McILROY, Ned Leroy	1964
*MITCHELL, George F.	1924
	1928
NORRIS, James Leo	1952
*NORTON, John D.	1924
&O'CONNOR, James Wallace	1924
(see also Swimming)	1928
	1932
	1936
*PARKER, John Michael	1968
	1972
@ROSS, Norman DeMille	1920
(see also Swimming)	
ROSS, William Donald	1956
SAARI, Robert Paul	1964
SAMSON, Paul Curkeet	1928
(see also Swimming)	
*SCHROTH, George Edward	1924
	1928

SEVERA, Ronald Duane	1956
	1960
*SHEERER, Gary Peter	1968
	1972
*SLATTON, James Walter	1972
SPARGO, John Arthur	1952
STANGE, Peter J.	1952
STEIGER, Preston M.	1920
STRANSKY, George Charles	1964
*STRONG, Calvert	1932
TAYLOR, George Herbert	1920
TISUE, Fred E., Jr.	1960
TOPP, Herbert R.	1928
Van DORP, Anton Ludwig	1964
	1968
*VOLLMER, Herbert Eberhard	1920
	1924
VOLMER, Ronald L.	1960
VOSBURGH, William R.	1920
*WEBB, Russell Irving	1968
	1972
&WEISSMULLER, Peter John	1924
(see also Swimming)	1928
*WEITZENBERG, Charles Barry	1968
	1972
WHITNEY, Ralph John	1964
*WILDMAN, Herbert Henry	1932
	1936
WILLEFORD, Leslie Dean	1968
@WOLF, Wallace Perry	1956
(see also Swimming)	1960

1904 "Olympic" Teams

New York Athletic Club [1]David BRATTON, [1]Leo G. "Budd" GOODWIN, [1]Louis de Breda HANDLEY, [1]David HESSER, [1]Joseph RUDDY, James STEEN, [3]George A. Van CLEAF.

Chicago Athletic Association Rex E. BEACH, [1]David HAMMOND, Charles HEALY, [2]Frank KEHOE, Jerome STEEVER, [1]Edwin Paul SWATEK, [1]William TUTTLE.

Missouri Athletic Club [1]Gwynne EVANS, [1]Augustus M. GOESSLING, [1]John C. MEYERS, [1]William Robert ORTHWEIN, [1]Amedee V. REYBURN, Fred SCHREIN-ER, Manfred TOEPPEN.

[1]see also Swimming
[2]see also Diving
[3]see also Swimming and Track & Field

WEIGHTLIFTING (65)

With the exception of 1900, 1908, and 1912, weightlifting events have been held at every Olympic Games. The United States first competed in 1904, but did not appear in Olympic weightlifting again until 1932, since which time they have always competed.

Because weight limitations on the various classes have undergone frequent changes through the years, the weight classes are coded by name (featherweight, etc.) rather than weight limit.

B = Bantamweight	L = Lightweight
BB = Barbell event (open division)	LH = Light-heavyweight
DB = Dumbbell event (open division)	M = Middleweight
F = Featherweight	MH = Middle-heavyweight
H = Heavyweight	SH = Super-heavyweight

*ANDERSON, Paul Edward	1956 H
BACHTELL, Richard Earl	1932 F
BALL, Alan Jerome	1972 H
BARTHOLOMEW, Robert	1968 MH
*BERGER, Isaac	1956
	1960 F
	1964 F
BIGLER, Samuel L.	1976 LH
*BRADFORD, James Edward	1952 H
	1960 H
CAMERON, Mark	1976 H
CANTORE, Daniel Michael	1972 L
	1976 L
CAPSOURAS, Frank Richard	1972 H
CLEVELAND, Gary Gayin	1964 LH
*DAVIS, John Henry, Jr.	1948 H
	1952 H
*DePIETRO, Joseph Nicholas	1948 B
DRINNON, Gary Lynn	1976 H
*DUBE, Joseph D.	1968 H
*DUEY, Henry Ludwig	1932 LH
EMRICH, Clyde Bryan	1952 LH
GARCY, Anthony Michael	1964 L
*GEORGE, James D.	1956 LH
	1960 LH
*GEORGE, Peter T.	1948 M
	1952 M
	1956 M
GOOD, Walter L.	1936 M
GOOD, William L.	1932 LH
	1936 LH
GRIMEK, John Carl	1936 H

GRIPPALDI, Philip	1968 MH
	1972 MH
	1976 MH
GUBNER, Gary Jay	1964 H
HOLBROOK, Patrick Joseph	1972 MH
ISHIKAWA, Kotaro Emerick	1948 F
*JAMES, Lee R., Jr.	1976 MH
KARCHUT, Michael	1972 LH
KNIPP, Russell Lowell	1968 M
	1972 M
*KONO, Tommy Tamio	1952 L
	1956 LH
	1960 M
KRATKOWSKI, Stanley Joseph	1932 M
	1936 M
&KUNGLER, Frank	1904 DB, BB
(see also Wrestling and Track & Field)	
LOWE, Frederick Harland	1968 M
	1972 M
	1976 M
MANGER, Albert Henry	1932 H
MARCH, William Frederick	1964 MH
MAYOR, David	1936 H
MILLER, John Henry	1936 LH
MITCHELL, Robert Marion	1936 L
@OLSON, Oscar G.	1904 BB
(see also Track & Field)	
*OSTHOFF, Oscar Paul	1904 DB, BB
PATERA, Kenneth Wayne	1972 SH
PICKETT, George Ernest	1968 H
PITMAN, Joseph Prescott	1948 L
PULEO, Joseph Robert	1968 LH
PULSKAMP, John Robert	1960 MH
RIECKE, Louis George, Jr.	1964 MH
*SAKATA, Harold T.	1948 LH
*SCHEMANSKY, Norbert	1948 H
	1952 MH
	1960 H
	1964 H
*SHEPPARD, David Joseph	1956 MH
*SPELLMAN, Frank Isaac	1948 M
*STANCZYK, Stanley Anthony	1948 LH
	1952 LH
SUNDBERG, Arnie	1932 L
*TERLAZZO, Anthony	1932 F
	1936 F
TERMINE, Sam	1932 M
TERPAK, John Basil	1936 L
	1948 L
TERRY, John F.	1936 F
*TOM, Richard W. S.	1948 B
TOMITA, Richard K.	1948 F
TURBYFILL, Howard	1932 H
*VINCI, Charles Thomas, Jr.	1956 B
	1960 B

WALKER, Sam	1976 SH
WILHELM, Bruce Douglas	1976 SH
*WINTERS, Frederick	1904 DB
ZAGURSKI, Walter	1932 L

WRESTLING (195)
(138 Freestyle; 50 Greco-Roman; 7 Both)

Wrestling has appeared in every Olympic Games except 1900. There are two distinct styles of competition—freestyle (used since 1924 and similar though not exactly identical to the older Olympic style of catch-as-catch-can), and Greco-Roman. Because the weight limits for the varying classes have undergone many changes, the classes are coded by their names rather than weight limits.

A class code with no letter after it indicates that it is in the freestyle or the catch-as-catch-can style. All Greco-Roman classes are followed by the small letter "g."

g = Greco-Roman	LF = Light-flyweight
B = Bantamweight	LH = Light-heavyweight
FE = Featherweight	M = Middleweight
FL = Flyweight	S = Super-heavyweight
H = Heavyweight	W = Welterweight
L = Lightweight	

*ACKERLY, Charles Edwin	1920 FE
ALEXANDER, Gary Joseph	1976 FEg
ALLEN, Lee Dale	1956 B
	1960 FEg
*APPLETON, Lloyd Otto	1928 W
AUBLE, David Camillo	1964 B
BABCOCK, J. C.	1904 FE
*BAUER, Gustav	1904 FL
BAUGHMAN, Richard Wayne	1964 Mg
	1968 Mg
	1972 LHg
*BECKMANN, William	1904 W
*BEHM, Donald	1968 B
BERRYMAN, Clarence Iven	1928 L
BETCHESTOBILL, A. J.	1904 W
*BLAIR, Peter Steele	1956 LH
*BLUBAUGH, Douglas Morton	1960 W
BORDERS, William D.	1952 B
*BRADSHAW, Benjamin Joseph	1904 FE
*BRAND, Daniel Oliver	1960 LH
	1964 M
*BRAND, Glen	1948 M
BRIAN, Adrian Robert	1920 FEg
BURKE, James Edward	1964 Lg

BUZZARD, Robert	1972 Lg
CAMILLERI, Russell Anthony	1960 Mg
	1964 Wg
CARDWELL, J. M.	1904 B
CARR, James	1972 FL
CHANDLER, Daniel Christie	1976 Mg
*CLAPPER, Charles E.	1904 FE
CLEMONS, Raymond	1936 LH
CLODFELTER, Marvin Carl	1932 L
COMBS, Steven Paul	1968 W
CONINE, Gerald Guy	1964 LH
CORSO, Joe Marion	1976 B
CRAIGE, John H.	1908 M
*CURRY, Robert	1904 LF
*DAVIS, Gene	1972 FE
	1976 FE
DEADRICH, Buck	1972 Hg
DELGADO, Richard Alfredo	1956 FL
DeWITT, Edward J.	1960 M
DILG, Joseph Edward	1904 H
*DOLE, George Stuart	1908 FE
DOUGLAS, Bobby Eddie	1964 FE
	1968 FE
DUNN, Roy Harvey	1936 H
*DZIEDZIC, Stanley, Jr.	1976 W
EDWARDS, Heywood Lane	1928 LH
ENG, Charles	1904 L
*ERICKSEN, Charles F.	1904 W
*EVANS, Jay Thomas	1952 L
	1956 L, Lg
FARINA, Michael Charles	1976 LFg
FERGUSON, Frederick C.	1904 B, FE
FILLER, S. A.	1904 W
FINLEY, Ronald Leslie	1964 FEg
FISCHER, William Ernest T.	1956 W
FITCH, Andrew	1964 Bg
FIVIAN, Fritz	1960 Wg
FLANDERS, Roger Lee	1924 H
*FLOOD, Aaron Ross	1936 B
FRANTZ, Angus MacDonald	1920 M
*GABLE, Danny Mack	1972 L
GALLERY, Daniel Vincent	1920 FEg
GEORGE, Edward Donald	1928 H
GEORGE, Howard R.	1960 LHg
*GERSON, Samuel Norton	1920 FE
GIANI, Louis Domenico	1960 FE
GONZALEZ, Sergio Steven	1972 LF
@HABERKORN, Charles	1904 L
(see also Track & Field)	
HAINES, James Allen	1976 FL
HAMMONDS, Ralph Waldo	1928 M
*HANSEN, Bernhuff	1904 H
HAZEWINKEL, David G.	1968 Bg
	1972 Bg
HAZEWINKEL, James A.	1968 FEg
	1972 FEg
*HEIN, John C.	1904 LF
*HELLICKSON, Russell Owen	1976 H
HENNESSY, William Joseph	1904 L, W, H
*HENSON, Josiah	1952 FE
HESS, Robert William	1932 M
HEWITT, Robert Donald	1928 B
*HINES, Bryan	1924 B
*HODGE, Daniel Allen	1952 M
	1956 M
HOLGATE, Claude	1904 LF
HOLMES, Wayne A.	1972 LFg
HOLT, James Jay	1956 Wg
HOLZER, Werner P.	1968 Lg
HUSSMAN, Fred	1904 L
HUTTON, Richard Heron Avis	1948 H
JACKSON, Jimmy	1976 S
JERNIGAN, William S.	1948 FL
*JOHNSON, Charles F.	1920 M
JOHNSON, James Evan	1976 LHg
JOHNSON, William Byron	1924 W
*KEASER, Lloyd Weldon	1976 L
KERSLAKE, William Roy	1952 H
	1956 H
	1960 H
KOENIG, Frederick Augustus	1904 L
KOLL, William	1948 L
KRISTOFF, Larry Dean	1964 H
	1968 H
KRUG, John H.	1908 L
&KUNGLER, Frank	1904 H
(see also Track & Field and Weightlifting)	
LAUCHLE, Larry E.	1960 Bg
LEE, William Marlin "Pete"	1976 Sg
*LEEMAN, Gerald Grant	1948 B
LEWIS, Dale Folsom	1956 Hg
	1960 Hg
*LEWIS, Frank Wyatt	1936 W
LEWIS, Jesse Thomas	1968 LH
LOOKABOUGH, Guy Howard	1924 W
LOVELL, William Patrick	1964 LHg
LYDEN, Larry	1968 Wg
LYSHON, William Jones	1912 FEg
MacWILLIAM, Charles Milton	1924 B
MAICHLE, Frank Martin	1920 LHg
MARCY, Patrick J.	1976 Lg
MARTTER, Perry Francis	1924 L
MATTHEWS, John Kelly	1976 Wg
*MAURER, Walter S.	1920 LH
*McCANN, Terrence John	1960 B
*McLEAR, Theodore J.	1904 FE
*MEHNERT, George Nicholas	1904 FL
	1908 B
*MEHRINGER, Peter Joseph	1932 LH
MELLINGER, A.	1904 W
*MERRILL, Leland Gilbert, Jr.	1948 W
METROPOULOS, George	1920 L, Lg

*MEYER, Fred Julius	1920 H
*MILLARD, Francis Edward	1936 FE
MILLER, Max	1904 FE
MOORE, Hal L.	1948 FE
*MORRISON, Allie Roy	1928 FE
NARGANES, Frederico	1908 M
NEIST, Gary	1972 Wg
*NELSON, William L.	1904 FL
*NEMIR, Edgar	1932 FE
*NEWTON, Chester Willard	1924 FE
*NIFLOT, Isidor "Jack"	1904 B
	1906 Lg
NORTHRUP, Benjamin Alfred	1960 Lg
*PEARCE, Robert Edward	1932 B
PECKHAM, James Cameron	1956 Mg
PECKHAM, Roy Thomas	1968 M
PEERY, Robert Hugh	1952 FL
*PENDLETON, Nathanael Greene	1920 H, LHg
*PETERSON, Benjamin Lee	1972 LH
	1976 LH
*PETERSON, John Allan	1972 M
	1976 M
PICKENS, Robert James	1964 Hg
REDMAN, John Roland	1920 LH
*REED, Robin	1924 FE
RETZER, George Washington, Jr.	1912 FEg
RHEINGANS, Bradley Bert	1976 Hg
RICE, Alan H.	1956 FEg
*RILEY, John Horn	1932 FE
ROBINSON, Jay Paul	1972 Mg
RODERICK, Myron Willis	1956 FE
*ROEHM, Otto F.	1904 L, W
ROOP, Robert	1968 Hg
ROSADO, William John	1976 LF
RUTH, Gregory Koch	1964 L
SADE, Joseph Earl	1976 Bg
*SANDERS, Richard Joseph	1968 FL
	1972 B
SCHAEFER, William	1904 W
SCHENK, Henk	1968 LHg
	1972 H
SHIMMON, Joseph Malek	1920 L
SIMONS, Elliott Gray	1960 FL
	1964 FL
SMITH, Herschel Albert	1924 M
*SMITH, William Thomas	1952 W
*SPELLMAN, John Franklin	1924 LH
*STEEL, Harry Dwight	1924 H
STEVENS, Charles	1904 B
STRACK, Charles William	1924 LH
*STREBLER, Z. B.	1904 B, FE
STRONG, Harley DeWitt, Jr.	1936 L
SULLIVAN, Daniel Albert (see also Track & Field)	1906 Mg
SWIGERT, Oral Raymond	1920 Lg
SZYMANSKI, Henry Ignatius	1920 Mg

TALBOT, Leander James, Jr. (see also Track & Field)	1908 H
TAMBLE, Richard	1968 FLg
*TAYLOR, Chris J.	1972 S, Sg
*TESING, Rudolph	1904 L
*THIEFENTHALER, Gustav	1904 LF
THOMAS, Dale Oren	1956 LHg
THOMPSON, Bruce Jerome	1976 FLg
TOEPPEN, Hugo	1904 FE, W
TOWNLEY, Kent Harold	1956 Bg
TRIBBLE, Charles Edward	1964 W
*VanBEBBER, Jack Francis	1932 W
*VIS, Russell John	1924 L
*VOLIVA, Richard Lawrence	1936 M
*WARMBOLDT, Fred Charles	1904 H
*WELLS, Wayne Turner	1968 L
	1972 W
*WESTER, August, Jr.	1904 B
WEYAND, Alexander Mathias	1920 Hg
WHITEHURST, Milton Morris	1904 B
WILLKIE, Edward Everett	1920 Hg
WILSON, John Richard	1956 FLg
	1960 FLg
	1964 FLg
*WILSON, Shelby A.	1960 L
*WINHOLTZ, Jerry	1904 L, W
*WITTENBERG, Henry	1948 LH
	1952 LH
WOLKEN, Rudolph	1904 L
WORTMANN, Dietrich	1904 FE
WRIGHT, Walter David, Jr.	1924 M
ZANOLINE, Paul D.	1920 Mg
*ZIRKEL, Albert	1904 L

YACHTING (132: 129 Men; 3 Women)

Yachting events were held at the Paris Olympics of 1900, but were absent until London in 1908, since which time they have always frequented the Olympic program. The United States had competitors in 1900 but did not make another appearance until 1928, although we have always been represented since.

The number of different events in yachting is almost beyond description; it seems the program undergoes a change at every Olympics. There have been many events other than those listed below, but those listed are the only events in which the United States has been represented.

In yachting, men and women compete against one another. Consequently we have not included a separate list for the women but have marked them with a "#" for easy reference.

Abbreviation	Meaning	Abbreviation	Meaning
3–10	= 3 to 10 ton class	55	= 5.5 meter class
6	= 6 meter class	8	= 8 meter class
470	= 470 class	DR	= Dragon class
FD	= Flying Dutchman	FF	= Firefly class
FM	= Finn monotype	SH	= Sharpie class
SO	= Soling class	ST	= Star class
SW	= Swallow class	TE	= Tempest class
TO	= Tornado class	Open	= Open class

ADAMS, Morgan Orland	1936 6	
ALLAN, Scott Hazzard	1972 FD	
*ALLEN, William Charles	1972 SO	
*ASHBROOK, Temple W.	1932 6	
*BARRETT, Peter Jones	1960 FM	
	1964 FM	
	1968 ST	
BARTHOLOMAE, William A., Jr.	1936 6	
*BATCHELDER, Joseph Laws	1964 55	
BENNETT, Edward Grant	1972 FM	
*BENTSEN, William Bruce	1964 FD	
	1972 SO	
*BIBY, John Edward, Jr.	1932 8	
*BURNAND, Alphonse A., Jr.	1932 8	
CAREY, Kenneth A.	1932 8	
*CARLSON, Robert	1932 6	
*CHANCE, Britton	1952 55	
#CHURCHILL, Antonia	1936 8	
*CHURCHILL, Owen Porter	1928 8	
	1932 8	
	1936 8	
*COHAN, Donald Smith	1972 DR	
COLGATE, Stephen	1968 55	
COMMETTE, Peter Michael	1976 FM	
*CONANT, Frederic Warren	1932 6	
*CONNER, Dennis W.	1976 TE	
*COOPER, William H.	1932 8	
COX, Frank Gardner, Jr.	1968 55	
CURRY, Manfred	1928 FM	
*DAVIS, Emmett S.	1932 6	
*DAVIS, Pierpont	1932 8	
*DEAN, Peter Sweetser	1972 TE	
*DEAVER, Richard Burke	1964 DR	
*DORSEY, Karl James	1932 8	
	1936 8	
*DOUGLAS, Donald Wills, Jr.	1932 6	
DUYS, Henry Meursinge, Jr.	1948 DR	
ECHEVARRIA, Carlos Porfirio, Jr.	1956 DR	
*ENDT, Everard C.	1952 6	
*EVANS, Ralph L., Jr.	1948 FF	
&FINDLAY, Conn Francis	1976 TE	
(see also Rowing)		
*FOSTER, Glen Seward, II	1972 TE	
FREEMAN, Norman Douglas	1976 FD	
*FRIEDRICHS, George Shelby, Jr.	1968 DR	

GARNER, Charles Speed	1936 6	
GATES, Richard Redwine	1972 ST	
*GLASGOW, Walter	1976 SO	
*GRAY, Gilbert T.	1932 ST	
*HALPERIN, Robert Sherman	1960 ST	
HEKMA, Frank	1928 8	
HEKMA, Nicholas Barry	1928 8	
*HOEPFNER, Richard H.	1976 SO	
HOLT, Alan Christian	1972 ST	
*HORTER, Charles John	1972 DR	
#HORTON, Joyce	1952 DR	
HORTON, William Landon	1952 DR	
HORTON, William Landon, Jr.	1952 DR	
HUETTNER, John E.	1932 8	
*HUNT, James Hawley	1960 55	
*JAHNCKE, Barton Williams Benedict	1968 DR	
JAMES, David Nowell	1968 FD	
JAMES, Robert Lee, Jr.	1968 FD	
JESSUP, Richard N.	1948 DR	
JEWETT, Frank Baldwin, Jr.	1936 FM	
KEANE, William Patrick, Jr.	1936 8	
KOHLER, Claude Lazard, II	1960 DR	
*KOLIUS, John Waldrip	1976 SO	
*LIBANO, Andrew J., Jr.	1932 ST	
*LOOMIS, Alfred Lee, Jr.	1948 6	
*LOW, Lawrence Edgar	1956 ST	
LYON, Charles	1932 FM	
MacHENRY, M.	1900	
	3–10	
*MARSHALL, John Knox	1972 DR	
*MARVIN, John	1956 FM	
MATHIAS, John G., Jr.	1976 FD	
McCLURE, Allen W., Jr.	1960 DR	
*McFAULL, David Rockwell	1976 TO	
*McNAMARA, John Joseph, Jr.	1964 55	
MELAIKA, Edward A.	1952 FM	
*MELGES, Harry Clemens "Buddy," Jr.	1964 FD	
	1972 SO	
METCALF, Woodbridge	1936 ST	
*MOONEY, Michael	1948 6	
MOORE, Richard	1932 8	
MORGAN, Alan C.	1932 8	
*MORGAN, John Adams	1952 6	
MORRIS, Frederick Wistar, III	1928 6	
*NORTH, Lowell Orton	1964 DR	
	1968 ST	
*O'DAY, George Dwyer	1960 55	
OLMSTEAD, Conway H.	1928 6	
OLSEN, C. Eric, Jr.	1956 SH	
OUTERBRIDGE, J. Willetts	1928 6	
*PARKS, William Wilson	1960 ST	
PAUL, Carl	1936 6	
*PIRIE, Lockwood	1948 SW	
*PRICE, John Wesley	1952 ST	
*REID, John S.	1952 ST	
RENEHAN, William N. Stanley	1956 SH	

*RIDDER, Eric	1952 6	
*ROGERS, Charles Sinclair	1964 DR	
*ROOSEVELT, Julian Kean	1948 DR	
	1952 6	
*ROTHWELL, Michael	1976 TO	
SCHICK, Frederick William	1936 8	
SCHOETTLE, Ferdinand Paul, Jr.	1956 55	
SCHOETTLE, Michael Beaver	1952 55	
*SCHRECK, Gerald Click	1968 DR	
*SCULLY, Francis Paul, Jr.	1964 55	
SHERONAS, Victor Frank	1956 55	
SINDLE, Harry Robert	1960 FD	
*SMART, Hilary Hurlburt	1948 ST	
*SMART, Paul Hurlburt	1948 ST	
*SMITH, Charles E.	1932 6	
*SMITH, David J.	1960 55	
*SMITH, James Hopkins, Jr.	1948 6	
STEARN, Smith "Tim"	1972 FD	
*STEARNS, Richard Irving	1964 ST	
STINSON, Robert, Jr.	1956 55	
SUTTON, Robert Mandel	1932 8	
	1936 8	
THOMPSON, James W. H.	1928 6	
*TORREY, Owen Cates, Jr.	1948 SW	
*Van BURGEN, Harry A.	1900	
	Open	
Van DUYNE, Carl III	1968 FM	
WALET, Eugene Henry, Jr.	1956 DR	
WALET, Eugene Henry, III	1956 DR	
	1960 DR	
WALKER, Stuart Hodge	1968 55	
WALLACE, John Donald	1936 6	
WATERHOUSE, William Glenn	1936 ST	
WEBSTER, Thomas C.	1932 8	
*WEEKES, James Higginson	1948 6	
WESTON, Benjamin F.	1928 8	
*WHITE, Edgar Pardee Earle	1952 55	
*WHITE, Sumner Wheeler, III	1952 55	
WHITEHURST, Robert	1976 470	
WHITEHURST, Thomas	1976 470	
#WHITON, Emelyn Thatcher Leonard	1952 6	
*WHITON, Herman Frasch	1928 6	
	1948 6	
	1952 6	
*WILLIAMS, Herbert Philip	1956 ST	
*WILLIAMS, Lynn Alfred, III	1964 ST	
WOOD, Robert Morford	1960 FD	

ABOUT THE AUTHORS

Bill Mallon

Ian Buchanan

Bill Mallon holds an M.D. degree from Duke University. Formerly a pro golfer on the PGA Tour, Mallon's hobby for many years has been collecting books about the Olympics. He has written several articles for various American magazines (*Golf Digest, Golf Journal, World Tennis, The Olympian*) and also for *Olympic Review,* the magazine of the International Olympic Committee. He is also the author of a monograph of the 1904 Olympics. The German Olympic magazine, *Olympischen Feuer,* recently described Mallon as "the foremost American expert on the history of the Olympics."

Ian Buchanan, British by birth, lives in Hong Kong and is an expert on track and field and on the Olympics in general. He has authored several books on track and field, notably *A History of British Athletic Records* (with Norris and Ross McWhirter, of Guinness fame) and *A Handbook of Far Eastern and Asian Games Track and Field Athletics.* In addition he has written *The Guinness Book of British Olympic Champions,* to be published shortly. For *Quest for Gold* Buchanan prepared the section on track and field.

Jeffrey Tishman lives in Glen Rock, New Jersey, and is known as the world's foremost fencing historian. He has written several articles on fencing for *The Olympian,* the magazine of the U.S. Olympic Committee. He is a frequent contributor to *American Fencing,* the magazine of the Amateur Fencing League of America. Tishman compiled the sections on fencing and the modern pentathlon for *Quest for Gold.*